CHILD RIGHTS & REMEDIES

Child Rights
&
Remedies

by

Robert C. Fellmeth

and

Jessica K. Heldman

Clarity Press, Inc.

Clarity Press, Inc.
2625 Piedmont Rd. NE, Ste. 56
Atlanta, GA. 30324

Table of Contents

Table of Cases

Acknowledgments

We are indebted to our colleagues in the child advocacy movement—the members of the National Association of Counsel for Children, the Partnership for America's Children, the former Voices for America's Children, First Star, the Children's Defense Fund, the Child Welfare League of America, the ABA Center on Children and the Law, the Maternal and Child Health Access Project, Campaign for Tobacco-Free Kids, Children Now, Children's Rights, the American Academy of Pediatrics, Children's Hospitals, teachers, social workers, child care providers, and the many other advocates who attempt to advance the interests of children. Those advocates include many attorneys from the heroic efforts of the *Castano* lawyers to protect children from tobacco addiction, to the juvenile courts and legal aid attorneys who work one on one to help children day after day. They are joined by important foundations, including the Price Philanthropies Foundation, the May and Stanley Smith Charitable Trust, the William D. Lynch Foundation for Children, The Barbara McDowell and Jerry Hartman Foundation, Casey Family Programs, The California Wellness Foundation, the ConAgra Foundation, the Rosenberg Foundation, the David and Lucile Packard Foundation, the Robert Wood Johnson Foundation, the Sierra Health Foundation, the San Diego County Bar Foundation, Price Charities, the Cox Kids Foundation, the Simon-Strauss Foundation, the Maximilian E. & Marion O. Hoffman Foundation, the Weingart Foundation, the Mattel Foundation, the Annie E. Casey Foundation, The Patio Group Foundation, The Robert and Allison Price Family Foundation, and the large number of anonymous givers who care about children and contribute for their effective representation.

We are grateful for the review and comments on early drafts of this work by Deborah Stein, then with the National Association of Child Advocates, and by Nancy Fellmeth of Families for Early Autism Treatment. We are also grateful for the help and assistance from Public Citizen and other public interest advocates throughout the nation from Ralph Nader to Scott Harshbarger, Joshua Rosenkranz, and Charles Lewis—whose assistance in the first chapter of this work has been invaluable.

Our special thanks goes to Margaret Dalton, Associate Dean and Professor of Law at the University of San Diego (USD) School of Law; Prof. Dalton is one of the nation's leading experts in special education law, and her contributions on the update of Chapter 6 were invaluable.

We also acknowledge the contribution of the pro bono department of the law firm Morrison & Foerster for facilitating the discovery of facts informing parts of Chapter 8, including their service as co-counsel in the *Wagner* case therein. In addition, USD School of Law Dean Stephen Ferruolo and former Deans Daniel B. Rodriguez and Kevin Cole; the faculty of the University of San Diego (USD) School of Law; USD Presidents James T. Harris, Alice Hayes, and Mary Lyons, and USD Provosts Gail F. Baker, Frank Lazarus, and Julie Sullivan have been important supporters of our work over the years.

We are grateful for the editorial and publishing assistance of Elisa Weichel, Administrative Director of the Children's Advocacy Institute (CAI) and Katie Gonzalez, Assistant Director of Public Interest Law Communications for CAI and its parent organization, the Center for Public Interest Law (CPIL). Also, this book would have been impossible without the intellectual contribution and dedicated support of Julie D'Angelo Fellmeth, Staff Counsel and former Administrative Director of CPIL. Further, we are indebted to all of the other current and prior staff of CAI and CPIL, including Mercedes Alcoser, Lupe Alonzo-Diaz, Debra Back, Steve Barrow, Brianna Blanchard, June Brashares, Tina Calvert, Collette Cavalier, Lillian Clark, Terry Coble, Leanne Cotham, Margaret Dalton, Cindy Dana, Melanie Delgado, Alicia Dienst, Kriste Draper, Kathryn Dresslar, Gene Erbin, Christina Falcone, Cheryl Forbes, Barry Fraser, Beth Givens, Bridget Gramme, Aarika Guerrero, John Hardesty, Amy Harfeld, Inez Hope, Ed Howard, Jim Jacobson, Louise Jones, the Hon. Sharon Kalemkiarian, Lynn Kersey, Joy Kolender, Christine Harbs Mailloux, Rebecca Licavoli, Kathleen Murphy Mallinger, Marissa Martinez, Mark McWilliams, Claudia Terrazas Mellon, Betty Mulroy Mohr, Rusty Nichols, Carl Oshiro, Tom Papageorge, Kim Parks, Kathleen Quinn, Stephanie Reighley, Randy Reiter, Christina Riehl, Diana Roberts, Alecia Sanchez, Kathy Self, Kate Turnbull, Jim Wheaton, and Ellen Widess. We thank Christine Basic, Hanna Gibson, Catherine Learned, Molly Selway, Melissa Stewart, Amanda Moreno, Kristy Gill, Evangeline Woo, Tiffany Salayer, Michelle Butler, Karen Prosek, Haley Frasca, Alex Calero, Victoria Furman, Elizabeth Rodriguez, Sarah Shelvy, Nicole Smith, Natalie Valdes, Mary Elizabeth Grant, Desiree Serrano, Mittal Shah, Erin Davis, Ho Kon Yoo, Jaclyn Mraz, Lisa Storing, Daniel Richardson, Alyson Hayden, Yangkyoung Lee, Aliz Nagyvaradi, Helen Lockett, Nancy Tran, Heather Morse, Helene Mayer, and Nilmini Silva-Send for their comments, research, proofing, cite checks or other assistance. And we thank Mary Massoud and Sydney D'Angelo for their help in preparing the third edition that preceded this 4th iteration and that substantially benefits it. We also acknowledge the help and assistance of David Bender and Matthew Boulay in assisting our research into the higher education challenges of youth.

We are thankful for the enduring support of some of our leading child advocates in their service on CAI's Council for Children. These leaders in pediatrics, education, social work, business, and law serve without compensation and spend many hours helping to guide the Children's Advocacy Institute. They currently include Bill Bentley, Denise Moreno Ducheny, Anne Fragasso, Dr. John Goldenring, the Hon. Leon Kaplan, David Meyers, Tom Papageorge, Gary Redenbacher, Dr. Gary Richwald, Gloria Perez Samson, Anne Segal, and John Thelan, as well as emeritus members Dr. Robert Black, Dr. Birt Harvey, Dr. Louise Horvitz, James McKenna, Paul Peterson, Blair Sadler, Dr. Alan Shumacher, and Owen Smith. Past members of and/or special consultants to the Council have included Frank Alessio, Nancy Daly, Martin Fern, Robert Frandzel, Theodore Hurwitz, Ralph Jonas, the Hon. Sharon Kalemkiarian, Christine Kehoe, Quynh Kieu, Harvey Levine, Mary O'Connor, the Hon. Robert Presley, and W. Willard Wirtz. In addition, we thank Deborah Stein, now the leader of the Partnership for America's Children, Kim Dvorchak of the National Association of Counsel for Children, Cathy Krebs of the American Bar

Association (ABA), and Howard Davidson, founder of the ABA's Center on Children and the Law, for their years of assistance and leadership.

Finally, the spiritual underpinning for this book and for our child advocacy comes from our original mentors: the late Sol and Helen Price.

Dedication

Robert C. Fellmeth: To Michael Q. and Aaron X. Fellmeth, to the memories of Robert B. and Jane Z., and also to the memories of our models: Jimmy D., and Sol, Helen and Aaron P.

Jessica K. Heldman: To Noah, Ethan, Lucas, Mom (Denise) and Dad (Joel)

Preface

Scholarship on children and the law reflects a movement from a view of children as property, to children as a protected underclass, to children as rights-based citizens. The first English book on children and the law, *Law, Both Ancient and Modern Relating to Infants,* published in 1697, described children as paternal chattel. Subsequent scholarship from Elizabethan England to 20th Century America reflected changes in the status of children as they gradually came to be viewed as worthy of society's protection. This publication, *Child Rights & Remedies,* represents the next step in our evolving understanding of the place of children in society.

The evolutionary component of this work is found in its treatment of rights-based versus welfare-based thinking, and how that distinction dictates law and public policy. While it may be agreed that society as a whole probably cares about children, it can be more important to ask how we care about them. Whether we provide for children out of a benevolent sense of care-taking (a welfare-based approach) or because we believe children are entitled to certain treatment (a rights-based approach), these motives serve as ideological principles that guide our law and policy.

In the context of the legal representation of children, where we are situated on that ideological continuum determines in large part which type of legal representation we provide. If we take a welfare-based view, we are inclined to protect children by providing advocate-directed representation where the representative determines the best interests of a child (as is currently the norm in child abuse and neglect proceedings) and then advocates for it. If we take a rights-based approach, we are inclined toward client-directed representation where the child client is given an independent voice (as is the case in juvenile justice / delinquency proceedings).

It can be argued that as we review the history of juvenile law, we see progress toward better outcomes for children through the movement from welfare-based systems toward rights-based systems. At one time, the only protection children could receive from parental abuse was to see their parents prosecuted in criminal court. Children were not entitled to care or services; as one 19th century court wrote, "[t]he state, through its criminal laws, will give the minor child protection from parental violence and wrongdoing, *and this is all the child can be heard to demand.*" At the turn of the 20th century, however, with the advent of juvenile courts, society began to provide special care for children as part of the "child saving" movement. Ultimately, that child saving welfare-based movement was struck down (for delinquent children) by a Supreme Court which, having reviewed the history of the care-taking experiment, created a rights-based juvenile court in which youth would be *entitled* to the protections of due process of law. The Court wrote, "[j]uvenile court history has again demonstrated that unbridled discretion, however benevolently motivated, is frequently a poor substitute for principle and procedure."

But just how evolved was the new juvenile court? Did a rights-based due process court produce better outcomes for children? In many instances yes, but at the same time it can be argued that in actuality it tipped the balance too far away from beneficence and toward autonomy; resulting in a juvenile court that is essentially an adult criminal court which fails to treat children as children, and by so doing, actually infringes upon their rights.

So should we follow this evolutionary trend in the abuse and neglect court or other areas of law affecting children? Do we truly serve children by empowering them or does empowerment ultimately lead to the diminution of children's protected status? That is the question that serves as context for this book and gives us an analytical structure for responding.

It is also a theme that enables Professors Fellmeth and Heldman to unite so many areas of law and policy affecting children. Children have historically been treated by legal scholars as either delinquent or dependent, but the all-important picture of the whole child—as determined not only by personal and familial circumstances, but also by the gamut of social policies through which governments seek to regulate or affect the socio-economic environment—has eluded them. By including not only delinquency and dependency, but also health care, education and property rights, poverty, mental health, civil liberties and reproductive law, *Child Rights & Remedies* provides a uniquely holistic analysis of children's law and policy.

With this comprehensive systemic analysis, Professors Fellmeth and Heldman have made an important contribution to the growth of the field of children and the law.

Marvin Ventrell
Founder and Director, Juvenile Law Society (JLS)
Executive Director, National Association of Counsel for Children, 1994–2009

ENDNOTES

[1] Juvenile Court historian Sanford J. Fox believed this to be the first English book on law relating to children.
[2] *Hewlett v. George*, 68 Miss. 703, 711, 9 So. 885, 887 (1891) (emphasis added).
[3] *In re Gault*, 387 U.S. 1 (1967).
[4] *Id.*, at 18.

Introduction

This text is intended for use in law school, political science, social science, and social work/public health graduate courses. The book focuses on the leading court cases interpreting and defining American law pertaining to children. It is supplemented with important data, brief commentaries, and questions to stimulate discussion.

The subject matter is deliberately broad, covering the political/legal context of rights and remedies available to children, and thirteen substantive areas. Three themes tie together all of the issues and discussion of this work. First is a pervasive dichotomy underlying child-related public policies. On the one hand, children are all persons entitled to the rights and privileges of any citizen. Indeed, our affection for them gives them special status. In a sense, the status of adults is believed by many to be a floor above which children are properly elevated. On the other hand, however, children are immature. They are not merely "little adults" and cannot be relied upon to always judge their own self-interest. Rather, they require protection and guidance. This dualism underlies much public policy affecting children and has often worked to their disadvantage, as the materials to follow indicate. Sometimes children are not granted the minimum floor of rights reserved for adults. Their inferior status does not always relate to their immaturity or to their protection.

Second, children represent the politically weakest grouping of persons. Adults have organized across a wide spectrum of characteristics, from disabled status to sexual preference. To offend any grouping is to risk quick approbation. This status is reflected in many ways; for example, the media coverage of school shootings failed to report the marked diminution of youth crime and the fact that violence against children occurs hundreds of times more often than the reverse. Would similar reporting have occurred based on shootings by an Hispanic, a Lutheran, a gay man, or a senior citizen? A more critical reflection of this lack of status can be found in our attitude toward adult reproductive rights (which are expansively defended) as opposed to a posited right of a child simply to be intended by two adults. The statistical correlation between this rather simple stated "right" and child welfare is remarkable. But it brooks virtually no weight against the prerogatives of adult groupings. This political power deficit is exacerbated by their lack of organization, lobbying presence, ability to vote, lack of campaign finance resources, and limited access to court redress. How would the rights and remedies of children differ were they to have the organization and resources of energy corporations, trade associations, or senior citizens?

The final feature binding all of the chapters of this work is a cliché. But like many clichés, it covers a seminal truth. Children are our future, what we shall leave behind. One of the marks of civilization is the recognition of the sacrifices of our parents and of their parents—for us, and the ethical imperative to pass that legacy onto our own legatees. These sentiments cut across many cultures, from the People of Israel ("I have drunk from wells I did not dig, and warmed by fires I did not build") to the Native American ("I did not inherit this earth from my parents, I have borrowed it from my grandchildren").

CHAPTER ONE

The Underlying Context: Access to Political/Legal Remedies

INTRODUCTION: REPRESENTATION OF THE LONG-TERM PUBLIC INTEREST

Rights and remedies inevitably depend upon the political system that enacts laws, and then interprets and enforces them. Elected and appointed public officials decide federal, state, and local budgets, and prohibit or reward private acts affecting children. Given the complexity of modern society, the public officials who make decisions necessarily depend upon outside advocacy to bring matters to their attention, frame issues, present alternatives, and provide information. Even the legislature, designedly the most proactive of the three branches, largely responds to advocacy before it. Who provides that advocacy? Is the result likely to reflect the ethical aspirations of the citizenry?

Child advocates argue that if decisions were made on their merits by those applying the underlying ethical mandate of the body politic, children would fare well. However, such a crucible for decisions may be distorted where public institutions are dominated by advocacy from those organized around a short-term profit stake in public policy.

An examination of the rights and remedies available to children properly begins with a review of the underlying process creating them. Such creation and subsequent change depend upon the political process within the three branches at the local, state, and federal levels, respectively. To what extent can children—or those who advocate on their behalf—participate in the process and achieve an appropriate impact on resulting policy?

Child advocates have undertaken two approaches to current advocacy imbalance. The first is to alter the rules to give interests without a proprietary profit stake (such as children) greater access and weight *vis-à-vis* public decision-making. One theory holds that reforms to lessen the influence of organized special interests necessarily enhance the prospects of those currently excluded, as the tinkling of a glass at a dinner may quiet the crowd so a soft voice can be heard. Political reformers argue that children and other diffuse interests will achieve a seat at the table only if decisions are driven more "on the merits" and less based on influence from the organized and those with a financial stake in the outcome. Accordingly, lessening dependence on private campaign contributors, on those able to provide employment to public officials, or on the information provided by organized interests may stimulate decisions that are more responsive to accepted public values which are otherwise overridden or entirely absent.

Such reform efforts vary from public financing of campaigns, providing incentives for more balanced advocacy before legislatures, increasing the independence of agencies, enhancing access to courts, and exposing governmental decisions to public examination. Such measures are intended to counterbalance the advantage of organization and money by raising considerations important to those interests—children's first among them—which otherwise are muffled and unheard.

The second approach is to work within whatever system exists to maximize the influence of children by using available resources—however disadvantageous the structural setting. Hence, child advocates have increased their political involvement (*e.g.*, formulating "report cards" on legislator votes, organizing to pose questions to candidates, etc.). Other child advocates devote resources to lobbying to the limited extent now feasible, and attempt to enlist powerful lobbyists with a tangential interest in policy benefiting children. Some child advocates use class action and mandamus tools in the courts. Others propose rules before federal and state agencies.

This Chapter explores the major political/structural impediments to child-sensitive public policies within the three branches, paying attention to the distorted "rules of the game" impeding balanced decision making, and identifying some of the successful tactics employed by child advocates to overcome existing barriers.

A. CHILDREN AND CAMPAIGN CONTRIBUTIONS

All three branches of government are necessarily affected by political elections. All legislators and many major executive branch officials are elected. Judges are often appointed and confirmed by elected officials, and many must run for subsequent election in most states. Campaigns have become increasingly expensive and most candidates depend upon private contributions to provide that funding. Such contributions often come from those with a vested profit stake in the decisions of the contested office. The extent to which such contributions influence later official acts varies, but few dispute that it provides an advantage, particularly in terms of access to elected officials. Such access can be a critical determinant of the decisions made. Understandably, large contributors tend to have a financial interest in those decisions. Large contributions are made or organized by corporations, unions, or trade associations across a spectrum of economic actors. However, three features often predominate: the defense of existing capital investment or occupational prerogatives, an advantage to those organized around their financial stake, and a focus on immediate economic consequences as opposed to longer range consequences. In contrast, children, who may benefit from new and different investment (capital) decisions, are inherently unorganized and incapable of direct political organization, and have an interest in longer term future impacts.

Children lack the policy leverage and access that often attends financial campaign support. On occasion, those who provide services to children may be organized and may contribute. But such organized support is insubstantial compared to vested profit stake interests which dominate campaign giving. Such "surrogate" giving on behalf of the interests of children is hampered by three factors: (1) many who serve children are relatively unorganized and are paid close to minimum wage (*e.g.*, child care providers); (2) political giving by charitable interests (*e.g.*, foundations, churches, charities) organized around the interests of children is legally barred; and (3) such providers may not always place the interests of children above their own economic stake when the two conflict.

1. Facts: How Much, From Whom, To Whom

Current campaign regulation generally takes two forms: amount limitations per election on contributions to candidates (including an outright prohibition on corporate contributions for federal elections), and widespread required public identification of contributors. However, stated regulatory goals have been partially thwarted by the increased use of political action committees (PACs) by organized interests, U.S. Supreme Court cases, and the rise of the "Super PACs," political action committees allegedly operating independent from a particular candidate.

The purpose of a PAC is to raise and spend money to elect candidates aligned with particular business, labor, or ideological interests. PACs can give up to $5,000 to an individual candidate's committee per election, or up to $15,000 to any national party committee per year.[1]

Direct contributions to candidates themselves (controlled by his or her campaign committee) are still subject to limitations and disclosures—to some extent. The races for non-federal offices are governed by state and local law. Over half the states allow some level of corporate and union contributions. Some states have limits on contributions from individuals that are lower than the national limits, while eleven states have no limits at all.[2]

In terms of federal law applicable to Congressional and Presidential private campaign contributions, an individual may contribute as much as $2,800 to a candidate (once for the primary and then again for the general election), $5,000 to a multicandidate PAC, $10,000 to a state or local party committee, and $35,500 to a national party committee per election.[3] Corporations and unions are still banned from making direct contributions in federal elections.

However, substantial money is routed through PACs and political party systems for local, state, and federal elections. These operate to cloak the identity of actual donors by candidates who benefit. The top ten spending PACs in 2017–18 were as follows:[4]

PAC Name	Total Amount	Dem %	Rep %
National Beer Wholesalers Ass'n	$3,444,000	48%	52%
National Ass'n of Realtors	$3,407,777	51%	49%
AT&T Inc.	$3,108,200	40%	60%
Northrop Grumman	$2,848,740	43%	57%
Sheet Metal, Air, Rail & Transportation Union	$2,792,950	88%	12%
National Air Traffic Controllers Ass'n	$2,787,000	56%	44%
American Bankers Ass'n	$2,779,580	23%	77%
Operating Engineers Union	$2,746,409	80%	19%
National Auto Dealers Ass'n	$2,683,400	23%	77%
International Brotherhood of Electrical Workers	$2,600,274	96%	4%

These entities are not notably focused on children or our future.

The Center for Responsive Politics reported in 2018 that "The candidate who spends the most usually wins." The most recent 2018 data reveal that in 88% of House races, the top spending candidate won; the same was true in 85.7% of Senate races.[5]

The same Center for Responsive Politics collected total campaign spending in 2017–18 from the Federal Elections Commission as follows:[6]

House: Financial total for all House candidates, 2017–18:

Party	No. of Candidates	Total Raised	Total Spent	Total Cash on Hand	Total from PACs	Total from Indivs
All	2905	$1,682,489,486	$1,652,710,902	$305,845,445	$405,020,525	$1,060,683,028
Dem	1511	$1,016,006,417	$974,256,767	$181,243,073	$181,047,341	$714,626,007
Rep	1220	$661,431,215	$673,517,381	$124,125,024	$223,945,494	$343,941,310

Senate: Financial total for all Senate candidates, 2017–18:

Party	No. of Candidates	Total Raised	Total Spent	Total Cash on Hand	Total from PACs	Total from Indivs
All	478	$1,086,010,175	$1,034,289,811	$288,251,984	$109,076,368	$756,333,503
Dem	160	$598,882,765	$576,848,550	$110,214,697	$54,863,016	$492,760,438
Rep	257	$456,469,061	$432,360,274	$108,438,038	$52,869,640	$247,166,952

In terms of the identities of the PAC grouping, the 2018 data reveal the following sectors by highest amount.[7]

Sector	Total	To Incumbents	To Challengers	To Open Seats
Agribusiness	$27,751,688	93.8%	1.8%	4.3%
Communications/Electronics	$28,488,664	96.2%	0.5%	3.3%
Construction	$16,621,667	89.3%	3.7%	7.0%
Defense	$18,108,018	96.7%	0.6%	2.7%
Energy/Natural Resource	$31,248,577	89.8%	3.6%	6.6%
Finance/Insurance/Real Estate	$88,833,201	94.3%	1.3%	4.4%
Health	$54,486,961	93.1%	1.8%	5.2%
Lawyers & Lobbyists	$13,776,517	88.9%	5.0%	6.1%
Transportation	$27,673,331	93.3%	2.1%	4.7%
Miscellaneous Business	$42,242,128	93.0%	2.4%	4.6%
Labor	$58,108,510	73.1%	14.3%	12.6%
Ideology/Single-Issue	$91,589,143	57.5%	23.3%	19.2%

Separate and apart from the spending through the candidate's own campaign committees and as outlined above, is even "darker" money expended through the Super PACs. These Super PACs are allegedly separate from a candidate-controlled campaign, and avoid the above limitations entirely. These entities effectively make up almost half of all current campaign spending—and tend to dominate races where there is a particular economic interest for the underlying contributor. Given the Super PAC dispensation, individual, union, or corporate contributions have no practical contribution or spending limits, nor do they effectively identify the sources of monies so collected and spent.

Super PACs tend to be more ideological, or based on the extreme wealth of super-funders. The Center for Responsive Politics' 2018 data reveals that 2,395 Super PACS were in operation, with $1.5 billion raised and $817.6 million expended. Conservative Super PACs spent $428.2 million in 2018, with liberal Super PACs spending $342.4 million. More than $23 million of Super PAC spending was done without disclosing donors, with another $365.8 million spent with only partial disclosure of donors.

2. Applicable Precedents

The leading case casting a long shadow over all post-1976 regulatory efforts is *Buckley v. Valeo*, 424 U.S. 1 (1976), where the Supreme Court distinguished between campaign contributions (which may be regulated in amount) and campaign expenditures. The Court reasoned that unlike contribution limits, spending limits do not have the same "compelling state interest" in corruption diminution. Limiting campaign spending, including the amount a candidate could spend from her own assets, became problematical. Accordingly, campaign finance reformers developed a "quid pro quo" strategy: give the candidates something in return for a promise to limit spending. Different arrangements have allowed a public declaration that a candidate has "abided by a limitation" (sometimes placed on the ballot itself), or have allowed public financing (usually public funds to match small private contributions on a 1–to–1 or higher ratio), or have allowed a larger contribution limitation to candidates who agree to an expenditure ceiling.

The most prominent example of such a strategy is the Presidential election, financed through Form 1040 IRS tax check-off monies to political parties receiving more than 5% of the vote in the previous election, and whose candidates agree to abide by specified spending limitations. At the state level, fourteen states utilize some method of partial public financing to allow candidates to run without complete reliance on private funding from self-interested groups. One method, known as clean election programs, gives each candidate who chooses to participate a fixed amount of money. To qualify for this subsidy, the candidates must collect a specified number of signatures and small (usually $5) contributions. The candidates are not allowed to accept outside donations or to use their own personal money if they receive this public funding. Candidates who choose to raise money privately rather than accept the government subsidy are subject to some restrictions involving disclosures.[8] This procedure has been in place in races for all statewide and legislative offices in Arizona and Maine since 2000, where a majority of officials were elected without spending any private contributions on their campaigns. Connecticut passed a Clean Elections law in 2005, along with the cities of Portland, Oregon and Albuquerque, New Mexico. In 2006, in *Randall v. Sorrell*, 548 U.S. 230, the Supreme Court held that large parts of Vermont's Clean Elections law were unconstitutional. As discussed below, in 2008, the Supreme Court's decision in *Davis v. Federal Election*

Commission, 554 U.S. 724, suggested that a key part of most Clean Election laws—a provision granting extra money (or "rescue funds") to participating candidates who are being outspent by non-participating candidates—is unconstitutional. In 2011, in *Arizona Free Enterprise Club's Freedom Club PAC v. Bennett*, 564 U.S. 721, the Supreme Court struck down the matching funds provision of Arizona's law on First Amendment grounds.

Massachusetts has had a hybrid public funding system for statewide offices since 1978. Taxpayers are allowed to contribute $1 to the statewide election fund by checking a box on their annual income tax returns. Candidates who agree to spending limits are eligible for money from this fund. Non-participating candidates are required to estimate spending, and this will raise the limit for participating opponents if higher than the agreed-to limit.[9] This Massachusetts option is analogous to the Presidential Tax Return check off for presidential candidate partial financing, which has also been upheld, but which has been substantially overshadowed by the scale and scope of internet-driven and private Super PAC financing.

The consequences of campaign contributions include radically enhanced access to the elected public official receiving funds or benefitting from an allied campaign. Lobbyist access to members of Congress or other officials is critical to influence. Lobbying does not occur in a public setting of argument and rebuttal. Private conversations with unchecked claims and contentions are their hallmark. The Supreme Court decision in *Nixon v. Shrink Missouri Government PAC*, 528 U.S. 377 (2000), upheld a contribution limit of $1,075 imposed by Missouri on statewide races, noting that money is not directly equivalent to speech, and recognizing the legitimate public interest not only to prevent bribery, but "extending to the broader threat from politicians too compliant with the wishes of large contributors." Heartened by the judgment that money is not necessarily speech, reform efforts were initiated, including the following:

1) "Clean Money Campaign Reform" where candidates qualify for public campaign funds through signatures or a minimum number of $5 contributions from registered voters in their jurisdiction, with private contributions limited to $100 per person.

2) "Matching funds" allowing candidates to receive anywhere from a 1–to–1 match to 4–to–1 in public funds for every $250 in private contributions from a registered voter in the jurisdiction.

3) Refundable tax credits for contributions to candidates who have agreed to spending limits.

4) A system called "patriot dollars" where citizens are each given $200 in vouchers to commit to candidates for public office.

5) Subsidized or free required time from the media for campaign messages by candidates, debates, and other means to lessen the increasing costs of candidate communications.

6) A local charter provision enacted by citizen initiative in three California cities (San Francisco, Santa Monica, and Pasadena) which provides that where a local official has conferred a "public benefit" beyond a specified level to a corporation or

person, that beneficiary may not give anything of value to the official for five years after the decision is made, or two years after leaving office, whichever is longer. Campaign contributions (as well as gifts and employment) may not be received by such an official during that period from such a beneficiary.

Note on 2002 Bipartisan Campaign Reform Act and Subsequent Cases on Campaign Contributions

On March 27, 2002, the President signed the "Bipartisan Campaign Reform Act of 2002" (also known as the McCain-Feingold Act),[10] addressing the rapid "soft money" growth in campaign finance through the 1990s. As noted above, that soft money consisted of large contributions from corporations, unions, and wealthy individuals to the respective political parties. The monies were then channeled into the Presidential and Congressional campaigns, facilitating disproportionate influence by a small group of givers. Those givers also were able to effectively avoid disclosure of their identities as financiers of particular candidates as required by law due to the middleman role of the party. However, critics charged that party leaders knew well who the big givers were and would facilitate their influence on those public officials their funds helped to elect. In addition, the nation's political action committees began to use "independent expenditure" campaigns to influence elections—alleged public mailing and media advertising for and against candidates for office run by special interests independent of the candidates' political campaigns. These campaigns avoided the contribution limitations and contributor identification provisions of law applicable to the candidates.

As noted above, the law imposed some limitations on soft money contributions to political parties, prohibiting unions and corporations (already limited in federal candidate campaign giving) from making contributions for candidates through party giving. In addition, corporations and unions cannot fund ads for or against candidates for federal office within sixty days of a general election or thirty days of a primary election from their general treasury. Although addressing some important abuses, five factors limit its ability to redress campaign finance imbalance working to the disadvantage of children: (1) Independent expenditures immediately prior to an election remain lawful where funded by a political action committee. The law simply prohibits funding from the membership treasury where contributions presumably are not given voluntarily for that particular political purpose. Such PAC funding may still be substantial. (2) Corporations and unions may be able to tap their general treasuries for campaign spending outside the thirty and sixty-day prohibitory period, including substantial spending for ads attacking public officials with whom they disagree and who shortly face election. (3) The law may not apply fully to Internal Revenue Code § 527 organizations.[11] (4) The law does not apply at all to state and local office. Moreover, it does not prevent unlimited corporate or union soft money giving to state political parties, who can then funnel it into expenditure campaigns to assist state candidates allied with their federal counterparts. Most states do not have the federal limitation on corporate or union campaign funding, and the decried abuses leading to this legislation all remain largely unaddressed at the state level. (5) The law raised the limit on so-called "hard money" contributions (made by individuals to candidates directly) from $1,000 per person per election to $2,000, to be adjusted in the future by inflation.[12] Hence, a married couple can together give $8,000 to a candidate, $4,000 to the primary campaign, and $4,000 to the general. These limits are subject to increase where a candidate spends substantial personal funds for his or her own election; such spending above two times the law's specified threshold will raise the $8,000 limit for the couple in the example above to $24,000. At a very high level of personal spending by a candidate on his or her own campaign, the individual limits are waived entirely for the opponents in that election. (6) As noted above, none of these limitations, such as they are, apply to Super PACs.

In *McConnell v. Federal Election Commission*, 540 U.S. 93 (2003), the Court upheld most of this 2002 Reform Act. The Court applied a "heightened scrutiny" test (less than "strict scrutiny" but more rigorous than "rational relation") to limitations on contributions. As discussed above, the Court distinguished between "expenditures" where one is spending one's own money on one's speech (and subject to strict scrutiny) and "contributions" that involve giving money to another to finance his/ her electoral speech. The test enunciated by the Court for contribution control is whether there is a "sufficiently important interest" at stake and whether the restriction is "closely drawn" to avoid unnecessary abridgement of First Amendment interests. Applying this test, the Court upheld the new statute's restrictions on soft money contributions via political parties, political advertising rate ceilings at the "lowest unit charge" for that class of advertising normally charged, and record keeping requirements imposed on broadcasters.

One aspect of the new statute suffered reversal—its prohibition on contributions by minor children. The government's justification that the restriction was necessary to prevent circumvention of limits based on family size was rejected as too attenuated given the lack of evidence presented of such abuse and the existing and still applicable general prohibition on giving or receiving contributions "in the name of another person."

The soft money restriction on the pre-2003 common use of contributions to state and local parties—who then give to federal candidates free from otherwise applicable limitations on amount limitations, allowing avoidance of source disclosure—was upheld by a 5–4 margin, with Justice O'Connor providing the swing vote. The statute as upheld does not address the five tactics discussed above.

Since *McConnell*, political spending by the so-called Section 527 groups has increased dramatically—undermining the limitation and disclosure purposes of campaign regulation. Indeed, unlimited spending that is not controlled by or coordinated by a candidate (or his/her party under the expanded terms of the new statute) cannot be easily circumscribed given the Court's view of the First Amendment speech and association rights connection.

In *Speechnow.org v. FEC*, 599 F.3d 686 (D.C. Cir. 2010), the court held that contributions made to "independent" political committees, including Section 527 entities, could not be limited as to donation amount. The decision hence departed from the *Buckley* criterion distinguishing expenditures—that involved one's own First Amendment expression and could not be limited in amount, from donations to another entity that could be subject to maximums. The decision did not preclude disclosure requirements on such expenditures, but such disclosures are not effectively required at present, as discussed below.

The *Speechnow* decision followed three Supreme Court opinions substantially altering political campaign law. In *Randall v. Sorrell*, 548 U.S. 230 (2006), the Supreme Court struck the Vermont "Act 64" limitations on individual contributions to state political office. The Court concluded that the limits burden protected interests "in a manner disproportionate to the public purpose they were enacted to advance." The Vermont statute limited individual contributions to $200 to $400 for individuals and political parties to candidates. The decision does not preclude contribution limits, but holds that these maximums (in combination with other factors such as counting the expenses incurred by volunteers as a contribution and lack of a CPI inflator on the maximum) invalidated the limitations. Although the Vermont limits are below most federal and state maximums, which still may survive, many local elections historically have imposed contribution limits in the range of the Vermont maximums.

Then the Court decided *Davis v. FEC*, 554 U.S. 724 (2008), striking the so-called "Millionaire's Amendment" of the federal McCain-Feingold Act. This provision was intended to limit the advantage of a wealthy candidate who spends more than $350,000 of his/her own money on a campaign. Such a threshold triggered an increase in maximum donations to challengers from $2,300 to $6,900. The law was consistent with the "adjustment" approach to high expenditures of one's own—recognizing that they could not be limited given their direct manifestation of First Amendment exercise by *Buckley*. The wealthy candidate is not limited in the financing of his/her "speech," but it may trigger revised maximums or other consequences (*e.g.*, disclosure on voter ballots that a candidate exceeded a specified advisory maximum). However, the Court struck that consequence as an "asymmetrical" regulatory consequence to such a spending decision, and rejected the argument of "leveling" or "diversity" of information in political campaigns as a sufficient "state interest." This decision calls into some question the longstanding strategy of public finance political reformers to allow a higher allocation of public monies for candidates where opponents self-finance at high levels.

The most serious Supreme Court decision altering political finance law is *Citizens United v. FEC*, 130 S.Ct. 876 (2010). Corporations have been viewed as entities that may collectively associate into combinations. Although such combinations are limited by federal and state antitrust law, the First Amendment and its "freedom of association" allow coalescence for the purpose of "petitioning government" under the so-called "*Noerr-Pennington*" doctrine. The *Citizens United* decision extended First Amendment rights more directly to individual corporate entities as they may seek to influence elections. First, the decision reverses *Austin v. Michigan Chamber of Commerce*, 494 U.S. 652 (1990)—that had allowed requiring for-profit corporations to use political action committees funded only by individuals (not from corporate funds) when engaging in express electoral advocacy. These expenditures have historically taken the form federally of either contributions to a party then distributed to candidates, or contributions of individuals to PACs. Although such monies may derive indirectly from corporate assets, they previously were funded through individuals to such PACs—2,000 of which already exist to promulgate corporate political messages.

Second, the decision revises *McConnell*, above, that allowed the McCain-Feingold restrictions on "electioneering communications" by corporations—*e.g.*, election eve broadcasts that have clear election-influence intent and effect. *Citizens United* imbues corporations with the previously granted privileges of sentient persons. They now have the First Amendment right to expend funds for political purposes without limitation in any and all elections—where theoretically separate and apart from a candidate's campaign. That is, the Court first ties First Amendment rights to political free speech, entitled to "strict scrutiny" protection. Corporations previously enjoyed clearly a less expansive commercial free speech right subject to "heightened scrutiny." Then it confers on corporations the right to fund their own political speech (not the giving of it to a candidate but for its own political purposes). Such spending is, in this new formulation, an "expenditure" and not a "contribution to another," and is therefore an unlimited First Amendment "expenditure" for speech right of the corporation.

The Court writes: "[the] prohibition on corporate independent expenditures is thus a ban on speech. As a 'restriction on the amount of money a person or group can spend on political communication during a campaign,' that statute 'necessarily reduces the quantity of expression by restricting the number of issues discussed, the depth of their exploration, and the size of the audience reached'" (at 898). The majority opinion rests on the premise that although every person has political First Amendment rights as individuals (including all corporate officers and stockholders), the corporate "persons" created by statute are also so imbued, separate and apart from individuals.

The Stevens dissent argues that the *Citizens United* case, involving a corporation funding an anti-Hillary Clinton video just before the primary presidential election of 2008, merely required that the company used its multimillion dollar PAC rather than corporate monies to fund an electorally intended publication within 60 days of an election. Justice Stevens writes: "In the context of election to public office, the distinction between corporate and human speakers is significant. Although they make enormous contributions to our society, corporations are not actually members of it. They cannot vote or run for office. Because they may be managed and controlled by nonresidents, their interests may conflict in fundamental respects with the interests of eligible voters. The financial resources, legal structure, and instrumental orientation of corporations raise legitimate concerns about their role in the electoral process. Our lawmakers have a compelling constitutional basis, if not also a democratic duty, to take measures designed to guard against the potentially deleterious effects of corporate spending in local and national races. The majority's approach to corporate electioneering marks a dramatic break from our past. Congress has placed special limitations on campaign spending by corporations ever since the passage of the Tillman Act in 1907..." (at 930).

The U.S. Supreme Court then created another huge loophole beyond *Citizens United* and the rise of Super PAC limit and disclosure abnegation. In *McCutcheon v. FEC*, 572 U.S. 185 (2014), it held that the two-year limits on amounts that can be contributed to national party and federal candidate committees were unconstitutional.

The concern of child advocates involves democratic decision-making along three spectra: (a) organized versus diffuse interests, (b) defense of prior investment versus new options, and (c) short-term horizon versus long-run consequence. The interests of children are often aligned with the diffuse, new, and long-range end of these spectra. And individuals have sentiments that allow these latter factors much weight—concern over impacts in general and on others, and the legacy left for our children and grandchildren. In contrast, a corporation is a created entity with a legitimate interest in defending its assets. A corporation collects investment from stockholders and loans from bondholders to purchase a capital asset for production. That production yields a return to repay bondholders and provide a return on investment to the shareholders who own the corporation. The officers of the corporation have a fiduciary duty to those owners to advance that corporate interest. Such a description is not pejorative; it is the legitimate and expected function of corporate capital. But it necessarily involves a commitment to maximum profit from the capital investment that is the essence of a corporation. Hence, for example, an energy company purchases oil assets, creates pipelines, constructs refineries. It has a commitment to provide a return to those who funded those assets—that is its prime directive. In contrast, energy policy in the interests of children may involve consideration of nonrenewable oil exhaustion, pollution from the refinery, and oil consumption. The corporation properly looks at relatively short-term and narrow consequences, and to the extent it is politically influential will rationally oppose the assessment of external costs (*e.g.*, pollution) it may be able to pass onto others, or long-term impacts on future generations (*e.g.*, resource exhaustion or global warming).

Those groups opposing *Citizens United* and *McCutcheon*, including Common Cause and Public Citizen, have proposed a constitutional amendment to reverse it. They also support one or more of the six options to lessen the private money influence discussed above. And they have proposed four more limited avenues of statutory change to ameliorate its effects that may withstand constitutional challenge before the existing Supreme Court:

1) a shareholders protection provision would require approval prior to corporate spending for political purposes. Reformers argue that monies given to a corporation for investment are not properly diverted to political purposes that may contravene the views of the investor providing it. In theory, shareholders invest in a corporation for limited purposes, and long-term collateral effects on children may lead many stockholders to oppose the maximum, short-term return on an investment where offending deeply held values.

2) a limitation on contributions from or through corporate lobbyists (which tend to allow more explicit *quid pro quo* tie of public votes with money receipt) and from major government contractors.

3) a prohibition on independent expenditures by foreign corporations or their subsidiaries.

4) new transparency rules requiring public disclosure of corporate campaign expenditures, whether made directly or through election committees, nonprofits, or trade associations.

The current system of election financing confers substantial influence on three types of actors. First, seniors are by far the largest source of individual campaign contributions. The median age of large contributors to campaigns is typically over 65. Such persons are often able to contribute substantial sums, particularly in the funding of PACs and political parties or candidate committees. Second, the continuation of individual campaign contributions at the $1,000 to $5,000 range in many states gives substantial power to horizontally-organized trade and professional associations able to gather a large number of such contributions for extraordinary political influence. Third, the corporation has now arisen as a direct and substantially anonymous funder of political mass messaging.

Of some additional concern beyond these sources dominating executive and legislative elections is growing private funding influence on judicial elections. From 2000 to the present, groups with some interest in judicial decisions have contributed hundreds of millions to state supreme court candidates. Former Justice Sandra Day O'Connor has devoted much of her post-retirement advocacy to opposing this growing threat to court independence and integrity. The *Citizens United* decision may open the door to a dramatic increase in "independent expenditures" by corporations with an interest in judicial decisions with child impact—particularly in areas such as environmental protection and product liability.

Also exacerbating the possible imbalance from profit-stake domination of elections is the lack of media attention achievable by children. Such transparency is one of the few politically potent assets available to child advocates. That attention is undermined by legally-required confidentiality—including the understandable privacy needs in medical treatment and education, and the excessive secrecy surrounding the fate of foster children being directly raised by the state (see discussion in Chapter 8). The decline of newspapers and investigative reporting and the rise of the anonymous and eye bite format of the internet contribute to less attention paid by the general public to the long-range education, health, and protection status of children.

Child advocates argue that achieving decisions based on the merits, such as giving proper weight to the interests of children (and other diffuse, long-term interests), requires more substantial reduction of reliance on private giving, probably via some system of public financing as suggested by the six options listed above.

Questions for Discussion

1. Is a financial stake in public policy a surrogate measure of legitimate "intensity of interest?" At what point does influence based on a relatively short-term economic interest improperly compromise broader, long-range interests, such as the environment and children?

2. Does the disclosure of many campaign contributors counterbalance the alleged disproportionate influence of profit stake interests? Will the banning of soft money significantly lessen reliance on those organized around a proprietary profit stake?

3. As noted above, those making large individual campaign contributions are disproportionately seniors. Does such dependence influence public policies in the direction of senior citizen benefits as opposed to investment in children (e.g., private pension subsidies, property tax relief, Medicare, prescription drug coverage, Social Security)? How much public discourse occurs on the extreme deferral of trillions of dollars paid for the benefit of current seniors—the cost of which must be borne by our grandchildren?

4. Some groups that provide services to children may be organized enough to provide campaign assistance, votes, and even independent expenditures on their behalf. Do the interests of such groups always correspond to the long-range interests of children in their respective economic territories?

5. Even if public financing of campaigns removed substantial private dependence and enhanced competitive elections, would the interests of children secure adequate attention? Do lobbying resources—which frame public policy debates, employment of public officials, and other sources of influence based on proprietary stake—also contribute to public policies focusing on short-term profit and the protection of highly organized interests?

6. Does the rise of the internet and the chance to organize massive campaign funds from small contributions provide some counterbalance to existing trade associations, corporate, and wealthy individual influence? Obama's campaigns gathered substantial resources from this more diffuse mechanism, but he was also the first to decline the IRS check-off public financing of presidential campaigns, thus removing the campaign finance limitations in that law and shifting away from public finance. If the major plausible reform is not small voluntary contributions but increased public financing of campaigns, does this decision have long-term benefits for political elections? Is it feasible for many federal, state, and local campaigns? What role does the decline in child coverage by the media play in the efficacy of such a widely-solicited source? Does the fact that internet communications allow the concealment of the sender not facilitate special interest domination of even this diffuse source of citizen contribution?

B. CHILDREN, LEGISLATURES, AND LOBBYING

In addition to a lack of campaign contribution assets, children lack substantial lobbying presence in Washington, D.C., and especially in state capitols. Lobbying maximizes the impact of campaign contributions or independent expenditures by providing advocacy tied to givers. Children are not represented in terms of direct campaign givers, and are minimally represented through surrogate givers. Similarly, they are under-represented in the lobbying of public officials in the executive and legislative branches.

The most prevalent lobbying presence on behalf of children comes from horizontally-organized interests that provide services for them, such as social workers, child care providers, and teachers. However, except in limited degree for teachers, such lobbying is not often supported by campaign finance assets. In addition, such advocacy by child service providers may serve the interests of members as a priority. Political scientists have noted that political advocacy (PAC lobbying) for a group tends to focus on the defense or expansion of the client's "territory." Less attention may be given to prevention, competition, or alternatives that may benefit children. For example, a child care providers' association may oppose increased inspections or remedies for safety violations by its licensed members. Or a teachers' association may focus more on member employee benefits than on class size reduction, or may want dismissals and rehiring to be based solely on seniority without regard to teaching efficacy or subject area need. To cite another real example, it may advocate that public funding for schools be taken away from high priority pre-school preparation or special education where not taught by its membership.[13]

However, differences between child service providers and the interests of children may be less problematical than the domination of lobbying advocacy by commercial and organized interests. The imbalance mirrors the power of high campaign contributing industries nationally (e.g., oil and gas, manufacturing, pharmaceuticals, Wall Street, telecommunications, powerful unions, the elderly). These interests are joined at the state level by effectively organized counterparts, including the alcohol and insurance industries, organized physicians, trial lawyers, and others much affected by state law. While not consciously hostile to the interests of children, the preoccupation of these groups with their own immediate self-interests often influences public policy adversely to those not so represented.

In terms of lobbying in D.C., the Center for Responsive Politics collects applicable data, finding $1.45 billion expended for 10,419 lobbyists in 1998. Those totals increased in 2018 to $3.42 billion and 11,586 lobbyists.[14] That amounts to 21 lobbyists for each member of Congress. One scholar has calculated the total monies expended on Congressional lobbying by all advocates representing just the interests of children, including the Children's Defense Fund, Voices for America's Children, The Partnership for America's Children, First Focus, Every Child Matters, Fight Crime—Invest in Kids and others total approximately $1 million.[15] That sum amounts to 3/100th of 1% of total lobbying expenditures. To be sure, some lobbying by professional associations and other groups will take positions in the interests of present and future children—but conflicts and priorities limit the scope of that contribution. Nor does the disparity in direct lobbying fully account for the substantial monies spent on legislative and executive branch influence not considered a "lobbying expense." These include publications, press releases, media influence, litigation and other advocacy not counted as part of the relatively narrow "lobbying" category.

Nor is the disparity confined to commercial interests. The American Association of Retired Persons alone spends from $6 million to $20 million per year on lobbying.[16] The spending of other groups representing the elderly and those receiving funds from Medicare and Social Security spending overwhelm expenditures on behalf of children—who, as noted above, and discussed below, will add two other sources to the obligations to be transferred to our children: 1) high public employee pensions and retirement medical coverage, and 2) a rising federal budget spending deficit generally. While these expenditures may have merit, the issue of who should pay is a seminal ethical concern central to any discussion of child rights and remedies. The major lobbying interests ranked in order of expenditures and including those spending over $45 million in 2018 include the following:[17]

Pharmaceuticals/Helth Products	$280,305,523
Insurance	$156,867,044
Electronics Mfg & Equip	$144,870,718
Business Associations	$141,539,249
Oil & Gas	$124,492,199
Electric Utilities	$120,725,148
Real Estate	$117,334,792
Hospitals/Nursing Homes	$99,686,787
Securities & Investment	$98,576,572
Misc. Manufacturing & Distributing	$95,519,395
Telecom Services	$92,851,826
Air Transport	$91,346,438
Health Professionals	$89,724,045
Health Services/HMOs	$79,352,992
Education	$77,443,167
Internet	$77,202,866
Civil Servants/Public Officials	$74,504,292
Automotive	$67,774,786
Commercial Banks	$64,022,918
Defense Aerospace	$64,014,043

High on the list of specific trade associations are the American Medical Association, the Pharmaceutical Research and Manufacturers, and the American Hospital Association—each spending over $20 million per year. This is not a new or temporary dynamic. The Center for Responsive Politics analyzed federal lobbying disclosure forms in the area of health care and found 4,525 paid lobbyists—eight for each member of Congress—to influence the health reform bill in 2009.[18] Public

Citizen released an earlier report counting 673 lobbyists from the drug industry spending $91 million in reported expenses, plus over $50 million in direct mail and telemarketing. Among those lobbyists were 26 former members of Congress. About one-half of the lobbyists (342) have "revolving door" connections to the federal government (e.g., Congressional or agency staffs).[19]

The financial industry lobbying reports reveal that 1,447 of their individual lobbyists in 2009 were previous government employees, including 73 former members of Congress. The 43 House and Senate members negotiating the financial industry reform legislation in 2010 were lobbied by 56 of their former staffers. Another 59 industry lobbyists previously worked for the House or Senate Banking Committees[20] (see Chapter 14 discussion of the implications of dangers such as the 2008–10 international financial meltdown on child-related future interests).

Current law requires a one-year waiting period before contacting Congress and personally lobbying after hire. But those members serve as "consultants" during that period and are well able to wend influence even then.[21] The combination of private communications without balanced presentation of all sides, the absence of advocacy on behalf of non-profit future interests, and the prospect of discussions of future employment while still in public office or on Congressional staffs, all coalesce in a manner inimical to balanced decision-making in the interests of current and future children.

1. Legislative Passivity

State legislatures and Congress became more professional during the 20th century. Such advancement implies an independent, proactive entity able to exercise its own prerogatives on behalf of its constituents and their values. However, the size and sophistication of private lobbies have also grown, while substantial legislative resources focus on constituent services. The drafting of bills, amendments, supporting documentation, and public advocacy is dominated by the private side. In many states, legislators serve on a part-time basis while maintaining relatively full-time employment elsewhere, are in session only several months a year, and have minimal staff to help with policy decisions. The term limits movement has further increased the power of private lobbies in states where short terms are imposed. Campaign money becomes more important as new offices must be won, more power is delegated to private lobbies, and higher legislative staff turnover means more former legislative staff are hired by profit interests to influence their previous legislative committees.

Washington, D.C. is home to approximately 12,000 registered lobbyists as well as thousands of unregistered attorneys and other advocates. The percentage of full-time, professional lobbyists representing the interests of children—and only children—is estimated to be approximately one-tenth of one percent of that number. The states are similarly balanced. For example, California has more than 1,800 registered lobbyists (15 for every legislator). Two of those lobbyists represent the interests of children exclusively. The formal nomenclature of the state assigns the term "sponsor" not to the legislator carrying a bill, but to the private group proposing and supporting it.

2. Structural Problems

To be clear, the issue of decisions on the merits is not an issue that need turn on Democrat vs. Republican, or liberal vs. conservative factors. The size and degree of governmental activity is a variable separate and apart from the substantive neutrality of state actors. But that is a separate issue from the proper *bona fides* of state actors. However large and involved the "state" is, those who govern are properly not compromised by self-interest, adult group allegiances, or other extraneous factors. Ideally, they combine two necessary features—expertise sufficient to know the likely consequences of their decision, and a focus not on immediate financial impact on themselves or their friends, but long-term impact on the People they represent in a democracy.

As noted above, child advocates argue that children benefit where public decisions are made "on the merits." Such decisions are more likely to be made in the long-range public interest where other considerations do not unduly interfere with such a *bona fide* attempt. One such variable is the domination of information and advocacy by those with a vested economic stake in the policy to be decided, buttressed by campaign finance influence. Another variable may be direct economic benefit to the decision maker arranged by similar interests, including direct conflicts of interest (*e.g.*, where legislators continue law practice or other occupations that allow for financial gain from those affected by decisions made), honoraria, or job interchange (where lobbyists, legislators, and legislative staff interchange hiring and make implied or explicit job offers while public officials are still in office). These avenues of influence potentially distort decisions away from the merits.

Although published 20 years ago, the disturbing revelations of Charles Lewis remain not only applicable today, but his examples understate the degree of dubious transactions that appear to compromise decisions on the merits.

Everything I'm Telling You is Entirely Legal
by Charles Lewis[22]
The Center for Public Integrity

In 1991, the Center issued a report called "Saving for a Rainy Day." We found that 112 former members of Congress had pocketed $10 million in leftover campaign funds. Some of them bought themselves Cadillacs or Lincoln Continentals. Others used the money to pay their legal bills after being prosecuted for various ethical transgressions. But my personal favorite is that one fellow [Gene Taylor] actually opened up a museum about himself [in Sarcoxie, Mo.]

* * *

In 1994, 17 researchers, writers and editors at the Center put out an investigative report ("Well-Healed") about the lobbying for and against the Clinton health care plan, in which we tracked the Washington activities of 660 interest groups trying to influence the legislative process. We found that 80 former U.S. officials had tripled, quadrupled, quintupled their salaries by going to work for health care-related interests.

Health care companies had contributed $30 million to congressional campaigns in the two years leading up to the Clinton health care legislation. They took members of Congress on 181 all-expenses-paid trips to nice locales such as Honolulu, the Caribbean and, well, Tampa, to "educate" them about health care, of course.

Forty members of Congress sitting on the five key committees with jurisdiction over health care reform legislation owned stock in various companies that would be affected by any new laws—some members actually were buying and selling pharmaceutical and other health care-related stocks during the mark-up sessions. One interest group, the people that brought America the "Harry and Louise" commercials, the Health Insurance Association of America, made a deal with then-House Ways and Means Committee Chairman Dan Rostenkowski. HIAA would pull the highly effective TV ads critical of the proposed reform legislation from the airwaves if the committee would make substantive policy concessions to the insurance industry. It was a done deal. The only reason it fell apart is that Rostenkowski was indicted on unrelated federal charges.

Remember, everything that I am telling you is entirely legal. "The Buying of the Congress"

Some politicians and their patrons would have you believe that all of this money and fund raising does not affect public policies that are enacted. Well, in 1998, 36 researchers, writers and editors at the Center for Public Integrity produced a book, *The Buying of the Congress.* It showed in stunning example after example that, on important health, safety, environmental and financial issues that affect every American's daily life, Congress frequently sides with powerful special interests, to our detriment. This book, unfortunately, was released in Washington the same day that Kenneth Starr released his report about Monica Lewinsky. I hate when that happens.

But we looked at the cost of groceries and how certain items cost more because of various deals with donors in Congress. Cable TV rates are higher because of legislation pushed by the cable industry....

Pay attention to state capitols

For example, Americans need to pay more attention to what's happening in their state capitols. Last year, state governments enacted 25,000 bills and collected $470 billion in taxes....

We called and wrote to every state legislator in the U.S., asking about his or her personal financial interests. One state lawmaker was so angry that we were asking these basic, public interest questions that he actually had his mother call us: "Why are you calling my son?" And then he had the state Senate majority leader call us, and he asked, "Why are you harassing one of my members?" We were just asking simple, clarifying-type questions about his disclosure form.

Roughly 10 people at the Center for Public Integrity worked on this project for more than two years. What did we find? That literally hundreds of state lawmakers are engaged in unabashed self-dealing, all legal, of course, because they write the laws. That more than one in five state legislators today sits on a legislative committee that regulates his or her professional or business interest. At least 18 percent of state lawmakers have financial ties to businesses or organizations that lobby state government. Nearly one in four state legislators receives income from a government agency other than the state legislature.

* * *

Questions for Discussion

1. Courts have *ex parte* contact restrictions to prohibit one party in a proceeding from privately communicating with a judge. The concept is to allow open examination of a matter where all parties hear what others say, with the right to cross-examine and rebut. Should some of these elements be introduced into the legislative branch, at least as to bills currently before a committee? Would such a

change elevate the importance of open hearings and lessen the disproportionate influence of special interests meeting privately with legislators?

2. Should Congress and state legislators be restricted from working for industries with business before their bodies for at least one or two years after they leave office? Should the moratorium be longer? Should they be limited in the direct lobbying of their former colleagues?

3. Currently, we allow profit stake interests to deduct lobbying expenses as a "normal business expense." We also exempt industry and trade groups of competitors organized to influence government from antitrust laws. Such groups have formed political action committees, institutes, and joint lobbying enterprises under first amendment dispensation and as an exception to federal and state antitrust laws (the "*Noerr-Pennington*" doctrine). Accordingly, many such associations assess themselves sums for lobbying and those costs are passed on to consumers as a *de facto* industry-wide assessment. At the same time, we prohibit or limit charities with a lesser profit stake in public policy from lobbying legislatures or agencies. What are the arguments for and against the reversal of those two social policies: tax profit stake lobbying expenses, but permit charities or others without a profit stake in public policy to participate free from tax status penalty or other sanction? What would be the long-range effect of such a change on the influence of children and other future interests before legislatures and agencies?

C. CHILD ADVOCACY AND THE COURTS

1. Children and Standing to Litigate

Contrary to common belief, children theoretically have standing to sue and to be sued in court---that is, their property, liberty, and interests may be adjudicated. However, for the same reason immaturity limits the enforcement of a contract against child signators, their ability to gain access to courts is limited. Children are grouped with incompetent adults in their presumed incapacity to understand legal procedures. Accordingly, they require adult assistance to initiate or defend lawsuits. Historically, a plaintiff child sued through a "*prochein ami*" or "next friend," while a child defendant was guided by the "*guardian ad litem*"—the term now most commonly used for all child court representation. Most states model child rules of representation after Federal Rule of Civil Procedure 17(c). Typically, parents perform this function, although a court may appoint another representative for a child—usually where parents have a conflict of interest. The usual rule is that where a court appoints such a person, compensatory fees may be awarded as well.[23]

A court-appointed *guardian ad litem* may or may not be an attorney. Courts have discretion to make or not to make such appointments. Usually, a court must be shown that "prejudice" to a child will result from the failure to make such an appointment. Precedents vest with the court the responsibility of monitoring a case to assure the welfare of child litigants, with the charge of representing the "child's best interests."

Much controversy has surrounded the role of such a *guardian ad litem* (who may decline to represent a child's expressed preferences) *vis-a-vis* a traditional attorney (who has a fiduciary duty to the client first and foremost and is more obligated to represent the expressed desires of the client). The typical conundrum is framed as follows: Where the *guardian ad litem* is an attorney, but believes that the child's preferences are irrational or not in his best interests, what is the proper course of action?

But larger questions are raised by the *guardian ad litem* mechanism for child representation. As discussed in Chapters 8 and 10, children who are accused of crimes and face punishment by the state are entitled to an attorney. But otherwise, representation of children is limited. Most states require representation of an allegedly abused or neglected child by a *guardian ad litem*, but many states do not require that person to be an attorney. This is in contrast to the universal practice of appointing counsel for all parents whose parental rights are adjudicated. Some jurisdictions devolve child representation onto volunteers. Others designate the attorney for the state agency removing the child to serve as the *guardian ad litem*. However, this practice is problematic given the federally-established obligation of the local agencies represented by the same office to provide "reasonable services" for parents to facilitate reunification and to protect children who may be returned (see Chapter 8). Such agencies often have budgetary constraints, and the same legal office representing them as counsel may be placed in an irreconcilable conflict between the interests of their agency client (*e.g.*, to avoid imposition of expense) and their child client who needs services for health and safety protection.

Courts are generally authorized to appoint *guardians ad litem* to represent children where a child is an "indispensable party" or has a substantial interest in the outcome of a suit (*e.g.*, insurance policy beneficiary, inheritee, survivorship claimant). Where such a guardian is not an attorney, he or she has intrinsic authority to manage the lawsuit, including the retention of counsel. However, few jurisdictions appoint compensated counsel for children outside of juvenile court. For example, although critical to a child's future, family court disputes involving custody, probate court disputes involving inheritance, and other proceedings do not in the normal course result in a *guardian ad litem* appointment.[24] Some jurisdictions will appoint counsel in special circumstances, but even where court rules may so allow, actual representation is problematical. For example, California has a court rule to provide counsel for children in Family Court where issues arise important to them—but those appointments are not in fact made unless the parents can provide remuneration for that representation.[25]

Children suffer substantial practical barriers to court access beyond eligibility for court-appointed *guardians ad litem*. Those impediments include: (1) the catch-22 problem of gaining access to a court to enable the appointment of such a representative; (2) the anti-solicitation standards applicable to the bar which inhibit attorney-initiated contact; (3) the lack of sophistication or contacts to arrange representation for themselves; (4) the confidentiality of juvenile court proceedings—particularly in dependency court where children are victims and visibility may serve their interests in court and outside of it; (5) the lack of financial resources available to children to compensate counsel; and (6) the limitation of legal authority to speak for a child outside of parental consent or even, perhaps, to bring a matter to court to allow the court to make an appointment.

Cases involving children reach the courts in one of three ways: First, a parent or guardian may bring an action on behalf of children (usually arranging for counsel). Second, children may be brought before the court by other persons (as in juvenile, family, or probate court, or when a child is sued). Third, children may benefit from an *en masse* suit which may include or assist them. The third category of lawsuit in turn depends upon access to the courts for class actions, petitions for writs of mandate, civil rights injunctive actions, or other remedies which operate to change underlying policies (as discussed below). The class or categorical court access opportunity is particularly important for children given the inherent weaknesses in the first two avenues of judicial redress.

In general, the doctrine of *stare decisis* applies to court holdings, allowing a single case to have a mass impact on similar disputes or issues. However, the courts are passive. They entertain only such actions as are brought before them by litigants with the standing, ability and resources to litigate. Such individual cases need to be brought in order to reach appellate resolution and inclusion into the body of American law. Where a given group has limited access, relatively few such decisions will be rendered to adjudicate their interests and hence to produce a *stare decisis* benefit.

Mass remedy court options that include children as intended beneficiaries may allow effective court decisions defining their rights and providing remedies where these rights are abridged.

2. Right to Sue *En Masse*

a. Legal Aid Actions

"None of the funds appropriated...to the Legal Services Corporation may be used to provide financial assistance to any person or entity...that initiates or participates in a class action suit."[26] This 1996 federal restriction was copied by Texas and other states. The attorneys it affects constitute the primary source of legal representation in civil matters for impoverished citizens.

The Legal Services Corporation restriction was revised slightly after 1996 to allow class actions, but only where approved by the administration (the Corporation's appointed officials nationally). The 1996 statute also included three additional measures which in effect restrict access to the courts on behalf of impoverished children. First, Congress provided that "None of the funds appropriated...to the Legal Services Corporation may be used to provide financial assistance to any person or entity...unless such person or entity agrees...not [to] accept employment resulting from in-person unsolicited advice...[to] take legal action."[27] The Legal Services Corporation then expanded this anti-personal outreach provision to prohibit counsel from communicating about available legal rights by telephone or through the mail

(45 CFR Section 1638.2). These restrictions go beyond the "solicitation" limitation applicable to attorneys, and may be unconstitutional.[28]

Second, the 1996 statute provided that "None of the funds appropriated... may be used to provide financial assistance to any person or entity...that claims... or collects and retains, attorneys' fees pursuant to federal or state law permitting or requiring ...such fees."[29] In other words, successful counsel may not collect fees from a defendant even where state or federal law otherwise allows or requires it. Children are generally unable to pay legal costs or to contribute to their legal representation. The possibility of recompense from the other party (which requires the beneficiary to prevail) may allow substantially more such actions to be brought. The possibility that such actions will provide their own costs and fees makes them feasible beyond the limited appropriations provided to the Legal Services Corporation.

A third provision was enacted applicable to any court challenge of federal welfare statutes. Congress was particularly concerned with eliminating judicial challenges to the welfare reform provisions of the Personal Responsibility and Work Opportunity Reconciliation Act of 1996. That statute changed the Aid for Families with Dependent Children (AFDC) entitlement safety net for children to a capped, conditional, and time-limited Temporary Assistance to Needy Families (TANF) system which began in 1997 and remains in effect. Approximately 70% of TANF beneficiaries are children. Together with the food stamp program, TANF provides the basic safety net for the majority of children living in families below the federal poverty line (see discussion in Chapter 3). As to this statutory scheme, an individual client may seek specific relief, but no challenge may be brought to the law, including a constitutional challenge. This provision raises the same objections as do the class action and broad outreach bans. Its constitutionality was tested in *Velazquez*, below. The issues framed for court review pertained to access, the First Amendment, and the separation of powers doctrine. Can one branch prohibit another from checking it? Or is the Legal Services Corporation a discretionary benefit which may be provided or not—and accordingly may be, conditioned on the surrender of judicial review?

Legal Services Corporation v. Carmen Velazquez
531 U.S. 533 (2001)

JUSTICE KENNEDY delivered the opinion of the Court.

In 1974, Congress enacted the Legal Services Corporation Act, 88 Stat. 378, 42 U.S.C. § 2996 et seq. The Act establishes the Legal Services Corporation (LSC) as a District of Columbia nonprofit corporation. LSC's mission is to distribute funds appropriated by Congress to eligible local grantee organizations "for the purpose of providing financial support for legal assistance in noncriminal proceedings or matters to persons financially unable to afford legal assistance." § 2996b(a).

LSC grantees consist of hundreds of local organizations governed, in the typical case, by local boards of directors. In many instances the grantees are funded by a combination of LSC funds and other public or private sources. The grantee organizations hire and supervise lawyers to provide free legal assistance to indigent clients. Each year LSC appropriates funds to grantees or recipients that hire and supervise lawyers for various professional activities, including representation of indigent clients seeking welfare benefits.

This suit requires us to decide whether one of the conditions imposed by Congress on the use of LSC funds violates the First Amendment rights of LSC grantees and their clients. For purposes of our decision, the restriction, to be quoted in further detail, prohibits legal representation funded by recipients of LSC moneys if the representation involves an effort to amend or otherwise challenge existing welfare law. As interpreted by the LSC and by the Government, the restriction prevents an attorney from arguing to a court that a state statute conflicts with a federal statute or that either a state or federal statute by its terms or in its application is violative of the United States Constitution.

...We agree that the restriction violates the First Amendment, and we affirm the judgment of the Court of Appeals.

* * *

The restrictions at issue were part of a compromise set of restrictions enacted in the Omnibus Consolidated Rescissions and Appropriations Act of 1996 (1996 Act), § 504, 110 Stat. 1321-53, and continued in each subsequent annual appropriations Act. The relevant portion of § 504(a)(16) prohibits funding of any organization

"that initiates legal representation or participates in any other way, in litigation, lobbying, or rulemaking, involving an effort to reform a Federal or State welfare system, except that this paragraph shall not be construed to preclude a recipient from representing an individual eligible client who is seeking specific relief from a welfare agency if such relief does not involve an effort to amend or otherwise challenge existing law in effect on the date of the initiation of the representation."

The prohibitions apply to all of the activities of an LSC grantee, including those paid for by non-LSC funds. §§ 504(d)(1) and (2). We are concerned with the statutory provision which excludes LSC representation in cases which "involve an effort to amend or otherwise challenge existing law in effect on the date of the initiation of the representation."

In 1997, LSC adopted final regulations clarifying § 504(a)(16). 45 CFR pt. 1639 (1999). LSC interpreted the statutory provision to allow indigent clients to challenge welfare agency determinations of benefit ineligibility under interpretations of existing law. For example, an LSC grantee could represent a welfare claimant who argued that an agency made an erroneous factual determination or that an agency misread or misapplied a term contained in an existing welfare statute. According to LSC, a grantee in that position could argue as well that an agency policy violated existing law. § 1639.4. Under LSC's interpretation, however, grantees could not accept representations designed to change welfare laws, much less argue against the constitutionality or statutory validity of those laws....Even in cases where constitutional or statutory challenges became apparent after representation was well under way, LSC advised that its attorneys must withdraw. *Ibid.*

* * *

....[T]he LSC program was designed to facilitate private speech, not to promote a governmental message. Congress funded LSC grantees to provide attorneys to represent the interests of indigent clients. In the specific context of § 504(a)(16) suits for benefits, an LSC-funded attorney speaks on the behalf of the client in a claim against the government for welfare benefits. The lawyer is not the government's speaker. The

attorney defending the decision to deny benefits will deliver the government's message in the litigation. The LSC lawyer, however, speaks on the behalf of his or her private, indigent client. Cf. *Polk County v. Dodson*, 454 U.S. 312, 321-322... (1981) (holding that a public defender does not act "under color of state law" because he "works under canons of professional responsibility that mandate his exercise of independent judgment on behalf of the client" and because there is an "assumption that counsel will be free of state control").

The Government has designed this program to use the legal profession and the established Judiciary of the States and the Federal Government to accomplish its end of assisting welfare claimants in determination or receipt of their benefits. The advice from the attorney to the client and the advocacy by the attorney to the courts cannot be classified as governmental speech even under a generous understanding of the concept. In this vital respect this suit is distinguishable from *Rust.*

The private nature of the speech involved here, and the extent of LSC's regulation of private expression, are indicated further by the circumstance that the Government seeks to use an existing medium of expression and to control it, in a class of cases, in ways which distort its usual functioning.

* * *

By providing subsidies to LSC, the Government seeks to facilitate suits for benefits by using the State and Federal courts and the independent bar on which those courts depend for the proper performance of their duties and responsibilities. Restricting LSC attorneys in advising their clients and in presenting arguments and analyses to the courts distorts the legal system by altering the traditional role of the attorneys in much the same way broadcast systems or student publication networks were changed in the limited forum cases we have cited. Just as government in those cases could not elect to use a broadcasting network or a college publication structure in a regime which prohibits speech necessary to the proper functioning of those systems, see *Arkansas Ed. Television Comm'n, supra,* and *Rosenberger, supra* it may not design a subsidy to effect this serious and fundamental restriction on advocacy of attorneys and the functioning of the judiciary.

LSC has advised us, furthermore, that upon determining a question of statutory validity is present in any anticipated or pending case or controversy, the LSC-funded attorney must cease the representation at once. This is true whether the validity issue becomes apparent during initial attorney-client consultations or in the midst of litigation proceedings. A disturbing example of the restriction was discussed during oral argument before the Court. It is well understood that when there are two reasonable constructions for a statute, yet one raises a constitutional question, the Court should prefer the interpretation which avoids the constitutional issue. *Gomez v. United States,* 490 U.S. 858, 864...(1989); *Ashwander v. TVA,* 297 U.S. 288, 346-348...(1936) (Brandeis, J., concurring). Yet, as the LSC advised the Court, if, during litigation, a judge were to ask an LSC attorney whether there was a constitutional concern, the LSC attorney simply could not answer. Tr. of Oral Arg. 8-9.

Interpretation of the law and the Constitution is the primary mission of the judiciary when it acts within the sphere of its authority to resolve a case or controversy. *Marbury v. Madison,* 5 U.S. 137... (1803) ("It is emphatically the province and the duty of the judicial department to say what the law is"). An informed, independent judiciary presumes an informed, independent bar. Under § 504(a)(16), however, cases would be presented by LSC attorneys who could not advise the courts of serious questions of statutory validity. The disability is inconsistent with the proposition that attorneys should present all the reasonable and well-grounded arguments necessary for proper resolution of the case. By seeking to prohibit the analysis of certain legal issues and to truncate presentation to the courts, the enactment under review prohibits speech and expression upon which courts must depend for the proper exercise of the judicial power. Congress cannot wrest the law from the Constitution which is its source. "Those then who controvert the principle that the constitution is to be considered, in court, as a paramount law, are reduced to the necessity of maintaining that courts must close their eyes on the constitution, and see only the law." *Id.* at 178.

The restriction imposed by the statute here threatens severe impairment of the judicial function. Section 504(a)(16) sifts out cases presenting constitutional challenges in order to insulate the Government's laws from judicial inquiry. If the restriction on speech and legal advice were to stand, the result would be two tiers of cases. In cases where LSC counsel were attorneys of record, there would be lingering doubt whether the truncated representation had resulted in complete analysis of the case, full advice to the client, and proper presentation to the court. The courts and the public would come to question the adequacy and fairness of professional representations when the attorney, either consciously to comply with this statute or unconsciously to continue the representation despite the statute, avoided all reference to questions of statutory validity and constitutional authority. A scheme so inconsistent with accepted separation-of-powers principles is an insufficient basis to sustain or uphold the restriction on speech.

* * *

The restriction on speech is even more problematic because in cases where the attorney withdraws from a representation, the client is unlikely to find other counsel. The explicit premise for providing LSC attorneys is the necessity to make available representation "to persons financially unable to afford legal assistance." 42 § 2996(a)(3). There often will be no alternative source for the client to receive vital information respecting constitutional and statutory rights bearing upon claimed benefits. Thus, with respect to the litigation services Congress has funded, there is no alternative channel for expression of the advocacy Congress seeks to restrict.

Congress was not required to fund an LSC attorney to represent indigent clients; and when it did so, it was not required to fund the whole range of legal representations or relationships. The LSC and the United States, however, in effect ask us to permit Congress to define the scope of the litigation it funds to exclude certain vital theories and ideas. The attempted restriction is designed to insulate the Government's interpretation of the Constitution from judicial challenge. The Constitution does not permit the Government to confine litigants and their attorneys in this manner. We must be vigilant when Congress imposes rules and conditions which in effect insulate its own laws from legitimate judicial challenge. Where private speech is involved, even Congress' antecedent funding decision cannot be aimed at the suppression of ideas thought inimical to the Government's own interest....

The judgment of the Court of Appeals is Affirmed.

JUSTICE SCALIA, with whom **THE CHIEF JUSTICE**, **JUSTICE O'CONNOR**, and **JUSTICE THOMAS** join, dissenting.

Section 504(a)(16) of the Omnibus Consolidated Rescissions and Appropriations Act of 1996 (Appropriations Act) defines the scope of a federal spending program. It does not directly regulate speech, and it neither establishes a public forum nor discriminates on the basis of viewpoint. The Court agrees with all this, yet applies a novel and unsupportable interpretation of our public-forum precedents to declare § 504(a)(16) facially unconstitutional. This holding not only has no foundation in our jurisprudence; it is flatly contradicted by a recent decision that is on all fours with the present case. Having found the limitation upon the spending program unconstitutional, the Court then declines to consider the question of severability, allowing a judgment to stand that lets the program go forward under a version of the statute Congress never enacted. I respectfully dissent from both aspects of the judgment.

* * *

The LSC Act is a federal subsidy program, not a federal regulatory program, and "there is a basic difference between [the two]." *Maher v. Roe*, 432 U.S. 464, 475... (1977) Regulations directly restrict speech; subsidies do not. Subsidies, it is true, may indirectly abridge speech, but only if the funding scheme is "manipulated" to have a "coercive effect" on those who do not hold the subsidized position....

In *Rust v. Sullivan, supra,* the Court applied these principles to a statutory scheme that is in all relevant respects indistinguishable from § 504(a)(16). The statute in Rust authorized grants for the provision of family planning services, but provided that "none of the funds...shall be used in programs where abortion is a method of family planning." *Id.* at 178. Valid regulations implementing the statute required funding recipients to refer pregnant clients "for appropriate prenatal...services by furnishing a list of available providers that promote the welfare of mother and unborn child," but forbade them to refer a pregnant woman specifically to an abortion provider, even upon request. *Id.* at 180. We rejected a First Amendment free-speech challenge to the funding scheme, explaining that "the Government can, without violating the Constitution, selectively fund a program to encourage certain activities it believes to be in the public interest, without at the same time funding an alternative program which seeks to deal with the problem another way." *Id.* at 193. This was not, we said, the type of "discrimination on the basis of viewpoint" that triggers strict scrutiny, ibid., because the "decision not to subsidize the exercise of a fundamental right does not infringe the right," *ibid.* (quoting *Regan v. Taxation With Representation of Wash., supra,* at 549).

The same is true here...

* * *

The Court's "nondistortion" principle is also wrong on the facts, since there is no basis for believing that § 504(a)(16), by causing "cases [to] be presented by LSC attorneys who cannot advise the courts of serious questions of statutory validity," *ante,* at 11, will distort the operation of the courts. It may well be that the bar of § 504(a)(16) will cause LSC-funded attorneys to decline or to withdraw from cases that involve statutory validity. But that means at most that fewer statutory challenges to welfare laws will be presented to the courts because of the unavailability of free legal services for that purpose. So what? The same result would ensue from excluding LSC-funded lawyers from welfare litigation entirely....

Nor will the judicial opinions produced by LSC cases systematically distort the interpretation of welfare laws. Judicial decisions do not stand as binding "precedent" for points that were not raised, not argued, and hence not analyzed....

Finally, the Court is troubled "because in cases where the attorney withdraws from a representation, the client is unlikely to find other counsel."....That is surely irrelevant, since it leaves the welfare recipient in no worse condition than he would have been in had the LSC program never been enacted. Respondents properly concede that even if welfare claimants cannot obtain a lawyer anywhere else, the Government is not required to provide one.

Questions for Discussion

1. What if the political consequence of *Velazquez* was Congressional termination of the Legal Services Corporation? Could the Court prevent such an outcome?

2. Some Legal Aid offices formed separate voluntary entities to file class actions where warranted; would the dissenters allow Congress to foreclose that alternative option?

3. Legal Aid attorneys argued that if they are prohibited from a mass remedy, or from constitutional challenge to a welfare provision, children are effectively deprived of the societal check provided by the courts for other persons, implying equal protection breach. What is the status of children for Fourteenth Amendment equal protection purposes? Would a "due process" argument be stronger?

4. In 2010, the Ninth Circuit upheld the other three Congressional 1996 restrictions from a First Amendment constitutional challenge. The 2–1 decision in *Legal Services of Oregon v. Legal Services Corporation,* 608 F.3d 1084 (2010), upheld the statute's provisions that prohibit federal legal services funded entities from soliciting clients, seeking fees (even where statutorily authorized), or bringing (or participating in) class actions. Why are the class action and attorney fee bars not voided by separation of powers principles? Class action procedure and public interest attorneys fees implicate how the cases before the courts are to be organized and how counsel is to be compensated for reasonable access. Why is that not the province of the courts, and not subject to Congressional co-equal branch dictation? Is not the class action governed by Rule 23 of the Supreme Court-adopted Federal Rules of Civil Procedure?

b. Current Barriers to Class Actions for Children

Federal Rule of Civil Procedure 23 provides the basis for class actions in federal court, and is roughly replicated in most states. The rule is divided into three kinds of class actions as specified by Rule 23(b)(1), (b)(2), and (b)(3), respectively. All three forms of class action require a class representative who is a part of the class and who is an "adequate class representative." There must be questions of fact and law common to all members of the class to allow the outcome to apply to all those within it. There must be an adequate number of class members ("numerosity") to make a consolidated suit naming each member impractical. The class must be "certified" by the court as qualifying, and limited discovery may be allowed on issues such as adequate commonality, adequacy of representation, and other requirements.

Once certified, the representative must give court-approved notice of the class to those included within it to allow members to "opt out" of the case in order to pursue their remedies separately if they wish to do so. Any final settlement or judgment will only occur after additional notice and public proceedings. These basic requirements are necessary to give the final judgment binding effect on all members of the class. Absent these elements, the action would potentially foreclose the due process rights of absent class members by persons with different claims, not adequately representing their interests, or by failing to provide notice of the case or its possible outcome.

The third of these three specified types—the Rule 23(b)(3) class action—has suffered from "add-on" requirements which have limited its application. This third type of class action authorizes damage actions at law on behalf of a class of persons. That common judicial remedy not only requires common questions of fact and law, but that such questions "predominate." Such actions must be "manageable," and must be "superior" to alternative remedies capable of redressing the stated grievance. Finally, in most cases, notice must be to individuals rather than by publication or other indirect means and must be financed by the plaintiff.

These add-on requirements do not apply as stringently to the common fund and injunctive (e.g., civil rights) actions respectively authorized by Rule 23(b)(1) and (b)(2).[30] Nevertheless, any class certification will require an adequate class representative who is a part of the class and whose claims are typical of the class claims. As such, many of the six impediments to individual access to the courts by children discussed above can also inhibit the bringing of actions on behalf of children. However, where a parent or *guardian ad litem* may be willing to vindicate the rights of a child, or where an organization has standing to bring suit, the class action mechanism may allow the direct application of a judgment outcome to a large number of children similarly affected.

The bringing of a single action to vindicate the rights of a group of children across state lines is possible where multi-district assignment allows it. In addition, some authority exists for a state to include within its class action case members who reside in other states if the cause of action arose within its borders and the statutes of other states where class members reside are consistent with the state law invoked in the host state, subject to some new limitations by the Class Action Fairness Act of 2005, discussed below.[31]

Marisol A. v. Giuliani

126 F.3d 372 (2d Cir. 1997)

OPINION: **PER CURIAM FEINBERG WALKER LEVAL**, Circuit Judges

...The defendants claim that certification of the plaintiff class was improper because the plaintiffs failed to demonstrate that the certified class adhered to the strictures of Fed. R. Civ. P. 23. Because we find that the district court, in certifying the class at this point in the litigation, has not abused its discretion, we affirm the decision of the district court.

BACKGROUND

Familiarity with the painful allegations of the named plaintiffs, eleven children who claim they were deprived of the services of the New York City child welfare system to their extreme detriment, is presumed....Briefly, in December 1995, the named plaintiffs brought this action by and through their adult next friends seeking declaratory and injunctive relief against the defendants to redress injuries caused by the alleged systemic failures of the City's child welfare system....The complaint charged that the manner in which the defendants operate that system violates a diverse array of federal and state laws, namely, the First, Ninth and Fourteenth Amendments to the United States Constitution; the Adoption Assistance and Child Welfare Act of 1980, 42 U.S.C. §§ 620-628, 670-679a; the Child Abuse Prevention and Treatment Act, 42 U.S.C. §§ 5101-5106a; the Early and Periodic Screening, Diagnosis and Treatment program of the Medicaid Act, 42 U.S.C. §§ 1396a, 1396d(a) & (r); the Multiethnic Placement Act of 1994, 42 U.S.C. § 622(b)(9); the Americans with Disabilities Act, 42 U.S.C. §§ 12101 et seq.; the Rehabilitation Act of 1973, 29 U.S.C. §§ 794, 794a; Article XVII of the New York State Constitution; the New York State Social Services Law Articles 2, 3, 6 & 7,; the New York State Family Court Act, Articles 6 & 10; and various state regulations, 18 N.Y.C.R.R. §§ 400-484.

Pursuant to Rule 23(b)(2) of the Federal Rules of Civil Procedure, the plaintiffs asked the district court to certify a class of similarly situated children who are the legal responsibility of the child welfare system. The defendants, maintaining that the requirements of Rule 23 were not met, opposed class certification. In an order dated July 3, 1996, the district court certified a plaintiff class consisting of

> All children who are or will be in the custody of the New York City Administration for Children's Services ("ACS"), and those children who, while not in the custody of ACS, are or will be at risk of neglect or abuse and whose status is or should be known to ACS.

DISCUSSION

* * *

The defendants argue that, except at the grossest level of generality, there are no questions of law or fact common to the class and that no named plaintiff may convincingly assert that his or her claim is typical of the class. See *K.L. ex rel. Dixon v. Valdez,* 167 F.R.D. 688, 691 (D.N.M. 1996) (refusing to certify similar class bringing variety of legal claims where "no named Plaintiff and no putative class member has allegedly suffered violations of all or even most of the statutory and constitutional rights listed."). The defendants point out that each named plaintiff challenges a different aspect of the child welfare system. These include allegations of inadequate training and supervision of foster parents, the failure to properly investigate reports of suspected neglect and abuse, unconscionable delay in removing children from abusive homes, and the inability to secure appropriate placements for adoption, see *Marisol A.,* 929 F. Supp. at 669-72. The claimed deficiencies implicate different statutory, constitutional and regulatory schemes. Further, the defendants note that no single plaintiff (named or otherwise) is affected by each and every legal violation alleged in the complaint, and that no single specific legal claim identified by the plaintiffs affects every member of the class. Thus, in light of the broad range of injuries which the named plaintiffs allegedly have suffered, defendants argue that the commonality and typicality requirements have not been satisfied.

* * *

We find that the district court did not abuse its discretion by certifying this class at this time, notwithstanding our view, expressed in Section III, infra, that the creation of subclasses will be necessary. Three considerations compel this conclusion. First, "Rule 23 is given liberal rather than restrictive construction, and courts are to adopt a standard of flexibility ...." *Sharif ex rel. Salahuddin v. New York State Educ. Dep't.*, 127 F.R.D. 84, 87 (S.D.N.Y. 1989). The rule's inherent flexibility, and the district court's ability to manage the litigation as it develops, counsel against decertification.

Second, although the district court's generalized characterization of the claims raised by the plaintiffs stretches the notions of commonality and typicality, we simply cannot say that these claims are so unrelated that their aggregation necessarily violates Rule 23. The plaintiffs allege that their injuries derive from a unitary course of conduct by a single system, and the district court agreed. At this stage of the litigation, we see no basis for finding that the district court abused its discretion in this regard.

Finally, we note that the only other circuit court which has considered this very question has held that it was an abuse of discretion not to certify a class nearly identical to the one considered here. See *Baby Neal*, 43 F.3d at 64-65; cf. *Jeanine B. ex rel. Blondis v. Thompson*, 877 F. Supp. 1268, 1287 (E.D. Wisc. 1995) (certifying two subclasses, one of children in foster care and one of children not in foster care about whom the county had received reports of neglect or abuse, where plaintiffs "challenged the operating practices of the...foster-care system, and generally alleged that the...program is systematically depriving children of their legal rights."). Although we believe that the district court is near the boundary of the class action device, we are not prepared to say that it has crossed into forbidden territory.

D. Rule 23(b)(2)

Class certification is appropriate where the defendant has acted or refused to act on grounds generally applicable to the class, thereby making injunctive or declaratory relief appropriate. Fed. R. Civ. P. 23(b)(2). Defendants argue that because the plaintiffs have alleged differing harms requiring individual remedies, no injunction will be appropriate for the entire class. Defendants further claim that due to the unique circumstances of each plaintiff's experience with the child welfare system, the defendants have not acted on grounds generally applicable to the class.

and systemic failures, the district court did not abuse its discretion in certifying a 23(b)(2) class at this stage of the litigation. See *Comer v. Cisneros*, 37 F.3d at 796 (Rule 23(b)(2) satisfied "because the plaintiffs seek injunctive relief and they predicate the lawsuit on the defendants' acts and omissions with respect to" the class); *Jeanine B.*,

We disagree. Insofar as the deficiencies of the child welfare system stem from central 877 F. Supp. at 1288 ("civil rights cases seeking broad declaratory or injunctive relief for a large and amorphous class...fall squarely into the category" of 23(b)(2) actions); Advisory Committee Note to Subdivision (b)(2) ("Illustrative are various actions...where a party is charged with discriminating unlawfully against a class, usually one whose members are incapable of specific enumeration.").

* * *

As presently certified, the class certified by the district court implicitly consists of two large subclasses. The first is comprised of "children who are or will be in the custody of the New York City Administration for Children's Services ("ACS");" the second is comprised of "those children who, while not in the custody of ACS, are or will be at risk of neglect or abuse and whose status is or should be known to ACS." *Marisol A.*, 95 Civ 10533 at 3 (A628). But in reality, each of these subclasses consists of smaller groups of children, each of which has separate and discrete legal claims pursuant to particular federal and state constitutional, statutory, and regulatory obligations of the defendants. Each claim, in turn, is based on one or more specific alleged deficiencies of the child welfare system.

> Well in advance of trial, the district court must engage in a rigorous analysis of the plaintiffs' legal claims and factual circumstances in order to ensure that appropriate subclasses are identified, that each subclass is tied to one or more suitable representatives, and that each subclass satisfies Rule 23(b)(2)....

* * *

Castano v. American Tobacco Co.
84 F.3d 734 (5th Cir. 1996)

OPINION: **JERRY E. SMITH**, Circuit Judge:

In what may be the largest class action ever attempted in federal court, the district court in this case embarked "on a road certainly less traveled, if ever taken at all,"...and entered a class certification order. The court defined the class as:

(a) All nicotine-dependent persons in the United States...who have purchased and smoked cigarettes manufactured by the defendants;

(b) the estates, representatives, and administrators of these nicotine-dependent cigarette smokers; and

(c) the spouses, children, relatives and "significant others" of these nicotine-dependent cigarette smokers as their heirs or survivors.

Id. at 560-61. The plaintiffs limit the claims to years since 1943.[1]

This matter comes before us on interlocutory appeal, under *28 U.S.C. § 292(b)*, of the class certification order. Concluding that the district court abused its discretion in certifying the class, we reverse.

I.
A. The Class Complaint

The plaintiffs...filed this class complaint against the defendant tobacco companies... and the Tobacco Institute, Inc., seeking compensation solely for the injury of nicotine addiction. The gravamen of their complaint is the novel and wholly untested theory that the defendants fraudulently failed to inform consumers that nicotine is addictive and manipulated the level of nicotine in cigarettes to sustain their addictive nature. The class complaint alleges nine causes of action: fraud and deceit, negligent misrepresentation, intentional infliction of emotional distress, negligence and negligent infliction of emotional distress, violation of state consumer protection statutes, breach of express warranty, breach of implied warranty, strict product liability, and redhibition pursuant to the Louisiana Civil Code.

The plaintiffs seek compensatory[4] and punitive damages[5] and attorneys' fees.[6] In addition, the plaintiffs seek equitable relief for fraud and deceit, negligent misrepresentation, violation of consumer protection statutes, and breach of express and implied warranty. The equitable remedies include a declaration that defendants are financially responsible for notifying all class members of nicotine's addictive nature, a declaration that the defendants manipulated nicotine levels with the intent to sustain the addiction of plaintiffs and the class members, an order that the defendants disgorge any profits made from the sale of cigarettes, restitution for sums paid for cigarettes, and the establishment of a medical monitoring fund.

The plaintiffs initially defined the class as "all nicotine dependent persons in the United States," including current, former and deceased smokers since 1943. Plaintiffs conceded that addiction would have to be proven by each class member; the defendants argued that proving class membership will require individual mini-trials to determine whether addiction actually exists.

In response to the district court's inquiry, the plaintiffs proposed a four-phase trial plan.[7] In phase 1, a jury would determine common issues of "core liability." Phase 1 issues would include...(1) issues of law and fact relating to defendants' course of conduct, fraud, and negligence liability (including duty, standard of care, misrepresentation and concealment, knowledge, intent); (2) issues of law and fact relating to defendants'

[margin annotation: πs claim]

[margin annotation: πs claimed damages]

alleged conspiracy and concert of action; (3) issues of fact relating to the addictive nature/dependency creating characteristics and properties of nicotine; (4) issues of fact relating to nicotine cigarettes as defective products; (5) issues of fact relating to whether defendants' wrongful conduct was intentional, reckless or negligent; (6) identifying which defendants specifically targeted their advertising and promotional efforts to particular groups (e.g., youths, minorities, etc.); (7) availability of a presumption of reliance; (8) whether defendants' misrepresentations/suppression of fact and/or of addictive properties of nicotine preclude availability of a "personal choice" defense; (9) defendants' liability for actual damages, and the categories of such damages; (10) defendants' liability for emotional distress damages; and (11) defendants' liability for punitive damages.

* * *

B. The Class Certification Order

Following extensive briefing, the district court granted, in part, plaintiffs' motion for class certification, concluding that the prerequisites of FED. R. CIV. P. 23(a) had been met.[9] The court rejected certification, under FED. R. CIV. P. 23(b)(2), of the plaintiffs' claim for equitable relief, including the claim for medical monitoring. 160 F.R.D. at 552. Appellees have not cross-appealed that portion of the order.

The court did grant the plaintiffs' motion to certify the class under FED. R. CIV. P. 23(b)(3),[10] organizing the class action issues into four categories: (1) core liability; (2) injury-in-fact, proximate cause, reliance and affirmative defenses; (3) compensatory damages; and (4) punitive damages. *Id.* at 553-58. It then analyzed each category to determine whether it met the predominance and superiority requirements of rule 23(b)(3). Using its power to sever issues for certification under FED. R. CIV. P. 23(c)(4), the court certified the class on core liability and punitive damages, and certified the class conditionally pursuant to FED. R. CIV. P. 23(c)(1).

1. Core Liability Issues

The court defined core liability issues as "common factual issues [of] whether defendants knew cigarette smoking was addictive, failed to inform cigarette smokers of such, and took actions to addict cigarette smokers. Common legal issues include fraud, negligence, breach of warranty (express or implied), strict liability, and violation of consumer protection statutes." 160 F.R.D. at 553.

The court found that the predominance requirement of rule 23(b)(3) was satisfied for the core liability issues....

* * *

II

* * *

The district court erred in its analysis in two distinct ways. First, it failed to consider how variations in state law affect predominance and superiority. Second, its predominance inquiry did not include consideration of how a trial on the merits would be conducted.

Each of these defects mandates reversal. Moreover, at this time, while the tort is immature, the class complaint must be dismissed, as class certification cannot be found to be a superior method of adjudication....

* * *

A. Variations in State Law

* * *

In a multi-state class action, variations in state law may swamp any common issues and defeat predominance....

* * *

The able opinion in *School Asbestos* demonstrates what is required from a district court when variations in state law exist. There, the court affirmed class certification, despite variations in state law, because:

To meet the problem of diversity in applicable state law, class plaintiffs have undertaken an extensive analysis of the variances in products liability among the jurisdictions. That review separates the law into four categories. Even assuming additional permutations and combinations, plaintiffs have made a creditable showing, which apparently satisfied the district court, that class certification does not present insuperable obstacles. Although we have some doubt on this score, the effort may nonetheless prove successful.

A thorough review of the record demonstrates that, in this case, the district court did not properly consider how variations in state law affect predominance. The court acknowledged as much in its order granting class certification, for, in declining to make a choice of law determination, it noted that "the parties have only briefly addressed the conflict of laws issue in this matter." 160 F.R.D. at 554. Similarly, the court stated that "there has been no showing that the consumer protection statutes differ so much as to make individual issues predominate." *Id.*....

The Castano class suffers from many of the difficulties that the Georgine court found dispositive. The class members were exposed to nicotine through different products, for different amounts of time, and over different time periods. Each class member's knowledge about the effects of smoking differs, and each plaintiff began smoking for different reasons. Each of these factual differences impacts the application of legal rules such as causation, reliance, comparative fault, and other affirmative defenses.

Variations in state law magnify the differences. In a fraud claim, some states require justifiable reliance on a misrepresentation, while others require reasonable reliance States impose varying standards to determine when there is a duty to disclose facts. Products liability law also differs among states. Some states do not recognize strict liability. Differences in affirmative defenses also exist. Assumption of risk is a complete defense to a products claim in some states. In others, it is a part of comparative fault analysis. Others follow a "greater fault bar, and still others use an "equal fault bar."

Despite these overwhelming individual issues, common issues might predominate. We are, however, left to speculate. The point of detailing the alleged differences is to demonstrate the inquiry the district court failed to make.

The court also failed to perform its duty to determine whether the class action would be manageable in light of state law variations. The court's only discussion of manageability is a citation to Jenkins and the claim that "while manageability of the liability issues in this case may well prove to be difficult, the Court finds that any such difficulties pale in comparison to the specter of thousands, if not millions, of similar trials of liability proceeding in thousands of courtrooms around the nation." *Id.* at 555-56.

...In summary, whether the specter of millions of cases outweighs any manageability problems in this class is uncertain when the scope of any manageability problems is unknown. Absent considered judgment on the manageability of the class, a comparison to millions of individual trials is meaningless.

B. Predominance

* * *

In addition to the reasons given above, regarding the district court's procedural errors, this class must be decertified because it independently fails the superiority requirement of rule 23(b)(3). In the context of mass tort class actions, certification dramatically affects the stakes for defendants. Class certification magnifies and strengthens the number of unmeritorious claims. *Agent Orange*, 818 F.2d at 165-66 Aggregation of claims also makes it more likely that a defendant will be found liable and results in significantly higher damage awards.

In addition to skewing trial outcomes, class certification creates insurmountable pressure on defendants to settle, whereas individual trials would not. See Peter H. Schuck, Mass Torts: An Institutional Evolutionist Perspective, 80 Cornell L. Rev. 941, 958 (1995). The risk of facing an all-or-nothing verdict presents too high a risk, even when the probability of an adverse judgment is low. *Rhone-Poulenc*, 51 F.3d at 1298. These settlements have been referred to as judicial blackmail.

It is no surprise then, that historically, certification of mass tort litigation classes has been disfavored....The traditional concern over the rights of defendants in mass tort class actions is magnified in the instant case. Our specific concern is that a mass tort cannot be properly certified without a prior track record of trials from which the district court can draw the information necessary to make the predominance and superiority requirements required by rule 23. This is because certification of an immature tort results in a higher than normal risk that the class action may not be superior to individual adjudication.

* * *

The plaintiffs' claim also overstates the defendants' ability to outspend plaintiffs. Assuming arguendo that the defendants pool resources and outspend plaintiffs in individual trials, there is no reason why plaintiffs still cannot prevail. The class is represented by a consortium of well-financed plaintiffs' lawyers who, over time, can develop the expertise and specialized knowledge sufficient to beat the tobacco companies at their own game. See Francis E. McGovern, An Analysis of Mass Torts for Judges, 73 Tex. L. Rev. 1821, 1834-35 (1995) (suggesting that plaintiffs can overcome tobacco defendants' perceived advantage when a sufficient number of plaintiffs have filed claims and shared discovery). Courts can also overcome the defendant's alleged advantages through coordination or consolidation of cases for discovery and other pretrial matters....

Severe manageability problems and the lack of a judicial crisis are not the only reasons why superiority is lacking. The most compelling rationale for finding superiority in a class action—the existence of a negative value suit—is missing in this case...

As he stated in the record, plaintiffs' counsel in this case has promised to inundate the courts with individual claims if class certification is denied. Independently of the reliability of this self-serving promise, there is reason to believe that individual suits are feasible...

* * *

...For the forgoing reasons, we REVERSE and REMAND with instructions that the district court dismiss the class complaint.

[1] The court defined "nicotine-dependent" as: (a) All cigarette smokers who have been diagnosed by a medical practitioner as nicotine-dependent; and/or (b) All regular cigarette smokers who were or have been advised by a medical practitioner that smoking has had or will have adverse health consequences who thereafter do not or have not quit smoking. *Id. at 561.* The definition is based upon the criteria for "dependence" set forth in AMERICAN PSYCHIATRIC ASSOCIATION, DIAGNOSTIC AND STATISTICAL MANUAL OF MENTAL DISORDERS (4th ed.).

[4] The plaintiffs seek compensatory damages for fraud and deceit, negligent misrepresentation, intentional infliction of emotional distress, breach of express and implied warranty, strict products liability, and redhibition.

[5] The plaintiffs seek punitive damages for fraud and deceit, intentional infliction of emotional distress, negligence, and negligent infliction of emotional distress.

[6] The plaintiffs seek attorneys' fees for violations of consumer protection statutes and redhibition.

[7] The district court did not adopt the plaintiffs' trial plan, but its order certifying the class incorporates many elements of it.

[9] Rule 23(a) states: One or more members of a class may sue or be sued as representative parties on behalf of all only if (1) the class is so numerous that joinder of all members is impracticable, (2) there are questions of law or fact common to the class, (3) the claims or defenses of the representative parties are typical of the claims or defenses of the class, and (4) the representative parties will fairly and adequately protect the interests of the class.

[10] Rule 23(b)(3) states, in pertinent part, that a class action may be maintained if the court finds that the questions of law or fact common to the members of the class predominate over any questions affecting only individual members, and that a class action is superior to other available methods for the fair and efficient adjudication of the controversy.

The relevance of *Castano* to child health includes the successful addiction of tobacco smokers at a median age of under 16 years, with most youthful smokers allegedly induced by industry promotion and peer pressure to begin smoking at between twelve and fifteen years of age. Note that, notwithstanding the certification denial, the plaintiff in *Castano* did not dismiss her action as an individual. That maintenance allowed a court order to remain in effect barring any destruction of documents by the industry. The early timing of that order and its continuation was propitious given subsequent events in the litigation.

Questions for Discussion

1. The *Castano* court's first reason for certification denial is the district court's failure to examine differences between states. Although states may have different rules regarding fraud and affirmative defenses, are there wide variations between the states relevant to misleading advertising (where the common test is simply "tendency to mislead"—with reliance, intent and other variations between states absent)? Is deliberate manipulation of addiction treated markedly different between states? Are they more varied than state statutes dealing with asbestos contamination? Why did the court not simply remand the matter to the district court to examine state statute variations?

2. Would the case have fared differently if confined to youth addiction, targeting, and sales? Are these child-related policies markedly different among the several states?

3. Would this case have been certified if brought within a single state as a class action? Note that following *Castano*, plaintiff attorneys associated with that group filed class actions in 22 states. Except for California (relying on a private attorney general theory discussed below) and Louisiana, class action status failed for lack of adequate commonality or related objections where the certification issue was decided.

4. The *Castano* court acknowledges that a class action may be "superior" if a plethora of individual actions result from class denial and inefficiently swamp the courts in repetitive adjudication of similar issues of fact and law. It argues that such a proliferation of lawsuits is unlikely. But which way should such a finding cut? If individualized remedies for a wrong are unlikely and court enforcement of the law is only viable on a class action basis, does not that condition argue for certification rather than against it? How does such a basis for class denial (if we deny class status, individual vindication of rights is unlikely) impact children's rights as victims with a relative lack of individualized access to the courts?

5. The *Castano* court also argues that defendants do not overwhelm plaintiffs in legal resources and that counsel for the latter can pursue trials against the tobacco industry via individual trials. Is this a realistic option? Note that fourteen states have punitive damage provisions which might apply to the allegations of plaintiff *Castano*. Those circumstances may provide inducement for such individual actions. During 2001, one jury made an award of $3 billion on behalf of a single individual, see *Boeken v. Philip Morris*, Los Angeles County Superior Court Case No. BC226593, later reduced on appeal to $100 million. In a 2001 Florida case, an unusual class action punitive damage award of $144.8 billion was handed down, see

Engle v. R.J. Reynolds Tobacco Co., et al., No. 94-08273 CA-22 (Fla. Cir. Ct., 11th Dist., Dade County).[32] Would it be "superior" and "more manageable" to distribute such a punitive penalty not to one or several plaintiffs who come to judgment first, or to those in a single state, but to the broader group of persons damaged by the practice (*e.g.*, through de-addiction services and child anti-smoking expenditures)?

6. One of the major allegations of *Castano* was the manipulation of nicotine by tobacco firms to create and enhance addiction, and to target children. Would the case be strengthened if it confined its scope to such marketing *and* pursued its claims in equity under 23(b)(2) as did the *Marisol* class (seeking only an injunction and restitution, disgorgement of profits from sales to minors, or the payment for de-addiction services for persons addicted as children)? In fact, are not the differences in abuses, impact, and defenses substantially more significant among the *Marisol* class than would be the case in targeting children for nicotine addiction? Why did the *Castano* decision not remand to certify the injunctive aspects of the proposed class under Rule 23(b)(2)?

3. Current Status of the Class Action Option

a. *Concepcion* and Class Action Remedy Decline

This use of the important class action to vindicate rights now encounters difficulties in addition to the *Castano* example of too much variation to qualify for adequate "commonality" among the class or insufficient "typicality" by the class representative. In addition to those threshold requirements, a controversial decision has eliminated a large percentage of class actions for both adults and children. In *AT&T Mobility v. Concepcion*, 563 U.S. 333 (2011), a 5–4 Supreme Court holding expansively applied the Federal Arbitration Act to allow commercial or other parties to specify in a contract that any related dispute involving them must be decided by individual arbitration and could bar both class and court actions to vindicate wrongs. These "*Concepcion*" clauses have quickly become a little noticed part of every "term and condition" in commercial contracts (or advance document sign offs). They are generally unread but are checked off by consumers in the normal course. This apparent misapplication of the Federal Arbitration Act (focusing on Admiralty disputes) has now been applied to prevent realistic access to the courts for many kinds of disputes most needing that group remedy. The same internet platform of mass communications that warrant class remedies ironically also facilitates the mass application of this clause negating those remedies.

Exacerbating the problem have been additional decisions upholding *Concepcion* against court findings of unconscionability in the "term and condition" contract setting. In a purported contract world requiring a "meeting of the minds" to form an actionable contract, an adhesive and unread provision is increasingly upheld. One puzzling aspect of this revision of contract principles is its application to children to whom contract terms are normally not applied as with adults, and where such adhesive terms and conditions are here fully enforceable without actual conscious review by them or by their parents.[33]

b. The Class Action Fairness Act (CAFA) and Recent Decisions Constrict Child Class Actions

Many of the successful child class action cases have been brought in state court, avoiding some federal precedents applying Federal Rule of Civil Procedure 23 impediments to certification. However, some securities and consumer law class actions filed in pro-plaintiff state court jurisdictions won certification for national classes, conferring powerful leverage for settlements in venues disadvantageous to defendants. Citing these abuses, corporate interests won passage of the Class Action Fairness Act of 2005, which alters federal class action jurisdiction. Historically, state class actions were removed to federal court only where there was absolute diversity (parties from different states) and class members suffered a loss in excess of $75,000 each. The new law gives any defendant the right to remove class actions to federal court unless virtually all parties are from the same state and the total amount in dispute is over $5 million. If more than one-third of the class is from one state and the defendant operates primarily in that state, remand to state court may be possible. As noted above, after the decertification decision of the Fifth Circuit above, the *Castano* case was refiled in 22 states. However, such state refilings under the 2005 Act would be problematical. The removal provisions of the Act do not apply to many class actions where the reach of the class is limited or the defendants opt not to remove.

Perhaps more germane to child class action remedies are the recent decisions requiring more extensive and early proof of class qualification. In the case of *Wal-Mart Stores, Inc. v. Dukes*, 131 S.Ct. 2541 (2011), the Supreme Court emphasized that the claims of each class member must "depend upon a common contention." Further, the court must now make a finding that a plaintiff has met the burden of qualification; as a practical matter this means that such discovery to meet the new burden must precede the certification decision. As noted above, some stricter certification qualification is already required for the 23(b)(3) actions for damages—including that common questions "predominate" and that the case be "manageable." But the new and stricter court criteria in *Wal-Mart* applies to 23(b)2 actions in equity which lack those add-ons and have traditionally allowed judicial enforcement of the law in ordering compliance *vis-à-vis* victim groupings. Children are a particular grouping warranting some flexibility in gaining access to the courts. Individual civil actions or arbitrations are not as feasible for those with limited finances, organization, legal knowledge, or attorney contacts. Nevertheless, the additional access barriers of *Wal-Mart* and other recent decisions for children were so applied in *M.D. et al. v. Perry et al.,* where the Fifth Circuit writes:[34]

> Before *Wal-Mart*, the rule in this circuit provided that in order to satisfy commonality "[t]he interests and claims of the various plaintiffs need not be identical. Rather, the commonality test is met when there is 'at

least one issue whose resolution will affect all or a significant number of the putative class members.'" *Forbush v. J.C. Penney Co., Inc.*, 994 F.2d 1101, 1106 (5th Cir. 1993)....

However, in *Wal-Mart*, the Court expounded on the meaning of its precedent providing that "[c]ommonality requires the plaintiff to demonstrate that the class members 'have suffered the same injury.'... After *Wal-Mart*,...[the] commonality requirement demands more than the presentation of questions that are common to the class because "'any competently crafted class complaint literally raises common questions.'"...Further, the members of a proposed class do not establish that "their claims can productively be litigated at once," merely by alleging a violation of the same legal provision by the same defendant....

...("'What matters to class certification...is not the raising of common 'questions'—even in droves—but, rather the capacity of a classwide proceedings to generate common answers apt to drive the resolution of the litigation.'")...Thus, the commonality test...requires that all of the class member's claims depend on a common issue of law or fact whose resolution "will resolve an issue that is central to the validity of each one of the [class member's] claims in one stroke."...

The Court further clarified that a trial court's obligation to perform a "rigorous analysis" before concluding that a class has satisfied the requirements of Rule 23(a) "[f]requently...will entail some overlap with the merits of the plaintiff's underlying claim."...([S]ometimes it may be necessary for the court to probe behind the pleadings before coming to rest on the certification question.")...

Lastly, after the [*Wal-Mart*] Court concluded that "proof of commonality necessarily overlap[ped] with the [purported class members'] merits contention that Wal-Mart engaged in a *pattern or practice* of discrimination," the Court probed beyond the plaintiffs' pleadings in an effort to decide if an "examination of all the class member's claims for relief will produce a common answer to the crucial [merits] question *why was I disfavored*."...

Children's Rights, counsel for the class in this Texas case, was able to narrow the contentions and create specific subclasses (each one of which had to have a "typical class representative" as well as an applicable remedy that would apply very similarly to each member of the class). But the breadth and difficulty of the class remedy from the recent *Wal-Mart* precedent is going to apply to child classes and affect access to this remedy even where all that is sought is an order compelling compliance with the Constitution or federal statutory floors. *Query*, how would this new requirement impact the *Marisol* precedent above involving different violations of many different statutes? How many subclasses would be required?

c. Alternatives to the Traditional Class Action

One alternative to the class representative elements of the private class action is a similar action brought by a state attorney general, district attorney, or other authorized public counsel in *parens patriae* for citizens within their respective jurisdiction, including children. Such status may overcome the need to find a parent willing to have his or her child serve as class representative and then meet the various requirements of such class representatives, including the "adequacy of representation" and related requirements noted above.

There are several areas where civil court remedies may still be tenable on behalf of a class of parents on behalf of children or through a class of child plaintiffs represented through parents, counsel or "next friend" mechanism. First, where the wrong is from a governmental entity, there is less likelihood of a qualifying "term and condition" foreclosing a group remedy. Further, a declaratory relief action or a writ of mandamus (discussed below) can apply to a governmental body and effectively alter policy, thus providing a group remedy for those to whom the policy might apply.

Second, in the area of commercial abuses, a few states allow their citizens to serve as a "private attorney general" and bring actions on behalf of the general public, including children. Such actions are brought in equity, but may yield disgorgement of ill-gotten gains and restitution. Most important, in some states they may be brought by any person, whether a part of the group aggrieved or not. That status allows public interest groups, or any litigant, to represent the interests of children without obtaining a child plaintiff. Such actions cannot be defeated based on lack of commonality since a right to sue for all who are injured or for the "general public" is explicitly authorized. And many of the defenses discussed above which undermine traditional class actions, such as inadequate commonality among the class for certification, are also not available (*e.g.*, assumption of risk, reliance, and intent elements are irrelevant to an unfair competition action based on misleading advertising). Such actions focus on unlawful or unfair marketplace practices, and often seek the disgorgement of "unjust enrichment," which is assigned to a "fund" and which may allow attorney's fees to prevailing counsel for plaintiffs on a "private attorney general fee award" basis, or alternatively on a "common fund" fee sharing theory (see discussion below).

California's Unfair Competition Law (Cal. Bus. & Prof. Code § 17200 *et seq.*), historically the prime example of such an option, was used in *Committee on Children's Television, Inc. v. General Foods* (35 Cal. 3d 197 (1983)) to sustain a private attorney general action against Fruity Pebbles and other cereals produced by the defendant for misleading advertising to children representing cereal consisting primarily of sugar as healthy. But the enactment in 2004 of Proposition 64 ended the private attorney general option and reimposed traditional class action requirements consistent with Federal Rule of Civil Procedure 23 and also with typical Unfair Competition laws at the state level (sometimes called "Little FTC Acts"). California traditionally had the most liberal statute to accommodate unfair competition actions against private businesses on a private attorney general basis.

There is one other area where a private attorney general structure can exist, providing financial rewards to those who reveal fraud perpetrated on the government by a company or an individual. These "*qui tam*" actions are authorized federally through the False Claims Act[35] and through similar state-level acts in 29 states.[36] In such actions, a whistleblower commonly serves as a private attorney general and submits a prospective case to the Attorney General or the U.S. Attorney. If it is not taken by the office, he or she may proceed with the case on behalf of the public with attorney fees paid and a possible reward to the private citizen.

Third, some grievances against a private entity are not amenable to "term and condition" imposition. Many acts of questionable legality affecting children do not occur in a setting where there is a chance for an advance "check off" via internet or paper or other means prior to an interaction. In these cases *Concepcion* will not apply, although the other criteria for class certification discussed above must still be met.

Fourth, a primary source of rights vindication for Unfair Competition or other commercial abuses victimizing children may apply—suit by a public prosecutor. For example, in most states Unfair Competition Laws and other consumer protection statutes relevant to children can be enforced by the Attorney General, district attorneys, or even city attorneys in some situations. These actors under their state constitutions represent "the People" and accomplish class or group representation as a matter of law. And at the federal level, the U.S. Attorneys and Federal Trade Commission, as well as other agencies, have similar powers to litigate in civil court on behalf of all alleged victims of a violation of law within their respective domains. There can also be some interaction betwPolitical processeen such public prosecutors and private class action counsel. The latter may be able to operate on behalf of the "People" where so authorized by a public prosecutor and applicable law—thus avoiding the *Concepcion* bar even where a "term and condition" barring a class action is involved. Although rare and with attendant difficulties involving delegation of public power to a private litigator requiring public supervision and limitations on attorneys' fees that would otherwise be available, in some situations the *Concepcion* bar may be overcome.

d. Use of Mandamus

Most states allow a special kind of pleading, often called a "petition for ordinary mandamus." It lies in equity (court trial without a jury) and is based on an alleged "abuse of discretion" by a public official. Accordingly, it does not normally help to vindicate a commercial violation of child rights. The abuse of discretion occurs where such an official (in any of the three branches) violates a ministerial duty to act, or not to act. An action which violates statutory intent, or a failure to act notwithstanding a statutory duty to do so, is such an abuse. In many states, trial and appellate courts may have coextensive original jurisdiction to hear such writs (allowing possible leapfrogging to appellate or Supreme Court levels). Such an approach may result in an order directing the agency to act as prayed. Even if only one petitioner is named, it is not realistic that an agency will apply different policies to litigants. Accordingly, the petition acts as a class action. However, few of the impediments to class actions discussed above apply. There is no delay to certify a class or to explore class or counsel adequacy. The petition is generally entitled to calendar preference. Such an approach may afford child advocates more useful access to court redress where the grievance is with a public official. The petition for writ of mandate only applies to abuses of discretion by government officials. Query, can it be used where children are victimized by private parties to force government officials to act? See *DeShaney v. Winnebago County Dep't of Social Services*, 489 U.S. 189 (1989), discussed in Chapter 12.

4. Fees and Incentives to Sue

Attorney fee recovery by successful plaintiffs facilitates access to courts for children. Such contingent recompense allows attorneys to proceed on behalf of clients lacking resources.

a. Private Attorney General Fees

Some states have allowed what are termed "private attorney general" fees where an attorney prevails in a public interest action. In the leading case of *Serrano v. Priest*, 32 Cal. 3d 621 (1982), attorneys brought an action on behalf of California's children to alter the system of school finance (see Chapter 4). The Court held that where an attorney represents an interest substantially beyond the pecuniary stake of his named client, and successfully vindicates a right of such general application, attorneys' fees may be awarded at market rates. In addition, the court enunciated criteria for the enhancement of that market level figure by a "multiplier" based on the difficulty of the case and other enumerated factors. Many states have codified private attorney general fee recompense arrangements similar to the *Serrano* holding (*see, e.g.*, Cal. Code Civ. Proc. § 1021.5).

The U.S. Supreme Court has formulated a very different rule for generic private attorney general recovery, requiring plaintiffs to rely on specific attorney fee recovery provisions in federal statutes.

Alyeska Pipeline Service Co. v. Wilderness Society, et al.
421 U.S. 240 (1975)

OPINION BY: **MR. JUSTICE WHITE**

This litigation was initiated by respondents Wilderness Society, Environmental Defense Fund, Inc., and Friends of the Earth in an attempt to prevent the issuance of permits by the Secretary of the Interior which were required for the construction of the trans-Alaska oil pipeline. The Court of Appeals awarded attorneys' fees to respondents against petitioner Alyeska Pipeline Service Co. based upon the court's equitable powers and the theory that respondents were entitled to fees because they were performing the services of a "private attorney general." Certiorari was granted, 419 U.S. 823 (1974), to determine whether this award of attorneys' fees was appropriate. We reverse.

* * *

With the merits of the litigation effectively terminated by this legislation, the Court of Appeals turned to the questions involved in respondents' request for an award of attorneys' fees.[13] 161 U.S. App. D.C. 446, 495 F. 2d 1026 (1974) (en banc). Since there was no applicable statutory authorization for such an award, the court proceeded to consider whether the requested fee award fell within any of the exceptions to the general "American rule" that the prevailing party may not recover attorneys' fees as costs or otherwise. The exception for an award against a party who had acted in bad faith was inapposite, since the position taken by the federal and state parties and Alyeska "was manifestly reasonable and assumed in good faith...." *Id.*, at 449, 495 F. 2d, at 1029. Application of the "common benefit" exception which spreads the cost of litigation to those persons benefiting from it would "stretch it totally outside its basic rationale...."

Ibid.[14] The Court of Appeals nevertheless held that respondents had acted to vindicate "important statutory rights of all citizens...," *id.*, at 452, 495 F. 2d, at 1032; had ensured that the governmental system functioned properly; and were entitled to attorneys' fees lest the great cost of litigation of this kind, particularly against well-financed defendants such as Alyeska, deter private parties desiring to see the laws protecting the environment properly enforced. Title 28 U.S.C. § 2412....was thought to bar taxing any attorneys' fees against the United States, and it was also deemed inappropriate to burden the State of Alaska with any part of the award....But Alyeska, the Court of Appeals held, could fairly be required to pay one-half of the full award to which respondents were entitled for having performed the functions of a private attorney general. Observing that "[t]he fee should represent the reasonable value of the services rendered, taking into account all the surrounding circumstances, including, but not limited to, the time and labor required on the case, the benefit to the public, the skill demanded by the novelty or complexity of the issues, and the incentive factor," 161 U.S. App. D.C., at 456, 495 F. 2d, at 1036, the Court of Appeals remanded the case to the District Court for assessment of the dollar amount of the award.[17]

In the United States, the prevailing litigant is ordinarily not entitled to collect a reasonable attorneys' fee from the loser. We are asked to fashion a far-reaching exception to this "American Rule"; but having considered its origin and development, we are convinced that it would be inappropriate for the Judiciary, without legislative guidance, to reallocate the burdens of litigation in the manner and to the extent urged by respondents and approved by the Court of Appeals.

At common law, costs were not allowed; but for centuries in England there has been statutory authorization to award costs, including attorneys' fees. Although the matter is in the discretion of the court, counsel fees are regularly allowed to the prevailing party.

* * *

Congress has not repudiated the judicially fashioned exceptions to the general rule against allowing substantial attorneys' fees; but neither has it retracted, repealed, or modified the limitations on taxable fees contained in the 1853 statute and its successors. Nor has it extended any roving authority to the Judiciary to allow counsel fees as costs or otherwise whenever the courts might deem them warranted. What Congress has done, however, while fully recognizing and accepting the general rule, is to make specific and explicit provisions for the allowance of attorneys' fees under selected statutes granting or protecting various federal rights....These statutory allowances are now available in a variety of circumstances, but they also differ considerably among themselves. Under the antitrust laws, for instance, allowance of attorneys' fees to a plaintiff awarded treble damages is mandatory....Under Title II of the Civil Rights Act of 1964, 42 U.S.C. § 2000a-3 (b),[35] the prevailing party is entitled to attorneys' fees, at the discretion of the court, but we have held that Congress intended that the award should be made to the successful plaintiff absent exceptional circumstances. *Newman v. Piggie Park Enterprises, Inc.*, 390

U.S. 400, 402 (1968) See also *Northcross v. Board of Education of the Memphis City Schools*, 412 U.S. 427 (1973) Under this scheme of things, it is apparent that the circumstances under which attorneys' fees are to be awarded and the range of discretion of the courts in making those awards are matters for Congress to determine....

It is true that under some, if not most, of the statutes providing for the allowance of reasonable fees, Congress has opted to rely heavily on private forcement to implement public policy and to allow counsel fees so as to encourage private litigation. Fee shifting in connection with treble-damages awards under the antitrust laws is a prime example; cf. *Hawaii v. Standard Oil Co.*, 405 U.S. 251, 265-266 (1972); and we have noted that Title II of the Civil Rights Act of 1964 was intended "not simply to penalize litigants who deliberately advance arguments they know to be untenable but, more broadly, to encourage individuals injured by racial discrimination to seek judicial relief under Title II." *Newman, supra,* at 402 (footnote omitted). But congressional utilization of the private-attorney-general concept can in no sense be construed as a grant of authority to the Judiciary to jettison the traditional rule against nonstatutory allowances to the prevailing party and to award attorneys' fees whenever the courts deem the public policy furthered by a particular statute important enough to warrant the award.

Congress itself presumably has the power and judgment to pick and choose among its statutes and to allow attorneys' fees under some, but not others. But it would be difficult, indeed, for the courts, without legislative guidance, to consider some statutes important and others unimportant and to allow attorneys' fees only in connection with the former. If the statutory limitation of right-of-way widths involved in this case is a matter of the gravest importance, it would appear that a wide range of statutes would arguably satisfy the criterion of public importance and justify an award of attorneys' fees to the private litigant. And, if any statutory policy is deemed so important that its enforcement must be encouraged by awards of attorneys' fees, how could a court deny attorneys' fees to private litigants in actions under 42 U.S.C. § 1983 seeking to vindicate constitutional rights? Moreover, should courts, if they were to embark on the course urged by respondents, opt for awards to the prevailing party, whether plaintiff or defendant, or only to the prevailing plaintiff?[37] Should awards be discretionary or mandatory?...Would there be a presumption operating for or against them in the ordinary case?...

* * *

The decision below must therefore be reversed.

[13] Respondents' bill of costs includes a total of 4,455 hours of attorneys' time spent on the litigation. App. 209-219.

[14] "[T]his litigation may well have provided substantial benefits to particular individuals and, indeed, to every citizen's interest in the proper functioning of our system of government. But imposing attorneys' fees on Alyeska will not operate to spread the costs of litigation proportionately among these beneficiaries...." 161 U.S. App. D.C., at 449, 495 F. 2d, at 1029.

[17] The Court of Appeals also directed that "[t]he fee award need not be limited... to the amount actually paid or owed by [respondents]. It may well be that counsel serve organizations like [respondents] for compensation below that obtainable in the market because they believe the organizations further a public interest. Litigation of this sort should not have to rely on the charity of counsel any more than it should rely on the charity of parties volunteering to serve as private attorneys general. The attorneys who worked on this case should be reimbursed the reasonable value of their services, despite the absence of any obligation on the part of [respondents] to pay attorneys' fees." Id., at 457, 495 F. 2d, at 1037.

[35] "In any action commenced pursuant to this subchapter, the court, in its discretion, may allow the prevailing party, other than the United States, a reasonable attorney's fee as part of the costs, and the United States shall be liable for costs the same as a private person."

[37] Congress in its specific statutory authorizations of fee shifting has in some instances provided that either party could be given such an award depending upon the outcome of the litigation and the court's discretion, see, e.g., 35 U.S.C. § 285 (patent infringement) Civil Rights Act of 1964, 42 U.S.C. §§ 2000a-3 (b), 2000e-5 (k), while in others it has specified that only one of the litigants can be awarded fees. See, e.g., the antitrust laws, 15 U.S.C. § 15; Fair Labor Standards Act, 29 U.S.C. § 216 (b).

MR. JUSTICE DOUGLAS and **MR. JUSTICE POWELL** took no part in the consideration or decision of this case.

* * *

MR. JUSTICE MARSHALL, dissenting.

In reversing the award of attorneys' fees to the respondent environmentalist groups, the Court today disavows the well-established power of federal equity courts to award attorneys' fees when the interests of justice so require. While under the traditional American Rule the courts ordinarily refrain from allowing attorneys' fees, we have recognized several judicial exceptions to that rule for classes of cases in which equity seemed to favor fee shifting. See *Sprague v. Ticonic National Bank*, 307 U.S. 161 (1939); *Mills v. Electric Auto-Lite Co.*, 396 U.S. 375, 391-392 (1970); *Hall v. Cole* 412 U.S. 1, 5, 9 (1973) By imposing an absolute bar on the use of the "private attorney general" rationale as a basis for awarding attorneys' fees, the Court today takes an extremely narrow view of the independent power of the courts in this area—a view that flies squarely in the face of our prior cases.

The Court relies primarily on the docketing-fees-and court-costs statute, 28 U.S.C. §1923 in concluding that the American Rule is grounded in statute and that the courts may not award counsel fees unless they determine that Congress so intended. The various exceptions to the rule against fee shifting that this Court has created in the past are explained as constructions of the fee statute. *Ante*, at 257. In addition, the Court notes that Congress has provided for attorneys' fees in a number of statutes, but made no such provision in others. It concludes from this selective treatment that where award of attorneys' fees is not expressly authorized, the courts should deny them as a matter of course. Finally, the Court suggests that the policy questions bearing on whether to grant attorneys' fees in a particular case are not ones that the Judiciary is well equipped to handle, and that fee shifting under the private-attorney-general rationale would quickly degenerate into an arbitrary and lawless process. Because the Court concludes that granting attorneys' fees to private attorneys general is beyond the equitable power of the federal courts, it does not reach the question whether an award would be proper against Alyeska in this case under the private-attorney-general rationale.

On my view of the case, both questions must be answered. I see no basis in precedent or policy for holding that the courts cannot award attorneys' fees where the interests of justice require recovery, simply because the claim does not fit comfortably within one of the previously sanctioned judicial exceptions to the American Rule. The Court has not in the past regarded the award of attorneys' fees as a matter reserved for the Legislature, and it has certainly not read the docketing-fees statute as a general bar to judicial fee shifting. The Court's concern with the difficulty of applying meaningful standards in awarding attorneys' fees to successful "public benefit" litigants is a legitimate one, but in my view it overstates the novelty of the "private attorney general" theory. The guidelines developed in closely analogous statutory and nonstatutory attorneys' fee cases could readily be applied in cases such as the one at bar. I therefore disagree with the Court's flat rejection of the private-attorney-general rationale for fee shifting. Morover, in my view the equities in this case support an award of attorneys' fees against Alyeska.

Accordingly, I must respectfully dissent.

* * *

...The cases plainly establish an independent basis for equity courts to grant attorneys' fees under several rather generous rubrics. The Court acknowledges as much when it says that we have independent authority to award fees in cases of bad faith or as a means of taxing costs to special beneficiaries. But I am at a loss to understand how it can also say that this independent judicial power succumbs to Procrustean statutory restrictions—indeed, to statutory silence—as soon as the far from bright line between common benefit and public benefit is crossed. I can only conclude that the Court is willing to tolerate the "equitable" exceptions to its analysis, not because they can be squared with it, but because they are by now too well established to be casually dispensed with.

B
* * *

Starting with the early common-fund cases, the Court has consistently read the fee-bill statute of 1853 narrowly when that Act has been interposed as a restriction on the Court's equitable powers to award attorneys' fees. In *Trustees v. Greenough*, 105 U.S. 527 (1881), the Court held that the statute imposed no bar to an award of

attorneys' fees from the fund collected as a result of the plaintiff's efforts, since: "[The fee bill statute addressed] only those fees and costs which are strictly chargeable as between party and party, and [did not] regulate the fees of counsel and other expenses and charges as between solicitor and client.... And the act contains nothing which can be fairly construed to deprive the Court of Chancery of its long-established control over the costs and charges of the litigation, to be exercised as equity and justice may require...." *Id.*, at 535-536...

* * *

In sum, the Court's primary contention—that Congress enjoys hegemony over fee shifting because of the docketing-fee statute and the occasional express provisions for attorneys' fees—will not withstand even the most casual reading of the precedents. The Court's recognition of the several judge-made exceptions to the American rule demonstrates the inadequacy of its analysis. Whatever the Court's view of the wisdom of fee shifting in "public benefit" cases in general, I think that it is a serious misstep for it to abdicate equitable authority in this area in the name of statutory construction.

II

The statutory analysis aside, the Court points to the difficulties in formulating a "private attorney general" exception that will not swallow the American Rule. I do not find the problem as vexing as the majority does. In fact, the guidelines to the proper application of the private-attorney-general rationale have been suggested in several of our recent cases, both under statutory attorneys' fee provisions and under the common-benefit exception...

* * *

...[I]t is possible to discern with some confidence the factors that should guide an equity court in determining whether an award of attorneys' fees is appropriate.[7] The reasonable cost of the plaintiff's representation should be placed upon the defendant if (1) the important right being protected is one actually or necessarily shared by the general public or some class thereof; (2) the plaintiff's pecuniary interest in the outcome, if any, would not normally justify incurring the cost of counsel; and (3) shifting that cost to the defendant would effectively place it on a class that benefits from the litigation.

[7] These teachings have not been lost on the lower courts in which the elements of the private-attorney-general rationale have been more fully explored. See, e.g., Souza v. Travisono, 512 F. 2d 1137 (CA1 1975); Hoitt v. Vitek, 495 F. 2d 219 (CA1 1974); Knight v. Auciello, 453 F. 2d 852 (CA1 1972); Cornist v. Richland Parish School Board, 495 F. 2d 189 (CA5 1974); Fairley v. Patterson, 493 F. 2d 598 (CA5 1974); Cooper v. Allen, 467 F. 2d 836 (CA5 1972); Lee v. Southern Home Sites Corp., 444 F. 2d 143 (CA5 1971); Taylor v. Perini, 503 F. 2d 899 (CA6 1974); Morales v. Haines, 486 F. 2d 880 (CA7 1973); Donahue v. Staunton, 471 F. 2d 475 (CA7 1972), cert. denied, 410 U.S. 955 (1973); Fowler v. Schwarzwalder, 498 F. 2d 143 (CA8 1974); Brandenburger v. Thompson, 494 F. 2d 885 (CA9 1974); La Raza Unida v. Volpe, 57 F.R.D. 94 (N.D. Cal. 1972); Wyatt v. Stickney, 344 F. Supp. 387 (MD Ala. 1972); NAACP v. Allen, 340 F. Supp. 703 (M.D. Ala. 1972).

b. The Common Fund Doctrine

The private attorney general basis for fees is considered a "fee shifting" approach because it takes fees from the losing party separate and apart from damages or restitutionary funds obtained for alleged victims. In contrast, a separate basis for fees has evolved out of the "common fund" doctrine. This concept takes funds not from the defendant, but from the proceeds due the victims represented by counsel. As such, it is considered a "fee sharing" approach, as named litigants do not bear the full cost of providing a fund benefiting a large group—rather, the entire group receiving an advantage share in paying attorney compensation, i.e., it comes from the fund recovered.

Although rejecting fee shifting without a specific statute, the federal courts allow such common fund fee sharing. Moreover, in many cases where financial recovery is substantial, plaintiff attorneys favor a common fund recovery because it may allow for a percentage of the large fund comparable to market contingent fee arrangements in an amount above compensation for hours times a multiplier—particularly given a tradition of multipliers in the 1.2 to 3.6 range.

Lealao v. Beneficial California, Inc.

82 Cal. App. 4th 19 (2000)

KLINE, P. J.

Appellants Richard U. Lealao and his wife Sese Lealao, who commenced this successful consumer class action, claim that the attorney fees awarded class counsel were unreasonably low. The questions before us are whether, under the circumstances of this case, the trial court had discretion to award a fee based solely on a percentage of the class benefit or, in the alternative, to measure an award calculated under the lodestar methodology by a percentage-of-the-benefit yardstick and to adjust the lodestar upward or downward on that basis. Our answers are no to the first question and yes to the second.

* * *

DISCUSSION
* * *

II

The parties' dispute centers on the validity and continuing jurisprudential viability of the distinction between "fee shifting" and "fee spreading."

In so-called fee shifting cases, in which the responsibility to pay attorney fees is statutorily or otherwise transferred from the prevailing plaintiff or class to the defendant, the primary method for establishing the amount of "reasonable" attorney fees is the lodestar method. The lodestar (or touchstone) is produced by multiplying the number of hours reasonably expended by counsel by a reasonable hourly rate. Once the court has fixed the lodestar, it may increase or decrease that amount by applying a positive or negative "multiplier" to take into account a variety of other factors, including the quality of the representation, the novelty and complexity of the issues, the results obtained, and the contingent risk presented....

Fee spreading occurs when a settlement or adjudication results in the establishment of a separate or so-called common fund for the benefit of the class. Because the fee awarded class counsel comes from this fund, it is said that the expense is borne by the beneficiaries. Percentage fees have traditionally been allowed in such common fund cases, although, as will be seen, the lodestar methodology may also be utilized in this context.

Respondent maintains that, because the settlement in this case did not result in the establishment of a traditional common fund, the percentage-of-the-benefit approach cannot be utilized, even in connection with the lodestar formulation. Appellant, conceding a conventional common fund does not exist, answers with federal cases suggesting that the distinction between "fee shifting" and "fee spreading" is an illusory jurisprudential construct, and that unless the fee award is in some fashion considered as a percentage of the monetary benefit received by the class the law will create counterproductive economic incentives and disincentives that should no longer be tolerated.

Δ's Arg.

* * *

Despite its primacy, the lodestar method is not necessarily utilized in common fund cases. The common fund or "fund-in-court" doctrine, first articulated by the United States Supreme Court in *Trustees v. Greenough* (1881) 105 U.S. 527..., is a venerable exception to the general American rule disfavoring attorney fees in the absence of statutory or contractual authorization. (Code Civ. Proc., § 1021.5) The exception "is grounded in 'the historic power of equity to permit the trustee of a fund or property, or a party preserving or recovering a fund for the benefit of others in addition to himself, to recover his costs, including his attorneys' fees, from the fund of property itself or directly from the other parties enjoying the benefit.'" (*Serrano III, supra,* 20 Cal. 3d at p. 35, quoting *Alyeska Pipeline Co. v. Wilderness Society* (1975) 421 U.S. 240, 257).

Because the common fund doctrine "rest[s] squarely on the principle of avoiding unjust enrichment" ...attorney fees awarded under this doctrine are not assessed directly against the losing party (fee shifting), but come out of the fund established by the litigation, so that the beneficiaries of the litigation, not the defendant, bear this cost (fee spreading). Under federal law, the amount of fees awarded in a common fund case may be determined under either the lodestar method or the percentage-of-the-benefit approach although, about a decade ago, as the Ninth Circuit then noted, there commenced a "ground swell of support for mandating the percentage-of-the-fund approach in common fund cases."...

III

Class counsel's argument rests heavily on federal cases. During the nearly quarter of a century since *Serrano III,* many federal courts, heavily burdened with the class and derivative actions that give rise to the need to adjudicate fee issues, became disillusioned with the lodestar method. This shift is perhaps most dramatically exemplified by the Third Circuit, whose 1973 opinion in *Lindy I, supra,* 487 F.2d 161, which was relied upon in *Serrano III* (20 Cal. 3d at p. 49, fn. 23), pioneered adoption of the lodestar methodology. (See also *Lindy Bros. Builders, Inc. v. Am. Radiator, etc.* (3d Cir. 1976) 540 F.2d 102 (Lindy II).) The so-called "Lindy lodestar' technique quickly gained wide acceptance among the federal circuits, sometimes in modified fashion...and was eventually approved by the United States Supreme Court. (*Hensley v. Eckerhart* (1983) 461 U.S. 424, 433) ....[2]

However, in 1985, concerned about increasing criticism of the lodestar method, the Third Circuit reexamined the concept it is credited with inventing in *Lindy I* and concluded it was seriously deficient and subject to abuse when applied in cases resulting in the creation of a fund. A task force commissioned by the Third Circuit concluded that the lodestar approach (1) "increases the workload of an already overtaxed judicial system," (2) is "insufficiently objective and produce[s] results that are far from homogenous," (3) "creates a sense of mathematical precision that is unwarranted in terms of the realities of the practice of law," (4) "is subject to manipulation by judges who prefer to calibrate fees in terms of percentages of the settlement fund or the amounts recovered by the plaintiffs or of an overall dollar amount," (5) "encourages lawyers to expend excessive hours, and...engage in duplicative and unjustified work," (6) "creates a disincentive for the early settlement of cases," (7) deprives trial courts of "flexibility to reward or deter lawyers so that desirable objectives, such as early settlement, will be fostered," (8) "works to the particular disadvantage of the public interest bar," and (9) results in "confusion and lack of predictability."...[3] Due to these perceived deficiencies, the Report of the Third Circuit Task Force concluded that the lodestar technique is a "cumbersome, enervating, and often surrealistic process of preparing and evaluating fee petitions that now plagues the Bench and Bar"... and recommended a return to the percentage of the recovery fee formula in cases involving a settlement fund.

...This now widely shared view has stimulated greater judicial willingness to evaluate a fee award as a percentage of the recovery....It is for present purposes significant, as class counsel are at great pains to emphasize, that the federal trend in favor of the percentage-of-the-benefit approach has been extended to cases in which (1) the "fund" that results from an adjudication or settlement is not deposited in a separate account; (2) the value of the "fund" depends on the number of valid claims presented or is imprecise for other reasons; and (3) attorney fees are not deducted from monies made available to the class, but are paid by the defendant directly. All that has been required in many such cases is that the benefits received by the class, or the range thereof, can be monetized without undue speculation.

* * *

IV

The cases just described reflect the growing willingness of federal courts to disregard the strict theoretical distinction between fee shifting and fee spreading in cases in which fees are not authorized by statute, no separate fund is established, and fees are paid directly by the defendant—provided, of course, that the monetary value of the class recovery is reasonably ascertainable.

* * *

...What constitutes a reasonable fee in a representative action has been shown to be a far more complex question than the judiciary once thought it to be. There are no easy answers. The lodestar methodology originated as an alternative to percentage recoveries, which often resulted in exorbitant fee awards clearly unjustified by the contributions of counsel, which in turn undermined public confidence in the bench and bar....Considering the fee only as a percentage of the benefit would simply resurrect that problem. Refusing ever to take that consideration into account, however, would, as we have indicated, create equally pernicious problems. The federal judicial experience teaches that the "reasonableness" of a fee in a representative action will often require some consideration of the amount to be awarded as a percentage of the class recovery. How much weight that factor should receive may well be, as an experienced trial judge has said, "the most difficult question in present-day jurisprudence concerning attorney's fees.' (Grady, Reasonable Fees: A Suggested *Value-Based Analysis for Judges, supra,...*) However difficult this question, it cannot be avoided; and the ability of California courts to intelligently address it would not be enhanced by diminishing the tools with which they have to work.

VI

The order denying the motion for new trial as to fees is reversed and the matter remanded to the trial court for reconsideration of the reasonable fee to which class counsel is entitled.

HAERLE, J., and **LAMBDEN, J.**, concurred.

[2] Adoption of the lodestar methodology in the early 1970's was stimulated by the view that awards based on a reasonable percentage of the fund, historically the preferred method of fee setting in common fund cases, was yielding fee awards that were excessive and unrelated to the work actually performed by counsel....

[3] The task force concluded that fund cases should be treated differently from the conventional statutory fee case, involving the declaration or enforcement of rights or relatively modest sums of money. It felt the lodestar method necessary in statutory fee cases "because it is reasonably objective, neutral, and does not require making monetary assessments of intangible rights that are not easily equated with dollars and cents." (Report of the Third Circuit Task Force, *supra*, 108 F.R.D. at p. 255.) The task force felt "these protections were not...needed in the traditional fund case or in those statutory fee cases likely to produce a sizeable fund from which counsel fees could be paid." (*Ibid.*)

Attorneys' fees are available to child advocates in federal court under the following circumstances: (1) a diversity case in federal court where state causes of action are pled and that state allows such fees; (2) the specific statute litigated authorizes or mandates fees; and (3) a common fund is created to allow "fee sharing."

Statutory attorneys' fees are common in many areas of public interest practice: environmental law, sunshine statutes (such as public records act statutes), taxpayer waste (*qui tam*) actions, antitrust, and civil rights cases. But note that most statutes giving rights or benefits to children lack such clauses, at both state and federal levels. In some cases, a child rights case may invoke civil rights concepts. But unlike groups delineated by race, religion, or gender, children are not a suspect class entitled to strict or heightened scrutiny (see Chapters 3 to 13).

Many child rights cases are brought under 42 U.S.C. § 1983, particularly where relevant to foster children who are within state custody and to whom its civil rights provisions will apply. As discussed above, the "multiplier" or augmentation above the "lodestar" of actual hours at market rate is common within California and other states that recognize the "private attorney general" basis for attorneys' fees. As noted above, the federal jurisdiction does not recognize such a generic right under *Alyeska*. However, will it award an "enhancement" of an amount where statutory fees are authorized and must be paid at least to that level? The Court answered that question in *Sonny Perdue v. Kenny A.*, 130 S. Ct. 1662 (2010), denying the awarded enhancement in that case (see presentation and discussion of underlying *Kenny A.* case in Chapter 8 below). However, the Court did not preclude such an enhancement. It rather set forth a much more difficult barrier to it, holding that the record at the district court did not support a 75% enhancement of the lodestar amount. *Kenny A.* is a major case vindicating the right of 3,000 children to counsel—and setting a national precedent of that right. It was a case on contingency with the possibility of no recovery for counsel, it benefitted many children beyond counsels' clients, and counsel advanced costs over the three years of the litigation. The district court made specific findings about the extraordinary effort and skill of counsel. The case would clearly justify a multiplier—not of the 75% awarded by the district court (1.75), but of 3.5 or more under California law (Cal. Code Civ. Proc. § 1021.5) and in other states and under other precedents. However, the Supreme Court would confine such multipliers in federal cases to extremely extraordinary situations, and tied to such factors as unusual cost advancement or payment delay (that are actually properly included in the lodestar calculation).

Questions for Discussion

1. As Justice Kline describes, federal policy permits liberal allowance of fees as a percentage of a recovery fund (often millions of dollars). Is it current federal policy to make such awards where monetary benefits are conferred to a fund beyond the named plaintiffs, but to categorically deny fees where a momentous non-economic benefit is conferred to a large societal group? What is the policy rationale to stimulate representation of an economic interest, but exclude interests not translatable into immediate financial recovery?

2. One common form of suit on behalf of children is a filing to compel state authorities to comply with minimum federal standards. Such cases have been brought on behalf of foster care children and others. The outcome of such a case may require redistribution of millions of dollars for the benefit of ignored children, but no direct fund is created for private collection. Few such statutes directly allow for attorney fees to prevailing plaintiffs. Is there a basis for an attorney fee claim in such cases under civil rights law (42 U.S.C. § 1983)? Where courts grant immunity or deny standing to preclude such civil rights statute invocation, what alternative is available for attorney recompense and effective court access (see discussion below)?

3. How important are these questions where the Legal Services Corporation (LSC), including a substantial portion of the nation's attorneys able to sue without compensation, is precluded by federal law from bringing class actions? Where the LSC is precluded by federal law from collecting fees if it prevails in an action? (See discussion above.)

4. In the *Kenny A.* case, the Supreme Court severely restricts fee enhancement above normal billing rates. This restriction, unlike many state court policies, applies in any federal "fee shift" case, where Congress has expressed an intent to provide private court enforcement by requiring fee compensation to successful counsel. The Court's holding denies any incentive beyond regular, secure compensation notwithstanding their skill, risk, or beneficial outcome in reaching the courts to vindicate the rights of many. Interestingly, the reward under the "common fund" percentage situation discussed above commonly allows substantial fee compensation beyond such a lodestar. What are the implications of such a disproportionate attorney reward/incentive where a financial fund is created *vis-à-vis* a case involving constitutional rights or statutory enforcement?

5. Constitutional Remedies: Limitations and a Proposed New Amendment

The U.S. Constitution provides the primary court-enforced standard entitled to supersession within federalist constraints. State constitutions provide theoretical cover where federal constitutional standards may be precluded by notions of state sovereignty. However, two major factors impede application of constitutional protection for the benefit of children. First, as noted above, children are not considered a "suspect" classification—thus, discrimination against them invokes neither the "strict scrutiny" test nor a "heightened scrutiny" test. In general, the state need only show a "rational relation" between a legitimate state interest and the practice that the complaint addresses.

The second impediment is the focus of constitutional rights on "state action." This occurs in the context of limiting the state *vis-à-vis* an individual subject to police power intrusion or abuse. The assumption is that the state is the only power capable of organized abuse, and by limiting it we preserve the individual liberty it may threaten. However, abuse may emanate from private power as well—as the residents of a one-company town, victims of a trust or cartel, or members of a corrupt union may attest. Children are among the weakest of private groupings. Indeed, one primary role of the state has been the protection of the weak from private power abuse, whether from labor conditions, institutional exploitation, or parental neglect. To the extent that constitutional standards are applied, they are asymmetrical. They limit the state—which may be the only check on private power disadvantage available to children. Hence, for example, constitutional police power limitations to protect individuals from state intrusion where there is suspected child abuse has consequences beyond the simple state vs. individual (adult) paradigm. From the child's perspective, a proper analysis must be tripartite and include the state, the strong private entity, and the weak private entity.

Over the past two decades, many have undertaken to add the "Equal Rights Amendment" to more specifically secure the rights of women. Some child advocates argue that the rationale for constitutional protection for children is *a fortiori* to any competing interest. They argue, as noted above, that children lack protected constitutional status, are politically and financially weak, and warrant protection written into the governmental structure. One advocate has proposed a constitutional amendment directed at protecting children's rights.[37] In amended form, it would read:

> We, the citizens of the United States, declare that our highest societal priority is the long term welfare of children and of the earth which shall be their home. We declare our interest in the welfare of children of all nations, recognizing that the suffering of any child diminishes all of us. Our commitment to our own children, to whom we have special responsibility, includes the following rights, which are here constitutionally secured against infringement by the state, and is an affirmative obligation of the state to preserve wherever abridged:

> All children residing within the United States shall enjoy the right to live in a home which is safe and secure, to adequate nutrition and health care, to protection from abuse, injury and environmental harm, and to meaningful educational opportunity.

> All children under the age of 16 years shall enjoy the right to publicly provided counsel in any legal proceeding that substantially affects their interests.

In all governmental actions, the best interests of children shall be a primary consideration.

These rights may be secured and protected by all means afforded for the vindication of constitutionally based civil rights under existing law.[38]

6. Statutorily Implied Remedies

Chapters 2 through 13 discuss the specific, substantive statutes conferring rights and benefits to children and forming the basis for court redress. And most cases litigated involve the invocation of statutory remedies.

a. Federal Education Law

Franklin v. Gwinnett County Public Schools
503 U.S. 60 (1992)

JUSTICE WHITE delivered the opinion of the Court.

This case presents the question whether the implied right of action under Title IX of the Education Amendments of 1972, 20 U.S.C. § 1681–1688 (Title IX),[1] which this Court recognized in *Cannon v. University of Chicago*, 441 U.S. 677 (1979), supports a claim for monetary damages.

Petitioner Christine Franklin was a student at North Gwinnett High School in Gwinnett County, Georgia, between September 1985 and August 1989. Respondent Gwinnett County School District operates the high school and receives federal funds. According to the complaint filed on December 29, 1988 in the United States District Court for the Northern District of Georgia, Franklin was subjected to continual sexual harassment beginning in the autumn of her tenth grade year (1986) from Andrew Hill, a sports coach and teacher employed by the district. Among other allegations, Franklin avers that Hill engaged her in sexually-oriented conversations in which he asked about her sexual experiences with her boyfriend and whether she would consider having sexual intercourse with an older man,...that Hill forcibly kissed her on the mouth in the school parking lot,...that he telephoned her at her home and asked if she would meet him socially,...and that, on three occasions in her junior year, Hill interrupted a class, requested that the teacher excuse Franklin, and took her to a private office where he subjected her to coercive intercourse....The complaint further alleges that though they became aware of and investigated Hill's sexual harassment of Franklin and other female students, teachers and administrators took no action to halt it and discouraged Franklin from pressing charges against Hill....On April 14, 1988, Hill resigned on the condition that all matters pending against him be dropped....The school thereupon closed its investigation....

In this action,[3] the District Court dismissed the complaint on the ground that Title IX does not authorize an award of damages. The Court of Appeals affirmed.

* * *

II

In *Cannon v. University of Chicago*, 441 U.S. 677 (1979), the Court held that Title IX is enforceable through an implied right of action. We have no occasion here to reconsider that decision. Rather, in this case we must decide what remedies are available in a suit brought pursuant to this implied right. As we have often stated, the question of what remedies are available under a statute that provides a private right of action is "analytically distinct" from the issue of whether such a right exists in the first place....Thus, although we examine the text and history of a statute to determine whether Congress intended to create a right of action,...we presume the availability of all appropriate remedies unless Congress has expressly indicated otherwise....This principle has deep roots in our jurisprudence.

A

"Where legal rights have been invaded, and a federal statute provides for a general right to sue for such invasion, federal courts may use any available remedy to make good the wrong done." *Bell v. Hood*, 327 U.S. 678 (1946). The Court explained this longstanding rule as jurisdictional, and upheld the exercise of the federal courts' power to award appropriate relief so long as a cause of action existed under the Constitution or laws of the United States...

The *Bell* Court's reliance on this rule was hardly revolutionary. From the earliest years of the Republic, the Court has recognized the power of the judiciary to award appropriate remedies to redress injuries actionable in federal court, although it did not always distinguish clearly between a right to bring suit and a remedy available under such a right. In *Marbury v. Madison*, 1 Cranch 137, 163 (1803), for example, CHIEF JUSTICE MARSHALL observed that our government "has been emphatically termed a government of laws, and not of men. It will certainly cease to deserve this high appellation, if the laws furnish no remedy for the violation of a vested legal right." This principle originated in the English common law, and Blackstone described "it is a general and indisputable rule, that where there is a legal right, there is also a legal remedy, by suit or action at law, whenever that right is invaded." 3 W. Blackstone, Commentaries 23 (1783). See also *Ashby v. White*, 1 Salk. 19, 21, 87 Eng. Rep. 808, 816 (Q.B. 1702) ("If a statute gives a right, the common law will give a remedy to maintain that right...").

* * *

The general rule, therefore, is that absent clear direction to the contrary by Congress, the federal courts have the power to award any appropriate relief in a cognizable cause of action brought pursuant to a federal statute.

* * *

IV

Respondents and the United States nevertheless suggest three reasons why we should not apply the traditional presumption in favor of appropriate relief in this case.

A

First, respondents argue that an award of damages violates separation of powers principles because it unduly expands the federal courts' power into a sphere properly reserved to the Executive and Legislative Branches....In making this argument, respondents misconceive the difference between a cause of action and a remedy. Unlike the finding of a cause of action, which authorizes a court to hear a case or controversy, the discretion to award appropriate relief involves no such increase in judicial power....Federal courts cannot reach out to award remedies when the Constitution or laws of the United States do not support a cause of action. Indeed, properly understood, respondents' position invites us to abdicate our historic judicial authority to award appropriate relief in cases brought in our court system. It is well to recall that such authority historically has been thought necessary to provide an important safeguard against abuses of legislative and executive power,...as well as to insure an independent judiciary....Moreover, selective abdication of the sort advocated here would harm separation of powers principles in another way, by giving judges the power to render inutile causes of action authorized by Congress through a decision that no remedy is available.

B

Next, consistent with the Court of Appeals's reasoning, respondents and the United States contend that the normal presumption in favor of all appropriate remedies should not apply because Title IX was enacted pursuant to Congress's Spending Clause power. In *Pennhurst State School and Hospital v. Halderman*, 451 1, 28–29 (1981), the Court observed that remedies were limited under such Spending Clause statutes when the alleged violation *was unintentional*. Respondents and the United States maintain that this presumption should apply equally to *intentional violations*. We disagree. The point of not permitting monetary damages for an unintentional violation is that the receiving entity of federal funds lacks notice that it will be liable for a monetary award....This notice problem does not arise in a case such as this, in which intentional discrimination is alleged. Unquestionably, Title IX placed on the Gwinnett County Schools the duty not to discriminate on the basis of sex, and "when a supervisor sexually harasses a subordinate because of the subordinate's sex, that supervisor discriminate[s] 'on the basis of sex.'....We believe the same rule should apply when a teacher sexually harasses and abuses a student. Congress surely did not intend for federal monies to be expended to support the intentional actions it sought by statute to proscribe....

* * *

V

In sum, we conclude that a damages remedy is available for an action brought to enforce Title IX. The judgment of the Court of Appeals, therefore, is reversed and the case is remanded for further proceedings consistent with this opinion.

So ordered.

[1] This statute provides in pertinent part that "No person in the United States shall, on the basis of sex, be excluded from participation in, be denied the benefits of, or be subjected to discrimination under any education program or activity receiving Federal financial assistance." 20 U.S.C. § 1681(a).

[3] Prior to bringing this lawsuit, Franklin filed a complaint with the Office of Civil Rights of the United States Department of Education (OCR) in August 1988. After investigating these charges for several months, OCR concluded that the school district had violated Franklin's rights by subjecting her to physical and verbal sexual harassment and by interfering with her right to complain about conduct proscribed by Title IX. OCR determined, however, that because of the resignations of Hill and respondent William Prescott and the implementation of a school grievance procedure, the district had come into compliance with Title IX. It then terminated its investigation. First Amended Complaint, Exh. A, pp. 7–9.

Questions for Discussion

1. In *Franklin*, the Court found an "implied" right of action for enforcement of the statute, including damages—although no remedy is explicitly provided in the statute. In 2005, the Ninth Circuit held in *Sanchez v. Johnson*, 416 F.3d 1051 (9th Cir. 2005) that an attempt to enforce Medicaid standards lacked private remedy recourse without clear Congressional statement of intent to include it. Substantively, the case involved the federal statutory mandate that federally-financed medical services not discriminate against any particular patient group. Pediatric specialists in many states, including California, Oklahoma, and Pennsylvania suffer Medicaid rates at less than one-half the levels paid under Medicare for identical services for the elderly. Providers serving impoverished children are allegedly in short supply for orthopod, neurosurgery, and other specialties. Suits in the latter two states contend that the statute is violated, with long delays and service unavailability a common result. If the *Sanchez* case stands and no private remedy is available, by what means are the statute's terms enforced?

2. How does the *Sanchez* conclusion that the lack of explicit Congressional remedy invokes a default rule of "no private remedy" comport with the *Franklin* holding of an implied private remedy—not only to compel prospective injunctive compliance, but to obtain private damages?

b. Violation of Federal Standards as a Civil Rights Violation

In addition to possible generic remedy available where federal statutes are violated, it also may be possible to invoke coverage of broad federal civil rights statutes, potentially applying their remedies on behalf of children. Although some cases have succeeded in that invocation, *Suter v. Artist M.* sets forth a major limiting line.

Suter v. Artist M.

503 U.S. 347 (1992)

THE CHIEF JUSTICE delivered the opinion of the Court.

This case raises the question whether private individuals have the right to enforce by suit a provision of the Adoption Assistance and Child Welfare Act of 1980 (Adoption Act or Act), 42 U.S.C. §§ 620–628, 670–679a, either under the Act itself or through an action under 42 U.S.C. § 1983. The Court of Appeals for the Seventh Circuit held that 42 U.S.C. § 671(a)(15) contained an implied right of action, and that respondents could enforce this section of the Act through an action brought under § 1983 as well. We hold that the Act does not create an unenforceable right on behalf of the respondents.

The Adoption Act establishes a federal reimbursement program for certain expenses incurred by the States in administering foster care and adoption services. The Act provides that States will be reimbursed for a percentage of foster care and adoption assistance payments when the State satisfies the requirements of the Act. 42 U.S.C. §§ 672–674, 675(4)(A)....

* * *

Petitioners in this action are Sue Suter and Gary T. Morgan, the Director and the Guardianship Administrator, respectively, of the Illinois Department of Children and Family Services (DCFS). DCFS is the state agency responsible for, among other things, investigating charges of child abuse and neglect and providing services to abused and neglected children and their families. DCFS is authorized under Illinois law,...to gain temporary custody of an abused or neglected child after a hearing and order by the Juvenile Court. Alternatively, the court may order that a child remain in his home under a protective supervisory order entered against his parents....

Respondents filed this class-action suit seeking declaratory and injunctive relief under the Adoption Act....They alleged that petitioners, in contravention of 42 U.S.C. § 671(a)(15) failed to make reasonable efforts to prevent removal of children from their homes and to facilitate reunification of families where removal had occurred....This failure occurred, as alleged by respondents, because DCFS failed promptly to assign caseworkers to children placed in DCFS custody and promptly to reassign cases when caseworkers were on leave from DCFS....The District Court, without objection from petitioners, certified two separate classes seeking relief, including all children who are or will be wards of DCFS and are placed in foster care or remain in their homes under a judicial protective order....The District Court denied a motion to dismiss filed by petitioners, holding, as relevant here, that the Adoption Act contained an implied cause of action and that suit could also be brought to enforce the Act under 42 U.S.C. § 1983....[the generic federal civil rights statute]

The District Court then entered an injunction requiring petitioners to assign a caseworker to each child placed in DCFS custody within three working days of the time the case is first heard in Juvenile Court, and to reassign a caseworker within three working days of the date any caseworker relinquishes responsibility for a particular case....

We granted certiorari, and now reverse....

In *Maine v. Thiboutot*, 448 U.S. 1...(1980), we first established that § 1983 is available as a remedy for violations of federal statutes as well as for constitutional violations. We have subsequently recognized that § 1983 is not available to enforce a violation of a federal statute "where Congress has foreclosed such enforcement of the statute in the enactment itself and where the statute did not create enforceable rights, privileges, or immunities within the meaning of § 1983." *Wright v. Roanoke Redevelopment and Housing Authority*, 479 U.S. 418, 423...(1987).

* * *

In both *Wright* and *Wilder* the word "reasonable" occupied a prominent place in the critical language of the statute or regulation, and the word "reasonable" is similarly involved here. But this, obviously, is not the end of the matter. The opinions in both *Wright* and *Wilder* took pains to analyze the statutory provisions in detail, in light of the entire legislative enactment, to determine whether the language in question created "enforceable rights, privileges, or immunities within the meaning of § 1983."....And in *Wilder*, we caution that "section 1983 speaks in terms of 'rights, privileges, or immunities,' not violations of federal law."....

Did Congress, in enacting the Adoption Act, unambiguously confer upon the child beneficiaries of the Act a right to enforce the requirement that the State make "reasonable efforts" to prevent a child from being removed from his home, and once removed to reunify the child with his family? We turn now to that inquiry.

As quoted above, 42 U.S.C. § 671(a)(15) requires that to obtain federal reimbursement, a State have a plan which "provides that, in each case, reasonable efforts will be made...to prevent or eliminate the need for removal of the child from his home, and...to make it possible for the child to return to his home...."....In the present case, however, the term "reasonable efforts" to maintain an abused or neglected child in his home, or return the child to his home from foster care, appears in quite a different context. No further statutory guidance is found as to how "reasonable efforts" are to be measured. This directive is not the only one which Congress has given to the States, and it is a directive whose meaning will obviously vary with the circumstances of each individual case. How the State was to comply with this directive, and with the other provisions of the Act, was, within broad limits, left up to the State....

The regulations promulgated by the Secretary to enforce the Adoption Act do not evidence a view that § 671(a) places any requirement for state receipt of federal funds other than the requirement that the State submit a plan to be approved by the Secretary....The regulations provide that to meet the requirements of § 671(a)(15) the case plan for each child must "include a description of the services offered and the services provided to prevent removal of the child from the home and to reunify the family."....Another regulation, entitled "requirements and submittal," provides that a state plan must specify "which preplacement preventive and reunification services are available to children and families in need." 1357.15(e)(1).14 What is significant is that the regulations are not specific, and do not provide notice to the States that failure to

do anything other than submit a plan with the requisite features, to be approved by the Secretary, is a further condition on the receipt of funds from the Federal Government. Respondents contend that "neither [petitioners] nor amici supporting them present any legislative history to refute the evidence that Congress intended 42 U.S.C. § 671(a)(15) to be enforceable."....To the extent such history may be relevant, our examination of it leads us to conclude that Congress was concerned that the required reasonable efforts be made by the States, but also indicated that the Act left a great deal of discretion to them....

Careful examination of the language relied upon by respondents, in the context of the entire Act, leads us to conclude that the "reasonable efforts" language does not unambiguously confer an enforceable right upon the Act's beneficiaries. The term "reasonable efforts" in this context is at least as plausibly read to impose only a rather generalized duty on the State, to be enforced not by private individuals, but by the Secretary in the manner previously discussed.

* * *

Reversed.

¹ Section 1983 provides, in relevant part: "Every person who, under color of any statute, ordinance, regulation, custom, or usage, of any State or Territory or the District of Columbia, subjects or causes to be subjected, any citizen of the United States or other person within the jurisdiction thereof to the deprivation of any rights, privileges, or immunities, secured by the Constitution and laws, shall be liable to the party injured in an action at law, suit in equity, or other proper proceeding for redress."

¹⁴ The regulation, 45 CFR § 1357.15(e)(2) (1990), goes on to provide a list of which services may be included in the State's proposal: "Twenty-four hour emergency caretaker, and homemaker services; day care; crisis counseling; individual and family counseling; emergency shelters; procedures and arrangements for access to available emergency financial assistance; arrangements for the provision of temporary child care to provide respite to the family for a brief period, as part of a plan for preventing children's removal from home; other services which the agency identifies as necessary and appropriate such as home-based family services, self-help groups, services to unmarried parents, provision of, or arrangements for, mental health, drug and alcohol abuse counseling, vocational counseling or vocational rehabilitation; and post adoption services."

JUSTICE BLACKMUN, with whom **JUSTICE STEVENS** joins, dissenting.

The Adoption Assistance and Child Welfare Act of 1980 (Adoption Act) conditions federal funding for state child welfare, foster care, and adoption programs upon, inter alia, the State's express commitment to make, "in each case, reasonable efforts" to prevent the need for removing children from their homes and "reasonable efforts," where removal has occurred, to reunify the family....The Court holds today that the plaintiff children in this case may not enforce the State's commitment in federal court either under 42 U.S.C. § 1983 or under the Act itself.

In my view, the Court's conclusion is plainly inconsistent with this Court's decision just two Terms ago in *Wilder v. Virginia Hospital Assn.*, 496 U.S. 498,...(1990), in which we found enforceable under § 1983 a functionally identical provision of the Medicaid Act requiring "reasonable" reimbursements to health care providers. More troubling still, the Court reaches its conclusion without even stating, much less applying, the principles our precedents have used to determine whether a statute has created a right enforceable under § 1983. I cannot acquiesce in this unexplained disregard for established law. Accordingly, I dissent.

I

A

Section 1983 provides a cause of action for the "deprivation of any rights, privileges, or immunities, secured by the Constitution and laws" of the United States. We recognized in *Maine v. Thiboutot*, 448 U.S. 1,...(1980), that § 1983 provides a cause of action for violations of federal statutes, not just the Constitution. Since *Thiboutot*, we have recognized two general exceptions to this rule. First, no cause of action will lie where the statute in question does not "create enforceable rights, privileges, or immunities within the meaning of § 1983." *Wilder*, 496 U.S. at 508... Second, § 1983 is unavailable where "Congress has foreclosed enforcement of the statute in the enactment itself."...

In determining the scope of the first exception—whether a federal statute creates an "enforceable right"—the Court has developed and repeatedly applied a three-part test. We have asked (1) whether the statutory provision at issue "was intended to benefit the putative plaintiff."....If so, then the provision creates an enforceable right unless (2) the provision "reflects merely a congressional preference for a certain kind of conduct rather than a binding obligation on the governmental unit,"...or unless (3) the plaintiff's interest is so "vague and amorphous" as to be "beyond the competence of the judiciary to enforce."....The Court today has little difficulty concluding that the plaintiff children in this case have no enforceable rights, because it does not mention—much less apply—this firmly established analytic framework.

* * *

C

These principles, as we applied them in *Wilder*, require the conclusion that the Adoption Act's "reasonable efforts' clause¹ establishes a right enforceable under § 1983. Each of the three elements of our three-part test is satisfied. First, and most obvious, the plaintiff children in this case are clearly the intended beneficiaries of the requirement that the State make "reasonable efforts" to prevent unnecessary removal and to reunify temporarily removed children with their families.

Second, the "reasonable efforts" clause imposes a binding obligation on the State because it is "cast in mandatory rather than precatory terms," providing that a participating State "*shall* have a plan approved by the Secretary which...*shall be in effect* in all political subdivisions of the State, and, if administered by them, *mandatory* upon them." Further, the statute requires the plan to "provide that, in each case, reasonable efforts *will be made.*" Moreover, as in *Wilder*, the statutory text expressly conditions federal funding on state compliance with the plan requirement and requires the Secretary to reduce payments to a State, if "in the administration of [the State's] plan there is a substantial failure to comply with the provisions of the plan." 42 U.S.C. § 671(b). Under our holding in *Wilder*, these provisions of the Adoption Act impose a binding obligation on the State. Indeed, neither the petitioner state officials nor amicus United States dispute this point....

* * *

Petitioners also argue that the right to "reasonable efforts" is "vague and amorphous" because of substantial disagreement in the child-welfare community concerning appropriate strategies. Furthermore, they contend, because the choice of a particular strategy in a particular case necessarily will depend upon the facts of that case, a court-enforced right to reasonable efforts either will homogenize very different situations or else will fragment into a plurality of "rights" that vary from State to State. For both of these reasons, petitioners contend, Congress left the question of what efforts are "reasonable" to state juvenile courts, the recognized experts in such matters.

Here again, comparison with *Wilder* is instructive. The Court noted the lack of consensus concerning which of various possible methods of calculating reimbursable costs would best promote efficient operation of health care facilities....The Court further noted that Congress chose a standard that leaves the States considerable autonomy in selecting the methods they will use to determine which reimbursement rates are "reasonable and adequate." *Id.*, at 506–508, 515. The result, of course, is that the "content" of the federal right to reasonable and adequate rates—the method of calculating reimbursement and the chosen rate—varies from State to State. And although federal judges are hardly expert either in selecting methods of Medicaid cost reimbursement or in determining whether particular rates are "reasonable and adequate," neither the majority nor the dissent found that the right to reasonable and adequate reimbursement was so vague and amorphous as to be "beyond the competence of the judiciary to enforce."....

* * *

Even assuming that it is accurate to call the statute and regulations involved in that case "detailed,"[4] the Court has misread *Wilder*. The Court there referred to the relative specificity of the statute and regulations not to demonstrate that the health-care providers enjoyed a substantive right to reasonable and adequate rates—we had already concluded that the State was under a binding obligation to adopt such rates,...but only to reinforce our conclusion that the providers' interest was not so "vague and amorphous" as to be "beyond the competence of judicial enforcement.".... Under our three-part test, the Court would not have inquired whether that interest was "vague and amorphous" unless it had already concluded that the State was required to do more than simply file a paper plan that lists the appropriate factors.

Second, the Court emphasizes: "Other sections of the [Adoption] Act provide enforcement mechanisms for the reasonable efforts clause of § 671(a)(15).".... Such "mechanisms" include the Secretary's power to cut off or reduce funds for noncompliance with the State plan, and the requirement of a state judicial finding that "reasonable efforts" have been made before federal funds may be used to reimburse foster care payments for a child involuntarily removed.

The Court has apparently forgotten that ever since *Rosado v. Wyman*, 397 U.S. 397...(1970), the power of the Secretary to enforce congressional spending conditions by cutting off funds has not prevented the federal courts from enforcing those same conditions....Indeed, we reasoned in Wilder that a similar "cutoff" provision supports the conclusion that the Medicaid Act creates an enforceable right, because it puts the State "on notice" that it may not simply adopt the reimbursement rates of its choosing.... As for the Court's contention that § 671(a)(15) should be enforced through individual removal determinations in state juvenile court, the availability of a state judicial forum can hardly deprive a § 1983 plaintiff of a federal forum. *Monroe v. Pape*, 365 U.S. 167,... (1961). The Court's reliance on enforcement mechanisms other than § 1983, therefore, does not support its conclusion that the "reasonable efforts" clause of the Adoption Act creates no enforceable right.

The Court, without acknowledgement, has departed from our precedents in yet another way. In our prior cases, the existence of other enforcement mechanisms has been relevant not to the question whether the statute at issue creates an enforceable right, but to whether the second exception to § 1983 enforcement applies—whether, that is, "Congress has foreclosed enforcement of the statute in the enactment itself." *Wilder*, 496 U.S. at 508...In determining whether this second exception to § 1983 enforcement applies, we have required the defendant not merely to point to the existence of alternative means of enforcement, but to demonstrate "by express provision or other specific evidence from the statute itself that Congress intended to foreclose [§ 1983] enforcement." 496 U.S. at 520–521. We have said repeatedly that we will not "lightly" conclude that Congress has so intended....In only two instances, where we concluded that "the statute itself provides a comprehensive remedial scheme which leaves no room for additional private remedies under § 1983," have we held that Congress has intended to foreclose § 1983 enforcement...

The Court does not find these demanding criteria satisfied here....Instead, it simply circumvents them altogether: The Court holds that even if the funding cutoff provision in the Adoption Act is not an "express provision" that "provides a comprehensive remedial scheme" leaving "no room for additional private remedies under § 1983,"...that provision nevertheless precludes § 1983 enforcement. In so holding, the Court has inverted the established presumption that a private remedy is available under § 1983 unless "Congress has affirmatively withdrawn the remedy."....

III

In sum, the Court has failed, without explanation, to apply the framework our precedents have consistently deemed applicable; it has sought to support its conclusion by resurrecting arguments decisively rejected less than two years ago in *Wilder*; and it has contravened 22 years of precedent by suggesting that the existence of other "enforcement mechanisms" precludes § 1983 enforcement. At least for this case, it has changed the rules of the game without offering even minimal justification, and it has failed even to acknowledge that it is doing anything more extraordinary than "interpreting" the Adoption Act "by its own terms."....Readers of the Court's opinion will not be misled by this hollow assurance. And, after all, we are dealing here with children....I dissent.

[1] "In order for a State to be eligible for payments under this part, it shall have a plan approved by the Secretary which—...(3) provides that the plan shall be in effect in all political subdivisions of the State, and, if administered by them, mandatory upon them; [and]...(15)... provides that, in each case, reasonable efforts will be made (A) prior to the placement of a child in foster care, to prevent or eliminate the need for removal of the child from his home, and (B) to make it possible for the child to return to his home." 42 U.S.C. § 671(a).

[4] Petitioners suggest a sharp contrast between the implementing regulations considered in *Wilder* and the implementing regulation for the Adoption Act "reasonable efforts" provision: The former, they say, require the State to consider certain factors, but the latter merely provides "a laundry list of services the States may provide." Brief for Petitioners 34 (citing 45 CFR § 1357.15(e) (1991)). Further, petitioners emphasize HHS's remark during rulemaking that States must retain flexibility in administering the Adoption Act's "reasonable efforts" requirement....

Neither of these factors marks a significant difference between Wilder and the present case. The difference between requiring States to consider certain factors, as in Wilder, and permitting States to provide certain listed services, as in the present case, is hardly dramatic. As for the second asserted difference, Wilder itself emphasized that States must retain substantial discretion in calculating "reasonable and adequate" reimbursement rates.

Questions for Discussion

1. The *Suter* Court implies that the general nature of the "reasonable efforts" requirement is critical to its holding that there is no implied private enforcement remedy. Can this defect be cured by enumerating specific standards in federal law, and invoking the many precedents finding implied private enforcement remedies where such specificity exists? If the statute deliberately delegates such specificity

to a federal agency (DHHS), and such specificity is produced by its rules, would that suffice?

2. Would it suffice if Congress intended such specificity to exist, but delegated the precise line drawing to a state? Does broad discretion to a state to fashion substantive policy preclude enforcement of the standard thus selected?

3. The civil authority under the federal civil rights statute 42 USC § 1983 is subject to the *Blessing* three-prong test (*Blessing v. Freestone*, 520 U.S. 329 (1992)): 1) whether the plaintiff is an intended beneficiary of the statute; (2) whether the plaintiff's asserted interests are not so vague and amorphous as to be beyond the competence of the judiciary to enforce; and (3) whether the statute imposes a binding obligation on the State. *See, e.g., Wilder v. Virginia Hospital Assn.*, 496 U.S. 498, 509 (1990). Even if a plaintiff demonstrates such a right, however, there is only a rebuttable presumption that it is enforceable under § 1983. Dismissal is proper if Congress specifically foreclosed a § 1983 remedy, *Smith v. Robinson*, 468 U. S. 992, 1005, n.9, 1003 (1984), either expressly, by forbidding recourse to § 1983 in the statute itself, or impliedly, by creating a comprehensive enforcement scheme that is incompatible with individual § 1983 enforcement. Given the above, would *Suter* be decided differently if the federal rights involved were amended to make more specific the obligations (beyond "reasonable") to address "too vague for judicial competence in fashioning a remedy" problem? Note that the Child Welfare Act was amended after *Suter* to more clearly describe some required floor provisions (sometimes called the "Suter Fix"). Does that federal court hesitation reflect judicial humility or lack of concern?

4. The federal Sherman Act only specifies the illegality of "unreasonable restraints of trade." Actual violative conduct has been judicially created in thousands of decisions defining exactly what is and what is not a reasonable restraint of trade, including the creation of "*per se*" categories, such as collusion to artificially affect prices. None of it is in these general statutes that are not only subject to orders of enforcement, but yield treble damages and are felony criminal offenses. How does one engage in 140 years of judicial interpretation of "reasonable restraints" in the economic sector, but then refuse to intervene on behalf of children to enforce a law that is rather markedly easier to understand and to apply?

5. Assume a federal court denies that there is a civil remedy for federal enforcement of a standard for whatever reason—lack of Congressional intent, vagueness requiring inappropriate judicial discretion, or abstention. Most states copy closely the wording of federal statutes that confer matching funds to be certain they qualify for them, including replication of Congressionally-enacted standards in state law. What would prevent a lawsuit to compel compliance with such a state standard in state court?

Note on Enforcement of Federal Standards Through Funding Cut-Off

Many of the rights and benefits of children derive from publicly-funded programs. Their federal enabling statutes often reflect liberal legislative intent to provide benefits, and are fleshed out in federal agency rulemaking. This body of federal law forms a minimum standard for state and local compliance. How are such standards to be enforced? Commonly, suit is brought by public interest counsel against state or local officials for failure to meet those standards, often by denying assistance to children in violation of federal law. The facial remedy sought is necessarily the termination of federal assistance to the state. Such redress involves a certain game of "chicken," since the plaintiffs do not want the remedy sought. They rather rely on the desire of the state to retain federal funding (or to avoid the embarrassment of losing federal funds to other states). As discussed above, these cases may raise attorney fee uncertainty and are the target of 1996 Congressional limitations on court challenge by federally funded attorneys representing the impoverished.

Such cases have been particularly successful where enforcing minimum standards in federal statute that may be a "condition subsequent" to continued federal funding. The Child Welfare Act and additional legislation discussed in Chapter 8 have minimum requirements that serve as a required floor for the much larger sums in Social Security Act IV-B and IV-E matching funds sent to states for child protective services and foster care in general. An example of such federal standard enforcement is *California Foster Parents Association v. Wagner*, 624 F.3d 974 (9th Cir. 2010), brought by the Children's Advocacy Institute (CAI), holding California's family foster care rates to be in violation of federal minimum required levels (failing to meet the eight specific out-of-pocket costs enumerated in federal law). The plaintiffs alleged that compensation was 43% below cost, while the group homes received nine times the compensation rate of families caring for foster children, resulting in a steep diminution in supply and in adoptions that more commonly occur from family placements.[39] Two national child advocacy groups, the National Center for Youth Law based in San Francisco and Children's Rights based in New York, have each filed numerous successful cases against state foster care systems to enforce constitutional and statutory standards implicating federal funding.[40]

Chapter 8 summarizes part of CAI's *Shame on U.S.* report, pertaining to the failure of federal agencies to deny federal funding or to otherwise enforce mandatory floors in the area of child welfare (child abuse prevention child protection).[41]

7. Federal Spending Standards Applicable to State Recipients and Possible "Sovereign Immunity" Bar

Child advocates commonly utilize 42 U.S.C. § 1983 civil rights actions to compel state compliance with federal standards. Such actions are brought on three bases: (1) a state action is unconstitutional; (2) a federal statute entitled to supremacy is violated; or (3) a federal precondition for federal funding is breached. In each of these cases states have invoked the Eleventh Amendment to the Constitution, raising "state sovereign immunity" doctrine to avoid federal court jurisdiction. The concept here is that the Constitution does not provide for federal jurisdiction over suits against non-consenting states. However, the leading case of *Ex Parte Young*, 209 U.S. 123 (1908), and its progeny have held that where state officials act in violation of the Constitution, or where federal statutes are entitled to supremacy,[42] state actors enjoy no such immunity. The Fourteenth Amendment to the Constitution, adopted after the Eleventh Amendment, refines the former. To the extent state and local officials act in violation of the federal constitution or effective federal law, they are shorn of the protective cloak of the state. Such a basis for suit has been broadly interpreted to allow for prospective injunctive relief where state officials violate effective federal mandates, including those requirements preconditioning the receipt of federal funds. See *Joseph A. v. Ingram*, 275 F.3d 1253 (10th Cir. 2002).

In addition to the Fourteenth Amendment/*Ex Parte Young* basis for such suit in federal court, a state (or its officials) may also be sued where it has "consented" to such federal jurisdiction. Arguably, such consent is implied where the federal jurisdiction provides funds on the condition that the state expend those funds as stipulated, and the state accepts the funding on those terms.

In *Will v. Michigan Department of State Police*, 491 U.S. 58 (N.D. Ill. 2002), the Court held that municipalities and local government units which are not part of the "state" are not covered by Eleventh Amendment immunity, citing the leading case of *Monell v. New York City Dept. of Social Services*, 436 U.S. 658 (1978). However, cities administer few child-related programs; most are administered by the state, or by counties considered to be "political subdivisions" of the state. *Will* otherwise affirmed the immunity of the state, and of state officials sued in their official capacity, from damage actions in federal court. It distinguished actions for prospective injunctive relief, holding that they are not "actions against the state" within the meaning of the Eleventh Amendment. In *Hafer v. Melo*, 502 U.S. 21 (1991), the Court narrowed *Will*, holding that state officials sued in their individual capacities are "persons" for purposes of 42 U.S.C. § 1983, and are subject to suit, reasoning that their violation of federal law strips them of the protective cloak of state immunity. In *Patterson v. McLean Credit Union*, 491 U.S. 164 (1989), the Court had already limited the reach of the related 42 U.S.C. § 1981 (guaranteeing the "same right" to all persons "to make and enforce contracts").

In *Jett v. Dallas Independent School District*, 491 U.S. 701 (1989), the Court went further and held that § 1981 creates no remedy against a "state actor," effectively foreclosing remedy for § 1981 civil rights actions to state civil rights or related statutes, or to allegations of constitutional breach. Congress responded to the 1989 *Jett* decision by amending 42 USC § 1981(c) to state: "The rights protected by this section are protected against impairment by nongovernmental discrimination *and impairment under color of State law* (emphasis added)." However, despite this apparent Congressional repudiation, *Jett* has been cited in a substantial number of federal court opinions as controlling while a small minority of decisions have held that it is effectively reversed by this amendment. In *Joseph A. v. Ingram*, 275 F.3d 1253 (10th Cir. 2002), the court upheld a case brought by a class of New Mexico foster children who had suffered excessive movement between placements and other violations of applicable federal law. The court held that where the remedy sought was "prospective" injunctive relief, immunity would not lie to protect state officials under the *Younger* (or other) doctrine.[43] The *Joseph A.* litigation consumed twenty years of proceedings and consent decree oversight. However, in repeated cases federal appellate courts have contradicted such a holding to preclude access to federal judicial remedy for violations of federal standards—particularly for children.[44]

Two years after *Joseph A.*, the Eleventh Circuit decided *31 Foster Children v. Jeb Bush*, 329 F.3d 1255 (10th Cir., 2003), a class action brought by Florida foster children to require compliance with the law. The court narrowly construed standing, denying it to children who had left the foster care system, and then barred even prospective relief for those currently suffering violations. The court held that as Congress did not clearly manifest an unambiguous intent for those provisions of the Adoption Assistance and Child Welfare Act of 1980 to provide a basis for private enforcement, there were no individual rights to be pursued under 42 U.S.C. § 1983. The court went on to hold that continuing state dependency proceedings involving each of the plaintiffs "were ongoing state proceedings for the purposes of *Middlesex* abstention analysis" and that the requested declaratory judgment and injunction "would interfere with the state proceedings in numerous ways." Since several forms of relief existed at the state level, including the state courts' protective order and contempt powers, the court held that such a theoretical state remedy (in an action against state officials) effectively bars federal remedy under the *Younger* doctrine.

Similarly, in *Olivia Y. v. Barbour*, 351 F.Supp.2d 543 (2004), the court manifested new and creative judicial obstacles to federal standards enforcement for children. There, plaintiffs sought to represent two classes, consisting of children who were in the Mississippi Division of Family and Children's Services (DFCS) custody, and children who were not in DFCS custody—but had been or were at risk of being abused or neglected. Granting defendants' motion in part, the court held, *inter alia*, that (1) there was no protectable liberty interest in that state's protective measures for foster children because they did not guarantee a specific substantive outcome; (2) the equal protection claim failed because plaintiffs failed to allege that defendants' action toward them was based on an illegitimate *animus* directed against them individually or as an identifiable class; (3) the substantive due process claim on behalf of the protective services class was subject to dismissal because the U.S. Court of Appeals for the Fifth Circuit had declined to adopt the "state-created danger" theory of liability; (4) plaintiffs' allegations did not support a conclusion of deliberate indifference; and (5) none of the provisions of the Adoption Assistance and Child Welfare Act of 1980 created an individual federal right enforceable under 42 U.S.C. § 1983.

The problems confronting child access to the courts for statutory compliance are illustrated in *Laurie Q. v. Contra Costa County*, 304 F.Supp.2d 1185 (2004), where the plaintiff class of disabled foster children filed under 42 U.S.C. § 1983. The class alleged that the county applied federal benefits to purposes unrelated to the children and violated state and federal mandates for that spending. The county claimed state sovereign immunity from damages and also argued that ongoing judicial oversight of the county's foster care activities required abstention which precluded injunctive relief, and that injunctive relief was moot as to children who were now adopted. The court found mootness as to adopted children and upheld immunity as to the remainder because state courts had jurisdiction over the children until their adoptions and held ultimate review authority over the case plans providing for the children's care. Hence, abstention was warranted since any injunctive relief concerning case plan management would constitute unwarranted federal intervention in state judicial proceedings.

A recent example of such "abstention" invocation is the Ninth Circuit case of *E.T. v. George*, No. 10-15248, where the plaintiff class challenged the California caseloads of up to 380 children per attorney representing them in Sacramento County juvenile dependency court. The case contends that such caseloads exceed the *Kenny A.* standard of 100 maximum and the state's own purported ceiling of 188, with substantial violation of federal and state statutes and constitutional guarantees resulting. The complaint outlined the many rights of foster children that are not vindicated, services not provided, and issues not presented because of the stifling number of cases per attorney. It also included allegations about court caseloads, where courts serve as the legal parent of removed children—exceeding 1,000 children per judge. The Ninth Circuit upheld the dismissal of the case based on "abstention," noting that the budgetary agency setting attorney compensation in the relevant counties in California is the Supreme Court's administrative arm, and that the federal courts do not properly intrude into state judicial processes. The plaintiffs contend that the state court is here not functioning judicially but as a budgeting agency, and that federal courts properly check unlawful/unconstitutional acts by states—without regard to which branch is engaged in the violation.[45]

While state immunity doctrine would appear to leave intact at least a 42 U.S.C. § 1983 claim against state officials for prospective relief for violation of constitutional substantive due process rights by those foster children in state custody, the creative invocation of collateral immunity concepts increasingly inhibits access to federal court for aggrieved children. As indicated above, these doctrines include standing impediments (*e.g.*, foster children are now over 18 years of age—not normally a basis for rejection where the issue is "likely to reoccur"). Indeed, the seminal case of *Roe v. Wade* (discussed in Chapter 2) was decided years after the pregnancy giving rise to the case. Other judicially extended obstacles include deference to the state where it may offer a theoretical remedy, or the recitation, as in *Laurie Q.*, of the theoretical jurisdiction of juvenile courts (a jurisdiction that does not include practically the issue here contested—appropriation of funds powers). Since juvenile courts in every state exercise purported jurisdiction over foster children, such an immunity concept may effectively bar access to federal court for foster children victimized by federal constitutional or statutory violations.

8. Federal Statutory Minimum Standards to Protect Children and Possible Contraction of Federal Supremacy and Jurisdiction

The expansion of state immunity barring federal jurisdiction over federal spending standards may not apply to direct federal statutes entitled to supremacy. Accordingly, child advocates here commonly use 42 U.S.C. § 1983 and other tools to compel compliance with such directly stated national minimum terms. However, in *U.S. v. Lopez*, 514 U.S. 549 (1995), the Supreme Court invalidated the Gun-Free School Zones Act of 1990, raising a possible new obstacle to enforcement of direct federal statutory minimums. The challenged statute made it a federal crime to carry a concealed handgun and bullets onto or within 1,000 feet of a school property. The Court held 5–4 that because the regulation was not of "commerce" (an "economic activity"), it did not "affect interstate commerce" sufficiently to confer federal jurisdiction under Article I, § 8 of the Constitution (see also discussion of *Lopez* in Chapter 4).[46]

The context of the decision is significant—occurring after five decades of expansive interpretation of "affecting interstate commerce" federal jurisdiction. For example, racial discrimination in local restaurants has been held to confer federal jurisdiction.[47] The presence of automobiles from other states in the parking lot of a motel justifies federal jurisdiction to prohibit accommodations discrimination.[48] In *McLain v. Real Estate Board*, 444 U.S. 232 (1980), the Court found an effect on interstate commerce in real estate sales—perhaps the ultimate local and untransportable commodity—because sales may involve title insurance and some title insurance firms conduct business across state lines.

Lopez may be overcome by the inclusion of "Congressional findings" in federal legislation explicating the impact on commerce of a measure (lacking with the Gun-Free School Zones Act). Such findings may persuade the Court that a given statute has a commercial impact sufficient to confer federal jurisdiction and possible supremacy.[49] However, the *Lopez* holding is a concern for child advocates because statutory protections for children are more often of a "social" nature than of a "commerce regulating" character. Hence, minimum federal standards may here involve public health and medical care, child abuse and foster care standards, special needs children, nutrition, education opportunity, *et al.* Query, under the *Lopez* rationale, can Congress mandate immunizations to protect children? Is that sufficiently "commercial?" To the extent *Lopez* is not surmountable, it could relegate federal health and social minimums to the states and inhibit a direct national health, safety, or other mandated floor for children.

D. CHILD ADVOCACY AND THE EXECUTIVE BRANCH

Within the Executive Branch, agencies carry out the intent of legislative enactments and budget decisions. However, the work of agencies is not purely ministerial. The trend has been to enact broad enabling statutes and to allow executive branch rulemaking to flesh out specific standards.

1. Executive Branch Advocacy

Two sets of statutes facilitate procedural advocacy for children before executive branch agencies. The first are administrative procedure acts (APAs) at the federal and state level. These statutes govern how agencies adopt rules and generally require a public process, including notice, opportunity for public comment, public hearings, and public vote (where the agency is governed by a multi-member board or commission). In addition, the federal and most state APAs not only assure a public process and opportunity for public comment, but also allow proposals for new rules or amendments under liberal standing criteria. See, for example, 5 U.S.C. § 500 *et seq.*, which requires federal agencies to give an interested person the right to petition for the issuance, amendment, or repeal of a rule.

The other set of relevant laws are generally termed "sunshine statutes" and require multi-member boards and commissions to conduct business in open meetings, with advance agenda notice of items to be acted upon. In addition, the federal Freedom of Information Act (5 U.S.C. § 552) and most state public records acts give citizens access to all documents held by agencies unless specifically exempt. These statutes generally do not impose standing requirements on those requesting documents. Further, they place the burden of non-disclosure on the agency. Both types of sunshine statutes (open meetings and public records) generally provide for attorney's fees for plaintiffs successfully vindicating their terms.

The formal requirements of broad public visibility and disclosure provide an opportunity for child advocates. Those with a vested profit stake in the business of public agencies are generally well represented and aware of prospective agency action. Accordingly, wider exposure provides some counterbalance to otherwise unchecked influence from profit stake advocates alone. However, the size of the public bureaucracy and its esoteric proceedings, combined with insubstantial resources and presence from child advocates in that forum marginalize their influence.

The imbalance of advocacy before agencies is exacerbated by continuing conflicts of interest similar to those discussed above and applicable to legislators. Such conflicts undermine "decisions on the merits" and can further bias public decisions in the direction of short term economic advantage for those with a stake in agency decisions. The primary current checks on such conflicts are federal (and common state) requirements applicable to high agency officials to (1) disclose holdings in industries regulated, (2) recuse themselves from participating in decisions where they have a material financial interest, and (3) to a limited extent, refrain for a period of time from accepting employment as a lobbyist before their previous agency. However, common problems undermining such conflict checks include:

- Many regulatory agencies (particularly at the state level) are literally governed by persons currently in the trade or profession their agency regulates;[50]
- Job interchange between executive agencies and private industry is common, even prevalent, at both the state and federal levels;

- Those with a vested profit stake in agency policies engage in extensive socialization with agency officials, including banquets, conferences, trips, entertainment, and awards;
- *Ex parte* contact (private communications between agency officials and private industry) is common and is generally not prohibited outside of adjudications and some rate proceedings; and
- External information and advocacy on pending issues is dominated by profit stake interests, and many agencies (particularly at the state and local levels) lack independent professional staffs capable of advancing internal agendas on behalf of diffuse and long term interests.

Two mechanisms have demonstrated success in providing some counterbalance on behalf of broader constituencies. First is the reform of creating an internal advocate with some structural independence.[51] For example, the California Public Utilities Commission (PUC) has an "Office of Ratepayer Advocacy" charged with independently representing consumers in agency proceedings. Second is the award of intervenor compensation on behalf of public interest organizations that represent broad and otherwise unrepresented interests and who prevail or contribute to the outcome of an agency proceeding. Both the California PUC and its Department of Insurance regularly make such awards. These two checks on profit stake interest domination of agency proceedings have most often been invoked on behalf of consumer interests, but could be extended to or could collaterally benefit those advocating for children. In addition, measures to ameliorate any of the five compromising factors above may elevate the merits in such decision-making, such as minimizing or disclosing *ex parte* contacts, preventing immediate employment with a regulatory industry upon leaving public office (as noted above), or assuring decision-making by a multi-member board or commission required to make decisions publically—with prior notice and opportunity for public comment and subject to Open Meeting laws—rather than a bureau or department structure governed by a single official particularly subject to concealed lobbying without check.

Perhaps the most significant recent case involving this conflict of interest antithetical to the general and future interests of children is the important case of *North Carolina Board of Dental Examiners v. FTC*, 135 S. Ct. 1101 (2015). This 6–3 decision holds that any state regulatory board controlled by what the Court describes as "active participants" in the trade or profession regulated lacks "sovereign status." That holding has serious implications because much of what state agencies do restrains trade and would be a violation of federal antitrust law but for the "sovereign state status" of an agency so acting. Lacking that status, its decisions that restrain trade in violation of federal law have no "state action" defense and are fully liable for treble damages, and for criminal felony prosecution. Hence, this case represents an unusual federal court line drawing to limit unchecked decisions by special interests. These decisions tend to favor the economic interests of the grouping controlling them and are often antithetical to the interest of children and the future. In fact, the vast majority of state regulatory agencies are controlled by boards and commissions where a majority of voting members are current practitioners of the area of business purportedly regulated by them. [52]

2. Standard Setting and Children

Most regulatory agencies operate through the issuance of "rules" to guide private action or the government's own allocation of services. Rules often set standards to protect the health and safety of the citizenry. To what extent do such standards take into account the physiological characteristics of children? The medical profession has recognized the importance of such developmental differences in its creation of the separate branch of pediatrics, with separate hospitals, practitioners, and procedures substantially attending to their special needs. Similarly, research has documented extraordinary dangers applicable to children which may not be as manifest when applied to adults, ranging from the impact of alcohol and drugs *in utero* to relatively minute lead contaminant damage to developing brains. (See Chapter 5 for detailed discussion of the differences between children and adults for regulatory purposes and the current state of the law in acknowledging them.)

E. CHILD ADVOCACY AND PUBLIC BUDGETS

Child service providers are sometimes organized to advocate for public spending on behalf of the children they serve. That advocacy is more effective for some accounts than for others. For example, education spending is promoted by organized teacher groups, and covers a subject matter of concern across the electorate. However, in areas such as child welfare (child abuse/neglect and foster children), special education, or child care, the practitioners are less organized. The children they serve may lack media visibility and come disproportionately from impoverished families. In general, budget advocacy for children implicates the priority distortions from the under-representation of diffuse, long run interests discussed above. To the extent that structural political reforms are implemented (*e.g.*, public financing of campaigns, reductions in conflicts of interest, less reliance on information/lobbying from profit stake interests), the consideration of children is enhanced.

Currently, the budget process varies widely between the federal jurisdiction and the states, and among the states. At the federal level, public spending is first "authorized" by legislation. Then monies are "appropriated" in a separate budgetary process. Where revenue does not match total sums appropriated, Congress engages in deficit spending, borrowing from buyers of treasury instruments or adding to the money supply. Such a deficit may benefit children if its proceeds are invested effectively in their future; but where expended for current adults, it constitutes a taking for the present from revenues to be generated by today's children, who must repay or pay interest on these amounts.

Almost all federal spending for children is in the form of either (1) capped grants to states or (2) entitlement spending that is open-ended—expended based on numbers who qualify for that spending. Both forms of spending often require a state or local contribution.

Such federal matches relative to children include as major accounts: Temporary Assistance for Needy Families (TANF) (see Chapter 3), Medicaid and the State Child Health Insurance Program (see Chapter 5), special education funding (see Chapter 6), and foster care costs (see Chapter 8). The major direct federal spending programs (not channeled through state agencies and budgets) are the Supplemental Nutrition Assistance Program (SNAP, formerly the Food Stamp Program) (see Chapter 2), higher education loans (see Chapter 4), and the Head Start child care/school preparation program (see Chapter 7).

Although the above accounts include substantial investment, the largest public spending accounts expended on children is for K–12 education from state governments. Total federal spending for children is a relatively small percentage and is in decline.[53] That decline is steepened by increased costs for youth emancipating into adulthood, particularly for higher education tuition and housing—where amounts have risen and are rising much more than the general inflation rate.

In 2010, the federal budget included 10.6% expended on children, including all accounts with identifiable child benefits (school lunches, child Medicaid coverage, education, special education, nutrition (SNAP), TANF, child abuse protection, social services, housing, *et al.*).[54] Those totals include not only spending but the tax credits and even the dependency deduction allowed. That total declined by 1.2%—to 9.4%—in 2017. It is projected to decline to 6.9% in nine years (by 2028). In contrast, the adult portion of Medicaid, plus Social Security and Medicare totals 45% of the budget and is projected to reach 50% by 2028. Note that interest on the national debt, now at 7% of the total budget, is projected to reach 13% by that date. In fact, by 2020 the debt interest will amount to more than all federal spending on children. That trend is important because although virtually all citizens contribute to Medicare and Social Security accounts, they are each passing huge deficits into future budgets beyond those contributions. In addition, these calculations do not fully include the cost of public employee pensions and medical coverage, which total a surprisingly large obligation going forward. Finally, none of these calculations fully include the momentous 2018 federal tax cuts—which do not benefit children in significant amount.[55]

The 2018 budget did add funds through the Child Care Development Block Grant and increased some spending for student programs, childhood lead poisoning prevention, and adoption incentives. But Congress has adopted a system of "budget caps" based on a dishonest concept of "revenue neutrality"—mandating that spending amounts be the same raw number year to year. Such "neutrality" is actually an annual automatic and cumulatively growing reduction, as discussed below. Perhaps more significantly is that those "budget caps" waived for those 2018 expenditures are set for ceiling reapplication in 2020 and at a $55 billion reduced amount.[56]

About 65% of public spending on children comes from state and local governments—primarily for education and health.[57] In fact, school related spending amounting to about 88% of all non-federal expenditures. But this sourcing raises two issues. First, where a child lives becomes a major factor in level of public investment. States vary widely. More importantly, school districts—often in extremely local settings with hundreds of school districts typically within a state, have very different wealth and budgetary circumstances. Accordingly, the local financing of schools, including the *Serrano* decision discussed in Chapter 4, become a major variable. To what extent does our public spending afford equal opportunity where schools are financed by property or other taxes in a relatively impoverished neighborhood where a child resides?

Second, unlike the federal jurisdiction, states are unable to engage in substantial deficit spending. Budgets must balance. Hence, an unexpected revenue downturn imposes special problems and hard choices, particularly where new taxation is politically foreclosed. States often devolve services for children to counties and school districts similar to federal spending devolution to the states. Local governments actually administer most programs affecting children, receiving funds based on population, need, or other criteria. Although local budgets must balance, they often lack broad revenue generating authority (taxation power).

1. Issues and Problems

a. Proper Adjusters

Official governmental budgets often compare amounts proposed to prior years' budgets in terms of raw numbers ("current dollars"). Child advocates argue that all figures should be adjusted by the proper measure of inflation, and by population. Only "adjusted" dollars are relevant when looking at trends over time. More money may be printed and the population of taxpayers (as well as those requiring services) changes year to year. Hence, the common claim that "spending for education is at or above previous levels" may often be misleading. It is not uncommon for official press releases to claim 2–3% increases each year, while in actuality constant dollar/child spending reductions have been effectuated.

b. Block Grants and Supplantation

Federal to state devolution through block grants rather than entitlement spending for qualified children raises the danger of state "supplantation"—referring to the dynamic of accepting new funds intended to supplement an existing purpose, then removing a similar amount from monies already addressing that function. For example, the federal jurisdiction may give the states $10 million for a given purpose only to find that states subtract a similar amount from current spending in the subject area, effectively diverting the intended sum to another purpose. The same process may occur within a state where counties and school districts undermine an intended *additive* effect of state directed funds by reducing their own current spending for the same project or purpose. Supplantation occurs commonly unless there is strong "anti-supplantation" language, usually in the form of "maintenance of effort" (MOE) requirements on the jurisdiction receiving the intended augmenting funds.

c. State "Suspense File" Referrals

State legislation that requires measurable public funding is normally referred to appropriations committees after passing out of one or more substantive committees in each legislative house. A typical initiative or reform intended to benefit children will be introduced by legislative authors, often with press release announcement. Such measures will be voted out of the one or more policy committees where they are initially referred, pass out of appropriations, and then may pass the floor of the house where introduced. Such legislation may then go to the second house, pass out of one or more policy committees and then be referred to the appropriations committee of the second house. During this travail, some measures enjoy strong public support and pass through public votes with few and sometimes no negative votes. However, as they reach the first or the second appropriations committee, they will commonly be referred to what is termed a "suspense file." In many states, unless a measure is affirmatively brought out of "suspense" by the decision of the appropriations committee chair (usually in consultation with the Governor or the Department of Finance), it is effectively defeated. Accordingly, where a legislative body whose appropriations committee is holding a measure in suspense is controlled by the same political party holding the Governorship, these bills are commonly killed. The spending they would authorize is defeated entirely through inaction and without public vote.[58]

d. Intra-State Realignment

Many states have replicated the federal Personal Responsibility Act's (PRA) format within their boundaries. Called "devolution" or "realignment," state requirements or mandates to provide minimum services are removed, and counties are assigned what were previously state responsibilities. Again, as with the PRA at the federal level, the state may create or designate a special fund to finance locally administered state programs. The assigned fund may be capped or have a source unrelated to the services allocated to it. In addition, the money from the state for such child related accounts may be "supplanted" locally, as discussed above with state supplantation of federal money intended for children.

Supplantation may often be stimulated by other financial pressure on states or counties. The local entity administering a program may lack control over the revenue source assigned, and lack realistic alternative funding. For example, in California, mental health spending for children comes from a pre-set fund fed by motor vehicle registration fees, which may not relate to mental health spending needs.

Child advocates argue that the result of such devolution is the severance of policy from appropriately-related funding sources, resulting in cuts which occur in fragmented fashion, and increasing variations between states and locales as time passes—implicating equality of opportunity goals.

e. Entitlement Status

Federal "entitlement status" means that children meeting statutory qualification for a service are entitled to it. Appropriations vary with need. Within states, such a status may be delineated with slightly different terminology, *e.g.,* "state mandate" or "mandated service." In either case, financing is provided so long as the standards and requirements of the funder are met. Such mandatory language gives child advocates the legal tool to compel performance—the teeth of court-ordered enforcement. The public record on spending for children includes many examples of spending shortfall and service cut-offs, and some examples of litigation to compel compliance with promises made. Historical examples include the failure of Medicaid state accounts to meet EPSDT requirements benefiting children, the failure to provide required "reunification" services to protect children in foster care, and the denial of JOBS child care subsidies to TANF mothers.

f. Tax Expenditures

The tax side of public budgets is a form of spending. Federal and state tax codes include numerous tax deductions and credits allowing taxpayers to forego or reduce tax burdens. That dispensation is regarded by economists as a form of spending, often termed a "tax expenditure." Unlike straight spending, however, such benefits are often not examined. They are not reappropriated annually, but rather continue indefinitely unless affirmatively terminated. In addition, some states require a supermajority legislative vote to raise taxes, and the ending of such a tax benefit is technically an increase requiring such a vote. Hence, tax expenditures are understandable targets for lobbyists. Each year additional tax expenditures are enacted to add to those currently in place. They tend to subtract future revenue from the federal and state general funds, which are the sources of most child-related funding. Some tax expenditures may themselves benefit children, but except for the Earned Income Tax Credit assisting impoverished working families, few are "refundable credits." In other words, they only serve to offset tax liability and hence provide no benefit for those who meet their conditions, but who earn too little to have a sufficient tax liability to offset.

g. Disinvestment in Children and Obligation Deferral to Their Future Detriment

The Congressional Budget Office reports on our federal deficit. It is projected at a record $985 billion in 2019 and over $1 trillion in 2020, to then increase substantially without pause. Its proportion of our Gross Domestic Product (GDP) is a critical measure because it adjusts for population and other factors to gauge effect. In the 1930s the deficit was 35% of GDP. It rose to a record 78% in 2018 and is now projected to reach 152% by 2048. At this level, the many trillions of dollars that must be committed for the provision of prior benefits will create an untenable burden on our children and grandchildren.

Some of the increase has come from post 2016 policies, especially Public Law 115-97 (originally called the Tax Cuts and Jobs Act, the Bipartisan Budget Act of 2018 (P.L. 115-123), and the Consolidated Appropriations Act, 2018 (P.L. 115-141). These acts have significantly reduced revenues and increased outlays. But the problem is deeper, with social security promised benefits at levels that are untenable from its revenue collected, and Medicare—with dramatically increasing projected costs from politically compelled coverage and drug/medical costs that are the highest in the world.[59]

There are three major elements to the debt currently destined for our children:

1. Defense spending. It has risen from $437 billion in 2003 to $855 billion in 2011 to $886 billion in 2019. It has been exempted from the "sequestration policy" that limits most accounts to the previous year's raw numbers, accomplishing a 3%–5% annual reduction from the failure to adjust for inflation and population. U.S. military spending is greater than the next ten largest government expenditures combined, and is four times greater than China's military budget and ten times bigger than Russia's defense spending. While a strong military may be necessary to protect the nation and our children, the relevance of these expenditure choices, e.g., billions of dollars for fighter planes with a dubious connection to current threats, eight military bases in Germany, and other projects of the "Military–Industrial Complex" were explicitly cautioned about in the famous address to the nation by then President Dwight David Eisenhower, previously the Allied Supreme Commander in World War II.

2. Impact of tax cuts. The argument made for these decreases is that they "trickle down" and produce benefits greater than their cost. But the National Bureau of Economic Research found that only 17% of the revenue from income tax cuts it has measured enjoyed a compensating gain. It also found that 50% of the revenue from corporate tax cuts was lost.[60] Going forward, the Trump tax cut will reduce revenue totaling $1.5 trillion over the next ten years. The Joint Committee on Taxation claims that the cuts would stimulate growth by 0.7% annually, which would—even if true—mean a deficit increase of $1 trillion over the next decade.[61]

3. Unfunded elements of mandatory spending. Social Security is funded through payroll taxes until 2035.

After that, promised increased benefits and the steeper population pyramid (more elderly from the baby boomers with fewer young adults to contribute) will create a serious shortfall. Importantly, Social Security is a "defined benefit" program, not a "defined contribution" plan, so although benefits are set, contributions do not have to provide them. Medicare will cost $625 billion in FY 2019. Payroll taxes and premiums pay for some of it, but not a large and growing 49% that will add to the deficit. The prescription drug benefits added to Medicare for seniors is adding $85 billion per year, yet Congress has not acted to lower the extraordinary profits from pharmaceutical patent system machinations. Adding to the future abyss facing our children is the cost of local, state, and federal public employees who often enjoy substantial pensions, and generous medical coverage and as with Social Security and Medicare, for a population living longer and more medically expensive lives.

The point to be made is not that all of these expenditures are unwarranted, but that their effects are properly gauged not only for the present, but as a future burden. The related point is that their provision is the obligation of the generation enjoying their fruits to provide, not those who follow and must pay, and are hence likely to be perhaps radically limited in such benefits.[62]

2. Strategies for Public Investment in Children

Child advocates have employed diverse and creative tactics to stimulate public investment in children, including:

- **A Minimum Floor.** A minimum percentage of general fund spending, or a special fund may be allocated for children. San Francisco's Children's Amendment (Proposition J) and California's Proposition 98 are examples of such alternatives. Sponsors of floors warn that such a floor may well become an effective ceiling. Further, any newly directed spending faces the risk of supplantation, as discussed above.
- **Special District or Other Special Fund Financing.** Florida allows for this format by local vote of special districts to fund children's services.
- **Use of 501(c)(3) Status.** Most jurisdictions employ public counsel to represent abused children in court. That structure allows tax benefits to flow to private contributors, and removes conflicts of interest common where counsel employed by a county to represent a child also represents county agencies.
- **Bonds/Debt Instruments.** Bond financing is a substantial source of public capital investment—even to build prisons and other facilities which generate no return. Could one create a bond-financed social service system, which demonstrably saves money through prevention? Why shouldn't such ventures be funded through general revenue bond sales, with the return on public savings designated for repayment?
- **Crime Victim Restitution Funds.** Almost every state has a crime victim restitution fund fed by court assessed fines *et al.* and the federal jurisdiction adds funds to each state's fund, declaring child victims to be of high priority for recompense, see 42 U.S.C. § 10601 *et seq.* Such funds finance medical treatment and assistance for injured and traumatized youngsters. Many states impede child access, *e.g.*, by requiring traditional police reports when much child abuse is investigated civilly by child protective services. Expanding eligibility beyond police reports opens funding for children.
- **Leveraging Maximum Federal Dollars.** Most federal funding for children comes with a state match requirement. Federal funds tend not to supply the outreach monies needed to maximize participation. State investment in full participation leverages maximum use of available federal funds. For example, summer school, school breakfasts, and child care nutrition programs for impoverished children are underutilized. Typically, state spending in these areas is less than 10% of the federal program dollars at issue. Often, additional state outreach dollars can

yield a better than 5–1 ratio in additional federal dollars. Perhaps the most extreme example of a failure to so leverage is the decision of numerous governors not to join in Medicaid expansion of particular benefit to children—despite the fact that 90% is financed federally.

- **New Grants.** There are new grant opportunities emerging from the federal administration and from the private sector. From the latter: a new fund from Hewlett, a strong continuing commitment from the Annie E. Casey Foundation, a major effort from Carnegie, a Center for the Future of Children from Packard, a new Ford Foundation initiative, investment by the MacArthur Foundation in juvenile justice reform, and others. Advocacy funding is growing as a foundation priority given the leveraged impact it has demonstrated.

- **Required Bulk Purchasing.** In the 1980s, national pharmaceutical companies successfully sponsored legislation within states to prohibit state bulk purchase of vaccines at a discount. Some states have won reversal of that policy and such bulk purchasing of products directed at impoverished children (such as vaccines and WIC nutritional supplements) saves substantial public monies, allowing more extensive coverage without appropriations increase.

- **Use of Existing Bureaucracy and Legal Regimes.** Even where paternity is known and child support orders are entered, child support collection is paltry. Over 20% of America's children are eligible for child support from an absent parent. Although collections have been increasing, they remain relatively trivial, with children of unwed parents receiving an average of $137 per month per child.[63] A large percentage live below the poverty line. This monthly figure contrasts starkly with the $800 to $1000 per month received by foster parents for each child in their care—an amount calculated to include the basic eight out-of-pocket costs federal law (the Child Welfare Act) requires. See the *Wagner* case and discussion in Chapter 8 below. One possible improvement puts existing bureaucracies to work collecting support. For example, some states have given their state tax collection agencies the authority to collect support payments delinquent over 90 days. The advantages include the use of an existing bureaucracy already engaged in money collection, agency tie-in to the IRS sources of information for collection, and legal status as a "tax lien" which is not dischargeable.

- **Tax Expenditures**. As discussed above, tax expenditures have focused on organized interests, the elderly, and middle class adults. One major exception is the federal earned income tax credit (EITC) which provides substantial income to working poor parents earning near the poverty line. As a refundable tax credit, it is paid to an eligible family regardless of income or tax liability. That is, since it is fully "refundable" it does not just subtract from tax liability but will produce an affirmative check from the government where income is too low to create a tax obligation. The ceiling 2018 amount of the annual EITC goes up to $3,461 with one child, $5,716 with two, and $6,431 with more than two.[64] Related to this credit is the evolving Child Care Tax Credit (CTTC). The amount here is 15% of earnings above $2,500— up to $2,000 per child in care expenses. Importantly, it is now partially refundable. That is, if your income is too low for significant taxes that would benefit from that subtraction, up to $1,400 per child may be affirmatively provided.[65]

- **The Federal EITC** can currently add up to $2,353 to the income of a working family with one child and up to $3,888 for families with two or more children. Only a few states have enacted state supplemental credits (*e.g.*, calculated at 10%–30% of the federal credit). Such additions create substantial benefits for impoverished children, helping working families at the margin. Aside from allowances for dependents, the other major source of federal assistance is child care credits, but— as noted above—these have generally not been refundable and tend to benefit middle class families rather than children living in families near the poverty line.

- **Interest Deferral and Forgiveness**. Many states provide limited scholarships for students admitted to higher education institutions. The federal government and many states also provide loan assistance, including low interest loans, and interest deferral until after graduation. Expansion of these programs can leverage opportunity for youth.

- **Tuition Reductions**. In addition to providing additional funds for children, another alternative is to reduce costs which serve as a barrier to their advancement. Low tuition for community colleges and state university systems provides such a child-related public benefit.

- **Regulatory Cross Subsidies and Incentives.** Public investment in children can take the form of little discussed regulatory subsidies. Such subsidies are often not a part of the continuing budget process, are not always subject to wide public debate, and continue automatically unless affirmatively ended. Such subsidies often involve rate or insurance systems which socialize costs for the benefit of those especially in need. Expansion of health insurance for children, or lower utility rates for the first increment of power usage by families with children are examples.

- **Industry Fees.** Legislatures may address a social harm by allowing the financial assessment of an industry responsible for it. For example, in 1991 the California legislature enacted AB 2038 (Connelly), the Childhood Lead Poisoning Prevention Act, which assesses the paint and oil industries based on their contribution to environmental lead to pay for monitoring of children and mitigation. Although many of the firms in the assessed industries are reconstituted or different from those contributing to lead contamination, the court has upheld the fee's constitutionality.[66]

- *Cy Pres* **Funds.** Class action or private attorney general cases may allow for the creation of a residuary fund after all identifiable claimants are paid damages or restitution or where payment to victims directly may be impractical. *Cy pres* ("as close as possible") relief allows courts to direct such sums disgorged from wrongdoers to the general benefit of the aggrieved group, or to a charity serving them. Organizations serving children can be eligible for such funds.

- **Punitive Damage Awards.** The primary purpose of punitive damages is to sanction a wrongdoer and to deter similar future conduct. But the incentive for a plaintiff or his counsel to add such a claim may not require its entire award to them. The named plaintiff may be one of many injured by the defendant. A statute allowing allocation of a portion of punitive damage awards to the broader group harmed, and/ or to children's programs on a *cy pres* basis could spread their benefits to a larger population.
- **Special Products.** In 1992, the Children's Advocacy Institute sponsored legislation to create the California Kids' Plates Program, which added four symbols to customized vehicle license plates (a child's handprint, a star, a heart, and a plus sign). Revenues from the sales of these special license plates, now reaching millions of dollars annually, are directed to a special fund for child facility inspections, poison control centers, safety, child abuse prevention, and related purposes.

F. ADVOCACY FOR CHILDREN AND THE MEDIA

1. Story Selection: Setting the Public Agenda

Notwithstanding the disappointment of many child advocates with the evolution of news toward entertainment, it remains the major tool available to them given general public sympathy for children. Those public sentiments are of marginal use in direct public policy negotiations because of the skill of special interest public relations experts in framing their arguments around other commonly revered points of agreement. However, to the extent the media pays attention to issues and reports on the actions of public officials, underlying public priorities can affect public decisions. Media attention requires that the subject matter for attention relate somehow to the needs of children, that the "media agenda" as reflected in subject matter (story selection) includes their issues.

THE MEDIA AND THE COVERAGE OF CHILDREN

Kathie Lee Gifford faces the camera dramatically, her hair is uncharacteristically disheveled; she looks a mess. She speaks in tremulous tones, about her outrage over accusations that the clothes sold under her name come from exploited children. Her appearance was preceded and followed by substantial attention to the issue of child labor. The trigger for the increased attention could have been the GATT treaty, but that was not a trigger. Nor was the trigger the gradual increase in child labor over the last decade—as international firms gravitate to the lowest common denominator for market advantage. Rather, it was a celebrity caught in a bind, boy bites dog—the "petty irony."

What the media chooses to cover may determine public policies. Our values are largely shaped by what we are thinking about. It is the subject matter of our thought—how much time and attention we devote to a problem that determines our priorities. They are especially important for the diffuse and future interests not well represented in Washington or state capitols. Although representing ethical sensibilities (to provide a better life for those who follow us)—these interests may depend on the bright light of repeated media attention.

The bias of story selection by journalists is not a matter of "liberal" or "conservative." It is a cultural phenomenon operating by predictable profession-specific rules. Journalists can be defensive about these biases, and often deny they exist. They not only exist, but can be catalogued.

The factors counting strongly toward "news" coverage include: (1) events involving a celebrity; (2) naughty sex or nudity (often at an adolescent-sniggering level); (3) violence; (4) a "contest," or an event involving a record; (5) something "cute" (e.g., animals); (6) a story involving strong sentiment (e.g., an individual rescue or sacrifice); (7) anything with an unexpected "twist," the petty irony noted above (e.g., the EPA Director driving gas guzzling car); and (8) a story recently or contemporaneously covered elsewhere, or where there is a photograph or video tape available.

Increasingly, TV news has added coverage of the fictional characters of their respective network's entertainment offerings and characters—as actual news events Does what is put "on our table" by news editors define what is important for us to know among the thousands of events which occurred on a given day? Were scientific discoveries surveyed? Substantial acts of charity? A momentous institutional achievement by a foundation, or government agency or corporation? Most important, the abandonment of impoverished children by some mothers, many fathers?

One problem is that the media is not good at covering anything gradual, even if massive. There is no "handle." To cover it implies that the journalist *has* bias, has made a *substantive* judgment that something warrants attention; believe it or not, such a judgment apart from the eight factors listed above, is commonly considered unprofessional.

We have to find a way to pay attention to a gradual process affecting the people we care the most about, to declare some subjects "stories" on some rational basis. And I do not mean the occasional feature or oblique try for the Pulitzer—I mean coverage, the kind of coverage that was given to Hugh Grant's tryst with a hooker (4 of the 7 factors: celebrity, sex, the petty irony of a leading man paying for sex, and coverage elsewhere). The kind of coverage given to Tom Cruise and Jennifer Lopez and to every insult uttered by President Trump or by his detractors -- without any significant coverage of actual child effects and prospects.[67]

2. Child Advocacy Media Strategies

A child advocate engaged in media relations must be aware of the need for a recognized "handle" for story coverage or opinion piece entry. In general, such a handle must correspond to one or more of the factors listed above. For example, a story must be spun around an "event" which is a "record" or involves "conflict or a contest." A personal profile with pathos must be found. Such management is not dishonest, nor are all of the biases of the media irrational. The media depend upon market interest and whatever is featured must be *interesting* or somehow noteworthy.

One child advocate known for her media skill is Margaret Brodkin of Coleman Advocates for Children in San Francisco. During a recent December she had a parade of school children dragging their little red wagons to city hall to present their "wish list" to the Mayor. Santa Claus accompanied them, along with television cameras from the local news. When they arrived at the Mayor's office, apparently unexpected, Santa was seen trying to arrange for a short visit with the Mayor. "I'm sorry," said his secretary in the high ceilinged anteroom, "he is very busy and can't see you." Without missing a beat, Brodkin's Santa turned full face to the camera and intoned, "gee that's too bad, because, you see, this is Santa's busy time also." Coverage was pervasive and children's needs were on the table for discussion.

Questions for Discussion

1. Many child advocates argue that current juvenile dependency court confidentiality disadvantages child abuse victims. They point out that where an offense is committed by an adult against another adult, the entire process is public, but when a child is the victim most states invoke strong presumptive confidentiality. Allegedly, that secrecy impedes public coverage of the conditions leading to abuse and neglect, and to the plight of children in the foster care system. Other child advocates argue that confidentiality is important to protect the privacy of children. Is it possible to have a presumptively open system where counsel for the child (or perhaps other parties) can petition for a protective order in cases where the best interests of the child warrant confidentiality? What would be the political implications of more extensive coverage of these children?

2. Some political scientists are critical of legislative enactments (or other public policy decisions) driven by a single dramatic incident (statutes may be enacted based on (and even named after) a highly publicized child victim). The political scientists argue that such drama may skew outcomes to address what may be an unusual wrong, while creating injustices in more prevalent circumstances. On the other hand, the human consequences of public policies are important, and without the public attention they bring, child advocates argue that it is difficult to gain attention to counterbalance financially dominant special interest advocacy. How can these two concerns be reconciled?

3. Public officials who advocate new revenue for child investment—even when an economic downturn chokes off general fund spending for children in need—are ostentatiously labeled "tax and spenders." Does the media bear any responsibility for the common anathema to a tax increase to benefit children? Does a new tax expenditure for commercial interests depleting the general fund warrant equivalent public attention? Does it receive it? Do the consequences of not spending for children in need properly yield media discussion?

ENDNOTES

[1] See www.opensecrets.org.

[2] See National Conference of State Legislators at http://www.ncsl.org/research/elections-and-campaigns/state-limits-on-contributions-to-candidates.aspx.

[3] See Federal Election Commission at https://www.fec.gov/help-candidates-and-committees/candidate-taking-receipts/contribution-limits/.

[4] See https://www.opensecrets.org/pacs/toppacs.php?cycle=2018&party=A, retrieved on February 22, 2019.

[5] See https://www.opensecrets.org/elections-overview/did-money-win, retrieved on February 22, 2019.

[6] See https://www.opensecrets.org/overview/, retrieved on February 22, 2019.

[7] See https://www.opensecrets.org/overview/pac2cands.php?cycle=2018, retrieved on February 22, 2019.

[8] National Conference of State Legislatures, *Overview of State Laws on Public Financing* at http://www.ncsl.org/research/elections-and-campaigns/public-financing-of-campaigns-overview.aspx.

[9] M.G.L. Chapter 55C.

[10] 2001 H.R. 2356 (Shays, Meehan).

[11] For a discussion of the § 527 evasion of soft money reform, see Public Citizen, *Deja Vu Soft Money: Outlawed Contributions Likely to Flow to Shadowy 527 Groups that Skirt Flawed Disclosure Law* (Washington, D.C.; April 2002).

[12] The statute prohibits contributions from persons under 18 years of age to avoid multiplication of the limits for families with children. Would the same basic purpose be accomplished through a tighter maximum limit for children, *e.g.*, $100 for children 14 to 18 years of age and $20 for children from 5 to 14 years of age? Some child advocates argue that such limits would correspond more to possible contributions from child earnings without unduly expanding the maximum $2,000 limit for adults through the artifice of counting children. Would such a compromise provide opportunity to some children for the civics lesson benefit of contributing to candidates they support? Is a categorical ban constitutional, given this or other less restrictive alternatives?

[13] See *California Teachers Association v. Hayes*, 5 Cal. App. 4th 1513 (1992).

[14] See www.opensecrets.org/lobby/, retrieved on February 22, 2019.

[15] Charles H. Bruner, PhD., *Philanthropy, Advocacy, Vulnerable Children, and Federal Policy, Working Paper*, National Center for Service Integration, NCSI Clearinghouse and the Child and Family Policy Center, 2009, at 66–67.

[16] *Id.*

[17] See https://www.opensecrets.org/lobby/top.php?showYear=2018&indexType=i, retrieved on February 22, 2019.

[18] Joe Eaton and M.B. Pell, *Lobbyists Swarm Capitol to Influence Health Reform*, Center for Public Integrity (February 23, 2010) at 1.

[19] Congress Watch, *The Other Drug War 2003*, Public Citizen (June 2003) at 1; see Appendix A listing the lobbyists and their former positions.

[20] *Conference Klatch*, Center for Responsive Politics and Public Citizen (June 11, 2010) at 5–6.

[21] See https://www.opensecrets.org/lobby/lobby00/former.php, retrieved on February 22, 2019.

[22] See Remarks at the 22nd annual conference of the Council on Governmental Ethics Laws in Tampa, Fla., Dec. 5, 2000. See www.public-i.org/report.aspx?aid=440.

[23] See *Friends for All Children, Inc. v. Lockheed Aircraft*, 533 F. Supp. 895 (D. D.C. 1982).

[24] See *contra* the states of New Hampshire and Wisconsin, which require appointment of a guardian ad litem for a child in all disputed custody cases. Montana and several other states require a court to consider such an appointment and state for the record why one is not made.

[25] Robert Noel Jacobs, Christina Riehl, *Doing More for Children with Less: Multidisciplinary Representation of Poor Children in Family Court and Probate Court*, 50 LOYOLA OF LOS ANGELES L. REV. (2016).

[26] Omnibus Consolidated Rescissions and Appropriations Act of 1996, Pub. L. No. 104-134, § 504(a)(7).

[27] *Id.* at § 504(a)(18).

[28] In the 1950s, the state of Virginia attempted to prohibit the NAACP from encouraging African-American parents to file suits against segregated school systems. Its ban, which includes attorneys and non-attorneys (as does the Legal Services prohibition above), was overturned by the Supreme Court as an infringement on free speech. See *NAACP v. Button*, 371 U.S. 415 (1963).

[29] Omnibus Consolidated Rescissions and Appropriations Act of 1996, *supra* note 26, at § 504(a) (13).

[30] The (b)(1) class includes cases where the defendant is obliged to treat class members alike, or where members claim money from a fund insufficient to satisfy all claimants. The 23(b)(2) provision focuses on cases where broad, injunctive or declaratory relief is sought. Note that under some circumstances such injunctive relief may include restitution.

[31] See *Phillips Petroleum Co. v. Shutts*, 472 U.S. 797 (1985); see also *Norwest Mortgage, Inc. v. Superior Court of San Diego County*, 72 Cal. App. 4th 214 (1999). See also *In Re Asbestos Sch. Litig.*, 104 F.R.D. 422, 434 (E.D. Pa. 1984) (discussing the similarity of negligence and strict liability in U.S. jurisdictions) *aff'd in part and reversed in part sub nom School Dist. of Lancaster v. Lake Asbestos, Ltd. (In re Sch. Asbestos Litig.)*, 789 F.2d 996, 1010 (3d Cir. 1986), cert. denied, 479 U.S. 852 (1986).

[32] Defendants filed an appeal of this decision in November 2001. However, in order to avoid posting $145 billion in escrow until all appeals are complete, the defendants agreed to pay the plaintiff class almost $710 million—which the plaintiff class will keep regardless of the outcome. See Terri Somers, *Tobacco Appeals Record Payout*, Sun-Sentinel (Nov. 27, 2001) at 1B. Query if one or more cases exhaust all or most of the tobacco companies' resources, is the resulting distribution adequately wide? The disproportionate remedy problem is even more pronounced in cases brought by individuals.

[33] See *Fraley v. Facebook*, discussed in Chapter 13.

[34] *M.D. v. Perry*, 675 F.3d 832, 840-41 (5th Cir. 2012).

[35] 31 U.S.C. 3729 *et seq.*

[36] Shauna Itri, *An Introduction to Whistleblower/Qui Tam Claims* (American Bar Association; 2013) at https://www.americanbar.org/groups/young_lawyers/publications/the_101_201_practice_series/an_introduction_to_whistleblower_qui_tam_claims/.

[37] For discussion of the need for such an amendment, with several additional provisions, see Hon. Charles D. Gill, *Essay on the Status of the American Child, 2000 AD: Chattel or Constitutionally Protected Child-Citizen?*, Children's Law Manual Series 1998, National Association of Counsel for Children, at 337.

[38] For a more extensive list of potential constitutional rights, see the excerpts of the United Nations' Convention on the Rights of the Child in Chapter 14.

[39] See http://www.caichildlaw.org/Misc/9thCir_Opinion.pdf.

[40] See http://www.youthlaw.org/litigation/ and http://www.childrensrights.org/reform-campaigns/legal-cases/.

[41] Children's Advocacy Institute, *Shame on U.S.* (University of San Diego, San Diego CA; 2015) at http://www.caichildlaw.org/Shame_on_US.htm.

[42] Although *Ex Parte Young* concerned allegedly unconstitutional state actions, the doctrine has been extended to violations of federal statute; *see, e.g., Idaho v. Coeur d'Alene Tribe*, 521 U.S. 261, 281 (1997).

[43] *Younger v. Harris*, 401 U.S. 37 (1971) established a doctrine of federal court abstention from the criminal enforcement of state statutes or other state matters, absent a federal constitutional or other overriding issue.

[44] *E.g.*, in the recent case of *Sprint Communications v. Jacobs*, 134 S. Ct. 584 (2013), involving a telecommunications dispute, the U.S. Supreme Court unanimously "reined in" that holding to apply only for state criminal proceedings, civil proceedings, and certain orders that are uniquely within state judicial functioning.

[45] See *E.T. v. George*, 637 F.3d 902 (2012). The alleged impact of some caseload limit in California's dependency court proceedings was a major factor, exacerbated by the inclusion of the California Supreme Court as defendant (since they arrange payment and decide caseloads for these attorneys). However, unless an objection is made during a proceeding (*e.g.*, "counsel cannot competently represent this child given other burdens"), it is deemed waived on appeal. Note the contrast between judicial deference in this abstention decision and the SCOTUS precedent of *In Re Gault* discussed in Chapter 9, where the federal courts required radical changes in the state court proceedings of virtually every juvenile delinquency case in the nation, requiring counsel for each child, confrontation, testimony under oath, a transcript and appeal rights. That case, yielding no abstention, threatened the outcomes of hundreds of thousands of adjudications in 50 states. How does one reconcile these two decisions? For the decision and court filings see http://www.caichildlaw.org/caseload.htm. Beyond the issue of an alleged constitutional due process breach in *E.T.*, the *Younger* doctrine apparently relied upon has been moderated in *Sprint Communications v. Jacobs*, as noted above, and decided the year after *E.T.*

[46] The dissent in *Lopez* advanced two arguments: (1) gun sales, possession, and use by youth have significant effects on interstate commerce (including a lengthy appendix listing studies, reports and references of those impacts); and (2) the distinction that federal jurisdiction should depend on a direct "commercial character" is not a useful basis for federal supremacy line-drawing. *Query*, how does the

Court find gun regulation insufficiently in "commerce" (a matter of local health and safety precluding federal activity), and then invalidate state law allowing limited, local marijuana use for medicinal purposes? See *Gonzales v. Angel McClary Raich*, 125 S.Ct. 2195 (2005).

[47] See *supra* note 42.

[48] *Heart of Atlanta Motel v. U.S.*, 379 U.S. 241 (1964).

[49] Note that the criminal format of the statute was noted by and may have also influenced the majority, although if the "commercial" or "non-commercial" characterization is determinative—as the majority opinion implies, it is unclear how the criminal or civil format of the statute would be influential.

[50] For example, state bars exercising public police powers over attorneys commonly are governed by boards of practicing lawyers selected by a vote of their peers. Similarly, state medical boards include primarily practicing physicians, etc.

[51] Another option could be an independent advocacy office within state government empowered to intervene and represent children before different child-related agencies.

[52] See discussion at http://www.sandiego.edu/cpil/current-initiatives/north-carolina.php.

[53] See https://www.urban.org/research/publication/kids-share-2016federal-expenditures-children-through-2015-and-future-projections/view/full_report.

[54] For an updated analysis of child related spending by major account, see the repeated reports of First Focus at https://firstfocus.org/resources/report/childrens-budget-2018.

[55] See Urban Institute, *Spending on Children*, at https://apps.urban.org/features/public-spending-on-children/, based on Office of Management and Budget reports for Fiscal Year 2019 at 2-6.

[56] *Id.* at 2.

[57] *Id.*

[58] *See, e.g.*, Robert Fellmeth, *California's Legislative Graveyard for Children*, SACRAMENTO BEE (Oct. 8, 2000).

[59] See Congressional Budget Office, *The Budget and Economic Outlook: 2018 to 2028* (April 2018) at https://www.cbo.gov/publication/53651.

[60] See www.nber.org/papers/w1035 and other papers by the National Bureau of Economic Research.

[61] See https://www.jct.gov/publications.html?func=startdown&id=5045.

[62] See https://www.thebalance.com/current-u-s-federal-budget-deficit-3305783.

[63] See https://www.acf.hhs.gov/sites/default/files/programs/css/2017_infographic_national_updated_0821.pdf. For more explanation, see endnote 2 of Chapter 2 below.

[64] 2018 data applicable to 2019. See https://www.cbpp.org/research/federal-tax/policy-basics-the-earned-income-tax-credit.

[65] For more information, see https://www.cbpp.org/research/federal-tax/policy-basics-the-child-tax-credit.

[66] See *Sinclair Paint Co. v. State Board of Equalization*, 15 Cal. 4th 866 (1997).

[67] Revised and excerpted from Robert C. Fellmeth, "Budget Advocacy for Children," *Children's Law, Policy and Practice*, National Association of Counsel for Children (1995) Chapter 14, at 323–34.

CHAPTER TWO

Reproductive Rights, Reproductive Responsibilities

A. POVERTY AND CHILDBEARING DECISIONS

Reproductive rights relate to deeply held views of morality, religion, and human purpose. How we decide to have children profoundly determines the world we create. Whereas most children born in the 1960s were born to a married couple during a first marriage, today's children are born into a far more diverse set of family circumstances, with no one dominant family form.[1]

1. Unintended Pregnancy and Birth

Child advocates argue that currently too many children occur as the happenstance byproduct of adult sexual activity. It is reported that nearly half of all pregnancies are unintended.[2] This rate, most recently reported in 2011, is actually lower than in recent decades, with a significant decrease in the number of adolescents reporting unintended pregnancies (44%) and births (47%). However, the continuing high number of unintended pregnancies has an impact on the quality of life for many children. The rate of unintended pregnancy among women with incomes less than 100% of the poverty line is five times the rate among women with incomes twice as high. These women also tend to be younger, with the highest rate being among women ages 20–24. When only considering the rate among girls and women who are sexually active, the rate is highest for adolescents age 15–19. Forty-two percent of unintended pregnancies were terminated, leaving 58% percent resulting in birth.[3]

2. Single Parent Families, Unwed Births

a. Incidence and Trends

There has been a trend over many decades away from births within married households. The percentage of all births to unwed mothers was 39.8% in 2017, down slightly from the peak of 41% occurring in 2009. In 2017, non-marital births made up 69.4% of African American births, 52.1% of Hispanic births, 11.8% of Asian births, and 28.4% of White births. Non-marital birth rates for women under 35 decreased, including among adolescents, while the birth rate among unmarried women ages 35–39 reached a record high.[4] The growth in unwed births (and single parenthood in general) over the course of the past few generations is not confined to the poor, but has occurred across all income groups.

Because of continuing high rates of divorce and unwed births, more than a quarter of children in America will live with only one of their biological parents for most of their childhood—usually a mother.[5] National data from 2018 finds 50.9 million children living with two parents, while 16.4 million live with only their mother and 3.3 million live only with their father.[6] As discussed below, the financial assistance paid by absent parents for child support amounts to $137 per month per child,[7] less than one-fifth the average out-of-pocket cost of caring for a child.[8]

b. Relation to Poverty

Two-parent families consistently have median household incomes more than twice the amount of female-headed single-parent households. The disparity holds for all ethnic groups.[9] The 2017 median income of households with married couples was $90,386, compared to $60,843 for households headed by a male, no wife present, and $41,703 in households headed by a female, no husband present.[10] The 2018 data indicate poverty for a large proportion of children in single parent households (over 30%), with under 10% living below the poverty line in two-parent households.[11]

In female-headed single-parent households, 50.3% of the women giving birth have never been married, 29.3% are divorced, 16.8% are separated, and 3.6% are widowed.[12] For those who have never been married, the poverty rate is a record 56.3%, divorced 20.8%, separated 20.5%, and widowed 2.3%, according to 2017 data.[13] Younger children fare the worst in these groupings, with the poverty rate at 48.4% for related children under the age of six in an unmarried single mother family.[14] The close correlation between unwed births and child poverty holds true for all ethnic groups.

c. Unwed Births Among Teens and Adults

Studies during the 1990s found almost one in ten teenage females became pregnant each year. Since 1991, however, the teen birth rate dropped 64%.[15] This decline is likely due to greater use of contraceptives and increased abstinence. In 2015, 24% of 9th graders, 36% of 10th graders, 50% of 11th graders, and 58% of 12th graders reported having had sex capable of producing a child absent effective birth control. The differences between racial groupings are insubstantial.[16] The data supports the conclusion that the minority not using contraception, or those using it improperly or inconsistently, account for an extraordinary fertility rate— still considerably higher than among other western industrialized countries— notwithstanding lack of pregnancy intent. This has significant consequences, given the finding that only about half of teen mothers obtain their high school diploma, and that their children are more likely to have low school achievement and drop out of high school as well.[17]

The finding that unwed teen births are down must be placed in the context of the much higher teen pregnancy rates in the 1960s and 1970s. These rates and other data make clear that while teen pregnancy remains a serious problem, child poverty is driven substantially beyond the purview of that issue—by births to unwed mothers in general. High unmarried incidence applies to all income and age groups. Counts of families on welfare consistently find fewer than 2% headed by a mother under 18 years of age, and fewer than 5% under 20 years of age.[18] A somewhat larger percentage receiving support may have had their first child as a teen, thus placing themselves in economic jeopardy for later Temporary Assistance for Needy Families (TANF) need, particularly where they have additional children. National surveys identifying the age of a mother at first birth find the mean age increasing gradually, and reaching a record high of 26.6 years in 2015. By race, the mean age of first birth is 27.4 for White women, 24.8 for African American women, and 24.7 for Hispanic women.[19]

d. Family Fragility

In the United States today, a large number of children born outside of marriage are born to cohabitating parents rather than to single mothers. By the age of 12, about 40% of children will have experienced being part of a cohabitating household.[20] These families tend to be less stable, with the average length of a cohabitating union lasting an average of eighteen months.[21] Research indicates this instability has negative impacts on a child's cognitive and social-emotional development. Of course, not every married union guarantees stability, and many single parents or separated co-parents do effectively parent; however, generally speaking, research shows that children fare better in two-parent families. It is less clear why this is the case. A number of factors are at play, giving rise to a variety of potential strategies to promote the well-being of children.

In late 2010, the Woodrow Wilson School of Public and International Affairs and the Brookings Institution published the findings of a major longitudinal study of 5,000 (mostly minority) children born in the late 1990s. One surprising finding was that 80% of poor, unmarried biological parents were, in fact, "romantically involved" and 50% were living together at the time of their child's birth. Most of the unmarried fathers visited mother and child in the hospital and contributed financial support. But within five years, only 15% had married, and 60% had entirely separated. At this early point, only 36% of the children lived with their fathers, and half of the other 64% had not even seen their fathers in the most recent month. About 60% of the absent fathers provided little or no financial support at the five-year mark. The parental break-up experienced by so many children is augmented by "multipartner fertility," i.e., by the time the children were 5, 20% of their mothers had delivered children with other biological fathers, and 27% of the kids were living with their mother's new live-in partner. These new relationships tended to further reduce biological father contacts with the child. Interestingly, the addition of new males in the household reduced rather than added to total family support available—with support substantially higher in families where the children are fathered by one man.

The Wilson/Brookings study also found counterpart effects where original fathers leave and then father additional children with other women—an increasing dynamic. These fathers have new children and predictably spend less time with their previous issue. The study found that the "quality of co-parenting" declines with the entry of new intimate partners. Most important, the study found hat behavioral problems were more common and substantial in single mother homes—beyond those associated with its statistical poverty implications. Further, those problems measurably worsen with every "transition" that occurs (every new relationship and break-up). And the presence of a non-biological father or boyfriend in the home correlates with higher rates of abuse.[22]

Those who handle substantial numbers of cases in dependency court see examples of sacrificial and devoted stepparents in the lives of many children. Such a stepparent role is fraught with difficulties as a newcomer to a family, and as someone perhaps seen as testing the child's loyalty to another person now absent, or as someone to whom the mother now gives high priority. Those new entrant difficulties are not easily surmounted in family dynamics, as the 2010 updated study documents. And experience in child abuse litigation confirms the implication that at least statistically, new adult entrants into households with children pose an enhanced risk of child molestation, beatings, and other abuse.

B. REPRODUCTIVE RESPONSIBILITY

1. Media and Culture

Cultural influences on personal decisions are momentous, and are substantially driven by the media, the entertainment industry, and commercial discourse—the sources of much public discussion in the modern era. In a 2009 survey, adolescents reported learning about sex most frequently from friends (74.9%), teachers (62.2%), and media (57%). Among those identifying media as a source, television and movies were most commonly cited (24.1% and 18.4%, respectively) with 7.5% citing the internet as a source.[23] The increased reliance on television, movies, and online entertainment as adolescence begins is significant, particularly given its influence on the other leading source (friends).

A Children Now study of the incidence and content of sexual messages during television's "family hour" compared three-week periods of 8:00–9:00 p.m. major network programming in 1976, 1986, and 1996, finding sexual content in 43% of the shows in 1976, rising to 65% in 1986, and 75% in 1996. Most importantly, the study found little mention of the potential consequences of sex: pregnancy, a new human being with rights, at least 18 years of costs and support, and a lifetime of obligation.[24] Consistent with Children Now's findings, child advocates argue that the underlying problem with television, the entertainment industry, the internet, and commercial advertising as they have evolved culturally is not that sex is discussed, but that its domination of story lines cumulatively imbalances developing priorities, and that its omissions are irresponsibly misleading. A more recent study found an even higher percentage of prime time programming that included sexual content (77%), with 6.7 sex-related scenes per hour within the top teen programs. Again, references to the risks and responsibilities associated with sex were few (10% among shows with sexual content). Alarmingly, a longitudinal study of more than 1,700 adolescents indicated that those who consumed this content in heavy concentrations were twice as likely to initiate sex than those viewing the least amount of such content.[25]

Child advocates contend that the culture emphasizes the importance of allure to females and denigrates the traditional paternal male role. Data from 2002 shows the average age of fathers of babies born to teen girls in California was 21.5. In that year, of the 51,000 births to teen mothers, 17,500 were fathered by teen boys and 25,200 by men between 20–24.[26] Many of these babies are born as a result of rape or abuse, with a majority of young teens who had sex reporting to have been forced to do so.[27] Advocates argue that the problem indicated by these numbers is reflected in the comic book "macho-bravado" values promoted by action adventure entertainment and manifested in youth gang behavior. It is also the failure to emphasize as a legitimate image those male traits that are valuable to children, starting with a commitment to marriage and fatherhood.

Of particular concern in recent decades is the private and concealed transmission and receipt of sexual messaging through modern phone and computer technology. Photo sharing, solicitations, flirting, and sexting have become endemic through a variety of online platforms, such as Snapchat, Instagram, Facebook, text messages, and e-mails. The majority of teens have access to these communication systems. Meanwhile, direct and flagrant pornography is available to children and youth through countless outlets—online and otherwise—explicitly displaying a variety of sexual acts.

The impact of the cultural dissonance between how we are entertained and informed and how we should live—particularly *vis-à-vis* our reproductive decisions—is not confined to the adolescent population. The unwed birth rates to older women and paternal abandonment at all ages suggest a similar effect on the older audience. Those making incremental decisions as to what will be the news, entertainment, and advertising subject matter do not consider the cumulative effect of thousands of individual but similar decisions to focus on sexual allure. Child advocates argue that those decisions affect what adults and children think about—a matter arguably of greater import than the transmitted message itself.

2. The Reproductive Rights Debate

Competing political ideologies interact in a manner disadvantageous to the long-range interests of children, as follows: (1) Most groups regard a direct state role in adult reproductive decisions as dangerous "social engineering." (2) However, liberals support state intervention to provide birth control and abortion options—including the public subsidy for the poor of both, but they oppose state measures to discourage unwed births—with the limited exception of teen pregnancies, which are politically correct to condemn. (3) Neo-conservatives favor policies that require mothers eligible for welfare assistance to work (at least within two years), limit lifetime cash safety net assistance to sixty months, and deny further assistance to a second child born to a woman receiving assistance. While these measures are intended to serve as an incentive for responsible adult procreation (children born to those able to afford their cost), they may gratuitously injure children. (4) Sexual conservatives oppose the abortion option and do not support birth control options other than sexual abstinence. (5) Some judicial conservatives focus on the political process leading to reproductive policies, opposing judicial line-drawing due to the unelected status of judges and because the courts provide a poor forum for broad policy debate.

The contention between these and other points of view has informed constitutional argument in repeated cases. As sexual conservatives and neo-conservatives have sporadically obtained criminal prohibitions against birth control and abortion, those who disagree (liberals, libertarians) have argued that sexual matters are an area of privacy intended by the framers to be free from state intrusion, while judicial conservatives argue that the matters are constitutionally irrelevant and should be properly determined by electoral and legislative vote.

The context of reproductive rights and public policy now includes the rescission of child statutory "entitlement" to assured safety net support, and reductions or cut-off. What are the implications of child sustenance diminution? Would it be a more effective deterrent to pregnancies without financial means if the work requirement were not delayed two or more years and the cut-off not imposed after five years, but immediately? How would this affect the innocent children who would be penalized by such a regime? How would the various political groupings respond to an immediate means test (if you lack the means to provide for a child, he or she will be taken at birth for adoption)? Is there merit to the conclusion that the current delayed means test is the worst possible alternative for children, *i.e.*, that the delay removes substantial deterrent impact on adult procreation decisions, while the cut off two to five years after birth will have permanent detrimental effects on impoverished children, who are then unlikely to be adopted elsewhere?

More generally, do future children have a stake in the reproductive rights of adults? What is that stake, and is it considered in the leading adjudications considering fundamental rights? What is the policy underpinning of constitutional holdings relating to adult procreative decisions? Are they based on a neutral "zone of privacy" concept? On the merits of the particular state intervention at issue? What part do the interests (and constitutional rights) of children play in the equations produced?

Griswold v. Connecticut
381 U.S. 479 (1965)

MR. JUSTICE DOUGLAS delivered the opinion of the Court.

Appellant Griswold is Executive Director of the Planned Parenthood League of Connecticut. Appellant Buxton is a licensed physician and a professor at the Yale Medical School who served as Medical Director for the League at its Center in New Haven—a center open and operating from November 1 to November 10, 1961, when appellants were arrested.

They gave information, instruction, and medical advice to *married* persons as to the means of preventing conception. They examined the wife and prescribed the best contraceptive device or material for her use. Fees were usually charged, although some couples were serviced free.

The statutes whose constitutionality is involved in this appeal are §§ 53-32 and 54-196 of the General Statutes of Connecticut.... The former provides:

"Any person who uses any drug, medicinal article or instrument for the purpose of preventing conception shall be fined not less than fifty dollars or imprisoned not less than sixty days nor more than one year or be both fined and imprisoned."

Section 54-196 provides:

"Any person who assists, abets, counsels, causes, hires or commands another to commit any offense may be prosecuted and punished as if he were the principal offender."

The appellants were found guilty as accessories and fined $100 each, against the claim that the accessory statute as so applied violated the Fourteenth Amendment.

* * *

Coming to the merits, we are met with a wide range of questions that implicate the Due Process Clause of the Fourteenth Amendment. Overtones of some arguments suggest that *Lochner v. New York,* 198 U.S. 45, should be our guide. But we decline that invitation as we did in *West Coast Hotel Co. v. Parrish,* 300 U.S. 379;...We do not sit as a super-legislature to determine the wisdom, need, and propriety of laws that touch economic problems, business affairs, or social conditions. This law, however, operates directly on an intimate relation of husband and wife and their physician's role in one aspect of that relation.

The association of people is not mentioned in the Constitution nor in the Bill of Rights. The right to educate a child in a school of the parents' choice—whether public or private or parochial—is also not mentioned. Nor is the right to study any particular subject or any foreign language. Yet the First Amendment has been construed to include certain of those rights.

By *Pierce v. Society of Sisters supra,* the right to educate one's children as one chooses is made applicable to the States by the force of the First and Fourteenth Amendments. By *Meyer v. Nebraska supra,* the same dignity is given the right to study the German language in a private school. In other words, the State may not, consistently with the spirit of the First Amendment, contract the spectrum of available knowledge. The right of freedom of speech and press includes not only the right to utter or to print, but the right to distribute, the right to receive, the right to read (*Martin v. Struthers,* 319 U.S. 141, 143) and freedom of inquiry, freedom of thought, and freedom to teach (see *Wieman v. Updegraff,* 344 U.S. 183, 195)—indeed the freedom of the entire university community....Without those peripheral rights the specific rights would be less secure....

* * *

The foregoing cases suggest that specific guarantees in the Bill of Rights have penumbras, formed by emanations from those guarantees that help give them life and substance....Various guarantees create zones of privacy. The right of association contained in the penumbra of the First Amendment is one, as we have seen. The Third Amendment in its prohibition against the quartering of soldiers "in any house" in time of peace without the consent of the owner is another facet of that privacy. The Fourth Amendment explicitly affirms the "right of the people to be secure in their persons, houses, papers, and effects, against unreasonable searches and seizures." The Fifth Amendment in its Self-Incrimination Clause enables the citizen to create a zone of privacy which government may not force him to surrender to his detriment. The Ninth Amendment provides: "The enumeration in the Constitution, of certain rights, shall not be construed to deny or disparage others retained by the people."

The present case, then, concerns a relationship lying within the zone of privacy created by several fundamental constitutional guarantees. And it concerns a law which, in forbidding the *use* of contraceptives rather than regulating their manufacture or sale, seeks to achieve its goals by means having a maximum destructive impact upon that relationship. Such a law cannot stand in light of the familiar principle, so often applied by this Court, that a "governmental purpose to control or prevent activities constitutionally subject to state regulation may not be achieved by means which sweep unnecessarily broadly and thereby invade the area of protected freedoms." *NAACP v. Alabama*, 377 U.S. 288, 307. Would we allow the police to search the sacred precincts of marital bedrooms for telltale signs of the use of contraceptives? The very idea is repulsive to the notions of privacy surrounding the marriage relationship.

We deal with a right of privacy older than the Bill of Rights—older than our political parties, older than our school system. Marriage is a coming together for better or for worse, hopefully enduring, and intimate to the degree of being sacred. It is an association that promotes a way of life, not causes; a harmony in living, not political faiths; a bilateral loyalty, not commercial or social projects. Yet it is an association for as noble a purpose as any involved in our prior decisions.

Reversed.

* * *

MR. JUSTICE BLACK, with whom MR. JUSTICE STEWART joins, dissenting.

I agree with my Brother STEWART's dissenting opinion. And like him I do not to any extent whatever base my view that this Connecticut law is constitutional on a belief that the law is wise or that its policy is a good one....

* * *

Had the doctor defendant here, or even the nondoctor defendant, been convicted for doing nothing more than expressing opinions to persons coming to the clinic that certain contraceptive devices, medicines or practices would do them good and would be desirable, or for telling people how devices could be used, I can think of no reasons at this time why their expressions of views would not be protected by the First and Fourteenth Amendments, which guarantee freedom of speech.... But speech is one thing; conduct and physical activities are quite another....The two defendants here were active participants in an organization which gave physical examinations to women, advised them what kind of contraceptive devices or medicines would most likely be satisfactory for them, and then supplied the devices themselves, all for a graduated scale of fees, based on the family income. Thus these defendants admittedly engaged with others in a planned course of conduct to help people violate the Connecticut law. Merely because some speech was used in carrying on that conduct—just as in ordinary life some speech accompanies most kinds of conduct—we are not in my view justified in holding that the First Amendment forbids the State to punish their conduct....

The Court talks about a constitutional "right of privacy" as though there is some constitutional provision or provisions forbidding any law ever to be passed which might abridge the "privacy" of individuals. But there is not. There are, of course, guarantees in certain specific constitutional provisions which are designed in part to protect privacy at certain times and places with respect to certain activities. Such, for example, is the Fourth Amendment's guarantee against "unreasonable searches and seizures." But I think it belittles that Amendment to talk about it as though it protects nothing but "privacy.".…

One of the most effective ways of diluting or expanding a constitutional guarantee another word or words, more or less flexible and more or less restricted in meaning. This fact is well illustrated by the use of the term "right of privacy" as a comprehensive substitute for the Fourth Amendment's guarantee against "unreasonable searches and seizures." "Privacy" is a broad, abstract and ambiguous concept which can easily be shrunken in meaning but which can also, on the other hand, easily be interpreted as a constitutional ban against many things other than searches and seizures...

* * *

The first ten amendments to the federal constitution do not address private action. They were drafted because of the framers' suspicion of centralized governmental power—"state action." Since the primary fear in 1787 was the possible coercive power of the newly-formed federal authority, the framers explicitly focused on the limitation of federal powers *vis-a-vis* the citizenry. In order to impede the power of the sovereign states, protections must be considered to be within the due process and equal protection guarantees of the Fourteenth Amendment—an amendment which explicitly applies to the states as well. Hence, until the 1960s, constitutional law was unclear as to whether one or all of the traditional constitutional guarantees of speech, search and seizure protection, *et al.* (the first eight amendments) would be considered a part of the Fourteenth Amendment and hence limit state as well as federal acts.

This setting explains the references of Douglas to the inclusion or exclusion of various amendments and protections, including marital privacy interests of *Griswold* within the Fourteenth Amendment. Such inclusion was required for such a "penumbral" privacy right to apply to the state of Connecticut. Justice Goldberg's concurring opinion argued that the mention of eight enumerated freedoms did not imply an exhaustive list. They are framed in light of the specific grievances of 1787. The Ninth Amendment implies a recognition of such additional freedoms and Goldberg would include the freedom to make marital decisions within such an *a fortiori*.

Questions for Discussion

1. What are the implications of a declared reservoir of presumed basic rights within the constitution and applicable to the states *vis-à-vis* children? Clearly, a child is a person entitled to some constitutional protection; is that protection different given the helplessness of the child? Do those rights include only speech, privacy, and belief rights? What about state action that deprives citizens of life or health? Can the state be affirmatively obligated to protect endangered children? To provide sustenance? Emergency medical care? What would trigger such affirmative obligations for the state under current constitutional doctrine?

2. Is it reasonable to cite the precise language of the founders as the outer limit of state intrusion or minority protection? Are the first eight amendments limited to their precise subject matter in protecting individuals from state intrusion, or do they imply that other, more egregious, intrusions are similarly prohibited?

3. Do many of our criminal prohibitions have an ethical base shared by religious leaders? If a religious doctrine is hostile to sexual liberties, does that preclude society from dealing with the same issue? Assuming that there is a legitimate social issue and impact apart from religious beliefs, and that persons are not compelled to engage affirmatively in the practice of religions other than their own, may not the "religion based" moral precepts of the majority be reflected in the criminal code? Do not many criminal prohibitions relate to the Ten Commandments? Does their enforcement thereby violate the religious rights of "nonbelievers" who violate their terms?

4. If the list of freedoms cited in the Constitution is to be expanded based on rights of "privacy," where is the bright line to demark the limits of majority rule? Is it based on the perceived wisdom of a particular state requirement? By its degree

of coercion? By its intrusiveness? By its connection with religious values? By its infringement on the conflicting rights or legitimate needs of others, particularly vulnerable groups?

Roe v. Wade
410 U.S. 113 (1973)

MR. JUSTICE BLACKMUN delivered the opinion of the Court.

* * *

We forthwith acknowledge our awareness of the sensitive and emotional nature of the abortion controversy, of the vigorous opposing views, even among physicians, and of the deep and seemingly absolute convictions that the subject inspires. One's philosophy, one's experiences, one's exposure to the raw edges of human existence, one's religious training, one's attitudes toward life and family and their values, and the moral standards one establishes and seeks to observe, are all likely to influence and to color one's thinking and conclusions about abortion.

* * *

...[W]e have inquired into, and in this opinion place some emphasis upon, medical and medical-legal history and what that history reveals about man's attitudes toward the abortion procedure over the centuries. We bear in mind, too, Mr. Justice Holmes' admonition in his now-vindicated dissent in Lochner v. New York, 198 U.S. 45, 76 (1905):

> "[The Constitution] is made for people of fundamentally differing views, and the accident of our finding certain opinions natural and familiar or novel and even shocking ought not to conclude our judgment upon the question whether statutes embodying them conflict with the Constitution of the United States."

I

The Texas statutes that concern us here...make it a crime to "procure an abortion," as therein defined, or to attempt one, except with respect to "an abortion procured or attempted by medical advice for the purpose of saving the life of the mother." Similar statutes are in existence in a majority of the States....

Texas first enacted a criminal abortion statute in 1854....This was soon modified into language that has remained substantially unchanged to the present time....The final article in each of these compilations provided the same exception, as does the present Article 1196, for an abortion by "medical advice for the purpose of saving the life of the mother."

* * *

V

The principal thrust of appellant's attack on the Texas statutes is that they improperly invade a right, said to be possessed by the pregnant woman, to choose to terminate her pregnancy. Appellant would discover this right in the concept of personal "liberty" embodied in the Fourteenth Amendment's Due Process Clause; or in personal, marital, familial, and sexual privacy said to be protected by the Bill of Rights or its penumbras, see Griswold v. Connecticut, 381 U.S. 479 (1965)....

VI

It perhaps is not generally appreciated that the restrictive criminal abortion laws in effect in a majority of States today are of relatively recent vintage. Those laws, generally proscribing abortion or its attempt at any time during pregnancy except when necessary to preserve the pregnant woman's life, are not of ancient or even of common-law origin. Instead, they derive from statutory changes effected, for the most part, in the latter half of the 19th century.

* * *

...The American law. In this country, the law in effect in all but a few States until mid-19th century was the pre-existing English common law. Connecticut, the first State to enact abortion legislation, adopted in 1821 that part of Lord Ellenborough's Act that related to a woman "quick with child."...The death penalty was not imposed. Abortion before quickening was made a crime in that State only in 1860....In 1828, New York enacted legislation...that, in two respects, was to serve as a model for early anti-abortion statutes. First, while barring destruction of an unquickened fetus as well as a quick fetus, it made the former only a misdemeanor, but the latter second-degree manslaughter. Second, it incorporated a concept of therapeutic abortion by providing that an abortion was excused if it "shall have been necessary to preserve the life of such mother, or shall have been advised by two physicians to be necessary for such purpose." By 1840, when Texas had received the common law,...only eight American States had statutes dealing with abortion....It was not until after the War between the States that legislation began generally to replace the common law. Most of these initial statutes dealt severely with abortion after quickening but were lenient with it before quickening. Most punished attempts equally with completed abortions. While many statutes included the exception for an abortion thought by one or more physicians to be necessary to save the mother's life, that provision soon disappeared and the typical law required that the procedure actually be necessary for that purpose.

Gradually, in the middle and late 19th century the quickening distinction disappeared from the statutory law of most States and the degree of the offense and the penalties were increased. By the end of the 1950's, a large majority of the jurisdictions banned abortion, however and whenever performed, unless done to save or preserve the life of the mother....

It is thus apparent that at common law, at the time of the adoption of our Constitution, and throughout the major portion of the 19th century, abortion was viewed with less disfavor than under most American statutes currently in effect. Phrasing it another way, a woman enjoyed a substantially broader right to terminate a pregnancy than she does in most States today. At least with respect to the early stage of pregnancy, and very possibly without such a limitation, the opportunity to make this choice was present in this country well into the 19th century. Even later, the law continued for some time to treat less punitively an abortion procured in early pregnancy.

* * *

VII

Three reasons have been advanced to explain historically the enactment of criminal abortion laws in the 19th century and to justify their continued existence.

It has been argued occasionally that these laws were the product of a Victorian social concern to discourage illicit sexual conduct. Texas, however, does not advance this justification in the present case, and it appears that no court or commentator has taken the argument seriously....The appellants and amici contend, moreover, that this is not a proper state purpose at all and suggest that, if it were, the Texas statutes are overbroad in protecting it since the law fails to distinguish between married and unwed mothers.

A second reason is concerned with abortion as a medical procedure. When most criminal abortion laws were first enacted, the procedure was a hazardous one for the woman....Thus, it has been argued that a State's real concern in enacting a criminal abortion law was to protect the pregnant woman, that is, to restrain her from submitting to a procedure that placed her life in serious jeopardy.

Modern medical techniques have altered this situation. Appellants and various amici refer to medical data indicating that abortion in early pregnancy, that is, prior to the end of the first trimester, although not without its risk, is now relatively safe. Mortality rates for women undergoing early abortions, where the procedure is legal, appear to be as low as or lower than the rates for normal childbirth.... Consequently, any interest of the State in protecting the woman from an inherently hazardous procedure, except when it would be equally dangerous for her to forgo it, has largely disappeared. Of course, important state interests in the areas of health and medical standards do remain. The State has a legitimate interest in seeing to it that abortion, like any other medical procedure, is performed under circumstances that insure maximum safety for the patient. This interest obviously extends at least to the performing physician and his staff, to the facilities involved, to the availability of after-care, and to adequate provision for any complication or emergency that might arise. The prevalence of high mortality rates at illegal "abortion mills" strengthens, rather than weakens, the State's interest in regulating the conditions under which abortions are performed. Moreover, the risk to the woman increases as her pregnancy continues. Thus, the State retains a definite interest in protecting the woman's own health and safety when an abortion is proposed at a late stage of pregnancy.

The third reason is the State's interest—some phrase it in terms of duty—in protecting prenatal life. Some of the argument for this justification rests on the theory that a new human life is present from the moment of conception....The State's interest and general obligation to protect life then extends, it is argued, to prenatal life. Only when the life of the pregnant mother herself is at stake, balanced against the life she carries within her, should the interest of the embryo or fetus not prevail. Logically, of course, a legitimate state interest in this area need not stand or fall on acceptance of the belief that life begins at conception or at some other point prior to live birth. In assessing the State's interest, recognition may be given to the less rigid claim that as long as at least potential life is involved, the State may assert interests beyond the protection of the pregnant woman alone.

Parties challenging state abortion laws have sharply disputed in some courts the contention that a purpose of these laws, when enacted, was to protect prenatal life.... Pointing to the absence of legislative history to support the contention, they claim that most state laws were designed solely to protect the woman. Because medical advances have lessened this concern, at least with respect to abortion in early pregnancy, they argue that with respect to such abortions the laws can no longer be justified by any state interest. There is some scholarly support for this view of original purpose....The few state courts called upon to interpret their laws in the late 19th and early 20th centuries did focus on the State's interest in protecting the woman's health rather than in preserving the embryo and fetus. Proponents of this view point out that in many States, including Texas, by statute or judicial interpretation, the pregnant woman herself could not be prosecuted for self-abortion or for cooperating in an abortion performed upon her by another. They claim that adoption of the "quickening" distinction through received common law and state statutes tacitly recognizes the greater health hazards inherent in late abortion and impliedly repudiates the theory that life begins at conception.

It is with these interests, and the weight to be attached to them, that this case is concerned.

VIII

The Constitution does not explicitly mention any right of privacy. In a line of decisions, however, going back perhaps as far as *Union Pacific R. Co. v. Botsford*, 141 U.S. 250, 251 (1891), the Court has recognized that a right of personal privacy, or a guarantee of certain areas or zones of privacy, does exist under the Constitution. In varying contexts, the Court or individual Justices have, indeed, found at least the roots of that right in the First Amendment,...in the Fourth and Fifth Amendments,...in the penumbras of the Bill of Rights,...or in the concept of liberty guaranteed by the first section of the Fourteenth Amendment.... These decisions make it clear that only personal rights that can be deemed "fundamental" or "implicit in the concept of ordered liberty,"... are included in this guarantee of personal privacy. They also make it clear that the right has some extension to activities relating to marriage...; procreation...; contraception...; family relationships...; and child rearing and education....

This right of privacy, whether it be founded in the Fourteenth Amendment's concept of personal liberty and restrictions upon state action, as we feel it is, or, as the District Court determined, in the Ninth Amendment's reservation of rights to the people, is broad enough to encompass a woman's decision whether or not to terminate her pregnancy. The detriment that the State would impose upon the pregnant woman by denying this choice altogether is apparent. Specific and direct harm medically diagnosable even in early pregnancy may be involved. Maternity, or additional offspring, may force upon the woman a distressful life and future. Psychological harm may be imminent. Mental and physical health may be taxed by child care. There is also the distress, for all concerned, associated with the unwanted child, and there is the problem of bringing a child into a family already unable, psychologically and otherwise, to care for it. In other cases, as in this one, the additional difficulties and continuing stigma of unwed motherhood may be involved. All these are factors the woman and her responsible physician necessarily will consider in consultation.

On the basis of elements such as these, appellant and some amici argue that the woman's right is absolute and that she is entitled to terminate her pregnancy at whatever time, in whatever way, and for whatever reason she alone chooses. With this we do not agree. Appellant's arguments that Texas either has no valid interest at all in regulating the abortion decision, or no interest strong enough to support any limitation upon the woman's sole determination, are unpersuasive. The Court's decisions recognizing a right of privacy also acknowledge that some state regulation in areas protected by that right is appropriate. As noted above, a State may properly assert important interests in safeguarding health, in maintaining medical standards, and in protecting potential life. At some point in pregnancy, these respective interests become sufficiently compelling to sustain regulation of the factors that govern the abortion decision. The privacy right involved, therefore, cannot be said to be absolute. In fact, it is not clear to us that the claim asserted by some amici that one has an unlimited right to do with one's body as one pleases bears a close relationship to the right of privacy previously articulated in the Court's decisions. The Court has refused to recognize an unlimited right of this kind in the past. *Jacobson v. Massachusetts*, 197 U.S. 11 (1905) (vaccination); *Buck v. Bell*, 274 U.S. 200 (1927) (sterilization).

We, therefore, conclude that the right of personal privacy includes the abortion decision, but that this right is not unqualified and must be considered against important state interests in regulation.

* * *

Where certain "fundamental rights" are involved, the Court has held that regulation limiting these rights may be justified only by a "compelling state interest,"...and that legislative enactments must be narrowly drawn to express only the legitimate state interests at stake....

* * *

The Constitution does not define "person" in so many words. Section 1 of the Fourteenth Amendment contains three references to "person." The first, in defining "citizens," speaks of "persons born or naturalized in the United States." The word also appears both in the Due Process Clause and in the Equal Protection Clause. "Person" is used in other places in the Constitution....But in nearly all these instances, the use of the word is such that it has application only postnatally. None indicates, with any assurance, that it has any possible pre-natal application.[54]

All this, together with our observation, *supra*, that throughout the major portion of the 19th century prevailing legal abortion practices were far freer than they are today, persuades us that the word "person," as used in the Fourteenth Amendment, does not include the unborn....This is in accord with the results reached in those few cases where the issue has been squarely presented....

* * *

B. The pregnant woman cannot be isolated in her privacy. She carries an embryo and, later, a fetus, if one accepts the medical definitions of the developing young in the human uterus....The situation therefore is inherently different from marital intimacy, or bedroom possession of obscene material, or marriage, or procreation, or education, with which *Eisenstadt* and *Griswold, Stanley, Loving, Skinner,* and *Pierce* and *Meyer* were respectively concerned. As we have intimated above, it is reasonable and appropriate for a State to decide that at some point in time another interest, that of health of the mother or that of potential human life, becomes significantly involved. The woman's privacy is no longer sole and any right of privacy she possesses must be measured accordingly.

Texas urges that, apart from the Fourteenth Amendment, life begins at conception and is present throughout pregnancy, and that, therefore, the State has a compelling interest in protecting that life from and after conception. We need not resolve the difficult question of when life begins. When those trained in the respective disciplines of medicine, philosophy, and theology are unable to arrive at any consensus, the judiciary, at this point in the development of man's knowledge, is not in a position to speculate as to the answer.

* * *

In areas other than criminal abortion, the law has been reluctant to endorse any theory that life, as we recognize it, begins before live birth or to accord legal rights to the unborn except in narrowly defined situations and except when the rights are contingent upon live birth. For example, the traditional rule of tort law denied recovery for prenatal injuries even though the child was born alive....That rule has been changed in almost every jurisdiction. In most States, recovery is said to be permitted only if the fetus was viable, or at least quick, when the injuries were sustained, though few courts have squarely so held....In a recent development, generally opposed by the commentators, some States permit the parents of a stillborn child to maintain an action for wrongful death because of prenatal injuries....Such an action, however, would appear to be one to vindicate the parents' interest and is thus consistent with the view that the fetus, at most, represents only the potentiality of life. Similarly, unborn children have been recognized as acquiring rights or interests by way of inheritance or other devolution of property, and have been represented by *guardians ad litem*. Perfection of the interests involved, again, has generally been contingent upon live birth. In short, the unborn have never been recognized in the law as persons in the whole sense.

X

In view of all this, we do not agree that, by adopting one theory of life, Texas may override the rights of the pregnant woman that are at stake. We repeat, however, that the State does have an important and legitimate interest in preserving and protecting the health of the pregnant woman, whether she be a resident of the State or a nonresident who seeks medical consultation and treatment there, and that it has still another important and legitimate interest in protecting the potentiality of human life. These interests are separate and distinct. Each grows in substantiality as the woman approaches term and, at a point during pregnancy, each becomes "compelling."

With respect to the State's important and legitimate interest in the health of the mother, the "compelling" point, in the light of present medical knowledge, is at approximately the end of the first trimester. This is so because of the now-established medical fact, referred to above at 149, that until the end of the first trimester mortality in abortion may be less than mortality in normal childbirth. It follows that, from and after this point, a State may regulate the abortion procedure to the extent that the regulation reasonably relates to the preservation and protection of maternal health. Examples of permissible state regulation in this area are requirements as to the qualifications of the person who is to perform the abortion; as to the licensure of that person; as to the facility in which the procedure is to be performed, that is, whether it must be a hospital or may be a clinic or some other place of less-than-hospital status; as to the licensing of the facility; and the like.

This means, on the other hand, that, for the period of pregnancy prior to this "compelling" point, the attending physician, in consultation with his patient, is free to determine, without regulation by the State, that, in his medical judgment, the patient's pregnancy should be terminated. If that decision is reached, the judgment may be effectuated by an abortion free of interference by the State.

With respect to the State's important and legitimate interest in potential life, the "compelling" point is at viability. This is so because the fetus then presumably has the capability of meaningful life outside the mother's womb. State regulation protective of fetal life after viability thus has both logical and biological justifications. If the State is interested in protecting fetal life after viability, it may go so far as to proscribe abortion during that period, except when it is necessary to preserve the life or health of the mother.

* * *

[54] When Texas urges that a fetus is entitled to Fourteenth Amendment protection as a person, it faces a dilemma. Neither in Texas nor in any other State are all abortions prohibited. Despite broad proscription, an exception always exists. The exception contained in Art. 1196, for an abortion procured or attempted by

medical advice for the purpose of saving the life of the mother, is typical. But if the fetus is a person who is not to be deprived of life without due process of law, and if the mother's condition is the sole determinant, does not the Texas exception appear to be out of line with the Amendment's command?

There are other inconsistencies between Fourteenth Amendment status and the typical abortion statute. It has already been pointed out,....that in Texas the woman is not a principal or an accomplice with respect to an abortion upon her. If the fetus is a person, why is the woman not a principal or an accomplice? Further, the penalty for criminal abortion specified by Art. 1195 is significantly less than the maximum penalty for murder prescribed by Art. 1257 of the Texas Penal Code. If the fetus is a person, may the penalties be different?

MR. JUSTICE REHNQUIST, dissenting.

* * *

II

Even if there were a plaintiff in this case capable of litigating the issue which the Court decides, I would reach a conclusion opposite to that reached by the Court. I have difficulty in concluding, as the Court does, that the right of "privacy" is involved in this case. Texas, by the statute here challenged, bars the performance of a medical abortion by a licensed physician on a plaintiff such as Roe. A transaction resulting in an operation such as this is not "private" in the ordinary usage of that word. Nor is the "privacy" that the Court finds here even a distant relative of the freedom from searches and seizures protected by the Fourth Amendment to the Constitution, which the Court has referred to as embodying a right to privacy..., 389 U.S. 347 (1967).

If the Court means by the term "privacy" no more than that the claim of a person to be free from unwanted state regulation of consensual transactions may be a form of "liberty" protected by the Fourteenth Amendment, there is no doubt that similar claims have been upheld in our earlier decisions on the basis of that liberty. I agree with the statement of MR. JUSTICE STEWART in his concurring opinion that the "liberty," against deprivation of which without due process the Fourteenth Amendment protects, embraces more than the rights found in the Bill of Rights. But that liberty is not guaranteed absolutely against deprivation, only against deprivation without due process of law. The test traditionally applied in the area of social and economic legislation is whether or not a law such as that challenged has a rational relation to a valid state objective.... The Due Process Clause of the Fourteenth Amendment undoubtedly does place a limit, albeit a broad one, on legislative power to enact laws such as this. If the Texas statute were to prohibit an abortion even where the mother's life is in jeopardy, I have little doubt that such a statute would lack a rational relation to a valid state objective under the test stated in *Williamson, supra.* But the Court's sweeping invalidation of any restrictions on abortion during the first trimester is impossible to justify under that standard, and the conscious weighing of competing factors that the Court's opinion apparently substitutes for the established test is far more appropriate to a legislative judgment than to a judicial one.

* * *

The fact that a majority of the States reflecting, after all, the majority sentiment in those States, have had restrictions on abortions for at least a century is a strong indication, it seems to me, that the asserted right to an abortion is not "so rooted in the traditions and conscience of our people as to be ranked as fundamental," *Snyder v. Massachusetts*, 291 U.S. 97, 105 (1934). Even today, when society's views on abortion are changing, the very existence of the debate is evidence that the "right" to an abortion is not so universally accepted as the appellant would have us believe.

To reach its result, the Court necessarily has had to find within the scope of the Fourteenth Amendment a right that was apparently completely unknown to the drafters of the Amendment. As early as 1821, the first state law dealing directly with abortion was enacted by the Connecticut Legislature....By the time of the adoption of the Fourteenth Amendment in 1868, there were at least 36 laws enacted by state or territorial legislatures limiting abortion....While many States have amended or updated their laws, 21 of the laws on the books in 1868 remain in effect today.... Indeed, the Texas statute struck down today was, as the majority notes, first enacted in 1857 and "has remained substantially unchanged to the present time."....

There apparently was no question concerning the validity of this provision or of any of the other state statutes when the Fourteenth Amendment was adopted. The only conclusion possible from this history is that the drafters did not intend to have the Fourteenth Amendment withdraw from the States the power to legislate with respect to this matter.

III

Even if one were to agree that the case that the Court decides were here, and that the enunciation of the substantive constitutional law in the Court's opinion were proper, the actual disposition of the case by the Court is still difficult to justify. The Texas statute is struck down *in toto*, even though the Court apparently concedes that at later periods of pregnancy Texas might impose these selfsame statutory limitations on abortion. My understanding of past practice is that a statute found to be invalid as applied to a particular plaintiff, but not unconstitutional as a whole, is not simply "struck down" but is, instead, declared unconstitutional as applied to the fact situation before the Court...

For all of the foregoing reasons, I respectfully dissent.

Planned Parenthood of Southeastern Pennsylvania v. Casey
505 U.S. 833 (1992)

JUSTICE O'CONNOR, JUSTICE KENNEDY, and JUSTICE SOUTER announced the judgment of the Court and delivered the opinion of the Court with respect to Parts I, II, III, V-A, V-C, and VI, an opinion with respect to Part V-E, in which JUSTICE STEVENS joins, and an opinion with respect to Parts IV, V-B, and V-D.

I

Liberty finds no refuge in a jurisprudence of doubt. Yet 19 years after our holding that the Constitution protects a woman's right to terminate her pregnancy in its early stages, *Roe v. Wade*, 410 U.S. 113 (1973), that definition of liberty is still questioned. Joining the respondents as *amicus curiae*, the United States, as it has done in five other cases in the last decade, again asks us to overrule *Roe*....

At issue in these cases are five provisions of the Pennsylvania Abortion Control Act of 1982 as amended in 1988 and 1989....The Act requires that a woman seeking an abortion give her informed consent prior to the abortion procedure, and specifies that she be provided with certain information at least 24 hours before the abortion is performed....For a minor to obtain an abortion, the Act requires the informed consent of one of her parents, but provides for a judicial bypass option if the minor does not wish to or cannot obtain a parent's consent....Another provision of the Act requires that, unless certain exceptions apply, a married woman seeking an abortion must sign a statement indicating that she has notified her husband of her intended abortion.... The Act exempts compliance with these three requirements in the event of a "medical emergency," which is defined in § 3203 of the Act....In addition to the above provisions regulating the performance of abortions, the Act imposes certain reporting requirements on facilities that provide abortion services....

* * *

After considering the fundamental constitutional questions resolved by *Roe*, principles of institutional integrity, and the rule of stare decisis, we are led to conclude this: the essential holding of *Roe v. Wade* should be retained and once again reaffirmed.

It must be stated at the outset and with clarity that *Roe's* essential holding, the holding we reaffirm, has three parts. First is a recognition of the right of the woman to choose to have an abortion before viability and to obtain it without undue interference from the State. Before viability, the State's interests are not strong enough to support a prohibition of abortion or the imposition of a substantial obstacle to the woman's effective right to elect the procedure. Second is a confirmation of the State's power to restrict abortions after fetal viability, if the law contains exceptions for pregnancies which endanger a woman's life or health. And third is the principle that the State has legitimate interests from the outset of the pregnancy in protecting the health of the woman and the life of the fetus that may become a child. These principles do not contradict one another; and we adhere to each.

II

Constitutional protection of the woman's decision to terminate her pregnancy derives from the Due Process Clause of the Fourteenth Amendment. It declares that no State shall "deprive any person of life, liberty, or property, without due process of law." The controlling word in the case before us is "liberty." Although a literal reading of the Clause might suggest that it governs only the procedures by which a State may deprive persons of liberty, for at least 105 years, at least since *Mugler v. Kansas*, 123 U.S. 623, 660-661 (1887), the Clause has been understood to contain a substantive component as well, one "barring certain government actions regardless of the fairness of the procedures used to implement them." *Daniels v. Williams*, 474 U.S. 327, 331 (1986)....

The most familiar of the substantive liberties protected by the Fourteenth Amendment are those recognized by the Bill of Rights. We have held that the Due Process Clause of the Fourteenth Amendment incorporates most of the Bill of Rights against the States....It is tempting, as a means of curbing the discretion of federal judges, to suppose that liberty encompasses no more than those rights already guaranteed to the individual against federal interference by the express provisions of the first eight amendments to the Constitution...But of course this Court has never accepted that view.

* * *

Neither the Bill of Rights nor the specific practices of States at the time of the adoption of the Fourteenth Amendment marks the outer limits of the substantive sphere of liberty which the Fourteenth Amendment protects....

Our law affords constitutional protection to personal decisions relating to marriage, procreation, contraception, family relationships, child rearing, and education. *Carey v. Population Services International*, 431 U.S. at 685. Our cases recognize "the right of the *individual*, married or single, to be free from unwarranted governmental intrusion into matters so fundamentally affecting a person as the decision whether to bear or beget a child." *Eisenstadt v. Baird supra*, at 453 (emphasis in original). Our precedents "have respected the private realm of family life which the state cannot enter." *Prince v. Massachusetts*, 321 U.S. 158, 166,...(1944). These matters, involving the most intimate and personal choices a person may make in a lifetime, choices central to personal dignity and autonomy, are central to the liberty protected by the Fourteenth Amendment. At the heart of liberty is the right to define one's own concept of existence, of meaning, of the universe, and of the mystery of human life. Beliefs about these matters could not define the attributes of personhood were they formed under compulsion of the State.

These considerations begin our analysis of the woman's interest in terminating her pregnancy but cannot end it, for this reason: though the abortion decision may originate within the zone of conscience and belief, it is more than a philosophic exercise. Abortion is a unique act. It is an act fraught with consequences for others: for the woman who must live with the implications of her decision; for the persons who perform and assist in the procedure; for the spouse, family, and society which must confront the knowledge that these procedures exist, procedures some deem nothing short of an act of violence against innocent human life; and, depending on one's beliefs, for the life or potential life that is aborted. Though abortion is conduct, it does not follow that the State is entitled

to proscribe it in all instances. That is because the liberty of the woman is at stake in a sense unique to the human condition and so unique to the law. The mother who carries a child to full term is subject to anxieties, to physical constraints, to pain that only she must bear. That these sacrifices have from the beginning of the human race been endured by woman with a pride that ennobles her in the eyes of others and gives to the infant a bond of love cannot alone be grounds for the State to insist she make the sacrifice. Her suffering is too intimate and personal for the State to insist, without more, upon its own vision of the woman's role, however dominant that vision has been in the course of our history and our culture. The destiny of the woman must be shaped to a large extent on her own conception of her spiritual imperatives and her place in society.

It should be recognized, moreover, that in some critical respects the abortion decision is of the same character as the decision to use contraception, to which *Griswold v. Connecticut, Eisenstadt v. Baird*, and *Carey v. Population Services International*, afford constitutional protection. We have no doubt as to the correctness of those decisions. They support the reasoning in *Roe* relating to the woman's liberty because they involve personal decisions concerning not only the meaning of procreation but also human responsibility and respect for it. As with abortion, reasonable people will have differences of opinion about these matters. One view is based on such reverence for the wonder of creation that any pregnancy ought to be welcomed and carried to full term no matter how difficult it will be to provide for the child and ensure its well-being. Another is that the inability to provide for the nurture and care of the infant is a cruelty to the child and an anguish to the parent. These are intimate views with infinite variations, and their deep, personal character underlay our decisions in *Griswold*, *Eisenstadt*, and *Carey*. The same concerns are present when the woman confronts the reality that, perhaps despite her attempts to avoid it, she has become pregnant.

* * *

To eliminate the issue of reliance that easily, however, one would need to limit cognizable reliance to specific instances of sexual activity. But to do this would be simply to refuse to face the fact that for two decades of economic and social developments, people have organized intimate relationships and made choices that define their views of themselves and their places in society, in reliance on the availability of abortion in the event that contraception should fail. The ability of women to participate equally in the economic and social life of the Nation has been facilitated by their ability to control their reproductive lives....The Constitution serves human values, and while the effect of reliance on *Roe* cannot be exactly measured, neither can the certain cost of overruling *Roe* for people who have ordered their thinking and living around that case be dismissed.

* * *

We have seen how time has overtaken some of *Roe's* factual assumptions: advances in maternal health care allow for abortions safe to the mother later in pregnancy than was true in 1973..., and advances in neonatal care have advanced viability to a point somewhat earlier....But these facts go only to the scheme of time limits on the realization of competing interests, and the divergences from the factual premises of 1973 have no bearing on the validity of *Roe's* central holding, that viability marks the earliest point at which the State's interest in fetal life is constitutionally adequate to justify a legislative ban on nontherapeutic abortions. The soundness or unsoundness of that constitutional judgment in no sense turns on whether viability occurs at approximately 28 weeks, as was usual at the time of *Roe*, at 23 to 24 weeks, as it sometimes does today, or at some moment even slightly earlier in pregnancy, as it may if fetal respiratory capacity can somehow be enhanced in the future. Whenever it may occur, the attainment of viability may continue to serve as the critical fact, just as it has done since *Roe* was decided; which is to say that no change in *Roe's* factual underpinning has left its central holding obsolete, and none supports an argument for overruling it.

* * *

...But whatever the premises of opposition may be, only the most convincing justification under accepted standards of precedent could suffice to demonstrate that a later decision overruling the first was anything but a surrender to political pressure, and an unjustified repudiation of the principle on which the Court staked its authority in the first instance. So to overrule under fire in the absence of the most compelling reason to reexamine a watershed decision would subvert the Court's legitimacy beyond any serious question....

* * *

We conclude the line should be drawn at viability, so that before that time the woman has a right to choose to terminate her pregnancy....

* * *

The trimester framework no doubt was erected to ensure that the woman's right to choose not become so subordinate to the State's interest in promoting fetal life that her choice exists in theory but not in fact. We do not agree, however, that the trimester approach is necessary to accomplish this objective. A framework of this rigidity was unnecessary and in its later interpretation sometimes contradicted the State's permissible exercise of its powers.

Though the woman has a right to choose to terminate or continue her pregnancy before viability, it does not at all follow that the State is prohibited from taking steps to ensure that this choice is thoughtful and informed. Even in the earliest stages of pregnancy, the State may enact rules and regulations designed to encourage her to know that there are philosophic and social arguments of great weight that can be brought to bear in favor of continuing the pregnancy to full term and that there are procedures and institutions to allow adoption of unwanted children as well as a certain degree of state assistance if the mother chooses to raise the child herself. "'The Constitution does not forbid a State or city, pursuant to democratic processes, from expressing a preference for normal childbirth.'"...

* * *

These principles control our assessment of the Pennsylvania statute, and we now turn to the issue of the validity of its challenged provisions.

V

The Court of Appeals applied what it believed to be the undue burden standard and upheld each of the provisions except for the husband notification requirement. We agree generally with this conclusion,...

A

* * *

Because it is central to the operation of various other requirements, we begin with the statute's definition of medical emergency. Under the statute, a medical emergency is

"that condition which, on the basis of the physician's good faith clinical judgment, so complicates the medical condition of a pregnant woman as to necessitate the immediate abortion of her pregnancy to avert her death or for which a delay will create serious risk of substantial and irreversible impairment of a major bodily function."...

* * *

...We...conclude that, as construed by the Court of Appeals, the medical emergency definition imposes no undue burden on a woman's abortion right.

B

We next consider the informed consent requirement....Except in a medical emergency, the statute requires that at least 24 hours before performing an abortion a physician inform the woman of the nature of the procedure, the health risks of the abortion and of childbirth, and the "probable gestational age of the unborn child." The

physician or a qualified nonphysician must inform the woman of the availability of printed materials published by the State describing the fetus and providing information about medical assistance for childbirth, information about child support from the father, and a list of agencies which provide adoption and other services as alternatives to abortion. An abortion may not be performed unless the woman certifies in writing that she has been informed of the availability of these printed materials and has been provided them if she chooses to view them.

Our prior decisions establish that as with any medical procedure, the State may require a woman to give her written informed consent to an abortion.... In this respect, the statute is unexceptional....

* * *

It cannot be questioned that psychological well-being is a facet of health. Nor can it be doubted that most women considering an abortion would deem the impact on the fetus relevant, if not dispositive, to the decision. In attempting to ensure that a woman apprehend the full consequences of her decision, the State furthers the legitimate purpose of reducing the risk that a woman may elect an abortion, only to discover later, with devastating psychological consequences, that her decision was not fully informed. If the information the State requires to be made available to the woman is truthful and not misleading, the requirement may be permissible.

* * *

C

Section 3209 of Pennsylvania's abortion law provides, except in cases of medical emergency, that no physician shall perform an abortion on a married woman without receiving a signed statement from the woman that she has notified her spouse that she is about to undergo an abortion. The woman has the option of providing an alternative signed statement certifying that her husband is not the man who impregnated her; that her husband could not be located; that the pregnancy is the result of spousal sexual assault which she has reported; or that the woman believes that notifying her husband will cause him or someone else to inflict bodily injury upon her. A physician who performs an abortion on a married woman without receiving the appropriate signed statement will have his or her license revoked, and is liable to the husband for damages.

* * *

This information and the District Court's findings reinforce what common sense would suggest. In well-functioning marriages, spouses discuss important intimate decisions such as whether to bear a child. But there are millions of women in this country who are the victims of regular physical and psychological abuse at the hands of their husbands. Should these women become pregnant, they may have very good reasons for not wishing to inform their husbands of their decision to obtain an abortion. Many may have justifiable fears of physical abuse, but may be no less fearful of the consequences of reporting prior abuse to the Commonwealth of Pennsylvania. Many may have a reasonable fear that notifying their husbands will provoke further instances of child abuse; these women are not exempt from § 3209's notification requirement. Many may fear devastating forms of psychological abuse from their husbands, including verbal harassment, threats of future violence, the destruction of possessions, physical confinement to the home, the withdrawal of financial support, or the disclosure of the abortion to family and friends. These methods of psychological abuse may act as even more of a deterrent to notification than the possibility of physical violence, but women who are the victims of the abuse are not exempt from § 3209's notification requirement. And many women who are pregnant as a result of sexual assaults by their husbands will be unable to avail themselves of the exception for spousal sexual assault, § 3209(b)(3), because the exception requires that the woman have notified law enforcement authorities within 90 days of the assault, and her husband will be notified of her report once an investigation begins. § 3128(c). If anything in this field is certain, it is that victims of spousal sexual assault are extremely reluctant to report the abuse to the government; hence, a great many spousal rape victims will not be exempt from the notification requirement imposed by § 3209.

The spousal notification requirement is thus likely to prevent a significant number of women from obtaining an abortion. It does not merely make abortions a little more difficult or expensive to obtain; for many women, it will impose a substantial obstacle. We must not blind ourselves to the fact that the significant number of women who fear for their safety and the safety of their children are likely to be deterred from procuring an abortion as surely as if the Commonwealth had outlawed abortion in all cases.

* * *

...Respondents speak of the one percent of women seeking abortions who are married and would choose not to notify their husbands of their plans. By selecting as the controlling class women who wish to obtain abortions, rather than all women or all pregnant women, respondents in effect concede that § 3209 must be judged by reference to those for whom it is an actual rather than irrelevant restriction.

* * *

...If this case concerned a State's ability to require the mother to notify the father before taking some action with respect to a living child raised by both, therefore, it would be reasonable to conclude as a general matter that the father's interest in the welfare of the child and the mother's interest are equal.

Before birth, however, the issue takes on a very different cast. It is an inescapable biological fact that state regulation with respect to the child a woman is carrying will have a far greater impact on the mother's liberty than on the father's. The effect of state regulation on a woman's protected liberty is doubly deserving of scrutiny in such a case, as the State has touched not only upon the private sphere of the family but upon the very bodily integrity of the pregnant woman....

* * *

D

We next consider the parental consent provision. Except in a medical emergency, an unemancipated young woman under 18 may not obtain an abortion unless she and one of her parents (or guardian) provides informed consent as defined above. If neither a parent nor a guardian provides consent, a court may authorize the performance of an abortion upon a determination that the young woman is mature and capable of giving informed consent and has in fact given her informed consent, or that an abortion would be in her best interests.

We have been over most of this ground before. Our cases establish, and we reaffirm today, that a State may require a minor seeking an abortion to obtain the consent of a parent or guardian, provided that there is an adequate judicial bypass procedure.... Under these precedents, in our view, the one-parent consent requirement and judicial bypass procedure are constitutional.

* * *

JUSTICE BLACKMUN, concurring in part, concurring in the judgment in part, and dissenting in part.

* * *

C

Application of the strict scrutiny standard results in the invalidation of all the challenged provisions. Indeed, as this Court has invalidated virtually identical provisions in prior cases, stare decisis requires that we again strike them down.

* * *

The 24-hour waiting period following the provision of the foregoing information is also clearly unconstitutional. The District Court found that the mandatory 24-hour delay could lead to delays in excess of 24 hours, thus increasing health risks, and that it would require two visits to the abortion provider, thereby increasing travel time, exposure to further harassment, and financial cost. Finally, the District Court found that the requirement would pose especially significant burdens on women living in rural areas and those women that have difficulty explaining their whereabouts....In *Akron* this Court invalidated a similarly arbitrary or inflexible waiting period because, as here, it furthered no legitimate state interest.[8]

* * *

III
* * *

THE CHIEF JUSTICE'S criticism of *Roe* follows from his stunted conception of individual liberty. While recognizing that the Due Process Clause protects more than simple physical liberty, he then goes on to construe this Court's personal-liberty cases as establishing only a laundry list of particular rights, rather than a principled account of how these particular rights are grounded in a more general right of privacy....This constricted view is reinforced by THE CHIEF JUSTICE's exclusive reliance on tradition as a source of fundamental rights....

Even more shocking than THE CHIEF JUSTICE's cramped notion of individual liberty is his complete omission of any discussion of the effects that compelled childbirth and motherhood have on women's lives. The only expression of concern with women's health is purely instrumental—for THE CHIEF JUSTICE, only women's psychological health is a concern, and only to the extent that he assumes that every woman who decides to have an abortion does so without serious consideration of the moral implications of their decision....In short, THE CHIEF JUSTICE's view of the State's compelling interest in maternal health has less to do with health than it does with compelling women to be maternal.

* * *

V

In one sense, the Court's approach is worlds apart from that of THE CHIEF JUSTICE and JUSTICE SCALIA. And yet, in another sense, the distance between the two approaches is short—the distance is but a single vote.

I am 83 years old. I cannot remain on this Court forever, and when I do step down, the confirmation process for my successor well may focus on the issue before us today. That, I regret, may be exactly where the choice between the two worlds will be made.

[8] The Court's decision in *Hodgson v. Minnesota*, 497 U.S. 417 (1990), validating a 48-hour waiting period for minors seeking an abortion to permit parental involvement does not alter this conclusion. Here the 24-hour delay is imposed on an adult woman....Moreover, the statute in Hodgson did not require any delay once the minor obtained the affirmative consent of either a parent or the court.

CHIEF JUSTICE REHNQUIST, with whom JUSTICE WHITE, JUSTICE SCALIA, and JUSTICE THOMAS join, concurring in the judgment in part and dissenting in part.

The joint opinion, following its newly-minted variation on stare decisis, retains the outer shell of *Roe v. Wade*, 410 U.S. 113,...(1973), but beats a wholesale retreat from the substance of that case. We believe that *Roe* was wrongly decided....

* * *

In *Roe v. Wade*, the Court recognized a "guarantee of personal privacy" which "is broad enough to encompass a woman's decision whether or not to terminate her pregnancy." 410 U.S., at 152–153. We are now of the view that, in terming this right fundamental, the Court in *Roe* read the earlier opinions upon which it based its decision much too broadly. Unlike marriage, procreation and contraception, abortion "involves the purposeful termination of potential life." *Harris v. McRae*, 448 U.S. 297, 325,...(1980). The abortion decision must therefore "be recognized as sui generis, different in kind from the others that the Court has protected under the rubric of personal or family privacy and autonomy."...One cannot ignore the fact that a woman is not isolated in her pregnancy, and that the decision to abort necessarily involves the destruction of a fetus....

* * *

JUSTICE SCALIA, with whom THE CHIEF JUSTICE, JUSTICE WHITE, and JUSTICE THOMAS join, concurring in the judgment in part and dissenting in part.

* * *

...The States may, if they wish, permit abortion-on-demand, but the Constitution does not require them to do so. The permissibility of abortion, and the limitations upon it, are to be resolved like most important questions in our democracy: by citizens trying to persuade one another and then voting....

* * *

The emptiness of the "reasoned judgment" that produced *Roe* is displayed in plain view by the fact that, after more than 19 years of effort by some of the brightest (and most determined) legal minds in the country, after more than 10 cases upholding abortion rights in this Court, and after dozens upon dozens of amicus briefs submitted in this and other cases, the best the Court can do to explain how it is that the word "liberty" must be thought to include the right to destroy human fetuses is to rattle off a collection of adjectives that simply decorate a value judgment and conceal a political choice. The right to abort, we are told, inheres in "liberty" because it is among "a person's most basic decisions,"...; it involves a "most intimate and personal choice,"....it is "central to personal dignity and autonomy,"...; it "originates within the zone of conscience and belief,"...; it is "too intimate and personal" for state interference,...; it reflects "intimate views" of a "deep, personal character,"...; it involves "intimate relationships," and notions of "personal autonomy and bodily integrity,"...; and it concerns a particularly "'important decision,'"....[2] But it is obvious to anyone applying "reasoned judgment" that the same adjectives can be applied to many forms of conduct that this Court (including one of the Justices in today's majority,...) has held are not entitled to constitutional protection—because, like abortion, they are forms of conduct that have long been criminalized in American society. Those adjectives might be applied, for example, to homosexual sodomy, polygamy, adult incest, and suicide, all of which are equally "intimate" and "deeply personal" decisions involving "personal autonomy and bodily integrity," and all of which can constitutionally be proscribed because it is our unquestionable constitutional tradition that they are proscribable. It is not reasoned judgment that supports the Court's decision; only personal predilection.... Liberty finds no refuge in a jurisprudence of doubt."...

One might have feared to encounter this august and sonorous phrase in an opinion defending the real *Roe v. Wade*, rather than the revised version fabricated today by the authors of the joint opinion. The shortcomings of *Roe* did not include lack of clarity: Virtually all regulation of abortion before the third trimester was invalid. But to come across this phrase in the joint opinion—which calls upon federal district judges to apply an "undue burden" standard as doubtful in application as it is unprincipled in origin—is really more than one should have to bear.

* * *

The joint opinion explains that a state regulation imposes an "undue burden" if it "has the purpose or effect of placing a substantial obstacle in the path of a woman seeking an abortion of a nonviable fetus."...An obstacle is "substantial," we are told, if it is "calculated, [not] to inform the woman's free choice, [but to] hinder it."[4]...This latter statement cannot possibly mean what it says. Any regulation of abortion that is intended to advance what the joint opinion concedes is the State's "substantial" interest in protecting unborn life will be "calculated [to] hinder" a decision to have an abortion. It thus seems more accurate to say that the joint opinion would uphold abortion regulations only if they do not unduly hinder the woman's decision. That, of course, brings us right back to square one....

* * *

The Imperial Judiciary lives. It is instructive to compare this Nietzschean vision of us unelected, life-tenured judges—leading a Volk who will be "tested by following," and whose very "belief in themselves" is mystically bound up in their "understanding" of a Court that "speaks before all others for their constitutional ideals"—with the somewhat more modest role envisioned for these lawyers by the Founders.

"The judiciary...has...no direction either of the strength or of the wealth of the society, and can take no active resolution whatever. It may truly be said to have neither FORCE nor WILL but merely judgment...." The Federalist No. 78, 393–394...

* * *

...The only principle the Court "adheres" to, it seems to me, is the principle that the Court must be seen as standing by *Roe*. That is not a principle of law (which is what I thought the Court was talking about), but a principle of Realpolitik—and a wrong one at that.

I cannot agree with, indeed I am appalled by, the Court's suggestion that the decision whether to stand by an erroneous constitutional decision must be strongly influenced—against overruling, no less—by the substantial and continuing public opposition the decision has generated. The Court's judgment that any other course would "subvert the Court's legitimacy" must be another consequence of reading the error-filled history book that described the deeply divided country brought together by *Roe*. In my history book, the Court was covered with dishonor and deprived of legitimacy by *Dred Scott v. Sandford*, 60 U.S. 393,...(1857), an erroneous (and widely opposed) opinion that it did not abandon,....

But whether it would "subvert the Court's legitimacy" or not, the notion that we would decide a case differently from the way we otherwise would in order to show that we can stand firm against public disapproval is frightening. It is a bad enough idea, even in the head of someone like me, who believes that the text of the Constitution, and our traditions, say what they say and there is no fiddling with them. But when it is in the mind of a Court that believes the Constitution has an evolving meaning,...that the Ninth Amendment's reference to "other" rights is not a disclaimer, but a charter for action, *ibid*; and that the function of this Court is to "speak before all others for [the people's] constitutional ideals" unrestrained by meaningful text or tradition—then the notion that the Court must adhere to a decision for as long as the decision faces "great opposition" and the Court is "under fire" acquires a character of almost czarist arrogance. We are offended by these marchers who descend upon us, every year on the anniversary of Roe, to protest our saying that the Constitution requires what our society has never thought the Constitution requires. These people who refuse to be "tested by following" must be taught a lesson. We have no Cossacks, but at least we can stubbornly refuse to abandon an erroneous opinion that we might otherwise change—to show how little they intimidate us.

* * *

We should get out of this area, where we have no right to be, and where we do neither ourselves nor the country any good by remaining.

[2] JUSTICE BLACKMUN's parade of adjectives is similarly empty: Abortion is among "the most intimate and personal choices,"...; it is a matter "central to personal dignity and autonomy,"...; and it involves "personal decisions that profoundly affect bodily integrity, identity, and destiny,"... JUSTICE STEVENS is not much less conclusory: The decision to choose abortion is a matter of "the highest privacy and the most personal nature,"...; it involves a "difficult choice having serious and personal consequences of major importance to [a woman's] future,"...; the authority to make this "traumatic and yet empowering decision" is "an element of basic human dignity,"...; and it is "nothing less than a matter of conscience,"...

[4] The joint opinion further asserts that a law imposing an undue burden on abortion decisions is not a "permissible" means of serving "legitimate" state interests....This description of the undue burden standard in terms more commonly associated with the rational-basis test will come as a surprise even to those who have followed closely our wanderings in this forsaken wilderness...

Questions for Discussion

1. Justice O'Connor recognizes in her opinion that a husband has a "deep and proper concern and interest...in his wife's pregnancy." Why is that interest more easily overcome than the interest of the parents of a pregnant minor? The parents of the minor may have an enhanced stake should a child be born to their dependent child, but doesn't a husband have a similar stake? Does the likely genetic contribution and possible affective interest of the husband constitutionally allow a permissible role (to be informed)? Is it relevant that a woman may end her marital status on a no-fault basis (divorce) while the state will likely return a runaway child to his or her parents?

2. Defenders of the parental consent requirement for an abortion by a minor point out that there is a medical emergency exception that a single parent may consent and is obligated to make a decision considering the child's "best interests." The law also allows the child to appear in the court of common pleas where she resides and petition the court to allow an abortion without notice (or where consent was denied). The court shall grant the petition where the woman is "mature and capable of giving informed consent," and if the court cannot make such a finding, where "in the best interests of the woman" in his or her judgment. Would a roughly parallel set of provisions for wives reasonably afraid of spousal abuse make required spousal consent constitutional?

3. According to the record, states (such as Massachusetts) with judicial redress for abortions by minors in lieu of parental consent approve those requests at close to a 100% rate; does the apparently gratuitous nature of such a hoop make it an "undue barrier"?

4.   Justice Blackmun would allow none of the provisions of the Pennsylvania law to stand. Does it make sense to prohibit a 24-hour waiting period on a decision as momentous—and irreversible—as is an abortion, while upholding required two-day rescission rights on all door-to-door sales, or on all loans secured by real property under the federal Truth-in-Lending law? Numerous statutes and rules require physician or hospital disclosures to patients. What would make such a legislatively determined informational or "cooling off" requirement unconstitutional here?

5.   If a description of the fate of the aborted fetus (as Pennsylvania requires) is accurate, on what basis should its recitation be barred as an intrusion? Can the mere disclosure of truthful information interfere with and hence violate a constitutional right to decide a personal matter? Is our free will so sensitive that mere mention of adverse consequences threatens its exercise? On the other hand, what if the "truthful information" is on the other side of the issue—consisting of a detailed presentation on the implications of parenting—particularly single parenting—for future income levels and personal freedom, and on non-surgical options for terminating a pregnancy? Should the state take a side in its selection of which truths to disclose? Does it matter if the issue is steeped in religious belief?

6.   Rehnquist would reverse *Roe* entirely, finding no liberty interest in a woman's decision as to a fetus within her prior to viability. Should protection depend upon the redcoats being un-British enough to issue edicts about colonial sexual practices? Should we be tied to the happenstance customs of 1787, or rather to the values and zones of privacy impliedly addressed?

7.   Another rationale of Chief Justice Rehnquist's opinion is the distinction that abortion involves the "purposeful termination of potential life." But does not birth control in any form involve the purposeful termination of potential life? The dissent states that the constitution should "get out of this area," referring to all of the birth control privacy decisions of the Court. Would it make sense to allow a state to make the use of condoms by a married couple a criminal offense but declare that an officer investigating a murder cannot intrude into the property of a citizen without a warrant? Should we defend the "reasonable expectation of privacy" protected by the Fourth Amendment against such a compelling interest (homicide prevention), but allow the state to imprison those who do not have sex with their spouses as prescribed by the state? Is that the reasonable privacy line intended by the founding fathers?

8.   Justice Scalia's dissent argues that the plurality opinion creates the notion of "undue burden" out of whole cloth, attacking it as objectionably vague— allowing excessive judicial discretion. How does this lack of specificity comport with constitutional jurisprudence extensively defining concepts such as "free speech," "reasonable expectation of privacy," "equal protection of the laws," *et al.* How does it comport with the extensive body of judicially created law interpreting

the "combination in restraint of trade" prohibition in antitrust law? Do not courts draw such lines inevitably and as a matter of course?

9. How different is "undue burden" as a standard from traditional "strict scrutiny" involving a fundamental liberty (requiring a "compelling state interest" and a least restrictive alternative approach)? Is it close to the "heightened scrutiny" approach the Court has taken as a middle ground, short of the more permissive "rational relation" test? On the other hand, if the concepts are similar to either strict or heightened scrutiny, is O'Connor's invocation of different nomenclature gratuitous and confusing?

10. If Justice Scalia would simply confine constitutional limitation on the states to the precise words of the first eight amendments, what does the term "liberty" mean in the 14th Amendment? Is a general term to be ignored because it is difficult to interpret? If drawing such lines should be done with care and only at the extremes, does that excuse not drawing them at all? Justice Scalia partly quotes Lord Acton's famous dictum that "power corrupts, absolute power corrupts absolutely" to apply to the judiciary. But if the judiciary removes itself as the check on majoritarian legislative imposition (often with criminal sanctions) related to sacrosanct aspects of individual conscience, who is left to check such abuses of power against a minority?

11. Justice Scalia would extend fundamental liberty interests to those traditionally protected by society. How would such criteria have been applied in the *Dred Scott* case? In *Brown v. Board of Education*? Does the Constitution only apply to halt changes in *status quo* tradition?

Note on Reproductive Rights of Minors

As discussed in *Casey*, it is constitutional for a state to impose some restrictions on the ability of a minor to obtain an abortion—specifically a requirement to obtain parental consent, as long as the state provides an exception referred to as "judicial bypass." This standard was established in 1979, in the U.S. Supreme Court case of *Belotti v. Baird*, 443 U.S. 622 (1979), in which the Court considered a Massachusetts statute requiring minors to get parental consent for an abortion. The Court considered the statute in light of its history of jurisprudence regarding the rights of minors. The Court first explained that regarding "minors' claims to constitutional protection against deprivations of liberty or property interests by the State...we have concluded that the child's right is virtually coextensive with that of an adult." The Court then reflected on its holdings concluding that "the States validly may limit the freedom of children to choose for themselves in the making of important, affirmative choices with potentially serious consequence." Finally, the Court reiterated its view that "the guiding role of parents in the upbringing of their children justifies limitation on the freedoms of minors." With this context, the Court attempted to reconcile the interests of the State, minors, and parents, as affected by the Massachusetts statute. The Court concluded that a state may require parental consent, but then it must also allow for an alternative procedure. In such a statutory scheme, a pregnant minor is entitled to go before a judge for a determination of whether she is: 1) "mature enough and well enough informed" to make the decision to have an abortion in consultation with her physician without the input of her parents; or 2) if she is deemed not mature enough to make this decision, whether it is nevertheless within her best interests to have the abortion without her parent's knowledge. *Casey* confirmed that such a statute did not create an "undue burden." Currently, 38 states have such parental consent laws that include "judicial bypass."[28]

Notwithstanding the judicial bypass alternative, there can be a number of obstacles for minors seeking an abortion. First, the criteria with which a judge determines whether the minor is "mature enough and well enough informed" to decide on an abortion without parental input can be unclear or arbitrary, leaving judges with wide discretion and potential for bias. Second, the logistics involved in the bypass procedure can be time-consuming, risking putting the minor into later stages of pregnancy before resolution. Finally, recent legislative measures have created additional procedural barriers such as a 2014 Alabama law requiring notification of the District Attorney to allow an opportunity to defend the interests of the fetus. This can involve the ability of the District Attorney to call witnesses—including those who may be the reason the minor is seeking judicial bypass in the first place.[29] Recently, the DC Circuit considered the case of an immigrant child in federal custody who was being denied the ability to obtain an abortion, with the government maintaining that she had "the burden of extracting herself from custody"—a logistical impossibility—in order to exercise her acknowledged constitutional right to the abortion. The court eventually granted an order making it possible for her to obtain the abortion, after a seven-week delay that put her into her second trimester.[30]

3. State Interest in Protection of the Fetus

A 1992 National Institute of Drug Abuse study surveyed admitted use of alcohol/drugs/tobacco during pregnancy. The survey of four million women who gave birth found that 5.5% used illicit drugs while they were pregnant.[31] The self-reporting of alcohol or cigarette use involves somewhat less stigma and 18.8% of pregnant women admitted to exposing their fetuses to alcohol, and 20.4% to cigarette smoking.[32] A 2017 update found 8.5% using illicit drugs while pregnant (compared to 14% of those not pregnant), 13.8% smoking while pregnant (compared to 18.7% of those not pregnant). Interestingly, the one area of informed cultural caution is alcohol, with 5.2% drinking (compared to 29% who were not pregnant).[33]

Using medical and other records, CDC studies have identified 0.2 to 1.5 infants with Fetal Alcohol Syndrome (FAS) for every 1,000 live births in the U.S. But the records understate the problem, with some studies indicating a FAS rate of 6 to 9 out of every 1,000 births, and no study has examined the full range of FAS issues. Some experts estimate that the FAS rate in the United States and Western Europe is far higher—somewhere between 1% and 5% of all births.[34] The most recent study from 2010 to 2016 surveyed 13,146 first graders in four regions of the country and concluded that a "conservative" estimate for FAS prevalence based on related disorder incidence ranged from 31.1 to 98.5 per 1000 children—that is, from 3% to 10% of the populations sampled.[35] Babies born with FAS suffer central nervous system dysfunction, including delayed motor development, mild to profound mental retardation, and learning disabilities.[36] FAS also causes problems that affect speech, language, swallowing, and hearing development.[37]

Another statistical indicator of potential abuse/neglect has been low birthweights. Although not indicative of direct abuse *in utero,* they statistically correlate closely with later child neglect risk. Delicate health and enhanced family stress are associated with neglect and/or abuse problems. The rate differs greatly for African American babies, with 2016 data indicating a low birth weight rate of about 11% underweight compared to a 5% rate among White babies.[38]

Whitner v. State of South Carolina
328 S.C. 1 (1997)

Opinion by TOAL, JUSTICE.

This case concerns the scope of the child abuse and endangerment statute in the South Carolina Children's Code (the Code)....[1] We hold the word "child" as used in that statute includes viable fetuses.

FACTS

On April 20, 1992, Cornelia Whitner (Whitner) pled guilty to criminal child neglect, S.C.Code Ann. § 20-7-50 (1985), for causing her baby to be born with cocaine metabolites in its system by reason of Whitner's ingestion of crack cocaine during the third trimester of her pregnancy. The circuit court judge sentenced Whitner to eight years in prison. Whitner did not appeal her conviction.

Thereafter, Whitner filed a petition for Post Conviction Relief (PCR), pleading the circuit court's lack of subject matter jurisdiction to accept her guilty plea as well as ineffective assistance of counsel. Her claim of ineffective assistance of counsel was based upon her lawyer's failure to advise her the statute under which she was being prosecuted might not apply to prenatal drug use. The petition was granted on both grounds. The State appeals.

LAW/ANALYSIS

A. Subject Matter Jurisdiction

* * *

S.C.Code Ann. § 20-7-50 (1985) provides: Any person having the legal custody of any child or helpless person, who shall, without lawful excuse, refuse or neglect to provide, as defined in § 20-7-490, the proper care and attention for such child or helpless person, so that the life, health or comfort of such child or helpless person is endangered or is likely to be endangered, shall be guilty of a misdemeanor and shall be punished within the discretion of the circuit court....

The State contends this section encompasses maternal acts endangering or likely to endanger the life, comfort, or health of a viable fetus.

Under the Children's Code, "child" means a "person under the age of eighteen." S.C.Code Ann. § 20-7-30(1) (1985). The question for this Court, therefore, is whether a viable fetus is a "person" for purposes of the Children's Code.

In interpreting a statute, this Court's primary function is to ascertain the intent of the legislature....South Carolina law has long recognized that viable fetuses are persons holding certain legal rights and privileges. In 1960, this Court decided *Hall v. Murphy*, 236 S.C. 257, 113 S.E.2d 790 (1960). That case concerned the application of South Carolina's wrongful death statute to an infant who died four hours after her birth as a result of injuries sustained prenatally during viability. The Appellants argued that a viable fetus was not a person within the purview of the wrongful death statute, because, *inter alia*, a fetus is thought to have no separate being apart from the mother.

We found such a reason for exclusion from recovery "unsound, illogical and unjust," and concluded there was "no medical or other basis" for the "assumed identity" of mother and viable unborn child. *Id.* at 262. In light of that conclusion, this Court unanimously held: "We have no difficulty in concluding that a fetus having reached that period of prenatal maturity where it is capable of independent life apart from its mother is a person." *Id.* at 263....

Four years later, in *Fowler v. Woodward*...we interpreted *Hall* as supporting a finding that a viable fetus injured while still in the womb need not be born alive for another to maintain an action for the wrongful death of the fetus.

Since a viable child is a person before separation from the body of its mother and since prenatal injuries tortiously inflicted on such a child are actionable, it is apparent that the complaint alleges such an 'act, neglect or default' by the defendant, to the injury of the child....

* * *

Once the concept of the unborn, viable child as a person is accepted, we have no difficulty in holding that a cause of action for tortious injury to such a child arises immediately upon the infliction of the injury....

More recently, we held the word "person" as used in a criminal statute includes viable fetuses. *State v. Horne*...concerned South Carolina's murder statute,...The defendant in that case stabbed his wife, who was nine months' pregnant, in the neck, arms, and abdomen. Although doctors performed an emergency caesarean section to deliver the child, the child died while still in the womb. The defendant was convicted of voluntary manslaughter and appealed his conviction on the ground South Carolina did not recognize the crime of feticide.

This Court disagreed. In a unanimous decision, we held it would be "grossly inconsistent ... to construe a viable fetus as a 'person' for the purposes of imposing civil liability while refusing to give it a similar classification in the criminal context."... Accordingly, the Court recognized the crime of feticide with respect to viable fetuses.

Similarly, we do not see any rational basis for finding a viable fetus is not a "person" in the present context. Indeed, it would be absurd to recognize the viable fetus as a person for purposes of homicide laws and wrongful death statutes but not for

purposes of statutes proscribing child abuse. Our holding in *Hall* that a viable fetus is a person rested primarily on the plain meaning of the word "person" in light of existing medical knowledge concerning fetal development. We do not believe that the plain and ordinary meaning of the word "person" has changed in any way that would now deny viable fetuses status as persons.

The policies enunciated in the Children's Code also support our plain meaning reading of "person."...[It] expressly states: "It shall be the policy of this State to concentrate on the prevention of children's problems as the most important strategy which can be planned and implemented on behalf of children and their families." (emphasis added). The abuse or neglect of a child at any time during childhood can exact a profound toll on the child herself as well as on society as a whole. However, the consequences of abuse or neglect which takes place after birth often pale in comparison to those resulting from abuse suffered by the viable fetus before birth. This policy of prevention supports a reading of the word "person" to include viable fetuses. Furthermore, the scope of the Children's Code is quite broad. It applies "to all children who have need of services."...

* * *

Whitner also argues an interpretation of the statute that includes viable fetuses would lead to absurd results obviously not intended by the legislature. Specifically, she claims if we interpret "child" to include viable fetuses, every action by a pregnant woman that endangers or is likely to endanger a fetus, whether otherwise legal or illegal, would constitute unlawful neglect under the statute. For example, a woman might be prosecuted under section 20-7-50 for smoking or drinking during pregnancy. Whitner asserts these "absurd" results could not have been intended by the legislature and, therefore, the statute should not be construed to include viable fetuses.

We disagree for a number of reasons. First, the same arguments against the statute can be made whether or not the child has been born. After the birth of a child, a parent can be prosecuted under section 20-7-50 for an action that is likely to endanger the child without regard to whether the action is illegal in itself. For example, a parent who drinks excessively could, under certain circumstances, be guilty of child neglect or endangerment even though the underlying act—consuming alcoholic beverages—is itself legal. Obviously, the legislature did not think it "absurd" to allow prosecution of parents for such otherwise legal acts when the acts actually or potentially endanger the "life, health or comfort" of the parents' born children. We see no reason such a result should be rendered absurd by the mere fact the child at issue is a viable fetus.

Moreover, we need not address this potential parade of horribles advanced by Whitner. In this case, which is the only case we are called upon to decide here, certain facts are clear. Whitner admits to having ingested crack cocaine during the third trimester of her pregnancy, which caused her child to be born with cocaine in its system. Although the precise effects of maternal crack use during pregnancy are somewhat unclear, it is well documented and within the realm of public knowledge that such use can cause serious harm to the viable unborn child....There can be no question here Whitner endangered the life, health, and comfort of her child. We need not decide any cases other than the one before us.

We are well aware of the many decisions from other states' courts throughout the country holding maternal conduct before the birth of the child does not give rise to criminal prosecution under state child abuse/endangerment or drug distribution statutes. [citations omitted] Many of these cases were prosecuted under statutes forbidding delivery or distribution of illicit substances and depended on statutory construction of the terms "delivery" and "distribution." Obviously, such cases are inapplicable to the present situation. The cases concerning child endangerment statutes or construing the terms "child" and "person" are also distinguishable, because the states in which these cases were decided have entirely different bodies of case law from South Carolina [citations omitted]. In *Reyes v. Superior Court*, the California Court of Appeals noted California law did not recognize a fetus as a "human being" within the purview of the state murder and manslaughter statutes, and that it was thus improper to find the fetus was a "child" for purposes of the felonious child endangerment statute. *Reyes*, 75 Cal.App.3d at 217.

Massachusetts, however, has a body of case law substantially similar to South Carolina's, yet a Massachusetts trial court has held that a mother pregnant with a viable fetus is not criminally liable for transmission of cocaine to the fetus. See *Commonwealth v. Pellegrini* [superior court decision, no citation]. Specifically, Massachusetts law allows wrongful death actions on behalf of viable fetuses injured in utero who are not subsequently born alive....Similarly, Massachusetts law permits homicide prosecutions of third parties who kill viable fetuses. See *Commonwealth v. Cass*,...(ruling a viable fetus is a person for purposes of vehicular homicide statute);...(viable fetus is a person for purposes of common law crime of murder)....In *Pellegrini*, the Massachusetts Superior Court found that state's distribution statute does not apply to the distribution of an illegal substance to a viable fetus. The statute at issue forbade distribution of cocaine to persons under the age of eighteen. Rather than construing the word "distribution," however, the superior court found that a viable fetus is not a "person under the age of eighteen" within the meaning of the statute. In so finding, the court had to distinguish *Lawrence* and *Cass supra*, both of which held viable fetuses are "persons" for purposes of criminal laws in Massachusetts.

The Massachusetts trial court found *Lawrence* and *Cass* "accord legal rights to the unborn only where the mother's or parents' interest in the potentiality of life, not the state's interest, are sought to be vindicated." [citation omitted] In other words, a viable fetus should only be accorded the rights of a person for the sake of its mother or both its parents. Under this rationale, the viable fetus lacks rights of its own that deserve vindication....

First, *Hall, Fowler* and *Horne* were decided primarily on the basis of the meaning of "person" as understood in the light of existing medical knowledge, rather than based on any policy of protecting the relationship between mother and child. As a homicide case, *Horne* also rested on the State's—not the mother's—interest in vindicating the life of the viable fetus. Moreover, the United States Supreme Court has repeatedly held that the states have a compelling interest in the life of a viable fetus. See *Roe v. Wade*...; see also *Planned Parenthood v. Casey*..., *Webster v. Reproductive Health Servs*....If, as Whitner suggests we should, we read *Horne* only as a vindication of the mother's interest in the life of her unborn child, there would be no basis for prosecuting a mother who kills her viable fetus by stabbing it, by shooting it, or by other such means, yet a third party could be prosecuted for the very same acts. We decline to read *Horne* in a way that insulates the mother from all culpability for harm to her viable child. Because the rationale underlying our body of law—protection of the viable fetus—is radically different from that underlying the law of Massachusetts, we decline to follow the decision of the Massachusetts Superior Court in *Pellegrini*.

* * *

...[W]e do not believe the statute is ambiguous and, therefore, the rule of lenity does not apply. Furthermore, our interpretation of the statute is based primarily on the plain meaning of the word "person" as contained in the statute. We need not go beyond that language. However, because our prior decisions in *Murphy, Fowler*, and *Horne* support our reading of the statute, we have discussed the rationale underlying those holdings. We conclude that both statutory language and case law compel the conclusion we reach. We see no ambiguity.

* * *

C. Constitutional Issues

1. Fair Notice/Vagueness

Whitner argues that section 20-7-50 does not give her fair notice that her behavior is proscribed.[6] We disagree.

The statute forbids any person having legal custody of a child from refusing or neglecting to provide proper care and attention to the child so that the life, health, or comfort of the child is endangered or is likely to be endangered. As we have found above, the plain meaning of "child" as used in this statute includes a viable fetus. Furthermore, it is common knowledge that use of cocaine during pregnancy can harm the viable unborn child....

2. Right to Privacy

Whitner argues that prosecuting her for using crack cocaine after her fetus attains viability unconstitutionally burdens her right of privacy, or, more specifically, her right to carry her pregnancy to term. We disagree.

Whitner argues that section 20-7-50 burdens her right of privacy, a right long recognized by the United States Supreme Court. *See, e.g., Eisenstadt v. Baird* [citations omitted], as standing for the proposition that the Constitution protects women from measures penalizing them for choosing to carry their pregnancies to term.

In *LaFleur* ...the United States Supreme Court...found that "by acting to penalize the pregnant teacher for deciding to bear a child, overly restrictive maternity leave regulations can constitute a heavy burden on the exercise of these protected freedoms." The Court then scrutinized...the policies to determine whether "the interests advanced in support of" the policy could "justify the particular procedures [the School Boards] ha[d] adopted." [ed. note: using the rational relationship test; citation omitted] Although it found that the purported justification for the policy—continuity of instruction—was a "significant and legitimate educational goal," the Court concluded that the "absolute requirement[ ] of termination at the end of the fourth or fifth month of pregnancy" was not a rational means for achieving continuity of instruction and that such a requirement "may serve to hinder attainment of the very continuity objectives that they are purportedly designed to promote." Finding no rational relationship between the purpose of the maternity leave policy and the means crafted to achieve that end, the Court concluded the policy violated the Due Process Clause of the Fourteenth Amendment.

Whitner argues that the alleged violation here is far more egregious than that in *LaFleur*. She first suggests that imprisonment is a far greater burden on her exercise of her freedom to carry the fetus to term than was the unpaid maternity leave in *LaFleur*. Although she is, of course, correct that imprisonment is more severe than unpaid maternity leave, Whitner misapprehends the fundamentally different nature of her own interests and those of the government in this case as compared to those at issue in *LaFleur*.

First, the State's interest in protecting the life and health of the viable fetus is not merely legitimate. It is compelling. The United States Supreme Court in *Casey* recognized that the State possesses a profound interest in the potential life of the fetus, not only after the fetus is viable, but throughout the expectant mother's pregnancy....

Even more importantly, however, we do not think any fundamental right of Whitner's—or any right at all, for that matter—is implicated under the present scenario. It strains belief for Whitner to argue that using crack cocaine during pregnancy is encompassed within the constitutionally recognized right of privacy. Use of crack cocaine is illegal, period. No one here argues that laws criminalizing the use of crack cocaine are themselves unconstitutional. If the State wishes to impose additional criminal penalties on pregnant women who engage in this already illegal conduct because of the effect the conduct has on the viable fetus, it may do so. We do not see how the fact of pregnancy elevates the use of crack cocaine to the lofty status of a fundamental right.

Moreover, as a practical matter, we do not see how our interpretation of section 20-7-50 imposes a burden on Whitner's right to carry her child to term. In *LaFleur*, the Supreme Court found that the mandatory maternity leave policies burdened women's rights to carry their pregnancies to term because the policies prevented pregnant teachers from exercising a freedom they would have enjoyed but for their pregnancies. In contrast, during her pregnancy after the fetus attained viability, Whitner enjoyed the same freedom to use cocaine that she enjoyed earlier in and predating her pregnancy— none whatsoever. Simply put, South Carolina's child abuse and endangerment statute as applied to this case does not restrict Whitner's freedom in any way that it was not already restricted. The State's imposition of an additional penalty when a pregnant woman with a viable fetus engages in the already proscribed behavior does not burden a woman's right to carry her pregnancy to term; rather, the additional penalty simply recognizes that a third party (the viable fetus or newborn child) is harmed by the behavior.

* * *

For the foregoing reasons, the decision of the PCR Court is REVERSED.

[1] Section 20-7-50 was amended in 1993 to make violation of the section a felony and to make the maximum term of imprisonment conform to the new crime classification system....

[6] In a related argument, Whitner suggests section 20-7-50 is void for vagueness. This argument lacks merit. As we noted in our interpretation of section 20-7-50, supra the same argument could be made about the statute as applied to a child who has already been born.

WALLER and **BURNETT, JJ.**, concur.

FINNEY, C.J., and **MOORE, J.**, dissenting in separate opinions.

FINNEY, CHIEF JUSTICE:

I respectfully dissent, and would affirm the grant of post-conviction relief to respondent Whitner.

The issue before the Court is whether a fetus is a "child" within the meaning of S.C.Code Ann. § 20-7-50 (1985), a statute which makes it a misdemeanor...for a "person having legal custody of any child or helpless person" to unlawfully neglect that child or helpless person. Since this is a penal statute, it is strictly construed against the State and in favor of respondent....

The term child for purposes of § 20-7-50 is defined as a "person under the age of eighteen" unless a different meaning is required by the circumstances. S.C.Code Ann. § 20-7-30(1) (1985). We have already held that this same definition found in another part of the Children's Code means a child in being and not a fetus. *Doe v. Clark* [citation omitted] It would be incongruous at best to hold the definition of "child" in the civil context of Doe is more restrictive than it is in the criminal context we consider today.

More importantly, it is apparent from a reading of the entire statute that the word child in § 20-7-50 means a child in being and not a fetus. [citation omitted] A plain reading of the entire child neglect statute demonstrates the intent to criminalize only acts directed at children, and not those which may harm fetuses. First, § 20-7-50 does not impose criminal liability on every person who neglects a child, but only on a person having legal custody of that child. The statutory requirement of legal custody is evidence of intent to extend the statute's reach only to children, because the concept of legal custody is simply inapplicable to a fetus. [citation omitted] Second, ...the vast majority of acts which constitute statutory harm under § 20-7-490 are acts which can only be directed against a child, and not towards a fetus.[2]...

At most, the majority only suggests that the term "child" as used in § 20-7-50 is ambiguous. This suggestion of ambiguity is created not by reference to our decisions under the Children's Code or by reference to the statutory language and applicable rules of statutory construction, but by reliance on decisions in two different fields of the law, civil wrongful death and common law feticide. Here, we deal with the Children's Code, and the meaning of language used in a criminal statute under that Code. We have already indicated that a child within the meaning of § 20-7-90(A) (1985), which criminalizes non-support, must be one already born. *State v. Montgomery* [citations omitted] Even if these wrongful death, common law, and Children's Code decisions are sufficient to render the term child in § 20-7-50 ambiguous, it is axiomatic that the ambiguity must be resolved in respondent's favor. [citation omitted]

I would affirm.

[2] Examples include condoning delinquency, using excessive corporal punishment, committing sexual offenses against the child, and depriving her of adequate food, clothing, shelter or education.

MOORE, JUSTICE:

I concur with the dissent in this case but write separately to express my concerns with today's decision.

In my view, the repeated failure of the legislature to pass proposed bills addressing the problem of drug use during pregnancy is evidence that the child abuse and neglect statute is not intended to apply in this instance. This Court should not invade what is clearly the sole province of the legislative branch. At the very least, the legislature's failed attempts to enact a statute regulating a pregnant woman's conduct indicate the complexity of this issue. While the majority opinion is perhaps an argument for what the law should be, it is for the General Assembly, and not this Court, to make that determination by means of a clearly drawn statute. With today's decision, the majority not only ignores legislative intent but embarks on a course of judicial activism rejected by every other court to address the issue.

* * *

In construing this statute to include conduct not contemplated by the legislature, the majority has rendered the statute vague and set for itself the task of determining what conduct is unlawful. Is a pregnant woman's failure to obtain prenatal care unlawful? Failure to quit smoking or drinking? Although the majority dismisses this issue as not before it, the impact of today's decision is to render a pregnant woman potentially criminally liable for myriad acts which the legislature has not seen fit to criminalize. To ignore this "down-the-road" consequence in a case of this import is unrealistic. The majority insists that parents may already be held liable for drinking after a child is born. This is untrue, however, without some further act on the part of the parent. A parent who drinks and then hits her child or fails to come home may be guilty of criminal neglect. The mere fact of drinking, however, does not constitute neglect of a child in being.

> The majority attempts to support an overinclusive construction of the child abuse and neglect statute by citing other legal protections extended equally to a viable fetus and a child in being. The only law, however, that specifically regulates the conduct of a mother toward her unborn child is our abortion statute under which a viable fetus is in fact treated differently from a child in being....
>
> The majority argues for equal treatment of viable fetuses and children, yet its construction of the statute results in even greater inequities. If the statute applies only when a fetus is "viable," a pregnant woman can use cocaine for the first twenty-four weeks...of her pregnancy, the most dangerous period for the fetus, and be immune from prosecution under the statute so long as she quits drug use before the fetus becomes viable. Further, a pregnant woman now faces up to ten years in prison for ingesting drugs during pregnancy but can have an illegal abortion and receive only a two-year sentence for killing her viable fetus....
>
> Because I disagree with the conclusion § 20-7-50 includes a viable fetus, I would affirm the grant of post-conviction relief.

Questions for Discussion

1. Does the federal constitutional right of a biological mother to abort a fetus imply a lesser included right to injure his or her child? Does it include a right to injure a fetus *in utero* to whom the mother intends to give birth?

2. South Carolina's neglect statute only covers "viable fetuses" (presumably well into the second trimester). Where a mother intends to give birth, can South Carolina protect a fetus during its first four months from illegal drug use which will demonstrably produce a baby with severe disabilities?

3. Does this "child neglect" case turn on the illegal nature of the contaminant threatening the child? How is child neglect vitiated because the chemical is legal to ingest, but has the same devastating effect on the child as an illegal drug?

4. Can the legislature protect a child from threatened severe Fetal Alcohol Syndrome injury *in utero*? Can the state regulate other actions hazardous to a child *in utero*, such as ingestion of foods hazardous to a fetus, frequenting rooms with heavy second-hand tobacco smoke, or extreme weight gain jeopardizing the health of the fetus? Does it matter that recent research discounts the long-term harm to children from moderate cocaine use during pregnancy? If evidence of harm is stronger as to tobacco or alcohol use, can "child neglect" be a constitutional basis for criminal penalties where cocaine is found at birth?

5. What is the assumption in *Whitner* about the status of the unborn child? Is the fetus considered a "person" capable of constitutional protection? If not a competing constitutional right *vis-à-vis* the mother, is its health nevertheless a "compelling state interest" warranting possible limitation on her constitutional rights? Because such a status may invoke "strict scrutiny," the state may be required to choose the least restrictive alternative to advancing that state interest. What measures would pass constitutional muster under both Blackmun's and O'Connor's acknowledged right of the state to protect the health of a fetus who will be born?

6. As the opinion indicates, a third party who intentionally injures a child *in utero* may be criminally prosecuted, or may be civilly liable where the injury was inflicted due to negligence. Usually, the parents are the recovering plaintiffs. Can the state constitutionally recover against a negligent mother who injures her child *in utero* and imposes substantial costs of care on the public?

7. Note that in *Ferguson v. City of Charleston*, 532 U.S. 67 (2001), the Supreme Court invalidated the South Carolina hospital practice of testing pregnant women suspected of drug use. Where samples tested positive during the first 27 weeks of pregnancy, the woman was charged with possession of an unlawful drug. Where testing positive after 27 weeks of pregnancy, she would be charged with possession and "distribution to a person under the age of 18." Where testing positive during delivery, she could be charged with unlawful neglect of a child. The Court held that where hospital employees take samples with the intent to obtain evidence for a criminal prosecution, they must obtain a knowing waiver (and patients must be informed of their constitutional right to refuse such a sample). Would *Ferguson* be decided differently if there is "probable cause" that such a mother is using drugs? Is a search warrant required? Would the bar the Court imposes here apply if the remedy were civil rather than criminal? What kind of remedy might protect a fetus which is viable or where birth is intended? Does the viable fetus have any constitutional rights whatever? If not, to what extent is his or her protection a "compelling state interest" and what are the alternatives available to the state to constitutionally protect that interest?

Note on the State Interest in Protecting the Fetus from Injury

The right to abort a fetus (to the point of its viability separate from the mother) remains settled law. But *Roe v. Wade* recognizes a state interest in protecting "potential life." Such a life does not appear to capture the rights of "person-hood" under the constitution until birth, but what of protecting an unborn child that is intended to be born as a "compelling state interest?" As a "legitimate state interest?" In *International Union v. Johnson Controls*, 499 U.S. 187 (1991), the Supreme Court addressed the problem of lead contamination in manufacturing—a disproportionate and dangerous contaminant correlated to permanent disability for the fetus and infants. Employer Johnson Controls makes batteries with lead as a primary ingredient. Eight employees working at the plant became pregnant and measured blood-lead levels in excess of limits set by the Occupational Safety and Health Administration (OSHA) for a woman who was planning to have a family. The employer announced a policy barring all women, except those whose inability to bear children was medically documented, from jobs involving exposure or potential exposure to lead at a level exceeding OSHA standards.

The policy was voided by the Supreme Court as a sex discrimination violation of Title VII of the Civil Rights Act of 1964. The Court held: (1) the policy was facially discriminatory by requiring only a female employee to prove that she was not capable of reproducing; (2) under the Pregnancy Discrimination Act of 1978

(PDA), the employer's choice to treat all female employees as potentially pregnant evinced sex discrimination; (3) the beneficence of the employer's purpose did not undermine the conclusion that the employer's policy was sex discrimination, and thus could be defended only as a "bona fide occupational qualification"; and (4) the policy did not come within such an exception because it is not reasonably necessary to the normal operation of the employer's particular business—since (a) fertile women, according to the record, participated in the manufacture of batteries as efficiently as anyone else, (b) through Title VII, as amended by the PDA, Congress mandated that decisions about the welfare of future children be left to the parents who conceive, bear, support, and raise them, and (c) concerns about the next generation were not part of the essence of the employer's business (*Johnson Controls, supra*, at 195–207).

Questions for Discussion

1. In *Johnson Controls*, the Court confined its "*bona fide* occupational qualification" that would allow the policy to issues involving production efficiency and profit impact. There was discussion of the issue of tort liability for the employer as a possible business cost (if its contaminants were the court proven cause of a permanent disability of a child). But the Court reasoned that so long as women are notified of the danger, tort liability would be unlikely. The majority and Scalia's concurring opinion essentially dismissed the effect on the fetus as irrelevant. The decision did not balance or analyze the danger and review all alternative methods to ameliorate it in order to insist on the least restrictive. Is he Court's analysis reflective of a "compelling state interest" in the health of children who will be born? Did the fetus even receive a "heightened scrutiny" analysis? Is protection of the fetus even a "legitimate state interest" balanced under "rational relation"?

2. Would the restriction pass muster were it to apply also to men? Does it matter that contamination danger differs between its effect on male sperm and its effect on those who are pregnant and carrying a fetus sharing the mother's blood? Would it help if it applied only to those who were actually pregnant—and who were intending to deliver the baby (not planning an abortion)?

3. How does the exclusion from work exposure to lead contamination correlate with the *criminal* "child abuse" prosecution in *Whitner* for ingesting a contaminant endangering a child? Does it matter that Cal-OSHA blood level safety limits were violated? Would it matter if Cal-OSHA made it a civil violation yielding a penalty if workers were exposed to levels increasing blood levels to its maximum limit? Would it matter if federal law made it a criminal offense to subject a pregnant woman to lead levels above such levels as a condition of employment?

4. In *Urbano v. Continental Airlines*, 138 F.3d 204 (5th Cir. 1998), a woman whose duties included lifting heavy objects became pregnant. The employer refused to allow her a "light lifting" work assignment because it made such adjustments

only for an "on the job" caused disability, forcing her into an uncompensated medical leave. The court rejected her claim of discrimination, citing *Johnson* for the proposition that pregnancy should make no difference and the employer properly did not distinguish pregnant females. The court indicates that distinguishing in favor of a pregnant female may be permissible, and that the employer may be allowed to confer a light load, but to require it to do so would be "discriminatory." What weight does the health of "potential life" play in such formulations?

5. Can licensed female boxers be required to include a pregnancy test in their pre-fight physicals? Note that California has prohibited such tests as "discriminatory" by statute because they are not required of male boxers. Would objections cease if the state were to also test male boxers for pregnancy? Would it be constitutional and compliant with federal employment law to not allow a pregnant woman to box, and hence receive potential blows of extreme danger to the fetus? Would it matter if she were seven months pregnant?

Reproductive Responsibility and Child Poverty in America
Robert C. Fellmeth
Originally Printed in the American Bar Association's
Human Rights Magazine (Winter 2005)

Johnny S. was eleven years old and his homeless mother had his five-year-old sister to worry about. So she left him on a street corner in Ocean Beach, a neighborhood in San Diego. Johnny looked for his mom for four days before he was picked up by social workers. He scrounged for odd jobs and conned a restaurant manager into letting him wash dishes for three hours a night, earning just over $135. When the social workers found him, he had every penny in his pockets. He had confined himself to just one meal at the restaurant because "Mom needs [the money]." Johnny is a bright-eyed boy with above average intelligence. However, he has a slight stoop due to a correctable bone malformation, and his teeth have painful cavities. He has not been to school for two years. He presents a microcosm of child poverty in America: a child with strong potential and admirable character but with health problems, an educational deficit, and likely relegation to group home foster care or to the streets. Regrettably, Johnny is not unique. He lives in our wealthiest state and, until gathered up, was sleeping under bushes by the beach, in the shadows of $5 million homes.

For two decades, child poverty has been fluctuating between 10-20% of the population, with an overall upward trend. It declined somewhat during the late 1990s, and welfare rolls fell substantially. But those hopeful signs obscure three caveats: (1) the increase appears to have resumed since 2000, and in the context of a now-limited and reduced welfare reform safety net; (2) "severe poverty," that is, income less than half of the federal poverty line, has increased (but is not precisely measured); and (3) large numbers of children are living below or near the poverty line. This last grouping now represents 37% of all American children, 42% of its infants and toddlers, 58% of its African American children, and 62% of its Latino children. National Center for Children in Poverty, Columbia University, *Low Income Children in the United States–2004*, at www.nccp.org.

Child advocates are concerned about both ends of this spectrum: the severe poverty, portending permanent damage, and the imminent creation of a large Third World underclass of intractable poverty. The latter concern is reflected in overall increasing income disparities, with the upper 1% of Americans now earning as much as the bottom 38% combined. And the concern is underlined by barriers to upward mobility driven not only by childhood poverty but by preclusive real estate and rent inflation; growing energy, gasoline, and healthcare costs; and small increases in the higher education capacity—including community college and technical training—that most will need for employment in the international economic labor niche of the United States. This effective contraction is joined by many years of tuition increases well above inflation. Impediments to mobility for the young include unprecedented economic solicitude for older adults and a record federal deficit for the future taxpayers who are now our children. Add to this deficit more ominous Social Security and Medicare obligations. Harvard Law School's Howell Jackson projects an obligation of more than $30 trillion, $300,000 for each child over the next generation. Unless policies radically change, it will double and perhaps quadruple the regressive and already substantial payroll deductions for the youth who secure employment. Child advocates increasingly decry our unique cross-generational taking. Instead of the long-standing American tradition of older adults investing in the young, which particularly represents an opportunity for the impoverished, we are burdening our children with unprecedented debts and future costs.

A Closer Look

Contrary to public perception, the parents of impoverished children are not consuming beer while watching soap operas, engaging in what some call "welfare as a way of life." Data reveal that 56% of these low-income families have at least one full-time working parent, 28% work part time, and only 16% are unemployed, many of whom would be willing to work if employment were available. *Id.* However, the single most striking variable underlying child poverty is single parenthood, caused by divorce and unwed births. The latter have risen over the last thirty years from below 10% of all births to over 30%. Contrary to the common view, these births are not to teenagers; the vast majority are to adult women. Paternal support for these children is minimal, with average payments amounting to less than $35 per month per child, and almost half of that going not to families but to repay state and federal governments for welfare payments. See Children's Advocacy Institute, *California Children's Budget 2004-05*, Ch. 2, at www.caichildlaw.org. Most of these children live below the poverty line. Perhaps the most remarkable number from the U.S. Census reports is the difference between the median income of a female single head of household with two or more young children (about $11,000 in annual income) and the median for those children in a family of a married couple (well over $50,000). *Id.*

The conundrum for children like Johnny is the need for two incomes to support high rents and other rising costs of living. His mother is caught between the rock of child care obligations for her children—which she either provides or finds $5,000 per year per child to finance—and the hard place of a single wage earner unlikely to net much more than her child care costs for two or more children. Current federal policy makes the hard place harder because she is limited to sixty months of Temporary Aid to Needy Families and, even if working part time, is given no credit for those months of income where she works less than thirty-two hours.

Child poverty involves both private decisions and public disinvestment. Hence, the causes mentioned by commentators tend to turn on their respective political leanings. Conservatives cite reproductive irresponsibility, sexual license, lack of paternal commitment, as well as deficits and unfair burdens imposed on the young by the old, limiting their future aspirations. Liberals cite reduction of the safety net, a minimum wage that is not adjusted to inflation and has declined to below the poverty level for parents of two or more children, and education disinvestment that jeopardizes future employability for an impoverished class. Is it possible that both are correct?

According to many child advocates, the problem facing children is the truce silently in force between these traditional political antagonists. Each appears to have surrendered its agenda favorable to impoverished children in return for the surrender of the other's. Hence, popular culture now purveys with impunity the notion that single parenthood is simply a different and somehow charming choice, with those dozens of sit-com and other adult models (from Rachel on *Friends* to Roz on *Frasier*) suffering no financial repercussions, child care dilemmas, or worries. Indeed, our fantasy parents in the media often do not seem to work for a living; the rent is magically paid. No male appears to pay child support, nor does any child appear to need it. Rather, our media flood us with sexual stimulation and commendation without apparent negative childbirth consequences, replete with Cialis and Viagra ads for hours of male "hardening" while hypocritically eschewing condom ads. Child advocates contend that liberal adults have surrendered (or been overborne) in the direction of momentous public disinvestment in children, especially impoverished children, with safety net support and education opportunity suffering the largest cuts. And child advocates complain that both adult political groupings (although purportedly deeply divided) have conspired to violate through deficits and huge obligations to the elderly the one pact always drawn in favor of children: that adults do not take from their children, but give to them.

A Search for Answers

If these complaints have merit, what is the answer? One prescription is to reverse the trade-off between private license and child disinvestment into the opposite proposition, one demanded from the body politic. The Honorable Charles D. Gill has advanced the public commitment aspect in a proposed constitutional amendment. NACC CHILDREN'S LAW MANUAL, *Essay on the Status of the American Child—2000 AD: Chattel or Constitutionally Protected Child-Citizen?* at 337 (1998). The U.S. Constitution is oriented to inhibit the coercive power of the state vis-à-vis private, individual liberties. However, the constitutions of most developed nations also interpose some affirmative obligations on the state, obligations that need not impede checks on state coercion. Similarly, the UN Convention on the Rights of the Child, signed and ratified by every nation except the United States and Somalia, posits some minimal affirmative obligations to our children. Such a compact may properly specify only those obligations that are clearly commended as a common floor: that our children will not be homeless, will receive adequate care and nutrition to develop healthy brains, will have minimal health coverage and educational opportunity so they may provide for themselves and their children in turn. What is the opposition to such a constitutional amendment, spelled out with sufficient specificity to be enforceable? Is it that we, unlike our less affluent contemporaries in Europe, cannot afford it?

We reserve for our Constitution measures that may be politically unpopular but are a consensus "rule of the game" underlying our society. Although denied "suspect class" status in equal protection cases, what group is more politically impotent than impoverished children? And what commitment do we have more basic than this one?

Would support for such a formalized pledge benefit from a cultural sea change that private decisions to have children warrant the preparation and respect that the miracle of childbirth implies? That the decision includes the simple and minimal obligation of parents simply to intend a child, and of a father to provide for his children? Assume such a commitment were an acknowledged part of our culture and became as politically incorrect to transgress as would an insult to a gay person or someone dependent on a wheelchair. What would be the prospects for such a constitutional commitment, and to child investment in general, in such an altered environment?

One need not have a long conversation with Johnny to appreciate the merits of both a constitutional amendment and a cultural commitment to children.

ENDNOTES

[1] Pew Research Center, *Parenting in America: Outlook, worries, aspirations are strongly linked to financial situation* (December 2015) at http://www.pewsocialtrends.org/2015/12/17/1-the-american-family-today/.

[2] Guttmacher Institute, *Unintended Pregnancy in the United States: Fact Sheet* (January 2019) at https://www.guttmacher.org/sites/default/files/factsheet/fb-unintended-pregnancy-us.pdf.

[3] *Id.*

[4] Centers for Disease Control and Prevention, *National Vital Statistics Reports, Births: Final Data for 2017*, Vol. 67, Number 8 (2018) at https://www.cdc.gov/nchs/data/nvsr/nvsr67/nvsr67_08-508.pdf.

[5] See Table CH-1 at https://www.census.gov/data/tables/time-series/demo/families/children.html.

[6] See Table C2 at https://www.census.gov/data/tables/2018/demo/families/cps-2018.html.

[7] See https://www.acf.hhs.gov/sites/default/files/programs/css/fy_2016_annual_report.pdf for 2016 data. For 2017, see https://www.acf.hhs.gov/sites/default/files/programs/css/fy/2017_infographic_national_updated_0821.pdf. The latter discloses $28.8 billion distributed to 15.562 million children with child support orders. However, only 87%of eligible children have such orders. Accordingly, of the 17.584 million with absent mothers or fathers theoretically obliged to support their children, in 2016 $28.83 billion was distributed, bringing the annual total per child to $1,640 per year, or $137 per month; see also discussion in Chapter 1 above.

[8] See discussion in Chapter 1, and note that the *Wagner* case litigated by CAI included an extensive record of national data on child costs and foster care payments to provide relevant payments, including an extensive study by the University of Maryland. See http://www.caichildlaw.org/FC_Litig.htm.

[9] Kayla Fontenot, *et al., Income and Poverty in the United States: 2017* (U.S. Census Bureau; 2018) at https://www.census.gov/content/dam/Census/library/publications/2018/demo/p60-263.pdf.

[10] *Id.*

[11] See Table C8 at https://www.census.gov/data/tables/2018/demo/families/cps-2018.html.

[12] See https://www.census.gov/data/tables/2017/demo/families/cps-2017.html.

[13] *Id.*

[14] Fontenot, *supra* note 9.

[15] See https://www.cdc.gov/teenpregnancy/about/index.htm.

[16] See https://www.childtrends.org/indicators/sexual-activity-among-teens.

[17] *Id.*

[18] See U.S. Department of Health and Human Services, *Characteristics and Financial Circumstances of TANF Recipients Fiscal Year 2017* (2018) at https://www.acf.hhs.gov/sites/default/files/ofa/fy17_characteristics.pdf. For example, 96.6% of TANF parents in California are over 19 years of age, and one quarter of these are married. See California Department of Social Services, *TANF Characteristics Survey 1998* (Sacramento, CA; 1999) Tables 18 and 19 at 34.

[19] For 2016 data, see Centers for Disease Control, *National Vital Statistics Reports*, Volume 67, Number 1, at https://www.cdc.gov/nchs/data/nvsr/nvsr67/nvsr67_01.pdf.

[20] Wendy Manning, *Cohabitation and Child Wellbeing*, 25 FUTURE CHILD (Fall 2015).

[21] *Id.*

[22] Woodrow Wilson School of Public and International Affairs at Princeton University and Brookings Institute, *Fragile Families*, THE FUTURE OF CHILDREN, Vol. 20, No. 2 (2010) at 99; see http://futureofchildren.org/futureofchildren/publications/docs/20_02_FullJournal.pdf.

[23] A. Bleakley, *How Sources of Sexual Information Relate to Adolescents' Beliefs about Sex*, 22 AM. J. HEALTH BEHAV. (2009).

[24] Children Now and the Kaiser Family Foundation, *Sex, Kids and the Family Hour: A Three-Part Study of Sexual Content on Television* (San Francisco, CA; 1996).

[25] Kaiser Family Foundation, *Sex on TV 4*, (Washington DC; 2005), executive summary at https://kaiserfamilyfoundation.files.wordpress.com/2013/01/sex-on-tv-4-executive-summary.pdf.

[26] Michael Males, *Teens and older Partners*, (2004) at http://recapp.etr.org/recapp/index.cfm?fuseaction=pages.CurrentResearchDetail&PageID=393&PageTypeID=18#who.

[27] *Id.*

[28] Advocates for Youth, *Judicial Bypass Procedures: Policy Brief* (Washington DC; 2015).

[29] *Id.*

[30] *Garza v. Hargan*, 874 F.3d 735 (D.C. Cir., 2017).

[31] Robert Mathias, National Institute on Drug Abuse, *NIDA Survey Provides First National Data on Drug Use During Pregnancy*, NIDA NOTES (Bethesda, MD; Jan./Feb. 1995).

[32] *Id.*

[33] See www/samhsa.gov/data/report/2017-nsduh-detailed-tables.

[34] See https://www.cdc.gov/ncbddd/fasd/data.html.

[35] Philip May, Christina Chambers, and Wendy Kalberg, *Prevalence of Fetal Alcohol Spectrum Disorders in 4 US Communities*, JOURNAL OF THE AMERICAN MEDICAL ASSOCIATION, 319(5):474-482 (2018).

[36] American Speech-Language-Hearing Association, *Fetal Alcohol Syndrome* (1996). See also CDC, *supra* note 34.

[37] *Id.*

[38] Centers for Disease Control and Prevention, *NCHS Data Brief No. 306* (March 2018) at https://www.cdc.gov/nchs/products/databriefs/db306.htm.

CHAPTER THREE

Child Poverty and Safety Net Sustenance

A. CHILD POVERTY

Child poverty correlates with critical health measures: low birthweights, undernutrition, lower cognitive development and IQ, and low height for age. It also correlates with child neglect and delinquency incidence. Perhaps most profoundly, it has a close relationship to long-term educational achievement and economic opportunity.

As of 2019, the federal poverty line for the contiguous 48 states was $16,910 for a family of two (usually a mother and child) and $21,330 for the benchmark family of three.[1] The official poverty rate for all Americans in 2017 was 12.3%; for children, the poverty rate was 17.5%, and for the elderly (age 65 and older) the rate was 9.2%.[2] While the official child poverty rate of 17.5% is lower than the 23% level in the late 1970s, over thirty nations—including all of Europe, Hungary, Australia, New Zealand, Canada, and Estonia—presently have lower child poverty rates than does the United States. Most of them have substantially lower rates—less than half of U.S. figures—although with substantially lower Gross Domestic Product levels.[3]

A breakdown of the poverty groupings is available from the 2019 Report from the National Academies of Sciences, Engineers and Medicine, using the more detailed data available from 2015–16.[4] That report estimates that just over two million children live in "deep poverty"—less than one-half of the poverty line. Without the Supplemental Nutrition Assistance Program (SNAP or "food stamps"), that number would double to about four million.[5] The benefits provided by SNAP are particularly important since the brain is vulnerable to damage from undernutrition far short of gross physical symptoms, particularly for children under six years of age. Even where noticeable emaciation may occur from severe malnutrition, preschool children who are most vulnerable are not commonly seen by the "mandated reporters" relied upon to detect child abuse and neglect (e.g., school nurses, teachers, school counselors). For pregnant women and young children, such undernutrition correlates statistically with low birthweight babies, delayed physical growth, higher infant mortality, brain underdevelopment, cognitive disability, language dysfunction, and other long-run costs (see below for a discussion of consequences). It also correlates with measurable cognitive and concentration shortfall, in turn reflected in school performance.[6]

In general, high poverty and deep poverty rates afflict four major groupings: Black (18%), Hispanic (22%), single parent (22%) and immigrant (21%) families. While SNAP is most relevant to deep poverty amelioration, two tax credits have played the largest role in lowering overall poverty rates: the Earned Income Tax Credit and the Child Tax Credit, discussed below.

B. CHILD POVERTY-RELATED PUBLIC POLICIES

Child poverty in the United States has been driven by a mix of factors: unemployment, wage depression below self-sufficiency for families, increased births to unwed mothers and more single-parent households, continued low rate of child support collection, tax policies, and substantial cuts in the safety net for impoverished children.

Other factors commonly cited include high unemployment among the young and the poor; high housing costs, requiring two incomes to maintain a household with children; decline in blue collar compensation and job opportunities; disinvestment in trade schools, community colleges, and university opportunities combined with fee increases and loan reductions; a minimum wage below the poverty line for full-time work for a family of three (after its 1996 increase); lack of assured and adequate medical coverage; substantial decline in public safety net assistance for children; and the isolation of the poor into neighborhoods where connections for upper mobility are lacking. International migration has also been a factor in some states, although less so than the negative impact of wage, education, regressive tax, and safety net policies.[7]

Current students face highly escalating tuition costs—even at public colleges and universities, and now bear unprecedented levels of debt upon graduation. Many of the loan programs for students are currently suffering reductions, precluding advanced education for some who would have advanced in prior years. Those who do graduate with higher debts and seek to purchase a home face unprecedented housing costs. Senior citizens are likely to have purchased their homes at a fraction of current market value. Under property tax systems such as California's, older citizens are locked into those low market values—and pay only a fraction of the property taxes of a young person purchasing his or her first house.

The major tax reform backed by both political parties since 1996 is to forgive capital gains entirely on home sales and in 2018 to radically lower corporate taxation benefitting relatively older, wealthy stockholders, and to reduce the taxation of the inheritance of wealthy estates.

1. Minimum Wage and Employment

In 1997, the federal minimum wage was $5.15 per hour. On July 24, 2009 it was set at $7.25, where it has remained into 2019. This floor has moved down in constant dollars over the past thirty years, and would have risen to over $12 by 2019 if adjusted for inflation. Some states impose higher minimum wages on workers in their respective domains, varying from the common replication of the federal minimum wage to some with levels in the $8.25 to $11 range. Only the 2019 level of $12 in effect in California has matched the declining value of the dollar due to inflation. In fact, if the minimum wage matched productivity increases over the past fifty years, it would be over $20 per hour in 2019.[8] Those working at the current floor will earn less than the federal poverty line for a family of two, and about 60% of the $25,750 poverty line for a family of four. The take-home pay, after subtraction of Social Security and other payroll deductions, will lower net income to 40–50% of poverty levels.

Advocates for the poor and children have argued for a minimum wage which allows a parent who works full-time to at least reach—and ideally surpass—the poverty level. Objections to such increases center on job losses at the low-wage end, possibly focusing on youth unemployment. However, these fears were somewhat undermined in California, where the minimum wage increased markedly from $4.25 to $5.75 from September 1996 to April 1998 and to $12 in 2019—with substantial new job creation statistics notwithstanding such increases.

Of those who would benefit from minimum wage increases, fewer than 10% are under twenty, and 28% are adult parents supporting children.[9] National studies find that single mothers benefit disproportionately from minimum wage increases, making up 5.7% of the total workforce, but 10% of those who would benefit directly. In particular, African American and Hispanic workers would benefit, with 38% and 33% respectively affected by minimum wage hikes.[10] Experts calculate that in addition to those earning under the minimum wage, those at or near that level also enjoy a boost in earnings (termed the "spillover effect").[11]

2. Tax Policies

Federal and state tax statutes and rules provide a variety of tax policies, such as deductions, credits, and forbearances (termed "tax expenditures") (see Chapter 1). While the activity stimulated by a tax deduction or credit may ameliorate child poverty, tax expenditures reduce general fund revenues upon which impoverished children rely for assistance. More generally, taxes affect income distribution. Taxation policies, including inheritance or estate transfers from the wealthy to their heirs, and tax rates imposed on various income levels, can either stimulate or impede equality of opportunity and upward mobility.

Tax subsidies are commonly arranged in three ways. First, a refundable tax credit allows a payment in the specified subsidy amount where the behavior to be subsidized occurs. Such credits benefit the poor as well as the wealthy. Second, a non-refundable tax credit does not benefit those who do not pay taxes, but it does benefit equally all taxpayers who owe taxes at or above the level of the credit. Hence, a state tax credit of $300 can be subtracted from taxes owed of $300 or more. If poverty reduces a parent's tax liability to $150, he or she will be able to benefit from only one-half of the subsidy. And those below the poverty line who pay no personal income taxes will receive no benefit whatsoever from a non-refundable tax credit.

The third type of subsidy, a deduction from taxable income, does not benefit the poor, and rewards in direct proportion to the tax bracket of the taxpayer. Hence, a taxpayer subtracting a $1,000 tax deduction from taxable income who is in the 35% bracket receives a $350 benefit while a taxpayer in the 5% bracket receives a $50 benefit.

a. Earned Income Tax Credit (EITC)—Refundable

The largest current tax benefit directed to impoverished children is the refundable federal Earned Income Tax Credit (EITC), which as of 2019 can provide up to $5,716 per year for a working family with two children and $6,431 for those with more than two children. The credit adds a percentage of income to a working adult above a certain level and then phases out as earned income increases. Hence, a parent with one child will start to receive a refundable tax credit after achieving income of a certain level that will gradually decrease as income rises above a "phase out" level that varies depending upon the number of children in the household (one, two, or more than two). This assistance allows many working poor parents to reach at least marginally above the poverty line.

b. Child and Dependent Tax Credit

The Child Tax Credit under the 2017 Tax Cut and Jobs Act is worth up to $2,000 per qualifying child. The age cut-off remains at 17 (the child must be under 17 at the end of the year for taxpayers to claim the credit). The refundable portion of the credit is limited to $1,400. This amount will be adjusted for inflation after 2018.

c. Post-2001 Federal Tax Changes

Federal tax changes during 2001 and 2003, with additional measures in 2017 and 2018, have included the phased abolition of federal taxation on estates—where the first $1 million was already exempt prior to these changes. A study of African American families found that inheritance opportunities for that group were a small fraction of the inheritance expected by the children of White Americans,[12] with the median wealth of the former at $11,030 and the latter at $134,230.[13] In addition, impoverished children generally do not live with parents able to take proportionate advantage of pension plan subsidies. The focus on pension benefits continues the trend of subsidy increase for older Americans.

Long-term tax expenditure resulting from tax changes deprives the government of resources to invest in children and the future, which will be difficult to regenerate politically. According to one source, the cost of the eleven-year tax reduction plan from 2001–12, estimated at $1.35 trillion, actually amounts to $2.3 trillion when the eleventh year totals are properly included and increased interest payments are counted.[14] In the following 2012–21 ten-year period, the cost will rise to $4.3 trillion, excluding substantially increased interest payments.[15] The 2017 tax change noted above includes an increase in the child tax credit. But other changes, then joined by 2018 changes for corporate tax and accelerated estate exemption, may likely more than double that wealth transfer by 2025. As discussed in Chapter 1, these tax expenditures, deficits, and even larger deferred obligations for Medicare, Social Security and public employee pensions/retired medical coverage, create an unprecedented burden for future taxpayers—*i.e.*, our current children.

3. Safety Net Assurance

a. History

Historically, the nation has had two major programs to address the basic shelter, clothing and food needs of its poorest children: Aid to Families with Dependent Children (AFDC) and food stamps. Nearly seventy percent of the recipients of funds expended on these two programs are children.[16]

Unlike the case in much of Europe, the U.S. Constitution does not address economic rights, including an assured safety net for children. However, since the 1960s federal statutes established both AFDC and food stamps as entitlements for children whose parents' income falls below a level likely to allow minimal housing and adequate nutrition. The states have been required roughly to match the AFDC contribution from the federal jurisdiction, but were allowed to individually set the total benefit levels. During the 1980s many states began to reduce AFDC benefits—often by failing to adjust for inflation over an extended period—with total safety net provision (AFDC plus food stamps) commonly declining to below 75% of the poverty line. This trend was limited by the federal entitlement status of AFDC. States could be granted "waivers" to experiment with terms separate and apart from federal minimums (in order to test theses for possible improvement or to reflect local conditions). However, after 1989 states were required to maintain their respective benefit levels per person at least at their chosen 1989 level unless granted a federal waiver. That limit was based on the raw numbers, allowing an effective 2–3% per annum further real spending reduction as inflation occurred thereafter. However, the 1989 floor provided some restraint on cuts below those levels during the early 1990s (see *Beno v. Shalala*, below).

During the mid-1990s, the opponents of AFDC contended that it stimulated "welfare as a way of life," *e.g.*, unwed births funded by the state without paternal involvement. Critics contended that the program discouraged work and suffered widespread abuse, including teen pregnancies, movement of claimants between states seeking higher benefits (and immigrants from other nations), and sequential children for higher grants. Although some of these criticisms may have some merit, the overall demographics of recipients reveals the typical parental recipient to be a mother, over thirty years old, white, with two children, averaging under $50 per month per child in support from the father. This typical welfare recipient works part-time and would work more if child care and employment were available. Fewer than 5% are unwed teens, and fewer than 2% have been in the state less than one year. None are undocumented immigrants. Studies indicate that the major causes of caseload include unemployment, divorce, paternal abandonment, and declining wage levels. The available evidence suggests that changes in benefit levels (beyond extremes) do not influence caseloads substantially.[17]

b. Personal Responsibility and Work Opportunity Reconciliation Act of 1996 (PRA)

As Congress changed composition in 1996, it enacted the Personal Responsibility and Work Opportunity Reconciliation Act of 1996 (PRA). The new statute removed Aid to Families with Dependent Children (AFDC) as an entitlement, replacing it with "Temporary Assistance to Needy Families (TANF)", and capped it (and other safety net programs) under several "block grants" with specified amounts.

For a family with dependent children to receive benefits under TANF (as with prior AFDC), most states impose asset limits, *e.g.*, no more than $2,250 (in California) and an auto allowance that varies widely by state. Recipients must be U.S. citizens or qualified legal aliens. If eligible, a family may receive monthly cash grants based on family size and income. If a family has earned income, the grant is reduced by the amount of earnings; but to encourage employment, recipients may disregard certain expenses, including actual child care expenses up to a set level.[18] In addition, states have JOBS training programs through which TANF parents may receive education, training, and child care assistance to achieve independent employment (see below).

The block grant could not be increased for at least five years (in fact, extended to ten and thereafter at a relatively static level), accomplishing assured reductions of 3–5% each year from inflation and population gain. The state must meet a Maintenance of Effort (MOE) requirement to obtain TANF funding, meaning that the state must spend some of its own funds on programs for needy families. However, the state contribution is no longer a match of federal monies—which were themselves once based on the safety net needs of children. Instead, both are capped through the block grant format and the general "sequestration" concept of Congress that keeps funding at similar raw number levels as an alleged "neutral" adjuster. It is, rather, a cumulatively constricting adjustment. In 2016, the amount spent by states was about half of what was spent in 1994, after adjusting for inflation.[19]

As originally framed, the five states most successful at reducing unwed births receive a bonus from the federal jurisdiction. A bonus is also possible for "high performance" (to be determined by the Secretary of the Department of Health and Human Services), based on the movement of TANF recipients into work. The state must assess the skills, work experience, and employability of each adult recipient. Under the Act, a specific percentage of families must participate in work activities. If it fails to comply, a state may lose up to 5% of its block grant. In addition, families face a five-year lifetime limit on use of block grant funds. The state may exempt up to 20% of families from the five-year limit, and from work requirements for "hardship" (*e.g.*, disabled or abused recipients).

Under the Act, teen parents may not receive TANF unless they attend school and live with their parents or in another approved adult setting. The state may deny benefits for additional children born while the parent is receiving TANF. The state may deny cash assistance to non-citizens legally residing in the state. The statute also provided that a state may limit benefits for persons from another state to the grant level of the former state (a provision struck by the U.S. Supreme Court in 1999, see discussion below).

The Act imposed work requirements on TANF families. For a two-parent family to count as "working," the adults must work at least a combined 35 hours per week. A single parent must work at least 30 hours per week in 2000 and beyond. A parent is "working" if employed or participating in on-the-job training, vocational education, job search, or community service. The state may exempt families with children under the age of one from TANF's work requirements.

The Act requires a 25% reduction in TANF benefits (and allows states to cut more) where a parent "fails to cooperate" in identifying and finding the non-custodial biological parent, usually an absent father. It is not clear what constitutes a "failure to cooperate." But it clearly requires the identification of the biological father. The law also includes a confusing requirement that the state's plan "require a parent... receiving assistance under the program to engage in work (as defined by the State) once the State determines the parent...is ready to engage in work, or once the parent...has received assistance under the program for 24 months [whether or not consecutive], whichever is earlier."[20] The "ready to engage" clause indicates that where a parent receiving TANF is able to work and is offered employment, it must be accepted. The second clause requires work after 24 months of total assistance (after January 1, 1998) as an outside limit. However, this requirement is not imposed on individuals, but on states. That is, states must have a mechanism in place to assure employment of all recipients after no more than 24 months of assistance after January 1, 1998. The mechanism to enforce state compliance with its plan requiring work within 24 months is unclear—few large states have fully complied as of 2006.

i.   PRA Consequences

The initial study of New York's TANF population reflected a national trend of substantial roll reductions after 1996. However, only about one-third of those dropped from TANF rolls from July 1996 to March 1997 achieved wages beyond $100 in total over three months after departure; most were driven by sanctions or new qualification or paperwork requirements into deep poverty without any employment whatever—and with dire implications for involved children.[21] Studies during 1997 and 1998 partly confirmed these findings. Summarizing from eleven state studies, experts concluded that approximately 50–60% of those who left welfare jobs, only slightly higher than the percentage leaving welfare for jobs prior to 1996. Most of the jobs obtained paid less than enough to lift families out of poverty, and far less than required for short of self-sufficiency. Child care and transportation remain major barriers to economic improvement for families.[22]

The Urban Institute's initial study released in August 1999 found that about two-thirds of those exiting welfare had found jobs, and generally achieved more income than TANF grants in their respective states. However, the average wage for those so employed was $6.61 per hour—still below the poverty line for a family of three. Studies published after 2000 indicate young children may benefit in terms of academic achievement and other indices where parents work *and* family income increases, although the lessening of parental attention has some negative impacts on adolescents. The positive results appear to correlate with quality child care and education/training investment in parents.[23] An economic downturn without concomitant employment assistance (less likely with lower tax revenues) will subject many recently employed parents to lay-off and reliance on safety net provision to the extent eligible.

Recent national studies (discussed below) attribute the expansion of the Earned Income Tax Credit as a substantial mitigation of what would otherwise have been a further deepening of poverty. Nevertheless, as discussed above, both child poverty and deep child poverty—below 50% of the line—remain at high levels.

ii. PRA Future Implications

As indicated, the PRA reverses federal policy from a required floor to a required ceiling. The ceiling terms raise two dominant concerns:

1) The law imposes a lifetime five-year (sixty-month) limit on all such assistance. Any month where any assistance amount is received counts against the maximum. Hence, if a parent works half-time for five years and receives a small TANF amount, then loses her job, her family is cut off entirely. Except for a few states (*e.g.*, Illinois), credit is not provided for part-time work. About one-half of parents receiving TANF traditionally work ten hours per week or more.

2) The statute requires that "adequate child care be provided," but supply is unavailable to many impoverished parents, and most who obtain jobs suffer the cut-off of all such child care help at the one- or two-year mark of post-TANF employment.

These concerns are supported by a major study by the University of California and Yale University, released in February 2000. The study focuses on three major states. Compared to control groups, the study found: (1) young children move into low-quality child care as their mothers move from welfare to work; (2) child care centers are in short supply in the neighborhoods where needed and almost half of working parents are compelled to leave children with family or friends; (3) the early development of young children is limited by uneven parenting practices and high rates of maternal depression; and (4) although a sizable percentage are moving into jobs, wages are low and income remains below the poverty line. About one-third of the mothers surveyed admitted that they had difficulty buying enough food for their children "often or sometimes."[24]

Some TANF parents entering employment post-1998 are achieving somewhat higher wages—close to the poverty line for the benchmark family of three.[25] However, payroll taxes push most back below the poverty line in take-home pay. Some do not receive medical coverage through their employer, and may be denied Medicaid coverage due to their income. Their children may be eligible for the State Child Health Insurance Program, but coverage requires co-payments difficult for many to afford (see Chapter 5).

The coverage of impoverished children from this safety net measure has declined consistently. In 2017, for every 100 families in poverty, only 23 received direct financial assistance from TANF, down from 68 families in 1996. This "TANF-to-poverty ratio" (TPR) reached its lowest point in 2014 and has remained there since.[26]

c. Supplemental Nutrition Assistance Program (SNAP)—Food Stamps

As of 2008, Supplemental Nutrition Assistance Program (SNAP) is the new name for the federal Food Stamp Program, which provides low-income households with an Electronic Benefits Transfer (EBT) card that can be used to purchase food at retail food stores.[27] The federal government pays for 100% of the benefits. The program is administered on the federal level by the U.S. Department of Agriculture (USDA) and in most states through departments of social services, usually at the county level. Most states pay about 60% of the limited "administrative costs" of the program, but the benefits themselves are federally-funded.

Food stamps are generally considered the nation's broadest and most basic safety net program, because there are no eligibility restrictions other than income, assets, and citizenship. The program includes TANF recipients by operation of law, but is more expansive. Hence, some parents leaving TANF for employment, or who are disqualified from TANF, may qualify for food stamp assistance for their children. Food stamps are available to any household with a gross income at or below 130% of the federal poverty line, a net income at or below the poverty line, and less than $2,250 in disposable assets (higher for the disabled and those over 65). Benefits have never been claimable by undocumented immigrants.

In a typical month, SNAP helps 40 million low-income individuals, including nearly 20 million children, purchase basic food.[28] That amounts to 25% of the children in the nation. Nearly 44% of SNAP benefits go to children directly and another 21% go to parents with children. SNAP provided some $44 billion in 2016 to help families with children buy groceries—more than half of this amount went to families that included young children under five years of age. A 2015 study estimated that 83% of eligible persons received SNAP benefits.[29] Studies indicate that SNAP increases the nutritional intake of impoverished children by 20–40%.[30]

i. Benefit Levels

The basis for food stamp allotments, USDA's Thrifty Food Plan, has been judged to be inadequate to meet nutritional needs, and to significantly underestimate the actual costs of purchasing the necessary component foods. As noted above, SNAP benefits are based on income, and thusly increase at least somewhat as TANF benefits decline. However, these increases only amount to $3 for every $10 in TANF reduction. In sum, SNAP benefits, although inadequate to assure proper nutrition by child beneficiaries, has deep application into impoverished child population and as discussed below, together with the Earned Income Tax Credit, are the major forces at least moderating child poverty consequences.

ii.   Personal Responsibility Act (PRA) Food Stamp Changes

Traditionally, food stamp recipients have been required to "register for work." The PRA allows states to require recipients with children over the age of one to work in order to receive benefits. However, the amounts appropriated will not fund training for an appreciable percentage of out-of-work recipients. Some states disqualify persons from food stamps who refuse to work or voluntarily quit "without cause"—a disqualification the PRA allows. The PRA provision authorizing work requirements for able-bodied adults without children within 90 days would affect children indirectly by adding substantially to the pool of persons competing for a limited number of jobs, thereby driving down wages, and potentially burdening counties to provide yet more workfare.

The PRA also gives states the option to disqualify individuals from food stamps aid who are delinquent in court-ordered child support, and to disqualify parents who do not cooperate with the child support program. Finally, where TANF aid is cut down, normally there is a partial increase in food stamps, as discussed above. However, this partial food stamp increase is prohibited if the TANF reduction is due to a failure to comply with a requirement, including reductions "until paternity is established," or failure to meet the 32-hour and other work requirements. The full measure of any such TANF reduction must be absorbed without mitigation from food stamps.

The PRA mandated food stamp cut-offs for many legal immigrants. One impetus for this ban was the perception that persons were moving to the United States to abusively take advantage of public benefits. However, data from California—where almost half of the nation's immigrants settle—indicate that less than 2% of its TANF recipients had less than twelve months tenure in the state (from another nation or another state) when first applying for aid. Of special concern is the group of legal immigrants arriving post-1996, whose children are barred from most safety net protection. Although citizenship makes these families eligible, there is a five-year mandatory waiting period applicable to immigrants during which federal food stamp assistance is categorically barred for adults and children.[31] California and several other states have established state-only funded food stamps for children excluded from federal coverage.[32]

iii.   2008 Changes

After the 1996 PRA changes, the food stamp system remained problematical as a sufficient safety net for impoverished children. The system remains a straight federal benefit system, requiring no state matching funds. The federal budgetary amount includes benefits and a small amount for state administrative expenses to administer it.

The Food and Nutrition Act of 2008 made some changes to the system. As noted above, the program's name was changed from the Food Stamp Program to the Supplemental Nutrition Assistance Program (SNAP). The 2008 Farm Bill was then enacted over a June 18, 2008 presidential veto. It added $10 billion to nutrition programs overall over the 2008–17 period, of which $7.8 billion was allocated to the new SNAP program. Although an impressive sounding cumulative amount, advocates for the poor argue that it represents a minuscule percentage of the federal budget (or in relation to adequate nutrition need). The addition amounted to about a 4% annual increase over 2009 current spending of $30 billion annually—less than 5% of the 2010 defense budget. The 2008 changes were relatively minor but did include indexing benefits to inflation for the first time. Although not having immediate impact, that change altered what had been a gradual annual real spending reduction in benefits as food stamps did not make CPI adjustments to food price changes.

d. Other Federal Safety Net Related Programs

i.   Special Child Meal Programs

In addition to food stamps, the federal government's Food and Nutrition Service within the Department of Agriculture funds the National School Lunch Program, School Breakfast Program, Child and Adult Care Food Program, Summer Food Service Program, Fresh Fruit and Vegetable Program, and Special Milk Program. Administered by state agencies, each of these programs helps fight hunger and obesity by reimbursing organizations such as schools, child care centers, and after-school programs for providing healthy meals to children. These accounts are funded almost entirely from federal dollars. The dominant program is the National School Lunch Program, which has grown to 30.4 million children receiving free or reduced price lunches daily, while school is in session.

Current federal law requires that the National School Lunch Program be available free to every child with income up to 130% of the poverty line, and that it provide children with at least one-third of their daily nutritional requirements. Studies indicate that the noon meal is important to children's health.[33] In addition, smaller programs provide summer food service to children, school breakfasts, and a child care food program. Children from families below 130% of the poverty line are subsidized with a free meal; children from families below 185% of the poverty line receive a reduced-price meal. The programs are administered nationally by USDA, and by state departments of education. The lunch program started in 1946, after the Army found high levels of nutritional problems in its recruiting pool. Beginning in the 1960s, the scope was expanded to include—for a limited number of children—breakfasts, summer lunches, and child care meals.

These federal meal programs remain as entitlements; all meal providers who have applied and are qualified may be reimbursed for meals provided to eligible children. In addition to the federal funding, which underwrites over 90% of the meal benefits, some states provide a supplement targeted for meals for the neediest children. Where applicable, this state money adds about 5 to 15 cents per meal for local providers serving free meals to the lowest-income children.

ii.   WIC Nutrition

The Special Supplemental Food Program for Women, Infants, and Children (WIC) provides vouchers for nutritious foods, assessment, counseling, and health care referrals for low-income pregnant, breastfeeding, and post-partum women, their infants, and children under the age of five, based on income level at or below 185% of the federal poverty line and an assessment of being at nutritional risk.

WIC is widely regarded as one of the most successful federal benefit programs in terms of benefits conferred and costs saved. An early USDA study concluded that for every WIC dollar spent on prenatal care, between $1.92 and $4.21 is saved in later Medicaid expenses during the first few months after birth.[34] A U.S. General Accounting Office study concluded that the $296 million spent by the federal government during 1990 on WIC prenatal assistance will save more than $1 billion in health-related costs over an eighteen-year period. Savings to states are estimated at 31% of that total.[35] The WIC program has continued to be evaluated as successful in preventing poor birth outcomes (such as infant mortality and low birthweight) and facilitating earlier use of prenatal care—leading to healthier pregnancies, births, and infants.[36]

WIC is a categorical program, funded from an annual federal appropriation. States' shares are allocated based on a distributional formula. WIC's national enrollment in 2016 was over 7.5 million. In general, 17% of participants are pregnant or breastfeeding women, 6% postpartum non-breastfeeding women, 24% infants, and 52% young children (1–5 years of age). The racial composition is 58.6 White, 20.8% African American, 10.3% American Indian or Alaska Native, and 4.4% Asian. For ethnicity, 41.8% of participants were Hispanic.[37]

e. Employment Development for Parents

i.   JOBS History

The federal Family Support Act of 1988 established a Jobs Opportunities and Basic Skills (JOBS) program, requiring states to set up an employment, training, and education program for TANF recipients. At least 11% of a state's TANF families not exempt from work were required to be enrolled by 1992–93. About two-thirds of state JOBS spending had been traditionally from the federal jurisdiction. The PRA merges the federal funding of this account into the broad TANF block grant, to be frozen for at least five years.

ii.   2014 Workforce Innovation and Opportunity Act

Separate and apart from Welfare-to-Work funding, the federal Department of Labor also provides funds to states through another vehicle, the Workforce Innovation and Opportunity Act (WIOA). This 2014 enactment repealed a preceding statute (the Federal Workforce Investment Act of 1998). WIOA is designed to be a demand driven workforce development system. This system is supposed to provide employment and training services that are responsive to the demands of local area employers. It provides local control to officials administering programs under it. Under the state formula grant portion of WIOA, which accounts for nearly 60% of total WIOA Title I funding, the majority of funds are allocated locally, providing a system of One-Stop centers: a single location for individuals seeking employment and training services. The new format is relatively untested. It is relevant to facilitate employment in general, but is not youth or child-centric. The Congressional Budget Office estimates that implementation of this measure cost $26 billion during the 2014–18 period.

f. Higher Education Necessity

As discussed in Chapter 4, there is a strong correlation between one's level of educational attainment and earnings in the United States. Higher educational attainment corresponds to higher wages and lower rates of unemployment. Many young parents earn somewhat above the current minimum wage. However, the income trend for those working at low-skill levels has been downward. The international economic niche of the United States is in technology and advanced services, not in assembly line or agricultural employment. Both demand for high-skill jobs and the corresponding wages have increased, whereas low-skill job wages continue to stagnate.

Investment in higher education—from community colleges to universities—is critical to child poverty amelioration over the next two decades. The nation has an extensive program of college loan assistance, but strong countervailing trends include rising tuition, higher living costs, and a general failure to invest in higher education capacity. The number of "slots" or seats available in higher education has increased in raw numbers nationally, but has decreased in relation to youth population[38]—the important measure.

g. The Barrier to Self-Sufficiency at the Poverty Line

For those who are able to obtain work, the EITC and higher minimum wage promise to move large numbers of parents and families to around $1,000–$1,400 per month in take-home income. But the various subsidies for impoverished parents—some designed to protect children—here interact to create a difficult barrier to increasing income from the poverty line to a "liveable wage" of above $2,000 per month to allow modest shelter, adequate nutrition, and child care without public subsidy. As the income of a single mother of two begins to exceed $1,000 per month, she sequentially loses TANF, food stamps, subsidized child health care, and Medicaid coverage.

Meanwhile, two economic trends post-2000 have exacerbated child poverty. Rental vacancy rates are low and are unlikely to increase markedly; accordingly, rent increases are likely to outpace inflation over the long term. In addition, two basic commodities are projected for substantial long-term price increases: energy (electricity and natural gas) and gasoline for automobiles.

C. INTERPRETING ELIGIBILITY

1. AFDC (TANF) Assistance Standards

Townsend v. Swank

404 U.S. 282 (1971)

MR. JUSTICE BRENNAN delivered the opinion of the Court.

Appellants, two college students and their mothers, brought this class action in the District Court for the Northern District of Illinois alleging that...the Illinois Public Aid Code...and the implementing Illinois Public Aid Regulation 150 violate the Equal Protection Clause of the Fourteenth Amendment, and, because inconsistent with...the Social Security Act, 42 U.S.C. § 606 (a)(2)(B), also violate the Supremacy Clause of the Constitution.[1] Under the Illinois statute and regulation needy dependent children 18 through 20 years of age who attend high school or vocational training school are eligible for benefits under the federally assisted Aid to Families With Dependent Children (AFDC) program, 42 U.S.C. § 601 *et seq.* but such children who attend a college or university are not eligible.[2] Section 406 (a)(2) of the Social Security Act, on the other hand, defines "dependent child" to include a child "...(B) under the age of twenty-one and (as determined by the State in accordance with standards prescribed by the Secretary) a student regularly attending a school, college, or university, or regularly attending a course of vocational or technical training designed to fit him for gainful employment."....

I

Section 402 (a)(10) of the Social Security Act provides that state participatory plans submitted under the AFDC program for the approval of the Secretary of the Department of Health, Education, and Welfare (HEW) must provide "that aid to families with dependent children shall be furnished with reasonable promptness to *all eligible* individuals." (Emphasis supplied.) In *King v. Smith*, 392 U.S. 309 (1968), we considered whether a State participating in an AFDC program may, consistently with the Supremacy Clause, adopt eligibility standards that exclude from benefits needy dependent children eligible for benefits under applicable federal statutory standards. There was before us in that case a regulation of the Alabama Department of Pensions and Security that treated a man who cohabited with the mother of needy dependent children in or outside the home as a nonabsent "parent" within the federal statute. Since aid can be granted under § 406 (a) of the Federal Act only if a "parent" of the needy child is continually absent from the home, Alabama's regulation resulted in the ineligibility of the children for benefits. We held that the Alabama regulation defined "parent" in a manner inconsistent with § 406 (a) of the Social Security Act and therefore that in "denying AFDC assistance to [children] on the basis of this invalid regulation, Alabama has breached its federally imposed obligation to furnish 'aid to families with dependent children...with reasonable promptness to all eligible individuals....'" 392 U.S., at 333.

Thus, *King v. Smith* establishes that, at least in the absence of congressional authorization for the exclusion clearly evidenced from the Social Security Act or its legislative history, a state eligibility standard that excludes persons eligible for assistance under federal AFDC standards violates the Social Security Act and is therefore invalid under the Supremacy Clause....

II

It is next argued that in the case of 18–20-year-old needy dependent children, Congress authorized the States to vary eligibility requirements from federal standards. In other words, it is contended that Congress authorized the States to discriminate between these needy dependent children solely upon the basis of the type of school attended. Our examination of the legislative history has uncovered no evidence that Congress granted the asserted authority. On the contrary, we are persuaded that the history supports the conclusion that Congress meant to continue financial assistance for AFDC programs for the age group only in States that conformed their eligibility requirements to the federal eligibility standards.

* * *

...Notwithstanding the view of the majority of the District Court, 314 F.Supp., at 1088–1089, we think there is a serious question whether the Illinois classification can withstand the strictures of the Equal Protection Clause. The majority justified the classification as designed to attain the twin goals of aiding needy children to become employable and self-sufficient, and of insuring fiscal integrity of the State's welfare program. We doubt the rationality of the classification as a means of furthering the goal of aiding needy children to become employable and self-sufficient ... we are not told what basis in practical experience supports the proposition that children with a vocational training are more readily employable than children with a college education. And a State's interest in preserving the fiscal integrity of its welfare program by economically allocating limited AFDC resources may not be protected by the device of adopting eligibility requirements restricting the class of children made eligible by federal standards. That interest may be protected by the State's "undisputed power to set the level of benefits...." *King v. Smith*, 392 U.S., at 334. See *Dandridge v. Williams*, 397 U.S. 471 (1970).[8]

Reversed.

[1]Section 4-1.1 of the Illinois Public Aid Code, Ill. Rev. Stat., c. 23, § 4-1.1 (1967), provides:

"Child Age Eligibility. The child or children must be under age 18, or age 18 or over but under age 21 if in regular attendance in high school or in a vocational or technical training school. 'Regular Attendance,' as used in this Section, means attendance full time during the regular terms of such schools, or attendance part time during such regular terms as may be authorized by rule of the Illinois Department for the purpose of permitting the child to engage in employment which supplements his classroom instruction or which otherwise enhances his development toward a self-supporting status."

Illinois Department of Public Aid Regulation 150 provides: "Age Requirements:

"A.D.C. Dependent children under 18 years of age, unless 18 through 20 years of age and in regular attendance in high school or vocational or technical training school. (This does not include 18 through 20 year old children in college.)"

[2] Appellant Loverta Alexander lives with her son Jerome in Chicago. Jerome reached his 18th birthday in August 1968 and enrolled in junior college about a month later. In early October a Cook County welfare officer notified Mrs. Alexander that the AFDC benefits received by her since 1963 would be terminated as of November 1, 1968. Though Mrs. Alexander was able to obtain general assistance benefits from the State, the termination of AFDC payments resulted in a loss of $23.52 per month in the family's income. The only reason given by the State for the termination was that Jerome had reached his 18th birthday and was not attending high school or vocational school.

Appellant Georgia Townsend is the sole support of Omega Minor, her only child. Mrs. Townsend, who is disabled, received AFDC benefits for herself and her daughter from 1953 through 1960. Thereafter she received an AFDC grant for Omega, and benefits for herself under the Aid to the Disabled provisions of the Social Security Act, 42 U.S.C. § 1351 *et seq.* In September 1966, Omega enrolled in junior college. Two months later a Cook County welfare officer notified Mrs. Townsend that Omega's monthly AFDC payment would be canceled as of January 1967. While Mrs. Townsend's disability payments were increased to meet her own needs, the loss of AFDC benefits resulted in a reduction of $47.94 per month in family income. Again the only reason given was the failure to comply with the Illinois statute and regulation.

[8] The concurring opinion below acknowledged that the reasonable basis for the classification would not be apparent if incentives to learn white- and blue-collar trades and the supply and demand for professional and labor positions were the same. The opinion concluded, however, that the classification could be reasonable in the context of a labor market in which "the skills of manual laborers are in short supply," because in such a market, "as a means of utilizing limited state funds in an effort to channel persons into those employment positions for which the society has great need, the statutory discrimination between college students and post-high school vocational trainees is not purely arbitrary or invidious, but rather, a rational approach designed to correct a perceived problem." 314 F.Supp., at 1091. Apart from the fact that nothing appears about the nature of the market, a classification that channels one class of people, poor people, into a particular class of low-paying, low-status jobs would plainly raise substantial questions under the Equal Protection Clause.

MR. CHIEF JUSTICE BURGER, concurring in the result.

I concur in the result reached by the Court, but add this brief comment. In dealing with these cases—and the other AFDC cases on the Court's docket—it seems appropriate to keep clearly in mind that Title IV of the Social Security Act governs the dispensation of federal funds and that it does no more than that. True, Congress has used the "power of the purse" to force the States to adhere to its wishes to a certain extent; but adherence to the provisions of Title IV is in no way mandatory upon the States under the Supremacy Clause. The appropriate inquiry in any case should be, simply, whether the State has indeed adhered to the provisions and is accordingly entitled to utilize federal funds in support of its program....I agree that the answer to that inquiry here must be in the negative; I therefore concur in the result reached by the Court.

Questions for Discussion

1. Under current federal law, states are permitted to vary aid based on the "type of institution" attended, among other locally determined factors. If the equal protection issue (which would apply notwithstanding federal statutes on spending) were to reach the Supreme Court, how would it be decided? Is there a suspect classification here, or a fundamental liberty interest to trigger strict scrutiny? The Court explicitly "doubts the rationality" of the limitation and implies that it might be unconstitutional even under a "rational relation" test. Would the current Supreme Court agree?

2. In terms of a "rational relation" policy argument, are college-educated youth likely to earn more money and hence need less federal assistance? On the other hand, how many will be academically qualified but compelled to sacrifice college to contribute to family income if TANF help is subtracted from their impoverished family? Can we rely on generic college aid, such as loan interest deferral, to facilitate entry? What is the return on investment for the public where a youth attends college who would otherwise be foreclosed? Are these questions well suited to court findings?

3. Note that this case assumes an age of majority of 21. Given the current 18-year-old age of majority, will the family qualify for TANF support for children in school (in any form) after that age?

4. This decision does not merely rest on compliance with a federal statute to receive federal monies. It purports to rest directly on Supremacy Clause supersession (generating a concurring note in disagreement from the Chief Justice). If the state sought to exclude college attendees from state-only assistance, would this holding apply? Would the current Supreme Court apply the Supremacy Clause here (beyond a federal funding precondition) to require state compliance?

Bowen v. Gilliard
483 U.S. 587 (1987)

JUSTICE STEVENS delivered the opinion of the Court.

As part of its major effort to reduce the federal deficit through the Deficit Reduction Act of 1984, 98 Stat. 494, Congress amended the statute authorizing Federal Aid to Families with Dependent Children (AFDC)...to require that a family's eligibility for benefits must take into account, with certain specified exceptions, the income of all parents, brothers, and sisters living in the same home....The principal question presented in this litigation is whether that requirement violates the Fifth Amendment to the United States Constitution when it is applied to require a family wishing to receive AFDC benefits to include within its unit a child for whom child support payments are being made by a noncustodial parent.

I

This litigation began in 1970. At that time the federal statute did not require that all parents and siblings be included in an AFDC filing unit. Thus, for example, if a teenage child had significant income of her own, perhaps from wages or perhaps in support payments from an absent parent, the other members of her family could exclude her from the filing unit in order to avoid disqualifying the entire family from benefits or reducing its level of benefits.

Beaty Mae Gilliard, one of the named class members in the 1970 suit,... began receiving public assistance from North Carolina under AFDC in 1962. In February 1970, after her seventh child was born, the State automatically included him in the filing unit, thereby increasing the family's monthly allotment from $217 to $227 to reflect the difference between the benefit for a family of seven and the benefit for a family of eight. Gilliard was, however, also receiving $43.33 each month in child support from the baby's father. When a formal parental support order was entered in April 1970, the State credited the support payments against her account and reduced her monthly benefit to $184. Gilliard sued, contending that she had a statutory right to exclude her seventh child from the unit and thus to continue to receive the $217 benefit for a family of seven and also to retain the $43.33 paid by her youngest child's father. A three-judge District Court agreed with her reading of the statute and entered an order requiring the State to reinstate her benefits at the $217 level and to reimburse her for the improper credits of $43 per month....

Congress amended the AFDC program in 1975 to require, as a condition of eligibility, that applicants for assistance must assign to the State any right to receive child support payments for any member of the family included in the filing unit....In response, North Carolina amended its laws to provide that the acceptance of public assistance on behalf of a dependent child would constitute an assignment of any right to support for that child....These amendments, however, did not harm recipients like Gilliard because they did not affect the right to define the family unit covered by an application and thereby to exclude children with independent income, such as a child for whom support payments were being made.

In 1983, the Secretary of Health and Human Services proposed certain amendments to the Social Security Act to "assure that limited Federal and State resources are spent as effectively as possible."....One of the Secretary's proposals was "to establish uniform rules on the family members who must file together for AFDC, and the situations in which income must be counted. In general, the parents, sisters, and brothers living together with a dependent child must all be included; the option of excluding a sibling with income, for example, would no longer be available.".... The Secretary stressed that the improvements would result in an AFDC allocation program that "much more realistically reflects the actual home situation."....

* * *

Because the 1984 amendment forced families to include in the filing unit children for whom support payments were being received, the practical effect was that many families' total income was reduced.[6] The burden of the change was mitigated somewhat by a separate amendment providing that the first $50 of child support collected by the State must be remitted to the family and not counted as income for the purpose of determining its benefit level.[7]....Thus, the net effect of the 1984 amendments for a family comparable to Gilliard's would include three changes: (1) the addition of the child receiving support would enlarge the filing unit and entitle the family to a somewhat larger benefit; (2) child support would be treated as family income and would be assigned to the State, thereby reducing the AFDC benefits by that amount; and (3) the reduction would be offset by $50 if that amount was collected from an absent parent. In sum, if the assigned support exceeded $50 plus the difference in the benefit level caused by adding the child or children receiving support, the family would suffer; if less than $50 and the difference in the benefit level was collected as support, it would not.

* * *

III

* * *

Appellees argue (and the District Court ruled),...that finding that Congress acted rationally is not enough to sustain this legislation. Rather, they claim that some form of "heightened scrutiny" is appropriate because the amendment interferes with a family's fundamental right to live in the type of family unit it chooses.[16] We conclude that the District Court erred in subjecting the DEFRA amendment to any form of heightened scrutiny. That some families may decide to modify their living arrangements in order to avoid the effect of the amendment, does not transform the amendment into an act whose design and direct effect are to "intrud[e] on choices concerning family living arrangements." *Moore v. East Cleveland*, 431 U.S. 494, 499 (1977).[17] As was the case with the marriage-related provision upheld in *Califano v. Jobst*, 434 U.S. 47 (1977), "Congress adopted this rule in the course of constructing a complex social welfare system that necessarily deals with the intimacies of family life. This is not a case in which government seeks to foist orthodoxy on the unwilling."....

* * *

IV

Aside from holding that the amendment violated the Due Process Clause of the Fifth Amendment and its equal protection component, the District Court invalidated the DEFRA amendments as a taking of private property without just compensation. The court based this holding on the premise that a child for whom support payments are made has a right to have the support money used exclusively in his or her "best interest." Yet, the court reasoned, the requirements (1) that a custodial parent who applies for AFDC must include a child's support money in computing family income, and (2) that the support must be assigned to the State, effectively converts the support funds that were once to be used exclusively for the child's best interests into an AFDC check which, under federal law, must be used for the benefit of all the children. § 405, 42 U.S.C. § 605. Therefore, the District Court held that the State was "taking" that child's right to exclusive use of the support money....

...Congress is not, by virtue of having instituted a social welfare program, bound to continue it at all, much less at the same benefit level. Thus, notwithstanding the technical legal arguments that have been advanced, it is imperative to recognize that the amendments at issue merely incorporate a definitional element into an entitlement program. It would be quite strange indeed if, by virtue of an offer to *provide* benefits to needy families through the entirely voluntary AFDC program, Congress or the States were deemed to have *taken* some of those very family members' property.

The basic requirement that the AFDC filing unit must include all family members living in the home, and therefore that support payments made on behalf of a member of the family must be considered in determining that family's level of benefits, does not even arguably take anyone's property. The family members other than the child for whom the support is being paid certainly have no takings claim, since it is clear that they have no protected property rights to continued benefits at the same level....Nor does the simple inclusion of the support income in the benefit calculation have any legal effect on the child's right to have it used for his or her benefit. To the extent that a child has the right to have the support payments used in his or her "best interest," he or she fully retains that right. Of course, the effect of counting the support payments as part of the filing unit's income often reduces the family's resources, and hence increases the chances that sharing of the support money will be appropriate....But given the unquestioned premise that the Government has a right to reduce AFDC benefits generally, that result does not constitute a taking of private property without just compensation.

The only possible legal basis for appellees' takings claim, therefore, is the requirement that an applicant for AFDC benefits must assign the support payments to the State, which then will remit the amount collected to the custodial parent to be used for the benefit of the entire family. This legal transformation in the status of the funds, the argument goes, modifies the child's interest in the use of the money so dramatically that it constitutes a taking of the child's property. As a practical matter, this argument places form over substance, and labels over reality. Although it is true that money which was earmarked for a specific child's or children's "best interest" becomes a part of a larger fund available for all of the children, the difference between these concepts is, as we have discussed, more theoretical than practical.[20]

* * *

The law does not require any custodial parent to apply for AFDC benefits. Surely it is reasonable to presume that a parent who does make such an application does so because she or he is convinced that the family as a whole—as well as each child committed to her or his custody—will be better off with the benefits than without. In making such a decision, the parent is not taking a child's property without just compensation; nor is the State doing so when it responds to that decision by supplementing the collections of support money with additional AFDC benefits.

* * *

[6] For example, under the July 1985 levels of payment in North Carolina, a family of four with no other income would have received $269. A child's support income of $100 would therefore reduce the family's AFDC payment to $169 if that child was included in the filing unit. The family would have a net income of $269. But if the family were permitted to exclude the child from the unit and only claim the somewhat smaller benefit of $246 for a family of three, it could have collected that amount plus the excepted child's $100 and have a net income of $346. See App. 85.

[7] Therefore, under our example, n. 6, *supra*, the net income with the child included in the unit would have been $319.

[16] For example, the District Court had before it an affidavit from one mother who stated that she had sent a child to live with the child's father in order to avoid the requirement of including that child, and the support received from the child's father, in the AFDC unit. 633 F.Supp., at 1537–1538.

[17] If the DEFRA amendment's indirect effects on family living arrangements were enough to subject the statute to heightened scrutiny, then the entire AFDC program might also be suspect since it generally provides benefits only to needy families without two resident parents. Surely this creates incentive for some needy parents to live separately. The answer, of course, is that these types of incentives are the unintended consequences of many social welfare programs, and do not call the legitimacy of the programs into question.

[20] In analyzing the effect of the assignment it is again instructive to ask what would happen to the support payments if there were no AFDC program at all. In that case, it would appear that custodial parents would have to use a much greater portion of the support payments to sustain the family unit, since it could hardly be deemed in the child's best interest for his custodial parent and siblings to have no funds whatsoever. The overall practical effect of the AFDC program (even after the 1984 amendment), therefore, is to enhance the probability that a child whose custodial parent is receiving support payments in the child's behalf will obtain direct economic benefit from those funds, in addition to the benefits that result from preserving the family unit. A reduction in that enhancement is no more a taking than any other reduction in a Social Security program.

JUSTICE BRENNAN, with whom JUSTICE MARSHALL joins, dissenting.

* * *

The very pervasiveness of modern government,...creates an unparalleled opportunity for intrusion on personal life. In a society in which most persons receive some form of government benefit, government has considerable leverage in shaping individual behavior. In most cases, we acknowledge that government may wield its power even when its actions likely influence choices involving personal behavior. On certain occasions, however, government intrusion into private life is so direct and substantial that we must deem it intolerable if we are to be true to our belief that there is a boundary between the public citizen and the private person.

This is such a case. The Government has told a child who lives with a mother receiving public assistance that it cannot both live with its mother and be supported by its father. The child must either leave the care and custody of the mother, or forgo the support of the father and become a Government client. The child is put to this choice not because it seeks Government benefits for itself, but because of a fact over which it has no control: the need of *other* household members for public assistance. A child who lives with one parent has, under the best of circumstances, a difficult time sustaining a relationship with both its parents. A crucial bond between a child and its parent outside the home, usually the father, is the father's commitment to care for the material needs of the child, and the expectation of the child that it may look to its father for such care. The Government has thus decreed that a condition of welfare eligibility for a mother is that her child surrender a vital connection with either the father or the mother.

The Court holds that the Government need only show a rational basis for such action. This standard of review has regularly been used in evaluating the claims of applicants for Government benefits, since "a noncontractual claim to receive funds from the public treasury enjoys no constitutionally protected status." *Weinberger v. Salfi*, 422 U.S. 749, 772 (1975). Plaintiff child support recipients in this case, however, are children who wish *not* to receive public assistance, but to continue to be supported by their noncustodial parent. Their claim is *not* that the Government has unfairly denied them benefits, but that it has intruded deeply into their relationship with their parents. More than a mere rational basis is required to withstand this challenge, and, as the following analysis shows, the Government can offer no adequate justification for doing such damage to the parent-child relationship.

I

A

The family is an institution "deeply rooted in this Nation's history and tradition." *Moore v. East Cleveland*, 431 U.S. 494, 503 (1977). Our society's special solicitude for the family reflects awareness that "it is through the family that we inculcate and pass down many of our most cherished values, moral and cultural." *Id.* at 503–504 (footnote omitted).[2] As a result, we have long recognized that "freedom of personal choice in matters of family life is a fundamental liberty interest protected by the Fourteenth Amendment."....Therefore, "when the government intrudes on choices concerning family living arrangements, this Court must examine carefully the importance of the governmental interests advanced and the extent to which they are served by the challenged regulation."....

A fundamental element of family life is the relationship between parent and child...

...When parents make a commitment to meet those responsibilities, the child has a right to rely on the unique contribution of each parent to material and emotional support. The child therefore has a fundamental interest in the continuation of parental care and support, and a right to be free of governmental action that would jeopardize it. As the next section discusses, a child in modern society faces perhaps more difficulty than ever before in sustaining a relationship with both parents.

B

It is increasingly the case that a child in contemporary America lives in a household in which only one parent is present. The percentage of households headed by one parent has doubled since 1970, from 13% to 26%....[5] Researchers predict that "close to half of all children living in the United States today will reach age 18 without having lived continuously with both biological parents." Furstenberg, Nord, Peterson, & Zill, The Life Course of Children of Divorce: Marital Disruption and Parental Contact, 48 Am. Sociological Rev. 656, 667 (1983).

Almost 90% of single-parent households are headed by women,[6] and a considerable percentage of them face great financial difficulty. One prominent reason is that divorce "produces a precipitous decline in women's household incomes.".... In 1977, one-half of *all* related children under age 18 in female-headed households were below the poverty level....Not surprisingly, many such households must rely on public assistance.[8]

Increasing numbers of children in this country thus reside only with their mother, in a household whose financial condition is precarious. These children have a fundamental interest in sustaining a relationship with their mother, since she is their primary source of daily emotional support. They also have a fundamental interest, of course, in sustaining a relationship with their father, whose absence from the household does not diminish the protection that must be afforded this parent-child relationship. The need for connection with the father is underscored by considerable scholarly research, which indicates that "the optimal situation for the child is to have both an involved mother and an involved father." H. Biller, Paternal Deprivation 10 (1974).[9] Research indicates that maintenance of a relationship with both parents is particularly important for children whose parents have divorced: "By his or her presence or absence, the visiting parent remains central to the psychic functioning of the children."....

In short, "training, nurture, and loving protection...are at the heart of the parental relationship protected by the Constitution,"...and a child's relationship with a father outside the home can be an important source of these benefits.

C

The Government's insistence that a child living with an AFDC mother relinquish its child support deeply intrudes on the father-child relationship, for child support is a crucial means of sustaining the bond between a child and its father outside the home. A father's support represents a way in which the father can make an important contribution to raising the child, and the benefits to the child are both financial and emotional.

* * *

...[T]he Government in these cases has...told children who live with mothers who need AFDC that they cannot both live with their mothers and receive child support from their fathers. Rather than terminate either relationship itself, the Government requires the *child* to choose between them. It has declared that, for an indigent mother with a child receiving child support, a condition of *her* AFDC eligibility is that *her child* relinquish its fundamental constitutional interest in maintaining a vital bond with either her or the child's father.

On the one hand, if the child stays with its mother, the father is told that henceforth the Government, not he, will support the child. Unless he is wealthy enough to support the entire household, all but $50 of any support payment that the father makes will be used to reimburse the Government for making a welfare payment for use by the whole family. This conversion of the father's support payment into Government reimbursement means that the father is rendered powerless in most cases to respond to the special financial needs of his child.

It is important to illustrate why this is the case. Let us suppose that a couple with one child obtains a divorce, that the mother has a child by a previous marriage, and that the mother has custody of the two children. The mother has no source of income, but the father from whom she obtained her recent divorce provides $150 a month to support his child. If the mother desires to keep both her children, the $150 in child support must be assigned to the State. In return, the three-person household receives, let us say, $400 a month in AFDC. Of the $150 in child support assigned to the State, $50 is returned for use of the child for whom it was paid, and $100 is kept by the State as reimbursement for its welfare payment.

If the father wanted to increase the amount of child support, say to $200, because of the child's special needs, *none of the extra money would go to the child.* The family would still receive $400 in AFDC, and the child would still receive $50 of the support payment. The only difference would be that the State would now get to keep $150 as reimbursement for the welfare payment. By continuing to live with the mother, the child has lost not only the financial benefit of the father's support, but a father-child relationship founded on the father's commitment to care for the material needs of his child. If the child has a conscientious father who has shouldered his paternal duty, that father will be enlisted to help defray the cost of providing for *other* children whose fathers are not so responsible. A child thus must pay a high price for continuing to live with its mother.

This price is not merely speculative. The affidavits in these cases establish it....

* * *

B

The nature of the interest asserted in these cases, as well as the direct disruption produced by the Government, distinguishes this litigation from typical challenges to the operation of Government benefit programs.

* * *

Finally, the disruption directly produced by the household filing requirement distinguishes these cases from cases in which we have upheld Government benefit provisions from a challenge that they interfered with family life. In *Lyng supra* for instance, we upheld the food stamp program's presumption that parents, children, and siblings who live together constitute a single "household," so that such persons could not individually apply for benefits as separate households. We noted that the definition "does not order or prevent any group of persons from dining together. Indeed, in the overwhelming majority of cases it probably has no effect at all." *Id.* at 638. In *Califano v. Jobst*, 434 U.S. 47 (1977), we upheld a provision whereby a recipient of dependent

Social Security benefits lost those benefits upon marriage to anyone other than another beneficiary, even though we acknowledged that the provision "may have an impact on a secondary beneficiary's desire to marry, and may make some suitors less welcome than others." *Id.*, at 58. These cases reflect recognition that the extensive activities of Government in modern society inevitably have the potential for creating incentives and disincentives for certain behavior. By itself, plausible speculation about the effect of Government programs generally cannot provide the basis for a constitutional challenge.

In these cases, however, the impact of Government action is not speculative, but direct and substantial. If a child support recipient lives with a mother who needs public assistance, AFDC will be provided *only* if the child either leaves the household or gives up its right to support from its father. Determining whether other eligibility requirements for Government assistance will influence family choices may call for subtle inquiry into the nuances of human motivation. Here, however, the burden on family life is inescapable, because it is *directly required* by the Government as a condition of obtaining benefits. "'Governmental imposition of such a choice puts the same kind of burden upon [the child's rights] as would a fine imposed against'" the child for living with its mother or being supported by its father....

* * *

IV

In The Republic and in The Laws, Plato offered a vision of a unified society, where the needs of children are met not by parents but by the government, and where no intermediate forms of association stand between the individual and the state....The vision is a brilliant one, but it is not our own:

* * *

"Happy families," wrote Tolstoy, "are all alike; every unhappy family is unhappy in its own way." L. Tolstoy, Anna Karenina 1....Contemporary life offers countless ways in which family life can be fractured and families made unhappy. The children who increasingly live in these families are entitled to the chance to sustain a special relationship with both their fathers and their mothers, regardless of how difficult that may be. Parents are entitled to provide both daily emotional solace and to meet their child's material needs; the fact that in some families a different parent may take on each role does not diminish the child's right to the care of both parents. The Government could not prohibit parents from performing these duties, and what it cannot do by direct fiat it should not be able to do by economic force. The Government has decreed that the only way a child can live with its mother and be supported by its father is if the mother is wealthy enough not to require public assistance. A child cannot be held responsible for the indigency of its mother, and should not be forced to choose between parents because of something so clearly out of its control. No society can assure its children that there will be no unhappy families. It can tell them, however, that their Government will not be allowed to contribute to the pain.

I dissent.

[2] See also *Smith v. Organization of Foster Families for Equality and Reform*, 431 U.S. 816, 844 (1977) (importance of the family "stems from the emotional attachments that derive from the intimacy of daily association, and from the role it plays in 'promot[ing] a way of life' through the instruction of children, as well as from the fact of blood relationship") (citation omitted).

[5] Almost 60% of all black families with children are headed by one parent, compared with only 36% in 1970. While only 1 in 10 white families were headed by a single parent in 1970, the figure is now 1 in 5. Current Population Reports, at 5.

[6] Families headed by women accounted for 25% of the households added from 1980 to 1984, compared to 18% of the households added from 1970 to 1980....

[8] In May 1982, of all AFDC families, only 9.4% had a father present in the home.

[9] "Paternal deprivation, including patterns of inadequate fathering as well as father absence, is a highly significant factor in the development of serious psychological and social problems." H. Biller, Paternal Deprivation 1 (1974)....

Questions for Discussion

1. AFDC (TANF) assistance increases with the number of children, with the increment declining per child added. *Bowen* asks: If the seventh child costs the state an additional $10 but his absent father pays $43, does the family keep the $33 the state is not spending on that child? If the state takes all $43, is the father's right to contribute to his child abridged? If he had nothing to do with the other six children, and he wants to contribute to his own child beyond the state's contribution for him, on what basis can the state take his money for his child?

2. If the mother refuses the AFDC (TANF) for the seventh child, knowing child support will be paid in a larger amount, can North Carolina say "you can't exclude a child from our assistance"? What if the father takes voluntary custody of his child, necessarily making the mother's family one child less for assistance? If the only way the father can give more to his son is to take custody of him, how does that impact the right of the child to live with his siblings? The right of the mother to have custody of children without state impediment?

3. Can the state argue that the seventh child benefits from the overall support of the family and accordingly all income generated by the family—however tied to a member—is owed back to the state for state assistance up to the total amount given by the state?

4. Can the state argue that the children within the family with outside child support will receive disproportionate income, which interferes with the mother's right to manage the family equitably? Or does the father have the right to give his child an advantage over his child's siblings who are biologically unrelated to him?

5. Assume a state gives "child only" benefits of $341 for a single child living with her grandmother (*e.g.*, kin foster care) as a "one person assistance unit" (AU). Assume the grandmother then accepts two nieces into her care from different parents, constituting a separate "child only" AU of two children at $561 per month for a $902 total. Can California refuse to acknowledge these separate units, but consider all three children as a single AU eligible for total support substantially below that level? See the affirmative answer in interpreting federal law and rules implementing AFDC in *Anderson v. Edwards*, 514 U.S. 143 (1995). If another person receives the two nieces, total payment received for the care of the three children will be $902. How is this California rule likely to affect custody decisions? Much has been written about the "marriage penalty" of federal income taxation—which has historically imposed lower taxes to two unmarried people filing separately than for a joint return as a married couple. The political upheaval has led to adjustment in federal tax rates. Does the welfare payment design effect on child custody decisions warrant similar attention?

6. The Court rejects impoverished children or the poor as a suspect class or even for heightened scrutiny, noting that it is not powerless but that "the opposite is true"? What is the evidence that impoverished children are politically powerful?

Saenz v. Roe
526 U.S. 489 (1999)

JUSTICE STEVENS delivered the opinion of the Court.

In 1992, California enacted a statute limiting the maximum welfare benefits available to newly arrived residents. The scheme limits the amount payable to a family that has resided in the State for less than 12 months to the amount payable by the State of the family's prior residence. The questions presented by this case are whether the 1992 statute was constitutional when it was enacted and, if not, whether an amendment to the Social Security Act enacted by Congress in 1996 affects that determination.

I

California is not only one of the largest, most populated, and most beautiful States in the Nation; it is also one of the most generous. Like all other States, California has participated in several welfare programs authorized by the Social Security Act and partially funded by the Federal Government. Its programs, however, provide a higher level of benefits and serve more needy citizens than those of most other States. In one year the most expensive of those programs, Aid to Families with Dependent Children (AFDC), which was replaced in 1996 with Temporary Assistance to Needy Families (TANF), provided benefits for an average of 2,645,814 persons per month at an annual cost to the State of $2.9 billion. In California the cash benefit for a family of two—a mother and one child—is $456 a month, but in the neighboring State of Arizona, for example, it is only $275.

In 1992, in order to make a relatively modest reduction in its vast welfare budget, the California Legislature enacted § 11450.03 of the state Welfare and Institutions Code. That section sought to change the California AFDC program by limiting new residents, for the first year they live in California, to the benefits they would have received in the State of their prior residence....Because in 1992 a state program either had to conform to federal specifications or receive a waiver from the Secretary of Health and Human Services in order to qualify for federal reimbursement, § 11450.03 required approval by the Secretary to take effect. In October 1992, the Secretary issued a waiver purporting to grant such approval.

* * *

PRWORA replaced the AFDC program with TANF. The new statute expressly authorizes any State that receives a block grant under TANF to "apply to a family the rules (including benefit amounts) of the [TANF] program...of another State if the family has moved to the State from the other State and has resided in the State for less than 12 months." 42 U.S.C. § 604(c) (1994 ed., Supp. II)....The California Department of Social Services therefore issued an "All County Letter" announcing that the enforcement of § 11450.03 would commence on April 1, 1997.

The All County Letter clarifies certain aspects of the statute. Even if members of an eligible family had lived in California all of their lives, but left the State "on January 29th, intending to reside in another state, and returned on April 15th," their benefits are determined by the law of their State of residence from January 29 to April 15, assuming that that level was lower than California's....Moreover, the lower level of benefits applies regardless of whether the family was on welfare in the State of prior residence and regardless of the family's motive for moving to California. The instructions also explain that the residency requirement is inapplicable to families that recently arrived from another country.

II

* * *

The State relied squarely on the undisputed fact that the statute would save some $10.9 million in annual welfare costs—an amount that is surely significant even though only a relatively small part of its annual expenditures of approximately $2.9 billion for the entire program. It contended that this cost saving was an appropriate exercise of budgetary authority as long as the residency requirement did not penalize the right to travel. The State reasoned that the payment of the same benefits that would have been received in the State of prior residency eliminated any potentially punitive aspects of the measure. Judge Levi concluded, however, that the relevant comparison was not between new residents of California and the residents of their former States, but rather between the new residents and longer term residents of California. He therefore again enjoined the implementation of the statute.

* * *

III

The word "travel" is not found in the text of the Constitution. Yet the "constitutional right to travel from one State to another" is firmly embedded in our jurisprudence....

...We [have] squarely held that it was "constitutionally impermissible" for a State to enact durational residency requirements for the purpose of inhibiting the migration by needy persons into the State....We further held that a classification that had the effect of imposing a penalty on the exercise of the right to travel violated the Equal Protection Clause "unless shown to be necessary to promote a compelling governmental interest,"... and that no such showing had been made.

In this case California argues that § 11450.03 was not enacted for the impermissible purpose of inhibiting migration by needy persons and that, unlike the legislation reviewed in *Shapiro*, it does not penalize the right to travel because new arrivals are not ineligible for benefits during their first year of residence. California submits that, instead of being subjected to the strictest scrutiny, the statute should be upheld if it is supported by a rational basis and that the State's legitimate interest in saving over $10 million a year satisfies that test. Although the United States did not elect to participate in the proceedings in the District Court or the Court of Appeals, it has participated as amicus curiae in this Court. It has advanced the novel argument that the enactment of PRWORA allows the States to adopt a "specialized choice-of-law-type provision" that "should be subject to an intermediate level of constitutional review," merely requiring that durational residency requirements be "substantially related to an important governmental objective."...The debate about the appropriate standard of review, together with the potential relevance of the federal statute, persuades us that it will be useful to focus on the source of the constitutional right on which respondents rely.

IV

The "right to travel" discussed in our cases embraces at least three different components. It protects the right of a citizen of one State to enter and to leave another State, the right to be treated as a welcome visitor rather than an unfriendly alien when temporarily present in the second State, and, for those travelers who elect to become permanent residents, the right to be treated like other citizens of that State.

It was the right to go from one place to another, including the right to cross state borders while en route, that was vindicated in *Edwards v. California*, 314 U.S. 160...(1941), which invalidated a state law that impeded the free interstate passage of the indigent....

The second component of the right to travel is...expressly protected by the text of the Constitution. The first sentence of Article IV, § 2, provides:

"The Citizens of each State shall be entitled to all Privileges and Immunities of Citizens in the several States."

Thus, by virtue of a person's state citizenship, a citizen of one State who travels in other States, intending to return home at the end of his journey, is entitled to enjoy the "Privileges and Immunities of Citizens in the several States" that he visits.... This provision removes "from the citizens of each State the disabilities of alienage in the other States."...Those protections are not "absolute," but the Clause "does bar discrimination against citizens of other States where there is no substantial reason for the discrimination beyond the mere fact that they are citizens of other States." 334 U.S. at 396. There may be a substantial reason for requiring the nonresident to pay more than the resident... to enroll in the state university, see *Vlandis v. Kline,* 412 U.S. 441...(1973), but our cases have not identified any acceptable reason for qualifying the protection afforded by the Clause for "the 'citizen of State A who ventures into State B' to settle there and establish a home.'"...

What is at issue in this case, then, is this third aspect of the right to travel—the right of the newly arrived citizen to the same privileges and immunities enjoyed by other citizens of the same State. That right is protected not only by the new arrival's status as a state citizen, but also by her status as a citizen of the United States.[15]... That additional source of protection is plainly identified in the opening words of the Fourteenth Amendment:

"All persons born or naturalized in the United States, and subject to the jurisdiction thereof, are citizens of the United States and of the State wherein they reside. No State shall make or enforce any law which shall abridge the privileges or immunities of citizens of the United States...."[16]

Despite fundamentally differing views concerning the coverage of the Privileges or Immunities Clause of the Fourteenth Amendment, most notably expressed in the majority and dissenting opinions in the *Slaughter-House Cases,* 83 U.S. 36, 16 Wall. 36, 21 L. Ed. 394 (1873), it has always been common ground that this Clause protects the third component of the right to travel....

* * *

V

Because this case involves discrimination against citizens who have completed their interstate travel, the State's argument that its welfare scheme affects the right to travel only "incidentally" is beside the point. Were we concerned solely with actual deterrence to migration, we might be persuaded that a partial withholding of benefits constitutes a lesser incursion on the right to travel than an outright denial of all benefits.... But since the right to travel embraces the citizen's right to be treated equally in her new State of residence, the discriminatory classification is itself a penalty.

It is undisputed that respondents and the members of the class that they represent are citizens of California and that their need for welfare benefits is unrelated to the length of time that they have resided in California. We thus have no occasion to consider what weight might be given to a citizen's length of residence if the bona fides of her claim to state citizenship were questioned. Moreover, because whatever benefits they receive will be consumed while they remain in California, there is no danger that recognition of their claim will encourage citizens of other States to establish residency for just long enough to acquire some readily portable benefit, such as a divorce or a college education, that will be enjoyed after they return to their original domicile....

...To justify § 11450.03, California must...explain not only why it is sound fiscal policy to discriminate against those who have been citizens for less than a year, but also why it is permissible to apply such a variety of rules within that class.

These classifications may not be justified by a purpose to deter welfare applicants from migrating to California for three reasons. First, although it is reasonable to assume that some persons may be motivated to move for the purpose of obtaining higher benefits, the empirical evidence reviewed by the District Judge, which takes into account the high cost of living in California, indicates that the number of such persons is quite small—surely not large enough to justify a burden on those who had no such motive.... Second, California has represented to the Court that the legislation was not enacted for any such reason.[19] Third, even if it were, as we squarely held in *Shapiro v. Thompson*, 394 U.S. 618...(1969), such a purpose would be unequivocally impermissible.

Disavowing any desire to fence out the indigent, California has instead advanced an entirely fiscal justification for its multitiered scheme. The enforcement of § 11450.03 will save the State approximately $10.9 million a year. The question is not whether such saving is a legitimate purpose but whether the State may accomplish that end by the discriminatory means it has chosen. An evenhanded, across-the-board reduction of about 72 cents per month for every beneficiary would produce the same result. But our negative answer to the question does not rest on the weakness of the State's purported fiscal justification. It rests on the fact that the Citizenship Clause of the Fourteenth Amendment expressly equates citizenship with residence: "That Clause does not provide for, and does not allow for, degrees of citizenship based on length of residence." *Zobel*, 457 U.S. at 69. It is equally clear that the Clause does not tolerate a hierarchy of 45 subclasses of similarly situated citizens based on the location of their prior residence.... Thus § 11450.03 is doubly vulnerable: Neither the duration of respondents' California residence, nor the identity of their prior States of residence, has any relevance to their need for benefits. Nor do those factors bear any relationship to the State's interest in making an equitable allocation of the funds to be distributed among its needy citizens. As in *Shapiro*, we reject any contributory rationale for the denial of benefits to new residents:

> "But we need not rest on the particular facts of these cases. Appellants' reasoning would logically permit the State to bar new residents from schools, parks, and libraries or deprive them of police and fire protection. Indeed it would permit the State to apportion all benefits and services according to the past tax contributions of its citizens."

394 U.S. at 632-633.

VI

The question that remains is whether congressional approval of durational residency requirements in the 1996 amendment to the Social Security Act somehow resuscitates the constitutionality of § 11450.03. That question is readily answered, for we have consistently held that Congress may not authorize the States to violate the Fourteenth Amendment....Moreover, the protection afforded to the citizen by the Citizenship Clause of that Amendment is a limitation on the powers of the National Government as well as the States.

* * *

The Solicitor General does not unequivocally defend the constitutionality of § 11450.03. But he has argued that two features of PRWORA may provide a sufficient justification for state durational requirements to warrant further inquiry before finally passing on the section's validity, or perhaps that it is only invalid insofar as it applies to new arrivals who were not on welfare before they arrived in California....

He first points out that because the TANF program gives the States broader discretion than did AFDC, there will be significant differences among the States which may provide new incentives for welfare recipients to change their residences. He does not, however, persuade us that the disparities under the new program will necessarily be any greater than the differences under AFDC, which included such examples as the disparity between California's monthly benefit of $673 for a family of four with Mississippi's benefit of $144 for a comparable family. Moreover, we are not convinced that a policy of eliminating incentives to move to California provides a more permissible justification for classifying California citizens than a policy of imposing special burdens on new arrivals to deter them from moving into the State. Nor is the discriminatory impact of § 11450.03 abated by repeatedly characterizing it as "a sort of specialized choice-of-law rule."...California law alone discriminates among its own citizens on the basis of their prior residence.

The Solicitor General also suggests that we should recognize the congressional concern addressed in the legislative history of PRWORA that the "States might engage in a 'race to the bottom' in setting the benefit levels in their TANF programs."[24] Again, it is difficult to see why that concern should be any greater under TANF than under AFDC. The evidence reviewed by the District Court indicates that the savings resulting from the discriminatory policy, if spread equitably throughout the entire program, would have only a minuscule impact on benefit levels. Indeed, as one of the legislators apparently interpreted this concern, it would logically prompt the States to reduce benefit levels sufficiently "to encourage emigration of benefit recipients."...But speculation about such an unlikely eventuality provides no basis for upholding § 11450.03.

Finally, the Solicitor General suggests that the State's discrimination might be acceptable if California had limited the disfavored subcategories of new citizens to those who had received aid in their prior State of residence at any time within the year before their arrival in California. The suggestion is ironic for at least three reasons: It would impose the most severe burdens on the neediest members of the disfavored classes; it would significantly reduce the savings that the State would obtain, thus making the State's claimed justification even less tenable; and, it would confine the effect of the statute to what the Solicitor General correctly characterizes as "the invidious purpose of discouraging poor people generally from settling in the State."...

* * *

Citizens of the United States, whether rich or poor, have the right to choose to be citizens "of the State wherein they reside." U.S. Const., Amdt. 14, § 1. The States, however, do not have any right to select their citizens.[27] The Fourteenth Amendment, like the Constitution itself, was, as Justice Cardozo put it, "framed upon the theory that the peoples of the several states must sink or swim together, and that in the long run prosperity and salvation are in union and not division." *Baldwin v. G. A. F. Seelig, Inc.*, 294 U.S. 511...(1935).

The judgment of the Court of Appeals is affirmed.

It is so ordered.

[5] The Framers of the Fourteenth Amendment modeled this Clause upon the "Privileges and Immunities" Clause found in Article IV. Cong. Globe, 39th Cong., 1st Sess., 1033-1034 (1866) (statement of Rep. Bingham). In *Dred Scott v. Sandford*, 60 U.S. 393 (1857), this Court had limited the protection of Article IV to rights under state law and concluded that free blacks could not claim citizenship. The Fourteenth Amendment overruled this decision. The Amendment's Privileges and Immunities Clause and Citizenship Clause guaranteed the rights of newly freed black citizens by ensuring that they could claim the state citizenship of any State in which they resided and by precluding that State from abridging their rights of national citizenship.

[16] U.S. Const., Amdt. 14, § 1. The remainder of the section provides: "nor shall any State deprive any person of life, liberty, or property, without due process of law; nor deny to any person within its jurisdiction the equal protection of the laws."

[19] The District Court and the Court of Appeals concluded, however, that the "apparent purpose of § 11450.03 was to deter migration of poor people to California." *Roe v. Anderson*, 134 F.3d 1400, 1404 (CA9 1998).

[24] *Id.*, at 8. See H. R. Rep. No. 104-651, p. 1337 (1996) ("States that want to pay higher benefits should not be deterred from doing so by the fear that they will attract large numbers of recipients from bordering States").

[27] As Justice Jackson observed, "it is a privilege of citizenship of the United States, protected from state abridgment, to enter any State of the Union, either for temporary sojourn or for the establishment of permanent residence therein and for gaining resultant citizenship thereof. If national citizenship means less than this, it means nothing." *Edwards v. California*, 314 U.S. 160, 183, 86 L. Ed. 119, 62 S. Ct. 164 (1941) (concurring opinion).

CHIEF JUSTICE REHNQUIST, with whom **JUSTICE THOMAS** joins, dissenting.

The Court today breathes new life into the previously dormant Privileges or Immunities Clause of the Fourteenth Amendment....It uses this Clause to strike down what I believe is a reasonable measure falling under the head of a "good-faith residency requirement." Because I do not think any provision of the Constitution—and surely not a provision relied upon for only the second time since its enactment 130 years ago—requires this result, I dissent.

I
* * *

...I cannot see how the right to become a citizen of another State is a necessary "component" of the right to travel, or why the Court tries to marry these separate and distinct rights. A person is no longer "traveling" in any sense of the word when he finishes his journey to a State which he plans to make his home. Indeed, under the Court's logic, the protections of the Privileges or Immunities Clause recognized in this case come into play only when an individual stops traveling with the intent to remain and become a citizen of a new State....

No doubt the Court has, in the past 30 years, essentially conflated the right to travel with the right to equal state citizenship in striking down durational residence requirements similar to the one challenged here....

Instead, the Court in these cases held that restricting the provision of welfare benefits, votes, or certain medical benefits to new citizens for a limited time impermissibly "penalized" them under the Equal Protection Clause of the Fourteenth Amendment for having exercised their right to travel....The Court thus settled for deciding what restrictions amounted to "deprivations of very important benefits and rights" that operated to indirectly "penalize" the right to travel. See *Attorney General of N.Y. v. Soto-Lopez*, 476 U.S. 898... (1986) (plurality opinion). In other cases, the Court recognized that laws dividing new and old residents had little to do with the right to travel and merely triggered an inquiry into whether the resulting classification rationally furthered a legitimate government purpose. See *Zobel v. Williams*, 457 U.S. 55...(1982); *Hooper v. Bernalillo County Assessor*, 472 U.S. 612...(1985)....While *Zobel* and *Hooper* reached the wrong result in my view, they at least put the Court on the proper track in identifying exactly what interests it was protecting; namely, the right of individuals not to be subject to unjustifiable classifications as opposed to infringements on the right to travel.

The Court today tries to clear much of the underbrush created by these prior right-to-travel cases, abandoning its effort to define what residence requirements deprive individuals of "important rights and benefits" or "penalize" the right to travel.... Under its new analytical framework, a State, outside certain ill-defined circumstances, cannot classify its citizens by the length of their residence in the State without offending the Privileges or Immunities Clause of the Fourteenth Amendment. The Court thus departs from *Shapiro* and its progeny, and, while paying lipservice to the right to travel, the Court does little to explain how the right to travel is involved at all. Instead, as the Court's analysis clearly demonstrates..., this case is only about respondents' right to immediately enjoy all the privileges of being a California citizen in relation to that State's ability to test the good-faith assertion of this right. The Court has thus come full circle by effectively disavowing the analysis of *Shapiro*, segregating the right to travel and the rights secured by Article IV from the right to become a citizen under the Privileges or Immunities Clause, and then testing the residence requirement here against this latter right. For all its misplaced efforts to fold the right to become a citizen into the right to travel, the Court has essentially returned to its original understanding of the right to travel.

II

In unearthing from its tomb the right to become a state citizen and to be treated equally in the new State of residence, however, the Court ignores a State's need to assure that only persons who establish a bona fide residence receive the benefits provided to current residents of the State....

...[T]he Court has consistently recognized that while new citizens must have the same opportunity to enjoy the privileges of being a citizen of a State, the States retain the ability to use bona fide residence requirements to ferret out those who intend to take the privileges and run....

While the physical presence element of a bona fide residence is easy to police, the subjective intent element is not. It is simply unworkable and futile to require States to inquire into each new resident's subjective intent to remain. Hence, States employ objective criteria such as durational residence requirements to test a new resident's resolve to remain before these new citizens can enjoy certain in-state benefits. Recognizing the practical appeal of such criteria, this Court has repeatedly sanctioned the State's use of durational residence requirements before new residents receive in-state tuition rates at state universities....The Court has done the same in upholding a 1-year residence requirement for eligibility to obtain a divorce in state courts..., and in upholding political party registration restrictions that amounted to a durational residency requirement for voting in primary elections....

If States can require individuals to reside in-state for a year before exercising the right to educational benefits, the right to terminate a marriage, or the right to vote in primary elections that all other state citizens enjoy, then States may surely do the same for welfare benefits. Indeed, there is no material difference between a 1-year residence requirement applied to the level of welfare benefits given out by a State, and the same requirement applied to the level of tuition subsidies at a state university. The welfare payment here and in-state tuition rates are cash subsidies provided to a limited class of people, and California's standard of living and higher education system make both subsidies quite attractive. Durational residence requirements were upheld when used to regulate the provision of higher education subsidies, and the same deference should be given in the case of welfare payments....

* * *

In one respect, the State has a greater need to require a durational residence for welfare benefits than for college eligibility. The impact of a large number of new residents who immediately seek welfare payments will have a far greater impact on a State's operating budget than the impact of new residents seeking to attend a state university. In the case of the welfare recipients, a modest durational residence requirement to allow for the completion of an annual legislative budget cycle gives the State time to decide how to finance the increased obligations.

The Court tries to distinguish education and divorce benefits by contending that the welfare payment here will be consumed in California, while a college education or a divorce produces benefits that are "portable" and can be enjoyed after individuals return to their original domicile....But this "you can't take it with you" distinction is more apparent than real, and offers little guidance to lower courts who must apply this rationale in the future. Welfare payments are a form of insurance, giving impoverished individuals and their families the means to meet the demands of daily life while they receive the necessary training, education, and time to look for a job. The cash itself will no doubt be spent in California, but the benefits from receiving this income and having the opportunity to become employed or employable will stick with the welfare recipient if they stay in California or go back to their true domicile...

I therefore believe that the durational residence requirement challenged here is a permissible exercise of the State's power to "assure that services provided for its residents are enjoyed only by residents."...

Finally, Congress' express approval in 42 U.S.C. § 604(c) of durational residence requirements for welfare recipients like the one established by California only goes to show the reasonableness of a law like § 11450.03. The National Legislature, where people from Mississippi as well as California are represented, has recognized the need to protect state resources in a time of experimentation and welfare reform. As States like California revamp their total welfare packages,... they should have the authority and flexibility to ensure that their new programs are not exploited. Congress has decided that it makes good welfare policy to give the States this power. California has reasonably exercised it through an objective, narrowly tailored residence requirement. I see nothing in the Constitution that should prevent the enforcement of that requirement.

* * *

Questions for Discussion

1. If California provides $645 a month in AFDC (TANF) safety-net assistance for a mother and two children based on a legislative intent to assure rent, utilities and basic necessities for child protection, how is that intent effectuated for newly-arrived children whose benefit is cut to $145 per month based on the rent extant in another state? Assuming parental responsibility, does not such a policy necessarily implicate a right to travel from such a state to California? Note that the "portability" discussion of *Saenz* suggests that California may restrict its benefits to only those children who are currently living in California and subject to its higher rents.

2. The dissent argues that the California policy is simply a variation of a commonly approved state "residency" requirement to assure state presence and prevent fraud. Is this posited *bona fide* residency intent actually the purpose or

effect of the policy? How is that state interest consistent with California's stated primary motivation to save $10 million in public funds?

3. Would it be permissible for California to set its tuition for out-of-state students based on the average tuition charged by each student's previous state of residence?

4. Is it important that the total number of TANF applicants in California who have been in the state less than one year before applying for assistance amounts to less than 2% of those enrolled? If such is the case, where is the empirical basis that the reduction policy is needed to discourage welfare movement between states seeking lucrative California benefits? Does that fact undermine the dissent's argument that the restriction is akin to a residency requirement for divorce, *i.e.*, intended to prevent fraud? Is the argument that such a condition prevents evasion of the divorce requirements of the real state of residency applicable at all to welfare benefits received only while a family is in California?

5. Assume that the purpose of the AFDC (TANF) program is to provide basic sustenance for the safety net protection of children, primarily money for rent to avoid homelessness. Is it consistent with such Congressional intent for one state to set benefit levels at median rent levels, while another state sets them at one-third its median rent? If a child in one state receives enough to pay for his family's rent, while a child in another state is rendered homeless, is the latter child receiving the "equal protection" of federal law?

6. Assume that a state does not use the "state of origin" level approach of California, but simply lowers its benefits so that its impoverished families are compelled to leave. The Court holds that California cannot influence families in Mississippi to stay put by refusing to allow them better benefits if they enter its domain. Is there a "freedom of travel" difference between impeding travel by sanctioning new entrants, and compelling travel by sanctioning your own impoverished population to force their departure?

7. Do the low benefits of a state such as Mississippi set at a small fraction of local median rent impede entry into that state from a California family receiving full median rent assistance? The Court might argue that equal protection principles are not violated where Mississippi treats all of its own residents similarly and that the difference is based on permissibly varying state policies. But does such a wide disparity between states implicate interstate "freedom of travel," regardless of benefit level consistency within a state?

8. What would be the equal protection implications of a holding that children had a "fundamental liberty interest" in shelter and food for minimal health and safety? What would be the equal protection implications for *Saenz* of a holding

that as with race, religion, and gender, children as a group have suffered historical discrimination and lack political power sufficiently to constitute a protected class, thus invoking "strict scrutiny"?

2. Foster Care Assistance Standards

Miller v. Youakim

440 U.S. 125 (1979)

MR. JUSTICE MARSHALL delivered the opinion of the Court.

At issue in this appeal is whether Illinois may exclude from its Aid to Families with Dependent Children-Foster Care program children who reside with relatives.

The Aid to Families with Dependent Children-Foster Care program (AFDC-FC) authorizes federal financial subsidies for the care and support of children removed from their homes and made wards of the State pursuant to a judicial determination that the children's homes were not conducive to their welfare. 42 U.S.C. §§ 608 (a)(1), (2).... To qualify for Foster Care assistance, these children must be placed in a "foster family home or child-care institution."...The basic AFDC program, already in existence when the Foster Care program was enacted in 1961, provides aid to eligible children who live with a parent or with a relative specified in § 406 (a) of the Act....In administering these programs, Illinois distinguishes between related and unrelated foster parents. Children placed in unrelated foster homes may participate in the AFDC-FC program. But those who are placed in the homes of relatives listed in § 406 (a), and who are entitled to basic AFDC benefits, cannot receive AFDC-FC assistance because the State defines the term "foster family home" as a facility for children unrelated to the operator....Foster children living with relatives may participate only in Illinois' basic AFDC program, which provides lower monthly payments than the Foster Care program.[5] The specific question presented here is whether Illinois has correctly interpreted the federal standards for AFDC-FC eligibility set forth in § 408 (a) of the Act to exclude children who, because of placement with related rather than unrelated foster parents, qualify for assistance under the basic AFDC program.

I

Appellees are four foster children, their older sister (Linda Youakim), and her husband (Marcel Youakim). In 1969, Illinois removed the children from their mother's home and made them wards of the State following a judicial determination of neglect. The Department of Children and Family Services (Department), which became responsible for the children,...placed them in unrelated foster care facilities until 1972. During this period, they each received full AFDC-FC benefits of $ 105 a month. In 1972, the Department decided to place two of the children with the Youakims, who were under no legal obligation to accept or support them....The Department investigated the Youakim home and approved it as meeting the licensing standards established for unrelated foster family homes, as required by state law.[8] Despite this approval, the State refused to make Foster Care payments on behalf of the children because they were related to Linda Youakim.

The exclusion of foster children living with related caretakers from Illinois' AFDC-FC program reflects the State's view that the home of a relative covered under basic AFDC is not a "foster family home" within the meaning of § 408 (a)(3), the federal AFDC-FC eligibility provision at issue here. Interpreting that provision, Illinois defines a "foster family home" as

> "a facility for child care in residences of families who receive no more than 8 children *unrelated to them*...for the purpose of providing family care and training for the children on a full-time basis...."....

Homes that do not meet the definition may not be licensed,...and under state law, only licensed facilities are entitled to Foster Care payments....

Although Illinois refused to make Foster Care payments, it did provide each child basic AFDC benefits of approximately $63 a month, substantially less than the applicable $105 AFDC-FC rate.[12] The Youakims, however, believed that these payments were insufficient to provide proper support, and declined to accept the other two children. These children remain in unrelated foster care facilities and continue to receive AFDC-FC benefits.

In 1973, the Youakims and the four foster children brought a class action under 42 U.S.C. § 1983 for themselves and persons similarly situated, challenging Illinois' distinction between related and unrelated foster parents as violative of the Equal Protection Clause of the Fourteenth Amendment....

* * *

II

A participating State may not deny assistance to persons who meet eligibility standards defined in the Social Security Act unless Congress clearly has indicated that the standards are permissive....Congress has specified that programs, like AFDC-FC, which employ the term "dependent child" to define eligibility must be available for "all eligible individuals."...Section 408 (e) reinforces this general rule by requiring States to provide Foster Care benefits to "any" child who satisfies the federal eligibility criteria of § 408 (a). Thus, if foster care in related homes is encompassed within § 408, Illinois may not deny AFDC-FC benefits when it places an eligible child in the care of a relative.

In arguing that related foster care does not fall within § 408's definition of "foster family home," appellants submit that Congress enacted the Foster Care program solely for the benefit of children not otherwise eligible for categorical assistance. We disagree. The purpose of the AFDC-FC program was not simply to duplicate the AFDC program for a different class of beneficiaries. As the language and legislative history of § 408 demonstrate, the Foster Care program was designed to meet the particular needs of all eligible neglected children, whether they are placed with related or unrelated foster parents.

A

Had Congress intended to exclude related foster parents from the definition of "foster family home," it presumably would have done so explicitly, just as it restricted the definition of "child-care institution."[15] Instead, the statute plainly states that a foster family home is the home of any individual licensed or approved by the State as meeting its licensing requirements, and we are unpersuaded that the provisions on which appellants rely implicitly limit that expansive definition.

* * *

III
* * *

...Accordingly, we hold that the AFDC-FC program encompasses foster children who, pursuant to a judicial determination of neglect, have been placed in related homes that meet a State's licensing requirements for foster homes.

The judgment below is

Affirmed.

* * *

[5] Illinois, like most other States, has consistently authorized substantially greater AFDC-FC payments than basic AFDC benefits....

[8] Ch. 23, §§ 4-1.2 and 2217...; Illinois Department of Children and Family Services, Child Welfare Manual 2.8.2 (1976).... The DCFS Welfare Manual recently has been revised to conform to the decisions below

The Agency documented its approval in two "Relative Home Placement Agreements" which were identical, both in form and in obligations imposed, to those used for unrelated foster care placements, except that the term "foster" was sometimes crossed out, two references were made to the familial relationship among appellees, and the usual promise of AFDC-FC benefits was deleted. See 431 F.Supp. 40, 43–44, and nn. 4, 5 (ND Ill. 1976); App. 20–23.

[12] As an exception to this benefit differential, the State has authorized special supplemental payments, upon an adequate showing of need by related foster parents, to bring basic AFDC related foster care assistance up to $105 per month. Brief for Appellants 5; 374 F.Supp. 1204, 1206 (ND III. 1974). Since September 1, 1974, the Youakims have received these need-based payments for their foster children. This Court previously held that receipt of the supplemental benefits does not render the case moot. *Youakim v. Miller*, 425 U.S. 231, 236 n. 2 (1976) (*per curiam*).

[15] In contrast to the broad definition of "foster family homes," the term "child-care institution" is explicitly qualified to exempt private institutions operated for profit and public institutions....

Unlike generic TANF, the AFDC-foster care program was not altered by the PRA and remains an entitlement, involving a higher benefit than straight AFDC (or TANF presently) provided in Illinois. States vary in their compensation for TANF versus "kin-care" versus regular licensed foster care. Usually TANF compensation is the lowest and licensed foster care the highest, particularly where multiple children are involved (unlike TANF parents, foster care rates are generally fully multiplied by number of children under care). Between 40–50% of foster care children are cared for by relatives. Some kin are given "formal" foster care status, achieving what amounts to licensed status at full foster care rates. But most such providers are simply relatives helping out, and states vary in their compensation from traditional TANF benefits to full foster care-level compensation. Where receiving TANF benefits, they may receive a family grant if their income is low enough to qualify, or alternatively may qualify for a lower "child only" coverage amount. If they choose the family grant, however, they will be subject to the PRA restrictions listed above, including the work requirement and the sixty-month absolute time limit.

The PRA creates a potential incentive shift in state funding by removing TANF as an entitlement and capping it as a block grant. Since foster care funds remain a federally matched entitlement without a lid, states can move children into foster care compensation (through "kin care" foster status), and use the TANF block grant money thus saved and already "in-hand" for other purposes.

Questions for Discussion

1. Can the state argue that a child's relative has a duty of care and that state compensation is inappropriate? Is such a duty to support enforceable? Could a statute theoretically impose such an obligation (similar to the obligation of parental support)? Assuming it could impose such a duty constitutionally, can it do so through a policy of non-payment for care by relatives where it imposes upon them no statutory duty of care? Does the state opportunity to save money by assigning foster children to relatives at no or lower compensation provide an economic incentive to do so apart from the merits (*e.g.*, where relatives are highly marginal or risky placements)?

2. Can the state pay higher foster care compensation to licensed providers? If so, can it enforce foster care by relatives on an unlicensed, and hence uncompensated, basis? What if the relatives could qualify for licensure?

3. Does a higher grant for foster care than for TANF in-home care provide an incentive for parents to abandon children to relatives who will receive more for them than will they? Note that TANF is to be cut off after sixty months, and may be reduced by up to one-half (the "parent's share" cut sanction). Will that drive large numbers of children into foster care with relatives (where either foster care or TANF compensation may be more available), when the sixty months will begin to expire for the parents of many children? How else will these children be supported absent other alternatives?

D. STATE WAIVERS AND BENEFIT LEVELS

Beno v. Shalala

30 F.3d 1057 (9th Cir. 1994)

GOODWIN, Circuit Judge:

Plaintiffs, California residents who receive Aid to Families with Dependant [sic] Children ("AFDC"), appeal the denial of their request for a preliminary injunction enjoining California's public benefits experiment. Plaintiffs object to a statewide benefits cut enacted as part of an experimental work-incentive project and challenge the Secretary of Health and Human Services' ("Secretary of HHS")...waiver of certain federal laws related to the project. They argue that the Secretary's waiver violates the Administrative Procedures Act, ("APA"), 5 U.S.C. § 701 *et seq.* and § 211 of the HHS Appropriations Act, 42 U.S.C. § 3515b, which prohibits HHS from spending federal money on experimental projects which pose a danger to human research subjects without their informed consent. In addition, they contend that California's project violates the Americans with Disabilities Act ("ADA"), 42 U.S.C. §§ 12131–12213, by failing to make reasonable accommodations for AFDC recipients with disabilities. We reverse.

I. CALIFORNIA'S PROGRAM

The benefits cut at issue in this appeal is part of a five-year Assistance Payments Demonstration Project ("APDP") enacted at Cal. Welf. & Inst. Code § 11450.01 *et seq.* APDP includes both a "residency requirement" and a "work-incentive" program. The former, which has been preliminarily enjoined on constitutional grounds, aims to discourage poor families from moving to California by limiting recent entrants' AFDC benefits to the amount received in their state of former residence. See *Green v. Anderson*, 811 F. Supp. 516 (E.D. Cal. 1993), *aff'd* 26 F.3d 95 (9th Cir. 1994). The latter, which is the subject of this appeal, aims to encourage AFDC recipients to find work by decreasing benefits and allowing recipients to keep more of their earned income.[2]

The work-incentive benefits cut affects all California AFDC families (approximately 826,000 families and 2.4 million persons,...) without regard to family composition or disabilities,[3] except for a "control group" of 5,000 families randomly selected from four counties. The control group receives AFDC benefits at their former levels and is subject to the old income-disregard rules. In order to assess the impact of the work-incentive program, the state plans to compare data about these control group families with data on 10,000 families randomly selected from the same four counties. The state does not plan to study most of the other approximately 800,000 families affected by the cut.

II. THE FEDERAL WAIVERS

The benefits program at issue, AFDC, is a cooperative federalism program created by the Social Security Act of 1935, 42 U.S.C. §§ 601–687. Participating states and the federal government jointly finance the program and state governments administer it under plans approved by the Secretary of Health and Human Services. *Id.* While states are not required to participate, participating states must comply with a variety of federal requirements....

California concedes that APDP violates several of these requirements, including the "Maintenance of Effort" requirement of 42 U.S.C. § 1396a(c)(1).[4] This section provides that:

> the Secretary shall not approve any State plan for medical assistance if—(1) the state has in effect [AFDC] payment levels that are less than the payment levels in effect under such plan on May 1, 1988.

42 U.S.C. § 1396a(c)(1). California's experiment reduces AFDC benefits to below their May 1988 levels. Thus, absent a waiver, the state could not implement the experiment without jeopardizing federal funding of its $14 billion Medicaid program. The California statutes enacting APDP, therefore, refer explicitly to obtaining HHS approval, and do not become effective until thirty days after state officials receive such approval....

* * *

(2) The Plain Language of § 1315

Moreover, § 1315(a) plainly requires the Secretary to review state proposals. On its face, the statute allows waivers only (1) for experimental, demonstration or pilot projects, which (2) in the judgment of the Secretary are likely to assist in promoting the objectives of the Social Security Act and only (3) for the extent and period she finds necessary. Thus, while the Secretary has considerable discretion to decide which projects meet these criteria, she must, at a minimum, examine each of these issues.

* * *

As this statute, its legislative history, and courts have made clear, the AFDC program's main objective is to support needy children....Thus, in determining that a state project is "likely to further the goals of the Act," the Secretary must obviously consider the impact of the state's project on the children and families the AFDC program was enacted to protect....

* * *

D. The Administrative Record

Plaintiffs have indisputably shown that California's experiment has serious problems, both as an experiment and as an attempt at welfare reform. The actors in this case—including the Secretary, the district court, and impressively credentialed *amici*[39]—agree that both the statewide scope of the benefits cut as well as the decision to cut benefits to individuals who cannot work appear wholly unjustified by any legitimate experimental goal. State officials have advanced no such experimental goal, and we are unable to explain how it would advance social science to cut benefits to recipients who are not even included in the study. *Amici* accurately observe that such a design is "methodologically indefensible" in that it exposes a large number of subjects to potential harm, yet studies only a few....

Moreover, the idea of imposing a work-incentive benefits cut on individuals whose disabilities preclude work can only be called absurd. As the district court found, "the Demonstration Project was intended to create work-incentives for recipients able to work; the effect of the project on those disabled recipients who are unable to work appears unintended and serves no stated goal of the project."...."The State could exclude from the benefit cut those of the disabled who are unable to work" and "it would be humane to do so." *Id.* at 35....

Nearly everyone also agrees that California's experiment will put "child-only" AFDC families, AFDC families headed by adults who are too disabled to work, and families whose heads are unable to find work—or cannot work due to child-care, transportation, and other difficulties—at increased risk of homelessness, inadequate nutrition, and a variety of emotional and physical problems....The program offers no work-training, child-care, or any other assistance designed to enable recipients to find and keep jobs. Moreover, given the minimum level of benefits already paid to AFDC families, it is difficult to imagine that the benefits cut would radically change the existing incentives to work. As plaintiffs point out, California could have accomplished its goal of increasing recipients' incentive to work without cutting AFDC benefits at all, by simply allowing recipients to keep more of their earned income.

Given these various problems, plaintiffs' expert contends that California's experiment is "utterly unconscionable,"...and *amici* argue that it "flagrantly disregards the basic norms of research."...

* * *

In the present case, the record contains a rather stunning lack of evidence that the Secretary gave plaintiffs' objections any...consideration. Except for the Secretary's conclusory letter to plaintiffs' counsel and possibly her decision to limit California's authority to cut benefits, the record contains no evidence that the Secretary ever considered the danger California's benefits cut would pose to recipients, the state's decision to impose a statewide benefits cut, the need for cutting benefits as a work-incentive, the merits of imposing a work-incentive cut on individuals whose disabilities preclude work, or the feasibility of excluding individuals who receive federal disability benefits or have already been adjudged unable to work in the context of other government programs such as California's Greater Avenue for Independence ("GAIN") program. Neither the Secretary nor California ever responded to the substance of plaintiffs' objections, and the Secretary did not revise the Terms and Conditions at all in response to plaintiffs' comments.

* * *

Here, the record contains no evidence that the Secretary considered the materials plaintiffs submitted. While the state and HHS exchanged detailed drafts of the Terms and Conditions, these drafts did not address any of plaintiffs' objections. Even if these drafts show, as the district court found, that a "good deal of thought went into approval of the research design," ...they do not show that HHS gave any such thought to plaintiffs' objections or proposed alternatives. If anything, the timing of the waiver approval—HHS's final changes to the draft Terms were made on the very day it received plaintiffs' objections—suggests the opposite....

* * *

...The Secretary's waiver of 42 U.S.C. § 1396a(c)(1) is VACATED...and the case is REMANDED to the district court with instructions to remand to the Secretary for additional consideration of plaintiffs' objections....

REVERSED AND REMANDED.

[2] Specifically, the Project reduces the 1992 Maximum Aid Payments ("MAP") (*i.e.*, the benefits) provided to needy families, but retains the 1992 Minimum Basic Standard of Adequate Care ("MBSAC") (with cost of living adjustments in 1992–96). Cal. Welf. & Inst. Code § 11452. Families are permitted to "fill the gap" between the MAP and the MBSAC by working and keeping their earnings as long as their total income does not exceed the MBSAC.

[3] Thus, the "work-incentive" benefits cut will affect not only AFDC families headed by "able-bodied" adults, but also families headed by adults who cannot work because of their disabilities and "child-only" AFDC families which contain no adult recipient.

[4] APDP also conflicts with (1) federal rules prohibiting states from basing AFDC benefits on the length of state residency; (2) federal income-disregard rules, including the "100 hour rule" which prohibits AFDC recipients from working more than 100 hours a month, 45 C.F.R.

§§ 233.100(a)(1)(i), 233.100(c)(1)(iii) and the "thirty dollars and one-third earnings disregard" which restrict AFDC recipients' ability to retain earned income without losing benefits, 45 C.F.R. §§ 233.20(a)(11)(i)(D), 233.20(a)(11)(ii)(B); and (3) rules requiring states to provide uniform benefit payments statewide.

[39] *Amici* include 19 biomedical and social scientists, physicians and other health care professionals, philosophers, and lawyers who served on the National Commission for the Protection of Human Subjects of Biomedical and Behavioral Research or its staff or on the President's Commission for the Study of Ethical Problems in Medicine and Biomedical and Behavioral Research or its staff.

O'SCANNLAIN, Circuit Judge, dissenting:

I respectfully dissent. For the reasons expressed in Judge Levi's well-crafted memorandum of decision and order (unpublished), I would affirm. Given the extremely deferential standard under which we review the Secretary's decisions under 42 U.S.C. § 1315, I believe that the agency record provides more than sufficient support for the Secretary's waiver.

* * *

...[T]he instant proceeding is very similar to *Aguayo v. Richardson*, 473 F.2d 1090 (2d Cir. 1973), the only other appellate case to review the Secretary's waiver of federal requirements under Section 1315 and approval of an experimental welfare project. In *Aguayo*, as here, the Secretary approved New York's proposed welfare program without a statement of the grounds for its decision. *Id.* at 1103...

The majority attempts to distinguish *Aguayo* because the *Aguayo* agency record included not only the plaintiffs' objections to the welfare plan, but also a memorandum prepared by the state responding to these objections. This is both true and irrelevant. Although California did not similarly respond to the appellants' objections, the agency record does include extensive information on the proposed program. Besides California's application for the waiver, the Secretary had before her the appellants' "voluminous materials" about the claimed harms the program would cause...

* * *

Because the extremely deferential standard for reviewing the agency's process controls the decision in this case, I need not comment on other issues discussed in the court's opinion.

Questions for Discussion

1. Assuming one wants to engage in an experiment with a control group, why would one test 2.4 million children and use 5,000 as the control group rather than vice versa? Would the state's experiment qualify as acceptable under "human subjects" ethical scrutiny?

2. Are state experiments acceptable where there is already an existing body of data on the impact of benefit reductions on percentage of recipients working? AFDC benefits at the time of *Beno* were about $7,000 per year for the benchmark mother and two children; does that assistance remove her incentive to work for more income? Are a substantial number of parents going to work hard at $6,000 per year in assistance, but reject additional work if receiving $7,000?

3. Is it relevant that from 1989 to 1994, AFDC benefits in California were already cut in constant dollars by over 15% by excluding any cost of living adjustment? Hadn't the state been experimenting with benefit reductions for the prior five years (during which numbers of claimants increased markedly)?

4. Would the state have a stronger case for reductions to test unwed birth rates at different compensation levels? Or the degree to which child support is generated from absent parents to make up for public aid subtractions?

1. Current Proposals to Reduce Child Poverty

Children's Defense Fund. In 2015, the Children's Defense Fund released its proposal to significantly reduce child poverty in America. It was repeated in 2019 and included the following eight elements: (1) add to current investments in housing assistance for poor families; (2) increase the value of SNAP benefits for improved child nutrition; (3) make the Child Tax Credit fully refundable so more low-income families benefit; (4) increase wages for working families and expand subsidized jobs; (5) provide access to quality, affordable child care; (6) assure comprehensive physical and behavioral health care; (7) provide access to high-quality early development and learning opportunities as well as high performing schools and colleges; and (8) assure the safety of families and neighborhoods from violence.[39]

National Academies of Sciences, Engineering, and Medicine (National Academies). In 2015, Congress included in its Omnibus Appropriations Bill a provision for a comprehensive study of child poverty in America by the National Academies. The three designated tasks were to (1) research linkages between child poverty and child wellbeing; (2) analyze major assistance programs aimed at children and families; and (3) recommend policies and programs to reduce overall child poverty and deep child poverty by one half of their current levels within ten years.

In 2019 the National Academies released a 580-page initial draft report entitled "A Roadmap to Reducing Child Poverty." Its major findings, consistent with the evidence presented in this text, include the following:

- Federal Earned Income Tax Credit increases have improved child educational and health outcomes;
- The SNAP program has improved birth outcomes as well as child and adult health;
- Expansion of public health insurance for pregnant women, infants and children has resulted in substantial improvements in both child and adult "health, educational attainment, employment and earnings"; and
- Housing assistance benefits have produced mixed results, but were positive where they allowed movement of families with children into less impoverished neighborhoods.[40]

The Roadmap suggested that even if the targeted 50% reduction in child poverty is not met, substantial improvements would occur if specified steps are taken, at a rough estimated public cost of $100 billion annually (a small percentage of the calculated public cost of child poverty in the U.S., which the Report calculates at between $800 billion and 1.1 trillion based on 2018 calculations).[41] The ten policy and program approaches recommended in the Roadmap are modifications to (1) the EITC, (2) child care subsidies, (3) the federal minimum wage, (4) Work Advance (a promising training and employment program), (5) SNAP, (6) the Housing Choice Voucher Program, and (7) Supplemental Security Income (specifically, increases to current child benefit levels), as well as (8) a child allowance (similar to the federal child tax credit but delivered monthly rather than annually), (9) a child support assurance program that sets guaranteed minimum child support payments per child per month, and (10) changes to immigrant provisions in safety net programs.[42]

2. Issues Beyond Current Advocacy or Consideration

The longstanding American commitment to succeeding generations has included a notion of egalitarianism—the chance for children born in poverty to advance, and with two hallmark promises from the previous generation: meaningful opportunities for employment and home ownership. Chapter 1 discusses the growth of regressive taxation and the deferral of obligation onto future generations that may affect these aspirations. In particular, regressive payroll taxes are relied upon to fund both Social Security and Medicare, together imposing a projected debt of over $30 trillion to be borne by the next generation, in addition to budget deficit and public employee retirement and medical coverage extending the projected debt passed onto the generation after the next at a $60 trillion level, over $400,000 for every future family at current population rates (see discussion in Chapter 1).

Other public policies and private costs amplify these trends to the disadvantage of child opportunity. Discussed above are some of them—*e.g.*, effective minimum wage decline. But there are four others that have substantial impact on child poverty and its effects, although they lack court precedents for text inclusion and are generally not a part of political or even academic discourse.

a. Inheritance/Extreme Wealth Taxation

In 2001 Congress voted to exempt the first $1.5 million in each estate from taxation. Half of all estate taxes are currently paid by the 2,400 largest estates, and the elimination of this tax confers a benefit on their heirs averaging $3.5 million each. The defenders of the abolition claim that family-owned businesses or farms are lost to family succession, but only 3% of taxed estates have such assets, and these paid less than one-half of one percent of existing estate taxes. Then starting in 2015, an increasingly larger share of estates were made entirely exempt from tax, with $5.4 million inheritable with no tax whatever, growing to $11.8 million in 2018.[43] African American children inherit less than one-fifth the average amount of white children. Child advocates argue that modest inheritance taxes allow a small sharing of unearned wealth by those born to privilege to other children—serving egalitarian principles of opportunity equity and meritocracy.

Related to this consideration is the advanced idea of a "wealth tax" on those with assets of over some substantial sum. The concept has a long precedent through real property taxation, also based on market value. To be sure, such an assessment must be minimal and judicious; it advisedly would not approach the socialist model of state seizure and control of private capital. The benefits of private capital and competitive markets are substantial and are demonstrated by the strength of the American economy and its history.

Assuming, hypothetically, an assessment of no more than 1% and with warranted exclusions for legitimately charitable asset commitment, inability to sell *et al.*, there are four aspects to such proposals warranting consideration. First, a small assessment may somewhat stimulate more socially beneficial use of assets—commitment to production and research, rather than their more passive sequestration. Second, in terms of equity, each one of us receives untold benefits from our society and public expenditures that are rarely discussed or acknowledged. Very few who have achieved great wealth did so in a vacuum, but were given everything from military defense to roads, libraries, trash collection, water, and electricity/gas, in addition to protection from crime, fire, and natural disasters. It is a long list before we get to education and copyright systems and courts. Third, the trend in wealth disparity is growing to radical levels and perhaps some modest check on extreme disproportionality is warranted—albeit a check preserving the vast brunt of incentive to profit. Finally, we fought a revolution against a system that passed political power onto children through inheritance. We rebelled, and that revulsion has included at least to some extent, disapproval of a caste model where prior family wealth determines assets of succeeding generations unrelated to the merits or contributions of those legatees. Our model was that we all have opportunity and no one grouping should start as a reviled caste at the bottom, nor as a privileged class at the top—particularly based primarily on the economic circumstances of their parents.

There is a serious counter consideration—the right of a parent or any person to make a gift or to spend monies for persons and purposes of their choosing. That is part of the right of possession. The question raised is, recognizing the merits of considerations in these various directions, where should the line be drawn? Is 1–2% of wealth, in a world where inflation alone will increase value annually by that much, a serious abridgement of the gift right to favored persons? Data from 2016 indicates that the wealthiest 10% of individuals control 65% of the nation's private wealth. Moreover, the bottom 50% control 0%, because their debts match their assets.[44] Amplifying the disproportionality is its extreme nature and trend. A Stanford study found that the wealthiest 0.1% (one-tenth of 1%) control 22% of the national wealth as of 2013, up from 7% in 1978.[45] The issue of child poverty and opportunity properly includes the consideration of wealth distribution in assuring opportunity for all children, a circumstance likely to allow a wider set of skills from new contributors conferring a cumulative benefit to the nation.

b. Prevention Through Parental Responsibility

The above discussion avoids one of the major factors contributing to child impoverishment that is generally undiscussed—the responsibility of parents to choose to bring a child into the world and to prepare for that profound arrival. The major aspect of this issue to generate public discussion occurred during the 1980 and 1990s AFDC years. It involved the stereotyping of "welfare queens," who allegedly choose motherhood as a remunerative occupation to be financed by taxpayers. That allegation, and Newt Gingrich's lobbying to reinforce that characterization, led to the end of impoverished child assistance as an entitlement into a PRA block grant structure with a five-year total limit, required identification of biological fathers for child support, required work within two years if available, *at al.* However, as discussed above, the facts regarding typical AFDC recipients—now magnified for the increasingly limited beneficiaries under the current TANF system—are at odds with that representation. Indeed, in the 1990s AFDC provided about $105 in additional monthly welfare benefits per added child—covering just 15–20% of the costs of that child. Although the *public persona* advanced was inaccurate, there is an aspect to these anti-welfare sentiments that warrants consideration—and more objective and thoughtful discussion than is offered by either party.

That undiscussed argument may be stated as follows: there is an obvious relationship between having unplanned children and child poverty incidence. Certainly unemployment and adverse events are not uncommon, but the fact remains that children deserve to be intended by adults who have secured sufficient resources for their optimum development and opportunity. They are collectively our future as a nation and planet. Should not our culture respect this decision as one properly made volitionally after due consideration, and with preparation for the challenge of parenting that will follow?

Beyond this cultural issue is the role of our public school system in preparing our youth for their most important life decisions by teaching them how to both succeed personally and facilitate the success of their children. *Query,* why is parenting education not required in public high schools? It need not be a full course; it can consist of various modules for inclusion in existing courses, to explain the basics of child development, the costs and expenses of raising a child, *et al.* How much more useful would such a course be for most students *vis-à-vis* shop or trigonometry? One critical way to reduce child poverty and advance opportunity is to teach the basic lesson that American culture and schools assiduously ignore: to intend and prepare for our children, and understand the financial obligations that parenthood involves.

c. Affordable Higher Education

Parents have historically taken pride in seeing their children attend a university and enjoy wealth and life options unavailable to them or their forbearers. Higher education tuition has joined energy and housing costs in a twenty-year rise well beyond CPI increases. Undergraduate college education costs nationally continue to rise rapidly above inflation. In 1987, public college tuition cost an average of $3,190 per year. That figure was $10,230 in 2018–19 for in-state students. Over the same period, tuition and fees at private non-profit colleges climbed from $15,160 to $35,830 per year.[46] Accordingly, the standard four-year undergraduate tuition burden rose from $12,760 to $40,920 for public in-state students during the same period—more than a 300% increase. For private non-profit schools, the total has risen from $60,640 to $143,340.[47] Room and board has also increased, from $5,840 per year in 1987 to $11,140 per year in 2018–19 for public schools and from $7,330 per year in 1987 to $12,680 in 2018–19 for private non-profits.

Including only basic tuition and room and board, costs for college now commonly amount to $85,480 at an in-state four-year public university, $149,720 at an out-of-state four-year public school, and $194,040 at a private non-profit school. This is two to three times what students paid a generation ago in constant dollars. And these figures exclude other often substantial costs that have also suffered major increases beyond inflation over the last thirty years, including transportation, communications, clothing, books, and food—beyond what a college would provide.

Public college assistance has also increased over this period. All monies for undergraduate students, including state and institutional grants, non-federal loans, and private and employer grants, now total $250 billion, up from $178 billion in 2006–

07. This assistance has included Pell Grants, Federal Supplemental Educational Opportunity Grants, the Leveraging Educational Assistance Partnership (LEAP) Program, Academic Competitiveness Grants, National Science and Mathematics Access to Retain Talent (SMART) grants, and GI bill (federal Title 38) assistance for veterans. However, the total increases here represent a small percentage of the tuition and cost increases extant. Critically, a large share of these amounts are on the loan side, amounting to $110 billion of the $250 billion in current total assistance.[48] Finally, as discussed below, a large and increasing share of this assistance consists of grants and loans for private, for-profit colleges that may award degrees of dubious economic value. Public assistance to these businesses too often yields questionable value for students or taxpayers, as studies, disclosures and litigation have documented over the past decade.[49]

College education today puts an unprecedented burden on families. Students and their parents are borrowing and sacrificing pensions to pay for education. In contrast to the dramatic rise of college costs, median family income in constant dollars nationally went up marginally from $51,973 in 1987 to $57,617 in 2016— the most recent Census Department figure. Basic college costs have increased from 20.4% of median income in 1971 to 51.8% today.[50] This college degree must precede an advanced degree for any youth intending to be an engineer, doctor, businessman, attorney, or other professional that normally requires one to five years of education after college. Increasingly, these categories of employment become more important as unskilled jobs are assumed by automation or where related products are imported. Taking the three additional years of law school as an illustration, and adding this cost to the undergraduate tuition and housing, the seven-year median cost as of 2018 was roughly $190,000 at public schools for in-state students, and $388,000 if attending private non-profits.[51] These 2018 figures exclude clothing, transportation, books, and other expenses. Because tuition increases are increasingly not subject to effective competitive check, further increases well above inflation may be anticipated (see Chapter 4 discussion).

d. Home Ownership

Beyond educational opportunity for meaningful employment, American tradition has also provided a second intergenerational promise: home ownership. The median price of homes is about $300,000, and surpasses $500,000 in coastal states and for most of the California population. The prices are now at a level inhibiting home ownership. The barrier will grow for the vast majority of children not positioned to inherit real property. Of special concern is the possibility of mortgage rate increases, or the possible reappearance of the "bait and switch" mortgages of 2000–08 that offered an initial token interest for three to five years followed by a "switch" to an interest rate based on an amount over the fed rate. Should those rates increase, the most important issue for youth opportunity to own a home will be that revised percentage. During the 2007 economic bust, those rates caused the foreclosure of a high percentage of home mortgages—with young homeowners subject to foreclosure at unprecedented levels.[52]

ENDNOTES

[1] See https://aspe.hhs.gov/poverty-guidelines.

[2] See https://www.census.gov/library/publications/2018/demo/p60-265.html at Figure 3.

[3] 2015–16 data at http://www.oecd.org/social/family/Poor-children-in-rich-countries-Policy-brief-2018.pdf, Figure 1, citing OECD Income Distribution Database at http://oe.cd/idd.

[4] National Academies of Sciences, Engineering, and Medicine, *A Roadmap to Reducing Child Poverty* (The National Academies Press, Washington D.C.; 2019); see https://doi.org/10.17226/25246.

[5] *Id.*, at S-3–4.

[6] Linda Neuhauser, Doris Disbrow, and Sheldon Margen, University of California at Berkeley School of Public Health, *Hunger and Food Insecurity in California*, California Policy Seminar Brief (Berkeley, CA; April 1995) at 2.

[7] See Mary C. Daly, Deborah Reed, and Heather N. Royer, *Population Mobility and Income Inequality in California*, Public Policy Institute of California, California Counts, Vol. 2, No. 4 (May 2001) at 1–2. The Institute places the impact of immigration as accounting for one-third of the income inequality growth in California, but adds: "However, other forces explain the bulk of the growth in inequality. The rising value of skills such as schooling and labor market experience has been one of the most important factors behind the growing inequality. Thus, the concern over the economic opportunities available to low-income families, particularly those headed by low-skilled workers, is well-founded" (at 2). In addition, since 2000 when these conclusions were reached, immigration across the southern border has declined to one-fifth the high levels of the early 2000s.

[8] See Economic Policy Institute, *Why America Needs a $15 Minimum Wage: Fact Sheet* (February 5, 2019) at https://www.epi.org/files/pdf/127246.pdf.

[9] *Id.*

[10] *Id.*

[11] Some cities (*e.g.*, Baltimore and San Francisco) have implemented "living wage" policies boosting hourly rates for city and other employees to above $10 per hour, attempting to target a higher percentage of working poor.

[12] See Tom Shapiro, Northeastern University, *Black Wealth, White Wealth* (1995).

[13] See https://www.epi.org/blog/the-racial-wealth-gap-how-african-americans-have-been-shortchanged-out-of-the-materials-to-build-wealth/.

[14] Joel Friedman, Richard Kogan, and Robert Greenstein, *Final Tax Bill Ultimately Costs as Much as Bush Plan*, Center for Budget and Policy Priorities (Washington, D.C.; May 29, 2001) at 1–3; see http://www.cbpp.org.

[15] *Id.*

[16] See https://www.cbpp.org/research/food-assistance/snap-helps-millions-of-children. Note that the percentage of child recipients varies from 69%–72% for the largest TANF category "family groups"; the percentage of child recipients for the smaller TANF unemployed category is 61%–63%. See Children's Advocacy Institute, *California Children's Budget 2001–02* (San Diego, CA; June 2001) at Chapter 2.

[17] Reducing TANF (AFDC) levels would have little impact on impoverishment caused by divorce, or by male abandonment or rejection. Proponents of reduction argue that it would stimulate employment. There may be some relationship between benefit levels and incentive to work, but the analyses of poverty incidence and TANF caseloads do not correlate closely with benefit levels, either over time or between states with very different benefit systems. Rather, TANF claims correlate with unemployment levels and prevailing wages for the working poor. See *e.g.*, Tufts University School of Nutrition Science and Policy, Center on Hunger and Poverty, *Statement on Key Welfare Reform Issues, The Empirical Evidence* (Medford, MA; 1995), referencing 73 studies and statistical sources.

[18] For example, in California the 2002 level was $175 per month ($200 for children younger than two) and $90 of work-related expenses. In addition, the first $30 earned each month for up to one year is not counted, and an additional one-third of earnings is disregarded (termed the "30 and one-third rule" to encourage work). If received, the first $50 per month in child support is also not counted. The first $225 in earnings each month plus 50% of what is earned may be kept, with TANF assistance reduced as the counted 50% of earnings raises income. These numbers are subject to some adjustment.

[19] See https://www.cbpp.org/research/policy-basics-an-introduction-to-tanf.

[20] Pub. L. No. 104-193, § 103 of the Act, 42 U.S.C. § 602.

[21] See Raymond Hernandez, *Most Dropped from Welfare Don't Get Jobs*, N.Y. TIMES (Mar. 22, 1998) at 1 (survey by New York State Office of Temporary and Disability Assistance).

[22] Staff of NGA, NCSL, and APWA, *Tracking Recipients after They Leave Welfare, July 1998*, at 1; see http://www.nga.org/welfare/statefollowup.htm.

[23] See Brooks, J. L., Hair, E. C. & Zaslow, M. J., *Welfare Reform's Impact on Adolescents: Early Warning Signs, Child Trends Research Brief* (Washington, D.C.; July 2001); see also Duncan, G. J. & Chase-Lansdale, P.L., *Welfare Reform and Children's Well-Being*, in R. Blank and R. Haskins (eds.), The New World of Welfare (Washington, D.C.; 2001) at 391–417; see also Hamilton, G., Freedman, S., Gennetian, L., Michalopoulos, C., Walter, J., Adams-Ciardullo, D., Gassman-Pines, A., McGroder, S., Zaslow, M., Ahluwalia, S., and Brooks, J., *How Effective Are Different Welfare-to-Work Approaches? Five-Year Adult and Child Impacts for Eleven Programs*, U.S. Department of Health and Human Services (Washington, D.C.; Dec. 2001); see also Morris, P. A., Huston, A.C., Duncan, G. J., Crosby, D. A., & Bos, J. M., *How Welfare and Work Policies Affect Children: A Synthesis of Research, Manpower Demonstration Research Corporation* (New York, NY; March 2001); see also Morris, P., Knox, V., and Gennetian, L. A., *Welfare Policies Matter for Children and Youth: Lessons for TANF Reauthorization*, MDRC Policy Brief (New York, NY; March 2002); see also Shields, M.K. (Ed.), *Children and Welfare Reform*, THE FUTURE OF CHILDREN, Vol. 12, No. 1 (2002); see also Zaslow, M., Brooks, J. L., Moore, K. A., Morris, P., Tout, K., and Redd, Z., *Impact on Children in Experimental Studies of Welfare-to-Work Programs*, Child Trends (Washington, D.C.; 2001). Note that earnings increases for some parents benefit their children, and for young children the increased hours employed do not correlate with measurable indices of child well-being. However, supporters of welfare reform have largely relied on welfare caseload reductions as the criterion for success. Impacts on children are rarely discussed or closely examined, and have had little impact on reauthorization of the PRA—now proposing minimum work requirements of 38 to 40 hours per week and permission to pay "workfare" at levels below minimum wage, *et al.*

[24] Bruce Fuller, Sharon Lynn Kagan, *Remember the Children: Mothers Balance Work and Child Care Under Welfare Reform, Growing Up in Poverty Project 2000, Wave 1 Findings: California, Connecticut, Florida* (U.C. Berkeley and Yale University; Feb. 2000) at 3–6.

[25] See Research Development Division, Department of Social Services, *Characteristics and Employment of Current and Former CalWORKs Recipients: What We Know From Statewide Administrative Data* (June 6, 2000) at 16–17.

[26] Floyd, Burnside and Schott, *TANF Reaching Few Poor Families*, Center on Budget and Policy Priorities (November 22, 2018) at https://www.cbpp.org/research/family-income-support/tanf-reaching-few-poor-families.

[27] The terms "SNAP benefits" and "food stamps" will both be used in this publication and they refer to the same program and benefits.

[28] Center on Budget and Policy Priorities, *SNAP Works for America's Children* (September 29, 2016) at https://www.cbpp.org/research/food-assistance/snap-works-for-americas-children.

[29] See https://fns-prod.azureedge.net/sites/default/files/ops/Reaching2015.pdf.

[30] Barbara Howell and Lynette Engelhardt, *Bread for the World, Elect to End Childhood Hunger "Childhood Hunger Facts"* (Silver Spring, MD; Feb. 1996) at 4 (citing USDA).

[31] Marriage to a citizen can shorten the waiting period to three years. Note also that veterans and those serving in the active duty military are exempt from the legal immigrant PRA bar to public assistance. Children who are born in the United States may be eligible for food stamp and TANF assistance because they are U.S. citizens at birth. However, many legal immigrants have withdrawn from TANF (and food stamp) assistance because of fears that accepting such help, even where needed for their children, will cause them to be designated a likely "public charge" and preclude their citizenship in their new country. According to the federal Immigration and Naturalization Service, the definition of public charge focuses on cash assistance *(e.g.,* TANF) and is supposed to measure future dependency on public funds, not prior use based on need not likely to recur.

[32] See AB 1576 (Bustamante) (Chapter 287, Statutes of 1997), which—effective August 18, 1997— added section 18930 *et seq.* to the Cal. Welfare & Institutions Code.

[33] See Laurie True, *Hunger in the Balance: The Impact of the Proposed AFDC Cuts on Childhood Hunger in California* (San Francisco, CA; March 1992) at 14.

[34] See Center on Budget and Policy Priorities and Center for the Study of the States, *The States and the Poor: How Budget Decisions Affected Low-Income People in 1992* (Washington, D.C.; 1993) at 67.

[35] *Id.*

[36] See Steven Carlson and Zoe Neuberger, *WIC Works: Addressing the Nutrition and Health Needs of Low-Income Families for 40 Years* (March 29, 2017) at https://www.cbpp.org/research/food-assistance/wic-works-addressing-the-nutrition-and-health-needs-of-low-income-families. For a discussion (and critique) of positive WIC research findings, see Douglas Besharov and Peter Germanis, *Is WIC as Good as They Say?*, THE PUBLIC INTEREST (Jan. 1, 1999). Note that although the authors state a strong case for more extensive and properly blind tested measurement of WIC, the evidence is substantial that it has important health benefits for the children in circumstances of extreme poverty. Direct familiarity with the program and its workings—what it provides to women and infants that they are otherwise not reliably

receiving indicates a substantial beneficial effect in light of double blind tested literature correlating the effect of nutrients on child development.

[37] U.S. Department of Agriculture, *WIC Participant and Program Characteristics 2016 Final Report* (April 2018) at https://fns-prod.azureedge.net/sites/default/files/ops/WICEligibles2016-Summary.pdf.

[38] See, *e.g.*, the California data indicating a failure to match population increase over the past decade, at Children's Advocacy Institute, *California Children's Budget 2001–02* (San Diego, CA; June 2001) at Chapter 7 (http://www.caichildlaw.org).

[39] See https://www.childrensdefense.org/policy/policy-priorities/child-poverty/.

[40] National Academies of Sciences, Engineering, and Medicine, *A Roadmap to Reducing Child Poverty* (The National Academy Press, Washington D.C.; 2019) at S-3; see https://doi.org/10.17226/25246.

[41] *Id.,* at S-2.

[42] *Id.,* at S-2 to S-14 for summary discussion and references to more detailed text discussion.

[43] See https://www.forbes.com/sites/ashleaebeling/2017/10/19/irs-announces-2018-estate-and-gift-tax-limits-11-2-million-per-couple/#361d65ac4a4b.

[44] Credit Suisse, *Global Wealth Databook 2018* (October 2018) at 16; see https://www.credit-suisse.com/corporate/en/research/research-institute/global-wealth-report.html.

[45] Gabriel Zucman, *Wealth Inequality* (The Stanford Center on Poverty and Inequality; 2016) at https://inequality.stanford.edu/sites/default/files/Pathways-SOTU-2016-Wealth-Inequality-3.pdf.

[46] See https://trends.collegeboard.org/college-pricing/figures-tables/published-prices-national#Published%20Charges%20over%20Time.

[47] These figures use 2017 dollars to adjust for inflation.

[48] This includes non-federal loans and Perkins, Stafford, Parent PLUS, Grad PLUS. Note also that most of the $110 billion in federal loans are unsubsidized Stafford loans. See https://trends.collegeboard.org/student-aid/figures-tables.

[49] See Delgado, *Failing U*, Children's Advocacy Institute (San Diego, CA; Jan. 2018), including underlying citations to the Harkin Report *et al.* and analyzing practices and problems; see http://www.caichildlaw.org/FailingU.html.

[50] See https://college-education.procon.org/view.resource.php?resourceID=005532, note that these figures are gathered by gender and these are the median percentages as to males. The percentages as to females, with somewhat lower median income, are measurably higher.

[51] For tuition, see https://data.lawschooltransparency.com/costs/tuition/?sgye=national. For living expenses, see https://data.lawschooltransparency.com/costs/living-expenses/.

[52] For full discussion of the causes of the mortgage crisis and economic problems of that era, see Papageorge and Fellmeth, CALIFORNIA WHITE COLLAR CRIME (Tower Publishing, 5th Edition, 2016) at Chapter 6, Sections 6.24-6.30.

CHAPTER FOUR

Education Rights and Investment

A. EDUCATION AND EQUALITY OF OPPORTUNITY

The educational level of children correlates with their future success. Table 4-A indicates the continuing strong and positive relationship between education and earnings in the United States.

Educational Attainment	Median Weekly Earnings	Unemployment Rate
Professional Degree	$1,836	1.5%
Doctoral Degree	$1,743	1.5%
Master's Degree	$1,401	2.2%
Bachelor's Degree	$1,173	2.5%
Associate Degree	$836	3.4%
Some College, No Degree	$774	4.0%
High School Diploma, No College	$712	4.6%
Less than a High School Diploma	$520	6.5%

Source: U.S. Bureau of Labor Statistics, Current Population Survey[1]

Table 4-A. Median Weekly Income and Unemployment Rate by Highest Educational Attainment, 2017

In 2014, almost 30% of individuals over the age of 25 without a high school diploma, and more than 14% of high school graduates without a college degree, were in poverty.[2] The number of "high skill" jobs within the U.S. labor market has significantly increased over the past several decades, strongly outpacing growth in "low skill" job sectors. It is projected that by 2020, 65% of all U.S. jobs will require postsecondary education, and the three fastest growing sectors—STEM, healthcare, and community services—generally call for education beyond high school.[3] Not only has the demand for high-skill jobs grown, but the wages associated with these jobs continue to increase at a higher rate than low-skill job wages. Since 1990, jobs utilizing analytical skills have experienced a wage increase of 19%, whereas wages of workers in jobs requiring primarily physical skills have increased by only 7%.[4]

Access to quality education throughout childhood is fundamental to achieving future educational success and, ultimately, economic stability and self-sufficiency. Thus, ensuring access regardless of race, ethnicity, language, or economic status has long been a priority of child advocates.

1. Public School Segregation

Brown v. Board of Education of Topeka
347 U.S. 483 (1954)

MR. CHIEF JUSTICE WARREN delivered the opinion of the Court.

Today, education is perhaps the most important function of state and local governments. Compulsory school attendance laws and the great expenditures for education both demonstrate our recognition of the importance of education to our democratic society. It is required in the performance of our most basic public responsibilities, even service in the armed forces. It is the very foundation of good citizenship. Today it is a principal instrument in awakening the child to cultural values, in preparing him for later professional training, and in helping him to adjust normally to his environment. In these days, it is doubtful that any child may reasonably be expected to succeed in life if he is denied the opportunity of an education. Such an opportunity, where the state has undertaken to provide it, is a right which must be made available to all on equal terms.

* * *

We come then to the question presented: Does segregation of children in public schools solely on the basis of race, even though the physical facilities and other "tangible" factors may be equal, deprive the children of the minority group of equal educational opportunities? We believe that it does.

In *Sweatt v. Painter*,...in finding that a segregated law school for Negroes could not provide them equal educational opportunities, this Court relied in large part on "those qualities which are incapable of objective measurement but which make for greatness in a law school." In *McLaurin v. Oklahoma State Regents* the Court, in requiring that a Negro admitted to a white graduate school be treated like all other students, again resorted to intangible considerations: "...his ability to study, to engage in discussions and exchange views with other students, and, in general, to learn his profession." Such considerations apply with added force to children in grade and high schools. To separate them from others of similar age and qualifications solely because of their race generates a feeling of inferiority as to their status in the community that may affect their hearts and minds in a way unlikely ever to be undone. The effect of this separation on their educational opportunities was well stated by a finding in the Kansas case by a court which nevertheless felt compelled to rule against the Negro plaintiffs:

> "Segregation of white and colored children in public schools has a detrimental effect upon the colored children. The impact is greater when it has the sanction of the law; for the policy of separating the races is usually interpreted as denoting the inferiority of the negro group. A sense of inferiority affects the motivation of a child to learn. Segregation with the sanction of law, therefore, has a tendency to [retard] the educational and mental development of negro children and to deprive them of some of the benefits they would receive in a racial[ly] integrated school system."[10]

Whatever may have been the extent of psychological knowledge at the time of *Plessy v. Ferguson*, this finding is amply supported by modern authority.[11] Any language in *Plessy v. Ferguson* contrary to this finding is rejected.

We conclude that in the field of public education the doctrine of "separate but equal" has no place. Separate educational facilities are inherently unequal. Therefore, we hold that the plaintiffs and others similarly situated for whom the actions have been brought are, by reason of the segregation complained of, deprived of the equal protection of the laws guaranteed by the Fourteenth Amendment. This disposition makes unnecessary any discussion whether such segregation also violates the Due Process Clause of the Fourteenth Amendment...

Because these are class actions, because of the wide applicability of this decision, and because of the great variety of local conditions, the formulation of decrees in these cases presents problems of considerable complexity. On reargument, the consideration of appropriate relief was necessarily subordinated to the primary question—the constitutionality of segregation in public education. We have now announced that such segregation is a denial of the equal protection of the laws. In order that we may have the full assistance of the parties in formulating decrees, the cases will be restored to the docket, and the parties are requested to present further argument on Questions 4 and 5 previously propounded by the Court for the reargument this Term.[13] The Attorney General of the United States is again invited to participate. The Attorneys General of the states requiring or permitting segregation in public education will also be permitted to appear amici curiae upon request to do so by September 15, 1954, and submission of briefs by October 1, 1954....

It is so ordered.

[10] A similar finding was made in the Delaware case: "I conclude from the testimony that in our Delaware society, State-imposed segregation in education itself results in the Negro children, as a class, receiving educational opportunities which are substantially inferior to those available to white children otherwise similarly situated." 87 A. 2d 862, 865.

[11] K.B. Clark, Effect of Prejudice and Discrimination on Personality Development (Midcentury White House Conference on Children and Youth, 1950); Witmer and Kotinsky, Personality in the Making (1952), c. VI; Deutscher and Chein, The Psychological Effects of Enforced Segregation: A Survey of Social Science Opinion, 26 J. Psychol. 259 (1948); Chein, What are the Psychological Effects of Segregation Under Conditions of Equal Facilities?, 3 Int. J. Opinion and Attitude Res. 229 (1949); Brameld, Educational Costs, in Discrimination and National Welfare (MacIver, ed., 1949), 44–48; Frazier, The Negro in the United States (1949), 674–681. And see generally Myrdal, An American Dilemma (1944).

[13] "4. Assuming it is decided that segregation in public schools violates the Fourteenth Amendment
(a) would a decree necessarily follow providing that, within the limits set by normal geographic school districting, Negro children should forthwith be admitted to schools of their choice, or
(b) may this Court, in the exercise of its equity powers, permit an effective gradual adjustment to be brought about from existing segregated systems to a system not based on color distinctions?
"5. On the assumption on which questions 4 (a) and (b) are based, and assuming further that this Court will exercise its equity powers to the end described in question 4(b)
(a) should this Court formulate detailed decrees in these cases;
(b) if so, what specific issues should the decrees reach;
(c) should this Court appoint a special master to hear evidence with a view to recommending specific terms for such decrees;
(d) should this Court remand to the courts of first instance with directions to frame decrees in these cases, and if so what general directions should the decrees of this Court include and what procedures should the courts of first instance follow in arriving at the specific forms of more detailed decrees?"

Questions for Discussion

1. Was it important that *Brown* was a unanimous decision of the Court? Why?

2. Is the judgment that separation is itself prima facie discriminatory an insult to minorities? Does it imply that minority children cannot achieve academic excellence except with the help of white children and their teachers? Does it portend the absorption of a viable African-American culture into a homogenous whole? If a black community were predominantly Muslim and did not want its children to be subject to outside influence, how would that situation differ from *Wisconsin v. Yoder* (Chapter 13 below), allowing the Amish to segregate as a constitutional right?

3. Have we conferred similar constitutional education integration rights to Native American children? Should we?

4. If opportunity involves social connections, and if the dominant race tends to obtain the most skilled teachers and extensive facilities, is integration then necessary for a more level playing field? What remedies did the federal courts then impose to accomplish integration? Was their detailed oversight of public education, including busing orders, calculation of percentage of minority students, et al. an appropriate court function? If relegated to a legislative decision, is it likely that a legislature dominated by the majority race would represent the interests of another group to raise the floor, at the partial expense of its own group?

5. Would housing integration be more effective at equalizing opportunity since it could act to integrate schools, as well as other institutions?

2. English Language Learners

Bilingual students and others with English language difficulties are referred to as Limited English Proficiency (LEP) students or English Language Learners (ELLs). They currently make up 9.4% of public school students nationwide, but some major states have an extraordinary proportion, *e.g.*, California's percentage is at 21%.[5]

Lau v. Nichols

414 U.S. 563 (1974)
MR. JUSTICE DOUGLAS delivered the opinion of the Court.

The San Francisco, California, school system was integrated in 1971 as a result of a federal court decree, 339 F.Supp. 1315....The District Court found that there are 2,856 students of Chinese ancestry in the school system who do not speak English. Of those who have that language deficiency, about 1,000 are given supplemental courses in the English language.[1] About 1,800, however, do not receive that instruction.

This class suit brought by non-English-speaking Chinese students against officials responsible for the operation of the San Francisco Unified School District seeks relief against the unequal educational opportunities, which are alleged to violate, inter alia, the Fourteenth Amendment. No specific remedy is urged upon us. Teaching English to the students of Chinese ancestry who do not speak the language is one choice. Giving instructions to this group in Chinese is another. There may be others. Petitioners ask only that the Board of Education be directed to apply its expertise to the problem and rectify the situation.

* * *

The Court of Appeals reasoned that "every student brings to the starting line of his educational career different advantages and disadvantages caused in part by social, economic and cultural background, created and continued completely apart from any contribution by the school system," 483 F.2d, at 797. Yet in our view the case may not be so easily decided. This is a public school system of California and § 71 of the California Education Code states that "English shall be the basic language of instruction in all schools." That section permits a school district to determine "when and under what circumstances instruction may be given bilingually." That section also states as "the policy of the state" to insure "the mastery of English by all pupils in the schools." And bilingual instruction is authorized "to the extent that it does not interfere with the systematic, sequential, and regular instruction of all pupils in the English language."

Moreover, § 8573 of the Education Code provides that no pupil shall receive a diploma of graduation from grade 12 who has not met the standards of proficiency in "English," as well as other prescribed subjects. Moreover, by § 12101 of the Education

Code...children between the ages of six and 16 years are (with exceptions not material here) "subject to compulsory full-time education."

Under these state-imposed standards there is no equality of treatment merely by providing students with the same facilities, textbooks, teachers, and curriculum; for students who do not understand English are effectively foreclosed from any meaningful education.

Basic English skills are at the very core of what these public schools teach. Imposition of a requirement that, before a child can effectively participate in the educational program, he must already have acquired those basic skills is to make a mockery of public education. We know that those who do not understand English are certain to find their classroom experiences wholly incomprehensible and in no way meaningful.

We do not reach the Equal Protection Clause argument which has been advanced but rely solely on § 601 of the Civil Rights Act of 1964, 42 U.S.C. § 2000d, to reverse the Court of Appeals.

That section bans discrimination based "on the ground of race, color, or national origin," in "any program or activity receiving Federal financial assistance." The school district involved in this litigation receives large amounts of federal financial assistance. The Department of Health, Education, and Welfare (HEW),...in 1968 issued one guideline that "school systems are responsible for assuring that students of a particular race, color, or national origin are not denied the opportunity to obtain the education generally obtained by other students in the system."....In 1970 HEW made the guidelines more specific, requiring school districts that were federally funded "to rectify the language deficiency in order to open" the instruction to students who had "linguistic deficiencies,"...

* * *

Discrimination is barred...even though no purposeful design is present: a recipient "may not...utilize criteria or methods of administration which have the effect of subjecting individuals to discrimination" or have "the effect of defeating or substantially impairing accomplishment of the objectives of the program as respect individuals of a particular race, color, or national origin."....

It seems obvious that the Chinese-speaking minority receive fewer benefits than the English-speaking majority from respondents' school system which denies them a meaningful opportunity to participate in the educational program—all earmarks of the discrimination banned by the regulations....

Reversed and remanded.

* * *

[1] A report adopted by the Human Rights Commission of San Francisco and submitted to the Court by respondents after oral argument shows that, as of April 1973, there were 3,457 Chinese students in the school system who spoke little or no English. The document further showed 2,136 students enrolled in Chinese special instruction classes, but at least 429 of the enrollees were not Chinese but were included for ethnic balance. Thus, as of April 1973, no more than 1,707 of the 3,457 Chinese students needing special English instruction were receiving it.

Note on Disparate Impact Claims following *Lau*

The decision in *Lau* relied upon the Court's judgment that Title VI of the Civil Rights Act could apply to acts in which discriminatory intent was lacking, but the effect was racially adverse. Furthermore, the *Lau* Court interpreted Title VI as conferring a private right of action on individuals to challenge such acts. However, following the *Lau* decision, the Supreme Court has retreated from these views, ultimately eliminating private rights of action for claims arising from disparate impact under Title VI. In deciding *Alexander v. Sandoval*, 532 U.S. 275, in 2001, the Court concluded that Congress did not clearly establish a private right of action based on disparate impact. Therefore, in order to bring an action under Title VI, private plaintiffs must allege intentional discrimination. Only federal agencies themselves can file actions based on adverse effect. This leaves individuals reliant on regulatory agencies to investigate and plead their case where disparate impact claims lie.

Questions for Discussion

1. Is the state policy to ensure "the mastery of English by all pupils" constitutionally compelled?

2. The Court does not address the equal protection issue, but notes that education is compulsory and that the Chinese will be deprived of meaningful education if they cannot understand the lessons. Does the Constitution or Section 601 of the Civil Rights Act require the state to bring each child to the same level of English proficiency? To some minimum level? Is equal protection provided where an equivalent effort is made as to each that is sufficient for some to achieve it? If some students start with languages particularly disparate from English (*e.g.*, an Asian language) is additional effort required on their behalf?

3. In the 1990s, several states enacted statutes reducing bilingual education, with some states requiring that English be learned on an "immersion" basis (*e.g.*, by limiting bilingual opportunity to a single year or less). Does that limitation discriminate against children whose primary languages are so disparate from English that they cannot learn sufficient English within one year and are unable to learn other subjects? Are these students deprived of educational opportunity in violation of the 14th Amendment or Section 601 of the Civil Rights Act? If such difficulties are particularly marked for Asian children, does their race afford them strict scrutiny protection, since race is a "suspect" classification?

4. A more recent trend allows for greater flexibility in the teaching of ELL students, with dual language education programs gaining popularity. These programs teach literacy and academic content in both English and a second language. Research suggests that these programs result in higher academic achievement for ELLs as compared to other bilingual programming. These programs appeal not only to ELLs but also to white, English-speaking families who find that the programs offer a uniquely contemporary emphasis on bilingualism and global awareness. In fact, the gentrification of urban neighborhoods where these programs first developed, along with the shortage of teachers with the skill set required to teach a dual immersion program, have led to concerns that ELL children are unable to access these programs originally designed to serve them. To what extent should these programs, if they continue to yield superior results for ELLs, be reserved for ELLs? Would such a preferential policy trigger equal protection concerns?

3. Public School Funding

Serrano v. Priest

5 Cal. 3d 584 (1971)

OPINION: SULLIVAN, J.

We are called upon to determine whether the California public school financing system, with its substantial dependence on local property taxes and resultant wide disparities in school revenue, violates the equal protection clause of the Fourteenth Amendment. We have determined that this funding scheme invidiously discriminates against the poor because it makes the quality of a child's education a function of the wealth of his parents and neighbors. Recognizing as we must that the right to an education in our public schools is a fundamental interest which cannot be conditioned on wealth, we can discern no compelling state purpose necessitating the present method of financing. We have concluded, therefore, that such a system cannot withstand constitutional challenge and must fall before the equal protection clause.

Plaintiffs, who are Los Angeles County public school children and their parents, brought this class action for declaratory and injunctive relief against certain state and county officials charged with administering the financing of the California public school system. Plaintiff children claim to represent a class consisting of all public school pupils in California, "except children in that school district, the identity of which is presently unknown, which school district affords the greatest educational opportunity of all school districts within California." Plaintiff parents purport to represent a class of all parents who have children in the school system and who pay real property taxes in the county of their residence.

* * *

The complaint sets forth three causes of action. The first cause alleges in substance as follows: Plaintiff children attend public elementary and secondary schools located in specified school districts in Los Angeles County. This public school system is maintained throughout California by a financing plan or scheme which relies heavily on local property taxes and causes substantial disparities among individual school districts in the amount of revenue available per pupil for the districts' educational programs. Consequently, districts with smaller tax bases are not able to spend as much money per child for education as districts with larger assessed valuations.

* * *

I

We begin our task by examining the California public school financing system which is the focal point of the complaint's allegations. At the threshold we find a fundamental statistic—over 90 percent of our public school funds derive from two basic sources: (a) local district taxes on real property and (b) aid from the State School Fund.[2]

By far the major source of school revenue is the local real property tax. Pursuant to Article IX, section 6 of the California Constitution, the Legislature has authorized the governing body of each county, and city and county, to levy taxes on the real property within a school district at a rate necessary to meet the district's annual education budget. (Ed. Code, § 20701 et seq.)....The amount of revenue which a district can raise in this manner thus depends largely on its tax base—i.e. the assessed valuation of real property within its borders. Tax bases vary widely throughout the state; in 1969–1970, for example, the assessed valuation per unit of average daily attendance of elementary school children[3] ranged from a low of $103 to a peak of $952,156—a ratio of nearly 1 to 10,000....

The other factor determining local school revenue is the rate of taxation within the district. Although the Legislature has placed ceilings on permissible district tax rates (§ 20751 et seq.), these statutory maxima may be surpassed in a "tax over-ride" election if a majority of the district's voters approve a higher rate. (§ 20803 et seq.) Nearly all districts have voted to override the statutory limits. Thus the locally raised funds which constitute the largest portion of school revenue are primarily a function of the value of the realty within a particular school district, coupled with the willingness of the district's residents to tax themselves for education.

Most of the remaining school revenue comes from the State School Fund pursuant to the "foundation program," through which the state undertakes to supplement local taxes in order to provide a "minimum amount of guaranteed support to all districts...." (§ 17300.) With certain minor exceptions,[6] the foundation program ensures that each school district will receive annually, from state or local funds, $355 for each elementary school pupil (§§ 17656, 17660) and $488 for each high school student. (§ 17665.)

The state contribution is supplied in two principal forms. "Basic state aid" consists of a flat grant to each district of $125 per pupil per year, regardless of the relative wealth of the district...."Equalization aid" is distributed in inverse proportion to the wealth of the district.

To compute the amount of equalization aid to which a district is entitled, the *[computing equalization aid]* State Superintendent of Public Instruction first determines how much local property tax revenue would be generated if the district were to levy a hypothetical tax at a rate of $1 on each $100 of assessed valuation in elementary school districts and $.80 per $100 in high school districts.[7]....To that figure, he adds the $125 per pupil basic aid grant. If the sum of those two amounts is less than the foundation program minimum for that district, the state contributes the difference....Thus, equalization funds guarantee to the poorer districts a basic minimum revenue, while wealthier districts are ineligible for such assistance.

An additional state program of "supplemental aid" is available to subsidize particularly poor school districts which are willing to make an extra local tax effort. An elementary district with an assessed valuation of $12,500 or less per pupil may obtain up to $125 more for each child if it sets its local tax rate above a certain statutory level. A high school district whose assessed valuation does not exceed $24,500 per pupil is eligible for a supplement of up to $72 per child if its local tax is sufficiently high....

Although equalization aid and supplemental aid temper the disparities which result from the vast variations in real property assessed valuation, wide differentials remain in the revenue available to individual districts and, consequently, in the level of educational expenditures. For example, in Los Angeles County, where plaintiff children attend school, the Baldwin Park Unified School District expended only $577.49 to educate each of its pupils in 1968–1969; during the same year the Pasadena Unified School District spent $840.19 on every student; and the Beverly Hills Unified School District paid out $1,231.72 per child....The source of these disparities is unmistakable: in Baldwin Park the assessed valuation per child totaled only $3,706; in Pasadena, assessed valuation was $13,706; while in Beverly Hills, the corresponding figure was $50,885—a ratio of 1 to 4 to 13....Thus, the state grants are inadequate to offset the inequalities inherent in a financing system based on widely varying local tax bases.

Furthermore, basic aid, which constitutes about half of the state educational funds...actually widens the gap between rich and poor districts....Such aid is distributed on a uniform per pupil basis to all districts, irrespective of a district's wealth. Beverly Hills, as well as Baldwin Park, receives $125 from the state for each of its students.

* * *

III

...[W]e take up the chief contention underlying plaintiffs' complaint, namely that the California public school financing scheme violates the Equal Protection Clause of the Fourteenth Amendment to the United States Constitution...

* * *

A

Wealth as a Suspect Classification

In recent years, the United States Supreme Court has demonstrated a marked antipathy toward legislative classifications which discriminate on the basis of certain "suspect" personal characteristics. One factor which has repeatedly come under the close scrutiny of the high court is wealth. "Lines drawn on the basis of wealth or property, like those of race [citation], are traditionally disfavored.".... Invalidating the Virginia poll tax in *Harper*, the court stated: "To introduce wealth or payment of a fee as a measure of a voter's qualifications is to introduce a capricious or irrelevant factor.".... "[A] careful examination on our part is especially warranted where lines are drawn on the basis of wealth...[a] factor which would independently render a classification highly suspect and thereby demand a more exacting judicial scrutiny...."

* * *

...[W]e reject defendants' underlying thesis that classification by wealth is constitutional so long as the wealth is that of the district, not the individual. We think that discrimination on the basis of district wealth is equally invalid. The commercial and industrial property which augments a district's tax base is distributed unevenly throughout the state. To allot more educational dollars to the children of one district than to those of another merely because of the fortuitous presence of such property is to make the quality of a child's education dependent upon the location of private commercial and industrial establishments.[16] Surely, this is to rely on the most irrelevant of factors as the basis for educational financing.

Defendants, assuming for the sake of argument that the financing system does classify by wealth, nevertheless claim that no constitutional infirmity is involved because the complaint contains no allegation of purposeful or intentional discrimination....Thus, defendants contend, any unequal treatment is only de facto, not de jure. Since the United States Supreme Court has not held de facto school segregation on the basis of race to be unconstitutional, so the argument goes, de facto classifications on the basis of wealth are presumptively valid.

We think that the whole structure of this argument must fall for want of a solid foundation in law and logic....[N]one of the wealth classifications previously invalidated by the United States Supreme Court or this court has been the product of purposeful discrimination. Instead, these prior decisions have involved "unintentional" classifications whose impact simply fell more heavily on the poor.

* * *

We turn now to defendants' related contention that the instant case involves at most de facto discrimination. We disagree. Indeed, we find the case unusual in the extent to which governmental action is the cause of the wealth classifications. The school funding scheme is mandated in every detail by the California Constitution and statutes. Although private residential and commercial patterns may be partly responsible for the distribution of assessed valuation throughout the state, such patterns are shaped and hardened by zoning ordinances and other governmental land-use controls which promote economic exclusivity....

Finally, even assuming arguendo that defendants are correct in their contention that the instant discrimination based on wealth is merely de facto, and not de jure,...such discrimination cannot be justified by analogy to de facto racial segregation. Although the United States Supreme Court has not yet ruled on the constitutionality of de facto racial segregation, this court eight years ago held such segregation invalid, and declared that school boards should take affirmative steps to alleviate racial imbalance, however created. (*Jackson v. Pasadena City School Dist.* (1963) 59 Cal.2d 876, 881)....

B
Education as a Fundamental Interest

* * *

Until the present time wealth classifications have been invalidated only in conjunction with a limited number of fundamental interests—rights of defendants in criminal cases...and voting rights....Plaintiffs' contention—that education is a fundamental interest which may not be conditioned on wealth—is not supported by any direct authority.[22]

We, therefore, begin by examining the indispensable role which education plays in the modern industrial state. This role, we believe, has two significant aspects: first, education is a major determinant of an individual's chances for economic and social success in our competitive society; second, education is a unique influence on a child's development as a citizen and his participation in political and community life. "[The] pivotal position of education to success in American society and its essential role in opening up to the individual the central experiences of our culture lend it an importance that is undeniable."....Thus, education is the lifeline of both the individual and society.

The fundamental importance of education has been recognized in other contexts by the United States Supreme Court and by this court. These decisions— while not legally controlling on the exact issue before us—are persuasive in their accurate factual description of the significance of learning....

The classic expression of this position came in *Brown v. Board of Education* (1954) 347 U.S. 483..., which invalidated de jure segregation by race in public schools...

* * *

When children living in remote areas brought an action to compel local school authorities to furnish them bus transportation to class, we stated: "We indulge in no hyperbole to assert that society has a compelling interest in affording children an opportunity to attend school. This was evidenced more than three centuries ago, when Massachusetts provided the first public school system in 1647. [Citation.] And today an education has become the *sine qua non* of useful existence....In light of the public interest in conserving the resource of young minds, we must unsympathetically examine any action of a public body which has the effect of depriving children of the opportunity to obtain an education." (Fn. omitted.)....

And long before these last mentioned cases, in *Piper v. Big Pine School Dist.*, *supra*, 193 Cal. 664, where an Indian girl sought to attend state public schools, we declared: "[The] common schools are doorways opening into chambers of science, art, and the learned professions, as well as into fields of industrial and commercial activities. Opportunities for securing employment are often more or less dependent upon the rating which a youth, as a pupil of our public institutions, has received in his school work. These are rights and privileges that cannot be denied." (*Id.* at p. 673;...) Although Manjares and Piper involved actual exclusion from the public schools, surely the right to an education today means more than access to a classroom.[24]

* * *

We are convinced that the distinctive and priceless function of education in our society warrants, indeed compels, our treating it as a "fundamental interest."...

First, education is essential in maintaining what several commentators have termed "free enterprise democracy"—that is, preserving an individual's opportunity to compete successfully in the economic marketplace, despite a disadvantaged background. Accordingly, the public schools of this state are the bright hope for entry of the poor and oppressed into the mainstream of American society....

Second, education is universally relevant. "Not every person finds it necessary to call upon the fire department or even the police in an entire lifetime. Relatively few are on welfare. Every person, however, benefits from education ...."

Third, public education continues over a lengthy period of life—between 10 and 13 years. Few other government services have such sustained, intensive contact with the recipient.

Fourth, education is unmatched in the extent to which it molds the personality of the youth of society....

Finally, education is so important that the state has made it compulsory—not only in the requirement of attendance but also by assignment to a particular district and school....

C
The Financing System Is Not Necessary to Accomplish a Compelling State Interest

* * *

[E]ven assuming arguendo that local administrative control may be a compelling state interest, the present financial system cannot be considered necessary to further this interest. No matter how the state decides to finance its system of public education, it can still leave this decision-making power in the hands of local districts.

The other asserted policy interest is that of allowing a local district to choose how much it wishes to spend on the education of its children. Defendants argue: "[If] one district raises a lesser amount per pupil than another district, this is a matter of choice and preference of the individual district, and reflects the individual desire for lower taxes rather than an expanded educational program, or may reflect a greater interest within that district in such other services that are supported by local property taxes as, for example, police and fire protection or hospital services."

We need not decide whether such decentralized financial decision-making is a compelling state interest, since under the present financing system, such fiscal freewill is a cruel illusion for the poor school districts. We cannot agree that Baldwin Park residents care less about education than those in Beverly Hills solely because Baldwin Park spends less than $600 per child while Beverly Hills spends over $1,200....

* * *

Defendants' second argument boils down to this: if the equal protection clause commands that the relative wealth of school districts may not determine the quality of public education, it must be deemed to direct the same command to all governmental entities in respect to all tax-supported public services;...and such a principle would spell the destruction of local government. We unhesitatingly reject this argument. We cannot share defendants' unreasoned apprehensions of such dire consequences from our holding today. Although we intimate no views on other governmental services,[31] we are satisfied that, as we have explained, its uniqueness among public activities clearly demonstrates that education must respond to the command of the equal protection clause.

* * *

By our holding today we further the cherished idea of American education that in a democratic society free public schools shall make available to all children equally the abundant gifts of learning. This was the credo of Horace Mann, which has been the heritage and the inspiration of this country. "I believe," he wrote, "in the existence of a great, immortal immutable principle of natural law, or natural ethics,—a principle antecedent to all human institutions, and incapable of being abrogated by any ordinance of man...which proves the absolute right to an education of every human being that comes into the world, and which, of course, proves the correlative duty of every government to see that the means of that education are provided for all...."

* * *

[2] California educational revenues for the fiscal year 1968–1969 came from the following sources: local property taxes, 55.7 percent; state aid, 35.5 percent; federal funds, 6.1 percent; miscellaneous sources, 2.7 percent.

[3] Most school aid determinations are based not on total enrollment, but on "average daily attendance" (ADA), a figure computed by adding together the number of students actually present on each school day and dividing that total by the number of days school was taught. (§§ 11252, 11301, 11401.) In practice, ADA approximates 98 percent of total enrollment....When we refer herein to figures on a "per pupil" or "per child" basis, we mean per unit of ADA.

[6] Districts which maintain "unnecessary small schools" receive $10 per pupil less in foundation funds...Certain types of school districts are eligible for "bonus" foundation funds. Elementary districts receive an additional $30 for each student in grades 1 through 3; this sum is intended to reduce class size in those grades....Unified school districts get an extra $20 per child in foundation support....

[7] This is simply a "computational" tax rate used to measure the relative wealth of the district for equalization purposes. It bears no relation to the tax rate actually set by the district in levying local real property taxes.

[16] Defendants contend that different levels of educational expenditure do not affect the quality of education. However, plaintiffs' complaint specifically alleges the contrary, and for purposes of testing the sufficiency of a complaint against a general demurrer, we must take its allegations to be true.

Although we recognize that there is considerable controversy among educators over the relative impact of educational spending and environmental influences on school achievement... we note that the several courts which have considered contentions similar to defendants' have uniformly rejected them.

In *McInnis v. Shapiro* (N.D.Ill. 1968) 293 F.Supp. 327, *affd. mem. sub nom. McInnis v. Ogilvie* (1969) 394 U.S. 322...heavily relied on by defendants, a three-judge federal court stated: "Presumably, students receiving a $1,000 education are better educated that [sic] those acquiring a $600 schooling."....

Spending differentials of up to $130 within a district were characterized as "spectacular" in *Hobson v. Hansen supra*, 269 F.Supp. 401. Responding to defendants' claim that the varying expenditures did not reflect actual educational benefits, the court replied: "To a great extent...defendants' own evidence verifies that the comparative per pupil figures do refer to actual educational advantages in the high cost schools, especially with respect to the caliber of the teaching staff."....

[22] In *Shapiro v. Thompson* (1969) 394 U.S. 618..., in which the Supreme Court invalidated state minimum residence requirements for welfare benefits, the high court indicated, in dictum, that certain wealth discrimination in the area of education would be unconstitutional: "We recognize that a State has a valid interest in preserving the fiscal integrity of its programs. It may legitimately attempt to limit its expenditures, whether for public assistance, public education, or any other program. But a State may not accomplish such a purpose by invidious distinctions between classes of its citizens. It could not, for example, reduce expenditures for education by barring indigent children from its schools."....Although the high court referred to actual exclusion from school, rather than discrimination in expenditures for education, we think the constitutional principle is the same. (*See* fn. 24, and accompanying text.)

A federal Court of Appeals has also held that education is arguably a fundamental interest. In *Hargrave v. McKinney* (5th Cir. 1969) 413 F.2d 320, the Fifth Circuit ruled that a three-judge district court must be convened to consider the constitutionality of a Florida statue which limited the local property tax rate which a county could levy in raising school revenue. Plaintiffs contended that the statute violated the equal protection clause because it allowed counties with a high per-pupil assessed valuation to raise much more local revenue than counties with smaller tax bases. The court stated: "The equal protection argument advanced by plaintiffs is the crux of the case. Noting that lines drawn on wealth are suspect [fn. omitted] and that we are here dealing with interests which may well be deemed fundamental, [fn. omitted] we cannot say that there is no reasonably arguable theory of equal protection which would support a decision in favor of the plaintiffs. [Citations.]" (*Id.* at p. 324.)

On remand, a three-judge court held the statute unconstitutional because there was no rational basis for the discriminatory effect which it had in poor counties. Having invalidated the statute under the traditional equal protection test, the court declined to consider plaintiffs' contention that education was a fundamental interest, requiring application of the "strict scrutiny" equal protection standard. (*Hargrave v. Kirk supra*, 313 F.Supp. 944.) On appeal, the Supreme Court vacated the district court's decision on other grounds, but indicated that on remand the lower court should thoroughly explore the equal protection issue. (*Askew v. Hargrave* (1971) 401 U.S. 476)

[24] *Cf. Reynolds v. Sims* (1964) 377 U.S. 533, 562–563..., where the Supreme Court asserted that the right to vote is impaired not only when a qualified individual is barred from voting, but also when the impact of his ballot is diminished by unequal electoral apportionment: "It could hardly be gainsaid that a constitutional claim had been asserted by an allegation that certain otherwise qualified voters had been entirely prohibited from voting for members of their state legislature. And, if a State should provide that the votes of citizens in one part of the State should be given two times, or five times, or ten times the weight of votes of citizens in another part of the State, it could hardly be contended that the right to vote of those residing in the disfavored areas had not been effectively diluted....Of course, the effect of state legislative districting schemes which give the same number of representatives to unequal numbers of constituents is identical....One must be ever aware that the Constitution forbids 'sophisticated as well as simpleminded modes of discrimination.' [Citation.]" (Fn. omitted.)

[31] We note, however, that the Court of Appeals for the Fifth Circuit has recently held that the equal protection clause forbids a town to discriminate racially in the provision of municipal services. In *Hawkins v. Town of Shaw, Mississippi supra*, 437 F.2d 1286, the court held that the town of Shaw, Mississippi had an affirmative duty to equalize such services as street paving and lighting, sanitary sewers, surface water drainage, water mains and fire hydrants. The decision applied the "strict scrutiny" equal protection standard and reversed the decision of the district court which, relying on the traditional test, had found no constitutional infirmity.

Although racial discrimination was the basis of the decision, the court intimated that wealth discrimination in the provision of city services might also be invalid: "Appellants also alleged the discriminatory provision of municipal services based on wealth. This claim was dropped on appeal. It is interesting to note, however, that the Supreme Court has stated that wealth as well as race renders a classification highly suspect and thus demanding of a more exacting judicial scrutiny. [Citation.]" (*Id.* at p. 1287, fn. 1.)

Questions for Discussion

1. The court writes that wealth is a "suspect classification" where a "fundamental interest" is at issue. Does that apply to free speech or to media access? Precedents have applied this concept to the right to vote, and to an attorney in a criminal matter; is education a different kind of application?

2. The court recognizes that local democracy is a "compelling state interest" warranting some variations based on wealth. Under what circumstances can that justify spending more on children? Can it be based on factors unrelated to need? Simply on the enhanced property values available to a school and its students? If everyone is assured a minimum floor of educational resources, can some parents/communities add to their floor? Does it matter if students from poorer neighborhoods are barred entry? What is the difference between such favoritism and the disparity created when the wealthy send their children to well-financed private schools?

Note on the Aftermath of *Serrano*: Federal Denial of Applicable Constitutional Right

In *San Antonio Independent School District v. Rodriguez*, 411 U.S. 1 (1973), the U.S. Supreme Court was presented with a Texas system of school finance similar to California's. Wide disparities in funding meant that students in poor areas would receive a fraction of the public investment committed to children in wealthier neighborhoods. As with California, locally financed schools meant that wealthy parents paid a lower property tax rate on their higher valued homes and were able to provide substantially more per student in K–12 spending. Nevertheless, the Court held that poor children were not a suspect classification. The Court wrote that no one is "absolutely precluded" from education, and concluded that "the class (impoverished children) is not saddled with such disabilities, or subjected to such a history of purposeful unequal treatment, or relegated to such a position of political powerlessness as to command extraordinary protection from the majoritarian political process." Hence, the Court found that strict scrutiny did not apply, and further held that the rational relation test was met because of the state's interest in "local participation and control." Accordingly, the means of funding chosen is not "invidiously discriminatory." The Court added that school taxation was a complex concept and that reforms in such areas "are matters reserved for the legislative processes of the various States."

Questions for Discussion

1. Can we rely on majority decisions of legislatures where a minority of impoverished children are disadvantaged *vis-à-vis* a majority? If a majority wishes to relegate such a group to an inferior public education system, who but the Court will draw a line for its protection? Is it a purpose of constitutional protections to limit the exploitation of the weak by the majority?

2. Is the cited fact that the poor are not "absolutely precluded" from education an appropriate criterion for constitutional acceptability? Are impoverished children not "saddled with" disabilities?

3.   Is education spending based explicitly on neighborhood wealth a form of "unequal treatment" as to the unwealthy? Is such inequality permissible so long as it is not "purposeful," as the Court suggests in *Rodriguez*? The state is purposefully basing school funding on the wealth of real property, knowing that substantial unequal funding will result. The Court might argue that the state's purpose is not unequal treatment, but "local control." But local control to do what? One could draw local lines to include the wealthy and poor together in a district, and have local control and little unequal treatment within the state. Where the state draws lines with substantial wealth disparity, knowing it will produce unequal education spending, is not unequal funding one (if not the central) purpose?

4.   Are questions of school finance impossibly complex? Has *Serrano* been impossible to implement in California? Is a command that financing not be based on the wealth of parents or neighborhoods, or commanding basic equality based on children served, that difficult of a concept? Has the Court used the complexity concern to eschew complex judgments in patent cases? In civil rights busing cases? In antitrust cases?

5.   Could the University of Texas spend less on the education of an admittee (or demand a higher tuition payment) because he grew up in a poor Texas town? Could it spend more on the education of a Texas student from a wealthy family for that reason? Could it discount his tuition? What is the difference between such a policy and the financing disparities found constitutional in *Rodriguez*?

6.   Is "local control" a factor with sufficient weight to vary education resources and opportunity based on wealth? Could the University of Texas, in the example above, argue that those citizens from the poorer areas do not contribute as much to the state budget financing the University and therefore their children should not receive the same educational value as those whose parents contribute more? What if the University operates a major online educational program for students who remain in their home towns, and charges less or offers more courses for students from wealthy towns? If such a University policy would be struck, would not twelve years of financial discrimination in basic, required public education—based on the wealth of parents, or on the locale of residence—be *a fortiori* objectionable?

7.   Would it be constitutionally permissible for a state to issue a contract to build a road, but pay workers less who come from poorer communities? To pay workers less for construction through poorer neighborhoods? On the other hand, if a poor town builds a road, must it pay wages at the same level a wealthier community would offer? Must a wealthier town deny itself an extensive fancy local library because a poor town cannot afford one? Must it cross-subsidize libraries throughout the state if it wishes to build one for its own residents?

8. Do the answers to the questions above suggest that the decisions in *Serrano/Rodriguez* turn on one's vision of whose children these are? Are they the children of a town, with understandable variations based on local preferences, traditions, and wealth variations, or are they all properly children of California and Texas, respectively, entitled to equal educational opportunity before the sovereign state? Would such a judgment change if the local entity receiving deference is not a town, but a school district? Does it matter that states commonly have from 200 to 1,200 such districts, with separate boundaries from other jurisdictions and usually performing only the function of school finance and control under the mandatory guidelines of the state?

9. The difference between *Serrano* and *Rodriguez* also necessarily turns on the weight given to K–12 education as a right/opportunity. Child advocates cite three features commending its elevated status: (a) its provision by the state or its subdivisions, (b) its compulsory nature, and (c) its direct relationship to higher education opportunity, future income, and livelihood. Can a strong argument be made for equal provision of many public services, *e.g.*, water, sewage, parks, trash collection? Many of these services are financed by special districts similar in structure to school districts and allowed relative financial autonomy. Those in the district pay fees and finance what is provided to those who pay for it. Is education different, or does the equality principle of *Serrano* (where the state or its agencies provide a basic service) properly apply beyond education? What factors should dictate line drawing for equal protection application?

Note on State Actions Following the *Rodriguez* Refusal to Federally Follow *Serrano*

As noted above, the federal jurisdiction refused to follow *Serrano*. However, California subsequently reaffirmed its holding, stating that it rested on California's constitution (on "state grounds") regardless of federal constitutional status.[6] Since 1971, similar court challenges to school funding schemes have occurred in forty-two states, with funding systems overturned in twenty-eight.[7]

The successful challenges in states such as New Jersey, New York, Arkansas, and Massachusetts turned to state constitutions and statutes and to state courts to challenge education inadequacy and disparities, particularly affecting impoverished children and minorities. The emphasis turned more to inadequacy in recent years, rather than relying solely on a "strict scrutiny" equal protection theory, particularly based on funding variations per se or on relatively lower funding for more impoverished children. A particularly dramatic case challenging school financing on such an "inadequacy" basis is *Connecticut Coalition for Justice in Education Funding v. Rell*, 327 Conn. 650 (2018). In 2010, the appellate court issued a lengthy opinion rejecting justiciability defenses, noting that the plaintiffs merely sought declaratory relief that the system was unlawful and that deference to the other two branches for political solutions as to "how" the illegal/inadequate funding would be resolved is properly dealt with as may be subsequently necessary. When the case returned to the trial court, the judge issued a scathing 90-page ruling which he read for more than two hours from the bench. Although he found that the state spent an adequate amount on education, he excoriated the current system, finding its funding formulas and educational standards irrational, leaving "rich school districts to flourish and poor school districts to flounder." He then ordered a near-total revamping of educational policy in the state.[8] In 2018, the Connecticut Supreme Court overturned the ruling, determining that any deficiencies and needed reforms were within the purview of the legislature, stating that "[i]t is not the function of the courts…to create educational policy or to attempt by judicial fiat to eliminate all of the societal deficiencies that continue to frustrate the state's educational efforts."[9]

Although the Connecticut Supreme Court brought an end to longstanding litigation in its state, the Kansas Supreme Court continues to maintain a role in assessing the sufficiency of legislative efforts to achieve adequate education funding. In 2017, the Kansas Supreme Court, in *Gannon v. State*, 306 Kan. 1170 (2017), issued its fifth ruling in litigation originally filed in 2010. The court there determined that the state legislature had not met its constitutional obligation to adequately and equitably fund the state's public schools. The court ordered the legislature to develop a new funding system by the following year, stating that "after that date we will not allow ourselves to be placed in the position of being complicit actors in the continuing deprivation of a constitutionally adequate and equitable education owed to hundreds of thousands of Kansas school children."[10] On June 25, 2018, the court found that the state's remediation plan had met the equity requirement but not the adequacy requirement under its constitution. In finding the state's spending on education inadequate, the court elected to retain jurisdiction to ensure constitutional infirmities are ultimately resolved.[11]

In California, child advocates filed *Williams v. State* in 2000 (San Francisco County Superior Court, Case No. 312236). The complaint charged that tens of thousands of children were "being deprived of basic educational opportunities available to more privileged children" because their schools lacked "the bare essentials required of a free and common school education." The plaintiffs contended that the schools lacked sufficient classrooms, desks, qualified teachers, books, healthy and safe facilities and even functioning bathrooms, and that some schools were infested with rats and cockroaches. Contentions included a description of Balboa High School in San Francisco infested with mice, a class of fifty-four students had only thirty desks, and the 1,200-student school had only one bathroom with four stalls available for girls, in which "[a] soiled feminine napkin and a moldy ice cream bar remained" for an entire school year. At San Francisco's Bryant Elementary School, thirty-seven fifth-grade students shared twenty social studies textbooks, and temperatures in some classrooms reached ninety-two degrees, while on cold days students had to wear coats and mittens in class. Some students at Susan Miller Dorsey Senior High School in Los Angeles had to stand or sit on counters for the entire school year because of the lack of desks, some classes did not have any books at all, and broken windows sat exposed for two years.

The plaintiffs, almost entirely minorities, also noted that in forty-two of the forty-six schools named, "nonwhite students constitute far more than half the student body." The complaint contended that the conditions violated "minimal education tools needed to pass mandatory graduation tests" and violated "every concept of fundamental fairness and due process" as well as Article I, Sections 7(a) and 15 of the California Constitution, the state's equal protection clauses and the California Constitution's imposed state duty to provide to the Plaintiff class the opportunity to obtain a basic education," and that the schools' conditions violated Article IX, section 5 of the state Constitution, which requires the state to provide a free education in a system of common schools. The complaint adds federal law civil rights violations and provisions of California law that obligate the state to "ensure that every child in California has an opportunity to obtain a basic education" and "ensure that no child is compelled to attend a fundamentally unequal school that lacks those requirements of a basic education that are provided to most children." The case was settled at the trial court level in 2005 for $1 billion in additional state funding for relevant schools.

In 2010, plaintiffs in *Campaign for Quality Education v. State of California* (Alameda County Superior Court, Case No. RG10524770) sought to challenge the adequacy of California education financing, arguing that current resources allocated to public schools—among the lowest in the nation—denied children the opportunity to obtain a meaningful education. In 2016, the California Court of Appeal ruled that despite the California Supreme Court's recognition of education as a fundamental right in *Serrano*, the state constitution does not guarantee any particular level of educational quality.[12] The California Supreme Court elected not to review the appellate court ruling.

A recent tactic in school finance litigation is to argue that students have a constitutional right to literacy predicated on the idea that the exercise of all other constitutional rights rely on the ability to read. The first case to pose this argument, filed in federal court in 2016, was ultimately dismissed. However, a companion case in California arguing for the right to evidence-based literary instruction on the same grounds has been allowed to proceed.[13]

Recent research indicates that increased per pupil spending leads to more completed years of education, higher wages, and a reduction in the incidence of adult poverty, with greater impact among children from low-income families.[14] However, millions of American children remain in schools where equality of opportunity is denied in the most basic sense: the state allows unequal K–12 education spending, based on the wealth of parents. The discrimination disfavors impoverished children. Nationwide, the school districts with the highest poverty rate receive about $1,000 less per student than the districts with the lowest poverty rates. This disparity exists despite research showing that it can cost at least twice as much to educate an impoverished student to the same level as a more affluent student.[15]

4. Undocumented Children

Plyler v. Doe

457 U.S. 202 (1982)
JUSTICE BRENNAN delivered the opinion of the Court.

The question presented by these cases is whether, consistent with the Equal Protection Clause of the Fourteenth Amendment, Texas may deny to undocumented school-age children the free public education that it provides to children who are citizens of the United States or legally admitted aliens.

I

Since the late 19th century, the United States has restricted immigration into this country. Unsanctioned entry into the United States is a crime, 8 U.S.C. § 1325, and those who have entered unlawfully are subject to deportation...But despite the existence of these legal restrictions, a substantial number of persons have succeeded in unlawfully entering the United States, and now live within various States, including the State of Texas.

In May 1975, the Texas Legislature revised its education laws to withhold from local school districts any state funds for the education of children who were not "legally admitted" into the United States. The 1975 revision also authorized local school districts to deny enrollment in their public schools to children not "legally admitted" to the country.... These cases involve constitutional challenges to those provisions.

* * *

...[T]he District Court made extensive findings of fact. The court found that neither § 21.031 nor the School District policy implementing it had "either the purpose or effect of keeping illegal aliens out of the State of Texas." 458 F.Supp. 569, 575 (1978). Respecting defendants' further claim that § 21.031 was simply a financial measure designed to avoid a drain on the State's fisc, the court recognized that the increases in population resulting from the immigration of Mexican nationals into the United States had created problems for the public schools of the State, and that these problems were exacerbated by the special educational needs of immigrant Mexican children. The court noted, however, that the increase in school enrollment was primarily attributable to the admission of children who were legal residents....It also found that while the "exclusion of all undocumented children from the public schools in Texas would eventually result in economies at some level,"... funding from both the State and Federal Governments was based primarily on the number of children enrolled. In net effect then, barring undocumented children from the schools would save money, but it would "not necessarily" improve "the quality of education."....The court further observed that the impact of § 21.031 was borne primarily by a very small subclass of illegal aliens, "entire families who have migrated illegally and—for all practical purposes—permanently to the United States." *Id.* at 578 [3] Finally, the court noted that under current laws and practices "the illegal alien of today may well be the legal alien of tomorrow,"[4] and that without an education, these undocumented children, "[already] disadvantaged as a result of poverty, lack of English-speaking ability, and undeniable racial prejudices,...will become permanently locked into the lowest socio-economic class." *Id.* at 577.

* * *

II

The Fourteenth Amendment provides that "[no] State shall...deprive any person of life, liberty, or property, without due process of law; nor deny to any person within its jurisdiction the equal protection of the laws." (Emphasis added.) Appellants argue at the outset that undocumented aliens, because of their immigration status, are not "persons within the jurisdiction" of the State of Texas, and that they therefore have no right to the equal protection of Texas law. We reject this argument. Whatever his status under the immigration laws, an alien is surely a "person" in any ordinary sense of that term. Aliens, even aliens whose presence in this country is unlawful, have long been recognized as "persons" guaranteed due process of law by the Fifth and Fourteenth Amendments.[9]

* * *

Sheer incapability or lax enforcement of the laws barring entry into this country, coupled with the failure to establish an effective bar to the employment of undocumented aliens, has resulted in the creation of a substantial "shadow population" of illegal migrants—numbering in the millions—within our borders.[17] This situation raises the specter of a permanent caste of undocumented resident aliens, encouraged by some to remain here as a source of cheap labor, but nevertheless denied the benefits that our society makes available to citizens and lawful residents.[18] The existence of such an underclass presents most difficult problems for a Nation that prides itself on adherence to principles of equality under law.[19]

The children who are plaintiffs in these cases are special members of this underclass. Persuasive arguments support the view that a State may withhold its beneficence from those whose very presence within the United States is the product of their own unlawful conduct. These arguments do not apply with the same force to classifications imposing disabilities on the minor children of such illegal entrants. At the least, those who elect to enter our territory by stealth and in violation of our law should be prepared to bear the consequences, including, but not limited to, deportation. But the children of those illegal entrants are not comparably situated. Their "parents have the ability to conform their conduct to societal norms," and presumably the ability to remove themselves from the State's jurisdiction; but the children who are plaintiffs in these cases "can affect neither their parents' conduct nor their own status."....Even if the State found it expedient to control the conduct of adults by acting against their children, legislation directing the onus of a parent's misconduct against his children does not comport with fundamental conceptions of justice.

* * *

Public education is not a "right" granted to individuals by the Constitution.... But neither is it merely some governmental "benefit" indistinguishable from other forms of social welfare legislation. Both the importance of education in maintaining our basic institutions, and the lasting impact of its deprivation on the life of the child, mark the distinction. The "American people have always regarded education and [the] acquisition of knowledge as matters of supreme importance."....We have recognized "the public schools as a most vital civic institution for the preservation of a democratic system of government,"....In addition, education provides the basic tools by which individuals might lead economically productive lives to the benefit of us all. In sum, education has a fundamental role in maintaining the fabric of our society. We cannot ignore the significant social costs borne by our Nation when select groups are denied the means to absorb the values and skills upon which our social order rests.

In addition to the pivotal role of education in sustaining our political and cultural heritage, denial of education to some isolated group of children poses an affront to one of the goals of the Equal Protection Clause: the abolition of governmental barriers presenting unreasonable obstacles to advancement on the basis of individual merit. Paradoxically, by depriving the children of any disfavored group of an education, we foreclose the means by which that group might raise the level of esteem in which it is held by the majority. But more directly, "education prepares individuals to be self-reliant and self-sufficient participants in society."....Illiteracy is an enduring disability. The inability to read and write will handicap the individual deprived of a basic education each and every day of his life. The inestimable toll of that deprivation on the social, economic, intellectual, and psychological well-being of the individual, and the obstacle it poses to individual achievement, make it most difficult to reconcile the cost or the principle of a status-based denial of basic education with the framework of equality embodied in the Equal Protection Clause.[20]

* * *

...In determining the rationality of § 21.031, we may appropriately take into account its costs to the Nation and to the innocent children who are its victims. In light of these countervailing costs, the discrimination contained in § 21.031 can hardly be considered rational unless it furthers some substantial goal of the State.

* * *

To be sure, like all persons who have entered the United States unlawfully, these children are subject to deportation....But there is no assurance that a child subject to deportation will ever be deported. An illegal entrant might be granted federal permission to continue to reside in this country, or even to become a citizen.... In light of the discretionary federal power to grant relief from deportation, a State cannot realistically determine that any particular undocumented child will in fact be deported until after deportation proceedings have been completed. It would of course be most difficult for the State to justify a denial of education to a child enjoying an inchoate federal permission to remain.

We are reluctant to impute to Congress the intention to withhold from these children, for so long as they are present in this country through no fault of their own, access to a basic education....

V

Appellants argue that the classification at issue furthers an interest in the "preservation of the state's limited resources for the education of its lawful residents."[21].... Of course, a concern for the preservation of resources standing alone can hardly justify the classification used in allocating those resources....The State must do more than justify its classification with a concise expression of an intention to discriminate...

First, appellants appear to suggest that the State may seek to protect itself from an influx of illegal immigrants. While a State might have an interest in mitigating the potentially harsh economic effects of sudden shifts in population,[23] § 21.031 hardly offers an effective method of dealing with an urgent demographic or economic problem. There is no evidence in the record suggesting that illegal entrants impose any significant burden on the State's economy. To the contrary, the available evidence suggests that illegal aliens underutilize public services, while contributing their labor to the local economy and tax money to the state fisc. 458 F.Supp. at 578; 501 F.Supp. at 570–571. The dominant incentive for illegal entry into the State of Texas is the availability of employment; few if any illegal immigrants come to this country, or presumably to the State of Texas, in order to avail themselves of a free education.[24] Thus, even making the doubtful assumption that the net impact of illegal aliens on the economy of the State is negative, we think it clear that "[charging] tuition to undocumented children constitutes a ludicrously ineffectual attempt to stem the tide of illegal immigration," at least when compared with the alternative of prohibiting the employment of illegal aliens....

* * *

VI

If the State is to deny a discrete group of innocent children the free public education that it offers to other children residing within its borders, that denial must be justified by a showing that it furthers some substantial state interest. No such showing was made here. Accordingly, the judgment of the Court of Appeals in each of these cases is

Affirmed.

[3] The court contrasted this group with those illegal aliens who entered the country alone in order to earn money to send to their dependents in Mexico, and who in many instances remained in this country for only a short period of time. 458 F.Supp., at 578.

[4] Plaintiffs' expert, Dr. Gilbert Cardenas, testified that "fifty to sixty per cent...of current legal alien workers were formerly illegal aliens."....A defense witness, Rolan Heston, District Director of the Houston District of the Immigration and Naturalization Service, testified that "undocumented children can and do live in the United States for years, and adjust their status through marriage to a citizen or permanent resident."....The court also took notice of congressional proposals to "legalize" the status of many unlawful entrants. *Id.* at 577–578....

[9] It would be incongruous to hold that the United States, to which the Constitution assigns a broad authority over both naturalization and foreign affairs, is barred from invidious discrimination with respect to unlawful aliens, while exempting the States from a similar limitation. *See* 426 U.S., at 84-86.

[17] The Attorney General recently estimated the number of illegal aliens within the United States at between 3 and 6 million. In presenting to both the Senate and House of Representatives several Presidential proposals for reform of the immigration laws—including one to "legalize" many of the illegal entrants currently

residing in the United States by creating for them a special status under the immigration laws—the Attorney General noted that this subclass is largely composed of persons with a permanent attachment to the Nation, and that they are unlikely to be displaced from our territory:

"We have neither the resources, the capability, nor the motivation to uproot and deport millions of illegal aliens, many of whom have become, in effect, members of the community. By granting limited legal status to the productive and law-abiding members of this shadow population, we will recognize reality and devote our enforcement resources to deterring future illegal arrivals."....

[19] We reject the claim that "illegal aliens" are a "suspect class." No case in which we have attempted to define a suspect class,...Unlike most of the classifications that we have recognized as suspect, entry into this class, by virtue of entry into this country, is the product of voluntary action. Indeed, entry into the class is itself a crime. In addition, it could hardly be suggested that undocumented status is a "constitutional irrelevancy." With respect to the actions of the Federal Government, alienage classifications may be intimately related to the conduct of foreign policy, to the federal prerogative to control access to the United States, and to the plenary federal power to determine who has sufficiently manifested his allegiance to become a citizen of the Nation. No State may independently exercise a like power. But if the Federal Government has by uniform rule prescribed what it believes to be appropriate standards for the treatment of an alien subclass, the States may, of course, follow the federal direction....

[20] Because the State does not afford noncitizens the right to vote, and may bar noncitizens from participating in activities at the heart of its political community, appellants argue that denial of a basic education to these children is of less significance than the denial to some other group. Whatever the current status of these children, the courts below concluded that many will remain here permanently and that some indeterminate number will eventually become citizens. The fact that many will not is not decisive, even with respect to the importance of education to participation in core political institutions. "[The] benefits of education are not reserved to those whose productive utilization of them is a certainty...." 458 F.Supp., at 581, n. 14. In addition, although a noncitizen "may be barred from full involvement in the political arena, he may play a role—perhaps even a leadership role—in other areas of import to the community." Nyquist v. Mauclet, 432 U.S. 1, 12 (1977). Moreover, the significance of education to our society is not limited to its political and cultural fruits. The public schools are an important socializing institution, imparting those shared values through which social order and stability are maintained.

[21] Appellant School District sought at oral argument to characterize the alienage classification contained in § 21.031 as simply a test of residence. We are unable to uphold § 21.031 on that basis. Appellants conceded that if, for example, a Virginian or a legally admitted Mexican citizen entered Tyler with his school-age children, intending to remain only six months, those children would be viewed as residents entitled to attend Tyler schools....It is thus clear that Tyler's residence argument amounts to nothing more than the assertion that illegal entry, without more, prevents a person from becoming a resident for purposes of enrolling his children in the public schools. A State may not, however, accomplish what would otherwise be prohibited by the Equal Protection Clause, merely by defining a disfavored group as nonresident. And illegal entry into the country would not, under traditional criteria, bar a person from obtaining domicile within a State....Appellants have not shown that the families of undocumented children do not comply with the established standards by which the State historically tests residence. Apart from the alienage limitation, §21.031(b) requires a school district to provide education only to resident children. The school districts of the State are as free to apply to undocumented children established criteria for determining residence as they are to apply those criteria to any other child who seeks admission.

[23] Although the State has no direct interest in controlling entry into this country, that interest being one reserved by the Constitution to the Federal Government, unchecked unlawful migration might impair the State's economy generally, or the State's ability to provide some important service. Despite the exclusive federal control of this Nation's borders, we cannot conclude that the States are without any power to deter the influx of persons entering the United States against federal law, and whose numbers might have a discernible impact on traditional state concerns....

[24] The courts below noted the ineffectiveness of the Texas provision as a means of controlling the influx of illegal entrants into the State....("The evidence demonstrates that undocumented persons do not immigrate in search for a free public education. Virtually all of the undocumented persons who come into this country seek employment opportunities and not educational benefits....There was overwhelming evidence...of the unimportance of public education as a stimulus for immigration")....

JUSTICE MARSHALL, concurring.

While I join the Court opinion,...I continue to believe that an individual's interest in education is fundamental, and that this view is amply supported "by the unique status accorded public education by our society, and by the close relationship between education and some of our most basic constitutional values."...

* * *

CHIEF JUSTICE BURGER, with whom **JUSTICE WHITE**, **JUSTICE REHNQUIST** and **JUSTICE O'CONNOR** join, dissenting.

Were it our business to set the Nation's social policy, I would agree without hesitation that it is senseless for an enlightened society to deprive any children—including illegal aliens—of an elementary education. I fully agree that it would be folly—and wrong—to tolerate creation of a segment of society made up of illiterate persons, many having a limited or no command of our language.[1] However, the Constitution does not constitute us as "Platonic Guardians" nor does it vest in this Court the authority to strike down laws because they do not meet our standards of desirable social policy, "wisdom," or "common sense." See TVA v. Hill 437 U.S. 153, 194–195 (1978). We trespass on the assigned function of the political branches under our structure of limited and separated powers when we assume a policymaking role as the Court does today.

The Court makes no attempt to disguise that it is acting to make up for Congress' lack of "effective leadership" in dealing with the serious national problems caused by the influx of uncountable millions of illegal aliens across our borders.[2] The failure of enforcement of the immigration laws over more than a decade and the inherent difficulty and expense of sealing our vast borders have combined to create a grave socioeconomic dilemma. It is a dilemma that has not yet even been fully assessed, let alone addressed. However, it is not the function of the Judiciary to provide "effective leadership" simply because the political branches of government fail to do so.

The Court's holding today manifests the justly criticized judicial tendency to attempt speedy and wholesale formulation of "remedies" for the failures—or simply the laggard pace—of the political processes of our system of government. The Court employs, and in my view abuses, the Fourteenth Amendment in an effort to become an omnipotent and omniscient problem solver. That the motives for doing so are noble and compassionate does not alter the fact that the Court distorts our constitutional function to make amends for the defaults of others.

* * *

In the end, we are told little more than that the level of scrutiny employed to strike down the Texas law applies only when illegal alien children are deprived of a public education,...[3] If ever a court was guilty of an unabashedly result-oriented approach, this case is a prime example.

(1)

The Court first suggests that these illegal alien children, although not a suspect class, are entitled to special solicitude under the Equal Protection Clause because they lack "control" over or "responsibility" for their unlawful entry into this country....Similarly, the Court appears to take the position that § 21.031 is presumptively "irrational" because it has the effect of imposing "penalties" on "innocent" children....[4]

* * *

(2)

The second strand of the Court's analysis rests on the premise that, although public education is not a constitutionally guaranteed right, "neither is it merely some governmental 'benefit' indistinguishable from other forms of social welfare legislation." ....Whatever meaning or relevance this opaque observation might have in some other context,[8] it simply has no bearing on the issues at hand. Indeed, it is never made clear what the Court's opinion means on this score.

The importance of education is beyond dispute. Yet we have held repeatedly that the importance of a governmental service does not elevate it to the status of a "fundamental right" for purposes of equal protection analysis....Moreover, the Court points to no meaningful way to distinguish between education and other governmental benefits in this context. Is the Court suggesting that education is more "fundamental" than food, shelter, or medical care?

* * *

189

Without laboring what will undoubtedly seem obvious to many, it simply is not "irrational" for a state to conclude that it does not have the same responsibility to provide benefits for persons whose very presence in the state and this country is illegal as it

does to provide for persons lawfully present. By definition, illegal aliens have no right whatever to be here, and the state may reasonably, and constitutionally, elect not to provide them with governmental services at the expense of those who are lawfully in the state.[11]

* * *

Denying a free education to illegal alien children is not a choice I would make were I a legislator. Apart from compassionate considerations, the long-range costs of excluding any children from the public schools may well outweigh the costs of educating them. But that is not the issue; the fact that there are sound policy arguments against the Texas Legislature's choice does not render that choice an unconstitutional one.

II

The Constitution does not provide a cure for every social ill, nor does it vest judges with a mandate to try to remedy every social problem.

* * *

The solution to this seemingly intractable problem is to defer to the political processes, unpalatable as that may be to some.

[1] It does not follow, however, that a state should bear the costs of educating children whose illegal presence in this country results from the default of the political branches of the Federal Government. A state has no power to prevent unlawful immigration, and no power to deport illegal aliens; those powers are reserved exclusively to Congress and the Executive. If the Federal Government, properly chargeable with deporting illegal aliens, fails to do so, it should bear the burdens of their presence here. Surely if illegal alien children can be identified for purposes of this litigation, their parents can be identified for purposes of prompt deportation.

[2] The Department of Justice recently estimated the number of illegal aliens within the United States at between 3 and 6 million....

[3] The Court implies, for example, that the Fourteenth Amendment would not require a state to provide welfare benefits to illegal aliens.

[4] Both the opinion of the Court and JUSTICE POWELL's concurrence imply that appellees are being "penalized" because their parents are illegal entrants....However, Texas has classified appellees on the basis of their own illegal status, not that of their parents. Children born in this country to illegal alien parents, including some of appellees' siblings, are not excluded from the Texas schools. Nor does Texas discriminate against appellees because of their Mexican origin or citizenship. Texas provides a free public education to countless thousands of Mexican immigrants who are lawfully in this country.

[8] In support of this conclusion, the Court's opinion strings together quotations drawn from cases addressing such diverse matters as the right of individuals under the Due Process Clause to learn a foreign language, *Meyer v. Nebraska*, 262 U.S. 390 (1923); the First Amendment prohibition against state-mandated religious exercises in the public schools, *Abington School District v. Schempp*, 374 U.S. 203 (1963); and state impingements upon the free exercise of religion, *Wisconsin v. Yoder*, 406 U.S. 205 (1972). However, not every isolated utterance of this Court retains force when wrested from the context in which it was made.

[11] The Court suggests that the State's classification is improper because "[a]n illegal entrant might be granted federal permission to continue to reside in this country, or even to become a citizen."....However, once an illegal alien is given federal permission to remain, he is no longer subject to exclusion from the tuition-free public schools under § 21.031. The Court acknowledges that the Tyler Independent School District provides a free public education to any alien who has obtained, or is in the procession of obtaining, documentation from the United States Immigration and Naturalization Service. Thus, Texas has not taken it upon itself to determine which aliens are or are not entitled to United States residence....

Questions for Discussion

1. In 1994, California voters approved Proposition 187, barring undocumented immigrants from public school attendance. The initiative was struck by a federal district court judge and its appeal was dropped by the administration of Governor Gray Davis in 2000. However, if the state could demonstrate its purpose was not

to save money, but to discourage unlawful immigration by accommodating the children of parental violators, would it pass constitutional muster if reviewed today? If the state could show some inducement impact from free public education, would *Plyler* be decided differently?

2. Assume that the undocumented immigrants who are lawfully here (*e.g.*, "permanent residents under color of law" or PRUCOL residents) are excluded from the education ban. Would that make it constitutional?

3. Is it relevant that undocumented parents pay sales and other taxes, but their children would be deprived of public services they help finance?

4. The Court notes that undocumented immigrants are "persons" under the Constitution. Is it relevant that the sanction punishes children who have no control over the immigration status of their parents? If the immigration statutes could be enforced directly with greater efficacy than using denial of schooling for their children as a disincentive, would that be relevant? If undocumented immigrant parents are working the fields, caring for the yards, and supervising the children of upper class Americans, what are the ethical implications of education denial for children in lieu of enforcing immigration at point of employment? If such school denial were to be examined under strict scrutiny, can the state satisfy the least restrictive alternative requirement if it were shown to be avoiding enforcement through employer sanctions and that such employment is the primary inducement for immigration?

5. Are undocumented immigrant children a suspect class entitled to strict scrutiny? The *Serrano* case labeled education a fundamental right—is that status confirmed in *Plyler*? Blackmun's concurring opinion argues that although education is not a fundamental right, its denial must be based on more than rational relation. Is this a "heightened scrutiny" standard? What is its basis?

6. Is the denial of education to the undocumented so steeped in federal immigration policy that the states' options are pre-empted? Can they be required to fund the schooling of persons unlawfully in the state (and nation) insofar as the federal jurisdiction has failed to stop them at the border?

7. Under federal law, undocumented immigrants are not eligible for federal financial assistance for higher education. In addition, federal law denies state residency status to undocumented individuals, limiting options for more affordable in-state tuition. Given the correlation between level of education and level of income, is it rational to deny financial assistance for higher education to undocumented immigrants? In *Plyer*, the Court reasoned that undocumented children brought to the U.S. by their parents should not be held accountable for their parent's illegal action. Should this principle be applied to high school graduates seeking higher education?

B. CHILD LABOR

Child labor problems may involve issues of child neglect, abuse and exploitation due to the onerous nature of assigned work. However, beyond the working conditions themselves, the time demanded for substantial child employment may foreclose educational opportunity and limit a child's potential. Accordingly, the extent to which a child may work has been limited by law in the United States. The Fair Labor Standards Act of 1938 (FLSA, 29 U.S.C. § 201 *et seq.*) includes a ceiling on such employment, with states permitted to lower that ceiling further. *U.S. v. Darby*, 312 U.S. 100 (1941), upheld the constitutionality of this state interference with parental and contract rights of adults, *et al.* Many states have enacted stricter standards to protect children from work exploitation beyond applicable federal standards. However, in recent years, states have proposed rolling back child labor protections.

In *Prince v. Massachusetts*, 321 U.S.158 (1944), the Supreme Court upheld the conviction of an aunt (given parental status in the decision) for violating state child labor law where she took her nine-year-old niece to help her sell Jehovah's Witness periodicals on the street. The prohibition was upheld against the invocation of constitutional religious and parental rights. On the other hand, *Wisconsin v. Yoder*, 406 U.S. 205 (1972), upheld a religion-based limitation on public education, allowing Amish children to leave public school at the age of 16, even though they were subject to long hours of work, and most of the affected children thus leave Amish communities without traditional schooling beyond the 8th grade (see discussion in Chapter 13).

The federal FLSA prohibits "oppressive child labor," defined as the employment of a child under 16 years of age (except by a parent or guardian). Even a parent or guardian cannot employ a child in "manufacturing or mining," or in work listed by the Secretary of Labor as "particularly hazardous" (*e.g.*, explosives, meat packing, roofing, and excavation). As to the hazardous list, child labor is considered unlawfully oppressive to age 18. However, it is not "oppressive" to employ children down to the age of 14 outside of hazardous work, manufacturing or mining, if not interfering with education or jeopardizing child health and safety. In addition, work on farms is permitted for children down to the age of 12.

Remedy for violation of the FLSA rests with criminal and civil remedies available to the Secretary of Labor, primarily against employers. However, enforcement of these limited standards is rare. The Act provides for no private enforcement of its standards, and courts have refused to imply such a remedy, leaving enforcement to parallel state enactments.

State laws generally protect children from excessive work where they are under 18 years of age, are not emancipated by court order or marriage, are not parents, and have not graduated from high school. The states may and do add to the federal FLSA a list of jobs unacceptably hazardous for children, including dangerous machinery and sometimes construction.

Hours are commonly limited by the week and for school nights while children are in school. Most states also require work permits from a school (or other) official where children work during the school year. The federal statute includes no such requirement and so the terms vary among the states. The permit may require attestation that the child is satisfactorily attending school. It usually includes a description of the work and hours, and commonly requires a physician's attestation that the child is able to perform the assigned tasks without health risk. Finally, it requires a signature indicating parental or guardian consent.

The agricultural exemption affords unusual latitude for child labor (and education avoidance) beyond that granted to the Amish in *Yoder* (see Chapter 13 below). The agricultural exemptions in federal and state statutes allow children to be used for labor with little limitation. While the exemption may have envisioned children helping with the harvest on a family farm, it also applies to the highly mechanized farm operations of the modern era. Child labor and educational foreclosure are particularly prevalent among the children of undocumented agricultural workers. Pay is often below poverty levels in such families, safety net support (TANF and food stamps) is barred, and children are conscripted as workers to assist their families to survive. This work may involve dangerous machinery, pesticide exposure with enhanced child susceptibility to harm, and long hours. Although *Plyler* rejected the categorical exclusion of undocumented immigrants from public education (see discussion above), movement between fields may further preclude educational opportunity.

Exemptions also often apply to children working for their own parents or guardians, including employment in family-owned businesses, such as restaurants. Moreover, some states define "work" and "labor" as restricted to remunerative work, and fail to limit child employment at all for so-called "volunteer" work that is not compensated.

The lack of private federal remedy places substantial burden on state enforcement of child labor violations. State worker compensation statutes commonly bar private tort causes of action separate and apart from the compensation statute extant—if the law includes child labor prohibitions and hence occupies that field. Where the statute is silent about such requirements, a private tort action against an employer may generally lie. However, most such statutes include or address unlawful child labor sufficiently to foreclose private tort remedies. Hence, enforcement against employers where there is injury (usually the context) is usually confined to the remedies enumerated in that law. Often, violation of a child related provision may trigger an enhanced award from 150% to 300% of the remedy for other violations, but that enhancement is from the low base allowed for worker's compensation. It does not include pain and suffering, nor lost future wages, nor punitive damages. It often covers only medical or funeral expenses, and perhaps lost wages while unable to work, often a non-existent sum for a child legally barred from that work in the first place.

Worker compensation statutes may bar remedies outside their confines against employers, but traditional tort actions remain viable against other actors where injury or death has occurred to children who are unlawfully employed. Where such causes of action are allowed, they serve as an important deterrent to stimulate compliance. The standard defenses of contributory negligence, assumption of risk, or consent are unavailable.

State "Unfair Competition Acts" may be the most potent enforcement alternative. The hiring of underage labor may provide a business with a competitive advantage in violation of law and give rise to injunctive and restitutionary relief. Here, suit is not brought by the child or employees, but by a competitor, or by a public prosecutor in many states under unfair competition statutes.

C. PUBLIC SCHOOL DISCIPLINE

Goss v. Lopez
419 U.S. 565 (1975)

MR. JUSTICE WHITE delivered the opinion of the Court.

This appeal by various administrators of the Columbus, Ohio, Public School System (CPSS) challenges the judgment of a three-judge federal court, declaring that appellees—various high school students in the CPSS—were denied due process of law contrary to the command of the Fourteenth Amendment in that they were temporarily suspended from their high schools without a hearing either prior to suspension or within a reasonable time thereafter, and enjoining the administrators to remove all references to such suspensions from the students' records.

I

Ohio law, Rev. Code Ann. § 3313.64 (1972), provides for free education to all children between the ages of six and 21. Section 3313.66 of the Code empowers the principal of an Ohio public school to suspend a pupil for misconduct for up to 10 days or to expel him. In either case, he must notify the student's parents within 24 hours and state the reasons for his action. A pupil who is expelled, or his parents, may appeal the decision to the Board of Education and in connection therewith shall be permitted to be heard at the board meeting. The Board may reinstate the pupil following the hearing. No similar procedure is provided in § 3313.66 or any other provision of state law for a suspended student....

* * *

The proof below established that the suspensions arose out of a period of widespread student unrest in the CPSS during February and March 1971. Six of the named plaintiffs, Rudolph Sutton, Tyrone Washington, Susan Cooper, Deborah Fox, Clarence Byars, and Bruce Harris, were students at the Marion-Franklin High School and were each suspended for 10 days on account of disruptive or disobedient conduct committed in the presence of the school administrator who ordered the suspension. One of these, Tyrone Washington, was among a group of students demonstrating in the school auditorium while a class was being conducted there. He was ordered by the school principal to leave, refused to do so, and was suspended. Rudolph Sutton, in the presence of the principal, physically attacked a police officer who was attempting to remove Tyrone Washington from the auditorium. He was immediately suspended. The other four Marion-Franklin students were suspended for similar conduct. None was given a hearing to determine the operative facts underlying the suspension, but each, together with his or her parents, was offered the opportunity to attend a conference, subsequent to the effective date of the suspension, to discuss the student's future.

Two named plaintiffs, Dwight Lopez and Betty Crome, were students at the Central High School and McGuffey Junior High School, respectively. The former was suspended in connection with a disturbance in the lunchroom which involved some physical damage to school property. Lopez testified that at least 75 other students were suspended from his school on the same day. He also testified below that he was not a party to the destructive conduct but was instead an innocent bystander. Because no one from the school testified with regard to this incident, there is no evidence in the record indicating the official basis for concluding otherwise. Lopez never had a hearing.

Betty Crome was present at a demonstration at a high school other than the one she was attending. There she was arrested together with others, taken to the police station, and released without being formally charged. Before she went to school on the following day, she was notified that she had been suspended for a 10-day period. Because no one from the school testified with respect to this incident, the record does not disclose how the McGuffey Junior High School principal went about making the decision to suspend Crome, nor does it disclose on what information the decision was based. It is clear from the record that no hearing was ever held.

There was no testimony with respect to the suspension of the ninth named plaintiff, Carl Smith. The school files were also silent as to his suspension, although as to some, but not all, of the other named plaintiffs the files contained either direct references to their suspensions or copies of letters sent to their parents advising them of the suspension.

On the basis of this evidence, the three-judge court declared that plaintiffs were denied due process of law because they were "suspended without hearing prior to suspension or within a reasonable time thereafter,"....

* * *

II

* * *

...School authorities here suspended appellees from school for periods of up to 10 days based on charges of misconduct. If sustained and recorded, those charges could seriously damage the students' standing with their fellow pupils and their teachers as well as interfere with later opportunities for higher education and employment.[3] It is apparent that the claimed right of the State to determine unilaterally and without process whether that misconduct has occurred immediately collides with the requirements of the Constitution.

Appellants proceed to argue that even if there is a right to a public education protected by the Due Process Clause generally, the Clause comes into play only when the State subjects a student to a "severe detriment or grievous loss." The loss of 10 days, it is said, is neither severe nor grievous and the Due Process Clause is therefore of no relevance....

A short suspension is, of course, a far milder deprivation than expulsion. But, "education is perhaps the most important function of state and local governments," *Brown v. Board of Education*, 347 U.S. 483, 493 (1954), and the total exclusion from the educational process for more than a trivial period, and certainly if the suspension is for 10 days, is a serious event in the life of the suspended child. Neither the property interest in educational benefits temporarily denied nor the liberty interest in reputation, which is also implicated, is so insubstantial that suspensions may constitutionally be imposed by any procedure the school chooses, no matter how arbitrary....

III

"Once it is determined that due process applies, the question remains what process is due." We turn to that question, fully realizing as our cases regularly do that the interpretation and application of the Due Process Clause are intensely practical matters and that "[the] very nature of due process negates any concept of inflexible procedures universally applicable to every imaginable situation." [citation omitted] We are also mindful of our own admonition:

"Judicial interposition in the operation of the public school system of the Nation raises problems requiring care and restraint....By and large, public education in our Nation is committed to the control of state and local authorities."...

* * *

The difficulty is that our schools are vast and complex. Some modicum of discipline and order is essential if the educational function is to be performed. Events calling for discipline are frequent occurrences and sometimes require immediate, effective action. Suspension is considered not only to be a necessary tool to maintain order but a valuable

educational device. The prospect of imposing elaborate hearing requirements in every suspension case is viewed with great concern, and many school authorities may well prefer the untrammeled power to act unilaterally, unhampered by rules about notice and hearing. But it would be a strange disciplinary system in an educational institution if no communication was sought by the disciplinarian with the student in an effort to inform him of his dereliction and to let him tell his side of the story in order to make sure that an injustice is not done.[9]

We do not believe that school authorities must be totally free from notice and hearing requirements if their schools are to operate with acceptable efficiency. Students facing temporary suspension have interests qualifying for protection of the Due Process Clause, and due process requires, in connection with a suspension of 10 days or less, that the student be given oral or written notice of the charges against him and, if he denies them, an explanation of the evidence the authorities have and an opportunity to present his side of the story. The Clause requires at least these rudimentary precautions against unfair or mistaken findings of misconduct and arbitrary exclusion from school....

There need be no delay between the time "notice" is given and the time of the hearing. In the great majority of cases the disciplinarian may informally discuss the alleged misconduct with the student minutes after it has occurred. We hold only that, in being given an opportunity to explain his version of the facts at this discussion, the student first be told what he is accused of doing and what the basis of the accusation is....Since the hearing may occur almost immediately following the misconduct, it follows that as a general rule notice and hearing should precede removal of the student from school. We agree with the District Court, however, that there are recurring situations in which prior notice and hearing cannot be insisted upon. Students whose presence poses a continuing danger to persons or property or an ongoing threat of disrupting the academic process may be immediately removed from school. In such cases, the necessary notice and rudimentary hearing should follow as soon as practicable, as the District Court indicated.

In holding as we do, we do not believe that we have imposed procedures on school disciplinarians which are inappropriate in a classroom setting. Instead we have imposed requirements which are, if anything, less than a fair-minded school principal would impose upon himself in order to avoid unfair suspensions. Indeed, according to the testimony of the principal of Marion-Franklin High School, that school had an informal procedure, remarkably similar to that which we now require, applicable to suspensions generally but which was not followed in this case....

We stop short of construing the Due Process Clause to require, country-wide, that hearings in connection with short suspensions must afford the student the opportunity to secure counsel, to confront and cross-examine witnesses supporting the charge, or to call his own witnesses to verify his version of the incident. Brief disciplinary suspensions are almost countless. To impose in each such case even truncated trial-type procedures might well overwhelm administrative facilities in many places and, by diverting resources, cost more than it would save in educational effectiveness. Moreover, further formalizing the suspension process and escalating its formality and adversary nature may not only make it too costly as a regular disciplinary tool but also destroy its effectiveness as part of the teaching process.

* * *

We should also make it clear that we have addressed ourselves solely to the short suspension, not exceeding 10 days. Longer suspensions or expulsions for the remainder of the school term, or permanently, may require more formal procedures. Nor do we put aside the possibility that in unusual situations, although involving only a short suspension, something more than the rudimentary procedures will be required.

IV

The District Court found each of the suspensions involved here to have occurred without a hearing, either before or after the suspension, and that each suspension was therefore invalid and the statute unconstitutional insofar as it permits such suspensions

without notice or hearing. Accordingly, the judgment is

Affirmed.

[3] Appellees assert in their brief that four of 12 randomly selected Ohio colleges specifically inquire of the high school of every applicant for admission whether the applicant has ever been suspended. Appellees also contend that many employers request similar information.

[9] The facts involved in this case illustrate the point. Betty Crome was suspended for conduct which did not occur on school grounds, and for which mass arrests were made—hardly guaranteeing careful individualized factfinding by the police or by the school principal. She claims to have been involved in no misconduct. However, she was suspended for 10 days without ever being told what she was accused of doing or being given an opportunity to explain her presence among those arrested. Similarly, Dwight Lopez was suspended, along with many others, in connection with a disturbance in the lunchroom. Lopez says he was not one of those in the lunchroom who was involved. However, he was never told the basis for the principal's belief that he was involved, nor was he ever given an opportunity to explain his presence in the lunchroom. The school principals who suspended Crome and Lopez may have been correct on the merits, but it is inconsistent with the Due Process Clause to have made the decision that misconduct had occurred without at some meaningful time giving Crome or Lopez an opportunity to persuade the principals otherwise....

Dissent: MR. JUSTICE POWELL, with whom THE CHIEF JUSTICE, MR. JUSTICE BLACKMUN, and MR. JUSTICE REHNQUIST join, dissenting.

The Court today invalidates an Ohio statute that permits student suspensions from school without a hearing "for not more than ten days."[1] The decision unnecessarily opens avenues for judicial intervention in the operation of our public schools that may affect adversely the quality of education. The Court holds for the first time that the federal courts, rather than educational officials and state legislatures, have the authority to determine the rules applicable to routine classroom discipline of children and teenagers in the public schools. It justifies this unprecedented intrusion into the process of elementary and secondary education by identifying a new constitutional right: the right of a student not to be suspended for as much as a single day without notice and a due process hearing either before or promptly following the suspension.[2]

...In my view, a student's interest in education is not infringed by a suspension within the limited period prescribed by Ohio law. Moreover, to the extent that there may be some arguable infringement, it is too speculative, transitory, and insubstantial to justify imposition of a constitutional rule.

* * *

The Ohio suspension statute allows no serious or significant infringement of education. It authorizes only a maximum suspension of eight school days, less than 5% of the normal 180-day school year. Absences of such limited duration will rarely affect a pupil's opportunity to learn or his scholastic performance. Indeed, the record in this case reflects no educational injury to appellees. Each completed the semester in which the suspension occurred and performed at least as well as he or she had in previous years....Despite the Court's unsupported speculation that a suspended student could be "seriously [damaged]" there is no factual showing of any such damage to appellees.

* * *

II

In prior decisions, this Court has explicitly recognized that school authorities must have broad discretionary authority in the daily operation of public schools. This includes wide latitude with respect to maintaining discipline and good order....

The Court today turns its back on these precedents. It can hardly seriously be claimed that a school principal's decision to suspend a pupil for a single day would "directly and sharply implicate basic constitutional values."...

Moreover, the Court ignores the experience of mankind, as well as the long history of our law, recognizing that there are differences which must be accommodated in determining the rights and duties of children as compared with those of adults. Examples of this distinction abound in our law: in contracts, in torts, in criminal law and procedure, in criminal sanctions and rehabilitation, and in the right to vote and to hold office. Until today, and except in the special context of the First Amendment issue in *Tinker*, the educational rights of children and teenagers in the elementary and secondary schools

have not been analogized to the rights of adults or to those accorded college students. Even with respect to the First Amendment, the rights of children have not been regarded as "co-extensive with those of adults." *Tinker, supra*, at 515 (STEWART, J., concurring).

A

* * *

The facts set forth in the margin[10] leave little room for doubt as to the magnitude of the disciplinary problem in the public schools, or as to the extent of reliance upon the right to suspend. They also demonstrate that if hearings were required for a substantial percentage of short-term suspensions, school authorities would have time to do little else.

* * *

C

One of the more disturbing aspects of today's decision is its indiscriminate reliance upon the judiciary, and the adversary process, as the means of resolving many of the most routine problems arising in the classroom. In mandating due process procedures the Court misapprehends the reality of the normal teacher-pupil relationship. There is an ongoing relationship, one in which the teacher must occupy many roles—educator, adviser, friend, and, at times, parent-substitute....It is rarely adversary in nature except with respect to the chronically disruptive or insubordinate pupil whom the teacher must be free to discipline without frustrating formalities....

* * *

If, as seems apparent, the Court will now require due process procedures whenever such routine school decisions are challenged, the impact upon public education will be serious indeed. The discretion and judgment of federal courts across the land often will be substituted for that of the 50 state legislatures, the 14,000 school boards,... and the 2,000,000 teachers who heretofore have been responsible for the administration of the American public school system. If the Court perceives a rational and analytically sound distinction between the discretionary decision by school authorities to suspend a pupil for a brief period, and the types of discretionary school decisions described above, it would be prudent to articulate it in today's opinion. Otherwise, the federal courts should prepare themselves for a vast new role in society.

IV

...In recent years the Court, wisely in my view, has rejected the "wooden distinction between 'rights' and 'privileges,'" [citation omitted] and looked instead to the significance of the state-created or state-enforced right and to the substantiality of the alleged deprivation. Today's opinion appears to abandon this reasonable approach by holding in effect that government infringement of any interest to which a person is entitled, no matter what the interest or how inconsequential the infringement, requires constitutional protection. As it is difficult to think of any less consequential infringement than suspension of a junior high school student for a single day, it is equally difficult to perceive any principled limit to the new reach of procedural due process...

---

[1] The Ohio statute actually is a limitation on the time-honored practice of school authorities themselves determining the appropriate duration of suspensions. The statute allows the superintendent or principal of a public school to suspend a pupil *"for not more than ten days..."* (italics supplied); and requires notification to the parent or guardian in writing within 24 hours of any suspension.

[2] Section 3313.66 also provides authority for the expulsion of pupils, but requires a hearing thereon by the school board upon request of a parent or guardian. The rights of pupils expelled are not involved in this case, which concerns only the limited discretion of school authorities to suspend for not more than 10 days. Expulsion, usually resulting at least in loss of a school year or semester, is an incomparably more serious matter than the brief suspension, traditionally used as the principal sanction for enforcing routine discipline. The Ohio statute recognizes this distinction.

[10] An amicus brief filed by the Children's Defense Fund states that at least 10% of the junior and senior high school students in the States sampled were suspended one or more times in the 1972–1973 school year....

Questions for Discussion

1. The majority in *Goss* argues that students subject to a sanction of less than ten days of school suspension must receive two elements of due process: notice and a chance to be heard. They are not entitled to a hearing, right to counsel, testimony under oath, right to cross-examine, transcript, neutral adjudicator, or other formal due process rights. Are these elements sufficient to assure consistency? Is more impractical?

2. The dissent would not require these elements, and rejects formal due process even for permanent expulsion. How is the dissent's view of expulsion due process consistent with the complete panoply of procedural due process rights (including notice, hearing before a neutral adjudicator, right to confront, testimony under oath, right to present evidence, transcript, right to appeal) offered adults where: (a) an employer wishes to garnish wages (*see Sniadach v. Family Finance Corp. of Bay View*, 395 U.S. 337 (1969)); (b) a state agency cuts off welfare payments (*see Goldberg v. Kelly*, 397 U.S. 254 (1970) and *Board of Regents v. Roth*, 408 U.S. 564 (1972)); (c) a state university denies tenure (*see Garnel v. Bunzel*, 68 Cal. App. 3d 999 (1977)); or (d) a state agency disciplines a trade licensee (contractor, pharmacist)? As to licensure discipline, the full panoply of due process also includes a burden on the state to prove its case by "clear and convincing evidence," and applies short of revocation and to cases where the sanction is a fine or short suspension. Yet other cases find due process procedures constitutionally-compelled where official charges, "however informal,..threaten to stain [a] personal or professional future" (*Endler v. Schutzbank*, 68 Cal. 2d 162 (1968)). What would be the dissenters' explanation for the differences between due process requirements imposed for adult takings or sanctions in (a) through (d) above and those required for the state to expel a student from school?

3. Assume, as the majority implies, that a suspension from school for alleged misconduct must be disclosed and may be given substantial weight by universities and employers. Is the loss to a student of admission to the college he or she has hoped to attend a significant consequence warranting some safeguards? Are the safeguards enumerated sufficient?

4. If there is a serious reputational impact, why doesn't the majority consider allowing the quick decision with only the two due process elements it imposes, but then allow a student a traditional due process hearing after the suspension has been served—so an unjust, inaccurate, or arbitrary stain on reputation may be removed or adjusted? Assuming that only those students who were damaged and feel it was incorrect factually or unjust will request such a remedy, why not provide some hearing opportunity?

5. How would a demonstration of substantial future reputational harm (with real impact on college and job prospects) affect the dissent's judgment that a suspension is categorically different from an expulsion? What if expulsions do not result in the loss of a school year, but merely require a student to attend school elsewhere or at a county-administered facility (as is commonly the case)?

6. The majority finds a property interest and liberty interest implicated in "the total exclusion from the educational process for more than a trivial period...." What constitutes "total exclusion?" Does an in-school suspension equate to exclusion? Is it relevant whether the student is required to do schoolwork during the suspension or not?

7. The dissent argues that "the interests here implicated—of the State through its schools and of the pupils—are essentially congruent." Are the interests of an accused child to be suspended and the principal suspending him congruent? Are the interests of the police and the citizenry at large "essentially congruent?" Similarly, the dissent cites the large number of students subject to suspension. Would the dissenters agree that a rising or high crime rate justifies the abrogation of criminal justice system due process?

8. Should the dissent have considered the range of discipline available to a school short of suspension (e.g., a required assignment related to the offense, after-hours detention, loss of privileges)? If such measures are available, would that tend to place a suspension in a qualitatively different category warranting some due process as imposed by the majority, although perhaps substantially less than a formal hearing for expulsion?

Note on Zero-Tolerance

In the 1990s, rising anxiety over youth gangs and violence spurred a wave of "tough on crime" rhetoric among politicians and policymakers. This rhetoric included the branding of juvenile "superpredators"—a population of youth who were supposedly violent, remorseless, and irredeemable. Schools responded to this new concern by developing hard-lined policies that sought to increase school safety by removing students from school for any violation of school rules regardless of the seriousness of the behavior or any mitigating circumstances. Under these "zero-tolerance" policies, students often suffer significant consequences such as long-term suspensions, expulsion from school, and/or arrest and referral to juvenile or adult court.[16]

Zero-tolerance policies have been applied very broadly, punishing students for a wide range of behaviors, many non-serious. The result has been a considerable increase in suspensions and expulsions, with a substantial number of students thus deprived of education services or diverted to substandard alternative schools.[17] These policies have disproportionately impacted poor children, students with disabilities, and youth of color, especially African American students. In addition, these policies have significantly contributed to what is known as the "school-to-prison-pipeline." With more schools having campus-based police officers (often referred to as School Resource Officers), the number of school-based arrests has increased, often in response to discipline issues traditionally handled without law enforcement involvement. Ultimately, zero-tolerance policies have not proven effective in improving student behavior or school safety.[18]

Despite the decision in *Goss*, students challenging zero-tolerance policies as a due process issue find that lower courts consistently defer to the schools, choosing not to entertain constitutional issues. In 1999, a middle school student, Benjamin Ratner, removed a bookbinder with a knife in it from the locker of a friend who was threatening suicide. When asked about it by the school principal, Benjamin reported that he had the knife in his locker and turned it in to the principal. The school promptly suspended Benjamin for the entirety of the school year as per the district's zero-tolerance policy. Ratner brought suit and the district court dismissed the claim. In affirming the decision, the Fourth Circuit Court of Appeals concluded "[h]owever harsh the result in this case, the federal courts are not properly called upon to judge the wisdom of a zero tolerance policy...."[19]

D. GENDER DISCRIMINATION IN SCHOOLS

Title IX of the Education Amendments of 1972 protects students from discrimination based on sex in education programs that receive federal financial assistance. Violations of Title IX can include sexual harassment or sexual violence, gender-based bullying, and disproportionate offerings of athletic programs or activities based on gender. Numerous lawsuits have focused on ensuring equal access to athletics for girls on school campuses. In 2014, the Ninth Circuit in *Ollier v. Sweetwater Union High School District*, 768 F.3d 843, affirmed a lower court ruling that the school district violated Title IX in all three of its mandates for equality in athletics, including failing to provide equal opportunities for girls to play, equal treatment and benefits for female athletes (*e.g.*, facilities, coaching, and publicity), and protection against retaliation for reporting violations.

More recently, Title IX claims have accompanied equal protection claims in cases asserting the right of transgender students to use the school bathroom that comports with the student's gender identity. Several cases have been filed, garnering considerable media attention. In 2016, the Seventh Circuit Court of Appeals upheld an injunction in *Whitaker v. Kenosha Unified Sch. Dist. No. 1 Bd. of Educ.*, 858 F.3d 1034, requiring a school district to allow high school senior Ashton Whitaker, who identifies as a boy, to use the boy's bathroom. The court found that the school district discriminated against Whitaker in violation of Title IX in that it subjected him to different rules, sanctions, and treatment than non-transgender students. In relation to the equal protection claim, the court found that the school's bathroom policy was based on a sex classification and therefore applied heightened scrutiny, which the school district's interest in student privacy failed to meet.

E. U.S. EDUCATION POLICIES AND INVESTMENT

1. Demographics of K–12 Education: Enrollment and Dropouts

A pattern of annual increases in K–12 public school enrollment began in 1985, rising 28% to 50.6 million enrollees in 2017. Private school attendance grew more slowly during this period, increasing 6% to 5.9 million, constituting about 10% of total school enrollment.[20] In 2015, 75% of these private school students were enrolled in religiously affiliated schools.[21] The National Center on Education Statistics forecasts a continued increase of another 3% for public elementary enrollment and 2% increase for public secondary enrollment by 2027.[22]

About 3.6 million students graduated from U.S. high schools in 2017–18, including 355,000 from private schools. In 2015–16, 84% of public high school graduates earned diplomas on schedule, an increase from 79% in 2010–11.[23] The number of individuals who did not complete high school but earned a General Equivalency Diploma (GED) increased by 40% between 2003 and 2013, from 387,000 to 541,000.[24]

The percentage of students dropping out of school has declined over the past twenty years. This reduction is controversial, with some education critics suggesting that statistical infirmities hide a large number of actual dropouts from traditionally compiled statistics. The accepted definition of a "dropout" is a person age 16–24 who is not in school and has no high school diploma. As of 2016, such youth make up 6% of the 16–24-year-old population. Despite the reported decline in the dropout rate, students of color continue to dropout at higher rates than their white peers. In 2016, the dropout rate for Hispanics was higher (9%) than for Whites (5%) and African Americans (6%).[25] Dropouts are subject to the income levels indicated above, with incomes below the federal poverty line for a family of three for about one half of this group. Although certainly many dropouts achieve remarkably, the group as a whole correlates with unemployment, criminal justice involvement, and homelessness. Notwithstanding their circumstances, a substantial percentage become parents, with high rates of single parent poverty for involved children, discussed above, and disproportionate intervention by child protective services, discussed in Chapter 8.

Some states have started experimenting with measures to ameliorate truancy—the common first step toward dropout status. These include arrests of parents for child neglect (albeit usually not with a harsh punitive result, but to remind parents of their duties and the consequences of school failure). They also include varying attention paid to truancy as a "status offense" that may invoke the jurisdiction of either child protective services on the juvenile court dependency side, or of the probation services of the juvenile delinquency system—depending on the state.

2. Kindergarten to Grade 12 State and Local Investment

In 2014–15, expenditures for K–12 education nationally totaled $668 billion. About 47% came from state budgets, another 45% from local sources, and 8% from the federal jurisdiction. Eighty-one percent of local revenues for public elementary and secondary school districts came from local property taxes.[26] Total spending per K–12 student has increased at rates just above the Consumer Price Index since 1990. In 2014–15, approximately 80% of expenditures went toward salaries and benefits for staff.[27] The average teacher salary in 2015–16 was $58,353 in current dollars. In the fall of 2016, about 3.6 million full-time equivalent teachers were engaged in classroom instruction throughout the nation. Of that total, 3.2 million taught in public schools and 400,000 in private schools.[28] Over the past decade, public school enrollment has increased while the number of public school teachers has slightly decreased, resulting in a ratio of 16.1 pupils per teacher in 2016, higher than the 15.6 ratio in 2006.[29]

The shortfall and remaining disparities between wealthy and impoverished districts (particularly in those states rejecting the *Serrano* equality of opportunity spending mandate) produce troubling outcomes. For example, in 2015 more than 75% of lower-income fourth and eighth grade public school students could not read or compute at grade level compared with less than 55% of higher income students. The disparity is particularly striking when taking race into account. In 2015, more than 73% of fourth and eighth grade African-American and Hispanic public school students could not read or compute at grade level compared with less than 60% of White students. Further, less than 80% of minority students graduated on time as compared to 87% of White students.[30] These students of color are more likely to attend high poverty schools, as measured by the percentage of students eligible for free or reduced-price lunch.[31] Although 9 out of 10 public school students were taught by certified teachers, those who were not were more likely to be African-American, Hispanic, students in high-minority schools, and students eligible for the National School Lunch Program. These students were also less likely to be taught by teachers having more than 5 years of teaching experience and with a degree in the subject area they are teaching.[32]

Since 2014, teacher shortages have been increasing nationwide. This is a result of both a decline in new entrants into teaching as well as high rates of teachers leaving the field. Low-income schools have been disproportionately disadvantaged by teacher attrition. Turnover rates are highest in Title I schools, which serve larger numbers of impoverished students. Turnover rates are also 70% higher for teachers in schools with the highest concentrations of students of color.[33] In recent years, teachers in several states have engaged in protests to highlight many of the issues contributing to the high rates of attrition, including uncompetitive salaries, lack of new teacher support, and poor working conditions.[34] In fact, when adjusted for inflation, salaries have actually decreased for the average teacher in 39 states, and according to a Department of Education survey, 94% of teachers have resorted to paying for school supplies out-of-pocket.[35]

Demand for teachers continues to grow given the increase in school-age population. Investment in teacher compensation and education to meet that need has not matched that need and is not proposed in most state budgets. Rather, and with rare exception, state officials view new taxation for such investment in children as politically untenable, and likely to raise the feared "tax and spend" label.

In contrast, public opinion polls reflect a strong public commitment to children and in particular to their education—including additional taxation for that purpose. Elected officials have reconciled this dichotomy by campaigning vigorously as "pro-education," with candidates and newly-elected officials throughout the nation commonly adopting the informal title "the Education Governor," or the "Education President." However, those claims have not always produced significant investment in education for public K–12 or for higher education (see discussion below).

3. **Underlying Major Federal K–12 and Vocational Education Funding Programs**

The federal contribution for K–12 education spending increased from 6% in the 1990s to a high of 12.7% in 2009–10. This percentage has since decreased with federal contributions comprising 8.5% in 2014–15.[36] The FY2018 federal budget commitment to education was $48.3 billion (not including the higher education Pell grants discussed below), which falls far below the 2010 level.[37] Investment in education consistently accounts for less than 2% of the federal budget.

Outside of nutrition and special education, the largest single federal contribution for K–12 education has been basic education Title I funds to improve the educational outcomes of impoverished children. This program, started in 1965 as part of President Johnson's "War on Poverty," has increased over the years, with a $15.8 billion allocation in 2018. In 2016, two-thirds of all elementary schools and half of all public schools received Title I funds.[38] More than 75% of all Title I schools operated programs that served students school-wide in higher-poverty settings rather than targeting assistance to students identified as eligible for services based on low achievement. The majority of Title I funds were spent by schools on personnel. In school-wide programs, teachers made up 41% of Title I funded staff in 2016. Paraprofessionals, such as school aides and teacher's assistants, made up 29% of the personnel.[39]

The results of Title I spending are in dispute, with the overall gap in reading and math scores between the impoverished and average student populations virtually unchanged over the past two decades, notwithstanding increases in the account from its original $1 billion to its current level. However, adjusting the original amount in 1965 for population and inflation indicates very little actual spending power increase. Further, the growth of ELL populations, and bouts of increasing poverty over the past several decades, may have led to a substantially larger gap but for this continuing investment. Finally, the initial impact of the program from 1965 to 1980 correlated with a marked improvement in test scores of impoverished children, with about one-third of the pre-1965 gap made up during the early years of the war on poverty. Final judgment about the program's efficacy is limited by a lack of control group comparison.

Whatever the historical or theoretical advantages of the Title I program, there is wide agreement that the funding is spread too thinly, that it is too often used to fund low-return activities, and that complicated grant formulations result in funds being funneled away from the program's intended recipients, ending up in wealthier than average districts. This occurs because the formula places more weight on the number of poor students in a district than on the percentage of such students in a district. Therefore larger districts, even if wealthier on the whole, may receive more funding per pupil than a smaller, poorer district. A recent survey found that Title I spending in a high-poverty school amounted to $558 per student, while per student Title I funding in a low-poverty school was $763.[40] In addition, the formula results in additional funding directed to states that have small populations. This may be appropriate in smaller rural states with remote schools, but wealthy small states such as Connecticut still qualify for additional funding regardless of it being a prosperous state.

Education has been a stated priority of several recent presidential administrations, resulting in significant policy initiatives undertaken to bolster educational success, particularly among low-income students. In 2001, George W. Bush declared that education reform would be a primary focus of his administration, and within a year he had signed into law the No Child Left Behind Act. The initiative emphasized competition and accountability in the quest for 100% proficiency among U.S. students. One of the political judgments made was that powerful teacher unions had created tenured privilege for their members, allowing poor teachers to remain in employ indefinitely, while parents were deprived of school choice where schools or teachers were not performing satisfactorily.

The approach under No Child Left Behind required testing of students in elementary, middle school, and for graduation (eliminating "social" diplomas based on four years of attendance). It also provided for the publication of test score results (required school report cards); incentives and sanctions to be applied to low-scoring schools; enhanced competition and parental choice, including allowance of school transfers for students from underperforming schools within a district; and stimulation of charter school alternatives. The law required the nation's 98,000 public schools to make "adequate yearly progress" as measured by the scores of required student tests. Schools that miss their targets in reading and math must offer students the opportunity to transfer to other schools and free after-school tutoring. Schools that repeatedly miss targets face harsher sanctions, which can include staff dismissals and closings.

The Administration favored the various "voucher" system alternatives, including application to parochial schools. However, the charter school option has been more substantially implemented, with many new schools experimenting with different teaching techniques. The efficacy of the charter schools is in some dispute, with apparent and perhaps unsurprising variation between them, both the students attending them and in outcomes. The public school supporters argue that the charter and other private schools "skim the cream" of the students lacking disability or special challenge, leaving more difficult students to the limited resources of public schools. But others argue that many charter schools—such as the famous Harlem "Children's Zone" education work of Geoffrey Canada—target impoverished students and demonstrate extraordinary success. Most child advocates agree that the challenge is not so much to find a successful strategy, as to measure what is working and to generalize it through merit-based and accountable federal (or state) funding.

4. Post-2009 Federal Programs and Investment

In 2009, as part of the economic stimulus package known as the American Recovery and Reinvestment Act, $77 billion was allocated to K–12 education. In addition, the Act established a competitive $4.35 billion grant program for states called Race to the Top.[41] These grants provided incentives for states to follow the education policies of the Obama Administration, with the stated goals of improving teacher efficacy, adopting proficiency standards, assisting low-performing schools, and enhancing data systems. The grant program was voluntary, but it came at a time at which many states were suffering the effects of recession and were desperate for additional funding for education. In the end, 46 states and the District of Columbia applied. At the same time, the Obama administration financed the development of standardized tests to measure new college and career ready standards. This effort, coupled with the Race to the Top standards, encouraged the widespread adoption of the controversial Common Core Standards.[42]

Race to the Top revised the No Child Left Behind Act, but retained much of its core—an emphasis on testing and accountability. Critics contend that the emphasis on testing detracts from necessary learning time in the classroom and that measuring student achievement through standardized test scores fails to give sufficient weight to other meaningful measures of success. These Bush and Obama era programs have garnered significant criticism for granting the federal government too much authority over education policy, constraining state and local innovation. Ultimately, critics argue, the law failed to address the systemic problems of inequality among school systems. In an effort to address these issues, Congress passed and President Obama signed the Every Student Succeeds Act (ESSA) in 2015. The intent of the law is to allow for greater flexibility, putting states more in control of their education policymaking. For example:

- Student testing is still required, but schools will have the power to design and implement tests. Schools are allowed to explore testing options to ensure that testing provides a more accurate measure of what students are learning.
- Although ESSA maintains the same testing requirements as No Child Left Behind, states will be responsible for creating their own accountability plans, to be reviewed and approved by the U.S. Department of Education.
- School performance will be measured using a system that now incorporates non-academic indicators.
- Under No Child Left Behind, schools that underperformed were subject to a limited number of options for addressing deficiencies, including widespread firings, conversion to a charter school, lengthening the school day or year, or even closing down. ESSA provides more specific measures by which to define a failing school, but leaves it to the states to take control of these schools.

- ESSA supports early childhood education and preschool readiness in particular. Preschool Development Grants were included to transform discretionary grants into a permanent component of the education system.

Despite the bipartisan support for ESSA and the fanfare that accompanied its passage, the legislation is not without its critics. Some point out that ESSA still relies primarily on testing as criteria by which to measure school effectiveness. Without specific federal guidance on what constitutes a "take over" of a failing school, it is likely that many of the same severe sanctions will be applied, but now by states rather than the federal government. Education advocates point out that regardless of any changes, ESSA, like No Child Left Behind, is underfunded. Changing outcomes for students and specifically closing the achievement gap between high- and low-poverty students will ultimately require a greater commitment to funding on the federal, state, and local level.

Questions for Discussion

1. ESSA has been celebrated as a return to state and local accountability and control for education. Yet, as the tortured history of school finance litigation illustrates, states have far from mastered how to ensure equity and adequacy of education for all students. Is the federal government abdicating responsibility for ensuring equal opportunity in education to those who have, in the words of Thurgood Marshall, "proved singularly unsuited to the task of providing a remedy"[43]?

2. The federal funding pattern in the modern era has had a fragmented "earmark" flavor to it—with catchy phrased titles for competitive grants to states, often of amounts large in national total, but quite small in individual school allocation. What are the total costs involved in the federal system of administration—both in federal approval and in school and state application? What are the reliable outcome measures of respective grants? Does their cessation, continuation, or enhancement relate to such demonstrated outcomes? Should it?

F. U.S. HIGHER EDUCATION INVESTMENT

The 2018 federal budget included $2.5 billion for all of higher education (non-loan) state grant assistance. The largest single account is the approximately $1 billion currently expended on federal TRIO programs, aimed at individuals from disadvantaged backgrounds, including Talent Search, Upward Bound, and Student Support Services as the major elements. Other grants include $681 million for Title III funding for disadvantaged students—primarily African-American or tribal beneficiaries at some colleges and in some disciplines (e.g., science and engineering).[44]

The major federal role to assist youth into higher education is providing grants and loan help for tuition and living expenses. In fiscal year 2017, the federal government provided approximately $100 billion in loans, $30 billion in need-based grants, and $30 billion in income tax preferences.[45] A major source of federal support for low-income students has long been the Pell grants, which provided $28.2 billion in 2018, serving seven million students.[46] The maximum grant provided to students for the 2017–18 academic year was $5,820, with grant amounts tied to student need. The maximum grant for the 2018–19 academic year is $6,095, which is essentially the same as the year prior after adjusting for the increase in the Consumer Price Index.[47] However, the current maximum does not assist students as much as in years prior. In 1998–99, the maximum Pell Grant would cover 92% of public university in-state tuition and fees; in 2018–19, the maximum covers only 60% of these costs. Furthermore, only 27% of recipients are actually awarded the maximum grant.[48] In addition, Pell Grants are underutilized by those who qualify. This is likely due to both the complicated application process and the fact that students must first enroll in college before learning the amount of their grant.[49]

As future funding levels for student aid remain uncertain, the cost of higher education has most certainly continued to increase. Since 2005, tuition, fees, room and board at public colleges have risen more than 35% and prices at private institutions rose more than 25%. In 2018–19, the average cost of yearly in-state tuition plus room and board at a public four-year college is $21,370; out-of-state costs at these institutions average $37,430. Private, non-profit, four-year institutions average an astounding $48,510 for the same.[50] Consequently, a college education at a public university will total, on average, $85,480 for an in-state student and $149,720 for an out of state student. Four years at a private institution comes with an average price tag of $194,040.[51] And these figures exclude additional costs such as transportation, clothing, and books.

The increases mean less access to higher education, particularly for the middle class that may be ineligible for available state higher education grants. The post-graduation burdens are unprecedented for those currently graduating and as projected forward. The particularly high price tag associated with advanced degrees results in the exclusion of middle- and low-income students from professions such as law and medicine, or inclusion with the burden of overwhelming debt.

The low amount limits on subsidized loans—including those common at the state level—means that students must seek other assistance, including extremely high interest credit card debt and other loans. Six-figure debt, now enhanced for many from years of accrued debt to be added onto balances at graduation, severely limit choices of students and preclude many from employment in public interest or any job lacking high remuneration. Those debts also compromise the ability of even college graduates to own their own homes, and to save well in advance for the college expenses of their own children.

One area of increasing concern in higher education is the expanding share of federal and state loans going to "for-profit" vocational and higher education institutions. These entities advertise aggressively, including common representations about future earnings after obtaining their degree or certificate. Some of these entities spend more per student on marketing and recruitment than on actual instruction.[52] A large and increasing share of federal higher education loans is now expended for students of these institutions. Some of the schools may afford special opportunities for advancement to their students and fully warrant loan inclusion, but for-profit schools are now the largest source of student loan defaults. Such defaults may become more common as tuition and interest rates on these loans rise.

The for-profit higher education/vocational training sector is not closely regulated, with some states lacking any oversight, contrary to systems of public education. A recent report from the Children's Advocacy Institute found that despite increased attention to this issue, states continue to lack effective laws that would prevent abuse by these institutions and/or provide recourse for impacted students.[53] Court cases have challenged successfully the advertising representations of some, but the business model they represent, selling the promise of advancement and success, has generated many entrepreneurs. Where false promises or economic decline results in less-than anticipated employment, the negative outcome is more profound than the public economic losses. Collection may be onerous and the consequences devastating for involved youth, with credit bureaus maintaining an effective bar to future loans for up to seven years of subsequent reliable debt payment. The credit ruination effect of loan default is furthered by the inability to discharge education loans in bankruptcy.

The federal government has not significantly assisted the needed capacity expansion of public postsecondary institutions, either in the regions with projected severe shortfalls or nationally. Child advocates argue that this relative disinvestment in our children contrasts with the massive "GI Bill of Rights" and other federal and state higher education opportunity provided for today's adults by their parents and grandparents.

ENDNOTES

[1] Elka Torpey, *Measuring the value of education*, Career Outlook,U.S. Bureau of Labor Statistics (April 2018), at https://www.bls.gov/careeroutlook/2018/data-on-display/education-pays.htm.

[2] U.S. Census Bureau, *Income and Poverty in the United States: 2014* (Washington, D.C.; 2015).

[3] Anthony P. Carnevale, Nicole Smith, and Jeff Strohl, *Recovery: Job Growth and Education Requirements Through 2020*, Center on Education and the Workforce, Georgetown Public Policy Institute, Georgetown University (Washington, D.C.; June 2013) at cew.georgetown.edu/recovery2020.

[4] Pew Research Center, *The State of American Jobs* (Washington, D.C.; October 2016) at http://www.pewsocialtrends.org/2016/10/06/1-changes-in-the-american-workplace/.

[5] U.S. Department of Education, National Center for Education Statistics, *The Condition of Education 2018: English Language Learners in Public Schools* (Washington, D.C.; 2018) at https://nces.ed.gov/programs/coe/indicator_cgf.asp.

[6] See *Serrano v. Priest*, 18 Cal. 3d 728 (1976), *cert. denied*, 432 U.S. 907 (1977) (adhering to decision in Serrano I on state equal protection grounds).

[7] Matthew M. Chingos & Kristin Blagg, *Making Sense of State School Funding Policy*, Urban Institute (Washington, D.C.; November 2017). See also Michael A. Rebell, *Courts & Kids: Pursuing Educational Equity Through The State Courts* (University of Chicago Press; 2009), and the 2017 Supplement for a comprehensive compilation of cases and rulings.

[8] See https://www.jud.ct.gov/HomePDFs/CCJEFvRell.pdf.

[9] *Conn. Coalition for Justice in Educ. Funding, Inc. v. Rell*, 327 Conn. 650, 658 (Conn. 2018).

[10] *Gannon v. State*, 306 Kan. 1170 (Kan. 2017).

[11] *Gannon v. State*, 08 Kan. 372 (Kan. 2018).

[12] *Campaign for Quality Education v. State of California*, 246 Cal. App. 4th 896 (2016).

[13] See https://www.mofo.com/special-content/ca-literacy/.

[14] C. Kirabo Jackson, Rucker C. Johnson, Claudia Persico; *The Effects of School Spending on Educational and Economic Outcomes: Evidence from School Finance Reforms*, 131 Q. J. Econ. 1, 157-218 (February 2016).

[15] Ivy Morgan and Ary Amerikaner, *Funding Gaps 2018: An Analysis of School Funding Equity Across the U.S. and Within Each State* (Washington, D.C.; The Education Trust; 2018).

[16] See Anthony J. Nocella II, Priya Parmar, and David Stovall, *From Education to Incarceration: Dismantling the School to-Prison Pipeline* (2014) at 11–36.

[17] *Id.*

[18] American Psychological Association Zero Tolerance Task Force, *Are Zero Tolerance Policies Effective in the Schools?*, 63 Am. Psychol. 9, 852-862 (December 2008) at https://www.apa.org/pubs/info/reports/zero-tolerance.pdf.

[19] *Ratner v. Loudoun County Pub. Sch.*, 16 Fed. Appx. 140 (4th Cir. 2001).

[20] U.S. Department of Education, National Center for Education Statistics, *Mobile Digest of Education Statistics, 2017* (Washington, DC.; 2018) at https://nces.ed.gov/pubs2018/2018138.pdf.

[21] U.S. Department of Education, National Center for Education Statistics, *The Condition of Education 2018: Private School Enrollment* (Washington, D.C.; 2018) at https://nces.ed.gov/programs/coe/indicator_cgc.asp.

[22] *Mobile Digest*, *supra* note 20.

[23] *Id.*

[24] U.S. Department of Education, National Center for Education Statistics, *Table 219.60: Number of People Taking the GED Test and Percentage Distribution of Those Who Passed, by Age Group, 1971 through 2013* (Washington, D.C.; 2015) at https://nces.ed.gov/programs/digest/d15/tables/dt15_219.60.asp?refer=dropout.

[25] *Mobile Digest*, *supra* note 20.

[26] *Id.*

[27] U.S. Department of Education, National Center for Education Statistics, *The Condition of Education 2018: Public School Revenue Sources* (Washington, D.C.; 2018) at https://nces.ed.gov/programs/coe/indicator_cma.asp.

[28] U.S. Department of Education, National Center for Education Statistics, *Digest of Education Statistics: 2016* (Washington, D.C.; February 2018) at https://nces.ed.gov/programs/digest/d16/index.asp.

[29] *Id.*

[30] Children's Defense Fund, *The State of American's Children 2017* (Washington D.C.; 2018) at https://www.childrensdefense.org/wp-content/uploads/2018/06/Education.pdf.

[31] U.S. Department of Education, National Center for Education Statistics, *The Condition of Education 2018: Concentration of Public School Students Eligible for Free or Reduced-Price Lunch* (Washington, D.C.; 2018) at https://nces.ed.gov/programs/coe/indicator_clb.asp.

[32] U.S. Department of Education, National Center for Education *Statistics, Certification Status and Experience of U.S. Public School Teachers* (Washington, D.C.; 2017) at https://nces.ed.gov/pubs2017/2017056.pdf.

[33] D. Carver-Thomas & L. Darling-Hammond, Teacher turnover: *Why it matters and what we can do about It, Learning Policy Institute* (Palo Alto, CA; 2017).

[34] A. Podolsky, T. Kini, J. Bishop, & I. Darling-Hammond, *Solving the Teacher Shortage: How to Attract and Retain Excellent Educators, Learning Policy Institute* (Palo Alto, CA; 2016).

[35] See Kaitlin Mulhere, *These 7 Charts Explain the Fight for Higher Teacher Pay*, MONEY (April 11, 2008) at http://time.com/money/5228237/teacher-pay-charts/.

[36] *Mobile Digest, supra* note 20.

[37] Committee for Education Funding, *Fiscal Year 2018 Funding for Selected Department of Education and Related Programs* (Washington, D.C.; 2018) at https://cef.org/charts-and-resources/charts/.

[38] U.S. Department of Education, Office of Planning, Evaluation and Policy Development, Policy and Program Studies Service, *Study of Title I Schoolwide and Targeted Assistance Programs: Final Report* (Washington, D.C.; 2018).

[39] *Id.*

[40] Mary Dynarski and Kirsten Kainz, *Why federal spending on disadvantaged students (Title I) doesn't work*, Brookings Institution, 1 Evidence Speaks Reports 7 (Washington, D.C.; November 2015) at https://www.brookings.edu/wp-content/uploads/2016/07/Download-the-paper-2.pdf.

[41] Joseph P. Viteritti, *The Federal Role in School Reform: Obama's Race to the Top*, 87 NOTRE DAME L.REV. 2087 (2013).

[42] See *id.*

[43] *San Antonio Independent School District v. Rodriguez*, 411 U.S. 1, 71 (1973).

[44] See https://www2.ed.gov/about/overview/budget/budget19/19action.pdf.

[45] U.S. Congressional Budget Office, *Federal Aid for Postsecondary Students* (Washington, D.C.; 2018).

[46] The College Board, *Total Pell Grant Expenditures and Number of Recipients over Time*, at https://trends.collegeboard.org/student-aid/figures-tables/pell-grants-total-expenditures-maximum-and-average-grant-and-number-recipients-over-time.

[47] The College Board, *Maximum Pell Grant and Published Prices at Four-Year Institutions over Time*, at https://trends.collegeboard.org/student-aid/figures-tables/maximum-pell-grant-and-published-prices-four-year-institutions-over-time.

[48] *Id.*

[49] U.S. Congressional Budget Office, *supra* note 45.

[50] The College Board, *Trends in College Pricing 2018*, at 9 (New York, NY; 2018) at https://trends.collegeboard.org/sites/default/files/2018-trends-in-college-pricing.pdf.

[51] *Id.*

[52] Comm. on Health, Educ., Labor, and Pension, *For Profit Higher Education: The Failure to Safeguard the Federal Investment and Ensure Student Success*, S. Rep. No. 112-37 (2d Sess. 2012).

[53] Melanie Delgado, *Failing U: Do State Laws Protect Our Veterans and Other Students from For-Profit Postsecondary Predators?* (Children's Advocacy Institute, San Diego, CA; 2018).

CHAPTER FIVE

Health, Medical Care, and Safety

A. CHILD RIGHT TO TREATMENT

Public policy obligating parents to medically care for their children is reflected in the common civil requirement to provide "necessaries." Failure to so provide is a basis for juvenile dependency court termination of parental rights. In addition, criminal liability for involuntary manslaughter may lie where death is the result of gross negligence. Some states have a "poverty exemption" to civil neglect charges where parents are not financially able to provide medical care or other necessities for their children.[1] However, the most extensive source of asserted parental exemption rests with the *bona fide* religious beliefs of parents in faith healing. The courts have ruled consistently that First Amendment religious or other parental constitutional rights do not cover allowing harm to befall a child. In one early leading case, the U.S. Supreme Court upheld mandatory vaccination laws against a parental religious challenge.[2] In perhaps the leading state case, Mississippi held in 1979 that "innocent children, too young to decide for themselves" should not be denied the protection against disability or death that immunization provides because of a religious belief adhered to by a parent.[3]

However, over the past thirty years partial, often confusing, religious exemption statutes have been enacted in all fifty states. They tend not to cover diagnosis and vaccination, but rather medical treatment for existing and known illness. In possibly applicable *dictum*, the U.S. Supreme Court held in *Prince v. Massachusetts* that a Jehovah's Witness could not compel her daughter to sell literature on the streets in violation of child labor laws,[4] writing: "The right to practice religion freely does not include liberty to expose the community or child to communicable disease or the latter to ill health or death....Parents may be free to become martyrs themselves. But it does not follow that they are free, in identical circumstances, to make martyrs of their children before they have reached the age of full and legal discretion when they can make that choice for themselves."[5]

However, notwithstanding this *Prince* reference, since the 1970s most states have enacted some religious exemption to civil dependency or neglect charges,[6] and/or a religious defense to a criminal charge involving the care of their children. Nine states have religious exemptions for negligent homicide, manslaughter, or capital murder.[7] These exemptions permit parents to pray and otherwise use faith healing to address a child's illness. Most are not intended to exempt from civil or criminal liability a failure to medically treat a child where his or her life is in danger; however their ambiguous wording has created some effective barrier to criminal prosecution—even in relatively egregious failures to treat.[8] The extent of harm is unknown but child advocates in Idaho have documented 185 child deaths in that state over the past 40 years since its exemption was enacted in the 1970s.[9]

One aspect of parental refusal is the failure to inoculate. This failure has grown since 1995, particularly after 2015.[10] The current policy in most states is to allow a "medical exemption" because a small number of children may face particular risks from a given vaccine. But some parents are abusing that allowance, aided by some physicians granting exemptions—without basis and for a fee.[11]

Some child advocates contend that the religious exemption itself is a constitutional affront to the equal protection and due process rights of children.[12] They contend that adults' failure to provide assistance where a duty lay should not be excused on religious grounds, and that the religion defense rests on the premise that the child is the property of the parent. The problem is complicated by the inclusion within parental rights of the prerogative to raise a child in the parent's religion, including to compel practice of that religion. It is clear that where a child's life is threatened, the state may supervene the religion-based decision of a parent not to treat a child and compel that treatment. What is less certain is the termination of parental rights or criminal sanctions for such failures where they do not occur *in extremis*. Some child advocates argue that a broad spectrum of sanctions is necessary to protect children.[13]

In Re Phillip B.

92 Cal. App. 3d 796 (1979)

OPINION: CALDECOTT P.J

A petition was filed by the juvenile probation department in the juvenile court, alleging that Phillip B., a minor, came within the provision of Welfare and Institutions Code section 300, subdivision (b),...because he was not provided with the "necessities of life."

The petition requested that Phillip be declared a dependent child of the court for the special purpose of ensuring that he receive cardiac surgery for a congenital heart defect. Phillip's parents had refused to consent to the surgery. The juvenile court dismissed the petition. The appeal is from the order.

Phillip is a 12-year-old boy suffering from Down's Syndrome.[2] At birth, his parents decided he should live in a residential care facility. Phillip suffers from a congenital heart defect—a ventricular septal defect[3] that results in elevated pulmonary blood pressure. Due to the defect, Phillip's heart must work three times harder than normal to supply blood to his body. When he overexerts, unoxygenated blood travels the wrong way through the septal hole reaching his circulation, rather than the lungs.

If the congenital heart defect is not corrected, damage to the lungs will increase to the point where his lungs will be unable to carry and oxygenate any blood. As a result, death follows. During the deterioration of the lungs, Phillip will suffer from a progressive loss of energy and vitality until he is forced to lead a bed-to-chair existence.

Phillip's heart condition has been known since 1973. At that time Dr. Gathman, a pediatric cardiologist, examined Phillip and recommended cardiac catheterization to further define the anatomy and dynamics of Phillip's condition. Phillip's parents refused.

In 1977, Dr. Gathman again recommended catheterization and this time Phillip's parents consented. The catheterization revealed the extensive nature of Phillip's septal defect, thus it was Dr. Gathman's recommendation that surgery be performed.

Dr. Gathman referred Phillip to a second pediatric cardiologist, Dr. William French of Stanford Medical Center. Dr. French estimates the surgical mortality rate to be 5 to 10 percent, and notes that Down's Syndrome children face a higher than average risk of postoperative complications. Dr. French found that Phillip's pulmonary vessels

213

have already undergone some change from high pulmonary artery pressure. Without the operation, Phillip will begin to function less physically until he will be severely incapacitated. Dr. French agrees with Dr. Gathman that Phillip will enjoy a significant expansion of his life span if his defect is surgically corrected. Without the surgery, Phillip may live at the outside 20 more years. Dr. French's opinion on the advisability of surgery was not asked.

I

It is fundamental that parental autonomy is constitutionally protected....

Inherent in the preference for parental autonomy is a commitment to diverse lifestyles, including the right of parents to raise their children as they think best. Legal judgments regarding the value of child rearing patterns should be kept to a minimum so long as the child is afforded the best available opportunity to fulfill his potential in society.

Parental autonomy, however, is not absolute. The state is the guardian of society's basic values. Under the doctrine of *parens patriae*, the state has a right, indeed, a duty, to protect children. (See, *e.g., Prince v. Massachusetts, supra*, 321 U.S. 158 at p. 166....) State officials may interfere in family matters to safeguard the child's health, educational development and emotional well-being.

One of the most basic values protected by the state is the sanctity of human life. (U.S. Const., 14th Amend., § 1.) Where parents fail to provide their children with adequate medical care, the state is justified to intervene. However, since the state should usually defer to the wishes of the parents, it has a serious burden of justification before abridging parental autonomy by substituting its judgment for that of the parents.

Several relevant factors must be taken into consideration before a state insists upon medical treatment rejected by the parents. The state should examine the seriousness of the harm the child is suffering or the substantial likelihood that he will suffer serious harm; the evaluation for the treatment by the medical profession; the risks involved in medically treating the child; and the expressed preferences of the child. Of course, the underlying consideration is the child's welfare and whether his best interests will be served by the medical treatment.

Section 300, subdivision (b), permits a court to adjudge a child under the age of 18 years a dependent of the court if the child is not provided with the "necessities of life."

* * *

Turning to the facts of this case, one expert witness testified that Phillip's case was more risky than the average for two reasons. One, he has pulmonary vascular changes and statistically this would make the operation more risky in that he would be subject to more complications than if he did not have these changes. Two, children with Down's Syndrome have more problems in the postoperative period. This witness put the mortality rate at 5 to 10 percent, and the morbidity would be somewhat higher. When asked if he knew of a case in which this type of operation had been performed on a Down's Syndrome child, the witness replied that he did, but could not remember a case involving a child who had the degree of pulmonary vascular change that Phillip had. Another expert witness testified that one of the risks of surgery to correct a ventricular septal defect was damage to the nerve that controls the heartbeat as the nerve is in the same area as the defect. When this occurs a pacemaker would be required.

The trial judge, in announcing his decision, cited the inconclusiveness of the evidence to support the petition.

On reading the record we can see the trial court's attempt to balance the possible benefits to be gained from the operation against the risks involved. The court had before it a child suffering not only from a ventricular septal defect but also from Down's Syndrome, with its higher than average morbidity, and the presence of pulmonary vascular changes. In light of these facts, we cannot say as a matter of law that there was no substantial evidence to support the decision of the trial court.

II

In denying the petition the trial court ruled that there was no clear and convincing evidence to sustain the petition. The state contends the proper standard of proof is by a preponderance of the evidence and not by the clear and convincing test. The state asserts

[margin handwritten note: Factors assessed by the state]

that only when a permanent severance of the parent-child relationship is ordered by the court must the clear and convincing standard of proof be applied. Since the petition did not seek permanent severance but only authorization for corrective heart surgery, the state contends the lower standard of proof should have been applied.

* * *

The order dismissing the petition is affirmed.

[2] "Down's syndrome or mongolism is a chromosomal disorder producing mental retardation caused by the presence of 47 rather than 46 chromosomes in a patient's cells, and marked by a distinctively shaped head, neck, trunk, and abdomen." (Robertson, Involuntary Euthanasia of Defective Newborns: A Legal Analysis (1975) 27 Stan.L.Rev. 213, fn. 5.)

[3] In other words, a hole between his right and left ventricles.

Questions for Discussion

1. This case involves the invocation of a parent's fundamental right to make a decision about his or her child's health. Would it matter if the decision were based on a *bona fide* religious belief that the proposed treatment was against a Divine directive?

2. Is this fundamental right to parent mentioned in the Constitution? How do the literalist Justices (such as Scalia) find it to be implied?

3. If the child is a "person" under the Constitution, do the rights to "life, liberty, and the pursuit of happiness" mentioned in the Declaration of Independence apply to him or her? Are the words of the Declaration of Independence relevant to constitutional doctrine?

4. Can the parents argue that as the procreators, parents, and caretakers of Phillip, they best determine what his happiness involves, and what risks it should entail, even including the risk of death? Don't parents make decisions about their children which commonly involve some measure of risk? Does it matter that these parents may have a conflict of interest with regard to care obligations? Does it matter that they have placed Phillip in substantial state care and the state bears the expense of caring for him? Should the economics matter?

B. PUBLIC COVERAGE AND SUBSIDY

1. Child Health Objectives

Several years ago, the U.S. Department of Health and Human Services (DHHS) established a number of child health objectives as part of its "Healthy People" program. The objectives contained in the Healthy People 2010[14] effort sought to improve a variety of child health indicators from 1998 baseline figures. In December 2010, DHHS announced the Healthy People 2020 effort, which included objectives to improve from baseline figures from 2007 or 2008.[15] Table 5-A presents the 2010 and 2020 objectives and baseline data for some key child-related health issues. This data reveals that although some progress was made in reducing child deaths in all five of the child-age brackets, the 2010 objectives were not met for any of the brackets. For all of the other child health issues presented in Table 5-A, in addition to not meeting the 2010 objectives, the country actually fared worse in 2007 or 2008 than in 1998, according to the data.

Health Issue	1998 Baseline	Year 2010 Objective	2007/2008 Baseline	Year 2020 Objective
Reduce all infant deaths (within 1 year)	7.2 per 1,000 of live births	4.5 per 1,000 of live births	6.7 per 1,000 of live births	6.0 per 1,000 of live births
Reduce child deaths, ages 1–4	34.6 per 100,000	18.6 per 100,000	28.6 per 100,000	25.7 per 100,000
Reduce child deaths, ages 5–9	17.7 per 100,000	12.3 per 100,000	13.7 per 100,000	12.3 per 100,000
Reduce child deaths, ages 10–14	22.1 per 100,000	16.8 per 100,000	16.9 per 100,000	15.2 per 100,000
Reduce child deaths, ages 15–19	70.6 per 100,000	39.8 per 100,000	61.9 per 100,000	55.7 per 100,000
Reduce preterm births	11.6% of live births	7.6% of live births	12.7% of live births	11.4% of live births
Increase use of child restraints in vehicles	92% of motor vehicle occupants aged 4 & under	100% of motor vehicle occupants aged 4 & under	86% of children aged 0–12 months 72% of children aged 1–3	95% of children aged 0–12 months 79% of children aged 1–3
Reduce measles breakouts	74 cases	0 cases	115 cases	30 cases
Increase number of children aged 19–35 months who received all recommended vaccines	73%	80%	68%	80%
Reduce preterm births first trimester of pregnancy	83% of live births	90% of live births	70.8% of live births	77.9% of live births
Reduce low birth weight	7.6% of live births	5.0% of live births	8.2% of live births	7.8% of live births
Reduce very low birth weight	1.4% of live births	0.9% of live births	1.5% of live births	1.4% of live births

Table 5-A. Selected Year 2010 and 2020 Objectives for Child Health[16]

2. Child Health Coverage Correlations

Research has shown that having health insurance coverage contributes to positive long-term outcomes related to health, education, and economic success.[17] Uninsured children lack a regular medical professional to monitor their development—and are far more likely than covered children to lack a regular source of care. They are less likely to have regular health examinations for early detection of problems. Timely treatment of children for infectious and chronic diseases such as strep throat, asthma, and ear infections is important to prevent the development of more serious medical conditions. Fewer immunizations, well baby checks, and genetic/chronic disease screening are related consequences. Lower rates of adolescent sexual health care, failed responses to fluid loss and diarrhea, and expensive or debilitating outcomes occur more frequently where coverage is lacking.

Figure 5-A below includes relatively recent 2016 data on child access to health care from the Kaiser Family Foundation Study. It reflects the close relationship between medical service access and insurance incidence, either from employer coverage or Medicaid and other public sources.

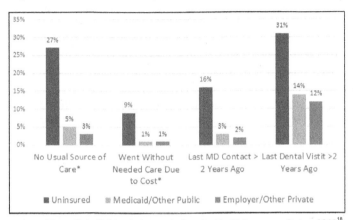

Figure 5–A. Children's Access to Care by Health Insurance Status, 2016[18]

3. Child Health Public Insurance Costs

Medicaid has long been the primary federal program covering the health of impoverished children (as well as adults). The program generally requires a 50% state match and covers all persons living below the poverty line. Medicaid expansion was implemented during the Obama Administration to cover persons up to 138% of the poverty line (as of 2019). Further, 90% of the costs for those subject to that expanded coverage is borne by the federal government. As of 2019, thirteen states have refused to participate in that additional coverage notwithstanding minimal state cost, including Texas, Florida, Wyoming, South Dakota, Wisconsin, Kansas, Missouri, Oklahoma, Mississippi, Tennessee, Georgia, and Alabama. The overall setting for adult coverage is complicated given these variations between states, as well as the related impact of the Affordable Care Act that is implemented in many states and covers a substantial number of adults. However, the recent rescission of the penalties for failure to participate in coverage and other trends make its continuation uncertain. On the other hand, as of 2019 a substantial political effort is underway, usually labelled "Medicare for All" that may change, expand, and simplify the overall coverage.

As for children, they have more inclusive coverage than do adults, without substantial state variations. Nationally, children now make up 43% of Medicaid enrollment, but because of their less expensive cost incur only 19% of its budget as of 2015.[19] Critical to its growth was the development of the Children's Health Insurance Program (CHIP), discussed below, that covers children living in families up to 250% of the poverty line in most states.

4. Extent of Child Medical Coverage

Unlike Medicaid coverage relied upon by impoverished children, the children of middle class and wealthy parents tend to be covered by private employer coverage. Working poor families whose parents earn above the federal poverty line (and work for employers who do not provide dependency coverage) account for most of the nation's uncovered children. In 2017, 77% of uninsured individuals had at least one family member working full-time.[20] A substantial number of uncovered children have parents who work for small businesses of fewer than fifty employees that do not provide coverage or where hours are reduced to avoid the obligation of employer coverage.

The extent of child coverage has increased due to the CHIP noted above. Together, CHIP and Medicaid provide health care coverage to more than 46 million children—Medicaid for 37 million and CHIP for another 9 million children.[21] CHIP was created in 1997 with strong bipartisan support to provide coverage for children who fell above Medicaid eligibility levels but lacked access to other options. CHIP was specifically designed to include child-appropriate benefits, access to pediatric providers, and cost-sharing limits. Children have been able to win unusual bipartisan support for medical coverage. On Jan. 22, 2018, Congress passed a six-year CHIP extension, including funding for the Pediatric Quality Measures program (PQMP)— the only significant federal investment in pediatric health care quality. On Feb. 9, 2018, Congress acted again to extend CHIP for an additional four years. This extension continued important beneficiary protections and funding for the PQMP. Beginning in 2024, states will also be required to report on the pediatric quality measures in the Child Core Set as part of PQMP above.

The federal percentage of CHIP is enhanced above the 50% share it provides to states for Medicaid. It is based on a Federal Medical Assistance Percentage (FMAP) calculation, with most states receiving close to 65% in federal assistance. The 2018 federal budget allocates $2.85 billion for its funding.

Figure 5-B below presents the current distribution of health insurance for children by race, including type or source of coverage. The data underscore two points: 1) the continued importance of private (usually employer-based) coverage for all children and 2) the enhanced importance of public coverage for minority children.

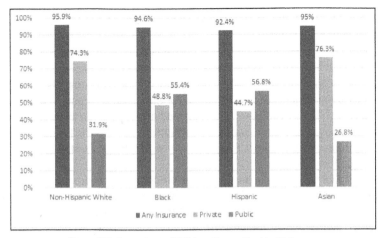

Figure 5-B. Percentage of Children Covered by Health Insurance
At Any Point in the Past Year, by Race and Hispanic Origin:* 2016[22]

5. Other Public Child Health Programs

Beyond generic Medicaid or CHIP coverage, many federal and state health programs have been created to address specific health care needs (e.g., prenatal care and immunizations). Each reflects public policy judgments that those eligible should have access to at least a specified set of services. The result is the current "system" of from nine to sixteen incrementally added programs—each with its own administration, eligibility, funding criteria, benefits, set of providers, payment sources and mechanisms, reporting requirements, and constituency. Each is subject to ongoing contention for political support and available public dollars.

Most of these programs provide direct clinical and/or educational services to a defined group. In addition, states operate a variety of programs to fulfill the public health functions of quality assurance, policy development, and assessment. Health programs are funded by federal, state, and county money. Their mix has been changing in recent years, but one common state strategy is to shift costs to the federal or to the county level.

One such specialized program operates within Medicaid: Early Preventive Screening, Diagnosis, and Treatment (EPSDT), available for eligible children. Most states also have special programs outside Medicaid to cover children with severe and chronic disabilities or diseases. Almost all states have a program called Child Health and Disability Prevention (CHDP), which provides health screens for low-income children not eligible for Medicaid. Funding for Maternal and Child Health Programs (MCH) is allocated to states to promote health care for mothers and children and provide it to those with inadequate access.[23] State Genetic Disease Testing Programs conduct screening, diagnosis, education, and prevention programs for genetic diseases. The Childhood Immunization Program assists state and local programs to immunize children against vaccine-preventable diseases. The Preventive Health and Health Services Block Grant supports a variety of state programs in health prevention. Migrant and Community Health Centers grants are administered directly by the federal Health Resources and Services Administration (HRSA) to the health centers.

The array of categorical programs presents a complex landscape of public programs to families trying to meet their needs. A child eligible for services one year may be ineligible the next, based on age, income status, length of residence, school enrollment, health needs, or changing program requirements. A parent may have different children in different programs and may herself be in yet another—if indeed all are covered. The annual budget struggles over funding levels and policy goals may cause program slots to open or close and program staff to disappear or suffer high turnover.

Some child advocates point out that the proportion of children uncovered and not eligible for public coverage is small. A foundational California study concluded that if coverage were raised to 250% of the poverty line, only 3.3% of those privately uncovered would be ineligible for public coverage. An additional 2.4% are undocumented children and are ineligible for that reason, bringing the total ineligible proportion to 5.7%. Accordingly, the numbers warrant deeming all children covered, with the *post hoc* billing of parents making over 250% of the poverty line on a sliding scale where significant expenses are incurred for their children. Such a change would result in both efficient universal child public health measures and considerable savings in paperwork, qualification, delay, and inconvenience. A further argument in favor: This is not a cash benefit amenable to abuse, and the current fragmented system of barriers is more expensive than the amount necessary to cover the small percentage of ineligible children. Thus far, no state has enacted such a paradigm shift, although California is considering similar changes in 2019.

6. Post-2010 Health Insurance Reform and Children

Two 2010 health reform federal statutes revised health care generally, with child-related impacts—The Patient Protection and Affordable Care Act and the Health Care and Education Reconciliation Act. Although broad in scope, the 2010 changes had the following implications for child health coverage:

- States are required to maintain Medicaid and CHIP coverage, now with assured coverage 2025.
- Private insurers cannot deny coverage for pre-existing conditions (including those of children), must cover children as dependents up to age 26 (the median age of acquired self-sufficiency by youth), cannot impose lifetime limits or drop coverage for illness, and child-only health insurance policies must be offered.
- Somewhat increased spending was authorized for "home visits" to help monitor high risk new parents ($1.5 billion total from 2010 to 2015).
- Funds were added for community health centers that might treat uncovered children ($12 billion total from 2010–15).

- Starting in 2014, individuals must purchase coverage or pay a sum "for maintenance" for themselves and their dependents under the Affordable Care Act (ACA).

The ACA rejected the single payer model of Canada and also the "public option" proposed by some reform groups. It does authorize states to create "exchanges" which allow enrollment by consumers through an entity that pools their market power for private insurance coverage. Historically, consumers who lack employer or public (Medicaid, Medicare, CHIP) coverage must purchase individual policies without group bargaining power and at much higher (often unaffordable) rates, particularly with disabled children or any preexisting condition for any person to be covered. The new exchanges do not pay insurers more than publicly paid rates, and include rules prohibiting rejection or cancellation. Most important for child coverage was the required post-2014 purchase of coverage for individuals and dependents, or the assessment of amounts though the federal income tax systems in lieu (see Section 5000(A)) of the Act. However, that mandatory aspect was struck by the Congress in revoking any penalty for its breach in 2017. Court cases challenging other elements of it remain pending. Some states, such as California, have aggressively implemented the new system, with substantial adult and some child additional coverage resulting. One area where such coverage can be increased would be for the population of children whose parents are deprived coverage by employers scheduling them for work under thirty hours a week or defining them as contractors rather than employees. That concern is heightened by the removal of the ACA penalties for refusing coverage under its terms.

A related factor not effectively addressed by the statute is the smaller supply of physicians and longer waiting periods given discriminatorily low public rates for pediatric services through CHIP or Medicaid. The new statute does require pediatric rates to at least match the Medicare rates for "primary care." But most of the large disparity in pediatric Medicaid compensation is for all or most of the "specialty rates"—orthopod, psychiatry, neurosurgery, and other rates in some states are a fraction of Medicare rates for the same procedures, resulting in long waiting periods or effective unavailability for critical treatment for children. This discrimination against medical services provided to children violates other longstanding provisions of federal law not altered by the ACA that more generally requires Medicare and Medicaid and other federal medical funding to not discriminate in price between disparate patient groupings. In fact, monies paid on behalf of Medicare recipients are commonly 30–50% higher than is paid to pediatricians for the same procedures performed for children. Litigation has not yet occurred to challenge this discriminatory pattern. Notwithstanding these issues of physician supply, scope of coverage, and price discrimination, full implementation of the ACA, if it were to occur, could increase child coverage.

C. CHILD PUBLIC MEDICAL COVERAGE INTERPRETATION AND STANDARDS

Stanton v. Bond

504 F.2d 1246 (7th Cir.1974)

OPINION: SPRECHER, Circuit Judge.

We are asked to determine whether failure of a state to comply with the requirements of the early and periodic screening, diagnosis and treatment (for persons under 21 years of age) provisions of the Social Security Act justifies injunctive relief.

Plaintiffs, representing the class of persons under age 21 who are eligible for medical benefits under Title XIX of the Social Security Act, brought this action under 42 U.S.C. § 1983, against various Indiana state officials, challenging their failure to implement a mandatory federal health program for needy children.

On March 22, 1974, the district court partially granted plaintiffs' motion for summary judgment and enjoined the state officials from continuing to administer the state program in violation of the statute and regulations, and ordered that a complying program be instituted by July 1, 1974. The defendants have appealed.

I

In 1965 Congress added Title XIX to the Social Security Act, which created a comprehensive program of medical assistance for the needy (popularly called Medicaid).[1] The medical assistance program is administered by the states...with the federal government participating through financial grants to the states....States are not required to operate medical assistance plans, but if they elect to do so they must comply with the requirements of Title XIX....

Title XIX requires...that each state plan provide five basic services: inpatient hospital services, outpatient hospital services, laboratory and x-ray services, skilled nursing home services and physicians' services....Originally nine other medical services were optional with the states,[7] and additional optional categories of care have been added by Congress from time to time.

In 1967 Congress amended one of the five mandatory requirements to, in effect, require each participating state to furnish a sixth basic service....

Effective July 1, 1969, such early and periodic screening and diagnosis of individuals who are eligible under the plan and are under the age of 21 to ascertain their physical or mental defects, and such health care, treatment, and other measures to correct or ameliorate defects and chronic conditions discovered thereby, as may be provided in regulations of the Secretary.

The addition of "early and periodic screening and diagnosis" and "treatment" (EPSDT) of persons under the age of 21 was the result of a growing need for child health care among the needy....

* * *

Most childhood handicaps can be prevented or cured or corrected if detected early enough. One-third of the chronically handicapped conditions of children in the United States could be corrected or prevented by preschool care, and continuing care to age eighteen would correct or prevent 60 percent.[14]

* * *

The regulations seek "to assure that individuals under 21 years of age who are eligible for medical assistance may receive the services of such facilities..."....and "assuring that such individuals are informed of such services...."....States are required to enter into "agreements to assure maximum utilization of existing screening, diagnostic, and treatment services provided by other public and voluntary agencies...."...State plans are to assure that the necessary services "will be available to all eligible individuals under 21 years of age...."...

[handwritten margin note: states responsibility]

* * *

The mandatory obligation upon each participating state to aggressively notify, seek out and screen persons under 21 in order to detect health problems and to pursue those problems with the needed treatment is made unambiguously clear by the 1967 act and by the interpretative regulations and guidelines.

Indiana is a participating state....

* * *

In defendants' reply brief, they summarize the nature of Indiana's compliance with EPSDT:

Any of the eligible children in this state can secure all of the requested services merely by requesting them from their local health provider....[Recipients] need merely take their children to the health providers of their choice and obtain for their children the required services.

On March 22, 1974, the district court in its memorandum opinion granting in part plaintiffs' motion for summary judgment, found:

A careful reading of the original and supplemental materials filed in this case indicates, in a clear and convincing fashion, that little, if any, headway has been made by the State as far as the implementation of the EPSDT program is concerned. From the information supplied by the Lake County Welfare Department as well as that supplied by the state, it appears to a certainty that the welfare procedures are nearly the same as they were last year. No special training is required for the caseworkers and there have been only minimal attempts to communicate this program to either the caseworkers or to the ultimate recipients. A few letters and directives, clothed in bureaucratic prose, have been issued to the local units of the Department of Public Welfare of Indiana. In fact, there is no evidence of a comprehensive EPSDT program, nor even any semblance of any screening program however minimal.

The court enjoined defendants "from continuing to administer EPSDT in violation of 42 U.S.C., Section 1396d (a)(4)(B) and the regulations established thereunder" and ordered defendants to have a program meeting the minimum standards of, and in substantial compliance with, the regulations and guidelines, "in effect in every county in Indiana by July 1, 1974."

There is no genuine issue as to any material fact and the plaintiffs were entitled to judgment as a matter of law.

Indiana's somewhat casual approach to EPSDT hardly conforms to the aggressive search for early detection of child health problems envisaged by Congress. It is difficult enough to activate the average affluent adult to seek medical assistance until he is virtually laid low. It is utterly beyond belief to expect that children of needy parents will volunteer themselves or that their parents will voluntarily deliver them to the providers of health services for early medical screening and diagnosis. By the time an Indiana child is brought for treatment it may too often be on a stretcher. This is hardly the goal of "early and periodic screening and diagnosis." EPSDT programs must be brought to the recipients; the recipients will not ordinarily go to the programs until it is too late to accomplish the congressional purpose.

* * *

JUDGMENT IS AFFIRMED.

[1] 42 U.S.C. §§ 1396–1396g.

[7] The nine original optional services were (1) medical or remedial care furnished by state licensed practitioners; (2) home health care services; (3) private duty nursing services; (4) clinic services; (5) dental services; (6) physical therapy; (7) prescribed drugs, dentures, prosthetic devices and eyeglasses; (8) other diagnostic, screening, preventive and rehabilitative services; and (9) tubercular and mental institution services for the aged. Id §§ 1396d(a)(6)—(14).

[14] White House Conference on Children, Report to the President, 184 (1970). Routine throat screening of children age 5—15 with respiratory illness or unexplained fever could prevent 75 percent of rheumatic fever cases....Early detection and treatment of lead poisoning, which leads to mental retardation, seizure disorder, kidney diseases and other handicaps, can reduce blood lead to safe levels before permanent handicaps occur....

Questions for Discussion

1. Indiana announced that EPSDT was "available"—what more should it have done? Is the court engaged in micro-management? If the court does not intervene, what other remedies are available?

2. Can Indiana be forced to engage in outreach if the underlying program is not federally funded? What if its failure incurs additional federal Medicaid dollars because of the state's failure to screen and prevent?

Note on *Sanchez* Case Prior to *Fogarty* Tenth Circuit Decision

Two years prior to the published Tenth Circuit opinion in *Fogarty* (below), the Ninth Circuit decided *Sanchez v. Johnson*, 416 F.3d 1051 (9th Cir. 2005). *Sanchez* was a challenge by the California Medical Association of Medicaid compliance in rate setting for the developmentally disabled. The Ninth Circuit weighed whether the Medicaid statute created a private remedy under 42 U.S.C. § 1983 (the civil rights statute commonly used to vindicate federal constitutional and statutory rights). The court cited the leading case of *Blessing* (520 U.S. 329 (1997)) for the three-part applicable test: (1) Congressional intent to benefit the plaintiff, (2) the right is not so vague and amorphous that it would "strain judicial competence," and (3) the statute unambiguously imposes an obligation on the states. The court held that because the state had in place a "comprehensive deinstitutionalization scheme, which, in light of existing budgetary constraints and the competing demands of other services that the State provides, including the maintenance of institutional care facilities… is 'effectively working'...the courts will not tinker with that scheme." Commenting that Congress did not "unambiguously create an enforceable right," it applied the *Blessing* test in a way to deny remedy—candidly admitting that its concern was not to "disrupt" the complex California system to deal with the developmentally disabled, including children. In *Fogarty*, the Tenth Circuit was confronted by pediatricians and allegations of different (and arguably less ambiguous) provisions of federal Medicaid law pertaining to pediatric rates. The plaintiffs argued that *Sanchez* is distinguishable, as indicated by the district court's findings (see below). In essence, *Fogarty* was not a challenge as to "how" the state should treat the developmentally disabled as part of a complex system, but dealt simply with pediatric Medicaid rates in Oklahoma and their effects on physician supply for children—in relation to the statute's provision requiring those rates not to discriminate against any particular patient grouping.

Oklahoma Chapter of the American Academy of Pediatrics v. Fogarty

472 F. 3d 1208 (10th Cir, 2007)

[Note that the record of the Fogarty case included the following relevant findings of fact and conclusions of law from district court judge Claire Eagan.]

FINDINGS OF FACT AND CONCLUSIONS OF LAW

Introduction

Plaintiff Oklahoma Chapter of the American Academy of Pediatrics is a non-profit professional organization of pediatricians and pediatric specialists....The individual named plaintiffs are thirteen children and their parents; they also serve as representatives of the class certified by the Court. Defendants are officials of the State of Oklahoma and Oklahoma Health Care Authority ("OHCA"), the designated agency responsible for implementing and administering Oklahoma's program to provide eligible children with the health and medical services at issue in this case.

Plaintiffs filed this action in March 2001, alleging essentially that defendants' policies and procedures denied or deprived eligible children of the health and medical care to which those children are entitled by federal law. Plaintiffs seek injunctive relief to ensure that eligible children receive that care. After the Court ruled on motions to dismiss, plaintiffs filed an amended complaint in May 2002. The Court defined and certified the plaintiff class of children on May 30, 2003. The Court then held a non jury trial for 19 days in April and May 2004.

* * *

Findings of Fact:

* * *

17. The United States is one of twenty-five countries with established market economies—so-called developed nations. Of all nations, the United States, at $5,440 per capita, spends more on health care per person than any other country. The rest of the market-economy nations spend about $ 2,400 per capita for health care. The United States, however, is near the bottom of the market economies in the health of its population, as measured by life expectancy, infant mortality, age-adjusted death rates, and other health standards.

18. Among the fifty states, Oklahoma ranks third highest in per capita cost of health insurance premiums. Despite these health insurance premiums, Oklahoma is the only state whose health status has worsened since 1990, as measured by life expectancy and age-adjusted death rates. In other words, poor health is a problem in Oklahoma for both Medicaid and non-Medicaid recipients. The health status of Oklahoma's poor children, in particular, has declined since 1990....

* * *

25. From 1995 through December 31, 2003, provider reimbursement under Oklahoma's Medicaid's fee-for-service schedule never exceeded 72% of Medicare.

* * *

27. Under commercial plans, Oklahoma physicians are reimbursed at rates of 130% to 180% of Medicare

28. While most of the medical services provided by Primary Care Physicians are included in a monthly capitated rate...the medical services provided by non-pediatrician specialists and sub-specialists are paid for on a fee-for-service basis...and are paid approximately 72% of Medicare for most of their services....

* * *

45. According to a 2003 survey conducted by the AAP, only 34% of Oklahoma's pediatricians participate fully in the Medicaid program by accepting all new Medicaid patients. At the same time, 69% of Oklahoma's pediatricians accept all new privately-insured patients....

* * *

49. The lack of pediatricians denies children needed diagnostic and treatment services. A pediatric cardiologist testified that he sees an "extraordinary number" of Medicaid children who find themselves in the hospital when their undiagnosed congenital heart disease becomes malignant....

* * *

53. Children living in rural Oklahoma counties often do not have access to pediatricians for primary care....

* * *

56. ...PCPs are experiencing difficulty in locating speciality providers for their SoonerCare Choice patients....The proportion of Medicaid specialty providers that are willing to accept their patients has steadily dropped since the inception of the program...

[Findings 57 to 91 concern insufficient supply of pediatric orthopods, ENT specialists, neurologists, psychiatrists, urologists, electrophysiologists (specialists who treat children with congenital heart deformities), nephrology, pediatric ER, cardiology, pediatric surgery. Findings 135 to 199 concern failures to provide require Early Periodic Screening, Diagnosis and Treatment (EPSDT) required under federal Medicaid law.]

* * *

Conclusions of Law

* * *

6. ...The "equal access" provision, 42 U.S.C. § 1396a(a)(30)(A), has been a part of the Medicaid Act since 1989. As codified, it requires that a State plan...assure that payments are consistent with efficiency, economy, and quality of care and are sufficient to enlist enough providers so that care and services are available under the plan at least to the extent that such care and services are available to the general population in the geographic area;....

* * *

9. The Court finds that those authorities holding that providers do not have enforceable rights under 1396a(a)(30)(A)....Accordingly, the Court concludes that [the Oklahoma Chapter of the American Academy of Pediatrics...does not have enforceable rights under § 1396a(a)(30)(A), and should be dismissed from this lawsuit....However, the Court concludes that the individual class members continue to have standing to enforce § 1396a(a)(30) as Medicaid recipients....

* * *

19. The second "major factor" which the Clark court considered in assessing compliance with the equal access mandate was the level of reimbursement....In deciding that California's dental rates were inadequate, the Clark court considered the fact that the rates there fell well short of the defendant's stated goal of "90% of the average allowance of private insurers." [In the instant case], the effect of defendants' rate-setting and implementation speaks for itself.

* * *

21. While there is no established percentage for sufficient Medicaid reimbursement rates under federal law, rates which consistently fall well below what is allowed under Medicare, let alone under private insurance, have been shown to be inadequate to attract enough providers so that health care services are available to Medicaid recipients to the same extent as those services are available to the general population....

* * *

39. As discussed above, the United States Supreme Court subsequently held that, in order for a statute to be individually enforceable under § 1983, the statutory language at issue must unambiguously confer a right. *Gonzaga University v. Doe*, 536 U.S. 273 (2002). After *Gonzaga*, at least four courts have found that the EPSDT provisions of the Medicaid Act are enforceable by private right of action under 42 U.S.C. § 1983....The Court concludes that the EPSDT provisions of the Medicaid Act unambiguously confer rights upon the class members in this case.

* * *

BRISCOE, Circuit Judge

...On May 19, 2005, after the parties submitted the agreed proposed injunctive order, the district court issued a Final Judgment and Permanent Injunction. Therein, the district court reiterated its legal conclusions and, based upon the two alleged violations outlined above, directed defendants to:

"institute a fee schedule for fee-for-service physician . . . reimbursement for covered, medically necessary physician services provided to minor children" under the Medicaid program "at the rate for each Current Procedural Terminology . . . Code that equals one hundred percent (100%) of the rate paid by Medicare for physician services as soon as possible within the strictures of" state and federal law;....[and] institute a fee-for-service schedule determined by the consulting firm as necessary to assure reasonably prompt access to health care for minor children in the Oklahoma Medicaid program...

* * *

The district court also erred, given our holding in Mandy R., in concluding that defendants violated § 1396a(a)(8)'s "reasonable promptness" requirement by paying providers insufficient rates for services rendered to Medicaid beneficiaries. Although the district court apparently concluded, and perhaps correctly so, that low rates of reimbursement reduce the number of providers available to Medicaid beneficiaries, and in turn increase the time Medicaid beneficiaries must wait to receive medical services from available providers, this conclusion does not mean that defendants failed (or will fail in the future) to be reasonably prompt in paying for services actually rendered by available providers, as required by § 1396a(a)(8). Indeed, if the district court's theory were correct, it would broaden [it] far beyond its intended scope, and would require federal courts to engage in what the Third Circuit has described as the "onerous" task of "evaluating whether a state's Medicaid reimbursement rates are 'reasonable and adequate.'" Chiles, 136 F.3d at 717. Thus, we agree with defendants that the district court erred when it directed defendants to conduct a study of rates, costs and services, and then to use the study to correct what the district court concluded were too-low rates of reimbursement. Likewise, we agree with defendants that the district court erred in requiring rates to be set at a level that would ensure a two-thirds "level of participation" among physicians in the State of Oklahoma....

* * *

Finally, plaintiffs' "substantial compliance" arguments are clearly wrong because they hinge on the mistaken view that the above-quoted provisions of the Medicaid Act "clearly and unambiguously require states to furnish EPSDT services to all eligible individuals under the age of 21." ... As we have discussed, the term "medical assistance," as used throughout the Medicaid Act, refers to the payment of all or part of the cost of the care and services specifically described in the act. That is, as noted in Mandy R., the Medicaid Act requires participating states to provide beneficiaries financial assistance rather than actual medical services. Thus, not only do the statutes cited by plaintiffs not obligate defendants to ensure that EPSDT services are "fully" delivered to the plaintiff class, those statutes impose no obligation whatsoever on defendants to deliver any medical services. Rather, as we concluded in Mandy R., defendants' obligation under these statutes is to pay promptly for the medical services outlined in the Medicaid Act, including EPSDT services.

* * *

In a supplemental brief filed after the issuance of Mandy R., plaintiffs argue for the first time on appeal that 42 U.S.C. § 1396a(a)(43) "create[s] enforceable rights" in favor of Medicaid recipients, "including the right to receive actual [EPSDT] services." ... We conclude these arguments are not properly before us. Absent authorization from this court, a party is generally precluded from raising issues in a supplemental brief that were not addressed in the opening brief."

* * *

Questions for Discussion

1. Is it reasonable for the court to distinguish that "medical assistance" under the Medicaid statute means actual delivery of services, not payment for them? Do not almost all federal statutes provide funding as the mechanism to accomplish stated goals? Assuming that funding is related to delivery of services, is not the inadequacy of the former in the marketplace not a direct deprivation of the latter?

2. Is the onerous task of examining rate adequacy one beyond the capacity of a court? Can the court not simply declare that a given compensation level does not meet the statutory requirement due to its effects contrary to that statute, without engaging in a new, complex judicial rewrite? Is not the relationship between compensation and supply a relatively simple matter of economic expert evidence? How does this complexity compare with historical court orders in areas ranging from antitrust to anti-discrimination statutes?

D. CHILD SAFETY

1. Causes of Child Deaths and Injuries

The leading non-disease causes of death of children have remained consistent since the late 1980s: for very young children to age four, drownings, auto accidents, homicides and accidental suffocations are the four leading causes. For children 5–15, auto accidents, homicides (especially those involving firearms), and accidental drownings head the list. For children 16–20, causes shift markedly to homicide (especially those involving firearms and knives) as the leading cause, followed by traffic accidents and suicides.[24]

Unintentional injuries (primarily motor vehicle accidents) are the leading cause of death for all boys and girls after age one. Among boys, homicide is the second leading cause for children age 1–4 and is the third leading cause among boys aged 15–19.[25] Improvements in infectious disease control and unintentional injury prevention may be offset by increases in violence, especially homicides, suicides, and injuries by firearms.[26]

2. Auto Safety

All states require that infants in a moving vehicle be in a child restraint car seat. However, coverage does not extend to all types of vehicles, with commercial and even school vehicles commonly excluded. Amendments in 2005 to the Code of Federal Regulations (49 CFR 571.213) and in effect from 2007, require restraint systems in vehicle manufacture that protect infants and small children. But actual use is dependent upon parental decisions, and studies commonly find the seat belt anchor of child car seats attached by parents is substantially looser than required for effective restraint. They also indicate that older children over five are the grouping with particularly deficient child accommodation.

Ideally, parents employ a rear facing car seat to age two and a forward facing seat from ages two to five, followed by a "booster seat" until an adult seat belt fits properly. These choices may also interact with the results of an airbag deployment, leading placement in the back seat as often the advisable choice. And the booster seat for children ages five to eight is the largest area of protection omission. A 2017 study found that increased use of the underutilized booster seats for those children increased their restraint use by almost 300%, and decreased injuries and incapacitations from accidents by 17%.[27]

The Centers for Disease Control recently cautioned that motor vehicle injuries are a leading cause of death among children in the United States and that many can be prevented. The CDC cited three relevant factual findings: (1) In the United States, 723 children ages twelve years and younger died as occupants in motor vehicle crashes during 2016,[4] and more than 128,000 were injured in 2016; (2) One CDC study found that, in one year, more than 618,000 children from newborn up to age twelve rode in vehicles without the use of a child safety seat or booster seat or a seat belt at least some of the time; and (3) Of the children ages twelve years and younger who died in a crash in 2016 (for which restraint use was known), 35% were not buckled up.[28]

3. Motor Vehicle Operations

Almost all American children begin to drive just after reaching the age of sixteen. The auto accident incidence among youth is extraordinary, and is reflected in disparate insurance rates that will often amount to five times or more the rates extant for adults over 25 years of age.

Most states prohibit youth motor vehicle driving until the age of fifteen or sixteen, with higher ages required for commercial vehicles. States increasingly regulate the details of license qualification, including the imposition of a graduated license, with an initial "learner's permit" allowing driving only where being tutored by a parent, driving instructor, or other qualified adult. This is followed by a restricted or probationary license including additional training and testing, before a standard license is issued, usually at age seventeen or eighteen.

Some states require parental (or other qualified adult) sponsorship and assumption of joint liability for youth licensure. A parent may avoid liability by reporting a possibly dangerous youth to the state department of motor vehicles for license revocation. In addition, states are increasingly using the revocation of the license privilege as a sanction to deter undesirable youth behavior, including truancy, school drop-outs, or the commission of specified crimes (including tobacco purchase, graffiti offenses or other violations unrelated to driving). Most states will suspend the license of a person under 21 for possessing or using drugs or alcohol even if not connected to vehicle operation.

4. Firearm Safety

The Gun-Free Schools Act of 1990 made it a federal crime to carry a concealed handgun or ammunition on or within 1,000 feet of a school. In *U.S. v. Lopez*, 514 U.S. 549 (1995), the Supreme Court struck the statute as insufficiently "commercial" in character to confer federal interstate commerce jurisdiction. Such a prohibition must rest exclusively with the states (see discussion of *Lopez* in Chapter 1).

Congress has enacted two major statutes since 1994 that strike a more "commercial" format. The Violent Crime Control and Law Enforcement Act of 1994 prohibits sale or transfer to a person reasonably known or believed to be under the age of eighteen as a federal offense.[29] States are permitted to detain juveniles arrested or convicted of possessing handguns in "secure" juvenile facilities. The amended Gun-Free Schools Act of 1994 requires that local schools receiving federal funds have a "zero tolerance" firearm policy requiring a minimum one year expulsion for any student bringing a firearm to school.[30] These approaches purport to regulate commerce or use federal funding conditions to avoid *Lopez* problems.

In addition, almost all states have policies consistent with these federal statutes, including prohibitions on possession of firearms on school grounds. Many states also include liability where negligent storage allows juveniles to obtain weapons. California, for example, imposes liability for "criminal storage of the first degree" where an individual stores a loaded firearm at a location he or she reasonably knows is accessible to a child and such a weapon is discharged with death or serious injury resulting. "Criminal storage of a firearm in the second degree" applies to such keeping where the result is any injury or the firearm is discharged at all or is carried to a public place.[31] Defenses to the crime include the illegal entry of the child to obtain the weapon, that it is in a locked container reasonably believed to be secure, or that it had a trigger lock.

Child advocates generally support restrictions on hand gun sales to minors, firearm registration, and most important, required trigger locks.

5. Alcohol Use

Alcohol consumption by youth occurs at a higher incidence than illegal drug use and correlates closely with violence related delinquency (and firearm fatalities) where victims are most often other youth.

Alcohol is also ubiquitous where fatal automobile accidents occur, especially those involving youth. When the Twenty-First Amendment to the Constitution was repealed, ending prohibition of alcohol sales, most states set 21 years of age as the minimum age to lawfully imbibe. However, the lowering of the voting age to 18 years of age and other youth advocacy efforts of the 1960s and 1970s led to the lowering of the drinking age in almost half of the states. In reaction to this reduction, Congress enacted the National Minimum Drinking Age Act in 1984,[32] withholding federal highway funds from states allowing alcohol purchase or possession by persons under 21 years of age. This spending power standard was upheld in

South Dakota v. Dole, 483 U.S. 203 (1987), and all fifty states have now raised the minimum age to 21.

Some states allow prescription of alcohol by physicians and religious use of alcohol by clergy. Some states go further and exempt parental provision of alcohol to their own children—which may trigger enhanced parental tort liability should an intoxicated child thus injure a third party. Further, where this parental exemption is used to permit excessive youth intoxication, the parent may suffer criminal or civil liability for parental neglect, for "contributing to the delinquency of a minor," reckless endangerment or other state law violations.

Federal law now reflects a national theoretical "zero tolerance" policy for underage drinking. As of 1995, federal highway funds are jeopardized to states failing to enact statutes setting the prohibited blood alcohol concentration for "driving under the influence" (DUI) by those under 21 years of age at or below 0.02% per liter of blood.[33] That level represents the effect of approximately one can of beer, glass of wine, or shot of hard liquor on a person of average body weight, and is one-third to one-fifth the typical level establishing DUI for adults.

6. Accident Injury Prevention

Most states have a program directed at injury prevention. In some states, it is called an Emergency Preparedness and Injury Control Program (EPIC), or a similar title. These agencies conduct epidemiological investigations and control programs for prevention of unintentional and intentional injuries. They generally include programs, education, an advisory task force and a state injury control plan.

These injury prevention programs are structured differently from state to state. However, they are eligible for MCH Title V block grant funds (see discussion above) and are sometimes administered as part of a state MCH office. Unintentional injuries remain the leading cause of death for all youth from ages one to twelve. Given the costs of such injuries, spending for prevention from federal or state sources is low, even in major states.[34]

Federal standards have been imposed historically to address some lethal dangers. For example, Federal Trade Commission standards altered flammable fabric use in child night clothing and blankets after some horrendous deaths of children by fire in the 1960s.[35] The widespread use of smoke alarms in homes since the 1980s has also saved increasing numbers of children from fire death or injury. Child proof medicine bottles, some household product safety lids, and the crib and other standards of the Consumer Product Safety Commission have evolved over the past two decades to contribute to child safety.

However, the incidence of serious injury and deaths to children remains high. Beyond automobile accidents, firearms, and alcohol as discussed above, death or unintentional injury to children particularly arise from eight preventable causes: drownings (most notably in home swimming pools), bicycle accidents, playground injuries (from unsafe equipment or surfaces), electrocution, parental shaking, being left unattended in cars, and strangulation or suffocation from such things as window blind cords or thin dry cleaner bags. Except for the last instance, most public sector prevention initiatives have come primarily from the state or local levels.

A Phoenix ordinance, enacted into law in California, has reduced child swimming pool drownings by requiring a fence with lockable gate, a secure cover, or a buzzer on the back doors leading to the pool.[36] States increasingly require children who ride bicycles to wear helmets given the devastating impact of head injuries on pavement.[37] Some states have adopted statewide public playground safety standards.[38] Many states have created a system of "poison control centers" including a hotline to call for immediate antidote information. Devices to block infant access to wall sockets and to provide additional circuit breakers have become common. Some states have initiated education campaigns on the theme "never, never shake a baby" to stress the danger, given the weak necks and vulnerable heads of infants. And an increasing number of states are addressing the problem of babies left unattended in cars without consideration of the often startling and sometimes fatal temperature effect of sunlight on a closed vehicle.[39] However, these measures, notwithstanding some evidence of preventive impact, provide protection in only a minority of states covering a fraction of the nation's children.

E. ENVIRONMENTAL HEALTH

Research has identified five common environmental dangers disproportionately endangering children: lead, air pollution, pesticides, environmental tobacco smoke, and drinking water contamination. As to each of these sources, children are not merely "little adults," but suffer more harm from levels of exposure which adults can tolerate. Child health advocates contend that federal and state regulatory officials have set standards based on danger to adults without adequately factoring in impacts on children, who are more vulnerable.

Environmental Policy: Increasing Focus on Children's Health
The George Washington University Medical Center 4:1 HEALTH POLICY: CHILD HEALTH
(Winter 1997)

For decades, the federal government has registered, regulated and sometimes restricted potential environmental pollutants, from industrial chemicals to lawn fertilizers. Yet, until very recently, the potential adverse effects of these substances on the health of children had rarely been addressed. This is largely the result of environmental policy that has generally emphasized protection of the environment over the health of the public.

Recently, however, environmental policy took a new turn with the enactment of the Food Quality Protection Act of 1996 and the Safe Drinking Water Act of 1996. Both of these new laws pay special attention to the health considerations of children and other vulnerable populations in defining food and water quality standards.

A trend toward growing concern for pediatric environmental health is further evidenced by proponents who tout the benefits to children's health of other environmental measures. Among these are proposed Environmental Protection Agency (EPA) regulations to lower ozone levels and particulate matter emissions, as well as legislation introduced to reform the Superfund and possible legislation to reauthorize the Clean Water Act.

Still, critics contend that the methodologies employed to assess the risks of various materials, even if increasingly sensitive to the dangers to children, remain inadequate and lead to unjustifiable consequences for children.

Children Are Not "Little Adults"

Children are more susceptible than adults to environmental pollutants due to physiological differences and developmental factors. At each stage of development, a child faces exposure to external hazards that may be harmful to her health.

The fetus, for example, is exposed to the same harmful substances to which the mother herself is exposed. An example is exposure to polychlorinated biphenyls (PCBs), which were produced in the U.S. between 1929 and 1977 to serve as insulating liquids in electrical transformers and capacitators.

Although no longer produced, PCBs released into the environment long ago are still present, as they take several decades to decompose. Measurable amounts of PCBs have been detected in soil, water, fish, milk and human tissues. Several studies show that pregnant women who chronically ingested PCBs through their food gave birth to babies with low birth weights, small head circumferences, and signs of developmental delay that persist over time.

Likewise, newborns can be exposed to harmful substances in milk, whether it be breast milk or cow's milk used in infant formula, polluted indoor air, and contaminated tap water. Infants are often placed on floors, carpets and lawns where they are more vulnerable to exposure to chemicals associated with these surfaces. And because of their greater proximity to the source, infants are more likely to inhale toxic fumes from such sources.

Toddlers engage in sucking and mouthing behaviors which increase their chances of ingesting environmental pollutants. A clear relationship has been established between these behaviors and increased blood lead levels, for example. A common source of lead is paint dust and chips in older homes which children eat directly or lick from their hands.

The most important adverse health effect of a high concentration of lead in children is cognitive deficiencies. One study shows that the higher the level of lead concentration in blood, the lower the IQ of the child.

Preschool and school-aged children consume more fluids and food, have higher rates of breathing and blood flow, and are in contact with the outside environment more often than adults. These factors expose children to an increased quantity of environmental pollutants and put them at greater risk of toxicity than any other age group.

Accumulation of pesticides from food, particularly fruits and vegetables, and the outside environment, such as treated lawns, is particularly high during childhood

* * *

Risk Assessment vs. the "Precautionary Principle"

...One major point of contention revolves around "risk assessment," the methodology used to evaluate the dangers of any given chemical substance. Risk assessment is a technique used to determine whether the risks associated with the use of a pollutant are outweighed by the environmental, social and economic benefits associated with its use. If the net benefit is positive, a pollutant is deemed safe and therefore allowed for general use. Safety is defined as "a reasonable certainty of no harm" or "negligible risk," often determined to be a probability of less than "a one in a million lifetime risk of cancer."

This approach, therefore, promotes the greater good at the expense of the few people who may be harmed. Under EPA policy and new federal law, determination of safety must now take into account whether a permissible pollutant is safe, not just for adults, but for infants and children as well..... [however, such risk assessment] is flawed for two main reasons.

First, it is based on assumptions of acceptable levels of harm set by regulators and imposed on unconsenting people. Second, it is based on data that are very limited, particularly when it comes to children.

Rather, these critics argue, a stricter methodology known as the "precautionary principle" or the "zero risk standard" should be used. This approach justifies the prohibition of the use of a pollutant if it can not be proven to be totally safe. In other words, as long as some individuals run the risk of being harmed from the use of a specific pollutant, that pollutant should be banned altogether.

...In 1988, Congress requested the National Academy of Sciences (NAS) to examine the issue of pesticide residues in food and children's health. The examination resulted in a 1993 report, Pesticides in the Diets of Infants and Children, which pointed to the need for a comprehensive strengthening of pesticide qualifications. Specifically, the report called for more stringent pesticide regulations to protect children's inherent vulnerabilities to toxic substances. It recommended that all testing for pesticide registration include children's dietary patterns.

The report also suggested improving the monitoring and tracking of pesticide residue found in children's food and establishing a full assessment of its distinctive risks to children's cognitive and physical development....

Postings of the EPA in 2017–19 indicate that the 1997 report above remains a relevant analysis of child safety regulation issues. The EPA has developed regulatory guides to implement Executive Order 13045, a 1997 Presidential Order commanding priority attention by the EPA and other federal agencies to child health and safety risks.[40] That Order requires that each federal agency: "(a) shall make it a high priority to identify and assess environmental health risks and safety risks that may disproportionately affect children; and (b) shall ensure that its policies, programs, activities, and standards address disproportionate risks to children that result from environmental health risks or safety risks." In addition, the Children's Health Policy requires EPA "to consider the risks to infants and children consistently and explicitly as a part of risk assessments generally." In 2003, it developed a Handbook reference tool of continued relevance in 2019.[41]

F. JUDICIAL REVIEW OF CHILD HEALTH AND SAFETY REGULATION

Aqua Slide 'N' Dive Corp. v. Consumer Product Safety Commission
569 F.2d 831 (5th Cir. 1978)

OPINION: RONEY, Circuit Judge:

In this proceeding for review authorized by the Consumer Product Safety Act, 15 U.S.C.A. §§ 2051 et seq., Aqua Slide 'N' Dive Corporation, an interested manufacturer, challenges the legality of a "Safety Standard for Swimming Pool Slides" adopted by the Consumer Product Safety Commission.

The primary issue is whether substantial evidence supports the Commission's finding, required by statute, that this standard is "reasonably necessary to eliminate or reduce an unreasonable risk of injury." § 2058(c)(2)(A). The Commission demonstrated that adults who slide into the water headfirst encounter a one in 10 million risk of spinal injury and paralysis. The Commission, however, has only an untested theory to support its conclusion that the warnings required by the standard to be affixed to slides will actually reduce such injuries, and has failed to produce adequate evidence to show the chain required by the standard to be fixed to the slide ladder will avert drownings which might result from the installation of slides in deep water, and has further failed to consider adequately the effect of these standards on slide purchasers. Accordingly, we grant the petition for review and set aside challenged sections of the standard relating to warning signs, a ladder chain, and installation instructions.

I. INTRODUCTION

Congress created the Consumer Product Safety Commission, an independent regulatory agency, in 1972. Among the purposes of the Commission are protection of the public "against unreasonable risks of injury associated with consumer products" and assistance to consumers "in evaluating the comparative safety" of such products....

* * *

The Act took effect in late 1972. In mid-1973 both a trade association known as the National Swimming Pool Institute and the plaintiff in this action, Aqua Slide, petitioned the Commission under § 2059 seeking promulgation of a safety standard for swimming pool slides. Aqua Slide's admitted motive was to prevent a product ban or forced repurchase threatened by the Bureau of Product Safety, a predecessor of the Commission,...

The Commission granted the petition and sought offers to develop the requested standard....The Institute appointed a committee and hired an engineering consultant, Weiner Associates, Inc., to assist it. Members of the committee included two pool builders, an orthopedic surgeon specializing in sports injuries, the president of Aqua Slide...[and others].

The Commission modified the Institute's proposal in several respects. It rewrote the warning signs, and included a specific mention of the danger of paralysis....The Commission decided it did not have jurisdiction to regulate slide installation, and so it substituted required instructions which recommended appropriate installation depths.... The ladder chain provision, however, remained mandatory....The Commission published its proposed rule on September 15, 1975. An oral proceeding took place in Washington, D.C., on October 10. Aqua Slide did not participate, and during the course of the comment period, which closed on October 15, submitted only a brief written criticism of the rule....

Aqua Slide brought a timely petition for review to this Court. The Court denied Aqua Slide's motion to stay enforcement and the standard became effective on July 17, 1976.

II. STANDARD OF REVIEW

* * *

[T]he Court will defer to Commission fact-finding expertise, but it can do so only when the record shows the Commission has made an actual judgment concerning the significance of the evidence....Also, the extent to which data and views in the record have been exposed to public comment will affect their reliability. Technical studies which have survived scrutiny of the scientific community and the public provide sounder footing for an inexpert judiciary to base its decision on than do facts which first see the light of day in a court proceeding....

* * *

III. "REASONABLE NECESSITY"

The Act requires a finding that the standard is "reasonably necessary to eliminate or reduce an unreasonable risk of injury."....Aqua Slide argues that substantial evidence does not support the Commission's conclusion,...that this standard is "reasonably necessary," in two particulars: (i) the warning signs have not been tested, may not work, and may be so explicit as to deter slide use unnecessarily, (ii) the ladder chain has not been shown effective.

* * *

The Act does not define the term "reasonably necessary," and apparently Congress intended the Commission and the courts to work out a definition on a case-by-case basis....The legislative history, and the holdings of other cases decided under similar statutes, do discuss the meaning of "unreasonable risk," and indicate that term is interrelated with the "reasonably necessary" requirement. The necessity for the standard depends upon the nature of the risk, and the reasonableness of the risk is a function of the burden a standard would impose on a user of the product.

* * *

The Senate Report provides an example of the kind of analysis Congress had in mind. It said a sharp knife might pose a reasonable risk of injury, because dulling the blade to make it safe would also make it useless. A sharp knife in a child's silverware set, however, might be unreasonable....In the *Forester* case, the D.C. Circuit found the Commission failed to show the risk of protrusions on a bicycle frame was unreasonable because it had not considered the extent to which a regulation which banned the protrusions would impair the bicycle's utility....In *Clever Idea Company v. Consumer Product Safety Commission*, 385 F. Supp. 688, 694 (E.D.N.Y.1974), another Federal Hazardous Substances Act case, the Commission failed to prove a risk of injury from plastic toy mouthpieces was unreasonable. There the risk was never shown to exist. No injuries had been reported, and the Commission's simulated "bite test" was not shown reliable. The Commission does not have to conduct an elaborate cost-benefit analysis....It does, however, have to shoulder the burden of examining the relevant factors and producing substantial evidence to support its conclusion that they weigh in favor of the standard.

In this case, the severity of the risk is so terrible that virtually any standard which actually promised to reduce it would seem to be "reasonably necessary." Both the Commission and the Institute concentrated their fact-gathering efforts on an attempt to identify the precise nature of the risk. After surveying slide accidents,... and considering the result of scientific studies of slide dynamics,...the Commission identified a risk of "quadriplegia and paraplegia resulting from users (primarily adults using the swimming pool slide for the first time) sliding down the slide in a head first position and striking the bottom of the pool."....The risk is greater than an inexperienced "belly-slider" would anticipate, because improper headfirst entry can cause an uncontrollable "snap rotation of the body" that "allows the arms to clear the bottom prior to head impact."....Also, a curved slide can disorient persons who are using it for the first time....Without question, paraplegia is a horrible injury....

The risk of paraplegia from swimming pool slides, however, is extremely remote. More than 350,000 slides are in use, yet the Commission could find no more than 11 instances of paraplegia over a six-year period. According to Institute figures, the risk, for slide users, is about one in 10 million, less than the risk an average person has of being killed by lightning. App. 583. The standard faces an initial difficulty because it is not easy to predict where paraplegia will next occur, and to burden all slide manufacturers, users, and owners with requirements that will only benefit a very few, is questionable. Remote risks have been found "unreasonable," but the context was one in which the safety standard promised to eliminate the danger entirely...see *Bunny Bear v. Peterson*, 473 F.2d 1002 (1st Cir. 1973) (risk of crib mattress fires, Flammable Fabrics Act, 15 U.S.C.A. § 1193)....

A. Warning Signs

Given the infrequency of the risk, it was incumbent upon the Institute and the Commission to produce evidence that the standard actually promised to reduce the risk. Instead, both the Institute and the Commission gave the matter short shrift. To begin with, the standard only applies to new slides. It does not affect slides now in use, despite an Institute finding that "there are many more slides in use than produced per year by a factor of ten to one."....It is odd that the Commission chose this limited method of addressing the risk rather than deciding to use its power to conduct a public education campaign, which could reach far more slide users.... A Red Cross representative told the Institute that its safety courses could inform 3,000,000 people a year of the risk of slide injury....

Furthermore, the record contains only the most ambiguous of indications that the warning signs would actually be heeded by slide users. The Commission did not test the signs....The only testing was done at the last minute by one Institute committee member, who conducted experiments for two days. The letter describing the tests, although it concluded that the signs "would seem capable of effecting significant risk reduction," also indicated that the test subjects "claimed they understood the belly slide message, but this seemed questionable," the message was "long," few readers "did more than glance" at it, and "it should be cautioned that the signs will not be a strong countermeasure to unsafe acts, but of limited effectiveness.".....

...While it is no doubt rational to assume the warning signs would be heeded, mere rationality is not enough. The statute requires substantial evidence to support the Commission's ultimate conclusion that the signs are a reasonably necessary means of reducing an unreasonable risk....Unarticulated reliance on Commission "experience" may satisfy an "arbitrary, capricious" standard of review,... but it does not add one jot to the record evidence....

In short, the Commission provided little evidence that the warning signs would benefit consumers. The risk is remote. The evidence that the signs would reduce the risk rests more on inference than it does on proof. In weighing the "reasonable necessity" for the signs, the crucial question then, is whether the benefit has a reasonable relationship to the disadvantages the sign requirement imposes.

In this case, the prime disadvantage to which Aqua Slide points is the warning's effect on the availability of the slides. Because the Commission did not test the signs, it provided little evidence of whether the signs were so explicit and shocking in their portrayal of the risk of paralysis as to constitute an unwarranted deterrent to the marketing of slides, and, hence, their availability to users. The record provides only scant assurance that purchasers would not be so alarmed by the warning signs that they would unnecessarily abstain. The signs do not indicate paralysis is a one in 10 million risk....

Certainly, on this record, the economic finding is crucial. The only way to tell whether the relationship between the advantages and disadvantages of the signs is reasonable is to know exactly what those disadvantages are. Yet the Commission's study of the standard's economic impact lacks the indicia of reliability. At the same time, the proof that signs will significantly reduce the risk is weak. We consequently hold that the Commission has failed to provide substantial evidence to demonstrate the reasonable necessity of the warning signs. We set aside the warning sign requirement and the mandatory intended use instructions which repeat the warning,....

B. *Ladder Chain*

The one aspect of the standard which does promise to reduce the risk of paraplegia is the placement of large slides in deep water....The Commission concluded it did not have jurisdiction over slide placement, so it included placement "recommendations" in the standard, and made them a part of the required intended use instructions....Deep water placement, however, presented the Commission with an increased risk of child drownings.

* * *

The Commission took two steps to reduce the risk of drowning associated with deep water slides. It redrew the warning sign to include a drowning figure, and it required all such slides to have a ladder chain. That warning sign, however, was never tested for effectiveness. The only tests performed on the ladder chain were done by Institute consultant Robert Weiner, who tried one out on his neighbors' children at a pool in his own back yard....The scant five pages of Institute committee discussion, which provides the only support for the chain cited by the Government, does not provide persuasive evidence that the chain would prevent children from using the slides....Weiner thought the chain would serve as a warning device, but he apparently did not think it would prevent a child from climbing the ladder....One Institute committee member, who had observed chains in use, said the chains would "create some difficulty."....The Commission concluded the chain's presence "should, on balance, create a safer product."....

This is not the stuff of which substantial evidence is made...

...Because the Commission failed to produce substantial evidence to show the ladder chain and warning sign would work, its balance collapses and all of 16 C.F.R. § 1207.6 must be set aside.

* * *

WISDOM, Judge, concurring.

... As I read the record, there was substantial evidence to support a conclusion that warning signs would reduce the risk, although the majority says that the Commission was operating on an "untested theory." This theory was that some people will read and be affected by warning signs. When the group for whom the message is intended is

first-time adult and teenage sliders, such a theory needs little, if any, empirical support to meet the substantial evidence standard. In this case the theory was supported, not only by the Commission, but by the National Swimming Pool Institute. The petitioner does not disagree. It has not pressed the question of the effectiveness of the signs; it questions only the relationship between the effectiveness and its economic cost. The changes the Commission made in the Institute's signs could only have strengthened them, as far as effectiveness is concerned.

Furthermore, there was a study made of the effectiveness of the Institute's signs. The majority properly notes that the researcher concluded that signs provided only a qualified benefit, but he did decide that they would be beneficial. His research dealt with children, rather than with the adults and teenagers at whom the Commission aimed its signs. That should make even stronger his conclusion that "they seem a desirable behavior modification device, but no panacea."....

The majority responds by pointing to evidence in the record that shows the signs will not solve the problem. Yet that evidence does not prove that signs will not work; it shows only that their effectiveness is limited....

* * *

Questions for Discussion

1. Assume that the Commission's *Aqua-Slide* order was upheld and thereafter violated. Can the Commission effectively void its own standards through non-enforcement? Note that the Consumer Product Safety Act (15 U.S.C. §§ 2051–2084) includes a right of private action for damages (15 U.S.C. § 2072) where rules are violated. Such a federal cause of action is concurrent with existing state tort or product liability damage actions. Is such enforcement viable through class actions given the commonality and other requirements now imposed for federal class certification? (See discussion in Chapter 1.) Is there adequate incentive for counsel to file such an action on an individual case basis where attorney's fees must be taken from a fund which may require a large group of victims (class format)?

2. Assume that the Commission had rejected the proposed *Aqua-Slide* order as to both a warning and a ladder sign. If a private tort action were filed in state court based partly on the failure to have such warnings, with an offer of proof that such warnings would have prevented an injury, what impact would the Commission's rejection have on the case? Could the defense use the Commission's rejection to bar liability for that notice failure?[42]

Anheuser-Busch, Inc. v. Mayor and City Council of Baltimore City
101 F.3d 325 (4th Cir. 1996)

NIEMEYER, Circuit Judge:

I

In Anheuser-Busch I, we upheld against a constitutional challenge a city ordinance prohibiting the placement of stationary, outdoor advertising that advertises alcoholic beverages in certain areas of *Baltimore City*. ...The ordinance was designed to promote the welfare and temperance of minors exposed to advertisements for alcoholic beverages by banning such advertisements in particular areas where children are expected to walk

to school or play in their neighborhood....Applying the four-prong test for evaluating commercial speech announced in *Central Hudson Gas & Elec. Corp. v. Public Serv. Comm'n*, 447 U.S. 557...(1980), we concluded, in respect to the disputed prongs, that the ban of outdoor advertising of alcoholic beverages in limited areas directly and materially advances Baltimore's interest in promoting the welfare and temperance of minors....

* * *

If the target is simply higher prices generally to discourage consumption, the regulation imposes too great, and unnecessary, a prohibition on speech in order to achieve it...."The objective of lowering consumption of alcohol by banning price advertising could be accomplished by establishing minimum prices and/or by increasing sales taxes on alcoholic beverages." *Id.* at 1521-22 (O'Connor, J., concurring in the judgment) (quoting 44 *Liquormart, Inc. v. Rhode Island*, 39 F.3d 5, 7 (1st Cir. 1994)....

III

While Rhode Island's blanket ban on price advertising failed *Central Hudson* scrutiny, Baltimore's attempt to zone outdoor alcoholic beverage advertising into appropriate areas survived our "close look" at the legislature's means of accomplishing its objective in Anheuser-Busch I. Baltimore's ordinance expressly targets persons who cannot be legal users of alcoholic beverages, not legal users as in Rhode Island. More significantly, Baltimore does not ban outdoor advertising of alcoholic beverages outright but merely restricts the time, place, and manner of such advertisements. And Baltimore's ordinance does not foreclose the plethora of newspaper, magazine, radio, television, direct mail, Internet, and other media available to Anheuser-Busch and its competitors.

* * *

...Baltimore's interest is to protect children who are not yet independently able to assess the value of the message presented. This decision thus conforms to the Supreme Court's repeated recognition that children deserve special solicitude in the First Amendment balance because they lack the ability to assess and analyze fully the information presented through commercial media. In the context of cable television, the Supreme Court recently upheld restrictions on programming imposed by the Cable Television Consumer Protection and Competition Act as a means of protecting children from indecent programming....The underlying reason for the special solicitude of children was articulated long ago: "A democratic society rests, for its continuance, upon the healthy, well-rounded growth of young people into full maturity as citizens." *Prince v. Massachusetts*, 321 U.S. 158, 168...(1944).

DISSENT: **BUTZNER**, Senior Circuit Judge, dissenting:

I dissent because I believe we should vacate the district courts' judgments and remand these cases for evidentiary hearings. I address in this dissent both the cases pertaining to advertising of alcoholic beverages and the case pertaining to the advertising of cigarettes.

* * *

...Even assuming, as common sense might suggest, that Baltimore's restrictions will reduce underage drinking to some degree, without any findings of fact we cannot determine whether the effect will be significant....

Baltimore must also show that its speech regulation is narrowly tailored. Anheuser-Busch argued that the city could implement other measures that would reduce underage drinking as effectively as the advertising restrictions without regulating speech. The company specifically suggested education programs and increased law enforcement efforts....The company's argument should be evaluated on the strength of the facts that support and negate it. The parties should be given the opportunity to present and contest those facts.

The same reasoning applies to Baltimore's restriction on cigarette advertising. Whether that restriction advances the asserted governmental interest and whether it is unnecessarily extensive raise factual questions that only an evidentiary hearing can answer. For example, Baltimore's transit buses, which carry children as well as adults, are exempted from the ordinance that restricts advertising of cigarettes. The ordinance permits such advertising at a ball park where minors watch games. What effect these and similar facts have on the validity of the city ordinance should be weighed by a court.

Lorillard Tobacco Co. v. Reilly

533 U.S. 525 (2001)

JUSTICE O'CONNOR delivered the opinion of the Court.

In January 1999, the Attorney General of Massachusetts promulgated comprehensive regulations governing the advertising and sale of cigarettes, smokeless tobacco, and cigars....Petitioners, a group of cigarette, smokeless tobacco, and cigar manufacturers and retailers, filed suit in Federal District Court claiming that the regulations violate federal law and the United States Constitution. In large measure, the District Court determined that the regulations are valid and enforceable.... The first question presented for our review is whether certain cigarette advertising regulations are pre-empted by the Federal Cigarette Labeling and Advertising Act (FCLAA), 79 Stat. 282, as amended, 15 U.S.C. § 1331 *et seq.* The second question presented is whether certain regulations governing the advertising and sale of tobacco products violate the First Amendment.

I

In November 1998, Massachusetts, along with over 40 other States, reached a landmark agreement with major manufacturers in the cigarette industry. The signatory States settled their claims against these companies in exchange for monetary payments and permanent injunctive relief.... At the press conference covering Massachusetts' decision to sign the agreement, then-Attorney General Scott Harshbarger announced that as one of his last acts in office, he would create consumer protection regulations to restrict advertising and sales practices for tobacco products. He explained that the regulations were necessary in order to "close holes" in the settlement agreement and "to stop Big Tobacco from recruiting new customers among the children of Massachusetts."

In January 1999, pursuant to his authority to prevent unfair or deceptive practices in trade, Mass. Gen. Laws, ch. 93A, § 2 (1997), the Massachusetts Attorney General (Attorney General) promulgated regulations governing the sale and advertisement of cigarettes, smokeless tobacco, and cigars. The purpose of the cigarette and smokeless tobacco regulations is "to eliminate deception and unfairness in the way cigarettes and smokeless tobacco products are marketed, sold and distributed in Massachusetts in order to address the incidence of cigarette smoking and smokeless tobacco use by children under legal age....[and] in order to prevent access to such products by underage consumers."...

The cigarette and smokeless tobacco regulations being challenged before this Court provide:

> "(2) Retail Outlet Sales Practices. Except as otherwise provided in [§ 21.04(4)], it shall be an unfair or deceptive act or practice for any person who sells or distributes cigarettes or smokeless tobacco products through a retail outlet located within Massachusetts to engage in any of the following retail outlet sales practices:

* * *

> "(c) Using self-service displays of cigarettes or smokeless tobacco products;

> "(d) Failing to place cigarettes and smokeless tobacco products out of the reach of all consumers, and in a location accessible only to outlet personnel." §§ 21.04(2)(c)-(d).

> "(5) Advertising Restrictions. Except as provided in [§ 21.04(6)], it shall be an unfair or deceptive act or practice for any manufacturer, distributor or retailer to engage in any of the following practices:

"(a) Outdoor advertising, including advertising in enclosed stadiums and advertising from within a retail establishment that is directed toward or visible from the outside of the establishment, in any location that is within a 1,000 foot radius of any public playground, playground area in a public park, elementary school or secondary school;

"(b) Point-of-sale advertising of cigarettes or smokeless tobacco products any portion of which is placed lower than five feet from the floor of any retail establishment which is located within a one thousand foot radius of any public playground, playground area in a public park, elementary school or secondary school, and which is not an adult-only retail establishment." §§ 21.04(5)(a)-(b).

* * *

II

Before reaching the First Amendment issues, we must decide to what extent federal law pre-empts the Attorney General's regulations. The cigarette petitioners contend that the FCLAA, 15 U.S.C. § 1331 *et seq.*, pre-empts the Attorney General's cigarette advertising regulations.

A

Article VI of the United States Constitution commands that the laws of the United States "shall be the supreme Law of the Land;...any Thing in the Constitution or Laws of any State to the Contrary notwithstanding." Art. VI, cl. 2....In the FCLAA, Congress has crafted a comprehensive federal scheme governing the advertising and promotion of cigarettes. The FCLAA's pre-emption provision provides:

"(a) Additional statements

"No statement relating to smoking and health, other than the statement required by section 1333 of this title, shall be required on any cigarette package.

"(b) State regulations

"No requirement or prohibition based on smoking and health shall be imposed under State law with respect to the advertising or promotion of any cigarettes the packages of which are labeled in conformity with the provisions of this chapter." 15 U.S.C. § 1334.

The FCLAA's pre-emption provision does not cover smokeless tobacco or cigars.

In this case, our task is to identify the domain expressly pre-empted,... we "work on the assumption that the historic police powers of the States are not to be superseded by the Federal Act unless that [is] the clear and manifest purpose of Congress."...Our analysis begins with the language of the statute....In the pre-emption provision, Congress unequivocally precludes the requirement of any additional statements on cigarette packages beyond those provided in § 1333.... Congress further precludes States or localities from imposing any requirement or prohibition based on smoking and health with respect to the advertising and promotion of cigarettes. § 1334(b). Without question, the second clause is more expansive than the first; it employs far more sweeping language to describe the state action that is pre-empted....

* * *

B

...Although they support the Court of Appeals' result, the Attorney General and United States as amicus curiae do not fully endorse that court's textual analysis of the pre-emption provision. Instead, they assert that the cigarette advertising regulations are not pre-empted because they are not "based on smoking and health." The Attorney General and the United States also contend that the regulations are not pre-empted because they do not prescribe the content of cigarette advertising and they fall squarely within the State's traditional powers to control the location of advertising and to protect the welfare of children.

* * *

JUSTICE STEVENS finds it ironic that we conclude that "federal law precludes States and localities from protecting children from dangerous products within 1,000 feet of a school," in light of our prior conclusion that the "Federal Government lacks the constitutional authority to impose a similarly-motivated ban" in *United States v. Lopez*, 514 U.S. 549 (1995)....Our holding is not as broad as the dissent states; we hold only that the FCLAA pre-empts state regulations targeting cigarette advertising. States remain free to enact generally applicable zoning regulations, and to regulate conduct with respect to cigarette use and sales....The reference to *Lopez* is also inapposite. In *Lopez*, we held that Congress exceeded the limits of its Commerce Clause power in the Gun-Free School Zones Act of 1990, which made it a federal crime to possess a firearm in a school zone....This case, by contrast, concerns the Supremacy Clause and the doctrine of pre-emption as applied in a case where Congress expressly precluded certain state regulations of cigarette advertising. Massachusetts did not raise a constitutional challenge to the FCLAA, and we are not confronted with whether Congress exceeded its constitutionally delegated authority in enacting the FCLAA.

In sum, we fail to see how the FCLAA and its pre-emption provision permit a distinction between the specific concern about minors and cigarette advertising and the more general concern about smoking and health in cigarette advertising, especially in light of the fact that Congress crafted a legislative solution for those very concerns. We also conclude that a distinction between state regulation of the location as opposed to the content of cigarette advertising has no foundation in the text of the pre-emption provision. Congress pre-empted state cigarette advertising regulations like the Attorney General's because they would upset federal legislative choices to require specific warnings and to impose the ban on cigarette advertising in electronic media in order to address concerns about smoking and health. Accordingly, we hold that the Attorney General's outdoor and point-of-sale advertising regulations targeting cigarettes are pre-empted by the FCLAA.

* * *

III

By its terms, the FCLAA's pre-emption provision only applies to cigarettes. Accordingly, we must evaluate the smokeless tobacco and cigar petitioners' First Amendment challenges to the State's outdoor and point-of-sale advertising regulations. The cigarette petitioners did not raise a pre-emption challenge to the sales practices regulations. Thus, we must analyze the cigarette as well as the smokeless tobacco and cigar petitioners' claim that certain sales practices regulations for tobacco products violate the First Amendment.

A

For over 25 years, the Court has recognized that commercial speech does not fall outside the purview of the First Amendment....

Petitioners urge us to reject the *Central Hudson* analysis and apply strict scrutiny. But...we see "no need to break new ground. *Central Hudson*, as applied in our more recent commercial speech cases, provides an adequate basis for decision." 527 U.S. at 184.

Only the last two steps of *Central Hudson's* four-part analysis are at issue here. The Attorney General has assumed for purposes of summary judgment that petitioners' speech is entitled to First Amendment protection....With respect to the second step, none of the petitioners contests the importance of the State's interest in preventing the use of tobacco products by minors....

The third step of *Central Hudson* concerns the relationship between the harm that underlies the State's interest and the means identified by the State to advance that interest. It requires that

> "the speech restriction directly and materially advance the asserted governmental interest. 'This burden is not satisfied by mere speculation or conjecture; rather, a governmental body seeking to sustain a restriction on commercial speech must demonstrate that the harms it recites are real and that its restriction will in fact alleviate them to a material degree.'"

We do not, however, require that "empirical data come...accompanied by a surfeit of background information....We have permitted litigants to justify speech restrictions by reference to studies and anecdotes pertaining to different locales altogether, or even, in a case applying strict scrutiny, to justify restrictions based solely on history, consensus, and 'simple common sense.'"...

B

* * *

1.

The smokeless tobacco and cigar petitioners contend that the Attorney General's regulations do not satisfy *Central Hudson's* third step.... In previous cases, we have acknowledged the theory that product advertising stimulates demand for products, while suppressed advertising may have the opposite effect.... The Attorney General cites numerous studies to support this theory in the case of tobacco products.

* * *

Our review of the record reveals that the Attorney General has provided ample documentation of the problem with underage use of smokeless tobacco and cigars. In addition, we disagree with petitioners' claim that there is no evidence that preventing targeted campaigns and limiting youth exposure to advertising will decrease underage use of smokeless tobacco and cigars. On this record and in the posture of summary judgment, we are unable to conclude that the Attorney General's decision to regulate advertising of smokeless tobacco and cigars in an effort to combat the use of tobacco products by minors was based on mere "speculation [and] conjecture." *Edenfield v. Fane*, 507 U.S. at 770.

2.

Whatever the strength of the Attorney General's evidence to justify the outdoor advertising regulations, however, we conclude that the regulations do not satisfy the fourth step of the *Central Hudson* analysis. The final step of the *Central Hudson* analysis, the "critical inquiry in this case," requires a reasonable fit between the means and ends of the regulatory scheme. 447 U.S. at 569. The Attorney General's regulations do not meet this standard. The broad sweep of the regulations indicates that the Attorney General did not "carefully calculate the costs and benefits associated with the burden on speech imposed" by the regulations....

The outdoor advertising regulations prohibit any smokeless tobacco or cigar advertising within 1,000 feet of schools or playgrounds. In the District Court, petitioners maintained that this prohibition would prevent advertising in 87% to 91% of Boston, Worcester, and Springfield, Massachusetts. 84 F. Supp. 2d at 191. The 87% to 91% figure appears to include not only the effect of the regulations, but also the limitations imposed by other generally applicable zoning restrictions.... The Attorney General disputed petitioners' figures but "conceded that the reach of the regulations is substantial."...Thus, the Court of Appeals concluded that the regulations prohibit advertising in a substantial portion of the major metropolitan areas of Massachusetts...

The substantial geographical reach of the Attorney General's outdoor advertising regulations is compounded by other factors. "Outdoor" advertising includes not only advertising located outside an establishment, but also advertising inside a store if that advertising is visible from outside the store....

* * *

The State's interest in preventing underage tobacco use is substantial, and even compelling, but it is no less true that the sale and use of tobacco products by adults is a legal activity. We must consider that tobacco retailers and manufacturers have an interest in conveying truthful information about their products to adults, and adults have a corresponding interest in receiving truthful information about tobacco products. In a case involving indecent speech on the Internet we explained that "the governmental interest in protecting children from harmful materials . . . does not justify an unnecessarily broad suppression of speech addressed to adults." *Reno v. American Civil Liberties Union*, 521 U.S. 844, 875 ...(1997) (citations omitted).

* * *

C

Massachusetts has also restricted indoor, point-of-sale advertising for smokeless tobacco and cigars. Advertising cannot be "placed lower than five feet from the floor of any retail establishment which is located within a one thousand foot radius of" any school or playground....

We conclude that the point-of-sale advertising regulations fail both the third and fourth steps of the *Central Hudson* analysis. A regulation cannot be sustained if it "'provides only ineffective or remote support for the government's purpose,'"... or if there is "little chance" that the restriction will advance the State's goal,...As outlined above, the State's goal is to prevent minors from using tobacco products and to curb demand for that activity by limiting youth exposure to advertising. The 5 foot rule does not seem to advance that goal. Not all children are less than 5 feet tall, and those who are certainly have the ability to look up and take in their surroundings....

Massachusetts may wish to target tobacco advertisements and displays that entice children, much like floor-level candy displays in a convenience store, but the blanket height restriction does not constitute a reasonable fit with that goal....

D

The Attorney General also promulgated a number of regulations that restrict sales practices by cigarette, smokeless tobacco, and cigar manufacturers and retailers. Among other restrictions, the regulations bar the use of self-service displays and require that tobacco products be placed out of the reach of all consumers in a location accessible only to salespersons....[These] sales practices provisions regulate conduct that may have a communicative component, but Massachusetts seeks to regulate the placement of tobacco products for reasons unrelated to the communication of ideas. We conclude that the State has demonstrated a substantial interest in preventing access to tobacco products by minors and has adopted an appropriately narrow means of advancing that interest...

Unattended displays of tobacco products present an opportunity for access without the proper age verification required by law. Thus, the State prohibits self-service and other displays that would allow an individual to obtain tobacco products without direct contact with a salesperson. It is clear that the regulations leave open ample channels of communication. The regulations do not significantly impede adult access to tobacco products.

* * *

JUSTICE STEVENS, with whom JUSTICE GINSBURG and JUSTICE BREYER join, and with whom JUSTICE SOUTER joins as to Part I, concurring in part, concurring in the judgment in part, and dissenting in part.

This suit presents two separate sets of issues. The first—involving preemption—is straightforward. The second — involving the First Amendment—is more complex. Because I strongly disagree with the Court's conclusion that the Federal Cigarette Labeling and Advertising Act of 1965 (FCLAA or Act), 15 U.S.C. § 1331 et seq. as amended, precludes States and localities from regulating the location of cigarette advertising, I dissent from Parts II-A and II-B of the Court's opinion. On the First Amendment questions, I agree with the Court both that the outdoor advertising restrictions imposed by Massachusetts serve legitimate and important state interests and that the record does not indicate that the measures were properly tailored to serve those interests. Because the present record does not enable us to adjudicate the merits of those claims on summary judgment, I would vacate the decision upholding those restrictions and

remand for trial on the constitutionality of the outdoor advertising regulations. Finally, because I do not believe that either the point-of-sale advertising restrictions or the sales practice restrictions implicate significant First Amendment concerns, I would uphold them in their entirety.

* * *

...To this day, the stated federal policies in this area are (1) to inform the public of the dangers of cigarette smoking and (2) to protect the cigarette companies from the burdens of confusing and contradictory state regulations of their labels and advertisements....The retention of this provision unchanged is strong evidence that Congress' only intention in expanding the preemption clause was to capture forms of content regulation that had fallen through the cracks of the prior provision—for example, state laws prohibiting cigarette manufacturers from making particular claims in their advertising or requiring them to utilize specified layouts or include particular graphics in their marketing.[4]

* * *

I am firmly convinced that, when Congress amended the preemption provision in 1969, it did not intend to expand the application of the provision beyond content regulations.[6] I, therefore, find the conclusion inescapable that the zoning regulation at issue in this suit is not a "requirement or prohibition...with respect to... advertising" within the meaning of the 1969 Act....Even if I were not so convinced, however, I would still dissent from the Court's conclusion with regard to preemption, because the provision is, at the very least, ambiguous. The historical record simply does not reflect that it was Congress'" 'clear and manifest purpose,'"...to preempt attempts by States to utilize their traditional zoning authority to protect the health and welfare of minors. Absent such a manifest purpose, Massachusetts and its sister States retain their traditional police powers.[8]

II

...[N]oble ends do not save a speech-restricting statute whose means are poorly tailored. Such statutes may be invalid for two different reasons. First, the means chosen may be insufficiently related to the ends they purportedly serve. See, e.g., Rubin v. Coors Brewing Co., 514 U.S. 476...(1995) (striking a statute prohibiting beer labels from displaying alcohol content because the provision did not significantly forward the government's interest in the health, safety, and welfare of its citizens). Alternatively, the statute may be so broadly drawn that, while effectively achieving its ends, it unduly restricts communications that are unrelated to its policy aims. See, e.g., United States v. Playboy Entertainment Group, Inc., 529 U.S. 803, 812...(2000) (striking a statute intended to protect children from indecent television broadcasts, in part because it constituted "a significant restriction of communication between speakers and willing adult listeners"). The second difficulty is most frequently encountered when government adopts measures for the protection of children that impose substantial restrictions on the ability of adults to communicate with one another...

To my mind, the 1,000-foot rule does not present a tailoring problem of the first type. For reasons cogently explained in our prior opinions and in the opinion of the Court, we may fairly assume that advertising stimulates consumption and, therefore, that regulations limiting advertising will facilitate efforts to stem consumption. Furthermore, if the government's intention is to limit consumption by a particular segment of the community—in this case, minors—it is appropriate, indeed necessary, to tailor advertising restrictions to the areas where that segment of the community congregates—in this case, the area surrounding schools and playgrounds.

However, I share the majority's concern as to whether the 1,000-foot rule unduly restricts the ability of cigarette manufacturers to convey lawful information to adult consumers. This, of course, is a question of line-drawing. While a ban on all communications about a given subject would be the most effective way to prevent children from exposure to such material, the state cannot by fiat reduce the level of discourse to that which is "fit for children."...On the other hand, efforts to protect children from exposure to harmful material will undoubtedly have some spillover effect on the free speech rights of adults....

Finding the appropriate balance is no easy matter. Though many factors plausibly enter the equation when calculating whether a child-directed location restriction goes too far in regulating adult speech, one crucial question is whether the regulatory scheme leaves available sufficient "alternative avenues of communication." Because I do not think the record contains sufficient information to enable us to answer that question, I would vacate the award of summary judgment upholding the 1,000-foot rule and remand for trial on that issue.

* * *

The Sales Practice and Indoor Advertising Restrictions

* * *

Second,…I would…uphold the regulation limiting tobacco advertising in certain retail establishments to the space five feet or more above the floor.[11] When viewed in isolation, this provision appears to target speech. Further, to the extent that it does target speech it may well run into constitutional problems, as the connection between the ends the statute purports to serve and the means it has chosen are dubious. Nonetheless, I am ultimately persuaded that the provision is unobjectionable because it is little more than an adjunct to the other sales practice restrictions. As the Commonwealth of Massachusetts can properly legislate the placement of products and the nature of displays in its convenience stores, I would not draw a distinction between such restrictions and height restrictions on related product advertising. I would accord the Commonwealth some latitude in imposing restrictions that can have only the slightest impact on the ability of adults to purchase a poisonous product and may save some children from taking the first step on the road to addiction.

* * *

[4] Because of the nature of magazine publishing and distribution, it is conceivable that a State or locality might cause the kind of regulatory confusion the statute was drafted to prevent by adopting a law prohibiting the advertising of cigarettes in any publication distributed within its boundaries. There is at least a modicum of support for the suggestion that Congress may have intended the preemption of such restrictions. See *id.* at 515, n. 11 (noting that California was considering such a ban at the time Congress was considering the 1969 Act). However, the concerns posed by the diverse regulation of national publications are not present with regard to the local regulation of the location of signs and billboards….

[6] Petitioners suggest in passing that Massachusetts' regulation amounts to a "near-total ban," Brief for Petitioners Lorillard Tobacco Co. *et al.* 22, and thus is a de facto regulation of the content of cigarette ads. But we need not consider today the circumstances in which location restrictions approximating a total ban might constitute regulation of content and thus be preempted by the Act, because petitioners have failed to introduce sufficient evidence to create a genuine issue as to that claim. Petitioners introduced maps purporting to show that cigarette advertising is barred in 90.6% of Boston proper, 87.8% of Worcester, and 89.8% of Springfield. See App. 165-167. But the maps do not distinguish between the area restricted due to the regulation at issue here and the area restricted due to pre-existing regulations, such as general zoning requirements applicable to all outdoor advertising. Nor do the maps show the percentage (with respect to either area or population) of the State that is off limits to cigarette advertising; they cover only three cities containing approximately 14% of the State's population.....And even on the interpretation of this data most favorable to petitioners, the Massachusetts regulation still permits indoor and outdoor cigarette advertising in at least 10% of the geographical area of the State. In short, the regulation here is not the equivalent of a total ban on cigarette advertising.

[8] The Court's holding that federal law precludes States and localities from protecting children from dangerous products within 1,000 feet of a school is particularly ironic given the Court's conclusion six years ago that the Federal Government lacks the constitutional authority to impose a similarly-motivated ban. See *United States v. Lopez,* 514 U.S. 549 (1995). Despite the absence of any identified federal interest in creating "an invisible federal zone extending 1,000 feet beyond the (often irregular) boundaries of the school property," as the majority construes it today, the "statute now before us forecloses the States from experimenting and exercising their own judgment in an area to which States lay claim by right of history and expertise," *Id.* at 583 (KENNEDY, J., concurring). I wonder why a Court sensitive to federalism concerns would adopt such a strange construction of statutory language whose quite different purpose Congress took pains to explain.

[11] This ban only applies to stores located within 1,000-feet of a school or playground and contains an exception for adult-only establishments….

Note on Tobacco Case Aftermath

The median age for initial tobacco addiction is under 16 years of age. Although most of its debilitating and lethal health consequences occur in adulthood, public health officials contend that youth-targeted advertising and nicotine manipulation for early addiction make it a child health problem. In early 1994, a combine of plaintiff lawyers organized nationally to challenge tobacco marketing practices, and successfully certified a federal class action in Louisiana, alleging addiction manipulation (see the *Castano* case and discussion in Chapter 1). These *Castano* attorneys obtained an immediate order prohibiting destruction of documents, and obtained a critical early settlement from defendant Liggett. Their work from 1994 to 1999 developed insiders willing to testify, created a depository of over one million documents, developed expert witnesses, and deposed witnesses. After the national class was decertified, they filed similar class action suits in over twenty states, often including "targeting youth" allegations. Various state attorneys general, spurred by Mississippi, joined or filed parallel state lawsuits.

A negotiated settlement with the remaining tobacco defendants required Congressional approval and was narrowly rejected in 1998, but that same year the industry nevertheless settled with forty state attorney generals to create a "Master Settlement Agreement" (MSA), including $196 billion to be paid to states over twenty years for tobacco-related prevention and amelioration (although some states facing budget shortfalls have allocated these sums for their general funds). It also requires tobacco funding of charities to reduce teen smoking, prohibits targeting of youth or cartoon use in ads, bans all outdoor advertising (except at the site of a sponsored event), limits retail ad signs outside of retail stores to fourteen square feet, bans transit ads, bans brand name apparel (caps, t-shirts, backpacks), limits tobacco companies to only one brand name sponsorship per year, prohibits brand name sponsorship of events with a significant youth audience, or sponsorship of team sports, allows corporate sponsorship of athletic, musical, and other events as long as the brand name is not used, stops free samples unless underage safeguards are in place, prohibits gifts based on tobacco purchases without proof of age, disbands the Council for Tobacco Research (CTR), the Tobacco Institute (TI), and the Council for Indoor Air Research (CIAR), and purports to prohibit tobacco industry political opposition to state or local laws intended to deter youth tobacco use. The restrictions do not apply to the foreign sales and promotion activities of American tobacco firms, which continue to promote their products to youth overseas.

After 2015, the termination of marijuana illegality in some states, although not applying to children, is likely to accelerate similar problems revealed in tobacco marketing. General availability makes such products easily available to children, with attendant problems—perhaps not cancer or other long-term tobacco consequences, but addiction and impact on automobile safety are of particular concern. Related to the increased incidence of "vaping" and other means of absorption, there are more indirect but nevertheless consequential effects on the reduction of drive and constructive ambition. Beyond marijuana, alcohol and tobacco is the growing scourge of cocaine, opioids, and meth—all afflicting increasing numbers of children and youth.

Questions for Discussion

1. Two of the three child safety regulatory cases above shift the burden to the state to show the efficacy of its health and safety protections for children. In the two advertising cases, this shift occurs because of the stated commercial free speech rights of advertisers. The Court acknowledges that the First Amendment provides no protection to misleading commercial messages. Can it be argued that messages on behalf of alcohol and tobacco are inherently misleading as applied to children?

2. Neither the Court's opinion nor the dissent in *Lorillard* acknowledge that the Master Settlement Agreement (MSA) entered into by the tobacco industry and state attorneys general (including Massachusetts) prohibits virtually all outdoor sign advertising, not merely advertising near schools and playgrounds (see Note above). How should that fact affect the "commercial free speech" impact and "tailoring" discussion of the majority and dissent?

3. The First Amendment analysis of *Lorillard* and *Anheuser-Busch* implies a presumptive right to advertise without regulatory impediment. Such impediments may be created by the state, but they must not merely be rationally related to a compelling state interest, they must demonstrably and materially advance such an interest; further, the state must consider other alternatives. Is the Court the ideal forum to decide the efficacy of regulatory measures to protect children? Should the burden on such regulation be "show me it works and you can do it," or should it be "if it might work do it, but stop it if it turns out to have no substantial impact"?

4. In *Lorillard*, Justice O'Connor rejects a Massachusetts restriction on tobacco advertising located below the five-foot level in retail stores because "not all children are less than five feet tall and those who are certainly have the ability to look up...." What evidence underlies her implied conclusion that locating this advertising above five feet does not advance a governmental interest by reducing to some degree child exposure? Is she equipped to make her own findings about child exposure to messages closer to their height level than above it? Is a state assumption that children are generally shorter and that the advertising of an addictive substance that produces illness and death should be made less noticeable to children reasonable? Is tobacco advertising that does not disclose its addictive and dangerous qualities misleading? Can the state prohibit all tobacco advertising that does not ostentatiously so warn?

5. Some states have a different mix of constitutional guarantees than the federal Constitution includes. For example, California's constitution enumerates safety as a primary right (Cal. Const. Art. I, Sec. 1). If this right (or a hypothetical child's right to safety) is coextensive with First Amendment rights, would the analyses of the courts above differ?

Association of American Physicians and Surgeons, Inc.v.
U.S. Food and Drug Administration
226 F. Supp. 2d 204 (D.C. District, 2002)

HENRY H. KENNEDY JR., United States District Judge:

The Federal Food Drug and Cosmetic Act ("FDCA"), 21 U.S.C. § 321 *et seq.* provides a systematic scheme for the approval of new drugs and new drug formulations intended to be marketed for use in interstate commerce. Under the FDCA, a new drug product cannot be marketed unless the FDA approves the product and determines that it is safe and effective for its intended use. See 21 U.S.C. § 355(a). When the FDA approves a drug, it approves the drug only for the particular use for which it was tested, but after the drug is approved for a particular use, the FDCA does not regulate how the drug may be prescribed. Thus, a drug that has been tested and approved for adult use only can be prescribed by a physician for her pediatric patients.

Because of the expense and difficulty in finding substantial pediatric populations to undergo tests, along with the ethical complications associated with testing new drugs on children, many drugs are tested for safety and effectiveness in adults only. As a result, even though there are many diseases and ailments that are common to both children and adults, physicians with pediatric patients often find their treatment options limited. Some physicians, forced "to choose between prescribing drugs without well-founded dosing and safety information or utilizing other, potentially less effective, therapy" respond by prescribing adult-approved drugs to children, but in a smaller dose. *See* Regulations Requiring Manufacturers to Assess the Safety and Effectiveness of New Drugs and Biological Products in Pediatric Patients, 62 Fed. Reg. 43,900 (Aug. 15, 1997).

Prescribing adult-approved drugs to children is often referred to as going "off-label." An off-label use is the prescription of a drug by a doctor for a condition not indicated on the label or for a dosing regimen or patient population not specified on the label. Off-label use of pharmaceuticals appears to be "generally accepted" in the medical community. ... While it is a common practice for physicians to prescribe to children pharmaceuticals only approved for adult use, by doing so, they can expose children to various hazards. Children may be given an ineffective dose or an overdose, and they face an increased risk of side effects. ...This happens because correct pediatric dosing cannot necessarily be extrapolated from adult dosing information using an equivalence based either on weight...or body surface area....Potentially significant differences in pharmacokinetics may alter a drug's effect in pediatric patients. The effects of growth and maturation of various organs, maturation of the immune system, alterations in metabolism throughout infancy and childhood, changes in body proportions, and other developmental changes may result in significant differences in the doses needed by pediatric patients and adults...

In the face of insufficient information about a new medication, pediatricians do not merely prescribe inexact doses, however. Physicians sometimes prescribe for their young patients older, less effective, but well-tested medication—as opposed to newer, more effective, medication that has not been subjected to rigorous study on pediatric populations. This practice keeps children from benefitting from state-of-the-art medication....In response to these concerns, in 1994, the FDA issued a regulation requiring manufacturers of marketed drugs to survey existing data and determine whether the data was sufficient to support pediatric use information on the drug's labeling. If so, the FDA required manufacturers to submit a supplemental new drug application seeking the FDA's approval of the labeling change. If the drug had not been sufficiently tested on children, the rule required the manufacturer to include in the product's labeling a statement to read: "Safety and effectiveness in pediatric patients have not been established."

Also in an effort to encourage pediatric testing, in 1997, Congress passed the Food and Drug Administration Modernization Act ("FDAMA")....This Act established a five-year experimental program to encourage pediatric drug-testing. Under this Act, the FDA could request (but never require) manufacturers of new drugs to conduct studies on pediatric patients. Drug manufacturers that agreed to conduct these pediatric tests could receive six months of market exclusivity for their products.

Finding that the voluntary incentive provisions of FDAMA did not increase pediatric testing as much as the FDA had hoped, after proper notice-and-comment, the FDA issued the "Pediatric Rule" in 1998. This Rule's legitimacy is challenged here.

In application, the Pediatric Rule distinguishes new drugs from already- marketed drugs. Manufacturers of new drugs "may be required to submit an application containing data adequate to assess whether the drug is safe and effective in pediatric populations. The application may be required to contain adequate evidence to support dosage and administration in some or all pediatric subpopulations, including neonates, infants, children, and adolescents...."...This means, in effect, drug manufacturers may now be obligated to study their product on pediatric populations, even if the product is not explicitly marketed for children's use. In addition, the "applicant may also be required to develop a pediatric formulation for a drug product that represents a meaningful therapeutic benefit to such patients over existing therapies."

The FDA presumes that sponsors will study all new drugs in pediatric patients unless the applicant can show that waiver is appropriate. Waivers are granted if: (1) necessary studies are impossible or highly impractical because, *e.g.*, the number of such patients is so small or geographically dispersed; or (2) there is evidence strongly suggesting that the product would be ineffective or unsafe in all pediatric age groups.

* * *

For already-marketed drugs, the Pediatric Rule still applies, but it has a more narrow sweep. For such drugs, the FDA may still require a manufacturer to submit an application containing adequate evidence to support dosage and administration in some or all pediatric subpopulations, and the FDA may also still require an applicant to develop a pediatric drug formulation. In this context, however, the burden is on the FDA show that such testing and analysis is required. The FDA satisfies this burden only if the absence of adequate labeling could pose significant risks to pediatric patients; and either (1) the drug is "used in a substantial number of pediatric patients for the labeled indications;" or (2) there is "reason to believe that the drug product would represent a meaningful therapeutic benefit over existing treatments for pediatric patients for one or more of the claimed indications." This Rule's application, for both new and existing drugs, is limited in three other respects as well. First, the Rule does not require a manufacturer to study its product for unapproved or unclaimed indications, even if the product is widely used in pediatric patients for those indications. This means that a drug marketed as a cure for one disease in adults does not need to be tested for its ability to cure an entirely different disease in children. Second, the Pediatric Rule allows drug manufacturers to defer pediatric testing until after the FDA has approved the product for adult use. Third, the Rule only requires testing of new "innovator" drugs. The Rule does not apply to generic copies of previously-approved drugs or for suitability petitions for a change in dosage strength.

* * *

Since the filing of this lawsuit, Congress has passed, and the President has signed into law, the "Best Pharmaceuticals for Children Act," Public Law No. 107-109, 115 Stat. 1408 (2002) ("BPCA"). This Act reauthorized and expanded the pediatric testing incentives set forth in FDAMA. The BPCA endorses the goal of increasing the number of drugs studied in pediatric populations but does not authorize FDA to require manufacturers to conduct pediatric testing. Instead, the Act establishes a legislative framework to encourage voluntary testing. Under the Act, a manufacturer receives an additional six months of market exclusivity on a new or marketed drug if: (1) FDA determines that pediatric testing of the drug "may produce health benefits in that population;" (2) FDA makes a written request to the manufacturer to conduct such testing; (3) the manufacturer agrees to test the drug within an appropriate time-frame; (4) the manufacturer conducts the tests and submits reports of these tests to the FDA; and (5) the FDA accepts the testing reports.

* * *

...We first turn to the FDCA, which the FDA claims serves as the basis for its authority. The FDA claims that its authority to promulgate the Pediatric Rule comes, generally, from 21 U.S.C. § 371(a). This Section provides: "The authority to promulgate regulations for the efficient enforcement of this chapter...is vested with the Secretary." As the Second Circuit has provided "'the validity of a regulation promulgated'" under § 371 "will be sustained so long as it is 'reasonably related to the purposes of the enabling legislation.'"

* * *

The FDA bases the Pediatric Rule, in part, on its authority under 21 U.S.C. §§ 352(a), 352(f), 355(d)(7), and 321(n), which pertain to labeling....Section 352(a) provides that drugs or devices are misbranded if they contain false or misleading labels, and Section 352(f) requires labels to contain adequate directions for use. Section 321(n) defines labeling as misleading if it "fails to reveal facts...material with respect to consequences which may result" from the use of the product as labeled or "from use of the article...under such conditions of use as are customary or usual."

Plaintiffs claim that § 352(n) and the other labeling provisions cannot support the Pediatric Rule because,...the FDA's ability to require manufacturers to include "adequate directions for use," simply permits the FDA to ensure that a product bears adequate directions for its *claimed* uses. In addition, plaintiffs contend that these provisions give the FDA limited power—power that truly extends to only "labeling and reporting" matters. According to plaintiffs, these provisions only authorize the FDA to require manufacturers to "(a) include in their labeling certain *known* material facts about products and (b) report to FDA on the use of the drugs in certain circumstances."...The question is a close one, however. Section 321(n) plainly provides that, in determining whether a label is misleading, the agency should look to whether the "labeling fails to reveal [material] facts...under such conditions of *customary or usual*" (emphasis added). In adopting the Pediatric Rule, the FDA relied on extensive evidence demonstrating that at least some drugs are "commonly" or "usually" used by children, despite the absence of pediatric labeling. In addition, there is authority for the proposition that a label can be misleading based on what it fails to say, in addition to what is actually said. (Citations omitted).

Although § 201(n) and the other sections regarding labeling speak to some of the matters at issue here, FDA's power to promulgate the Pediatric Rule cannot rest solely on these provisions. Most problematic are those Pediatric Rule provisions that require manufacturers to (1) conduct studies of drugs for unclaimed uses or (2) devise formulations of the drug tailored to those uses. It is simply difficult to see how such power can be wholly derived from the FDA's power over drug labeling. Moreover, if Congress had intended for these sections to authorize the FDA to require manufacturers to test their drugs for unclaimed uses, Congress would likely have spoken more clearly, especially since "Congress can reasonably be expected to be quite precise in defining critical jurisdictional terms going to the very power of the agency to regulate." The FDCA's labeling provisions, therefore, do not provide a clear basis for the Pediatric Rule.

* * *

The FDA also relies upon 21 U.S.C. §§ 321(p), 331(a) and (d), and 355(a), (j), and (d). Section 321(p) defines "new drugs" as those not recognized to be safe and effective under conditions "prescribed, recommended, or suggested" in product labeling. Section 355(a) forbids new drugs' distribution. Section 352(j), provides that a drug shall be deemed misbranded if it is "dangerous to health when used in the dosage or manner, or with the frequency or duration prescribed, recommended, or suggested in the labeling thereof." § 352(j). Sections 331(a) and (d) proscribe misbranded drugs' sale or introduction into interstate commerce. Finally, § 355(d) provides that manufacturers seeking to market a new drug must demonstrate that the product is safe "for use under the conditions prescribed, recommended, or suggested in the proposed labeling thereof."

The applicability of the above provisions all turns on what is "prescribed, recommended, or suggested" in a product's labeling. Thus, the import of those three words must be scrutinized, and the analysis may apply to all....To begin,...the Act defines "labeling" to include "all labels and other written, printed, or graphic matter (1) upon any article or any of its containers or wrappers, or (2) accompanying such article." The FDA argues, in essence, that notwithstanding the plain meaning of the statutory language, these provisions give the agency the authority to regulate drugs for pediatric uses even when such uses are not explicitly claimed by a drug manufacturer in a product's labeling.

* * *

FDA counters by claiming that the Pediatric Rule does not so expand its reach. FDA argues that the Rule "simply requires, in some instances, data on a reasonable sample of patients likely to be given a drug or biological product."... FDA provides that, since there is uncontroverted evidence that many drugs officially indicated for adult use are *routinely* used by pediatric patients, "such pediatric use is 'suggested.'"...This is true, according to the FDA, even if pediatric use is specifically disclaimed on the product's labeling.

* * *

In *Weinberger*, the plaintiffs challenged an FDA regulation restricting the distribution of methadone. The FDA promulgated the regulation because the agency feared that methadone was being diverted from its intended use—that of a "safe, useful, and effective agent in the treatment of severe pain." See *Weinberger*, 377 F. Supp. at 825. The question for the court was whether, under the FDCA, the FDA had the authority to enact the regulation....The *Weinberger* court found that "the term 'safe' was intended to refer to a determination of the inherent safety or lack thereof of the drug under consideration [only] when used for its intended purposes." After this determination, the court went on to conclude "that FDA has overstepped the bounds of its authority in purporting to limit the distribution of methadone in the manner contemplated by its regulations."...This court concludes that use of a drug nowhere indicated by the label and, in fact, specifically disclaimed by the label is, quite simply, not "suggested" by that label. For that reason, the court finds that the FDA's expansive interpretation of the FDCA lacks firm support in law.

* * *

Lastly, given that the court is to examine the statute in context, the court must consider the effects of 21 U.S.C. § 355(c) and (d), if any. These sections provide that once the FDA has determined that the new drug is safe and effective "for use under the conditions prescribed, recommended, or suggested in the proposed labeling thereof," and once the manufacturer meets certain other requirements not at issue here, the FDA "*shall* issue an order approving the application." (emphasis added).. While approval appears nondiscretionary once certain congressionally-prescribed conditions are satisfied, under the Pediatric Rule, the FDA can withhold approval merely because a manufacturer has failed to test the drug on children. This tension between § 355(c) and (d) and the Pediatric Rule suggests at least some inconsistency between the Pediatric Rule and the broader context of the FDCA.

For the foregoing reasons, this court concludes that the Pediatric Rule does not have a sound statutory basis in the FDCA.

* * *

...[M]ilitating in the Pediatric Rule's favor is the fact that, when enacting the BPCA, Congress failed to expressly reject the Pediatric Rule, even though Congress was well aware of its existence. Generally, Congress' "failure to revise or repeal the agency's interpretation is persuasive evidence that the interpretation is the one intended by Congress." ....[In addition]some affirmative legislative history does support the Pediatric Rule,...the Senate Report accompanying the BPCA... provides:

> [The Pediatric Rule] requires the manufacturers of certain new and marketed drugs and biological products to provide adequate labeling for the use of the products in children. The rule is both broader and narrower than the pediatric exclusivity provision enacted by congress in 1997. When their scopes overlap, Congress provided that pediatric studies required under the rule could also satisfy the requirements for market exclusivity.

S. Rep. No. 107-79, at 4 (2001). This language demonstrates some desire for the Pediatric Rule to exist along-side Congress' scheme, and it is somewhat persuasive. However, given that the relevant legislative history is contradictory,...this statement shall not be accorded undue weight.

* * *

b. BPCA and the Pediatric Rule are Incompatible

Congress adopted an incentive scheme while the FDA adopted a command and control approach. The two schemes differ in almost every possible regard. First, as far as drug approval, the Pediatric Rule gives the FDA the authority to refuse to approve new drug applications if manufacturers refuse to conduct pediatric studies. The BPCA does not. Second, in terms of drug testing on pediatric populations, the Pediatric Rule provides that the FDA may "require" manufacturers to tests new drugs on pediatric populations. In contrast, the BPCA provides these tests may be merely "requested," and the BPCA establishes a public fund to pay for third parties to conduct pediatric tests if the FDA determines that such tests are necessary but the manufacturer elects not to conduct them....For already-marketed drugs, the BPCA, unlike the Pediatric Rule, allows manufacturers to decline to conduct pediatric testing without any risk that their products will be deemed mis-branded and pulled off the market. As for labeling changes, the BPCA sets up an elaborate scheme to force labeling changes if, as a result of what was unearthed during pediatric testing, the FDA determines that such changes are necessary. In contrast, the Pediatric Rules gives the FDA the authority to simply declare a drug misbranded. In regard to pediatric formulations, the Pediatric Rule requires their development, but the BPCA provides that the FDA "shall send a nonbinding letter" recommending a change in formulation "if a pediatric study completed under public contract indicates that a formulation change is necessary and the Secretary agrees."...Finally, the very thrust of the BPCA—providing marketing incentives to encourage voluntary testing—is entirely anomalous with the very thrust of the Pediatric Rule—requiring such tests in the absence of a deferral or waiver.

Far from complementing Congress' voluntary incentive scheme, the Pediatric Rule usurps it by superimposing an often-incompatible regime.

Questions for Discussion

1. The court holds that the BCPA and the Pediatric rule are incompatible. Are they? What requirement cited by the court contradicts FDA authority to include child testing where it finds treatment of children is likely or is occurring? As the court acknowledges, Congress was well aware of the pediatric rule when it enacted the BCPA. What indication is there of its intent to abrogate it?

2. The court refers to the 2002 Best Pharmaceuticals for Children Act as using an "incentives" approach (e.g., it authorized six month patent extensions) to persuade pharmaceutical companies to test on children. But note that the 1997 previous Act prior to the FDA rule also conferred similar incentives for the same purpose—but with a cut-off date of 2001. Is the fact that the 2002 Act was not new, but merely the reauthorization (continuation) of the previous patent incentive, consistent with a finding that the 2002 Act evinces a new Congressional intent to use a novel and exclusive "incentives approach?"

3. The labels on new drugs are drafted by the pharmaceutical company holding the relevant patent. Must that label specifically instruct use on a particular patient group for that group's safety to be a part of required testing? Does it matter that children are over 20% of the population and that they often have different responses to drugs than do adults—particularly infants and young children (as the court acknowledges)? Does it matter if the illness addressed by the drug as stated occurs often in children? Are these factors relevant to the existing regulatory structure? To Congressional intent?

4. The court holds that the labeling authority of the FDA does not extend to pediatric testing because new drugs used on children do not have "customary or usual use" as noted in the statute. But does any new drug have such customary or usual use—whether prescribed to children or adults? Doesn't the phrase parsed by the court simply mean in such a prospective context the "usual" use as intended or as specified or as likely?

5. If a drug is developed that combats infections common with sickle-cell anemia victims (who are predominantly African American) would the FDA lack the authority to require the drug testing to include persons of that racial background? Does it lack that authority unless the label specifies "to be used by African Americans" or "use to treat sickle cell anemia"?

6. Perhaps the major historical event informing Congressional intent in enacting FDA related statutes was the thalidomide scandal of the 1960s, where women in Europe took the drug, leading to tens of thousands of deformed babies for those who were pregnant. Can the FDA require testing for mutagenesis (birth defect properties) of drugs that might be prescribed for pregnant women under this decision's prescribed charter for the agency?

7. Is the methadone case partly relied upon by the court applicable to a decision denying authority to protect children from off-label uses that the agency finds occur?

8. The plaintiffs challenging the FDA's rule to protect children argued that even where use on children is explicitly disclaimed the rule might require testing on that population—delaying the introduction of needed drugs to adult patients for whom they are intended. Would an FDA rule that applies only to drugs that are not so disclaimed pass muster with this court? What of a rule that requires such testing where the drug's target or features would likely lead to substantial child use or which does lead to such use (off-label or not)? How does the Pediatric rule described by the court differ from such a regime?

9. According to the Tufts Center for the Study of Drug Development, pediatric drug testing costs $3.87 million per drug. The pediatric tests for the 188 drugs granted six months of extra patent monopoly in the 2002 reauthorization would cost $727 million. But those extensions would bring in $29.6 billion in compensatory revenue, much of it profit.[43] What are the implications to Congressional intent of an "incentive" that is argued to be the exclusive provision for pediatric drug testing— where that benefit is wildly in excess of the costs of such testing? Why would the Congress intend only for the pediatric testing of the drugs on the pharmacy industry list for patent extension? Is it reasonable that Congress only wanted these drugs tested? Are such drugs correlated with those appropriately tested (*i.e.*, those likely to be used on children as the FDA rule provides)? Would it imply the expectation that the pharmaceutical industry, in receiving such a windfall, should use some portion of the excess profit to test drugs that would be administered to children— under the perhaps more relevant criteria of the FDA rule?

Note: The 2002 Best Pharmaceuticals for Children Act interpreted by the district court judge Kennedy was reauthorized in 2007 and then again in 2012 under the FDA Safety and Innovation Act. The reauthorizations continued the enriching grant of six additional months of patent protection to allow a longer term for monopoly-power pricing. The Act as reauthorized also directed the National Institute of Health to prioritize and sponsor (at government cost) child clinical trials of drugs (both patented drugs and herbal products exempt from regulation and efficacy trials).[44]

ENDNOTES

[1] See, *e.g.*, Iowa Code Ann. § 232.68(2)(d) (West 1998).

[2] *Jacobson v. Massachusetts*, 197 U.S. 11 (1905).

[3] *Brown v. Stone*, 378 So. 2d 218 (Miss 1979).

[4] *Prince v. Massachusetts*, 321 U.S. 158 (1944).

[5] *Id.*, at 165, 169.

[6] For a breakdown of states allowing and not allowing exemptions as of 2017, see https://www.childusa.org/medicalneglect/.

[7] See *id.*

[8] The problems attending the religious exemption are illustrated in *Lybarger v. People*, 807 P.2d 570 (Colo. 1991); see also *Walker v. Keldgord*, No. CIV S-93-0616 LKK JFM P (Cal. 1996).

[9] See *supra*, note 6.

[10] See https://www.nytimes.com/roomfordebate/2015/03/10/parents-beliefs-vs-their-childrens-health/religious-freedom-balanced-with-responsibility.

[11] See https://www.sacbee.com/opinion/editorials/article215404630.html.

[12] Note that one circuit declined to dispositively decide the Fourteenth Amendment equal protection issue raised by the plaintiffs in *Children's Healthcare Is a Legal Duty, Inc. v. Deters*, 92 F.3d 1412 (6th Cir. 1996). No other federal case has directly addressed the issue of the constitutional rights of affected children where medical care is denied and they are treated differently than are other persons in the state's response to that failure.

[13] See A. Massie, *The Religion Clauses and Parental Health Care Health Policy Research, The Consequences of Being Uninsured in California* (Policy Brief) (Los Angeles, CA: Feb. 1998) at 2.

[14] U.S. Department of Health and Human Services, *Healthy People 2010*, available at www.healthypeople.gov/2010/.

[15] U.S. Department of Health and Human Services, *Healthy People 2020*, available at www.healthypeople.gov.

[16] Source: U.S. Department of Health and Human Services, Office of Disease Prevention and Health Promotion, *Healthy People 2010 and Healthy People 2020 Programs*, at https://www.cdc.gov/nchs/healthy_people/hp2010.htm and https://www.cdc.gov/nchs/healthy_people/hp2020.htm.

[17] Samantha Artiga and Petry Ubri, *Key Issues in Children's Health Coverage* (February 2017) at https://www.kff.org/medicaid/issue-brief/key-issues-in-childrens-health-coverage/.

[18] Source: Kaiser Family Foundation analysis of the 2016 National Health Insurance Survey. Notes: *In past 12 months. Questions about dental care were analyzed for children ages 2–17. All other questions were analyzed for all children ages 0–17. MD contact includes other health professionals. Respondents who said usual source of care was the emergency room were included among those not having a usual source of care. All differences between the uninsured and the two insurance groups are statistically significant ($p<0.05$).

[19] See https://www.cbpp.org/research/health/policy-basics-introduction-to-medicaid.

[20] Kaiser Family Foundation, *Key Facts about the Uninsured Population: Fact Sheet* (December 2018) at http://files.kff.org/attachment//fact-sheet-key-facts-about-the-uninsured-population.

[21] See www.medicaid.gov/chip/index.html.

[22] See childtrends.org. Source of figure: U.S. Census Bureau (2017), CPS Table Creator (Data tool), Retrieved from http://www.census.gov/cps/data/cpstablecreator.html. Beginning in 2002, the Census allowed respondents to select more than one racial category. The white, black, and Asian categories refer to those respondents who selected only one race. Hispanic children may be of any race, while white children in this chart do not include Hispanic youth.

[23] The majority of MCH funds come from the federal Social Security Act Title V Block Grant. Current law requires that a portion of this funding be spent to assure child and adolescent access to preventive and primary care, another share for children with special needs (part for perinatal access), and places a 10% cap on administration. The incremental parts of a typical state MCH program vary somewhat in terminology, but generally include physician residency training, an MCH Epidemiology Unit for surveillance of health indicators, and various projects in which local health departments participate, such as Comprehensive Perinatal Services Program (CPSP), Adolescent Family Life Program (AFLP), High-Risk Infant Follow-Up (HRIF), Perinatal Regionalization (PERI) programs, in some states an African American Infant Death Program, Perinatal Substance Abuse Project, the Sudden Infant Death Syndrome (SIDS) programs, and Childhood Injury Prevention Programs (MCH-CHIPP).

[24] See https://www.cdc.gov/injury/images/lc-charts/leading_causes_of_death_by_age_group_unintentional_2017_1100w850h.jpg.

[25] See https://www.cdc.gov/healthequity/lcod/men/2015/all-males/index.htm.

[26] G. K. Singh, S. M. Yu, *U.S. Childhood Mortality, 1950 through 1993: Trends and Socioeconomic Differentials*, 86:4 Am. J. Pub. Health 505-13 (Apr. 1996); C. W. Sells, R. W. Blum, *Morbidity and Mortality among U.S. Adolescents: An Overview of Data and Trends*, 86:4 Am. J. Pub. Health 513-19 (Apr. 1996); G. K. Singh, S. M. Yu, *Trends and Differentials in Adolescent and Young Adult Mortality in the United States, 1950 through 1993*, 86:4 Am. J. Pub. Health 560-65 (Apr. 1996).

[27] See https://www.cdc.gov/motorvehiclesafety/child_passenger_safety/cps-factsheet.html.

[28] *Id.*

[29] 18 U.S.C. § 922 *et seq.*

[30] 20 U.S.C. § 8921 *et seq.*

[31] See, *e.g.*, Cal. Pen. Code § 25100(a)–(c), 25200(a)–(b).

[32] 23 U.S.C. § 158.

[33] 23 U.S.C. § 161(a)(3).

[34] For example, the total appropriation in California for its EPIC account, of which 46% derived from federal sources, ranged from $3 to $4 million during the 1990s falling to $600,000 in total by 2001–02, see Children's Advocacy Institute, *California Children's Budget 2001–02* (San Diego, CA; June 2001) at 4–62.

[35] See Flammable Fabrics Act of 1953, as amended by Pub. L. No. 90-189, then administered by the FTC.

[36] See AB 3305 (Setencich and Speier) (Chapter 925, Statutes of 1996) adding § 115920 *et seq.* to the Cal. Health & Safety Code; the measure also includes disclosures of options for safety additions in escrow for all real property sold with a pool in place.

[37] See AB 2268 (Caldera) (Chapter 1000, Statutes of 1993), adding § 21212 to the Cal. Vehicle Code; the provision was based on a successful law in Victoria, Australia to require approved helmets (meeting the standards of the American National Standards Institute) for children riding bicycles. A first offense yields a warning, with a further offense yielding a $25 fine. The law has increased helmet use substantially among children.

[38] See http://www.playgroundsafety.org/standards/cpsc. California was the first state to adopt comprehensive public playground safety standards. The rules were mandated by statute enacted in 1990 (Chapter 1163, Statutes of 1990), which required the California Department of Health Services (DHS) to adopt the regulations by January 1, 1992. Following years of delay and in response to litigation brought by the Children's Advocacy Institute, DHS adopted the standards in December 1999; the promulgated rules are largely based on recommendations of the National Consumer Product Safety Commission.

[39] See, *e.g.*, Texas Penal Code § 22.10, prohibiting the leaving of a child younger than seven not attended by someone 14 years of age or over for more than five minutes; approximately twelve other states have varying prohibitions, usually with citation or misdemeanor sanctions. See also extensive data regarding incidence and state responses at http://www.kidsncars.org.

[40] See *Guide to Considering Children's Health When Developing EPA Actions: Implementing Executive Order* 13045 and EPA's Policy on Evaluating Health Risks to Children.

[41] *Children's Health Valuation Handbook* (October 2003).

[42] Note that the Act also allows private injunctive enforcement by "any interested person" after advance notice is given to the Commission and the Attorney General and where neither then files a pre-emptive case.

[43] *E.g.*, note that the estimated cost of testing one of the drugs on children, Prilosec, was between $2 and $4 million while the patent protection extension would produce $1.4 billion in additional revenue to patent holder AstraZeneca. See detailed report and citations in Public Citizen, *Patently Offensive: Congress Set to Extend Monopoly Patents for Cipro and other Drugs* (Nov. 9, 2001) at 1–2, available at http://www. citizen.org/congress/article_redirect.cfm?ID=6435.

[44] See https://bpca.nichd.nih.gov/Pages/default.aspx.

CHAPTER SIX

Children with Special Needs

A. DEMOGRAPHIC BACKGROUND

Children with special needs vary widely by disability and circumstance. They include children injured prenatally, genetically disabled, or subject to post-birth injury or illness. Disabilities may be physical in nature, or may include mental illness, learning disabilities, or severe emotional problems. States provide services to these children directly and through federally-funded programs administered through the Social Security Administration (SSA), the Department of Education, or the Department of Health and Human Services.

U.S. Census data from 2014 indicate that about 17% of children under age 18 had a disability, totaling 12.6 million children. Approximately half of those—7.2 million—had a disability qualifying as severe. Most common among school-age children was Attention Deficit Hyperactivity Disorder (ADHD), with 6% of school-age children medicated or treated for the disorder. Learning disabilities, which include dyslexia, occurred in 2.2% of school-age children. Developmental disabilities, which include autism, occurred in 2.1% of school-age children, while 4.5% received treatment for another developmental condition.[1] Findings from the National Health Interview Survey reveal that during 2014–16, the prevalence of children who had ever been diagnosed with a developmental disability increased, although the prevalence of autism spectrum disorders did not significantly change.[2]

Almost 3% of school-age children are diagnosed with a mental illness, affective or personality disorder,[3] or conduct disorder. Related to mental stability, recent data reveals that suicide is the second leading cause of death among those ages 10–34.[4] In 2015, 1.82% of all children's hospital visits were due to either suicide attempts or suicidal thoughts, compared to 0.66% in 2008. The largest increases were seen among adolescents ages 12–14 and 15–17, and among girls.[5] The rate for girls ages 15–19 reached a 40-year peak in 2015.[6]

Disabilities can impact a child's ability to engage and succeed in school. Almost 3% of children have a disability that limits the ability to physically take part in all sport and game activities, and almost 4% of children have a disability that makes completing regular schoolwork a challenge. Children with disabilities are more likely to repeat a grade and to be suspended or expelled than their peers without disabilities.[7]

B. CAUSAL CORRELATIONS

1. Malnutrition

Longstanding research has established a strong connection between nutrition and optimum brain development. One leading source concluded that even moderate but chronic undernutrition correlates with lower scores in cognitive function tests, and found "substantial relations between nutrition and mental development."[8] A decades-long longitudinal study of diet and mental development from 1968 into the 1990s found that nutrition is highly correlated with cognitive competence, especially between ages 3 and 7, including language test performance results.[9] Recent studies have also found that poor nutrition and obesity during pregnancy poses a risk to the healthy development of a fetus's brain.[10]

Some harm is permanent—particularly where malnutrition occurs during the first five years of brain development. Recent research shows that even low levels of malnutrition for various nutrients harm children in a variety of ways; some—but not all—are irreversible. These developmental, growth, health, and educational effects are all preventable—and some can be wholly or partly reversed—if children are properly fed.[11] Yet, food insecurity is prevalent in many countries, including the United States, where 1 in 6 children live in a household with an inadequate supply of food.[12] A recent survey in California found 16.6% of mothers who gave birth reported food insecurity during pregnancy. The rate was 1 in 5 among mothers age 15–19.[13] Underscoring the importance of this issue, the American Academy of Pediatrics recently developed a toolkit for use by pediatricians in screening for food insecurity.[14] Identifying food-insecure children can ensure referrals to programs such as the Special Supplemental Nutrition Program for Women, Infants, and Children (WIC).

2. Fetal Drug Injury and Fetal Alcohol Syndrome

Parental abuse and neglect is a cause of child disability across a range of injuries. Children are particularly vulnerable *in utero*, where permanent damage can come from alcohol ingestion or drug use. The chemicals here of concern—alcohol, tobacco-borne substances, opiates, amphetamines, and cocaine—are not blocked by the placenta, and may infuse the small body-weight fetus at effective concentrations many times the level felt by the mother. A 2017 national survey found that among pregnant women, 8.5% reported using illicit drugs during the previous month, 11.5% drank alcohol, and 14.7% smoked cigarettes. This results in at least 194,000 babies exposed to drugs, 261,000 exposed to alcohol, and 334,000 exposed to tobacco before birth. The survey found drug use increasing among pregnant women, with a significant increase in the number of pregnant women reporting daily or near daily use of marijuana. This has important implications, with research suggesting that marijuana use in pregnancy may be associated with neurological development, leading to hyperactivity and poor cognitive function.[15]

Use of opiates in pregnancy has increased significantly since the early 1990s. Among pregnant women seeking substance abuse treatment, those who reported using opioids increased from 2% in 1992 to 28% in 2012. The rise in opioid use has inevitably led to an increase in the incidence of Neonatal Abstinence Syndrome (NAS), a drug withdrawal syndrome experienced by opioid-exposed newborns. Astoundingly, a baby is born with NAS every hour, affecting more than 10,000 infants each year.[16] Long-term studies of outcomes among children who suffer NAS are scant, but recent research suggests possible vision problems, motor issues, and behavioral and cognitive problems.

The health problems resulting from perinatal alcohol abuse are categorized as Fetal Alcohol Spectrum Disorders (FASD), the most severe of which is Fetal Alcohol Syndrome (FAS). The CDC found that the rate of American babies born with diagnosed FAS rose almost sixfold from 1979 through 1993. A 2004 study found that each day as many as 6–22 infants are born with FAS and as many as 87–103 more are born with other alcohol-related impairments, resulting in an estimated $4 billion in costs to the U.S. annually.[17] Recent studies estimate that as many as 5% of children suffer from FASD.[18] Babies born with FASD suffer central nervous system dysfunction and can have problems with learning, attention span, and communication, causing difficulties in school and social interactions.[19] Behavior and attention problems are associated with Neurobehavioral Disorder Associated with Prenatal Alcohol Exposure (ND-PAE), another FASD that can result from significant alcohol use in pregnancy.[20] Studies of outcomes among individuals with FASD reveal ongoing life difficulties, including:

- Those diagnosed with FAS were more likely to be unemployed;
- 61% of those with FASD had disrupted school experiences—53% had been suspended, 29% expelled, and 25% dropped out;
- 60% with FASD had trouble with the law, with 50% experiencing confinement; and
- 35% with FASD experienced alcohol or drug problems.[21]

The most effective strategy for avoiding the above adverse outcomes is early diagnosis and connection to appropriate services. Unfortunately, researchers note that many children with FASD go undiagnosed or are misdiagnosed. A recent study found that only 2 out of 222 children with FASD had previously received a diagnosis.[22]

3. Lead Contamination/Environmental Injury

As discussed briefly in Chapter 5, several environmental contaminants are disproportionately dangerous to children, particularly lead. Although blood lead levels in children have been declining for decades, elevated levels remain more common among low-income and minority children who are more likely to live in older housing that contains lead paint.[23] Substantial lead-based paint remains in fragile condition in older buildings. Lead remains environmentally common due to decades of leaded gasoline, and most ominously, there are signs of excessive lead in some drinking water supplies. Lead can leach into water through the corrosion of lead service lines, of which there are between 5.5 and 10 million providing water to approximately 15–22 million individuals.[24] Alarmingly, several studies have found extremely high levels of lead in water at schools, where children spend a large portion of their day. Test results from more than 3,700 California schools indicate that 150 schools had water lead levels above the federal limit and another 754 schools had levels considered dangerous by pediatricians and health advocates.[25] Lead from factories and power plants can also reach children by contaminating soil, which children may ingest or track into their homes. Again, at greatest risk of such exposure are minority children in low-income communities.[26]

For young children, serious brain damage—including IQ diminution and ability to read and write—correlate in the research to low exposure levels (well short of visible lead poisoning symptoms). It is widely accepted that there is no safe level of lead in blood. Most important, intake of lead poses a cumulative danger—each exposure adds to an overall tolerance threshold which must not be exceeded. Effects of lead exposure are permanent, unable to be reversed or diminished through treatment. There is evidence that lead exposure in childhood has long-term cognitive effects that impact an individual's occupational potential and consequently their socioeconomic status in adulthood.[27] Foundational studies established that elevated blood-lead levels are strongly linked with decreased intelligence and impaired neurobehavioral development.[28] A leading study concludes that the result of current "low level" exposure "could be a tripling of the number of youngsters who need specialized educational services."[29] Emotional and behavioral problems are also associated with exposure to lead, even at low levels. These problems can manifest in both externalizing problems such as aggressiveness and delinquent behavior, as well as internalizing problems such as anxiety and depression.[30]

Policies aimed at prevention have been extremely effective but the problem has not been eliminated. National surveys conducted from 2007–10 indicate that low levels of lead were found in approximately 2.6% of preschoolers—equivalent to about 535,000 children. This represents an enormous cost to our society—upwards of $50 billion annually.[31]

4. Causes Unknown: Autism Spectrum Disorder

The precise cause remains unknown for a substantial number of child disabilities. Garnering recent attention and concern are autism and related disabilities, collectively referred to as autism spectrum disorder (ASD).[32] ASD is a neurological variation that occurs in about one percent of the population and is considered a developmental disability. Typical characteristics of autism include different sensory experiences, non-standard ways of learning, difficulties in understanding and expressing typical social interaction, and difficulties in understanding and expressing language as used in typical communication.

The Centers for Disease Control (CDC) began tracking the prevalence of ASD among 8-year-old children in 1998 through the monitoring of eleven representative sites. In 2000–02, the prevalence was estimated at approximately 1 in 150. By 2010–12 this rate had doubled. Estimates as of 2014 show an increase of 150% since 2000, with a rate of 1 in 59 children.[33] Research shows that ASD is approximately four times more likely to occur in boys than in girls.[34] ASD affects all racial, ethnic, and socioeconomic groups, although rates are highest for White children. The gap between races has recently narrowed, possibly due to increased diagnoses among minority populations that are traditionally underdiagnosed. For example, recent data show that African American pre-school aged children with ASD were less likely than their White peers to be evaluated for developmental concerns by age three.[35] This skews prevalence data and is concerning in light of the importance of early identification to ensure access to supportive services that can significantly improve outcomes for children with ASD. Failing to provide early intervention has both a human and a fiscal toll. Lifetime support for an individual with ASD with an intellectual disability is estimated at $2.4 million in the United States; aggregated national costs are estimated at $236–$262 billion per year. These costs are due to special education, residential accommodation, and medical care needs, as well as productivity losses in adulthood.[36]

The increase in prevalence over the last two decades is largely attributed to increased awareness leading to improved diagnosis and identification. However, there may biological factors at play as well, such as increasing numbers of individuals having children at an older age and increased survival rates for prematurely born infants. These are among a set of factors believed to contribute to ASD, although all the causes of ASD are yet unknown.

The Children's Health Act of 2000 requires annual reports to Congress on the status of autism incidence and response. In 2007, existing research networks established to meet the Act's requirement were merged into the Centers of Excellence at the CDC and National Institutes for Health to coordinate and intensify research on causes and treatments. In 2017, the National Institutes of Health awarded grants totaling almost $100 million to fund the Centers over the next five years.[37] These grants have been awarded every five years, with 2017 being the third cycle. In 2006, the Combating Autism Act was passed, establishing a federal advisory committee to develop a plan for ASD research. In August 2014, the Committee was reauthorized in the Autism Collaboration, Accountability, Research, Education and Support (CARES) Act, which remains effective until September 30, 2019.[38]

The level of federal support for various research activities related to autism reached $245 million in FY2017, $260 million in FY2018 enactments, and is estimated to total $241 million in 2019.[39] Although monitoring and research spending has grown, child advocates contend that it represents less than half the sum needed for prevention and cause related research, based on the severity and incidence of the problem. And the funds devoted to treatment—largely through the Individuals with Disabilities Education Act (IDEA)—are a small fraction of sums needed for amelioration.

C. MAJOR PUBLIC PROGRAMS ADDRESSING DISABILITY

The programs designed to help children with special needs are scattered widely through governmental departments in most states. The pattern has been to provide special attention to children in various "categories" of need, primarily developmental disabilities, mental health needs, and learning disabilities.

As displayed below, programs for disabled children originate from a variety of different and substantially unconnected programs. In addition to those listed below, the Medicaid program discussed in Chapter 5 covered nearly 73 million impoverished persons in September 2018, including 35.3 million children. In 2016, Medicaid and the Children's Health Insurance Program (CHIP) covered about half of children with special health care needs.[40] Under the Affordable Care Act, children in impoverished families must be provided with Medicaid, which covers a number of children with special needs.[41] And as discussed in Chapter 7, just under one million children were enrolled in the federal Head Start Program in 2017, of whom 13%—almost 130,000—were categorized as disabled.[42] Others may come to the attention of the state because of criminal acts, an arrest, and "ward of the court" status. Children with special needs may generate SSI assistance, special education, special regular hospital services, outpatient counseling, drug testing, treatment at a "regional" mental health center, forced confinement in a mental health hospital or facility operated by the state, or other services.

Major Federal Child Disability Programs Serving Children with Special Needs

- **Supplemental Security Income (SSI)**
  - Law: Social Security Act, Title XVI, 42 US Code § 1381, 20 CFR Part 416
  - Agency: Social Security Administration
  - Purpose: To assure a minimum level of income to persons with income and resources below specified levels
- **Special Education—State Grants Program for Children with Disabilities**
  - Law: Individual with Disabilities Education Act (IDEA), Part B, 20 U.S. Code § 1411, 34 CFR § 300
  - Agency: U.S. Department of Education, Office of Special Education Programs
  - Purpose: To ensure that all children with disabilities receive a free, appropriate public education (FAPE)
- **Early Intervention Program for Infants and Toddlers with Disabilities**
  - Law: IDEA, Part C, 20 U.S. Code § 1431, et seq. 34 CFR § 303
  - Agency: U.S. Department of Education, Office of Special Education Programs
  - Purpose: To provide a statewide system of comprehensive, multi-disciplinary, coordinated services to infants and toddlers with disabilities and to their families
- **Comprehensive Community Mental Health Services for Children with Serious Emotional Disturbances Program**
  - Law: Public Health Service Act, Title V, 42 U.S. Code § 290ff

- ◦ Agency: U.S. Department of Health and Human Services, Center for Mental Health Services
- ◦ Purpose: Provides grants to public entities in order to provide comprehensive community mental health services to children with serious emotional disturbances
- **Section 811, Supportive Housing for Persons with Disabilities**
  - ◦ Law: 42 U.S. Code § 8013, 24 CFR § 890
  - ◦ Agency: U.S. Department of Housing and Urban Development (HUD), Office of Multifamily Housing Development
  - ◦ Purpose: To expand supply of housing that enables persons with disabilities to live independently
- **Protection and Advocacy for Individuals with Developmental Disabilities**
  - ◦ Law: Developmental Disabilities Assistance and Bill of Rights Act of 2000, 42 U.S. Code § 15043
  - ◦ Agency: U.S. Department of Health and Human Services, Administration for Community Living
  - ◦ Purpose: To protect the legal and human rights of individuals with developmental disabilities
- **Maternal and Child Health Services**
  - ◦ Law: Social Security Act, Title V, 42 U.S. Code § 701, 45 CFR § 96
  - ◦ Agency: U.S. Department of Health and Human Services, Maternal and Child Health Bureau
  - ◦ Purpose: To provide basic public health functions to improve the health of mothers and children

Major Federal Programs Affecting Children with Special Needs

- **Foster Care Program**
  - ◦ Law: Social Security Act, Title IV-E, Section 470, 42 U.S. Code § 671, 45 CFR § 1356
  - ◦ Agency: U.S. Department of Health and Human Services, Children's Bureau
  - ◦ Purpose: To assist states with the costs of foster care maintenance, administrative costs, training for staff and foster parents, and private agency staff
- **Adoption Assistance**
  - ◦ Law: Social Security Act, Title IV-E, Section 470, 42 U.S. Code §671, 45 CFR 1356
  - ◦ Agency: U.S. Department of Health and Human Services, Children's Bureau
  - ◦ Purpose: To assist states in paying maintenance costs for adopted children with special needs (disabled or older youths) and prevent inappropriate stays in foster care

- **Workforce Innovation and Opportunity Act Youth Program**
  - Law: 29 U.S. Code §3162, 20 CFR 681
  - Agency: U.S. Department of Labor, Employment and Training; U.S. Department of Education
  - Purpose: To provide services that focus on assisting youth with one or more barriers to employment prepare for post-secondary education and employment opportunities
- **State Vocational Rehabilitation Services Program**
  - Law: The Rehabilitation Act of 1973, Title I, as amended, 29 U.S. Code §720, 34 CFR Part 361
  - Agency: U.S. Department of Education, Rehabilitation Services Administration
  - Purpose: To prepare persons with disabilities to engage in competitive employment
- **State Supported Employment Services Program**
  - Law: The Rehabilitation Act of 1973, Title IV, as amended, 34 CFR Part 363
  - Agency: U.S. Department of Education, Rehabilitation Services Administration
  - Purpose: Employment for disabled individuals who require support and supervision
- **Client Assistance Programs (CAPs)**
  - Law: The Rehabilitation Act of 1973, Title I, Part B, 29 U.S. Code § 732, 34 CFR § 30
  - Agency: U.S. Department of Education, Rehabilitation Services Administration
  - Purpose: To provide information and assist Vocational Rehabilitation clients in identifying and accessing services
- **Protection and Advocacy for Individual Rights (PAIR)**
  - Law: The Rehabilitation Act of 1973, 29 U.S. Code § 794e, 34 CFR § 381
  - Agency: U.S. Department of Education, Rehabilitation Services Administration
  - Purpose: To enable persons with disabilities to function and continue by protecting their legal rights

D. TWO MAJOR FEDERAL BENEFIT PROGRAMS

Among the list of programs available to prevent and mitigate child disability, two programs cover the largest number of children and expend the most in public funding: SSI and the IDEA statute (see the bullets points above).

1. Federal Supplemental Security Income/State Supplementary Program (SSI/SSP)

The Supplementary Security Income (SSI) Program provides cash grants to aged, blind, or disabled persons, including children. A 2017 bulletin identified approximately 27% of SSI/SSP recipients as aged 65 or older, 59% as blind or disabled ages 18–64, and 15% as blind or disabled under age 18.[43] Whether a child is eligible for benefits is based on the severity of his or her disability as well as the family's income and savings. The criteria is strict, significantly limiting the number of eligible children. Among the 11 million children with special health care needs in the United States, 1.2 million receive SSI benefits. The benefits for those who do qualify average $650 per month, a modest sum that nevertheless provides an essential mechanism for families to avoid poverty, particularly deep poverty.[44] The program is administered by the federal Social Security Administration. Some states supplement federal SSI payment with a State Supplementary Payment (SSP).

Sullivan v. Zebley

493 U.S. 521 (1990)

JUSTICE BLACKMUN delivered the opinion of the Court.

This case concerns a facial challenge to the method used by the Secretary of Health and Human Services to determine whether a child is "disabled" and therefore eligible for benefits under the Supplemental Security Income Program, Title XVI of the Social Security Act...42 U.S.C. § 1381 *et seq*....

The program went into effect January 1, 1974. Currently, about 2 million claims for SSI benefits are adjudicated each year. Of these, about 100,000 are child-disability claims....

A person is eligible for SSI benefits if his income and financial resources are below a certain level, § 1382(a), and if he is "disabled." Disability is defined in § 1382c(a) (3) as follows:

"(A) An individual shall be considered to be disabled for purposes of this subchapter if he is unable to engage in any substantial gainful activity by reason of any medically determinable physical or mental impairment which can be expected to result in death or which has lasted or can be expected to last for a continuous period of not less than twelve months (or, in the case of a child under the age of 18, if he suffers from any medically determinable physical or mental impairment of comparable severity).

"(B) For purposes of subparagraph (A), an individual shall be determined to be under a disability only if his physical or mental impairment or impairments are of such severity that he is not only unable to do his previous work but cannot, considering his age, education, and work experience, engage in any other kind of substantial gainful work which exists in the national economy....

"(C) For purposes of this paragraph, a physical or mental impairment is an impairment that results from anatomical, physiological, or psychological abnormalities which are demonstrable by medically acceptable clinical and laboratory diagnostic techniques."

This statutory definition of disability was taken from Title II of the Social Security Act, 70 Stat. 815, as amended, 42 U.S.C. § 423 *et seq*....

Pursuant to his statutory authority to implement the SSI Program,...the Secretary has promulgated regulations creating a five-step test to determine whether *adult* claimant is disabled....

The Secretary's test for determining whether a *child* claimant is disabled is an abbreviated version of the adult test. A child qualifies for benefits if he "is not doing any substantial gainful activity,"...if his impairment meets the duration requirement,...and if it matches or is medically equal to a listed impairment,...In evaluating a child's claim, both the general listings and a special listing of children's impairments,...are considered. If a child cannot qualify under these listings, he is denied benefits. There is no further inquiry corresponding to the fourth and fifth steps of the adult test.

II

Respondent Brian Zebley, a child who had been denied SSI benefits, brought a class action in the United States District Court for the Eastern District of Pennsylvania to challenge the child-disability regulations....His complaint alleges that the Secretary

"has promulgated regulations and issued instructions...whereby children have their entitlement to SSI disability benefits based solely on the grounds that they have a listed impairment or the medical equivalent of a listed impairment...in contravention of the Act's requirement that a child be considered disabled 'if he suffers from any medically determinable physical or mental impairment of comparable severity' to that which disables an adult under the program."

* * *

I

Since the Social Security Act expressly grants the Secretary rulemaking power,..."'our review is limited to determining whether the regulations promulgated exceeded the Secretary's statutory authority and whether they are arbitrary and capricious."'....

The statute generally defines "disability" in terms of an individualized, functional inquiry into the effect of medical problems on a person's ability to work....

The statutory standard for child disability is explicitly linked to this functional, individualized standard for adult disability. A child is considered to be disabled "if he suffers from any...impairment of comparable severity" to one that would render an adult "unable to engage in any substantial gainful activity." 42 U.S.C. § 1382c(a)(3)(A)...The next paragraph of the statute elaborates on the adult disability standard, providing that an adult is considered unable to engage in substantial gainful activity, and is therefore disabled, if he is unable to do either his own past work or other work. § 1382c(a)(3)(B). In plain words, the two provisions together mean that a child is entitled to benefits if his impairment is as severe as one that would prevent an adult from working.

The question presented is whether the Secretary's method of determining child disability conforms to this statutory standard. Respondents argue, and the Third Circuit agreed, that it does not, because the regulatory requirement that a child claimant's impairment must match or be equivalent to a listed impairment denies benefits to those children whose impairments are severe and disabling even though the impairments are not listed and cannot meaningfully be compared with the listings....

IV

The listings set out at 20 CFR pt. 404, subpt. P, App. 1 (pt. A)..., are descriptions of various physical and mental illnesses and abnormalities, most of which are categorized by the body system they affect.[6] Each impairment is defined in terms of several specific medical signs, symptoms, or laboratory test results.[7] For a claimant to show that his impairment matches a listing, it must meet *all* of the specified medical criteria. An impairment that manifests only some of those criteria, no matter how severely, does not qualify.[8]

For a claimant to qualify for benefits by showing that his unlisted impairment, or combination of impairments, is "equivalent" to a listed impairment, he must present medical findings equal in severity to *all* the criteria for the one most similar listed impairment.[10] 20 CFR § 416.926(a) (1989) (a claimant's impairment is "equivalent" to a

266

listed impairment "if the medical findings are at least equal in severity" to the medical criteria for "the listed impairment most like [the claimant's] impairment");...when a person has a combination of impairments, "the medical findings of the combined impairments will be compared to the findings of the listed impairment most similar to the individual's most severe impairment").[11] A claimant cannot qualify for benefits under the "equivalence" step by showing that the overall functional impact of his unlisted impairment or combination of impairments is as severe as that of a listed impairment....

* * *

When the Secretary developed the child-disability listings, he set their medical criteria at the same level of severity as that of the adult listings....

Thus, the listings in several ways are more restrictive than the statutory standard. First, the listings obviously do not cover all illnesses and abnormalities that actually can be disabling. The Secretary himself has characterized the adult listing as merely containing "over 100 *examples* of medical conditions which ordinarily prevent" a person from working, and has recognized that "it is difficult to include in the listing all the sets of medical findings which describe impairments severe enough to prevent any gainful work."....Similarly, when the Secretary published the child-disability listings for comment in 1977, he described them as including only the "more common impairments" affecting children.[13]

* * *

For *adults*, these shortcomings of the listings are remedied at the final, vocational steps of the Secretary's test. A claimant who does not qualify for benefits under the listings, for any of the reasons described above, still has the opportunity to show that his impairment in fact prevents him from working....

For children, however, there is no similar opportunity. Children whose impairments are not quite severe enough to rise to the presumptively disabling level set by the listings; children with impairments that might not disable any and all children, but which actually disable *them*, due to symptomatic effects such as pain, nausea, side effects of medication, etc., or due to their particular age, educational background, and circumstances; and children with unlisted impairments or combinations of impairments[16] that are not equivalent to any one listing—all these categories of child claimants are simply denied benefits, even if their impairments are of "comparable severity" to ones that would actually (though not presumptively) render an adult disabled.

The child-disability regulations are simply inconsistent with the statutory standard of "comparable severity."[18]

V
* * *

The Secretary's claim that a functional analysis of child-disability claims is not feasible is unconvincing. The fact that a *vocational* analysis is inapplicable to children does not mean that a *functional* analysis cannot be applied to them....

VI   Conclusion

We conclude that the Secretary's regulations and rulings implementing the child-disability statute simply do not carry out the statutory requirement that SSI benefits shall be provided to children with "any...impairment of comparable severity" to an impairment that would make an adult "unable to engage in any substantial gainful activity."...

The judgment of the Court of Appeals, vacating in part the District Court's grant of summary judgment in the Secretary's favor as to the claims of the plaintiff class, is affirmed.

It is so ordered.

[6] There are 125 impairments defined in the adult listings, and an additional 57 in the child listings. The body system categories in the adult listings are: musculoskeletal, special senses and speech, respiratory, cardiovascular, digestive, genito-urinary, hemic and lymphatic, skin, and endocrine. In addition, there are four groups of listings not categorized by body system: multiple body system impairments, neurological impairments, mental disorders, and malignant neoplastic diseases. The child-disability listings include, in addition to all these, a category for growth impairment.

[7] For example, under the "growth impairment" category of the child-disability listings, 20 CFR pt. 404, subpt. P, App. 1 (pt. B), § 100.00 *et seq.* (1989), there is a listing the medical criteria of which require the claimant to show both a "[f]all of greater than 25 percentiles in height which is sustained" and "[b]one age greater than two standard deviations...below the mean for chronological age." § 100.03. Another example is the listing for "mental retardation," which requires that a child claimant show "achievement of only those developmental milestones generally acquired by children no more than one-half the child's chronological age," or "IQ of 59 or less," or "IQ of 60–69, inclusive, and a physical or other mental impairment imposing additional and significant restriction of function or developmental progression." § 112.05.

[9] For example, in the growth impairment listing described in n. 7, *supra,* a child claimant whose "bone age" was slightly less than two standard deviations below normal would not qualify under the listing, even if his height was much more than 25 percentiles below normal.

[10] For example, a child claimant with Down syndrome (which currently is not a listed impairment), a congenital disorder usually manifested by mental retardation, skeletal deformity, and cardiovascular and digestive problems, would have to fulfill the criteria for whichever single listing his condition most resembled....

[11] For example, if a child has both a growth impairment slightly less severe than required by listing § 100.03, and is mentally retarded but has an IQ just above the cut-off level set by § 112.04, he cannot qualify for benefits under the "equivalence" analysis—no matter how devastating the combined impact of mental retardation and impaired physical growth.

[13] There are, as yet, no specific listings for many well-known childhood impairments, including spina bifida, Down syndrome, muscular dystrophy, autism, AIDS, infant drug dependency, and fetal alcohol syndrome....The Secretary, however, has proposed new listings for "Down syndrome and other Hereditary, Congenital, and Acquired Disorders."....

[16] As the dissent points out,...42 U.S.C. § 1382c(a)(3)(F)...requires that "the combined impact of [multiple] impairments shall be considered throughout the disability determination process," and 20 CFR § 416.923...promises that "we will consider the combined effect of all your impairments." This assurance may be of value to adult claimants, but not to children, for whom the combined effect of multiple impairments is considered *only* within the confines of the equivalence determination, "whether the combination of your impairments is medically equal to *any listed impairment*."...As the Court of Appeals noted, *if* children are afforded the Benefits (1988).

A telling example of the effect of the listings-only approach is found in *Wilkinson ex rel. Wilkinson v. Bowen,* 847 F.2d 660 (CA11 1987) (child with rare liver disorder causing severe swelling, food allergies, and fever, and requiring constant care and confinement at home, does not qualify for benefits because his impairment does not meet or equal the criteria for any listing); see also *Zebley ex rel. Zebley v. Bowen,* 855 F.2d 67 (CA3 1988) (plaintiff Zebley denied benefits, despite evidence of congenital brain damage, mental retardation, development delay, eye problems, and musculoskeletal impairment, because his condition did not meet or equal any listing).

The disparity in the Secretary's treatment of child and adult claimants is thrown into sharp relief in cases where an unsuccessful child claimant, upon reaching age 18, is awarded benefits on the basis of the impairment deemed insufficient to qualify him for child disability benefits....

[18] The dissent proposes that children who fail to qualify for benefits under the Secretary's current approach can simply "make their case before the Secretary, and take the case to court if their claims are rejected."...We fail to see why each child denied benefits because his impairment falls within the several categories of impairments that meet the statutory standard but do not qualify under the Secretary's listings-only approach should be compelled to raise a separate, as-applied challenge to the regulations, or why a facial challenge is not a proper response to the systemic disparity between the statutory standard and the Secretary's approach to child-disability claims.

JUSTICE WHITE, with whom **THE CHIEF JUSTICE** joins, dissenting.

Only two Terms ago, when reviewing an aspect of the Secretary's methodology for evaluating disability applications under this Act, we emphasized that "Congress has 'conferred on the Secretary exceptionally broad authority'" in this context, and we stated that the Secretary's regulations were therefore entitled to great deference....Because the majority has failed to abide by this principle, I respectfully dissent.

* * *

At the end of 42 U.S.C. § 1382c(a)(3)(A)..., with its definition of disability, is a parenthetical provision defining that term in the case of persons under 18: "or, in the case of a child under the age of 18, if he suffers from any medically determinable physical or mental impairment of comparable severity." There is no reference to nonmedical factors in this definition and no references to specific consequences that an impairment must or should produce. Furthermore, neither "comparable," "severity," nor the two words together are there or elsewhere defined in the Act, and their meaning is anything but clear. The severity of an impairment that disables an adult is measured by its effects on the ability to engage in gainful employment. But that yardstick is not useful with respect to children, whose inability to work is not due to mental or physical impairment, but to the stage of their development and the labor market. Given this task of comparing apples and oranges, it is understandable that the Secretary implemented the statute with respect to children in a somewhat different manner than he did for adults, and surely there is no direction in the statute to employ the same methodology for both groups.

* * *

...Surely it cannot be said that the regulations, insofar as they use the Part A and Part B listings, singly or in combination, to identify disability in children, are inconsistent with the statute and void on their face. And as I understand it, no one claims that they are. What is submitted is, first, that the listings do not identify all of the specific medical impairments that should be considered disabling, and second, that each child not deemed disabled under Parts A and B must be evaluated in terms of both his or her medical impairments and nonmedical factors, as are adults.

These alleged deficiencies are said to be sufficient to invalidate the regulations on their face. But surely these claims, if true, only would demonstrate that the regulations do not go far enough. Furthermore, the claims purport to be supported by descriptions of various unlisted impairments and anecdotal evidence, none of which, it seems to me, has been adjudged by a court to be sufficient to demonstrate that the Part B impairments, or their equivalents, fail to identify impairments that will have comparably severe effects on a child's development as the disabling impairments for an adult will have on an adult's ability to engage in substantial gainful employment. If there are medically determinable diseases or impairments that should be considered disabling because of comparable severity to those affecting adults, the children suffering from them should claim disability, make their case before the Secretary, and take the case to court if their claims are rejected....

I also note that the majority faults the regulations on the grounds that they do not adequately provide for considering multiple impairments together...[H]owever, the regulations expressly provide that impairments in combination may add up to qualify for benefits....The Court of Appeals recognized that the Secretary's regulations faithfully implement the statutory mandate "by providing generally that the combined effect of all of a claimant's impairments will be considered throughout the disability determination process." *Zebley v. Bowen*, 855 F.2d 67, 76 (CA3 1988). There is no cross-petition challenging this aspect of the judgment below, and the Court should therefore not expand the relief obtained in the Court of Appeals.

In sum, because I cannot conclude that the Secretary's method for evaluating child-disability claims is an impermissible construction of the Act, I dissent. The Social Security Administration processes over 100,000 child-disability claims a year. The agency has a finite amount of funds with which to work. By requiring the Secretary to conduct unspecified individualized determinations in cases where an applicant fails to satisfy the agency that he is otherwise disabled, the majority imposes costs on the agency that surely will detract from the pool of benefits available to the unfortunate children that Congress has sought to protect through the Supplemental Security Income Program.

Note on Developments After *Sullivan v. Zebley* PRA Contraction

Six years after the *Zebley* decision, Congress enacted the Personal Responsibility and Work Opportunity Reconciliation Act (PRA), adversely affecting child eligibility for SSI/SSP. The new guidelines changed the definition of disability. Under post-*Zebley* standards, children were eligible for SSI benefits if an impairment existed that prevented them from performing age-appropriate activities.[45] The PRA and implementing rules eliminated references to the "comparable severity standard," the "individual functional assessment," and "maladaptive behavior."[46]

The new rules adopted by the Social Security Administration included a set of "medical listings."[47] All children who qualified on the basis of comparable severity, the individual functional assessment, or maladaptive behavior had to be reevaluated under the new PRA criteria.[48] SSI critics contended that some adults were "coaching" children to elicit a disabled diagnosis. However, the U.S. General Accounting Office independently investigated SSI child claimants to ascertain the prevalence of fabricated or coached child symptoms. In 1995, GAO released its report, concluding that the coaching and fabrication allegations regarding child claimants were not supported by the evidence.[49] Grant monies for children are not as susceptible to discretionary spending for non-medical purposes as they are for adults; their regimen is more likely to involve SSI-financed therapy, special diets, or rehabilitation after a third-party diagnosis.

As of May 30, 1998, 245,349 children had been reevaluated out of the country's 998,280 child recipients of SSI. Of that number, 147,933 (54%) were continued and 125,740 (46%) were terminated from SSI. In addition, 56.7% of the 61,402 adolescents turning age 18 were removed from SSI based on adult criteria even though many had been qualified previously under the strict "listings" criteria.[50] The two largest categories of SSI/SSP withdrawal for children appear to be those who qualified based on non-medical referrals: "maladaptive behavior," as noted above, and children with respiratory problems. The former often involves seriously mentally disabled, ADD, or ADHD children who were born drug-addicted. While the disabilities are clear and serious, there is no organ dysfunction, illness, or traditionally treatable medical condition involved. The conditions do not meet the "list" oriented to common adult illness and injury which dominate qualification.

The second group suffering withdrawal of assistance, those with respiratory problems, confronts the same adult-oriented list. Under its terms, children must often show respiratory failure in a Forced Expiratory Volume Test in a doctor's office. Unfortunately, the often serious asthma disability of children can be episodic and may not be reflected in an office test while no asthma attack is occurring. However, for children with the affliction, living with the suffocating feeling of not being able to breathe for many hours during an attack can be a serious and dangerous disability—often requiring close monitoring and expensive medicine.[51]

Adding to the concern over the withdrawal of SSI/SSP is the record of those cases reviewed by independent administrative law judges. Over the first two years of review, 63% of the terminations were reversed.[52] This extraordinary rate suggests a pattern of broad-brush denial, followed by reinstatement of those able to obtain independent review. In addition to the issue of terminations, the same new strict criteria are used to deny new child claimants since the effective date of the PRA (August 22, 1996); here, the rejection rate nationally has risen to 56%.

Over the past decade, the rate of children receiving SSI rose somewhat before ultimately leveling off. The rise can be attributed to two factors: 1) increased screening and diagnosis, as noted above related to autism, and 2) the rise in poverty rates from 2010–12 associated with the Great Recession. Such economic conditions brought more children into the sphere of eligibility. However, current rates have lowered again since recovery.[53]

Washington State Department of Social and Health Services
v. Guardianship Estate of Danny Keffeler

537 U.S. 371 (2003)

JUSTICE SOUTER delivered the opinion of the Court:

At its own expense, the State of Washington provides foster care to certain children removed from their parents' custody, and it also receives and manages Social Security benefits for many of the children involved, as permitted under the Social Security Act and regulations. The question here is whether the State's use of Social Security benefits to reimburse itself for some of its initial expenditures violates a provision of the Social Security Act protecting benefits from "execution, levy, attachment, garnishment, or other legal process."...We hold that it does not.

...A child may get OASDI payments if, say, the minor is unmarried and was dependent on a wage earner entitled to OASDI benefits..., including children, whose income and assets fall below specified levels (the level for the latter currently being $ 2,000). Although the Social Security Administration generally pays OASDI and SSI benefits directly, it may distribute them "for [a beneficiary's] use and benefit" to another individual or entity as the beneficiary's "'representative payee.'"...In the exercise of its rulemaking authority,...the Administration has given priority to a child's parent, legal guardian, or relative when considering such an appointment. While the Act and regulations allow social service agencies and custodial institutions to serve in this capacity, such entities come last in order of preference....Whoever the appointee may be,

the Commissioner of Social Security must be satisfied that the particular appointment is "in the interest of" the beneficiary. Detailed regulations govern a representative payee's use of benefits. Generally, a payee must expend funds "only for the use and benefit of the beneficiary," in a way the payee determines "to be in the [beneficiary's] best interests."...The regulations get more specific in providing that payments made for "current maintenance" are deemed to be "for the use and benefit of the beneficiary," defining "current maintenance" to include "costs incurred in obtaining food, shelter, clothing, *[cannot]* medical care, and personal comfort items."...Although a representative payee "may *[be used]* not be required to use benefit payments to satisfy a debt of the beneficiary" that arose *[to]* before the period the benefit payments are certified to cover, a payee may discharge *[discharge]* such a debt "if the current and reasonably foreseeable needs of the beneficiary are *[a debt]* met" and it is in the beneficiary's interest to do so. Finally, if there are any funds left over after a representative payee has used benefits for current maintenance and other authorized purposes, the payee is required to conserve or invest the funds and to hold them in trust for the beneficiary.

* * *

The State of Washington, through petitioner Department of Social and Health Services, makes foster care available to abandoned, abused, neglected, or orphaned children who have no guardians or other custodians able to care for them adequately.... Although the department provides foster care without strings attached to any child who needs it, the State's policy is "to attempt to recover the costs of foster care from the parents of [the] children,"...and to use "moneys and other funds" of the foster child to offset "the amount of public assistance otherwise payable,".... The department accordingly adopted a regulation providing that public benefits for a child, including benefits under SSI or OASDI, "shall be used on behalf of the child to help pay for the cost of the foster care received."...When the department receives Social Security benefits as representative payee for children in its care, it generally credits them to a special Foster Care Trust Fund Account kept by the state treasurer, which includes subsidiary accounts for each child beneficiary. When these accounts are debited, it is only rarely for a direct purchase by the State of a foster child's food, clothing, and shelter. The usual purchaser is a foster care provider, who is then paid back by the department according to a fixed compensation schedule. Every month, the department compares its payments to the provider of a child's care with the child's subsidiary account balance, on which the department then draws to reimburse itself. Since the State's outlay customarily exceeds a child's monthly Social Security benefits, the reimbursement to the State usually leaves the account empty until the next federal benefit check arrives.

* * *

As of September 1999, there were 10,578 foster children in the department's care, some 1,500 of them receiving OASDI or SSI benefits. The Commissioner had appointed the department to serve as representative payee for almost all of the latter children,.... who are among respondents in this action brought on behalf of foster care children in the State of Washington who receive or have received OASDI or SSI benefits and for whom the department serves or has served as representative payee. In their 1995 class action filed in state court, they alleged, among other things, that the department's use of their Social Security benefits to reimburse itself for the costs of foster care violated,...commonly called the Act's "antiattachment" provision, provides that "the right of any person to any future payment under this subchapter shall not be transferable or assignable, at law or in equity, and none of the moneys paid or payable or rights existing under this subchapter shall be subject to execution, levy, attachment, garnishment, or other legal process, or to the operation of any bankruptcy or insolvency law."

* * *

For obvious reasons, respondents do not contend that the department's activities involve any execution, levy, attachment, or garnishment. These legal terms of art refer to formal procedures by which one person gains a degree of control over property otherwise subject to the control of another, and generally involve some form of judicial authorization....Thus, the case boils down to whether the department's manner of gaining control of the federal funds involves "other legal process," as the statute uses that term....On this restrictive understanding of "other legal process," it is apparent that

the department's efforts to become respondents' representative payee and its use of respondents' benefits in that capacity involve nothing of the sort. Whereas the object of the processes specifically named is to discharge, or secure discharge of, some enforceable obligation, the State has no enforceable claim against its foster children. And although execution, levy, attachment, and garnishment typically involve the exercise of some sort of judicial or quasi-judicial authority to gain control over another's property, the department's reimbursement scheme operates on funds already in the department's possession and control, held on terms that allow the reimbursement.

* * *

The regulations previously quoted specify that payments made for a beneficiary's "current maintenance" are deemed to be "for the use and benefit of the beneficiary," and define "current maintenance" to include "costs incurred in obtaining food, shelter, clothing, medical care, and personal comfort items."...There is no question that the state funds to be reimbursed were spent for items of "current maintenance," and although the State typically makes the accounting reimbursement two months after spending its own funds, this practice is consistent with the regulation's definition of "current maintenance" as "costs incurred" for food and the like. That the State is dealing with the funds consistently with Social Security regulations is confirmed by the Commissioner's own interpretation of those regulations as allowing reimbursement by a representative payee for maintenance costs, at least for costs incurred after the first benefit payment is made to the payee.

* * *

Although it is true that the State could not directly compel the beneficiary or any other representative payee to pay Social Security benefits over to the State, that fact does not render the appointment of a self-reimbursing representative payee at odds with the Commissioner's mandate to find that a beneficiary's "interest...would be served" by the appointment....Respondents' premise that promoting the "best interests" of a beneficiary requires maximizing resources from left-over benefit income ignores the settled principle of administrative law that an open-ended and potentially vague term is highly susceptible to administrative interpretation subject to judicial deference....Under her statutory authority, the Commissioner has read the "interest" of the beneficiary in light of the basic objectives of the Act: to provide a "minimum level of income" to children who would not "have sufficient income and resources to maintain a standard of living at the established Federal minimum income level,"..., and to provide workers and their families the "income required for ordinary and necessary living expenses,"....The Commissioner, that is, has decided that a representative payee serves the beneficiary's interest by seeing that basic needs are met, not by maximizing a trust fund attributable to fortuitously overlapping state and federal grants.

* * *

...If respondents had their way, however, public offices like the department might well not be there to serve as payees even as the last resort, for there is reason to believe that if state agencies could not use Social Security benefits to reimburse the State in funding current costs of foster care, many States would be discouraged from accepting appointment as representative payees by the administrative costs of acting in that capacity...many eligible children would either obtain no Social Security benefits or need some very good luck to get them. With a smaller total pool of money for their potential use, the chances of having funds for genuine needs beyond immediate support would obviously shrink, to the children's loss. Respondents' position, in sum, would tend to produce worse representative payees in these cases, with less money to spend.

Questions for Discussion

1. If a foster child gets a paper route or otherwise earns money for his college education, should his parents take those earnings from the child's account to recompense them for rent, utilities, and food expenses of the child? Under current law, the child is entitled to a cumulative total of $2,000 in assets from such sources, but under this Court's decision is effectively entitled to no monies from SSI funds due and payable to him. For these foster children, the state exercises "parental jurisdiction." Is the taking of monies earned by (or due to) a child by a parent to pay for the living expenses of the child at home reflective of a responsible parent? Is it a typical approach of parents in our culture?

2. As the opinion discusses, the Social Security Act provisions on SSI benefits to children require the appointment of someone to act as the fiduciary of the child. The Court argues that the state does act in the best interests of the child in taking away these payments because the Commissioner has determined that paying the state is in the child's interests. Repayment of foster care benefits both the state and federal jurisdictions who may receive recompense. Is the taking of money due a person to whom one is owed a fiduciary duty—for the benefit of the fiduciary's employer—the proper discharge of that duty? Does the agreement to that diversion by an agent of the other beneficiary (the federal jurisdiction) provide convincing support for fiduciary compliance? The Court then argues that if the state cannot take the child's money, it will be unable to pay for the fiduciary payee to act for the child. Are there no alternative payees to serve as financial fiduciaries for foster children? If the state functions as the child's parent, does it not have the independent duty to seek funds for the child and to preserve monies due that child for the child's future use?

3. The purpose of SSI disability and OASDI death benefits is to supplement the other income or wealth of the recipient—for reasons of qualification separate and apart from foster care status. Does the child in foster care "owe" the state the cost of his care? Ironically, if the state openly declared that such a "debt" existed and could be enforced by garnishment or other legal process, *Keffeler* would hold that it could not be taken from the child because such "debt" payments are barred. Why does the direct taking of monies due a child warrant approval, while

its classification as a debt subject to procedural due process would allow the child to keep the funds? Is this the intent of the Congress?

4. *Keffeler* lacked a dissent and was buttressed by a puzzling brief by the Children's Defense Fund advancing the arguments of the state that these monies are properly (and advantageously) taken from the child and paid to it as recompense for child foster care expenses. What does this advocacy and this unanimous decision indicate about the political and legal status of children in American law? (See discussion of child protection in Chapter 8; *see also Parham v. J.R.*, 442 U.S. 584 (1979) and *Deshaney v. Winnebago County,* 489 U.S. 189 (1989), discussed in chapters 10 and 12, respectively.)

2. Individuals with Disabilities Education Act (IDEA)[54]

The Individuals with Disabilities Education Act (IDEA) guides the federal government's spending for special education. Congress last amended and reauthorized the IDEA statute through the Individual with Disabilities Education Improvement Act of 2004.[55] One important finding in the amended statute emphasizes that "the education of children with disabilities can be made more effective by having high expectations in the regular classroom" and "ensuring their access to the general education curriculum" so as to meet, "to the maximum extent possible, the challenging expectations that have been established for all children."[56] Likewise, Congress focused on the importance of well-trained professional staff "to improve the academic achievement and functional performance of children with disabilities... to the maximum extent possible."[57] Some of the changes were supported by child advocates, including the following:

- New language instructs use of "research-based teaching methods" allowing empirical results as a guidepost.
- The amendments give new importance to the Individualized Education Program (IEP) team, which must consider "the child's academic, *developmental,* and *functional needs*" (emphasis added). The IEP team must consider functional goals (life skills) whenever appropriate.[58]
- The mandate now includes preparing students for "further education" beyond Grade 12.[59]
- A foster child's foster parent is a "parent" for IDEA purposes, ending denials of services based on confusion over who had the authority to speak for these children—although still leaving uncertain in some jurisdictions who speaks for the child in the group home foster setting. The amendment also broadened "parent" for IDEA to specifically include any person acting in place of a parent, including a grandparent, stepparent, and other relatives with whom a child is living.[60]
- Early intervening services are authorized (eliminating the "wait first for the child to fail" problem) for "students in kindergarten through grade 12 (with a particular emphasis on students in kindergarten

through grade 3) who have not been identified as needing special education and related services but who need additional academic and behavioral support to succeed in a general education environment."[61] Early intervening services are distinct from early intervention services, which assist infants and toddlers under age 3, and were first established back in 1986.[62]

Early involvement by the school for these at-risk students not yet identified has burgeoned since the passage of the 2004 reauthorization. In 2007, about 25% of school districts had implemented what is now called "Response to Intervention" or "RTI" programs, to determine whether children have qualified learning disabilities, and to respond quickly. Currently, the majority of states have such programs.[63] The elements to this approach include "universal screening" to identify those with current or imminent academic problems—commonly focusing on early reading skills. Progress is closely monitored, and if intervention does not succeed, the intervention intensifies. If it persists, the student should be routed to a comprehensive special education assessment. This approach conflicts with the previous method based on "IQ deficit" based intervention. Under that previous method, children were given IQ tests, and intervention occurred primarily if performance was well below levels anticipated from those scores. Otherwise, intervention typically did not occur until students repeatedly failed and were so substantially behind that catch-up became problematic.

The new approach has some critics, including those arguing that it is over-inclusive and wastes substantial resources because a student with a "D" aptitude is performing consistent with that aptitude—which additional teaching may not efficiently remedy. But defenders argue that IQ is only one element in measuring aptitude and potential, is given excessive weight, and delays or excludes intervention that does, in fact, raise performance substantially, particularly during the early building block years. But the approach has many elements and variations—with a clear need for rigorous and sophisticated outcome measurement.

Three aspects of the 2004 statutory changes were opposed by child advocates:

- The changes appeared to add wide latitude for school districts to change placements where students violate the applicable "code of student conduct." However, this generally has not occurred, and advocates believe that is likely prevented by the "Stay Put" protections.[64]
- A new layer of administrative delay was interposed after the request for hearing by the parent. Instead of a 45-day timeline for hearing on the IEP, a "resolution" session must be held within 15 days at the request of the parent. That adds 15 days to the front end of the timeline, which means parents are subject to a 60-day wait for an administrative decision. Note that this does not apply when a school district files for a hearing. More importantly, a hearing officer may not award attorney fees to a prevailing parent for these sessions (unless the session is the result of a court or administrative order)—discouraging

- legal representation of children at that point and facilitating possible adhesive influence by school districts.
- Of related and greater concern, the amendments allow the school authorities to seek attorney's fees from the child's counsel or parents where the child does not prevail. Such fees are limited to circumstances where the school district can show that the request for hearing was frivolous, unreasonable or without foundation, or if the child's attorney is shown to have litigated beyond what was needed, or presented issues for an improper purpose. Child advocates argue that it is relatively easy for a prevailing school district (or any party) to argue that the rejected case presented by the child's attorney was "without foundation" or was litigated "beyond what was needed." After all, if the attorney's position is rejected, was its advocacy "founded" or "needed"? Child advocates note that under previous IDEA law, those attorneys representing parents without wealth undertook substantial work with the prospect of fees only if they prevailed. The added element of out-of-pocket loss to a state agency based on its substantial hourly fees to its counsel is not a common feature of American law where citizens challenge government, and serves to markedly chill the representation of children in these settings.

The original IDEA statute included a minimum guidepost of $1,500 per annum per child in Section 619 (over $2,200 in current dollars), spending that would be approximately three times actual appropriations as of 2004–05. Prior to the 2004 reauthorization, Congress enacted substantial amendments to the statute in 1997. The changes added federal funds and, when that addition surpassed $4.9 billion, changed the distribution formula for additional money to schools. Instead of their respective numbers of "identified" children with disabilities, distribution is based on broader population and poverty characteristics. States were required to "maintain" effort by spending the same per child as was previously expended. In FY2018, $13.4 billion was appropriated for IDEA.[65]

Part B of IDEA covers special education programs for children age three through 21 or a high school diploma, while Part C of IDEA governs early intervention services for infants and toddlers under age three. Some key provisions in Part B include the following:

- Parents are to participate in all eligibility and placement decisions, and school districts must "ensure" that parents participate in placement decisions;
- Parents must have access to all educational records concerning their child;
- If the child is in a regular education classroom for any part of the day, a regular education teacher is a mandatory member of the IEP team formulating the goals and services that will be provided;

- Students with disabilities under IDEA must be allowed to participate in districtwide assessments, or the district must explain its reasons for excluding them;
- IEPs must outline how a disability affects a student's performance in the general education curriculum, include goals tied to specific needs as identified in assessments, teacher input, and parent participation; and
- IEPs must identify the support needed to participate in general education.

Under Part C of IDEA, "[E]arly intervention services must be designed to meet the child's developmental needs, including physical, cognitive, communication, social and emotional, and adaptive areas, and must be provided by qualified personnel."[66] This may begin at birth; all infants and toddlers under 3 years of age are covered by this section. The 2004 amendments also provided states with a choice to continue Part C services (child-centered) as opposed to Part B services (education-focused) "until such children enter, or are eligible under State law to enter, kindergarten or elementary school, as appropriate...."[67] Grants are provided "to assist States to provide special education and related services...to children with disabilities aged 3 through 5, inclusive; and at the State's discretion, to 2-year-old children with disabilities who will turn 3 during the school year."[68] States who opt to continue services under Part C are eligible for special grants; the requirements and allocation formulas are found in Part B.[69]

Only a small percentage of the parents of children with disabilities can afford legal representation. Critics contend that school districts commonly ignore special education requests until contacted by counsel for a child. A growing number of legal practitioners now specialize in securing special education benefits. They are paid under the current arrangement only if they prevail, limiting fee-for-service attorney attraction to marginal cases. The 1997 federal changes preclude compensation for IEP meetings, where the presence of counsel may often resolve matters short of litigation. This likely reduces incentives to pursue cases, including meritorious cases.

E. IDEA KEY CONCEPTS AND CASES

1. FAPE: Free Appropriate Public Education

FAPE is part of every special education challenge—or it should be. IDEA defines FAPE as special education and related services that are provided at public expense (without charge) and under public supervision; meet state standards; include an appropriate preschool, elementary school, or secondary school education; and are provided in conformity with the IEP.[70]

Board of Education v. Rowley[71] is the seminal case establishing the parameters of FAPE. In *Rowley*, the U.S. Supreme Court established that an IEP must provide personalized instruction with support services to permit the child to benefit from the instruction.

Board of Education v. Rowley
458 U.S. 176 (1982)

JUSTICE REHNQUIST delivered the opinion of the Court.

* * *

II

This case arose in connection with the education of Amy Rowley, a deaf student at the Furnace Woods School in the Hendrick Hudson Central School District, Peekskill, N.Y. Amy has minimal residual hearing and is an excellent lipreader. During the year before she began attending Furnace Woods, a meeting between her parents and school administrators resulted in a decision to place her in a regular kindergarten class in order to determine what supplemental services would be necessary to her education. Several members of the school administration prepared for Amy's arrival by attending a course in sign-language interpretation, and a teletype machine was installed in the principal's office to facilitate communication with her parents who are also deaf. At the end of the trial period it was determined that Amy should remain in the kindergarten class, but that she should be provided with an FM hearing aid which would amplify words spoken into a wireless receiver by the teacher or fellow students during certain classroom activities. Amy successfully completed her kindergarten year.

As required by the Act, an IEP was prepared for Amy during the fall of her first-grade year. The IEP provided that Amy should be educated in a regular classroom at Furnace Woods, should continue to use the FM hearing aid, and should receive instruction from a tutor for the deaf for one hour each day and from a speech therapist for three hours each week. The Rowleys agreed with parts of the IEP but insisted that Amy also be provided a qualified sign-language interpreter in all her academic classes in lieu of the assistance proposed in other parts of the IEP. Such an interpreter had been placed in Amy's kindergarten class for a 2-week experimental period, but the interpreter had reported that Amy did not need his services at that time. The school administrators likewise concluded that Amy did not need such an interpreter in her first-grade classroom. They reached this conclusion after consulting the school district's Committee on the Handicapped, which had received expert evidence from Amy's parents on the importance of a sign-language interpreter, received testimony from Amy's teacher and other persons familiar with her academic and social progress, and visited a class for the deaf.

When their request for an interpreter was denied, the Rowleys demanded and received a hearing before an independent examiner. After receiving evidence from both sides, the examiner agreed with the administrators' determination that an interpreter was not necessary because "Amy was achieving educationally, academically, and socially" without such assistance....The examiner's decision was affirmed on appeal by the New York Commissioner of Education on the basis of substantial evidence in the record.... Pursuant to the Act's provision for judicial review, the Rowleys then brought an action in the United States District Court for the Southern District of New York, claiming that the administrators' denial of the sign-language interpreter constituted a denial of the "free appropriate public education" guaranteed by the Act.

The District Court found that Amy "is a remarkably well-adjusted child" who interacts and communicates well with her classmates and has "developed an extraordinary rapport" with her teachers....It also found that "she performs better than the average child in her class and is advancing easily from grade to grade,"...but "that she understands considerably less of what goes on in class than she could if she were not deaf" and thus "is not learning as much, or performing as well academically, as she would without her handicap,"....This disparity between Amy's achievement and her potential led the court to decide that she was not receiving a "free appropriate public education," which the court defined as "an opportunity to achieve [her] full potential commensurate with the opportunity provided to other children."...According to the District Court, such a standard "requires that the potential of the handicapped child be measured and compared to his or her performance, and that the resulting differential or 'shortfall' be compared to the shortfall experienced by non-handicapped children."...The District Court's definition arose from its assumption that the responsibility for "[giving] content to the requirement of an 'appropriate education'" had "been left entirely to the [federal] courts and the hearing officers."...A divided panel of the United States Court of Appeals for the Second Circuit affirmed. The Court of Appeals "[agreed] with the [District] [Court's] conclusions of law," and held that its "findings of fact [were] not clearly erroneous."...

What is meant by the Act's requirement of a "free appropriate public education"?

* * *

We think...that the requirement that a State provide specialized educational services to handicapped children generates no additional requirement that the services so provided be sufficient to maximize each child's potential "commensurate with the opportunity provided other children." Respondents and the United States correctly note that Congress sought "to provide assistance to the States in carrying out their responsibilities under...the Constitution of the United States to provide equal protection of the laws."...But we do not think that such statements imply a congressional intent to achieve strict equality of opportunity or services.

* * *

The District Court and the Court of Appeals thus erred when they held that the Act requires New York to maximize the potential of each handicapped child commensurate with the opportunity provided non-handicapped children. Desirable though that goal might be, it is not the standard that Congress imposed upon States which receive funding under the Act. Rather, Congress sought primarily to identify and evaluate handicapped children, and to provide them with access to a free public education.

Implicit in the congressional purpose of providing access to a "free appropriate public education" is the requirement that the education to which access is provided be sufficient to confer some educational benefit upon the handicapped child. It would

do little good for Congress to spend millions of dollars in providing access to a public education only to have the handicapped child receive no benefit from that education. The statutory definition of "free appropriate public education," in addition to requiring that States provide each child with "specially designed instruction," expressly requires the provision of "such...supportive services...as may be required to assist a handicapped child to benefit from special education." § 1401(17) (emphasis added). We therefore conclude that the "basic floor of opportunity" provided by the Act consists of access to specialized instruction and related services which are individually designed to provide educational benefit to the handicapped child....

* * *

When the language of the Act and its legislative history are considered together, the requirements imposed by Congress become tolerably clear. Insofar as a State is required to provide a handicapped child with a "free appropriate public education," we hold that it satisfies this requirement by providing personalized instruction with sufficient support services to permit the child to benefit educationally from that instruction. Such instruction and services must be provided at public expense, must meet the State's educational standards, must approximate the grade levels used in the State's regular education, and must comport with the child's IEP. In addition, the IEP, and therefore the personalized instruction, should be formulated in accordance with the requirements of the Act and, if the child is being educated in the regular classrooms of the public education system, should be reasonably calculated to enable the child to achieve passing marks and advance from grade to grade....

* * *

Applying these principles to the facts of this case, we conclude that the Court of Appeals erred in affirming the decision of the District Court. Neither the District Court nor the Court of Appeals found that petitioners had failed to comply with the procedures of the Act, and the findings of neither court would support a conclusion that Amy's educational program failed to comply with the substantive requirements of the Act. On the contrary, the District Court found that the "evidence firmly establishes that Amy is receiving an 'adequate' education, since she performs better than the average child in her class and is advancing easily from grade to grade." ....In light of this finding, and of the fact that Amy was receiving personalized instruction and related services calculated by the Furnace Woods school administrators to meet her educational needs, the lower courts should not have concluded that the Act requires the provision of a sign-language interpreter. Accordingly, the decision of the Court of Appeals is reversed, and the case is remanded for further proceedings consistent with this opinion....

Questions for Discussion

1. What spurred the federal government's entrance into special education?

2. In the opinion, the Supreme Court established a "floor of opportunity" for students with disabilities. Does this meet the letter of the law? The spirit of the law?

3. The *Rowley* court describes the school district's duty as "education sufficient to ensure some educational benefit." How much benefit is enough? How will a school district know if it is meeting the threshold?

4. What is the test *Rowley* uses to establish whether or not the school district provided FAPE to Amy Rowley? Are those factors relevant for every student?

Endrew F. v. Douglas County School Districe RE-1
137 S. Ct. 988 (2017)

CHIEF JUSTICE ROBERTS delivered the opinion of the Court.

Thirty-five years ago, this Court held that the Individuals with Disabilities Education Act establishes a substantive right to a "free appropriate public education" for certain children with disabilities....We declined, however, to endorse any one standard for determining "when handicapped children are receiving sufficient educational benefits to satisfy the requirements of the Act."...That "more difficult problem" is before us today....

* * *

This Court first addressed the FAPE requirement in *Rowley*.... Even though "Congress was rather sketchy in establishing substantive requirements" under the Act,... the Court nonetheless made clear that the Act guarantees a substantively adequate program of education to all eligible children....We explained that this requirement is satisfied, and a child has received a FAPE, if the child's IEP sets out an educational program that is "reasonably calculated to enable the child to receive educational benefits." .... For children receiving instruction in the regular classroom, this would generally require an IEP "reasonably calculated to enable the child to achieve passing marks and advance from grade to grade."...

In view of Amy Rowley's excellent progress and the "substantial" suite of specialized instruction and services offered in her IEP, we concluded that her program satisfied the FAPE requirement. But we went no further. Instead, we expressly "confine[d] our analysis" to the facts of the case before us.... Observing that the Act requires States to "educate a wide spectrum" of children with disabilities and that "the benefits obtainable by children at one end of the spectrum will differ dramatically from those obtainable by children at the other end," we declined "to establish any one test for determining the adequacy of educational benefits conferred upon all children covered by the Act."...

* * *

Endrew attended school in respondent Douglas County School District from preschool through fourth grade. Each year, his IEP Team drafted an IEP addressed to his educational and functional needs. By Endrew's fourth grade year, however, his parents had become dissatisfied with his progress....As Endrew's parents saw it, his academic and functional progress had essentially stalled: Endrew's IEPs largely carried over the same basic goals and objectives from one year to the next, indicating that he was failing to make meaningful progress toward his aims. His parents believed that only a thorough overhaul of the school district's approach to Endrew's behavioral problems could reverse the trend. But in April 2010, the school district presented Endrew's parents with a proposed fifth grade IEP that was, in their view, pretty much the same as his past ones. So his parents removed Endrew from public school and enrolled him at Firefly Autism House, a private school that specializes in educating children with autism.

Endrew did much better at Firefly. The school developed a "behavioral intervention plan" that identified Endrew's most problematic behaviors and set out particular strategies for addressing them....Firefly also added heft to Endrew's academic goals. Within months, Endrew's behavior improved significantly, permitting him to make a degree of academic progress that had eluded him in public school.

In November 2010, some six months after Endrew started classes at Firefly, his parents again met with representatives of the Douglas County School District. The district presented a new IEP. Endrew's parents considered the IEP no more adequate than the one proposed in April, and rejected it. They were particularly concerned that the stated plan for addressing Endrew's behavior did not differ meaningfully from the plan in his fourth grade IEP, despite the fact that his experience at Firefly suggested that he would benefit from a different approach.

In February 2012, Endrew's parents filed a complaint with the Colorado Department of Education seeking reimbursement for Endrew's tuition at Firefly. To qualify for such relief, they were required to show that the school district had not provided Endrew a FAPE in a timely manner prior to his enrollment at the private school....Endrew's parents contended that the final IEP proposed by the school district was not "reasonably calculated to enable [Endrew] to receive educational benefits" and that Endrew had therefore been denied a FAPE....An Administrative Law Judge (ALJ) disagreed and denied relief....[T]he District Court affirmed. The court acknowledged that Endrew's performance under past IEPs "did not reveal immense educational growth."...But it concluded that annual modifications to Endrew's IEP objectives were "sufficient to show a pattern of, at the least, minimal progress."...

The Tenth Circuit affirmed. The Court of Appeals recited language from *Rowley* stating that the instruction and services furnished to children with disabilities must be calculated to confer "*some* educational benefit."...The court noted that it had long interpreted this language to mean that a child's IEP is adequate as long as it is calculated to confer an "educational benefit [that is] merely...more than *de minimis*."...Applying this standard, the Tenth Circuit held that Endrew's IEP had been "reasonably calculated to enable [him] to make *some* progress."...Accordingly, he had not been denied a FAPE.

* * *

While *Rowley* declined to articulate an overarching standard to evaluate the adequacy of the education provided under the Act, the decision and the statutory language point to a general approach: To meet its substantive obligation under the IDEA, a school must offer an IEP reasonably calculated to enable a child to make progress appropriate in light of the child's circumstances.

* * *

...After all, the essential function of an IEP is to set out a plan for pursuing academic and functional advancement. This reflects the broad purpose of the IDEA, an "ambitious" piece of legislation enacted "in response to Congress' perception that a majority of handicapped children in the United States 'were either totally excluded from schools or [were] sitting idly in regular classrooms awaiting the time when they were old enough to "drop out."'"...A substantive standard not focused on student progress would do little to remedy the pervasive and tragic academic stagnation that prompted Congress to act.

That the progress contemplated by the IEP must be appropriate in light of the child's circumstances should come as no surprise. A focus on the particular child is at the core of the IDEA. The instruction offered must be "*specially* designed" to meet a child's "*unique* needs" through an "[*i*]*ndividualized* education program."...An IEP is not a form document. It is constructed only after careful consideration of the child's present levels of achievement, disability, and potential for growth.

* * *

Rowley had no need to provide concrete guidance with respect to a child who is not fully integrated in the regular classroom and not able to achieve on grade level. That case concerned a young girl who was progressing smoothly through the regular curriculum. If that is not a reasonable prospect for a child, his IEP need not aim for grade-level advancement. But his educational program must be appropriately ambitious in light of his circumstances, just as advancement from grade to grade is appropriately ambitious for most children in the regular classroom. The goals may differ, but every child should have the chance to meet challenging objectives.

Of course this describes a general standard, not a formula. But whatever else can be said about it, this standard is markedly more demanding than the "merely more than *de minimis*" test applied by the Tenth Circuit. It cannot be the case that the Act typically aims for grade-level advancement for children with disabilities who can be educated in the regular classroom, but is satisfied with barely more than *de minimis* progress for those who cannot.

When all is said and done, a student offered an educational program providing "merely more than *de minimis*" progress from year to year can hardly be said to have been offered an education at all. For children with disabilities, receiving instruction that aims so low would be tantamount to "sitting idly...awaiting the time when they were old enough to 'drop out.'" ... The IDEA demands more. It requires an educational program reasonably calculated to enable a child to make progress appropriate in light of the child's circumstances.

* * *

Questions for Discussion

1. Justice Roberts begins by acknowledging that in *Rowley*, the Court elected not to provide a standard by which to measure sufficiency of educational benefit. Near the end of the opinion, he offers what he describes as a "general standard." Does the *Endrew F.* opinion provide substantially more guidance for schools, parents, and lower courts in determining whether educational programs are sufficiently in compliance with IDEA?

2. Who determines what constitutes "appropriate progress" for a student? Will courts be likely to defer to the expertise of schools in assessing progress? Will parents be expected to provide credible expert testimony in order to successfully argue that their child is capable of making greater progress? Does this significantly disadvantage parents in light of the *Arlington Central* case below?

3. How did the changes to IDEA in its 2004 reauthorization and amendments likely impact the Court's decision in *Endrew F.*? Did the new emphasis on the value of having "high expectations" for all children provide a stronger basis for the Court

to require an arguably more robust standard? Would *Rowley* have been decided differently under the most current version of the statute?

2. LRE: Least Restrictive Environment

IDEA requires that schools educate all children with disabilities in the least restrictive environment to the maximum extent appropriate where they can achieve educational benefit. The analysis should always begin with the regular education classroom, and the law's requirement is that children should only be placed in a more restrictive environment when the nature and severity of the needs is such that education cannot be achieved satisfactorily *even with supplemental aids and services.*[72]

Sacramento City Unified Sch. Dist., Bd. Of Educ. v. Rachel H.

14 F.3d 1398 (1994)

SNEED, Circuit Judge

...The court found that the appropriate placement for Rachel under the Individuals with Disabilities Act ("IDEA") was full-time in a regular second grade classroom with

some supplemental services. The District contends that the appropriate placement for Rachel is half-time in special education classes and half-time in a regular class....

I.   FACTS AND PRIOR PROCEEDINGS

Rachel Holland is now 11 years old and is moderately mentally retarded. She was tested with an I.Q. of 44. She attended a variety of special education programs in the District from 1985-89. Her parents sought to increase the time Rachel spent in a regular classroom, and in the fall of 1989, they requested that Rachel be placed full-time in a regular classroom for the 1989-90 school year. The District rejected their request and proposed a placement that would have divided Rachel's time between a special education class for academic subjects and a regular class for non-academic activities such as art, music, lunch, and recess. The district court found that this plan would have required moving Rachel at least 6 times each day between the two classrooms....The Hollands instead enrolled Rachel in a regular kindergarten class at the Shalom School, a private school. Rachel remained at the Shalom School in regular classes and at the time the district court rendered its opinion, was in the second grade....

* * *

The Hollands appealed the District's placement decision to a state hearing officer pursuant to 20 U.S.C. § 1415(b)(2). They maintained that Rachel best learned social and academic skills in a regular classroom and would not benefit from being in a special education class. The District contended Rachel was too severely disabled to benefit from full-time placement in a regular class. The hearing officer concluded that the District had failed to make an adequate effort to educate Rachel in a regular class pursuant to the IDEA. The officer found that (1) Rachel had benefitted from her regular kindergarten class - that she was motivated to learn and learned by imitation and modeling; (2) Rachel was not disruptive in a regular classroom; and (3) the District had overstated the cost of putting Rachel in regular education - that the cost would not be so great that it weighed against placing her in a regular classroom. The hearing officer ordered the District to place Rachel in a regular classroom with support services, including a special education consultant and a part-time aide.

* * *

In considering whether the District proposed an appropriate placement for Rachel, the district court examined the following factors: (1) the educational benefits available to Rachel in a regular classroom, supplemented with appropriate aids and services, as compared with the educational benefits of a special education classroom; (2) the non-academic benefits of interaction with children who were not disabled; (3) the effect of Rachel's presence on the teacher and other children in the classroom; and (4) the cost of mainstreaming Rachel in a regular classroom.

1.   Educational Benefits

The district court found the first factor, educational benefits to Rachel, weighed in favor of placing her in a regular classroom….[T]he District's evidence focused on Rachel's limitations, but did not establish that the educational opportunities available through special education were better or equal to those available in a regular classroom….

The district court found that Rachel received substantial benefits in regular education and that all of her IEP goals could be implemented in a regular classroom with some modification to the curriculum and with the assistance of a part-time aide.

2.   Non-academic Benefits

The district court next found that the second factor, nonacademic benefits to Rachel, also weighed in favor of placing her in a regular classroom….The court found the testimony of Rachel's mother and her current teacher to be the most credible. These witnesses testified regarding Rachel's excitement about school, learning, and her new friendships, and Rachel's improved self-confidence.

3.   Effect on the Teacher and Children in the Regular Class

The district court next addressed the issue of whether Rachel had a detrimental effect on others in her regular classroom. The court looked at two aspects, (1) whether

there was detriment because the child was disruptive, distracting or unruly, and (2) whether the child would take up so much of the teacher's time that the other students would suffer from lack of attention. The witnesses of both parties agreed that Rachel followed directions, was well-behaved and not a distraction in class. The court found the most germane evidence on the second aspect came from Rachel's second grade teacher, Nina Crone, who testified that Rachel did not interfere with her ability to teach the other children and in the future would require only a part-time aide. Accordingly, the district court determined that the third factor weighed in favor of placing Rachel in a regular classroom.

4.   Cost

Finally, the district court found that the District had not offered any persuasive or credible evidence to support its claim that educating Rachel in a regular classroom with appropriate services would be significantly more expensive than educating her in the District's proposed setting.

* * *

III.   STANDARDS OF REVIEW

…The district court's findings of fact are reviewed for clear error….The clearly erroneous standard applies to the district court's factual determinations regarding (1) whether Rachel was receiving academic and non-academic benefits in the regular classroom; (2) whether her presence was a detriment to others in the classroom; and (3) whether the District demonstrated that the cost of placing her in a regular classroom would be significantly more expensive….

IV.   DISCUSSION

A.   Mootness

* * *

...As the district court noted, the District and the Hollands have conflicting educational philosophies and perceptions of the District's mainstreaming obligation. The District has consistently taken the view that a child with Rachel's I.Q. is too severely disabled to benefit from full-time placement in a regular class, while the Hollands maintain that Rachel learns both social and academic skills in a regular class and would not benefit from being in a special education class....

B.   *Mainstreaming Requirements of the IDEA*

1. *The Statute*

The IDEA provides that each state must establish:

Procedures to assure that, to the maximum extent appropriate, children with disabilities...are educated with children who are not disabled, and that special classes, separate schooling, or other removal of children with disabilities from the regular educational environment occurs only when the nature or severity of the disability is such that education in regular classes with the use of supplementary aids and services cannot be achieved satisfactorily....

20 U.S.C. § 1412 (5)(B).

This provision sets forth Congress's preference for educating children with disabilities in regular classrooms with their peers....

2. *Burden of Proof*

...[I]n this case the District, which was challenging the agency decision, had the burden of demonstrating in the district court that its proposed placement provided mainstreaming to "the maximum extent appropriate."

3. *Test for Determining Compliance with the IDEA's Mainstreaming Requirement*

* * *

Although the district court relied principally on *Daniel R.R.* and *Greer*, it did not specifically adopt the *Daniel R.R.* test over the *Roncker* test. Rather, it employed factors found in both lines of cases in its analysis. The result was a four factor balancing test in which the court considered (1) the educational benefits of placement full-time in a regular class; (2) the nonacademic benefits of such placement; (3) the effect Rachel had on the teacher and children in the regular class, and (4) the costs of mainstreaming Rachel. This analysis directly addresses the issue of the appropriate placement for a child with disabilities under the requirements of 20 U.S.C. § 1412(5)(b). Accordingly, we approve and adopt the test employed by the district court.

4. *The District's Contentions on Appeal*

The District strenuously disagrees with the district court's findings that Rachel was receiving academic and non-academic benefits in a regular class and did not have a detrimental effect on the teacher or other students. It argues that the court's findings were contrary to the evidence of the state Diagnostic Center, and that the court should not have been persuaded by the testimony of Rachel's teacher, particularly her testimony that Rachel would need only a part-time aide in the future. The district court, however, conducted a full evidentiary hearing and made a thorough analysis. The court found the Hollands' evidence to be more persuasive. Moreover, the court asked Rachel's teacher extensive questions regarding Rachel's need for a part-time aide. We will not disturb the findings of the district court.

The District is also not persuasive on the issue of cost. The District now claims that it will lose up to $ 190,764 in state special education funding if Rachel is not enrolled in a special education class at least 51% of the day. However, the District has not sought a waiver pursuant to California Education Code § 56101. This section provides that (1) any school district may request a waiver of any provision of the Education Code if the waiver is necessary or beneficial to the student's IEP, and (2) the Board may grant the waiver when failure to do so would hinder compliance with federal mandates for a free appropriate education for children with disabilities. Cal. Ed. Code § 56101(a) & (b)....

Finally, the District, citing *Wilson v. Marana Unified Sch. Dist.*, 735 F.2d 1178 (9th Cir. 1984), argues that Rachel must receive her academic and functional curriculum in special education from a specially credentialed teacher. Wilson does not stand for this proposition. Rather, the court in *Wilson* stated:

The school district argues that under state law a child who qualifies for special education must be taught by a teacher who is certificated in that child's particular area of disability. We do not agree and do not reach a decision on that broad assertion. We hold only, under our standard of review, that the school district's decision was a reasonable one under the circumstances of this case.

...More importantly, the District's proposition that Rachel must be taught by a special education teacher runs directly counter to the congressional preference that children with disabilities be educated in regular classes with children who are not disabled. See 20 U.S.C. § 1412(5)(B).

We affirm the judgment of the district court....

* * *

Questions for Discussion

1. Can the district argue that economies of scale dictate the movement of children with significant disabilities into a special day class, where arguably they will have a lower student-to-teacher ratio?

2. If special education and related services cost substantial monies, will it lessen services to other students? What obligation do we owe other students in terms of balanced resources? Do students who demonstrate genius potential warrant special investment? Are they likely to manifest a special return on such an investment? Is it necessary to make such choices?

3. Is mainstreaming appropriate in every case? In Rachel's case? What benefits accrue to other children from contact with their special needs peers? How do you balance those benefits against possible educational distraction?

4. What evidence does Rachel's attorney use that made her case successful? Why did the district not prevail? Considering the district's strategy/arguments, would you have done anything differently?

5. The Appellate Court created a four-part test that is used in a number of circuits throughout the country. Does the test always favor a student like Rachel, who has an intellectual disability? What factors, if changed, would have produced a different result using this test? Should the factors weigh differently depending on the age of the student? Elementary v. Secondary considerations?

3. Related Services

Related services are transportation and developmental, corrective, and other supportive services *as may be required to assist a child with a disability to benefit from special education.*[73] IDEA offers examples of related services that are not exclusive—any service needed to enable a child with a disability to receive FAPE should be considered by the IEP team. Some of the enumerated examples are speech-language, interpreting, psychological services, physical and occupational therapy, counseling services, and mobility services. The statute specifically excludes medical services, except those for diagnostic and evaluation purposes only.

Cedar Rapids Community School District v. Garret F.
526 U.S. 66 (1999)

MR. JUSTICE STEVENS delivered the opinion of the Court, JUSTICES THOMAS and KENNEDY dissenting.

...The question presented in this case is whether the definition of "related services" in [the Individuals with Disabilities Education Act (IDEA)][1] requires a public school district in a participating State to provide a ventilator-dependent student with certain nursing services during school hours.

I

Respondent Garret F. is a friendly, creative, and intelligent young man. When Garret was four years old, his spinal column was severed in a motorcycle accident. Though paralyzed from the neck down, his mental capacities were unaffected. He is able to speak, to control his motorized wheelchair through use of a puff and suck straw,

and to operate a computer with a device that responds to head movements. Garret is currently a student in the Cedar Rapids Community School District (District), he attends regular classes in a typical school program, and his academic performance has been a success. Garret is, however, ventilator dependent,[2] and therefore requires a responsible individual nearby to attend to certain physical needs while he is in school.[3]

During Garret's early years at school his family provided for his physical care during the school day. When he was in kindergarten, his 18-year-old aunt attended him; in the next four years, his family used settlement proceeds they received after the accident, their insurance, and other resources to employ a licensed practical nurse. In 1993, Garret's mother requested the District to accept financial responsibility for the health care services that Garret requires during the school day. The District denied the request, believing that it was not legally obligated to provide continuous one-on-one nursing services.

Relying on both the IDEA and Iowa law, Garret's mother requested a hearing before the Iowa Department of Education. An Administrative Law Judge (ALJ) received extensive evidence concerning Garret's special needs, the District's treatment of other disabled students, and the assistance provided to other ventilator-dependent children in other parts of the country. In his 47-page report, the ALJ found that the District has about 17,500 students, of whom approximately 2,200 need some form of special education or special services. Although Garret is the only ventilator-dependent student in the District, most of the health care services that he needs are already provided for some other students.[4] "The primary difference between Garret's situation and that of other students is his dependency on his ventilator for life support."

The ALJ explained that federal law requires that children with a variety of health impairments be provided with "special education and related services" when their disabilities adversely affect their academic performance, and that such children should be educated to the maximum extent appropriate with children who are not disabled. In addition, the ALJ explained that applicable federal regulations distinguish between "school health services," which are provided by a "qualified school nurse or other qualified person," and "medical services," which are provided by a licensed physician. [cites omitted] The District must provide the former, but need not provide the latter (except, of course, those "medical services" that are for diagnostic or evaluation purposes,..) According to the ALJ, the distinction in the regulations does not just depend on "the title of the person providing the service"; instead, the "medical services" exclusion is limited to services that are "in the special training, knowledge, and judgment of a physician to carry out." The ALJ thus concluded that the IDEA required the District to bear financial responsibility for all of the services in dispute, including continuous nursing services.

The District challenged the ALJ's decision in Federal District Court, but that Court approved the ALJ's IDEA ruling and granted summary judgment against the District.... The Court of Appeals affirmed....

...The District pointed out that some federal courts have not asked whether the requested health services must be delivered by a physician, but instead have applied a multi-factor test that considers, generally speaking, the nature and extent of the services at issue.

II

The text of the "related services" definition, see n.1, *supra*, broadly encompasses those supportive services that "may be required to assist a child with a disability to benefit from special education." As we have already noted, the District does not challenge the Court of Appeals' conclusion that the in-school services at issue are within the covered category of "supportive services." As a general matter, services that enable a disabled child to remain in school during the day provide the student with "the meaningful access to education that Congress envisioned." *Tatro*, 468 U.S. at 891,...

* * *

...The continuous character of certain services associated with Garret's ventilator dependency has no apparent relationship to "medical" services, much less a relationship of equivalence. Continuous services may be more costly and may require additional school personnel, but they are not thereby more "medical." Whatever its imperfections, a rule that limits the medical services exemption to physician services is unquestionably a reasonable and generally workable interpretation of the statute....

Finally, the District raises broader concerns about the financial burden that it must bear to provide the services that Garret needs to stay in school. The problem for the District in providing these services is not that its staff cannot be trained to deliver them; the problem, the District contends, is that the existing school health staff cannot meet all of their responsibilities and provide for Garret at the same time.[9] Through its multi-factor test, the District seeks to establish a kind of undue-burden exemption primarily based on the cost of the requested services....

The District may have legitimate financial concerns, but our role in this dispute s to interpret existing law. Defining "related services" in a manner that accommodates the cost concerns Congress may have had, is altogether different from using cost itself as the definition....

This case is about whether meaningful access to the public schools will be assured, not the level of education that a school must finance once access is attained. It is undisputed that the services at issue must be provided if Garret is to remain in school. Under the statute, our precedent, and the purposes of the IDEA, the District must fund such "related services" in order to help guarantee that students like Garret are integrated into the public schools.

The judgment of the Court of Appeals is accordingly

Affirmed

[1] "The term 'related services' means transportation, and such developmental, corrective, and other supportive services (including speech pathology and audiology, psychological services, physical and occupational therapy, recreation, including therapeutic recreation, social work services, counseling services, including rehabilitation counseling, and medical services, except that such medical services shall be for diagnostic and evaluation purposes only) as may be required to assist a child with a disability to benefit from special education, and includes the early identification and assessment of disabling conditions in children." 20 U.S.C. § 1401(a)(17)....

[2] In his report in this case, the Administrative Law Judge explained that "being ventilator dependent means that [Garret] breathes only with external aids, usually an electric ventilator, and occasionally by someone else's manual pumping of an air bag attached to his tracheotomy tube when the ventilator is being maintained. This later procedure is called ambu bagging."...

[3] "He needs assistance with urinary bladder catheterization once a day, the suctioning of his tracheotomy tube as needed, but at least once every six hours, with food and drink at lunchtime, in getting into a reclining position for five minutes of each hour, and ambu bagging occasionally as needed when

the ventilator is checked for proper functioning. He also needs assistance from someone familiar with his ventilator in the event there is a malfunction or electrical problem, and someone who can perform emergency procedures in the event he experiences autonomic hyperreflexia. Autonomic hyperreflexia is an uncontrolled visceral reaction to anxiety or a full bladder. Blood pressure increases, heart rate increases, and flushing and sweating may occur. Garret has not experienced autonomic hyperreflexia frequently in recent years, and it has usually been alleviated by catheterization. He has not ever experienced autonomic hyperreflexia at school. Garret is capable of communicating his needs orally or in another fashion so long as he has not been rendered unable to do so by an extended lack of oxygen.".…

⁴ "Included are such services as care for students who need urinary catheterization, food and drink, oxygen supplement positioning, and suctioning.".…

⁹ …The District, however, will not necessarily need to hire an additional employee to meet Garret's needs. The District already employs a one-on-one teacher associate (TA) who assists Garret during the school day. At one time, Garret's TA was a licensed practical nurse (LPN). In light of the state Board of Nursing's recent ruling that the District's registered nurses may decide to delegate Garret's care to an LPN, the dissent's future-cost estimate is speculative.…

DISSENT: **JUSTICE THOMAS**, with whom **JUSTICE KENNEDY** joins, dissenting.

The majority, relying heavily on our decision in *Irving Independent School Dist. v. Tatro*, 468 U.S. 883 (1984), concludes that the Individuals with Disabilities Education Act (IDEA), 20 U.S.C. § 1400 *et seq.*, requires a public school district to fund continuous, one-on-one nursing care for disabled children. Because *Tatro* cannot be squared with the text of IDEA, the Court should not adhere to it in this case. Even assuming that *Tatro* was correct in the first instance, the majority's extension of it is unwarranted and ignores the constitutionally mandated rules of construction applicable to legislation enacted pursuant to Congress' spending power.

* * *

The primary problem with *Tatro*, and the majority's reliance on it today, is that the Court focused on the provider of the services rather than the services themselves. We do not typically think that automotive services are limited to those provided by a mechanic, for example. Rather, anything done to repair or service a car, no matter who does the work, is thought to fall into that category. Similarly, the term "food service" is not generally thought to be limited to work performed by a chef. The term "medical" similarly does not support *Tatro's* provider-specific approach, but encompasses services that are "of, relating to, or concerned with physicians or the practice of medicine." See Webster's Third New International Dictionary 1402 (1986) (emphasis added); see also *id.* at 1551 (defining "nurse" as "a person skilled in caring for and waiting on the infirm, the injured, or the sick; specif: one esp. trained to carry out such duties under the supervision of a physician").

IDEA's structure and purpose reinforce this textual interpretation. Congress enacted IDEA to increase the educational opportunities available to disabled children, not to provide medical care for them.….As such, where Congress decided to require a supportive service—including speech pathology, occupational therapy, and audiology— that appears "medical" in nature, it took care to do so explicitly. See §1401(a)(17). Congress specified these services precisely because it recognized that they would otherwise fall under the broad "medical services" exclusion. Indeed, when it crafted the definition of related services, Congress could have, but chose not to, include "nursing services" in this list.

B

Tatro was wrongly decided even if the phrase "medical services" was subject to multiple constructions, and therefore, deference to any reasonable Department of Education regulation was appropriate.…

* * *

II

Assuming that *Tatro* was correctly decided in the first instance, it does not control the outcome of this case.…We have repeatedly emphasized that, when Congress places conditions on the receipt of federal funds, "it must do so unambiguously. [Cites omitted]… [W]e must interpret Spending Clause legislation narrowly, in order to avoid saddling the States with obligations that they did not anticipate.

The majority's approach in this case turns this Spending Clause presumption on its head. We have held that, in enacting IDEA, Congress wished to require "States to educate handicapped children with nonhandicapped children whenever possible," *Rowley*, 458 U.S. at 202. Congress, however, also took steps to limit the fiscal burdens that States must bear in attempting to achieve this laudable goal. These steps include requiring States to provide an education that is only "appropriate" rather that requiring them to maximize the potential of disabled students,... recognizing that integration into the public school environment is not always possible,...and clarifying that, with a few exceptions, public schools need not provide "medical services" for disabled students...

For this reason, we have previously recognized that Congress did not intend to "impose upon the States a burden of unspecified proportions and weight" in enacting IDEA. *Rowley, supra*, at 176, n. 11. These federalism concerns require us to interpret IDEA's related services provision, consistent with *Tatro*, as follows: Department of Education regulations require districts to provide disabled children with health-related services that school nurses can perform as part of their normal duties. This reading of *Tatro*, although less broad than the majority's, is equally plausible and certainly more consistent with our obligation to interpret Spending Clause legislation narrowly....

Unlike clean intermittent catheterization, however, a school nurse cannot provide the services that respondent requires, see *ante*, at 3, n. 3, and continue to perform her normal duties. To the contrary, because respondent requires continuous, one-on-one care throughout the entire school day, all agree that the district must hire an additional employee to attend solely to respondent. This will cost a minimum of $ 18,000 per year.

Although the majority recognizes this fact, it nonetheless concludes that the "more extensive" nature of the services that respondent needs is irrelevant to the question whether those services fall under the medical services exclusion. Ante, at 9. This approach disregards the constitutionally mandated principles of construction applicable to Spending Clause legislation and blindsides unwary States with fiscal obligations that they could not have anticipated.

* * *

For the foregoing reasons, I respectfully dissent.

Questions for Discussion

1. The dissent argues that since we do not define car repair services in terms of what an auto mechanic does, we should not define medical services in terms of what a licensed physician does. However, isn't a licensed physician exclusively authorized to "practice medicine?" Here, a body of law prohibits others from "unauthorized practice of medicine." Does such a "scope of practice" definition apply to auto mechanics? Or to the other dissent example: food preparation?

2. The dissent proposes an alternative test: that medical services exempt from IDEA funding be broadly defined, but that it include those services provided to non-handicapped students which are medical in nature, such as those provided by school nurses. However, what is the "medical services" definition proposed by the dissent? Is it ascertainable? What if a school does not have a school nurse, or the only nurse is busy with non-handicapped children and the extensive services provided by the handicapped will require hiring additional nurses?

3. If you were drafting amendments to IDEA, would you want to consider allowing IDEA "medical service funding" where it affirmatively saved education funds otherwise required? For example, assume that a special needs student

could eliminate a disability with a major operation and hence save all future special education costs. Assume that the operation (or other medical cure) costs less than the special education costs to be saved. Assume that the child's parents do not qualify for public medical subsidy and cannot afford the operation. Should those medical expenses then be included within the scope of IDEA?

4. Reimbursement

Cases involving even small amounts of monies to parents for reimbursement of out-of-pocket expenses are often heavily litigated. But parents often feel they have no choice other than to provide for their child when the school district does not meet the need for services.

Florence County School District Four v. Carter
510 U.S. 7 (1993)

JUSTICE O'CONNOR delivered the opinion of the Court.

The Individuals with Disabilities Education Act (IDEA),...20 U.S.C. § 1400 et seq..., requires States to provide disabled children with a "free appropriate public education,"... This case presents the question whether a court may order reimbursement for parents who unilaterally withdraw their child from a public school that provides an inappropriate education under IDEA and put the child in a private school that provides an education that is otherwise proper under IDEA, but does not meet all the requirements of § 1401(a) (18). We hold that the court may order such reimbursement, and therefore affirm the judgment of the Court of Appeals.

I

Respondent Shannon Carter was classified as learning disabled in 1985, while a ninth grade student in a school operated by petitioner Florence County School District Four. School officials met with Shannon's parents to formulate an individualized education program (IEP) for Shannon, as required under IDEA....The IEP provided that Shannon would stay in regular classes except for three periods of individualized instruction per week, and established specific goals in reading and mathematics of four months' progress for the entire school year. Shannon's parents were dissatisfied, and requested a hearing to challenge the appropriateness of the IEP....Both the local educational officer and the state educational agency hearing officer rejected Shannon's parents' claim and concluded that the IEP was adequate. In the meantime, Shannon's parents had placed her in Trident Academy, a private school specializing in educating children with disabilities. Shannon began at Trident in September 1985 and graduated in the spring of 1988.

Shannon's parents filed this suit in July 1986, claiming that the school district had breached its duty under IDEA to provide Shannon with a "free appropriate public education,"...and seeking reimbursement for tuition and other costs incurred at Trident. After a bench trial, the District Court ruled in the parents' favor....

* * *

II

In *School Comm. of Burlington v. Department of Ed. of Mass.*, 471 U.S. 359... (1985), we held that IDEA's grant of equitable authority empowers a court "to order school authorities to reimburse parents for their expenditures on private special education for a child if the court ultimately determines that such placement, rather than a proposed IEP, is proper under the Act." Congress intended that IDEA's promise of a "free appropriate public education" for disabled children would normally be met by an IEP's provision for education in the regular public schools or in private schools chosen jointly by school officials and parents. In cases where cooperation fails, however, "parents who disagree with the proposed IEP are faced with a choice: go along with the IEP to the detriment of their child if it turns out to be inappropriate or pay for what they consider to be the appropriate placement."....For parents willing and able to make the latter choice, "it would be an empty victory to have a court tell them several years later that they were right but that these expenditures could not in a proper case be reimbursed by the school officials."....Because such a result would be contrary to IDEA's guarantee of a "free appropriate public education," we held that "Congress meant to include retroactive reimbursement to parents as an available remedy in a proper case."....

As this case comes to us, two issues are settled: 1) the school district's proposed IEP was inappropriate under IDEA, and 2) although Trident did not meet the § 1401(a)(18) requirements, it provided an education otherwise proper under IDEA. This case presents the narrow question whether Shannon's parents are barred from reimbursement because the private school in which Shannon enrolled did not meet the § 1401(a)(18) definition of a "free appropriate public education."* We hold that they are not, because § 1401(a)(18)'s requirements cannot be read as applying to parental placements.

Section 1401(a)(18)(A) requires that the education be "provided at public expense, under public supervision and direction." Similarly, § 1401(a)(18)(D) requires schools to provide an IEP, which must be designed by "a representative of the local educational agency,"...and must be "established," "revised," and "reviewed" by the agency, § 1414(a)(5). These requirements do not make sense in the context of a parental placement. In this case, as in all *Burlington* reimbursement cases, the parents' rejection of the school district's proposed IEP is the very reason for the parents' decision to put their child in

a private school. In such cases, where the private placement has necessarily been made over the school district's objection, the private school education will not be under "public supervision and direction." Accordingly, to read the § 1401(a)(18) requirements as applying to parental placements would effectively eliminate the right of unilateral withdrawal recognized in *Burlington*. Moreover, IDEA was intended to ensure that children with disabilities receive an education that is both appropriate and free....To read the provisions of § 1401(a)(18) to bar reimbursement in the circumstances of this case would defeat this statutory purpose.

Nor do we believe that reimbursement is necessarily barred by a private school's failure to meet state education standards. Trident's deficiencies, according to the school district, were that it employed at least two faculty members who were not state-certified and that it did not develop IEPs....

* * *

III

The school district also claims that allowing reimbursement for parents such as Shannon's puts an unreasonable burden on financially strapped local educational authorities. The school district argues that requiring parents to choose a state-approved private school if they want reimbursement is the only meaningful way to allow States to control costs; otherwise States will have to reimburse dissatisfied parents for any private school that provides an education that is proper under the Act, no matter how expensive it may be.

There is no doubt that Congress has imposed a significant financial burden on States and school districts that participate in IDEA. Yet public educational authorities who want to avoid reimbursing parents for the private education of a disabled child can do one of two things: give the child a free appropriate public education in a public setting, or place the child in an appropriate private setting of the State's choice. This is IDEA's mandate, and school officials who conform to it need not worry about reimbursement claims.

* * *

Accordingly, we affirm the judgment of the Court of Appeals.

So ordered.

* Section 1401(a)(18) defines "free appropriate public education" as, "special education and related services that

(A) have been provided at public expense, under public supervision and direction, and without charge,

(B) meet the standards of the State educational agency,

(C) include an appropriate preschool, elementary, or secondary school education in the State involved, and

(D) are provided in conformity with the individualized education program...."

Questions for Discussion

1. The *Florence* child was given an IEP for ninth grade in 1985. The decision was handed down in 1993. Given this timing, how important is the parental option to provide required services immediately and obtain recompense? How does the *Florence* precedent work for the vast majority of parents who cannot afford to up-front finance a private alternative?

2. Can parents receive a "blank check" where the school district fails to provide a program fully complying with IDEA? Should parents be required to pursue IDEA specified remedies prior to the pursuit of a private alternative with *post hoc* public funding? Should administrative/court remedies include timelines for expeditious resolution? Should such timelines bind the courts in their review?

3. What discretion do parents have to choose their private alternative? Should a district failing to provide required services be strictly liable for alternative expenses? In *Florence* the Trident school allegedly failed to meet some state standards. What if the child had not done well? Do we know that the child may have achieved better results in other settings? Do we know whether the child would have done as well under the District's plans?

Note on *Forest Grove School District*

The Supreme Court again considered the Florence County issue of private school tuition recompense under IDEA in *Forest Grove School District v. T.A.*, 129 S. Ct. 2484 (2009). In *Forest Grove* the child was not subject to a deficient IEP, but chose a private school option even though no special education eligibility had been approved by the school district. The opinion described the factual setting as follows:

> In June 2003, the District engaged a school psychologist to assist in determining whether respondent had a disability that significantly interfered with his educational performance. Respondent's parents cooperated with the District during the evaluation process. In July 2003, a multidisciplinary team met to discuss whether respondent satisfied IDEA's disability criteria and concluded that he did not because his ADHD did not have a sufficiently significant adverse impact on his educational performance. Because the School District maintained that respondent was not eligible for special-education services and therefore declined to provide an individualized education program (IEP), respondent's parents left him enrolled at the private academy for his senior year....The administrative review process resumed in September 2003. After considering the parties' evidence,

including the testimony of numerous experts, the hearing officer issued a decision in January 2004 finding that respondent's ADHD adversely affected his educational performance and that the School District failed to meet its obligations under IDEA in not identifying respondent as a student eligible for special-education services. Because the District did not offer respondent a FAPE [Free Appropriate Public Education] and his private-school placement was appropriate under IDEA, the hearing officer ordered the District to reimburse respondent's parents for the cost of the private-school tuition (at 2488).

The Supreme Court noted that the IDEA statute had been altered in 1997, after the *Florence* case, and did not alter the relevant language (generally allowing a court to award "such relief as it may deem appropriate")—thus implying Congressional consent to private school tuition liability.

Schaffer v. Jerry Weast
546 U.S. 49 (2005)

JUSTICE O'CONNOR delivered the opinion of the Court:

The Individuals with Disabilities Education Act (IDEA or Act), 84 Stat. 175, as amended,...is a Spending Clause statute that seeks to ensure that "all children with disabilities have available to them a free appropriate public education,"....Under IDEA, school districts must create an "individualized education program" (IEP) for each disabled child....If parents believe their child's IEP is inappropriate, they may request an "impartial due process hearing."...The Act is silent, however, as to which party bears the burden of persuasion at such a hearing. We hold that the burden lies, as it typically does, on the party seeking relief.

This case concerns the educational services that were due, under IDEA, to petitioner Brian Schaffer. Brian suffers from learning disabilities and speech-language impairments. From prekindergarten through seventh grade he attended a private school and struggled academically. In 1997, school officials informed Brian's mother that he needed a school that could better accommodate his needs. Brian's parents contacted respondent Montgomery County Public Schools System (MCPS) seeking a placement for him for the following school year.

MCPS evaluated Brian and convened an IEP team. The committee generated an initial IEP offering Brian a place in either of two MCPS middle schools. Brian's parents were not satisfied with the arrangement, believing that Brian needed smaller classes and more intensive services. The Schaffers thus enrolled Brian in another private school, and initiated a due process hearing challenging the IEP and seeking compensation for the cost of Brian's subsequent private education.

In Maryland, IEP hearings are conducted by administrative law judges (ALJs).... After a 3-day hearing, the ALJ deemed the evidence close, held that the parents bore the burden of persuasion, and ruled in favor of the school district. The parents brought a civil action challenging the result.

* * *

The term "burden of proof" is one of the "slipperiest members of the family of legal terms."... Part of the confusion surrounding the term arises from the fact that historically, the concept encompassed two distinct burdens: the "burden of persuasion," *i.e.*, which party loses if the evidence is closely balanced, and the "burden of production," *i.e.*, which party bears the obligation to come forward with the evidence at different points in the proceeding....We note at the outset that this case concerns only the burden of persuasion.

* * *

We therefore begin with the ordinary default rule that plaintiffs bear the risk of failing to prove their claims....

* * *

Petitioners contend first that a close reading of IDEA's text compels a conclusion in their favor. They urge that we should interpret the statutory words "due process" in light of their constitutional meaning, and apply the balancing test established by *Mathews Eldridge*, 424 U.S. 319 (1976). Even assuming that the Act incorporates constitutional due process doctrine, *Eldridge* is no help to petitioners, because "outside the criminal law area, where special concerns attend, the locus of the burden of persuasion is normally not an issue of federal constitutional moment."

* * *

Petitioners also urge that putting the burden of persuasion on school districts will further IDEA's purposes because it will help ensure that children receive a free appropriate public education. In truth, however, very few cases will be in evidentiary equipoise. Assigning the burden of persuasion to school districts might encourage schools to put more resources into preparing IEPs and presenting their evidence. But IDEA is silent about whether marginal dollars should be allocated to litigation and administrative expenditures or to educational services. Moreover, there is reason to believe that a great deal is already spent on the administration of the Act. Litigating a due process complaint is an expensive affair, costing schools approximately $ 8,000- to $12,000 per hearing....Congress has also repeatedly amended the Act in order to reduce its administrative and litigation-related costs....

Petitioners in effect ask this Court to assume that every IEP is invalid until the school district demonstrates that it is not. The Act does not support this conclusion. IDEA relies heavily upon the expertise of school districts to meet its goals. It also includes a so-called "stay-put" provision, which requires a child to remain in his or her "then-current educational placement" during the pendency of an IDEA hearing.... Congress could have required that a child be given the educational placement that a parent requested during a dispute, but it did no such thing. Congress appears to have presumed instead that, if the Act's procedural requirements are respected, parents will prevail when they have legitimate grievances....Petitioners' most plausible argument is that "the ordinary rule, based on considerations of fairness, does not place the burden upon a litigant of establishing facts peculiarly within the knowledge of his adversary."...But this "rule is far from being universal, and has many qualifications upon its application."... School districts have a "natural advantage" in information and expertise, but Congress addressed this when it obliged schools to safeguard the procedural rights of parents and to share information with them....As noted above, parents have the right to review all records that the school possesses in relation to their child....They also have the right to an "independent educational evaluation of their child." The regulations clarify this entitlement by providing that a "parent has the right to an independent educational evaluation at public expense if the parent disagrees with an evaluation obtained by the public agency."...IDEA thus ensures parents access to an expert who can evaluate all the materials that the school must make available, and who can give an independent opinion. They are not left to challenge the government without a realistic opportunity to access the necessary evidence, or without an expert with the firepower to match the opposition.

Additionally, in 2004, Congress added provisions requiring school districts to answer the subject matter of a complaint in writing, and to provide parents with the reasoning behind the disputed action, details about the other options considered and rejected by the IEP team, and a description of all evaluations, reports, and other factors that the school used in coming to its decision....

* * *

We hold no more than we must to resolve the case at hand: The burden of proof in an administrative hearing challenging an IEP is properly placed upon the party seeking relief. In this case, that party is Brian, as represented by his parents. But the rule applies with equal effect to school districts: If they seek to challenge an IEP, they will in turn bear the burden of persuasion before an ALJ.

JUSTICE GINSBURG, dissenting:

...The IDEA is atypical in this respect: It casts an affirmative, beneficiary-specific obligation on providers of public education. School districts are charged with responsibility to offer to each disabled child an individualized education program (IEP) suitable to the child's special needs.... The proponent of the IEP, it seems to me, is properly called upon to demonstrate its adequacy.

Familiar with the full range of education facilities in the area, and informed by "their experiences with other, similarly-disabled children,"..."the school district is...in a far better position to demonstrate that it has fulfilled [its statutory] obligation than the disabled student's parents are in to show that the school district has failed to do so,"...."In practical terms, the school has an advantage when a dispute arises under the Act: the school has better access to relevant information, greater control over the potentially more persuasive witnesses (those who have been directly involved with the child's education), and greater overall educational expertise than the parents."...[The] parent's obligation "should be merely to place in issue the appropriateness of the IEP. The school board should then bear the burden of proving that the IEP was appropriate. In reaching that result, we have sought to implement the intent of the statutory and regulatory schemes."...

Understandably, school districts striving to balance their budgets, if "left to [their] own devices," will favor educational options that enable them to conserve resources.... Saddled with a proof burden in administrative "due process" hearings, parents are likely to find a district-proposed IEP "resistant to challenge."...Placing the burden on the district to show that its plan measures up to the statutorily mandated "free appropriate public education,"...will strengthen school officials' resolve to choose a course genuinely tailored to the child's individual needs.[7]

The Court acknowledges that "assigning the burden of persuasion to school districts might encourage schools to put more resources into preparing IEPs."...Curiously, the Court next suggests that resources spent on developing IEPs rank as "administrative expenditures" not as expenditures for "educational services."...Costs entailed in the preparation of suitable IEPs, however, are the very expenditures necessary to ensure each child covered by IDEA access to a free appropriate education. These outlays surely relate to "educational services." Indeed, a carefully designed IEP may ward off disputes productive of large administrative or litigation expenses.

This case is illustrative. Not until the District Court ruled that the school district had the burden of persuasion did the school design an IEP that met Brian Schaffer's special educational needs....

Notably, nine States, as friends of the Court, have urged that placement of the burden of persuasion on the school district best comports with IDEA's aim....If allocating the burden to school districts would saddle school systems with inordinate costs, it is doubtful that these States would have filed in favor of petitioners....It bears emphasis that "the vast majority of parents whose children require the benefits and protections provided in the IDEA" lack "knowledge about the educational resources available to their [child]" and the "sophistication" to mount an effective case against a district-proposed IEP....In this setting, "the party with the 'bigger guns' also has better access to information, greater expertise, and an affirmative obligation to provide the contested services."...Policy considerations, convenience, and fairness, I think it plain, point in the same direction. Their collective weight warrants a rule requiring a school district, in "due process" hearings, to explain persuasively why its proposed IEP satisfies IDEA's standards. I would therefore reverse the judgment of the Fourth Circuit.

* * *

[7] The Court observes that decisions placing "the entire burden of persuasion on the opposing party at the outset of a proceeding...are extremely rare."...In cases of this order, however, the persuasion burden is indivisible. It must be borne entirely by one side or the other: Either the school district must establish the adequacy of the IEP it has proposed or the parents must demonstrate the plan's inadequacy.

Questions for Discussion

1. The majority opinion concludes that whoever challenges the IEP—whether parents or the local educational agency (LEA)—should bear the burden of persuasion, implying symmetry. How often does a school district challenge an IEP that is generally formulated by its own agents?

2. Justice O'Connor emphasizes the collaborative nature of the IDEA process and the costs of litigation. Do these factors commend a burden of persuasion on the child (or parents) or on the LEA? If litigation is expensive, is it not generally more expensive for parents than for the LEA? What should be the impact of the 2004 amendments discussed above (including the lack of payment for parents' counsel at pre-hearing proceedings, and possible assessment of LEA fees against parents) on the burden of persuasion? Does it signal Congressional intent to rely on LEA judgment? Or does it signal Congressional assumption that obstacles to child (parental) legal access further commend a burden of persuasion on the LEA when a challenge does reach hearing?

3. Is the fact emphasized by Ginsburg of an *amicus* filing by nine states in favor of an LEA burden of persuasion significant? Is it fair to conclude from such a filing that putting the burden of persuasion on the LEA will not involve inordinate costs?

4. The dissent disputes the majority view that IDEA proceedings involve administrative costs, characterizing the development of the IEP as determining the educational content of a child's program. But doesn't this case concern the legal proceedings challenging the IEP, properly characterized as a transaction or process cost separate from the actual delivery of services? How much does the LEA spend per hour on counsel to meet the burden of persuasion before an ALJ or in court, versus the amount per hour for a child's special education tutor?

Arlington Central School District Board of Education v. Murphy
548 U.S. 291 (2006)

JUSTICE ALITO, for the majority.

The Individuals with Disabilities Education Act (IDEA or Act) provides that a court "may award reasonable attorneys' fees as part of the costs" to parents who prevail in an action brought under the Act....We granted certiorari to decide whether this fee-shifting provision authorizes prevailing parents to recover fees for services rendered by experts in IDEA actions. We hold that it does not.

* * *

The governing provision of the IDEA... provides that "[i]n any action or proceeding brought under this section, the court, in its discretion, may award reasonable attorneys' fees as part of the costs" to the parents of "a child with a disability" who is the "prevailing party." While this provision provides for an award of "reasonable attorneys' fees," this provision does not even hint that acceptance of IDEA funds makes a State responsible for reimbursing prevailing parents for services rendered by experts.

Respondents contend that we should interpret the term "costs" in accordance with its meaning in ordinary usage and that § 1415(i)(3)(B) should therefore be read to "authorize reimbursement of all costs parents incur in IDEA proceedings, including expert costs." Brief for Respondents 17.

This argument has multiple flaws. For one thing, as the Court of Appeals in this case acknowledged, "'costs' is a term of art that generally does not include expert fees."...The use of this term of art, rather than a term such as "expenses," strongly suggests that § 1415(i)(3)(B) was not meant to be an open-ended provision that makes participating States liable for all expenses incurred by prevailing parents in connection with an IDEA case--for example, travel and lodging expenses or lost wages due to time taken off from work. Moreover, contrary to respondents' suggestion, 1415(i)(3)(B) does not say that a court may award "costs" to prevailing parents; rather, it says that a court may award reasonable attorney's fees "as part of the costs" to prevailing parents. This language simply adds reasonable attorney's fees incurred by prevailing parents to the list of costs that prevailing parents are otherwise entitled to recover. This list of otherwise recoverable [costs] is [obviously] the list set out in 28 U.S.C. § 1920, the general statute governing the taxation of costs in federal court, and the recovery of witness fees under § 1920 is strictly limited by §1821, which authorizes travel reimbursement and a $40 per diem. Thus, the text of 20 U.S.C. § 1415(i)(3)(B) does not authorize an award of any additional expert fees, and it certainly fails to provide the clear notice that is required under the Spending Clause.

* * *

JUSTICE BREYER, joined by JUSTICE SOUTER and JUSTICE STEVENS, dissenting.

The Individuals with Disabilities Education Act (IDEA or Act), 20 U.S.C. § 1400 et seq. (2000 ed. and Supp. V), says that a court may "award reasonable attorneys' fees as part of the costs to the parents" who are prevailing parties. § 1415(i)(3)(B). Unlike the Court, I believe that the word "costs" includes, and authorizes payment of, the costs of experts. The word "costs" does not define its own scope. Neither does the phrase "attorneys' fees as part of costs." But Members of Congress did make clear their intent by, among other things, approving a Conference Report that specified that "the term 'attorneys' fees as part of the costs' include[s] reasonable expenses and fees of expert witnesses and the reasonable costs of any test or evaluation which is found to be necessary for the preparation of the parent or guardian's case in the action or proceeding." H. R. Conf. Rep. No. 99-687, p 5 (1986), Appendix A....No Senator or Representative voiced any opposition to this statement in the discussion preceding the vote on the Conference Report--the last vote on the bill before it was sent to the President. I can find no good reason for this Court to interpret the language of this statute as meaning the precise opposite of what Congress told us it intended.

I

There are two strong reasons for interpreting the statutory phrase to include the award of expert fees. First, that is what Congress said it intended by the phrase. Second, that interpretation furthers the IDEA's statutorily defined purposes.

A

Congress added the IDEA's cost-shifting provision when it enacted the Handicapped Children's Protection Act of 1986 (HCPA), 100 Stat. 796. Senator Lowell Weicker introduced the relevant bill in 1985. 131 Cong. Rec. 1979-1980 (1985). As introduced, it sought to overturn this Court's determination that the then-current version of the IDEA (and other civil rights statutes) did not authorize courts to award attorney's fees to prevailing parents in IDEA cases... The bill provided that "'[i]n any action or proceeding brought under this subsection, the court, in its discretion, may award a reasonable attorney's fee as part of the costs to a parent or legal representative of a handicapped child or youth who is the prevailing party.'" (cite omitted).

After hearings and debate, several Senators introduced a new bill in the Senate that would have put a cap on attorney's fees for legal services lawyers, but at the same time would have explicitly authorized the award of "a reasonable attorney's fee, reasonable witness fees, and other reasonable expenses of the civil action, in addition to the costs to a parent...who is the prevailing party." *Id* , at 7 (some emphasis deleted). While no Senator objected to the latter provision, some objected to the cap. See, *e.g.*, *id.*, at 17-18 (additional views of Sens. Kerry, Kennedy, Pell, Dodd, Simon, Metzenbaum, and

Matsunaga) (accepting cost-shifting provision, but objecting to cap and other aspects of the bill). A bipartisan group of Senators, led by Senators Hatch and Weicker, proposed an alternative bill that authorized courts to award "'a reasonable attorney's fee in addition to the costs to a parent'" who prevailed. *Id.*, at 15-16 (additional views of Sens. Hatch, Weicker, Stafford, Dole, Pell, Matsunaga, Simon, Kerry, Kennedy, Metzenbaum, Dodd, and Grassley); 131 Cong. Rec. 21389.

* * *

Members of the House and Senate (including all of the primary sponsors of the HCPA) then met in conference to work out certain differences. At the conclusion of those negotiations, they produced a Conference Report, which contained the text of the agreed-upon bill and a "Joint Explanatory Statement of the Committee of Conference." See H. R. Conf. Rep. No. 99-687, at 5, Appendix A,.. The Conference accepted the House bill's GAO provision with "an amendment expanding the data collection requirements of the GAO study to include information regarding the amount of funds expended by local educational agencies and state educational agencies on civil actions and administrative proceedings." *Id.*, at 7....And it accepted (with minor changes) the cost-shifting provisions provided in both the Senate and House versions. The conferees explained:

> "With slightly different wording, both the Senate bill and the House amendment provide for the awarding of attorneys' fees in addition to costs.

> "The Senate recedes to the House and the House recedes to the Senate with an amendment clarifying that 'the court, in its discretion, may award reasonable attorneys' fees as part of the costs . . .' This change in wording incorporates the Supreme Court['s] *Marek v. Chesny*, decision.

> *The conferees intend that the term 'attorneys' fees as part of the costs' include reasonable expenses and fees of expert witnesses and the reasonable costs of any test or evaluation which is found to be necessary for the preparation of the parent or guardian's case in the action or proceeding, as well as traditional costs incurred in the course of litigating a case* " *Id.* at 5, Appendix A....

The Conference Report was returned to the Senate and the House. A motion was put to each to adopt the Conference Report, and both the Senate and the House agreed to the Conference Report by voice votes....

* * *

The Act's basic purpose further supports interpreting the provision's language to include expert costs. The IDEA guarantees a "free" and "appropriate" public education for "all" children with disabilities. ... see also § 1401(9)(A) (defining "free appropriate public education" as one "provided at public expense," "without charge"); § 1401(29) (defining "special education" as "specially designed instruction, at *no cost* to parents, to meet the unique needs of a child with a disability" (emphasis added)).

Parents have every right to become involved in the Act's efforts to provide that education; indeed, the Act encourages their participation. (IDEA "ensur[es] that families of [disabled] children have meaningful opportunities to participate in the education of their children at school"). It assures parents that they may question a school district's decisions about what is "appropriate" for their child. And in doing so, they may secure the help of experts.§ 1415(h)(1) (parents have "the right to be accompanied and advised by counsel and by individuals with special knowledge or training with respect to the problems of children with disabilities")....

The practical significance of the Act's participatory rights and procedural protections may be seriously diminished if parents are unable to obtain reimbursement for the costs of their experts. In IDEA cases, experts are necessary....

* * *

To read the word "costs" as requiring successful parents to bear their own expenses for experts suffers from the same problem. Today's result will leave many parents and guardians "without an expert with the firepower to match the opposition," ... a far cry from the level playing field that Congress envisioned.

* * *

Questions for Discussion

1. Would it be relevant if most state courts regard "costs" as generically including "expert witness" fees in a case? If the federal definition of "costs" does not include such expenses, should Congress not specify that they are included? Does the legislative history cited by the dissent about the approving reference to expert fees in the conference report suffice?

2. The practical effect of a "no expert fee" recovery means that parents must—even if they prevail—bear the full costs. What impact does that have on the availability of hearing access or judicial review for impoverished families versus the wealthy?

3. Other changes in IDEA now confer no attorneys' fees where the matter is resolved through negotiation or mediation (see *P.N. v. Seattle School District No. 1*, 474 F.3d 1165 (9th Cir. 2007)). Is an attorney whose fees are now so limited going to be able to front costs, or be willing to pursue cases from impoverished parents who themselves cannot fund needed experts?

4. All agree that expert testimony can be critical in providing persuasive on point evidence in IDEA cases. The school district has substantial resources from the public treasury to retain experts. Many parents do not. Should that imbalance be relevant to the *Schaffer* calculation that a tie goes to the District?

5. In *Winkelman v. Parma City Schools*, 550 U.S. 516 (2007), the school district had challenged the parents' right to appeal on behalf of their child, unrepresented by counsel. While parents may represent their child in due process hearings, the common law rule of *pro per* representation does not include non-lawyer parents representing their minor child. The Supreme Court, however, issued no holding on the actual issue in the case (whether parents could represent their child's interest in appeals at district court, the appeals court, or beyond). Rather, the Court determined that the parents had independent, enforceable rights under IDEA that are derivative of the child's claim. Therefore, the Court held that non-attorney parents may represent a child with a disability in federal court. Does the now-allowed circumstance of the school district represented by counsel and assisted by experts, comport with the *Schaffer* balance favoring the school district, where the child is so represented (by a non-attorney parent) and may have no access to expert testimony?

ENDNOTES

[1] Danielle M. Taylor, *Americans With Disabilities: 2014* (November 2018) at https://www.census.gov/content/dam/Census/library/publications/2018/demo/p70-152.pdf.

[2] Benjamin Zablotsky, *et al., Estimated Prevalence of Children with Diagnosed Developmental Disabilities in the United States, 2014-16* (November 2017) at https://www.cdc.gov/nchs/data/databriefs/db291.pdf.

[3] See *Taylor, supra* note 1.

[4] See https://www.nimh.nih.gov/health/statistics/suicide.shtml.

[5] G. Plemmons, *et al., Hospitalization for Suicide Ideation or Attempt: 2008–2015.* 141 PEDIATRICS (June 2018).

[6] See *QuickStats: Suicide Rates for Teens Aged 15-19 years*, by Sex–United States, 1975–2015, at https://www.cdc.gov/mmwr/volumes/66/wr/mm6630a6.htm#suggestedcitation.

[7] See *Taylor, supra* note 1.

[8] A. B. Wilson, *Longitudinal Analysis of Diet, Physical Growth*, Verbal Development and School Performance, in Balderston, et al. (eds.) MALNOURISHED CHILDREN OF THE RURAL POOR (Auburn House, Boston) at 40.

[9] See, *e.g.*, H. E. Freeman, *et al., Nutritional and Cognitive Development Among Rural Guatemalan Children*, AM. J. PUB. HEALTH (1980) at 1277–85.

[10] Sarah E. Cusick and Michael K Georgieff, *"The Role of Nutrition in Brain Development: The Golden Opportunity of the "First 1000 Days"* 175 JOURNAL OF PEDIATRICS 16 (2016).

[11] Information about the effects of nutrition deficits on children's development are summarized in Tufts University School of Nutrition Science and Policy, Center on Hunger, Poverty and Nutrition Policy, *The Link Between Nutrition and Cognitive Development in Children* (Medford, MA; 1995). See also J. Larry Brown and Ernesto Pollitt, *Malnutrition, Poverty and Intellectual Development*, SCIENTIFIC AMERICAN (February 1996) at 38–43.

[12] *Cusick, supra* note 10.

[13] California Department of Public Health, Maternal, Child and Adolescent Health Division, *MIHA Report, 2013–2014: Data from the Maternal and Infant Health Assessment (MIHA) Survey* (Sacramento CA; 2016).

[14] The toolkit can be accessed at http://www.frac.org/wp-content/uploads/frac-aap-toolkit.pdf.

[15] See https://www.samhsa.gov/data/sites/default/files/nsduh-ppt-09-2018.pdf.

[16] Denise Maguire *et al., Long-term Outcomes of Infants with Neonatal Abstinence Syndrome*, 35 NEONATAL NETWORK (September/October 2016).

[17] C. Lupton, Larry Burd, and Rick Harwood, 127C *Cost of Fetal Alcohol Syndrome Disorders*, AM. J. MED. GENETICS (2004).

[18] Philip May, *et al. Prevalence and characteristics of fetal alcohol spectrum disorders*, 134 Pediatrics 5 (2014): 855-66. See also Philip May et al., *Prevalence of Fetal Alcohol Spectrum Disorders in 4 US Communities*, 319 J. AM. MED. ASSN. 474 (2018).

[19] See https://www.cdc.gov/ncbddd/fasd/facts.html.

[20] *Id.*

[21] A. Streissguth *et al. Risk Factors for Adverse Life Outcomes in Fetal Alcohol Syndrome and Fetal Alcohol Effects*, 25 DEVELOPMENTAL AND BEHAVIORAL PEDICATRICS 228 (2004); see also J. Ragmar *et al., Psychosocial outcomes of fetal alcohol syndrome in adulthood* 135 PEDICATRICS (2015).

[22] See *Prevalence of Fetal Alcohol Spectrum Disorders in 4 US Communities, supra* note 18.

[23] Vanessa Sacks and Susan Balding, *The United States can and should eliminate childhood lead exposure* (Child Trends; 2018) at https://www.childtrends.org/publications/united-states-can-eliminate-childhood-lead-exposure.

[24] *Id.*

[25] Nico Savidge and Daniel J. Willis, *Gaps in California law requiring schools to test for lead could leave children at risk, Edsource Special Report* (September 24, 2018) at https://edsource.org/2018/gaps-in-california-law-requiring-schools-to-test-for-lead-could-leave-children-at-risk/602756.

[26] *Sacks, supra* note 23.

[27] A. Rueben *et al., Association of Childhood Blood Lead Levels With Cognitive Function and Socioeconomic Status at Age 38 Years and With IQ Change and Socioeconomic Mobility Between Childhood and Adulthood.* 317(12) J. AM. MED. ASSN. 1244 (2017).

[28] See Lawrie Mott, *Natural Resources Defense Council, Our Children at Risk: The Five Worst Environmental Threats to Their Health* (New York, NY; 1997) at 12, citing P. Mushak, et al., *Prenatal and Postnatal Effects of Low-Level Lead Exposure: Integrated Summary of a Report to the U.S. Congress on Childhood Lead Poisoning*, 50 ENV. RES. (1989) at 11–36; see also P. Baghurst, et al., *Exposure*

to *Environmental Lead and Visual-Motor Integration at Age 7 Years: The Port Pirie Cohort Study*, 6:2 EPIDEMIOLOGY (March 1995) at 104–09.

[29] See *Our Children at Risk, supra* note 28, at 13.

[30] J. Liu J, *et al. Blood lead levels and children's behavioral and emotional problems: a cohort study.* 168 J. AM. MED. ASSN. PED. 737 (2014).

[31] AAP Council on Environmental Health, *Prevention of Childhood Lead Toxicity.* 38 PEDIATRICS (2017).

[32] Autistic spectrum disorders include autism, Aspergers Disorder, and PDD-NOS (Pervasive Developmental Disorder–Not Otherwise Specified).

[33] J. Baio, *et al. Prevalence of Autism Spectrum Disorder Among Children Aged 8 years – Autism and Developmental Disabilities Monitoring Network*, 11 Sites, United States, 2014, MMWR Survel. Summ 2018, at https://www.cdc.gov/mmwr/volumes/67/ss/ss6706a1.htm?s_cid=ss6706a1_w.

[34] See https://www.cdc.gov/ncbddd/autism/facts.html.

[35] D. Christensen, *et al. Prevalence and Charateristics of Autism Spectrum Disorder among 4-year-old Children in the Autism and Developmental Disabilities Monitoring Network*, J. DEVELOPMENTAL AND BEHAVIORAL PED. (2015) at https://www.cdc.gov/ncbddd/autism/features/characteristics.html.

[36] A. Buescher, *et al. Costs of Autism Spectrum Disorders in the United Kingdom and the United States*, J. AM. MED. ASSN. PED. (2014).

[37] See https://www.nichd.nih.gov/newsroom/releases/090717-ACE.

[38] See http://www.ncsl.org/research/health/autism-policy-issues-overview.aspx.

[39] U.S. Department of Health and Human Services, *Estimates of Funding for Various Research, Condition, and Disease Categories* (May 18, 2018) at https://report.nih.gov/categorical_spending.aspx.

[40] MaryBeth Musumeci and Julia Foutz, *Medicaid's Role for Children with Special Health Care Needs: A Look at Eligibility, Services, and Spending*, (February 22, 2018) at https://www.kff.org/medicaid/issue-brief/medicaids-role-for-children-with-special-health-care-needs-a-look-at-eligibility-services-and-spending/.

[41] *Id.*

[42] U.S. Department of Health and Human Services, *Head Start Program Facts: 2017*, at https://eclkc.ohs.acf.hhs.gov/about-us/article/head-start-program-facts-fiscal-year-2017.

[43] Annual Statistical Supplement to the Social Security Bulletin, 2017 at https://www.ssa.gov/policy/docs/statcomps/supplement/2017/supplement17.pdf.

[44] Kathleen Roming, *SSI: A Lifeline for Children with Disabilities* (Center on Budget and Policy Priorities; 2017) at https://www.cbpp.org/sites/default/files/atoms/files/5-11-17ss.pdf.

[45] See Legislative Analyst's Office, *Federal Welfare Reform* (H.R. 3734): *Fiscal Effect on California* (Sacramento, CA; Aug. 20, 1996) at 19.

[46] See Judge David L. Bazelon Center for Mental Health Law, *New Rules for Children's SSI Program* (Washington, D.C.; Feb. 11, 1997) at 2.

[47] *Id.*, at 1–2.

[48] *Id.*, at 5.

[49] See U.S. General Accounting Office, *Social Security: New Functional Assessments for Children Raise Eligibility Questions* (GAO/HEHS-95-66) (Washington, D.C.; March 1995) at 18; see also *Study: Kids on SSI Not Faking*, SACRAMEMTO BEE, May 8, 1995, at A-9 (separate study by National Academy of Social Insurance contradicts claims that parents are coaching children to gain eligibility for SSI).

[50] Prepared Statement of Robert E. Cooke, MD, *Before the Senate Finance Committee/Social Security and Family Policy Subcommittee*, July 7, 1998.

[51] For a detailed discussion of the elimination of children with serious asthmatic conditions, see Chris Palamountain, National Center for Youth Law, *Children with Asthma Prove Vulnerable to SSI Cuts*, XIX:1 YOUTH LAW NEWS (San Francisco, CA; January–February 1998) at 1–8.

[52] See David Lash, *Cease Fire* L.A. DAILY J. (Jan. 22, 1998) at 6.

[53] *Roming, supra* note 44.

[54] The section was authored in part by Margaret Dalton, Associate Dean and Professor of Law at the University of San Diego School of Law.

[55] Note that Congress previously enacted substantial amendments to the statute in 1997.

[56] 20 U.S.C. § 1400 (c)(5)(A).

[57] 20 U.S.C. § 1400 (c)(5)(E).

[58] 20 U.S.C. § 1414 (d)(3)(A).

[59] Often, students with serious developmental disabilities will not earn a high school diploma. For those youth and any other students with an IEP who do not yet earn the diploma by the end of grade 12, they have a right to FAPE until approximately age 22 (depending on the birthday). These placements can be very challenging, as typical education ends at grade 12; thus, school districts must develop programs

for these students or contract for them.

[60] 20 U.S.C. § 1401 (23).

[61] 20 U.S.C. § 1413 (f)(1).

[62] 20 U.S.C. § 1431-1444. Part C, which authorizes early intervention services, was first established as Part H of the Amendments to the Education of the Handicapped Act in October of 1986 [Public Law No. 99-457, 100 Stat. 1145]. When IDEA was amended in 1997, Part H was revised and was renamed under new Part C [Public Law No. 105-17, 111 Stat. 37].

[63] American Institutes for Research, Using a Response to Intervention Framework to Improve Student Learning (Washington DC; 2013) at https://rti4success.org/sites/default/files/Response_to_Intervention_Pocket_Guide_2.pdf.

[64] "Stay Put" is the term used for the IDEA provision that requires maintenance of the student's current educational placement until all legal proceedings are completed. Thus, the school cannot expel most students with an IEP absent an administrative proceeding order. The only exceptions are for weapons, drugs or serious bodily injury. 20 U.S.C. § 1415 (j).

[65] Congressional Research Service, The Individuals with Disabilities Education Act (IDEA) Funding: A Primer (Washington DC; 2018).

[66] Peter W.D. Wright and Pamela Darr Wright, *Special Education Law*, Second Edition (2007), p. 34.

[67] 20 U.S.C. §1432(5).

[68] 20 U.S.C. §1419(a).

[69] 20 U.S.C. § 1419, also referred to as §619 in Public Law No. 108-446.

[70] 20 U.S.C. § 1401 (9).

[71] *Bd. of Educ. v. Rowley*, 458 U.S. 176 (1982).

[72] 20 U.S.C. § 1412(a)(5)(emphasis added). Advocates arguing for LRE often argue that the school has not tried sufficient aids and services, if any.

[73] 20 U.S.C. §1401(26)

CHAPTER SEVEN

Child Care

A. CHILD CARE DEMOGRAPHICS

1. Demand

Child care is divided into two markets: full-time child care for children under five years of age, and part-time (usually after school) care for older children. Full-time child care is in turn divided into two submarkets: full-day infant care and full-day toddler care. In addition, there is a demand for "preschool" education, particularly for four-year-olds and increasingly, for three-year-olds. These programs have a child care aspect but also seek to give students, particularly those in impoverished families, a better chance to enter elementary school on a more even footing with other children.

a. Full-Time Infant and Toddler Care

Children may enter organized child care as early as six weeks of age and remain in full-time day care until kindergarten, sometimes with the option of nursery or preschool for three- or four-year-olds. The growth of preschool has been driven by the radical change in demographics partly discussed in Chapter 2, including the growth of unwed births and other single parent families, higher real estate (and rent) costs requiring more than one income in a two-parent household, and the concomitant growth in the employment of mothers. Currently, 65% of mothers with children under six are in the labor force.[1] Among married couple families with children, over 56% have both parents employed.[2]

In 2016, 40% of U.S. children under six were cared for primarily by a parent, leaving 60% primarily in the care of others. Almost 30% were cared for in child care centers, 18.5% were cared for in a relative's home, 10% were in non-relative home-based care, and just under 2% were cared for through multiple arrangements. This amounts to approximately 12.8 million children under age six in the U.S. routinely in non-parental child care. On average, parents of these children required 30.6 hours of child care per week.[3] The quality of care varies greatly and many working families struggle with the costs.[4] The costs are often above those required to attend a college (see discussion below). In addition, child care options can be scarce. Among young children with employed mothers, African American children are least often in parental care, and most likely to be in center-based care, while Hispanic children are the most likely to be cared for by a parent and least likely to be in child care centers.

b. Part-Time Care for School-age Children

Part-time child care for children in school is also driven by maternal employment. Children ages 5–17 spend the majority of their day supervised in their school setting, with the afterschool hours spent in supervised care or taking care of themselves. The National Center for Education Statistics reported in 2005 that relatives provided afterschool care for 23% of K–2 students, 19% of students in grades 3–5, and 12% of students in grades 6–8. This care was provided by grandparents in the majority of families. Siblings provided care in 23% of families.[5]

Data from 2014 indicates that one in four school-age children participated in an afterschool program.[6] Surveyed parents with a child in afterschool care overwhelmingly agree that the availability of an afterschool program helps the parent maintain employment. Yet there is significant and increasing unmet demand for afterschool programs, with a recent survey revealing that 41% of children not in an afterschool program (approximately 19.4 million children) would be enrolled in one if programming were available.[7] Hispanic and African-American children are more likely to participate in an afterschool program than White children, and unmet demand is higher among these families as well. Families with low incomes indicate that cost and transportation to care are primary obstacles, and more than 40% of these parents reported that afterschool programs were not available in their community. A 2009 report found that the total capacity for non-relative school-age child care totals only 2.4 million spaces.[8] This leaves more than 800,000 elementary school and 2.2 million middle school children without supervision between 3–6pm.[9] The lack of supervision has consequences in terms of delinquency and early gang attraction (see Chapter 10).

A notable effort by California to increase availability of afterschool programming was mounted with the passage of Proposition 49 in 2002—proposed by Governor Arnold Schwarzenegger prior to his gubernatorial candidacy, and sold to the electorate based on (a) the existing public investment in school buildings and grounds that are otherwise unused after school and (b) the need for afterschool care for millions of children, with those useful facilities in place. The initiative allocates $550 million per year to fund before and afterschool programs that include tutoring and homework assistance as well as educational enrichment activities such as arts, physical activity, and recreation.

c. Demand from Federal Welfare Reform Requiring Employment

In addition to the child care demand created by households where both parents work outside the home, additional demand comes from unemployed parents who live below the poverty line and who would require child care in order to work. Federal welfare reform (the 1996 Personal Responsibility and Work Opportunity Reconciliation Act or "PRA") requires such employment by most parents receiving Temporary Assistance to Needy Families (TANF), formerly Aid to Families with Dependent Children (AFDC).

The PRA includes a two-year maximum period before just under 80% of those receiving TANF theoretically must be in a "work activity," and a sixty-month lifetime limit on safety net assistance for their children. For the vast majority of parents receiving aid, work will require child care, which the PRA requires states to provide.[10] Literal compliance with the law requires an extraordinary bolus of child care capacity and subsidy when an economic downturn increases unemployment and reinflates TANF rolls.

2. Distribution of Supply

The distribution of supply versus demand is another concern. Most parents report difficulty in finding child care, with 83% of parents of children under five surveyed indicating that finding affordable, quality care was a "serious problem" in their community.[11] The Center for American Progress recently determined that 51% of Americans live in what they term "child care deserts"—areas with an inadequate supply of licensed child care.[12] This dearth of supply hits rural areas the hardest, with three of five rural communities meeting the definition of a child care desert. Urban communities also suffer from an undersupply of child care options, being more likely than not to qualify as a child care desert. While urban communities may have a higher number of child care centers, it is also costlier in cities, pricing out a significant number of residents with need.[13]

The shortage of licensed spaces is most severe in minority neighborhoods. Almost 60% of Hispanic families live in areas with too few licensed child care options. With projections that one-third of the U.S. child population will be Hispanic by 2050, the difficulty for these families in securing child care is of significant concern. Although it has been long-assumed that Hispanic families have a cultural preference for relative care, some research suggests that Hispanic families' child care preferences are not dissimilar to those of other ethnicities, and that lack of demand does not account for the high rate of child care deserts within largely Hispanic neighborhoods. Neighborhoods with high concentrations of immigrant families are also more likely to be child care deserts, and several studies show that these parents desire the same child care opportunities but experience more obstacles to access, including inadequate translation and interpretation services and distrust of government institutions. Young children of immigrant families have been shown to benefit from high-quality early care and education.[14]

The Center for American Progress also reports that child care is more difficult to find for infants and toddlers than preschoolers, due to the higher expense associated with the care of these very young children. Parents who work nontraditional hours also find child care challenging to secure. A very small proportion of child care centers (8%) and only one-third of home-based providers provide care at night or on weekends. Where child care is scarce, parental employment is in jeopardy. A recent survey found more than three-fourths of parents of young children experienced negative employment impacts within their families related to child care circumstances.[15]

In October of 2000 the Human Services Alliance released a report on the current undersupply of child care slots in Los Angeles. The report surveyed 500 low-income parents and put a human face on the numbers. Virtually all of those surveyed qualify for child care subsidies, but supply does not exist for their use. Of concern, 52% reported that a lack of child care caused them to lose a job, and 68% reported that it impeded them from attempting employment. One half of those surveyed did not have a provider outside the family of any type, although 87% of those without placement were actively seeking it. As the data for California indicates, parents stay home and eschew employment (now required for safety net assistance) or count on family or friends.[16]

3. Child Care Costs

Child care is unaffordable for most U.S. parents, both married and single. For afterschool care, the 2005 National Association of Education Statistics survey found that fees paid by parents averaged $7.09-$7.29 per hour for relative-, center- or school-based care, and $9.30 per hour for non-relative outside care.[17] Such costs total from $3,600 to $5,000 per year at the common utilization of two hours a day and up to $7,200 if before school care is required at the rate of one hour per day. In 2016, the average cost of hourly infant or toddler center-based care was $7.60, $6.54 for nonrelative care, and $4.99 for relative care. Compared to costs in 2001, the 2016 costs were 72% higher, 48% higher, and 70% higher, respectively.[18] Full-day child care for a preschool toddler totals from over $7,000 to $10,000 per year; infant care costs from $8,000 to over $11,000.[19] In general, the cost of center-based child care is equal to or greater than the cost of annual tuition for public college. In the suburbs of Los Angeles, one infant in child care can cost $10,000 more a year than in-state tuition at the local university.[20] And college tuition is often largely subsidized by state and federal funds, whereas families pay about 60% of childcare costs out of pocket.

The U.S. Department of Health and Human Services advises that any child care costing in excess of 7% of a family's income is deemed unaffordable. By this standard, the cost of center-based care in 49 states and D.C. is thus considered unaffordable. A family with two young children and both parents working full-time at minimum wage would have to pay over two-thirds of their take-home pay in such costs. In 35 states, the cost of child care for two children is greater than what is paid in mortgage costs, and in every state such fees exceed annual median rent payment. Families spend more on average on child care than they do on food and transportation combined. More than four million young parents—millennials born between 1980 and 1996—live below the federal poverty line. Recognizing the high cost of child care, 64% of millennials cite this as the primary reason they plan to have smaller families.[21]

The average cost of infant care in a child care center ranges from a staggering 27% to 91% of the median income of a single parent.[22] A single parent earning minimum wage with a single toddler would pay about 60% of her net pay for child care—leaving just over $6,000 to finance total shelter, food, clothing, and other costs for herself and her child for an entire year.

B. MAJOR FEDERAL STATUTES

1. Generic Federal Child Care Programs

In FY2016, federal and state spending on child care assistance totaled $11.6 billion, an overall decline of 2% from the year prior.[23] The major sources of assistance are the Child Care and Development Block Grant (CCDBG), the Temporary Assistance to Needy Families (TANF) block grant, and the Social Services Block Grant. The CCDBG is the largest source of federal funding to states to assist with the provision of quality child care to low-income families. In 2016, federal funding for CCDBG totaled $5.7 billion, through which 1.37 million children received child care. This represents the lowest number of children served by CCDBG since its creation.[24] In 2012, the Office of the Assistant Secretary for Planning and Evaluation found that only 15% of children eligible for CCDBG subsidies received them.[25] These historical withdrawals of assistance are related to their means of delivery. The block-grant structure commonly sets a static ceiling on monies available to states for at least five years, and commonly for longer periods. They do not usually adjust for inflation and population, accomplishing a gradual, constricting cut of 2%–5% per annum in per capita spending power (see discussion of budget policy in Chapter 1). Further complications affect the TANF block grant source. This grant includes child care grouped with obligations to pay for job search, training, and safety net assistance payments under the PRA. In 2017, states spent 16% of their TANF funds on child care. When adjusting for inflation, TANF child care spending in 2017 was 44% less than it was in 2000.[26] Overall, child care assistance has been underfunded on both the federal and state level for decades, which has diminished the number of quality options.

2. Federal Head Start

The federal Head Start program is not a part of the state budget, but is one of the few child-related federal programs administered and funded directly by a federal agency. The program provides additional "catch-up" preparation for preschool children who live in families making under 100% of the federal poverty line or who are categorically eligible due to homelessness or foster care status, or who have a disability.[27] In 2016–17, enrollment for Head Start was at a record low of 848,000. This represents less than half of all children eligible for the program.[28] About 54% of eligible African American preschoolers were served, along with 38% of eligible Hispanic children. Approximately 13% of the enrollment consists of children with disabilities. Ninety-six percent of Head Start teachers have an AA or higher degree in early childhood education or a related field. Large numbers of parents participate as volunteers in Head Start classes. Traditionally, Head Start has been a part-day, four-days-per-week program for four-year-olds. It has been expanding its scope gradually to provide full-day coverage to assist parents who need to work full-time, with about 50% of the programs now offering such care.[29] National-level evaluation of Head Start programming indicates that participation benefitted children in several areas, including their preschool experiences and school readiness. However, not all of the advantages gained during Head Start and up to age four translated to statistically significant improved outcomes at the end of 1st grade.[30]

Another area of expansion is the inclusion of children under four years of age. An "Early Head Start" program was initiated by Congress with the reauthorization of the Head Start Act in 1994. However, this program for young children from birth through age two remains unsubstantial in scope, with just 5% of eligible children served.[31] Yet, a national evaluation found positive effects on a range of developmental skills among participating children.[32]

As noted, federal Head Start is one of the few programs that is not channeled through a state budget or state administration. It is a direct federal program. The 2018 Appropriations Act provided $9.86 billion for Head Start programming, with $775 million for Early Head Start grants.[33] Some states have their own preschool child care accounts—intended to cover four-year-olds not reached by Head Start for school preparation purposes. Sometimes called "child development" programs, they have been under pressure post-2007 and are unlikely to provide a source of coverage gain.

3. Other Federal Programs: 21st Century Learning Center Grants

One substantial federal program approved and expanded after 1998 provides indirect resources to facilitate afterschool activities to ease child care burdens to some extent: the 21st Century Learning Centers Program. This program was established by Congress to award grants to rural and inner-city public schools, or consortia of such schools, for projects that benefit the educational, health, and related needs of the community. It is administered by the U.S. Department of Education, but states manage the competition for funding. The program is designed to target funds to high-need, low-achieving students where there are high rates of juvenile crime, school violence, and student drug abuse, but where resources for afterschool centers are lacking. Evaluations indicate that students participating in the Centers improved school attendance and behavior, as well as achievement scores and grades.[34]

By statute, a 21st Century Community Learning Center grant cannot exceed three years. The grants are highly competitive, and only one in three requests for funding have historically been awarded. Annual costs are approximately $122,000 per center, depending on the array of proposed activities and the availability of additional resources. Funding had been static at $999 million for several years, effectuating a 3%–5% adjusted reduction each year. This account increased to $1.2 billion as of 2011, with allocations through 2019 remaining essentially the same.[35] The initiative serves almost two million children and families, although more than 21 million youth are eligible to attend Centers.[36]

4. Tax Subsidies

Public subsidies are also provided through federal and state tax credits for child care, based on income eligibility. A family can claim costs of up to $3,000 for the care of one child and $6,000 for the care of two or more. The maximum credit is 35% of those costs for the care of one child, and twice that for two or more. As income increases, the percentage range drops from a credit of 35% to 20% of allowable costs.[37] However, it is a nonrefundable credit—that is, it merely offsets tax liability. The working poor who pay little in income taxes receive limited benefit from it. It is distinguishable from the "child tax credit" unrelated to child care costs and which is refundable up to a designated amount. (See discussion in Chapter 3 above.) Studies of the federal system indicate that the child care credit benefits relatively few poor families, and extends into the middle class more than do the direct subsidy programs.[38] Some states have similar credit or deduction allowances for child care, but most are modest in amount, are not refundable, and provide little assistance for the children of the working poor.

C. THE PROBLEM OF CHILD CARE PROVISION FOR THE WORKING POOR

Among low-income families, studies have shown that child care subsidies allowing access to high-quality child care provide benefits to low-income families in several domains. For example, a 2010 study in Los Angeles showed that those families receiving subsidized child care reported higher rates of employment stability as well as overall economic stability within their families. In addition, these parents were able to spend more time with their children and observed their children doing better in their social and academic activities.[39]

In 2018, Congress significantly increased federal funding for child care. However, due to the many years of flat funding and failure to account for inflation, the new funding level still falls below that of FY2001 after adjusting for inflation.[40] Moreover, two serious problems remain. First, as discussed above, quality child care is not available in the areas where the PRA creates the most need. Accordingly, the work requirement is imposed without the assurance of "adequate child care" notwithstanding the theoretical appropriation of funds. As the data show, impoverished parents use relatives and neighbors to supervise their children, or leave them unsupervised. Currently, 19 states have waiting lists or no availability whatsoever for their child care programs.[41] In addition, African American families are more likely than White families to live in states that spend the lowest amounts on child care. In fact, Louisiana and Texas, with 12% of the country's African American population, spent among the least of their TANF funds on child care—Louisiana spent 5% and Texas spent *none*.[42] This leaves African American families particularly challenged to meet the work requirements of TANF.

The second problem is the actual diminution of child care for the working poor. In many states, child care is divided into three stages: Stage 1 is six months of child care while a parent is in training for employment; Stage 2 covers those who have obtained work and are transitioning off aid; and Stage 3 consists of those who have been employed more than one year (more than two years in some states). Child care subsidy is provided in theory to meet the full need (assuming availability as noted above) for Stages 1 and 2. But Stage 3 child care is excluded from assured provision. TANF recipients, who receive assistance to leave welfare rolls and for one year post-employment, do not achieve a sudden pay raise of $4,000 to $10,000 in net pay at the one- or two-year mark to pay for child care. Under current practice, most are then cut off from assured child care help under the TANF block grant. They then depend on eligibility as part of the general working poor population from another child care funding source, such as CCDBG. However, as noted above, only a small portion of children eligible for such assistance actually receive it.

Those who receive help from other accounts generally qualify based on income. Those who have been on the TANF rolls are subject to a difficult choice— because where welfare to work has succeeded, their income may be too high to qualify for subsidy, but is likely to be far short of the amount allowing them to pay the full cost of licensed care for even one young child and remain above the poverty line. Those who are forced back (or newly) onto welfare rolls because they are unwilling to leave their children unsupervised and lack relatives or other alternatives to provide care now also face a lifetime limit of sixty months of safety net TANF assistance, as noted in Chapter 3.

The acknowledged goal of welfare reform is to lift families with children above the poverty line and to "self-sufficiency." However, in every community across the nation, a family needs an income above 200% of poverty ($41,560 annually for a family of three in 2018) in order to provide the basic necessities of housing, food, child care, health care, and transportation.[43] A single mother of two who begins to earn more than $1,000 per month sequentially loses TANF, begins to pick up federal (and some state) tax liability, loses food stamps, progressively loses the Earned Income Tax Credit (EITC), loses eligibility for subsidized school lunches, loses priority for subsidized child care (if available), and loses Medicaid (or picks up premium obligations for child coverage under federal SCHIP).

The major costs impeding self-sufficiency as subsidies drop off at the poverty line are housing and child care. Child care costs are the single largest expense for working parents with two or more young children. Private sector child care coverage for dependents is rare. Hence, the shortfall in public child care subsidies creates a ceiling in net income for living expenses for many working poor families. Assistance with this single expense makes self-sufficiency a more realistic prospect—allowing the drop-off of TANF, food stamps, school lunch subsidy, and the EITC, and gradually increasing in tax contribution.

D. SUBSIDY OPPORTUNITY: INTERPRETATION OF FEDERAL FAMILY SUPPORT ACT

Miller v. Carlson
768 F. Supp. 1331 (N.D. Cal. 1991)

STANLEY A. WEIGEL, UNITED STATES DISTRICT JUDGE

I. BACKGROUND

Plaintiffs are California recipients of Aid to Families with Dependent Children ("AFDC") who need child care in order to participate in educational or training activities likely to provide them opportunities to secure employment and remove themselves from the welfare rolls. Defendants include the California Department of Social Services ("DSS"), the United States Department of Health and Human Services ("HHS"), and the Directors of DSS, HHS, and the California Department of Finance.

At issue is a provision of the Family Support Act of 1988 which requires all states to guarantee child care to each recipient of AFDC who is participating satisfactorily in an education or training activity approved by the state. 42 U.S.C. § 602(g)(1)(A)(i)(II).

On March 3, 1991, plaintiffs filed a complaint for declaratory and injunctive relief, contending that defendants have violated their rights under the Family Support Act of 1988, 42 U.S.C. § 602(g)(1)(A)(i)(II)..., by limiting the guarantee of child care exclusively to AFDC recipients enrolled in the state sponsored employment and training program known as Greater Avenues to Independence ("GAIN"). Defendants maintain that such a policy is in compliance with the Act.

* * *

A. THE FAMILY SUPPORT ACT OF 1988

Congress enacted the Family Support Act of 1988...(codified in scattered sections of 42 U.S.C.), to "profoundly and fundamentally change the welfare system...[by creating] opportunities for recipients of Aid to Families with Dependent Children to further their education and job training and ultimately to remove themselves from the welfare rolls and gain self sufficiency through meaningful employment."....

The Act requires each state, as a condition of participation in the AFDC program, to create a "Job Opportunities and Basic Skills" ("JOBS") program in order to provide training, education, and work opportunities for AFDC recipients. 42 U.S.C. § 681 et seq. JOBS participants are entitled to support services necessary for participation, including costs of transportation and other work-related expenses....

A separate section of the Act requires the state to "guarantee" child care

for each individual [AFDC recipient] participating in an education and training activity (including participation in a program that meets the requirements of [the JOBS provision]) if the State agency approves the activity and determines that the individual is satisfactorily participating in the activity.

....Plaintiffs argue (1) that on its face, this child care guarantee includes, but is not limited to, JOBS participants; (2) that the structure of the Family Support Act confirms that the child care guarantee is not limited to JOBS participants; and (3) that the legislative history of this provision demonstrates that it extends beyond JOBS.

Yet HHS has promulgated a regulation which requires states to offer child care assistance to AFDC recipients only if they "participate in an approved education or training activity under JOBS."[2] 45 C.F.R. § 255.2(a)(2) (emphasis added). In reliance on this regulation, California has denied child care to AFDC recipients who are participating satisfactorily in education or training programs but who, due to capped GAIN [the name of California's JOBS' program] funds, have not been admitted into or have been terminated from GAIN. Both HHS and DSS defend their actions as consistent with the Family Support Act.

B. Plaintiffs' Predicament

Plaintiffs are recipients of AFDC who are currently participating or wish to participate in educational or training programs likely to lead to permanent employment. The named plaintiffs have chosen programs such as nursing, court reporting, and paralegal training. Their declarations indicate that lack of affordable child care is the primary obstacle to successful completion of their education and training.

Members of the class seeking preliminary injunctive relief were participating in training or education activities approved through the GAIN program until they were recently terminated from the program due to budget reductions. As a result, these plaintiffs lost their child care assistance....

In support of this motion, class members describe their inability to participate in training and educational activities without child care assistance. Their declarations indicate that they cannot afford to pay for child care without sacrificing basic necessities. The AFDC grant, which is their only source of income, is often insufficient even for essentials.[4] This money must be stretched to pay for housing, food, utilities, clothing, transportation, personal hygiene and miscellaneous necessities for the entire family. There is no money left to pay for child care....

* * *

As plaintiffs argue, the plain language of the Family Support Act provides that JOBS participants comprise one group of AFDC recipients entitled to child care. The use of the word "including" indicates Congress's intent to extend the child care guarantee *beyond* the JOBS program to *all* eligible AFDC recipients. Any other interpretation renders the word "including" meaningless. In construing a statute, courts are "obliged to give effect, if possible, to every word Congress used."....

* * *

The child care provisions of the statute are not only broadly delineated, but also mandatory. The Family Support Act dictates that a state "must guarantee" child care for each eligible individual. 42 U.S.C. § 602(g)(1)(A)(i). Child care for *all* eligible individuals is therefore a requirement, not an option. Congress established only two criteria that an AFDC recipient must meet in order to qualify for child care: satisfactory participation in an educational or training activity, and approval of this activity by the state....

California has no authority to deny child care to plaintiffs to whom a federal statute guarantees such assistance....

2. *Structure of the Family Support Act*

The plain meaning derived from the language of the Family Support Act is further supported by an examination of the structure of the Act....Title II of the Family Support Act, entitled "Job Opportunities and Basic Skills Program," contains the requirements for the JOBS program. Federal funding for JOBS is capped and each state's share determined by the state's percentage of the total national AFDC caseload. Funding for transportation and other work-related expenses, provided only to JOBS participants, is limited by this provision....

By contrast, the child care provisions are found in Title III of the Act, entitled "Supportive Services for Families" (not, significantly, "Supportive Services for JOBS Families"), and funding for child care is uncapped. 42 U.S.C. § 602(g)(3). States receive open-ended federal matching funds for child care provided to those who need it to accept employment or to remain employed, to JOBS participants, and to "each individual participating in an education and training activity...if the State agency approves the activity " 42 U.S.C. § 602 (g)(1)(A). Funding for child care, unlike JOBS funding, is therefore limited only by the number of eligible individuals.

* * *

C. Dispute Over What Constitutes a State Approved Activity
* * *

...Defendants admit that the educational or training activities of plaintiffs seeking preliminary relief were previously approved by the state under California's GAIN program. Defendants also admit that plaintiffs were removed from the program due to program reductions not because their activity was no longer approved.[11] Plaintiffs were terminated because they were not in the target population prioritized to remain in GAIN. The State has approved plaintiffs' educational and training activities pursuant to the only criteria it has developed for that purpose in connection with GAIN....

* * *

In addition, defendants imply that by granting plaintiffs child care assistance, the court would directly diminish GAIN funds. They assert that plaintiffs seek to deprive "more deserving" or higher priority recipients of their right to GAIN services. As plaintiffs argue, this claim is based on an erroneous construction of the Family Support Act. Plaintiffs do not seek entry or reentry into GAIN at the expense of participants who are in higher priority groups. They seek only the child care assistance to which they are entitled under the Family Support Act. Funding for this child care assistance is uncapped and separate from JOBS funding. Moreover, fiscal constraints cannot justify the state's failure to comply with its legal obligations.

* * *

[2] The regulation also provides that states may provide child care to AFDC recipients in non-JOBS areas (areas of the state which do not have a JOBS program). In California, there are no non-JOBS areas. California AFDC recipients who are unable to participate in GAIN [California's JOBS program] are denied child care.

[4] The AFDC grant for a parent and two children in California, for instance, is only $694 per month, or 74.8% of the federal poverty level....

[11] See notices of termination attached to Declaration of Tom Burke. For each of the named plaintiffs who were terminated from GAIN, the Notices read in relevant part:
As of December 31, 1990: Payment for your GAIN Child Care Will Stop. Here's Why:....
( ) Your child is 13 years old, which is over the age we can pay for.
( ) Your child care provider is your child's parent, legal guardian, or a member of your assistance unit.
( ) You are not attending an approved GAIN activity.
(x) other: Your GAIN Program Services are discontinued.

Questions for Discussion

1. Why would the state want to preclude private training if it works to qualify AFDC (TANF) parents for employment?

2. Could the state partially accomplish elimination of non-JOBS training programs by requiring special and strict licensure of all such private programs? Would some state controls on this vocational education be warranted based on possible abuse (tuition charges for dubious training)? Does the state's provision of child care give it a special stake in the quality of training provided?

3. As discussed above, the system described in *Miller* remains generally in place, buttressed by a two-year time limit to seek JOBS training, and a five-year lifetime TANF aid limit. What happens to a trainee who is educated for jobs which are not available? Can such parents seek new or additional training and another round of child care provision?

4. What happens after Miller obtains employment and her Stage 2 child care runs out? What if she is laid off within the first year of her employment due to economic downturn and her junior status? Can she re-enter TANF and obtain new and different training until her five years of lifetime aid reservoir is exhausted? Will she receive child care during this period, and for at least the first year of her subsequent employment?

E. CHILD CARE QUALITY

1. Safety

As discussed above, many parents entrust their children for most of the day to the care and facilities of strangers, either in a commercial center context, or in the home of a day care provider. Safety issues are of particular importance given the tendency of young children to test their environment, and the increase in allowable children per facility. In a January 2000 report, the General Accounting Office found that inspections of child care facilities were not generally assured and that caseloads were high.[44] As noted above, Congress passed the Child Care and Development Block Grant Act of 2014, reauthorizing the Act for the first time since 1996. The 2014 Act included new health and safety requirements for states receiving funds, including the following:

- Establishing health and safety requirements in 10 areas including prevention of sudden infant death syndrome, first aid, and CPR;
- Requiring pre-service and ongoing training of child care providers in the 10 health and safety areas;
- Conducting background checks for all child care staff members;
- Conducting pre-licensure and annual unannounced inspections of licensed providers; and
- Establishing standards for group size limits and child-to-provider ratios.[45]

The 2014 Act also required states to make available to the public information about providers, such as licensing and inspection history, annual number of deaths, injuries, and abuse, and quality information. The new standards apply to providers receiving public funding, but states have the ability to exempt from these and other health and safety requirements any providers not receiving such funds. Ultimately, states develop their own licensing regulations as well as standards for license-exempt providers. The result is that more than half of states do not require annual inspections of license-exempt providers.[46]

2. Quality of Care

Both adequacy and quality of child care have become a subject of extensive scholarship and commentary. Studies generally conclude that attention in the early developmental years is important and has lasting impact. They also find that the supply of subsidized child care is inadequate, and the quality is uneven and disappointing.[47] The quality of child care is generally measured by considering two types of features: 1) regulable features such as the adult-to-child ratio, group sizes, and provider education and training; and 2) process features that reflect the day-to-day social interactions and activities experienced in care. Such process features include whether the caregiver engages in positive caregiving (*e.g.*, shows a positive attitude, responds to the child's questions, asks the child age appropriate questions, encourages development, and supports social interaction among children).[48]

A 1995 four-state study of quality in child care centers found that only 14% could be rated as high in quality.[49] The Packard Foundation's Center for the Future of Children concluded in 1996 that "(1) the quality of services is mediocre, on average; (2) the cost of full-time care is high; (3) at the present time, the cost of increasing quality from mediocre to good is not great, about 10%; [and] (4) good child care is dependent on professionally approved staffing ratios, well-educated staff, low staff turnover...."[50] One of the leading authorities in the field concluded that the state of child care "reflect[s] the low priority given to children's care and women's work in American society."[51] Other recent studies have raised serious questions about the impact of low-quality child care on children, exacerbated by its substitution for parental time and attention.

The most substantial longitudinal study of child care was financed by the National Institute of Child Health and Human Development (NICHHD). The study started in 1991 with 1,364 children from ten cities who underwent detailed surveys and a follow-up study—including observation of classroom and social behavior. Three preliminary findings emerged from the first seven years of observation: (1) 17% of kindergartners who had been in child care showed more assertive and aggressive behaviors; (2) family relationships correlate more closely with measures of aggression than does child care; and (3) higher quality child care correlates with academic success in early school years. These early findings produced great controversy because of the political ramifications implicit in a message that child care was not beneficial to children. While the degree of aggression increase is not severe, it is statistically significant and not appropriately rejected based on notions of political correctness. Rather than view such findings as an assault on parental prerogative, it should trigger active further inquiry. What are the implications of the aggression measured? What is their relation to delinquency? What are the detailed characteristics of child care provided which correlate with such aggression, *e.g.*, age of child, extent of adult supervision, degree of cognitive stimulation?

A full-time parent is not an option for millions of children, and the findings of the NICHHD and other studies confirm the advantages of high quality child care where it is provided, with this study noting: "The quality of child care over the first three years of life is consistently but modestly associated with children's cognitive and language development. The higher the quality of child care (more positive language stimulation and interaction between the child and provider), the greater the child's language abilities at 15, 24, and 36 months, the better the child's cognitive development at age two, and the more school readiness the child showed at age three." The study also acknowledged that other variables were more influential, including family income, maternal vocabulary, home environment, and maternal cognitive stimulation.[52]

Later phases of the NICHHD study, observing children through elementary school years, confirm that the quality of child care impacts cognitive and academic functioning, that more time spent in care predicts more behavior issues, and that center care in particular is associated with both better academic outcomes as well as increased behavior problems in childhood. Most recently, researchers examined whether these early child care experiences had an effect on functioning into adolescence. Findings showed that the positive cognitive and academic effects of high quality child care did continue into the teen years. Similarly, behavior problems observed at younger ages among children who spent more time in care endured through adolescence. Teens who had spent more hours in early care engaged in more risk-taking and demonstrated more impulsivity. The effects were small, but statistically significant.[53]

Studies in the late 1990s presented additional evidence of the advantages of high-quality child care.[54] In 2001, the *Journal of the American Medical Association* published a peer-reviewed article which involved a long-term (17 year) study of 1,539 low-income children enrolled as three- and four-year-olds in Chicago Public Schools' Child-Parent Centers, with half-day care similar to Head Start, and some school-age services linked to elementary schools at ages six to nine. The results were more decisive than the NICHHD study discussed above, with those admitted in the program 33% less likely to be arrested, 41% less likely to be arrested for a violent crime, and 20% more likely to finish high school *vis-a-vis* control groups. The study concluded: "Participation in an established early childhood intervention for low-income children was associated with better educational and social outcomes up to age 20 years."[55] A 2015 review of such early interventions concluded that there is significant evidence that high-quality preschool programming can improve the later educational attainment and earnings among low-income children.[56]

The importance of child care quality is underlined by the fact that 80% of the brain develops in the first three years of life, and more than 60% of these infants and toddlers are now cared for over 35 plus hours a week by someone other than a parent, as discussed above. But recent findings about quality and teacher pay are troubling. One respected source cites 2009 surveys contrasting parental assumptions with the state of child care regulation and law:

> Almost 8 in 10 parents polled assume caregivers have training to work with children, but only 13 states require training in early childhood education before someone can lead a classroom in a child care center. More than 3/4 of parents believe that most child care programs are inspected regularly. Yet only 11 states license all child care programs and 8 inspect licensed programs, and those inspections are less than once a year (including building and fire safety inspections). Most parents believe that child care programs are licensed and that caregivers undergo a background check and are trained in first-aid, CPR and in recognizing and reporting signs of child abuse. Unfortunately, this is too often not the case and the situation varies widely state by state.[57]

Child care quality is compromised by three factors: (1) a general lack of any certification or other system to provide enhanced status to providers as a positive incentive to learn and improve;[58] (2) high staff turnover (now at 20% to 30% per annum), and (3) low pay. The last factor is of particular importance, and influences the first two. Some family day care workers do not earn minimum wage. In 2017, the median hourly wage for childcare workers was $10.72.[59] These workers, in whose hands children are placed, may live below the poverty line themselves.[60] Nationally, the median salary of a preschool teacher is $28,990 for twelve months of work. An elementary school teacher *starts* at $38,617 for a ten-month year with a realistic career track to earn approximately $56,000.[61] In contrast, the median pay of child care workers nationally is $22,290 per year—one of the lowest levels of any occupation tracked by the Department of Labor.[62] Their conditions of employment also generally exclude medical benefits, retirement accounts, paid leave, or other common compensation. These levels of pay contrast markedly with the higher levels (comparable to teacher salaries and benefits) extant in Western Europe.

On April 29, 2001, a University of California at Berkeley study focusing on California reported that salaries for child-care teachers had fallen over the previous six years in relation to inflation. The study focuses on child care centers in Santa Cruz, Santa Clara, and San Mateo counties, but its results appear to be fairly generalized. In examining centers, the study overstates income because of the much smaller compensation (generally close to minimum wage) available for licensed family day care providers. But the study found that "just 24% of teaching staff employed in 1996 were still on the job in 2000, more than half of the centers reporting turnover last year had not replaced the staff they lost, when teachers leave a center about one-half leave child care provision entirely, and wages for teachers decreased 6% adjusted for inflation since 1994."[63] The study found "the presence of a greater proportion of highly trained teaching staff in 2000 is the strongest predictor of whether a center can sustain quality improvements over time. Wages are also a significant predictor."[64]

The data from 2000 to the present shows no improvement, notwithstanding much discussion of underpayment and the importance of quality. The most recent (2017) national wage data of adults caring for children includes:

- 61,800 education/preschool and child care center administrator jobs, with an average annual wage of $46,890;[65]
- 478,500 preschool (non-special education) teacher jobs, with an average annual wage of $28,990;[66] and
- 562,420 child care provider jobs, with an average annual wage of $22,290[67] (more than $3,000 below the 2019 poverty line for a family of four).

ENDNOTES

[1] U.S. Department of Labor, Bureau of Labor Statistics, *Employment Characteristics of Families Summary* (Washington DC; April 19, 2018) at https://www.bls.gov/news.release/famee.nr0.htm.

[2] U.S. Department of Labor, Bureau of Labor Statistics, *Employment in Families with Children* (Washington DC; April 27, 2017) at https://www.bls.gov/opub/ted/2017/employment-in-families-with-children-in-2016.htm.

[3] National Center for Education Statistics, *Early Childhood Care Arrangements: Choices and Costs* (Washington DC; May 2018) at https://nces.ed.gov/programs/coe/indicator_tca.asp. See also Table 202.30 at https://nces.ed.gov/programs/digest/d17/tables/dt17_202.30.asp.

[4] *Id.*

[5] National Center for Education Statistics, After-School Programs and Activities: 2005 (Washington DC; 2006) at https://nces.ed.gov/pubs2006/afterschool/02.asp.

[6] Afterschool Alliance, *America After 3pm* (Washington DC; 2014) at http://www.afterschoolalliance.org/documents/aa3pm-2014/aa3pm_national_report.pdf.

[7] *Id.*

[8] National Association of Child Care Resource and Referral Agencies, *2008 Child Care Capacity* (March 2009) at 3.

[9] Afterschool Alliance, *supra* note 6.

[10] See discussion in Chapter 3.

[11] Rasheed Malik, *et al., America's Child Care Deserts in 2018*, (Center for American Progress; 2018) at https://www.americanprogress.org/issues/early-childhood/reports/2018/12/06/461643/americas-child-care-deserts-2018/.

[12] See https://www.americanprogress.org/issues/early-childhood/reports/2018/12/06/461643/americas-child-care-deserts-2018/.

[13] *Id.*

[14] *Id.*

[15] *Id.*

[16] Sam Mistrano, *Transforming Child Care from the Ground Up, Human Services Alliance* (Los Angeles, CA; Oct. 2000), *passim.*

[17] National Center for Education Statistics, *Early Childhood Care Arrangements: Choices and Costs* (May 2018) at https://nces.ed.gov/programs/coe/indicator_tca.asp.

[18] *Id.*

[19] Karen Schulman, *Issue Brief: The High Cost of Child Care* (Children's Defense Fund, Washington D.C.; 2000). See also Children's Defense Fund, *Green Book* (State of America's Children) 2005 at Chapter 3 (www.childrensdefense.org). See also Children's Advocacy Institute, *California Children's Budget 2004–05* (San Diego, CA; 2004) at Chapter 6 (www.caichildlaw.org) for discussion of the Regional Market Surveys of California tracking market charges for child care in urban and rural areas.

[20] Child Care Aware of America, *The US and the High Cost of Child Care: 2018* at http://usa.childcareaware.org/advocacy-public-policy/resources/research/costofcare/.

[21] *Id.*

[22] *Id.*

[23] Center for Law and Social Policy, *Child Care Assistance Spending and Participation in 2016* (2018) at https://www.clasp.org/sites/default/files/publications/2018/06/Child%20Care%20Assistance%20and%20Participation%20in%202016.pdf.

[24] Rasheed Malik, *supra* note 11.

[25] Center for Law and Social Policy, *Disparate Access* (Washington DC; February 2016) at https://www.clasp.org/sites/default/files/public/resources-and-publications/publication-1/Disparate-Access.pdf.

[26] Liz Schott, Ife Floyd, and Ashley Burnside, *How States Use Funds under the TANF Block Grant* (Center on Budget and Policy Priorities; February 19, 2019) at https://www.cbpp.org/research/family-income-support/how-states-use-funds-under-the-tanf-block-grant#_ftnref20. See also Karen Schulman, *Overdue for Investment: State Child Care Assistance Policies 2018* (National Women's Law Center; 2018), which notes that in FY 2018 dollars, states used only $2.8 billion in FY2017 compared to $6 billion in FY2000.

[27] Unlike most federal subsidy programs, Head Start is not channeled through a state agency but is dispensed through direct federal contracts with providers.

[28] Center for Law and Social Policy, *supra* note 23.

[29] U.S. Department of Health and Human Services, *Head Start Program Facts: Fiscal Year 2017* (Washington DC; 2018) at https://eclkc.ohs.acf.hhs.gov/sites/default/files/pdf/hs-program-fact-sheet-2017_0.pdf.

[30] U.S. Department of Health and Human Services, Office of Planning, Research and Evaluation, *Head Start Impact Study: Final Report* (Washington DC; 2010) at https://www.acf.hhs.gov/opre/research/project/head-start-impact-study-and-follow-up.

[31] Center for Law and Social Policy, *supra* note 30.

[32] See evaluation materials and publications at https://www.acf.hhs.gov/opre/research/project/early-head-start-research-and-evaluation-project-ehsre-1996-2010.

[33] See https://www.acf.hhs.gov/occ/resource/fiscal-year-2018-federal-child-care-and-related-appropriations.

[34] Afterschool Alliance, *21st Century Community Learning Centers* (April 2018) at http://afterschoolalliance.org/documents/21stCCLC-Overview-2018.pdf.

[35] See https://www2.ed.gov/programs/21stcclc/funding.html.

[36] Afterschool Alliance, *supra* note 34.

[37] A separate federal "Wee Tot" Earned Income Tax Credit (EITC) Supplement allowed a credit of 5% of earned income up to $388 for a parent who stays home to care for a newborn and in so doing loses eligibility for straight earned income tax credit benefits. That credit was repealed in 1994.

[38] A study by Harvard University's Professor Bruce Fuller surveyed 1,800 child care centers in 36 states and concluded that families with annual incomes over $50,000 pay just 6% of their incomes for child care, while families earning under $15,000 devote 23% of their income for child care. The tax credits provide a tax expenditure of $4 billion annually. One-third of the credit goes to families with incomes above $50,000 per year. For a discussion, see Diego Ribadeneira, *Day Care Credits Said to Favor Well Off*, BOSTON GLOBE, Sept. 18, 1992, at 3.

[39] Child Care Resource Center, *The Impact of Subsidized Child Care on Low-Income Families* (2010).

[40] See Schulman, *supra* note 19.

[41] See Schott, *supra* note 26.

[42] *Id.*

[43] See Schulman, *supra* note 19.

[44] General Accounting Office, *Child Care: State Efforts to Enforce Safety and Health Requirements*, GAO/HEHS-00-28 (Jan. 2000) at 19, 28, 37.

[45] See https://www.acf.hhs.gov/occ/resource/ccdbg-of-2014-plain-language-summary-of-statutory-changes.

[46] Center for American Progress, *The Importance of Child Care Safety Protections* (Washington DC; October, 2017) at https://www.americanprogress.org/issues/early-childhood/reports/2017/10/30/441748/the-importance-of-child-care-safety-protections/.

[47] *See, e.g.,* David Illig, California Research Bureau, *Birth to Kindergarten: The Importance of the Early Years* (Sacramento, CA; Feb. 1998) (conducted at the request of Senator Dede Alpert); Jane Knitzer and Stephen Page, Columbia University National Center for Children in Poverty, *Map and Track: State Initiatives for Young Children and Families* (New York; NY; 1998); Anne Mitchell, Louise Stoney, and Harriet Dichter, *Financing Child Care in the United States*, Ewing Marion Kauffman Foundation and The Pew Charitable Trusts (1997); Sharon L. Kagan and Nancy E. Cohen, Yale University, The Bush Center in Child Development and Social Policy, *Not By Chance: Creating an Early Care and Education System for America's Children* (New Haven, CT; 1997); Mary L. Culkin, Scott Groginsky, and Steve Christian, National Conference of State Legislatures, *Building Blocks: A Legislator's Guide to Child Care Policy* (Washington, D.C.; 1997); Children's Defense Fund, *Study Reveals Working Families Are Locked Out of Child Care*, 19:4/5 CDF REPORTS 1 (Washington, D.C.; April/May 1998); U.S. General Accounting Office, *Welfare Reform: Implications of Increased Work Participation for Child Care* (GAO/HEHS-97-75) (Washington, D.C.; 1997); Mark H. Greenberg, Center for Law and Social Policy, *The Child Care Protection Under TANF* (Washington, D.C.; 1998); U.S. General Accounting Office, *Welfare Reform: States' Efforts to Expand Child Care Programs* (GAO/HEHS-98-21) (Washington, D.C.; 1998); Center for the Future of Children, The David and Lucile Packard Foundation, THE FUTURE OF CHILDREN, *Financing Child Care* (Richard E. Behrman, M.D., ed.) (Los Angeles, CA; Summer/Fall 1996).

[48] U.S. Department of Health and Human Services, *The NICHD Study of Early Child Care and Youth Development: Findings for Children up to Age 4 ½ Years* (Washington DC; 2006).

[49] Suzanne W. Helburn, ed., University of Colorado, Center for Research in Economic and Social Policy, *Cost, Quality, and Child Outcomes in Child Care Centers: Technical Report* (Denver, CO; 1995).

[50] Suzanne W. Helburn and Carollee Howes, Center for the Future of Children, The David and Lucile Packard Foundation, *Child Care Cost and Quality* 6:2 THE FUTURE OF CHILDREN, *Financing Child Care* (Richard E. Behrman, M.D., ed.) (Los Angeles, CA; Summer/Fall 1996) at 79–80.

[51] *Id.*, at 80.

[52] See Robin Peth-Pierce, *Early Child Care: About the NICHD Study of Early Child Care* (2001) at 10.

[53] Deborah Lowe Vandell, *Do Effects of Early Child Care Extend to Age 15 Years? Results from the NICHD Study of Early Child Care and Youth Development*, 81 CHILD DEV. (May–Jun 2010).

[54] *Child Care Outcomes When Center Classes Meet Recommended Standards for Quality*, American Journal of Public Health, 1999; National Center for Early Development and Learning, *The Children of the Cost, Quality, and Outcomes Study Go to School* (1999); Nancy Kerrebrock, Eugene Lewitt, *Children in Self-Care*, THE FUTURE OF CHILDREN 9(2), Packard Foundation (1999), at 151–160; Jill Posner and Deborah Candell, *After-school Activities and the Development of Low-Income Urban Children: A Longitudinal Study*, DEVELOPMENTAL PSYCHOLOGY 35(3) (1999) at 868–879.

[55] Arthur J. Reynolds, PhD, Judy A. Temple, PhD, Dylan L. Robertson, Emily A. Mann MSSW, *Long-term Effects of an Early Childhood Intervention on Educational Achievement and Juvenile Arrest: A 15-Year Follow-up of Low-Income Children in Public Schools*, 285 JOURNAL OF THE AMERICAN MEDICAL ASSOCIATION 2339–2346 (May 9, 2001), see http://www.jama.com.

[56] Greg J. Duncan and Katherine Magnusson, *Early Childhood Interventions for Low-Income Children*, 31 FOCUS (Institute for Research on Poverty, University of Wisconsin-Madison; Fall/Winter 2014–15).

[57] National Association of Child Care Resource and Referral Agencies, *Child Care in America: 2009 State Fact Sheets* (April 2009) at 4.

[58] See the interesting study by William T. Gormley, Jr. and Jessica Lucas, Money, Accreditation and Child Care Center Quality, Foundation for Child Development, *Working Paper Series* (August 2000) *passim* (see http://www.ffcd.org). The study cites eighteen states providing certification to assure and demonstrate enhanced child care quality, and which also triggers enhanced compensation. Evidence is compelling that this incentive driven technique for enhancing quality works.

[59] See https://www.bls.gov/ooh/personal-care-and-service/childcare-workers.htm.

[60] For a discussion of labor commissioner protests by workers and rate levels extant, see Carla Rivera, *Day-Care Providers Say State Reimbursements Fail to Pay a Living Wage*, LOS ANGELES TIMES (May 19, 2000) at B-3.

[61] See http://www.nea.org/home/2016-2017-average-starting-teacher-salary.html.

[62] *Id.*

[63] See Marcy Whitebrook, Laura Sakai, Emily Gerber, Carollee Howes, *Then & Now: Changes in Child Care Staffing, 1994–2000*, Institute of Industrial Relations (Berkeley, CA; April 2001) *passim*.

[64] *Id.*, summary at 4.

[65] See https://www.bls.gov/ooh/management/preschool-and-childcare-center-directors.htm.

[66] See https://www.bls.gov/ooh/education-training-and-library/preschool-teachers.htm.

[67] See https://www.bls.gov/ooh/personal-care-and-service/childcare-workers.htm.

CHAPTER EIGHT

Child Protection from Abuse

The term "child welfare" does not refer to cash safety net assistance programs (AFDC or TANF) but to the system addressing child abuse and neglect. As described in Chapter 10 below, the juvenile courts evolved under a *parens patriae* concept that did not clearly distinguish between juvenile law violators and juvenile child abuse victims. Many of those subject to the "House of Refuge Movement" were impoverished children who had committed no criminal offense. Many were abandoned, orphaned, or neglected. Most suffered extreme poverty.

Illinois established a juvenile court to similarly group minor offenders and child abuse victims into a single system designedly to aid children in trouble. The Illinois Act defined "dependency and neglect" to include "(1) any child...destitute or homeless or abandoned, (2) or [without] proper parental care or guardianship, (3) or who habitually begs or receives alms, (4) or who is found living in any house of ill fame or with any vicious or disreputable person, (5) or whose home, by reason of neglect, cruelty, or depravity on the part of its parents, guardian or other person in whose care it may be, is an unfit place for such a child, (6) or [who is] under the age of 8 years who is found peddling or selling any article or singing or playing any musical instrument upon the street or giving any public entertainment."[1]

Current notions of child abuse based on excessive corporal punishment, failure to treat for medical ailments, or even molestation were not ascendant in the early formation of juvenile courts. Parental authority over children was close to absolute and the system focused on children effectively abandoned or orphaned by parents. Over time, the delinquency system discussed in Chapter 10 evolved to incorporate some adult criminal justice procedures, particularly after the *Gault* decision. Meanwhile, the "dependency" jurisdiction of juvenile court separated into a system where children enjoyed broader state protection. That protection covered physical abuse, psychological abuse (where *in extremis*), sexual abuse, medical neglect, and general neglect. In addition, "status offenses" marked the entry of juvenile court jurisdiction for runaways, truants, curfew violators, "incorrigible" children, and those with intractable drug addiction problems. As discussed below, mandated reporting and investigations have increased caseloads markedly in most states. Much of the increase and many of the problems of children relate to poverty and parental drug and alcohol abuse, both at high incidence, as the data presented below reflect.

A. NATIONAL INCIDENCE OF ABUSE AND NEGLECT

National data gathered in 2017 on child abuse reports and disposition found:[2]

Reports, Victims, Perpetrators

- 4.1 million child abuse referrals were received by Child Protection Services (CPS), involving approximately 7.5 million children. The national rate of referral in 2017 was 55.7 per 1,000 children in the population, an increase from the rate of 48.4 per 1,000 in 2013.
- 57.6% of referrals (2.4 million) were "screened-in," meaning the referral resulted in either an investigation or an alternative response. This represents a 10% increase since 2013.
- 65.7% of reports (screened-in referrals) were received from professionals, meaning that the person had contact with the alleged child victim as part of his or her job (*e.g.*, teachers or pediatricians). The remaining reports were submitted by friends, neighbors, relatives, or those wishing to remain anonymous.
- Most states have established time standards for initiating the investigation of reports. The median response time to initiate a report investigation is 65 hours or 2.7 days.
- 17% of children whose referrals were investigated were found to be victims of child abuse or neglect while 83% were found to be non-victims. This amounts to approximately 674,000 victims of child abuse and neglect, with a rate of 9.1 victims per 1,000 children.
- 74.9% of all victims suffered neglect, 18.3% physical abuse, and 8.6% sexual abuse. In addition, 7.1% are victims of other types of maltreatment, such as lack of supervision.
- The highest victimization rate is for children in their first year of life, with rates declining with the age of the child.
- The victimization rate for American Indian or Alaska Native children is the highest at 14.3 per 1,000 children in the same race or ethnicity; African American children had the second highest rate at 13.9 per 1,000 children in the same race or ethnicity.
- More than 91% of victims are maltreated by a parent. Approximately 69% of perpetrators are the child's mother; 40% of these mothers acted alone, and 28% acted with a father and/or non-parent.

Fatalities

- 1,720 children died of abuse or neglect (2.32 per 100,000 child population), marking an 11% increase since 2013. Just under one half of these victims were less than one year of age. Almost 72% were younger than three years old.
- The rate of fatalities among African-American children is 2.6 times higher than the rate of White children.

- More than 27% of reported fatalities had at least one prior contact with child protection agencies within three years of the date of death.

Services

- Approximately 1.9 million children received preventive services.
- Approximately 1.3 million children received post-response services from a child welfare agency.
- More than 23% of victims were removed from their homes following investigation. Just under 2% of non-victims, including siblings of victims and some children who are voluntarily placed, were removed from their homes as well.
- 21.6% of victims were reported to have a court-appointed representative.[3]
- 15.1% of victims had received family preservation services within the previous five years, while 5.1% had been removed previously and reunited with their families.[4]
- Average annual caseload for a Child Protective Service (CPS) investigation/assessment worker was 72 investigations.

The data above is generated from the National Child Abuse and Neglect Data System (NCANDS), which is a voluntary program that collects child maltreatment data from child protection services agencies across the nation. Due to its voluntary nature, it is widely understood to represent only a fraction of the incidence of child maltreatment.

The number of children in foster care had been steadily declining throughout the early 2000s. However, the number entering foster care began to increase again in 2012.

Year	Children in Foster Care
2011	397,605
2012	397,301
2013	400,394
2014	414,129
2015	427,328
2016	436,551
2017	442,995

Table 8-A. Children in Foster Care in the United States 2011–17[5]

The numbers in Table 8-A include those children in foster care at a given point in time. Note that nationally, just under 700,000 children experience the foster care system each year, but because of the large number in and out within a year, a single day snapshot count is in the mid-400,000 range. The 2017 data[6] provides more detail about the demographics of these removed children:

- The median age of a foster child is 7.7, with 24% age two or under; 52% are male.

- The median age of foster care entry is 6.1 years old.
- 44% of foster children are White, 23% African American, 21% Hispanic, and 9% are mixed or not determined.
- The average length of stay in foster care is 20.1 months. The median is much lower at 12.9 months because of the substantial number generally returned to parents within the first year.
- Placement settings in foster care are 45% non-relative foster family home, 32% relative family home, 7% in a public institution, 6% in a group home, 5% in a trial visit back home, 4% in a pre-adoptive home, 1% in "supervised independent living" (over 18 years of age), and 1% (4,660) are classified as runaways.
- Case goals are reunification with parent or primary caretaker for 56% of removed children, adoption for 27%, live with other relative for 3%, guardianship for 4%, long-term foster care for 2%, emancipation for 4%, and goal not yet established for 5%.
- 250,248 children exited foster care during fiscal year 2017 for the following reasons: 49% parental reunification, 24% adoption, 8% emancipation, 7% living with a non-parent relative, 10% in a guardianship, 1% transferred to another agency, and less than 1% (766) ran away. Another 386 children died in foster care during 2016.

Public agencies helped facilitate the adoption of 59,430 children in fiscal year 2017—most but not all of them were foster children. Those adopted from foster care had a median age of 5.2. It took an average of 11.6 months after termination of parental rights for adoptions to be finalized. Sixty-eight percent of those adopting are married couples, 25% are single females, 3% single males, and 3% an unmarried couple. Thirty-five percent of adopting families are related to the child (often grandparents), but 51%—the largest source—are family foster care providers, not related to the child by blood. The families of 93% of the adopted children receive Adoption Assistance Payments to provide some of the costs of care (covering 52,795 children).

The number of children awaiting adoption on September 30, 2017 was 123,437, with the average waiting time within continuous foster care at 30.9 months. Those children awaiting adoption were at a median age of 6.8 and a median age of 4.2 when first removed from their homes. Forty-four percent of those waiting are African American, Hispanic, or American Indian.[7]

B. CHILD ABUSE/NEGLECT CAUSAL CORRELATIONS

In 2010, the U.S. Department of Health and Human Services released the fourth national incidence study of child abuse and neglect which tested important correlations.[8] The Department's studies occur each decade, with the first study using data from 1979–80, the second study using data from 1986, and the third study using data from 1993. The most recent study collected data from 2005–06, and was based on surveys of 126 CPS agencies as well as 10,791 professionals working in 1,094 agencies serving 122 counties. The study compared the 2005–06 data with previous data, using two standards: "harm"—meaning experienced abuse or neglect, and "endangerment"—meaning at risk of harm. The study found an overall decrease in maltreatment, with the following specific findings:

- The total number of children who experienced abuse or neglect in 2005–06 was 19% lower than in 1993. However, the number of children endangered showed no statistically reliable change. This reflects counterbalancing increases and decreases within categories of abuse. For example, the estimated number of Endangerment Standard sexually abused children decreased while the estimated number of Endangerment Standard emotionally neglected children more than doubled.
- Girls were sexually abused five times more often than boys. This disparity is consistent with findings from earlier studies.
- African American children suffered maltreatment at a significantly higher rate than White or Hispanic children. Whereas the rate of maltreatment had generally declined, it had declined less so for African American and Hispanic children.
- The majority of maltreated children are not investigated by Child Protective services (CPS), a finding consistent with earlier studies.

The study found the following correlations between families and child abuse:

- The incidence of maltreatment and levels of harm increased since 1993 for children living with a single parent and decreased for those living with two parents.
- Incidence of maltreatment is highest for children in the largest families (four or more children).
- Children in rural counties were twice as likely to be maltreated by both definitional standards.
- Children in households with low socioeconomic status had significantly higher rates of maltreatment; they were more than three times more likely to be abused and about seven times more likely to be neglected.

Most studies find that parental substance abuse is a contributing factor for between one-third and two-thirds of children involved with the child welfare system; data from 2002–07 indicated that an estimated 8.3 million children in the U.S.—12% of all children in the country—live in households in which at least one parent is either an alcoholic or in need of substance abuse treatment.[9] As noted above, the number of children in foster care has increased since 2012. Many have associated this increase with the rise in drug overdose deaths and drug-related hospitalizations, particularly due to opioid abuse, during the same period. A recent study confirmed such a correlation, finding that counties with higher substance use indicators had higher rates of child maltreatment reports, substantiated reports, and foster care entry from 2011–16.[10]

C. FEDERAL STATUTES, FUNDING, MAJOR POLICY ISSUES

1. Evolution to the Current System

a. The Formative Statutes

In 1980, the Congress began to rationalize the nation's treatment of abused and neglected children through a system of funding assistance and minimum standards. In 1980, Congress passed the Adoption Assistance and Child Welfare Act[11] directed at state and local child protection and foster care systems. In 1981, Title XX of the Social Security Act was amended to include the Social Services Block Grant to provide child protective service funding for states. Federal funding has required state compliance with minimum standards. In 1983, the Act was amended to include required "reasonable efforts" before removing children from homes and to reunify them with parents after removal.

The Child Abuse Victims' Rights Act was enacted in 1986, giving child victims of federal sexual exploitation laws a private right of action. In 1991, Congress enacted the Victims of Child Abuse Act of 1990 to upgrade the investigation and prosecution of child abuse laws. As part of the Omnibus Budget and Reconciliation Act of 1993, the Congress provided funding to study performance of the Adoption Assistance and Child Welfare Act of 1980, particularly focusing on dependency court practices.

b. Brief Outline of Traditional Procedure

Spurred by federal statutes requiring some common elements between states to qualify for federal funds, states developed "child welfare" systems which mandated that certain professionals (such as teachers or physicians) report suspected child abuse or neglect, and established both hotline intake systems and emergency response protocols. For about three-fourths of the children from whom reports are deemed founded and response appropriate, the result is "family preservation" services in their homes. However, where the county contends that the child is in substantial danger, children are removed to a receiving facility or into temporary foster care.

When children are removed, the child protective services agency at the county level files a petition with the juvenile court to take "jurisdiction" of the child. Within a short time frame (less than one week), a "detention hearing" is held before a juvenile court (dependency) judge to determine if the state has an adequate basis for its initial removal. At this point counsel is appointed for parents at public cost if necessary, and counsel or a lay *"guardian ad litem"* is usually appointed for the child. A critical "jurisdictional" hearing is generally held within the subsequent thirty days to consider the county petition for court jurisdiction over the child. If granted, the child then becomes a "dependent" of the court and parental authority is supplanted *pendente lite.* A "dispositional" hearing will be held with or close to the jurisdictional hearing to determine where the child shall be placed pending further proceedings. As discussed below, federal policy—adopted by all of the states—requires the state to engage in reasonable efforts to accomplish the reunification of children who have been removed from parental custody and control. These services often include parenting classes, psychological counseling, alcohol or drug rehabilitation, or other programs, depending on the basis for removal. Generally, twelve months are allowed for such services to provide an acceptably safe home for the children, with review hearings scheduled at six-month intervals. At the end of that period (or sooner under extraordinary conditions) a "termination" hearing may consider a county agency petition to terminate parental authority. The burden is on the state to prove that a parent whose parental rights are terminated is "unfit" as a parent, under a "clear and convincing" evidentiary showing, as the leading cases presented below hold. A "permanent placement" hearing is coextensively or subsequently held to determine the child's future care and custody.

During the pendency of the dependency court proceedings (and often after), removed children are placed into foster care under the jurisdiction of the juvenile court. That care is usually provided by one of three types of entities: family foster care providers, foster care agencies, and more institutional group homes. Group homes can vary between a home-like setting with five or six children, to a larger facility associated in the public mind with traditional orphanages. Children may also be placed with relatives (so-called "kin-care") who may receive guardianship status from the courts in most states. Finally, children are eligible for adoption upon the termination of previously applicable parental rights. Such adoptions are most easily accomplished for younger, healthy white children, often through family foster care providers when they are so placed.

Children who are not adopted remain in foster care status, with the juvenile court supervising those assigned the parental role. At the age of 18, they are "emancipated" by age from the foster care system—at which point public assistance to foster care parents or agencies for their care generally stops, subject to assistance for some to age 21 under new legislation discussed below.

c. Current Major Federal Funding

Federal funding for abused or neglected children is distributed through the following vehicles:

1) Federal funding to states under Title IV-B of the Social Security Act[12] is provided through two subparts. Subpart 1 funding (the Stephanie Tubbs Jones Child Welfare Services Program), awarded by formula to states, is used to support a variety of child welfare services including abuse prevention, family preservation and reunification, and staff training. Subpart 2 (Promoting Safe and Stable Families Program) primarily funds programs aimed at family support and preservation as well as adoption-promotion activities. Targeted funds are awarded competitively to fund research, evaluation, and training, as well as specialized programming

to improve outcomes for youth affected by parental substance abuse. Through both subparts, states are provided funds to cover 75% of program costs, with the remaining 25% to be matched by the state.

2) The federal government subsidizes the costs of state foster care. Related to the pre-1996 Aid to Families with Dependent Children (AFDC) system of federal subsidies for impoverished families, and unlike the other categories of that aid, federal monies for the care of foster children remained an entitlement. The source of the important funds that are provided is now from Social Security Act Title IV-E. Accordingly, these federal matching funds are termed IV-E monies herein.[13]

The federal IV-E grants are expended for the out-of-home placement of children who (1) have been removed from parental or guardian custody or control for purposes of adoption or because of a court order or voluntary placement agreement, (2) a court determination that the child is a dependent or ward of the court (finding of delinquency), (3) are living with a non-related legal guardian, or (4) have been placed in foster care under the federal Indian Child Welfare Act.

Children eligible for federal IV-E funding are often placed in foster homes or licensed group homes as discussed above, and some may be placed in more intensive treatment facilities. These monies can pay 50–83% of the costs of care (compensation to providers of care for food, board, and other costs), and 50% of related administrative costs. These children may also receive benefits from other federal accounts, including Medicaid and mental health services. Discussed below are the exclusion of an increasing number of children from this assistance because the family they were removed from had an income above the federal poverty line as it existed in 1996 (the irrational "look back" exclusion), and the taking of federal funds due these children where in the form of survivor benefits (OASDI) or disability (SSI) benefits under the Social Security Act by states in violation of applicable fiduciary duty (see the *Keffeler* case in Chapter 6 above).

3) Less substantial federal grant programs include the Child Abuse/ Neglect Prevention and Treatment Act[14] (CAPTA) through which states receive modest grants to fund child abuse prevention and treatment efforts and which funded the National Center on Child Abuse and Neglect to serve as an information clearinghouse; small training grants for universities training social workers under Section 426 of the Social Security Act; the federal "Independent Living Program" through Title IV-E of the Social Security Act providing some children modest assistance as they reach 18 and are no longer eligible for foster care; and a small number of competitive grants under Title III of the Juvenile Justice Act to help homeless and runaway youth, and provide some emergency assistance to homeless youth under the McKinney-Vento Homeless Assistance Act.

Much of the spending relevant to child protection is routed through the five accounts of Table 8-B below.[15]

	FY 2012	FY 2013	FY 2014	FY 2015	FY 2016	FY 2017	FY 2018*
Title IV-E Foster Care	$4,180.0	$4,132.0	$4,746.0	$4,581.0	$4,581.0	$5,362.7	$5,277.8
Title IV-E Adoption Assistance	$2,296.0	$2,278.0	$2,450.0	$2,510.0	$2,674.0	$2,706.1	$2,861.0
Social Services Block Grant	$1,700.0	$1,613	$1,578	$1,576.0	$1,584.0	$1,583.0	$1,588.0
Promoting Safe & Stable Families	$408.1	$387.1	$379.8	$379.6	$381.3	$520.6	$381.6
Child Welfare Services	$280.7	$262.6	$268.7	$268.7	$268.7	$267.9	$266.9
Total, unadjusted.	$8,864.80	$8,672.70	$9,422.50	$9,315.30	$9,489.00	$10,440	$10,375
**Total as adjusted to 2018 $	$9,861.35	$9,496.21	$10,156.83	$10,050.26	$10,098.99	$10,840.12	$10,375

All figures are in millions. *Requested. **Adjusted to CPI (FY 2018=1.00).
Table 8-B. Major Federal Sources of Child Welfare Funding

d. Adoption Tax Expenditures

The Small Business Job Protection Act of 1996 included a new adoption tax credit to stimulate more adoptions and lessen the population of children in less secure foster care placement (see discussion below).[16] The law allows married couples filing a joint return to claim a credit for "adoption expenses" for an eligible child (a person under 18 years of age unable to care for himself or herself) through 2001. In 2013, the Federal Adoption Tax Credit became permanent. The maximum amount available in 2018 is $13,810, and families adopting children with "special needs" are allowed to claim that maximum credit. A child with "special needs" is defined as a citizen or resident of the United States for whom the state has determined assistance is needed to effectuate an adoption—that is, someone the state cannot place. The credit is limited to necessary adoption fees, court costs, legal fees, and similar costs, and it is not refundable; it may only be used to offset tax liability, and is accordingly of no value to those who lack tax liability. A similar credit is available to an employer who pays such costs for an employee seeking to adopt.[17]

2. Post-1996 Federal Legislation

a. The Federal Adoption and Safe Families Act of 1997

During 1997, Congress passed a conference committee bill (H.R. 327) which supplanted prior House and Senate initiatives to stimulate adoptions and further protect children.[18] The new statute was driven by highly publicized cases of children "reunified" with parents who subsequently murdered those children, as well as the following conditions: evidence of harm given the long 18-month period then allowed to parents to win reunification, use of procedures to extend beyond that period, and "permanency plans" which maintained children in unstable foster care settings, often with little subsequent court review.

The 1997 statute reauthorized the pre-existing Family Preservation and Support Services Act and imposed new requirements on the "state plan" necessary for federal funding. Changes included the "safety of children" as the paramount concern in state administration, and the following specific adjustments to prior law:

- "Reasonable efforts" to reunify are guided by "the child's health and safety" as the paramount concern, and 12 months instead of 18 months is allowed in the normal course to make the disposition decision, with even shorter time spans allowed under some circumstances.
- Reasonable efforts may not be required where there is abandonment, chronic abuse, torture, sexual abuse, the parent has seriously injured a child or sibling, or parental rights to a sibling have been terminated.
- Where the court has determined that no reasonable efforts are required, a permanency hearing is to be held within 30 days.
- Permanency planning and reasonable efforts to reunify with parents can proceed *concurrently,* to enable preparation for a permanent alternative (such as adoption) if reunification is denied.
- The "disposition hearing" is replaced by a "permanency hearing." The previous terminology appeared to sanction a continued "holding pattern" status for affected children. Permanency options include return to the parent(s), termination of parental rights and placement for adoption, referral for legal guardianship, or placement in another planned living arrangement.
- A petition for termination of parental rights must be filed for foster children who have been in state custody for 15 out of the most recent 22 months, and for all children for whom reasonable efforts to reunify are not required. However, exceptions are allowed where children are placed with a relative of a parent, where services have not been completed to allow safe return of a child (and that is the permanency plan), or where there is a compelling reason why it would not be in the best interests of the child to so terminate parental rights.
- Foster parents, pre-adoptive parents, or relatives providing care have a right to notice and opportunity to be heard in any review or hearing about a child, but do not have "party" status.
- States may receive an "adoption incentive payment." This is currently referred to as Adoption and Legal Guardianship Incentive Payments, provided to jurisdictions demonstrating improved performance in both adoptions and legal guardianship of children in foster care. The program was recently reauthorized through 2021 as part of the Family First Prevention Services Act (see below).

- To receive incentive payments, a state must provide health insurance coverage to any child with special needs who is subject to an adoption assistance agreement.

b. Chafee Foster Care Program for Successful Transition to Adulthood[19]

In 1999, Congress enacted the Federal Foster Care Independence Act, a statute focusing on youths from 18 to 21 years old who age out of the foster care program but are often not given the kind of support youths receive from their families, often leaving them without resources, prospects, or income for basic expenses once on their own. Renamed in 2018, the program provides federal funding for "independent living" programs. The funds can be used to help youths transition to independence by financing education, training in daily living skills, substance abuse and pregnancy prevention, and health services. In 2013, states reported that almost 100,000 youth and young adults received at least one such service, and 58% received three or more.[20] Services can begin as early as age 14 and recent amendments extend supports to age 23 under certain circumstances. States can use up to 30% of the funds for room and board for youth ages 18 and older. The program also provides Education and Training Vouchers, which are available to eligible youth up to age 26 to defray the costs of postsecondary education or training. The funds are available beginning at age 14, but youth cannot participate in the voucher program for more than 5 years. The maximum annual amount of the voucher is $5,000.[21]

Note that total funds provided to youth through this program amounts to a small proportion of the median funds provided by private parents for their own children through age 26, the median age of self-sufficiency. Although the 1999 Act increased the amount of assets allowable for children in foster care to retain foster care assistance from $1,000 to $10,000, there has been no increase in this amount since, including no adjustment to the CPI. This limitation means that hard earned savings to afford a car to get to work and several thousand in the bank results in the termination of basic sustenance support.

c. Fostering Connections to Success and Increasing Adoptions Act of 2008

The Fostering Connections to Success and Increasing Adoptions Act of 2008 (Fostering Connections) made four important changes for foster children. First, the statute provided federal IV-E matching federal monies for children who are placed in kin guardianships. Guardianships through probate court have been (and continue to be) an option for parents unable to care for their children. These voluntary arrangements (albeit sometimes driven by imminent child protective services intervention) allow parents some role in choosing the persons who will care for their children. If CPS acts to remove a child, the selection of the foster parent, or adoptive parent, may not be someone known to the parent, and may be less likely to allow future contact. Accordingly, often, these probate guardianships involve petitions joined in by biological parents.

But even for children who have been removed and are now within the jurisdiction of juvenile dependency courts, there has long been a similar option of guardianship with a relative of one of the parents. And they are often favored not only by parents who want to have a better chance to retain contact, but by the state and often counsel for the child, who often favor the continuity of care provided by someone the child already knows, and who knows the child. The guardianship option is often selected because the guardians do not want to insult the parent—to whom they are related—by assuming a full adoptive parental role. A guardian does have the authority of a parent, providing stability for the child. And in that parental role, the guardian may decide who the child will see. There may be guardianship conditions, however, and the court retains authority to terminate or alter a guardianship on criteria easier than parental rights termination. But lacking some affirmative intervention, these guardianships are generally regarded as a "permanent placement," and the children are usually taken off of court calendars and social worker monthly visit status.

The guardians have traditionally not received any of their expenses, providing a disincentive *vis-a-vis* compensated foster care or compensated adoption. Some states provided family foster care rate support for these guardians from state-only money. The Fostering Connections Act allows most children in such guardianships to receive a IV-E match, making this option more attractive to the states.

The second change increases adoption incentive payments to states that provide increased adoptions, especially for disabled and older children. However, the federal adoption incentives remain small in amount and do not appear historically to have influenced state adoption rates—which remain disappointing as the data above suggests.

The third change strengthens education continuity for children who have been removed. Currently, large numbers of children are moved between foster care placements—typically three to four times while in care. Often, these involve geographic moves that put them into different school districts. In addition, some group homes provide their own "non-public school" education programs for extra compensation from the state. These educational programs vary widely by state and county—from model programs such as San Diego's San Pasqual Academy for high school students to regrettably inadequate programs. Some states have enacted statutes making it a presumptive rule that foster children are to be "mainstreamed" in public schools unless clearly not in their best interests, and that schools must accept and facilitate foster child transfers between schools and districts. The Fostering Connections Act hooks into the federal McKinney-Vento Homeless Assistance Act (which applies to homeless children or those awaiting foster care placement) to provide increasing school stability as a federal policy. Both statutes establish the right to remain in their schools of origin, and transportation must be provided to facilitate that—often an expensive proposition. For the first time the law is clear that schools all must enroll foster children without delay for paperwork receipt.

The fourth change may be the most profound. When they turn 18, youth become legal adults. But they may still "remain in care" (albeit as adults) up until age 21, and the state may receive a federal IV-E matching payment to provide to the family or group home providing care. The continuation of "in care" help has been possible in a number of states. As of December 2017, 24 states and the District of Columbia had elected to provide continued care to foster youth after age 18 through the Fostering Connections Act.[22] California began providing extended foster care in 2012 launching the CalYOUTH evaluation of these efforts concomitantly. Current findings indicate that most youth choose to remain in extended foster care when given the opportunity and generally report being satisfied with the services they receive. However, despite this help, these youth continue to experience worse outcomes compared to peers their age in many domains, including educational attainment, employment, criminality, and health. These early findings suggest a need to ensure that support services are individualized, taking into account differences in circumstances, gender, race, ethnicity, and gender.[23]

d. Family First Prevention Services Act

The Family First Prevention and Services Act (Public Law 115-123) was signed into law in February 2018. It represents the most significant shift in child welfare financing since the establishment of the Title IV-E entitlement in 1980. The primary feature of the Act is that it opens up the Title IV-E entitlement to pay for services outside of foster care in order to keep children safely at home while their parents get the support they need to care for them. The central provision of the Family First Act allows for Title IV-E entitlement dollars, historically limited to payments for foster care and adoption assistance, to be used for three types of time-limited services for parents of children who are "candidates for foster care." Specifically, approved evidence-based programs for substance abuse, mental health, and parenting skills can be accessed for up to twelve months. Children who would otherwise be removed from care may remain at home for the duration of these services if deemed safe. Services can also be provided to pregnant and parenting foster youth. The new law does not provide financial assistance to relatives who care for children while these services are provided, but does propose to match state spending on kinship navigator programs that assist relative caregivers learn about, find, and access support and services to meet their needs and the needs of the children they are raising.

One of the Act's main goals was to reduce the excessive use of congregate care for foster youth. These facilities are exorbitantly expensive, poorly supervised and regulated, and over-utilized for long periods of time, which is unhealthy and damaging to children's psyches. The Act cuts off federal reimbursement for stays in these facilities after two weeks, with a few exceptions. The Act also requires states to address child abuse and neglect fatalities by working towards compiling complete and accurate information on maltreatment-related deaths and describing their efforts to develop and implement a multidisciplinary fatality prevention plan. This provision reflects recommendations made by the federal Commission to

Eliminate Child Abuse and Neglect Fatalities, as well as provisions in the Child Welfare Oversight and Accountability Act introduced in 2017.

Family First also has several important provisions relating to transition age foster youth. Eligibility for benefits through the Chafee Independent Living Program was extended from 21 to 23, and the age limit to access Chafee Education Training Vouchers was extended from 23 to 26. These changes were made without any increases in funding for the programs, which may result in states having to spread the same amount of money around a now-larger group of students—and many states are rightfully concerned about this.

This legislation has been celebrated, as it represents a shift in values, moving from fiscally incentivizing removals and foster care placements to promoting family preservation. However, the Act fails to cure the chronic underfunding of most child welfare programs or other programs that support the children and families that end up in child welfare. And although the services it covers are not subject to the restrictive eligibility determinations of the rest of Title IV-E funding, it does not cure the arcane and morally reprehensible "lookback" which makes any foster child removed from a family earning over the poverty line *as it existed in 1996* ineligible for federal foster care funding.

3. Current Policy Issues

Notwithstanding the evolution of state child protection, six problem areas concern child advocates, as follows:

a. Prevention/Early Intervention/Education Failure

Studies have found a correlation between non-marital childbearing and a risk for abuse and neglect, as well as a similar correlation involving unintended pregnancy.[24] Research indicates that children in single mother households may be more t risk of maltreatment. Studies suggest that poverty also correlates with maltreatment by single mothers.[25] This is of particular concern given the low levels of child support collection from absent fathers.

As discussed above, another highly correlated variable is alcohol/drug abuse. Numerous studies have confirmed this relationship, finding that as many as 7 of 10 child abuse and neglect reports indicate substance abuse as a factor.[26] The increasing prevalence of these cases is a significant cause for concern. A 2018 report from the U.S. Department of Health and Human Services revealed that across the nation, child abuse reports and foster care placements have increased in counties where drug-related deaths and hospitalizations have increased. Additionally, these substance use indicators are associated with more complex and severe child welfare cases.[27] Although the development of drug courts and other preventive measures has increased, as the budget figures outlined above indicate, this and related prevention measures remain a relatively low funding priority. Furthermore, effective treatment services are in short supply in many communities, resulting in delays in accessing services and consistent failure to match clients with the specific treatment program most effective for their particular needs.[28]

In addition to underlying prevention, there is a growing movement in support of "early preventive intervention." "Family preservation" is one alternative response to a report of abuse or neglect. A child is not removed from the home and the juvenile court does not formally assume jurisdiction over him or her. Rather, a parent signs an agreement to receive services (*e.g.*, drug rehabilitation, anger management, living skills) and such services are provided while the child remains at home. An early intervention model originated in Hawaii during the late 1980s (sometimes termed the "Hawaii model"). Rather than wait for an abuse report, new mothers who fit a profile for high-risk abuse are visited in their homes by social workers shortly after they give birth. These "house call" social and public health workers proactively check on the status of the new child and provide on-site individual instruction and advice. This model has enjoyed increasing political support and it has been implemented in many counties in varying forms over the last decade. In 2018, a study of a statewide home-visiting program for socially high-risk families in Connecticut indicated a 22% decrease in the likelihood of substantiated reports of neglect among participants.[29] However, "home visitation" to large numbers of new mothers without prior abuse reports is expensive. Nevertheless, the early intervention model shows substantial promise compared to the "report response" standard approach, since such reports may not occur, particularly for young pre-school children who do not come into contact often with mandated reporters.

The almost universal support for such intervention contrasts with opposition to an approach facially even more cost effective in preventing abuse/neglect: mandatory parenting education. Child advocates supporting such education argue that most children will become parents, and all are likely to perform some parenting functions. These advocates argue that this momentous task with profound social consequences is amenable to useful instruction. Young parents currently lack basic information about the care of an infant, dangers, and optimum child rearing practices. Parenting education advocates ask: Why should this critical information not be taught in classes where future parents are gathered in groups of 20 to 30—an apparently more efficient means of delivery than the one-on-one limited in-home format?

Such lessons need not sacrifice substantial time from important education in English, math, science, and other important subjects. They would include important information ranging from the difficulties and financial costs of parenthood to basic facts about infant care: nursing, food, physiology, development, health needs, etc. An educated parent would know not only that an infant must never be shaken, but would understand why—the weak neck and brain trauma from whiplash. Students would be taught about common hazards, from leaving children unattended in cars in hot weather to swimming pool dangers to the special vulnerability of young brains to lead contamination, *et al.* Future parents would learn why children cry, what they should eat, and when to seek medical attention. Social services departments would provide current material based on errors and abuses evident from their investigations.

Most high school curricula will include substantial coverage of a wide range of subjects from how to fill out a tax form, to Hannibal's conquests, to the trigonometric use of the cosign and tangent. But few include basic parenting information—notwithstanding three million reports of abuse/neglect annually, and the many child developmental benefits that follow from informed and skilled parenting. Parenting education opponents have thus far contended successfully that such information is properly confined to family, non-profit and religious instruction.[30]

b. Foster Care Drift and Adoption Failure

Removal from a home, even a dangerous and harmful one, can be a devastating disruption for a child. That disruption is exacerbated by the normal course of proceedings of dependency court and the foster care system. Only a minority of children achieve quick and certain stability, usually when a relative previously known to them is an acceptable alternative or they are reunited expeditiously with parents. Data from the National Survey of Child and Adolescent Well-Being (NSCAW II) indicated that half of the children placed out of home achieved permanency within three years, with more than 73% of those doing so through reunification. However, among those reunified, almost a quarter were re-reported to child protective services.[31] Among the children awaiting a permanent resolution in 2017, more than 50,000 were in a group home or institution, and more than three quarters were in a relative or non-relative foster home.[32]

Child advocates use the term "foster care drift" to refer to the repeated placement changes affecting many children in foster care. Children often are moved from an initial receiving facility to temporary foster care, to family foster care, then to one or more other families, and often to multiple group home placements. According to a national longitudinal study, children who spent at least 36 consecutive months in foster care (meeting the criteria for what is termed "long term foster care") most commonly had five placement changes, with some experiencing as many as nineteen. Foster children in care fewer than 36 months most commonly experienced three moves.[33] National statistics indicate that 35% of children in foster care in 2016 had experienced at least three placements.[34] Psychologists term one consequence of such drift "detachment syndrome" as children lack the reliable, certain anchor that a parent can provide.

Exacerbating foster care drift is the deliberate pacing of judicial proceedings. Although the federal Adoption and Safe Families Act of 1997 discussed above has reduced the normal course eighteen-month period for reunification to twelve months, it is in practice often well beyond one year. During this period, children are often in a temporary waiting status. Studies show that the possibility of reunification decreases as time in out of home care increases.[35] Less than half of the children awaiting adoption in 2014 found their permanent home in 2015. For those adopted the average length of stay in foster care prior to adoption was 32 months.[36] In some states, a large percentage of children in foster care are designated as "unadoptable" and are designated for permanent foster care status until emancipating out of the system at 18 years of age. Nationwide in 2017, almost 20,000 youth "aged out" of the system in this fashion.[37]

Adoptions are impeded by the confidentiality of the dependency system which advocates argue allows more effective exposure of canine adoption needs than human. They are also limited by the practice of many jurisdictions to refuse Adoption Assistance payments to adoptive parents who the state believes may be able to afford their costs.

Another impediment to adoption is racial preference, often reflected within child welfare agencies. Such bias is not at all confined to whites, but frequently is reflected in the attitudes of social workers of minority ethnicity, who are concerned about the adoption of a child by white parents. The placement of a child with an adoptive parent of his or her own ethnic group has advantages—including those which flow from appearance similarity between parent and child. But more than half of foster children are minorities and insistence on matching them with minority parents precludes adoption for many of these children. Paradoxically, child welfare agencies have little objection to foster care placement of children in homes of different races—placements that can well last until emancipation.

Congress has enacted two successive statutes to address racially-based adoptive rejection: the Multiethnic Placement Act of 1994, and the Interethnic Adoption Provisions of 1996, which further amended the law to prioritize interracial adoptions over foster care drift. Despite these legislative efforts, there is a disproportionate number of children of color within the foster care system and awaiting adoption.

c. Family Foster Care Supply and Quality

One of the impediments to foster care stability is low compensation paid to foster family care providers. There is no minimum rate established in federal law, nor is there a standard method for calculating what constitutes adequate rates ensuring coverage of the costs of foster care. Basic monthly rates vary widely among states, with a range from $232 in Wisconsin to $1003 in the District of Columbia.[38] What is consistent in most states, however, is that the basic rate provided to foster parents does not meet the out-of-pocket costs of children, particularly for families seeking just two or three children for possible adoption. In several states, basic foster care rates cover less than half of the estimated cost of care. These family foster care providers account for more than half of the adoptive parents of children who are adopted out of foster care.[39] In contrast, group homes, which generally produce poorer outcomes for children, can be paid as much as twelve times the foster care rate per month per child. The result has been a failure in the supply and quality of family foster care providers, who often lack the political representation in state capitols of the more organized and commercial group home providers (see discussion of lobbying and influence in Chapter 1). Child advocates within the states have argued, generally without success, for increased compensation for family foster care to stimulate supply, maintenance of compensation into adoption, and certification of advanced care skills (especially for special needs children) warranting augmented payment. In 2017, the state of Georgia responded to the dwindling supply of foster parents – at a time when the number of children in foster care was increasing – with its first increase in daily rates for foster parents in a decade. Other efforts have ultimately involved the courts, as in the *Wagner* case below.

California Foster Parents Association v. Wagner
624 F.3d 974 (9th Cir. 2010)

SCHROEDER, Circuit Judge.

The federal Child Welfare Act ("CWA" or "the Act") provides money to state governments to pay for children's foster care and adoption assistance programs. 42 USC § 670 et seq. The CWA spells out the specific foster care provider expenses that states' payments are supposed to cover. See 42 U.S.C. §§ 672 (a) and 675 (4)(a). ... In this case are three associations representing individual foster parents in the State of California....They brought this suit against officials of the State of California ("the State") under 42 U.S.C. § 1983 claiming a violation of their federal right to payments under the CWA and seeking declaratory and injunctive relief. Foster Parents seek to compel the State to revise its payment schedule upward in order to reflect Foster Parents' actual costs. The State moved to dismiss on the ground that the CWA does not create rights enforceable under § 1983. The district court denied the motion and ultimately entered judgment in favor of Foster Parents, finding that the CWA created a federal monetary entitlement and that the State violated the Act by setting rates without considering the CWA's mandatory cost factors....We recently decided *California Alliance of Child and Family Services v. Allenby*, 589 F.3d 1017 (9th Cir. 2009) ("*Allenby II*"), a similar case brought by institutional providers of foster care.

The district court in that case held that the CWA created a right enforceable under § 1983.....The district court viewed these plaintiffs as having an even stronger case on the merits than the institutional providers in *Allenby*. On summary judgment, the district court found that the State failed to provide evidence that the payments to individual foster care providers were ever based on the CWA's itemized list of costs, and that Foster Parents had provided uncontroverted evidence that their rates had "fallen further out of line with the cost of providing the enumerated terms than had the institutional rates" addressed in *Allenby* The court ordered a remedy that would bring about "substantial compliance" with the federal statute.... We are now therefore squarely faced with the issue of whether the CWA, at 42 U.S.C. §§ 672(a) and 675(4)(A), creates an enforceable federal right. We hold that it does. ...[T]his conclusion flows from the controlling Supreme Court and Ninth Circuit authority governing when federal statutes create federal rights enforceable through 42 U.S.C. § 1983. See *Gonzaga University v. Doe*, 536 U.S. 273... (2002); *Blessing v. Freestone*, 520 U.S. 329 ... (1997).

* * *

... State receipt of funds is conditioned upon submission of a plan for assistance to the Department of Health and Human Services for approval. 42 U.S.C. § 671(a). The CWA requires that participating states use the federal funds to reimburse foster parents for identified out-of-pocket costs. 42 U.S.C. §§ 671(a)-(b), 672, 675(4)(A)...."foster care maintenance payments" (are defined) as payments to cover the cost of (and the cost of providing) food, clothing, shelter, daily supervision, school supplies, a child's personal incidentals, liability insurance with respect to a child, reasonable travel to the child's home for visitation, and reasonable travel for the child to remain in the school in which the child is enrolled at the time of placement...

* * *

The inquiry into whether a statute creates a right enforceable under § 1983 is one of congressional intent. Congress's intent to benefit the plaintiff must be "unambiguous." *Gonzaga*, 536 U.S. at 283. The touchstone is "whether Congress *intended to create a federal right." Id.* The Court explained that "broader or vaguer 'benefits' or 'interests' " do not suffice. *Id.* The inquiry begins with the three-part test the Supreme Court established in *Blessing. Price,* 390 F.3d at 1109 & n.4. *Blessing's* test asks: (1) whether Congress intended the provision in question to benefit the plaintiff; (2) whether the plaintiff has demonstrated that the asserted right is not so vague and amorphous that its enforcement would strain judicial competence; and (3) whether the provision giving rise to the right is couched in mandatory, rather than precatory, terms.

The CWA similarly contains a provision creating a right, in § 672(a), and a provision "spelling out the content" of that right in § 675(4)(A). The asserted right under the statutory language in question, is therefore the right to foster care maintenance payments that cover the cost of the expenses enumerated in § 675(4)(A)....We conclude that Congress intended for §§ 672(a) and 675(4)(A) to benefit Foster Parents as the caregivers for foster children.

* * *

The second *Blessing* factor asks "whether the plaintiff has demonstrated that the asserted right is not so vague and amorphous that its enforcement would strain judicial competence." *Price,* 390 F.3d at 1109. The State argues that the CWA is too vague because it does not specify how rates should be set to cover the enumerated costs, and that no regulations governing the calculation of foster care maintenance payments fill the gap. We disagree. Our precedent strongly suggests, if not compels, the conclusion that the asserted right is sufficiently specific...We agree with Foster Parents that courts may review the State's compliance with a requirement to set rates that cover the costs of the enumerated expenditures. If a statute or applicable federal requirement does not prescribe a particular methodology for calculating costs, we give deference to a reasonable methodology employed by the State. *See Wilder,* 496 at 518-19. Though some deference may be owed to the State's methodology, the absence of a uniform federal methodology for setting rates "does not render the [statute] unenforceable by a court." *Id.* at 519.

* * *

The third and final *Blessing* factor requires that "the provision giving rise to the right is couched in mandatory, rather than precatory, terms." ...in this case, the State does not seriously contend that the § 672(a)'s language is precatory rather than mandatory. We therefore conclude that § 672(a)'s language is clearly mandatory, satisfying the third and final *Blessing* factor. There is, moreover, an additional important distinction between this case and *Gonzaga* that bolsters our conclusion... the CWA provides no administrative means through which a foster parent may ask the State to make foster care maintenance payments that cover the mandatory costs. The fact that Foster Parents have no administrative forum in which to raise their concerns lends additional support to our conclusion that Congress intended to create an enforceable right here, just as the presence of an administrative mechanism "buttressed" the Supreme Court's opposite conclusion in *Gonzaga.* See 536 U.S. at 289-90.

Questions for Discussion

1. The evidence in the *Wagner* case above indicated that the average rates of $530 per month for family foster care providers was about 43% below the out-of-pocket costs of foster care provision. In contrast, the group homes with substantial lobbying presence at the state capitol receive an average of over $4,000 per month per child, with the group home case mentioned by the *Wagner* decision compelling a 20% increase in 2010. What accounts for the quicker and more solicitous response to funding increases for the commercial centers? Did they suffer a greater degree of underpayment? Are their outcomes for children superior?

2. The number of children in family foster care had fallen in California from above 15,000 in 2001 to under 5,000 in 2011. The plaintiffs contended that this

supply diminution was caused by the inability to provide care without sacrificing personal pensions or having independent wealth. The plaintiffs note that family placements are the major source of cost saving and child beneficial adoptions. What are the arguments supporting such alleged underpayment where it puts more children into group homes at eight times the cost? If this rate disparity and supply diminution extends nationally, what are the political factors, if any, explaining it?

3. The four years of litigation in *Wagner* focused on the threshold question of a private right of remedy. No authority questions the clear authority of the federal executive branch to simply inform the state that it must comply with the statutory standard. Indeed, it would appear that the purpose of the executive branch is to carry out the legislative directions of the Congress. Why has the federal DHHS not simply told the state to raise its rates to lawful levels or suffer federal funding cut-off? Would a federal mandamus action lie against DHHS officials to compel enforcement (based on the failure to cut off federal funds where applicable statutes are violated as an "abuse of discretion"?).

4. State law includes provisions assuring compliance with applicable federal law, and also includes provisions that would arguably mandate compensatory rates to family foster parents. Would an action lie in state court to enforce a minimum standard? What form would it take and what are its advantages and disadvantages?

5. Federal and state statutes give taxpayers the right to bring *qui tam* or "taxpayer waste suits" against private parties who overcharge public accounts. Could such a concept apply to the underpayment of private parties directly leading to excessive public expenditures? How would such a law be structured?

Note on Cases after *Wagner*

Since the Ninth Circuit decision in *Wagner*, other federal appellate courts have considered the issue of whether the Child Welfare Act confers an individually enforceable right regarding foster care maintenance payments. In 2013, the Eighth Circuit split with the Ninth Circuit, finding that such a right did not exist. The Eighth Circuit reasoned that because the Act conditions funding on the development of a state plan, the statute has an "aggregate focus" rather than an intention to establish an enforceable individual right. The court concluded that the only remedy provided for a state's nonconformity with the statute is for the federal government to terminate provision of matching funds, an action the federal government has elected not to take.[40] In 2017, the Sixth Circuit in *D.O. v. Glisson*, 847 F.3d 374, rejected the Eighth Circuit's conclusion and rationale, disagreeing that the Act only addressed the state as regulated participants. The Sixth Circuit found that the Act focused on individual recipients by mandating payments "on behalf of each child." In conjunction with the mandatory language Congress included ("shall make") this gave rise to an individually enforceable right. Although some district courts have followed the reasoning of the Eighth Circuit,[41] the majority of lower courts considering the issue have found that the Act gives rise to an enforceable right.[42]

d. Independent, Quality Representation

The juvenile courts, as with the judiciary in general, are inherently passive. The affirmative supervision duties of the dependency court, however, are extraordinary given its direct parental function for the foster care children under its charge. Despite the cases presented below indirectly guaranteeing parents an attorney for legal representation, involved children have not been so universally advantaged. Approximately 40 states provide attorneys for children in dependency court, but a constitutional right to such representation has not yet been clearly established. In 2003, the federal Child Abuse Prevention and Treatment Act (CAPTA) providing state grants was amended to specify that:

> in every case involving a victim of child abuse or neglect which results in a judicial proceeding, a *guardian ad litem*, who has received training appropriate to the role…and who may be an attorney or a court appointed special advocate who has received training appropriate to that role (or both), shall be appointed to represent the child in such proceedings
>
> (I) to obtain first-hand, a clear understanding of the situation and needs of the child; and
>
> (II) to make recommendations to the court concerning the best interests of the child....[43]

Interpretations of who the "*guardian ad litem*" may be vary widely. Some contend that a Court Appointed Special Advocate (CASA) volunteer can fulfill such a role. These volunteers, often retired persons, monitor foster children in placements and independently report to the court on their status. Although an important contribution, child advocates concede that the CASA program is not a substitute for professional, competent representation of children before the court. An attorney is required to present evidence to the court—consistent with the legal basis for the court's decisions. An attorney is capable of filing a writ or otherwise contesting an action by the county or a parent. CASA volunteers, although important to many foster children, are usually not attorneys. They are often persons with trusted judgment and independence from the parties who give the judge additional factual insight about the child's situation. However, non-attorneys cannot effectively file legal motions, evaluate evidence admissibility, subpoena witnesses to the case, engage in assured confidential communications with the child, or file a writ or otherwise appeal a trial court decision, among other limitations.

Others argue that county counsel (or the attorney for the agency) may perform such a role. Still others contend that the social worker assigned to the case may qualify. The consensus view of child advocates is that a child pulled from a home is about to undertake a serious legal proceeding of far-reaching consequences. Accordingly, the child needs legal representation meeting minimal standards (as to qualification and performance),[44] as well as sufficiently low caseloads to adequately represent child clients.

In January of 2019, the federal government took an encouraging step by issuing a policy change that will now allow federal IV-E funds to be used to help pay for counsel for children (and parents) in dependency court. This will allow states that provide such representation to obtain partial reimbursement for these costs, and may incentivize other states to consider following suit. Notwithstanding this development, advocates continue to urge recognition of a constitutional right to counsel for children in dependency court.

The *Kenny A.* case positing a constitutional right to an attorney as the required *guardian ad litem* for children in juvenile dependency court is not universally followed, as discussed below. Its caseload standard for such counsel of no more than 100 suffers from rare compliance. A case filed before the Ninth Circuit Court of Appeals challenged a caseload of 380 extant in Sacramento County.[45] Other jurisdictions have caseloads of 500 or more. These burdens mean that counsel are barely able to talk with their client, and are typically unable to explore disability, tort, education, or medical rights of a client, and are even limited in appealing a dependency court decision.

Research on the benefits of providing counsel to children in these proceedings is scarce. The most widely referenced study was published in 2008 by the Chapin Hall Center for Children, based on a study in Palm Beach County, Florida. This report concluded that children with effective counsel in dependency cases were moved to permanency at about twice the rate of unrepresented children.[46] Such an outcome appears to benefit involved children, and save the state money by abbreviating the court case and the foster care stay.

The National Association of Counsel for Children (NACC) and the American Bar Association (ABA) are working to stimulate competent representation. In 2011, the American Bar Association (ABA) adopted the Model Act Governing Representation of Children in Abuse, Neglect, and Dependency Proceedings.[47] The Model Act provides a far more robust model of representation than the minimal standard included in CAPTA; however, it does not create requirements binding on the states. The NACC created a Child Welfare Law Specialist certification process through which more than 800 attorneys in more than 40 states have been certified. Practitioners in these states complete a rigorous examination and application process to demonstrate competence in child welfare law. In 2009, the Children's Bureau of the U.S Department of Health and Human Services awarded a six-year, $6 million grant to the University of Michigan Law School's Child Advocacy Clinic to establish a National Quality Improvement Center (QIC) to generate and disseminate knowledge on the representation of children and youth in the child welfare system.

Beyond lawyer involvement, competence assurance and caseloads, is the common controversy over the "model" of attorney child representation. Should it be the "attorney" model, where counsel represents the stated desires of the client, or a "best interests" model where the attorney represents his or her view of what is in the child's best interests? Those supporting the latter configuration cite the immaturity of children and the possibility of manipulation by adults. Those supporting the attorney model argue that children are not necessarily less mature than many adult clients, that it is arrogant for an attorney to presume to know the optimum outcome unilaterally, and that there are limits on representation of unlawful or self-destructive positions for attorneys whatever the age of a client. Those adherents also argue that children benefit where they know their views and preferences are presented and considered, and that the outcome is not dictated by the views of any single party or witness—many of whom may have bias and maturity issues. Many scholars believe that the attorney model is preferable at some point of child maturity, with views varying from a child with the equivalent judgment of a five-year-old, up to a fifteen-year-old.[48]

During 2012, First Star and the Children's Advocacy Institute (CAI) released the third edition of A Child's Right to Counsel, a national survey of child dependency court representation, evaluating each state's status. The report concluded that client-directed counsel to maltreated children has ethical dimensions, and is also economically prudent. If good legal representation results in resolving cases with children attaining permanency more quickly, the net result will be to reduce the amount of money that states spend on court costs and on foster care. The grading criteria of the First Star/CAI survey included whether children receive an attorney for dependency court; the duration of the appointment (e.g., some children have no appellate representation); the role of counsel (client-directed or best interests); required measures to assure competence (e.g., education for the child's counsel, including important multidisciplinary elements such as child development and education law); whether state law confers "party" status on children under court jurisdiction; and application of the Rules of Professional Conduct (or its equivalent) regarding confidentiality and immunity from liability. Extra credit was conferred where state law addresses caseload standards for child's counsel.

The third edition of A Child's Right to Counsel found that since the original 2007 survey, several states had improved their statutes and/or rules. But only three states earned 100%—Massachusetts, Connecticut, and Oklahoma. Over half of the 51 jurisdictions surveyed earned a grade of A or B, while one-third of the 51 jurisdictions surveyed scored a D or an F—with some major states not offering assured attorney representation at all. The results indicate continued wide disparities in child attorney representation among the states.[49]

e. Safety Net Cut-Off Endangerment

The Personal Responsibility and Work Opportunity Reconciliation Act of 1996 (PRA) did not directly alter child protection programs. The traditional requirements of the federal Adoption Assistance and Child Welfare Act remain in force. Eligibility, entitlement status, and funding for Title IV-E, Adoption Assistance, and Medicaid for foster and adopted children were substantially maintained. A child's eligibility for federal foster care and adoption assistance is based on the eligibility of the child's family for AFDC according to the rules in effect on June 1, 1995, rather than on the family's eligibility for the new TANF welfare block grant post 1996.

Overall, the PRA cut federal contribution for state safety-net (TANF) provision substantially. Funds for the Social Services Block Grant, which is used in part for child protection services, were reduced 15% in fiscal year 1997. It was authorized and funded in 2002 at $1.7 billion and remained at that level through FY2012.[50] It has since been reduced—even in raw, unadjusted numbers—declining from $1.7 billion in 2012 to less than $1.6 billion in 2018. Under TANF, states receive funds through a fixed block grant, the amount of which has not risen with inflation nor child population gain, thus reducing its value by more than a third since its creation.[51] The end result has been a decline in safety net support for those fully eligible from close to the poverty line in the 1970s, to 70% of the line in major states, and below half the poverty line in others.[52]

Some of the evidence of welfare reform outcomes is favorable to impoverished children. Employment has increased. Child poverty and unwed births appear to have leveled. However, the primary visible sign of success—substantial diminution in welfare rolls—is misleading. In 2017, 23 per 100 families in poverty received TANF cash assistance, which marks a two-thirds decline in those served since 1996. This reduction in the TANF-to-Poverty ratio[53] is due to a combination of factors, including state policy and administrative changes resulting in less accessibility to TANF. For example, several states have shortened time limits or tightened eligibility restrictions. The inability to access TANF has left families in deep poverty without a sufficient safety net. In 1995, AFDC lifted more than 2.7 children out of deep poverty. In 2015, TANF did the same for only 349,000 children.[54]

Studies indicate that at least one-third of those not receiving TANF have not found employment. Of those who have, few earn incomes above the poverty line. Moreover, as discussed in Chapter 7, child care financial assistance—necessary for continued work for these parents[55] is assured in many states for only one to two years after initial employment. The children of immigrants who arrived in the United States after 1996 are likely to be in particularly dire straits due to their ineligibility for most safety net assistance, including the Supplemental Nutrition Assistance Program (SNAP), SSI, TANF, and non-emergency Medicaid. Some states have limited state-only assistance for some children, but the evidence indicates that although the percentage of children living in poverty has declined slightly, a larger number are living in extreme poverty, defined as under one-half of the federal poverty line.

Punitive provisions of the federal statute which threaten children include lifetime cut-off of the "parent's share" (which could be up to one-half of the grant) from TANF and SNAP to any person convicted of a drug offense.[56] Children with parents attempting rehabilitation (or successfully accomplishing it) suffer safety net reductions to minimal levels (generally below one-half of the poverty line). Mothers are also required to assist in the identification of biological fathers for child support collection purposes. Child advocates argued unsuccessfully that alleged "parent share" reductions primarily impacted children. More ominous is the prospective cut-off of all assistance to any parent after sixty months of benefits. The limitation applies even for parents who have worked continuously on a part-time basis during this period and received only small public payments. While the federal law sets the limit at sixty months, some states have opted to set the limit even lower. Arizona has set the most severe limit, instituting a lifetime maximum of twelve months of assistance. Such limits have started to affect millions of children, with uncertain long-term consequences.

A state is allowed to use up to 30% of its TANF funds to carry out programs under the Social Services Block Grant and the Child Care and Development Block Grant, provided that not more than one-third of the transferred amount may be used for Title XX child welfare programs.[57] Hence, up to 10% of federal TANF funds may be used for child abuse/neglect spending—an important provision if TANF cut-downs produce substantial foster care demand increases as children are surrendered or taken from families unable to provide basic sustenance. However, reliance on the child welfare system as the final safeguard for children is problematical. Parental rights are normally not terminated based on poverty alone, but require *post hoc* proof of child endangerment. Further, even severe harm is not likely to be reported for children aged 0–5, who are less visible to teachers and other mandated child abuse reporters—at the same time, these children are at an age where nutritional deficiency can portend permanent damage.

Finally, reliance on child protective services is uneconomic given its substantially higher cost over denied TANF. The policy rationale of removing an otherwise competent and loving parent from a child (and vice versa) when the cost to do so is greater than public assistance in place is questionable. One explanation may be an unstated theory akin to "don't feed the pigeons"—if you deny help to impoverished adults, they will not have children they cannot afford. Child advocates argue that children are not pigeons, and that adult influence is best not accomplished through child deprivation. They contend that the political and media strength of children is so minimal that a direct discussion of adult reproductive responsibility, incentives, birth control, parenting education, or other subjects addressing decisions to have children is *verboten*, but cutting children to below one-half of the federal poverty line, with attendant nutritional shortfall and brain development implications, is not.

f. Confidentiality: Dependency Court, Foster Children, and Child Abuse Deaths

Most states conduct dependency proceedings confidentially. The public is not allowed to attend, they are not publicly reported or examined and few states use juries. Such confidentiality extends in practice to the entire foster care population under the jurisdiction of that dependency court, concealing it (and its omissions and the consequences for dependent children) from public examination. As discussed in Chapter 1, these children lack political power and a major factor in reform and responsiveness to their needs is public attention. On the other hand, many circumstances may commend confidentiality in the best interests of a child victim or other member of the family in an individual case. Some child advocates and courts favor what is termed "presumptively open" dependency courts, where the default rule is open, but with liberal allowance for the closing of a particular hearing or witness testimony "in the best interests" of involved children. Motions for such protective order may be brought by any party, with particular deference for motions brought by counsel for children.

One study by the National Center for State Courts of the Minnesota system of open dependency courts found no serious harm to involved children,[58] nor did a study of Arizona from a presumptively open system. Critics contend that these studies are flawed and instead emphasize the concern that already victimized children may be further traumatized by public exposure and that family's efforts at rehabilitation will be negatively impacted if their cases are public.[59] The case of *Globe Newspaper Co. v. Superior Court*, 457 U.S. 596 (1982), discussed in Chapter 9 below, voids a Massachusetts law prohibiting adult criminal trial testimony by minor sex abuse victims for being "overly broad" as applied. The Court notes the default rule of public trials. Child advocates favoring presumptively open dependency courts contend that their proceedings commend public disclosure given the onerous police power they exercise over children under their jurisdiction. It is not a single decision to be made, but a continuing jurisdiction touching where they will live, with whom, and their conditions of health and education. Historically, foster children have been much abused, and reforms consistently depend upon public disclosure.[60]

Related to dependency court and foster child confidentiality is the issue of child deaths and near deaths from abuse or neglect. At least 1,700 U.S. child deaths from abuse or neglect are reported each year; many more suffer near death injuries.[61] The federal Child Abuse Prevention and Treatment Act (CAPTA) explicitly requires states to disclose findings and information regarding the deaths or near deaths of children from abuse or neglect—whether in or not in foster care at the time. States must adopt "provisions which allow for public disclosure of the findings or information about the case of child abuse or neglect which has resulted in a child fatality or near fatality." In providing clarification as to proper state execution of this provision, the Child Welfare Policy Manual declares that a state "does not have discretion in whether to allow the public access to the child fatality or near fatality information; rather, the public has the discretion as to whether to access the information."[62] This means that the state is not required to provide information to the public unless it is requested. The legislative history underlying this requirement indicates the importance to the electorate of such extreme events and their possible relevance to public policies.

In 2012, the Children's Advocacy Institute released the second edition of its national report, *State Secrecy and Child Deaths in the U.S.*, evaluating each state's CAPTA-required public disclosure practices where there are child deaths or near deaths from abuse or neglect. The updated report found that while every state has now developed some identifiable public disclosure policy regarding child abuse or neglect deaths, some states lack policies to cover the disclosure of near fatalities. Furthermore, many existing state policies fail to fulfill the congressional goal of identifying systemic problems that can be addressed to prevent such tragedies. Finally, even in states where the public disclosure laws are relatively strong, there is concern among advocates that officials are not complying with the letter or spirit of the laws.[63]

The report compares the child death and near death disclosure laws and policies of the fifty states and the District of Columbia and grades them from "A" to "F," along the following criteria:

- Does the state have a public disclosure policy as mandated by CAPTA?
- Is the state's policy codified in statute, or is it contained in regulation or written (or oral) policy?
- What is the ease of access to the information (does the policy use mandatory or permissive language, and is the release of information contingent on conditions precedent)?
- What is the scope of information authorized for release, and are there exceptions that decrease the type of information that will be released?
- Does the state allow public access to dependency court (abuse/neglect) proceedings?

Since the release of the initial report in 2008, 21 states amended their public disclosure policies, with 10 states meaningfully improving their policies and a few states taking steps backwards. Twenty states still fall in the "C" range or below, including the three most populous states (California, Texas, and New York). However, six states earned an "A+" or "A" and only one state received a grade of F. The report notes that for a surprisingly high percentage of cases (over 70% in a California survey), deaths of children *not* in foster care from abuse or neglect involve prior reports to local child protective services. In half of the cases, the prior reports related to the later cause of death.

Questions for Discussion

1. Assume a 30-year-old man assaults his 22-year-old wife and injures her. Any proceedings in criminal or family court will be public. Preserving the "family" (or spousal reunification) is not a permitted basis for confidential proceedings. But if that same 30-year-old assaults a seven-year-old entrusted to his custody, the decision as to his parental status and where and under what conditions that child shall live—perhaps for the next eleven years or more—is cloaked in secrecy in many states. If such testimony would be painful for the child in a criminal case, should testimony be allowed in confidence?

2. Is the child psychological protection concern distinguishable in the criminal case *vis-a-vis* a dependency case? On the other hand, would it be possible to have a more tailored confidentiality arrangement that might apply in both settings?

3. Some states allow child testimony in criminal cases, particularly where the child is an abuse victim, outside of the physical presence of the defendant (*e.g.*, via one-way video where the defendant is in a different room). However, current laws require the child to demonstrate an inability to testify given threats or fear (see *Maryland v. Craig*, discussed in Chapter 9). The Supreme Court allows

such confrontation limitation in these circumstances. Can such a rule not also apply to dependency court? Can it be more solicitous of child sensitivity given its non-criminal setting?

4. Is it possible to strike a balance between sensitivity to psychological harms from emotional testimony in court in front of strangers, and broadly cloaking children from public knowledge about their conditions under effective state custody and control? How might such a balance be struck?

5. Where a social worker suspects physical abuse or danger to a child from a parent, the system provides multiple checks on improvident removal—detention, jurisdiction, and other hearings before a neutral judge; a burden on the state; appointed attorneys for parents; a "reasonable efforts" to reunify, et al. What is the check on errors in the other direction (the failure to remove a child in jeopardy of beatings or molestation)? Is it possible to create such checks outside of public disclosure, e.g., independent ombudsmen review?

g. Emancipation Abandonment

Foster children reaching 18 years of age are commonly sent into the world without the family platform that supports most children during their early years of adulthood. Historically these children "aging out" of the foster care system into young adulthood have fared poorly, particularly in comparison to their peers. Recent national surveys of youth transitioning out of foster care revealed that among 21 year old respondents, 23% were neither enrolled in an educational program nor employed either full or part time. Forty-three percent indicated having experienced homelessness. One-fifth reported a history of incarceration during the previous two years. Thirty-two percent reported having a child by age 21, while only 9% of those respondents indicated having been married at the time of the child's birth.[64] Studies have shown that although most foster children express a desire to attend college, only about 8% earn a four-year degree. By age 26, only 70% of former foster youth had income from employment over the past year, compared to 94% of the general population.[65] When employed, former foster youth earn less than half, on average, than their peers with no history of foster care. Many experience chronic health problems, with up to 85% experiencing mental health issues.[66] The outcomes for these approximately 25,000 youth aging out annually as the "children of the state" remains a major concern of child advocates.

For a little over two decades, Congress has slowly been making modest changes in the law relating to older foster youth. In 1986, Congress amended the Social Security Act (SSA) to include the Independent Living Initiative (ILI),[67] which provides funding to assist foster youth transitioning out of foster care to independent living. Until 1999, the ILI limited the funding to foster youth ages 16–18 and focused on teaching the skills necessary for self-sufficiency (such as cooking, opening a bank account, and paying taxes). It did not include funding to address the need for transitional housing for former foster youth. States had the option to continue services after the foster youth aged out, but had to pay for these services with state-only funding. It is and had been clear that simply teaching foster youth some domestic skills did not prepare these youth for living on their own past age 18.

As noted above, in 1999, Congress responded marginally to the mounting evidence and enacted the John H. Chafee Foster Care Independence Act (FCIA).[68] The purpose of the FCIA is to identify children who are likely to remain in foster care until 18 years of age and to help them make the transition to self-sufficiency by providing services beyond the mechanics of the ILI, which may include help to obtain a high school diploma, vocational training, job placement services, substance abuse prevention, preventive health activities (including smoking avoidance, nutrition education, and pregnancy prevention), preparation to enter postsecondary training and education institutions, and personal and emotional support through mentors and the promotion of interactions with dedicated adults. The law also authorizes financial, housing, counseling, employment, education, and other appropriate support and services to former foster care recipients between 18–21 years of age.[69]

FCIA doubled federal funding for independent living programs from $70 million to a still modest $140 million nationally, with a planned increase to $143 million in 2020.[70] FCIA significantly changed independent living services available to foster youth by also imposing a mandate, upon which federal funding is contingent, that states use a portion of FCIA funding to serve current and former foster youth up to age 21. Foster youth qualify under this law for the independent living services outlined above from age 16 until age 21. Updates to the Chafee program as part of the Family First Act include the extension of services to age 23 in states that have opted to extend foster care to age 21. States may use up to 30% of FCIA funding to provide housing assistance to youth who have left foster care and are between the ages 18–21 (or 23 in extended foster care states). Finally, FCIA provided states with the option to extend Medicaid eligibility to former foster youth to age 21. As with other Chafee programs, state laws differ on the age at which Medicaid eligibility ends. However, effective in 2014, the Affordable Care Act provided for Medicaid eligibility of older youth who were in foster care and receiving Medicaid at age 18 or on the date the youth aged out of foster care. Under this law, former foster youth remain eligible for Medicaid until their 26th birthday.

In 2002, amendments added Educational and Training Vouchers (ETV) to the Act.[71] Congress provided $60 million for this program that makes available up to $5,000 per year for former foster youth to help pay for qualifying college or vocational education expenses. As with previous FCIA funding, states must provide a 20% match for these federal funds. Youth who are participating in the ETV program on the date they turn 21 are eligible to continue participation until age 23 if they are enrolled in a postsecondary education program and making satisfactory progress toward completing that program. Importantly, the amount of a voucher may be disregarded for the purposes of determining the recipient's eligibility for, or the amount of, any federal or federally-funded assistance.

At any point in time, about 60,000 former foster youth are between the ages of 18–21. As of 2010, FCIA funding for Independent Living, discussed above, provides $140 million in total funding—with no more than $102 million allocable to post-emancipation help. Adding to this independent living assistance are direct education help (ETV grants of up to $5,000) discussed above. The average *annual* tuition and room/board costs for a public college in the United States in 2018–19 was $21,370 for in-state students; the average amount for out-of-state students was $37,430.[72] A maximum recipient of Chafee grants will receive less than a quarter of the funding necessary to cover tuition and expected living costs. As discussed in Chapter 4, Pell grants are capped at $6,095 per annum in 2018–19.

If a foster youth receives $6,120 in general assistance federal FCIA funding (with its 20% state match)[73] and receives the maximum $5,000 ETV grant for education each year over four years of college, the total public subsidy would total $26,120—or just over half the median amount private parents provide in monies to their children after age 18 (in addition to room and other assistance) to achieve self-sufficiency as adults. Moreover, most of this assistance is in the form of the ETV grants that are received by less than 18% of emancipating foster youth.

Independent Living funding and ETV provide assistance to youth who age out of the system, but the amount shortfall *vis-a-vis* both need and levels extant from private parents underlines the importance of state implementation of the federal Fostering Connections to Success Act after 2011, and state-only funded programs. The latter vary widely but sometimes include transitional housing help and education vouchers for foster youth. However, as discussed above, most suffer from underfunding and from "top down" administration by county-level officials, involving little youth input, no continued court involvement (the parent to point of adulthood) and a setting of what former foster youth describe as rules, applications and intrusive social worker visits.

Importantly, few former foster youth receive even this partial support. While private parents provide a median of just under $50,000 for their children after the age of 18, in addition to housing where needed, or many other forms of support, foster youth average less than one-fourth of this total in typical federal and state financial help, and those sums are skewed to the few able to finish high school and seek higher education.[74] Even for those who gain entrance into a college, as the date above indicate, obstacles to completion—including required, substantial employment while in school, remains a problem. Finally, and perhaps more important, these youth lack the nonfinancial continuing allegiance and safety net that other youth enjoy from their parents.

One proposal to provide reasonable opportunity for those emancipating from foster care is the "Transition Life Coach" (TLC) proposal of the Children's Advocacy Institute. That proposal recognizes the above obstacles and seeks a solution that is personal and not caseload-driven, is flexible, and most replicates what effective parents do for their children to achieve self-sufficiency. Under the TLC model, the median amount that private parents give to their young adult children (approximately $50,000) is put into trust, with the Court, which has been the legal parent of the child while in foster care and has information about him or her, serving as the trustor. The trustee is a person who assists the youth to obtain successful transition, with the name "coach" for these persons selected by a survey of foster children. This person is not a social worker with a caseload, but can be a CASA, relative, or other person who knows the youth and is trained for this parental function. The youth is the beneficiary and formulates a plan for education and employment and living arrangement in consultation with the trustee coach, and it is reviewed by the court. The money funds this plan, monitored and assisted with six-month reviews and changes as needed. It is not formulaic, nor does it involve applications and social workers supervising the youth as part of a large caseload.

The economics of the TLC proposal have been studied, with estimates by an expert economist that it will result in public expense savings that will substantially exceed its cost. The proposal has been theoretically authorized in California with the enactment of a statute giving juvenile dependency courts the authority to create a trust for any child ever in the foster care system to take effect at age 21. Thus far, the plan has not been implemented anywhere in the U.S., although it is hoped that in 2020 a five-year pilot may begin in San Diego County.[75]

h. The Failure to Enforce Federal Floors for Child Protection

Discussed above are many of the requirements of federal law, including the Child Welfare and the Child Abuse Prevention and Treatment Acts. These include the requirements to provide at least a *guardian ad litem* for children in dependency court, the duty to report child abuse deaths and near deaths, the requirement to provide compensation for eight enumerated categories of child costs to foster parents, and numerous other floors. As CAI reports and prior litigation have documented, violation of these floors is not only substantial, but prevalent. CAI's national 2015 report, *Shame on U.S.*, documents those offenses and catalogues the many civil suits by child advocacy organizations, including the renowned national litigator Children's Rights,[76] with court findings of violations.[77] However, the limited resources available to child advocacy legal entities only allows a small percentage of compliance failure to reach the courts. Many violations of federal law are well known to federal authorities who allocate to the states over $9 billion in related federal spending for the protection and sustenance of children endangered by abuse and neglect, as discussed above. Although federal authorities have insisted on compliance in certain limited areas, *e.g.*, child support collection failure where monies go substantially to federal accounts to compensate for TANF expenses, other examples are rare. Where child protection is the primary issue, there has been virtually no enforcement of the stated requirements of federal law.[78] This failure extends over the life of each of the statutes discussed above and includes every administration of both parties.[79]

i. Financing of the Child Welfare System

An overarching child welfare policy issue is the performance of the federal government in the financing of the child welfare system. In addition to the enforcement failures noted above, the Children's Advocacy Institute completed a study of this issue in 2018,[80] excerpts from the Executive Summary include the following:

A White Paper on America's Family Values

The Big Lie of Revenue Neutrality and the Arbitrary Lookback. Congress has been engaged in the big lie of so-called "revenue neutrality" for almost two decades. Promoted by Republicans, the doctrine falsely posits that keeping the raw numbers the same for child welfare accounts keeps their funding levels neutral. Of course, funding would only remain neutral if there were no inflation or population changes. Failing to adjust for these two essential elements over many years has strangled children's programs across the board, particularly child welfare spending—where the numbers of children and reports increase—as do the number of taxpayers. Although the large IV-E account has kept pace with these two necessary adjustors since 2012, the laudable inclusion of more foster youth from age 18 to 21 from this source should have increased beyond overall population change to accomplish steady per capita spending. That has not happened and per child spending has been in decline. Meanwhile, thirteen other major accounts have declined by 24.8% in the last seven years when properly adjusted for inflation and population changes.

Congress has also found a way to annually reduce the number of children eligible for Title IV-E foster care entitlement funding—the only existing federal entitlement in the child welfare arena, and which is supposed to represent a commitment to the children legally parented by the state. Even more reprehensible than the big lie of neutrality is the so-called "lookback" provision, which provides that any child removed from a home where the family income is above the poverty line as it existed in 1996 ($12,980 for a mother and two children) is not eligible to receive federal assistance for his/her basic foster care costs. Currently, more than half of the children brought into foster care receive no federal match for basic foster care—and the number and percentage of ineligible children increases each year. This results in increasing burdens and stresses for state budgets.

Other Critical Failures. Other critical failures of our current child welfare system include the following:

- the failure to meaningfully address actual underlying causes, instead of defining prevention as social worker attention to families post-abuse report;
- outrageous policies and practices even beyond the neutrality and lookback scandals, including allowing states and counties to embezzle Social Security benefits directed at foster care beneficiaries; and barring any child from federal foster care benefits if he/she has more than $10,000 in total assets and barring SSI benefits for any child with over $2,000 in total assets;
- the absence of evidence-based tests for major foster care programs, notwithstanding the addition of some now required by the 2018 enacted Family First statute;

- the failure of most states to provide appropriate reimbursements to family foster homes, with resulting diminution of supply;
- the inattention paid to the consequences of not removing a child, such as deaths and near deaths; and
- the writing off of youth aging out of foster care at 18 or 21. These youth should receive help and support to at least age 26—the median age of self-sufficiency for American youth.

* * *

Federal Child Welfare Financing Reform Proposals. Our recommendations for reforming the federal child welfare financing system include the following:

- Adjust the term revenue neutral to its proper definition and end the lookback. Require evidence-based and funded evaluation with sunset specifications.

- Achieve permanence through a federal incentive that provides an enhanced federal match for the Adoption Assistance and Kinship Guardianship programs. This new formula should add 15% to the current ratio applicable to each state for payments made to children who have achieved permanence.
- Adopt additional statutory changes, such as:

  * ending the irrational impediments that undermine the ability of young adults to attain self-sufficiency after leaving foster care;
  * unifying federal child welfare laws to create a comprehensive and cohesive framework that provides clear direction to DHHS and states, mandates robust oversight and enforcement by DHHS to ensure state compliance, requires Congressional monitoring of DHHS performance, and imposes consequences on DHHS for failing to engage in oversight and enforcement;
  * explicitly providing clear private remedies to allow the enforcement of all child welfare statutory mandates by the child beneficiaries;
  * cross-referencing all CAPTA and other child welfare statutory provisions to the Child Welfare Act so the full panoply of federal funding stands behind those requirements;
  * requiring the appointment of attorney GALs for every foster child, consistent with the caseload standard set forth in *Kenny A. v. Perdue*, in addition to the appointment of court appointed special advocates and requiring reasonable juvenile court caseloads, given their role as the legal parents of these children;
  * addressing the underlying causes of child abuse and neglect, including unplanned children, the collapse of marital commitment, and financial and other abandonment by many fathers, including studies that educate public officials and the body politic of correlations and of possible incentivizing policies for child welfare;
  * addressing child poverty and enacting the conservative and prudent recommendations to that end by the Children's Defense Fund;
  * expending meaningful resources on preventing and treating alcohol and drug abuse—particularly meth addiction—closely and increasingly related to serious child abuse; and
  * acknowledging the need for and subsidizing parenting education in high schools so future parents will understand what children need, how to keep them safe and healthy, and the financial commitment required to provide for them.
- Fully fund all federal child welfare programs at levels commensurate with the full and effective implementation of each provision.

* * *

...These children are the legal children of the state—governed by both parties. Our nation's performance to date in protecting them from abuse and neglect, ensuring their well-being while in state custody and managing their transition to self-sufficiency as adults—will determine their respective legacies, and ours.

j. Affirmative Obstacles to Foster Youth Self-Sufficiency

A final major public child welfare policy issue extends from the problematical foster care youth investment above—namely, the public policies that affirmatively undermine foster youth opportunity. Child advocates contend that the nonfeasance of abandonment is exacerbated by policies of confiscation and particularized barriers for new foster youth adults, including those discussed in a March 2011 report issued by the Children's Advocacy Institute and First Star. In summary, that report documented:[81]

The Fleecing of Foster Children

Diversion of Foster Children's OASDI/SSI Benefits. Thousands of children in foster care are eligible for benefits from the Old Age, Survivors and Disability Insurance Benefits program (OASDI) and/or the Supplemental Security Income for Aged, Blind and Disabled (SSI) program. Generally a child entitled to such benefits is required to have a "representative payee" appointed by the Social Security Administration (SSA) to manage his or her funds, and to ensure that the funds are used to serve the best interests of the child beneficiary. A duly appointed representative payee has a "fiduciary duty" (a duty of loyalty and fidelity) to that beneficiary.

For most child beneficiaries, SSA appoints the child's parent or guardian to serve as representative payee. However, for foster children, that is often not possible or appropriate. In such cases, SSA is required to identify and select the representative payee who will best serve the child's interests, using preference lists contained in federal regulations. Although the lists provide guidelines that are meant to be flexible, foster care agencies are ranked last in order of preference. However, in many jurisdictions, the assignment of the responsible child welfare agency as representative payee for a foster child is practically automatic....

Regrettably, most of those agencies then routinely confiscate foster children's SSI and OASDI money to pay the state share of foster care costs. The vast majority of states openly admit to—and actually defend—taking and using foster children's Social Security benefits to pay for child welfare services that these children are entitled to receive as a matter of right. Although *Washington State Dep't of Social and Health Services v. Keffeler* held that [such a confiscation] did not violate the Social Security Act's anti-attachment provision...,[it] *did not excuse foster care agencies serving as representative payees from their affirmative fiduciary duties to ensure that such use best serves the unique interests of each child beneficiary*—a determination that must be made on an individualized, case-by-case basis following a meaningful examination of each child's circumstances, special needs, age, etc.

Failure to Notify the Foster Child's Attorney/GAL that an Agency Has Applied to be or was Apointed as the Child's Representative Payee. Further, children usually have no idea that states have even applied for benefits on their behalf, let alone that the states are confiscating the funds. Before it selects a representative payee, SSA is required to notify the beneficiary and give the beneficiary an opportunity to appeal SSA's decision. Because of their age, foster children are typically not notified directly about the impending appointment, nor are most of them even told they are eligible for (or receiving) benefits.

Instead, for most foster youth, SSA provides notice solely to the child's legal guardian or legal representative—and this is often the same state or county agency that is applying to be the child's representative payee in the first place. Current federal law does not require the foster care agency to notify the child, the child's attorney/guardian ad litem (GAL) or the juvenile court (which is ultimately responsible for the child's well being) that it has applied to be or has been appointed as a foster child's representative payee. Without notification, the child, the child's attorney/GAL and the juvenile court

have no opportunity to notify SSA that there is a parent, relative, family friend, or other person in the child's life who might be a more appropriate choice. The result is a rather clandestine process in which the foster care agency applies to be representative payee, is appointed, and uses a child's benefits to benefit itself. Many youth leave foster care unaware that they had been receiving benefits—and for those receiving SSI, they leave care unprepared for the cumbersome redetermination process that awaits them.

Failure to Screen Foster Children for OASDI / SSI Eligibility and to Provide Assistance in Applying for Benefits. Unfortunately, foster children are not accessing all the government programs available to them while they are in care or after they age out of care. Among 25 states responding to a recent survey of state child welfare agencies, 7 indicated that SSI eligibility screening was not routine. This is particularly troubling because these are youth who, through no fault of their own and by institutional design, have only the government to act as their safety net.

Asset and Resource Caps: Limiting How Much Money Foster Youth Can Save for the Future. Most parents encourage their kids to save money that comes their way, perhaps from part-time employment, bequests, gifts, etc. Saving for the future is a basic value that all responsible parents imbue in their children. However, those who are eligible SSI benefits because of a qualifying disability are not allowed to accumulate resources that exceed $2,000—a figure that has been in place since 1989 and is not indexed for inflation. While the SSI cap applies to all SSI beneficiaries, not just foster kids, its impact is arguably more severe for children who lack a familial support system and will be expected to support themselves....

Further, many foster youth will need to rely temporarily on programs such as Temporary Assistance for Needy Families, Medicaid, and Supplemental Nutrition Assistance Program (Food Stamps) for support after they age out of foster care. In many states, they will be disqualified for some or all of these programs if their assets exceed certain levels—a disincentive to foster youth to save for their future....

Failure to Provide Dedicated Accounts to Hold Benefits for Each Youth. Where a representative payee lives with the child, that payee has firsthand knowledge of the long- and short-term needs of the child, and knows how the child's funds are being used to meet those needs. However, when governments act as representative payee for foster children, benefits are frequently dumped into an account and billed for services by someone who often has not met the child and has no direct knowledge of the best interest needs of the child. SSA's Office of the Inspector General (OIG) has found that oversight mechanisms are often not in place to ensure that a foster child's benefits are spent on that specific child and that unspent money is were saved for the child's use at a later date....

Failure to Require States to Check into Foster Youths' Credit Records and Repair Credit History Where Necessary. Identity theft is a common problem in the foster care system. Parents, grandparents, family members, foster parents, social workers, group home personnel and many others regularly have access to a foster youth's Social Security number and other personal information. Too often, this access is abused for everything from opening credit cards to fraudulently providing identification for criminal matters. Many foster youth do not learn that their identities have been stolen and their credit destroyed until they have exited care and apply for credit.

Identity theft can have devastating consequences. Former foster youth may face problems finding safe and adequate housing; they may be denied loans for cars and other larger necessities, and they may be denied financial aid and the opportunity to attend college, all as a result of identity theft that occurred while they were in foster care. Complicating the problem is the reality that repairing credit problems caused by identity theft can be a complex, expensive, and time consuming process.

Failure to Pass Conserved Funds—When They Do Exist—to the Youth.... Until very recently, when a representative payee who had conserved funds for a foster youth stopped serving as payee, the payee was required to return the conserved funds and any interest earned to SSA, which would then reissue the funds to the youth. The unfortunate result was a delay between when the youth left the system and when the youth received his/her own funds. Given the lack of a familial safety net, and the limited resources most foster youth have when they age out of the system, the delay had a very real potential for disastrous consequences.

Although SSA's Program Operations Manual System now specifies that the SSA may permit a former payee to transfer conserved funds directly to a new payee or to a capable beneficiary, it is not clear how a payee should proceed with requesting a direct transfer of funds to a beneficiary....

Slashing of State and County Social Services Budgets. Most of the problems discussed above are exacerbated by the fact that state and county social services budgets have been reduced over the last several years,... [leading to consideration of all options to raising revenue—even where in violation of a fiduciary role].

One notable federal policy regarding foster children unduly exacerbates the financial woes of states and counties. Eligibility for federal reimbursement of foster care benefits through Title IV-E funding is linked to the Aid to Families with Dependent

Children (AFDC) income requirements as they existed in 1996—with no adjustment to reflect inflation over the many years since. If a child does not meet the 1996 eligibility criteria, federal Title IV-E funds are not available to reimburse the state. According to one source, 53% of children in foster care were eligible for federal support in 1998, but by 2005 the percentage had declined to 46%—and the number was projected to decline by approximately 5,000 children each year thereafter. As long as the federal eligibility remains linked to the 1996 AFDC income requirements, the financial burden on states and counties will continue to grow...[with consequences for those who lack political power and public visibility].

4. The Special Problem of Child Sexual Abuse

a. Protection Difficulties

Sexual abuse of children presents special enforcement and prosecutorial problems. Such abuse usually involves a betrayal of trust by persons on whom a child relies. It does not occur in public. It may not leave unambiguous physical evidence. It involves an area of human function steeped in understandable privacy. It is often not reported, or not immediately disclosed by a victim, due to what is termed the "Child Sexual Abuse Accommodation Syndrome," which can be stimulated by threats from a perpetrator and/or by the underlying dependent position of the child, as well as the possibly embarrassing nature of the events. The syndrome also frequently produces common "retractions" of sexual abuse disclosures, even in cases where abuse is well documented from other evidence. Expert testimony as to the "syndrome" is normally not permitted to buttress the credibility of a child witness, unless the defense opens the door by challenging the failure of the child to report clearly and expeditiously, or raising statements of retraction.

Where children themselves report offenses, they are sometimes not believed. Tragically, they are often not believed by the other adult protectors of the child with a relationship to the offender. The most common such scenario is a mother's defense of a husband or boyfriend implicated in such an offense, even where the evidence may be substantial. That posture makes detection more difficult and subjects the child to the possible additional trauma of removal from the home due to that parent's "failure to protect" the child. The end result may be the loss of contact with the only parent a child victim has known and trusted.

Children suffer from the format and timing of societal response to alleged sexual offenses against them. First, the state may not only pursue a civil case to remove a child, but also a criminal prosecution against the suspected offender. The criminal case usually precedes the final civil determination but requires the high "proof beyond a reasonable doubt" burden of proof. An acquittal or plea to a lesser charge may have an impact on the civil dependency court proceedings. The criminal nature of such a prosecution also invokes due process rights of the accused, including the appointment of counsel, discovery rights, and cross examination. Although often assigned an attorney for the dependency court proceeding, children as victims or witnesses are not assured appointment of counsel on that basis or for those purposes.

The confluence of a criminal and civil case together thus raises problems for affected children. One such problem is the sequential interviews of a child by a relative, physician, police officer, Child Protective Service social worker, DA investigator, assigned attorney, attorney investigator, therapist, and others. These interviews may cause a child to relive a molestation or other offense repeatedly. In addition, they produce interview summaries that necessarily vary given the different styles of interviewing, and are subject to discovery. Such early questioning may include interviewers insensitive to the misleading consequences of excessive suggestion, thus weakening a meritorious case. To address this problem, some jurisdictions have instituted a "single interview" multi-disciplinary videotape technique. It provides for a single interview as early as possible by a trained professional in a child-friendly room, on videotape, and observed by a multidisciplinary group behind one-way mirrors. The child must talk about the events once, with others able to suggest to the interviewer questions they need answered, and with a videotape recording the nature of the questions and the answers, including precise tone and body language.[82] This format has enhanced the reliability and credibility of child victims, and reduces the number of sequential interviews.

Other problems for child victims attending the child sexual abuse civil/ criminal trials are discussed in Chapter 9 below, and include the difficulty in testifying against a powerful adult in his or her close physical proximity, particularly if prior threats have been made to the child and the allowance of one-way or two-way testimony by videotape;[83] the attempted discovery of psychological counseling records (even those occurring post-arrest) by defense counsel and involving the conflict between psychotherapist-patient confidentiality, and the due process rights of a criminal defendant to discovery; and the challenged credibility of child witnesses based on an alleged "False Memory Syndrome" or possible manipulation by biased adults.

b. Civil Commitment of Offenders

Reporting of sex crimes is notoriously low, making it difficult to measure the recidivism rates of sexual offenders. However, research indicates that among sex offenders, child molesters—particularly those who offend against boys—have the highest rates of recidivism.[84] The rights of child sexual molestation victims may be affected by the ability of the state to civilly commit such persons, or to track their presence and activities post-release. Some states have enacted statutes to accomplish such treatment/child protection on a civil basis. The Kansas Sexually Violent Predator Act provides for such commitment where a court finds that a "mental abnormality" makes a respondent "likely to engage" in future violent sexual predation. The statute covers those convicted of violent sexual offenses and awaiting release, those found so mentally defective they are incompetent to stand trial and those found not guilty by reason of a mental defect or disease. The Act was upheld in *Kansas v. Hendricks*, 521 U.S. 346 (1997).[85]

c. Sex Offender Registries

Many states require persons convicted of certain sexual offenses to register as "Mentally Disordered Sex Offenders" after their release, and even after their period of parole has expired. Such registration allows further monitoring of the location of such persons for public protection. The states providing for such registration increased substantially in number, and public notice of the location of such persons was added, following the brutal rape and murder of seven-year-old Megan Kanka in 1994 by a neighbor who, unknown to the Kankas, had two prior child sex-related convictions. Within two years most states had enacted "Megan's Law" statutes requiring registration with local police departments by persons previously convicted of criminal child-sexual offenses, and community notification of their presence and respective names and addresses—to theoretically allow parental safeguards. During 1994, Congress enacted the Jacob Wetterling Crimes Against Children and Sexually Violent Offender Registration Act[86] that financially sanctioned states (through a reduction in federal law enforcement assistance funding) where they failed to create a sex offender registration program. The Act was amended in 1996 to require an additional notification element for full federal funding, and most states now include both elements in their statutes, with some posting the information on the Internet.

In 2006, Congress passed the Adam Walsh Act, Title I of which is the Sex Offender Registration and Notification Act (SORNA). SORNA established minimum standards for sex offender registration and notification. States have struggled to comply with SORNA requirements, citing excessive costs, and in some states judicial opposition. A particularly challenging aspect of SORNA involves its requirement to have juvenile offenders register. Some states argue that this is incongruous with the trend of recognizing the adolescent's capacity for change and rehabilitation, and some jurisdictions have found courts unwilling to allow such registration. As technology develops, states have also had to consider how to regulate sex offenders' use of social media. Legislation in a number of states limits offender access. However, the U.S. Supreme Court in *Packingham v. North Carolina,* 137 S. Ct. 1730 (2017), considered a North Carolina law making it a felony for a registered sex offender to access social media where minors can create profiles. The Court ruled that the statute violated the free speech rights of sex offenders. The Court found the particular provision too broad, but left the door open for more narrowly-tailored laws.

d. Child Pornography

Child pornography is defined as "the possession, trade, advertising, and production of images that depict the sexual abuse of children."[87] In *New York v. Ferber,* 458 U.S. 747 (1982), the Court upheld the criminal conviction of a bookstore owner who sold films to an undercover officer of young boys masturbating. The holding rejected the proffered First Amendment defense, finding that apart from the issue of expression and viewing, depictions of the sexual activity of children was itself a form of child abuse as to those performing.[88] After *Ferber* and reflecting its holding, Congress expanded its 1977 Act in 1984 to criminalize the transportation across state lines of material depicting sexual activity by children even if not obscene and with or without profit motive. In 1986, Congress expanded the child sexual activity prohibition to include not merely transport or receipt across state lines, but production and advertising even if intra-state. It also created a civil remedy allowing private enforcement where personal injury occurs.[89]

The Supreme Court upheld the criminalization of private possession and viewing of non-obscene child pornography in the home and without any commercial intent—reflecting a generous reach as a "compelling state interest" of the *Ferber* protection for underage performers (*Osborne v. Ohio*, 495 U.S. 103 (1990)). The Court implicitly recognized the market incentive such possession provides for child sexual exploitation. In addition, many states enacted photo processor reporting statutes, requiring the reporting of child sexual activities on film given to processors for developing, and providing civil immunity for such reports where filed in good faith.

In 1996, Congress passed the Mandatory Restitution Provision, providing for restitution for victims in addition to any civil or criminal penalty.[90] In *Paroline v. United States*, 572 U.S. 434 (2014), the U.S. Supreme Court considered whether possessors of child pornography can be liable for restitution to those victimized under the provision, and if so, to what extent. The Court recognized that "every viewing of child pornography is a repetition of the victim's abuse," and held that restitution from possessors was proper. However, the Court concluded that individual defendants can only be liable to the extent to which they were a proximate cause of the victim's losses. The Court did not provide a formula for determining how that amount should be calculated, and the result has been that victims must pursue individual cases against individual possessors of the pornography in order to receive full restitution. Advocates argue that this was not Congress' intent and have urged Congress to amend the statute to establish a minimum amount of restitution to which victims are entitled in individual actions against possessors of their image. In 2018, Congress passed the "Amy, Vicky, and Andy Child Pornography Victim Assistance Act of 2018," which provided a fix to the issue of restitution, providing that victims receive a minimum of $3,000 from each defendant and are entitled to a one-time payment of $35,000 from the existing Crime Victims Fund. The bill also provided for victims to have access to the images in which they are depicted, in order to aid in victim identification, expert testimony, forensic review, and treatment.

The *Ferber* analysis and its related federal legislation leave open the possibility of First Amendment protection for "artificial" child pornography (*e.g.*, explicit sexual acts by persons who appear to be minors but who are in fact 18 years of age or older, or computer-generated images of young children). This technological advance has combined with the rapid growth of pornography sites on the Internet, a situs allowing intrusive entry of easily accessible or unsolicited pornography into homes with uncertain parental ability to block or oversee. In 1996, Congress enacted the Child Pornography Prevention Act[91] to extend the reach of prohibition beyond the use of underage performers condemned in *Ferber* and focusing upon the prurient effect on viewers. It prohibits "any visual depiction" (computer-generated or actors over 18 years of age who appear younger) where the appearance is created of a minor engaging in "sexually explicit conduct."[92]

However, on April 16, 2002, the Supreme Court decided *Ashcroft v. Free Speech Coalition*, 535 U.S. 234 (2002), a 7–2 decision invalidating the Child Pornography Act of 1996 as overly broad and violative of the First Amendment. The fact that the prohibition reached sexual acts by persons who were not children and extended beyond the definition of "obscenity" allegedly prohibited by separate statute[93] was determinative. The *Ferber* Court had upheld the 1984 prohibition as addressing images where the "creation of the speech is itself the crime of child abuse." The 1996 Act's prohibition is based on the content of the communication. The images may be (and increasingly are) altered photos of persons over 18 or are entirely computer-generated.[94] The Court noted that the 1996 Act's prohibition would apply to a picture in a psychology manual, or in a movie depicting the horrors of child sexual abuse; it could apply to a modern movie adaptation of Shakespeare's Romeo and Juliet, involving love between young teens, and might reach award-winning movies such as Traffic and American Beauty.[95] The Court noted that one section of the law prohibits advertising or promotion that vaguely "conveys the impression" that the product includes children engaging in sex. And the Court also found objectionable the alleged broad liability imposed by the law to "knowing" reproduction, distribution, sale, reception, or possession of such materials, which compounds its vagueness.

The Court's holding did not grant dispensation for child pornography, reiterating support of the separate federal obscenity statute which requires that the "work taken as a whole, appeals to the prurient interest, is patently offensive in light of community standards, and lacks serious literary, artistic, political, or scientific value."[96]

Questions for Discussion

1. The Court acknowledges the compelling state interest in preventing child sexual abuse. It finds the Government's evidence of connection between the prohibited depictions and child abuse incidence to be weak. Would the 1996 Act withstand scrutiny if the Government produced an evidentiary record indicating a strong correlation between the depiction of children engaged in sex and child molestation incidence?

2. If the law were to be rewritten to prohibit only the depiction of children appearing to be under the age of twelve engaged in sex acts, would the Court approve of that narrower category? If not, would it approve of a rebuttable presumption that depiction of children engaged in sex acts was obscene, allowing a defendant to then demonstrate that the three elements of "obscenity" listed above did not apply? Would it approve such a presumption shift where the objectionable depiction appeared to be children under the age of twelve? Under the age of six? Where the sex depicted also included violence?

3. Would the Court approve a similar statute but more narrowly prohibiting the viewing of child sexual depictions by children? A ban on depiction to persons without prior consent?

e. Commercially Sexually Exploited Children

The Commercial Sexual Exploitation of Children (CSEC) occurs in various forms, all involving the sexual abuse or exploitation of children for the financial benefit of a person or in exchange for something of value. This includes situations in which a child engages in sexual activity in exchange for non-monetary things such as food, housing, drugs, or protection, often referred to as "survival sex." The prevalence of CSEC is difficult to quantify, as these crimes against children are severely underreported and identifying victims is difficult for law enforcement, social services, and other typical mandated reporters. However, estimates are that a minimum of 100,000 children nationally are sexually exploited annually. Recent studies undertaken in local jurisdictions provide greater definition of the problem. In San Diego County, sex trafficking is estimated to be an $810 million dollar economy, largely promoted by local gangs.[97] In numerous locales, the vast majority of exploited children are found to have prior involvement with the child welfare system, with most having been subject to foster care placement, especially within group home facilities.[98] Exploiters commonly seek out children in placement, initially offering youth food, shelter, clothes, affection, and a sense of belonging. Exploiters find that these youth may be particularly vulnerable given their history of trauma and neglect and their lack of connection to a stable family. The National Center for Missing and Exploited Children found that in 2016, one in six endangered runaways reported were likely sex trafficking victims and 86% of these children were in the care of the child welfare system when they went missing.[99]

Internationally, minors who engage in sexual acts for compensation are formally designated as victims (see Chapter 14 for applicable conventions and more detailed discussion of child sex trafficking). Domestically, federal law also defines individuals under 18 years of age who engage in sex for compensation as victims. However, states have traditionally treated such youth as criminals, funneling them into the delinquency system. Law enforcement has historically supported the arrest, jailing, and prosecution of "child prostitutes" rather than responding to them as victims. The rationale is two-fold. First, the difficulty in prosecuting the adults who profit requires testimony from the victimized minors. The prosecution is viewed as necessary to provide pressure for youth to "roll over" on the more culpable adults. Second, many victimized youth have a significant emotional and pragmatic reliance upon their pimps. Exploited children are extremely likely to return to their exploiter. Treating the child solely as a victim removes the basis under which the court can control the youth, namely locking the child up, in order to maintain separation between her and those who victimize her.

Despite these concerns, a significant shift has taken place over the past decade. Researchers and advocates had long argued that a punitive approach to the issue of exploited children, particularly the locking up of youth, was counterproductive because it delays provision of necessary services and reduces the victim's willingness to participate in efforts to leave "the life." Instead, victim-centered services facilitated through a multidisciplinary approach held greater promise in preventing a return of a victim to her exploiter. Accordingly, by the end of 2015, two-thirds of states had passed some type of legislation to recognize and respond to these youth as victims rather than criminals. The scope of these "Safe Harbor" laws differ among states, however. Some ensure that youth are not prosecuted for prostitution, but do not address protection or services. Other states still allow arrest, while creating an opportunity for diversion to social services for arrested youth—sometimes mandatory, yet sometimes at the discretion of authorities. Other states have embraced both decriminalization as well as directed the development of targeted policy and programming to serve child victims. In California, home to three of the FBI's thirteen high intensity CSEC locales, decriminalization legislation passed in 2016. This followed legislation passed in 2014 dedicating funding to county child welfare departments to develop protocols to identify and respond to child victims of exploitation.

Courts have recognized and responded to this legislative trend. In 2010, the Texas Supreme Court considered the issue, ruling that a child below the legal age of consent—age fourteen in Texas—cannot be found guilty of prostitution. The court in *In re B.W.*, 313 S.W.3d 818 (2010), determined that because these children cannot lawfully consent to sex, they cannot "knowingly" engage in sexual conduct. Analogizing this situation to other circumstances in which age limitations are placed on the ability to consent—marriage and contracting—the court concluded that the Legislature made it clear that the child's consent to sex is void rather than voidable. The court also squarely addressed concerns that decriminalizing prostitution for youth under fourteen would hamper efforts to protect and treat these children by pointing out the responsibility of the child protection system and its ability to provide services in a purely rehabilitative setting.

Following the passage of safe harbor legislation, local juvenile courts have also had to rethink the approach to CSEC. Some jurisdictions, such as Los Angeles, Sacramento, and San Diego, have developed specialized courts utilizing a collaborative model. Thus far, most of these specialized courts remain in the delinquency arena, despite decriminalization. Some of these youth may be eligible for dependency court status, but dependency courts focus on the fitness of parents and its adjudication. There is a third option increasingly being entertained—not treating such youth as criminal offenders or as dependents, but creating a civil "status offense" category as "persons in need of supervision" (PINS). That option involves enforced isolation from the adults profiting from the criminal enterprise, treatment, and the offering of alternatives.

The greater focus for prosecutors in light of the trend of decriminalization is now to address demand and facilitation—"johns" and "pimps." Federal law makes trafficking of individuals a crime with severe penalties, as well as clarifies that buyers who solicit sex with a child are committing sex trafficking. Federal statutes also provide a federal civil right of action for victims to sue their traffickers. Advocates encourage states to ensure that statutes identify CSEC as a distinct offense from general sex offenses, utilize high penalties—like those in federal law—for buyers and traffickers including asset forfeiture and registration as sex offenders, and specify that use of the Internet or electronic communications to lure, entice, recruit or sell sex with a minor triggers an enhanced penalty.[100]

D. REPORTING CHILD ABUSE

People v. Stritzinger
34 Cal. 3d 505 (1983)

OPINION **Mosk, J**—Defendant appeals from a judgment convicting him of multiple counts of child molestation. He contends that certain evidentiary rulings at his trial violated his psychotherapist-patient privilege and his right to confrontation. As will appear, we conclude that both points are well taken and compel reversal of the judgment.

During a 15-month period ending May 1981 defendant allegedly engaged in various acts of fondling, mutual masturbation, and oral copulation with his stepdaughter Sarah.[1] When Sarah's mother—defendant's wife—learned of these activities she arranged for her daughter and her husband each to see Dr. Walker, a licensed clinical psychologist. During Sarah's counseling session on July 28, 1981, she revealed that she had engaged in sexual activity with her stepfather. Dr. Walker reported the conversation to the child welfare agency that same afternoon.[2] The agency in turn relayed the information to the sheriff's office.

The next day Deputy Buttell of the sheriff's office telephoned Dr. Walker to investigate the child abuse report. Dr. Walker told Buttell that he had seen Sarah the day before, and related the substance of her discussion of sexual relations with her stepfather. He also informed Buttell that he was scheduled to meet with defendant himself later that afternoon, July 29, and with Sarah's older sister two days later, July 31. The deputy asked the doctor to call back after his session with Sarah's sister because he was concerned that she might also be the victim of child abuse. However, he hesitated on the issue of defendant's communications, acknowledging there might be a "confidentiality" problem. This telephone conversation was tape recorded.

Defendant saw Dr. Walker as scheduled, and during his conversation with the psychotherapist discussed his sexual relations with Sarah. Deputy Buttell telephoned the doctor again the next day, July 30, to inquire further about the reported child abuse. When Dr. Walker expressed reservations about disclosing defendant's confidential communications, Buttell read him Penal Code section 11171, subdivision (b), part of the Child Abuse Reporting Act, which he described as providing an applicable exception to the psychotherapist-patient privilege. The doctor then recounted the substance of defendant's session of July 29. This telephone conversation was also tape recorded, and a written report summarizing the conversation was prepared.

At the opening of trial defendant moved that Dr. Walker's testimony be excluded on the basis of the psychotherapist-patient privilege. (Evid. Code, § 1014.) The court held that Penal Code section 11171, subdivision (b), provides an applicable exception to the privilege and ruled the testimony admissible.

* * *

Defendant was convicted of one count of lewd and lascivious conduct with a minor, a felony, in violation of Penal Code section 288a, subdivision (b)(2); one count of misdemeanor child molestation, a necessarily included lesser offense under this section, based on an act of oral copulation; and seven counts of misdemeanor child molestation in violation of Penal Code section 647a. The verdict on one of the latter counts was set aside on defendant's motion to dismiss. Defendant was sentenced to three year's probation with ninety days in the county jail.

I

The Psychotherapist-Patient Privilege and the Child Abuse Reporting Act.

Defendant first contends that Dr. Walker's testimony regarding the consultation of July 29 was erroneously admitted at trial in violation of the psychotherapist-patient privilege, a relationship subsumed in the right to privacy and defined by statutory provision. On the facts of this case, we agree that the doctor's testimony should have been excluded.

Evidence Code section 1014 provides in part that "the patient, whether or not a party, has a privilege to refuse to disclose, and to prevent another from disclosing, a confidential communication between patient and psychotherapist...." We acknowledged in *In re Lifschutz* (1970) 2 Cal.3d 415, 421..., "the growing importance of the psychiatric profession in our modern, ultracomplex society." Thus for reasons of policy the psychotherapist-patient privilege has been broadly construed in favor of the patient.... Confidential communications between psychotherapist and patient are protected in order to encourage those who may pose a threat to themselves or to others, because of some mental or emotional disturbance, to seek professional assistance....

The psychotherapist-patient privilege has been recognized as an aspect of the patient's constitutional right to privacy. (Cal. Const., art. I, § 1; *In re Lifschutz supra*, 2 Cal.3d at pp. 431–432, citing *Griswold v. Connecticut* (1965) 381 U.S. 479, 484....

* * *

To determine whether the psychotherapist-patient privilege embraced by the right to privacy has impermissibly been violated, we begin by considering the state's competing interest. Here that interest is the detection and prevention of child abuse, and is expressed in the recently enacted Child Abuse Reporting Act. (Pen. Code, § 11165 et seq.) Section 11166, subdivision (a), of the act provides in part that "any child care custodian, medical practitioner, nonmedical practitioner, or employee of a child protective agency who has knowledge of or observes a child in his or her professional capacity or within the scope of his or her employment whom he or she knows or reasonably suspects has been the victim of child abuse shall report the known or suspected instance of child abuse to a child protective agency immediately or as soon as practically possible by telephone and shall prepare and send a written report thereof within 36 hours of receiving the information concerning the incident." Section 11165 of the act provides the following: subdivision (g) defines "child abuse" to include "the sexual assault of a child..."; subdivision (i) defines "medical practitioner" to include licensed psychiatrists and psychologists...

Together these provisions impose on psychotherapists the affirmative duty to report to a child protective agency all known and suspected instances of child abuse. Lest there be any doubt that the Legislature intended the child abuse reporting obligation to take precedence over the physician-patient or psychotherapist-patient privilege, section 11171, subdivision (b), explicitly provides an exception to these very privileges: "Neither the physician-patient privilege nor the psychotherapist-patient privilege applies to information reported pursuant to this article in any court proceeding or administrative hearing."...

Defendant neither challenges the constitutionality of the child-abuse reporting exception to the psychotherapist-patient privilege, nor argues that the state's interest in protecting children is less than compelling. Rather, he contends that on the particular facts of his case the exception provided in Penal Code section 11171, subdivision (b), was unnecessarily and therefore erroneously applied to his confidential communications with Dr. Walker. We agree.

* * *

Dr. Walker was under no statutory obligation to make a second report concerning the same activity. Had he learned from defendant of possible further child abuse—whether additional incidents involving Sarah, or other incidents with another child—he

would, of course, have been required to report these new suspicions. Or, if Dr. Walker had first learned of the fondling incidents from defendant himself, he would have been bound to report that information as provided in the act. However, on the facts of this case, we conclude that Dr. Walker satisfied his statutory reporting obligation when he divulged Sarah's revelations; he was not required to reiterate his suspicion following consultation with defendant.

* * *

[1] Sarah turned 14 on July 13, 1980.

[2] Defendant concedes Evidence Code section 1027 provides an exception to the psychotherapist-patient privilege that allowed Dr. Walker to disclose Sarah's confidential communications. The section provides that "There is no [psychotherapist-patient] privilege under this article if all of the following circumstances exist:

"(a) The patient is a child under the age of 16.
"(b) The psychotherapist has reasonable cause to believe that the patient has been the victim of a crime and that disclosure of the communication is in the best interest of the child."

RICHARDSON, J —I respectfully dissent.

The majority finds prejudicial error was committed in admitting (1) Dr. Walker's testimony regarding defendant's admissions to him that he had sexually abused his stepdaughter Sarah, and (2) Sarah's own preliminary hearing testimony confirming that such abuse had occurred. In my view, both Dr. Walker's and Sarah's testimony were admissible and fully support defendant's conviction of child molestation.

1. *Dr. Walker's Testimony*

The majority concedes that Dr. Walker's initial report regarding his interview with Sarah was not rendered inadmissible by the psychotherapist-patient privilege.... Yet the majority holds that Dr. Walker's supplemental report, discussing his interview with defendant himself, was protected by that privilege. With due respect, this holding is patently incorrect.

The Child Abuse Reporting Act (Pen. Code, § 11165 *et seq.*) unequivocally provides that the psychotherapist-patient privilege shall not apply "to information reported pursuant to" the act....Thus, if Dr. Walker's supplemental report was made "pursuant to" the act's provisions, the report was unprivileged and Dr. Walker was free to testify regarding its contents.

The act's provisions impose on psychotherapists such as Dr. Walker an affirmative duty to report to a child protective agency all known or suspected instances of child abuse, even though they may learn of such incidents through otherwise confidential communications with their patients....

The majority holds that, because Dr. Walker initially reported Sarah's own communications with him regarding defendant's misconduct, Dr. Walker's statutory obligations were somehow satisfied and permanently discharged and, accordingly, the psychotherapist-patient privilege was revived. It is claimed that the privilege thereafter protected any further disclosure regarding the same incidents of sexual abuse.

With deference, I suggest that the majority's interpretation of the Child Abuse Reporting Act is erroneous. Under section 11171, subdivision (b), the privilege is rendered inapplicable to *any* information "reported pursuant to" the act. The provision is not limited merely to information *required* to be reported thereunder. Certainly Dr. Walker was *permitted* (if indeed, not required) to file a supplemental report which *corroborated* the victim's unsubstantiated charges by reporting admissions from the alleged offender himself. How can it reasonably be argued that such a critical follow-up report, confirming what otherwise might be deemed mere fantasy or fabrication by a young child, was not issued "pursuant to" the act? In my view, in order to carry out the act's salutary purposes, such confirmatory reports should be encouraged and the information contained therein made freely available for use in criminal proceedings. I have no doubt whatever that this was the legislative intent underlying section 11171, subdivision (b).

* * *

I would affirm the judgment.

Questions for Discussion

1. Should Dr. Walker be seeing both the defendant and his daughter, particularly after he knows of a conflict of interest? Would Dr. Walker be obligated to report the molestation if only the defendant were his patient and he confessed to

molestation? If the information of molestation only concerned prior events that were not continuing and in Dr. Walker's professional opinion were not likely to reoccur?

2. The court notes that the patient holds the psychotherapist-patient privilege. What would happen if Sara were to tell Dr. Walker that her disclosures to him were privileged and she wanted him to assert that privilege? Should the court recognize such a decision by Sara given her age? What if Sara's mother were loyal to the defendant (or doubted her daughter's allegations) and informed Dr. Walker that, speaking as Sara's parent, the privilege should be asserted?

3. What if a client informs an attorney that not only has he committed a crime, but that he is now in the course of planning and carrying out additional crimes? The "continuing crime exception" limits even the attorney-client privilege. Is this molestation a continuing crime?

4. The California Constitution buttresses the privilege with an explicit "right to privacy," which would possibly apply to the defendant's statements to Dr. Walker during the course of treatment. But the same section (Cal. Const. Art. I, Sec. 1) also confers a "right to safety." Does such a right apply to Sara, who may be facing rape within her own home? Is it a factor which is reflected in the court's decision? Should it be?

5. Is it persuasive that the initial report by Dr. Walker satisfies the statute and the majority implies that further reports may be gratuitous? What if the matter is disregarded by child protective services due to a lack of corroboration? Is confirmation not relevant? Is a mandated reporter excused from reporting if another report has been made by another reporter?

6. What happens if the child receives psychotherapy—with the privilege applied so she is not betrayed by another adult—and the defendant seeks those records to impeach her testimony? What if her disclosures were, in fact, exculpatory and would preclude his conviction—does he have a due process right to that information? Can these competing interests be reconciled through *in camera* review by a court to determine if exculpatory material is present and germane, and with confidentiality otherwise maintained?

Note on Child Protective Services Investigations and *Camreta v. Greene*

Over four million reports of possible abuse are received each year by local child protective service (CPS) agencies, 65% from mandated reporters like Dr. Walker in *Stritzinger* above. The inquiry by the state into such possible endangerment may intrude into deeply personal affairs and implicate the constitutional rights of involved adults. Those rights, including search and seizure limitations of the Fourth Amendment, due process rights, and the fundamental liberty interest of the "right to parent" may affect the investigation. On the other hand, states and some child advocates argue that the constitutional protection against the "state" seeking a possible criminal sanction against an individual is here somewhat different—it is a civil inquiry intended to protect a weak private party from the abuse of a stronger one.

Most courts do not apply the same standards of privacy that would require probable cause warrants or other obstacles to initial inquiry. The exclusionary rule does not typically apply in dependency court proceedings to state intrusions that do violate standards.[101] And the confrontation clause does not strictly apply as it does in criminal cases.[102] Nevertheless, there is often a difficult-to-draw line between protecting a child and parents who may suffer criminal exposure given broad potential application of assault, molestation, and parental neglect criminal prohibitions.

The Ninth Circuit's 2009 decision in *Camreta v. Greene*[103] addresses the status of CPS investigations under constitutional standards. In *Camreta*, a child was removed from class for an interview by CPS based on a report of alleged molestation by her stepfather. She was subjected to an involuntary two hours of questioning, with a peace officer present. The Ninth Circuit, in a controversial decision, held that this removal from class was a Fourth Amendment "seizure" and that it may only occur if there is parental permission or probable cause level court order or warrant.

Child advocacy groups were split on the Circuit holding, with many concerned about the civil liberty implications of removal of children and perhaps coercive (and psychologically harmful) cross-examination by the state. On the other hand, state agencies and many child advocates objected strongly to the two obstacles posited in the decision, noting first that 80% of child abuse offenders are parents, and that even if one parent is not a suspected offender, there is often a pattern of spouses protecting each other. Reliance on parental consent is problematical.

Objectors to the holding note that although a peace officer was present, he did not participate in the questioning, which was controlled by a social worker with a civil child protection mission. Those advocates also argue that the alternative probable cause standard is inappropriate, contending that the proper standard must be the alternative level of "reasonable suspicion." The difference between the two partly involves the degree of reliability of a source. In most probable cause affidavits for search warrants the "snitch" or other source of information is identified and prior information and its reliability are described, as an important element for probable cause qualification. But child abuse occurs in private and is not witnessed by a "reliable informant" with prior police contact, but by a neighbor or a mandated reporter without prior state contact history. Hence, probable cause is often not reached until the child is interviewed, and such a prerequisite to that interview would stymie many inquiries in a catch-22.

In 2011 the U.S. Supreme Court vacated the Ninth Circuit decision in *Camreta*, but then declined to rule beyond that eradication—based on the alleged mootness of the dispute (since the minor is now almost 18). The effect of the U.S. Supreme Court action is that the Fourth Amendment issue in this circumstance remains unresolved.

E. RIGHT TO COUNSEL

1. Parents

Lassiter v. Department of Social Services
452 U.S. 18 (1981)

JUSTICE STEWART delivered the opinion of the Court.

I

In the late spring of 1975, after hearing evidence that the petitioner, Abby Gail Lassiter, had not provided her infant son William with proper medical care, the District Court of Durham County, N.C., adjudicated him a neglected child and transferred him to the custody of the Durham County Department of Social Services, the respondent here. A year later, Ms. Lassiter was charged with first-degree murder, was convicted of second-degree murder, and began a sentence of 25 to 40 years of imprisonment.[1] In 1978 the Department petitioned the court to terminate Ms. Lassiter's parental rights because, the Department alleged, she "has not had any contact with the child since December of 1975" and "has willfully left the child in foster care for more than two consecutive years without showing that substantial progress has been made in correcting the conditions which led to the removal of the child, or without showing a positive response to the diligent efforts of the Department of Social Services to strengthen her relationship to the child, or to make and follow through with constructive planning for the future of the child."

* * *

A

The pre-eminent generalization that emerges from this Court's precedents on an indigent's right to appointed counsel is that such a right has been recognized to exist only where the litigant may lose his physical liberty if he loses the litigation....

* * *

B

The case of *Mathews v. Eldridge*, 424 U.S. 319, 335, propounds three elements to be evaluated in deciding what due process requires, viz., the private interests at stake, the government's interest, and the risk that the procedures used will lead to erroneous decisions. We must balance these elements against each other, and then set their net weight in the scales against the presumption that there is a right to appointed counsel only where the indigent, if he is unsuccessful, may lose his personal freedom.

This Court's decisions have by now made plain beyond the need for multiple citation that a parent's desire for and right to "the companionship, care, custody, and management of his or her children" is an important interest that "undeniably warrants deference and, absent a powerful countervailing interest, protection." *Stanley v. Illinois*, 405 U.S. 645, 651. Here the State has sought not simply to infringe upon that interest, but to end it. If the State prevails, it will have worked a unique kind of deprivation....A parent's interest in the accuracy and justice of the decision to terminate his or her parental status is, therefore, a commanding one.[3]

Since the State has an urgent interest in the welfare of the child, it shares the parent's interest in an accurate and just decision. For this reason, the State may share the indigent parent's interest in the availability of appointed counsel. If, as our adversary system presupposes, accurate and just results are most likely to be obtained through the equal contest of opposed interests, the State's interest in the child's welfare may perhaps best be served by a hearing in which both the parent and the State acting for the child are represented by counsel, without whom the contest of interests may become unwholesomely unequal. North Carolina itself acknowledges as much by providing that where a parent files a written answer to a termination petition, the State must supply a lawyer to represent the child....

The State's interests, however, clearly diverge from the parent's insofar as the State wishes the termination decision to be made as economically as possible and thus wants to avoid both the expense of appointed counsel and the cost of the lengthened proceedings his presence may cause. But though the State's pecuniary interest is legitimate, it is hardly significant enough to overcome private interests as important as those here, particularly in light of the concession in the respondent's brief that the "potential costs of appointed counsel in termination proceedings...is [sic] admittedly de minimis compared to the costs in all criminal actions."

Finally, consideration must be given to the risk that a parent will be erroneously deprived of his or her child because the parent is not represented by counsel...

* * *

Yet the ultimate issues with which a termination hearing deals are not always simple, however commonplace they may be. Expert medical and psychiatric testimony, which few parents are equipped to understand and fewer still to confute, is sometimes presented. The parents are likely to be people with little education, who have had uncommon difficulty in dealing with life, and who are, at the hearing, thrust into a distressing and disorienting situation. That these factors may combine to overwhelm an uncounseled parent is evident from the findings some courts have made....Thus, courts have generally held that the State must appoint counsel for indigent parents at termination proceedings....

C

The dispositive question, which must now be addressed, is whether the three *Eldridge* factors, when weighed against the presumption that there is no right to appointed counsel in the absence of at least a potential deprivation of physical liberty, suffice to rebut that presumption and thus to lead to the conclusion that the Due Process Clause requires the appointment of counsel when a State seeks to terminate an indigent's parental status. To summarize the above discussion of the *Eldridge* factors: the parent's interest is an extremely important one (and may be supplemented by the dangers of criminal liability inherent in some termination proceedings); the State shares with the parent an interest in a correct decision, has a relatively weak pecuniary interest, and, in some but not all cases, has a possibly stronger interest in informal procedures; and the complexity of the proceeding and the incapacity of the uncounseled parent could be, but would not always be, great enough to make the risk of an erroneous deprivation of the parent's rights insupportably high.

* * *

III

Here, as in *Scarpelli*, "[it] is neither possible nor prudent to attempt to formulate a precise and detailed set of guidelines to be followed in determining when the providing of counsel is necessary to meet the applicable due process requirements," since here, as in that case, "[the] facts and circumstances...are susceptible of almost infinite variation...." 411 U.S., at 790. Nevertheless, because child-custody litigation must be concluded as rapidly as is consistent with fairness,[7] we decide today whether the trial judge denied Ms. Lassiter due process of law when he did not appoint counsel for her.

The respondent represents that the petition to terminate Ms. Lassiter's parental rights contained no allegations of neglect or abuse upon which criminal charges could be based, and hence Ms. Lassiter could not well have argued that she required counsel for that reason. The Department of Social Services was represented at the hearing by counsel, but no expert witnesses testified, and the case presented no specially troublesome points of law, either procedural or substantive. While hearsay evidence was no doubt admitted, and while Ms. Lassiter no doubt left incomplete her defense that the Department had not adequately assisted her in rekindling her interest in her son, the weight of the evidence that she had few sparks of such an interest was sufficiently great that the presence of counsel for Ms. Lassiter could not have made a determinative difference. True, a lawyer might have done more with the argument that William should live with Ms. Lassiter's mother—but that argument was quite explicitly made by both Lassiters, and the evidence that the elder Ms. Lassiter had said she could not handle another child, that the social worker's investigation had led to a similar conclusion, and that the grandmother had displayed scant interest in the child once he had been removed from her daughter's custody was, though controverted, sufficiently substantial that the absence of counsel's guidance on this point did not render the proceedings fundamentally unfair.[8] Finally, a court deciding whether due process requires the appointment of counsel need not ignore a parent's plain demonstration that she is not interested in attending a hearing. Here, the trial court had previously found that Ms. Lassiter had expressly declined to appear at the 1975 child custody hearing, Ms. Lassiter had not even bothered to speak to her retained lawyer after being notified of the termination hearing, and the court specifically found that Ms. Lassiter's failure to make an effort to contest the termination proceeding was without cause. In view of all these circumstances, we hold that the trial court did not err in failing to appoint counsel for Ms. Lassiter.

* * *

For the reasons stated in this opinion, the judgment is affirmed.

* * *

[1] The North Carolina Court of Appeals, in reviewing the petitioner's conviction, indicated that the murder occurred during an altercation between Ms. Lassiter, her mother, and the deceased "Defendant's mother told [the deceased] to 'come on.' They began to struggle and deceased fell or was knocked to the floor. Defendant's mother was beating deceased with a broom. While deceased was still on the floor and being beaten with the broom, defendant entered the apartment. She went into the kitchen and got a butcher knife. She took the knife and began stabbing the deceased who was still prostrate. The body of deceased had seven stab wounds...." *State v. Lassiter*, No. 7614SC1054 (June 1, 1977).

After her conviction was affirmed on appeal, Ms. Lassiter sought to attack it collaterally. Among her arguments was that the assistance of her trial counsel had been ineffective because he had failed to "seek to elicit or introduce before the jury the statement made by [Ms. Lassiter's mother,] 'And I did it, I hope she dies.'" Ms. Lassiter's mother had, like Ms. Lassiter, been indicted on a first-degree murder charge; however, the trial court granted the elder Ms. Lassiter's motion for a nonsuit. The North Carolina General Court of Justice, Superior Court Division, denied Ms. Lassiter's motion for collateral relief....

[3] Some parents will have an additional interest to protect. Petitions to terminate parental rights are not uncommonly based on alleged criminal activity. Parents so accused may need legal counsel to guide them in understanding the problems such petitions may create.

[7] According to the respondent's brief, William Lassiter is now living "in a pre-adoptive home with foster parents committed to formal adoption to become his legal parents." He cannot be legally adopted, nor can his status otherwise be finally clarified, until this litigation ends.

[8] Ms. Lassiter's argument here that her mother should have been given custody of William is hardly consistent with her argument in the collateral attack on her murder conviction that she was innocent because her mother was guilty. See n. 1, *supra*.

JUSTICE BLACKMUN, with whom **JUSTICE BRENNAN** and **JUSTICE MARSHALL** join, dissenting.

The Court today denies an indigent mother the representation of counsel in a judicial proceeding initiated by the State of North Carolina to terminate her parental rights with respect to her youngest child. The Court most appropriately recognizes that the mother's interest is a "commanding one,"...and it finds no countervailing state interest of even remotely comparable significance, ...Nonetheless, the Court avoids what seems to me the obvious conclusion that due process requires the presence of counsel for a parent threatened with judicial termination of parental rights, and, instead, revives an ad hoc approach thoroughly discredited nearly 20 years ago in *Gideon v. Wainwright*, 372 U.S. 335 (1963). Because I believe that the unique importance of a parent's interest in the care and custody of his or her child cannot constitutionally be extinguished through formal judicial proceedings without the benefit of counsel, I dissent.

Questions for Discussion

1. What of the child's right to an attorney? Is a state order terminating a parental relationship any less of a constitutional taking for the child than for the parent? Can we assume that the attorney for the county represents the child's interests? Can an attorney for the county appeal or otherwise seek, on behalf of a child, review of a decision by a county official who is also that attorney's client?

2. The dissent believes the parent's right to counsel should be absolute. It is then left with the task of distinguishing *Parham*, where counsel (and hearing) are denied children subject to civil commitment (see Chapter 10). The dissent contends that (a) dependency court proceedings are complex, (b) error is more likely, and (c) the parent is not trained in the law. However, isn't the *Parham* civil commitment process less complex because there is virtually no due process? Is there more or less risk of error where an independent judge takes testimony than where medical professionals and parents make the final judgment (as in *Parham*)? Why would not the County "professionals" exercise the same neutrality in dependency court as the state psychiatrists who are relied on in *Parham*? Is the parent here less articulate than the child in *Parham*—who need not be apprised of the basis for his commitment?

3. The holding of *Lassiter* is that appointed counsel was not required for this parent. However, the case essentially requires the appointment of counsel in most proceedings where the right to parent is at risk. Why? The Court's failure to categorically recognize the right to counsel has led to a lack of uniformity across states regarding when and how counsel is appointed. Although most states—though not all—recognize the parents' right to counsel in termination proceedings through state constitutions, statutes, and case law, a number of states allow trial courts discretion in appointing counsel at earlier proceedings such as at the initial removal.[104]

4. Does the right to counsel in termination proceedings necessarily give rise to the right to *effective* counsel, meaning that a parent has the right to challenge a termination on the basis of ineffective assistance of counsel? Thirty-three states have considered this question and concluded that such a right does exist under a statutory claim of right to counsel. However, two states have found otherwise and the U.S. Supreme Court has declined to resolve the issue. Does not providing an opportunity for a parent to seek relief for ineffective representation render the requirement of counsel "an empty gesture" as noted in *In re Carrington H.*, 483 S.W.3d 507 (2008) (dissenting opinion)?

2. Children

Kenny A. v. Sonny Perdue
356 F. Supp. 2d 1353 (N.D. Ga. 2005)

MARVIN H. SHOOB, Senior Judge:

* * *

In both Fulton and DeKalb Counties, child advocate attorneys are responsible for representing allegedly deprived children in all of these proceedings. Fulton County employs four child advocate attorneys, while DeKalb County employs five.... As of March 2004, there were 1,757 plaintiff foster children in custody in Fulton County and 914 in DeKalb County. This equates to a caseload of 439.2 child clients per attorney in Fulton County, and 182.8 child clients per attorney in DeKalb County. The American

Bar Association, the United States Department of Health and Human Services, and the National Association of Counsel for Children (NACC) have each established standards of practice for lawyers who represent children in abuse and neglect cases. In light of the minimum requirements for effective advocacy set forth in these standards, the NACC recommends that no child advocate attorney should maintain a caseload of over 100 individual child clients at a time.

* * *

The Court concludes that plaintiff foster children have both a statutory and a constitutional right to counsel in all deprivation proceedings, including but not limited to TPR (termination of parental rights) proceedings. The Court further concludes that plaintiffs have presented sufficient evidence to create a genuine issue for trial as to whether they are threatened with irreparable harm because they are receiving, or face a substantial risk of receiving, ineffective assistance of counsel in such proceedings.... [T]he Court rejects County Defendants' argument that only the legislature has the authority to correct this problem. If plaintiffs prove their case at trial, then this Court has not only the authority but the obligation to grant appropriate injunctive relief.

* * *

...[T]he Court concludes that in a deprivation proceeding there is an inherent conflict of interests between the child and his or her parent, guardian, or custodian, which requires appointment of separate counsel for the child pursuant to [state law].... There is no conflict, however, in requiring the appointment of both an attorney and a guardian ad litem for the child. Indeed, the two Code sections expressly require the appointment of both an attorney and a guardian ad litem in cases where the child is not represented by his or her parent, guardian, or custodian....

* * *

III. Constitutional Right to Counsel

Even if there were not a statutory right to counsel for children in deprivation cases and TPR proceedings, the Court concludes that such a right is guaranteed under the Due Process Clause of the Georgia Constitution, Art. I, § 1, P 1. It is well settled that children are afforded protection under the Due Process Clauses of both the United States and Georgia Constitutions and are entitled to constitutionally adequate procedural due process when their liberty or property rights are at stake. *See, e.g., Goss v. Lopez*, 419 U.S. 565 (1975) (lack of adequate procedures used by school in suspending students violated due process); *In re Gault*, 387 U.S. 1 (1967) (holding that minors have due process right to counsel in delinquency proceedings)....The question, therefore, is whether plaintiff foster children have liberty or property interests at stake in deprivation and TPR proceedings, and, if so, what process is due when those interests are threatened.

The Court finds that children have fundamental liberty interests at stake in deprivation and TPR proceedings. These include a child's interest in his or her own safety, health, and well-being, as well as an interest in maintaining the integrity of the family unit and in having a relationship with his or her biological parents. On the one hand, an erroneous decision that a child is not deprived or that parental rights should not be terminated can have a devastating effect on a child, leading to chronic abuse or even death. On the other hand, an erroneous decision that a child is deprived or that parental rights should be terminated can lead to the unnecessary destruction of the child's most important family relationships.

Furthermore, a child's liberty interests continue to be at stake even after the child is placed in state custody. At that point, a "special relationship" is created that gives rise to rights to reasonably safe living conditions and services necessary to ensure protection from physical, psychological, and emotional harm....Thus, a child's fundamental liberty interests are at stake not only in the initial deprivation hearing but also in the series of hearings and review proceedings that occur as part of a deprivation case once a child comes into state custody.

Given the liberty interests at stake, the question becomes what process is constitutionally required to safeguard those interests. To determine what process is due under the Due Process Clause of the Georgia Constitution, Georgia courts apply the three-part federal test enunciated in *Mathews v. Eldridge*, 424 U.S. 319, 334-35 (1976):

[O]ur prior decisions indicate that identification of the specific dictates of due process generally requires consideration of three distinct factors: First, the private interest that will be affected by the official action; second, the risk of an erroneous deprivation of such interest through the procedures used, and the probable value, if any, of additional or substitute procedural safeguards; and finally, the Government's interest, including the function involved and the fiscal and administrative burdens that the additional or substitute procedural requirement would entail.

...Applying the Mathews test to this case, the Court concludes that plaintiff foster children have a right to counsel in deprivation and TPR proceedings under the Due Process Clause of the Georgia Constitution.

...[T]he evidence shows that foster children in state custody are subject to placement in a wide array of different types of foster care placements, including institutional facilities where their physical liberty is greatly restricted. Indeed, plaintiffs have pointed to evidence that foster children are often forced to live in such institutional settings because suitable family foster homes are not available. The Court concludes that the private liberty interests at stake support a due process right to counsel in deprivation and TPR proceedings.

Second, the Court finds that there is a significant risk that erroneous decisions will be made during the course of deprivation and TPR proceedings. As an initial matter, the standards employed by juvenile courts in deprivation and TPR proceedings allow wide room for judicial discretion and thus for subjective determinations....Such "imprecise substantive standards that leave determinations unusually open to the subjective values of the judge" serve "to magnify the risk of erroneous factfinding."...In addition, plaintiffs have pointed to strong empirical evidence that DFCS makes erroneous decisions on a routine basis that affect the safety and welfare of foster children.

Contrary to County Defendants' argument, juvenile court judges, court appointed special advocates (CASAs), and citizen review panels do not adequately mitigate the risk of such errors. Judges, unlike child advocate attorneys, cannot conduct their own investigations and are entirely dependent on others to provide them information about the child's circumstances. Similarly, citizen review panels must rely on facts presented to them by state and county personnel, including local DFCS offices. As a result, their reviews are only as good as the information provided to them by DFCS and other state and local agencies. CASAs are also volunteers who do not provide legal representation to a child. Moreover, CASAs are appointed in only a small number of cases. The Court concludes that only the appointment of counsel can effectively mitigate the risk of significant errors in deprivation and TPR proceedings.

Finally, the Court must consider the government's interest, including the function involved and the fiscal and administrative burdens that a right to counsel would entail. In this case, the function involved is that of the state as *parens patriae* which refers to "the state in its capacity as provider of protection to those unable to care for themselves."

* * *

Plaintiffs cite deposition testimony and documentary evidence showing that effective assistance of counsel by a child advocate attorney requires that he or she carry out certain minimum legal tasks as part of the representation. These tasks include meeting with the child prior to court hearings and when apprised of emergencies or significant events impacting the child; conducting investigations and discovery, including interviewing individuals involved with the child, such as caseworkers and foster parents, and reviewing all judicial, medical, social services, educational, and other records pertaining to the child; evaluating the child's need for particular services; monitoring the implementation of all court orders; participating in all hearings; and filing all relevant motions and appeals.

Plaintiffs also cite the NACC recommendation that, in order to perform these essential tasks, a child advocate attorney should represent no more than 100 individual clients at a time. The evidence shows that this recommendation is based on the assumption that a child advocate attorney will spend an average of 20 hours representing each child and will work 2000 hours in a year. The recommended caseload limit is meant to apply regardless of how many support staff an attorney might have and assumes that child advocate attorneys are not required to perform non-legal, administrative tasks. Based on his extensive experience in the child welfare area and his participation in the development of the NACC caseload limit, NACC Executive Director Marvin Ventrell testified that a child advocate attorney could not possibly provide effective representation if the attorney had a number of clients significantly above 100, and certainly not if the attorney had a caseload of 200 clients. The evidence shows that each of the four child advocate attorneys in Fulton County represent almost 450 clients, while the five child advocate attorneys in DeKalb County each represent approximately 200 clients.

In addition, plaintiffs have presented testimonial and documentary evidence showing that Fulton and DeKalb Counties' child advocate attorneys are overwhelmed by their caseloads and cannot provide effective representation to their child clients.... Plaintiffs also point to evidence from the named plaintiffs' own child advocate attorney files. This evidence shows that the child advocate attorneys often failed to meet with their clients, failed to monitor compliance with court orders, and failed to ensure that their clients' foster care placements were safe and appropriate. All of this evidence is more than sufficient to create a genuine issue for trial as to whether plaintiff foster children, including the named plaintiffs, are receiving, or face a substantial risk of receiving, ineffective assistance of counsel.

County Defendants argue that public policy considerations mandate that plaintiffs not be allowed to circumvent the Georgia legislature, which has sole authority to determine the appropriate amount of funding for child advocate attorneys. This argument is without merit. If this Court finds that plaintiff foster children's right to counsel is being violated, then it is the obligation of the Court to order an appropriate remedy even if such an order requires the state to appropriate additional funds to hire more child advocate attorneys. County Defendants cite no authority to the contrary.

Questions for Discussion

1. Is this published holding limited to Georgia on an independent state basis? Given the extensive discussion of federal constitutional standards (held to be here applicable as well), is this decision binding as a federal precedent? Is it being followed as to either its attorney representation or caseload limitation holding?

2. How has the U.S. Supreme Court holding in *Lassiter* influenced the jurisprudence regarding a child's right to counsel in child welfare proceedings? In Washington, the Supreme Court rejected the argument that children have a universal right to appointment of counsel at termination, holding that the case by case determination of the right, as articulated in *Lassiter*, is constitutionally adequate. See *In re Dependency of M.S.R.*, 174 Wn.2d 1 (2012). The court also reasoned that the right to counsel is protected by appellate review. Although the Court of Appeals found occasion to review and reverse a trial court denial of counsel (see *In re J.A.*, 2014 Wash. App. 1395 (2014)), does this rationale beg the question of who is likely to file an appeal when a child is unrepresented by counsel in the first instance? Furthermore, to what extent does an appellate opinion filed more than a year following the denial of counsel remedy the harms experienced by the child? Most recently, the Washington Supreme Court again rejected the argument for a categorical right to counsel for children, this time considering the issue of counsel at stages of the dependency process preceding termination. See *In re E.H.*, 2018 Wash. LEXIS 690 (2018).

3. Should standards allow higher caseloads where attorneys for children are given investigators or social workers to assist them? Will a jurisdiction meet the suggested 100 case per attorney maximum by dismissing existing support staff in order to finance new attorney hiring?

4. What of the status of child's counsel if provided? Are children parties in dependency court proceedings? For example, if the county bringing the case and the attorneys for the defense agree to dismiss, or to drop certain charges, does counsel for the child have standing to object? See *Allen M. v. Superior Court of San Diego County*, 6 Cal.App.4th 1069 (1992). If a child is given counsel at the trial level in juvenile court, does he or she have continuing rights to that representation on appeal? See *In re Josiah Z.*, 36 Cal.4th 664 (2005). Does the child even have the right to appeal? See *In the Interest of W.L.H.*, 292 Ga. 521 (2013), in which the Supreme Court of Georgia held that a child did not have standing to bring an appeal through an attorney (who represented his expressed interest) when his *guardian ad litem* (representing his best interest) did not seek appeal on the child's behalf. What is the role of a child's attorney as to ancillary legal needs outside of dependency court? Can the child's attorney represent the child for SSI benefits? Qualification for education disability benefits (*e.g.*, under the federal IDEA statute)? Medical coverage? Tort injury?

5. In January 2019, the Children's Bureau of the Office of Administration for Children and Families within DHHS announced a change in federal policy: Title IV-E funds may include as a federal match monies expended by states for the attorneys of parents and children. Previously these expenses had been barred a federal match. What is the likely impact of this funding change regarding the states that have thus far refused to provide counsel for children?

6. Although the *Kenny A.* case above states the 100 is the proper maximum caseload for child attorneys in dependency court, most states impose higher caseloads. In the case of *E.T. v. Tani Cantil Sakauye*, 657 F.3d 902 (9th Cir 2011), the Children's Advocacy Institute challenged the Sacramento caseload of 388 children per attorney, suing the state supreme court which arranges the major contracts determining compensation and caseloads for foster child attorneys. The 2012 Ninth Circuit Opinion refused to impose any standard, even though the state supreme court's own Commission on this subject found that caseloads above 188 were unacceptable. Instead, the Circuit invoked "equitable abstention" and refused to decide the case at all.[105] *Query*, is a violation of due process by a state court an appropriate subject for federal court "abstention"? What means are available to enforce reasonable caseloads for counsel in dependency court? The case also established that the courts in Sacramento County had caseloads of over 1,000—with the judge exercising "parental" jurisdiction over this number of children. What are the remedies available to lower those caseloads, and given the hesitation of the judiciary to challenge their own system before the legislature or any other court, how can it be accomplished?

F. TERMINATION OF PARENTAL RIGHTS: STANDARDS AND BURDEN

Santosky v. Kramer
455 U.S. 745 (1982)

JUSTICE BLACKMUN delivered the opinion of the Court

Under New York law, the State may terminate, over parental objection, the rights of parents in their natural child upon a finding that the child is "permanently neglected." N.Y. Soc. Serv. Law §§ 384-b.4.(d), 384-b.7.(a)...The New York Family Court Act § 622... requires that only a "fair preponderance of the evidence" support that finding. Thus, in New York, the factual certainty required to extinguish the parent-child relationship is no greater than that necessary to award money damages in an ordinary civil action.

Today we hold that the Due Process Clause of the Fourteenth Amendment demands more than this. Before a State may sever completely and irrevocably the rights of parents in their natural child, due process requires that the State support its allegations by at least clear and convincing evidence.

I

A

New York authorizes its officials to remove a child temporarily from his or her home if the child appears "neglected," within the meaning of Art. 10 of the Family Court Act....Once removed, a child under the age of 18 customarily is placed "in the care of an authorized agency,"...usually a state institution or a foster home. At that point, "the state's first obligation is to help the family with services to...reunite it...."...But if convinced that "positive, nurturing parent-child relationships no longer exist,"...the State may initiate "permanent neglect" proceedings to free the child for adoption.

* * *

B

Petitioners John Santosky II and Annie Santosky are the natural parents of Tina and John III. In November 1973, after incidents reflecting parental neglect, respondent Kramer, Commissioner of the Ulster County Department of Social Services, initiated a neglect proceeding under Fam. Ct. Act § 1022 and removed Tina from her natural home. About 10 months later, he removed John III and placed him with foster parents. On the day John was taken, Annie Santosky gave birth to a third child, Jed. When Jed was only three days old, respondent transferred him to a foster home on the ground that immediate removal was necessary to avoid imminent danger to his life or health.

In October 1978, respondent petitioned the Ulster County Family Court to terminate petitioners' parental rights in the three children.[4] Petitioners challenged the constitutionality of the "fair preponderance of the evidence" standard specified in Fam. Ct. Act § 622. The Family Court Judge rejected this constitutional challenge, App. 29–30, and weighed the evidence under the statutory standard. While acknowledging that the Santoskys had maintained contact with their children, the judge found those visits "at best superficial and devoid of any real emotional content." *Id.*, at 21. After deciding that the agency had made "'diligent efforts' to encourage and strengthen the parental relationship," *id.*, at 30, he concluded that the Santoskys were incapable, even with public assistance, of planning for the future of their children. *Id.*, at 33–37. The judge later held a dispositional hearing and ruled that the best interests of the three children required permanent termination of the Santoskys' custody.[5] *Id.*, at 39.

Petitioners appealed, again contesting the constitutionality of § 622's standard of proof....

* * *

II

* * *

...When the State moves to destroy weakened familial bonds, it must provide the parents with fundamentally fair procedures.[7]

mathews v Eldridge factors

In *Lassiter*, the Court and three dissenters agreed that the nature of the process due in parental rights termination proceedings turns on a balancing of the "three distinct factors" specified in *Mathews v. Eldridge*, 424 U.S. 319, 335 (1976): the private interests affected by the proceeding; the risk of error created by the State's chosen procedure; and the countervailing governmental interest supporting use of the challenged procedure....

* * *

Thus, while private parties may be interested intensely in a civil dispute over money damages, application of a "fair preponderance of the evidence" standard indicates both society's "minimal concern with the outcome," and a conclusion that the litigants should "share the risk of error in roughly equal fashion." 441 U.S., at 423...

* * *

This Court has mandated an intermediate standard of proof—"clear and convincing evidence"—when the individual interests at stake in a state proceeding are both "particularly important" and "more substantial than mere loss of money." *Addington v. Texas*, 441 U.S., at 424. Notwithstanding "the state's 'civil labels. and good intentions,'"... the Court has deemed this level of certainty necessary to preserve fundamental fairness in a variety of government-initiated proceedings that threaten the individual involved with "a significant deprivation of liberty" or "stigma." 441 U.S., at 425, 426....

* * *

III

In parental rights termination proceedings, the private interest affected is commanding; the risk of error from using a preponderance standard is substantial; and the countervailing governmental interest favoring that standard is comparatively slight. Evaluation of the three *Eldridge* factors compels the conclusion that use of a "fair preponderance of the evidence" standard in such proceedings is inconsistent with due process.

A

* * *

The factfinding does not purport—and is not intended—to balance the child's interest in a normal family home against the parents' interest in raising the child. Nor does it purport to determine whether the natural parents or the foster parents would provide the better home. Rather, the factfinding hearing pits the State directly against the parents. The State alleges that the natural parents are at fault....The questions disputed and decided are what the State did—"made diligent efforts,"...—and what the natural parents did not do—"maintain contact with or plan for the future of the child.".... The State marshals an array of public resources to prove its case and disprove the parents' case. Victory by the State not only makes termination of parental rights possible; it entails a judicial determination that the parents are unfit to raise their own children.[10]

At the factfinding, the State cannot presume that a child and his parents are adversaries. After the State has established parental unfitness at that initial proceeding, the court may assume at the dispositional stage that the interests of the child and the natural parents do diverge. See Fam. Ct. Act § 631 (judge shall make his order "solely on the basis of the best interests of the child," and thus has no obligation to consider the natural parents' rights in selecting dispositional alternatives). But until the State proves parental unfitness, the child and his parents share a vital interest in preventing erroneous termination of their natural relationship.[11] Thus, at the factfinding, the interests of the child and his natural parents coincide to favor use of error-reducing procedures.

* * *

B

Under *Mathews v. Eldridge*, we next must consider both the risk of erroneous deprivation of private interests resulting from use of a "fair preponderance" standard and the likelihood that a higher evidentiary standard would reduce that risk. See 424 U.S., at 335. Since the factfinding phase of a permanent neglect proceeding is an adversary contest between the State and the natural parents, the relevant question is whether a preponderance standard fairly allocates the risk of an erroneous factfinding between these two parties.

In New York, the factfinding stage of a state-initiated permanent neglect proceeding bears many of the indicia of a criminal trial....

At such a proceeding, numerous factors combine to magnify the risk of erroneous factfinding. Permanent neglect proceedings employ imprecise substantive standards that leave determinations unusually open to the subjective values of the judge....Because parents subject to termination proceedings are often poor, uneducated, or members of minority groups,...such proceedings are often vulnerable to judgments based on cultural or class bias.

The State's ability to assemble its case almost inevitably dwarfs the parents' ability to mount a defense. No predetermined limits restrict the sums an agency may spend in prosecuting a given termination proceeding. The State's attorney usually will be expert on the issues contested and the procedures employed at the factfinding hearing, and enjoys full access to all public records concerning the family. The State may call on experts in family relations, psychology, and medicine to bolster its case. Furthermore, the primary witnesses at the hearing will be the agency's own professional caseworkers whom the State has empowered both to investigate the family situation and to testify against the parents. Indeed, because the child is already in agency custody, the State even has the power to shape the historical events that form the basis for termination.[13]

* * *

C

Two state interests are at stake in parental rights termination proceedings—a *parens patriae* interest in preserving and promoting the welfare of the child and a fiscal and administrative interest in reducing the cost and burden of such proceedings. A standard of proof more strict than preponderance of the evidence is consistent with both interests.

"Since the State has an urgent interest in the welfare of the child, it shares the parent's interest in an accurate and just decision" at the factfinding proceeding. *Lassiter v. Department of Social Services*, 452 U.S., at 27. As *parens patriae*, the State's goal is to provide the child with a permanent home....Yet while there is still reason to believe that positive, nurturing parent-child relationships exist, the parens patriae interest favors preservation, not severance, of natural familial bonds.[17]...."[The] State registers no gain towards its declared goals when it separates children from the custody of fit parents." *Stanley v. Illinois*, 405 U.S., at 652.

* * *

Like civil commitment hearings, termination proceedings often require the factfinder to evaluate medical and psychiatric testimony, and to decide issues difficult to prove to a level of absolute certainty, such as lack of parental motive, absence of affection between parent and child, and failure of parental foresight and progress....The substantive standards applied vary from State to State. Although Congress found a "beyond a reasonable doubt" standard proper in one type of parental rights termination case, another legislative body might well conclude that a reasonable-doubt standard would erect an unreasonable barrier to state efforts to free permanently neglected children for adoption.

A majority of the States have concluded that a "clear and convincing evidence" standard of proof strikes a fair balance between the rights of the natural parents and the State's legitimate concerns....We hold that such a standard adequately conveys to the factfinder the level of subjective certainty about his factual conclusions necessary to satisfy due process. We further hold that determination of the precise burden equal to or greater than that standard is a matter of state law properly left to state legislatures and state courts....

* * *

It is so ordered.

[4] Respondent had made an earlier and unsuccessful termination effort in September 1976. After a factfinding hearing, the Family Court Judge dismissed respondent's petition for failure to prove an essential element of Fam. Ct. Act § 614.1.(d). See *In re Santosky*, 89 Misc. 2d 730, 393 N.Y.S. 2d 486 (1977). The New York Supreme Court, Appellate Division, affirmed, finding that "the record as a whole" revealed that petitioners had "substantially planned for the future of the children." *In re John W.*,...404 N.Y.S. 2d 717, 719 (1978).

[5] Since respondent Kramer took custody of Tina, John III, and Jed, the Santoskys have had two other children, James and Jeremy. The State has taken no action to remove these younger children. At oral argument, counsel for respondents replied affirmatively when asked whether he was asserting that petitioners were "unfit to handle the three older ones but not unfit to handle the two younger ones."....

[7] We therefore reject respondent Kramer's claim that a parental rights termination proceeding does not interfere with a fundamental liberty interest. See Brief for Respondent Kramer 11–18; Tr. of Oral Arg. 38. The fact that important liberty interests of the child and its foster parents may also be affected by a permanent neglect proceeding does not justify denying the natural parents constitutionally adequate procedures. Nor can the State refuse to provide natural parents adequate procedural safeguards on the ground that the family unit already has broken down; that is the very issue the permanent neglect proceeding is meant to decide.

[10] The Family Court Judge in the present case expressly refused to terminate petitioners' parental rights on a "non-statutory, no-fault basis."....Nor is it clear that the State constitutionally could terminate a parent's rights without showing parental unfitness. See *Quilloin v. Walcott*, 434 U.S. 246, 255 (1978) ("We have little doubt that the Due Process Clause would be offended '[if] a State were to attempt to force the breakup of a natural family, over the objections of the parents and their children, without some showing of unfitness and for the sole reason that to do so was thought to be in the children's best interest,'" quoting *Smith v. Organization of Foster Families*, 431 U.S. 816, 862–863 (1977)...

[11] For a child, the consequences of termination of his natural parents' rights may well be far-reaching. In Colorado, for example, it has been noted: "The child loses the right of support and maintenance, for which he may thereafter be dependent upon society; the right to inherit; and all other rights inherent in the legal parent-child relationship, not just for [a limited] period..., but forever."...

Some losses cannot be measured. In this case, for example, Jed Santosky was removed from his natural parents' custody when he was only three days old; the judge's finding of permanent neglect effectively foreclosed the possibility that Jed would ever know his natural parents.

[13] In this case, for example, the parents claim that the State sought court orders denying them the right to visit their children, which would have prevented them from maintaining the contact required by Fam. Ct. Act. § 614.1.(d)....The parents further claim that the State cited their rejection of social services they found offensive or superfluous as proof of the agency's "diligent efforts" and their own "failure to plan" for the children's future....

We need not accept these statements as true to recognize that the State's unusual ability to structure the evidence increases the risk of an erroneous factfinding. Of course, the disparity between the litigants' resources will be vastly greater in States where there is no statutory right to court-appointed counsel....

[17] Any *parens patriae* interest in terminating the natural parents' rights arises only at the dispositional phase, *after* the parents have been found unfit.

JUSTICE REHNQUIST with whom **THE CHIEF JUSTICE, JUSTICE WHITE** and **JUSTICE O'CONNOR** join, dissenting.

I believe that few of us would care to live in a society where every aspect of life was regulated by a single source of law, whether that source be this Court or some other organ of our complex body politic. But today's decision certainly moves us in that direction. By parsing the New York scheme and holding one narrow provision unconstitutional, the majority invites further federal-court intrusion into every facet of state family law. If ever there were an area in which federal courts should heed the admonition of Justice Holmes that "a page of history is worth a volume of logic,"...it is in the area of domestic relations. This area has been left to the States from time immemorial, and not without good reason.

Equally as troubling is the majority's due process analysis. The Fourteenth Amendment guarantees that a State will treat individuals with "fundamental fairness" whenever its actions infringe their protected liberty or property interests. By adoption of the procedures relevant to this case, New York has created an exhaustive program to assist parents in regaining the custody of their children and to protect parents from the unfair deprivation of their parental rights. And yet the majority's myopic scrutiny of the standard of proof blinds it to the very considerations and procedures which make the New York scheme "fundamentally fair."

* * *

II

As the majority opinion notes, petitioners are the parents of five children, three of whom were removed from petitioners' care on or before August 22, 1974. During the next four and one-half years, those three children were in the custody of the State and in the care of foster homes or institutions, and the State was diligently engaged in efforts to prepare petitioners for the children's return. Those efforts were unsuccessful, however, and on April 10, 1979, the New York Family Court for Ulster County terminated petitioners' parental rights as to the three children removed in 1974 or earlier. This termination was preceded by a judicial finding that petitioners had failed to plan for the return and future of their children, a statutory category of permanent neglect. Petitioners now contend, and the Court today holds, that they were denied due process of law, not because of a general inadequacy of procedural protections, but simply because the finding of permanent neglect was made on the basis of a preponderance of the evidence adduced at the termination hearing.

* * *

Parents subjected to temporary removal proceedings are provided extensive procedural protections. A summons and copy of the temporary removal petition must be served upon the parents within two days of issuance by the court... and the parents may, at their own request, delay the commencement of the factfinding hearing for three days after service of the summons. FCA § 1048.6 The factfinding hearing may not commence without a determination by the court that the parents are present at the hearing and have been served with the petition....At the hearing itself, "only competent, material and relevant evidence may be admitted," with some enumerated exceptions for particularly probative evidence....In addition, indigent parents are provided with an attorney to represent them at both the factfinding and dispositional hearings, as well as at all other proceedings related to temporary removal of their child...

An order of temporary removal must be reviewed every 18 months by the Family Court....Such review is conducted by hearing before the same judge who ordered the temporary removal, and a notice of the hearing, including a statement of the dispositional alternatives, must be given to the parents at least 20 days before the hearing is held.... As in the initial removal action, the parents must be parties to the proceedings, and are entitled to court-appointed counsel if indigent....

One or more years after a child has been removed temporarily from the parents' home, permanent termination proceedings may be commenced by the filing of a petition in the court which ordered the temporary removal. The petition must be filed by a state agency or by a foster parent authorized by the court, SSL § 384-b.3.(b), and must allege that the child has been permanently neglected by the parents....Notice of the petition and the dispositional proceedings must be served upon the parents at least 20 days before the commencement of the hearing,...must inform them of the potential consequences of the hearing,...and must inform them "of their right to the assistance of counsel, including [their] right...to have counsel assigned by the court [if] they are financially unable to obtain counsel."....

As in the initial removal proceedings, two hearings are held in consideration of the permanent termination petition....At the factfinding hearing, the court must determine, by a fair preponderance of the evidence, whether the child has been permanently neglected...."Only competent, material and relevant evidence may be admitted in a factfinding hearing."....The court may find permanent neglect if the child is in the care of an authorized agency or foster home and the parents have "failed for a period of more than one year...substantially and continuously or repeatedly to maintain contact with or plan for the future of the child, although physically. and financially able to do so."....In addition, because the State considers its "first obligation" to be the reuniting of the child with its natural parents,...the court must also find that the supervising state agency has, without success, made "diligent efforts to encourage and strengthen the parental relationship."....

Following the factfinding hearing, a separate, dispositional hearing is held to determine what course of action would be in "the best interests of the child."... A finding of permanent neglect at the factfinding hearing, although necessary to a termination of parental rights, does not control the court's order at the dispositional hearing. The court may dismiss the petition, suspend judgment on the petition and retain jurisdiction for a period of one year in order to provide further opportunity for a reuniting of the family, or terminate the parents' right to the custody and care of the child....The court must base its decision solely upon the record of "material and relevant evidence" introduced at the dispositional hearing,...and may not entertain any presumption that the best interests of the child "will be promoted by any particular disposition."....

As petitioners did in this case, parents may appeal any unfavorable decision to the Appellate Division of the New York Supreme Court. Thereafter, review may be sought in the New York Court of Appeals and, ultimately, in this Court if a federal question is properly presented.

As this description of New York's termination procedures demonstrates, the State seeks not only to protect the interests of parents in rearing their own children, but also to assist and encourage parents who have lost custody of their children to reassume their rightful role. Fully understood, the New York system is a comprehensive program to aid parents such as petitioners. Only as a last resort, when "diligent efforts" to reunite the family have failed, does New York authorize the termination of parental rights. The procedures for termination of those relationships which cannot be aided and which threaten permanent injury to the child, administered by a judge who has supervised the case from the first temporary removal through the final termination, cannot be viewed as fundamentally unfair. The facts of this case demonstrate the fairness of the system.

* * *

It is inconceivable to me that these procedures were "fundamentally unfair" to petitioners. Only by its obsessive focus on the standard of proof and its almost complete disregard of the facts of this case does the majority find otherwise.[11]...

B

In addition to the basic fairness of the process afforded petitioners, the standard of proof chosen by New York clearly reflects a constitutionally permissible balance of the interests at stake in this case. The standard of proof "represents an attempt to instruct the factfinder concerning the degree of confidence our society thinks he should have in the correctness of factual conclusions for a particular type of adjudication."....[12]

* * *

On the other side of the termination proceeding are the often countervailing interests of the child.[13] A stable, loving homelife is essential to a child's physical, emotional, and spiritual well-being. It requires no citation of authority to assert that children who are abused in their youth generally face extraordinary problems developing into responsible, productive citizens. The same can be said of children who, though not physically or emotionally abused, are passed from one foster home to another with no constancy of love, trust, or discipline. If the Family Court makes an incorrect factual determination resulting in a failure to terminate a parent-child relationship which rightfully should be ended, the child involved must return either to an abusive home[14] or to the often unstable world of foster care.[15] The reality of these risks is magnified by the fact that the only families faced with termination actions are those which have voluntarily surrendered custody of their child to the State, or, as in this case, those from which the child has been removed by judicial action because of threatened irreparable injury through abuse or neglect. Permanent neglect findings also occur only in families where the child has been in foster care for at least one year.

* * *

III

For the reasons heretofore stated, I believe that the Court today errs in concluding that the New York standard of proof in parental-rights termination proceedings violates due process of law. The decision disregards New York's earnest efforts to *aid* parents in regaining the custody of their children and a host of procedural protections placed around parental rights and interests. The Court finds a constitutional violation only by a tunnel-vision application of due process principles that altogether loses sight of the unmistakable fairness of the New York procedure.

Even more worrisome, today's decision cavalierly rejects the considered judgment of the New York Legislature in an area traditionally entrusted to state care. The Court thereby begins, I fear, a trend of federal intervention in state family law matters which surely will stifle creative responses to vexing problems. Accordingly, I dissent.

[1] The majority finds, without any reference to the facts of this case, that "numerous factors [in New York termination proceedings] combine to magnify the risk of erroneous factfinding."....In short, the majority characterizes the State as a wealthy and powerful bully bent on taking children away from defenseless parents....Such characterization finds no support in the record....

[6] The relatively short time between notice and commencement of hearing provided by § 1048 undoubtedly reflects the State's desire to protect the child. These proceedings are designed to permit prompt action by the court when the child is threatened with imminent and serious physical, mental, or emotional harm.

[12] It is worth noting that the significance of the standard of proof in New York parental termination proceedings differs from the significance of the standard in other forms of litigation. In the usual adjudicatory setting, the factfinder has had little or no prior exposure to the facts of the case. His only knowledge of those facts comes from the evidence adduced at trial, and he renders his findings solely upon the basis of that evidence. Thus, normally, the standard of proof is a crucial factor in the final outcome of the case, for it is the scale upon which the factfinder weighs his knowledge and makes his decision.

Although the standard serves the same function in New York parental termination proceedings, additional assurances of accuracy are present in its application. As was adduced at oral argument, the practice in New York is to assign one judge to supervise a case from the initial temporary removal of the child to the final termination of parental rights. Therefore, as discussed above, the factfinder is intimately familiar with the case before the termination proceedings ever begin. Indeed, as in this case, he often will have been closely involved in protracted efforts to rehabilitate the parents....

[13] The majority dismisses the child's interest in the accuracy of determinations made at the factfinding hearing because "[the] factfinding does not purport...to balance the child's interest in a normal family home against the parents' interest in raising the child," but instead "pits the State directly against the parents."....Only "[after] the State has established parental unfitness," the majority reasons, may the court "assume... that the interests of the child and the natural parents do diverge."....

This reasoning misses the mark. The child has an interest in the outcome of the factfinding hearing independent of that of the parent. To be sure, "the child and his parents share a vital interest in preventing termination of their natural relationship."....But the child's interest in a continuation of the family unit exists only to the extent that such a continuation would not be harmful to him. An error *in the factfinding hearing* that results in a failure to terminate a parent-child relationship which rightfully should be terminated may well detrimentally affect the child....

The preponderance-of-the-evidence standard, which allocates the risk of error more or less evenly, is employed when the social disutility of error *in either direction* is roughly equal—that is, when an incorrect finding of fault would produce consequences as undesirable as the consequences that would be produced by an incorrect finding of fault. Only when the disutility of error in one direction discernibly outweighs the disutility of error in the other direction do we choose, by means of the standard of proof, to reduce the likelihood of the more onerous outcome...

New York's adoption of the preponderance-of-the-evidence standard reflects its conclusion that the undesirable consequence of an erroneous finding of parental unfitness—the unwarranted termination of the family relationship—is roughly equal to the undesirable consequence of an erroneous finding of parental fitness—the risk of permanent injury to the child either by return of the child to an abusive home or by the child's continued lack of a permanent home....Such a conclusion is well within the province of state legislatures. It cannot be said that the New York procedures are unconstitutional simply because a majority of the Members of this Court disagree with the New York Legislature's weighing of the interests of the parents and the child in an error-free factfinding hearing.

[14] The record in this case illustrates the problems that may arise when a child is returned to an abusive home. Eighteen months after Tina, petitioners' oldest child, was first removed from petitioner's home, she was returned to the home on a trial basis. Katherine Weiss, a supervisor in the Child Protective Unit of the Ulster County Child Welfare Department, later testified in Family Court that "[the] attempt to return Tina to her home just totally blew up.".... When asked to explain what happened, Mrs. Weiss testified that "there were instances on the record in this court of Mr. Santosky's abuse of his wife, alleged abuse of the children and proven neglect of the children." *Ibid.* Tina again was removed from the home, this time along with John and Jed.

[15] The New York Legislature recognized the potential harm to children of extended, nonpermanent foster care. It found "that many children who have been placed in foster care experience unnecessarily protracted stays in such care without being adopted or returned to their parents or other custodians. Such unnecessary stays may deprive these children of positive, nurturing family relationships and have

deleterious effects on their development into responsible, productive citizens."....Subsequent studies have proved this finding correct. One commentator recently wrote of "the lamentable conditions of many foster care placements" under the New York system even today. He noted: "Over fifty percent of the children in foster care have been in this 'temporary' status for more than two years; over thirty percent for more than five years. During this time, many children are placed in a sequence of ill-suited foster homes, denying them the consistent support and nurturing that they so desperately need." Besharov, State Intervention To Protect Children: New York's Definition of "Child Abuse" and "Child Neglect," 26 N.Y.L.S.L. REV. 723, 770–771 (1981) (footnotes omitted). In this case, petitioners' three children have been in foster care for more than four years, one child since he was only three days old. Failure to terminate petitioners' parental rights will only mean a continuation of this unsatisfactory situation.

Questions for Discussion

1. The majority argues that the burden of "clear and convincing" is compelled by the extraordinary taking of a child. Can it be argued that the court's analysis treats the child as a valuable chattel which the state cannot take without an enhanced burden of proof beyond preponderance? That is, if the court were to represent the interests of a child who may be subject to unfit parents endangering his safety, and the contest is between the state on the one side and the parents on the other, would preponderance be the more likely test?

2. Is the clear and convincing burden required only for the final termination of parental rights? Should it apply at the detention and jurisdictional stages as well?

3. The majority writes that the "child and foster parent" are involved at the fact-finding stage but "the focus is not on them." What does that mean? The behavior of the parents may be a focus, but does that mean that the issue is simply state vs. parents? How is the child's interest in the proceeding and its outcome any less important than the outcome to the parent?

4. In terms of distribution of risk, what is the consequence of placing a child back with the Santoskys if they are a danger to the child? Imagine a parent who may be raping a child every night; if the evidence is more than 50% that the rapes have occurred and will continue, what burden should we impose for loss of custody? For termination of parental rights? If we impose a lesser standard for loss of custody, will the outcome of the "clear and convincing for termination" outcome preclude adoption for the child (and a parental relationship elsewhere)?

5. Is the solemnity with which the court considers parental rights consistent with the way adults decide to reproduce (with a substantial percentage of pregnancies unintended)?

6. The dissent argues that the confidence needed to warrant termination of parental rights may be provided by a variety of means, of which the burden of proof is one, and that states should be free to develop their own combination of notice, compensated counsel, hearing procedures, *et al.* How would the Supreme Court establish due process lines under such flexibility? Would a system which is less adversarial (more on the continental European model of active, neutral investigation by the court) warrant a preponderance type burden of proof?

G. FOSTER CARE REGULATION

Smith v. Organization of Foster Families For Equality & Reform

431 U.S. 816 (1977)

MR. JUSTICE BRENNAN delivered the opinion of the Court.

Appellees, individual foster parents...and an organization of foster parents, brought this civil rights class action pursuant to 42 U.S.C. § 1983 in the United States District Court for the Southern District of New York, on their own behalf and on behalf of children for whom they have provided homes for a year or more. They sought declaratory and injunctive relief against New York State and New York City officials,...alleging that the procedures governing the removal of foster children from foster homes provided in N.Y. Soc. Serv. Law...violated the Due Process and Equal Protection Clauses of the Fourteenth Amendment....The District Court appointed independent counsel for the foster children to forestall any possibility of conflict between their interests and the interests asserted by the foster parents....A group of natural mothers of children in foster care... were granted leave to intervene...on behalf of themselves and others similarly situated....

A divided three-judge District Court concluded that "the pre-removal procedures presently employed by the State are constitutionally defective," holding that "before a foster child can be peremptorily transferred from the foster home in which he has been living, be it to another foster home or to the natural parents who initially placed him in foster care, he is entitled to a hearing at which all concerned parties may present any relevant information to the administrative decisionmaker charged with determining the future placement of the child,"...We reverse.

* * *

Foster care has been defined as "[a] child welfare service which provides substitute family care for a planned period for a child when his own family cannot care for him for a temporary or extended period, and when adoption is neither desirable nor possible." Child Welfare League of America, Standards for Foster Family Care Service 5 (1959).[8] Thus, the distinctive features of foster care are, first, "that it is care in a *family*, it is noninstitutional substitute care," and, second, "that it is for a *planned* period—either temporary or extended. This is unlike adoptive placement, which implies a *permanent* substitution of one home for another."...

Under the New York scheme children may be placed in foster care either by voluntary placement or by court order. Most foster-care placements are voluntary.[9] They occur when physical or mental illness, economic problems, or other family crises make it impossible for natural parents, particularly single parents, to provide a stable home life for their children for some limited period.[10] Resort to such placements is almost compelled when it is not possible in such circumstance to place the child with a relative or friend, or to pay for the services of a homemaker or boarding school.

Voluntary placement requires the signing of a written agreement by...the natural parent or guardian, transferring the care and custody of the child to. an authorized child welfare agency.[11]....Although by statute the terms of such agreements are open to negotiation,...it is contended that agencies require execution of standardized forms....The agreement may provide for return of the child to the natural parent at a specified date or upon occurrence of a particular event, and if it does not, the child must be returned by the agency, in the absence of a court order, within 20 days of notice from the parent....

* * *

B

The provisions of the scheme specifically at issue in this litigation come into play when the agency having legal custody determines to remove the foster child from the foster home, either because it has determined that it would be in the child's best interests to transfer him to some other foster home, or to return the child to his natural parents in accordance with the statute or placement agreement.

Most children are removed in order to be transferred to another foster home.[23] The procedures by which foster parents may challenge a removal made for that purpose differ somewhat from those where the removal is made to return the child to his natural parent.

Section 383(2)...provides that the "authorized agency placing out or boarding [a foster] child...may in its discretion remove such child from the home where placed or boarded." Administrative regulations implement this provision. The agency is required, except in emergencies, to notify the foster parents in writing 10 days in advance of any removal....The notice advises the foster parents that if they object to the child's removal they may request a "conference" with the Social Services Department....The department schedules requested conferences within 10 days of the receipt of the request. § 450.10(b). The foster parent may appear with counsel at the conference, where he will "be advised of the reasons [for the removal of the child] and be afforded an opportunity to submit reasons why the child should not be removed."....The official must render a decision in writing within five days after the close of the conference, and send notice of his decision to the foster parents and the agency....The proposed removal is stayed pending the outcome of the conference....

If the child is removed after the conference, the foster parent may appeal to the Department of Social Services for a "fair hearing," that is, a full adversary administrative hearing, under Soc. Serv. Law § 400,...the determination of which is subject to judicial review...; however, the removal is not automatically stayed pending the hearing and judicial review....

This statutory and regulatory scheme applies statewide.[28] In addition, regulations promulgated by the New York City Human Resources Administration, Department of Social Services—Special Services for Children (SSC) provide even greater procedural safeguards there. Under SSC Procedure No. 5..., in place of or in addition to the conference provided by the state regulations, the foster parents may request a full trial-type hearing before the child is removed from their home. This procedure applies, however, only if the child is being transferred to another foster home, and not if the child is being returned to his natural parents....

One further preremoval procedural safeguard is available. Under Soc. Serv. Law § 392, the Family Court has jurisdiction to review, on petition of the foster parent or the agency, the status of any child who has been in foster care for 18 months or longer.[30]

* * *

Appellee foster parents as well as natural parents question the accuracy of the idealized picture portrayed by New York. They note that children often stay in "temporary" foster care for much longer than contemplated by the theory of the system....The District Court found as a fact that the median time spent in foster care in New York was over four years. 418 F.Supp., at 281. Indeed, many children apparently remain in this "limbo" indefinitely....The District Court also found that the longer a child remains in foster care, the more likely it is that he will never leave: "[T]he probability of a foster child being returned to his biological parents declined markedly after the first year in foster care." 418 F.Supp., at 279 n. 6....It is not surprising then that many children, particularly those that enter foster care at a very early age[38] and have little or no contact with their natural parents during extended stays in foster care[39] often develop deep emotional ties with their foster parents.[40]

Yet such ties do not seem to be regarded as obstacles to transfer of the child from one foster placement to another. The record in this case indicates that nearly 60% of the children in foster care in New York City have experienced more than one placement, and about 28% have experienced three or more....The intended stability of the foster-home management is further damaged by the rapid turnover among social work professionals who supervise the foster-care arrangements on behalf of the State....Moreover, even when it is clear that a foster child will not be returned to his natural parents, it is rare that he achieves a stable home life through final termination of parental ties and adoption into a new permanent family....

A

Our first inquiry is whether appellees have asserted interests within the Fourteenth Amendment's protection of "liberty" and "property." *Board of Regents v. Roth*, 408 U.S. 564, 571 (1972).

* * *

The appellees' basic contention is that when a child has lived in a foster home for a year or more, a psychological tie is created between the child and the foster parents which constitutes the foster family the true "psychological family" of the child....That family, they argue, has a "liberty interest" in its survival as a family protected by the Fourteenth Amendment....Upon this premise they conclude that the foster child cannot be removed without a prior hearing satisfying due process. Appointed counsel for the children,...however, disagrees, and has consistently argued that the foster parents have no such liberty interest independent of the interests of the foster children, and that the best interests of the children would not be served by procedural protections beyond those already provided by New York law. The intervening natural parents of children in foster care,...also oppose the foster parents, arguing that recognition of the procedural right claimed would undercut both the substantive family law of New York, which favors the return of children to their natural parents as expeditiously as possible,...and their constitutionally protected right of family privacy, by forcing them to submit to a hearing and defend their rights to their children before the children could be returned to them. *[margin note: appellees arg.]*

The District Court did not reach appellees' contention "that the foster home is entitled to the same constitutional deference as that long granted to the more traditional biological family." 418 F.Supp., at 281. Rather than "reach[ing] out to decide such novel questions," the court based its holding that "the pre-removal procedures presently employed by the state are constitutionally defective,"...not on the recognized liberty interest in family privacy, but on an independent right of the foster child "to be heard before being 'condemned to suffer grievous loss,' *Joint Anti-Fascist Committee v. McGrath*, 341 U.S. 123, 168...(1951)..."

The court apparently reached this conclusion by weighing the "harmful consequences of a precipitous and perhaps improvident decision to remove a child from his foster family,"... and concluding that this disruption of the stable relationships needed by the child might constitute "grievous loss." But if this was the reasoning applied by the District Court, it must be rejected.[43] *Meachum v. Fano*, 427 U.S. 215, 224 (1976), is authority that such a finding does not, in and of itself, implicate the due process guarantee. What was said in Board of *Regents v. Roth supra*, at 570–571, applies equally well here:

> "The District Court decided that procedural due process guarantees apply in this case by assessing and balancing the weights of the particular interests involved....[A] weighing process has long been a part of any determination of the *form* of hearing required in particular situations by procedural due process. But, to determine whether due process requirements apply in the first place, we must look not to the 'weight' but to the nature of the interest at stake.... We must look to see if the interest is within the Fourteenth Amendment's protection of liberty and property."... *[margin note: DC apply Matthews v Eldridge]*

* * *

B

....There does exist a "private realm of family life which the state cannot enter," *Prince v. Massachusetts*, 321 U.S. 158, 166 (1944), that has been afforded both substantive...and procedural...protection. But is the relation of foster parent to foster child sufficiently akin to the concept of "family" recognized in our precedents to merit similar protection?...

* * *

...[T]here are also important distinctions between the foster family and the natural family. First, unlike the earlier cases recognizing a right to family privacy, the State here seeks to interfere, not with a relationship having its origins entirely apart from the power of the State, but rather with a foster family which has its source in state law and contractual arrangements....Here, however, whatever emotional ties may develop between foster parent and foster child have their origins in an arrangement in which the State has been a partner from the outset. While the Court has recognized that liberty interests may in some cases arise from positive-law sources,...in such a case, and particularly where, as here, the claimed interest derives from a knowingly assumed contractual relation with the State, it is appropriate to ascertain from state law the expectations and entitlements of the parties. In this case, the limited recognition accorded to the foster family by the New York statutes and the contracts executed by the foster parents argue against any but the most limited constitutional "liberty" in the foster family.

* * *

Reversed.

[8] The term "foster care" is often used more generally to apply to any type of care that substitutes others for the natural parent in the parental role, including group homes, adoptive homes, and institutions, as well as foster family homes....Since this case is only concerned with children in foster family homes, the term will generally be used here in the more restricted sense defined in the text.

[9] The record indicates that as many as 80% of the children in foster care in New York City are voluntarily placed....

[10] Experienced commentators have suggested that typical parents in this situation might be "[a] divorced parent in a financial bind, an unwed adolescent mother still too immature to rear a child, or a welfare mother confronted with hospitalization and therefore temporarily incapable of caring for her child."....A leading text on child-care services suggests that "[family] disruption, marginal economic circumstances, and poor health" are principal factors leading to placement of children in foster care....Other studies suggest, however, that neglect, abuse, abandonment and exploitation of children, which presumably account for most of the children who enter foster care by court order,...are also involved in many cases of voluntary placement....

[11] "Authorized agency" is defined in N.Y. Soc. Serv. Law § 371(10) (McKinney 1976) and "includes any local public welfare children's bureau, such as the defendants New York City Bureau of Child Welfare and Nassau County Children's Bureau, and any voluntary child-care agency under the supervision of the New York State Board of Social Welfare, such as the defendant Catholic Guardian Society of New York." 418 F.Supp., at 278 n. 5.

An *amicus curiae* brief states that in New York City, 85% of the children in foster care are placed with voluntary child-care agencies licensed by the State, while most children in foster care outside New York City are placed directly with the local Department of Social Services.

[23] The record shows that in 1973–1974 approximately 80% of the children removed from foster homes in New York State after living in the foster home for one year or more were transferred to another foster placement. Thirteen percent were returned to the biological parents, and 7% were adopted.

[28] There is some dispute whether the procedures set out in 18 N.Y.C.R.R. § 450.10 and Soc. Serv. Law § 400 apply in the case of a foster child being removed from his foster home to be returned to his natural parents. Application of these procedures to children who have been placed voluntarily, for example, arguably conflicts with the requirement of § 384-a (2)(a) that children in that situation be returned to the natural parent as provided in the placement agreement or within 20 days of demand. Similarly, if the child has been ordered returned by a court, it is unclear what purpose could be served by an administrative conference or hearing on the correctness of the decision to remove the child from the foster home. Moreover, since the § 400 hearing takes place after removal of the child from the foster home, the hearing would have no purpose if the child has been returned to its parents, since the agency apparently has no authority to take the child back from its parents against their will without court intervention.

Nevertheless, nothing in either the statute or the regulations limits the availability of these procedures to transfers within the foster-care system. Each refers to the decision to child from the foster family home, and thus on its face each would seem to cover removal for the purpose of returning the child to its parents. Furthermore, it is undisputed on this record that the actual administrative practice in New York is to provide the conference and hearing in all cases where they are requested, regardless of the destination of the child. In the absence of authoritative state-court interpretation to the contrary, we therefore assume that these procedures are available whenever a child is removed from a foster family home.

[30] The agency is required to initiate such a review when a child has remained in foster care for 18 months, § 392(2)(a), and if the child remains in foster care, the court "shall rehear the matter whenever it deems necessary or desirable, or upon petition by any party entitled to notice in proceedings under this section, but at least every twenty-four months." § 392(10).

[38] In New York City, 23.1% of foster children enter foster care when under one year of age, and 43% at age three or under...(18% of foster-care children in Rhode Island study were under one year of age when they entered foster care, and 43% were under the age of three).

[39] One study of parental contacts in New York City found that 57.4% of all foster children had had no contact with their natural parents for the previous six months....

[40] The development of such ties points up an intrinsic ambiguity of foster care that is central to this case. The warmer and more homelike environment of foster care is intended to be its main advantage over institutional child care, yet because in theory foster care is intended to be only temporary, foster parents are urged not be become too attached to the children in their care....Indeed, the New York courts have upheld removal from a foster home for the very reason that the foster parents had become too emotionally

involved with the child. *In re Jewish Child Care Assn. (Sanders)*, 5 N.Y. 2d 222 (1959). See also the case of the Lhotans, named appellees in this case,...

On the other hand, too warm a relation between foster parent and foster child is not the only possible problem in foster care. Qualified foster parents are hard to find,...and very little training is provided to equip them to handle the often complicated demands of their role,...; it is thus sometimes possible that foster homes may provide inadequate care. Indeed, situations in which foster children were mistreated or abused have been reported. Wald 645. And the social work services that are supposed to be delivered to both the natural and foster families are limited, due to the heavy caseloads of the agencies....Given these problems, and given that the very fact of removal from even an inadequate natural family is often traumatic for the child,... it is not surprising that one commentator has found "rather persuasive, if still incomplete, evidence that throughout the United States, children in foster care are experiencing high rates of psychiatric disturbance."....

[43] The dissenting judge argued that the court's underlying premise was a holding "over the objection of the representative of the children...that the foster children have a 'liberty' interest in their relationship with the foster parents." 418 F.Supp., at 288. If this was in fact the reasoning of the District Court, we do not see how it differs from a holding that the foster family relationship is entitled to privacy protection analogous to the natural family—the issue the District Court purported not to reach.

MR. JUSTICE STEWART, with whom **THE CHIEF JUSTICE** and **MR. JUSTICE REHNQUIST** join, concurring in the judgment.

The foster parent-foster child relationship involved in this litigation is, of course, wholly a creation of the State. New York law defines the circumstances under which a child may be placed in foster care, prescribes the obligations of the foster parents, and provides for the removal of the child from the foster home "in [the] discretion" of the agency with custody of the child....

* * *

In these circumstances, I cannot understand why the Court thinks itself obliged to decide these cases on the assumption that either foster parents or foster children in New York have some sort of "liberty" interest in the continuation of their relationship.[1] Rather than tiptoeing around this central issue, I would squarely hold that the interests asserted by the appellees are not of a kind that the Due Process Clause of the Fourteenth Amendment protects.

* * *

...[U]nder New York's foster-care laws, any case where the foster parents had assumed the emotional role of the child's natural parents would represent not a triumph of the system, to be constitutionally safeguarded from state intrusion, but a failure. The goal of foster care, at least in New York, is not to provide a permanent substitute for the natural or adoptive home, but to prepare the child for his return to his real parents or placement in a permanent adoptive home by giving him temporary shelter in a family setting....

* * *

...The family life upon which the State "intrudes" is simply a temporary status which the State itself has created. It is a "family life" defined and controlled by the law of New York, for which New York pays, and the goals of which New York is entitled to and does set for itself.

For these reasons I concur in the judgment of the Court.

[1] The Court's opinion seems to indicate that there is no reason to distinguish between the claims of the foster parents and the foster children, either because the parents have standing to assert the rights of the children or because the parents' interest is identical to that of the children....I cannot agree.

First, it is by no means obvious that foster parents and foster children have the same interest in a continuation of their relationship. When the child leaves the foster family, it is because the agency with custody of him has determined that his interests will be better served by a new home, either with his natural parents, adoptive parents, or a different foster family. Any assessment of the child's alleged deprivation must take into account not only what he has lost, but what he has received in return. Foster parents, on the other hand, do not automatically receive a new child with whom they will presumably have a more profitable relationship.

Second, unlike the situation in *Craig v. Boren*, 429 U.S. 190, 195–196, this is not a case where the failure to grant the parents their requested relief will inevitably tend to "[dilute] or adversely [affect]" the alleged constitutional rights of the children. Denying the parents a hearing simply has no effect whatever on the children's separate claim to a hearing, and does not impair their alleged constitutional rights. There is therefore no standing in the parents to assert the children's claims...

I would nevertheless consider both the parents' and the children's claims in these cases, but only because the suit was originally brought on behalf of both the parents and the children, all of whom were parties plaintiff. While it is true that their interests may conflict, there was no reason not to allow counsel for the parents to continue to represent the children to the extent that their interests may be compatible. The conflict was avoided by the District Court's appointment of independent counsel, who took a position opposite to that of the foster parents as to where the children's welfare lay. The appointment of independent counsel, however, should not have left the children without advocacy for the position, right or wrong, that they are entitled to due process hearings. That position should have been left to be asserted by the counsel who originally brought the suit for the children. My view, therefore, is that the parents and the children are properly before the Court and entitled to assert their own separate claims, but that neither group has standing to assert the claims of the other.

Questions for Discussion

1. Do the majority or concurring opinions analyze the issues from the child's point of view?

2. Under New York law, foster parents may appeal to the local agency making the decision to remove a child from their care within the first eighteen months of their custody. What elements of traditional due process are missing from such a review?

3. The Court opines that there is no reason to assume bonding takes place before eighteen months. Is there any evidence to support this extraordinary finding? If one were to place a child or puppy or new car with the justices authoring that opinion, what would they say to summary retrieval after fifteen months? Six months? Three weeks? Does a young child bond with non-parents who may be performing the parental function before eighteen months transpires?

4. More than half of adoptions through a public agency come from family foster care providers. Only about half of children removed from their homes are reunified and many remain in foster care until emancipation (see discussion above). Do we want bonding to take place between foster parents and the children entrusted to them in such a setting? Or is the Court's footnote correct that such bonding violates public policy and can properly justify removal of children from foster parents? Or the concurring opinion's conclusion that such bonding constitutes a "failure" of foster care?

5. The Court's holding may apply not only to decisions to move a child from foster care back to a parent (reunification) but to the much more common case where the transfer is between foster care placements. What is the downside of a hearing on the issue of transfer as a check on possible local agency error (as well as gratuitous foster care drift)? If the foster. parent is the agent of the court in caring for the child, why would the court deny its own agent access to its offices to inform it of the status of children where the courts function as the *de jure* parents?

6. If the county agency decides to move a child from a foster parent who seeks adoption to a group home with delinquents who the foster parent believes would be detrimental for the child, what is the likelihood of court review or other check under the *OFFER* standard?

7. The concurring opinion notes that the issue is not the "weight of the loss" but its nature, and that its nature does not involve deprivation of life or property.

How does that square with *Lassiter,* where the parental loss of a child is a sufficient taking of something to warrant publicly financed counsel if it could make a difference in the outcome?

8. Is it relevant that in New York City, where a local rule permits some neutral hearings prior to removing children from objecting foster care parents, the local agency was reversed in 45% of its reviewed decisions?

9. Is any constitutional weight due to a child's reasonable perception that an adult has functioned as his or her parent? If a child is a "person" for purposes of constitutional rights, how is the "right to parent" a fundamental liberty interest, but the child's counterpart relationship entirely devoid of constitutional status? Since the *OFFER* case in 1977, state courts have increasingly entertained the status of *de facto* parents—delineating a person who may not have a parental claim from biology or marriage, but who has been a parent in the eyes of a child, and has functioned as such by community standards (*see, e.g., Webster v. Ryan* discussed in Chapter 11). Why would such *de facto* status (with the court access and due process rights increasingly conferred to it) not apply to a foster parent—particularly where the alternative is not parental return? If the distinction is a notion of "waiver" implicit or explicit in the foster arrangement "contract," how would that eliminate any right to a parent held by the child, who has not so agreed?

10. Is it clear from *OFFER* under what circumstances foster parents may in fact have a liberty interest in their relationship with their foster child? Does the analysis turn on whether the rights of the biological parents have yet been terminated? The Tenth Circuit held in 2012 that foster parents who had cared for a child for an extended period of time, who had been the only parents the child had ever known, and who had an adoption plan approved by the court, did indeed have a liberty interest in their relationship with the child, whose biological parents had had their rights terminated. See *Elwell v. Byers,* 699 F.3d 1208 (2012). However, the Seventh Circuit decided differently in a case in which a foster child had resided with foster parents since shortly after birth and was then returned to her biological parents at age five. Despite the foster parents' desire to adopt, the court held that they did not have a liberty interest that triggered due process. See *Procopio v. Johnson,* 994 F.2d 325 (1993).

H. PERMANENT PLACEMENT

Drummond v. Fulton County Department of Family & Children's Services

563 F.2d 1200 (5th Cir. 1977)

RONEY, Circuit Judge:

Plaintiffs, Robert and Mildred Drummond, a white couple, acted as state-designated foster parents of a mixed race child for over two years. When the defendant state adoption agency decided to remove the child for permanent placement in another home, plaintiffs commenced this action under 42 U.S.C.A. § 1983. Alleging denial of their rights under both the equal protection and the due process clauses of the Fourteenth Amendment, they sought preliminary and permanent injunctive relief, which was denied by the district court. Although a panel of this Court reversed, *Drummond v. Fulton County Department of Family & Children's Services*, 547 F.2d 835 (5th Cir. 1977), the full Court finds no deprivation of constitutional rights and affirms the dismissal of plaintiffs' complaint.

* * *

In December 1973 in an emergency situation, a one-month-old mixed race child named Timmy was placed for temporary care in the home of Mr. and Mrs. Drummond by the Fulton County children's service agency. Lengthy proceedings were commenced to determine whether the child should be permanently removed from his natural mother's custody and placed for adoption.

Within a year, the Drummonds had become sufficiently attached to Timmy to request permission to adopt him. The Drummonds had not signed an agreement that they would not try to adopt their foster child, as is common practice with many placement agencies. Although the level of care provided by them as foster parents had consistently been rated excellent, there was an emerging consensus within the defendant child placement agency charged with Timmy's care that it would be best to look elsewhere for a permanent adoptive home. When this was explained to the Drummonds in March 1975 they appeared to acquiesce. By August of that year, however, they had renewed their request to adopt Timmy.

The child was not legally freed for adoption by the Georgia courts until September 1975. Because this signaled the end of any attempt to return Timmy to his natural mother, the agency began a more focused consideration of what ultimate placement would be best for Timmy. After a number of discussions with the Drummonds, a final decision-making meeting was held in November 1975 with 19 agency employees present. Although the Drummonds were not present at this meeting, caseworkers who had dealt with them during the past two years did attend. As a result of that meeting a final agency decision was made to remove Timmy from the Drummond home and to deny the Drummonds' adoption application. It is clear that the race of the Drummonds and of Timmy and the racial attitudes of the parties were given substantial weight in coming to this conclusion. The agency employees were also aware that as Timmy grew older he would retain the characteristics of his black father. A few months later the plaintiffs filed suit.

* * *

The manner in which race was considered in this case frames the precise issue before us. The district court found that race was not used in an automatic fashion. The Drummonds' application was not automatically rejected on racial grounds. This finding may not be disturbed here because not clearly erroneous.... But can race be taken into account, perhaps decisively if it is the factor which tips the balance between two potential families, where it is not used automatically? We conclude, as did another court which grappled with the problem, that "the difficulties inherent in interracial adoption" justify the consideration of "race as a relevant factor in adoption,..."...

* * *

In concluding that there has been no denial of equal protection in these circumstances, we note the following factors.

First, consideration of race in the child placement process suggests no racial slur or stigma in connection with any race. It is a natural thing for children to be raised by parents of their same ethnic background.

Second, no case has been cited to the Court suggesting that it is impermissible to consider race in adoption placement. The only cases which have addressed this problem indicate that, while the automatic use of race is barred, the use of race as one of the factors in making the ultimate decision is legitimate....

Third, the professional literature on the subject of transracial child placement stresses the importance of considering the racial attitudes of potential parents. The constitutional strictures against racial discrimination are not mandates to ignore the accumulated experience of unbiased professionals. A couple has no right to adopt a child it is not equipped to rear, and according to the professional literature race bears directly on that inquiry. From the child's perspective, the consideration of race is simply another facet of finding him the best possible home. Rather than eliminating certain categories of homes from consideration it avoids the potentially tragic possibility of placing a child in a home with parents who will not be able to cope with the child's problems.

Fourth, in the analogous inquiry over the permissibility of considering the religion of would-be adoptive parents, numerous courts have found no constitutional infirmity.... Those cases make the same distinction as this Court makes in the racial context. So long as religion is not an automatic factor, its consideration as one of a number of factors is unobjectionable.

Finally, adoption agencies quite frequently try to place a child where he an most easily become a normal family member. The duplication of his natural biological environment is a part of that program. Such factors as age, hair color, eye color and facial features of parents and child are considered in reaching a decision. This flows from the belief that a child and adoptive parents can best adjust to a normal family relationship if the child is placed with adoptive parents who could have actually parented him. To permit consideration of physical characteristics necessarily carries with it permission to consider racial characteristics. This Court does not have the professional expertise to assess the wisdom of that type of inquiry, but it is our province to conclude, as we do today, that the use of race as one of those factors is not unconstitutional.

II

In order to make out a claim of deprivation of Fourteenth Amendment due process rights a plaintiff must demonstrate first, that he has been deprived of liberty or property in the constitutional sense, and second, that the procedure used to deprive him of that interest was constitutionally deficient. *Board of Regents v. Roth*, 408 U.S. 564 (1972).

A

The Drummonds assert two possible constitutional liberty and property interests. The first involves a concept which plaintiffs have denominated the "psychological family"; the second, a stigma to their reputation alleged to accrue upon the rejection by the agency of their application to adopt Timmy.

Plaintiffs maintain that during the period Timmy lived with them mutual feelings of love and dependence developed which are analogous to those found in most biological families....

* * *

We conclude that there is no such constitutionally protected interest in the context of this case. An understanding of the role of the foster parent in a child placement helps make this conclusion plain. In the search for adoptive parents, thorough investigations are made so that long range considerations may be given substantial weight....Potential adoptive parents are evaluated forward in the full family context through a child's adulthood, marriage, offspring, and backward to the "adoptive" grandparents, uncles, aunts, and cousins. The attitudes of other family members are examined. In short, the goal is to duplicate the relationship that most persons have with their natural parents during their entire lives.

* * *

Here, the only time potential parents could assert a liberty interest as psychological parents would be when they had developed precisely the relationship which state law warns against the foster context....The very fact that the relationship before us is a creature of state law, as well as the fact that it has never been recognized as equivalent to either the natural family or the adoptive family by any court, demonstrates that it is not a protected liberty interest, but an interest limited by the very laws which create it....

* * *

B

Independent counsel for Timmy claims a liberty right personal to Timmy which he asserts must be dealt with in constitutional due process terms. The interest upon which he bases this claim is one which he has chosen to call the "right to a stable environment." He argues that a child has a liberty right not to be moved from home to home, without a prior hearing, particularly in light of the significant literature which indicates a traumatic effect of such moves on young children. Counsel insists this right

[handwritten margin note: Timmy's counsel arg.]

exists regardless of whether the child is in a natural, adoptive or foster setting and in all other temporary care situations.

* * *

Given the nature of the interests at stake, and the inquiry involved, as well as the overwhelming need for flexibility in this situation and the complexity of the decision to be made, this Court holds that whatever process was due was rendered by the state agency in this case.

AFFIRMED.

* * *

TUTTLE, Circuit Judge, with whom **GOLDBERG**, Circuit Judge, joins, dissenting:

* * *

In view of the fact that the State of Georgia has "preremoval procedures" that will fit any concept of due process, a subject that will be discussed later, the case before us demands that a determination be made whether there is such protectable interest in the Drummonds.

As is sometimes the case, I believe that the concurring opinion, joined in by the Chief Justice and two of the Justices, dramatically emphasizes the importance which a majority of the court attributed to the question whether a liberty interest inheres in the relationship between the foster parents and children who have been in their care a substantial period of time....

* * *

...[T]he Court took considerable pains to analyze the assertion of the foster parents and foster children that they had a constitutionally protected liberty interest. A careful reading of the opinion indicates to me that but for the existence of the narrower ground in that case and but for the fact that the contest before the court was being waged between foster parents on the one hand and natural parents on the other, the court would readily have determined that such constitutionally protected liberty interest did exist. In the first place, the court recognized that, although "the usual understanding of 'family' implies biological relationships, and most decisions treating the relation between parent and child have stressed this element" and that "a biological relationship is not present in the case of the usual foster family" nevertheless "biological relationships are not exclusive determination of the existence of a family.".

* * *

II. TIMMY'S "LIBERTY" INTEREST

What has been said respecting the liberty interest of the Drummonds, of course, applies, possibly even more cogently, in the case of the small child whose entire life will be affected in large or small degree by his being taken away from the only parents he has known since his birth....

* * *

...[T]he defendants concede that the liberty interest exists, but that the Georgia adoptive system, taken as a whole, affords to Timmy the due process to which he is entitled and that all the process that Timmy is due at any stage of his temporary care, his foster family relationship and their terminations, the termination of parents' rights, and final adoption is that "the state structures a system *designed* to accommodate the child's best interest." In other words, appellees say that as long as the legislature decides in its wisdom that everything relating to an abandoned child's welfare and status can safely be left to the uncontrolled and unreviewable discretion of state and county employees that satisfies all due process requirements. This would include the action taken here by which the defendants seek to terminate irrevocably a relationship which the Supreme Court has, in the passages quoted above, recognized as parallel to that

of a biological family, without any opportunity of the child to be heard. In any event, it appears to be a concession by the state that Timmy has a protectable interest. The question whether this interest can be taken away from him by the sort of proceedings had here is discussed below.

III. WHAT PROCESS IS DUE?

....[I]n March 1976, a "staffing" of four caseworkers or supervisors, none of whom had either seen the Drummonds or Timmy at that time, concluded ex parte that the Drummonds should be told that Timmy was to be taken from their care and "that it would be in Timmy's best interest to be adopted by a black couple." Bearing in mind that this decision was made before any of the persons involved had seen the Drummonds and before the several investigations and studies of the Drummonds as potential adoptive parents were made,[2] it is obvious, it seems to me, that Mrs. Dallinger's effort to analyze at the trial what was meant by the action taken at the staffing is an afterthought, because the only purpose for approaching the Drummonds was to explain to them that the child was to be removed and awarded to black adoptive parents. I comment on this only because the decision on whether the procedures followed provided minimal due process must necessarily depend upon when the decision was made. Miss Osgood's statement that the question was raised "that if the Drummonds were not amenable to our plan, would we move Timmy to a black foster home feeling that, you know, it would be better if we were going to have him adopted by a black couple, to have him in a black foster home if there was going to be any length of time before he was free" clearly indicates that "our plan" was that "we were going to have him adopted by a black couple." It seems apparent that this was the decision because the undisputed testimony of Mrs. Drummond following the final "consensus" was that Mrs. Dallinger said to Mr. and Mrs. Drummond: "I am sure that you are both very anxious to know what has happened and we called you in to tell you that the decision still stands, that we feel that Timmy will be better off adopted by a black couple or a black family." [Emphasis added]. Of course, the only "decision" that Mrs. Dallinger could have referred to is the decision made at the March staffing which I have discussed above. I suppose no one would claim that if the Drummonds and Timmy are entitled to any process at all they had received it by the time this decision was made.

However, the matter did not end after the March meeting between the caseworkers and the Drummonds. The latter protested and requested a reconsideration. They were put off by statements that no action would be taken until after Timmy's mother's rights had been terminated by the Juvenile Court. This was done in September, and in the meantime, several inquiries and studies were made by caseworkers or other officials of the defendant Department, most of which discussed the merits, pro and con, of the relationship between Timmy and his foster parents.[3] Finally, without giving the Drummonds an opportunity to be present and without their having been notified of the standards by which the relationship would be judged, a group meeting of 19 employees of the Department was called to obtain a "consensus" as to what should be done with Timmy in relation to his foster parents.

A written report of this meeting states in its last paragraph:

"A vote was taken and it was a group decision that it would not be in Timmy's best interest to leave him in the Drummonds' home, and that we would begin immediately to look for an appropriate black adoptive home. Although this was a difficult decision it was felt that Timmy's long range best interest must be the focus."

The Drummonds were not present at the staffing of November 21. No physician or psychiatrist was present. There is no record of any testimony or statement made by any person present, except that we can assume that the documents heretofore referred to were available to the members of the group. The Drummonds were not given an opportunity to present any statements or evidence, much less to be represented by counsel or to present witnesses supporting their position nor were they given any notice of the basis on which the decision might rest. Of course, it is apparent from the face of the documents that no findings of fact were made as to any of the possible grounds of challenging their qualifications as adoptive parents. It is apparent from the record that they were attempting at all times merely to resist the removal of Timmy on the only ground which was explained to them, that is that it was the plan for "this type" of child to be adopted by black parents....

* * *

...[T]here is no statute and there are no regulations that cover the requirements which must be complied with by the Department before a relationship such as that enjoyed by the Drummonds and Timmy is terminated. In actual practice, moreover, there was nothing to compare with the provision described in the margin that "whenever the agency's tentative assessment of the beneficiary's condition differs from his own assessment, the beneficiary is informed that benefits may be terminated, provided a summary of the evidence upon which the proposed determination to terminate is based, and afforded an opportunity to review the medical reports and other evidence in his case file" nor was there anything remotely resembling the opportunity given, as described by the Supreme Court in its opinion which says "he also may respond in writing and submit additional evidence."

In the Mathews case, as the Supreme Court noted, the final determination by the agency is then "reviewed by an examiner in the SSA Bureau of Disability Insurance." 42 U.S.C. § 421(c);...If, as is usually the case, the SSA accepts the agency determination, it notifies the recipient in writing informing him of the reasons for the decision, and of his right to seek de novo reconsideration by the state agency ..." 424 U.S. at 338. [Emphasis added.]

All this is then followed if the recipient seeks reconsideration, by a federal appeal and an evidentiary hearing before an administrative law judge, as pointed out in the margin. In contrast, there is nothing in the Georgia law that permits any review, appeal or reconsideration by any tribunal or official or court of the "consensus judgment" made by this ad hoc committee.

The only kind of judicial review available is by the filing of a complaint in the United States Court where, as happened in this case, the district court had before it only an imperfect documentary record and the testimony of several of the actors in the proceeding who undertook to speak for the entire group of 19 and to explain what they had in their mind when they finally terminated Timmy's only known family relationship.

* * *

I know of no other situation under our laws in which the whole future life of a child of tender years can be gravely affected by the totally uncontrolled discretion of public officials without an opportunity for a hearing by those affected. I join in the assumption that I am sure underlies the opinion of the Court that the persons involved intended to do what they thought to be for the best of the child in the circumstances, but the law we announce today would deny relief to persons equally affected even though a strong showing could be made that the persons acting had done so capriciously, venally, or from definite racial bias, because the opinion says that the proceedings which produced the result in Timmy's case were adequate to satisfy the requirements of due process.

IV. THE RACIAL QUESTION

The complaint alleged that the action of the defendants in removing Timmy from custody of the Drummonds was motivated solely on racial grounds, that is it was done pursuant to a policy that black or part black children could not be placed for adoption with a white couple. One of the great defects in the proceeding here is the fact it is utterly impossible to determine whether or not this allegation is true. A careful reading of the documentary and oral testimony introduced at the trial gives me a strong belief that the decision made by the four or five workers in March to tell the Drummonds that they must give up Timmy so that he can be raised by a black couple was the one and only basis for all of the proceedings and the result that issued therefrom. In any event, there was no record, there was no transcript of testimony, there is no indication that any word about other reasons than Timmy's race went into any decision-making or was the basis for the final decision.

* * *

I would adhere to the mandate issued following the panel opinion of this Court.

[2] It is to be noted again here that each of the investigations resulted in fulsome praise of the Drummonds' relationship with the child.

[3] It should be noted again that most of these reports were extravagant in their praise of the manner in which the Drummonds had developed a genuine loving family with this child. See 547 F.2d 835.

Questions for Discussion

1. What elements of due process were missing from the procedure to decide Timmy's permanent placement? Are the Drummonds given a formal or informal hearing? An opportunity to be heard at all by the decision-makers? Is anyone independently speaking for Timmy?

2. The court opines that the State's "motive [is to move] Timmy to a better place." Is that a sufficient check on the executive branch of the state? If prosecutors are motivated to accomplish a just result, are judges, juries, or hearings rendered gratuitous?

3. If race is a legitimate factor in Timmy's permanent placement, why is he placed into foster care with the Drummonds (for two years)?

4. If Timmy is of mixed race (half black, half white), would a black couple be as racially disparate from Timmy as are the white Drummonds?

5. Can one argue that the child is living in Georgia in the 1970s and should not be subject to the torments of classmates or local discrimination because he is clearly of a different race than his parents? What is the response to the argument: "Take your liberal theories that race doesn't matter and fight your battles, but don't send a child to take the blows for you"?

6. If race is a legitimate factor in the proper placement of a child, can it be a factor in a parental rights hearing to find a white biological mother of a mixed race child unfit?

7. Timmy has been with the Drummonds from the age of one month to two years of age, when the permanent placement decision is to be made. Has Timmy bonded with these parents? Who does he call Mommy and Daddy? Who changes his diapers, feeds him, reads him books at night? Does Timmy have any procedural due process rights in the decision to permanently place him? Should constitutional doctrine permit such decisions to be made by the agency without review?

8. Supreme Court decisions have required the full panoply of procedural due process before a state taking of a welfare grant[106] and prior to the garnishment of wages by a creditor,[107] among other situations. What commends these situations for due process and judicial review over the permanent placement of Timmy?

Note on the Interstate Compact on the Placement of Children (ICPC)

The latter stages of a dependency case will involve possible permanent placement where parental rights will be terminated. This requires an evaluation of placement options, as the *Drummond* case and others discuss. Often, such placements may be with new care providers in other states, especially where long-term foster care, guardianships. or adoptions involve relatives of the child not living in the state of child residence and court jurisdiction. The Interstate Compact on the Placement of Children (ICPC) was established in 1960 to address this issue, allowing the original court (the "sending" state) to retain jurisdiction over the child. Under the Compact, which has been enacted in all fifty states, the "receiving" state is obligated to conduct a pre-placement "home study," and "post placement" supervision to assure safety. And they may occur under the ICPC where placements are arranged by courts, agencies or private persons.

In one detailed critique of the ICPC, Professor Vivek Sankaran identifies several areas of concern:[108]

> While this approach might make some sense in theory, in practice, this process is tearing families apart. First, it takes child welfare agencies months, if not longer, to conduct interstate home studies. While the process slowly unfolds, children languish in the homes of strangers. Courts and other stakeholders remain largely powerless to expedite home studies. Despite the fact that the ICPC is undermining the system's goal of keeping kids with extended family, stakeholders remain resigned to the reality that these inordinate delays will always exist.

> Second, caseworkers (many of whom are not actually licensed social workers) complete home studies using evaluation standards that are unclear and ill-defined. Does a relative need to be licensed as a foster parent? Does a prior criminal conviction render them unfit to care for a child? Does the size of their home matter? What about their employment status? Each jurisdiction seems to have differing— and conflicting standards—by which these decisions are made.

> Finally, the lack of clarity over placement standards is exacerbated by the fact that child welfare agencies—and not courts—have the sole discretion to determine whether the placement can be made. In other words, if the agency in the state in which the potential placement lives denies the home study, the placement cannot happen

> Think about that. One caseworker's unilateral decision can result in a child's permanent separation from his or her extended family. The judge, along with others who advocate for the family, remain powerless to act.

Professor Sankaran offers suggestions for reform:

> So how do we fix this mess? First, Congress should impose more stringent requirements as to how quickly home studies must be completed. Federal law currently requires home studies to be done within 60 days in interstate cases, and the Family First Prevention Services Act requires states to maintain an electronic interstate processing system by the year 2027. Stricter, enforceable deadlines are needed now. Absent compelling circumstances, they should be completed within 14 days of a request. A longer deadline only places the needs of the bureaucracy ahead of those of the child.

Second, federal law should clarify exactly what information caseworkers must collect in an ICPC home study, and who is entitled to a copy of that report. At a minimum, all parties in the child welfare case—along with the relatives seeking the placement—should receive a copy of an ICPC home study.

Third, and perhaps most importantly, the ICPC must be amended to put the ultimate decision about whether or not the placement can be made in the hands of the juvenile court judge who is presiding over the child welfare matter. The judge should make this decision after receiving the completed home study and hearing the arguments of everyone involved, including the caseworker who conducted the study.

Summary of Key Reforms in Child Protection[109]

As the "current policy discussion above in this chapter suggests, there are several priority areas for child advocates regarding reform of child protection, in addition to the overarching need to assure attorney representation of children in dependency court: (a) prevention through a higher percentage of intended births; (b) family foster care supply and quality enhancement; (c) refinement of excessive confidentiality for dependency court and foster care regulation; (d) a major commitment to combat parental drug abuse—particularly of amphetamines; and (e) state assistance to foster children (and those adopted from foster care) to age 26.

Prevention through a higher percentage of intended births. The unwed birth rate has reached almost 40%.[110] A substantial number of children are not intended by one or both parents. These children are disproportionately subject to abuse, neglect and removal into foster care. Public programs that stimulate the ethic of a child's simple right to be intended by those persons creating him or her—and support for any measure accomplishing it—from parenting education, to sex education, to abstinence encouragement, to stimulation of the old fashioned values of marriage and commitment are all properly considered (see discussion in Chapters 2 and 3). Parenting education that extends beyond reproductive responsibility and includes basic information about child development and dangers (from shaking babies to leaving children unattended in automobile car seats during the day) also has important prevention value. Parenting education advocates argue that few high school students will actually use their trigonometry lessons, or revisit the table of elements as adults. But most will become parents and the health of their children may depend upon what they know. To the extent such education is a part of the modern curriculum, it currently is concentrated in home economics classes eschewed by the male half of the population.

Family foster care supply and quality enhancement. Eighty percent of adoptions for foster children come through their family foster care providers. Historically, the demographics of stay-at-home moms produced a substantial supply of such homes. However, with real estate prices and child care costs, few adults below the upper-middle to upper classes can afford to provide a home for a child without at least receiving the cost of such care. But compensation remains low—usually in the $500 to $700 per month for a child. As a result, the supply of family foster care providers has not grown commensurate with foster child caseloads. Meanwhile, group homes are commonly paid $4,000 to $5,000 per month for each child—and more if educational services are provided. This distortion has stimulated group home placement with the lack of an intimate, permanent, committed family so essential to healthy child development. And it leaves tens of thousands of foster children eligible for and warranting adoption without the intimacy of a family. Where foster children have special needs, allowing substantial additional compensation to family foster care providers who obtain skills and training in their disabilities will increase supply in areas requiring special commitment.

Revision of confidentiality for dependency court and foster care regulation. Some cases may warrant a protective order, as with some molestation cases. But a policy of openness subject to confidentiality when and if so warranted will have advantages for involved children. Those children are not subject to public ridicule or calumny—they are more often the heroes in the stories coming before the court. But all that has happened, and the actions of the court, and of the departments of social services—are subject to presumptive confidentiality in most states. While it may be possible to waive that secrecy, the catch-22 of not knowing to file such a petition insulates the child welfare system from public visibility and democratic accountability. Hence, a 25-year-old can assault and injure a 20-year-old spouse or friend and the proceedings and outcome are public. But if the victim is 15 or 7 or 4, it is generally adjudicated in secret. Child advocates argue that even when children die while in foster care, the circumstances of their deaths are kept effectively from public examination. And they contend that those foster care children in group homes—and who might be adoptable if more visible—are subject to less exposure for that purpose than are the abandoned dogs in the local pound.

A major commitment to combat parental drug abuse. Attorneys who represent children in dependency court generally observe a high correlation between parental drug abuse and child neglect. Some drugs, particularly so-called "speed," seem to reduce maternal and paternal instinct and at the same time speed up metabolic reactions in ways harmful to involved children. The popular culture is ambivalent about such drug use—with notions of civil liberties and personal choice dampening societal response. Those who practice in juvenile dependency court know that they are not victimless crimes when children are involved.

State assistance to foster children to age 26. The median age of youth self-sufficiency is 26 years. Until that time, most youth do not fully earn their own keep. Responsible parents assist their children as they enter adulthood, helping them with education costs, room and board, and employment. However, child advocates argue that those foster children for whom the state serves as parent are commonly abandoned to the streets at age 18. "Independent Living," tuition assistance, and other programs have increased in number and resources since the late 1990s. However, these programs do not approach the transitional help a typical parent provides. They will assist a number of emancipating youth with rent for several years. However, these youth must work full time, even with this help, to pay rent and for food and other basics given the costs of the 21st century. That burden makes higher education (even with low or subsidized tuition) problematical for most of them. The reduction of emancipation age to 18 from 21 occurred during the late 1960s and the new cut-off did not distinguish between youth obligations and protections. When foster youth age out of care, they generally have nobody to answer basic questions about life's concerns. There is no opportunity to move back home when things get tough. They have nobody to ask for a loan. There is no family health insurance policy providing coverage. Their caseworker is no longer available. Their attorney (if they were lucky enough to have one) has closed their file. They are, quite literally, on their own.

The "continuation" approach of the 2008 Fostering Connections Act, or other bureaucratic "application for housing assistance models" are of only marginal advantage for many youth. These approaches rely on social worker control of youth, applications and qualification, submission to visits and control by public employees, and little assistance beyond shelter and food.

An alternative approach is to create "trusts" approved by the dependency courts who have been the legal parents of these children and who are effectively removed from involvement by the Fostering Connections approach.[111] Such trusts give the court continuing jurisdiction over the funds committed to it—ideally at the same levels provided by private parents. The trust agreement would be administered by a mentor known to the youth and monitored by the court. The youth would have input into the plan for self-sufficiency and it would be alterable and customized with spending not tied to foster provider payments or mental health treatment or any predetermined account. The administration of funding and assistance under this proposal is not dictated by regulations and administered by social workers where the youth are part of a "caseload."

ENDNOTES

[1] Act of April 21, 1899 [1899] III. Laws 131.

[2] U.S. Department of Health & Human Services, Children's Bureau, *Child Maltreatment 2017* (Washington DC; 2019). Available from https://www.acf.hhs.gov/cb/research-data-technology/ statistics-research/child-maltreatment.

[3] Numerous states are not included in this data due to variances in how court representation is reported. Furthermore, the Administration for Children and Families does not include state data if fewer than 5% of victims had a court-appointed representative.

[4] Administration for Children and Families indicates that states are continuing to work to improve the collection and reporting of this data.

[5] U.S. Department of Health and Human Services, Children's Bureau, *The AFCARS Report (25)*, at www.acf.hhs.gov/cb; see also U.S. Department of Health and Human Services, Children's Bureau, The AFCARS Report (23),at www.acf.hhs.gov/cb.

[6] U.S. Department of Health and Human Services, Children's Bureau, *The AFCARS Report (25)* at www.acf.hhs.gov/cb.

[7] *Id.*

[8] Andrea Sedlak, *et al., Fourth National Incidence Study of Child Abuse and Neglect (NIS–4): Report to Congress* (Washington DC; 2010) https://www.acf.hhs.gov/sites/default/files/opre/nis4_report_congress_full_pdf_jan2010.pdf.

[9] U.S. Department of Health and Human Services, Children's Bureau, Child Welfare Information Gateway, *Parental Substance Use and the Child Welfare System* (Washington DC; 2014) at https://www.childwelfare.gov/pubPDFs/parentalsubabuse.pdf.

[10] Robin Ghertner, *et al., The Relationship between Substance Use Indicators and Child Welfare Caseloads* (U.S. Department of Health and Human Services, Washington DC; 2018) at https://aspe.hhs.gov/system/files/pdf/258831/SubstanceUseCWCaseloads.pdf.

[11] Pub. L. No. 96-272 (42 U.S.C. § 420).

[12] 42 U.S.C. §§ 620-629m.

[13] Before 1996, there were three programs within Aid for Families with Dependent Children (AFDC): AFDC-U, AFDC-FG and AFDC-FC. The first two pertain to impoverished families and these programs were supplanted in the Personal Responsibility and Work Opportunity Reconciliation Act of that year, becoming the Temporary Assistance to Needy Families (TANF) program, funded through block grants. But the third grouping, AFDC-Foster Care or AFDC-FC, helped to pay foster children costs of car. This third fund was not transferred to a block grant structure with limits and with new qualifications. It remained an entitlement. Some states refer to their share of federal Foster Care payments as "TANF-FC." But others, including this text, refer to it most often as Social Security Act (SSA) "Title IV-E" funding—its current source.

[14] 42 U.S.C. § 5101 *et seq.*

[15] See Robert C. Fellmeth, *A White Paper on America's Family Values* (University of San Diego School of Law, San Diego, CA; 2018) at http://www.caichildlaw.org/Misc/WP.pdf.

[16] See Pub. L. No. 104-188.

[17] See Margot L. Crandall-Hollick, *Adoption Tax Benefits: An Overview* (Congressional Research Service, Washington DC; 2018) at https://fas.org/sgp/crs/misc/R44745.pdf.

[18] The enacted version was based on a compromise between H.R. 867 and the Senate's SAFE and PASS Acts. However, it omitted a number of important provisions sought by child advocates, including more money for permanency services and training for child protection case workers. The child protection system depends critically upon the professional judgment of social workers employed by county child protection agencies (working within county departments of social services). An incompetent or strongly biased social worker can influence decisions affecting the health, safety, and future of children. Child advocates contend that the competence and expertise of this group is uneven. Civil service protection makes weeding out those who consistently manifest bad judgment difficult.

[19] 42 U.S.C. 677.

[20] Fellmeth, *supra* note 15.

[21] *Id.*

[22] Mark Courtney, *et al., Planning a Next-Generation Evaluation Agenda for the John H. Chafee Foster Care Independency Program*, (U.S. Department of Health and Human Services, Washington DC; 2017). https://www.acf.hhs.gov/sites/default/files/opre/20180103_planning_a_next_generation_final508_newfinal2_b508.pdf.

[23] Mark Courtney, *et al., Findings from the California Youth Transitions to Adulthood Study (CalYOUTH): Conditions of Youth at Age 21* (Chapin Hall at the University of Chicago, Chicago IL; 2018).

[24] See Isabel Sawhill, Quentin Karpilow, and Joanna Venator, *The Impact of Unintended Childbearing on Future Generations* (The Brookings Institution: Washington DC; 2014) at. https://www.brookings.edu/wp-content/uploads/2016/06/12_impact_unintended_childbearing_future_sawhill.pdf.

[25] See William Schneider, *Single Mothers, the Role of Fathers, and the Risk for Child Maltreatment*, 81 CHILDREN AND YOUTH SERV. REV. 81–93 (2017).

[26] D.K. Smith, *et al.*, *Child Maltreatment and Foster Care: Unpacking the Effects of Prenatal and Postnatal Parental Substance Use*, 12 CHILD MALTREATMENT (2007).

[27] Laura Radel, *et al.*, *Substance Use, the Opioid Epidemic, and the Child Welfare System: Key Findings from a Mixed Methods Study (*March 7, 2018). https://aspe.hhs.gov/system/files/pdf/258836/SubstanceUseChildWelfareOverview.pdf.

[28] *Id.*

[29] B.H. Chaiyachati, *et al.*, *Preventing child maltreatment: Examination of an established statewide home-visiting program*, 79 CHILD ABUSE & NEGLECT, 476-484 (2018).

[30] In 1998, California Republican Governor Pete Wilson vetoed SB 2138 which would have implemented basic parenting education in high school, writing: "SB 2138 requires parental notification—but not consent. It...should offer to those parents and pupils who desire it, the option to satisfy the curricular requirement (here created) by alternatives...which could include church-based or home-teaching." In 1999, new Democratic California Governor Gray Davis then vetoed SB 305 to provide more modest parenting education. His veto message stated: "The primary responsibility of schools is to teach the basics....I do not believe the teaching of parenting skills is the appropriate role of schools. Rather, this is a subject that is rightfully the domain of parents, families, faith-based entities and non-profit organizations." See Children's Advocacy Institute, *Children's Legislative Report Card 1998* (San Diego, CA; October 1998) at 13; Children's Advocacy Institute, *Children's Legislative Report Card 1999* (San Diego, CA; October 1999) at 11 (http://www.sandiego.edu/childrensissues).

[31] U.S. Department of Health and Human Services, *Patterns of Foster Care Placement and Family Reunification Following Child Maltreatment Investigations* (2016) at https://aspe.hhs.gov/system/files/pdf/258526/Reunification.pdf.

[32] U.S. Department of Health and Human Services, *supra* note 6.

[33] H. Ringeisen, *et al.*, *Risk of long-term foster care placement among children involved with the child welfare system. OPRE Report #2013-30.* (U.S. Department of Health and Human Services, Washington, DC; 2013).

[34] See https://datacenter.kidscount.org/data/tables/8822-children-in-foster-care-with-more-than-two-placements?loc=1&loct=1#detailed/1/any/false/870,573,869,36,868,867,133,38,35,18/any/17680,17681.

[35] U.S. Department of Health and Human Services, *Patterns of Foster Care Placement and Family Reunification Following Child Maltreatment Investigations*, December 2016.

[36] See https://www.childtrends.org/wp-content/uploads/2017/01/United-States-Adoption-Factsheet_2015-1.pdf.

[37] U.S. Department of Health and Human Services, *supra* note 6.

[38] Haksoon Ahn, *et al.*, *Estimating minimum adequate foster care costs for children in the United States*, 84 CHILDREN AND YOUTH SERV. REV. 55-67 (2018).

[39] U.S. Department of Health and Human Services, *supra* note 6.

[40] *Midwest Foster Care & Adoption Ass'n v. Kincade*, 712 F.3d 1190 (8th Cir. 2013).

[41] See *New York State Citizens' Coalition for Children v. Carrion*, 31 F. Supp. 3d 512 (E.D.N.Y.2014).

[42] *See, e.g., C.H. v. Payne*, 683 F. Supp. 2d 865, 877 (S.D. Ind. 2010); *Cal. Alliance of Child and Family Servs. v. Allenby*, 459 F. Supp. 2d 919, 925 (N.D. Cal. 2006);. *Mo. Childcare Ass'n v. Martin*, 241 F. Supp. 2d 1032, 1040-41 (W.D. Mo. -2003); *Kenny A.*, 218 F.R.D, at 292; *LaShawn A.*, 762 F. Supp. at 989 (1991).

[43] 42 U.S.C. § 5106a(b)(2)(B)(xiii).

[44] See *ABA Standards of Practice for Lawyers Who Represent Children in Abuse and Neglect Cases*; see also NACC Recommendations for Representation of Children in Abuse and Neglect Cases at https://www.naccchildlaw.org/page/StandardsOfPractice.

[45] See *E.T. v. George*, Ninth Circuit Court of Appeals Case No. 10-15248, discussed briefly in Chapter 1, a class action on behalf of the foster children of Sacramento County. Although the federal district court acknowledged the constitutional right of dependent children to counsel, and the problems inherent in caseloads of 380 or more, it invoked the doctrine of "abstention" to refuse jurisdiction, characterizing the matter as one lying within the discretion of the state court system (see http://www.caichildlaw.org/Misc/Order_re_Motion_to_Dismiss.pdf). The Ninth Circuit found that abstention was proper and affirmed dismissal of the complaint. The U.S. Supreme Court subsequently denied Plaintiff's Cert Petition in 2012.

See pleadings, appellants' brief, and amicus brief of Voices for America's Children *et al.*, and of Children's Rights of New York, and other documents at http://www.caichildlaw.org/caseload.htm.

[46] A. Zinn & J. Slowriver, *Expediting Permanency: Legal Representation for Foster Children in Palm Beach County* (Chapin Hall Center for Children: Chicago, IL; 2008).

[47] For the text of the Act, see https://apps.americanbar.org/litigation/committees/childrights/docs/aba_model_act_2011.pdf.

[48] Age seven is viewed by some advocates as the appropriate separation between the need for a client-directed attorney and a best interests attorney. *See, e.g.,* Donald Duquette, *Special Issue on Legal Representation of Children: Responses to the Conference: Two Distinct Roles/Bright Line Test,* 6 NEV. L.J. 1240, (Spring 2006). See also research of John Anzelc, Melissa Cohen & Sarah Taylor, an interdisciplinary student group from the University of Michigan Law School who participated in the semester-long Lance J. Johnson Children in the Law Workshop and studied the capacity of children to participate in decisions affecting their welfare and provided to the American Bar Association Children's Rights Litigation Committee in a Memo dated April 24th, 2009, and titled, *Comment on the Committee's Model Act Governing Representation of Children in Abuse and Neglect Proceedings* (a child begins to have greater decision-making ability due to their increased problem-solving abilities and their greater understanding of the importance of a broader social sphere at approximately age seven).

[49] First Star and Children's Advocacy Institute, *A Child's Right to Counsel: A National Report Card on Legal Representation for Abused and Neglected Children,* Third Edition (2012); see http://www.caichildlaw.org/Misc/3rd_Ed_Childs_Right_to_Counsel.pdf.

[50] Congressional Research Office, *Social Services Block Grant: Background and Funding* (Washington DC; March 2016) at https://fas.org/sgp/crs/misc/94-953.pdf.

[51] Liz Schott, Ife Floyd, and Ashley Burnside, *How States Use Funds Under the TANF Block Grant* (Center on Budget and Policy Priorities, Washington DC; 2018).

[52] For calculation of total safety net reduction (TANF plus food stamps) to approximately 70% of the poverty line for the benchmark family of mother and two children in California by 2004–05, see Robert C. Fellmeth, *California Children's Budget 2004-05,* (Children's Advocacy Institute, San Diego, CA; June 2004) at Chapter 2. The trend since the 2004 report has not altered the previous decade of sequentially accruing cuts in this basic poverty ameliorating account.

[53] According to the Center on Budget and Policy Priorities, the falling of the TANF-to-Poverty Ratio indicates that TANF is less responsive to need. This can happen if the number of families receiving TANF drops while the number of families living in poverty does not, or if the number of families in poverty increases without an increase in the number of families receiving TANF. See Schott, *supra* note 51.

[54] Ife Floyd, Ashley Burnside, Liz Schott, *TANF Reaching Few Poor Families* (Center on Budget and Policy Priorities, Washington DC; 2018).

[55] Child care costs in states ranged from an average of $4,822 per year per child in Mississippi to $22,631 per year per child. Two children would consume virtually all of the net earnings of a single mother making minimum wage in most states.

[56] States are allowed to opt-out of this restriction. By 2001, eight states and D.C. had fully done so and another 20 states modified the restriction. As of 2017, about a dozen states continue the ban while half of all states have modified it to some degree.

[57] These funds must not be used for services to children or families with incomes below 200% of the poverty line. Note that a small additional percentage may now be transferred for any use if related to impoverished children. See Schott, *supra* note 51.

[58] Fred Cheesman, *Key Findings From the Evaluation of Open Hearings and Court Records in Juvenile Protection Matters, Final Report-Volume 1* (National Center for State Courts, Williamsburg, VA; 2001).

[59] Gregory Broberg & Vera Lopez, *Arizona Open Dependency Hearing Pilot Study: Final Report* (2006) at http://www.azcourts.gov/LinkClick.aspx?fileticket=MIqR1UH59Q4%3D&tabid=2023.

[60] For examples of such exposes leading to reforms in California, see http://www.caichildlaw.org/price-awards.htm. Note the consistent association of reform legislation and the publicly known circumstances of child victims (Chelsea's Law, Amber Alerts, *et al.*).

[61] Children's Advocacy Institute and First Star, *State Secrecy and Child Deaths in the U.S.,* 2nd ed. (April 2012); see http://www.caichildlaw.org/Misc/StateSecrecy2ndEd.pdf.

[62] See Child Welfare Policy Manual at https://www.acf.hhs.gov/cwpm/public_html/programs/cb/laws_policies/laws/cwpm/policy_dsp_pf.jsp?citID=68.

[63] Children's Advocacy Institute, *supra* note 61.

[64] U.S. Department of Health and Human Services, *Highlights from the National Youth in Transition Database Survey: Data Brief #5* (Washington DC; 2016) at https://www.acf.hhs.gov/sites/default/files/cb/nytd_data_brief_5.pdf.

[65] Courtney, *supra* note 23.

[66] Children's Advocacy Institute and First Star, *The Fleecing of Foster Children: How We Confiscate Their Assets and Undermine Their Financial Security* (Washington, D.C., 2011) at ES-1, www.caichildlaw.org.

[67] 42 U.S.C. § 677.

[68] *Id.*

[69] 42 U.S.C. § 677(a)(4). These services may be available to foster children who are 16 or older when they exit the system to kin guardianship or adoption as well.

[70] FCIA funding is a capped entitlement, and states are required to provide a 20% match on their total allotment, based on youth in federally-funded foster care.

[71] 42 U.S.C § 677(i)(4). Vouchers may be available to pay for the cost of attendance at an institution of higher education as defined at 20 U.S.C. § 1002. Vouchers shall not exceed the lesser of $5,000 per year or the total cost of attendance as defined at 20 U.S.C. § 1087.

[72] See https://trends.collegeboard.org/college-pricing/figures-tables/average-published-undergraduate-charges-sector-2018-19.

[73] Such youth receive on average $2,000 per annum from Chafee, with a state match of 20% bringing the amount up to $2,400. Accordingly, at current levels, the total average amount received over three years per emancipated youth is $7,200.

[74] Children's Advocacy Institute, *Expanding Transitional Services for Emancipating Foster Youth* (January 2007) at ii–iii. Note that California has an unusual new sum for a Transition Housing Program Plus (THP-Plus), but even with its total of $40 million added, and with other state and described federal resources, the fortunate few youth benefitting from the program receive less than one-half of the median amount private parents provide. The percentage is much lower for those foster youth not eligible for higher education assistance or suffering practical obstacles to application for further education. And it is negligible for youth who are not accepted for THP Plus help. See www.caichildlaw.org/TransitionalServices.htm for continuing data on emancipating foster youth and advocacy efforts on their behalf.

[75] See http://www.caichildlaw.org/Misc/TLC_Summary.pdf; for a summary of the Plan, background data and related studies and citations, see http://www.caichildlaw.org/TransitionalServices.htm#S.

[76] See https://www.childrensrights.org/.

[77] For the full report, see http://www.caichildlaw.org/Misc/Shame%20on%20U.S._FINAL.pdf.

[78] There has been no serious threat to withhold federal monies or to otherwise insist on compliance with federal law. Note that while child advocates do not encourage federal financial withdrawal, that threat has demonstrated efficacy in changing state policies prior to the actual withdrawal of such funds.

[79] For back up information and citations, see http://www.caichildlaw.org/Shame_on_US.htm.

[80] See http://www.caichildlaw.org/Misc/WP.pdf.

[81] Children's Advocacy Institute, *supra* note 66, at ES-1–5.

[82] California Attorney General's Office, *Child Victim Witness Investigative Pilot Projects: Research and Evaluation Final Report* (Sacramento, CA; July 1994).

[83] See the Child Victims' and Child Witness' Protection Act of 1990, 18 U.S.C. § 3509 allowing in federal court closed circuit two way testimony by child victims of sexual abuse, or of sexual exploitation (pornography production, prostitution), or children witnessing a crime against a third party. However, the procedure requires an evidentiary finding that such a child could not communicate reasonably in the close physical presence of the defendant. Over half of the nation's states have enacted statutes allowing either two-way, or one-way video testimony by such a qualifying child. Such arrangements commonly allow for cross examination of a child by defense counsel in a less intimidating room without the jury, or defendant physically present, but with prosecutor, defense counsel and usually the court in the room with the child, with all other persons able to see the testimony via video transmission into the regular court room. See *Maryland v. Craig* and related discussion in Chapter 9, *infra.*

[84] U.S. Department of Justice, *Recidivism of Adult Sexual Offenders* (2015) https://smart.gov/pdfs/RecidivismofAdultSexualOffenders.pdf.

[85] See also *Seling v. Young*, 531 U.S. 250 (2000), allowing such statutes to be characterized as "civil" rather than criminal, thus avoiding double jeopardy, double punishment, or *ex post facto* bars were the proceeding to be considered a continuation of the criminal case.

[86] 42 U.S.C. § 14071.

[87] U.S. Dep't of Justice, *The National Strategy for Child Exploitation Prevention and Interdiction: A Report to Congress* 8 (2010).

[88] The use of underage performers led to the Protection of Children Against Sexual Exploitation Act of 1977 adding 18 U.S.C. §§ 2251–2252. The first section makes it a federal crime to use children in "sexually explicit" productions, with sanctions for both the producer and applicable parents or guardians allowing such labor. Section 2252 prohibits the transportation or receipt in interstate commerce for profit

of such "obscene" visual or print material.

89 18 U.S.C. § 2255.

[90] 18 U.S.C. § 2259.

[91] 18 U.S.C. § 2251 *et seq.*

[92] 18 U.S.C. § 2256(8).

[93] 18 U.S.C. §§ 1460–1466.

[94] Dissenting Justice O'Connor would distinguish the two, striking the portion of the statute prohibiting depiction of those over 18 as under that age, but upholding the ban on entirely computer generated children engaged in sexual activity.

[95] Note that the statute defines prohibited "sexually explicit conduct" by apparent children, as: "actual or simulated...sexual intercourse, including genital-genital, oral-genital, anal-genital, or oral anal, whether between persons of the same or opposite sex...bestiality;...masturbation;...sadistic or masochistic abuse;... or lascivious exhibition of the genitals or pubic area of any person." 18 U.S.C. § 2256(2). Hence, the statute appears to ban specific depiction of sex acts by children; child nudity is prohibited only where "lascivious." Such nudity would require the prurient element of obscenity, but would not be subject to its "redeeming value" factor.

[96] The *Ashcroft* Court quoted from *Miller v. California*, 413 U.S. 15 (1973), discussing necessary elements for obscenity.

[97] Ami Carpenter and Jamie Gates, *The Nature and Extent of Gang Involvement in Sex Trafficking in San Diego County* (San Diego, CA; 2016).

[98] K. Walker & F. Quraishi, *From Abused and Neglected to Abused and Exploited: The Intersection Between the Child Welfare System and Child Sex Trafficking* (National Center for Youth Law, Oakland, CA; 2014).

[99] Shared Hope International, *Protected Innocence Challenge: Toolkit 2017* (Vancouver WA; 2017) at https://sharedhope.org/wp-content/uploads/2017/11/2017-PIC-Toolkit.pdf.

[100] See https://sharedhope.org/what-we-do/bring-justice/reportcards/protected-innocence-challenge-issue-briefs/#section1.

[101] *See, e.g., State ex rel HHS v. W.P. (In Re W.L.P.)*, 345 Ore. 657 (2009).

[102] *See, e.g., In re Taylor E.*, 958 A.2d 170 at 183 (Conn.App.Ct 2008). The Supreme Court application of confrontation rights from the Supreme Court decision in *Crawford v. Washington*, 541 U.S. 36 (2004) does not appear to apply. Nor are Miranda warnings required for statement admissibility in dependency court.

[103] 588 F.3d 1011 (9th Cir. 2009). For an amicus brief filed for neither party outlining one point of view, see www.caichildlaw.org/Misc/Camreta_CAI_Amicus_FINAL.pdf.

[104] See Vivek Sankaran, *Moving Beyond Lassiter: The Need for a Federal Statutory Right to Counsel for Parents in Child Welfare Cases*, 44 J. LEGIS. 1 (2017). See also www.civilrighttocounsel. org/map for a map of states indicating their approach to the right to counsel for parents and children in child welfare proceedings.

[105] See http://www.caichildlaw.org/caseload.htm.

[106] *Goldberg v. Kelly*, 397 U.S. 254 (1970).

[107] *Sniadach v. Family Finance Corp. of Bay View*, 395 U.S. 337 (1969).

[108] Vivek Sankaran, *Can We Please Fix the Interstate Placement of Children in Foster Care*, The Chronicle of Social Change (October 9, 2018) at https://chronicleofsocialchange.org/child-welfare-2/can-please-fix-interstate-placement-children-foster-care.

[109] For more on these issues, see Children's Advocacy Institute, *A White Paper on America's Family Values, supra* note 15, and *Shame on U.S., supra* note 77.

[110] See https://www.cdc.gov/nchs/data/nvsr/nvsr67_01.pdf; see also https://www.cdc.gov/nchs/data/nvsr/nvsr67nvsr67_01_tables.pdf#126.

[111] See http://www.caichildlaw.org/TransitionalServices.htm.

CHAPTER NINE

Child Rights as Abuse Victims/Witnesses

A. CHILD COMPETENCY TO TESTIFY

More than 100,000 children testify in court each year.[1] Competency to testify traditionally requires the ability to perceive, remember, and communicate; the ability to tell the difference between truth and a lie; and an understanding of the duty to tell the truth. These tests apply to the situation at trial, not when the events testified about occurred. An exception is sometimes drawn where a child is so young when the events occurred that he or she is incapable of their accurate recall. Yet, children as young as three have been found to be competent witnesses. In a recent example, a three-year-old alleged victim of molestation was deemed competent to testify based on her demonstrated ability to remember facts such as the names of her teachers and the judge from a previous trial, and her recognition of the importance of not telling a lie, which she noted "can get you in trouble with both man and God."[2] Witness competency is traditionally determined just before trial (through a motion *in limine*) or through *voir dire* at trial (out of the presence of the jury).

At common law, children below the age of 14 have been presumed incompetent to testify as witnesses in court while those who have reached 14 are presumed competent. In either case, the presumption may be rebutted with evidence to either allow or disallow testimony. Some states draw the line for presumption shift at 10 years of age. Evidence scholars have criticized the tendency of some courts to bar testimony of child witnesses, contending that it reflects a distrust of the primary jury role—to evaluate credibility of witnesses.[3] The trend has been to more liberally allow testimony, deferring to the jury its proper weight, consistent with Rule 601 of the Federal Rules of Evidence, which presumes that every person is competent to testify.

Historically, objections about child testimony have centered around four issues: perception, memory, narration, and truthfulness. Studies during the 1970s and 1980s rebutted much of that concern, finding that children were not more prone than adults to give false testimony.[4] Language limitations and complexity may require questions to be simplified, and leading questions are commonly permitted.

The primary concern evolving in the 1990s was that children are "suggestible" as witnesses—that a parent or other authority figure can plant detailed facts or stories which children can come to believe and testify about with dangerous efficacy. Sociologically, the emotional trauma during divorce and the regrettably common use of children by one parent against the other has led to increasing accusations of child abuse or molestation. Not all of these accusations have merit, and children have been enlisted by one or both parents to buttress a case against the other. The result has been added suspicion concerning the credibility of child testimony.

The Suggestibility of the Child Witness:An Historical Review and Synthesis

by
Stephen J. Ceci, Cornell University
Maggie Bruck, McGill University

More research on children's eyewitness testimony has been conducted in the past decade than in the rest of the twentieth century combined....A synthesis of this research posits three "families" of factors, cognitive, social, and biological, which must be taken into consideration if we are to understand seemingly contradictory interpretations of findings. It is concluded that there are reliable age differences in suggestibility, due to a variety of factors, but that even very young children are capable of recalling much that is forensically relevant.

* * *

The second aspect of children's testimonial credibility concerns their "suggestibility", and it is this aspect that is the focus of the present review. According to its broadest definition, suggestibility concerns the degree to which children's encoding, storage, and/or retrieval of events can be influenced by a range of internal and external factors...how easily one is influenced by both subtle suggestions and leading questions, as well as by explicit bribes, threats, and other forms of inducement. By broadening this definition of suggestibility to entail all forms of influence, not just mnemonic ones, this paper summarizes the literature that addresses the following two questions. First, are children more suggestible than adults? Second, to what degree does children's suggestibility reflect cognitive factors, social-motivated factors, and/or biological factors? The examination of these questions allows for a more precise understanding not only of the conditions under which children are suggestible, but more generally of the causal mechanisms that underlie their suggestibility.

Historical Review

* * *

During the final decade of the seventeenth century, a group of children known as the "circle girls" gave false testimony in the witchcraft trials of over 20 residents of Salem Village and Salem Farms, Massachusetts. The girls claimed to have seen the defendants flying on broom sticks, to have witnessed celestial apparitions in the form of speaking animals, and to have observed the defendants instructing insects to fly into their mouths and deposit bent nails and pins in their stomachs (which they subsequently vomited during their testimony). On the basis of their testimony, 20 defendants were convicted and put to death, and a dozen more were spared execution because they threw themselves on the mercy of the court, and admitted their participation in witchcraft. In the aftermath of the executions, some of the child witnesses publicly recanted their testimonies....

* * *

...Perhaps no other researcher has done more to redress the historical imbalance in favor of child witnesses than has Gail Goodman. After almost a century of research criticizing and belittling the accuracy and suggestibility of child witnesses, Goodman has presented a picture that is far more optimistic about children's abilities. Her work is animated in part by a desire to know whether non-abused children will make false claims of abuse in response to erroneous suggestions by adults. In order to examine this question, Goodman's strategy has been to interview nonabused children about sexual as well as non-sexual experiences.

As one example, Goodman, Rudy, Bottoms, and Aman (1990) studied eighteen pairs of same-age, same-sex 4- and 7-year-old children who were left in a trailer with a strange adult. One child played a game with the adult that involved being dressed in a clown's costume, being lifted and photographed, while the other child was encouraged to carefully observe this interchange. Approximately ten days later, both children were asked general and specific questions about the event by a different adult. During this interview, suggestive and non-suggestive questions about the event were asked. Some of these questions concerned actions that might lead to an accusation of child abuse, such as "He took your clothes off, didn't he?" Older children were more accurate on the suggestive questions. Overall, the older children also gave more accurate answers (93%) to the "abuse" questions than did the younger children (83%). However, Goodman *et al.* feel that these figures represent an overestimate of suggestibility in reference to courtroom issues, since a more detailed analysis of the incorrect answers to the suggestive abuse questions, revealed that there was only one false report of abuse (out of a possible 252) given by the seven-year-olds, and there were only 13 false reports given by the five-year-olds. Goodman, *et al.* claimed that under these circumstances child participants and bystanders are equally accurate in resisting the interviewer's erroneous suggestions about abusive actions. In fact, these children demonstrated surprise in response to the suggestive questions.

...A second study conducted by Goodman and her colleagues (Saywitz, *et al.*, 1989) examined 5- and 7-year-old girls' memories of medical examinations. Half of each age group had a scoliosis exam and half had a genital exam. Children were tested between one and four weeks following their exam. As was true in the Goodman *et al.* (1990) study just described, children were asked suggestive and non-suggestive questions which are abusive or nonabusive in nature. The older children's answers to the suggestive questions, and to the abuse-related questions were more accurate than those of the younger children. However, there was essentially no difference in resistance to suggestibility for "abuse related suggestive questions" (.96 vs. .99 for the 5- and 7-year-olds, respectively). Furthermore, the seven-year-old children never made a false report of abuse, and this occurred only three times (out of a possible 215 opportunities) for the five-year-olds. These findings led the investigators to conclude that, "...our findings indicated that there are important limits on children's suggestibility" (p. 9).

* * *

Although the studies just described highlight particular aspects of an interview that may influence children's reports, the experimental settings used by the researchers are pale versions of interviews carried out in legal settings (McGough, in press). In the latter context children are questioned, on average, eleven times prior to testifying in court, often by a number of different interviewers (*e.g.*, parents, police, therapists, child protection workers, lawyers) who usually do not have a specific set of written questions. Rather, interviewers generally employ a variety of on-line strategies before and during the interview to achieve the goal of obtaining the most detailed and accurate information about events that a child may have witnessed.

* * *

[Many] of the State's interviews in the Kelly Michaels' case [involved] highly suggestive use of props (spoons, forks, knives, dolls), and a relentless pursuit of only one hypothesis, often accompanied by bribes for the promise of disclosure (popsicles, trips to the jail, use of the tape recorder, gifts of toy police badges) and implied threats in the face of nondisclosure. For example, upon Child 43C's insistence that he had not observed any wrong-doing by Michaels, Folloneras admonished: "Don't be a baby. You're acting like a nursery school kid." (p.10 A266 in Kelly Michaels case). In a similar vein, when Child 40C requested to leave the interview to eat, McGrath asked: "You're hungry? Okay. You tell me why you want to hit the doll and I'll give you something to eat...Okay., then I'm gonna stay here and we're gonna keep on with this, its okay with me. Cause I'm here to help you, and I know you want to tell me something and I'll stay here all day 'till you tell me."

A similar pattern of threats, bribes, and strong insinuations that their friends had already told investigators of the defendant's abusive behavior can also be seen in other cases (Benedek, 1989). For example, in the celebrated McMartin Preschool sex abuse case, jurors eventually acquitted the two defendants, Peggy McMartin and Raymond Buckey, on all 65 counts against them, claiming that the videotaped interviews conducted by the social worker who headed the team revealed doubts as to what the children actually remembered versus what the interviewer had suggested to them. For example, the interviewer informed the children that other children had already told of being sexually abused by the defendants.

* * *

...Experts in psychology, social work, pediatrics, and psychiatry frequently claim in court that children are incapable of lying, or are not suggestible (*e.g., People v. Watson*, 1965; *Commonwealth v. Seese*, 1986; *Matter of Nicole V.*, 1987; also see Mason, in press; McGough, in press). It is rare to see experts presenting a careful summary of the research, because doing so would probably force them to attenuate their often strident claims for one side or another.

As a way of avoid this problem, legal jurisdictions traditionally adopted what is known as a "Frye Test" standard, or the Kelly-Frye standard, which stipulates that expert testimony is only permitted when the research that underpins the expert's testimony is "sufficiently established to have gained general acceptance in the particular field in which it belongs." (Frye v. the United States, 1923 § 1014). This ruling came about as a result of an attempt to introduce the results of an early form of polygraph testing into the record. Federal Rule 703 has diluted the Frye Test standard somewhat, allowing that the data base that expert witnesses use "must be reasonably relied upon by experts in a field in forming opinions or inferences on the subject." Hence it is permissible for experts to disagree about the meaning of research findings, as long as they are aware of them. Since we assume that this review will serve as a basis for the opinions of some who venture into court as expert witnesses on childhood suggestibility, then the following three conclusions would seem to meet a traditional Fry Test standard.

First, and foremost, preschool aged children are disproportionately more vulnerable to erroneous post-event suggestion than are older individuals, contrary to disclaimers made by some (e.g., Melton, 1990). This conclusion follows from the synopsis of past and current research, over 90% of which shows reliable age differences in children's accuracy in the aftermath of leading questions....

Differences of opinion exist as to the boundary conditions for younger children's greater suggestibility, with some researchers arguing that it is diminished or even nonexistent when the act in question concerns a child's own body, or when it is a central action (e.g., Goodman, et al., 1990; also see Amicus Brief in Wright v. Idaho No. 89-260):

Resistance to suggestion appears to be highest concerning the core aspects of events. Moreover, participation in an event, as opposed to mere observation, appears to lower children's suggestibility. (p. 80)

Others, however, have failed to provide support for these claims....

Second, contrary to some claims, children will lie when the motivational structure is tilted toward lying. In this sense they are probably no different than adults...

Extreme statements that some have proferred in the media (e.g., "Children never lie" vs. "children are incapable of getting it right because they cannot distinguish reality and fantasy") are not supported by the findings reviewed here. That children are found to lie at times ought not surprise anyone, save the rather extreme advocates who have made such baseless claims. Children are, after all, members of the human race, and as such they should be susceptible to the same influences that older members are. More research is needed into age-related shifts in motivational salience, so that we have a better understanding of whether fear of reprisals, honoring a promise, resisting bribes, for example are more or less influential for a given age group. Until such research becomes available, it is safe to conclude that sometimes children will lie, but certainly not all of the time, nor uniformly in response to all motivational forces. And when children do lie, there is some evidence that they are easier to detect than adults due to their greater leakage through nonverbal and verbal behaviors (Bussey, 1990; Goodman, 1990; Peters, 1990), though this research does not approximate the cases in which children have been rehearsed, threatened, or cajoled by powerful adults over long periods.

Third, notwithstanding the above two points, it is clear that children—even preschoolers—are capable of recalling much that is forensically relevant. That their reports are more vulnerable to post-event distortion than those of older persons, and that they can be induced to lie in response to certain motives, is not meant to imply that they are incapable of providing accurate testimony. In fact, in most of the studies that have been reported during the past decade, young children are able to accurately recollect the majority of the information that they observed, even when they did not recall as much as older children. They may be more likely to succumb to erroneous suggestions than older children and adults, but their vulnerability is a matter of degree only. Even adults are suggestible (Belli, 1989; Loftus, 1979; Loftus & Hoffman, 1989), so the question ought not be "Are children suggestible?", but rather "Is their level of suggestibility so much greater than an adult's as to: a) render them worthless as witnesses?, b) require competency hearings to determine if they ought to be allowed to provide testimony to juries?, and/or c) require judges to instruct juries about their special reliability risks?" Based on the evidence reviewed in this paper, the answer to the first two of these questions is a qualified "no."

* * *

Source: Ceci. S.J. & Bruck, M. (1993) The Suggestibility of the Child Witness: A Historical Review and Synthesis. Psychological Bulletin, 113, 403-439. See http:www.cogstud.cornell.edu.faculty/ ed.ceci.html.

State v. Michaels

136 N.J. 299 (1994)

The opinion of the Court was delivered by HANDLER, J.

* * *

I

In September 1984, Margaret Kelly Michaels was hired by Wee Care Day Nursery ("Wee Care") as a teacher's aide for preschoolers. Located in St. George's Episcopal Church, in Maplewood, Wee Care served approximately fifty families, with an enrollment of about sixty children, ages three to five.

Michaels, a college senior from Pittsburgh, Pennsylvania, came to New Jersey to pursue an acting career. She responded to an advertisement and was hired by Wee Care, initially as a teacher's aide for preschoolers, then, at the beginning of October, as a teacher. Michaels had no prior experience as a teacher at any level.

Wee Care had staff consisting of eight teachers, numerous aides, and two administrators. The nursery classes for the three-year-old children were housed in the basement, and the kindergarten class was located on the third floor. During nap time, Michaels, under the supervision of the head teacher and the director, was responsible for about twelve children in one of the basement classrooms. The classroom assigned to Michaels was separated from an adjacent occupied classroom by a vinyl curtain.

During the seven-month-period that Michaels worked at Wee Care, she apparently performed satisfactorily. Wee Care never received a complaint about her from staff, children, or parents. According to the State, however, between October 8, 1984, and the date of Michaels's resignation on April 26, 1985, parents and teachers began observing behavioral changes in the children.

On April 26, 1985, the mother of M.P., a four-year-old in Michaels's nap class, noticed while awakening him for school, that he was covered with spots. She took the child to his pediatrician and had him examined. During the examination, a pediatric nurse took M.P.'s temperature rectally. In the presence of the nurse and his mother, M.P. stated, "this is what my teacher does to me at nap time at school." M.P. indicated to the nurse that his teacher, Kelly (the name by which Michaels was known to the children), was the one who took his temperature. M.P. added that Kelly undressed him and took his temperature daily. On further questioning by his mother, M.P. said that Kelly did the same thing to S.R.

The pediatrician, Dr. Delfino, then examined M.P. He informed Mrs. P. that the spots were caused by a rash. Mrs. P. did not tell Dr. Delfino about M.P.'s remarks; consequently, he did not examine M.P.'s rectum. In response to further questioning from his mother after they had returned home, M.P., while rubbing his genitals, stated that "[Kelly] uses the white jean stuff." Although M.P. was unable to tell his mother what the "white jean stuff" was, investigators later found vaseline in Wee Care's bathroom and white cream in the first-aid kit. During the same conversation, M.P. indicated that Kelly had "hurt" two of his classmates, S.R. and E.N.

M.P.'s mother contacted the New Jersey Division of Youth and Family Services ("DYFS") and Ms. Spector, Director of Wee Care, to inform them of her son's disclosures. On May 1, 1985, the Essex County Prosecutor's office received information from DYFS about the alleged sexual abuse at Wee Care. The Prosecutor's office assumed investigation of the complaint.

The Prosecutor's office interviewed several Wee Care children and their parents, concluding their initial investigation on May 8, 1985. During that period of investigation, Michaels submitted to approximately nine hours of questioning. Additionally, Michaels consented to taking a lie detector test, which she passed. Extensive additional interviews and examinations of the Wee Care children by the prosecutor's office and DYFS then followed.

Michaels was charged on June 6, 1985, in a three-count indictment involving the alleged sexual abuse of three Wee Care boys. After further investigation, a second indictment was returned July 30, 1985, containing 174 counts of various charges involving twenty Wee Care boys and girls. An additional indictment of fifty-five counts was filed November 21, 1985, involving fifteen Wee Care children. Prior to trial the prosecution dismissed seventy-two counts, proceeding to trial on the remaining 163 counts.

After several pretrial hearings, the trial commenced on June 22, 1987. The bulk of the State's evidence consisted of the testimony of the children. That testimony referred extensively to the pretrial statements that had been elicited from the children during the course of the State's investigations. The State introduced limited physical evidence to support the contention that the Wee Care children had been molested.

By the time the trial concluded nine months later, another thirty-two counts had been dismissed, leaving 131 counts. On April 15, 1988, after twelve days of deliberation, the jury returned guilty verdicts on 115 counts, including aggravated sexual assault (thirty-eight counts), sexual assault (thirty-one counts), endangering the welfare of children (forty-four counts), and terroristic threats (two counts). The trial court sentenced Michaels to an aggregate term of forty-seven years imprisonment with fourteen years of parole ineligibility.

II

The focus of this case is on the manner in which the State conducted its investigatory interviews of the children. In particular, the Court is asked to consider whether the interview techniques employed by the state could have undermined the reliability of the children's statements and subsequent testimony, to the point that a hearing should be held to determine whether either form of evidence should be admitted at re-trial.

The question of whether the interviews of the child victims of alleged sexual-abuse were unduly suggestive and coercive requires a highly nuanced inquiry into the totality of circumstances surrounding those interviews. Like confessions and identification, the inculpatory capacity of statements indicating the occurrence of sexual abuse and the anticipated testimony about those occurrences requires that special care be taken to ensure their reliability.

The Appellate Division carefully examined the record concerning the investigatory interviews. It concluded that the interrogations that had been conducted were highly improper. The court determined from the record that the children's accusations were founded "upon unreliable perceptions, or memory caused by improper investigative procedures," and that testimony reflecting those accusations could lead to an unfair trial. Accordingly, it held that in the event of a re-trial, a pretrial hearing would be required to assess the reliability of the statements and testimony to be presented by those children to determine their admissibility....The State appeals that determination.

Woven into our consideration of this case is the question of a child's susceptibility to influence through coercive or suggestive questioning. As the Appellate Division noted, a constantly broadening body of scholarly authority exists on the question of children's susceptibility to improper interrogation. The expanse of that literature encompasses a variety of views and conclusions. Among the varying perspectives, however, the Appellate Division found a consistent and recurrent concern over the capacity of the

interviewer and the interview process to distort a child's recollection through unduly slanted interrogation techniques. The Appellate Division concluded that certain interview practices are sufficiently coercive or suggestive to alter irremediably the perceptions of the child victims....

A
* * *

Additional factors temper our consideration of whether children are susceptible to manipulative interrogation. This Court has been especially vigilant in its insistence that children, as a class, are not to be viewed as inherently suspect witnesses. We have specifically held that age per se cannot render a witness incompetent. We declined to require or allow, absent a strong showing of abnormality, psychological testing of child-victims of sexual abuse as a predicate to a determination of the credibility of the child-victim as a witness....We have also recognized that under certain circumstances children's accounts of sexual abuse can be highly reliable....Nevertheless, our common experience tells us that children generate special concerns because of their vulnerability, immaturity, and impressionability, and our laws have recognized and attempted to accommodate those concerns, particularly in the area of child sexual abuse....

The broad question of whether children as a class are more or less susceptible to suggestion than adults is one that we need not definitively answer in order to resolve the central issue in this case. Our inquiry is much more focused. The issue we must determine is whether the interview techniques used by the State in this case were so coercive or suggestive that they had a capacity to distort substantially the children's recollections of actual events and thus compromise the reliability of the children's statements and testimony based on their recollections.

We begin our analyses by noting, as did the Appellate Division, that the "investigative interview" is a crucial, perhaps determinative, moment in a child-sex-abuse case. A decision to prosecute a case of child sexual abuse often hinges on the information elicited in the initial investigatory interviews with alleged victims, carried out by social workers or police investigators....

That an investigatory interview of a young child can be coercive or suggestive and thus shape the child's responses is generally accepted. If a child's recollection of events has been molded by an interrogation, that influence undermines the reliability of the child's responses as an accurate recollection of actual events.

* * *

The use of incessantly repeated questions also adds a manipulative element to an interview. When a child is asked a question and gives an answer, and the question is immediately asked again, the child's normal reaction is to assume that the first answer was wrong or displeasing to the adult questioner. The insidious effects of repeated questioning are even more pronounced when the questions themselves over time suggest information to the children....

The explicit vilification or criticism of the person charged with wrongdoing is another factor that can induce a child to believe abuse has occurred....Similarly, an interviewer's bias with respect to a suspected person's guilt or innocence can have a marked effect on the accuracy of a child's statements....The transmission of suggestion can also be subtly communicated to children through more obvious factors such as the interviewer's tone of voice, mild threats, praise, cajoling, bribes and rewards, as well as resort to peer pressure.

The Appellate Division recognized the considerable authority supporting the deleterious impact improper interrogation can have on a child's memory....Other courts have recognized that once tainted the distortion of the child's memory is irremediable.... ("Once this tainting of memory has occurred, the problem is irredeemable. That memory is, from then on, as real to the child as any other."). The debilitating impact of improper interrogation has even more pronounced effect among young children. Maryann King and John C. Yuille, Suggestibility and the Child Witness, in Children's Eyewitness Memory, 29 (Stephen J. Ceci et al. eds., 1987) and Stephen J. Ceci, Age Differences in Suggestibility, in Children's Eyewitness Memory 82 (Stephen J. Ceci, et al. ed., 1987).

The critical influence that can be exerted by interview techniques is also supported by the literature that generally addresses the reliability of children's memories. Those studies stress the importance of proper interview techniques as a predicate for eliciting accurate and consistent recollection....

* * *

B

413

We next turn to an examination of the interrogations conducted in this case to determine if they were so suggestive or coercive that they created a substantial risk that the statements and testimony thereby elicited lack sufficient reliability to justify their admission at trial.

The interrogations undertaken in the course of this case utilized most, if not all, of the practices that are disfavored or condemned by experts, law enforcement authorities and government agencies.

The initial investigation giving rise to defendant's prosecution was sparked by a child volunteering that his teacher, "Kelly," had taken his temperature rectally, and that she had done so to other children. However, the overwhelming majority of the interviews and interrogations did not arise from the spontaneous recollections that are generally considered to be most reliable. See *Wright supra*, 497 U.S. at 826–27,... (implying that spontaneous recall is under normal conditions an accurate indicator of trustworthiness);...Few, if any, of the children volunteered information that directly implicated defendant. Further, none of the child victims related incidents of actual sexual abuse to their interviewers using "free recall." 264 N.J.Super. at 629,...Additionally, few of the children provided any tell-tale details of the alleged abuse although they were repeatedly prompted to do so by the investigators. We note further that the investigators were not trained in interviewing young children. The earliest interviews with children were not recorded and in some instances the original notes were destroyed.[1] Many of the interviewers demonstrated ineptness in dealing with the challenges presented by pre-schoolers, and displayed their frustration with the children.

Almost all of the interrogations conducted in the course of the investigation revealed an obvious lack of impartiality on the part of the interviewer. One investigator, who conducted the majority of the interviews with the children, stated that his interview techniques had been based on the premise that the "interview process is in essence the beginning of the healing process." He considered it his "professional and ethical responsibility to alleviate whatever anxiety has arisen as a result of what happened to them." A lack of objectivity also was indicated by the interviewer's failure to pursue any alternative hypothesis that might contradict an assumption of defendant's guilt, and a failure to challenge or probe seemingly outlandish statements made by the children.

The record is replete with instances in which children were asked blatantly leading questions that furnished information the children themselves had not mentioned. All but five of the thirty-four children interviewed were asked questions that indicated or strongly suggested that perverse sexual acts had in fact occurred. Seventeen of the children, fully one-half of the thirty-four, were asked questions that involved references to urination, defecation, consumption of human wastes, and oral sexual contacts. Twenty-three of the thirty-four children were asked questions that suggested the occurrence of nudity. In addition, many of the children, some over the course of nearly two years leading up to trial, were subjected to repeated, almost incessant, interrogation. Some children were re-interviewed at the urgings of their parents.

The record of the investigative interviews discloses the use of mild threats, cajoling, and bribing. Positive reinforcement was given when children made inculpatory statements, whereas negative reinforcement was expressed when children denied being abused or made exculpatory statements.

Throughout the record, the element of "vilification" appears. Fifteen of the thirty-four children were told, at one time or another, that Kelly was in jail because she had done bad things to children; the children were encouraged to keep "Kelly" in jail. For example, they were told that the investigators "needed their help" and that they could be "little detectives." Children were also introduced to the police officer who had arrested defendant and were shown the handcuffs used during her arrest; mock police badges were given to children who cooperated.

* * *

IV

This Court has a responsibility to ensure that evidence admitted at trial is sufficiently reliable so that it may be of use to the finder of fact who will draw the ultimate conclusions of guilt or innocence. That concern implicates principles of constitutional due process. "[R]eliability [is] the linchpin in determining admissibility" of evidence under a standard of fairness that is required by the Due Process Clause of the Fourteenth Amendment. *Manson v. Brathwaite*, 432 U.S. 98...Competent and reliable evidence remains at the foundation of a fair trial, which seeks ultimately to determine the truth about criminal culpability. If crucial inculpatory evidence is alleged to have been derived from unreliable sources due process interests are at risk....

A

We acknowledge that although reliability assessments with respect to the admissibility of out-of-court statements are commonplace,...assessing reliability as a predicate to the admission of in-court testimony is a somewhat extraordinary step. Nevertheless, it is not unprecedented. See *Manson supra*, 432 U.S. 98,...(authorizing hearing to determine admissibility of in-court identification testimony because of pretrial suggestiveness);...When faced with extraordinary situations in which police or prosecutorial conduct has thrown the integrity of the judicial process into question, we have not hesitated to use the procedural protection of a pretrial hearing to cleanse a potential prosecution from the corrupting effects of tainted evidence...

* * *

We are confronted in this case with pretrial events relating not to the identification of an offender but, perhaps more crucially, to the occurrence of the offense itself. Those events—investigatory interviews—are fraught with the elements of untoward suggestiveness and the danger of unreliable evidentiary results. We thus concur in the determination of the Appellate Division,...,that to ensure defendant's right to a fair trial a pretrial taint hearing is essential to demonstrate the reliability of the resultant evidence.

B

The pretrial hearing should be conducted pursuant to Evid.R. 104. The basic issue to be addressed at such a pretrial hearing is whether the pretrial events, the investigatory interviews and interrogations, were so suggestive that they give rise to a substantial likelihood of irreparably mistaken or false recollection of material facts bearing on defendant's guilt. See *Simmons v. United States*, 390 U.S. 377, 384 (1968)...

Consonant with the presumption that child victims are to be presumed no more or less reliable than any other class of witnesses, the initial burden to trigger a pretrial taint hearing is on the defendant. *Watkins v. Sowders*, 449 U.S. 341 (1981) (holding that no constitutional mandate exists for pretrial Wade hearing be held merely because counsel demands it). The defendant must make a showing of "some evidence" that the victim's statements were the product of suggestive or coercive interview techniques. *Id.*, 449 U.S. at 350,...

That threshold standard has been met with respect to the investigatory interviews and interrogations that occurred in this case. Without limiting the grounds that could serve to trigger a taint hearing, we note that the kind of practices used here—the absence of spontaneous recall, interviewer bias, repeated leading questions, multiple interviews, incessant questioning, vilification of defendant, ongoing contact with peers and references to their statements, and the use of threats, bribes and cajoling, as well as the failure to videotape or otherwise document the initial interview sessions— constitute more than sufficient evidence to support a finding that the interrogations created a substantial risk that the statements and anticipated testimony are unreliable, and therefore justify a taint hearing.

Once defendant establishes that sufficient evidence of unreliability exists, the burden shall shift to the State to prove the reliability of the proffered statements and testimony by clear and convincing evidence....Hence, the ultimate determination to be made is whether, despite the presence of some suggestive or coercive interview techniques, when considering the totality of the circumstances surrounding the interviews, the statements or testimony retain a degree of reliability sufficient to outweigh the effects of the improper interview techniques. The State may attempt to demonstrate that the investigatory procedures employed in a case did not have the effect of tainting an individual child's recollection of an event. To make that showing, the State is entitled to call experts to offer testimony with regard to the suggestive capacity of the suspect investigative procedures. The defendant, in countering the State's evidence, may also offer experts on the issue of the suggestiveness of the interrogations. However, the relevance of expert opinion focusing essentially on the propriety of the interrogation should not extend to or encompass the ultimate issue of the credibility of an individual child as a witness....

In choosing the burden of proof to be imposed on the State, we are satisfied that the clear-and-convincing-evidence standard serves to safeguard the fairness of a defendant's trial without making legitimate prosecution of child sexual abuse impossible....

* * *

C

In conclusion, we find that the interrogations that occurred in this case were improper and there is a substantial likelihood that the evidence derived from them is unreliable. We therefore hold that in the event the State seeks to re-prosecute this defendant, a pretrial hearing must be held in which the State must prove by clear and convincing evidence that the statements and testimony elicited by the improper interview techniques nonetheless retains a sufficient degree of reliability to warrant admission at trial. Given the egregious prosecutorial abuses evidenced in this record, the challenge that the State faces is formidable. If the statements and proffered testimony of any of the children survive the pretrial hearing, the jury will have to determine the credibility and probative worth of such testimony in light of all the surrounding circumstances.

* * *

The judgment of the Appellate Division is affirmed.

[1] As a matter of sound interviewing methodology, nearly all experts agree that initial interviews should be videotaped....We have recognized generally that the existence of a video or sound recording of a statement elicited through pretrial interrogation is a factor bearing on its reliability....

In this case, fully one-half of the earliest interviews at issue here were not audio or videotaped. The record indicates that the DYFS investigator did not begin taping interviews until June 19, 1985. The Court is aware of 39 transcripts of interviews with thirty-four children, or about one-half of those interviewed by DYFS. The rest were apparently unrecorded.

APPENDIX

This Appendix presents a detailed summary of several interviews....

* * *

3. B.M

On June 26, 1988, Investigator (I) interviewed B.M., a six year-old boy. The interview began in typical fashion with Investigator (I) asking B.M. to draw pictures of himself, his mother, his father and Kelly. After B.M. drew several pictures, Investigator (I) began asking B.M. about Kelly.

Investigator (I): I talked to all of [the kids in your class] and they were telling me how they didn't like the stuff Kelly was doing. Anyway I like talking to you older guys better because you're better to talk to, more like grownups than the little kids in the nursery school. So I'm asking you a favor—
B.M.: Why because they talked about Kelly because she did something bad to them?
Investigator (I): Uh, huh.
B.M.: What?
Investigator (I): She did bad stuff to them.
B.M.: Not me.

* * *

Investigator (I): She was hurting some kids in not some nice ways. So I'm wondering if you saw anything. You can help me to find out who some of the hurt kids are so that I can make it all better again. Because they must be pretty upset and pretty mad.
B.M.: What did she do?
Investigator (I): Well, I don't want to tell you exactly what she did because you may know something that I don't know yet, and that can really help....These are funny dolls. A little different from those you have seen before.

IB.M.: I want to leave
Investigator (I): Why.
B.M.: Because I don't like—
Investigator (I): Like what? You don't like being here. Well you'll be out of here in a couple of minutes. And you never have to come back if you don't want to. Anyway these are—what's different about these dolls, this one's a boy.

B.M.: Yeah
Investigator (I): Because he's got a what? What do you call this?
B.M.: I don't know

* * *

Investigator (I): I want to ask you something.
B.M.: No
Investigator (I): Don't be a baby. You're acting like a nursery school kid. Come here. Come here a second. B.M., come here. We're not finished yet. Sit down.
B.M.: No
Investigator (I): Come here. Seriously, we are going to need your help on this.
B.M.: No I'm not
Investigator (I): How do you think she would hurt boys and girls, with a fork? A fork in the face? Sticking on the legs? The arms or on the neck? Does that hurt?
B.M.: [Inaudible reply.]

> At that point in the questioning B.M. told Investigator (I) that he wanted to leave. Investigator (I), in an effort to put B.M. at ease, changed the tenor of the conversation and began to reassure B.M. that he was safe from Kelly.

* * *

Investigator (I): Did she try to bother you and you didn't let her?
B.M.: No

* * *

Investigator (I): That's o.k....Believe me she is not going to be coming out of jail. She's not going to be hurting you guys anymore. That's why I'm really proud of you, and E.N. and L.J. Which one got hurt the worst?
B.M.: None of them
Investigator (I): That's not what they told me.
B.M.: I never saw anybody get hurt.

Investigator (I): You never saw anybody get hurt? Did they ever tell you that they got hurt? See, the reason I think that you might have gotten hurt or seen them....is that you started to show me on the dolls just exactly what happened. And unless you saw it happen you wouldn't really know, would you?
B.M.: I didn't get hurt.
Investigator (I): No maybe you didn't, maybe you fought her off. Maybe you really didn't hurt then. Maybe you saw your other friends getting hurt and you didn't like it very much. You know.

* * *

B.M.: What did Kelly do?
Investigator (I): Oh I think you know. N.J. told me, and G.G. told me that she hurt them in the gym downstairs. And E.N. told me what he saw.
B.M.: What did he see?
Investigator (I): I don't want to tell you what they told me because I want to know if everybody is telling me the truth. If what you tell me goes along with what they said, then I know they were all telling the truth. You know what I mean, jellybean.
B.M.: I want to leave.—Now!

* * *

Investigator (I): Did you ever see Kelly locking any of the kids in the bathroom or closet?
B.M.: No
Investigator (I): If you did see her hurt any kids would you tell me?
B.M.: No

B.M. steadfastly refused to implicate Kelly in any way. The interview continued for a few more minutes, ending with Investigator (I)'s final attempts to gain "cooperation" from B.M.

* * *

Questions for Discussion

1. Why select children out for an advance hearing for admissibility? Are children more likely than adults to lie? The majority cites Stephen Ceci in support of its suspicion about child testimony. Do his conclusions support that use? Would they apply as to children who are over five years of age when testifying?

2. Do children have the adult motivations of greed, jealousy, or lust? Is the lie of a child somewhat easier to expose through cross-examination than the lie of an adult (who may be more able to fabricate consistent surrounding facts)?[5]

3. The *Michaels* court cites as a primary problem the "pursuit by the interviewer of a preconceived notion" implying that the questioner should believe in the "presumption of innocence." Why would the interviewer's state of mind be relevant? Do the police often have "preconceived notions" of possible guilt during investigations of adults? Do they ask leading questions? Make accusations?

4. Is the problem leading questions, or the suggestion of answers implying guilt with severe approval or disapproval based on guilt confirmation? Is the problem the court fears an adult authority figure imposing his views on a child's will and memory? Will cross-examination reveal a lack of specific facts, and inconsistencies between witnesses as to details?

5. Are children easily manipulated? The majority opinion included the most onerous interview techniques in its appendix (excerpted above). Did it indicate the children were highly responsive to suggestion?

6. The *Michaels* decision sets up an extraordinary potential pre-screening hearing to qualify a child's testimony, triggered by a showing of possible prejudice. How difficult would it be to meet the New Jersey "some evidence of pre-trial suggestion/coercion" test for pretrial hearing? Once it is met, the burden shifts to the People to show by "clear and convincing evidence" that the testimony is reliable. Where the issue is simply whether the jury will hear evidence, should the test be "clear and convincing" or "preponderance?" Or should it be "beyond a reasonable doubt"—the burden in the underlying case?

7. Criminal cases already normally involve a preliminary hearing at which children testify and are cross-examined. In the alternative, they involve sworn testimony before a grand jury, which can be challenged by motion and writ. If the *Michaels* decision forces a hearing to demonstrate truthful statements, is it effectively requiring child testimony in three formal proceedings in each case?

8. New Jersey has a liberal "tender years" hearsay exception[6] allowing admission of statements of a sexual abuse victim under the age of 12 where the prosecution notifies the defense of its intent to introduce the statement in advance;

the court finds it probable that the statement is trustworthy; and the child testifies at the proceeding, or if unavailable, puts forth corroborating evidence of the abuse. Does the extra round of qualification that the child is "trustworthy" under *Michaels* make such latitude more palatable? See *State v. R.B.*, 183 N.J. 308 (2005). Does such an intermediary "reliability" judgment satisfy the recent U.S. Supreme Court demand that hearsay not be admitted without opportunity for cross-examination? See *Crawford v. Washington*, 541 U.S. 36 (2004).

B. A CHILD'S OUT OF COURT STATEMENTS

Ohio v. Clark

135 S. Ct. 2173 (2015)

JUSTICE ALITO delivered the opinion of the Court.

* * *

Darius Clark, who went by the nickname "Dee," lived in Cleveland, Ohio, with his girlfriend, T. T., and her two children: L. P., a 3-year-old boy, and A. T., an 18-month-old girl. Clark was also T. T.'s pimp, and he would regularly send her on trips to Washington, D. C., to work as a prostitute. In March 2010, T. T. went on one such trip, and she left the children in Clark's care.

The next day, Clark took L. P. to preschool. In the lunchroom, one of L. P.'s teachers...observed that L. P.'s left eye appeared bloodshot....When they moved into the brighter lights of a classroom, Whitley noticed "'[r]ed marks, like whips of some sort,'" on L. P.'s face....She notified the lead teacher, Debra Jones, who asked L. P., "'Who did this? What happened to you?'"....According to Jones, L. P. "'seemed kind of bewildered'" and "'said something like, Dee, Dee.'"...Jones asked L. P. whether Dee is "big or little," to which L. P. responded that "Dee is big."...Jones then brought L. P. to her supervisor, who lifted the boy's shirt, revealing more injuries. Whitley called a child abuse hotline to alert authorities about the suspected abuse.

When Clark later arrived at the school, he denied responsibility for the injuries and quickly left with L. P. The next day, a social worker found the children at Clark's mother's house and took them to a hospital, where a physician discovered additional injuries suggesting child abuse. L. P. had a black eye, belt marks on his back and stomach, and bruises all over his body. A. T. had two black eyes, a swollen hand, and a large burn on her cheek, and two pigtails had been ripped out at the roots of her hair.

A grand jury indicted Clark on five counts of felonious assault (four related to A. T. and one related to L. P.), two counts of endangering children (one for each child), and two counts of domestic violence (one for each child). At trial, the State introduced L. P.'s statements to his teachers as evidence of Clark's guilt, but L. P. did not testify. Under Ohio law, children younger than 10 years old are incompetent to testify if they "appear incapable of receiving just impressions of the facts and transactions respecting which they are examined, or of relating them truly." Ohio Rule Evid. 601(A).... After conducting a hearing, the trial court concluded that L. P. was not competent to testify. But under Ohio Rule of Evidence 807, which allows the admission of reliable hearsay by child abuse victims, the court ruled that L. P.'s statements to his teachers bore sufficient guarantees of trustworthiness to be admitted as evidence.

Clark moved to exclude testimony about L. P.'s out-of-court statements under the Confrontation Clause. The trial court denied the motion, ruling that L. P.'s responses were not testimonial statements covered by the Sixth Amendment. The jury found Clark guilty on all counts except for one assault count related to A. T., and it sentenced him to 28 years' imprisonment. Clark appealed his conviction, and a state appellate court reversed on the ground that the introduction of L. P.'s out-of-court statements violated the Confrontation Clause.

In a 4-to-3 decision, the Supreme Court of Ohio affirmed. It held that, under this Court's Confrontation Clause decisions, L. P.'s statements qualified as testimonial because the primary purpose of the teachers' questioning "was not to deal with an existing emergency but rather to gather evidence potentially relevant to a subsequent criminal prosecution.".…The court noted that Ohio has a "mandatory reporting" law that requires certain professionals, including preschool teachers, to report suspected child abuse to government authorities.…In the court's view, the teachers acted as agents of the State under the mandatory reporting law and "sought facts concerning past criminal activity to identify the person responsible, eliciting statements that 'are functionally identical to live, in-court testimony, doing precisely what a witness does on direct examination.'"…

We granted certiorari…and we now reverse.

II

A

The Sixth Amendment's Confrontation Clause, which is binding on the States through the Fourteenth Amendment, provides: "In all criminal prosecutions, the accused shall enjoy the right…to be confronted with the witnesses against him." In *Ohio v. Roberts*, 448 U.S. 56, 66 (1980), we interpreted the Clause to permit the admission of out-of-court statements by an unavailable witness, so long as the statements bore "adequate 'indicia of reliability.'" Such indicia are present, we held, if "the evidence falls within a firmly rooted hearsay exception" or bears "particularized guarantees of trustworthiness." *Ibid.*

In *Crawford v. Washington*, 541 U.S. 36 (2004), we adopted a different approach. We explained that "witnesses," under the Confrontation Clause, are those "who bear testimony," and we defined "testimony" as "a solemn declaration or affirmation made for the purpose of establishing or proving some fact."…

Our more recent cases have labored to flesh out what it means for a statement to be "testimonial." In *Davis v. Washington* and *Hammon v. Indiana*, 547 U.S. 813 (2006), which we decided together, we dealt with statements given to law enforcement officers by the victims of domestic abuse. The victim in *Davis* made statements to a 911 emergency operator during and shortly after her boyfriend's violent attack. In *Hammon*, the victim, after being isolated from her abusive husband, made statements to police that were memorialized in a "'battery affidavit.'"…

We held that the statements in *Hammon* were testimonial, while the statements in *Davis* were not. Announcing what has come to be known as the "primary purpose" test, we explained: "Statements are nontestimonial when made in the course of police interrogation under circumstances objectively indicating that the primary purpose of the interrogation is to enable police assistance to meet an ongoing emergency. They are testimonial when the circumstances objectively indicate that there is no such ongoing emergency, and that the primary purpose of the interrogation is to establish or prove past events potentially relevant to later criminal prosecution."…

In *Michigan v. Bryant*, 562 U.S. 344 (2011), we further expounded on the primary purpose test. The inquiry, we emphasized, must consider "all of the relevant circumstances."…

One additional factor is "the informality of the situation and the interrogation."…A "formal station-house interrogation," like the questioning in *Crawford*, is more likely to provoke testimonial statements, while less formal questioning is less likely to reflect a primary purpose aimed at obtaining testimonial evidence against the accused.…

* * *

B

In this case, we consider statements made to preschool teachers, not the police. We are therefore presented with the question we have repeatedly reserved: whether statements to persons other than law enforcement officers are subject to the Confrontation Clause. Because at least some statements to individuals who are not law enforcement officers could conceivably raise confrontation concerns, we decline to adopt a categorical rule excluding them from the Sixth Amendment's reach. Nevertheless, such statements are much less likely to be testimonial than statements to law enforcement officers. And considering all the relevant circumstances here, L. P.'s statements clearly were not made with the primary purpose of creating evidence for Clark's prosecution. Thus, their introduction at trial did not violate the Confrontation Clause.

L. P.'s statements occurred in the context of an ongoing emergency involving suspected child abuse. When L. P.'s teachers noticed his injuries, they rightly became worried that the 3-year-old was the victim of serious violence. Because the teachers needed to know whether it was safe to release L. P. to his guardian at the end of the day, they needed to determine who might be abusing the child. Thus, the immediate concern was to protect a vulnerable child who needed help....

* * *

L. P.'s age fortifies our conclusion that the statements in question were not testimonial. Statements by very young children will rarely, if ever, implicate the Confrontation Clause. Few preschool students understand the details of our criminal justice system. Rather, "[r]esearch on children's understanding of the legal system finds that" young children "have little understanding of prosecution." Brief for American Professional Society on the Abuse of Children as *Amicus Curiae* 7, and n. 5 (collecting sources). And Clark does not dispute those findings. Thus, it is extremely unlikely that a 3-year-old child in L. P.'s position would intend his statements to be a substitute for trial testimony. On the contrary, a young child in these circumstances would simply want the abuse to end, would want to protect other victims, or would have no discernible purpose at all.

As a historical matter, moreover, there is strong evidence that statements made in circumstances similar to those facing L. P. and his teachers were admissible at common law. ... And when 18th-century courts excluded statements of this sort,...they appeared to do so because the child should have been ruled competent to testify, not because the statements were otherwise inadmissible....

Finally, although we decline to adopt a rule that statements to individuals who are not law enforcement officers are categorically outside the Sixth Amendment, the fact that L. P. was speaking to his teachers remains highly relevant. Courts must evaluate challenged statements in context, and part of that context is the questioner's identity.... Statements made to someone who is not principally charged with uncovering and prosecuting criminal behavior are significantly less likely to be testimonial than statements given to law enforcement officers....It is common sense that the relationship between a student and his teacher is very different from that between a citizen and the police. We do not ignore that reality. In light of these circumstances, the Sixth Amendment did not prohibit the State from introducing L. P.'s statements at trial.

* * *

Questions for Discussion

1. The Court finds the statements of a pre-schooler to his teacher in this case to be non-testimonial because the primary purpose of the communication was not to gather evidence for prosecution of a criminal act, but to address the threat of potential harm to the child. What is the primary purpose of a child protection worker's efforts to elicit statements from an allegedly abused child? Such a worker is certainly responding to a potentially ongoing emergency, but is she not also focused on gathering evidence to ultimately build a case against an alleged abuser? When there are dual purposes, does the Court explain how to determine which is primary?

2. A pediatrician in the course of examining a patient may elicit information from a child about suspected abuse. In determining whether the statements are testimonial, does it matter if the pediatrician happens upon the signs of abuse or

if the pediatrician is asked by the parent to specifically question the child to obtain information that could ultimately be used in a prosecution?

3. When conducting a "primary purpose" analysis, does one consider the primary purpose of the speaker in giving the statements, or the primary purpose of the recipient in receiving or eliciting the information? Or both? When Justice Alito concludes that statements by young children will usually not be testimonial because a child will rarely have a testimonial purpose, should that be interpreted as giving greater weight to the primary purpose of the speaker rather than the recipient? What if the purpose of each individual is different?

4. The Court notes that it is very unlikely for a three-year-old to have testimonial intent in giving his statement. Is there an age at which a child would have sufficient understanding of the legal system to potentially demonstrate a testimonial intent? See *State v. McLaughlin*, 246 N.C. App. 306 (2016), where the court found that even at the age of 15, the child abuse victim could not be presumed to know that statements given to a nurse would be used at trial.

5. Why is it allowable to admit statements of an individual who is otherwise deemed incompetent to testify? If a child does not meet the criteria to be a competent witness, how can his statements demonstrate sufficient indicia of trustworthiness to be admissible?

C. CHILD VICTIM/WITNESS PROTECTION

Maryland v. Craig

497 U.S. 836 (1990)

JUSTICE O'CONNOR delivered the opinion of the Court.

This case requires us to decide whether the Confrontation Clause of the Sixth Amendment categorically prohibits a child witness in a child abuse case from testifying against a defendant at trial, outside the defendant's physical presence, by one-way closed circuit television.

I

In October 1986, a Howard County grand jury charged respondent, Sandra Ann Craig, with child abuse, first and second degree sexual offenses, perverted sexual practice, assault, and battery. The named victim in each count was a 6-year-old girl who, from August 1984 to June 1986, had attended a kindergarten and prekindergarten center owned and operated by Craig.

In March 1987, before the case went to trial, the State sought to invoke a Maryland statutory procedure that permits a judge to receive, by one-way closed circuit television, the testimony of a child witness who is alleged to be a victim of child abuse. To invoke the procedure, the trial judge must first "determin[e] that testimony by the child victim in the courtroom will result in the child suffering serious emotional distress such that the child cannot reasonably communicate." Once the procedure is invoked, the child witness, prosecutor, and defense counsel withdraw to a separate room; the judge, jury, and defendant remain in the courtroom. The child witness is then examined and cross-examined in the separate room, while a video monitor records and displays the witness' testimony to those in the courtroom. During this time the witness cannot see the defendant. The defendant remains in electronic communication with defense counsel, and objections may be made and ruled on as if the witness were testifying in the courtroom.

In support of its motion invoking the one-way closed circuit television procedure, the State presented expert testimony that the named victim, as well as a number of other children who were alleged to have been sexually abused by Craig, would suffer "serious emotional distress such that [they could not] reasonably communicate,"...if required to testify in the courtroom. The Maryland Court of Appeals characterized the evidence as follows:

> "The expert testimony in each case suggested that each child would have some or considerable difficulty in testifying in Craig's presence. For example, as to one child, the expert said that what 'would cause him the most anxiety would be to testify in front of Mrs. Craig.' The child 'wouldn't be able to communicate effectively.' As to another, an expert said she 'would probably stop talking and she would withdraw and curl up.' With respect to two others, the testimony was that one would 'become highly agitated, that he may refuse to talk or if he did talk, that he would choose his subject regardless of the questions' while the other would 'become extremely timid and unwilling to talk.'"....

Craig objected to the use of the procedure on Confrontation Clause grounds, but the trial court rejected that contention, concluding that although the statute "take[s] away the right of the defendant to be face to face with his or her accuser," the defendant retains the "essence of the right of confrontation," including the right to observe, cross-examine, and have the jury view the demeanor of the witness....The trial court further found that, "based upon the evidence presented the testimony of each of these children in a courtroom will result in each child suffering serious emotional distress...such that each of these children cannot reasonably communicate."...The trial court then found the named victim and three other children competent to testify and accordingly permitted them to testify against Craig via the one-way closed circuit television procedure. The jury convicted Craig on all counts, and the Maryland Court of Special Appeals affirmed the convictions,...

* * *

II

The Confrontation Clause of the Sixth Amendment, made applicable to the States through the Fourteenth Amendment, provides: "In all criminal prosecutions, the accused shall enjoy the right...to be confronted with the witnesses against him."

* * *

The central concern of the Confrontation Clause is to ensure the reliability of the evidence against a criminal defendant by subjecting it to rigorous testing in the context of an adversary proceeding before the trier of fact. The word "confront," after all, also means a clashing of forces or ideas, thus carrying with it the notion of adversariness....

...[T]he right guaranteed by the Confrontation Clause includes not only a "personal examination," 156 U.S., at 242, but also "(1) insures that the witness will give his statements under oath—thus impressing him with the seriousness of the matter and guarding against the lie by the possibility of a penalty for perjury; (2) forces the witness to submit to cross-examination, the 'greatest legal engine ever invented for the discovery of truth'; [and] (3) permits the jury that is to decide the defendant's fate to observe the demeanor of the witness in making his statement, thus aiding the jury in assessing his credibility."....

The combined effect of these elements of confrontation—physical presence, oath, cross-examination, and observation of demeanor by the trier of fact—serves the purposes of the Confrontation Clause by ensuring that evidence admitted against an accused is reliable and subject to the rigorous adversarial testing that is the norm of Anglo-American criminal proceedings....

* * *

We have accordingly stated that a literal reading of the Confrontation Clause would "abrogate virtually every hearsay exception, a result long rejected as unintended and too extreme." *Roberts*, 448 U.S., at 63. Thus, in certain narrow circumstances, "competing interests, if 'closely examined,' may warrant dispensing with confrontation at trial." *Id.*, at 64...We have recently held, for example, that hearsay statements of nontestifying coconspirators may be admitted against a defendant despite the lack of any face-to-face encounter with the accused....Given our hearsay cases, the word "confronted," as used in the Confrontation Clause, cannot simply mean face-to-face confrontation, for the Clause would then, contrary to our cases, prohibit the admission of any accusatory hearsay statement made by an absent declarant—a declarant who is undoubtedly as much a "witness against" a defendant as one who actually testifies at trial.

In sum, our precedents establish that "the Confrontation Clause reflects a *preference* for face-to-face confrontation at trial," *Roberts supra*, at 63...,a preference that "must occasionally give way to considerations of public policy and the necessities of the case,"...

That the face-to-face confrontation requirement is not absolute does not, of course, mean that it may easily be dispensed with. As we suggested in *Coy* our precedents confirm that a defendant's right to confront accusatory witnesses may be satisfied absent a physical, face-to-face confrontation at trial only where denial of such confrontation is necessary to further an important public policy and only where the reliability of the testimony is otherwise assured....

III

Maryland's statutory procedure, when invoked, prevents a child witness from seeing the defendant as he or she testifies against the defendant at trial. We find it significant, however, that Maryland's procedure preserves all of the other elements of the confrontation right: The child witness must be competent to testify and must testify under oath; the defendant retains full opportunity for contemporaneous cross-examination; and the judge, jury, and defendant are able to view (albeit by video monitor) the demeanor (and body) of the witness as he or she testifies. Although we are mindful of the many subtle effects face-to-face confrontation may have on an adversary criminal proceeding, the presence of these other elements of confrontation—oath, cross-examination, and observation of the witness' demeanor—adequately ensures that the testimony is both reliable and subject to rigorous adversarial testing in a manner functionally equivalent to that accorded live, in-person testimony. These safeguards of reliability and adversariness render the use of such a procedure a far cry from the undisputed prohibition of the Confrontation Clause: trial by *ex parte* affidavit or inquisition,....Rather, we think these elements of effective confrontation not only permit a defendant to "confound and undo the false accuser, or reveal the child coached by a malevolent adult," *Coy supra*, at 1020, but may well aid a defendant in eliciting favorable testimony from the child witness. Indeed, to the extent the child witness' testimony may be said to be technically given out of court (though we do not so hold), these assurances of reliability and adversariness are far greater than those required for admission of hearsay testimony under the Confrontation Clause. We are therefore confident that use of the one-way closed circuit television procedure, where necessary to further an important state interest, does not impinge upon the truth-seeking or symbolic purposes of the Confrontation Clause.

The critical inquiry in this case, therefore, is whether use of the procedure is necessary to further an important state interest. The State contends that it has a substantial interest in protecting children who are allegedly victims of child abuse from the trauma of testifying against the alleged perpetrator and that its statutory procedure for receiving testimony from such witnesses is necessary to further that interest.

We have of course recognized that a State's interest in "the protection of minor victims of sex crimes from further trauma and embarrassment" is a "compelling" one....

We likewise conclude today that a State's interest in the physical and psychological well-being of child abuse victims may be sufficiently important to outweigh, at least in some cases, a defendant's right to face his or her accusers in court. That a significant majority of States have enacted statutes to protect child witnesses from the trauma of giving testimony in child abuse cases attests to the widespread belief in the importance of such a public policy....Thirty-seven States, for example, permit the use of videotaped testimony of sexually abused children;....24 States have authorized the use of one-way closed circuit television testimony in child abuse cases;....and 8 States authorize the use of a two-way system in which the child witness is permitted to see the courtroom and the defendant on a video monitor and in which the jury and judge are permitted to view the child during the testimony....

* * *

The requisite finding of necessity must of course be a case-specific one: The trial court must hear evidence and determine whether use of the one-way closed circuit television procedure is necessary to protect the welfare of the particular child witness who seeks to testify....

* * *

IV
* * *

...The trial court in this case, for example, could well have found, on the basis of the expert testimony before it, that testimony by the child witnesses in the courtroom in the defendant's presence "will result in [each] child suffering serious emotional distress such that the child cannot reasonably communicate,"....

It is so ordered.

JUSTICE SCALIA, with whom **JUSTICE BRENNAN**, **JUSTICE MARSHALL**, and **JUSTICE STEVENS** join, dissenting.

Seldom has this Court failed so conspicuously to sustain a categorical guarantee of the Constitution against the tide of prevailing current opinion. The Sixth Amendment provides, with unmistakable clarity, that "[i]n all criminal prosecutions, the accused shall enjoy the right...to be confronted with the witnesses against him." The purpose of enshrining this protection in the Constitution was to assure that none of the many policy interests from time to time pursued by statutory law could overcome a defendant's right to face his or her accusers in court....

Because of this subordination of explicit constitutional text to currently favored public policy, the following scene can be played out in an American courtroom for the first time in two centuries: A father whose young daughter has been given over to the exclusive custody of his estranged wife, or a mother whose young son has been taken into custody by the State's child welfare department, is sentenced to prison for sexual abuse on the basis of testimony by a child the parent has not seen or spoken to for many months; and the guilty verdict is rendered without giving the parent so much as the opportunity to sit in the presence of the child, and to ask, personally or through counsel, "it is really not true, is it, that I—your father (or mother) whom you see before you—did these terrible things?" Perhaps that is a procedure today's society desires; perhaps (though I doubt it) it is even a fair procedure; but it is assuredly not a procedure permitted by the Constitution.

Because the text of the Sixth Amendment is clear, and because the Constitution is meant to protect against, rather than conform to, current "widespread belief," I respectfully dissent.

I
* * *

..."[T]o confront" plainly means to encounter face to face, whatever else it may mean in addition. And we are not talking about the manner of arranging that face-to-face encounter, but about whether it shall occur at all. The "necessities of trial and the adversary process" are irrelevant here, since they cannot alter the constitutional text.

II

Much of the Court's opinion consists of applying to this case the mode of analysis we have used in the admission of hearsay evidence. The Sixth Amendment does not literally contain a prohibition upon such evidence, since it guarantees the defendant only the right to confront "the witnesses against him." As applied in the Sixth Amendment's context of a prosecution, the noun "witness"—in 1791 as today— could mean either (a) one "who knows or sees any thing; one personally present" or (b) "one who gives testimony" or who "testifies," *i.e.*, "[i]n *judicial proceedings* [one who] make[s] a solemn

425

declaration under oath, for the purpose of establishing or making proof of some fact to a court." 2 N. Webster, An American Dictionary of the English Language (1828) (emphasis added). See also J. Buchanan, Linguae Britannicae Vera Pronunciatio (1757). The former meaning (one "who knows or sees") would cover hearsay evidence, but is excluded in the Sixth Amendment by the words following the noun: "witnesses *against him.*" The phrase obviously refers to those who give testimony against the defendant at trial. We have nonetheless found implicit in the Confrontation Clause some limitation upon hearsay evidence, since otherwise the government could subvert the confrontation right by putting on witnesses who know nothing except what an absent declarant said. And in determining the scope of that implicit limitation, we have focused upon whether the reliability of the hearsay statements (which are not *expressly* excluded by the Confrontation Clause) "is otherwise assured."...The same test cannot be applied, however, to permit what is explicitly forbidden by the constitutional text; there is simply no room for interpretation with regard to "the irreducible literal meaning of the Clause."...

* * *

The Court's test today requires unavailability only in the sense that the child is unable to testify in the presence of the defendant.[1] That cannot possibly be the relevant sense. If unconfronted testimony is admissible hearsay when the witness is unable to confront the defendant, then presumably there are other categories of admissible hearsay consisting of unsworn testimony when the witness is unable to risk perjury, un-cross-examined testimony when the witness is unable to undergo hostile questioning, etc. *California v. Green*, 399 U.S. 149 (1970), is not precedent for such a silly system. That case held that the Confrontation Clause does not bar admission of prior testimony when the declarant is sworn as a witness but refuses to answer. But in *Green*, as in most cases of refusal, we could not know *why* the declarant refused to testify. Here, by contrast, we know that it is precisely because the child is unwilling to testify in the presence of the defendant....

III

The Court characterizes the State's interest which "out-weigh[s]" the explicit text of the Constitution as an "interest in the physical and psychological well-being of child abuse victims,"...an "interest in protecting" such victims "from the emotional trauma of testifying,"...That is not so. A child who meets the Maryland statute's requirement of suffering such "serious emotional distress" from confrontation that he "cannot reasonably communicate" would seem entirely safe. Why would a prosecutor want to call a witness who cannot reasonably communicate? And if he did, it would be the State's own fault. Protection of the child's interest—as far as the Confrontation Clause is concerned[2]—is entirely within Maryland's control. The State's interest here is in fact no more and no less than what the State's interest always is when it seeks to get a class of evidence admitted in criminal proceedings: more convictions of guilty defendants. That is not an unworthy interest, but it should not be dressed up as a humanitarian one.

And the interest on the other side is also what it usually is when the State seeks to get a new class of evidence admitted: fewer convictions of innocent defendants— specifically, in the present context, innocent defendants accused of particularly heinous crimes. The "special" reasons that exist for suspending one of the usual guarantees of reliability in the case of children's testimony are perhaps matched by "special" reasons for being particularly insistent upon it in the case of children's testimony. Some studies show that children are substantially more vulnerable to suggestion than adults, and often unable to separate recollected fantasy (or suggestion) from reality....The injustice their

erroneous testimony can produce is evidenced by the tragic Scott County investigations of 1983–1984, which disrupted the lives of many (as far as we know) innocent people in the small town of Jordan, Minnesota. At one stage those investigations were pursuing allegations by at least eight children of multiple murders, but the prosecutions actually initiated charged only sexual abuse. Specifically, 24 adults were charged with molesting 37 children. In the course of the investigations, 25 children were placed in foster homes. Of the 24 indicted defendants, one pleaded guilty, two were acquitted at trial, and the charges against the remaining 21 were voluntarily dismissed....There is no doubt that some sexual abuse took place in Jordan; but there is no reason to believe it was as widespread as charged....

* * *

The Court today has applied "interest-balancing" analysis where the text of the Constitution simply does not permit it. We are not free to conduct a cost-benefit analysis of clear and explicit constitutional guarantees, and then to adjust their meaning to comport with our findings. The Court has convincingly proved that the Maryland procedure serves a valid interest, and gives the defendant virtually everything the Confrontation Clause guarantees (everything, that is, except confrontation). I am persuaded, therefore, that

the Maryland procedure is virtually constitutional. Since it is not, however, actually constitutional I would affirm the judgment of the Maryland Court of Appeals reversing the judgment of conviction.

[1] I presume that when the Court says "trauma would impair the child's ability to communicate,"...it means that trauma would make it impossible for the child to communicate. That is the requirement of the Maryland law at issue here: "serious emotional distress such that the child cannot reasonably communicate." Md. Cts. & Jud. Proc. Code Ann. § 9-102(a)(1)(ii) (1989). Any implication beyond that would in any event be dictum.

[2] A different situation would be presented if the defendant sought to call the child. In that event, the State's refusal to compel the child to appear, or its insistence upon a procedure such as that set forth in the Maryland statute as a condition of its compelling him to do so, would call into question—initially, at least, and perhaps exclusively—the scope of the defendant's Sixth Amendment right "to have compulsory process for obtaining witnesses in his favor."

Questions for Discussion

1. Do the "confrontation" rights litigated in *Maryland v. Craig* similarly apply to a civil proceeding (a dependency court adjudication of parental rights)?

2. How important is the physical confrontation between a victim and the defendant in determining the truth? Justice Scalia argues that a child is less likely to tell falsehoods to a father asking "is it true I did all these terrible things?" in his physical presence. If a child had been brutally raped by a powerful adult, will the violator's close presence make the child's testimony more or less accurate? Is it permissible to assume the possibility of such guilt without violating the presumption of innocence?

3. The Maryland law requires a finding that the one-way closed circuit video is necessary for the child to testify (that she cannot reasonably communicate in the physical presence of the defendant). How does a requirement of physical confrontation serve the truth by producing more honest testimony—when it eliminates the testimony?

4. The dissent considers confrontation a categorical guarantee because it is enumerated in the Constitution as intended in 1787. Does the provision specify "face to face" confrontation? Was there video in 1787? Were children testifying in such matters during this period?

5. Justice Scalia implies that children are easily manipulated to lie, citing a case where 24 were indicted and children were interrogated 50 times. Would such interrogation and other flaws in the prosecution's case be available for defense exploitation without physical confrontation?

6. The dissent acknowledges that numerous hearsay exceptions allow evidence to be introduced with no chance for cross-examination at all, but makes the distinction: If a witness appears at the trial, then physical confrontation must be permitted. Aren't statements against the interest of a co-defendant admissible without cross-examination even if present? Would the dissenters be satisfied if all child molestation victim testimony at trial were to be by transcript from a preliminary proceeding (where cross-examination is allowed)? The witness is then not at trial at all.

7. Business records are admitted into evidence without cross-examination of the source, as well as statements against interest, dying statements, spontaneous declarations—because of a policy presuming some reliability excusing cross-examination. None of these exceptions are enumerated in the Constitution. Why is the defendant not deprived of his "confrontation" right in such cases, where he may be completely foreclosed from confronting the source of the evidence? Given this latitude to allow waiver of any confrontation, why would the substantial confrontation of the child, absent only the close physical proximity and presence of the defendant, be a breach of due process?

White v. Illinois
502 U.S. 346 (1992)

REHNQUIST, C. J., delivered the opinion of the Court.

In this case, we consider whether the Confrontation Clause of the Sixth Amendment requires that, before a trial court admits testimony under the "spontaneous declaration" and "medical examination" exceptions to the hearsay rule, the prosecution must either produce the declarant at trial or the trial court must find that the declarant is unavailable. The Illinois Appellate Court concluded that such procedures are not constitutionally required. We agree with that conclusion.

Petitioner was convicted by a jury of aggravated criminal sexual assault, residential burglary, and unlawful restraint....The events giving rise to the charges related to the sexual assault of S. G., then four years old. Testimony at the trial established that in the early morning hours of April 16, 1988, S. G.'s babysitter, Tony DeVore, was awakened by S. G.'s scream. DeVore went to S. G.'s bedroom and witnessed petitioner leaving the room, and petitioner then left the house. DeVore knew petitioner because petitioner was a friend of S. G.'s mother, Tammy Grigsby. DeVore asked S. G. what had happened. According to DeVore's trial testimony, S. G. stated that petitioner had put his hand over her mouth, choked her, threatened to whip her if she screamed and had "touched her in the wrong places." Asked by DeVore to point to where she had been touched, S. G. identified the vaginal area....

Tammy Grigsby, S. G.'s mother, returned home about 30 minutes later. Grigsby testified that her daughter appeared "scared" and a "little hyper." Grigsby proceeded to question her daughter about what had happened. At trial, Grigsby testified that S. G. repeated her claims that petitioner had choked and threatened her. Grigsby also testified that S. G. stated that petitioner had "put his mouth on her front part. Grigsby also noticed that S. G. had bruises and red marks on her neck that had not been there previously. Grigsby called the police.

Officer Terry Lewis arrived a few minutes later, roughly 45 minutes after S. G.'s scream had first awakened DeVore. Lewis questioned S. G. alone in the kitchen. At trial, Lewis' summary of S. G.'s statement indicated that she had offered essentially the same story as she had first reported to DeVore and to Grigsby, including a statement that petitioner had "used his tongue on her in her private parts."

After Lewis concluded his investigation, and approximately four hours after DeVore first heard S. G.'s scream, S. G. was taken to the hospital. She was examined first by Cheryl Reents, an emergency room nurse, and then by Dr. Michael Meinzen. Each testified at trial, and their testimony indicated that, in response to questioning, S. G. again provided an account of events that was essentially identical to the one she had given to DeVore, Grigsby, and Lewis.

S. G. never testified at petitioner's trial. The State attempted on two occasions to call her as a witness, but she apparently experienced emotional difficulty on being brought to the courtroom and in each instance left without testifying. The defense made no attempt to call S. G. as a witness, and the trial court neither made, nor was asked to make, a finding that S. G. was unavailable to testify. Petitioner objected on hearsay grounds to DeVore, Grigsby, Lewis, Reents, and Meinzen being permitted to testify regarding S. G.'s statements describing the assault. The trial court overruled each objection. With respect to DeVore, Grigsby, and Lewis the trial court concluded that the testimony could be permitted pursuant to an Illinois hearsay exception for spontaneous declarations.[1] Petitioner's objections to Reents' and Meinzen's testimony was similarly overruled, based on both the spontaneous declaration exception and an exception for statements made in the course of securing medical treatment.[2]

...[W]e granted certiorari, 500 U.S. 904 (1991) limited to the constitutional question whether permitting the challenged testimony violated petitioner's Sixth Amendment Confrontation Clause right.[3]

* * *

...[W]e observed that there is little benefit, if any, to be accomplished by imposing an "unavailability rule."[6] Such a rule will not work to bar absolutely the introduction of the out-of-court statements; if the declarant either is unavailable, or is available and produced for trial, the statements can be introduced. Nor is an unavailability rule likely to produce much testimony that adds meaningfully to the trial's truth-determining process.....

...We note first that the evidentiary rationale for permitting hearsay testimony regarding spontaneous declarations and statements made in the course of receiving medical care is that such out-of-court declarations are made in contexts that provide substantial guarantees of their trustworthiness.[8] But those same factors that contribute to the statements' reliability cannot be recaptured even by later in-court testimony. A statement that has been offered in a moment of excitement—without the opportunity to reflect on the consequences of one's exclamation—may justifiably carry more weight with a trier of fact than a similar statement offered in the relative calm of the courtroom. Similarly, a statement made in the course of procuring medical services, where the declarant knows that a false statement may cause misdiagnosis or mistreatment, carries special guarantees of credibility that a trier of fact may not think replicated by courtroom testimony. They are thus materially different from the statements at issue in *Roberts*, where the out-of-court statements sought to be introduced were themselves made in the course of a judicial proceeding, and where there was consequently no threat of lost evidentiary value if the out-of-court statements were replaced with live testimony.

The preference for live testimony in the case of statements like those offered in *Roberts* is because of the importance of cross-examination, "the greatest legal engine ever invented for the discovery of truth." *Green*, 399 U.S. at 158 Thus courts have adopted the general rule prohibiting the receipt of hearsay evidence. But where proffered hearsay has sufficient guarantees of reliability to come within a firmly rooted exception to the hearsay rule, the Confrontation Clause is satisfied.

We therefore think it clear that the out-of-court statements admitted in this case had substantial probative value, value that could not be duplicated simply by the declarant later testifying in court. To exclude such probative statements under the strictures of the Confrontation Clause would be the height of wrongheadedness, given that the Confrontation Clause has as a basic purpose the promotion of the "'integrity of the factfinding process.'"... We therefore see no basis in *Roberts* or *Inadi* for excluding from trial, under the aegis of the Confrontation Clause, evidence embraced within such exceptions to the hearsay rule as those for spontaneous declarations and statements made for medical treatment.

As a second line of argument, petitioner presses upon us two recent decisions involving child testimony in child sexual-assault cases....In *Craig* we upheld a conviction that resulted from a trial in which a child witness testified via closed circuit television after such a showing of necessity. Petitioner draws from these two cases a general rule that hearsay testimony offered by a child should be permitted only upon a showing of necessity—i.e., in cases where necessary to protect the child's physical and psychological well-being.

Petitioner's reliance is misplaced. *Coy* and *Craig* involved only the question of what in-court procedures are constitutionally required to guarantee a defendant's confrontation right once a witness is testifying. Such a question is quite separate from that of what requirements the Confrontation Clause imposes as a predicate for the introduction of out-of-court declarations....

For the foregoing reasons, the judgment of the Illinois Appellate Court is

Affirmed.

* * *

[1] The spontaneous declaration exception applies to "[a] statement relating to a startling event or condition made while the declarant was under the stress of excitement caused by the event or condition."

[2] "...statements made by the victim to medical personnel for purposes of medical diagnosis or treatment including descriptions of the cause of symptom, pain or sensations, or the inception or general character of the cause or external source thereof insofar as reasonably pertinent to diagnosis or treatment shall be admitted as an exception to the hearsay rule."

[3] "In all criminal prosecutions, the accused shall enjoy the right to...be confronted with the witnesses against him...." U.S. Const., Amdt. 6.

[6] By "unavailability rule," we mean a rule which would require as a predicate for introducing hearsay testimony either a showing of the declarant's unavailability or production at trial of the declarant.

[8] Indeed, it is this factor that has led us to conclude that "firmly rooted" exceptions carry sufficient indicia of reliability to satisfy the reliability requirement posed by the Confrontation Clause....There can be no doubt that the two exceptions we consider in this "firmly rooted." The exception for spontaneous declarations is at least two centuries old....The exception for statements made for purposes of medical diagnosis or treatment is similarly recognized in Federal Rule of Evidence 803(4), and is equally widely accepted among the States.

Questions for Discussion

1. The majority concedes that the statements at issue had "substantial probative value," and that cross-examination is the "greatest legal engine ever invented for the discovery of truth." Does the holding reflect these observations?

2. The majority rules that *Craig* merely concerned how children would testify once they do testify, but that out-of-court declarations have different rules. Under the *Craig* holding, the Sixth Amendment right to confront compels strict face-to-face confrontation between child and defendant unless "inability to communicate" is demonstrated by the state. Does it make sense that the Court would more easily allow total exclusion of a witness than limit the manner of cross-examination?

3. Although not a child-testimony case, the U.S. Supreme Court ruled in *Crawford v. Washington*, 541 U.S. 36 (2004) that the confrontation right of an adult criminal defendant requires that he be allowed to cross-examine witnesses at trial—and effectively limited hearsay exceptions for out-of-court statements where the witness is available. Such hearsay is commonly used in juvenile court proceedings on a variety of bases, including those discussed in *White*, a so-called

"tender years" exception, and others. The constitutional limitations on its use are apparently not applicable in that civil venue. However, what of its use against juvenile respondents in delinquency proceedings, where the result may be incarceration, and where the Court has required substantial adult-court due process (see *In Re Gault* and progeny discussed in Chapter 10)?

4. Is the *Crawford* holding distinguishable from *Craig* because the latter concerns not the right to cross-examine, but the physical layout and visibility? If so, how is it distinguishable from *White*, which concerns admission of hearsay statements against a criminal defendant and which rejects an "unavailability" rule?

D. CHILD VICTIM/WITNESS CONFIDENTIALITY

Globe Newspaper Co. v. Superior Court for the County of Norfolk
457 U.S. 596 (1982)

JUSTICE BRENNAN delivered the opinion of the Court.

Section 16A of Chapter 278 of the Massachusetts General Laws,[1] construed by the Massachusetts Supreme Judicial Court, requires trial judges, at trials for specified sexual offenses involving a victim under the age of 18, to exclude the press and general public from the courtroom during the testimony of that victim. The question presented is whether the statute thus construed violates the First Amendment as applied to the States through the Fourteenth Amendment.

I

The case began when appellant, Globe Newspaper Co. (Globe), unsuccessfully attempted to gain access to a rape trial conducted in the Superior Court for the County of Norfolk, Commonwealth of Massachusetts. The criminal defendant in that trial had been charged with the forcible rape and forced unnatural rape of three girls who were minors at the time of trial—two 16 years of age and one 17. In April 1979, during hearings on several preliminary motions, the trial judge ordered the courtroom closed.[2] Before the trial began, Globe moved that the court revoke this closure order, hold hearings on any future such orders, and permit appellant to intervene "for the limited purpose of asserting its rights to access to the trial and hearings on related preliminary motions."....

Within hours after the court had issued its exclusion order, Globe sought injunctive relief from a justice of the Supreme Judicial Court of Massachusetts....The next day the justice conducted a hearing, at which the Commonwealth, "on behalf of the victims," waived "whatever rights it [might] have [had] to exclude the press."...[5] Nevertheless, Globe's request for relief was denied. Before Globe appealed to the full court, the rape trial proceeded and the defendant was acquitted.

* * *

II

In this Court, Globe challenges that portion of the trial court's order, approved by the Supreme Judicial Court of Massachusetts, that holds that § 16A requires, under all circumstances, the exclusion of the press and general public during the testimony of a minor victim in a sex-offense trial....

* * *

III

A

The Court's recent decision in *Richmond Newspapers* firmly established for the first time that the press and general public have a constitutional right of access to criminal trials. Although there was no opinion of the Court in that case, seven Justices recognized that this right of access is embodied in the First Amendment, and applied to the States through the Fourteenth Amendment. 448 U.S., at 558–581 (plurality opinion);...

* * *

Two features of the criminal justice system, emphasized in the various opinions in *Richmond Newspapers*, together serve to explain why a right of access to *criminal trials* in particular is properly afforded protection by the First Amendment. First, the criminal trial historically has been open to the press and general public....

Second, the right of access to criminal trials plays a particularly significant role in the functioning of the judicial process and the government as a whole. Public scrutiny of a criminal trial enhances the quality and safeguards the integrity of the factfinding process, with benefits to both the defendant and to society as a whole. Moreover, public access to the criminal trial fosters an appearance of fairness, thereby heightening public respect for the judicial process....And in the broadest terms, public access to criminal trials permits the public to participate in and serve as a check upon the judicial process—an essential component in our structure of self-government. In sum, the institutional value of the open criminal trial is recognized in both logic and experience.

B

Although the right of access to criminal trials is of constitutional stature, it is not absolute....But the circumstances under which the press and public can be barred from a criminal trial are limited; the State's justification in denying access must be a weighty one. Where, as in the present case, the State attempts to deny the right of access in order to inhibit the disclosure of sensitive information, it must be shown that the denial is necessitated by a compelling governmental interest, and is narrowly tailored to serve that interest....[17] We now consider the state interests advanced to support Massachusetts' mandatory rule barring press and public access to criminal sex-offense trials during the testimony of minor victims.

IV
* * *

We agree with appellee that the first interest—safeguarding the physical and psychological well-being of a minor[19]—is a compelling one. But as compelling as that interest is, it does not justify a *mandatory* closure rule, for it is clear that the circumstances of the particular case may affect the significance of the interest. A trial court can determine on a case-by-case basis whether closure is necessary to protect the welfare of a minor victim.[20] Among the factors to be weighed are the minor victim's age, psychological maturity and understanding, the nature of the crime, the desires of the victim,[21] and the interests of parents and relatives. Section 16A, in contrast, requires closure even if the victim does not seek the exclusion of the press and general public, and would not suffer injury by their presence.[22] In the case before us, for example, the names of the minor victims were already in the public record,[23] and the record indicates

that the victims may have been willing to testify despite the presence of the press.... If the trial court had been permitted to exercise its discretion, closure might well have been deemed unnecessary. In short, § 16A cannot be viewed as a narrowly tailored means of accommodating the State's asserted interest: That interest could be served just as well by requiring the trial court to determine on a case-by-case basis whether the State's legitimate concern for the well-being of the minor victim necessitates closure. Such an approach ensures that the constitutional right of the press and public to gain access to criminal trials will not be restricted except where necessary to protect the State's interest.[25]

Nor can § 16A be justified on the basis of the Commonwealth's second asserted interest—the encouragement of minor victims of sex crimes to come forward and provide accurate testimony. The Commonwealth has offered no empirical support for the claim that the rule of automatic closure contained in § 16A will lead to an increase in the number of minor sex victims coming forward and cooperating with state authorities.[26]...

V

For the foregoing reasons, we hold that § 16A, as construed by the Massachusetts Supreme Judicial Court, violates the First Amendment to the Constitution.[27] Accordingly, the judgment of the Massachusetts Supreme Judicial Court is

Reversed.

* * *

[1] Massachusetts Gen. Laws Ann., ch. 278, § 16A..., provides in pertinent part: "At the trial of a complaint or indictment for rape, incest, carnal abuse or other crime involving sex, where a minor under eighteen years of age is the person upon, with or against whom the crime is alleged to have been committed,... the presiding justice shall exclude the general public from the court room, admitting only such persons as may have a direct interest in the case."

[2] "The court caused a sign marked 'closed' to be placed on the courtroom door, and court personnel turned away people seeking entry."....

[5] The Commonwealth's representative stated: "[Our] position before the trial judge [was], and it is before this Court, that in some circumstances a trial judge, where the defendant is asserting his right to a constitutional, public trial,...may consider that as outweighing the otherwise legitimate statutory interests, particularly where the Commonwealth [acts] on behalf of the victims, and this is literally on behalf of the victims in the sense that they were consulted fully by the prosecutor in this case. The Commonwealth waives whatever rights it may have to exclude the press."...Some time after the trial began, the prosecuting attorney informed the judge at a lobby conference that she had "[spoken] with each of the victims regarding... excluding the press."....The prosecuting attorney indicated that the victims had expressed some "privacy concerns" that were based on "their own privacy interests, as well as the fact that there are grandparents involved with a couple of these victims." But according to the prosecuting attorney, the victims "wouldn't object to the press being included" if "it were at all possible to obtain a guarantee" that the press would not attempt to interview them or publish their names, photographs, or any personal information. *Ibid.* In fact, their names were already part of the public record. See 383 Mass. 838, 849 (1981). It is not clear from the record, however, whether or not the victims were aware of this fact at the time of their discussions with the prosecuting attorney.

[17] Of course, limitations on the right of access that resemble "time, place, and manner" restrictions on protected speech,...would not be subjected to such strict scrutiny....

[19] It is important to note that in the context of § 16A, the measure of the State's interest lies not in the extent to which minor victims are injured by testifying, but rather in the incremental injury suffered by testifying in the presence of the press and the general public.

[20] Indeed, the plurality opinion in Richmond Newspapers suggested that individualized determinations are always required before the right of access may be denied: "Absent an overriding interest articulated in findings, the trial of a criminal case must be open to the public." 448 U.S., at 581 (footnote omitted) (emphasis added).

[21] "[I]f the minor victim wanted the public to know precisely what a heinous crime the defendant had committed, the imputed legislative justifications for requiring the closing of the trial during the victim's testimony would in part, at least, be inapplicable."....

[22] It appears that while other States have statutory or constitutional provisions that would allow a trial judge to close a criminal sex-offense trial during the testimony of a minor victim, no other State has a mandatory provision excluding both the press and general public during such testimony....

[23] The Court has held that the government may not impose sanctions for the publication of the names of rape victims lawfully obtained from the public record....

[25] Of course, for a case-by-case approach to be meaningful, representatives of the press and general public "must be given an opportunity to be heard on the question of their exclusion."...This does not mean, however, that for purposes of this inquiry the court cannot protect the minor victim by denying these representatives the opportunity to confront or cross-examine the victim, or by denying them access to sensitive details concerning the victim and the victim's future testimony. Such discretion is consistent with the traditional authority of trial judges to conduct in camera conferences....Without such trial court discretion, a State's interest in safeguarding the welfare of the minor victim, determined in an individual case to merit some form of closure, would be defeated before it could ever be brought to bear.

[26] To the extent that it is suggested that, quite apart from encouraging minor victims to testify, §16A improves the quality and credibility of testimony, the suggestion also is speculative. And while closure may have such an effect in particular cases, the Court has recognized that, *as a general matter, "[openness]* in court proceedings may *improve* the quality of testimony."...In the absence of any showing that closure would improve the quality of testimony of all minor sex victims, the State's interest certainly cannot justify a *mandatory* closure rule.

[27] We emphasize that our holding is a narrow one: that a rule of mandatory closure respecting the testimony of minor sex victims is constitutionally infirm. In individual cases, and under appropriate circumstances, the First Amendment does not necessarily stand as a bar to the exclusion from the courtroom of the press and general public during the testimony of minor sex-offense victims. But a mandatory rule, requiring no particularized determinations in individual cases, is unconstitutional.

It certainly cannot be said that the victims in this case consented to testifying in open court. During a lobby conference prior to trial, the prosecutor informed the trial judge that she had interviewed the victims, that they were concerned about publicity, and would agree to press attendance only if certain guarantees could be given:

"Each of [the three victims] indicated that they had the same concerns and basically they are privacy concerns.

"The difficulty of obtaining any kind of guarantee that the press would not print their names or where they go to school or any personal data or take pictures of them or attempt to interview them, those concerns come from their own privacy interests, as well as the fact that there are grandparents involved with a couple of these victims who do not know what happened and if they were to find out by reading the paper, everyone was concerned about what would happen then. And they stated that if it were at all possible to obtain a guarantee that this information would not be used, then they wouldn't object to the press being included. I explained that that is [a] very difficult guarantee to obtain because the Court cannot issue a conditional order, or anything like that, but I just wanted to put on the record what their concerns were and what they are afraid of." App. 48a.

It is clear that the victims would "waive" the exclusion of the press only if the trial court gave them guarantees of strict privacy, guarantees that were probably beyond the authority of the court and which themselves would raise grave constitutional problems....

CHIEF JUSTICE BURGER, with whom **JUSTICE REHNQUIST** joins, dissenting.

Historically our society has gone to great lengths to protect minors *charged* with crime, particularly by prohibiting the release of the names of offenders, barring the press and public from juvenile proceedings, and sealing the records of those proceedings. Yet today the Court holds unconstitutional a state statute designed to protect not the *accused*, but the minor *victims* of sex crimes. In doing so, it advances a disturbing paradox. Although states are permitted, for example, to mandate the closure of all proceedings in order to protect a 17-year-old charged with rape, they are not permitted to require the closing of part of criminal proceedings in order to protect an innocent child who has been raped or otherwise sexually abused.

The Court has tried to make its holding a narrow one by not disturbing the authority of state legislatures to enact more narrowly drawn statutes giving trial judges the discretion to exclude the public and the press from the courtroom during the minor victim's testimony....I also do not read the Court's opinion as foreclosing a state statute which mandates closure except in cases where the victim agrees to testify in open court.[1] But the Court's decision is nevertheless a gross invasion of state authority and a state's duty to protect its citizens—in this case minor victims of crime. I cannot agree with the Court's expansive interpretation of our decision in *Richmond Newspapers, Inc. v. Virginia*, 448 U.S. 555 (1980), or its cavalier rejection of the serious interests supporting Massachusetts' mandatory closure rule. Accordingly, I dissent.

* * *

...The Court's wooden application of the rigid standard it asserts for this case is inappropriate. The Commonwealth has not denied the public or the media access to information as to what takes place at trial. As the Court acknowledges, Massachusetts does not deny the press and the public access to the trial transcript or to other sources of information about the victim's testimony. Even the victim's identity is part of the public record, although the name of a 16-year-old accused rapist generally would not be a matter of public record....The Commonwealth does not deny access to information, and does nothing whatever to inhibit its disclosure. This case is quite unlike others in which we have held unconstitutional state laws which prevent the dissemination of information or the public discussion of ideas....

The purpose of the Commonwealth in enacting § 16A was to give assurance to parents and minors that they would have this moderate and limited protection from the trauma, embarrassment, and humiliation of having to reveal the intimate details of a sexual assault in front of a large group of unfamiliar spectators— and perhaps a television audience—and to lower the barriers to the reporting of such crimes which might come from the victim's dread of public testimony....

Neither the purpose of the law nor its effect is primarily to deny the press or public access to information; the verbatim transcript is made available to the public and the media and may be used without limit. We therefore need only examine whether the restrictions imposed are reasonable and whether the interests of the Commonwealth override the very limited incidental effects of the law on First Amendment rights....Our obligation in this case is to balance the competing interests: the interests of the media for instant access, against the interest of the State in protecting child rape victims from the trauma of public testimony. In more than half the states, public testimony will include television coverage.

III

For me, it seems beyond doubt, considering the minimal impact of the law on First Amendment rights and the overriding weight of the Commonwealth's interest in protecting child rape victims, that the Massachusetts law is not unconstitutional. The Court acknowledges that the press and the public have prompt and full access to all of the victim's testimony. Their additional interest in actually being present during the testimony is minimal....

* * *

...Section 16A is intended not to preserve confidentiality, but to prevent the risk of severe psychological damage caused by having to relate the details of the crime in front of a crowd which inevitably will include voyeuristic strangers.[6] In most states, that crowd may be expanded to include a live television audience, with reruns on the evening news. That ordeal could be difficult for an adult; to a child, the experience can be devastating and leave permanent scars.[7]

The Commonwealth's interests are clearly furthered by the mandatory nature of the closure statute. Certainly if the law were discretionary, most judges would exercise that discretion soundly and would avoid unnecessary harm to the child, but victims and their families are entitled to assurance of such protection....

IV

...Paradoxically, the Court today denies the victims the kind of protection routinely given to juveniles who commit crimes. Many will find it difficult to reconcile the concern so often expressed for the rights of the accused with the callous indifference exhibited today for children who, having suffered the trauma of rape or other sexual abuse, are denied the modest protection the Massachusetts Legislature provided.

* * *

[6] As one commentator put it: "Especially in cases involving minors, the courts stress the serious embarrassment and shame of the victim who is forced to testify to sexual acts or whose intimate life is revealed in detail before a crowd of the idly curious." Berger, Man's Trial, Woman's Tribulation: Rape Cases in the Courtroom, 77 Colum. L. Rev. 1, 88 (1977). The victim's interest in avoiding the humiliation of testifying in open court is thus quite separate from any interest in preventing the public from learning of the crime. It is ironic that the Court emphasizes the failure of the Commonwealth to seal the trial transcript and bar disclosure of the victim's identity. The Court implies that a state law more severely encroaching upon the interests of the press and public would be upheld.

[7] ...Holmstrom and Burgess report that nearly half of all *adult* rape victims were disturbed by the public setting of their trials. Certainly the impact on children must be greater.

Questions for Discussion

1. The Commonwealth purportedly "waived" confidentiality on behalf of the three juvenile rape victims; does it have standing to do so?

2. Does the defendant have a constitutional right to a "public" trial, including public exposure of his accusers? Should he? Does confidentiality for testimony of victims presume the guilt of the defendant?

3. If the defendant is provided an independent judge presiding, a right to a jury, publicly paid counsel, evidence against him under oath and pursuant to the rules of evidence, the right to cross-examine the witness, and appellate review, how much quantum of due process is added by general public attendance and/or

media coverage? Is it possible that widespread coverage could injure a fair trial for defendant? Should confidentiality be allowed only if the defendant requests it?

4. If the state has a compelling state interest in protecting the privacy rights of persons possibly subjected to humiliating crimes, is the measure here narrowly enough tailored to that interest? The majority contends that it is overly broad since it applies in all cases categorically, whether the names of victims are already known, and whether they do not object to public attendance. Note that dependency court proceedings are confidential. Is that policy overly broad? The categorical judgment of legislatures that all dependency court cases are to be confidential has been universally upheld. Can the Court reconcile broad confidentiality in all cases where minors have been abused (or molested) out of concern for the child, while constitutionally barring the more limited protection in *Globe*?

5. The Court argues that there is no "empirical support" that a courtroom bar deters crime while a transcript of the proceedings is still available. Would it pass muster if the transcript were sealed as well? Is there a rational distinction between public attendance/media coverage and later availability of a transcript in terms of the privacy interest of victims? If those who have been victims are routinely featured ostentatiously in the media during trials, will that stimulate or discourage crime reports by victims? What empirical support does the Court require? If the issue is empirically grounded, is the court (as opposed to the legislature) the optimum institution to receive evidence from a wide variety of sources to decide such a policy issue?

Pennsylvania v. Ritchie
480 U.S. 39 (1987)

JUSTICE POWELL announced the judgment of the Court and delivered the opinion of the Court with respect to Parts I, II, III-B, III-C, and IV, and an opinion with respect to Part III-A, in which THE CHIEF JUSTICE, JUSTICE WHITE, and JUSTICE O'CONNOR join.

The question presented in this case is whether and to what extent a State's interest in the confidentiality of its investigative files concerning child abuse must yield to a criminal defendant's Sixth and Fourteenth Amendment right to discover favorable evidence.

I

As part of its efforts to combat child abuse, the Commonwealth of Pennsylvania has established Children and Youth Services (CYS), a protective service agency charged with investigating cases of suspected mistreatment and neglect. In 1979, respondent George Ritchie was charged with rape, involuntary deviate sexual intercourse, incest, and corruption of a minor. The victim of the alleged attacks was his 13-year-old daughter, who claimed that she had been assaulted by Ritchie two or three times per week during the previous four years. The girl reported the incidents to the police, and the matter then was referred to the CYS.

During pretrial discovery, Ritchie served CYS with a subpoena, seeking access to the records concerning the daughter. Ritchie requested disclosure of the file related to the immediate charges, as well as certain records that he claimed were compiled in 1978, when CYS investigated a separate report by an unidentified source that Ritchie's children were being abused.[1] CYS refused to comply with the subpoena, claiming that the records were privileged under Pennsylvania law....

Ritchie moved to have CYS sanctioned for failing to honor the subpoena, and the trial court held a hearing on the motion in chambers. Ritchie argued that he was entitled to the information because the file might contain the names of favorable witnesses, as well as other, unspecified exculpatory evidence. He also requested disclosure of a medical report that he believed was compiled during the 1978 CYS investigation. Although the trial judge acknowledged that he had not examined the entire CYS file, he accepted a CYS representative's assertion that there was no medical report in the record.[3] The judge then denied the motion and refused to order CYS to disclose the files.[4]

At trial, the main witness against Ritchie was his daughter. In an attempt to rebut her testimony, defense counsel cross-examined the girl at length, questioning her on all aspects of the alleged attacks and her reasons for not reporting the incidents sooner. Except for routine evidentiary rulings, the trial judge placed no limitation on the scope of cross-examination. At the close of trial Ritchie was convicted by a jury on all counts, and the judge sentenced him to 3 to 10 years in prison.

On appeal to the Pennsylvania Superior Court, Ritchie claimed, *inter alia* that the failure to disclose the contents of the CYS file violated the Confrontation Clause of the Sixth Amendment, as applied to the States through the Due Process Clause of the Fourteenth Amendment.[5] The court agreed that there had been a constitutional violation, and accordingly vacated the conviction and remanded for further proceedings....

* * *

III

* * *

Ritchie argues that he could not effectively question his daughter because, without the CYS material, he did not know which types of questions would best expose the weaknesses in her testimony. Had the files been disclosed, Ritchie argues that he might have been able to show that the daughter made statements to the CYS counselor that were inconsistent with her trial statements, or perhaps to reveal that the girl acted with an improper motive. Of course, the right to cross-examine includes the opportunity to show that a witness is biased, or that the testimony is exaggerated or unbelievable....Because this type of evidence can make the difference between conviction and acquittal,...Ritchie argues that the failure to disclose information that might have made cross-examination more effective undermines the Confrontation Clause's purpose of increasing the accuracy of the truth-finding process at trial....

* * *

If we were to accept this broad interpretation...,the effect would be to transform the Confrontation Clause into a constitutionally compelled rule of pretrial discovery. Nothing in the case law supports such a view. The opinions of this Court show that the right to confrontation is a *trial* right, designed to prevent improper restrictions on the types of questions that defense counsel may ask during cross-examination....The ability to question adverse witnesses, however, does not include the power to require the pretrial disclosure of any and all information that might be useful in contradicting unfavorable testimony.[9] Normally the right to confront one's accusers is satisfied if defense counsel receives wide latitude at trial to question witnesses. In short, the Confrontation Clause only guarantees "an *opportunity* for effective cross-examination, not cross-examination that is effective in whatever way, and to whatever extent, the defense might wish."...

* * *

B

The Pennsylvania Supreme Court also suggested that the failure to disclose the CYS file violated the Sixth Amendment's guarantee of compulsory process. Ritchie asserts that the trial court's ruling prevented him from learning the names of the "witnesses in his favor," as well as other evidence that might be contained in the file. Although the basis for the Pennsylvania Supreme Court's ruling on this point is unclear, it apparently concluded that the right of compulsory process includes the right to have the State's assistance in uncovering arguably useful information, without regard to the existence of a state-created restriction—here, the confidentiality of the files.

1

* * *

437

This Court has never squarely held that the Compulsory Process Clause guarantees the right to discover the *identity* of witnesses, or to require the government to produce exculpatory evidence. Instead, the Court traditionally has evaluated claims such as those raised by Ritchie under the broader protections of the Due Process Clause...

2

It is well settled that the government has the obligation to turn over evidence in its possession that is both favorable to the accused and material to guilt or punishment. Although courts have used different terminologies to define "materiality," a majority of this Court has agreed, "[evidence] is material only if there is a reasonable probability that, had the evidence been disclosed to the defense, the result of the proceeding would have been different. A 'reasonable probability' is a probability sufficient to undermine confidence in the outcome."...

At this stage, of course, it is impossible to say whether any information in the CYS records may be relevant to Ritchie's claim of innocence, because neither the prosecution nor defense counsel has seen the information, and the trial judge acknowledged that he had not reviewed the full file. The Commonwealth, however, argues that no materiality inquiry is required, because a statute renders the contents of the file privileged. Requiring disclosure here, it is argued, would override the Commonwealth's compelling interest in confidentiality on the mere speculation that the file "might" have been useful to the defense.

Although we recognize that the public interest in protecting this type of sensitive information is strong, we do not agree that this interest necessarily prevents disclosure in all circumstances....

* * *

C

This ruling does not end our analysis, because the Pennsylvania Supreme Court did more than simply remand. It also held that defense counsel must be allowed to examine all of the confidential information, both relevant and irrelevant, and present arguments in favor of disclosure. The court apparently concluded that whenever a defendant alleges that protected evidence might be material, the appropriate method of assessing this claim is to grant full access to the disputed information, regardless of the State's interest in confidentiality. We cannot agree.

A defendant's right to discover exculpatory evidence does not include the unsupervised authority to search through the Commonwealth's files....Although the eye of an advocate may be helpful to a defendant in ferreting out information,...this Court has never held—even in the absence of a statute restricting disclosure—that a defendant alone may make the determination as to the materiality of the information. Settled practice is to the contrary. In the typical case where a defendant makes only a general request for exculpatory material under *Brady v. Maryland*, 373 U.S. 83 (1963), it is the State that decides which information must be disclosed. Unless defense counsel becomes aware that other exculpatory evidence was withheld and brings it to the court's attention,[16] the prosecutor's decision on disclosure is final. Defense counsel has no constitutional right to conduct his own search of the State's files to argue relevance....

We find that Ritchie's interest (as well as that of the Commonwealth) in ensuring a fair trial can be protected fully by requiring that the CYS files be submitted only to the trial court for *in camera* review. Although this rule denies Ritchie the benefits of an "advocate's eye," we note that the trial court's discretion is not unbounded. If a defendant is aware of specific information contained in the file (*e.g.*, the medical report), he is free to request it directly from the court, and argue in favor of its materiality. Moreover, the duty to disclose is ongoing; information that may be deemed immaterial upon original examination may become important as the proceedings progress, and the court would be obligated to release information material to the fairness of the trial.

To allow full disclosure to defense counsel in this type of case would sacrifice unnecessarily the Commonwealth's compelling interest in protecting its child abuse information. If the CYS records were made available to defendants, even through counsel, it could have a seriously adverse effect on Pennsylvania's efforts to uncover and treat abuse. Child abuse is one of the most difficult crimes to detect and prosecute, in large part because there often are no witnesses except the victim. A child's feelings of vulnerability and guilt and his or her unwillingness to come forward are particularly acute when the abuser is a parent. It therefore is essential that the child have a state-designated person to whom he may turn, and to do so with the assurance of confidentiality. Relatives and neighbors who suspect abuse also will be more willing to come forward if they know that their identities will be protected. Recognizing this, the Commonwealth—like all other States[17]—has made a commendable effort to assure victims and witnesses that they may speak to the CYS counselors without fear of general disclosure....

IV

...An *in camera* review by the trial court will serve Ritchie's interest without destroying the Commonwealth's need to protect the confidentiality of those involved in child-abuse investigations. The judgment of the Pennsylvania Supreme Court is affirmed in part and reversed in part, and the case is remanded for further proceedings not inconsistent with this opinion.

It is so ordered.

* * *

[1] Although the 1978 investigation took place during the period that the daughter claimed she was being molested, it is undisputed that the daughter did not tell CYS about the assaults at that time. No criminal charges were filed as a result of this earlier investigation.

[3] The trial judge stated that he did not read "50 pages or more of an extensive record."....The judge had no knowledge of the case before the pretrial hearing....

[4] There is no suggestion that the Commonwealth's prosecutor was given access to the file at any point in the proceedings, or that he was aware of its contents.

[5] The Sixth Amendment of the United States Constitution protects both the right of confrontation and the right of compulsory process: "In all criminal prosecutions, the accused shall enjoy the right to be confronted with the witnesses against him; [and] to have compulsory process for obtaining witnesses in his favor." Both Clauses are made obligatory on the States by the Fourteenth Amendment....

[9] This is not to suggest, of course, that there are no protections for pretrial discovery in criminal cases....We simply hold that with respect to this issue, the Confrontation Clause only protects a defendant's trial rights, and does not compel the pretrial production of information that might be useful in preparing for trial. Also, we hardly need say that nothing in our opinion today is intended to alter a trial judge's traditional power to control the scope of cross-examination by prohibiting questions that are prejudicial, irrelevant, or otherwise improper....

[16] See Fed. Rule Crim. Proc. 16(d)(2); Pa. Rule Crim. Proc. 305(E) ("If at any time during the course of the proceedings it is brought to the attention of the court that a party has failed to comply with this rule [mandating disclosure of exculpatory evidence], the court may...enter such...order as it deems just under the circumstances").

[17] The importance of the public interest at issue in this case is evidenced by the fact that all 50 States and the District of Columbia have statutes that protect the confidentiality of their official records concerning child abuse. See Brief for State of California ex rel. John K. Van de Kamp et al....

JUSTICE BRENNAN, with whom **JUSTICE MARSHALL** joins, dissenting.

...I write separately to challenge the Court's narrow reading of the Confrontation Clause as applicable only to events that occur at trial. That interpretation ignores the fact that the right of cross-examination also may be significantly infringed by events occurring outside the trial itself, such as the wholesale denial of access to material that would serve as the basis for a significant line of inquiry at trial. In this case, the trial court properly viewed Ritchie's vague speculations that the agency file might contain something useful as an insufficient basis for permitting general access to the file. However, in denying access to the prior statements of the victim the court deprived Ritchie of material crucial to any effort to impeach the victim at trial. I view this deprivation as a violation of the Confrontation Clause.

* * *

The creation of a significant impediment to the conduct of cross-examination thus undercuts the protections of the Confrontation Clause, even if that impediment is not erected at the trial itself. In this case, the foreclosure of access to prior statements of the testifying victim deprived the defendant of material crucial to the conduct of cross-examination. As we noted in *Jencks*, a witness' prior statements are essential to any effort at impeachment:

"Every experienced trial judge and trial lawyer knows the value for impeaching purposes of statements of the witness recording the events before time dulls treacherous memory. Flat contradiction between the witness' testimony and the version of the events given in his reports is not the only test of inconsistency. The omission from the reports of facts related at the trial, or a contrast in emphasis upon the same facts, even a different order of treatment, are also relevant to the cross-examining process of testing the credibility of a witness' trial testimony." 353 U.S., at 667.

The right of a defendant to confront an accuser is intended fundamentally to provide an opportunity to subject *accusations* to critical scrutiny....Essential to testing a witness' account of events is the ability to compare that version with other versions the witness has earlier recounted. Denial of access to a witness' prior statements thus imposes a handicap that strikes at the heart of cross-examination.

* * *

The Court today adopts an interpretation of the Confrontation Clause unwarranted by previous case law and inconsistent with the underlying values of that constitutional provision. I therefore dissent.

* * *

Questions for Discussion

1. Is full discovery an enumerated constitutional right? Is it implied by the confrontation clause, because of the need for facts to cross-examine? Does that discovery right reach beyond information directly possessed by the state, to information possessed by third parties? Does it apply if only relevant to witnesses who are not called by the People (and hence irrelevant to cross-examination)? Or does the possibility of exculpatory evidence discovery make its production more generally compelled by the right to due process—quite apart from the confrontation clause?

2. Why might the defense find the *in camera* court examination of records insufficient? Will the court know if statements are exculpatory? Should counsel also be allowed to review the statements under a protective order of confidentiality? Would defense counsel be in a conflict situation regarding disclosure of what he knows to his client?

3. Should the court distinguish the alleged victim's psychotherapy, which occurs post-arrest and is not known to or reviewed by the prosecutors putting on the People's case? Note the strong weight given to the psychotherapy privilege privacy right of the alleged molester in *Stritzinger* (Chapter 8). If the court disallows a mandated child abuse report by his psychotherapist because of the privacy importance of the privilege, should the alleged victim's privacy be similarly respected? Or does the due process and accuracy importance of the trial trump that consideration?

ENDNOTES

[1] Robert H. Pantell and AAP Committee on Psychosocial Aspects of Child and Family Health, *The Child Witness in the Courtroom,* 139 PEDIATRICS 3 (2017).

[2] *Tubbs v. State*, 195 So.3d 363 (Miss. 2016).

[3] C. McCormick Evidence 140 (2d Ed. 1972); see also J. Wigmore, *Evidence*, Sections 507, 509 (3d Ed. 1940).

[4] *See e.g.*, Milton, *Children's Competency to Testify*, 5 LAW & HUMAN BEHAVIOR 73 (1981).

[5] A classic example of unsophisticated guile is provided from an early article. A child wishing to skip school for a baseball game called his teacher, pretending to be his father to report his illness: "Hello, Miss Brown, my son is very ill, and I am sorry to say he cannot come to school today." "Who is talking?" asked the teacher. "My father," replied the boy. Stephen J. Ceci, Maggie Bruck, *The Suggestibility of the Child Witness: An Historical Review and Synthesis*, citing Krout (1931) at 23.

[6] N.J. R. Evid. 803.

CHAPTER TEN

Juvenile Crime and Delinquency

A. JUVENILE CRIME DEMOGRAPHIC BACKGROUND

1. Juvenile Crime Trends

Juvenile arrests have declined significantly over the past two decades. According to the Office of Juvenile Justice and Delinquency Prevention, the overall arrest rate for juveniles decreased 72% between 1996 and 2017. In actual numbers, 2017 saw the arrest of 809,700 juveniles, which marked a 59% decrease compared to 2008. Between 2008 and 2017, the number of arrests decreased in every offense category, including murder, burglary, assault (simple and aggravated) and arson.[1]

Offense	Number of Juveniles Arrested	Percent Change 2008–17	Percent Change 2013–17	Percent Change 2016–17
TOTAL	809,700	-59%	-25%	-5%
Murder/Negligent Manslaughter	910	-27%	23%	7%
Robbery	19,330	-45%	1%	1%
Aggravated assault	28,220	-49%	-9%	1%
Burglary	30,850	-63%	-28%	-4%
Larceny-theft	118,660	-63%	-36%	-12%
Motor Vehicle theft	16,300	-34%	40%	4%
Arson	2,240	-65%	-39%	-12%

Table 10A: Percent Change in Juvenile Arrests[2]

The proportion of serious violent crime committed by juveniles reached a high point in 1993 (26%) and reached a new historic low point in 2011 (10%). In 2016, 12% of all violent crimes were committed by juveniles.[3] The juvenile arrest rate for murder reached a low in 2012, 83% below the rate in 1993. Since 2012, the rate has modestly increased, from 2.2 to 2.7 per 100,000 youth.[4] In 2017, juveniles accounted for less than one in five arrests for all property crimes,[5] bringing the juvenile Property Crime Index arrest rate to a 35 year low.[6] Even the arrest rate for arson, which for several years was the only crime for which juveniles comprised the majority of arrestees, has steadily decreased. In 2017, juveniles comprised a quarter of the individuals arrested for that offense.[7]

Despite encouraging trends in overall juvenile offending and arrests, the demographics of juvenile arrests have long been, and still remain, troubling. In 2016, African American youth comprised 17% of the population age 10–17. However, 53% of all juvenile arrests for violent crimes—including 61% of arrests for murder/non-negligent manslaughter and 69% of robbery arrests—involved African American youth.[8] In 2016, 28% of juvenile arrests including 57% of juvenile arrests for arson, were of children under age 15.[9] Arrest rates for juvenile females have declined less than for males, increasing their proportion somewhat. Although boys account for more than half of all status offenses, including truancy and curfew violations, 55% of petitioned runaways are girls.[10]

2. Child Victim Incidence

For adolescents age 12–18, violent and serious violent victimization has significantly decreased since 1995.[11] In 2014, the violent victimization of adolescents was at an historic low, one-sixth of the incidence in the mid-1990s.[12] However, youth ages 12–17 remain more likely than adults to be victims of violent crimes. On average, those in this age group are 2.2 times more likely than adults to be victims of serious violent crime and 2.6 times more likely to be victims of simple assault.[13] In 2014, just over half of children of all ages surveyed nationally reported having been physically assaulted in their lifetime.[14] Although most of this violence is perpetrated by adults,[15] where juvenile violence does occur, other juveniles are most often the victims.[16]

In 2016, the Centers for Disease Control listed homicide as the fourth leading cause of death for children ages 1–4 and children ages 5–14, and third for young people ages 15–24.[17] In 2014, an average of 12 young people age 10–24 were victims of homicide each day. For African-American youth in this age range, homicide was the number one cause of death.[18] Of all juveniles under 18 murdered in 2016, 38% percent were younger than five. These very young children represented 31% percent of male victims, 52% of female victims, 45% of white victims, and 30% of black victims.[19] Eighty-six percent of homicide victims ages 10 to 24 were killed with a firearm. A recent study, conducted between 2012–14, indicated that among all ages, an average of nearly 700 children died and more than 4000 were treated for gunshot wounds annually.[20]

3. Risk Factors for Delinquency

In recent years, brain science and research on adolescent development have confirmed what has always been intuitive—children are different from adults. Specifically, adolescents are more impulsive, less able to regulate their behavior in emotionally charged situations, and less able to make decisions that take into account future consequences. Thus, many youth engage in what is considered "delinquent" activity. Whether a youth ultimately becomes involved in the juvenile justice system is driven by a number of factors, including the ways in which our society and systems operate. Policy considerations such as the overuse of detention, disparate treatment based on race, and ineffective punitive consequences are discussed later in this chapter. Other factors influencing delinquent behavior and system involvement are related to the risks and supports individual children experience in their lives.

Numerous studies have identified risk factors which in combination influence delinquent behavior. Not surprisingly, the presence of multiple risk factors increases the chance a child will commit a delinquent offense. Furthermore, exposure to risk factors early in a child's life is associated with offending at younger ages. Risk factors can be categorized into several domains: individual, family, peer, school and community. For younger children, the most salient factors are those related to the individual and family, while peer, school, and community factors have greater impact in later adolescence.[21] Although the existence of risk factors can help predict delinquent behavior, they do not exist in a vacuum. Additional factors, known as protective factors, work to mitigate risks. Falling into the same domains as risk factors, protective factors are characteristics or supports that build resilience and discourage offending. Following this framework, efforts to prevent and respond to delinquency involve both the reduction of risk factors and the promotion of protective factors.

a. Individual-Related Factors

A youth's personal characteristics as a result of genetics, personality traits, and early moral development can influence whether he or she will engage in delinquent behavior. Children with cognitive deficiencies, conduct disorders, antisocial personality, mental health disorders, substance abuse issues, or exposure to violence tend to be at greater risk for delinquency. Protective factors that mitigate the effect of individual risk factors include having a positive temperament, possessing problem-solving skills, and being committed to community and school.[22] Efforts to bolster protective factors in this domain center on the development of social and emotional competencies and problem-solving skills.

Studies show that up to 75% of youth within the delinquency system have a diagnosable mental health problem, compared with approximately 20% of the general population of youth.[23] Common among delinquent youth are diagnoses of mood disorders (e.g., depression), disruptive behavior disorders (e.g., conduct disorder), and anxiety disorders such as post-traumatic stress disorder (PTSD). In particular, traumatized youth who experience PTSD are prone to over-interpreting signs of danger and tend to respond impulsively and aggressively. This can increase the risk of engaging in acts that result in an arrest.[24]

A youth's tendency to use alcohol and drugs can also contribute to the risk of delinquency, in part because a good portion of juvenile crime directly involves these substances, and in part because the use of substances increases the potential of engaging in other types of offenses.[25] As juvenile crime has decreased over the past two decades, so has drug use in general. Findings from the Monitoring the Future annual national survey of students in 8th, 10th, and 12th grades reveal that current rates of drug use are far below peak levels of recent years. However, use of marijuana—the most commonly used illicit drug—rose in 2017 for the three grades combined. Alcohol has been and continues to be the most widely used substance among teenagers. Rates of alcohol use have greatly declined since the 1990s, but this long trend appeared to cease as of 2017, with a slight rise in rates of alcohol use during that year.[26]

Youth who struggle with addiction and substance use disorders are at increased risk of delinquency. Rates of substance abuse disorders among juvenile offenders are considerably higher than among youth in the general population—as much as 3 to 5 times higher.[27] Research indicates that more than 60% of justice-involved youth with a mental disorder also suffer from a substance abuse disorder. These youth generally experience poorer outcomes associated with recidivism and general functioning.[28] For youth struggling with substance abuse disorders, treatment services can be effective in both recovery and in reducing recidivism. However, despite the juvenile justice system being the largest publicly-funded source of treatment in the nation, many youth fail to receive treatment while system-involved.

b. Family-Related Factors

The risk of delinquency can be influenced by several factors related to the structure and functioning of the youth's family, including poor parental supervision, child maltreatment, poor family attachment, and parental use of harsh and erratic discipline.[29] In addition, large family size and parental antisocial history are among the strongest predictors of early-onset violent behavior among children.[30] Families can be a tremendous source of protective factors as well. Protective factors related to the family include family cohesion, parental monitoring and supervision, the presence of a good parent-child relationship, consistent discipline, and positive involvement in pro-social family activities.[31]

One key family risk factor is the absence of fathers in the home. Nearly half of all U.S. children will live apart from their father at some point, and this separation has been shown to have negative effects.[32] Youth in single-parent homes, most typically with only a mother present, are at greater risk of engaging in delinquent behavior as compared to teens living with both biological parents. In addition, paternal absence can be the genesis of other risk factors such as poverty, lack of supervision for children, and hostility within the relationship between the present parent and the child.[33] In particular, a parent's absence due to incarceration can increase financial and emotional stressors for a family. More than five million children, typically from low-income families of color, have had a parent absent in their lives due to parental incarceration. Even if parents were not living with their children prior to incarceration, they were likely to be the primary financial support for the child. A recent survey revealed that 65% of families of an incarcerated parent were unable to meet basic needs.[34]

Although parental absence can be a risk factor, parental presence is not necessarily a protective factor. The quality of the relationship is key to its impact. For example, having a father who is present but expresses hostility and harshness is associated with high rates of delinquency and offending behaviors among boys.[35] In fact, a recent study found that having a present father who is hostile and cold can be more damaging than having an absent father. At the same time, studies suggest that a secure attachment to one parent, typically the mother, serves as a strong protective factor that can significantly alter the likelihood of delinquency among youth with a nonresident or hostile father.[36]

Violence within families also contributes to delinquency risk. It is well established that childhood abuse and neglect are related to delinquent and criminal behavior. Research indicates that these adverse experiences increase the risk of

445

arrest as a juvenile by 59% and as an adult by 28%. Studies show that maltreated children begin engaging in crime earlier than other delinquent youth and commit nearly twice as many offenses. Experiences within the child welfare system can exacerbate the risk of delinquency for abused and neglected youth. Children who experience numerous out of home placements while in foster care as well as those placed in congregate care (*i.e.*, group homes) have an increased risk of delinquency.[37]

A child who is simply exposed to violence in the home, where the child herself is not the victim, is also at risk for aggression and conduct problems. Research suggests a relationship between a child's witnessing of parental violence and the development of delinquent behavior. This puts a substantial number of children at risk of delinquency. According to the second National Survey of Children's Exposure to Violence, more than 20% of children had witnessed an assault within their family at some point during their lifetime, and one in six witnessed such violence between parents or between a parent and a potential partner.[38]

c. School-Related Factors

Students with low academic achievement, a negative attitude toward school, and low commitment to school are at higher risk for delinquency.[39] Experiencing academic failure and dropping out of school are factors associated with violent behavior. These effects are often explained through social bond theory, which posits that bonding to social institutions will curb youth tendencies toward delinquent behavior.[40] It follows that stronger attachment to school through positive interactions between students and teachers, as well as participation in school-based activities, work as protective factors to reduce the risk of delinquency. Yet, when children experience low academic achievement, those bonds to school can be challenged, creating a cycle of failure and disengagement, thus increasing the risk of developing delinquent behaviors. Numerous studies conclude that poor academic performance has an impact on prevalence, frequency, and seriousness of delinquency.

Poorly functioning or stressful school environments are also associated with delinquent behavior.[41] In such environments, children observe oversized classes, decaying structures, and teachers struggling with fewer resources, and may conclude that education is not valued. Teachers in such schools report a lack of support in enforcing rules and social norms, resulting in chaotic or even violent environments.[42] Attachment to school is also challenging where students experience violence on campus. In a 2015 national survey, 10% of male students and 5% of female students reported fighting on school property, and overall 5.6% of students reported avoiding going to school due to feeling unsafe at or on their way to school.[43]

School discipline practices can exacerbate delinquency risk, leading to what is characterized as the "school-to-prison pipeline," discussed in chapter 4.

d. Peer-Related Factors

Adolescents are highly susceptible to the influence of their peers. Close relationships with non-delinquent peers can reduce the risk of delinquency and associated risk factors such as substance use. On the other hand, research indicates that having delinquent friends increases the likelihood of delinquency. Antisocial peers have been shown to promote a youth's engagement in more frequent and more serious crime.[44] Delinquent peers can exacerbate other risk factors as well by encouraging school disengagement or drug and alcohol use. This process of influence is referred to as "peer contagion."[45] Research suggests that this effect within the population of incarcerated youth contributes to negative outcomes, hypothesizing that moderately deviant youth will be negatively influenced by the more deviant among the incarcerated population, essentially learning how to be a "better" criminal.[46]

The presence of antisocial peers is a strong predictor of delinquency in a child's life, particularly when youth are lacking an attachment to parents.[47] This can lead to a child's association with a youth gang. Gangs can be attractive because they can fill an emotional need for belonging and meet a youth's social needs such as providing status among peers or access to the opposite sex. A national study of gangs estimated the existence of more than 30,000 gangs, primarily found in large urban areas. Juveniles generally accounted for 35–40% of gang members, with the peak age range for gang membership among juveniles falling between 14 and 15.[48] More recently, the National Crime Victimization Survey identified a decline in the number of students reporting gang activity at their schools. However, within urban areas the presence of gangs remains concerning, with 15% of students reporting gangs at school. Black students are more likely to report the presence of gangs at their schools (17%) compared to white students (7%).[49]

Although the negative influence of peers can contribute to the risk of delinquency, a positive influence can serve as a protective factor. An approach to delinquency prevention known as Positive Youth Development seeks to establish a youth's connections with positive peers and adults.[50]

e. Community-Related Factors

The environment in which children are raised can contribute to his or her risk for delinquency. More than 14 million children are categorized as "poor" and more than 6 million meet the definition of living in "deep poverty."[51] The largest portion of impoverished children are under the age of three. Research has shown that experiencing poverty as a very young child (0–5) can make future delinquency more likely. This may be due in part to the fact that that these young children may have lacked pre-natal and post-natal care that can prevent cognitive difficulties.[52] Persistent poverty has also been shown to increase the risk of delinquency.[53]

Poverty, crime, and instability within neighborhoods are relevant risk factors. It is theorized that where family poverty may create a risk for delinquency, living within an impoverished community can exacerbate the risk. Those residing within disorganized neighborhoods may be less willing to intervene with youth who are acting out, and children in these neighborhoods can find violence normalized.[54] Similar to the impact of witnessing parental violence, research suggests that exposure to violence in communities in which a child lives increases the risk of delinquency.[55] As evidenced by the finding of the third National Survey of Children's Exposure to Violence, almost 60% of all children reported having witnessed a community assault during their lifetime.[56]

Firearms are easy to come by in many communities, thus increasing the risk of serious violence. Youth most likely to perpetrate gun violence are those who have experienced or been exposed to violence themselves.[57] A recent study found that those at risk for future violent behavior were five times more likely to know where to obtain a gun than those not at risk. Adolescents with mental health diagnoses were twice as likely to report easy access to a gun than youth without such a diagnosis. Additional findings reveal that 39% of parents surveyed wrongly believed that their children did not know where their gun was stored and 22% mistakenly believed that their child had never handled their gun.[58]

Importantly, communities can be a source of important protective factors as well, and research suggests that neighborhoods can have a significant effect on deterring delinquent behavior. The presence of supportive and caring adults such as neighbors, coaches, or mentors can have a positive impact on the development of a youth. Providing pro-social activities and meaningful ways for youth to participate in their communities can mitigate many of the risk factors discussed above.

B. THE EVOLUTION OF THE JUVENILE COURT

Nineteenth Century America: The Rise of the Parens Patriae System[1]
by Marvin Ventrell

* * *

Major social change is a theme of the 19th century. Early 19th century America was dominated by the "rural-communitarian-protestant triad."...That triad began to come apart in the 19th century with the industrialization and urbanization of America. Additionally, the industrialized urban areas became populated with European and Asian immigrants. An 1824 report concluded, for example, that there were approximately 9,000 children under age 14 living in poverty in New York State, and that three-fourths of the children receiving public relief were immigrant children....

1. The House of Refuge Movement

In response to the creation of the underclass of urban poor children, the House of Refuge Movement...was launched....The movement began with the Society for Prevention of Pauperism, which believed that poverty was a cause, if not the primary cause, of crime committed by children. The Society issued a report in 1819 raising concern for the number of children confined with adults in Bellevue Prison, and in 1823 the Society issued a now famous statement describing the streets as overrun with pauper children in need of saving. On January 1, 1825, New York City opened the first "House of Refuge."...

The New York House of Refuge was authorized by New York Law...which provided a charter to the Society for the Reformation of Juvenile Delinquents, the successor to the Society for Prevention of Pauperism....The authorizing legislation allowed managers of the Society to take into the house children committed as vagrants or convicted of crimes by authorities. Criminal conviction was not a condition to incarceration in the House of Refuge. Children could even be committed by administrative order or application of their parents. Neither was there any right to indictment or jury trial,... as summary conviction of disorderly persons had previously been upheld in New York in the case *In re Goodhue*....

It is a mistake to assume that the House of Refuge served as a haven for youth otherwise guilty of serious crime. Those youth were still maintained in the adult system. In the first two years of operation of the New York House of Refuge, approximately 90% of the children were housed as a result of vagrancy or minor offenses....And it is unlikely that these children would have been consequented without a House of Refuge as such minor offenses tended to go unpunished by the law....

Neither, however, was the Refuge movement one to protect abused children from their caretaker's authority. There is no evidence that children were placed as a result of caretaker cruelty. To the contrary, severe corporal punishment was clearly part of the House of Refuge system. In fact, conditions in many Houses were quite abusive by modern standards, including solitary confinement and beatings.

* * *

The Refuge movement spread from New York to Boston (1826) to Philadelphia (1828) to New Orleans (1827) to Baltimore (1828) to Cincinnati (1850) to Pittsburgh and St. Louis (1854). By 1860, 16 Houses of Refuge were opened in the United States Legislation authorizing the intervention and placement of delinquent and dependent children similarly spread throughout the jurisdictions....

In addition to Houses of Refuge, Reformatories, which were entirely state-financed, began to emerge toward the middle of the century. John Watkins points out that the reformatory movement was initiated by a number of influential individuals who believed the House of Refuge system had now slowed the rate of delinquency....Reformatories were to be progressive institutions where, through civic and moral training, the youth would be reformed by his/her surrogate parent. In reality, Reformatories tended to be coercive, labor intensive incarceration....

Houses of Refuge dominated the first half, and Reformatories the last half of the century. They were characterized by an ultimate parent philosophy toward the poor, which ties the movement to the poor laws. Another link to the past was the use of apprenticeship in the Refuge movement. As Houses of Refuge became overcrowded, many children were "placed out" by being transported to rural areas of the state or placed on trains headed to the developing west where they were apprenticed to age 21. It was thought, or at least stated, that rural agrarian lifestyle would reform children from the effects of urban poverty....

2. *Ex parte Crouse* and *Parens Patriae*

The House of Refuge movement may not have had significant impact on the ultimate development of the juvenile court if the judicial system had not validated it. In a number of cases during this period, courts affirmed and authorized the practice of intervention into the lives of children through the English doctrine of *parens patriae*, which means ultimate parent or parent of the country. The courts accepted the Reformers' logic that they were entitled to take custody of a child, regardless of the child's status as victim or offender, without due process of law, because of the state's authority and obligation to save children from becoming criminal.

The 1839 Pennsylvania decision of *Ex parte Crouse*...is thought to be the first case upholding the Refuge System. The Child, Mary Ann Crouse, was committed to the Philadelphia House of Refuge by a Justice of the Peace Warrant. The warrant, executed by Mary Ann's mother essentially provided that it would be in Mary Ann's interests to be incarcerated in the House because she was "beyond her parent's control." The reported case is an appeal from a denial of the father's subsequent habeas corpus petition for his daughter's return. The father argued that the law allowing commitment of children without a trial was unconstitutional. The court summarily rejected the father's argument on the basis that the House was not a prison (even though Mary Ann was not free to leave), and the child was there for her own reformation, not punishment (even though Mary Ann was probably treated very harshly, a fact the court did not review). The court essentially accepted the rhetoric of the representatives of the House of Refuge. In doing so, the court acknowledged and sanctioned the state's authority to intervene into the family as ultimate parent via the doctrine of parens patriae. The case and the doctrine become the cornerstones of juvenile proceedings throughout the century and through the pre-Gault years of the juvenile court. The case was generally relied on to support "the right of the state to make coercive predictions about deviant children."...Although the distinction may have been irrelevant at the time, the case involved a dependent, not delinquent child, and in dicta, as Rendleman points out, the court argued that the state has authority to intervene into the parent-child relationship for the good of the child:

> To this end...may not the natural parents, when unequal to the task of education, or unworthy of it, be superseded by the parens patriae, or common guardian of the community?....That parents are ordinarily intrusted with it because it can seldom be put into better hands; but where they are incompetent or corrupt, what is there to prevent the public from withdrawing their faculties, held as they obviously are, at its sufferance? **The right of parental control is a natural, but not unalienable one....**
>
> * * *

The lead of the *Crouse* court was followed in a series of cases involving delinquent and dependent children. In Maryland, *Roth v. House of Refuge*,...in Ohio, *Prescott v. State*,...in New Hampshire, *State ex rel. Cunnigham v. Ray*,...in Wisconsin, *Milwaukee Indus. School v. Supervisors of Milwaukee County*,...and in Illinois, *In re Ferrier* ...courts adopted the *Crouse* policy that the state's *parens patriae* duty and authority permitted seemingly unlimited intervention into family autonomy, including the child's deprivation of liberty.

F. The Juvenile Court: Institutionalizing and Developing the Parens Patriae System

1. Founding and Dependency Philosophy

* * *

The legislation, which led to the creation of a special tribunal which came to be called the juvenile court, was "An Act to Regulate the Treatment and Control of Dependent, Neglected and Delinquent Children."...The Juvenile Court of Cook County, Illinois opened on July 1, 1899. Although it is accurate that the Cook County Court was the first fully formalized tribunal of its kind, Massachusetts in 1874, and New York in 1892 had actually passed laws separating minors' trials from adults. While it is a mistake to assume all subsequent juvenile courts simply copied the Illinois legislation, it did serve as a model, and in less than 20 years, similar legislation had been passed in all but three states....

The Illinois legislation was largely the product of a Progressive Era movement called Child Saving. The Child Savers were individuals who viewed their cause of saving " those less fortunately placed in the social order"...as a matter of morality. The Child Savers were dominated by bourgeois women, although many were considered liberals. The movement, which was supported by the propertied and powerful, "tried to do for the criminal justice system what industrialists and corporate leaders were trying to do for the economy—that is, achieve order, stability, and control, while preserving the existing class system and distribution of wealth."...The Child Savers' rhetoric envisioned a juvenile court which would serve children and society by removing children from the criminal law process and placing them in special programs...The movement in Chicago was supported by the Illinois Conference of Charities, The Chicago Bar Association and the Chicago Women's Club.

The Illinois act provided for jurisdiction in a special court for delinquent and dependent and neglected children. A delinquent child was any child under age 16 who violated a law or ordinance, except capital offenses....

There also appears to be little, if any, support for the proposition that the juvenile court began a system of benevolent caretaking of youth by substituting a kind of therapeutic jurisprudence for harsher and limiting criminal procedure. First, serious older offenders stayed in the adult criminal system. Second, the 19th century case law reveals that juveniles brought to court under delinquency and dependency concepts received no due process. Crouse served to inform us they were entitled to none.

Not to suggest the juvenile court was a step backward. It was progress in the form of codification and institutionalization of the 19th century *parens patriae* system. As an institution, the juvenile court stressed centrality for dependent children. Rather than being subject to random placements without follow up, it was believed that a court could function as a centralized agency responsible for all such children from start to finish. The new court implemented the concept of probation and the founders made minimal progress toward improving placement conditions for children. Dependent children could be placed with an agency or put on probation. To at least some extent, the Child Savers' mission of creating a juvenile "statutory, non-criminal, stigma-neutral, treatment-oriented" system was achieved....

The early years of the court were characterized by continued commingling of dependency and delinquency under the courts' *parens patriae* authority. Minimal numbers of appeals validated that authority. Families remained autonomous.

2. **Gault and the Transformation of Delinquency Out From *Parens Patriae***
The delinquency and dependency components of the juvenile court, historically connected by a "child saving" philosophy, began to separate into distinct functions in the 1960's. Driven by judicial process in delinquency, and social progress in dependency, both components were transformed.

The delinquency component of juvenile court was transformed in the late 1960s by two U.S. Supreme Court cases. In 1966, in *Kent v. United States* the court set the stage for dismantling the *parens patriae* authority of the juvenile delinquency court by holding that the action of transferring a juvenile to criminal court required procedural due process....Then, in 1967, the Court struck down the *parens patriae* authority of the juvenile court in the context of delinquency adjudication in *In re Gault*....

¹ Excerpts from *NACC Children's Law Manual Series – 1999 Edition*, National Association of Counsel for Children (Denver, CO; 1999) at 11-20.

C. JUVENILE JUSTICE CONSTITUTIONAL STANDARDS

1. Due Process Notice: Counsel, Confrontation, Self-Incrimination

In Re Gault
387 U.S. 1 (1966)

MR. JUSTICE FORTAS delivered the opinion of the Court.

...We begin with a statement of the facts.

I

On Monday, June 8, 1964, at about 10 a.m., Gerald Francis Gault and a friend, Ronald Lewis, were taken into custody by the Sheriff of Gila County. Gerald was then still subject to a six months' probation order which had been entered on February 25, 1964, as a result of his having been in the company of another boy who had stolen a wallet from a lady's purse. The police action on June 8 was taken as the result of a verbal complaint by a neighbor of the boys, Mrs. Cook, about a telephone call made to her in which the caller or callers made lewd or indecent remarks. It will suffice for purposes of this opinion to say that the remarks or questions put to her were of the irritatingly offensive, adolescent, sex variety.

At the time Gerald was picked up, his mother and father were both at work. No notice that Gerald was being taken into custody was left at the home. No other steps were taken to advise them that their son had, in effect, been arrested. Gerald was taken to the Children's Detention Home. When his mother arrived home at about 6 o'clock, Gerald was not there. Gerald's older brother was sent to look for him at the trailer home of the Lewis family. He apparently learned then that Gerald was in custody. He so informed his mother. The two of them went to the Detention Home. The deputy probation officer, Flagg, who was also superintendent of the Detention Home, told Mrs. Gault "why Jerry was there" and said that a hearing would be held in Juvenile Court at 3 o'clock the following day, June 9.

Officer Flagg filed a petition with the court on the hearing day, June 9, 1964. It was not served on the Gaults. Indeed, none of them saw this petition until the habeas corpus hearing on August 17, 1964. The petition was entirely formal. It made no reference to any factual basis for the judicial action which it initiated. It recited only that "said minor is under the age of eighteen years, and is in need of the protection of this Honorable Court; [and that] said minor is a delinquent minor." It prayed for a hearing and an order regarding "the care and custody of said minor." Officer Flagg executed a formal affidavit in support of the petition.

On June 9, Gerald, his mother, his older brother, and Probation Officers Flagg and Henderson appeared before the Juvenile Judge in chambers. Gerald's father was not there. He was at work out of the city. Mrs. Cook, the complainant, was not there. No one was sworn at this hearing. No transcript or recording was made. No memorandum or record of the substance of the proceedings was prepared. Our information about the proceedings and the subsequent hearing on June 15, derives entirely from the testimony of the Juvenile Court Judge,[1] Mr. and Mrs. Gault and Officer Flagg at the habeas corpus proceeding conducted two months later. From this, it appears that at the June 9 hearing Gerald was questioned by the judge about the telephone call. There was conflict as to what he said. His mother recalled that Gerald said he only dialed Mrs. Cook's number and handed the telephone to his friend, Ronald. Officer Flagg recalled that Gerald had admitted making the lewd remarks. Judge McGhee testified that Gerald "admitted making one of these [lewd] statements." At the conclusion of the hearing, the judge said he would "think about it." Gerald was taken back to the Detention Home. He was not sent to his own home with his parents. On June 11 or 12, after having been detained since June 8, Gerald was released and driven home.[2] There is no explanation in the record as to why he was kept in the Detention Home or why he was released. At 5 p.m. on the day of Gerald's release, Mrs. Gault received a note signed by Officer Flagg. It was on plain paper, not letterhead. Its entire text was as follows:

"Mrs. Gault:
"Judge McGHEE has set Monday June 15, 1964 at 11:00 A. M. as the date and time for further Hearings on Gerald's delinquency.

"/s/Flagg"

At the appointed time on Monday, June 15, Gerald, his father and mother, Ronald Lewis and his father, and Officers Flagg and Henderson were present before Judge McGhee. Witnesses at the habeas corpus proceeding differed in their recollections of Gerald's testimony at the June 15 hearing. Mr. and Mrs. Gault recalled that Gerald again testified that he had only dialed the number and that the other boy had made the remarks. Officer Flagg agreed that at this hearing Gerald did not admit making the lewd remarks.[3] But Judge McGhee recalled that "there was some admission again of some of the lewd statements. He—he didn't admit any of the more serious lewd statements."[4] Again, the complainant, Mrs. Cook, was not present. Mrs. Gault asked that Mrs. Cook be present "so she could see which boy that done the talking, the dirty talking over the phone." The Juvenile Judge said "she didn't have to be present at that hearing." The judge did not speak to Mrs. Cook or communicate with her at any time. Probation Officer Flagg had talked to her once—over the telephone on June 9.

At this June 15 hearing a "referral report" made by the probation officers was filed with the court, although not disclosed to Gerald or his parents. This listed the charge as "Lewd Phone Calls." At the conclusion of the hearing, the judge committed Gerald as a juvenile delinquent to the State Industrial School "for the period of his minority [that is, until 21], unless sooner discharged by due process of law." An order to that effect was entered. It recites that "after a full hearing and due deliberation the Court finds that said minor is a delinquent child, and that said minor is of the age of 15 years."

No appeal is permitted by Arizona law in juvenile cases. On August 3, 1964, a petition for a writ of habeas corpus was filed with the Supreme Court of Arizona and referred by it to the Superior Court for hearing.

At the habeas corpus hearing on August 17, Judge McGhee was vigorously cross-examined as to the basis for his actions. He testified that he had taken into account the fact that Gerald was on probation. He was asked "under what section of...the code you found the boy delinquent?"

His answer is set forth in the margin.[5] In substance, he concluded that Gerald came within ARS § 8-201-6 (a), which specifies that a "delinquent child" includes one "who has violated a law of the state or an ordinance or regulation of a political subdivision thereof." The law which Gerald was found to have violated is ARS § 13-377. This section of the Arizona Criminal Code provides that a person who "in the presence or hearing of any woman or child...uses vulgar, abusive or obscene language, is guilty of a misdemeanor...." The penalty specified in the Criminal Code, which would apply to an adult, is $5 to $50, or imprisonment for not more than two months. The judge also testified that he acted under ARS § 8-201-6(d) which includes in the definition of a "delinquent child" one who, as the judge phrased it, is "habitually involved in immoral matters."[6]

Asked about the basis for his conclusion that Gerald was "habitually involved in immoral matters," the judge testified, somewhat vaguely, that two years earlier, on July 2, 1962, a "referral" was made concerning Gerald, "where the boy had stolen a baseball glove from another boy and lied to the Police Department about it." The judge said there was "no hearing," and "no accusation" relating to this incident, "because of lack of material foundation." But it seems to have remained in his mind as a relevant factor. The judge also testified that Gerald had admitted making other nuisance phone calls in the past which, as the judge recalled the boy's testimony, were "silly calls, or funny calls, or something like that."

* * *

We do not in this opinion consider the impact of these constitutional provisions upon the totality of the relationship of the juvenile and the state. We do not even consider the entire process relating to juvenile "delinquents." For example, we are not here concerned with the procedures or constitutional rights applicable to the pre-judicial stages of the juvenile process, nor do we direct our attention to the post-adjudicative or dispositional process. See note 48, *infra*. We consider only the problems presented to us by this case. These relate to the proceedings by which a determination is made as to whether a juvenile is a "delinquent" as a result of alleged misconduct on his part, with the consequence that he may be committed to a state institution. As to these proceedings, there appears to be little current dissent from the proposition that the Due Process Clause has a role to play....The problem is to ascertain the precise impact of the due process requirement upon such proceedings.

From the inception of the juvenile court system, wide differences have been tolerated—indeed insisted upon—between the procedural rights accorded to adults and those of juveniles. In practically all jurisdictions, there are rights granted to adults which are withheld from juveniles. In addition to the specific problems involved in the present case, for example, it has been held that the juvenile is not entitled to bail, to indictment by grand jury, to a public trial or to trial by jury. It is frequent practice that rules governing the arrest and interrogation of adults by the police are not observed in the case of juveniles....

* * *

It is claimed that juveniles obtain benefits from the special procedures applicable to them which more than offset the disadvantages of denial of the substance of normal due process. As we shall discuss, the observance of due process standards, intelligently and not ruthlessly administered, will not compel the States to abandon or displace any of the substantive benefits of the juvenile process....But it is important, we think, that the claimed benefits of the juvenile process should be candidly appraised. Neither sentiment nor folklore should cause us to shut our eyes, for example, to such startling findings as that reported in an exceptionally reliable study of repeaters or recidivism conducted by the Stanford Research Institute for the President's Commission on Crime in the District of Columbia. This Commission's Report states:

"In fiscal 1966 approximately 66 percent of the 16- and 17-year-old juveniles referred to the court by the Youth Aid Division had been before the court previously. In 1965, 56 percent of those in the Receiving Home were repeaters. The SRI study revealed that 61 percent of the sample Juvenile Court referrals in 1965 had been previously referred at least once and that 42 percent had been referred at least twice before." *Id.*, at 773.

Certainly, these figures and the high crime rates among juveniles to which we have referred (*supra*, n. 26), could not lead us to conclude that the absence of constitutional protections reduces crime, or that the juvenile system, functioning free of constitutional inhibitions as it has largely done, is effective to reduce crime or rehabilitate offenders. We do not mean by this to denigrate the juvenile court process or to suggest that there are not aspects of the juvenile system relating to offenders which are valuable. But the features of the juvenile system which its proponents have asserted are of unique benefit will not be impaired by constitutional domestication. For example, the commendable principles relating to the processing and treatment of juveniles separately from adults are in no way involved or affected by the procedural issues under discussion.[30] Further, we are told that one of the important benefits of the special juvenile court procedures is that they avoid classifying the juvenile as a "criminal." The juvenile offender is now classed as a "delinquent." There is, of course, no reason why this should not continue. It is disconcerting, however, that this term has come to involve only slightly less stigma than the term "criminal" applied to adults.[31] It is also emphasized that in practically all jurisdictions, statutes provide that an adjudication of the child as a delinquent shall not operate as a civil disability or disqualify him for civil service appointment....There is no reason why the application of due process requirements should interfere with such provisions.

Beyond this, it is frequently said that juveniles are protected by the process from disclosure of their deviational behavior. As the Supreme Court of Arizona phrased it in the present case, the summary procedures of Juvenile Courts are sometimes defended by a statement that it is the law's policy "to hide youthful errors from the full gaze of the public and bury them in the graveyard of the forgotten past." This claim of secrecy, however, is more rhetoric than reality. Disclosure of court records is discretionary with the judge in most jurisdictions. Statutory restrictions almost invariably apply only to the court records, and even as to those the evidence is that many courts routinely furnish information to the FBI and the military, and on request to government agencies and even to private employers....Of more importance are police records. In most States the police keep a complete file of juvenile "police contacts" and have complete discretion as to disclosure of juvenile records. Police departments receive requests for information from the FBI and other law-enforcement agencies, the Armed Forces, and social service agencies, and most of them generally comply....Private employers word their application forms to produce information concerning juvenile arrests and court proceedings, and in some jurisdictions information concerning juvenile police contacts is furnished private employers as well as government agencies....

In any event, there is no reason why, consistently with due process, a State cannot continue, if it deems it appropriate, to provide and to improve provision for the confidentiality of records of police contacts and court action relating to juveniles....

Further, it is urged that the juvenile benefits from informal proceedings in the court. The early conception of the Juvenile Court proceeding was one in which a fatherly judge touched the heart and conscience of the erring youth by talking over his problems, by paternal advice and admonition, and in which, in extreme situations, benevolent and wise institutions of the State provided guidance and help "to save him from a downward career."...Then, as now, goodwill and compassion were admirably prevalent. But recent studies have, with surprising unanimity, entered sharp dissent as to the validity of this gentle conception. They suggest that the appearance as well as the actuality of fairness, impartiality and orderliness—in short, the essentials of due process—may be a more impressive and more therapeutic attitude so far as the juvenile is concerned. For example, in a recent study, the sociologists Wheeler and Cottrell observe that when the procedural laxness of the "parens patriae" attitude is followed by stern disciplining, the contrast may have an adverse effect upon the child, who feels that he has been deceived or enticed....

Ultimately, however, we confront the reality of that portion of the Juvenile Court process with which we deal in this case. A boy is charged with misconduct. The boy is committed to an institution where he may be restrained of liberty for years. It is of no constitutional consequence—and of limited practical meaning—that the institution to which he is committed is called an Industrial School. The fact of the matter is that, however euphemistic the title, a "receiving home" or an "industrial school" for juveniles is an institution of confinement in which the child is incarcerated for a greater or lesser time. His world becomes "a building with whitewashed walls, regimented routine and institutional hours....".…Instead of mother and father and sisters and brothers and friends and classmates, his world is peopled by guards, custodians, state employees, and "delinquents" confined with him for anything from waywardness....to rape and homicide.

In view of this, it would be extraordinary if our Constitution did not require the procedural regularity and the exercise of care implied in the phrase "due process."...

If Gerald had been over 18, he would not have been subject to Juvenile Court proceedings....For the particular offense immediately involved, the maximum punishment would have been a fine of $5 to $50, or imprisonment in jail for not more than two months. Instead, he was committed to custody for a maximum of six years. If he had been over 18 and had committed an offense to which such a sentence might apply, he would have been entitled to substantial rights under the Constitution of the United States as well as under Arizona's laws and constitution. The United States Constitution would guarantee him rights and protections with respect to arrest, search and seizure, and pretrial interrogation. It would assure him of specific notice of the charges and adequate time to decide his course of action and to prepare his defense. He would be entitled to clear advice that he could be represented by counsel, and, at least if a felony were involved, the State would be required to provide counsel if his parents were unable to afford it. If the court acted on the basis of his confession, careful procedures would be required to assure its voluntariness. If the case went to trial, confrontation and opportunity for cross-examination would be guaranteed. So wide a gulf between the State's treatment of the adult and of the child requires a bridge sturdier than mere verbiage, and reasons more persuasive than cliché can provide. As Wheeler and Cottrell have put it, "The rhetoric of the juvenile court movement has developed without any necessarily close correspondence to the realities of court and institutional routines."...

* * *

We now turn to the specific issues which are presented to us in the present case.

III. NOTICE OF CHARGES

* * *

We cannot agree with the court's conclusion that adequate notice was given in this case. Notice, to comply with due process requirements, must be given sufficiently in advance of scheduled court proceedings so that reasonable opportunity to prepare will be afforded, and it must "set forth the alleged misconduct with particularity."...It is obvious, as we have discussed above, that no purpose of shielding the child from the public stigma of knowledge of his having been taken into custody and scheduled for hearing is served by the procedure approved by the court below. The "initial hearing" in the present case was a hearing on the merits. Notice at that time is not timely.... Nor, in the circumstances of this case, can it reasonably be said that the requirement of notice was waived.[54]

IV. RIGHT TO COUNSEL
* * *

We conclude that the Due Process Clause of the Fourteenth Amendment requires that in respect of proceedings to determine delinquency which may result in commitment to an institution in which the juvenile's freedom is curtailed, the child and his parents must be notified of the child's right to be represented by counsel retained by them, or if they are unable to afford counsel, that counsel will be appointed to represent the child.

* * *

V. CONFRONTATION, SELF-INCRIMINATION, CROSS-EXAMINATION
* * *

...Neither Gerald nor his parents were advised that he did not have to testify or make a statement, or that an incriminating statement might result in his commitment as a "delinquent."

* * *

It is...urged, as the Supreme Court of Arizona here asserted, that the juvenile and presumably his parents should not be advised of the juvenile's right to silence because confession is good for the child as the commencement of the assumed therapy of the juvenile court process, and he should be encouraged to assume an attitude of trust and confidence toward the officials of the juvenile process. This proposition has been subjected to widespread challenge on the basis of current reappraisals of the rhetoric and realities of the handling of juvenile offenders.

In fact, evidence is accumulating that confessions by juveniles do not aid in "individualized treatment," as the court below put it, and that compelling the child to answer questions, without warning or advice as to his right to remain silent, does not serve this or any other good purpose. In light of the observations of Wheeler and Cottrell,...and others, it seems probable that where children are induced to confess by "paternal" urgings on the part of officials and the confession is then followed by disciplinary action, the child's reaction is likely to be hostile and adverse—the child may well feel that he has been led or tricked into confession and that despite his confession, he is being punished....

Further, authoritative opinion has cast formidable doubt upon the reliability and trustworthiness of "confessions" by children....

* * *

We conclude that the constitutional privilege against self-incrimination is applicable in the case of juveniles as it is with respect to adults. We appreciate that special problems may arise with respect to waiver of the privilege by or on behalf of children, and that there may well be some differences in technique—but not in principle—depending upon the age of the child and the presence and competence of parents. The participation of counsel will, of course, assist the police, Juvenile Courts and appellate tribunals in administering the privilege. If counsel was not present for some permissible reason when an admission was obtained, the greatest care must be taken to assure that the admission was voluntary, in the sense not only that it was not coerced or suggested, but also that it was not the product of ignorance of rights or of adolescent fantasy, fright or despair....

The " confession" of Gerald Gault was first obtained by Officer Flagg, out of the presence of Gerald's parents, without counsel and without advising him of his right to silence, as far as appears. The judgment of the Juvenile Court was stated by the judge to be based on Gerald's admissions in court. Neither "admission" was reduced to writing, and, to say the least, the process by which the "admissions" were obtained and received must be characterized as lacking the certainty and order which are required of proceedings of such formidable consequences....Apart from the "admissions," there was nothing upon which a judgment or finding might be based. There was no sworn testimony. Mrs. Cook, the complainant, was not present. The Arizona Supreme Court held that "sworn testimony must be required of all witnesses including police officers, probation officers and others who are part of or officially related to the juvenile court structure." We hold that this is not enough. No reason is suggested or appears for a different rule in respect of sworn testimony in juvenile courts than in adult tribunals. Absent a valid confession adequate to support the determination of the Juvenile Court, confrontation and sworn testimony by witnesses available for cross-examination were essential for a finding of "delinquency" and an order committing Gerald to a state institution for a maximum of six years.

* * *

VI. APPELLATE REVIEW AND TRANSCRIPT OF PROCEEDINGS

Appellants urge that the Arizona statute is unconstitutional under the Due Process Clause because, as construed by its Supreme Court, "there is no right of appeal from a juvenile court order...." The court held that there is no right to a transcript because there is no right to appeal and because the proceedings are confidential and any record must be destroyed after a prescribed period of time....Whether a transcript or other recording is made, it held, is a matter for the discretion of the juvenile court.

This Court has not held that a State is required by the Federal Constitution "to provide appellate courts or a right to appellate review at all."...In view of the fact that we must reverse the Supreme Court of Arizona's affirmance of the dismissal of the writ of habeas corpus for other reasons, we need not rule on this question in the present case or upon the failure to provide a transcript or recording of the hearings—or, indeed, the failure of the Juvenile Judge to state the grounds for his conclusion....

For the reasons stated, the judgment of the Supreme Court of Arizona is reversed and the cause remanded for further proceedings not inconsistent with this opinion. It is so ordered.

* * *

[1] Under Arizona law, juvenile hearings are conducted by a judge of the Superior Court, designated by his colleagues on the Superior Court to serve as Juvenile Court Judge....

[2] There is a conflict between the recollection of Mrs. Gault and that of Officer Flagg. Mrs. Gault testified that Gerald was released on Friday, June 12, Officer Flagg that it had been on Thursday, June 11. This was from memory; he had no record, and the note hereafter referred to was undated.

[3] Officer Flagg also testified that Gerald had not, when questioned at the Detention Home, admitted having made any of the lewd statements, but that each boy had sought to put the blame on the other. There was conflicting testimony as to whether Ronald had accused Gerald of making the lewd statements during the June 15 hearing.

[4] Judge McGhee also testified that Gerald had not denied "certain statements" made to him at the hearing by Officer Henderson.

[5] "Q. All right. Now, Judge, would you tell me under what section of the law or tell me under what section of—of the code you found the boy delinquent?

A. Well, there is a—I think it amounts to disturbing the peace. I can't give you the section, but I can tell you the law, that when one person uses lewd language in the presence of another person, that it can amount to—and I consider that when a person makes it over the phone, that it is considered in the presence, I might be wrong, that is one section. The other section upon which I consider the boy delinquent is Section 8-201, Subsection (d), habitually involved in immoral matters."

[6] ARS § 8-201-6, the section of the Arizona Juvenile Code which defines a delinquent child, reads:

"'Delinquent child' includes:

"(a) A child who has violated a law of the state or an ordinance or regulation of a political subdivision thereof

"(b) A child who, by reason of being incorrigible, wayward or habitually disobedient, is uncontrolled by his parent, guardian or custodian.

"(c) A child who is habitually truant from school or home.

"(d) A child who habitually so deports himself as to injure or endanger the morals or health of himself or others."

[30] Here again, however, there is substantial question as to whether fact and pretension, with respect to the separate handling and treatment of children, coincide. See generally *infra*. While we are concerned only with procedure before the juvenile court in this case, it should be noted that to the extent that the special procedures for juveniles are thought to be justified by the special consideration and treatment afforded them, there is reason to doubt that juveniles always receive the benefits of such a quid pro quo. As to the problem and importance of special care at the adjudicatory stage, *cf.* nn. 14 and 26, *supra.* As to treatment, see Nat'l Crime Comm'n Report, pp. 80, 87; D. C. Crime Comm'n Report, pp. 665–676, 686–687 (at p. 687 the Report refers to the District's "bankruptcy of dispositional resources"), 692–695, 700–718 (at p. 701 the Report observes that "The Department of Public Welfare currently lacks even the rudiments of essential diagnostic and clinical services");...The high rate of juvenile recidivism casts some doubt upon the adequacy of treatment afforded juveniles. See D. C. Crime Comm'n Report, p. 773; Nat'l Crime Comm'n Report, pp. 55, 78.

In fact, some courts have recently indicated that appropriate treatment is essential to the validity of juvenile custody, and therefore that a juvenile may challenge the validity of his custody on the ground that he is not in fact receiving any special treatment....

[31] "The word 'delinquent' has today developed such invidious connotations that the terminology is in the process of being altered; the new descriptive phrase is 'persons in need of supervision,' usually shortened to 'pins.'" HARVARD LAW REVIEW Note, p. 799, n. 140. The N. Y. Family Court Act § 712 distinguishes between "delinquents" and "persons in need of supervision."

[54] Mrs. Gault's "knowledge" of the charge against Gerald, and/or the asserted failure to object, does not excuse the lack of adequate notice. Indeed, one of the purposes of notice is to clarify the issues to be considered, and as our discussion of the facts, supra, shows, even the Juvenile Court Judge was uncertain as to the precise issues determined at the two "hearings." Since the Gaults had no counsel and were not told of their right to counsel, we cannot consider their failure to object to the lack of constitutionally adequate

notice as a waiver of their rights. Because of our conclusion that notice given only at the first hearing is inadequate, we need not reach the question whether the Gaults ever received adequately specific notice even at the June 9 hearing, in light of the fact they were never apprised of the charge of being habitually involved in immoral matters.

MR. JUSTICE HARLAN, concurring in part and dissenting in part.

* * *

II

...[O]nly three procedural requirements should, in my opinion, now be deemed required of state juvenile courts by the Due Process Clause of the Fourteenth Amendment: first, timely notice must be provided to parents and children of the nature and terms of any juvenile court proceeding in which a determination affecting their rights or interests may be made; second, unequivocal and timely notice must be given that counsel may appear in any such proceeding in behalf of the child and its parents, and that in cases in which the child may be confined in an institution, counsel may, in circumstances of indigency, be appointed for them; and third, the court must maintain a written record, or its equivalent, adequate to permit effective review on appeal or in collateral proceedings. These requirements would guarantee to juveniles the tools with which their rights could be fully vindicated, and yet permit the States to pursue without unnecessary hindrance the purposes which they believe imperative in this field....

* * *

...The Court has, even under its own premises, asked the wrong questions: the problem here is to determine what forms of procedural protection are necessary to guarantee the fundamental fairness of juvenile proceedings, and not which of the procedures now employed in criminal trials should be transplanted intact to proceedings in these specialized courts.

* * *

MR. JUSTICE STEWART, dissenting.

The Court today uses an obscure Arizona case as a vehicle to impose upon thousands of juvenile courts throughout the Nation restrictions that the Constitution made applicable to adversary criminal trials.[1] I believe the Court's decision is wholly unsound as a matter of constitutional law, and sadly unwise as a matter of judicial policy.

Juvenile proceedings are not criminal trials. They are not civil trials. They are simply not adversary proceedings. Whether treating with a delinquent child, a neglected child, a defective child, or a dependent child, a juvenile proceeding's whole purpose and mission is the very opposite of the mission and purpose of a prosecution in a criminal court. The object of the one is correction of a condition. The object of the other is conviction and punishment for a criminal act.

In the last 70 years many dedicated men and women have devoted their professional lives to the enlightened task of bringing us out of the dark world of Charles Dickens in meeting our responsibilities to the child in our society. The result has been the creation in this century of a system of juvenile and family courts in each of the 50 States. There can be no denying that in many areas the performance of these agencies has fallen disappointingly short of the hopes and dreams of the courageous pioneers who first conceived them....

I possess neither the specialized experience nor the expert knowledge to predict with any certainty where may lie the brightest hope for progress in dealing with the serious problems of juvenile delinquency. But I am certain that the answer does not lie in the Court's opinion in this case, which serves to convert a juvenile proceeding into a criminal prosecution.

The inflexible restrictions that the Constitution so wisely made applicable to adversary criminal trials have no inevitable place in the proceedings of those public social agencies known as juvenile or family courts. And to impose the Court's long catalog of requirements upon juvenile proceedings in every area of the country is to invite a long step backwards into the nineteenth century. In that era there were no juvenile proceedings, and a child was tried in a conventional criminal court with all the

trappings of a conventional criminal trial. So it was that a 12-year-old boy named James Guild was tried in New Jersey for killing Catharine Beakes. A jury found him guilty of murder, and he was sentenced to death by hanging. The sentence was executed. It was all very constitutional.[2]

A State in all its dealings must, of course, accord every person due process of law. And due process may require that some of the same restrictions which the Constitution has placed upon criminal trials must be imposed upon juvenile proceedings. For example, I suppose that all would agree that a brutally coerced confession could not constitutionally be considered in a juvenile court hearing. But it surely does not follow that the testimonial privilege against self-incrimination is applicable in all juvenile proceedings.[3] Similarly, due process clearly requires timely notice of the purpose and scope of any proceedings affecting the relationship of parent and child....But it certainly does not follow that notice of a juvenile hearing must be framed with all the technical niceties of a criminal indictment...

In any event, there is no reason to deal with issues such as these in the present case. The Supreme Court of Arizona found that the parents of Gerald Gault "knew of their right to counsel, to subpoena and cross examine witnesses, of the right to confront the witnesses against Gerald and the possible consequences of a finding of delinquency."…. It further found that "Mrs. Gault knew the exact nature of the charge against Gerald from the day he was taken to the detention home."...And, as Mr. Justice White correctly points out,...no issue of compulsory self-incrimination is presented by this case.

I would dismiss the appeal.

[1] I find it strange that a Court so intent upon fastening an absolute right to counsel upon nonadversary juvenile proceedings has not been willing even to consider whether the Constitution requires a lawyer's help in a criminal prosecution upon a misdemeanor charge....

[2] *State v. Guild*, 5 Halst. 163, 18 Am. Dec. 404 (N. J. Sup. Ct.).

"Thus, also, in very modern times, a boy of ten years old was convicted on his own confession of murdering his bed-fellow, there appearing in his whole behavior plain tokens of a mischievous discretion; and as the sparing this boy merely on account of his tender years might be of dangerous consequence to the public, by propagating a notion that children might commit such atrocious crimes with impunity, it was unanimously agreed by all the judges that he was a proper subject of capital punishment."...

[3] Until June 13, 1966, it was clear that the Fourteenth Amendment's ban upon the use of a coerced confession is constitutionally quite a different thing from the Fifth Amendment's testimonial privilege against self-incrimination. See, for example, the Court's unanimous opinion in *Brown v. Mississippi*, 297 U.S. 278, at 285–286, written by Chief Justice Hughes and joined by such distinguished members of this Court as Mr. Justice Brandeis, Mr. Justice Stone, and Mr. Justice Cardozo. See also *Tehan v. Shott*, 382 U.S. 406, decided January 19, 1966, where the Court emphasized the "contrast" between "the wrongful use of a coerced confession" and "the Fifth Amendment's privilege against self-incrimination." 382 U.S., at 416. The complete confusion of these separate constitutional doctrines in Part V of the Court's opinion today stems, no doubt, from *Miranda v. Arizona*, 384 U.S. 436, a decision which I continue to believe was constitutionally erroneous.

Questions for Discussion

1. Is the ideal juvenile justice system a mimic of the adult system? Does the adult model provide ideal parens patriae proceedings? Does it encourage a child to tell the truth? To apologize? To try to make it right? Does it introduce, as its critics contend, an element of gamesmanship with the goal of "getting off?"

2. Did the adoption of a more formal adversarial process in *Gault* soften the distinction between children and adults, setting the stage for the more punitive approach of the 1990s and the "tough on crime" policies embraced by politicians and the public that brought more juveniles into the adult court?

3. Is it possible to ascertain the truth without the adversary system, the right not to testify, appointed adversary counsel, *et al.*? Would a continental European "tribune" model be superior, where an independent investigation is conducted by the court? Is that closer to what a parent would do? If a state were to implement such a system, would it be constitutional under *Gault*? What is the majority's

answer to the concern of the dissents about the "lock-in" nature of the majority's constitutionally-based specifics?

4. On the other hand, how many states had implemented a system at least equivalent to *Gault's* safeguards for accuracy and fairness (by any means, adversary adult system or otherwise)? Was the penalty in *Gault* more or less severe than that for the same offense committed by an adult? Was the proceeding as likely to yield an accurate or consistent result as typical adult proceedings?

5. The dissents in *Gault* imply that the due process requirements it imposes may fall into two categories: those which enhance accuracy in determining guilt (notice, neutral investigation or adjudicator, right to present evidence), and those which are tied to an adversary *modus operandi* or promote ancillary social goals (right not to testify or the exclusionary rule discussed below). Is it possible to require a due process floor to assure accuracy and consistency without interposing the requirements for the latter ancillary goals?

6. The 5th Amendment guarantee against self-incrimination is intended to prevent involuntary and unreliable confessions. If a juvenile court proceeding is civil in nature, should the same right to remain silent without prejudice prevail? Would a parent advise his or her child suspected of wrongdoing that no explanation is necessary because of "a right to remain silent"? Does the right to remain silent frustrate the ability of the juvenile court to ascertain the risks and needs of a youth that can best inform a plan for effective rehabilitation?

7. Would denial of 5th Amendment right of refusal to testify be appropriate if the juvenile court decided as a threshold matter that confinement was not a remedy being considered? In such a setting, would a request to the child to explain himself or herself be permitted, with an inference of guilt allowed if the child refuses to talk?

8. How widely should *Gault* apply? To status offense proceedings (truancy, curfew, runaways)? To civil commitment cases? To school expulsion cases?

9. Despite the ruling in *Gault*, studies have shown that many juveniles proceed through juvenile court without legal representation. Why might this occur?

10. Should adult rules not covered by *Gault* also apply to make trials public, allow juries, or exclude evidence taken in violation of the 4th Amendment? (See cases and discussion below.)

2. Unreasonable Searches and the Exclusionary Rule

New Jersey v. T.L.O.

469 U.S. 325 (1985)

JUSTICE WHITE delivered the opinion of the Court.

We granted certiorari in this case to examine the appropriateness of the exclusionary rule as a remedy for searches carried out in violation of the Fourth Amendment by public school authorities. Our consideration of the proper application of the Fourth Amendment to the public schools, however, has led us to conclude that the search that gave rise to the case now before us did not violate the Fourth Amendment. Accordingly, we here address only the question of the proper standard for assessing the legality of searches conducted by public school officials and the application of that standard to the facts of this case.

I

On March 7, 1980, a teacher at Piscataway High School in Middlesex County, N.J., discovered two girls smoking in a lavatory. One of the two girls was the respondent T.L.O., who at that time was a 14-year-old high school freshman. Because smoking in the lavatory was a violation of a school rule, the teacher took the two girls to the Principal's office, where they met with Assistant Vice Principal Theodore Choplick. In response to questioning by Mr. Choplick, T.L.O.'s companion admitted that she had violated the rule. T.L.O., however, denied that she had been smoking in the lavatory and claimed that she did not smoke at all.

Mr. Choplick asked T.L.O. to come into his private office and demanded to see her purse. Opening the purse, he found a pack of cigarettes, which he removed from the purse and held before T.L.O. as he accused her of having lied to him. As he reached into the purse for the cigarettes, Mr. Choplick also noticed a package of cigarette rolling papers. In his experience, possession of rolling papers by high school students was closely associated with the use of marihuana. Suspecting that a closer examination of the purse might yield further evidence of drug use, Mr. Choplick proceeded to search the purse thoroughly. The search revealed a small amount of marihuana, a pipe, a number of empty plastic bags, a substantial quantity of money in one-dollar bills, an index card that appeared to be a list of students who owed T.L.O. money, and two letters that implicated T.L.O. in marihuana dealing.

Mr. Choplick notified T.L.O.'s mother and the police, and turned the evidence of drug dealing over to the police. At the request of the police, T.L.O.'s mother took her daughter to police headquarters, where T.L.O. confessed that she had been selling marihuana at the high school. On the basis of the confession and the evidence seized by Mr. Choplick, the State brought delinquency charges against T.L.O. in the Juvenile and Domestic Relations Court of Middlesex County.[1]..

* * *

Although we originally granted certiorari to decide the issue of the appropriate remedy in juvenile court proceedings for unlawful school searches, our doubts regarding the wisdom of deciding that question in isolation from the broader question of what limits, if any, the Fourth Amendment places on the activities of school authorities prompted us to order reargument on that question.[2] Having heard argument on the legality of the search of T.L.O.'s purse, we are satisfied that the search did not violate the Fourth Amendment.[3]

II

In determining whether the search at issue in this case violated the Fourth Amendment, we are faced initially with the question whether that Amendment's prohibition on unreasonable searches and seizures applies to searches conducted by public school officials. We hold that it does.

* * *

III

To hold that the Fourth Amendment applies to searches conducted by school authorities is only to begin the inquiry into the standards governing such searches. Although the underlying command of the Fourth Amendment is always that searches and seizures be reasonable, what is reasonable depends on the context within which a

search takes place. The determination of the standard of reasonableness governing any specific class of searches requires "balancing the need to search against the invasion which the search entails." *Camara v. Municipal Court supra*, 387 U.S., at 536-537. On one side of the balance are arrayed the individual's legitimate expectations of privacy and personal security; on the other, the government's need for effective methods to deal with breaches of public order.

* * *

Although this Court may take notice of the difficulty of maintaining discipline in the public schools today, the situation is not so dire that students in the schools may claim no legitimate expectations of privacy. We have recently recognized that the need to maintain order in a prison is such that prisoners retain no legitimate expectations of privacy in their cells, but it goes almost without saying that "[t]he prisoner and the schoolchild stand in wholly different circumstances, separated by the harsh facts of criminal conviction and incarceration." *Ingraham v. Wright, supra*, at 669. We are not yet ready to hold that the schools and the prisons need be equated for purposes of the Fourth Amendment.

Nor does the State's suggestion that children have no legitimate need to bring personal property into the schools seem well anchored in reality. Students at a minimum must bring to school not only the supplies needed for their studies, but also keys, money, and the necessaries of personal hygiene and grooming. In addition, students may carry on their persons or in purses or wallets such nondisruptive yet highly personal items as photographs, letters, and diaries. Finally, students may have perfectly legitimate reasons to carry with them articles of property needed in connection with extracurricular or recreational activities. In short, schoolchildren may find it necessary to carry with them a variety of legitimate, noncontraband items, and there is no reason to conclude that they have necessarily waived all rights to privacy in such items merely by bringing them onto school grounds.

Against the child's interest in privacy must be set the substantial interest of teachers and administrators in maintaining discipline in the classroom and on school grounds. Maintaining order in the classroom has never been easy, but in recent years, school disorder has often taken particularly ugly forms: drug use and violent crime in the schools have become major social problems....Even in schools that have been spared the most severe disciplinary problems, the preservation of order and a proper educational environment requires close supervision of schoolchildren, as well as the enforcement of rules against conduct that would be perfectly permissible if undertaken by an adult. "Events calling for discipline are frequent occurrences and sometimes require immediate, effective action."...Accordingly, we have recognized that maintaining security and order in the schools requires a certain degree of flexibility in school disciplinary procedures, and we have respected the value of preserving the informality of the student-teacher relationship....

How, then, should we strike the balance between the schoolchild's legitimate expectations of privacy and the school's equally legitimate need to maintain an environment in which learning can take place? It is evident that the school setting requires some easing of the restrictions to which searches by public authorities are ordinarily subject. The warrant requirement, in particular, is unsuited to the school environment: requiring a teacher to obtain a warrant before searching a child suspected of an infraction of school rules (or of the criminal law) would unduly interfere with the maintenance of the swift and informal disciplinary procedures needed in the schools. Just as we have in other cases dispensed with the warrant requirement when "the burden of obtaining a warrant is likely to frustrate the governmental purpose behind the search," *Camara v. Municipal Court*, 387 U.S., at 532-533, we hold today that school officials need not obtain a warrant before searching a student who is under their authority.

The school setting also requires some modification of the level of suspicion of illicit activity needed to justify a search. Ordinarily, a search—even one that may permissibly be carried out without a warrant—must be based upon "probable cause" to believe that a violation of the law has occurred....However, "probable cause" is not an irreducible requirement of a valid search. The fundamental command of the Fourth Amendment is that searches and seizures be reasonable, and although "both the concept of probable cause and the requirement of a warrant bear on the reasonableness of a search,... in certain limited circumstances neither is required."....Thus, we have in a number of cases recognized the legality of searches and seizures based on suspicions that, although "reasonable," do not rise to the level of probable cause....Where a careful balancing of governmental and private interests suggests that the public interest is best served by a Fourth Amendment standard of reasonableness that stops short of probable cause, we have not hesitated to adopt such a standard.

We join the majority of courts that have examined this issue in concluding that the accommodation of the privacy interests of schoolchildren with the substantial need of teachers and administrators for freedom to maintain order in the schools does not require strict adherence to the requirement that searches be based on probable cause to believe that the subject of the search has violated or is violating the law. Rather, the legality of a search of a student should depend simply on the reasonableness, under all the circumstances, of the search. Determining the reasonableness of any search involves a twofold inquiry: first, one must consider "whether the...action was justified at its inception,".... second, one must determine whether the search as actually conducted "was reasonably related in scope to the circumstances which justified the interference in the first place,"...Under ordinary circumstances, a search of a student by a teacher or other school official[7] will be "justified at its inception" when there are reasonable grounds for suspecting that the search will turn up evidence that the student has violated or is violating either the law or the rules of the school.[8] Such a search will be permissible in its scope when the measures adopted are reasonably related to the objectives of the search and not excessively intrusive in light of the age and sex of the student and the nature of the infraction...

This standard will, we trust, neither unduly burden the efforts of school authorities to maintain order in their schools nor authorize unrestrained intrusions upon the privacy of schoolchildren. By focusing attention on the question of reasonableness, the standard will spare teachers and school administrators the necessity of schooling themselves in the niceties of probable cause and permit them to regulate their conduct according to the dictates of reason and common sense. At the same time, the reasonableness standard should ensure that the interests of students will be invaded no more than is necessary to achieve the legitimate end of preserving order in the schools.

* * *

...[I]f Mr. Choplick in fact had a reasonable suspicion that T.L.O. had cigarettes in her purse, the search was justified despite the fact that the cigarettes, if found, would constitute "mere evidence" of a violation....

* * *

Our conclusion that Mr. Choplick's decision to open T.L.O.'s purse was reasonable brings us to the question of the further search for marihuana once the pack of cigarettes was located. The suspicion upon which the search for marihuana was founded was provided when Mr. Choplick observed a package of rolling papers in the purse as he removed the pack of cigarettes. Although T.L.O. does not dispute the reasonableness of Mr. Choplick's belief that the rolling papers indicated the presence of marihuana, she does contend that the scope of the search Mr. Choplick conducted exceeded permissible bounds when he seized and read certain letters that implicated T.L.O. in drug dealing. This argument, too, is unpersuasive. The discovery of the rolling papers concededly gave rise to a reasonable suspicion that T.L.O. was carrying marihuana as well as cigarettes in her purse. This suspicion justified further exploration of T.L.O.'s purse,...

Because the search resulting in the discovery of the evidence of marihuana dealing by T.L.O. was reasonable, the New Jersey Supreme Court's decision to exclude that evidence from T.L.O.'s juvenile delinquency proceedings on Fourth Amendment grounds was erroneous. Accordingly, the judgment of the Supreme Court of New Jersey is

Reversed.

* * *

[1] T.L.O. also received a 3-day suspension from school for smoking cigarettes in a nonsmoking area and a 7-day suspension for possession of marihuana. On T.L.O.'s motion, the Superior Court of New Jersey, Chancery Division, set aside the 7-day suspension on the ground that it was based on evidence seized in violation of the Fourth Amendment. *(T.L.O.) v. Piscataway Bd. of Ed.,* No. C.2865-79 (Super.Ct.N.J., Ch.Div., Mar. 31, 1980). The Board of Education apparently did not appeal the decision of the Chancery Division.

[2] State and federal courts considering these questions have struggled to accommodate the interests protected by the Fourth Amendment and the interest of the States in providing a safe environment conducive to education in the public schools. Some courts have resolved the tension between these interests by giving full force to one or the other side of the balance. Thus, in a number of cases courts have held that school officials conducting in-school searches of students are private parties acting in loco parentis and are therefore not subject to the constraints of the Fourth Amendment....At least one court has held, on the other hand, that the Fourth Amendment applies in full to in-school searches by school officials and that a search conducted without probable cause is unreasonable...; others have held or suggested that the probable-cause standard is applicable at least where the police are involved in a search...or where the search is highly intrusive....

The majority of courts that have addressed the issue of the Fourth Amendment in the schools have, like the Supreme Court of New Jersey in this case, reached a middle position: the Fourth Amendment applies to searches conducted by school authorities, but the special needs of the school environment require assessment of the legality of such searches against a standard less exacting than that of probable cause. These courts have, by and large, upheld warrantless searches by school authorities provided that they are supported by a reasonable suspicion that the search will uncover evidence of an infraction of school disciplinary rules or a violation of the law...

Although few have considered the matter, courts have also split over whether the exclusionary rule is an appropriate remedy for Fourth Amendment violations committed by school authorities....

[3] In holding that the search of T.L.O.'s purse did not violate the Fourth Amendment, we do not implicitly determine that the exclusionary rule applies to the fruits of unlawful searches conducted by school authorities. The question whether evidence should be excluded from a criminal proceeding involves two discrete inquiries: whether the evidence was seized in violation of the Fourth Amendment, and whether the exclusionary rule is the appropriate remedy for the violation. Neither question is logically antecedent to the other, for a negative answer to either question is sufficient to dispose of the case. Thus, our determination that the search at issue in this case did not violate the Fourth Amendment implies no particular resolution of the question of the applicability of the exclusionary rule.

[7] We here consider only searches carried out by school authorities acting alone and on their own authority. This case does not present the question of the appropriate standard for assessing the legality of searches conducted by school officials in conjunction with or at the behest of law enforcement agencies, and we express no opinion on that question. Cf. *Picha v. Wielgos,* 410 F.Supp. 1214, 1219-1221 (ND Ill.1976) (holding probable-cause standard applicable to searches involving the police).

[8] We do not decide whether individualized suspicion is an essential element of the reasonableness standard we adopt for searches by school authorities. In other contexts, however, we have held that although "some quantum of individualized suspicion is usually a prerequisite to a constitutional search or seizure[,]... the Fourth Amendment imposes no irreducible requirement of such suspicion."

JUSTICE BRENNAN with whom **JUSTICE MARSHALL** joins, concurring in part and dissenting in part.

* * *

...Today's decision sanctions school officials to conduct full-scale searches on a "reasonableness" standard whose only definite content is that it is not the same test as the "probable cause" standard found in the text of the Fourth Amendment. In adopting this unclear, unprecedented, and unnecessary departure from generally applicable Fourth Amendment standards, the Court carves out a broad exception to standards that this Court has developed over years of considering Fourth Amendment problems. Its decision is supported neither by precedent nor even by a fair application of the "balancing test" it proclaims in this very opinion.

I

* * *

...Such an exception, however, is not to be justified, as the Court apparently holds, by assessing net social value through application of an unguided "balancing test" in which "the individual's legitimate expectations of privacy and personal security" are weighed against "the government's need for effective methods to deal with breaches of public order."... The Warrant Clause is something more than an exhortation to this Court to maximize social welfare as we see fit. It requires that the authorities must obtain a warrant before conducting a full-scale search. The undifferentiated governmental interest in law enforcement is insufficient to justify an exception to the warrant requirement. Rather, some *special* governmental interest beyond the need merely to apprehend lawbreakers is necessary to justify a categorical exception to the warrant requirement. For the most part, special governmental needs sufficient to override the warrant requirement flow from "exigency"—that is, from the press of time that makes obtaining a warrant either impossible or hopelessly infeasible.... Only after finding an extraordinary governmental interest of this kind do we—or ought we— engage in a balancing test to determine if a warrant should nonetheless be required.[2]

* * *

In this case, such extraordinary governmental interests do exist and are sufficient to justify an exception to the warrant requirement. Students are necessarily confined for most of the schoolday in close proximity to each other and to the school staff. I agree with the Court that we can take judicial notice of the serious problems of drugs and violence that plague our schools....

B

I emphatically disagree with the Court's decision to cast aside the constitutional probable-cause standard when assessing the constitutional validity of a schoolhouse search. The Court's decision jettisons the probable- cause standard— the only standard that finds support in the text of the Fourth Amendment—on the basis of its Rohrschach-like "balancing test.".....

* * *

As compared with the relative ease with which teachers can apply the probable-cause standard, the amorphous "reasonableness under all the circumstances" standard freshly coined by the Court today will likely spawn increased litigation and greater uncertainty among teachers and administrators....

* * *

II

Applying the constitutional probable-cause standard to the facts of this case, I would find that Mr. Choplick's search violated T.L.O.'s Fourth Amendment rights. After escorting T.L.O. into his private office, Mr. Choplick demanded to see her purse. He then opened the purse to find evidence of whether she had been smoking in the bathroom. When he opened the purse, he discovered the pack of cigarettes. At this point, his search for evidence of the smoking violation was complete.

* * *

[2] Administrative search cases involving inspection schemes have recognized that "if inspection is to be effective and serve as a credible deterrent, unannounced, even frequent, inspections are essential. In this context, the prerequisite of a warrant could easily frustrate inspection ...."....

Questions for Discussion

1. The Court upholds juvenile school searches on "reasonable suspicion," allowing substantial state intrusion more easily than with the probable cause to arrest or exigent circumstance tests applicable to adults. Did the principal have probable cause under an adult standard given the teacher's credible report and the materials viewed in plain sight?

2. If normal course adult standards applied, would the principal be required to cease his search after an initial look fails to find cigarettes? If he saw cigarette papers and cash in plain sight during his initial search of the purse, could he use this discovery as a basis to search further and read the money-owed list?

3. The Court has already created numerous exigent circumstances justifying searches without warrants and not incident to a probable cause arrest, including: border searches, stop and frisk, murder scene, hot pursuit, traffic stops, regulatory searches, *et al.* Is there a difference in the relaxed "student search" standard here approved?

4. The Court contends that students in a school do not have as much of a "reasonable expectation of privacy" as do other citizens. To what extent is such a student expectation a reflection of the degree of intrusion traditionally exercised by school officials? Is there a self-fulfilling feature to this rationale (pattern and practice of intrusion removes an expectation of privacy which then makes the intrusion reasonable)?

5. Is there an alternative to creating broad exigent circumstance categories? What if the court were to balance four factors: (1) justification for intrusion, (2) degree of intrusion, (3) quantum of probable cause to search, and (4) opportunity for a warrant? Should a search to find a possible explosive or firearm in the school meet the same probable cause standards as one investigating a hall pass excuse? Does the majority decision allow such a balancing? Why not use such a balancing formula in lieu of the specific search and seizure doctrines created for more than twenty different types of exigent circumstances applicable to adult searches?

Note on *Vernonia School District 47J v. Acton*

Following *T.L.O.*, the Supreme Court decided *Vernonia School District 47J v. Acton*, 515 U.S. 646 (1995). The school district governing Vernonia High School in Oregon was concerned about increasing drug use on and about possible involvement of athletes as "leaders of the drug culture." A football and a wrestling coach believed that drug use was impeding the performance of some of their athletes. The District attempted drug education without improvement and turned to mandatory drug testing for all students seeking to participate in all interscholastic athletics at the start of a respective season, with 10% of participants then randomly selected for further testing each week thereafter. The policy was not framed as a law enforcement effort but to "prevent student athletes from using drugs, to protect their health and safety, and to provide drug users with assistance programs." Students were compelled to urinate under inspection (or within hearing) of an adult monitor of the same gender. A positive result (verified by a second test) would result in a choice of either a six-week assistance program with weekly testing, or suspension from the team. A further offense would lead to permanent suspension.

Justice Scalia, writing for a 6–3 majority, upheld the reasonableness of the search, citing the following three factors: decreased expectation of privacy, the relative unobtrusiveness of the search, and the severity of the need met by the search. The Court noted that it was not endorsing broadscale drug testing, distinguishing the school setting, where the institution acts as the "guardian and tutor of children entrusted to its care." The opinion noted that the searches are confined to optional athletics and the maximum sanction is a bar to participation. It also cited a district meeting with parents approving of the search, and the lack of substantial parental objection aside from the petitioner.

The dissent of Justice O'Connor, joined by Justices Stevens and Souter, argued that the search is prompted by no individualized probable cause or even suspicion, noting that "mass, suspicionless searches, however evenhanded, are generally unreasonable" in the criminal context, and that such searches have been permitted outside such a context only where they are not personally intrusive (such as searches of a closely regulated business), or arose out of unique contexts (such as a prison, which the dissent states is the apparent parallel). Justice O'Connor noted that the basis for generalized suspicion in the case arose from several specific students who were acting "in ways that plainly gave rise to reasonable suspicion...." Hence, the constitutional course of action would be to test those persons, not all students in a broad class without any factual basis.

Board of Education of Independent School District No. 92
of Pottawatomie County v. Earls
536 U.S. 822 (2002)

JUSTICE THOMAS delivered the opinion of the Court

The Student Activities Drug Testing Policy implemented by the Board of Education of Independent School District No. 92 of Pottawatomie County (School District) requires all students who participate in competitive extracurricular activities to submit to drug testing. Because this Policy reasonably serves the School District's important interest in detecting and preventing drug use among its students, we hold that it is constitutional.

* * *

The city of Tecumseh, Oklahoma, is a rural community located approximately 40 miles southeast of Oklahoma City. The School District administers all Tecumseh public schools. In the fall of 1998, the School District adopted the Student Activities Drug Testing Policy (Policy), which requires all middle and high school students to consent to drug testing in order to participate in any extracurricular activity. In practice, the Policy has been applied only to competitive extracurricular activities sanctioned by the Oklahoma Secondary Schools Activities Association, such as the Academic Team, Future Farmers of America, Future Homemakers of America, band, choir, pom pon, cheerleading, and athletics. Under the Policy, students are required to take a drug test before participating in an extracurricular activity, must submit to random drug testing while participating in that activity, and must agree to be tested at any time upon reasonable suspicion. The urinalysis tests are designed to detect only the use of illegal drugs, including amphetamines, marijuana, cocaine, opiates, and barbituates, not medical conditions or the presence of authorized prescription medications.

At the time of their suit, both respondents attended Tecumseh High School. Respondent Lindsay Earls was a member of the show choir, the marching band, the Academic Team, and the National Honor Society. Respondent Daniel James sought to participate in the Academic Team....Together with their parents, Earls and James brought a 42 U.S.C. § 1983 action against the School District, challenging the Policy both on its face and as applied to their participation in extracurricular activities....They alleged that the Policy violates the Fourth Amendment as incorporated by the Fourteenth Amendment and requested injunctive and declarative relief. They also argued that the School District failed to identify a special need for testing students who participate in extracurricular activities, and that the "Drug Testing Policy neither addresses a proven problem nor promises to bring any benefit to students or the school."

* * *

In the criminal context, reasonableness usually requires a showing of probable cause....The probable-cause standard, however, "is peculiarly related to criminal investigations" and may be unsuited to determining the reasonableness of administrative searches where the "Government seeks to *prevent* the development of hazardous conditions."...The Court has also held that a warrant and finding of probable cause are unnecessary in the public school context because such requirements "'would unduly interfere with the maintenance of the swift and informal disciplinary procedures [that are] needed.'"...

Given that the School District's Policy is not in any way related to the conduct of criminal investigations,...respondents do not contend that the School District requires probable cause before testing students for drug use. Respondents instead argue that drug testing must be based at least on some level of individualized suspicion. It is true that we generally determine the reasonableness of a search by balancing the nature of the intrusion on the individual's privacy against the promotion of legitimate governmental interests....But we have long held that "the Fourth Amendment imposes no irreducible requirement of [individualized] suspicion."...[I]n the context of safety and administrative regulations, a search unsupported by probable cause may be reasonable "when 'special needs, beyond the normal need for law enforcement, make the warrant and probable-cause requirement impracticable.'"...

Significantly, this Court has previously held that "special needs" inhere in the public school context....While schoolchildren do not shed their constitutional rights when they enter the schoolhouse,..."Fourth Amendment rights...are different in public schools than elsewhere; the 'reasonableness' inquiry cannot disregard the schools' custodial and tutelary responsibility for children."...In particular, a finding of individualized suspicion may not be necessary when a school conducts drug testing.

In *Vernonia*, this Court held that the suspicionless drug testing of athletes was constitutional. The Court, however, did not simply authorize all school drug testing, but rather conducted a fact-specific balancing of the intrusion on the children's Fourth Amendment rights against the promotion of legitimate governmental interests. Applying the principles of *Vernonia* to the somewhat different facts of this case, we conclude that Tecumseh's Policy is also constitutional.

* * *

We first consider the nature of the privacy interest allegedly compromised by the drug testing....A student's privacy interest is limited in a public school environment where the State is responsible for maintaining discipline, health, and safety. Schoolchildren are routinely required to submit to physical examinations and vaccinations against disease....Securing order in the school environment sometimes requires that students be subjected to greater controls than those appropriate for adults....

* * *

Respondents argue that because children participating in nonathletic extracurricular activities are not subject to regular physicals and communal undress, they have a stronger expectation of privacy than the athletes tested in *Vernonia*.... This distinction, however, was not essential to our decision in *Vernonia*, which depended primarily upon the school's custodial responsibility and authority....

In any event, students who participate in competitive extracurricular activities voluntarily subject themselves to many of the same intrusions on their privacy as do athletes....Some of these clubs and activities require occasional off-campus travel and communal undress. All of them have their own rules and requirements for participating students that do not apply to the student body as a whole....For example, each of the competitive extracurricular activities governed by the Policy must abide by the rules of the Oklahoma Secondary Schools Activities Association, and a faculty sponsor monitors the students for compliance with the various rules dictated by the clubs and activities.... This regulation of extracurricular activities further diminishes the expectation of privacy among schoolchildren...."Somewhat like adults who choose to participate in a closely regulated industry, students who voluntarily participate in school athletics have reason to expect intrusions upon normal rights and privileges, including privacy."...We therefore conclude that the students affected by this Policy have a limited expectation of privacy.

Next, we consider the character of the intrusion imposed by the Policy....Urination is "an excretory function traditionally shielded by great privacy."...But the "degree of intrusion" on one's privacy caused by collecting a urine sample "depends upon the manner in which production of the urine sample is monitored."...

Under the Policy, a faculty monitor waits outside the closed restroom stall for the student to produce a sample and must "listen for the normal sounds of urination in order to guard against tampered specimens and to insure an accurate chain of custody."... The monitor then pours the sample into two bottles that are sealed and placed into

a mailing pouch along with a consent form signed by the student. This procedure is virtually identical to that reviewed in *Vernonia*, except that it additionally protects privacy by allowing male students to produce their samples behind a closed stall. Given that we considered the method of collection in *Vernonia* a "negligible" intrusion,...the method here is even less problematic.

* * *

In addition, the Policy clearly requires that the test results be kept in confidential files separate from a student's other educational records and released to school personnel only on a "need to know" basis. Moreover, the test results are not turned over to any law enforcement authority. Nor do the test results here lead to the imposition of discipline or have any academic consequences...

...Rather, the only consequence of a failed drug test is to limit the student's privilege of participating in extracurricular activities. Indeed, a student may test positive for drugs twice and still be allowed to participate in extracurricular activities. After the first positive test, the school contacts the student's parent or guardian for a meeting. The student may continue to participate in the activity if within five days of the meeting the student shows proof of receiving drug counseling and submits to a second drug test in two weeks. For the second positive test, the student is suspended from participation in all extracurricular activities for 14 days, must complete four hours of substance abuse counseling, and must submit to monthly drug tests. Only after a third positive test will the student be suspended from participating in any extracurricular activity for the remainder of the school year, or 88 school days, whichever is longer....

Given the minimally intrusive nature of the sample collection and the limited uses to which the test results are put, we conclude that the invasion of students' privacy is not significant.

* * *

Finally, this Court must consider the nature and immediacy of the government's concerns and the efficacy of the Policy in meeting them....This Court has already articulated in detail the importance of the governmental concern in preventing drug use by schoolchildren....The drug abuse problem among our Nation's youth has hardly abated since *Vernonia* was decided in 1995. In fact, evidence suggests that it has only grown worse....As in *Vernonia*, "the necessity for the State to act is magnified by the fact that this evil is being visited not just upon individuals at large, but upon children for whom it has undertaken a special responsibility of care and direction."...The health and safety risks identified in *Vernonia* apply with equal force to Tecumseh's children. Indeed, the nationwide drug epidemic makes the war against drugs a pressing concern in every school.

Additionally, the School District in this case has presented specific evidence of drug use at Tecumseh schools. Teachers testified that they had seen students who appeared to be under the influence of drugs and that they had heard students speaking openly about using drugs....A drug dog found marijuana cigarettes near the school parking lot. Police officers once found drugs or drug paraphernalia in a car driven by a Future Farmers of America member. And the school board president reported that people in the community were calling the board to discuss the "drug situation."

* * *

...[T]he safety interest furthered by drug testing is undoubtedly substantial for all children, athletes and nonathletes alike. We know all too well that drug use carries a variety of health risks for children, including death from overdose.

We also reject respondents' argument that drug testing must presumptively be based upon an individualized reasonable suspicion of wrongdoing because such a testing regime would be less intrusive....Such a regime would place an additional burden on public school teachers who are already tasked with the difficult job of maintaining order and discipline. A program of individualized suspicion might unfairly target members of unpopular groups. The fear of lawsuits resulting from such targeted searches may chill enforcement of the program, rendering it ineffective in combating drug use....

Finally, we find that testing students who participate in extracurricular activities is a reasonably effective means of addressing the School District's legitimate concerns in preventing, deterring, and detecting drug use. While in *Vernonia* there might have been a closer fit between the testing of athletes and the trial court's finding that the drug problem was "fueled by the 'role model' effect of athletes' drug use," such a finding was not essential to the holding....

* * *

Within the limits of the Fourth Amendment, local school boards must assess the desirability of drug testing schoolchildren. In upholding the constitutionality of the Policy, we express no opinion as to its wisdom. Rather, we hold only that Tecumseh's Policy is a reasonable means of furthering the School District's important interest in preventing and deterring drug use among its schoolchildren. Accordingly, we reverse the judgment of the Court of Appeals.

JUSTICE GINSBURG, with whom **JUSTICE STEVENS, JUSTICE O'CONNOR**, and **JUSTICE SOUTER** join, dissenting:

Seven years ago, in *Vernonia School Dist. 47J v. Acton* 515 U.S. 646... (1995), this Court determined that a school district's policy of randomly testing the urine of its student athletes for illicit drugs did not violate the Fourth Amendment. In so ruling, the Court emphasized that drug use "increased the risk of sports-related injury" and that Vernonia's athletes were the "leaders" of an aggressive local "drug culture" that had reached "'epidemic proportions.'"...Today, the Court relies upon *Vernonia* to permit a school district with a drug problem its superintendent repeatedly described as "not... major,"...to test the urine of an academic team member solely by reason of her participation in a nonathletic, competitive extracurricular activity—participation associated with neither special dangers from, nor particular predilections for, drug use.

"The legality of a search of a student," this Court has instructed, "should depend simply on the reasonableness, under all the circumstances, of the search."... Although "'special needs' inhere in the public school context,"...those needs are not so expansive or malleable as to render reasonable any program of student drug testing a school district elects to install. The particular testing program upheld today is not reasonable, it is capricious, even perverse: Petitioners' policy targets for testing a student population least likely to be at risk from illicit drugs and their damaging effects. I therefore dissent.

* * *

A search unsupported by probable cause nevertheless may be consistent with the Fourth Amendment "when special needs, beyond the normal need for law enforcement, make the warrant and probable-cause requirement impracticable."...

"...Fourth Amendment rights, no less than First and Fourteenth Amendment rights, are different in public schools than elsewhere; the 'reasonableness' inquiry cannot disregard the schools' custodial and tutelary responsibility for children."...

The *Vernonia* Court concluded that a public school district facing a disruptive and explosive drug abuse problem sparked by members of its athletic teams had "special needs" that justified suspicionless testing of district athletes as a condition of their athletic participation.

This case presents circumstances dispositively different from those of *Vernonia*. True, as the Court stresses, Tecumseh students participating in competitive extracurricular activities other than athletics share two relevant characteristics with the athletes of Vernonia. First, both groups attend public schools. "Our decision in *Vernonia*," the Court states, "depended primarily upon the school's custodial responsibility and authority."...

Those risks, however, are present for *all* schoolchildren. *Vernonia* cannot be read to endorse invasive and suspicionless drug testing of all students upon any evidence of drug use, solely because drugs jeopardize the life and health of those who use them. Many children, like many adults, engage in dangerous activities on their own time; that the children are enrolled in school scarcely allows government to monitor all such activities. If a student has a reasonable subjective expectation of privacy in the personal items she brings to school,...surely she has a similar expectation regarding the chemical composition of her urine....

The second commonality to which the Court points is the voluntary character of both interscholastic athletics and other competitive extracurricular activities. "By choosing to 'go out for the team,' [school athletes] voluntarily subject themselves to a degree of regulation even higher than that imposed on students generally."...Comparably, the Court today observes, "students who participate in competitive extracurricular activities voluntarily subject themselves to" additional rules not applicable to other students....

The comparison is enlightening. While extracurricular activities are "voluntary" in the sense that they are not required for graduation, they are part of the school's educational program; for that reason, the petitioner (hereinafter School District) is justified in expending public resources to make them available. Participation in such activities is a key component of school life, essential in reality for students applying to college, and, for all participants, a significant contributor to the breadth and quality of the educational experience....Students "volunteer" for extracurricular pursuits in the same way they might volunteer for honors classes. They subject themselves to additional requirements, but they do so in order to take full advantage of the education offered them....

Voluntary participation in athletics has a distinctly different dimension: Schools regulate student athletes discretely because competitive school sports by their nature require communal undress and, more important, expose students to physical risks that schools have a duty to mitigate. For the very reason that schools cannot offer a program of competitive athletics without intimately affecting the privacy of students, *Vernonia* reasonably analogized school athletes to "adults who choose to participate in a closely regulated industry."...Interscholastic athletics similarly require close safety and health regulation; a school's choir, band, and academic team do not.

In short, *Vernonia* applied, it did not repudiate, the principle that "the legality of a search of a student should depend simply on the reasonableness, *under all the circumstances*, of the search."...Enrollment in a public school, and election to participate in school activities beyond the bare minimum that the curriculum requires, are indeed factors relevant to reasonableness, but they do not on their own justify intrusive, suspicionless searches. *Vernonia* accordingly, did not rest upon these factors; instead, the Court performed what today's majority aptly describes as a "fact-specific balancing."... Balancing of that order, applied to the facts now before the Court, should yield a result other than the one the Court announces today.

* * *

Vernonia initially considered "the nature of the privacy interest upon which the search [there] at issue intruded."...The Court emphasized that student athletes' expectations of privacy are necessarily attenuated:

"Legitimate privacy expectations are even less with regard to student athletes. School sports are not for the bashful. They require 'suiting up' before each practice or event, and showering and changing afterwards. Public school locker rooms, the usual sites for these activities, are not notable for the privacy they afford. The locker rooms in Vernonia are typical: No individual dressing rooms are provided; shower heads are lined up along a wall, unseparated by any sort of partition or curtain; not even all the toilet stalls have doors.... There is an element of communal undress inherent in athletic participation."...

Competitive extracurricular activities other than athletics, however, serve students of all manner: the modest and shy along with the bold and uninhibited. Activities of the kind plaintiff-respondent Lindsay Earls pursued—choir, show choir, marching band, and academic team—afford opportunities to gain self-assurance, to "come to know faculty members in a less formal setting than the typical classroom," and to acquire "positive social supports and networks [that] play a critical role in periods of heightened stress."...

* * *

Finally, the "nature and immediacy of the governmental concern,"...faced by the Vernonia School District dwarfed that confronting Tecumseh administrators. Vernonia initiated its drug testing policy in response to an alarming situation: "[A] large segment of the student body, particularly those involved in interscholastic athletics, was in a state

of rebellion...fueled by alcohol and drug abuse as well as the student[s'] misperceptions about the drug culture."...Tecumseh, by contrast, repeatedly reported to the Federal Government during the period leading up to the adoption of the policy that "types of drugs [other than alcohol and tobacco] including controlled dangerous substances, are present [in the schools] but have not identified themselves as major problems at this time."...

* * *

At the margins, of course, no policy of *random* drug testing is perfectly tailored to the harms it seeks to address. The School District cites the dangers faced by members of the band, who must "perform extremely precise routines with heavy equipment and instruments in close proximity to other students," and by Future Farmers of America, who "are required to individually control and restrain animals as large as 1500 pounds."...For its part, the United States acknowledges that "the linebacker faces a greater risk of serious injury if he takes the field under the influence of drugs than the drummer in the halftime band," but parries that "the risk of injury to a student who is under the influence of drugs while playing golf, cross country, or volleyball (sports covered by the policy in *Vernonia*) is scarcely any greater than the risk of injury to a student...handling a 1500-pound steer (as [Future Farmers of America] members do) or working with cutlery or other sharp instruments (as [Future Homemakers of America] members do)."...One can demur to the Government's view of the risks drug use poses to golfers,...for golfers were surely as marginal among the linebackers, sprinters, and basketball players targeted for testing in Vernonia as steer-handlers are among the choristers, musicians, and academic-team members subject to urinalysis in Tecumseh. Notwithstanding nightmarish images of out-of-control flatware, livestock run amok, and colliding tubas disturbing the peace and quiet of Tecumseh, the great majority of students the School District seeks to test in truth are engaged in activities that are not safety sensitive to an unusual degree. There is a difference between imperfect tailoring and no tailoring at all.

* * *

Nationwide, students who participate in extracurricular activities are significantly less likely to develop substance abuse problems than are their less-involved peers... (tenth graders "who reported spending no time in school-sponsored activities were...49 percent more likely to have used drugs" than those who spent 1–4 hours per week in such activities). Even if students might be deterred from drug use in order to preserve their extracurricular eligibility, it is at least as likely that other students might forgo their extracurricular involvement in order to avoid detection of their drug use. Tecumseh's policy thus falls short doubly if deterrence is its aim: It invades the privacy of students who need deterrence least, and risks steering students at greatest risk for substance abuse away from extracurricular involvement that potentially may palliate drug problems....

To summarize, this case resembles *Vernonia* only in that the School Districts in both cases conditioned engagement in activities outside the obligatory curriculum on random subjection to urinalysis. The defining characteristics of the two programs, however, are entirely dissimilar. The Vernonia district sought to test a subpopulation of students distinguished by their reduced expectation of privacy, their special susceptibility to drug-related injury, and their heavy involvement with drug use. The Tecumseh district seeks to test a much larger population associated with none of these factors. It does so, moreover, without carefully safeguarding student confidentiality and without regard to the program's untoward effects. A program so sweeping is not sheltered by *Vernonia*; its unreasonable reach renders it impermissible under the Fourth Amendment.

* * *

It is a sad irony that the petitioning School District seeks to justify its edict here by trumpeting "the schools' custodial and tutelary responsibility for children."...In regulating an athletic program or endeavoring to combat an exploding drug epidemic, a school's custodial obligations may permit searches that would otherwise unacceptably abridge students' rights. When custodial duties are not ascendant, however, schools' tutelary obligations to their students require them to "teach by example" by avoiding symbolic measures that diminish constitutional protections. "That [schools] are educating the young for citizenship is reason for scrupulous protection of Constitutional freedoms of the individual, if we are not to strangle the free mind at its source and teach youth to discount important principles of our government as mere platitudes.".

Questions for Discussion

1. Does the extensive categorical nature of the *Earls* search (as with the *Vernonia* search for athletes) actually help its constitutionality, in light of the court's historical concern over excessive discretion given to state officials (particularly the police) to search or not? The majority notes that such discretion (even on the "reasonable suspicion" standard approved in *TLO*) might allow school officials to "target members of unpopular groups," which the mechanical search of those in extra-curricular ventures avoids? But what would prevent school officials from also selectively searching such groups on the loose "reasonable suspicion" standard of *TLO*? How does the supplemental liberal allowance of *Earls* address that alleged danger cited by the majority?

2. The Pottawatomie policy preserves confidentiality, and drug results are not turned over to law enforcement. Would it make a difference if law enforcement were notified? Can that information be the basis for a "reasonable suspicion" search of the offender's locker? Can it be used for a search warrant (perhaps by sealed affidavit to preserve confidentiality)? On the one hand, the school becomes a potential agent of the police held to the higher standards applicable to criminal investigations. On the other hand, are not juvenile proceedings civil in nature—and designed to assist involved children? If a child is using dangerous amphetamines or opiates, should the only response be possible loss of chess club activities? If the drug problem is as serious as the majority claims, why would it not be permissible to use the information to more effectively detect the problem and treat the child?

3. Apart from the majority's stated purpose of "protecting" children from a danger, what are the implications of the concept that if a *crime* is being investigated, the state should be more constricted than if it is merely a *regulatory* matter? While precedents and both the majority opinion and dissent so assume, do not criminal offenses represent human activity of the greatest societal concern and damage? Are not most criminal acts by youth harmful to both themselves and to other children? Why should a strong justification for a search—signaled by the criminal activity addressed—justify more restrictions on investigations, rather than less?

4. Do you agree with Justice Scalia in *Vernonia* and Justice Thomas in *Earls* that the required production of urine under the monitoring of another person, including either listening for splash and feeling the warmth of the liquid, or visually inspecting genitalia while urinating—followed by the chemical testing of one's internal fluids—is a minimal intrusion by the state, as the majority opines? Is that

judgment consistent with the extraordinary privacy accorded persons in their medical treatment and histories by custom, statute, and other precedents? One might argue that there is a compelling state interest in assuring the public that Supreme Court justices are not addicted or chemically imbalanced given the force-of-law authority of their decisions. Accordingly, would the majority justices find that a similar urine analysis of each of them before every major decision (mechanically applied) constitutes only a minimal intrusion? Is it relevant that in 1998 the U.S. House of Representatives quietly rejected a drug testing proposal for themselves and their staffs, declaring it to be "insulting and undignified"?

5. Is death by overdose really a safety problem being addressed by comprehensive drug testing? Was there any evidence of such deaths, or of overdoses among the population here to be comprehensively tested? Justice Thomas cites teacher testimony about some students in school who were apparently on drugs and some conversations overheard about their use. Why not engage in a "reasonable suspicion" search of these students under *TLO*?

6. Is the "closely regulated industry" allowance for searches cited by the majority applicable here? Closely regulated industries are "clothed in the public interest"—a term of art implying monopoly power or "external costs" (such as the provision of medical services or hazardous activity implicating health and safety or involving extraordinary public reliance and possible irreparable harm). Would there be a basis to "closely regulate" these school clubs due to their possible external impact on the public? Is the school band, or the Future Homemakers of America club, such an entity? The chess club? The after school bible-study club? If they so qualify, who does not qualify? Why would the majority's logic not apply to students who choose to eat in the cafeteria when other options may be available, or who engage in the extra-curricular activity of attending a football game? What is the reach of the majority's allowance of searches lacking probable cause or reasonable suspicion if the major tether is "the drug problem"?

7. May school searches such as those allowed in *Vernonia* and *Earls* be prohibited by the states under the "independent state grounds" application of their separate constitutions?

Safford Unified School District v. April Redding
557 U.S. 364 (2009)

JUSTICE SOUTER delivered the opinion of the Court.

The issue here is whether a 13-year-old student's Fourth Amendment right was violated when she was subjected to a search of her bra and underpants by school officials acting on reasonable suspicion that she had brought forbidden prescription and over-the-counter drugs to school. Because there were no reasons to suspect the drugs presented a danger or were concealed in her underwear, we hold that the search did violate the Constitution, but because there is reason to question the clarity with which the right was established, the official who ordered the unconstitutional search is entitled to qualified immunity from liability.

I

The events immediately prior to the search in question began in 13-year-old Savana Redding's math class at Safford Middle School one October day in 2003. The assistant principal of the school, Kerry Wilson, came into the room and asked Savana to go to his office. There, he showed her a day planner, unzipped and open flat on his desk, in which there were several knives, lighters, a permanent marker, and a cigarette.

Wilson asked Savana whether the planner was hers; she said it was, but that a few days before she had lent it to her friend, Marissa Glines. Savana stated that none of the items in the planner belonged to her.

Wilson then showed Savana four white prescription-strength ibuprofen 400-mg pills, and one over-the-counter blue naproxen 200-mg pill, all used for pain and inflammation but banned under school rules without advance permission. He asked Savana if she knew anything about the pills. Savana answered that she did not. Wilson then told Savana that he had received a report that she was giving these pills to fellow students; Savana denied it and agreed to let Wilson search her belongings. Helen Romero, an administrative assistant, came into the office, and together with Wilson they searched Savana's backpack, finding nothing.

At that point, Wilson instructed Romero to take Savana to the school nurse's office to search her clothes for pills. Romero and the nurse, Peggy Schwallier, asked Savana to remove her jacket, socks, and shoes, leaving her in stretch pants and a T-shirt (both without pockets), which she was then asked to remove. Finally, Savana was told to pull her bra out and to the side and shake it, and to pull out the elastic on her underpants, thus exposing her breasts and pelvic area to some degree. No pills were found.

Savana's mother filed suit against Safford Unified School District #1, Wilson, Romero, and Schwallier for conducting a strip search in violation of Savana's Fourth Amendment rights. The individuals (hereinafter petitioners) moved for summary judgment, raising a defense of qualified immunity. * * *

II

... In *T.L.O.*, we recognized that the school setting "requires some modification of the level of suspicion of illicit activity needed to justify a search," and held that for searches by school officials "a careful balancing of governmental and private interests suggests that the public interest is best served by a Fourth Amendment standard of reasonableness that stops short of probable cause," *id.*, at 341.... We have thus applied a standard of reasonable suspicion to determine the legality of a school administrator's search of a student (at 342), and have held that a school search "will be permissible in its scope when the measures adopted are reasonably related to the objectives of the search and not excessively intrusive in light of the age and sex of the student and the nature of the infraction," (*id.*).

...Perhaps the best that can be said generally about the required knowledge component of probable cause for a law enforcement officer's evidence search is that it raise a "fair probability," or a "substantial chance,"...of discovering evidence of criminal activity. The lesser standard for school searches could as readily be described as a moderate chance of finding evidence of wrongdoing...

III

A.

A week before Savana was searched, another student, Jordan Romero (no relation of the school's administrative assistant), told the principal and Assistant Principal Wilson that "certain students were bringing drugs and weapons on campus," and that he had been sick after taking some pills that "he got from a classmate." App. 8a. On the morning of October 8, the same boy handed Wilson a white pill that he said Marissa Glines had given him. He told Wilson that students were planning to take the pills at lunch.

Wilson learned from Peggy Schwallier, the school nurse, that the pill was Ibuprofen 400 mg, available only by prescription. Wilson then called Marissa out of class. Outside the classroom, Marissa's teacher handed Wilson the day planner, found within Marissa's reach, containing various contraband items. Wilson escorted Marissa back to his office.

In the presence of Helen Romero, Wilson requested Marissa to turn out her pockets and open her wallet. Marissa produced a blue pill, several white ones, and a razor blade. Wilson asked where the blue pill came from, and Marissa answered, "'I guess it slipped in when she gave me the IBU 400s.'" *Id.*, at 13a. When Wilson asked whom she meant, Marissa replied, "'Savana Redding.'" *Ibid.* Wilson then enquired about the day planner and its contents; Marissa denied knowing anything about them. Wilson did not ask Marissa any followup questions to determine whether there was any likelihood that Savana presently had pills: neither asking when Marissa received the pills from Savana nor where Savana might be hiding them.

Schwallier did not immediately recognize the blue pill, but information provided through a poison control hotline indicated that the pill was a 200-mg dose of an antiinflammatory drug, generically called naproxen, available over the counter. At Wilson's direction, Marissa was then subjected to a search of her bra and underpants by Romero and Schwallier, as Savana was later on. The search revealed no additional pills.

It was at this juncture that Wilson called Savana into his office and showed her the day planner. Their conversation established that Savana and Marissa were on friendly terms: while she denied knowledge of the contraband, Savana admitted that the day planner was hers and that she had lent it to Marissa. Wilson had other reports of their friendship from staff members, who had identified Savana and Marissa as part of an unusually rowdy group at the school's opening dance in August, during which alcohol and cigarettes were found in the girls' bathroom. Wilson had reason to connect the girls with this contraband, for Wilson knew that Jordan Romero had told the principal that before the dance, he had been at a party at Savana's house where alcohol was served. Marissa's statement that the pills came from Savana was thus sufficiently plausible to warrant suspicion that Savana was involved in pill distribution.

This suspicion of Wilson's was enough to justify a search of Savana's backpack and outer clothing. If a student is reasonably suspected of giving out contraband pills, she is reasonably suspected of carrying them on her person and in the carryall that has become an item of student uniform in most places today. If Wilson's reasonable suspicion of pill distribution were not understood to support searches of outer clothes and backpack, it would not justify any search worth making. And the look into Savana's bag, in her presence and in the relative privacy of Wilson's office, was not excessively intrusive, any more than Romero's subsequent search of her outer clothing.

B

Here it is that the parties part company, with Savana's claim that extending the search at Wilson's behest to the point of making her pull out her underwear was constitutionally unreasonable. The exact label for this final step in the intrusion is not important, though strip search is a fair way to speak of it. Romero and Schwallier directed Savana to remove her clothes down to her underwear, and then "pull out" her bra and the elastic band on her underpants. *Id.*, at 23a. Although Romero and Schwallier stated that they did not see anything when Savana followed their instructions, ...we would not define strip search and its Fourth Amendment consequences in a way that would guarantee litigation about who was looking and how much was seen. The very fact of Savana's pulling her underwear away from her body in the presence of the two officials who were able to see her necessarily exposed her breasts and pelvic area to some degree, and both subjective and reasonable societal expectations of personal privacy support the treatment of such a search as categorically distinct, requiring distinct elements of justification on the part of school authorities for going beyond a search of outer clothing and belongings.

Savana's subjective expectation of privacy against such a search is inherent in her account of it as embarrassing, frightening, and humiliating. The reasonableness of her expectation (required by the Fourth Amendment standard) is indicated by the consistent experiences of other young people similarly searched, whose adolescent vulnerability intensifies the patent intrusiveness of the exposure....The common reaction of these adolescents simply registers the obviously different meaning of a search exposing the body from the experience of nakedness or near undress in other school circumstances. Changing for gym is getting ready for play; exposing for a search is responding to an accusation reserved for suspected wrongdoers and fairly understood as so degrading that a number of communities have decided that strip searches in schools are never reasonable and have banned them no matter what the facts may be (citing regulation of New York City Dept. of Education).

The indignity of the search does not, of course, outlaw it, but it does implicate the rule of reasonableness as stated in *T.L.O.*, that "the search as actually conducted [be] reasonably related in scope to the circumstances which justified the interference in the first place." (at 341). The scope will be permissible, that is, when it is "not excessively intrusive in light of the age and sex of the student and the nature of the infraction." (at 342)....

Here, the content of the suspicion failed to match the degree of intrusion. Wilson knew beforehand that the pills were prescription-strength ibuprofen and over-the-counter naproxen, common pain relievers equivalent to two Advil, or one Aleve. He must have been aware of the nature and limited threat of the specific drugs he was searching for, and while just about anything can be taken in quantities that will do real harm, Wilson had no reason to suspect that large amounts of the drugs were being passed around, or that individual students were receiving great numbers of pills.

IV.

A number of judges have read *T.L.O.* as the en banc minority of the Ninth Circuit did here. The Sixth Circuit upheld a strip search of a high school student for a drug, without any suspicion that drugs were hidden next to her body. *Williams v. Ellington*, 936 F.2d 881, 882-883, 887 (1991). And other courts considering qualified immunity for strip searches have read *T.L.O.* as "a series of abstractions, on the one hand, and a declaration of seeming deference to the judgments of school officials, on the other," *Jenkins v. Talladega City Bd. of Ed.*, 115 F.3d 821, 828 (CA11 1997) (en banc), which made it impossible "to establish clearly the contours of a Fourth Amendment right... [in] the wide variety of possible school settings different from those involved in *T.L.O* " itself. *Ibid.* See also *Thomas v. Roberts*, 323 F.3d 950 (CA11 2003) (granting qualified immunity to a teacher and police officer who conducted a group strip search of a fifth grade class when looking for a missing $26).

We think these differences of opinion from our own are substantial enough to require immunity for the school officials in this case. We would not suggest that entitlement to qualified immunity is the guaranteed product of disuniform views of the law in the other federal, or state, courts, and the fact that a single judge, or even a group of judges, disagrees about the contours of a right does not automatically render the law unclear if we have been clear. That said, however, the cases viewing school strip searches differently from the way we see them are numerous enough, with well-reasoned majority and dissenting opinions, to counsel doubt that we were sufficiently clear in the prior statement of law. We conclude that qualified immunity is warranted.

* * *

JUSTICE THOMAS, concurring in part and dissenting in part.

* * *

... For nearly 25 years this Court has understood that "[m]aintaining order in the classroom has never been easy, but in more recent years, school disorder has often taken particularly ugly forms: drug use and violent crime in the schools have become major social problems." *Ibid.* In schools, "[e]vents calling for discipline are frequent occurrences and sometimes require immediate, effective action." *Goss v. Lopez*, 419 U.S. 565, 580,..For this reason, school officials retain broad authority to protect students and preserve "order and a proper educational environment" under the Fourth Amendment... This authority requires that school officials be able to engage in the "close supervision of schoolchildren, as well as...enforc[e] rules against conduct that would be perfectly permissible if undertaken by an adult." *Ibid.* Seeking to reconcile the Fourth Amendment with this unique public school setting, the Court in *T.L.O* held that a school search is "reasonable" if it is "'justified at its inception'" and "'reasonably related in scope to the circumstances which justified the interference in the first place.'" *Id.*, at 341-342,.... The search under review easily meets this standard.

* * *

...As an initial matter, school officials were aware that a few years earlier, a student had become "seriously ill" and "spent several days in intensive care" after ingesting prescription medication obtained from a classmate. App. 10a. Fourth Amendment searches do not occur in a vacuum; rather, context must inform the judicial inquiry.... In this instance, the suspicion of drug possession arose at a middle school that had "a history of problems with students using and distributing prohibited and illegal substances on campus." App. 7a, 10a.

The school's substance-abuse problems had not abated by the 2003-2004 school year, which is when the challenged search of Redding took place. School officials had found alcohol and cigarettes in the girls' bathroom during the first school dance of the year and noticed that a group of students including Redding and Marissa Glines smelled of alcohol. *Ibid.* Several weeks later, another student, Jordan Romero, reported that Redding had hosted a party before the dance where she served whiskey, vodka, and tequila. *Id.*, at 8a, 11a. Romero had provided this report to school officials as a result of a meeting his mother scheduled with the officials after Romero "bec[a]me violent" and "sick to his stomach" one night and admitted that "he had taken some pills that he had got[ten] from a classmate." *Id.*, at 7a-8a, 10a-11a. At that meeting, Romero admitted that "certain students were bringing drugs and weapons on campus." *Id.* at 8a, 11a. One week later, Romero handed the assistant principal a white pill that he said he had received from Glines. *Id.*, at 11a. He reported "that a group of students [were] planning on taking the pills at lunch." *Ibid.*

School officials justifiably took quick action in light of the lunchtime deadline. The assistant principal took the pill to the school nurse who identified it as prescription-strength 400-mg Ibuprofen. *Id.*, at 12a. A subsequent search of Glines and her belongings produced a razor blade, a Naproxen 200-mg pill, and several Ibuprofen 400-mg pills. *Id.*, at 13a. When asked, Glines claimed that she had received the pills from Redding. *Ibid.* A search of Redding's planner, which Glines had borrowed, then uncovered "several knives, several lighters, a cigarette, and a permanent marker." *Id.*, at 12a, 14a, 22a. Thus, as the majority acknowledges,.. the totality of relevant circumstances justified a search of Redding for pills.

* * *

[The majority objects to the scope of the search but a] search of a student... is permissible in scope under *T.L.O.* so long as it is objectively reasonable to believe that the area searched could conceal the contraband. The dissenting opinion below correctly captured this Fourth Amendment standard, noting that "if a student brought a baseball bat on campus in violation of school policy, a search of that student's shirt pocket would be patently unjustified."531 F.3d at 1104 (opinion of Hawkins, J.).

The analysis of whether the scope of the search here was permissible under that standard is straightforward. Indeed, the majority does not dispute that "general background possibilities" establish that students conceal "contraband in their underwear." It acknowledges that school officials had reasonable suspicion to look in Redding's backpack and outer clothing because if "Wilson's reasonable suspicion of pill distribution were not understood to support searches of outer clothes and backpack, it would not justify any search worth making."...The majority nevertheless concludes that proceeding any further with the search was unreasonable. ("Any reasonable search for the pills would have ended when inspection of Redding's backpack and jacket pockets yielded nothing"). But there is no support for this conclusion. The reasonable suspicion that Redding possessed the pills for distribution purposes did not dissipate simply because the search of her backpack turned up nothing. It was eminently reasonable to conclude that the backpack was empty because Redding was secreting the pills in a place she thought no one would look. See *Ross, supra,* at 820, 102 S. Ct. 2157, 72 L. Ed. 2d 572 ("Contraband goods rarely are strewn" about in plain view; "by their very nature such goods must be withheld from public view").

Redding would not have been the first person to conceal pills in her undergarments. See Hicks, Man Gets 17-Year Drug Sentence, [Corbin, KY] Times-Tribune, Oct. 7, 2008, p. 1 (Drug courier "told officials she had the [Oxycontin] pills concealed in her crotch"); Conley, Whitehaven: Traffic Stop Yields Hydrocodone Pills, [Memphis] Commercial Appeal, Aug. 3, 2007, p. B3 ("An additional 40 hydrocodone pills were found in her

pants"); Caywood, Police Vehicle Chase Leads to Drug Arrests, [Worcester] Telegram & Gazette, June 7, 2008, p. A7 (25-year-old "allegedly had a cigar tube stuffed with pills tucked into the waistband of his pants"); Hubartt, 23-Year-Old Charged With Dealing Ecstasy, The [Fort Wayne] Journal Gazette, Aug. 8, 2007, p. C2 ("[W]hile he was being put into a squad car, his pants fell down and a plastic bag containing pink and orange pills fell on the ground")....Nor will she be the last after today's decision, which announces the safest place to secrete contraband in school.

* * *

Even accepting the majority's assurances that it is not attacking the rule's reasonableness, it certainly is attacking the rule's importance. This approach directly conflicts with *T.L.O.* in which the Court was "unwilling to adopt a standard under which the legality of a search is dependent upon a judge's evaluation of the relative importance of school rules."...Indeed, the Court in *T.L.O.* expressly rejected the proposition that the majority seemingly endorses -- that "some rules regarding student conduct are by nature too 'trivial' to justify a search based upon reasonable suspicion." ("The promulgation of a rule forbidding specified conduct presumably reflects a judgment on the part of school officials that such conduct is destructive of school order or of a proper educational environment. Absent any suggestion that the rule violates some substantive constitutional guarantee, the courts should as a general matter, defer to that judgment").

The majority's decision in this regard also departs from another basic principle of the Fourth Amendment: that law enforcement officials can enforce with the same vigor all rules and regulations irrespective of the perceived importance of any of those rules. "In a long line of cases, we have said that when an officer has probable cause to believe a person committed even a minor crime in his presence, the balancing of private and public interests is not in doubt. The arrest is constitutionally reasonable." *Virginia v. Moore*, 553 U.S. 164 (2008). The Fourth Amendment rule for searches is the same: Police officers are entitled to search regardless of the perceived triviality of the underlying law. As we have explained, requiring police to make "sensitive, case-by-case determinations of government need,"....

The majority has placed school officials in this "impossible spot" by questioning whether possession of Ibuprofen and Naproxen causes a severe enough threat to warrant investigation. Had the suspected infraction involved a street drug, the majority implies that it would have approved the scope of the search...(relying on the "limited threat of the specific drugs he was searching for"); (relying on the limited "power of the drugs" involved). In effect, then, the majority has replaced a school rule that draws no distinction among drugs with a new one that does. As a result, a full search of a student's person for prohibited drugs will be permitted only if the Court agrees that the drug in question was sufficiently dangerous. Such a test is unworkable and unsound. School officials cannot be expected to halt searches based on the possibility that a court might later find that the particular infraction at issue is not severe enough to warrant an intrusive investigation.

* * *

II

...If the common-law view that parents delegate to teachers their authority to discipline and maintain order were to be applied in this case, the search of Redding would stand. There can be no doubt that a parent would have had the authority to conduct the search at issue in this case. Parents have "immunity from the strictures of the Fourth Amendment" when it comes to searches of a child or that child's belongings. *T.L.O.*, 469 U.S., at 337,...(A parent's authority is "not subject to the limits of the Fourth Amendment"); *Griffin v. Wisconsin*, 483 U.S. 868, 876, ("[P]arental custodial authority" does not require "judicial approval for [a] search of a minor child's room").

> In the end, the task of implementing and amending public school policies is beyond this Court's function. Parents, teachers, school administrators, local politicians, and state officials are all better suited than judges to determine the appropriate limits on searches conducted by school officials. Preservation of order, discipline, and safety in public schools is simply not the domain of the Constitution. And, common sense is not a judicial monopoly or a Constitutional imperative.
>
> * * *

Questions for Discussion

1. In *Safford*, there is evidence that the student possesses and is distributing what may be dangerous unlawful prescription medicine. How does the line drawn by the Court compare to the holding in *Earls* allowing the testing (and production) of a urine sample of any student engaged in extra-curricular activity, without any particularized probable cause or reasonable suspicion? Would it be more acceptable were the school to require all students to pull down underwear and bras for inspection?

2. Would it help if the inspection of the child were by a young female? By a pediatrician brought to the school?

3. If the intrusion in *Safford* is objectionable in its scope and degree (in relation to the purpose of the search) would it be permitted were Savana thought to possess methamphetamine, heroin, or cocaine?

4. The dissent contends that the importance of the seizure is irrelevant once its object involves a violation of law. Does every violation of law justify a search with the same level of probable cause and the same justifiable degree of intrusion? Assume there is some suspicion of violations such as cigarette smoking (tobacco purchased underage) or alcohol on campus. Assume there is a similar concern over weapons (small firearms), *e.g.*, based on discovery of such weapons at a nearby school. Is the justification for a *Safford* search the same?

5. The dissent argues that schools are delegated parental authority, and that parents have the right to search their own children. Is the viewing of genitals by school officials using the power of the state, equivalent to such a parental search?

Note on the Exclusionary Rule and *U.S. v. Frederick Doe*

In *T.L.O.*, the Supreme Court originally granted certiorari to consider whether the exclusionary rule, which prohibits the use of illegally-obtained evidence in criminal proceedings, is applicable to juvenile proceedings. However, the Court elected to defer that question and instead consider the threshold issue of the legality of the search. The Court has not revisited the issue, leaving a decision of the U.S. District Court for the Eastern Division of Texas as the leading federal case on the matter. In *United States v. Frederick Doe*, 801 F. Supp. 1562 (1992), officers had seized drugs, a firearm, and a box of ammunition from the car of the defendant, an African American teen. The search of the car and seizure of the items were found to be in violation of the Fourth Amendment. The question that remained for the court was whether this necessitated suppression of the evidence as per the exclusionary rule. Having no direct Supreme Court precedent to rely upon, the Texas court considered the unanimous application of the rule among state courts that had considered the issue. The court also reflected upon the recognition in *Gault* that juvenile penalties can be as severe as criminal penalties.

Ultimately, the court employed a cost-benefit analysis in which it considered the central purpose of the exclusionary rule—to deter future unlawful conduct by the police. The court reasoned that this purpose would be frustrated were the rule not applied to juvenile proceedings. The court found that "the sole deterrent for violation of the Fourth Amendment rights of juveniles is the existence of the exclusionary rule." Absent a remedy for juveniles, police would essentially be free to conduct illegal search and seizure without consequence. In fact, the court viewed such a limit in the application of the rule to be a threat to the deterrent power of the rule in general. The court weighed this against costs of applying the rule, such as the imposition of an additional hearing and the risk that a guilty party may go unpunished. What the court did not consider is the potential cost in relation to the rehabilitative purpose of the juvenile justice system. As noted above, it can be argued that procedures permitting the exclusion of pertinent information in juvenile proceedings compromises the ability of the system to meet its goal of providing assistance to troubled youth. In the end, the court concluded that the rule should apply in federal delinquency adjudications, accordant with the prevailing view of state courts.

3. Juveniles and the Fifth Amendment

J.D.B. v. North Carolina
564 U.S. 261 (2011)

JUSTICE SOTOMAYOR delivered the opinion of the Court.

This case presents the question whether the age of a child subjected to police questioning is relevant to the custody analysis of *Miranda v. Arizona*, 384 U.S. 436 (1966). It is beyond dispute that children will often feel bound to submit to police questioning when an adult in the same circumstances would feel free to leave. Seeing no reason for police officers or courts to blind themselves to that commonsense reality, we hold that a child's age properly informs the *Miranda* custody analysis.

I

A

Petitioner J.D.B. was a 13-year-old, seventh-grade student attending class at Smith Middle School in Chapel Hill, North Carolina, when he was removed from his classroom by a uniformed police officer, escorted to a closed-door conference room, and questioned by police for at least half an hour.

This was the second time that police questioned J.D.B. in the span of a week. Five days earlier, two home break-ins occurred, and various items were stolen. Police stopped and questioned J.D.B. after he was seen behind a residence in the neighborhood where the crimes occurred. That same day, police also spoke to J.D.B.'s grandmother--his legal guardian--as well as his aunt.

Police later learned that a digital camera matching the description of one of the stolen items had been found at J.D.B.'s middle school and seen in J.D.B.'s possession. Investigator DiCostanzo...went to the school to question J.D.B. Upon arrival, DiCostanzo informed the uniformed police officer on detail to the school (a so-called school resource officer), the assistant principal, and an administrative intern that he was there to question

J.D.B. about the break-ins. Although DiCostanzo asked the school administrators to verify J.D.B.'s date of birth, address, and parent contact information from school records, neither the police officers nor the school administrators contacted J.D.B.'s grandmother.

The uniformed officer interrupted J.D.B.'s afternoon social studies class, removed J.D.B. from the classroom, and escorted him to a school conference room. There, J.D.B. was met by DiCostanzo, the assistant principal, and the administrative intern. The door to the conference room was closed. With the two police officers and the two administrators present, J.D.B. was questioned for the next 30 to 45 minutes. Prior to the commencement of questioning, J.D.B. was given neither Miranda warnings nor the opportunity to speak to his grandmother. Nor was he informed that he was free to leave the room.

* * *

After learning of the prospect of juvenile detention, J.D.B. confessed that he and a friend were responsible for the break-ins. DiCostanzo only then informed J.D.B. that he could refuse to answer the investigator's questions and that he was free to leave. Asked whether he understood, J.D.B. nodded and provided further detail, including information about the location of the stolen items. Eventually J.D.B. wrote a statement, at DiCostanzo's request. When the bell rang indicating the end of the schoolday, J.D.B. was allowed to leave to catch the bus home.

B

Two juvenile petitions were filed against J.D.B., each alleging one count of breaking and entering and one count of larceny. J.D.B.'s public defender moved to suppress his statements and the evidence derived therefrom, arguing that suppression was necessary because J.D.B. had been "interrogated by police in a custodial setting without being afforded *Miranda* warning[s]," ... and because his statements were involuntary under the totality of the circumstances test; see *Schneckloth v. Bustamonte*, 412 U.S. 218, 226 (1973) ("due process precludes admission of a confession where a defendant's will was overborne" by the circumstances of the interrogation). After a suppression hearing at which DiCostanzo and J.D.B. testified, the trial court denied the motion, deciding that J.D.B. was not in custody at the time of the schoolhouse interrogation and that his statements were voluntary...

A divided panel of the North Carolina Court of Appeals affirmed... The North Carolina Supreme Court held, over two dissents, that J.D.B. was not in custody when he confessed, "declin[ing] to extend the test for custody to include consideration of the age... of an individual subjected to questioning by police."...

We granted certiorari to determine whether the Miranda custody analysis includes consideration of a juvenile suspect's age.

II

A

* * *

By its very nature, custodial police interrogation entails "inherently compelling pressures." .... Even for an adult, the physical and psychological isolation of custodial interrogation can "undermine the individual's will to resist and . . . compel him to speak where he would not otherwise do so freely." ... Indeed, the pressure of custodial interrogation is so immense that it "can induce a frighteningly high percentage of people to confess to crimes they never committed." ... That risk is all the more troubling--and recent studies suggest, all the more acute--when the subject of custodial interrogation is a juvenile.

Recognizing that the inherently coercive nature of custodial interrogation "blurs the line between voluntary and involuntary statements," ...this Court in *Miranda* adopted a set of prophylactic measures designed to safeguard the constitutional guarantee against self-incrimination. ...

Because these measures protect the individual against the coercive nature of custodial interrogation, they are required "'only where there has been such a restriction on a person's freedom as to render him "in custody."'"...As we have repeatedly emphasized, whether a suspect is "in custody" is an objective inquiry.

"Two discrete inquiries are essential to the determination: first, what were the circumstances surrounding the interrogation; and second, given those circumstances, would a reasonable person have felt he or she was at liberty to terminate the interrogation and leave."...

* * *

B.

The State and its *amici* contend that a child's age has no place in the custody analysis, no matter how young the child subjected to police questioning. We cannot agree. In some circumstances, a child's age "would have affected how a reasonable person" in the suspect's position "would perceive his or her freedom to leave." ... That is, a reasonable child subjected to police questioning will sometimes feel pressured to submit when a reasonable adult would feel free to go. We think it clear that courts can account for that reality without doing any damage to the objective nature of the custody analysis.

* * *

The law has historically reflected the same assumption that children characteristically lack the capacity to exercise mature judgment and possess only an incomplete ability to understand the world around them....Like this Court's own generalizations, the legal disqualifications placed on children as a class--e.g., limitations on their ability to alienate property, enter a binding contract enforceable against them, and marry without parental consent--exhibit the settled understanding that the differentiating characteristics of youth are universal.

Indeed, even where a "reasonable person" standard otherwise applies, the common law has reflected the reality that children are not adults. In negligence suits, for instance, where liability turns on what an objectively reasonable person would do in the circumstances, "[a]ll American jurisdictions accept the idea that a person's childhood is a relevant circumstance" to be considered....

* * *

Reviewing the question *de novo* today, we hold that so long as the child's age was known to the officer at the time of police questioning, or would have been objectively apparent to a reasonable officer, its inclusion in the custody analysis is consistent with the objective nature of that test. This is not to say that a child's age will be a determinative, or even a significant, factor in every case. ...It is, however, a reality that courts cannot simply ignore.

* * *

JUSTICE ALITO, with whom the CHIEF JUSTICE, JUSTICE SCALIA, and JUSTICE THOMAS, join, dissenting.

The Court's decision in this case may seem on first consideration to be modest and sensible, but in truth it is neither. It is fundamentally inconsistent with one of the main justifications for the *Miranda* rule: the perceived need for a clear rule that can be easily applied in all cases. And today's holding is not needed to protect the constitutional rights of minors who are questioned by the police.

* * *

Today's decision shifts the *Miranda* custody determination from a one-size-fits-all reasonable-person test into an inquiry that must account for at least one individualized characteristic--age--that is thought to correlate with susceptibility to coercive pressures. Age, however, is in no way the only personal characteristic that may correlate with pliability, and in future cases the Court will be forced to choose between two unpalatable alternatives. It may choose to limit today's decision by arbitrarily distinguishing a suspect's age from other personal characteristics--such as intelligence, education, occupation, or prior experience with law enforcement--that may also correlate with susceptibility to coercive pressures. Or, if the Court is unwilling to draw these arbitrary lines, it will be forced to effect a fundamental transformation of the *Miranda* custody test--from a clear, easily applied prophylactic rule into a highly fact-intensive standard resembling the voluntariness test that the *Miranda* Court found to be unsatisfactory.

For at least three reasons, there is no need to go down this road. First, many minors subjected to police interrogation are near the age of majority, and for these suspects the one-size-fits-all *Miranda* custody rule may not be a bad fit. Second, many of the difficulties in applying the *Miranda* custody rule to minors arise because of the unique circumstances present when the police conduct interrogations at school. The *Miranda* custody rule has always taken into account the setting in which questioning occurs, and accounting for the school setting in such cases will address many of these problems. Third, in cases like the one now before us, where the suspect is especially young, courts applying the constitutional voluntariness standard can take special care to ensure that incriminating statements were not obtained through coercion.

Safeguarding the constitutional rights of minors does not require the extreme makeover of *Miranda* that today's decision may portend.

* * *

The Court's rationale for importing age into the custody standard is that minors tend to lack adults' "capacity to exercise mature judgment" and that failing to account for that "reality" will leave some minors unprotected under *Miranda* in situations where they perceive themselves to be confined. I do not dispute that many suspects who are under 18 will be more susceptible to police pressure than the average adult. As the Court notes, our pre-*Miranda* cases were particularly attuned to this "reality" in applying the constitutional requirement of voluntariness in fact...It is no less a "reality," however, that many persons over the age of 18 are also more susceptible to police pressure than the hypothetical reasonable person.... Yet the *Miranda* custody standard has never accounted for the personal characteristics of these or any other individual defendants.

Indeed, it has always been the case under *Miranda* that the unusually meek or compliant are subject to the same fixed rules, including the same custody requirement, as those who are unusually resistant to police pressure.... *Miranda's* rigid standards are both overinclusive and underinclusive. They are overinclusive to the extent that they provide a windfall to the most hardened and savvy of suspects, who often have no need for *Miranda's* protections.... And *Miranda's* requirements are underinclusive to the extent that they fail to account for "frailties," "idiosyncrasies," and other individualized considerations that might cause a person to bend more easily during a confrontation with the police... Members of this Court have seen this rigidity as a major weakness in *Miranda's* "code of rules for confessions." ...But if it is, then the weakness is an inescapable consequence of the *Miranda* Court's decision to supplement the more holistic voluntariness requirement with a one-size-fits-all prophylactic rule.

* * *

If *Miranda's* rigid, one-size-fits-all standards fail to account for the unique needs of juveniles, the response should be to rigorously apply the constitutional rule against coercion to ensure that the rights of minors are protected. There is no need to run *Miranda* off the rails.

Questions for Discussion

1. The dissent argues that age is only one of several personal characteristics that could influence a person's interpretation of whether they are in custody. Does the majority decision open the door to the consideration of other characteristics, such as intelligence or mental illness? How can age be distinguished from these other characteristics?

2. As the Court states, the age of the suspect is not a determinative factor in every case. What other factors are relevant in determining whether a minor was in custody for *Miranda* purposes? Does the location of the questioning affect whether

the youth is deemed in custody? Can the youth be considered in custody if the questioning occurs at the minor's home? At her school? Is questioning at a police station more likely to be considered custodial by virtue of the location? Does the duration of the questioning matter? If the officer specifically tells a youth that he or she is free to leave at any time, does that prove that the questioning was not a custodial interrogation?

3. In what other circumstances would it be appropriate to apply the concept of the "reasonable child" or "reasonable juvenile?" Would this standard make sense when considering seizure or consent to search under the 4th amendment? Would it make sense to require consideration of the "reasonable juvenile" when determining whether waiver of right to counsel is valid?

4. Studies indicate that many juveniles fail to fully comprehend the *Miranda* warnings. Key concepts and vocabulary used in the warnings are misunderstood by juveniles far more often than by adults. Research also reveals that the vast majority of juveniles waive their rights under *Miranda* when being interrogated. In light of these findings, does the administering of *Miranda* warnings adequately protect a child's rights in custodial situations? Should there be a requirement to have counsel, or a parent, present when a child is interrogated, or at least when waiver is given? See, for example, North Carolina G.S. §7B-2101(b) that makes inadmissible any in-custody admission or confession made outside of the presence of a juvenile's parent, guardian, or attorney. In 2017 California passed a similar bill, requiring that minors age 15 or under must consult with an attorney prior to custodial interrogation and before waiver of *Miranda* rights.[59]

4. Trial/Hearing Procedures

In Re Winship
397 U.S. 358 (1970)

MR. JUSTICE BRENNAN delivered the opinion of the Court.

Constitutional questions decided by this Court concerning the juvenile process have centered on the adjudicatory stage at "which a determination is made as to whether a juvenile is a 'delinquent' as a result of alleged misconduct on his part, with the consequence that he may be committed to a state institution." *In re Gault,* 387 U.S. 1, 13 (1967). *Gault* decided that, although the Fourteenth Amendment does not require that the hearing at this stage conform with all the requirements of a criminal trial or even of the usual administrative proceeding, the Due Process Clause does require application during the adjudicatory hearing of "'the essentials of due process and fair treatment.'"... This case presents the single, narrow question whether proof beyond a reasonable doubt is among the "essentials of due process and fair treatment" required during the adjudicatory stage when a juvenile is charged with an act which would constitute a crime if committed by an adult.[1]

* * *

The requirement that guilt of a criminal charge be established by proof beyond a reasonable doubt dates at least from our early years as a Nation. The "demand for a higher degree of persuasion in criminal cases was recurrently expressed from ancient times, [though] its crystallization into the formula 'beyond a reasonable doubt' seems to have occurred as late as 1798...

* * *

We turn to the question whether juveniles, like adults, are constitutionally entitled to proof beyond a reasonable doubt when they are charged with violation of a criminal law. The same considerations that demand extreme caution in factfinding to protect the innocent adult apply as well to the innocent child....

* * *

We conclude, as we concluded regarding the essential due process safeguards applied in *Gault*, that the observance of the standard of proof beyond a reasonable doubt "will not compel the States to abandon or displace any of the substantive benefits of the juvenile process."....

Finally, we reject the Court of Appeals' suggestion that there is, in any event, only a "tenuous difference" between the reasonable-doubt and preponderance standards. The suggestion is singularly unpersuasive. In this very case, the trial judge's ability to distinguish between the two standards enabled him to make a finding of guilt that he conceded he might not have made under the standard of proof beyond a reasonable doubt. Indeed, the trial judge's action evidences the accuracy of the observation of commentators that "the preponderance test is susceptible to the misinterpretation that it calls on the trier of fact merely to perform an abstract weighing of the evidence in order to determine which side has produced the greater quantum, without regard to its effect in convincing his mind of the truth of the proposition asserted."...[6]

III

In sum, the constitutional safeguard of proof beyond a reasonable doubt is as much required during the adjudicatory stage of a delinquency proceeding as are those constitutional safeguards applied in *Gault*—notice of charges, right to counsel, the rights of confrontation and examination, and the privilege against self-incrimination. We therefore hold, in agreement with Chief Judge Fuld in dissent in the Court of Appeals, "that, where a 12-year-old child is charged with an act of stealing which renders him liable to confinement for as long as six years, then, as a matter of due process...the case against him must be proved beyond a reasonable doubt."...

Reversed.

* * *

[1] Thus, we do not see how it can be said in dissent that this opinion "rests entirely on the assumption that all juvenile proceedings are 'criminal prosecutions,' hence subject to constitutional limitations." As in *Gault*, "we are not here concerned with...the pre-judicial stages of the juvenile process, nor do we direct our attention to the post-adjudicative or dispositional process."...In New York, the adjudicatory stage of a delinquency proceeding is clearly distinct from both the preliminary phase of the juvenile process and from its dispositional stage....Similarly, we intimate no view concerning the constitutionality of the New York procedures governing children "in need of supervision."...Nor do we consider whether there are other "essentials of due process and fair treatment" required during the adjudicatory hearing of a delinquency proceeding. Finally, we have no occasion to consider appellant's argument that § 744 (b) is a violation of the Equal Protection Clause, as well as a denial of due process.

[6] Compare this Court's rejection of the preponderance standard in deportation proceedings, where we ruled that the Government must support its allegations with "clear, unequivocal and convincing evidence."... Although we ruled in *Woodby* that deportation is not tantamount to a criminal conviction, we found that since it could lead to "drastic deprivations," it is impermissible for a person to be "banished from this country upon no higher degree of proof than applies in a negligence case."....

MR. CHIEF JUSTICE BURGER, with whom **MR. JUSTICE STEWART** joins, dissenting.

The Court's opinion today rests entirely on the assumption that all juvenile proceedings are "criminal prosecutions," hence subject to constitutional limitations. This derives from earlier holdings, which, like today's holding, were steps eroding the differences between juvenile courts and traditional criminal courts. The original concept of the juvenile court system was to provide a benevolent and less formal means than criminal courts could provide for dealing with the special and often sensitive problems of youthful offenders. Since I see no constitutional requirement of due process sufficient to overcome the legislative judgment of the States in this area, I dissent from further strait-jacketing of an already overly restricted system. What the juvenile court system needs is not more but less of the trappings of legal procedure and judicial formalism;

the juvenile court system requires breathing room and flexibility in order to survive, if it can survive the repeated assaults from this Court.

Much of the judicial attitude manifested by the Court's opinion today and earlier holdings in this field is really a protest against inadequate juvenile court staffs and facilities; we "burn down the stable to get rid of the mice." The lack of support and the distressing growth of juvenile crime have combined to make for a literal breakdown in many if not most juvenile courts. Constitutional problems were not seen while those courts functioned in an atmosphere where juvenile judges were not crushed with an avalanche of cases.

My hope is that today's decision will not spell the end of a generously conceived program of compassionate treatment intended to mitigate the rigors and trauma of exposing youthful offenders to a traditional criminal court; each step we take turns the clock back to the pre-juvenile-court era. I cannot regard it as a manifestation of progress to transform juvenile courts into criminal courts, which is what we are well on the way to accomplishing. We can only hope the legislative response will not reflect our own by having these courts abolished.

* * *

Questions for Discussion

1. How would a genuinely "rehabilitative" court formulate the burden of proof? If the juvenile court remedy were actually beneficial to the child, *e.g.*, involved special schooling and elevated his prospects, would that make a preponderance test more appropriate? If a state could demonstrate that such kind paternalism were involved in an individual case, would the adult standard of *Winship* be excused? Should it be?

2. Civil proceedings which threaten one's livelihood, such as disbarment or the revocation of a license to do business, generally require "clear and convincing" evidence, which constitutes an intermediate burden of proof between New York's juvenile court preponderance test and proof beyond a reasonable doubt. Would such an intermediate step be preferable to replication of the adult standard?

3. Many jurisdictions have adopted a punitive approach to juvenile justice proceedings, including counting juvenile court "true findings" as "prior convictions" for harsh three-strike minimum penalties. Does such use require the adult standard of proof in juvenile court?

5. Jury Trial

McKeiver v. Pennsylvania
403 U.S. 528 (1971)

MR. JUSTICE BLACKMUN announced the judgments of the Court and an opinion in which THE CHIEF JUSTICE, MR. JUSTICE STEWART, and MR. JUSTICE WHITE join.

These cases present the narrow but precise issue whether the Due Process Clause of the Fourteenth Amendment assures the right to trial by jury in the adjudicative phase of a state juvenile court delinquency proceeding.

* * *

II
...[W]e turn to the facts of the present cases:

No. 322. Joseph McKeiver, then age 16, in May 1968 was charged with robbery, larceny, and receiving stolen goods (felonies under Pennsylvania law, Pa. Stat. Ann., Tit. 18, §§ 4704, 4807, and 4817 (1963)) as acts of juvenile delinquency. At the time of the adjudication hearing he was represented by counsel.[2] His request for a jury trial was denied....

* * *

It suffices to say that McKeiver's offense was his participating with 20 or 30 youths who pursued three young teenagers and took 25 cents from them; that McKeiver never before had been arrested and had a record of gainful employment; [and] that the testimony of two of the victims was described by the court as somewhat inconsistent and as "weak"....

No. 128. Barbara Burrus and approximately 45 other black children, ranging in age from 11 to 15 years,...were the subjects of juvenile court summonses issued in Hyde County, North Carolina, in January 1969.

The charges arose out of a series of demonstrations in the county in late 1968 by black adults and children protesting school assignments and a school consolidation plan. Petitions were filed by North Carolina state highway patrolmen. Except for one relating to James Lambert Howard, the petitions charged the respective juveniles with wilfully impeding traffic. The charge against Howard was that he wilfully made riotous noise and was disorderly in the O. A. Peay School in Swan Quarter; interrupted and disturbed the school during its regular sessions; and defaced school furniture. The acts so charged are misdemeanors under North Carolina law...

The several cases were consolidated into groups for hearing before District Judge Hallett S. Ward, sitting as a juvenile court. The same lawyer appeared for all the juveniles. Over counsel's objection, made in all except two of the cases, the general public was excluded. A request for a jury trial in each case was denied.

The evidence as to the juveniles other than Howard consisted solely of testimony of highway patrolmen. No juvenile took the stand or offered any witness. The testimony was to the effect that on various occasions the juveniles and adults were observed walking along Highway 64 singing, shouting, clapping, and playing basketball. As a result, there was interference with traffic. The marchers were asked to leave the paved portion of the highway and they were warned that they were committing a statutory offense. They either refused or left the roadway and immediately returned. The juveniles and participating adults were taken into custody. Juvenile petitions were then filed with respect to those under the age of 16.

The evidence as to Howard was that on the morning of December 5, he was in the office of the principal of the O.A. Peay School with 15 other persons while school was in session and was moving furniture around; that the office was in disarray; that as a result the school closed before noon; and that neither he nor any of the others was a student at the school or authorized to enter the principal's office.

...The court...placed each juvenile on probation for either one or two years conditioned upon his violating none of the State's laws, upon his reporting monthly to the County Department of Welfare, upon his being home by 11 p.m. each evening, and upon his attending a school approved by the Welfare Director. None of the juveniles has been confined on these charges.

* * *

IV
The right to an impartial jury "in all criminal prosecutions" under federal law is guaranteed by the Sixth Amendment. Through the Fourteenth Amendment that requirement has now been imposed upon the States "in all criminal cases which— were they to be tried in a federal court—would come within the Sixth Amendment's guarantee." This is because the Court has said it believes "that trial by jury in criminal cases is fundamental to the American scheme of justice."....

This, of course, does not automatically provide the answer to the present jury trial issue, if for no other reason than that the juvenile court proceeding has not yet been held to be a "criminal prosecution," within the meaning and reach of the Sixth Amendment, and also has not yet been regarded as devoid of criminal aspects merely because it usually has been given the civil label....

Little, indeed, is to be gained by any attempt simplistically to call the juvenile court proceeding either "civil" or "criminal." The Court carefully has avoided this wooden approach. Before *Gault* was decided in 1967, the Fifth Amendment's guarantee against self-incrimination had been imposed upon the state criminal trial....So, too, had the Sixth Amendment's rights of confrontation and cross-examination....Yet the Court did not automatically and peremptorily apply those rights to the juvenile proceeding. A reading of *Gault* reveals the opposite. And the same separate approach to the standard-of-proof issue is evident from the carefully separated application of the standard, first to the criminal trial, and then to the juvenile proceeding, displayed in *Winship*....

Thus, accepting "the proposition that the Due Process Clause has a role to play," *Gault*, 387 U.S., at 13, our task here with respect to trial by jury, as it was in *Gault* with respect to other claimed rights, "is to ascertain the precise impact of the due process requirement."....

V

The Pennsylvania juveniles' basic argument is that they were tried in proceedings "substantially similar to a criminal trial." They say that a delinquency proceeding in their State is initiated by a petition charging a penal code violation in the conclusory language of an indictment; that a juvenile detained prior to trial is held in a building substantially similar to an adult prison; that in Philadelphia juveniles over 16 are, in fact, held in the cells of a prison; that counsel and the prosecution engage in plea bargaining; that motions to suppress are routinely heard and decided; that the usual rules of evidence are applied; that the customary common-law defenses are available; that the press is generally admitted in the Philadelphia juvenile courtrooms; that members of the public enter the room; that arrest and prior record may be reported by the press (from police sources, however, rather than from the juvenile court records); that, once adjudged delinquent, a juvenile may be confined until his majority in what amounts to a prison..., describing the state correctional institution at Camp Hill as a "maximum security prison for adjudged delinquents and youthful criminal offenders"); and that the stigma attached upon delinquency adjudication approximates that resulting from conviction in an adult criminal proceeding.

The North Carolina juveniles particularly urge that the requirement of a jury trial would not operate to deny the supposed benefits of the juvenile court system; that the system's primary benefits are its discretionary intake procedure permitting disposition short of adjudication, and its flexible sentencing permitting emphasis on rehabilitation; that realization of these benefits does not depend upon dispensing with the jury; that adjudication of factual issues on the one hand and disposition of the case on the other are very different matters with very different purposes; that the purpose of the former is indistinguishable from that of the criminal trial; that the jury trial provides an independent protective factor; that experience has shown that jury trials in juvenile courts are manageable; that no reason exists why protection traditionally accorded in criminal proceedings should be denied young people subject to involuntary incarceration for lengthy periods; and that the juvenile courts deserve healthy public scrutiny.

VI

* * *

Despite all these disappointments, all these failures, and all these shortcomings, we conclude that trial by jury in the juvenile court's adjudicative stage is not a constitutional requirement....

* * *

...There is a possibility, at least, that the jury trial, if required as a matter of constitutional precept, will remake the juvenile proceeding into a fully adversary process and will put an effective end to what has been the idealistic prospect of an intimate, informal protective proceeding.

* * *

...The Court specifically has recognized by dictum that a jury is not a necessary part even of every criminal process that is fair and equitable....

...The imposition of the jury trial on the juvenile court system would not strengthen greatly, if at all, the factfinding function, and would, contrarily, provide an attrition of the juvenile court's assumed ability to function in a unique manner. It would not remedy the defects of the system....

* * *

...There is, of course, nothing to prevent a juvenile court judge, in a particular case where he feels the need, or when the need is demonstrated, from using an advisory jury.

* * *

...Since *Gault* and since *Duncan* the great majority of States, in addition to Pennsylvania and North Carolina, that have faced the issue have concluded that the considerations that led to the result in those two cases do not compel trial by jury in the juvenile court....

* * *

...If the jury trial were to be injected into the juvenile court system as a matter of right, it would bring with it into that system the traditional delay, the formality, and the clamor of the adversary system and, possibly, the public trial....

...Finally, the arguments advanced by the juveniles here are, of course, the identical arguments that underlie the demand for the jury trial for criminal proceedings. The arguments necessarily equate the juvenile proceeding—or at least the adjudicative phase of it—with the criminal trial. Whether they should be so equated is our issue. Concern about the inapplicability of exclusionary and other rules of evidence, about the juvenile court judge's possible awareness of the juvenile's prior record and of the contents of the social file; about repeated appearances of the same familiar witnesses in the persons of juvenile and probation officers and social workers—all to the effect that this will create the likelihood of pre-judgment—chooses to ignore, it seems to us, every aspect of fairness, of concern, of sympathy, and of paternal attention that the juvenile court system contemplates.

If the formalities of the criminal adjudicative process are to be superimposed upon the juvenile court system, there is little need for its separate existence. Perhaps that ultimate disillusionment will come one day, but for the moment we are disinclined to give impetus to it.

Affirmed.

[2] At McKeiver's hearing his counsel advised the court that he had never seen McKeiver before and "was just in the middle of interviewing" him. The court allowed him five minutes for the interview. Counsel's office, Community Legal Services, however, had been appointed to represent McKeiver five months earlier....

* * *

MR. JUSTICE BRENNAN, concurring in the judgment in No. 322 and dissenting in No. 128.

I agree with the plurality opinion's conclusion that the proceedings below in these cases were not "criminal prosecutions" within the meaning of the Sixth Amendment. For me, therefore, the question in these cases is whether jury trial is among the "essentials of due process and fair treatment," *In re Gault*, 387 U.S. 1, 30 (1967), required during the adjudication of a charge of delinquency based upon acts that would constitute a crime if engaged in by an adult.... The Due Process Clause commands, not a particular procedure, but only a result: in my Brother BLACKMUN'S words, "fundamental fairness . . . [in] factfinding." In the context of these and similar juvenile delinquency proceedings, what this means is that the States are not bound to provide jury trials on demand so long as some other aspect of the process adequately protects the interests that Sixth Amendment jury trials are intended to serve.

In my view, therefore, the due process question cannot be decided upon the basis of general characteristics of juvenile proceedings, but only in terms of the adequacy of a particular state procedure to "protect the [juvenile] from oppression by the Government,"... and to protect him against "the compliant, biased, or eccentric judge." ...

Examined in this light, I find no defect in the Pennsylvania cases before us. The availability of trial by jury allows an accused to protect himself against possible oppression by what is in essence an appeal to the community conscience, as embodied in the jury that hears his case. To some extent, however, a similar protection may be obtained when an accused may in essence appeal to the community at large, by focusing public attention upon the facts of his trial, exposing improper judicial behavior to public view, and obtaining, if necessary, executive redress through the medium of public indignation. Of course, the Constitution, in the context of adult criminal trials, has rejected the notion that public trial is an adequate substitute for trial by jury in serious cases. But in the context of juvenile delinquency proceedings, I cannot say that it is beyond the competence of a State to conclude that juveniles who fear that delinquency proceedings will mask judicial oppression may obtain adequate protection by focusing community attention upon the trial of their cases. For, however much the juvenile system may have failed in practice, its very existence as an ostensibly beneficent and noncriminal process for the care and guidance of young persons demonstrates the existence of the community's sympathy and concern for the young. Juveniles able to bring the community's attention to bear upon their trials may therefore draw upon a reservoir of public concern unavailable to the adult criminal defendant.

* * *

MR. JUSTICE DOUGLAS, with whom **MR. JUSTICE BLACK** and **MR. JUSTICE MARSHALL** concur, dissenting.

These cases from Pennsylvania and North Carolina present the issue of the right to a jury trial for offenders charged in juvenile court and facing a possible incarceration until they reach their majority. I believe the guarantees of the Bill of Rights, made applicable to the States by the Fourteenth Amendment, require a jury trial.

In the Pennsylvania cases one of the appellants was charged with robbery..., larceny..., and receiving stolen goods...as acts of juvenile delinquency....He was found a delinquent and placed on probation. The other appellant was charged with assault and battery on a police officer...and conspiracy...as acts of juvenile delinquency. On a finding of delinquency he was committed to a youth center. Despite the fact that the two appellants, aged 15 and 16, would face potential incarceration until their majority,... they were denied a jury trial.

In the North Carolina cases petitioners are students, from 11 to 15 years of age, who were charged under one of three criminal statutes: (1) "disorderly conduct" in a public building,...(2) "wilful" interruption or disturbance of a public or private school,... or (3) obstructing the flow of traffic on a highway or street,...

Conviction of each of these crimes would subject a person, whether juvenile or adult, to imprisonment in a state institution. In the case of these students the possible term was six to 10 years; it would be computed for the period until an individual reached the age of 21. Each asked for a jury trial which was denied. The trial judge stated that the hearings were juvenile hearings, not criminal trials. But the issue in each case was whether they had violated a state criminal law....

* * *

...[T]he child, the same as the adult, is in the category of those described in the Magna Carta:

"No freeman may be...imprisoned. except by the lawful judgment of his peers, or by the law of the land."

These cases should be remanded for trial by jury on the criminal charges filed against these youngsters.

* * *

Questions for Discussion

1. Assuming confidentiality is important to juvenile rehabilitation goals, how much of a threat to it does a jury pose? Can juries be relied upon to maintain matters in confidence? Grand jury proceedings are universally secret, with large

numbers of citizens serving on them; have those jurors commonly disclosed on-going proceedings?

2. Is the existence of a jury "audience" a possible disadvantage in its encouragement of "performing" and appeals to emotion, as opposed to a parent-like judge?

3. If adult due process includes a jury to help determine the truth (what happened), is factual accuracy for an accused youth any less important? Is it fair to require a jury in a disturbing-the-peace case against a 22-year-old with maximum jeopardy of ten days, but deny it for a child facing 6 to 15 years in custody (as with the juveniles before the *McKeiver* Court)?

4. Where a young adult is convicted of a crime, can juvenile court non-jury "convictions" be used as prior strikes in applying a three-strike adult minimum sentence—which in some states requires a 25-year minimum prison term? *See, e.g., People v. Nguyen*, 46 Cal.4th 1007 (2009), holding that such priors while a juvenile may constitutionally count under California's "three strikes law" to substantially enhance an adult sentence. The Court in *Nguyen* cited the fact that the now-adult defendant in the subsequent prosecution is allowed jury consideration of whether or not he "suffered" a juvenile conviction. How does a jury right limited to verification of a prior conviction—one that did not itself allow a jury decision—pass muster? How does it satisfy the U.S. Supreme Court's post-*McKeiver* decision of *Apprendi v. New Jersey*, 530 U.S.466 (2000), finding that "any fact" crucial to the maximum punishment for a later offense must be subject to a jury trial requirement?

5. The Constitution explicitly guarantees right of trial by jury in criminal matters. If *Gault* acknowledged modern juvenile proceedings as criminal in nature, including involuntary custody as a common outcome, is *McKeiver* consistent?

6. The Court acknowledges that juveniles are persons under the Constitution. How can the *Gault* Court constitutionally require publicly-provided counsel (and other features of adult criminal court) not mentioned in the Constitution, but deprive accused juveniles of the one guarantee that is specifically enumerated?

7. Given the fact that the constitutional guarantee does not specify "twelve jurors," could states preserve juvenile court efficiency by authorizing nine-person, six-person, or even three-person juries? Do we balance such efficiency in applying jury requirements in adult proceedings?

8. The Court relied substantially on a task force report on juries. Was that report litigated or subject to cross examination? Is the Court the ideal forum to weigh such public policy evidence?

9. Justice Brennan raises a concern about the ability to curb judicial excess or abuse. In thirteen states, juvenile proceedings are presumptively closed to the press and public.[60] If the public is denied access, and juries are not required, by what mechanism can the community ensure a check on judicial power? Are these proceedings, transpiring outside of public view, ripe for judicial abuses such as those revealed in the "Kids for Cash" scandal in Pennsylvania, where two juvenile court judges sentenced low-level offenders to incarceration in a private placement facility that provided kickbacks to the judges?[61]

6. Sentencing

Roper v. Simmons
543 U.S. 551 (2005)

JUSTICE KENNEDY delivered the opinion of the Court.

This case requires us to address, for the second time in a decade and a half, whether it is permissible under the Eighth and Fourteenth Amendments to the Constitution of the United States to execute a juvenile offender who was older than 15 but younger than 18 when he committed a capital crime. In *Stanford v. Kentucky*, 492 U.S. 361 (1989), a divided Court rejected the proposition that the Constitution bars capital punishment for juvenile offenders in this age group. We reconsider the question.

I

At the age of 17, when he was still a junior in high school, Christopher Simmons, the respondent here, committed murder. About nine months later, after he had turned 18, he was tried and sentenced to death....

* * *

...As aggravating factors, the State submitted that the murder was committed for the purpose of receiving money; was committed for the purpose of avoiding, interfering with, or preventing lawful arrest of the defendant; and involved depravity of mind and was outrageously and wantonly vile, horrible, and inhuman. The State called Shirley Crook's husband, daughter, and two sisters, who presented moving evidence of the devastation her death had brought to their lives.

In mitigation, Simmons' attorneys first called an officer of the Missouri juvenile justice system, who testified that Simmons had no prior convictions and that no previous charges had been filed against him. Simmons' mother, father, two younger half brothers, a neighbor, and a friend took the stand to tell the jurors of the close relationships they had formed with Simmons and to plead for mercy on his behalf. Simmons' mother, in particular, testified to the responsibility Simmons demonstrated in taking care of his two younger half brothers and of his grandmother and to his capacity to show love for them.

During closing arguments, both the prosecutor and defense counsel addressed Simmons' age, which the trial judge had instructed the jurors they could consider as a mitigating factor. Defense counsel reminded the jurors that juveniles of Simmons' age cannot drink, serve on juries, or even see certain movies, because "the legislatures have wisely decided that individuals of a certain age aren't responsible enough." Defense counsel argued that Simmons' age should make "a huge difference to [the jurors] in deciding just exactly what sort of punishment to make." In rebuttal, the prosecutor gave the following response: "Age, he says. Think about age. Seventeen years old. Isn't that scary? Doesn't that scare you? Mitigating? Quite the contrary I submit. Quite the contrary."

The jury recommended the death penalty after finding the State had proved each of the three aggravating factors submitted to it. Accepting the jury's recommendation, the trial judge imposed the death penalty.

* * *

After these proceedings in Simmons' case had run their course, this Court held that the Eighth and Fourteenth Amendments prohibit the execution of a mentally retarded person. *Atkins v. Virginia*, 536 U.S. 304 (2002). Simmons filed a new petition for state postconviction relief, arguing that the reasoning of *Atkins* established that the Constitution prohibits the execution of a juvenile who was under 18 when the crime was committed.

* * *

II

The Eighth Amendment provides: "Excessive bail shall not be required, nor excessive fines imposed, nor cruel and unusual punishments inflicted." The provision is applicable to the States through the Fourteenth Amendment....

The prohibition against "cruel and unusual punishments," like other expansive language in the Constitution, must be interpreted according to its text, by considering history, tradition, and precedent, and with due regard for its purpose and function in the constitutional design. To implement this framework we have established the propriety and affirmed the necessity of referring to "the evolving standards of decency that mark the progress of a maturing society" to determine which punishments are so disproportionate as to be cruel and unusual....

In *Thompson v. Oklahoma*, 487 U.S. 815, (1988), a plurality of the Court determined that our standards of decency do not permit the execution of any offender under the age of 16 at the time of the crime....The plurality also observed that "[t]he conclusion that it would offend civilized standards of decency to execute a person who was less than 16 years old at the time of his or her offense is consistent with the views that have been expressed by respected professional organizations, by other nations that share our Anglo-American heritage, and by the leading members of the Western European community."...The opinion further noted that juries imposed the death penalty on offenders under 16 with exceeding rarity; the last execution of an offender for a crime committed under the age of 16 had been carried out in 1948, 40 years prior....

* * *

The next year, in *Stanford v. Kentucky*, 492 U.S. 361 (1989), the Court, over a dissenting opinion joined by four Justices, referred to contemporary standards of decency in this country and concluded the Eighth and Fourteenth Amendments did not proscribe the execution of juvenile offenders over 15 but under 18. The Court noted that 22 of the 37 death penalty States permitted the death penalty for 16-year-old offenders, and, among these 37 States, 25 permitted it for 17-year-old offenders. These numbers, in the Court's view, indicated there was no national consensus "sufficient to label a particular punishment cruel and unusual."...A plurality of the Court also "emphatically reject[ed]" the suggestion that the Court should bring its own judgment to bear on the acceptability of the juvenile death penalty....

* * *

III

A

The evidence of national consensus against the death penalty for juveniles is similar, and in some respects parallel, to the evidence *Atkins* held sufficient to demonstrate a national consensus against the death penalty for the mentally retarded. When *Atkins* was decided, 30 States prohibited the death penalty for the mentally retarded. This number comprised 12 that had abandoned the death penalty altogether, and 18 that maintained it but excluded the mentally retarded from its reach....By a similar calculation in this case, 30 States prohibit the juvenile death penalty, comprising 12 that have rejected the death penalty altogether and 18 that maintain it but, by express provision or judicial interpretation, exclude juveniles from its reach....*Atkins* emphasized that even in the 20 States without formal prohibition, the practice of executing the mentally retarded was infrequent. Since *Penry*, only five States had executed offenders known to have an IQ under 70....In the present case, too, even in the 20 States without a formal prohibition on executing juveniles, the practice is infrequent. Since *Stanford*, six States have executed prisoners for crimes committed as juveniles. In the past 10 years, only three have done so: Oklahoma, Texas, and Virginia....In December 2003 the Governor of Kentucky decided to spare the life of Kevin Stanford, and commuted his sentence to one of life imprisonment without parole, with the declaration that "'[w]e ought not be executing people who, legally, were children.'"...By this act the Governor ensured Kentucky would not add itself to the list of States that have executed juveniles within the last 10 years even by the execution of the very defendant whose death sentence the Court had upheld in *Stanford v. Kentucky*.

There is, to be sure, at least one difference between the evidence of consensus in *Atkins* and in this case. Impressive in *Atkins* was the rate of abolition of the death penalty for the mentally retarded. Sixteen States that permitted the execution of the mentally retarded at the time of *Penry* had prohibited the practice by the time we heard *Atkins*. By contrast, the rate of change in reducing the incidence of the juvenile death penalty, or in taking specific steps to abolish it, has been slower. Five States that allowed the juvenile death penalty at the time of *Stanford* have abandoned it in the intervening 15 years—four through legislative enactments and one through judicial decision....

Though less dramatic than the change from *Penry* to *Atkins*...we still consider the change from *Stanford* to this case to be significant. As noted in *Atkins* with respect to the States that had abandoned the death penalty for the mentally retarded since *Penry*, "[i]t is not so much the number of these States that is significant, but the consistency of the direction of change."...

* * *

As in *Atkins*, the objective indicia of consensus in this case—the rejection of the juvenile death penalty in the majority of States; the infrequency of its use even where it remains on the books; and the consistency in the trend toward abolition of the practice—provide sufficient evidence that today our society views juveniles, in the words *Atkins* used respecting the mentally retarded, as "categorically less culpable than the average criminal."...

* * *

Three general differences between juveniles under 18 and adults demonstrate that juvenile offenders cannot with reliability be classified among the worst offenders. First, as any parent knows and as the scientific and sociological studies respondent and his amici cite tend to confirm, "[a] lack of maturity and an underdeveloped sense of responsibility are found in youth more often than in adults and are more understandable among the young. These qualities often result in impetuous and ill-considered actions and decisions."...

The second area of difference is that juveniles are more vulnerable or susceptible to negative influences and outside pressures, including peer pressure....

The third broad difference is that the character of a juvenile is not as well formed as that of an adult. The personality traits of juveniles are more transitory, less fixed...

These differences render suspect any conclusion that a juvenile falls among the worst offenders. The susceptibility of juveniles to immature and irresponsible behavior means "their irresponsible conduct is not as morally reprehensible as that of an adult."...Their own vulnerability and comparative lack of control over their immediate surroundings mean juveniles have a greater claim than adults to be forgiven for failing to escape negative influences in their whole environment....The reality that juveniles still struggle to define their identity means it is less supportable to conclude that even a heinous crime committed by a juvenile is evidence of irretrievably depraved character. From a moral standpoint it would be misguided to equate the failings of a minor with those of an adult, for a greater possibility exists that a minor's character deficiencies will be reformed. Indeed, "[t]he relevance of youth as a mitigating factor derives from the fact that the signature qualities of youth are transient; as individuals mature, the impetuousness and recklessness that may dominate in younger years can subside."... (...Only a relatively small proportion of adolescents who experiment in risky or illegal activities develop entrenched patterns of problem behavior that persist into adulthood").

In *Thompson*, a plurality of the Court recognized the import of these characteristics with respect to juveniles under 16, and relied on them to hold that the Eighth Amendment prohibited the imposition of the death penalty on juveniles below that age....We conclude the same reasoning applies to all juvenile offenders under 18.

Once the diminished culpability of juveniles is recognized, it is evident that the penological justifications for the death penalty apply to them with lesser force than to adults. We have held there are two distinct social purposes served by the death penalty: "'retribution and deterrence of capital crimes by prospective offenders.'"...Retribution is not proportional if the law's most severe penalty is imposed on one whose culpability or blameworthiness is diminished, to a substantial degree, by reason of youth and immaturity.

As for deterrence, it is unclear whether the death penalty has a significant or even measurable deterrent effect on juveniles, as counsel for the petitioner acknowledged at oral argument....

* * *

...[Petitioners] assert that even assuming the truth of the observations we have made about juveniles' diminished culpability in general, jurors nonetheless should be allowed to consider mitigating arguments related to youth on a case-by-case basis, and in some cases to impose the death penalty if justified. A central feature of death penalty sentencing is a particular assessment of the circumstances of the crime and the characteristics of the offender. The system is designed to consider both aggravating and mitigating circumstances, including youth, in every case. Given this Court's own insistence on individualized consideration, petitioner maintains that it is both arbitrary and unnecessary to adopt a categorical rule barring imposition of the death penalty on any offender under 18 years of age.

We disagree. The differences between juvenile and adult offenders are too marked and well understood to risk allowing a youthful person to receive the death penalty despite insufficient culpability. An unacceptable likelihood exists that the brutality or cold-blooded nature of any particular crime would overpower mitigating arguments based on youth as a matter of course, even where the juvenile offender's objective immaturity, vulnerability, and lack of true depravity should require a sentence less severe than death. In some cases a defendant's youth may even be counted against him. In this very case, as we noted above, the prosecutor argued Simmons' youth was aggravating rather than mitigating....While this sort of overreaching could be corrected by a particular rule to ensure that the mitigating force of youth is not overlooked, that would not address our larger concerns.

It is difficult even for expert psychologists to differentiate between the juvenile offender whose crime reflects unfortunate yet transient immaturity, and the rare juvenile offender whose crime reflects irreparable corruption....

* * *

Our determination that the death penalty is disproportionate punishment for offenders under 18 finds confirmation in the stark reality that the United States is the only country in the world that continues to give official sanction to the juvenile death penalty. This reality does not become controlling, for the task of interpreting the Eighth Amendment remains our responsibility. Yet at least from the time of the Court's decision in *Trop*, the Court has referred to the laws of other countries and to international authorities as instructive for its interpretation of the Eighth Amendment's prohibition of "cruel and unusual punishments."

As respondent and a number of amici emphasize, Article 37 of the United Nations Convention on the Rights of the Child, which every country in the world has ratified save for the United States and Somalia, contains an express prohibition on capital punishment for crimes committed by juveniles under 18....

Respondent and his *amici* have submitted, and petitioner does not contest, that only seven countries other than the United States have executed juvenile offenders since 1990: Iran, Pakistan, Saudi Arabia, Yemen, Nigeria, the Democratic Republic of Congo, and China. Since then each of these countries has either abolished capital punishment for juveniles or made public disavowal of the practice. In sum, it is fair to say that the United States now stands alone in a world that has turned its face against the juvenile death penalty.

* * *

...The Eighth and Fourteenth Amendments forbid imposition of the death penalty on offenders who were under the age of 18 when their crimes were committed. The judgment of the Missouri Supreme Court setting aside the sentence of death imposed upon Christopher Simmons is affirmed.

JUSTICE SCALIA with whom THE CHIEF JUSTICE and JUSTICE THOMAS join, dissenting.

...What a mockery today's opinion makes of [Alexander] Hamilton's expectation, announcing the Court's conclusion that the meaning of our Constitution has changed over the past 15 years—not, mind you, that this Court's decision 15 years ago was wrong, but that the Constitution *has changed*. The Court reaches this implausible result by purporting to advert, not to the original meaning of the Eighth Amendment, but to "the evolving standards of decency,"...of our national society. It then finds, on the flimsiest of grounds, that a national consensus which could not be perceived in our people's laws barely 15 years ago now solidly exists. Worse still, the Court says in so many words that what our people's laws say about the issue does not, in the last analysis, matter: "[I]n the end our own judgment will be brought to bear on the question of the acceptability of the death penalty under the Eighth Amendment."...The Court thus proclaims itself sole arbiter of our Nation's moral standards—and in the course of discharging that awesome responsibility purports to take guidance from the views of foreign courts and legislatures. Because I do not believe that the meaning of our Eighth Amendment, any more than the meaning of other provisions of our Constitution, should be determined by the subjective views of five Members of this Court and like-minded foreigners, I dissent.

I

...Words have no meaning if the views of less than 50% of death penalty States can constitute a national consensus....Our previous cases have required overwhelming opposition to a challenged practice, generally over a long period of time....[W]e invalidated capital punishment imposed for participation in a robbery in which an accomplice committed murder, because 78% of all death penalty States prohibited this punishment....

* * *

Relying on...narrow margins is especially inappropriate in light of the fact that a number of legislatures and voters have expressly affirmed their support for capital punishment of 16- and 17-year-old offenders since *Stanford*. Though the Court is correct that no State has lowered its death penalty age, both the Missouri and Virginia Legislatures—which, at the time of *Stanford*, had no minimum age requirement—expressly established 16 as the minimum....The people of Arizona...and Florida...have done the same by ballot initiative. Thus, even States that have not executed an under-18 offender in recent years unquestionably favor the possibility of capital punishment in some circumstances.

The Court's reliance on the infrequency of executions, for under-18 murderers,... credits an argument that this Court considered and explicitly rejected in *Stanford*. That infrequency is explained, we accurately said, both by "the undisputed fact that a far smaller percentage of capital crimes are committed by persons under 18 than over 18,"...and by the fact that juries are required at sentencing to consider the offender's youth as a mitigating factor. Thus, "it is not only possible, but overwhelmingly probable, that the very considerations which induce [respondent] and [his] supporters to believe that death should be imposed on offenders under 18 cause prosecutors and juries to believe that it should *rarely* be imposed."...

It is, furthermore, unclear that executions of the relevant age group have decreased since we decided *Stanford*. Between 1990 and 2003, 123 of 3,599 death sentences, or 3.4%, were given to individuals who committed crimes before reaching age 18.... Thus, the numbers of under-18 offenders subjected to the death penalty, though low compared with adults, have either held steady or slightly increased since *Stanford*. These statistics in no way support the action the Court takes today.

* * *

Today's opinion provides a perfect example of why judges are ill equipped to make the type of legislative judgments the Court insists on making here. To support its opinion that States should be prohibited from imposing the death penalty on anyone who committed murder before age 18, the Court looks to scientific and sociological studies, picking and choosing those that support its position. It never explains why those particular studies are methodologically sound; none was ever entered into evidence or tested in an adversarial proceeding....

* * *

Even putting aside questions of methodology, the studies cited by the Court offer scant support for a categorical prohibition of the death penalty for murderers under 18. At most, these studies conclude that, *on average or in most cases* persons under 18 are unable to take moral responsibility for their actions. Not one of the cited studies opines that all individuals under 18 are unable to appreciate the nature of their crimes.

Moreover, the cited studies describe only adolescents who engage in risky or antisocial behavior, as many young people do. Murder, however, is more than just risky or antisocial behavior. It is entirely consistent to believe that young people often act impetuously and lack judgment, but, at the same time, to believe that those who commit premeditated murder are—at least sometimes—just as culpable as adults. Christopher Simmons, who was only seven months shy of his 18th birthday when he murdered Shirley Crook, described to his friends *beforehand*—"[i]n chilling, callous terms," as the Court puts it,...the murder he planned to commit. He then broke into the home of an innocent woman, bound her with duct tape and electrical wire, and threw her off a bridge alive and conscious....

* * *

That "almost every State prohibits those under 18 years of age from voting, serving on juries, or marrying without parental consent,"...is patently irrelevant—and is yet another resurrection of an argument that this Court gave a decent burial in *Stanford* (What kind of Equal Justice under Law is it that—without so much as a "Sorry about that"—gives as the basis for sparing one person from execution arguments *explicitly rejected* in refusing to spare another?) As we explained in *Stanford*,...it is "absurd to think that one must be mature enough to drive carefully, to drink responsibly, or to vote intelligently, in order to be mature enough to understand that murdering another human being is profoundly wrong, and to conform one's conduct to that most minimal of all civilized standards." Serving on a jury or entering into marriage also involve decisions far more sophisticated than the simple decision not to take another's life.

Moreover, the age statutes the Court lists "set the appropriate ages for the operation of a system that makes its determinations in gross, and that does not conduct individualized maturity tests." *Ibid.* The criminal justice system, by contrast, provides for individualized consideration of each defendant....

* * *

The Court's contention that the goals of retribution and deterrence are not served by executing murderers under 18 is also transparently false. The argument that "[r]etribution is not proportional if the law's most severe penalty is imposed on one whose culpability or blameworthiness is diminished,"...is simply an extension of the earlier, false generalization that youth always defeats culpability. The Court claims that "juveniles will be less susceptible to deterrence,"...because "'[t]he likelihood that the teenage offender has made the kind of cost-benefit analysis that attaches any weight to the possibility of execution is so remote as to be virtually nonexistent'"....The Court unsurprisingly finds no support for this astounding proposition, save its own case law. The facts of this very case show the proposition to be false. Before committing the crime, Simmons encouraged his friends to join him by assuring them that they could "get away with it" because they were minors....

* * *

Though the views of our own citizens are essentially irrelevant to the Court's decision today, the views of other countries and the so-called international community take center stage.

* * *

...[I]n addition to barring the execution of under-18 offenders, the United Nations Convention on the Rights of the Child prohibits punishing them with life in prison without the possibility of release. If we are truly going to get in line with the international community, then the Court's reassurance that the death penalty is really not needed, since "the punishment of life imprisonment without the possibility of parole is itself a severe sanction,"...gives little comfort.

It is interesting that whereas the Court is not content to accept what the States of our Federal Union say, but insists on inquiring into what they do (specifically, whether they in fact apply the juvenile death penalty that their laws allow), the Court is quite willing to believe that every foreign nation—of whatever tyrannical political makeup and with however subservient or incompetent a court system—in fact adheres to a rule of no death penalty for offenders under 18. Nor does the Court inquire into how many of the countries that have the death penalty, but have forsworn (on paper at least) imposing that penalty on offenders under 18, have what no State of this country can constitutionally have: a mandatory death penalty for certain crimes, with no possibility of mitigation by the sentencing authority, for youth or any other reason. I suspect it is most of them....

More fundamentally, however, the basic premise of the Court's argument—that American law should conform to the laws of the rest of the world—ought to be rejected out of hand. In fact the Court itself does not believe it. In many significant respects the laws of most other countries differ from our law—including not only such explicit provisions of our Constitution as the right to jury trial and grand jury indictment, but even many interpretations of the Constitution prescribed by this Court itself. The Court-pronounced exclusionary rule, for example, is distinctively American...

* * *

And let us not forget the Court's abortion jurisprudence, which makes us one of only six countries that allow abortion on demand until the point of viability....

* * *

The Court should either profess its willingness to reconsider all these matters in light of the views of foreigners, or else it should cease putting forth foreigners' views as part of the *reasoned basis* of its decisions. To invoke alien law when it agrees with one's own thinking, and ignore it otherwise, is not reasoned decisionmaking, but sophistry....

The Court responds that "[i]t does not lessen our fidelity to the Constitution or our pride in its origins to acknowledge that the express affirmation of certain fundamental rights by other nations and peoples simply underscores the centrality of those same rights within our own heritage of freedom."...To begin with, I do not believe that approval by "other nations and peoples" should buttress our commitment to American principles any more than (what should logically follow) disapproval by "other nations and peoples" should weaken that commitment. More importantly, however, the Court's statement flatly misdescribes what is going on here. Foreign sources are cited today, *not* to underscore our "fidelity" to the Constitution, our "pride in its origins," and "our own [American] heritage." To the contrary, they are cited *to set aside* the centuries-old American practice—a practice still engaged in by a large majority of the relevant States—of letting a jury of 12 citizens decide whether, in the particular case, youth should be the basis for withholding the death penalty....

* * *

However sound philosophically, this is no way to run a legal system. We must disregard the new reality that, to the extent our Eighth Amendment decisions constitute something more than a show of hands on the current Justices' current personal views about penology, they purport to be nothing more than a snapshot of American public opinion at a particular point in time (with the timeframes now shortened to a mere 15 years). We must treat these decisions just as though they represented *real* law, *real* prescriptions democratically adopted by the American people, as conclusively (rather than sequentially) construed by this Court. Allowing lower courts to reinterpret the Eighth Amendment whenever they decide enough time has passed for a new snapshot leaves this Court's decisions without any force—especially since the "evolution" of our Eighth Amendment is no longer determined by objective criteria....

Questions for Discussion

1. The majority argues that a bright line of age is used to limit the rights of children to vote, drive, drink, or otherwise enjoy adult privileges—all because of

the generalized judgment of immaturity. The dissent counters that these policies are in gross, but that criminal trials are already individualized—and that a jury can consider precisely all appropriate factors (including immaturity) in assigning blame. But the majority cites the prosecutor's statement that the defendant's age is an *aggravating* factor militating toward the death penalty as an example of the inconsistency and danger of the individualized approach. If such a comment violates the "mitigation" that the dissent acknowledges should be considered based on youth, why could *Roper* not be reversed on that narrow basis (improper prosecutorial argument)? What is the response to the argument that the major problem is solved if state legislatures must agree to the sanction, and juries may impose it only where *admissible* factors so warrant?

2. In general, a contract cannot be enforced against a child because of the bright line judgment of immaturity (see Chapter 12). Further, litigation to enforce a contract may be individualized and enforced in a particular case. Why is adequate maturity for contract execution not subject to individual determination? Would it not be possible to arrange individual exceptions to the bright line judgement that children cannot vote or drive? Aren't driving tests individualized? Are not juries selected by individual *voir dire* and examination? Is Scalia's distinction that these tasks are far more complex than the "decision not to take another's life" convincing? Is the decision to execute a youth—evaluating maturity and capacity—not complex? Is it less complex than deciding whether a 16-year-old should be allowed to marry— which in many states is forbidden without parental permission?

3. Does the majority know whether the death penalty has a deterrent impact on youth? Although the statement of the defendant that nothing would happen to him because of his youth may not be dispositive, what is the evidence of deterrent impact? Is the Court the optimum forum to make such judgments, or is Scalia right that the legislature should do so—considering a broad array of evidence—and not centered on a specific fact situation?

4. How many state legislatures must act before the Court finds a practice "unusual" within the meaning of the Eighth Amendment? Is it the number of legislatures that allow it? Is it the incidence of actual executions? Does it matter if the legislatures maintaining the death penalty represent relatively small populations? Does it matter if their legislative processes take time and condemned youth tend not to be a powerful political group forcing decision? If the Court must wait until virtually all state legislatures act to bar capital punishment, what is the relevance of the Court? Is it to act only when a few stragglers remain due to dilatory proceedings or inattention?

5. Is the "cruel and unusual" standard of the Eighth Amendment disjunctive, so both must occur for a violation? Scalia, both in the *Roper* dissent and in his *Stanford* majority opinion, argues that "rare" does not mean "unusual." He argues that not many children are arrested for capital crimes and that the circumstances

warranting a death penalty are "rare." The implication is that when the prerequisites exist for such an outcome its imposition would then not be "unusual." But aside from the circularity of such a definition, is not capital punishment empirically "rare"—even among the population of youth convicted for capital crimes? Why is such rarity not "unusual"? If concededly "unusual," would the dissent be more effectively framed as not "cruel"?

6. The dissent cites precedent holding the execution of one who committed crimes at under 16 as violative of the Eighth Amendment. Why does its reasoning about the skill of juries to make individualized decisions without arbitrary lines based on "averages" not apply to this age, or to earlier ages?

7. The dissent discounts the scientific evidence as untested by the adversary process, ambiguous, and producing generalized findings for which there are exceptions (appropriate for jury delineation). But what of the substantial evidence offered in *Roper* of brain and development change through the teen years—and cited by the majority? Do not these chemical and brain development stages apply to virtually every human as he or she grows and enters adolescence? If that evidence is weak, is not the state or its amici well-equipped to counter such findings with contrary studies or to otherwise impeach it?

8. Is Justice Scalia correct in his opening that the majority opinion purports to "change" the Constitution itself? Castration was an accepted mode of punishment in 1787 (and recommended by Jefferson) and is not prohibited explicitly by the Constitution—is it permissible? Should it be left to state decision and individual cases? What of torture? Is it explicitly mentioned in the Eighth Amendment?

9. Are the views of the rest of the world irrelevant to the "evolving standards" at issue? Is the strong world consensus against child capital punishment credibly dismissed as simply "the subjective views of five Members of the Court and like-minded foreigners," as the dissent writes?

10. The dissent mentions life without the possibility of parole as also an uncommon sanction for the criminal acts of children internationally. In fact, almost all of the defendants in the world so incarcerated based on crimes committed while children are in the United States. Does a term of what may be 60 or more years also conflict with the medical evidence presented in *Roper*? If there are documented stages of hormonal and brain development affecting persons through the teen years, is it not "cruel and unusual" to interpose a lifetime of incarceration, including fifty or more years after the body chemistry of adolescence has passed? Is such a policy consistent with the rehabilitation goals of juvenile justice? Is such a permanent judgment appropriate for the acts of a 15-year-old? For a 12-year-old?

Note on Life Without the Possibility of Parole (LWOP)

In 2010, the U.S. Supreme Court followed *Roper* with *Graham v. Florida*, 560 U.S. 48. The *Graham* decision did not fully answer Question for Discussion No. 10 above, but drew a limited line prohibiting Life without the Possibility of Parole (LWOP) for offenses of a juvenile less than homicide. The Court's 6–3 decision (written by Justice Kennedy) explicitly applies to all non-homicide cases in which the defendant was under the age of 18 at the time of the crime. The stated rationale for the Court's holding includes: (a) the LWOP sentence for juveniles is relatively rare in practice, (b) penological theory does not justify such a harsh sentence given the more limited culpability of the offender (an immature juvenile with ongoing brain development as discussed in *Roper*), (c) the more limited culpability where there is no intent to kill, and (d) the severity of the penalty is enhanced for juveniles who spend a longer time incarcerated because their sentences begin at an earlier age. The Court holds that the state is not required to guarantee eventual freedom for the offender, but must impose a sentence that provides "some meaningful opportunity for release based on demonstrated maturity and rehabilitation."[62]

The major dissent by Justice Thomas mirrors the objections to those in *Roper* above. It objects to a categorical proscription, particularly under a "proportionality" test which turns on individually varying factors which it contends is beyond the scope of the Eighth Amendment's prohibition. It would entrust such decisions to states—respecting their local democratic decision-making about crimes and punishment—and to juries and courts directly involved with the case and best able to measure culpability and rehabilitation prospects.

The decision cites the rejection of LWOP for juvenile offenders "the world over," noting that "this observation does not control our decision" but is "not irrelevant." The Court notes that only two nations of the world impose such sentences in practice: the United States and Israel, and the latter reserves those sentences only for homicides. The dissent repeats the same arguments rejecting categorically the relevance of international practices or standards in determining what is "unusual" under the Eighth Amendment or otherwise acceptable (see excerpts and analysis of *Roper* and *Graham* international standard discussion in Chapter 14).

In 2012, the Court continued its succession of cases on juvenile sentencing with *Miller v. Alabama*, 567 U.S. 460, holding that a *mandatory* sentence of LWOP for a juvenile convicted of homicide is unconstitutional. Relying on the same understanding of adolescent development and brain science that influenced *Roper* and *Graham*, the Court determined that a youth's age, background, and development must be considered to ensure a sentence proportionate to the crime committed. As a result, juveniles convicted of homicide are entitled to a sentencing hearing in which the following factors—known as "*Miller* factors"—are considered before LWOP can be imposed: 1) age and its "hallmark features—among them, immaturity, impetuosity, and failure to appreciate risks"; 2) the youth's family and home environment; 3) the circumstance of the offense, such as the extent of the youth's participation; 4) legal competency issues, meaning the inability of the youth to assist in his or her defense; and 5) the youth's potential for rehabilitation.[63] *Miller* did not foreclose the imposition of a juvenile LWOP sentence in a homicide case, but it may not occur absent consideration of the potentially mitigating factors listed above.

Following *Miller*, states were divided on whether the decision applied retroactively. Interpretation turned on whether the state viewed the *Miller* decision as issuing a procedural mandate or as establishing a substantive rule limiting sentences for juveniles. Such a substantive rule would require application to sentences previously imposed. Supreme courts in fourteen states interpreted the decision as retroactive, but seven other state supreme courts held otherwise. In 2016, the U.S. Supreme Court resolved the issue in *Montgomery v. Louisiana*, 136 S. Ct. 718, determining that the holding in *Miller* was substantive in nature and that it did in fact apply retroactively. The Court was careful to note that the decision did not require resentencing of all 2,100 individuals still serving sentences under mandatory regimes, offering instead that the constitutional violation could be remedied by providing parole hearings for inmates at which release would be considered. The Court in *Montgomery* re-emphasized the conclusion in *Miller* that juvenile LWOP should be uncommon, reserved only for the rare youth who is found to be permanently incorrigible. This effectively limits the application of juvenile LWOP to a very discrete population of youth—those convicted of homicide who are shown to be incapable of rehabilitation.

In a rather derisive dissent, Justice Scalia opined that the majority decision in *Montgomery* was a thinly veiled effort to put an end to LWOP for juveniles in any circumstance. Whether the Court intended such a result or not, the response to the decision among state legislatures and courts has in fact been a further limiting of the juvenile LWOP sentence. For example, in 2016, the Iowa Supreme Court held juvenile LWOP to be in violation of its state constitution. In 2017, California passed legislation prohibiting any future sentencing of juveniles to LWOP and ensuring that juveniles currently serving life sentences become eligible for release through a special hearing following their 25th year of incarceration. In 2018, the Washington Supreme Court similarly prohibited the sentence prospectively, joining 20 other states and the District of Columbia.

As momentum continues toward limiting, if not barring, the use of the juvenile LWOP sentence, advocates are pointing to the unresolved issue of "de facto" life sentences—sentences of such length that the juvenile is likely to live out the rest of his natural life before being released. Consider a case in which a defendant is sentenced to multiple and consecutive lengthy terms, totaling more than 70, 80, or 90 years before parole becomes an option. Does *Graham* prohibit such sentences for non-homicide juvenile offenders? Do *Miller* and *Montgomery* prohibit mandatory sentences for terms of years that effectively result in a life sentence for juvenile homicide offenders?

Several state and federal courts have considered these questions and have come to varying conclusions. The Sixth Circuit in *Bunch v. Smith*, 685 F.3d 546 (2012), held that a consecutive, fixed-term sentence that amounted to 89 years for a non-homicide juvenile offense was permissible, whereas the Tenth Circuit in *Budder v. Addison*, 851 F.3d 1047 (2017), concluded "the sentencing practice that was the Court's focus in *Graham* was any sentence that denies a juvenile non-homicide offender a realistic opportunity to obtain release in his or her lifetime, whether or not that sentence bears the specific label 'life without parole.'"[64] The California Supreme Court in *People v. Caballero*, 55 Cal. 4th 262 (2012), determined that a 110 years to life sentence for three attempted murder convictions was functionally equivalent to LWOP, thus violating *Graham*. In 2018, the California Supreme Court extended the rationale, ruling that a sentence of 50 years or more before consideration of parole for juveniles convicted of non-homicide offenses violates the Eighth Amendment.[65]

Most recently, the Third Circuit in *United States v. Grant* ruled that the Eighth Amendment prohibits such de facto life sentences in homicide cases without a finding of permanent incorrigibility. The Third Circuit also established that non-incorrigible juveniles should be provided with the opportunity for release before the "national age of retirement," in effect requiring courts to consider the life expectancy of the defendant before imposing a lengthy sentence.[66] The Supreme Court has declined to review cases that would resolve these issues.

Questions for Discussion

1. The dissent in *Graham* argues at length that death as a penalty has been a bright-line category appropriate for limitation because of its unique severity, and that Eighth Amendment application is properly so limited. Justice Thomas writes: "The Court's departure from the 'death is different' distinction is especially mystifying when one considers how long it has resisted crossing that divide." The dissent contends that to open the door to LWOP sentence reviews (the second most severe sentence), especially under a loosely-defined "proportionality" standard, opens the door to the challenge of "the third, fourth, fifth, or fiftieth most severe penalties as well." Presumably, sentences over 25 years in length could next be on the chopping block. But is not a penalty that precludes rehabilitation—or release during a lifetime from incarceration—also categorically different from other alternatives? The death penalty and LWOP are the only two sentences condemned by the International Covenant on the Rights of the Child. Is it really a "slippery slope," as the dissent argues?

2. The Thomas dissent in *Graham* poignantly notes: "...in the end, the Court does not even believe its pronouncements about the juvenile mind. If it did, the categorical rule it announces today would be most peculiar because it leaves intact state and federal laws that permit life-without-parole sentences for juveniles who commit homicides."[67] The dissent then asks how a juvenile who "pulls a trigger on a firearm" (resulting in a death) should be eligible for the severe LWOP penalty, while one who rapes and tortures a child left for dead would be precluded from that penalty. Though perhaps not intended, does that point also support the rejection of LWOP for homicides as well as other crimes? Does the factor turn on a death outcome? For example, a youth may be the youngest of a gang and asked to perform as a "lookout" in a store robbery. One of the gang is killed by the clerk, and under current law, that death is "felony murder"—a homicide offense for the youngest gang member not intending anyone's death. Or if the line were to be a

more sophisticated "intending someone to die"—a shooting with five bullets fired into a victim while screaming "die, die now!"—but without death—would not allow the LWOP sentence. If the critical factor in finding a lifetime punishment as "cruel and unusual" for a juvenile is its extraordinary length applied to one whose brain is still developing and is subject to change, why *does* the Court draw the line at non-homicide offenses?

3. In *Montgomery*, the Court was compelled by the disproportionality of a life sentence imposed on a child whose crime is a result of impermanent immaturity. The sentencing hearings required by *Miller* are intended to avoid such disproportionate sentences by separating children amenable to rehabilitation from children for whom rehabilitation is impossible. How effectively can a court make that distinction? As the Court in *Graham* recognized, it is even difficult for experts to differentiate between transient immaturity and permanent incorrigibility. What specific findings should be required, if any? Should courts assume that there is a presumption against imposing LWOP sentences and that the state has the burden to prove incorrigibility in order to impose the sentence? Must a prosecutor prove beyond a reasonable doubt that the sentence is appropriate? Is this determination a factual finding more properly made by a jury?

4. For many, a parole hearing is the mechanism through which an inmate sentenced as a juvenile is provided a meaningful opportunity for release as required by the U.S. Supreme Court. How meaningful is this opportunity if parole systems lack procedures many would argue are necessary for meaningful consideration—for example, allowing prisoners to appear before the parole board, or allowing prisoners to see or refute information given to the parole board? Does the infrequency with which parole is granted for juvenile offenders raise concern about the adequacy of a state's procedures? See *Haden v. Keller*, 134 F. Supp. 3d 1000 (2015), in which a North Carolina district court questioned the state process under which no juveniles had been paroled in four of the previous five years. Should there be a unique entity or specialized procedures to consider parole for prisoners sentenced as juveniles? In Connecticut, legislation established new parole eligibility and assessment criteria for juvenile offenders as well as required appointment of counsel in preparation for parole hearings. Louisiana now requires the assessment of the offender by an expert in adolescent brain development. Courts have also weighed in, requiring certain procedures to ensure a meaningful opportunity for release. The Massachusetts Supreme Judicial Court determined that juveniles serving life sentences have the right to representation at their initial parole hearings, access to funding for experts, and judicial review of a denial of release.[68]

5. How do the rulings requiring consideration of the mitigating factor of youth impact the imposition of mandatory minimum sentences of a term less than life? Do mandatory minimums in which sentencers are denied discretion run afoul of the principle underlying the U.S. Supreme Court sentencing cases? See *State v. Lyle*, 854 N.S.2d 378 (2014), in which the Iowa Supreme Court barred mandatory

minimum sentences, concluding that justice requires consideration of factors relating to the culpability of a juvenile in all cases.

D. STATUS OFFENSES

Juvenile Court jurisdiction covers children who have been abandoned (see emancipation discussion), abused or neglected, delinquent, or who commit status offenses. Status offenses are behaviors that would not be considered offenses if committed by an adult. These include curfew violations, running away, underage use of alcohol, and truancy. Most status offenders do not graduate to more significant delinquent behavior and do not require intervention by the juvenile court. In fact, some research indicates that involvement in the juvenile justice system can actually increase the risk of continued offending behavior.[69] On the other hand, some programs aimed at status offenders can target unaddressed needs and help promote protective factors, preventing the escalation of behavior issues. Providing services to meet a youth's needs without formal involvement in the juvenile justice system is a focus of juvenile justice reform advocates.

Curfews prohibiting juveniles from being in public and unaccompanied by an adult after certain evening hours have become common. Most are adopted by local ordinance, with over 80% of American cities of over 30,000 population so acting. Other curfews require school-age children to be "off the streets" during school hours. Courts have generally upheld such ordinances, while often finding more specific prohibitions unconstitutionally vague. For example, a Chicago prohibition on a street gang member "loitering in a public place" with one or more other such persons was so struck (see *City of Chicago v. Morales*, 527 U.S. 41 (1999)). A critical basis for rejection of such measures is the degree to which latitude is given to police authority to determine who is violating the law and who is not.

A wholesale limitation on youth movement, with defined exceptions that do not rely on police judgment, more often survives court challenge. *See, e.g., Hutchins v. District of Columbia*, 188 F.3d 531 (D.C. Cir. 1999), affirming the District of Columbia curfew for those sixteen years of age and under without adult supervision after 11 p.m. on weekdays, and after midnight on Friday, Saturday, and Sunday. As with most such ordinances, it included seven common exceptions: going on a parental errand without detour; going to or from a job without detour; an emergency; on the sidewalk abutting the residence or next door; attending an official school, religious, or youth activity itself supervised by adults; or exercising 1st Amendment rights of religion, speech, or assembly. The Supreme Court has allowed lower courts to strike such broad prohibitions on general activity for adults (see *Bykofsky v. Borough of Middletown*, 401 F. Supp. 1242 (M.D. Pa. 1975), *aff'd without opinion* 535 F.2d 1245 (3rd Cir. 1976), *cert denied* 429 U.S. 964 (1976)). However, the Court has not spoken dispositively about juvenile curfews, and the circuits vary substantially (compare *Schleifer v. City of Charlottesville*, 159 F.3d 843 (4th Cir. 1998), upholding Charlottesville's ordinance, and *Nunez v. City of San Diego*, 114 F.3d 935 (9th Cir. 1997), striking San Diego's).

Few studies find a strong correlation between curfews and crime reduction; a recent study suggests that in relation to gun violence, curfews may in fact increase the incidence by removing the deterrent effect of bystanders and witnesses being present on the streets.[70] Afterschool and other programs that occupy the attention of children during the 3 p.m. to 10 p.m. period may prove more effective at preventing juvenile violent crime, which is most common during the afterschool hours on school days and in the early evening on non-school days.[71]

Truancy is dealt with somewhat differently among the states, but California's approach is typical. In 1974, the state created School Attendance Review Boards (SARBs), which include parents, school administrators, and local mental health and law enforcement representatives. A minor who is deemed a habitual truant, or is irregular in attendance at school, or is habitually insubordinate, may be referred to a SARB. The SARB will refer the student and family to community services where appropriate. Where services are determined to be inappropriate, or if a family fails to follow a SARB directive, the matter may be referred to the district attorney for possible status offense petition *vis-à-vis* the minor, or criminal prosecution against a parent. Legal consequences for a student over age 13 found to be a habitual truant by the juvenile court can include fines, community service, participation in a truancy prevention program, or suspension or revocation of driving privileges. Penalties for parents under the Education Code include fines and court-ordered parent education or counseling programs.[72] As of 2011, parents can also be found guilty of a misdemeanor for failing to "reasonably supervise and encourage" school attendance for a chronically truant youth in Kindergarten through 8th grade.[73] Although the provision allows for the imposition of a fine or imprisonment, a court may instead establish a deferred entry of judgment program that provides parents with service referrals and case management aimed at addressing challenges within the family that contribute to the child's truancy.

The number of runaway youth is difficult to quantify given the transient nature of the population and the hesitancy of youth to report that they have left home. A federally-funded study out of Chapin Hall at the University of Chicago found that approximately 700,000 youth between ages 13 and 17, and 3.5 million young adults between ages 18 and 25 reported having been homeless within the past year.[74] The most often reported reason for running away is family conflict. In addition, experts calculate that approximately half of these children have not fled their families as much as they were "thrownaway"—either directly told to leave, or driven away through sexual abuse, beatings, or extreme neglect. Gay and lesbian young adults are twice as likely to be homeless as those who are heterosexual, often as a result of negative reactions from parents.[75] This problem is caused by private actors rather than the state directly. Since the Court has eschewed any affirmative duty of the state toward its children (see the leading *Deshaney* case, Chapter 12), and since the U.S. Constitution is directed toward state abuses, such abandoned children lack constitutional protection.

Congress and some states have enacted statutes aimed at addressing the issue of runaway and homeless youth. Federally, the Runaway and Homeless Youth Program provides modest grants to states in three areas: 1) Basic Center

Program, which provides temporary shelter and services to runaway and homeless youth and their families; 2) the Transitional Living Program, which serves older youth (16–22) by providing longer-term housing and services; and 3) the Street Outreach Program, which provides services and referrals to youth on the street.[76]

Youth in foster care experience high runaway incidence, often based on the desire to connect with their biological parents and siblings, to express their autonomy, or to escape abuse or neglect in placement.[77] The victimization experienced by these children and their lack of connection to a support system leaves them particularly vulnerable to commercial sexual exploitation. In 2014, President Obama signed into law the Preventing Sex Trafficking and Strengthening Families Act in part to protect and prevent children in foster care from such victimization. The law requires child welfare agencies to develop policies and procedures to locate children missing from foster care and determine the factors that led to running away and address those factors in subsequent placements. The National Center for Missing and Exploited Children has partnered with child welfare agencies to support efforts to locate and return children who have run from care.

E. COMMITMENT TO CIVIL INSTITUTIONS

Parham v. J.R.

442 U.S. 584 (1979)

MR. CHIEF JUSTICE BURGER delivered the opinion of the Court.

The question presented in this appeal is what process is constitutionally due a minor child whose parents or guardian seek state administered institutional mental health care for the child and specifically whether an adversary proceeding is required prior to or after the commitment.

I

(a) Appellee...J.R., a child being treated in a Georgia state mental hospital, was a plaintiff in this class action2 based on 42 U.S.C. § 1983, in the District Court for the Middle District of Georgia. Appellants are the State's Commissioner of the Department of Human Resources, the Director of the Mental Health Division of the Department of Human Resources, and the Chief Medical Officer at the hospital where appellee was being treated. Appellee sought a declaratory judgment that Georgia's voluntary commitment procedures for children under the age of 18, Ga. Code §§ 88-503.1, 88-503.2 (1975),[3] violated the Due Process Clause of the Fourteenth Amendment and requested an injunction against their future enforcement.

* * *

(b) J.L., a plaintiff before the District Court who is now deceased, was admitted in 1970 at the age of 6 years to Central State Regional Hospital in Milledgeville, Ga. Prior to his admission, J.L. had received outpatient treatment at the hospital for over two months. J.L.'s mother then requested the hospital to admit him indefinitely.

The admitting physician interviewed J.L. and his parents. He learned that J.L.'s natural parents had divorced and his mother had remarried. He also learned that J.L. had been expelled from school because he was uncontrollable. He accepted the parents' representation that the boy had been extremely aggressive and diagnosed the child as having a "hyperkinetic reaction of childhood."

J.L.'s mother and stepfather agreed to participate in family therapy during the time their son was hospitalized. Under this program, J.L. was permitted to go home for short stays. Apparently his behavior during these visits was erratic. After several months, the parents requested discontinuance of the program.

In 1972, the child was returned to his mother and stepfather on a furlough basis, *i.e.*, he would live at home but go to school at the hospital. The parents found they were unable to control J.L. to their satisfaction, and this created family stress. Within two months, they requested his readmission to Central State. J.L.'s parents relinquished their parental rights to the county in 1974.

Although several hospital employees recommended that J.L. should be placed in a special foster home with "a warm, supported, truly involved couple," the Department of Family and Children Services was unable to place him in such a setting. On October 24, 1975, J.L. (with J.R.) filed this suit requesting an order of the court placing him in a less drastic environment suitable to his needs.

(c) Appellee J.R. was declared a neglected child by the county and removed from his natural parents when he was 3 months old. He was placed in seven different foster homes in succession prior to his admission to Central State Hospital at the age of 7.

Immediately preceding his hospitalization, J.R. received outpatient treatment at a county mental health center for several months. He then began attending school where he was so disruptive and incorrigible that he could not conform to normal behavior patterns. Because of his abnormal behavior, J.R.'s seventh set of foster parents requested his removal from their home. The Department of Family and Children Services then sought his admission at Central State....

* * *

(d) Georgia Code § 88-503.1 (1975) provides for the voluntary admission to a state regional hospital of children such as J.L. and J.R. Under that provision, admission begins with an application for hospitalization signed by a "parent or guardian." Upon application, the superintendent of each hospital is given the power to admit temporarily any child for "observation and diagnosis." If, after observation, the superintendent finds "evidence of mental illness" and that the child is "suitable for treatment" in the hospital, then the child may be admitted "for such period and under such conditions as may be authorized by law."

Georgia's mental health statute also provides for the discharge of voluntary patients. Any child who has been hospitalized for more than five days may be discharged at the request of a parent or guardian. § 88-503.3 (a) (1975). Even without a request for discharge, however, the superintendent of each regional hospital has an affirmative duty to release any child "who has recovered from his mental illness or who has sufficiently improved that the superintendent determines that hospitalization of the patient is no longer desirable." § 88-503.2 (1975).

Georgia's Mental Health Director has not published any statewide regulations defining what specific procedures each superintendent must employ when admitting a child under 18. Instead, each regional hospital's superintendent is responsible for the procedures in his or her facility. There is substantial variation....

In holding unconstitutional Georgia's statutory procedure for voluntary commitment of juveniles, the District Court first determined that commitment to any of the eight regional hospitals...constitutes a severe deprivation of a child's liberty. The court defined this liberty interest in terms of both freedom from bodily restraint and freedom from the "emotional and psychic harm" caused by the institutionalization.[7] Having determined that a liberty interest is implicated by a child's admission to a mental hospital, the court considered what process is required to protect that interest. It held that the process due "includes at least the right after notice to be heard before an impartial tribunal."....

* * *

II

In requiring the prescribed hearing, the court rejected Georgia's argument that no adversary-type hearing was required since the State was merely assisting parents who could not afford private care by making available treatment similar to that offered in private hospitals and by private physicians. The court acknowledged that most parents who seek to have their children admitted to a state mental hospital do so in good faith. It, however, relied on one of appellees' witnesses who expressed an opinion that "some still look upon mental hospitals as a 'dumping ground.'"...[8] No specific evidence of such "dumping," however, can be found in the record.

The District Court also rejected the argument that review by the superintendents of the hospitals and their staffs was sufficient to protect the child's liberty interest. The court held that the inexactness of psychiatry, coupled with the possibility that the sources of information used to make the commitment decision may not always be reliable, made the superintendent's decision too arbitrary to satisfy due process....

III

...[W]e must consider first the child's interest in not being committed. Normally, however, since this interest is inextricably linked with the parents' interest in and obligation for the welfare and health of the child, the private interest at stake is a combination of the child's and parents' concerns.[11] Next, we must examine the State's interest in the procedures it has adopted for commitment and treatment of children. Finally, we must consider how well Georgia's procedures protect against arbitrariness in the decision to commit a child to a state mental hospital.

(a) It is not disputed that a child, in common with adults, has a substantial liberty interest in not being confined unnecessarily for medical treatment and that the state's involvement in the commitment decision constitutes state action under the Fourteenth Amendment....We also recognize that commitment sometimes produces adverse social consequences for the child because of the reaction of some to the discovery that the child has received psychiatric care....

* * *

(b) We next deal with the interests of the parents who have decided, on the basis of their observations and independent professional recommendations, that their child needs institutional care. Appellees argue that the constitutional rights of the child are of such magnitude and the likelihood of parental abuse is so great that the parents' traditional interests in and responsibility for the upbringing of their child must be subordinated at least to the extent of providing a formal adversary hearing prior to a voluntary commitment.

Our jurisprudence historically has reflected Western civilization concepts of the family as a unit with broad parental authority over minor children. Our cases have consistently followed that course; our constitutional system long ago rejected any notion that a child is "the mere creature of the State" and, on the contrary, asserted that parents generally "have the right, coupled with the high duty, to recognize and prepare [their children] for additional obligations." *Pierce v. Society of Sisters*, 268 U.S. 510, 535 (1925). See also *Wisconsin v. Yoder*, 406 U.S. 205, 213 (1972); *Prince v. Massachusetts*, 321 U.S. 158, 166 (1944); *Meyer v. Nebraska*, 262 U.S. 390, 400 (1923). Surely, this includes a "high duty" to recognize symptoms of illness and to seek and follow medical advice. The law's concept of the family rests on a presumption that parents possess what a child lacks in maturity, experience, and capacity for judgment required for making life's difficult decisions. More important, historically it has recognized that natural bonds of affection lead parents to act in the best interests of their children...

* * *

In defining the respective rights and prerogatives of the child and parent in the voluntary commitment setting, we conclude that our precedents permit the parents to retain a substantial, if not the dominant, role in the decision, absent a finding of neglect or abuse, and that the traditional presumption that the parents act in the best interests of their child should apply. We also conclude, however, that the child's rights and the nature of the commitment decision are such that parents cannot always have absolute and unreviewable discretion to decide whether to have a child institutionalized. They, of course, retain plenary authority to seek such care for their children, subject to a physician's independent examination and medical judgment.

(c) The State obviously has a significant interest in confining the use of its costly mental health facilities to cases of genuine need. The Georgia program seeks first to determine whether the patient seeking admission has an illness that calls for inpatient treatment. To accomplish this purpose, the State has charged the superintendents of each regional hospital with the responsibility for determining, before authorizing an

admission, whether a prospective patient is mentally ill and whether the patient will likely benefit from hospital care. In addition, the State has imposed a continuing duty on hospital superintendents to release any patient who has recovered to the point where hospitalization is no longer needed.

The State in performing its voluntarily assumed mission also has a significant interest in not imposing unnecessary procedural obstacles that may discourage the mentally ill or their families from seeking needed psychiatric assistance. The parens patriae interest in helping parents care for the mental health of their children cannot be fulfilled if the parents are unwilling to take advantage of the opportunities because the admission process is too onerous, too embarrassing, or too contentious. It is surely not idle to speculate as to how many parents who believe they are acting in good faith would forgo state-provided hospital care if such care is contingent on participation in an adversary proceeding designed to probe their motives and other private family matters in seeking the voluntary admission.

The State also has a genuine interest in allocating priority to the diagnosis and treatment of patients as soon as they are admitted to a hospital rather than to time-consuming procedural minuets before the admission....One factor that must be considered is the utilization of the time of psychiatrists, psychologists, and other behavioral specialists in preparing for and participating in hearings rather than performing the task for which their special training has fitted them. Behavioral experts in courtrooms and hearings are of little help to patients.

* * *

(d) We now turn to consideration of what process protects adequately the child's constitutional rights....

* * *

Due process has never been thought to require that the neutral and detached trier of fact be law trained or a judicial or administrative officer....Surely, this is the case as to medical decisions, for "neither judges nor administrative hearing officers are better qualified than psychiatrists to render psychiatric judgments." *In re Roger S.*, 19 Cal. 3d 92 (1977)....Thus, a staff physician will suffice, so long as he or she is free to evaluate independently the child's mental and emotional condition and need for treatment.

It is not necessary that the deciding physician conduct a formal or quasi-formal hearing. A state is free to require such a hearing, but due process is not violated by use of informal, traditional medical investigative techniques....

* * *

Here, the questions are essentially medical in character: whether the child is mentally or emotionally ill and whether he can benefit from the treatment that is provided by the state. While facts are plainly necessary for a proper resolution of those questions, they are only a first step in the process. In an opinion for a unanimous Court, we recently stated in *Addington v. Texas*, 441 U.S., at 429, that the determination of whether a person is mentally ill "turns on the meaning of the facts which must be interpreted by expert psychiatrists and psychologists."

* * *

Another problem with requiring a formalized, factfinding hearing lies in the danger it poses for significant intrusion into the parent-child relationship. Pitting the parents and child as adversaries often will be at odds with the presumption that parents act in the best interests of their child. It is one thing to require a neutral physician to make a careful review of the parents' decision in order to make sure it is proper from a medical standpoint; it is a wholly different matter to employ an adversary contest to ascertain whether the parents' motivation is consistent with the child's interests.

Moreover, it is appropriate to inquire into how such a hearing would contribute to the successful long-range treatment of the patient. Surely, there is a risk that it would exacerbate whatever tensions already exist between the child and the parents. Since the parents can and usually do play a significant role in the treatment while the child is hospitalized and even more so after release, there is a serious risk that an adversary confrontation will adversely affect the ability of the parents to assist the child while in

the hospital. Moreover, it will make his subsequent return home more difficult. These unfortunate results are especially critical with an emotionally disturbed child; they seem likely to occur in the context of an adversary hearing in which the parents testify. A confrontation over such intimate family relationships would distress the normal adult parents and the impact on a disturbed child almost certainly would be significantly greater.[18]

It has been suggested that a hearing conducted by someone other than the admitting physician is necessary in order to detect instances where parents are "guilty of railroading their children into asylums" or are using "voluntary commitment procedures in order to sanction behavior of which they [disapprove]."....It is unrealistic to believe that trained psychiatrists, skilled in eliciting responses, sorting medically relevant facts, and sensing motivational nuances will often be deceived about the family situation surrounding a child's emotional disturbance.[19] Surely a lay, or even law-trained, factfinder would be no more skilled in this process than the professional.

* * *

At the regional hospital an admissions team composed of a psychiatrist and at least one other mental health professional examines and interviews the child—privately in most instances. This team then examines the medical records provided by the clinic staff and interviews the parents. Based on this information, and any additional background that can be obtained, the admissions team makes a diagnosis and determines whether the child will likely benefit from institutionalized care. If the team finds either condition not met, admission is refused.

If the team admits a child as suited for hospitalization, the child's condition and continuing need for hospital care are reviewed periodically by at least one independent, medical review group. For the most part, the reviews are as frequent as weekly, but none are less often than once every two months. Moreover, as we noted earlier, the superintendent of each hospital is charged with an affirmative statutory duty to discharge any child who is no longer mentally ill or in need of therapy.[21]

* * *

IV

(a) Our discussion in Part III was directed at the situation where a child's natural parents request his admission to a state mental hospital. Some members of appellees' class, including J.R., were wards of the State of Georgia at the time of their admission. Obviously their situation differs from those members of the class who have natural parents. While the determination of what process is due varies somewhat when the state, rather than a natural parent, makes the request for commitment, we conclude that the differences in the two situations do not justify requiring different procedures at the time of the child's initial admission to the hospital.

* * *

Indeed, if anything, the decision with regard to wards of the State may well be even more reasonable in light of the extensive written records that are compiled about each child while in the State's custody. In J.R.'s case, the admitting physician had a complete social and medical history of the child before even beginning the diagnosis. After carefully interviewing him and reviewing his extensive files, three physicians independently concluded that institutional care was in his best interests. See *supra*, at 590.

Since the state agency having custody and control of the child in loco parentis has a duty to consider the best interests of the child with respect to a decision on commitment to a mental hospital, the State may constitutionally allow that custodial agency to speak for the child, subject, of course, to the restrictions governing natural parents. On this record, we cannot declare unconstitutional Georgia's admission procedures for wards of the State.

* * *

[2] The class certified by the District Court, without objection by appellants, consisted "of all persons younger than 18 years of age now or hereafter received by any defendant for observation and diagnosis and/or detained for care and treatment at any 'facility' within the State of Georgia pursuant to" Ga. Code § 88-503.1 (1975). Although one witness testified that on any given day there may be 200 children in the class, in December 1975 there were only 140.

[3] Section 88-503.1 provides: "The superintendent of any facility may receive for observation and diagnosis...any individual under 18 years of age for whom such application is made by his parent or guardian.... If found to show evidence of mental illness and to be suitable for treatment, such person may be given care and treatment at such facility and such person may be detained by such facility for such period and under such conditions as may be authorized by law."

Section 88-503.2 provides: "The superintendent of the facility shall discharge any voluntary patient who has recovered from his mental illness or who has sufficiently improved that the superintendent determines that hospitalization of the patient is no longer desirable."

Section 88-503 was amended in some respects in 1978, but references herein are to the provisions in effect at the time in question.

[7] In both respects, the District Court found strong support for its holding in this Court's decision in *In re Gault*, 387 U.S. 1 (1967). In that decision, we held that a state cannot institutionalize a juvenile delinquent without first providing certain due process protections.

[8] In light of the District Court's holding that a judicial or quasi-judicial body should review voluntary commitment decisions, it is at least interesting to note that the witness who made the statement quoted in the text was not referring to parents as the people who "dump" children into hospitals. This witness opined that some juvenile court judges and child welfare agencies misused the hospitals.

[11] In this part of the opinion, we will deal with the issues arising when the natural parents of the child seek commitment to a state hospital. In Part IV, we will deal with the situation presented when the child is a ward of the state.

[18] While not altogether clear, the District Court opinion apparently contemplated a hearing preceded by a written notice of the proposed commitment. At the hearing the child presumably would be given an opportunity to be heard and present evidence, and the right to cross-examine witnesses, including, of course, the parents. The court also required an impartial trier of fact who would render a written decision reciting the reasons for accepting or rejecting the parental application.

Since the parents in this situation are seeking the child's admission to the state institution, the procedure contemplated by the District Court presumably would call for some other person to be designated as a guardian ad litem to act for the child. The guardian, in turn, if not a lawyer, would be empowered to retain counsel to act as an advocate of the child's interest.

Of course, a state may elect to provide such adversary hearings in situations where it perceives that parents and a child may be at odds, but nothing in the Constitution compels such procedures.

[19] In evaluating the problem of detecting "dumping" by parents, it is important to keep in mind that each of the regional hospitals has a continuing relationship with the Department of Family and Children Services. The staffs at those hospitals refer cases to the Department when they suspect a child is being mistreated and thus are sensitive to this problem. In fact, J.L.'s situation is in point. The family conflicts and problems were well documented in the hospital records. Equally well documented, however, were the child's severe emotional disturbances and his need for treatment.

[21] While the record does demonstrate that the procedures may vary from case to case, it also reflects that no child in Georgia was admitted for indefinite hospitalization without being interviewed personally and without the admitting physician's checking with secondary sources, such as school or work records.

MR. JUSTICE BRENNAN, with whom MR. JUSTICE MARSHALL and MR. JUSTICE STEVENS join, concurring in part and dissenting in part.

I agree with the Court that the commitment of juveniles to state mental hospitals by their parents or by state officials acting *in loco parentis* involves state action that impacts upon constitutionally protected interests and therefore must be accomplished through procedures consistent with the constitutional mandate of due process of law. I agree also that the District Court erred in interpreting the Due Process Clause to require preconfinement commitment hearings in all cases in which parents wish to hospitalize their children. I disagree, however, with the Court's decision to pretermit questions concerning the postadmission procedures due Georgia's institutionalized juveniles. While the question of the frequency of postadmission review hearings may properly be deferred, the right to at least one postadmission hearing can and should be affirmed now. I also disagree with the Court's conclusion concerning the procedures due juvenile wards of the State of Georgia. I believe that the Georgia statute is unconstitutional in that it fails to accord preconfinement hearings to juvenile wards of the State committed by the State acting *in loco parentis*.

I

Rights Of Children Committed To Mental Institutions

Commitment to a mental institution necessarily entails a "massive curtailment of liberty,"...and inevitably affects "fundamental rights."...Persons incarcerated in mental hospitals are not only deprived of their physical liberty, they are also deprived of friends, family, and community. Institutionalized mental patients must live in unnatural surroundings under the continuous and detailed control of strangers. They are subject to intrusive treatment which, especially if unwarranted, may violate their right to bodily integrity. Such treatment modalities may include forced administration of psychotropic medication, aversive conditioning, convulsive therapy, and even psychosurgery. Furthermore, as the Court recognizes,...persons confined in mental institutions are stigmatized as sick and abnormal during confinement and, in some cases, even after release.

Because of these considerations, our cases have made clear that commitment to a mental hospital "is a deprivation of liberty which the State cannot accomplish without due process of law." *O'Connor v. Donaldson*, 422 U.S. 563, 580 (1975)....In the absence of a voluntary, knowing, and intelligent waiver, adults facing commitment to mental institutions are entitled to full and fair adversary hearings in which the necessity for their commitment is established to the satisfaction of a neutral tribunal. At such hearings they must be accorded the right of "be present with counsel, have an opportunity to be heard, be confronted with witnesses against [them], have the right to cross-examine, and to offer evidence of [their] own."....

These principles also govern the commitment of children. "Constitutional rights do not mature and come into being magically only when one attains the state-defined age of majority. Minors, as well as adults, are protected by the Constitution and possess constitutional rights...."

Indeed, it may well be argued that children are entitled to more protection than are adults. The consequences of an erroneous commitment decision are more tragic where children are involved. Children, on the average, are confined for longer periods than are adults....Moreover, childhood is a particularly vulnerable time of life...and children erroneously institutionalized during their formative years may bear the scars for the rest of their lives....Furthermore, the provision of satisfactory institutionalized mental care for children generally requires a substantial financial commitment that too often has not been forthcoming....Decisions of the lower courts have chronicled the inadequacies of existing mental health facilities for children....

In addition, the chances of an erroneous commitment decision are particularly great where children are involved. Even under the best of circumstances psychiatric diagnosis and therapy decisions are fraught with uncertainties. See *O'Connor v. Donaldson, supra*, at 584....These uncertainties are aggravated when, as under the Georgia practice, the psychiatrist interviews the child during a period of abnormal stress in connection with the commitment, and without adequate time or opportunity to become acquainted with the patient....These uncertainties may be further aggravated when economic and social class separate doctor and child, thereby frustrating the accurate diagnosis of pathology....

These compounded uncertainties often lead to erroneous commitments since psychiatrists tend to err on the side of medical caution and therefore hospitalize patients for whom other dispositions would be more beneficial....The National Institute of Mental Health recently found that only 36% of patients below age 20 who were confined at St. Elizabeths Hospital actually required such hospitalization....Of particular relevance to this case, a Georgia study Commission on Mental Health Services for Children and Youth concluded that more than half of the State's institutionalized children were not in need of confinement if other forms of care were made available or used. Cited in *J.L. v. Parham*, 412 F.Supp. 112, 122 (MD Ga. 1976).

II

Rights Of Children Committed By Their Parents

A

Notwithstanding all this, Georgia denies hearings to juveniles institutionalized at the behest of their parents. Georgia rationalizes this practice on the theory that parents act in their children's best interests and therefore may waive their children's due process rights. Children incarcerated because their parents wish them confined, Georgia contends, are really voluntary patients. I cannot accept this argument.

In our society, parental rights are limited by the legitimate rights and interests of their children. "Parents may be free to become martyrs themselves. But it does not follow they are free, in identical circumstances, to make martyrs of their children before they have reached the age of full and legal discretion when they can make that choice for themselves." *Prince v. Massachusetts*, 321 U.S. 158, 170 (1944)....

* * *

Additional considerations counsel against allowing parents unfettered power to institutionalize their children without cause or without any hearing to ascertain that cause. The presumption that parents act in their children's best interests, while applicable to most child-rearing decisions, is not applicable in the commitment context. Numerous studies reveal that parental decisions to institutionalize their children often are the results of dislocation in the family unrelated to the children's mental condition....Moreover, even well-meaning parents lack the expertise necessary to evaluate the relative advantages and disadvantages of inpatient as opposed to outpatient psychiatric treatment. Parental decisions to waive hearings in which such questions could be explored, therefore, cannot be conclusively deemed either informed or intelligent. In these circumstances, I respectfully suggest, it ignores reality to assume blindly that parents act in their children's best interests when making commitment decisions and when waiving their children's due process rights.

B

This does not mean States are obliged to treat children who are committed at the behest of their parents in precisely the same manner as other persons who are involuntarily committed. The demands of due process are flexible and the parental commitment decision carries with it practical implications that States may legitimately take into account. While as a general rule due process requires that commitment hearings precede involuntary hospitalization, when parents seek to hospitalize their children special considerations militate in favor of postponement of formal commitment proceedings and against mandatory adversary preconfinement commitment hearings.

First, the prospect of an adversary hearing prior to admission might deter parents from seeking needed medical attention for their children. Second, the hearings themselves might delay treatment of children whose home life has become impossible and who require some form of immediate state care. Furthermore, because adversary hearings at this juncture would necessarily involve direct challenges to parental authority, judgment, or veracity, preadmission hearings may well result in pitting the child and his advocate against the parents. This, in turn, might traumatize both parent and child and make the child's eventual return to his family more difficult.

Because of these special considerations, I believe that States may legitimately postpone formal commitment proceedings when parents seek inpatient psychiatric treatment for their children. Such children may be admitted, for a limited period, without prior hearing, so long as the admitting psychiatrist first interviews parent and child and concludes that short-term inpatient treatment would be appropriate.

Georgia's present admission procedures are reasonably consistent with these principles....To the extent the District Court invalidated this aspect of the Georgia juvenile commitment scheme and mandated preconfinement hearings in all cases, I agree with the Court that the District Court was in error.

C

I do not believe, however, that the present Georgia juvenile commitment scheme is constitutional in its entirety. Although Georgia may postpone formal commitment hearings, when parents seek to commit their children, the State cannot dispense with such hearings altogether....

The informal postadmission procedures that Georgia now follows are simply not enough to qualify as hearings—let alone reasonably prompt hearings. The procedures lack all the traditional due process safeguards. Commitment decisions are made ex parte. Georgia's institutionalized juveniles are not informed of the reasons for their commitment; nor do they enjoy the right to be present at the commitment determination, the right to representation, the right to be heard, the right to be confronted with adverse witnesses, the right to cross-examine, or the right to offer evidence of their own. By any standard of due process, these procedures are deficient....I cannot understand why the Court pretermits condemnation of these ex parte procedures which operate to deny Georgia's institutionalized juveniles even "some form of hearing," *Mathews v. Eldridge, supra,* at 333, before they are condemned to suffer the rigors of long-term institutional confinement.[21]

The special considerations that militate against preadmission commitment hearings when parents seek to hospitalize their children do not militate against reasonably prompt postadmission commitment hearings. In the first place, postadmission hearings would not delay the commencement of needed treatment. Children could be cared for by the State pending the disposition decision.

Second, the interest in avoiding family discord would be less significant at this stage since the family autonomy already will have been fractured by the institutionalization of the child. In any event, postadmission hearings are unlikely to disrupt family relationships. At later hearings, the case for and against commitment would be based upon the observations of the hospital staff and the judgments of the staff psychiatrists, rather than upon parental observations and recommendations...

* * *

Nor can the good faith and good intentions of Georgia's psychiatrists and social workers, adverted to by the Court,...excuse Georgia's *ex parte* procedures. Georgia's admitting psychiatrists, like the school disciplinarians described in *Goss v. Lopez,* 419 U.S. 565 (1975), "although proceeding in utmost good faith, frequently act on the reports and advice of others; and the controlling facts and the nature of the conduct under challenge are often disputed."...Here, as in *Goss,* the "risk of error is not at all trivial, and it should be guarded against if that may be done without prohibitive cost or interference with the...process....'[Fairness] can rarely be obtained by secret, one-sided determination of facts decisive of rights....'Secrecy is not congenial to truth-seeking and self-righteousness gives too slender an assurance of rightness. No better instrument has been devised for arriving at truth than to give a person in jeopardy of serious loss notice of the case against him and opportunity to meet it.'"...

III

Rights of Children Committed By Their State Guardians

Georgia does not accord prior hearings to juvenile wards of the State of Georgia committed by state social workers acting in loco parentis The Court dismisses a challenge to this practice on the grounds that state social workers are obliged by statute to act in the children's best interest....

* * *

To my mind, there is no justification for denying children committed by their social workers the prior hearings that the Constitution typically requires. In the first place, such children cannot be said to have waived their rights to a prior hearing simply because their social workers wished them to be confined. The rule that parents speak for their children, even if it were applicable in the commitment context, cannot be transmuted into a rule that state social workers speak for their minor clients....

* * *

IV

Children incarcerated in public mental institutions are constitutionally entitled to a fair opportunity to contest the legitimacy of their confinement. They are entitled to some champion who can speak on their behalf and who stands ready to oppose a wrongful commitment. Georgia should not be permitted to deny that opportunity and that champion simply because the children's parents or guardians wish them to be confined without a hearing. The risk of erroneous commitment is simply too great unless there is some form of adversary review. And fairness demands that children abandoned by their supposed protectors to the rigors of institutional confinement be given the help of some separate voice.

[21] The National Institute of Mental Health has reported: "[Thousands] upon thousands of elderly patients now confined on the back wards of...state [mental] institutions were first admitted as children thirty, forty, and even fifty years ago. A recent report from one state estimates that one in every four children admitted to its mental hospitals 'can anticipate being permanently hospitalized for the next 50 years of their lives.'" Joint Commission on Mental Health of Children, *supra* n. 9, at 5-6.

Questions for Discussion

1. Is *Parham* consistent with *Gault*? Is it appropriate to assume that parents and physicians interacting with children are acting in their best interests and do not require judicial check? Are not the police sworn to obey the law and apprehend the guilty, and are not public prosecutors sworn to seek a just resolution? Why do we not rely on their judgment in the adult criminal justice system? Why don't we rely solely on the judgment of caring relatives and physicians for the civil commitment of adults?

2. The majority opinion cites the "natural bonds of affection" which lead parents to act in the best interests of their children. Is such reliance consistent with the three million annual child abuse reports received? With the numerous adjudications of parental neglect and unfitness in juvenile dependency courts? Is it appropriate where the context is a parental attempt to remove a child from the family and place him into state institution confinement?

3. The opinion notes that there is no evidence of bad faith by the parents in *Parham*. If such bad faith were to exist, would it be detected under the Court's procedural rights holding?

4. The Court finds that many parents would forego mental health services if an adversary hearing were required. What is the empirical basis (evidence) for that finding? If accurate, is a check possible without a hostile adversarial approach? If an attorney is assigned to represent such a child and the parents are acting in the child's best interests, would not such an attorney be cooperative? Why should counsel be confrontational where all concerned care about and are trying to help his client?

5. The holding here finds sufficient constitutional check from the review of the hospital director. Is such an official adequately neutral? Is there a possible budgetary or other conflict that might compromise such a review? Do we allow the director of a mental hospital to serve as the primary check on adult admissions? Is it enough that an independent medical group "reviews" programs? How does such a review take place? Is the child heard? Does anybody speak for the child, separate from institution officials?

6.˙ The decision argues that the questions at issue are "medical" and properly left to psychiatrists. Do we delegate psychiatric judgments about diminished capacity in any adult context to such experts—as the final decision makers?

7. The dissent argues for at least one post-admission hearing, and complains that juveniles are not even told the reasons for their confinement. Is the dissent an ambitious defense of the rights of children? Does it reflect a high priority that the

involuntary confinement of children be considered seriously, that checks on abuse exist, and that care be taken to prevent error?

F. MAJOR FEDERAL DELINQUENCY-RELATED STATUTES AND PROGRAMS

There is no federal juvenile justice system. State and local governments operate their systems independently, developing their own policies and procedures. The federal government influences juvenile justice policy by setting standards that states are incentivized to meet through the provision of funds to compliant jurisdictions. The major federal statute establishing these standards—referred to as "core protections"—is the Juvenile Justice and Delinquency Prevention Act of 1974 (JJDPA).[78] The JJDPA established the Office of Juvenile Justice and Delinquency Prevention (OJJDP) within the Justice Department to administer state and local grants. The "core protections" outlined in the Act are: 1) the "deinstitutionalization" of status offenders, meaning that youth whose offenses would not constitute an adult crime are not to be detained or incarcerated; 2) prohibiting the placement of youth in a jail or lock-up intended for adults except under certain limited circumstances; 3) "sight and sound" separation from adults when juveniles are confined in facilities where adult inmates are present; and 4) a requirement for states to demonstrate how they are working to address the over-representation of youth of color in their juvenile justice systems.

The JJDPA was finally reauthorized in 2018, after sixteen years of inaction. While awaiting reauthorization, Congress continued to appropriate funds for some of the programs authorized under the Act as well as other programs outside of the JJDPA. These include:

- The State Formula Grant Program, known as Title II, which provides funds to states to support effective programs and to improve their juvenile justice systems. The formula to determine funding is based on the state's population of youth under 18. Sixty million dollars were appropriated for this program in 2018, compared to $75 million a decade ago.
- The Juvenile Accountability Block Grant Program (JABG), which provides funding to encourage states and local jurisdictions to implement accountability-based programs and services aimed at reducing juvenile offending. The Program is based on research showing that graduated sanctions—imposing consequences that correspond with the seriousness of the youth's offense—are effective in reducing recidivism. The Program was originally known as the Juvenile Accountability Incentive Block Grant and was renamed and revised as part of the Omnibus Crime Control and Safe Streets Act in 2002. This major source of funding for delinquency prevention and recidivism reduction has been completely eliminated from the federal budget since 2014.

- Title V Incentive Grants for Local Delinquency Prevention are grants made by OJJDP to states that are then distributed to units of local government to support programs to prevent delinquency. It is the only federal program that provides preventive funding at the local level, focusing on reducing risk and enhancing protective factors. The program targets first-time and non-serious offenders. Although authorization for this program expired in 2008, Congress continues to provide funding, although at levels far below previous allocations.
- The Juvenile Mentoring Program, authorized under the JJDPA to provide grants to local educational agencies to support mentoring programs aimed at reducing delinquency and improve educational performance of students. Funding for these programs has remained relatively steady and represents the largest single outlay of federal funds within the juvenile justice program sphere.
- Victims of Child Abuse Act Grants fund efforts to improve juvenile and family court handling of child abuse and neglect cases. These funds were authorized as part of the Violence Against Women Act reauthorization in 2013, allocating $2.3 million each year through 2018.[79]

When the JJDPA was reauthorized in 2002, Congress appropriated nearly $547 million for juvenile justice. Sixteen years later, federal funding for juvenile justice has dropped to just $283 million. The President's 2019 budget request called for a $17 million dollar decrease in juvenile justice spending, but the Senate-approved spending bill provided $15 million of additional funding for FY2019. Despite recent increases, overall funding remains low and advocates worry that states may lose the incentive to comply with the federal standards to which the funding is tied. Some states contend that the funding provided is not commensurate with the costs incurred in complying with the core protections and as a result these governments may simply elect not to receive the monies. For many years Wyoming alone chose to not participate in the JJDPA; recently Connecticut and Nebraska have joined its ranks.

Reauthorization efforts in recent years were stalled by opposition to attempts to phase out the Valid Court Order (VCO) exception, a loophole that allows children to be detained for a status offense if they have been court-ordered to refrain from such behavior. For example, a truant child who is required by a judge to attend school can be incarcerated for missing school notwithstanding the prohibition against locking up status offenders. Some states and local jurisdictions have already stopped utilizing the VCO exception, recognizing the harm to youth and the costs to communities. However, most states still employ the practice.

In December 2018, the Act was reauthorized, stabilizing its funding and core protections. The Act did not include ceasing or phasing-out the VCO exception, but it did include several updates to provisions of the Act, including requirements that states:

- Limit to seven days the detention of status offenders detained for violation of a VCO. Courts must issue a written order for any such detention, articulating the facts supporting the need for detention;
- Within three years, end the practice of placing youth under 18 who are transferred to adult court in adult facilities;
- Begin phasing out the use of restraints on girls who are pregnant or in post-partum recovery, except where "credible, reasonable grounds exist;"
- Coordinate with the education system to ensure the transfer of school records and credits for detained or committed youth; and
- Establish plans for the re-entry into the community of incarcerated youth.

The reauthorization also incorporated aspects of the Youth PROMISE Act (YPA), first introduced in 2009. The purpose of the Act was to reduce youth violence through the development of local councils charged with creating and implementing a community plan to prevent youth gang involvement and delinquency. The enacted elements include grants to states to fund local programs focused on a range of preventative services such as restorative justice programs, housing assistance, home visiting programs, and employment assistance. The Government Accountability Office will conduct a study after five years to evaluate the impact of the grants, providing an opportunity for future funding of a more expansive program. The reauthorization also includes more robust monitoring of state compliance and consequences for noncompliance with the requirements under the Act. Funding to states will be reduced for failure to comply with core requirements.

G. JUVENILE JUSTICE REFORM EFFORTS

Juvenile justice reform within the United States can be described as happening in four major waves:[80]

- The first wave is defined by the original development of the juvenile court, as described above.
- The second wave is characterized by the application of Constitutional due process protections to youth in juvenile court.
- The third wave came as a response to the increase in violent juvenile crime during the 1990s, resulting in the passage of harsh and punitive laws supplanting the rehabilitative aims of the court.
- The fourth wave emerged as juvenile crime subsided and research on adolescent development and brain science gained attention. New approaches took hold, emphasizing holding youth accountable in developmentally appropriate ways.

Within this "fourth wave," several priority policy areas have emerged, including: 1) reducing the detention and incarceration of juveniles and the harms associated with locking children up; 2) keeping youth in the juvenile justice system rather than transferring to the adult criminal system; 3) diverting low-risk youth from the juvenile justice system altogether; and 4) reducing racial and ethnic disparities within the juvenile justice system.

1. Reducing Detention and Incarceration and Associated Harms

In 2008, a multi-national study found that the United States had the highest incarceration rate among all the countries studied, which included Australia, France, Germany, Japan, and South Africa. In fact, the U.S. incarcerated children at a rate of 336 of every 100,000 youth, while South Africa, the next highest, incarcerated 69 of every 100,000.[81] Many of these ncarcerated youth have not committed violent offenses, and many are simply awaiting trial. In 1984, the Supreme Court upheld a New York statute permitting pre-trial detention of juveniles who posed a "serious risk" of committing a crime.[82] Endorsement of such discretionary use of pre-trial detention and the still reverberating policies of the 1990s "tough on crime" era have in part contributed to the uniquely high rate of detention in the United States. In addition, research shows that African American youth are detained at higher rates than white youth, contributing to the racial disparities within the juvenile justice system. In recent years, advocates have successfully argued that reducing juvenile detention and incarceration can actually save money without causing a rise in juvenile crime. The Juvenile Detention Alternatives Initiative (JDAI) is one programmatic effort that has led to the adoption of objective screening and assessment procedures to distinguish youth who demonstrate a high risk of reoffending from those who can be effectively monitored through alternatives to secure detention. A number of state governments have recently closed facilities and redirected funds toward community-based programs that more effectively treat and rehabilitate youth.

Of concern to advocates is not only the prevalence of detained and incarcerated children, but also the manner in which they are treated. Numerous media reports reveal overcrowded conditions, abusive staff, overuse of isolation and restraints, and the failure to provide needed health, mental health, and educational services. A 2011 report by the Annie E. Casey Foundation found that systemic maltreatment within juvenile correctional facilities has occurred in the vast majority of states, and 52 lawsuits since 1970 have resulted in court orders to address such issues. An updated 2015 report finds that such conditions have persisted even where states have entered into consent decrees with the obligation to improve conditions. For example, in 1998 Georgia entered into a consent decree with the U.S. Department of Justice to address conditions within the state's facilities. A federal study in 2013 found that these facilities had the highest rates of sexual abuse in the country and that more than 700 internal investigations of facilities had not been resolved. In Illinois, a monitoring report produced as part of a consent decree found that in 2012–13, facility youth were placed in isolation 1,170 times for an average of two and a half days each. Media reports in Iowa documented extensive stays in seclusion for incarcerated youth, up to months at a time. These youth were allowed out of their 12-by-10 cells, which had no furniture save a concrete slab with a thin mattress for a bed, for just one hour a day. In West Virginia, the state's primary training school was shuttered following findings by a state court that youth were kept in isolation excessively, with youth deemed suicidal locked in cells for several days before receiving a mental health assessment.[83]

2. Keeping Juveniles Out of Adult Court

As a result of the punitive approach of the 1990s, many youth were transferred from juvenile courts to adult criminal courts. During this era, the public, the courts, and lawmakers blurred the line between child and adult, focusing on the crime committed rather than the offender and his or her potential for rehabilitation. States gave prosecutors discretion to charge youths as adults in many circumstances. Laws were passed in almost every state lowering the age of criminal culpability, with children as young as ten eligible for transfer to the adult system. Such youth can be placed in adult jails and can be subject to lengthy sentences in adult facilities that lack educational, mental health, and other rehabilitative programming. This approach to public safety is questionable at best, with most studies indicating no reduction in crime rates as a result of transfer laws. Furthermore, studies have shown abysmal outcomes for juveniles leaving adult facilities. Several large studies have found greater recidivism rates among youth who were prosecuted as adults as compared to similarly situated youth who remained in the juvenile justice system.[84]

During the fourth wave of reform, a body of research returned the focus to recognizing how children are distinct from adults. Specifically, studies on adolescent development and brain science demonstrated that adolescents are less culpable than adults and have a greater capacity for change. As discussed above, this led to a series of U.S. Supreme Court cases endorsing these findings and creating the basis for policy that emphasizes the uniqueness and potential of young offenders. Some states have followed suit, passing laws making prosecution of juveniles as adults more difficult or limited. This has occurred through the rolling back of prosecutorial discretion to try youth as adults and/or the raising of the age of jurisdiction for the juvenile court. For example, Illinois eliminated the automatic transfer of youth to adult court for drug offenses; Arizona took the discretion to transfer youth away from prosecutors, instead giving district court judges this power; and some states have corrected the lowering of criminal court jurisdiction by raising the age to 18. Most recently, California passed SB 1391, which prohibits juveniles age 14 or 15 from prosecution in adult court. Despite these several examples, remnants of the punitive era exist in state laws that remain unchanged in many parts of the country.

3. Diverting Lower-Risk Youth from the Juvenile Justice System

At the other end of the spectrum from the serious offenders tried within the adult criminal system are the much more typical low- to moderate-risk youth who come into contact with law enforcement. Most children are going to engage in some type of "delinquent" behavior during their adolescence. However, the vast majority of youth will simply cease such behavior naturally as they mature.

When youth become involved with the juvenile justice system, however, research indicates that the system can do more harm than good, increasing their chance of future arrests.[85] Furthermore, the deeper into the system children go, the more their prospects diminish.

Advocates argue that an individualized approach to responding to delinquency is most effective. This approach is based on the use of risk assessments that indicate the level of risk for reoffending among delinquent youth. On this scientific basis, youth who are at lower risk can be diverted to programs that teach accountability outside of the juvenile justice system, thereby targeting the resources and efforts of the system on the higher risk youth. Such diversion programs include civil citation programs in which police can directly offer an offending youth the option of community service or counseling in lieu of prosecution; restorative justice programs in which offenders work to repair harms to victims resulting from their actions; and treatment and service provision to meet the behavioral health needs of youth.[86] Specialized mental health courts have been developed in several jurisdictions, the first of which was in Santa Clara, California.

Of particular importance are programs that interrupt the "school-to-prison-pipeline" that developed as a result of the harsh zero-tolerance policies adopted by schools in the 1990s. Many students were brought into juvenile court as a result of the criminalization of typical, albeit disruptive, adolescent behavior displayed at school. Entry into the juvenile justice system had significant consequences that impacted a youth's education and future prospects. In recent years, programs that limit the involvement of law enforcement and instead establish conflict mediation programs, for example, have begun to reduce arrests at school, notably without reducing school safety. Some state legislatures have revised their zero-tolerance laws and other states have required schools to train staff in discipline and adolescent behavior. Other special populations, such as dual status youth—youth who touch the child welfare and juvenile justice systems—and commercially sexually exploited children have been the focus of policy reform aimed at decriminalizing behaviors that are the result of a youth's victimization.[87]

4. Reducing Racial and Ethnic Disparities

Despite the inclusion of this issue as a core protection within the JJDPA, the overrepresentation of youth of color persists within the juvenile justice system. At each phase of a case—from arrest to confinement—minority youth are progressively more overrepresented. Studies have shown that youth of color are more often stopped and arrested by law enforcement than white youth; probation officers often view black youth as more culpable than white youth, and courts in urban areas—where there is a greater concentration of minority youth—tend to operate more formally and are more likely to impose severe sentences. Specifically, minority youth are disproportionately placed out of home rather than on probation and serve longer sentences than their white peers committing similar crimes.[88]

Several states have worked to address the issue of racial disparity through a variety of strategies including requiring a racial impact statement for proposed justice legislation that considers the potential impact on racial and ethnic minorities; requiring cultural competency training for system participants from law enforcement officers to judges; requiring data collection and committees to review the data and develop strategies specific to their community; and requiring that risk assessments used within the juvenile justice system are race neutral.[89] Nevertheless, disparities remain.

ENDNOTES

[1] U.S. Department of Justice, Office of Juvenile Justice and Delinquency Prevention, *OJJDP Statistical Briefing Book* (Washington, DC; October 2018) at https://www.ojjdp.gov/ojstatbb/crime/qa05101.asp?qaDate=2017.

[2] *Id.*

[3] U.S. Department of Justice, Office of Juvenile Justice and Delinquency Prevention, *OJJDP Statistical Briefing Book* (Washington DC; October 2018) at https://www.ojjdp.gov/ojstatbb/offenders/qa03202.asp?qaDate=2016.

[4] U.S. Department of Justice, Office of Juvenile Justice and Delinquency Prevention, *OJJDP Statistical Briefing Book* (Washington, DC; October 2018) at http://www.ojjdp.gov/ojstatbb/crime/JAR_Display.asp?ID=qa05202.

[5] U.S. Department of Justice, Office of Juvenile Justice and Delinquency Prevention, *OJJDP Statistical Briefing Book* (Washington DC; October 2018) at https://www.ojjdp.gov/ojstatbb/crime/qa05102.asp?qaDate=2017 (juvenile arrests).

[6] U.S. Department of Justice, Office of Juvenile Justice and Delinquency Prevention, *OJJDP Statistical Briefing Book* (Washington DC; October 2018) at https://www.ojjdp.gov/ojstatbb/crime/JAR_Display.asp?ID=qa05206 (juvenile arrest rate trends).

[7] U.S. Department of Justice, *supra*, note 5.

[8] U.S. Department of Justice, Office of Juvenile Justice and Delinquency Prevention, *Juvenile Arrests 2016*, Juvenile Justice Statistics, National Report Series Bulletin (Washington, DC; 2018) at https://www.ojjdp.gov/pubs/251861.pdf.

[9] U.S. Department of Justice, Office of Juvenile Justice and Delinquency Prevention, *OJJDP Statistical Briefing Book* (Washington, DC; October 2018) at https://www.ojjdp.gov/ojstatbb/crime/qa05104.asp?qaDate=2016&text=yes.

[10] Charles Puzzanchera and Samantha Ehrmann, National Center for Juvenile Justice, *Spotlight on Girls in the Juvenile Justice System* (Pittsburgh, PA; January 2018) at https://www.ojjdp.gov/ojstatbb/snapshots/DataSnapshot_GIRLS2015.pdf.

[11] U.S. Department of Justice, Office of Victims of Crime, *National Crime Victims' Rights Week Resource Guide: Youth Victimization Fact Sheet* (2017) at https://ovc.ncjrs.gov/ncvrw2017/images/en_artwork/Fact_Sheets/2017NCVRW_YouthVictimization_508.pdf.

[12] Child Trends, *Violent Crime Victimization* (Bethesda, MD; December 2015) at https://www.childtrends.org/wp-content/uploads/2015/12/71_Violent_Crime_Victimization.pdf.

[13] Melissa Sickmund and Charles Puzzanchera (eds.), *Juvenile Offenders and Victims: 2014 National Report*, at 39 (Pittsburgh, PA; 2014) at https://www.ojjdp.gov/ojstatbb/nr2014/.

[14] Child Trends, *Children's Exposure to Violence* (Bethesda, MD: 2016) at https://www.childtrends.org/indicators/childrens-exposure-to-violence.

[15] Sickmund & Puzzanchera, *supra* note 13, at 46.

[16] Carl McCurley and Howard N. Snyder, *Victims of Violent Juvenile Crime* (Washington, DC; 2004) at https://www.ncjrs.gov/pdffiles1/ojjdp/201628.pdf.

[17] Centers for Disease Control and Prevention, *10 Leading Causes of Death by Age Group 2016*, at https://www.cdc.gov/injury/wisqars/pdf/leading_causes_of_death_by_age_group_2016-508.pdf.

[18] Centers for Disease Control and Prevention, *Youth Violence Facts at a Glance: 2016*, at https://www.cdc.gov/violenceprevention/pdf/yv-datasheet.pdf.

[19] Charles Puzzanchera, National Center for Juvenile Justice, *Juvenile Arrests, 2016* (U.S. Department of Justice, Office of Juvenile Justice and Delinquency Prevention; 2018) at https://www.ojjdp.gov/pubs/251861.pdf.

[20] K.A. Fowler, *et al.*, *Childhood Firearm Injuries in the United States*. 140 PEDIATRICS 1 (2017).

[21] Development Services Group, Inc., *Risk Factors for Delinquency: Literature Review* (Washington, D.C., Office of Juvenile Justice and Delinquency Prevention; 2015) at https://www.ojjdp.gov/mpg/litreviews/Risk%20Factors.pdf.

[22] Development Services Group, Inc., *Protective Factors Against Delinquency: Literature Review* (Washington, DC, Office of Juvenile Justice and Delinquency Prevention; 2015) at https://www.ojjdp.gov/mpg/litreviews/Protective%20Factors.pdf.

[23] Liann Seiter, *Mental Health and Juvenile Justice: A Review of Prevalence, Promising Practices, and Areas for Improvement* (Washington, DC: National Technical Assistance Center for the Education of Neglected or Delinquent Children and Youth (2017) at https://neglected-delinquent.ed.gov/sites/default/files/NDTAC-MentalHealth-JJ-Brief-508.pdf.

[24] *Id.*

[25] Laurie Chassin, *et al.*, *Substance Use and Substance Use Disorders as Risk Factors for*

Juvenile Offending, Chapter 13, APA Handbook of Psychology and Juvenile Justice pp. 277–305 (2016).

[26] Lloyd D. Johnston et al., *Key Findings on Adolescent Drug Use: 2017 Overview, Monitoring the Future, National Survey Results on Drug Use 1975–2017* (2018) at http://monitoringthefuture.org/pubs/monographs/mtf-overview2017.pdf.

[27] Chassin, *supra* note 25.

[28] National Center for Mental Health and Juvenile Justice, *Co-Occurring Disorders Among Youth in Juvenile Justice* (2016) https://www.ncmhjj.com/wp-content/uploads/2016/09/Co-occurring-Disorders-Among-Youth-in-Juvenile-Justice-FOR-WEBSITE.pdf.

[29] Development Services Group, *supra* note 21.

[30] Gail Wasserman *et al.*, *Risk and Protective Factors of Child Delinquency*, U.S. Department of Justice, Office of Juvenile Justice and Delinquency Prevention (Washington, DC; 2003) at https://www.ncjrs.gov/pdffiles1/ojjdp/193409.pdf.

[31] Development Services Group, *supra* note 22.

[32] Anna J. Markowitz and Rebecca M. Ryan, *Father Absence and Adolescent Depression and Delinquency: A Comparison of Siblings Approach*, 78, J. MARRIAGE FAM 5 (2016).

[33] Cortney Simmons, et al., *The differential influence of absent and harsh fathers on juvenile delinquency*. 62 J. ADOL., pp. 9–17 (2018).

[34] Annie E. Casey Foundation, *A Shared Sentence* (Baltimore, MD; 2016).

[35] Simmons, *supra* note 33.

[36] *Id.*

[37] Janet K. Wiig, John A. Tuell, and Jessica K. Heldman, *Guidebook for Juvenile Justice and Child Welfare System Coordination and Integration*, 3rd ed., Robert F. Kennedy National Resource Center for Juvenile Justice (Boston, MA; 2013).

[38] David Finkelhor et al, *Children's Exposure to Violence, Crime, and Abuse: An Update, National Survey of Children's Exposure to Violence*, Juvenile Justice Bulletin (September 2015) at https://www.ojjdp.gov/pubs/248547.pdf.

[39] Wasserman, *supra* note 30.

[40] JP Hoffman, *Modeling the Association Between Academic Achievement and Delinquency: an Application of Interactional Theory*, 51 CRIMINOLOGY 3 (August 2013).

[41] *Id.*

[42] Wasserman, *supra* note 30.

[43] Centers for Disease Control and Prevention, *supra* note 18.

[44] Wasserman, *supra* note 30.

[45] TJ Dishion and JM Tipsord, *Peer contagion in child and adolescent social and emotional development*. 62 ANN. REV. PSYCHOL. 189–214 (2011).

[46] I. Lambie, *The impact of incarceration on juvenile offenders*, 33 CLIN. PSYCH. REV. 448–459 (2013).

[47] Michael Shader, *Risk Factors for Delinquency: An Overview* (Washington, DC, Office of Juvenile Justice and Delinquency Prevention; 2004).

[48] Development Services Group, Inc., *Gang Prevention: Literature review* (Washington, D.C., Office of Juvenile Justice and Delinquency Prevention, 2014) at https://www.ojjdp.gov/mpg/litreviews/Gang_Prevention.pdf; see also https://www.nationalgangcenter.gov/survey-analysis/measuring-the-extent-of-gang-problems.

[49] U.S. Department of Education, National Center for Education Statistics, *Indicator 8: Students' Reports of Gangs at School, Indicators of School Crime and Safety* (Washington, DC; May 2017) at https://nces.ed.gov/programs/crimeindicators/ind_08.asp.

[50] For more on Positive Youth Development research and programming, visit https://www.ojjdp.gov/mpg/litreviews/PositiveYouthDevelopment.pdf.

[51] Heather Koball & Yang Jiang, *Basic Facts about Low-Income Children: Fact Sheet* (National Center for Children in Poverty, Mailman School of Public Health, Columbia University, New York, NY; 2018) at http://www.nccp.org/publications/pub_1194.html.

[52] Roger Jarjoura, Ruth Triplett, & Gregory P. Brinker, *Growing Up Poor: Examining the Link Between Persistent Childhood Poverty and Delinquency*, 18 J. of QUANTITATIVE CRIMINOLOGY 2, 159-187 (2002).

[53] *Id.*

[54] Carter Hay, et al., *Compounded Risk: The Implications for Delinquency of Coming from a Poor Family that Lives in a Poor Community*, 36 J. YOUTH & ADOL. 5, 593–605 (2007).

[55] Heidi Zinzow, *Witnessed Community and Parental Violence in Relation to Substance Use and Delinquency in a National Sample of Adolescents*, 22 J. TRAUMA STRESS 6, 525–533 (2009).

[56] David Finkelhor, *et al.*, *Prevalence of Childhood Exposure to Violence, Crime, and Abuse* 169 JAMA PEDIATR. 8, p. 746-754 (2015).

[57] Developmental Services Group, Inc., *Gun Violence and Youth: Literature Review* (Washington DC, Office of Juvenile Justice and Delinquency Prevention; 2016) at https://www.ojjdp.gov/mpg/litreviews/gun-violence-and-youth.pdf.

[58] Kavita Parikh, *et al.*, *Pediatric Firearm-Related Injuries in the United States*, 7 HOSPITAL PEDIATRICS 6 (June 2017).

[59] See Cal. Welf. & Inst. Code §625.6 (2019).

[60] See https://www.ojjdp.gov/ojstatbb/structure_process/qa04125.asp?qaDate=2011.

[61] For more on the Kids for Cash scandal, see https://jlc.org/luzerne-kids-cash-scandal.

[62] *Graham v. Florida*, 560 U.S. 48, 75 (2010).

[63] *Miller v. Alabama*, 567 U.S. 460, at 477 (2012).

[64] *Budder v. Addison*, 851 F.3d 1047 at 1057 (2017).

[65] *People v. Contreras*, 4 Cal. 5th 349 (2018).

[66] This ruling was vacated and rehearing has been scheduled for February 2019.

[67] *Graham v. Florida*, 130 S. Ct. 2011, 2055 (2010) (Thomas dissent).

[68] Sarah Russell & Tracy Denholtz, *Procedures for Proportionate Sentences: The Next Wave of Eighth Amendment Noncapital Litigation*, 48 Conn. L. Rev 4. 1121 (2016).

[69] Gina M. Vincent, Laura S. Guy, and Thomas Grisso, *Risk Assessment in Juvenile Justice: A Guidebook for Implementation, Models for Change* (MacArthur Foundation, Chicago, IL: 2012).

[70] Jillian B. Carr & Jennifer L. Doleac, *Keep the Kids Inside? Juvenile Curfews and Urban Gun Violence*, 47 RESEARCH BRIEFS IN ECONOMIC POLICY (Cato Institute, 2016).

[71] See https://www.ojjdp.gov/ojstatbb/offenders/qa03301.asp?qaDate=2016.

[72] Cal. Educ. Code §48293(a).

[73] Cal. Penal Code § 270.1.

[74] Adrienne L. Fernandes-Alcantara, *Runaway and Homeless Youth: Demographics and Programs* (Congressional Research Service; 2018).

[75] *Id.*

[76] *Id.*

[77] Mark E. Courtney, *et al.*, *Youth who run away from out-of-home care* (Chicago, IL: Chapin Hall at the University of Chicago; 2005).

[78] 42 U.S.C. § 5601 *et seq.*

[79] Congressional Research Service, *Juvenile Justice Funding Trends* (May 1, 2018) at https://crsreports.congress.gov/product/pdf/R/R44879.

[80] National Campaign to Reform State Juvenile Justice Systems, *The Fourth Wave: Juvenile Justice Reforms for the Twenty-First Century* (2013).

[81] *Id.*

[82] See *Schall v. Martin*, 467 U.S. 253 (1984).

[83] Annie E. Casey Foundation, *Maltreatment of Youth in U.S. Juvenile Corrections Facilities: An Update* (Baltimore, MD; 2015).

[84] Patrick Griffin, et al., *Trying Juveniles as Adults: An Analysis of State Transfer Laws and Reporting*, U.S. Department of Justice, Office of Juvenile Justice and Delinquency Prevention (Washington DC; 2011) at https://www.ncjrs.gov/pdffiles1/ojjdp/232434.pdf.

[85] John A. Tuell, Jessica Heldman, and Kari Harp, *Translating the Science of Adolescent Development to Sustainable Best Practice* (Robert F. Kennedy National Resource Center for Juvenile Justice, Boston, MA; 2018).

[86] *Id.*

[87] See Wiig, Tuell, & Heldman, *supra* note 37.

[88] Barry Feld, *Competence and Culpability: Delinquents in Juvenile Courts, Youths in Criminal Courts*, 102 MINN. L. REV. 473 (2017).

[89] See http://www.ncsl.org/research/civil-and-criminal-justice/racial-and-ethnic-disparities-in-the-juvenile-justice-system.aspx.

CHAPTER ELEVEN

Child Rights to Custody, Family Support and Emancipation

A. CHILD CUSTODY

1. In General

Questions about child custody arise in a variety of contexts: adoption, divorce, abuse, parental death, incapacitation, or abandonment. The question of who is the parent, guardian, or custodian of a child may evolve from proceedings in general civil, probate, family, or juvenile court departments—each subject to its own rules.

One of the most important differences between the respective types of courts adjudicating child custody issues is the representation of the child. Commonly, a child has no assured separate counsel in general civil, probate, or family court— even where his or her rights and future are at issue. Children are generally given a *guardian ad litem* in juvenile dependency court—which can assume civil jurisdiction over allegedly abused or neglected children for their protection. Federal law requires such an appointment to receive child welfare funds from the Congress. Increasingly, such appointees are attorneys. In practice, parents are assured of counsel in juvenile dependency court where their basic right to parental status is implicated. They receive an attorney at public cost if they are indigent (see *Lassiter* case in Chapter 8).

2. Paternal Assertion of Parental Rights

Paternal rights are most commonly litigated in family court, where child support orders may be framed obligating biological or otherwise liable fathers to support children as part of a marriage dissolution proceeding. With marriage, the involvement of the family court in arranging for child custody upon divorce creates a system for tracking parental rights and maintaining some parental role upon the separation of parents. Apart from this divorce/custody circumstance is the difficult problem of paternal status where the birth is to an unwed mother. As discussed in Chapter 2, close to 40% of current births are to unwed mothers, with the annual number of such births increasing from 243,000 in 1960 to almost 2 million by 2007, although decreasing somewhat from that point to 2017. The rate among African-American women has not declined markedly and is at 69.8% in 2016—including 389,780 births.[1]

Here, assertion of paternal rights may take the form of a refusal to consent to a child's placement for adoption as sought by the child's mother, an attempt at visitation or some continuing role in the life of the child, or even a demand for full custody. This difficult context has raised emotional issues in highly publicized cases where adoptive parents were compelled to return children to the biological father even when the unwed mother had supported adoption by others. On occasion, such custody contests occur only after several years of care by prospective adoptive couples as the cases wind through the appellate courts.

The determination of paternity rights usually depends in the first instance on the "status of the father." That status is defined from a vocabulary created by applicable statutes and court decisions. The "terms of art" outline the following paternal categories:

- The term "alleged" father refers to a person who may be a biological father, but biological paternity has not been genetically or legally established.
- The term "biological" father (sometimes pejoratively referred to as a "mere biological" father in case law) refers to a person who has been confirmed as the biological father of a child, but who has not achieved "presumed" fatherhood status as defined in most state statutes.
- The term "*Kelsey*" father refers to a biological father who promptly attempted to assume his paternal responsibility as fully as circumstances allow under the criteria of *Adoption of Kelsey S.*, 1 Cal. 4th 816 (1992) (see below).
- The term "*de facto*" father (or parent) refers to a person who may be reasonably regarded as a parent by a child; such status is based on actual parental performance.
- The term "presumed" father refers to one who meets the criteria of state statutes allowing presumptive (but rebuttable) fatherhood status.

The Uniform Parentage Act (UPA),[2] a creation of the Uniform Law Commission, has been adopted in some form by all 50 states. Its early iteration has been amended in 2002 and 2017. Every version, however, provides for "presumed" fatherhood status where he and the child's natural mother are or have been married to each other *and* (a) the child is born during the marriage or within 300 days after the marriage is terminated by death, annulment, divorce, or separation decree; or (b) the man receives the child into his home and openly holds the child out as his own.

In general, presumed fatherhood status is rebuttable by clear and convincing evidence; a paternity judgment establishing another man as the biological father provides such a showing. However, a practical challenge to a presumptive father from another claimant may turn on legal standing to challenge the presumed status of another, as discussed below. A common conundrum occurs when a father does not welcome a child into his home (technically required for presumed father status) only because he is deprived of that placement over his objection. Where a paternal role is sought in good faith, some courts hold that "taking into the home" is not required and may be excused. Some courts give such fathers "*Kelsey*" father status just short of a presumed father, and still others would designate such a person an "equitable" father—meaning he is fulfilling the function but without all of the rights commonly ascribed to parents.

Over the past four decades, paternity rights and obligations have been much affected by:

- the withdrawal of marriage as a permissibly exclusive bright line test for parenthood status;
- the use of biology as a strong criterion for parental child support financial obligation (including repayment of the state for welfare paid for the children of biological fathers);
- the growth of single-parent families, and the increasing problem of paternal abandonment of children;
- the assertion and exercise of a woman's prerogative to abort, and to make decisions concerning the adoption of children;
- the growth of "surrogacy" fertilization by a man not intended to fulfill a paternal role; and
- the complexity of gay or lesbian parents, often through surrogacy or adoption, particularly in states that legally recognize only two parents for a child.

As noted, the UPA was amended in 2002 and in 2017. In 2002 it was updated to add a streamlined voluntary acknowledgement of paternity for non-marital children important to eligibility of beneficiaries for TANF benefits after 1996 discussed in Chapter 3. It also addressed the parentage of children born through surrogacy. The 2017 amendments made seven further refinements to the UPA: (1) removal of gender distinctions; (2) new methods for establishing parentage for non-biological parents; (3) the addition of a multi-factor assessment to resolve competing claims; (4) allowing for the optional recognition of more than two parents; (5) addressing parentage of children born from a sexual assault; (6) updates to the 2002 surrogacy circumstance; and (7) the addition of a new Article addressing the rights of children born through Assisted Reproductive Technology and gamete (sperm and ova) providers.

Where large numbers of children are born as a result of unintended pregnancies, what are the implications for the biological father's parental rights? We do not allocate children to the wealthiest or most able or most loving available adults; historically we start with biology and marriage as the two critical factors. How does biology alone work where there is little connection between impregnation and intent or ability to be a father (or mother)? What do we do when a mother wants the child adopted by a "better" family for the child's own good and believes the biological father to be dangerous? The legal status of "father" (as with "mother") invokes a constitutionally-protected "fundamental liberty interest" to parent. Is reliance on biology alone to confer that status over-inclusive? But is "marriage" as an alternative criterion under-inclusive where fathers in fact function as such without marrying the mothers of their children? What do we do when an otherwise able and willing unmarried father wanted to and would have so functioned but is deceived about his biological role and only learns of it well after the child's birth?

As with most legal questions, the answers are much influenced by whose shoes we occupy in answering. Are the child's shoes occupied in the decisions considering the rights and obligations of contesting parents? Is there an element viewing the child as a prize to be awarded to the adult less "in the wrong," as if an object subject to competing ownership claims? Does such an "in the wrong" analysis include recognition of children as fully participating parties?

Related questions also arise in the difficult adjudications determining these rights. Must the answer to custody questions be absolute (either "x" or "y" is the sole custodian)? In divorce, there is a trend to grant "joint custody" to both parents where possible—in the interest of the child. There is a compelled sharing. Is some role possible for a biological father, who may have delayed too long to be recognized as the father without removing a happy child from a successful adoptive family, but who still may have something to contribute? We celebrate uncles and cousins and extended family involvement in the lives of children; should we allow some role for the *bona fide* assertion of another adult wanting to care for a child—particularly in a society starved for paternal concern? But what if such a claimant is a bad influence, or a danger, in the rational view of those charged with the child's custody? How do the courts draw reasonably clear and predictable lines in such matters without becoming overly enmeshed in family disputes?

One variable, not much discussed, has to do with the impact of the legal process itself: where the major harm to a child caught in a custody dispute is to bond and then to be taken from loving arms, what responsibility does the judiciary have to make a timely decision? To what extent does physical custody during adjudication determine the outcome? Where it does not determine the outcome, what is the impact of a decision to disturb the custody arrangement after a delay of two to five years and after inevitable reliance by the child on the functioning parents *pendente lite*?

Stanley v. Illinois
405 U.S. 645 (1972)

MR. JUSTICE WHITE delivered the opinion of the Court.

Joan Stanley lived with Peter Stanley intermittently for 18 years, during which time they had three children...When Joan Stanley died, Peter Stanley lost not only her but also his children. Under Illinois law, the children of unwed fathers become wards of the State upon the death of the mother. Accordingly, upon Joan Stanley's death, in a dependency proceeding instituted by the State of Illinois, Stanley's children[3] were declared wards of the State and placed with court-appointed guardians. Stanley appealed, claiming that he had never been shown to be an unfit parent and that since married fathers and unwed mothers could not be deprived of their children without such a showing, he had been deprived of the equal protection of the laws guaranteed him by the Fourteenth Amendment. The Illinois Supreme Court accepted the fact that Stanley's own unfitness had not been established but rejected the equal protection

claim, holding that Stanley could properly be separated from his children upon proof of the single fact that he and the dead mother had not been married. Stanley's actual fitness as a father was irrelevant....

Stanley presses his equal protection claim here. The State continues to respond that unwed fathers are presumed unfit to raise their children and that it is unnecessary to hold individualized hearings to determine whether particular fathers are in fact unfit parents before they are separated from their children. We granted certiorari, 400 U.S. 1020 (1971), to determine whether this method of procedure by presumption could be allowed to stand in light of the fact that Illinois allows married fathers—whether divorced, widowed, or separated—and mothers—even if unwed—the benefit of the presumption that they are fit to raise their children.

I
* * *

...It is first urged that Stanley could act to adopt his children. But under Illinois law, Stanley is treated not as a parent but as a stranger to his children, and the dependency proceeding has gone forward on the presumption that he is unfit to exercise parental rights. Insofar as we are informed, Illinois law affords him no priority in adoption proceedings. It would be his burden to establish not only that he would be a suitable parent but also that he would be the most suitable of all who might want custody of the children. Neither can we ignore that in the proceedings from which this action developed, the "probation officer,"...the assistant state's attorney,...and the judge charged with the case,...made it apparent that Stanley, unmarried and impecunious as he is, could not now expect to profit from adoption proceedings....

...We must therefore examine the question that Illinois would have us avoid: Is a presumption that distinguishes and burdens all unwed fathers constitutionally repugnant? We conclude that, as a matter of due process of law, Stanley was entitled to a hearing on his fitness as a parent before his children were taken from him and that, by denying him a hearing and extending it to all other parents whose custody of their children is challenged, the State denied Stanley the equal protection of the laws guaranteed by the Fourteenth Amendment.

II

Illinois has two principal methods of removing nondelinquent children from the homes of their parents. In a dependency proceeding it may demonstrate that the children are wards of the State because they have no surviving parent or guardian....In a neglect proceeding it may show that children should be wards of the State because the present parent(s) or guardian does not provide suitable care....

The State's right—indeed, duty—to protect minor children through a judicial determination of their interests in a neglect proceeding is not challenged here. Rather, we are faced with a dependency statute that empowers state officials to circumvent neglect proceedings on the theory that an unwed father is not a "parent" whose existing relationship with his children must be considered.[4] "Parents," says the State, "means the father and mother of a legitimate child, or the survivor of them, or the natural mother of an illegitimate child, and includes any adoptive parent,"...but the term does not include unwed fathers.

Under Illinois law, therefore, while the children of all parents can be taken from them in neglect proceedings, that is only after notice, hearing, and proof of such unfitness as a parent as amounts to neglect, an unwed father is uniquely subject to the more simplistic dependency proceeding. By use of this proceeding, the State, on showing that the father was not married to the mother, need not prove unfitness in fact, because it is presumed at law. Thus, the unwed father's claim of parental qualification is avoided as "irrelevant."

* * *

The private interest here, that of a man in the children he has sired and raised, undeniably warrants deference and, absent a powerful countervailing interest, protection. It is plain that the interest of a parent in the companionship, care, custody, and management of his or her children "come[s] to this Court with a momentum for respect lacking when appeal is made to liberties which derive merely from shifting economic arrangements." *Kovacs v. Cooper*, 336 U.S. 77, 95 (1949) (Frankfurter, J., concurring).

The Court has frequently emphasized the importance of the family. The rights to conceive and to raise one's children have been deemed "essential," *Meyer v. Nebraska*, 262 U.S. 390, 399 (1923), "basic civil rights of man," *Skinner v. Oklahoma*, 316 U.S.

535, 541 (1942), and "rights far more precious...than property rights," *May v. Anderson*, 345 U.S. 528, 533 (1953)....

Nor has the law refused to recognize those family relationships unlegitimized by a marriage ceremony. The Court has declared unconstitutional a state statute denying natural, but illegitimate, children a wrongful-death action for the death of their mother, emphasizing that such children cannot be denied the right of other children because familial bonds in such cases were often as warm, enduring, and important as those arising within a more formally organized family unit. *Levy v. Louisiana*, 391 U.S. 68, 71–72 (1968). "To say that the test of equal protection should be the 'legal' rather than the biological relationship is to avoid the issue. For the Equal Protection Clause necessarily limits the authority of a State to draw such 'legal' lines as it chooses." *Glona v. American Guarantee Co.*, 391 U.S. 73, 75–76 (1968).

These authorities make it clear that, at the least, Stanley's interest in retaining custody of his children is cognizable and substantial.

For its part, the State has made its interest quite plain: Illinois has declared that the aim of the Juvenile Court Act is to protect "the moral, emotional, mental, and physical welfare of the minor and the best interests of the community" and to "strengthen the minor's family ties whenever possible, removing him from the custody of his parents only when his welfare or safety or the protection of the public cannot be adequately safeguarded without removal...."...These are legitimate interests, well within the power of the State to implement. We do not question the assertion that neglectful parents may be separated from their children.

But we are here not asked to evaluate the legitimacy of the state ends, rather, to determine whether the means used to achieve these ends are constitutionally defensible. What is the state interest in separating children from fathers without a hearing designed to determine whether the father is unfit in a particular disputed case? We observe that the State registers no gain towards its declared goals when it separates children from the custody of fit parents. Indeed, if Stanley is a fit father, the State spites its own articulated goals when it needlessly separates him from his family.

* * *

III

The State of Illinois assumes custody of the children of married parents, divorced parents, and unmarried mothers only after a hearing and proof of neglect. The children of unmarried fathers, however, are declared dependent children without a hearing on parental fitness and without proof of neglect. Stanley's claim in the state courts and here is that failure to afford him a hearing on his parental qualifications while extending it to other parents denied him equal protection of the laws. We have concluded that all Illinois parents are constitutionally entitled to a hearing on their fitness before their children are removed from their custody. It follows that denying such a hearing to Stanley and those like him while granting it to other Illinois parents is inescapably contrary to the Equal Protection Clause....

* * *

[3] Only two children are involved in this litigation.

[4] Even while refusing to label him a "legal parent," the State does not deny that Stanley has a special interest in the outcome of these proceedings. It is undisputed that he is the father of these children, that he lived with the two children whose custody is challenged all their lives, and that he has supported them.

MR. CHIEF JUSTICE BURGER, with whom **MR. JUSTICE BLACKMAN** concurs, dissenting.

* * *

In regard to the only issue that I consider properly before the Court, I agree with the State's argument that the Equal Protection Clause is not violated when Illinois gives full recognition only to those father-child relationships that arise in the context of family units bound together by legal obligations arising from marriage or from adoption proceedings. Quite apart from the religious or quasi-religious connotations that marriage has—and has historically enjoyed—for a large proportion of this Nation's citizens, it is in law an essentially contractual relationship, the parties to which have legally enforceable rights and duties, with respect both to each other and to any children born to them. Stanley and the mother of these children never entered such a relationship. The record is silent as to whether they ever privately exchanged such promises as would have bound them in marriage under the common law....In any event, Illinois has not recognized common-law marriages since 1905. Ill. Rev. Stat., c. 89, § 4. Stanley did not seek the burdens when he could have freely assumed them.

* * *

The Illinois Supreme Court correctly held that the State may constitutionally distinguish between unwed fathers and unwed mothers. Here, Illinois' different treatment of the two is part of that State's statutory scheme for protecting the welfare of illegitimate children. In almost all cases, the unwed mother is readily identifiable, generally from hospital records, and alternatively by physicians or others attending the child's birth. Unwed fathers, as a class, are not traditionally quite so easy to identify and locate. Many of them either deny all responsibility or exhibit no interest in the child or its welfare; and, of course, many unwed fathers are simply not aware of their parenthood.

Furthermore, I believe that a State is fully justified in concluding, on the basis of common human experience, that the biological role of the mother in carrying and nursing an infant creates stronger bonds between her and the child than the bonds resulting from the male's often casual encounter. This view is reinforced by the observable fact that most unwed mothers exhibit a concern for their offspring either permanently or at least until they are safely placed for adoption, while unwed fathers rarely burden either the mother or the child with their attentions or loyalties. Centuries of human experience buttress this view of the realities of human conditions and suggest that unwed mothers of illegitimate children are generally more dependable protectors of their children than are unwed fathers. While these, like most generalizations, are not without exceptions, they nevertheless provide a sufficient basis to sustain a statutory classification whose objective is not to penalize unwed parents but to further the welfare of illegitimate children in fulfillment of the State's obligations as *parens patriae*.[4]

Stanley depicts himself as a somewhat unusual unwed father, namely, as one who has always acknowledged and never doubted his fatherhood of these children. He alleges that he loved, cared for, and supported these children from the time of their birth until the death of their mother. He contends that he consequently must be treated the same as a married father of legitimate children. Even assuming the truth of Stanley's allegations, I am unable to construe the Equal Protection Clause as requiring Illinois to tailor its statutory definition of "parents" so meticulously as to include such unusual unwed fathers, while at the same time excluding those unwed, and generally unidentified, biological fathers who in no way share Stanley's professed desires.

Indeed, the nature of Stanley's own desires is less than absolutely clear from the record in this case. Shortly after the death of the mother, Stanley turned these two children over to the care of a Mr. and Mrs. Ness; he took no action to gain recognition of himself as a father, through adoption, or as a legal custodian, through a guardianship proceeding. Eventually it came to the attention of the State that there was no living adult who had any legally enforceable obligation for the care and support of the children; it was only then that the dependency proceeding here under review took place and that Stanley made himself known to the juvenile court in connection with these two children. [5] Even then, however, Stanley did not ask to be charged with the legal responsibility for the children. He asked only that such legal responsibility be given to no one else. He seemed, in particular, to be concerned with the loss of the welfare payments he would suffer as a result of the designation of others as guardians of the children.

[4] When the marriage between the parents of a legitimate child is dissolved by divorce or separation, the State, of course, normally awards custody of the child to one parent or the other. This is considered necessary for the child's welfare, since the parents are no longer legally bound together. The unmarried parents of an illegitimate child are likewise not legally bound together. Thus, even if Illinois did recognize the parenthood of both the mother and father of an illegitimate child, it would, for consistency with its practice in divorce proceedings, be called upon to award custody to one or the other of them, at least once it had by some means ascertained the identity of the father.

[5] As the majority notes, ante,....,Joan Stanley gave birth to three children during the 18 years Peter Stanley was living "intermittently" with her. At oral argument, we were told by Stanley's counsel that the oldest of these three children had previously been declared a ward of the court pursuant to a neglect proceeding that was "proven against" Stanley at a time, apparently, when the juvenile court officials were under the erroneous impression that Peter and Joan Stanley had been married....

Questions for Discussion

1. The *Stanley* Court held that the Illinois assumption that an unmarried father may have his parental rights terminated without hearing violates his due process rights. Such a father is entitled to a due process hearing. What will that hearing decide and on what basis? Is not the answer to these questions more important than the formalism of a hearing right alone? Although Illinois is required to grant Stanley a hearing, can it substantively weigh his failure to marry the mother of these children as a factor in terminating his parental rights? Can absence of marriage shift the burden from the state to Stanley to demonstrate his fitness as a parent? What if Stanley has functioned as the father, but has not married the mother of the children, *and* is not the biological father?

2. The dissent argues that the bright line distinction of marriage is constitutionally permissible as a determinant of parental rights. Arguably, children benefit from marriage incentives in a variety of ways, from inclusion in the employee health policies of fathers, to insurance and disability protections, to family court jurisdiction if the biological mother and father part ways. Parental status infirmity can be cured by the involved parents by marrying. However, the denial of parental rights to a father who has functioned as such can mean the permanent loss of that parent. From the child's perspective, that "taking" by the state may be momentous, and if marriage is to be the critical criterion, what opportunity do children have to determine the marital status of their parents? Is the child's loss of a parent entitled to the same constitutional cognizance as the right to parent? To any constitutional status? If so, is it appropriately abrogated based on circumstances over which affected children have no control?

3. Is the child's perspective discussed or considered by the majority opinion? By the dissent?

Lehr v. Robertson

463 U.S. 248 (1983)

JUSTICE STEVENS delivered the opinion of the Court.

The question presented is whether New York has sufficiently protected an unmarried father's inchoate relationship with a child whom he has never supported and rarely seen in the two years since her birth. The appellant, Jonathan Lehr, claims that the Due Process and Equal Protection Clauses of the Fourteenth Amendment, as interpreted in *Stanley v. Illinois,* 405 U.S. 645 (1972), and *Caban v. Mohammed,* 441 U.S. 380 (1979), give him an absolute right to notice and an opportunity to be heard before the child may be adopted. We disagree.

Jessica M. was born out of wedlock on November 9, 1976. Her mother, Lorraine Robertson, married Richard Robertson eight months after Jessica's birth....On December 21, 1978, when Jessica was over two years old, the Robertsons filed an adoption petition in the Family Court of Ulster County, New York. The court heard their testimony and received a favorable report from the Ulster County Department of Social Services. On March 7, 1979, the court entered an order of adoption....In this proceeding, appellant contends that the adoption order is invalid because he, Jessica's putative father, was not given advance notice of the adoption proceeding....

The State of New York maintains a "putative father registry."...A man who files with that registry demonstrates his intent to claim paternity of a child born out of wedlock and is therefore entitled to receive notice of any proceeding to adopt that child. Before entering Jessica's adoption order, the Ulster County Family Court had the putative father registry examined. Although appellant claims to be Jessica's natural father, he had not entered his name in the registry.

In addition to the persons whose names are listed on the putative father registry, New York law requires that notice of an adoption proceeding be given to several other classes of possible fathers of children born out of wedlock—those who have been adjudicated to be the father, those who have been identified as the father on the child's birth certificate, those who live openly with the child and the child's mother and who hold themselves out to be the father, those who have been identified as the father by the mother in a sworn written statement, and those who were married to the child's mother before the child was six months old.[5] Appellant admittedly was not a member of any of those classes. He had lived with appellee prior to Jessica's birth and visited her in the hospital when Jessica was born, but his name does not appear on Jessica's birth certificate. He did not live with appellee or Jessica after Jessica's birth, he has never provided them with any financial support, and he has never offered to marry appellee. Nevertheless, he contends that the following special circumstances gave him a constitutional right to notice and a hearing before Jessica was adopted.

On January 30, 1979, one month after the adoption proceeding was commenced in Ulster County, appellant filed a "visitation and paternity petition" in the Westchester County Family Court. In that petition, he asked for a determination of paternity, an order of support, and reasonable visitation privileges with Jessica. Notice of that proceeding was served on appellee on February 22, 1979. Four days later appellee's attorney informed the Ulster County Court that appellant had commenced a paternity proceeding in Westchester County; the Ulster County judge then entered an order staying appellant's paternity proceeding until he could rule on a motion to change the venue of that proceeding to Ulster County. On March 3, 1979, appellant received notice of the change of venue motion and, for the first time, learned that an adoption proceeding was pending in Ulster County.

On March 7, 1979, appellant's attorney telephoned the Ulster County judge to inform him that he planned to seek a stay of the adoption proceeding pending the determination of the paternity petition. In that telephone conversation, the judge advised the lawyer that he had already signed the adoption order earlier that day. According to appellant's attorney, the judge stated that he was aware of the pending paternity petition but did not believe he was required to give notice to appellant prior to the entry of the order of adoption.

* * *

Appellant has now invoked our appellate jurisdiction....He offers two alternative grounds for holding the New York statutory scheme unconstitutional. First, he contends that a putative father's actual or potential relationship with a child born out of wedlock is an interest in liberty which may not be destroyed without due process of law; he argues therefore that he had a constitutional right to prior notice and an opportunity to be heard before he was deprived of that interest. Second, he contends that the gender-based classification in the statute, which both denied him the right to consent to Jessica's adoption and accorded him fewer procedural rights than her mother, violated the Equal Protection Clause....

The Due Process Claim.

The Fourteenth Amendment provides that no State shall deprive any person of life, liberty, or property without due process of law. When that Clause is invoked in a novel context, it is our practice to begin the inquiry with a determination of the precise nature of the private interest that is threatened by the State....

I

The intangible fibers that connect parent and child have infinite variety. They are woven throughout the fabric of our society, providing it with strength, beauty, and flexibility. It is self-evident that they are sufficiently vital to merit constitutional protection in appropriate cases. In deciding whether this is such a case, however, we must consider the broad framework that has traditionally been used to resolve the legal problems arising from the parent-child relationship.

In the vast majority of cases, state law determines the final outcome....Rules governing the inheritance of property, adoption, and child custody are generally specified in statutory enactments that vary from State to State....Moreover, equally varied state laws governing marriage and divorce affect a multitude of parent-child relationships. The institution of marriage has played a critical role both in defining the legal entitlements of family members and in developing the decentralized structure of our democratic society....In recognition of that role, and as part of their general overarching concern for serving the best interests of children, state laws almost universally express an appropriate preference for the formal family....

* * *

The difference between the developed parent-child relationship that was implicated in *Stanley* and *Caban*, and the potential relationship involved in *Quilloin* and this case, is both clear and significant. When an unwed father demonstrates a full commitment to the responsibilities of parenthood by "[coming] forward to participate in the rearing of his child," *Caban*, 441 U.S., at 392, his interest in personal contact with his child acquires substantial protection under the Due Process Clause. At that point it may be said that he "[acts] as a father toward his children." *Id.*, at 389, n. 7. But the mere existence of a biological link does not merit equivalent constitutional protection. The actions of judges neither create nor sever genetic bonds. "[The] importance of the familial relationship, to the individuals involved and to the society, stems from the emotional attachments that derive from the intimacy of daily association, and from the role it plays in '[promoting] a way of life' through the instruction of children...as well as from the fact of blood relationship." *Smith v. Organization of Foster Families for Equality and Reform*, 431 U.S. 816, 844 (1977) (quoting *Wisconsin v. Yoder*, 406 U.S. 205, 231-233 (1972))....

The significance of the biological connection is that it offers the natural father an opportunity that no other male possesses to develop a relationship with his offspring. If he grasps that opportunity and accepts some measure of responsibility for the child's future, he may enjoy the blessings of the parent-child relationship and make uniquely valuable contributions to the child's development.[18] If he fails to do so, the Federal Constitution will not automatically compel a State to listen to his opinion of where the child's best interests lie.

In this case, we are not assessing the constitutional adequacy of New York's procedures for terminating a developed relationship. Appellant has never had any significant custodial, personal, or financial relationship with Jessica, and he did not seek to establish a legal tie until after she was two years old.[19] We are concerned only with whether New York has adequately protected his opportunity to form such a relationship.

II

The most effective protection of the putative father's opportunity to develop a relationship with his child is provided by the laws that authorize formal marriage and govern its consequences. But the availability of that protection is, of course, dependent on the will of both parents of the child. Thus, New York has adopted a special statutory scheme to protect the unmarried father's interest in assuming a responsible role in the future of his child.

* * *

Appellant argues, however, that even if the putative father's opportunity to establish a relationship with an illegitimate child is adequately protected by the New York statutory scheme in the normal case, he was nevertheless entitled to special notice because the court and the mother knew that he had filed an affiliation proceeding in another court. This argument amounts to nothing more than an indirect attack on the notice provisions of the New York statute. The legitimate state interests in facilitating the adoption of young children and having the adoption proceeding completed expeditiously that underlie the entire statutory scheme also justify a trial judge's determination to require all interested parties to adhere precisely to the procedural requirements of the statute. The Constitution does not require either a trial judge or a litigant to give special notice to nonparties who are presumptively capable of asserting and protecting their own rights.[23] Since the New York statutes adequately protected appellant's inchoate interest in establishing a relationship with Jessica, we find no merit in the claim that his constitutional rights were offended because the Family Court strictly complied with the notice provisions of the statute.

The Equal Protection Claim.

* * *

We have held that these statutes may not constitutionally be applied in that class of cases where the mother and father are in fact similarly situated with regard to their relationship with the child. In *Caban v. Mohammed*, 441 U.S. 380 (1979), the Court held that it violated the Equal Protection Clause to grant the mother a veto over the adoption of a 4-year-old girl and a 6-year-old boy, but not to grant a veto to their father, who had admitted paternity and had participated in the rearing of the children. The Court made it clear, however, that if the father had not "come forward to participate in the rearing of his child, nothing in the Equal Protection Clause [would] [preclude] the State from withholding from him the privilege of vetoing the adoption of that child." *Id.*, at 392.

Jessica's parents are not like the parents involved in Caban. Whereas appellee had a continuous custodial responsibility for Jessica, appellant never established any custodial, personal, or financial relationship with her. If one parent has an established custodial relationship with the child and the other parent has either abandoned...or never established a relationship, the Equal Protection Clause does not prevent a State from according the two parents different legal rights....

The judgment of the New York Court of Appeals is

Affirmed.

[5] At the time Jessica's adoption order was entered, N. Y. Dom. Rel. Law...provided:

"2. Persons entitled to notice, pursuant to subdivision one of this section, shall include: "(a) any person adjudicated by a court in this state to be the father of the child;

"(b) any person adjudicated by a court of another state or territory of the United States to be the father of the child, when a certified copy of the court order has been filed with the putative father registry, pursuant to section three hundred seventy-two-c of the social services law;

"(c) any person who has timely filed an unrevoked notice of intent to claim paternity of the child, pursuant to section three hundred seventy-two of the social services law;

"(d) any person who is recorded on the child's birth certificate as the child's father;

"(e) any person who is openly living with the child and the child's mother at the time the proceeding is initiated and who is holding himself out to be the child's father;

"(f) any person who has been identified as the child's father by the mother in written, sworn statement; and

"(g) any person who was married to the child's mother within six months subsequent to the birth of the child and prior to the execution of a surrender instrument or the initiation of a proceeding pursuant to section three hundred eighty-four-b of the social services law.

"3. The sole purpose of notice under this section shall be to enable the person served pursuant to subdivision two to present evidence to the court relevant to the best interests of the child."

[18] Of course, we need not take sides in the ongoing debate among family psychologists over the relative weight to be accorded biological ties and psychological ties, in order to recognize that a natural father who has played a substantial role in rearing his child has a greater claim to constitutional protection than a mere biological parent. New York's statutory scheme reflects these differences, guaranteeing notice to any putative father who is living openly with the child, and providing putative fathers who have never developed a relationship with the child the opportunity to receive notice simply by mailing a postcard to the putative father registry.

[19] This case happens to involve an adoption by the husband of the natural mother, but we do not believe the natural father has any greater right to object to such an adoption than to an adoption by two total strangers. If anything, the balance of equities tips the opposite way in a case such as this. In denying the putative father relief in *Quilloin v. Walcott*, 434 U.S. 246 (1978), we made an observation equally applicable here:

"Nor is this a case in which the proposed adoption would place the child with a new set of parents with whom the child had never before lived. Rather, the result of the adoption in this case is to give full recognition to a family unit already in existence, a result desired by all concerned, except appellant. Whatever might be required in other situations, we cannot say that the State was required in this situation to find anything more than that the adoption, and denial of legitimation, were in the 'best interests of the child.'" *Id.*, at 255.

[23] It is a generally accepted feature of our adversary system that a potential defendant who knows that the statute of limitations is about to run out has no duty to give the plaintiff advice. There is no suggestion in the record that appellee engaged in fraudulent practices that led appellant not to protect his rights.

JUSTICE WHITE, with whom JUSTICE MARSHALL and JUSTICE BLACKMAN join, dissenting.

The question in this case is whether the State may, consistent with the Due Process Clause, deny notice and an opportunity to be heard in an adoption proceeding to a putative father when the State has actual notice of his existence, whereabouts, and interest in the child.

I

* * *

According to Lehr, he and Jessica's mother met in 1971 and began living together in 1974. The couple cohabited for approximately two years, until Jessica's birth in 1976. Throughout the pregnancy and after the birth, Lorraine acknowledged to friends and relatives that Lehr was Jessica's father; Lorraine told Lehr that she had reported to the New York State Department of Social Services that he was the father.[2] Lehr visited Lorraine and Jessica in the hospital every day during Lorraine's confinement. According to Lehr, from the time Lorraine was discharged from the hospital until August 1978, she concealed her whereabouts from him. During this time Lehr never ceased his efforts to locate Lorraine and Jessica and achieved sporadic success until August 1977, after which time he was unable to locate them at all. On those occasions when he did determine Lorraine's location, he visited with her and her children to the extent she was willing to permit it. When Lehr, with the aid of a detective agency, located Lorraine and Jessica in August 1978, Lorraine was already married to Mr. Robertson. Lehr asserts that at this time he offered to provide financial assistance and to set up a trust fund for Jessica, but that Lorraine refused. Lorraine threatened Lehr with arrest unless he stayed away and refused to permit him to see Jessica. Thereafter Lehr retained counsel who wrote to Lorraine in early December 1978, requesting that she permit Lehr to visit Jessica and threatening legal action on Lehr's behalf. On December 21, 1978, perhaps as a response to Lehr's threatened legal action, appellees commenced the adoption action at issue here.

* * *

The "nature of the interest" at stake here is the interest that a natural parent has in his or her child, one that has long been recognized and accorded constitutional protection....

* * *

I reject the peculiar notion that the only significance of the biological connection between father and child is that "it offers the natural father an opportunity that no other male possesses to develop a relationship with his offspring."...A "mere biological relationship" is not as unimportant in determining the nature of liberty interests as the majority suggests.

* * *

II

In this case, of course, there was no question about either the identity or the location of the putative father. The mother knew exactly who he was and both she and the court entering the order of adoption knew precisely where he was and how to give him actual notice that his parental rights were about to be terminated by an adoption order.[5] Lehr was entitled to due process, and the right to be heard is one of

the fundamentals of that right, which "'has little reality or worth unless one is informed that the matter is pending and can choose for himself whether to appear or default, acquiesce or contest.'"....

* * *

...It makes little sense to me to deny notice and hearing to a father who has not placed his name in the register but who has unmistakably identified himself by filing suit to establish his paternity and has notified the adoption court of his action and his interest. I thus need not question the statutory scheme on its face. Even assuming that Lehr would have been foreclosed if his failure to utilize the register had somehow disadvantaged the State, he effectively made himself known by other means, and it is the sheerest formalism to deny him a hearing because he informed the State in the wrong manner....

* * *

Respectfully, I dissent.

[2] Under 18 NYCRR § 369.2(b) (1982), recipients of public assistance in the Aid to Families with Dependent Children program are required as a condition of eligibility to provide the name and address of the child's father. Lorraine apparently received public assistance after Jessica's birth; it is unclear whether she received public assistance after that regulation went into effect in 1977.

[5] Absent special circumstances, there is no bar to requiring the mother of an illegitimate child to divulge the name of the father when the proceedings at issue involve the permanent termination of the father's rights. Likewise, there is no reason not to require such identification when it is the spouse of the custodial parent who seeks to adopt the child. Indeed, the State now requires the mother to provide the identity of the father if she applies for financial benefits under the Aid to Families with Dependent Children Program....The State's obligation to provide notice to persons before their interests are permanently terminated cannot be a lesser concern than its obligation to assure that state funds are not expended when there exists a person upon whom the financial responsibility should fall.

Questions for Discussion

1. Is it relevant that in *Stanley* the alternative to paternal rights is foster care, but in *Lehr* (and in *Caban v. Mohammed*[3]) there is another person competing for fatherhood status? Would it matter if Lehr is (or is likely to be) a superlative parent? If he had remarried as well to provide two parents? If the prospective adoptive father Robertson is fit, but would not prevail in a choice merely between the two based on the best interests of the child?

2. Would it make a difference if there had not been a three-year delay? Did Lehr "seize" his paternal opportunity? Does it matter if the child's mother misled Lehr to preclude him from invoking his paternal rights? What obligations of due diligence should be required of Lehr? Is submitting his name to the New York registry arranged for this purpose excused by the actual public filing of Lehr for fatherhood status? If we find for Lehr, do we remove the bright line such a registry is intended to provide and remove the certainty that children need for secure status? If we find against Lehr, do we reward the deception of a mother in foreclosing paternal rights?

3. The context of *Lehr*, unlike current divorce custody decisions, is an absolute "yes" or "no," without the middle ground of joint custody or visitation. Would Jessica benefit from the allowance of additional caring adults in her life, including her biological father? But if parental status is granted to Robertson, should the court intervene to overrule the common judgment of her mother and father as to what persons should have contact with Jessica? *E.g.*, if they believe that Lehr is a bad influence or is disruptive to their marriage? Should it matter if Lehr had, in fact, served as a psychological father to his biological child for a substantial period of time and she regarded him as her "father?"

Michael H. v. Gerald D.

491 U.S. 110 (1989)

JUSTICE SCALIA, announced the judgment of the Court and delivered an opinion, in which THE CHIEF JUSTICE joins, and in all but footnote 6 of which JUSTICE O'CONNOR and JUSTICE KENNEDY join.

Under California law, a child born to a married woman living with her husband is presumed to be a child of the marriage. Cal. Evid. Code Ann. § 621....The presumption of legitimacy may be rebutted only by the husband or wife, and then only in limited circumstances....The instant appeal presents the claim that this presumption infringes upon the due process rights of a man who wishes to establish his paternity of a child born to the wife of another man, and the claim that it infringes upon the constitutional right of the child to maintain a relationship with her natural father.

I

The facts of this case are, we must hope, extraordinary. On May 9, 1976, in Las Vegas, Nevada, Carole D., an international model, and Gerald D., a top executive in a French oil company, were married. The couple established a home in Playa del Rey, California, in which they resided as husband and wife when one or the other was not out of the country on business. In the summer of 1978, Carole became involved in an adulterous affair with a neighbor, Michael H. In September 1980, she conceived a child, Victoria D., who was born on May 11, 1981. Gerald was listed as father on the birth certificate and has always held Victoria out to the world as his daughter. Soon after delivery of the child, however, Carole informed Michael that she believed he might be the father.

In the first three years of her life, Victoria remained always with Carole, but found herself within a variety of quasi-family units. In October 1981, Gerald moved to New York City to pursue his business interests, but Carole chose to remain in California. At the end of that month, Carole and Michael had blood tests of themselves and Victoria, which showed a 98.07% probability that Michael was Victoria's father. In January 1982, Carole visited Michael in St. Thomas, where his primary business interests were based. There Michael held Victoria out as his child. In March, however, Carole left Michael and returned to California, where she took up residence with yet another man, Scott K. Later that spring, and again in the summer, Carole and Victoria spent time with Gerald in New York City, as well as on vacation in Europe. In the fall, they returned to Scott in California.

In November 1982, rebuffed in his attempts to visit Victoria, Michael filed a filiation action in California Superior Court to establish his paternity and right to visitation. In March 1983, the court appointed an attorney and *guardian ad litem* to represent Victoria's interests. Victoria then filed a cross-complaint asserting that if she had more than one psychological or de facto father, she was entitled to maintain her filial relationship, with all of the attendant rights, duties, and obligations, with both. In May 1983, Carole filed a motion for summary judgment. During this period, from March through July 1983, Carole was again living with Gerald in New York. In August, however, she returned to California, became involved once again with Michael, and instructed her attorneys to remove the summary judgment motion from the calendar.

For the ensuing eight months, when Michael was not in St. Thomas he lived with Carole and Victoria in Carole's apartment in Los Angeles and held Victoria out as his daughter. In April 1984, Carole and Michael signed a stipulation that Michael was Victoria's natural father. Carole left Michael the next month, however, and instructed her attorneys not to file the stipulation. In June 1984, Carole reconciled with Gerald and joined him in New York, where they now live with Victoria and two other children since born into the marriage.

In May 1984, Michael and Victoria, through her *guardian ad litem*, sought visitation rights for Michael *pendente lite*. To assist in determining whether visitation would be in Victoria's best interests, the Superior Court appointed a psychologist to evaluate Victoria, Gerald, Michael, and Carole. The psychologist recommended that Carole retain sole custody, but that Michael be allowed continued contact with Victoria pursuant to a restricted visitation schedule. The court concurred and ordered that Michael be provided with limited visitation privileges *pendente lite*.

On October 19, 1984, Gerald, who had intervened in the action, moved for summary judgment on the ground that under Cal. Evid. Code § 621 there were no triable issues of fact as to Victoria's paternity. This law provides that "the issue of a wife cohabiting with her husband, who is not impotent or sterile, is conclusively presumed to be a child of the marriage." Cal. Evid. Code Ann. § 621(a)....The presumption may be rebutted by blood tests, but only if a motion for such tests is made, within two years from the date of the child's birth, either by the husband or, if the natural father has filed an affidavit acknowledging paternity, by the wife. §§ 621(c) and (d).

On January 28, 1985, having found that affidavits submitted by Carole and Gerald sufficed to demonstrate that the two were cohabiting at conception and birth and that Gerald was neither sterile nor impotent, the Superior Court granted Gerald's motion for summary judgment, rejecting Michael's and Victoria's challenges to the constitutionality of § 621. The court also denied their motions for continued visitation pending the appeal under Cal. Civ. Code § 4601, which provides that a court may, in its discretion, grant "reasonable visitation rights...to any...person having an interest in the welfare of the child." Cal. Civ. Code Ann. § 4601....It found that allowing such visitation would "violat[e] the intention of the Legislature by impugning the integrity of the family unit.".…

On appeal, Michael asserted, *inter alia*, that the Superior Court's application of § 621 had violated his procedural and substantive due process rights. Victoria also raised a due process challenge to the statute, seeking to preserve her *de facto* relationship with Michael as well as with Gerald. She contended, in addition, that as § 621 allows the husband and, at least to a limited extent, the mother, but not the child, to rebut the presumption of legitimacy, it violates the child's right to equal protection. Finally, she asserted a right to continued visitation with Michael under § 4601....

...Before us, Michael and Victoria both raise equal protection and due process challenges. We do not reach Michael's equal protection claim, however, as it was neither raised nor passed upon below....

II

The California statute that is the subject of this litigation is, in substance, more than a century old. California Code of Civ. Proc. § 1962(5), enacted in 1872, provided that "[t]he issue of a wife cohabiting with her husband, who is not impotent, is indisputably presumed to be legitimate."....In 1980, the legislature again amended the statute to provide the husband an opportunity to introduce blood-test evidence in rebuttal of the presumption,...and in 1981 amended it to provide the mother such an opportunity....

* * *

III

We address first the claims of Michael. At the outset, it is necessary to clarify what he sought and what he was denied. California law, like nature itself, makes no provision for dual fatherhood. Michael was seeking to be declared the father of Victoria. The immediate benefit he evidently sought to obtain from that status was visitation rights....But if Michael were successful in being declared the father, other rights would follow—most importantly, the right to be considered as the parent who should have custody....All parental rights, including visitation, were automatically denied by denying Michael status as the father. While Cal. Civ. Code Ann. § 4601 places it within the discretionary power of a court to award visitation rights to a nonparent, the Superior Court here, affirmed by the Court of Appeal, held that California law denies visitation, against the wishes of the mother, to a putative father who has been prevented by § 621 from establishing his paternity....

* * *

Michael contends as a matter of substantive due process that, because he has established a parental relationship with Victoria, protection of Gerald's and Carole's marital union is an insufficient state interest to support termination of that relationship. This argument is, of course, predicated on the assertion that Michael has a constitutionally protected liberty interest in his relationship with Victoria.

* * *

In an attempt to limit and guide interpretation of the Clause, we have insisted not merely that the interest denominated as a "liberty" be "fundamental" (a concept that, in isolation, is hard to objectify), but also that it be an interest traditionally protected by our society. As we have put it, the Due Process Clause affords only those protections "so rooted in the traditions and conscience of our people as to be ranked as fundamental."... Our cases reflect "continual insistence upon respect for the teachings of history [and] solid recognition of the basic values that underlie our society...." *Griswold v. Connecticut*, 381 U.S. 479, 501 (1965)....

This insistence that the asserted liberty interest be rooted in history and tradition is evident, as elsewhere, in our cases according constitutional protection to certain parental rights. Michael reads the landmark case of *Stanley v. Illinois*, 405 U.S. 645 (1972), and the subsequent cases of *Quilloin v. Walcott*, 434 U.S. 246 (1978), *Caban v. Mohammed*, 441 U.S. 380 (1979), and *Lehr v. Robertson*, 463 U.S. 248 (1983), as establishing that a liberty interest is created by biological fatherhood plus an established parental relationship—factors that exist in the present case as well. We think that distorts the rationale of those cases. As we view them, they rest not upon such isolated factors but upon the historic respect—indeed, sanctity would not be too strong a term—traditionally accorded to the relationships that develop within the unitary family.[3]

Thus, the legal issue in the present case reduces to whether the relationship between persons in the situation of Michael and Victoria has been treated as a protected family unit under the historic practices of our society, or whether on any other basis it has been accorded special protection. We think it impossible to find that it has. In fact, quite to the contrary, our traditions have protected the marital family (Gerald, Carole, and the child they acknowledge to be theirs) against the sort of claim Michael asserts.[4]

The presumption of legitimacy was a fundamental principle of the common law.... Traditionally, that presumption could be rebutted only by proof that a husband was incapable of procreation or had had no access to his wife during the relevant period....

We have found nothing in the older sources, nor in the older cases, addressing specifically the power of the natural father to assert parental rights over a child born into a woman's existing marriage with another man. Since it is Michael's burden to establish that such a power (at least where the natural father has established a relationship with the child) is so deeply embedded within our traditions as to be a fundamental right, the lack of evidence alone might defeat his case. But the evidence shows that even in modern times—when, as we have noted, the rigid protection of the marital family has in other respects been relaxed—the ability of a person in Michael's position to claim paternity has not been generally acknowledged....

* * *

IV

We have never had occasion to decide whether a child has a liberty interest, symmetrical with that of her parent, in maintaining her filial relationship. We need not do so here because, even assuming that such a right exists, Victoria's claim must fail. Victoria's due process challenge is, if anything, weaker than Michael's. Her basic claim is not that California has erred in preventing her from establishing that Michael, not Gerald, should stand as her legal father. Rather, she claims a due process right to maintain filial relationships with both Michael and Gerald. This assertion merits little discussion, for, whatever the merits of the guardian ad litem's belief that such an arrangement can be of great psychological benefit to a child, the claim that a State must recognize multiple fatherhood has no support in the history or traditions of this country. Moreover, even

if we were to construe Victoria's argument as forwarding the lesser proposition that, whatever her status vis-a-vis Gerald, she has a liberty interest in maintaining a filial relationship with her natural father, Michael, we find that, at best, her claim is the obverse of Michael's and fails for the same reasons.

Victoria claims in addition that her equal protection rights have been violated because, unlike her mother and presumed father, she had no opportunity to rebut the presumption of her legitimacy. We find this argument wholly without merit. We reject, at the outset, Victoria's suggestion that her equal protection challenge must be assessed under a standard of strict scrutiny because, in denying her the right to maintain a filial relationship with Michael, the State is discriminating against her on the basis of her illegitimacy....Illegitimacy is a legal construct, not a natural trait. Under California law,

Victoria is not illegitimate, and she is treated in the same manner as all other legitimate children: she is entitled to maintain a filial relationship with her legal parents.

We apply, therefore, the ordinary "rational relationship" test to Victoria's equal protection challenge. The primary rationale underlying § 621's limitation on those who may rebut the presumption of legitimacy is a concern that allowing persons other than the husband or wife to do so may undermine the integrity of the marital union. When the husband or wife contests the legitimacy of their child, the stability of the marriage has already been shaken. In contrast, allowing a claim of illegitimacy to be pressed by the child—or, more accurately, by a court-appointed guardian ad litem—may well disrupt an otherwise peaceful union. Since it pursues a legitimate end by rational means, California's decision to treat Victoria differently from her parents is not a denial of equal protection.

The judgment of the California Court of Appeal is

Affirmed.

[3] Justice Brennan asserts that only a "pinched conception of 'the family'" would exclude Michael, Carole, and Victoria from protection....We disagree. The family unit accorded traditional respect in our society, which we have referred to as the "unitary family," is typified, of course, by the marital family, but also includes the household of unmarried parents and their children. Perhaps the concept can be expanded even beyond this, but it will bear no resemblance to traditionally respected relationships—and will thus cease to have any constitutional significance—if it is stretched so far as to include the relationship established between a married woman, her lover, and their child, during a 3-month sojourn in St. Thomas, or during a subsequent 8-month period when, if he happened to be in Los Angeles, he stayed with her and the child.

[4] Justice Brennan insists that in determining whether a liberty interest exists we must look at Michael's relationship with Victoria in isolation, without reference to the circumstance that Victoria's mother was married to someone else when the child was conceived, and that that woman and her husband wish to raise the child as their own. We cannot imagine what compels this strange procedure of looking at the act which is assertedly the subject of a liberty interest in isolation from its effect upon other people—rather like inquiring whether there is a liberty interest in firing a gun where the case at hand happens to involve its discharge into another person's body. The logic of Justice Brennan's position leads to the conclusion that if Michael had begotten Victoria by rape, that fact would in no way affect his possession of a liberty interest in his relationship with her.

JUSTICE BRENNAN, with whom **JUSTICE MARSHALL** and **JUSTICE BLACKMUN** join, dissenting.

In a case that has yielded so many opinions as has this one, it is fruitful to begin by emphasizing the common ground shared by a majority of this Court. Five Members of the Court refuse to foreclose "the possibility that a natural father might ever have a constitutionally protected interest in his relationship with a child whose mother was married to, and cohabiting with, another man at the time of the child's conception and birth."...Five Justices agree that the flaw inhering in a conclusive presumption that terminates a constitutionally protected interest without any hearing whatsoever is a *procedural* one....Four Members of the Court agree that Michael H. has a liberty interest in his relationship with Victoria..., and one assumes for purposes of this case that he does,....

In contrast, only one other Member of the Court fully endorses Justice Scalia's view of the proper method of analyzing questions arising under the Due Process Clause...(O'Connor, J., concurring in part). Nevertheless, because the plurality opinion's exclusively historical analysis portends a significant and unfortunate departure from our prior cases and from sound constitutional decisionmaking, I devote a substantial portion of my discussion to it.

I

Once we recognized that the "liberty" protected by the Due Process Clause of the Fourteenth Amendment encompasses more than freedom from bodily restraint, today's plurality opinion emphasizes, the concept was cut loose from one natural limitation on its meaning. This innovation paved the way, so the plurality hints, for judges to substitute their own preferences for those of elected officials. Dissatisfied with this supposedly unbridled and uncertain state of affairs, the plurality casts about for another limitation on the concept of liberty.

It finds this limitation in "tradition." Apparently oblivious to the fact that this concept can be as malleable and as elusive as "liberty" itself, the plurality pretends that tradition places a discernible border around the Constitution. The pretense is seductive; it would be comforting to believe that a search for "tradition" involves nothing more idiosyncratic or complicated than poring through dusty volumes on American history. Yet, as Justice White observed in his dissent in *Moore v. East Cleveland*, 431 U.S. 494, 549 (1977): "What the deeply rooted traditions of the country are is arguable." Indeed, wherever I would begin to look for an interest "deeply rooted in the country's traditions," one thing is certain: I would not stop (as does the plurality) at Bracton, or Blackstone, or Kent, or even the American Law Reports in conducting my search. Because reasonable people can disagree about the content of particular traditions, and because they can disagree even about which traditions are relevant to the definition of "liberty," the plurality has not found the objective boundary that it seeks.

* * *

Thus, to describe the issue in this case as whether the relationship existing between Michael and Victoria "has been treated as a protected family unit under the historic practices of our society, or whether on any other basis it has been accorded special protection,"...is to reinvent the wheel. The better approach—indeed, the one commanded by our prior cases and by common sense—is to ask whether the specific parent-child relationship under consideration is close enough to the interests that we already have protected to be deemed an aspect of "liberty" as well. On the facts before us, therefore, the question is not what "level of generality" should be used to describe the relationship between Michael and Victoria,...but whether the relationship under consideration is sufficiently substantial to qualify as a liberty interest under our prior cases.

* * *

The evidence is undisputed that Michael, Victoria, and Carole did live together as a family; that is, they shared the same household, Victoria called Michael "Daddy," Michael contributed to Victoria's support, and he is eager to continue his relationship with her. Yet they are not, in the plurality's view, a "unitary family," whereas Gerald, Carole, and Victoria do compose such a family. The only difference between these two sets of relationships, however, is the fact of marriage. The plurality, indeed, expressly recognizes that marriage is the critical fact in denying Michael a constitutionally protected stake in his relationship with Victoria: no fewer than six times, the plurality refers to Michael as the "*adulterous* natural father" (emphasis added) or the like....However, the very premise of *Stanley* and the cases following it is that marriage is not decisive in answering the question whether the Constitution protects the parental relationship under consideration. These cases are, after all, important precisely because they involve the rights of unwed fathers. It is important to remember, moreover, that in *Quilloin, Caban,* and *Lehr,* the putative father's demands would have disrupted a "unitary family" as the plurality defines it; in each case, the husband of the child's mother sought to adopt the child over the objections of the natural father. Significantly, our decisions in those cases in no way relied on the need to protect the marital family. Hence the plurality's claim that *Stanley, Quilloin, Caban,* and *Lehr* were about the "unitary family," as that family is defined by today's plurality, is surprising indeed.

* * *

The plurality has wedged itself between a rock and a hard place. If it limits its holding to those situations in which a wife and husband wish to raise the child together, then it necessarily takes the State's interest into account in defining "liberty"; yet if it extends that approach to circumstances in which the marital union already has been dissolved, then it may no longer rely on the State's asserted interest in protecting the "unitary family" in denying that Michael and Victoria have been deprived of liberty.

* * *

III

Because the plurality decides that Michael and Victoria have no liberty interest in their relationship with each other, it need consider neither the effect of § 621 on their relationship nor the State's interest in bringing about that effect. It is obvious, however, that the effect of § 621 is to terminate the relationship between Michael and Victoria before affording any hearing whatsoever on the issue whether Michael is Victoria's father.

This refusal to hold a hearing is properly analyzed under our procedural due process cases, which instruct us to consider the State's interest in curtailing the procedures accompanying the termination of a constitutionally protected interest. California's interest, minute in comparison with a father's interest in his relationship with his child, cannot justify its refusal to hear Michael out on his claim that he is Victoria's father.

* * *

B

The question before us, therefore, is whether California has an interest so powerful that it justifies granting Michael no hearing before terminating his parental rights.

"Many controversies have raged about the cryptic and abstract words of the Due Process Clause but there can be no doubt that at a minimum they require that deprivation of life, liberty or property by adjudication be preceded by notice and opportunity for hearing appropriate to the nature of the case."...

The purported state interests here, however, stem primarily from the State's antagonism to Michael's and Victoria's constitutionally protected interest in their relationship with each other and not from any desire to streamline procedures. Gerald D. explains that § 621 promotes marriage, maintains the relationship between the child and presumed father, and protects the integrity and privacy of the matrimonial family.... It is not, however, § 621, but the best-interest principle, that protects a stable marital relationship and maintains the relationship between the child and presumed father. These interests are implicated by the determination of who gets parental rights, not by the determination of who is the father; in the hearing that Michael seeks, parental rights are not the issue. Of the objectives that Gerald stresses, therefore, only the preservation of family privacy is promoted by the refusal to hold a hearing itself. Yet § 621 furthers even this objective only partially.

Gerald D. gives generous proportions to the privacy protected by § 621, asserting that this provision protects a couple like Gerald and Carole from answering questions on such matters as "their sexual habits and practices with each other and outside their marriage, their finances, and their thoughts, beliefs, and opinions concerning their relationship with each other and with Victoria."...Yet invalidation of § 621 would not, as Gerald suggests, subject Gerald and Carole to public scrutiny of all of these private matters. Family finances and family dynamics are relevant, not to paternity, but to the best interests of the child—and the child's best interests are not, as I have stressed, in issue at the hearing that Michael seeks. The only private matter touching on the paternity presumed by § 621 is the married couple's sex life. Even there, § 621 as interpreted by California's intermediate appellate courts preempts inquiry into a couple's sexual relations, since "cohabitation" consists simply of living under the same roof together; the wife and husband need not even share the same bed....Admittedly, § 621 does not foreclose inquiry into the husband's fertility or virility—matters that are ordinarily thought of as the couple's private business. In this day and age, however, proving paternity by asking intimate and detailed questions about a couple's relationship would be decidedly anachronistic. Who on earth would choose this method of establishing fatherhood when blood tests prove it with far more certainty and far less fuss? The State's purported interest in protecting matrimonial privacy thus does not measure up to Michael's and Victoria's interest in maintaining their relationship with each other.[11]

Make no mistake: to say that the State must provide Michael with a hearing to prove his paternity is not to express any opinion of the ultimate state of affairs between Michael and Victoria and Carole and Gerald. In order to change the current situation among these people, Michael first must convince a court that he is Victoria's father, and even if he is able to do this, he will be denied visitation rights if that would be in Victoria's best interests. See Cal. Civ. Code Ann. § 4601....It is elementary that a determination

that a State must afford procedures before it terminates a given right is not a prediction about the end result of those procedures.[12]

IV

The atmosphere surrounding today's decision is one of make-believe. Beginning with the suggestion that the situation confronting us here does not repeat itself every day in every corner of the country,...moving on to the claim that it is tradition alone that supplies the details of the liberty that the Constitution protects, and passing finally to the notion that the Court always has recognized a cramped vision of "the family," today's decision lets stand California's pronouncement that Michael—whom blood tests show to a 98 percent probability to be Victoria's father—is not Victoria's father. When and if the Court awakes to reality, it will find a world very different from the one it expects.

* * *

[11] Thus, in concluding that § 621 "exclud[es] inquiries into the child's paternity that would be destructive of family integrity and privacy,"...the plurality exaggerates the extent to which these interests would be threatened by the elimination of § 621's presumption. On the other hand, if the State's foremost interest is in protecting the husband from discovering that he may not be the father of his wife's children, as the plurality suggests, see...at 120, n. 1, then § 621 is unhelpful indeed. Since "cohabitation" under California law includes sharing the same roof but not the same bed and since a person need only make a phone call in order to unsettle a husband's certainty in the paternity of his wife's children, § 621 will do little to prevent such discoveries.

[12] The plurality's failure to see this point causes it to misstate Michael's claim in the following way: "Michael contends as a matter of substantive due process that, because he has established a parental relationship with Victoria, protection of Gerald's and Carole's marital union is an insufficient state interest to support termination of that relationship."...Michael does not claim that the State may not, under any circumstance, terminate his relationship with Victoria; instead, he simply claims that the State may not do so without affording him a hearing on the issue—paternity—that it deems vital to the question whether their relationship may be discontinued. The plurality makes Michael's claim easier to knock down by turning it into such a big target.

The plurality's misunderstanding of Michael's claim also leads to its assertion that "to *provide* protection to an adulterous natural father is to *deny* protection to a marital father."...To allow Michael a chance to prove his paternity, however, in no way guarantees that Gerald's relationship with Victoria will be changed.

Questions for Discussion

1. The dissent would give Michael a due process hearing, but what would such a hearing decide and on what basis? If he demonstrates that he is the biological father, would that alone win him parental rights? What should he be required to show to win custody? Does he need parental rights status to be given court ordered visitation? (Note that Justice Stevens believes such visitation can be ordered without parental status under California law—even over the opposition of Carol and Gerald, but eight Justices disagree).

2. Should it be significant that Victoria has two half-siblings living with Carol and Gerald?

3. If, under the majority opinion, Michael is denied standing to demand paternity because Gerald was married to Carol at the time of conception and birth, what happens if Gerald and Carol divorce and *Gerald* demands a paternity test to escape child support in lieu of biological father Michael? Will he be able to transfer that obligation to Michael?

4. What if Carol divorces and then marries Michael so he has (1) substantially functioned as a father, (2) is the biological father, and (3) is married to the child's mother? Does that change the outcome under the plurality opinion?

5. Scalia's opinion rejects consideration of a child's constitutional right to a filial (or other parental) relationship because it lacks "support in history or tradition." On what basis is a child's loss of a parent of less constitutional significance than an adult's loss of a child? Scalia argues that to permit Michael's challenge would

disrupt the "peaceful union" of the marriage. Should the analysis be only of the "union," absent the children, or the "family," including them?

6. The Brennan dissent argues that biology plus a paternal relationship can trump the marriage bright line for parental status. If a wife has an affair and gives birth to a child by a third party, what are the likely outcomes of liberal paternity challenge for the survival of such marriages? For the involved children?

7. In *Michael*, both competing men have functioned to some extent as fathers. What happens where the biological father serves almost exclusively as the functioning father, and has exclusively bonded with the child. Would that make a difference to the plurality?

Note: The *Kelsey* case below presents a growing type of dispute for parental status, involving (1) a biological father unaware that he has fathered a child, or who has been misled by the mother; (2) the mother intends to place the child for adoption but regards the biological father is an unacceptable candidate; (3) the child is adopted into a family with whom the child bonds; and (4) the biological father learns of the child belatedly (through no fault of his own) and seeks to rescind the adoption and assert the due process rights of a father to block adoption and to claim parental status. Such a fact pattern is more easily resolved if a measure of due diligence is required of such fathers and it is absent. Courts now regard "mere biology" alone as overly-inclusive to confer upon such fathers constitutionally protected parental rights. In this context, California has attempted to fashion yet another basis for line drawing, which has been adopted in at least a substantial minority of the states.

Adoption of Kelsey S.
1 Cal. 4th 816 (1992)

OPINION BY: **BAXTER**

The primary question in this case is whether the father of a child born out of wedlock may properly be denied the right to withhold his consent to his child's adoption by third parties despite his diligent and legal attempts to obtain custody of his child and to rear it himself, and absent any showing of the father's unfitness as a parent. We conclude that, under these circumstances, the federal constitutional guarantees of equal protection and due process require that the father be allowed to withhold his consent to his child's adoption and therefore that his parental rights cannot be terminated absent a showing of his unfitness within the meaning of Civil Code section 221.20.

FACTS

Kari S. gave birth to Kelsey, a boy, on May 18, 1988. The child's undisputed natural father is petitioner Rickie M....He and Kari S. were not married to one another. At that time, he was married to another woman but was separated from her and apparently was in divorce proceedings. He was aware that Kari planned to place their child for adoption, and he objected to her decision because he wanted to rear the child.

Two days after the child's birth, petitioner filed an action in superior court under Civil Code section 7006 to establish his parental relationship with the child and to obtain custody of the child. (The petition erroneously stated that the child had not yet been born. His birth was earlier than expected, and petitioner had not been informed of it when he filed his action.) That same day, the court issued a restraining order that temporarily awarded care, custody, and control of the child to petitioner. The order also stayed all adoption proceedings and prohibited any contact between the child and the prospective adoptive parents.

Later that day, petitioner filed a copy of the order with law enforcement officials. He also personally attempted to serve it on the prospective adoptive parents at their home. He was unsuccessful.

On May 24, 1988, Steven and Suzanne A., the prospective adoptive parents, filed an adoption petition under Civil Code section 226....Their petition alleged that only the mother's consent to the adoption was required because there was no presumed father under section 7004, subdivision (a)....

* * *

On May 31, 1988, the prospective adoptive parents filed a petition under section 7017 to terminate petitioner's parental rights. The superior court consolidated that proceeding with the adoption proceeding. The court allowed petitioner to have supervised visitation with the child at the women's shelter where the child was living with his mother. The court also allowed the prospective adoptive parents to have unsupervised visitation at the shelter.

The parties subsequently stipulated that petitioner was the child's natural father. The superior court, however, ruled that he was not a "presumed father"....The court held four days of hearings...to determine whether it was in the child's best interest for petitioner to retain his parental rights and whether the adoption should be allowed to proceed. (The attorney appointed by the trial court to represent the child's interests advocated that petitioner should retain his parental rights.) On August 26, 1988, the court found "by a bare preponderance" of the evidence that the child's best interest required termination of petitioner's parental rights....

Petitioner appealed. He contended the superior court erred by: (1) concluding that he was not the child's presumed father; (2) not granting him a parental placement preference; and (3) applying a preponderance-of-the-evidence standard of proof. The Court of Appeal rejected each of his contentions and affirmed the judgment.

DISCUSSION

1. The statutory framework

* * *

This statutory scheme creates three classifications of parents: mothers, biological fathers who are presumed fathers, and biological fathers who are not presumed fathers (*i.e.*, natural fathers). A natural father's consent to an adoption of his child by third parties is not required unless the father makes the required showing that retention of his parental rights is in the child's best interest. Consent, however, is required of a mother and a presumed father regardless of the child's best interest. The natural father is therefore treated differently from both mothers and presumed fathers. With this statutory framework in mind, we now examine petitioner's contentions.

* * *

...We now turn to that difficult constitutional question.[6]

* * *

The most recent relevant high court decision arose in California. (*Michael H. v. Gerald D* (1989) 491 U.S. 110....) Michael H. claimed to be the father of a child and sought a declaration of paternity and visitation rights....Blood tests showed a 98.07 percent probability that Michael H. was the father....The mother, however, was married

to and living with another man at the time of conception. On grounds not relevant to the present case, the high court upheld the denial of Michael H.'s request for a declaration of paternity and visitation rights. (A plurality of the court found to be constitutional the conclusive presumption in California Evidence Code section 621 that the mother's husband was the child's father.) Of special significance for us, however, four justices agreed that the biological father had a protected liberty interest in his relationship with his child....Justice Stevens in concurrence assumed for purposes of the decision that the natural father's relationship was entitled to constitutional protection....

Although the foregoing high court decisions do not provide a comprehensive rule for all situations involving unwed fathers, one unifying and transcendent theme emerges. The biological connection between father and child is unique and worthy of constitutional protection if the father grasps the opportunity to develop that biological connection into a full and enduring relationship.

* * *

We agree that the courts have the authority under this state's Uniform Parentage Act to grant custody to the natural father despite the mother's objection. In the present case, the superior court had the authority to grant petitioner custody of his child so that he could qualify as a presumed father under section 7004, subdivision (a). Indeed, the superior court initially did so but shortly thereafter reversed itself after enforcement of its order was thwarted.

* * *

5. The constitutionally protected interest of an unwed, natural father

* * *

Respondents do not adequately explain how an unwed mother's control over a biological father's rights furthers the state's interest in the well-being of the child. The linchpin of their position, however, is clear although largely implicit: Allowing the biological father to have the same rights as the mother would make adoptions more difficult because the consent of both parents is more difficult to obtain than the consent of the mother alone. This reasoning is flawed in several respects.

A. Respondents' view too narrowly assumes that the proper governmental objective is adoption. As we have explained, the constitutionally valid objective is the protection of the child's well-being. We cannot conclude in the abstract that adoption is itself a sufficient objective to allow the state to take whatever measures it deems appropriate. Nor can we merely assume, either as a policy or factual matter, that adoption is necessarily in a child's best interest. This assumption is especially untenable in light of the rapidly changing concept of family. As recently as only a few years ago, it might have been reasonable to assume that an adopted child would be placed into a two-parent home and thereby have a more stable environment than a child raised by a single father. The validity of that assumption is now highly suspect in light of modern adoption practice. Recent statistics show that a significant percentage of children placed for independent adoption—7.7 percent—are adopted by a single parent....The figure is even higher—21.9 percent—for children placed with agencies for adoption....

If the possible benefit of adoption were by itself sufficient to justify terminating a parent's rights, the state could terminate an unwed mother's parental rights based on nothing more than a showing that her child's best interest would be served by adoption. Of course, that is not the law; nor do the parties advocate such a system. We simply do not in our society take children away from their mothers married—or otherwise— because a "better" adoptive parent can be found. We see no valid reason why we should be less solicitous of a father's efforts to establish a parental relationship with his child. Respondents seem to suggest that a child is inherently better served by adoptive parents than by a single, biological father but that the child is also inherently better served by a single, biological mother than by adoptive parents. The logic of this view is not apparent, and there is no evidence in the record to support such a counterintuitive view.

* * *

The anomalies under this statutory scheme become readily apparent. A father who is indisputably ready, willing, and able to exercise the full measure of his parental responsibilities can have his rights terminated merely on a showing that his child's best interest would be served by adoption. If the child's mother, however, were equally of the opposite character—unready, unwilling, and unable—her rights in the child could nevertheless be terminated only under the much more protective standards of section 221.20. Such a distinction bears no substantial relationship to protecting the well-being of children. Indeed, it has little rationality.

The system also leads to irrational distinctions between fathers. Based solely on the mother's wishes, a model father can be denied presumed father status, whereas a father of dubious ability and intent can achieve such status by the fortuitous circumstance of the mother allowing him to come into her home, even if only briefly—perhaps a single day. We cannot ignore reality. Parental unfitness is considerably more difficult to show than that the child's best interest is served by adoption. Under the statutory scheme, two fathers who are by all accounts equal in their ability and commitment to fulfill their parental missions can be treated differently based solely on the mothers' decisions whether to allow the father to become a presumed father.

The system also makes little sense from a child's perspective. A child may have a wholly acceptable father who wants to nurture it, but whose parental rights can be terminated under the best-interest standard because the mother has precluded the father from attaining presumed father status. Conversely, if a presumed father is highly questionable in every respect, he is nevertheless allowed to withhold consent absent proof by clear and convincing evidence that he is unfit. (§§ 221.20 and 232.) As a practical matter, the child's best interest is largely ignored by the statutory distinction between presumed fathers and those natural fathers who are willing to assume their parental responsibilities.

* * *

E. In summary, we hold that section 7004, subdivision (a) and the related statutory scheme violates the federal constitutional guarantees of equal protection and due process for unwed fathers to the extent that the statutes allow a mother unilaterally to preclude her child's biological father from becoming a presumed father and thereby allowing the state to terminate his parental rights on nothing more than a showing of the child's best interest. If an unwed father promptly comes forward and demonstrates a full commitment to his parental responsibilities—emotional, financial, and otherwise—his federal constitutional right to due process prohibits the termination of his parental relationship absent a showing of his unfitness as a parent. Absent such a showing, the child's well-being is presumptively best served by continuation of the father's parental relationship. Similarly, when the father has come forward to grasp his parental responsibilities, his parental rights are entitled to equal protection as those of the mother....

A court should consider all factors relevant to that determination. The father's conduct both before and after the child's birth must be considered. Once he knows or reasonably should know of the pregnancy, he must promptly attempt to assume his parental responsibilities as fully as the mother will allow and his circumstances permit. In particular, the father must demonstrate "a willingness himself to assume full custody of the child—not merely to block adoption by others."...A court should also consider the father's public acknowledgement of paternity, payment of pregnancy and birth expenses commensurate with his ability to do so, and prompt legal action to seek custody of the child....

We reiterate and emphasize the narrowness of our decision. The statutory distinction between natural fathers and presumed fathers is constitutionally invalid only to the extent it is applied to an unwed father who has sufficiently and timely demonstrated a full commitment to his parental responsibilities....

* * *

[6] The nature and scope of an unwed parent's rights are questions of enormous practical significance. The United States Census Bureau recently issued "Fertility of American Women," reporting that, for the most recent statistical year (July 1989 to June 1990), 913,000 of 3.9 million births—1 in 4—were out of wedlock.

Mosk, J., Concurring and Dissenting.

I concur in the result only. My concern for the welfare of the child in cases of this sort prevents me from joining the majority's reasoning. The majority declare that Civil Code section 7004, a provision of the Uniform Parentage Act enacted in 1975, is unconstitutional as applied. The soundness of their determination is open to serious question. Its potential for mischief is not. It creates needless uncertainty in the application of statutory categories that have been consistently employed for almost 20 years. Such uncertainty will redound to the disadvantage of all parties—but especially the child.

The majority yield to the lamentable temptation to invoke the Constitution when there is a perfectly simple legal solution to the factual problem of this case. It is settled law that we should not reach constitutional questions unless absolutely required....

* * *

Though the facts are disputed, assume, *arguendo*, that in this case they can be established at trial. The biological father engaged in an adulterous relationship with the mother. A child was born. Though he had rejected the mother and returned to his wife, the biological father conceded paternity, made reasonable efforts to ascertain the whereabouts of the child and indicated a willingness to take the child into his home and to support it. In short, the biological father allegedly sought to become a presumed father within the statutory requirements of Civil Code section 7004, subdivision (a)(4), but was thwarted from achieving that status through the purported devious actions of the mother.

Under those circumstances, if established by a preponderance of evidence in court, I would estop the mother and the proposed adoptive parents from denying that the biological father had assumed the status of a presumed father. These are paradigm circumstances for the imposition of an estoppel....

* * *

To my mind, the choice between a declaration of unconstitutionality and a use of the doctrine of equitable estoppel is clear. The latter will yield justice for the party if he deserves justice in this individual action without providing a precedent that has the potential to produce unfortunate results in countless other proceedings, even those previously concluded.

* * *

Questions for Discussion

1. The *Kelsey* case was in litigation for four years. During this period the child was in the custody of his mother, the one party who did not want him. Now the case is to be remanded for further proceedings. Does the court take responsibility for or comment upon the impact of a four-year delay before Kelsey achieves a permanent home and parents?

2. Assume that on remand the trial court finds that Rickie M. adequately attempted to assume a parental role with Kelsey and that he is not "unfit." He then blocks the proposed adoption. But he remains single and the court concludes that it is not in the best interests of the child to give him custody (only 8% of adoptive parents are single). What happens to Kelsey?

3. Scalia might argue that Rickie M. had an option to perfect his paternal rights: marry the mother of his child, and that a legislature may rationally require such a commitment prior to recognizing a father's parental rights given the ease of biology alone. What is the response of the majority to this argument?

4. Lacking marriage and presumptive father status, should "showing substantial interest" in a child by a biological father suffice to invoke constitutional parental rights? Does the vagueness of the *Kelsey* test raise problems in accomplishing expeditious adoptions?

5. Should a *Kelsey* father (a biological father who does not qualify as a "presumed" father) be held to a strong "due diligence" standard to monitor and learn about any possible pregnancies he may have caused in order to claim the significant constitutional right to parenthood that can (1) veto an adoption, (2)

claim custody, and (3) be extinguished only upon a showing of unfitness by clear and convincing evidence by the state at a full due process hearing, with counsel provided for him at public expense if needed?[4]

Note on Cases Post-*Kelsey:* Baby Richard, Surrender to Guardians and Related Problems

Following *Kelsey*, the Illinois Supreme Court decided the highly publicized case of Baby Richard (*In Re Petition of Doe*, 638 N.E.2d 181 (Ill. 1994)). The facts as found by that court include the following: (1) Otakar Kirchner impregnated Daniella Janikova while living with her, and intending to marry her and father their child. (2) While Otakar was visiting relatives in Czechoslovakia, Daniella received information that he may have been unfaithful to her in Europe; she then left the home two weeks before giving birth at a hospital unknown to the father, gave birth, and told Otakar the infant died at birth. (3) The mother then signed away her rights to the child, arranging for an adoption with a qualified couple (the Warburtons) who obtained custody of the child four days after his birth. (4) The father searched to verify the fate of the baby and learned 57 days after the birth that the child was alive; the father hired counsel and objected to the adoption. (5) The trial court and the appellate court considering the case found that it would be in the "best interests of the child" to remain with and be adopted by the Warburtons. (6) Otakar and Daniella then reunited and she reversed herself to support his assertion of paternal rights and to object to the adoption she had arranged. The Illinois Supreme Court granted review and issued an opinion granting a final order of habeas corpus to award the child to Otakar on approximately the child's fourth birthday.

Is Otakar a "presumed father" under the Uniform Parentage Act? Has he met the *Kelsey* standard? Is it relevant that he was misled by the mother and was prevented from bringing the child into his home or from assuming a paternal role earlier? Is it determinative? Is it relevant that four years have passed and the adoptive parents are the only parents the child has known?

Through the 1990s, a number of well-publicized cases were litigated involving biological fathers who did not marry nor live with the biological mothers, but who were interested in a parental role, and who appeared post-birth to contest adoptions arranged by the respective biological mothers. Many of them had contentions about the mother misleading them or hiding from them to prevent them from "seizing" the *Kelsey* opportunity. A substantial number sought parental rights and custody as single fathers of children who had been adopted for one to five years or more.

Justice Heiple of the Illinois Supreme Court was angry enough at the extensive press coverage of Baby Richard being torn from the arms of his adoptive parents to include an unusual emotional attack on the media's characterization of the case, accusing Chicago columnist Bob Greene of engaging in "journalistic terrorism" and bitterly criticizing the legislature, the Governor, and the Warburtons. He argued—consistent with precedent—that the "best interests" standard does not apply to deprive a fit parent of parental status. Some child advocates argued that his position begged the question in assuming that Otakar properly claimed constitutional parental status as a threshold matter. Of particular concern to child advocates was the opinion's discounting of the child's loss of his adoptive parents. Consistent with the majority rule to date, the child's right to the two parents serving this function for four years was not given constitutional dimension, in contrast to Otakar, who was afforded that status in full measure although he had not functioned as a father. The court opined that the removal from the Warburtons will not be an "insurmountable trauma," citing the deaths of some parents and the high incidence of divorce.[5] The Illinois Supreme Court also opined that the adoptive parents bear responsibility for the delay because of their extensive litigation to keep the child.[6]

The justices here stood in the shoes of Otakar, recognized his good faith, and empathized with the denigration of his parental rights by others. Indeed, where the abdication of paternal responsibility to children has become a major societal problem, child advocates welcome a father not only willing to raise his child, but exhibiting zeal to do so. On the other hand, they also argue that Baby Richard is not a prize to be awarded to the meritorious, but a sentient human with arguably the same rights to his parents as the courts readily grant parents to their children.

The dilemma in the case stems less from the decision between the Warburtons and Otakar than from the consequence of a four-year travail while the child is parented by adults who the state will then remove from him. Accordingly, and as the query in *Kelsey* above asks about the similar four-year period of that litigation, should the court take some responsibility for such a delay? Has the time period to decide these cases—arguably the source of much of the harm to involved children—ever been addressed in any pertinent court decision (other than here, where the court blames one of the parties for the decision to litigate)? How long should it take to establish the facts (1) through (7) above? The Illinois Court contends that the law applied to these facts is self-apparent and the decision reversing the trial and appellate court and awarding the child to Otakar was 7–0. Accordingly, and of import to child advocates, can the decision be made in thirty days? Ninety days? Due process takes time, but how many total hours were actually consumed with necessary fact gathering, trial, writing of briefs, and oral argument over the four years while the parents of Kelsey, Richard and many other children are being determined? Does a state's supreme court have the authority to impose tight timelines on itself and its lower courts where a child is in limbo? Can it make a preliminary decision to make it more likely the child will not be moved? Would the Illinois Legislature—which responded to the publicity by attempting to legislatively reverse the Court—not serve the interests of these children by statutorily imposing tight timelines if the court does not act through its rulemaking power to do so?

Child reliance over time on her *de facto* parents creates estoppel issues beyond the dilemma of the deceived father versus the functioning parents. In many jurisdictions, biological parents will join a petition for a guardianship, suspending their parental rights. This voluntary surrender is commonly ordered not by juvenile dependency courts, but by probate courts. A parent may opt for such a guardianship for her child because of a possibly pending Child Protective Service intervention. Where the parent initiates such an action he or she may be able to select the guardian—rather than having a court decide with social service workers' recommendations, and with counsel for the child. Such a guardianship can avoid a judgment that a parent is legally "unfit," and may allow placement with a person more likely to allow parental visitation. Accordingly, such petitions often seek to appoint grandparents as guardians. This option is more common for wealthy or middle class families since counsel must be retained privately and there is no "kin guardianship" or other compensation because this guardian is not caring for a child under the auspices of the state's child protection system (see discussion of the trend toward these guardianships in Chapter 8).

These arrangements may pose some risk for biological parental rights if some probate statutes and recent state cases are followed more generally. In the case of *Guardianship of Ann S.*, 45 Cal. 4th 1110 (2009), the California Supreme Court ruled that state law allowing the termination of parental rights after surrender to a guardian for more than two years (Cal. Prob. Code § 1516.5) was facially constitutional. Importantly, the court held that a showing of current unfitness was not always necessary to terminate biological parents' rights, particularly where those rights had been suspended during a probate guardianship. The court explicitly recognized the guardian's acquisition over time of an interest in the "care and custody" of the child. At least implicitly, the holding gives some force to the notion of the child's interest in continuing a parental relationship on an estoppel basis (the detrimental reliance of the child on the biological parents' failure to care for the child and surrender of the child for parental care to another person).

At the same time as the *Ann S.* case above, the California Supreme Court decided *In re Charlotte D.*, 45 Cal. 4th 1140 (2009). The court there rejected the claimed *Kelsey* father claims of the biological father, and balanced a rather weak factual record of parental performance in the context of paternal surrender of the children to his own parents as guardians. The court again upheld the same Probate Code provision allowing guardian transformation to parental status after two years and applied it to reject his claim to parental status.

These statutes and cases continue a general trend in the direction of recognizing *de facto* parental status, particularly outside of foster care providers. Those foster parents are in the dependency system with parental reunification part of the mandate and where, at least in theory, care is undertaken with the understanding that it may well be temporary. However, even here the trend at the state level is contrary to the controversial Supreme Court decision in *Smith v. OFFER* (discussed in Chapter 8) and is affording more voice to foster providers before juvenile dependency courts. These are the persons directly caring for the children, and commonly know more about their circumstances and needs than do social workers or counsel—with their large caseloads and episodic contact with the children. The foster parents are not given counsel—but are increasingly given the chance to at least be heard by the court. In addition, "concurrent permanency planning" is now commonly in place to begin adoption paperwork before the final parental termination decision is made, so there is not a typically long delay between that termination and permanent adoption. Since family foster care providers are the dominant source of such adoptions, their performance—and the reliance of the child on them as functioning parents—has some relevance and seems to be gaining traction in state statutes and precedents. At the same time, this desired role as parent involves a delicate tightrope for foster care providers and courts, since there may be a conflict of interest between a foster parent who becomes bonded to a child (and vice versa) and the statutory responsibility of "reasonable efforts" to reunify these children with their biological parents (as well as constitutional implications regarding the right to parent terminable only by a finding of "unfitness" by clear and convincing evidence).

Troxel v. Granville

530 U.S. 57 (2000)

OPINION: JUSTICE O'CONNOR announced the judgment of the Court and delivered an opinion, in which THE CHIEF JUSTICE, JUSTICE GINSBURG, and JUSTICE BREYER join.

Section 26.10.160(3) of the Revised Code of Washington permits "any person" to petition a superior court for visitation rights "at any time," and authorizes that court to grant such visitation rights whenever "visitation may serve the best interest of the child." Petitioners Jenifer and Gary Troxel petitioned a Washington Superior Court for the right to visit their grandchildren, Isabelle and Natalie Troxel. Respondent Tommie Granville, the mother of Isabelle and Natalie, opposed the petition. The case ultimately reached the Washington Supreme Court, which held that § 26.10.160(3) unconstitutionally interferes with the fundamental right of parents to rear their children.

I

Tommie Granville and Brad Troxel shared a relationship that ended in June 1991. The two never married, but they had two daughters, Isabelle and Natalie. Jenifer and Gary Troxel are Brad's parents, and thus the paternal grandparents of Isabelle and Natalie. After Tommie and Brad separated in 1991, Brad lived with his parents and regularly brought his daughters to his parents' home for weekend visitation. Brad committed suicide in May 1993. Although the Troxels at first continued to see Isabelle and Natalie on a regular basis after their son's death, Tommie Granville informed the Troxels in October 1993 that she wished to limit their visitation with her daughters to one short visit per month....

In December 1993, the Troxels commenced the present action by filing, in the Washington Superior Court for Skagit County, a petition to obtain visitation rights with Isabelle and Natalie. The Troxels filed their petition under two Washington statutes, Wash. Rev. Code §§ 26.09.240 and 26.10.160(3) (1994). Only the latter statute is at issue in this case. Section 26.10.160(3) provides: "Any person may petition the court for visitation rights at any time including, but not limited to, custody proceedings. The court may order visitation rights for any person when visitation may serve the best interest of the child whether or not there has been any change of circumstances." At trial, the Troxels requested two weekends of overnight visitation per month and two weeks of visitation each summer. Granville did not oppose visitation altogether, but instead asked

the court to order one day of visitation per month with no overnight stay....In 1995, the Superior Court issued an oral ruling and entered a visitation decree ordering visitation one weekend per month, one week during the summer, and four hours on both of the petitioning grandparents' birthdays....

Granville appealed, during which time she married Kelly Wynn. Before addressing the merits of Granville's appeal, the Washington Court of Appeals remanded the case to the Superior Court for entry of written findings of fact and conclusions of law....On remand, the Superior Court found that visitation was in Isabelle and Natalie's best interests.

"The Petitioners [the Troxels] are part of a large, central, loving family, all located in this area, and the Petitioners can provide opportunities for the children in the areas of cousins and music.

The court took into consideration all factors regarding the best interest of the children and considered all the testimony before it. The children would be benefitted from spending quality time with the Petitioners, provided that that time is balanced with time with the childrens' [sic] nuclear family. The court finds that the childrens' [sic] best interests are served by spending time with their mother and stepfather's other six children."....

Approximately nine months after the Superior Court entered its order on remand, Granville's husband formally adopted Isabelle and Natalie....

* * *

The Washington Supreme Court...agreed with the Court of Appeals' ultimate conclusion that the Troxels could not obtain visitation of Isabelle and Natalie pursuant to § 26.10.160(3). The court rested its decision on the Federal Constitution, holding that § 26.10.160(3) unconstitutionally infringes on the fundamental right of parents to rear their children. In the court's view, there were at least two problems with the nonparental visitation statute. First, according to the Washington Supreme Court, the Constitution permits a State to interfere with the right of parents to rear their children only to prevent harm or potential harm....Second, by allowing "'any person' to petition for forced visitation of a child at 'any time' with the only requirement being that the visitation serve the best interest of the child," the Washington visitation statute sweeps too broadly.... "It is not within the province of the state to make significant decisions concerning the custody of children merely because it could make a 'better' decision." *Ibid.*, 969 P.2d at 31. The Washington Supreme Court held that "parents have a right to limit visitation of their children with third persons," and that between parents and judges, "the parents should be the ones to choose whether to expose their children to certain people or ideas."....

We...affirm the judgment.

II

The demographic changes of the past century make it difficult to speak of an average American family. The composition of families varies greatly from household to household. While many children may have two married parents and grandparents who visit regularly, many other children are raised in single-parent households. In 1996, children living with only one parent accounted for 28 percent of all children under age 18 in the United States. U.S. Dept. of Commerce, Bureau of Census, Current Population Reports, 1997 Population Profile of the United States 27 (1998). Understandably, in these single-parent households, persons outside the nuclear family are called upon with increasing frequency to assist in the everyday tasks of child rearing. In many cases, grandparents play an important role. For example, in 1998, approximately 4 million children—or 5.6 percent of all children under age 18—lived in the household of their grandparents. U.S. Dept. of Commerce, Bureau of Census, Current Population Reports, Marital Status and Living Arrangements: March 1998 (Update), p. *i* (1998).

The nationwide enactment of nonparental visitation statutes is assuredly due, in some part, to the States' recognition of these changing realities of the American family. Because grandparents and other relatives undertake duties of a parental nature in many households, States have sought to ensure the welfare of the children therein by protecting the relationships those children form with such third parties. The States' nonparental visitation statutes are further supported by a recognition, which varies from State to State, that children should have the opportunity to benefit from relationships

with statutorily specified persons—for example, their grandparents. The extension of statutory rights in this area to persons other than a child's parents, however, comes with an obvious cost. For example, the State's recognition of an independent third-party interest in a child can place a substantial burden on the traditional parent-child relationship. Contrary to Justice Stevens' accusation, our description of state nonparental visitation statutes in these terms, of course, is not meant to suggest that "children are so much chattel." Rather, our terminology is intended to highlight the fact that these statutes can present questions of constitutional import. In this case, we are presented with just such a question. Specifically, we are asked to decide whether § 26.10.160(3), as applied to Tommie Granville and her family, violates the Federal Constitution.

* * *

The liberty interest at issue in this case—the interest of parents in the care, custody, and control of their children—is perhaps the oldest of the fundamental liberty interests recognized by this Court. More than 75 years ago, in *Meyer v. Nebraska*, 262 U.S. 390, 399, 401...(1923), we held that the "liberty" protected by the Due Process Clause includes the right of parents to "establish a home and bring up children" and "to control the education of their own."....

* * *

Section 26.10.160(3), as applied to Granville and her family in this case, unconstitutionally infringes on that fundamental parental right. The Washington nonparental visitation statute is breathtakingly broad. According to the statute's text, "*any person* may petition the court for visitation rights *at any time*," and the court may grant such visitation rights whenever "visitation may serve *the best interest of the child*." § 26.10.160(3) (emphases added). That language effectively permits any third party seeking visitation to subject any decision by a parent concerning visitation of the parent's children to state-court review. Once the visitation petition has been filed in court and the matter is placed before a judge, a parent's decision that visitation would not be in the child's best interest is accorded no deference. Section 26.10.160(3) contains no requirement that a court accord the parent's decision any presumption of validity or any weight whatsoever. Instead, the Washington statute places the best-interest determination solely in the hands of the judge. Should the judge disagree with the parent's estimation of the child's best interests, the judge's view necessarily prevails. Thus, in practical effect, in the State of Washington a court can disregard and overturn any decision by a fit custodial parent concerning visitation whenever a third party affected by the decision files a visitation petition, based solely on the judge's determination of the child's best interests. The Washington Supreme Court had the opportunity to give § 26.10.160(3) a narrower reading, but it declined to do so....

* * *

...[T]his case involves nothing more than a simple disagreement between the Washington Superior Court and Granville concerning her children's best interests. The Superior Court's announced reason for ordering one week of visitation in the summer demonstrates our conclusion well: "I look back on some personal experiences.... We always spent as kids a week with one set of grandparents and another set of grandparents, [and] it happened to work out in our family that [it] turned out to be an enjoyable experience....

* * *

Because we rest our decision on the sweeping breadth of § 26.10.160(3) and the application of that broad, unlimited power in this case, we do not consider the primary constitutional question passed on by the Washington Supreme Court—whether the Due Process Clause requires all nonparental visitation statutes to include a showing of harm or potential harm to the child as a condition precedent to granting visitation. We do not, and need not, define today the precise scope of the parental due process right in the visitation context. In this respect, we agree with Justice Kennedy that the constitutionality of any standard for awarding visitation turns on the specific manner in which that standard is applied and that the constitutional protections in this area are best "elaborated with care." *Post*, at 9 (dissenting opinion). Because much state-court adjudication in this context occurs on a case-by-case basis, we would be hesitant to hold that specific nonparental visitation statutes violate the Due Process Clause as a *per se* matter...

* * *

Accordingly, the judgment of the Washington Supreme Court is affirmed.

* * *

JUSTICE STEVENS, dissenting.

* * *

A parent's rights with respect to her child have thus never been regarded as absolute, but rather are limited by the existence of an actual, developed relationship with a child, and are tied to the presence or absence of some embodiment of family. These limitations have arisen, not simply out of the definition of parenthood itself, but because of this Court's assumption that a parent's interests in a child must be balanced against the State's long-recognized interests as parens patriae, *see, e.g., Reno v. Flores*, 507 U.S. 292, 303-304...(1993); *Santosky v. Kramer*, 455 U.S. at 766; *Parham*, 442 U.S. at 605; *Prince v. Massachusetts*, 321 U.S. 158, 166...(1944), and, critically, the child's own complementary interest in preserving relationships that serve her welfare and protection, *Santosky*, 455 U.S. at 760.

While this Court has not yet had occasion to elucidate the nature of a child's liberty interests in preserving established familial or family-like bonds, 491 U.S. at 130 (reserving the question), it seems to me extremely likely that, to the extent parents and families have fundamental liberty interests in preserving such intimate relationships, so, too, do children have these interests, and so, too, must their interests be balanced in the equation.[8] At a minimum, our prior cases recognizing that children are, generally speaking, constitutionally protected actors require that this Court reject any suggestion that when it comes to parental rights, children are so much chattel. See *ante*, at 5-6 (opinion of O'Connor, J.) (describing States' recognition of "an independent third-party interest in a child"). The constitutional protection against arbitrary state interference with parental rights should not be extended to prevent the States from protecting children against the arbitrary exercise of parental authority that is not in fact motivated by an interest in the welfare of the child.[9]

This is not, of course, to suggest that a child's liberty interest in maintaining contact with a particular individual is to be treated invariably as on a par with that child's parents' contrary interests. Because our substantive due process case law includes a strong presumption that a parent will act in the best interest of her child, it would be necessary, were the state appellate courts actually to confront a challenge to the statute as applied, to consider whether the trial court's assessment of the "best interest of the child" incorporated that presumption. Neither would I decide whether the trial court applied Washington's statute in a constitutional way in this case, although, as I have explained,...I think the outcome of this determination is far from clear. For the purpose of a facial challenge like this, I think it safe to assume that trial judges usually give great deference to parents' wishes, and I am not persuaded otherwise here.

But presumptions notwithstanding, we should recognize that there may be circumstances in which a child has a stronger interest at stake than mere protection from serious harm caused by the termination of visitation by a "person" other than a parent. The almost infinite variety of family relationships that pervade our ever-changing society strongly counsel against the creation by this Court of a constitutional rule that treats a biological parent's liberty interest in the care and supervision of her child as an isolated right that may be exercised arbitrarily....

* * *

[8] This Court has on numerous occasions acknowledged that children are in many circumstances possessed of constitutionally protected rights and liberties. See *Parham v. J. R.*, 442 U.S. 584, 600...(1979) (liberty interest in avoiding involuntary confinement); *Planned Parenthood of Central Mo. v. Danforth*, 428 U.S. 52, 74...(1976) ("Constitutional rights do not mature and come into being magically only when one attains the state-defined age of majority. Minors, as well as adults, are protected by the Constitution and possess constitutional rights"); *Tinker v. Des Moines Independent Community School Dist.*, 393 U.S. 503, 506-507...(1969) (First Amendment right to political speech); *In re Gault*, 387 U.S. 1, 13...(1967) (due process rights in criminal proceedings).

[9] *Cf., e.g., Wisconsin v. Yoder*, 406 U.S. 205, 241-246...(1972) (Douglas, J., dissenting) ("While the parents, absent dissent, normally speak for the entire family, the education of the child is a matter on which the child will often have decided views. He may want to be a pianist or an astronaut or an oceanographer.

To do so he will have to break from the Amish tradition. It is the future of the student, not the future of the parents, that is imperiled by today's decision. If a parent keeps his child out of school beyond the grade school, then the child will be forever barred from entry into the new and amazing world of diversity that we have today It is the student's judgment, not his parents', that is essential if we are to give full meaning to what we have said about the Bill of Rights and of the right of students to be masters of their own destiny."). The majority's disagreement with Justice Douglas in that case turned not on any contrary view of children's interest in their own education, but on the impact of the Free Exercise Clause of the First Amendment on its analysis of school-related decisions by the Amish community.

JUSTICE SCALIA, dissenting.

In my view, a right of parents to direct the upbringing of their children is among the "unalienable Rights" with which the Declaration of Independence proclaims "all Men...are endowed by their Creator." And in my view that right is also among the "other [rights] retained by the people" which the Ninth Amendment says the Constitution's enumeration of rights "shall not be construed to deny or disparage." The Declaration of Independence, however, is not a legal prescription conferring powers upon the courts; and the Constitution's refusal to "deny or disparage" other rights is far removed from affirming any one of them, and even farther removed from authorizing judges to identify what they might be, and to enforce the judges' list against laws duly enacted by the people. Consequently, while I would think it entirely compatible with the commitment to representative democracy set forth in the founding documents to argue, in legislative chambers or in electoral campaigns, that the state has *no power* to interfere with parents' authority over the rearing of their children, I do not believe that the power which the Constitution confers upon *as a judge* entitles me to deny legal effect to laws that (in my view) infringe upon what is (in my view) that unenumerated right.

* * *

Judicial vindication of "parental rights" under a Constitution that does not even mention them requires (as Justice Kennedy's opinion rightly points out) not only a judicially crafted definition of parents, but also—unless, as no one believes, the parental rights are to be absolute—judicially approved assessments of "harm to the child" and judicially defined gradations of other persons (grandparents, extended family, adoptive family in an adoption later found to be invalid, long-term guardians, etc.) who may have some claim against the wishes of the parents. If we embrace this unenumerated right, I think it obvious—whether we affirm or reverse the judgment here, or remand as Justice Stevens or Justice Kennedy would do—that we will be ushering in a new regime of judicially prescribed, and federally prescribed, family law. I have no reason to believe that federal judges will be better at this than state legislatures; and state legislatures have the great advantages of doing harm in a more circumscribed area, of being able to correct their mistakes in a flash, and of being removable by the people.[2]

For these reasons, I would reverse the judgment below.

* * *

[2] I note that respondent is asserting only, *on her own behalf*, a substantive due process right to direct the upbringing of her own children, and is not asserting, *on behalf of her children* their First Amendment rights of association or free exercise. I therefore do not have occasion to consider whether, and under what circumstances, the parent could assert the latter enumerated rights.

JUSTICE KENNEDY, dissenting.

* * *

The first flaw the State Supreme Court found in the statute is that it allows an award of visitation to a non-parent without a finding that harm to the child would result if visitation were withheld; and the second is that the statute allows any person to seek visitation at any time. In my view the first theory is too broad to be correct, as it appears to contemplate that the best interests of the child standard may not be applied in any visitation case. I acknowledge the distinct possibility that visitation cases may arise where, considering the absence of other protection for the parent under state laws and procedures, the best interests of the child standard would give insufficient protection to the parent's constitutional right to raise the child without undue intervention by the state; but it is quite a different matter to say, as I understand the Supreme Court of Washington to have said, that a harm to the child standard is required in every instance.

* * *

Turning to the question whether harm to the child must be the controlling standard in every visitation proceeding, there is a beginning point that commands general, perhaps unanimous, agreement in our separate opinions: As our case law has developed, the custodial parent has a constitutional right to determine, without undue interference by the state, how best to raise, nurture, and educate the child. The parental right stems from the liberty protected by the Due Process Clause of the Fourteenth Amendment...

The State Supreme Court sought to give content to the parent's right by announcing a categorical rule that third parties who seek visitation must always prove the denial of visitation would harm the child. After reviewing some of the relevant precedents, the Supreme Court of Washington concluded "'the requirement of harm is the sole protection that parents have against pervasive state interference in the parenting process.'"... For that reason, "short of preventing harm to the child," the court considered the best interests of the child to be "insufficient to serve as a compelling state interest overruling a parent's fundamental rights."...

While it might be argued as an abstract matter that in some sense the child is always harmed if his or her best interests are not considered, the law of domestic relations, as it has evolved to this point, treats as distinct the two standards, one harm to the child and the other the best interests of the child. The judgment of the Supreme Court of Washington rests on that assumption, and I, too, shall assume that there are real and consequential differences between the two standards.

* * *

My principal concern is that the holding seems to proceed from the assumption that the parent or parents who resist visitation have always been the child's primary caregivers and that the third parties who seek visitation have no legitimate and established relationship with the child. That idea, in turn, appears influenced by the concept that the conventional nuclear family ought to establish the visitation standard for every domestic relations case. As we all know, this is simply not the structure or prevailing condition in many households. *See, e.g., Moore East Cleveland*, 431 U.S. 494,...(1977). For many boys and girls a traditional family with two or even one permanent and caring parent is simply not the reality of their childhood. This may be so whether their childhood has been marked by tragedy or filled with considerable happiness and fulfillment.

Cases are sure to arise—perhaps a substantial number of cases—in which a third party, by acting in a caregiving role over a significant period of time, has developed a relationship with a child which is not necessarily subject to absolute parental veto. See *Michael H Gerald D.*, 491 U.S. 110,...(1989) (putative natural father not entitled to rebut state law presumption that child born in a marriage is a child of the marriage); *Quilloin v. Walcott*, 434 U.S. 246,...(1978) (best interests standard sufficient in adoption proceeding to protect interests of natural father who had not legitimated the child); see also Lehr Robertson,.. Some pre-existing relationships, then, serve to identify persons who have a strong attachment to the child with the concomitant motivation to act in a responsible way to ensure the child's welfare. As the State Supreme Court was correct to acknowledge, those relationships can be so enduring that "in certain circumstances where a child has enjoyed a substantial relationship with a third person, arbitrarily depriving the child of the relationship could cause severe psychological harm to the child," *In re Smith*, 137 Wn.2d at 20, 969 P.2d at 30; and harm to the adult may also ensue. In the design and elaboration of their visitation laws, States may be entitled to consider that certain relationships are such that to avoid the risk of harm, a best interests standard can be employed by their domestic relations courts in some circumstances.

Indeed, contemporary practice should give us some pause before rejecting the best interests of the child standard in all third-party visitation cases, as the Washington court has done. The standard has been recognized for many years as a basic tool of domestic relations law in visitation proceedings. Since 1965 all 50 States have enacted a third-party visitation statute of some sort. See *ante*, at 15, n. (plurality opinion). Each of these statutes, save one, permits a court order to issue in certain cases if visitation is found to be in the best interests of the child. While it is unnecessary for us to consider the constitutionality of any particular provision in the case now before us, it can be noted that the statutes also include a variety of methods for limiting parents' exposure to third-party visitation petitions and for ensuring parental decisions are given respect. Many States limit the identity of permissible petitioners by restricting visitation petitions to grandparents, or by requiring petitioners to show a substantial relationship with a child, or both....

* * *

Questions for Discussion

1. What are the proper criteria for court-ordered visitation against the wishes of a parent? Does it require a biological relationship (such as a grandparent)? Does it require a previous or existing parental role or function by the person granted such visitation—as Kennedy's dissent suggests might suffice?

2. Would it matter if their son Brad had custody at the time of his death? Would it have made a difference if the Troxel grandparents were the only parents this child had ever known?

3. The opinions in *Troxel* have much in common, even between the majority opinion and the dissents. How do the Kennedy and Stevens dissents differ from the majority? From each other? Kennedy implies and Stevens states that the loss of a parental relationship from a child's perspective is a cognizable interest. Does the majority find that interest to be of constitutional dimension?

4. Note that the interests of children are often cast as a "compelling state interest" of importance—but subservient to competing adult constitutional "fundamental liberties" (such as the right to parent a child). If a child's concomitant constitutional rights are recognized and competed in a "balancing" of those rights on the same level, what would be the implications for *Troxel*? For other leading constitutional cases involving children?

Webster v. Ryan
189 Misc. 2d 86 [729 N.Y.S.2d 315] (2001)

W. Dennis Duggan, J.

In this case, the Court holds that a child has an independent, constitutionally guaranteed right to maintain contact...with a person with whom the child has developed a parent-like relationship.[1]

That right is constitutionally guaranteed because it is a fundamental liberty encompassed within the freedom of association right of the First Amendment of the United States Constitution (see the intimate personal relationship rights of *Griswold v. Connecticut*, 381 US 479 (1965)), and article I, §§ 8 and 9 of the New York Constitution. This liberty is protected by the Due Process Clause of the Fourteenth Amendment and article I, § 6 of the New York Constitution. Because the state has provided no statutory basis for a child to assert such right of contact in a court of law, as it has for similar situations involving child contact with parents, grandparents and siblings, Alex Ryan, Jr., has been denied the equal protection of the laws guaranteed by the Fourteenth Amendment of the US Constitution and article I, § 11 of the New York Constitution....

* * *

...Alex, Jr., was born in 1995, with a positive toxicology for cocaine. He was removed from his mother's custody shortly after birth. Her parental rights were eventually terminated, as were the father's in 1999. Both parents' terminations were based on permanent neglect. During the time that the Department of Social Services (DSS) was providing services for the mother, the father was filing at least four custody proceedings. All of the father's petitions were dismissed by the Family Court judge without a hearing. According to the trial court, the petitions were "dismissed due to [the father's] unwillingness to partake in services recommended by [DSS]." For the years from 1995 to 1998, the father received one hour of DSS-supervised visitation each week. In reviewing the denial of the father's custody petitions, the Appellate Division held:

> "In fact, the records in these proceedings reveal no evidence that the father would not be a proper custodian for the child or that the child would be at risk in his custody. To the contrary, despite Family Court's limitation on the evidence received, the record generally supports a finding that the father is qualified to serve as a custodian for the child...."

Concerning the termination of parental rights finding, the Appellate Division held that DSS made no effort to satisfy its burden of showing that it had formulated a realistic plan that was tailored to fit the father's circumstances. It also held that the Family Court judge "repeatedly thwarted the father's efforts to establish the lack of any reasonable basis for the plan that was put in place.... Obviously, the petition should have been dismissed at the conclusion of DSS' case, if not earlier."...The Appellate Division, in finding that the Family Court judge had demonstrated hostility toward the father and his attorney, ordered that all further proceedings be conducted before a different judge.

Upon remand, in *Ryan III*, this Court returned custody of the child to the father and entered a series of visitation orders to facilitate the transition of the child back into the father's home. During this period of time, the foster mother filed petitions seeking visitation and custody rights to Alex, Jr. This Court, in *Ryan III*, rejected the foster mother's claims. It found that there was no statutory, common law or constitutional basis to grant visitation to a nonbiological, former custodian. The Court reserved on the question of whether the child has an independent constitutional right to seek visitation with his former foster mother and allowed the parties and the Law Guardian time to brief the issue. This decision answers that question in the affirmative. From Alex, Jr.'s birth in 1995 until April 2000, when he was returned to his father, the boy had lived with the foster mother for all of his life but for a few weeks.

II. Determination of Fundamental Rights

In this case, the Court has concluded that a child has a fundamental right to maintain contact, over the objection of a parent, with a person with whom the child has developed a parent-like relationship. The Court also holds that this right has constitutional protection but that this right must be balanced with the unquestionable fundamental right of the parent to raise his son without undue state interference.

The judicial determination (disparagingly described by some as "discovery") of fundamental rights has long been a subject of great debate in the legal and judicial professions.[2]...A judge, wading into the constitutional rights determination quicksand, must have an abiding concern that he not set himself up as a judicial legislature.... [But] proof that the People possess other rights, not contained in or derivative of the Constitution, comes from three powerful positive sources: the Declaration of Independence, the Constitution and the Bill of Rights.

* * *

...The Constitution, as first passed, had no bill of rights at all. The Delegates to the Convention did not believe one was necessary. It was not necessary, in the Framers' view, because the Constitution, as written, gave the Federal Government no power to abridge any fundamental rights....The final element of proof which establishes that all of our rights are not bestowed by or contained in the Constitution comes from the Bill of Rights itself—Amendment IX provides: "The enumeration in the Constitution, of certain rights, shall not be construed to deny or disparage others *retained by the people.*" (Emphasis added.)

Amendment X provides: "The powers not delegated to the United States by the Constitution, nor prohibited by it to the States, are reserved to the States respectively, *or to the people*" (emphasis added).

Amendment XIV, § 1 provides: "No State shall make or enforce any law which shall abridge the privileges or immunities of citizens of the United States."

These three Amendments all speak to rights held by the People that are not listed in the Constitution. Knowing that other rights exist, how are they to be determined and who should do the determining, the judiciary or the legislature? Most would readily agree that the legislature has the authority to determine rights or even create new rights. For example, the legislature could determine that the people have a right to universal health care. It is doubtful that the judiciary could make such a determination….The question to be asked here is, what is the judiciary's proper place in the rights determination business? It is clear that the Constitution does create some rights that would not be considered fundamental (*e.g.*, the prohibition against bills of attainder and ex post facto laws). It is also clear that the Constitution protects or guarantees many other rights, some of which are now (but were not always) universally regarded as fundamental (*e.g.*, freedom of speech and religion). Finally, it is clear that other rights determined by the courts to be possessed by the people are not specified in but are protected by the Constitution. For example, the rights to travel (*Edwards v California*, 314 US 160 [1941]), to marry (*Loving v Virginia*, 388 US 1 [1967]), and to privacy (*Griswold v Connecticut*, 381 US 479 [1965]) are rights protected by the Due Process and Equal Protection Clauses of the Fourteenth Amendment, but they are not listed anywhere in the Constitution.[3] The above discussion shows that if a right exists for a child to maintain contact with a person with whom he has developed a parent-like relationship, it will not be found explicitly or inferentially set forth in the Constitution, but it need not be. However, if such a right exists, and this Court holds that it does, that right has constitutional protection because it is a fundamental right and the Constitution protects our fundamental rights from unwarranted state intrusion or exclusion….The search for such a right must begin with the Supreme Court's Talmudic exposition of our Constitution.[4]

If one scans 200 years of Supreme Court decisions that define, determine or discover rights (however one defines the process)….and the work of legal scholars who have written on the subject, one is left quite disoriented from trying to find any consistently applied, generally agreed upon, theory of constitutional interpretation…. Despite the absence of a legislative road map or clearly defined constitutional sign posts or a generally accepted method of rights determinations to provide guidance, courts, since courts began, have been determining rights….These rights have been birthed from statutes, bills of rights, constitutions, natural law and the common law.

* * *

…*Griswold* was a substantive due process case and Justice Goldberg (with Chief Justice Burger and Justice Brennan concurring) [wrote]

"I do agree that the concept of liberty protects those personal rights that are fundamental, and is not confined to the specific terms of the Bill of Rights. My conclusion that the concept of liberty is not so restricted and that it embraces the right of marital privacy though that right is not mentioned explicitly in the Constitution is supported by both numerous decisions of this Court, referred to in the Court's opinion, and by the language and history of the Ninth Amendment. The Ninth Amendment…shows a belief of the Constitution's authors that fundamental rights exist that are not deemed exhaustive."…

* * *

However these liberty rights are found, the Supreme Court's progression of rulings on issues affecting family privacy rights does show a fairly consistent trend. This trend expands the rights of families and individual family members.

1. In *Meyer v Nebraska* (262 US 390 [1923]), the Supreme Court ruled unconstitutional a Nebraska law which prohibited the teaching of any foreign language in any elementary school.

2. In *Pierce v Society of Sisters* (268 US 510 [1925]), the Supreme Court ruled unconstitutional an Oregon statute which required all children to attend public schools.

3. In *Skinner v Oklahoma* (316 US 535 [1942]), the Supreme Court declared unconstitutional the Oklahoma Criminal Sterilization Act. It declared that Skinner, who had two convictions for robbery and one for stealing chickens, had a fundamental right to procreate

4. In *Griswold v Connecticut* (381 US 479 [1965]), the Court held unconstitutional a law which prohibited the dissemination of contraceptive materials to married couples.

5. In *Levy v Louisiana* (391 US 68 [1968]), the Court ruled unconstitutional a Louisiana law that prohibited illegitimate children from recovery for the wrongful death of their mother.

6. In *Glona v American Guar. & Liab. Ins. Co.* (391 US 73 [1968]), the Court ruled unconstitutional a Louisiana Law which denied the right of a mother to recover for the wrongful death of her child because the child was illegitimate.

7. In *Loving v Virginia* (388 US 1 [1967]), the Court held unconstitutional a Virginia law which prohibited interracial marriages.

8. In *Eisenstadt v Baird* (405 US 438 [1972]), the Court ruled unconstitutional a Massachusetts law which prohibited the distribution of contraceptives to unmarried people.

9. In *Weber v Aetna Cas. & Sur. Co.* (406 US 164 [1972]), the Court held unconstitutional a Louisiana law which denied workers' compensation benefits to an unacknowledged illegitimate child.

10. In *Carey v Population Servs. Intl.* (431 US 678 [1972]), the Court ruled unconstitutional a New York law which permitted only pharmacists to sell contraceptives to adults and a blanket prohibition on such sales to minors.

11. In *Wisconsin v Yoder* (406 US 205 [1972]), the Court held that the state could not require parents of the Amish Church to send their children to public school after the eighth grade.

12. In *Roe v Wade* (410 US 113 [1973]), the Court ruled that the state cannot prohibit a woman from terminating a pregnancy during the first two trimesters of her pregnancy because it violates her fundamental privacy right.

13. In *Gomez v Perez* (409 US 535 [1973]), the Court ruled unconstitutional a Texas law which prohibited illegitimate children from claiming child support from their father.

14. In *Cleveland Bd. of Educ. v LaFleur* (414 US 632 [1974]), the Court held unconstitutional mandatory maternity leaves.

15. In *Planned Parenthood v Danforth* (428 US 52 1976]), the Court held that the state could not require spousal consent as a predicate for a woman having an abortion or give a parent veto power over a minor's decision to have an abortion (a competing rights case).

16. In *Moore v City of E. Cleveland* (431 US 494 [1977]), the Court ruled unconstitutional a housing ordinance which prohibited a grandmother and her grandchildren from living together in a single dwelling unit.

17. In *Caban v Mohammed* (441 US 380 [1979]), the Court ruled unconstitutional New York's adoption consent statute which gave the unwed mother of a child an automatic right to veto an adoption, while the father had to show that the adoption would not be in the child's best interest.

18. In *Clark v Jeter* (486 US 456 [1988]), the Court held that a six-year statute of limitations in which to establish paternity violated the Equal Protection Clause.

Consistent with this progression of Supreme Court decisions that protect, extend and expand the liberty rights of individuals and families, and within the trajectory of the developed meaning of the Constitution, would be a holding that the state cannot deny (or in this case, refuse to enforce) the First Amendment rights of a child to associate with another person with whom the child has developed a parent-like relationship. If a child

has such a right, and the Court holds that he does, and the state extends a procedure to protect or enforce similar rights of similar persons in similar situations, but excludes the child from the due process that protects that right, then the child has been denied the equal protection of the laws.

It has been firmly established that children are persons within the meaning of the Constitution and accordingly possess constitutional rights. Precisely defining these rights has not been an easy task.

"The question of the extent of state power to regulate conduct of minors not constitutionally regulable when committed by adults is a vexing one, perhaps not susceptible of a precise answer. We have been reluctant to attempt to define 'the totality of the relationship of the juvenile and the state'....Certain principles, however, have been recognized. 'Minors, as well as adults, are protected by the Constitution and possess constitutional rights'....Watever [sic] may be their precise impact, neither the Fourteenth Amendment nor the Bill of Rights is for adults alone'....On the other hand, we have held in a variety of contexts that 'the power of the state to control the conduct of children reaches beyond the scope of its authority over adults'....Thus minors are entitled to constitutional protection for freedom of speech...equal protection against racial discrimination...due process in civil contexts...and a variety of rights of defendants in criminal proceedings." (*Carey v Population Servs.*, 431 US 678, 692 [1977].)

In this case, there is no claim that the state is intervening in a family relationship for regulatory or parens patriae purposes. The narrow holding in this case is that a statutory scheme that permits court intervention to order contact between a child and a parent or his sibling or grandparent is an unconstitutional denial of a child's right to equal protection of the laws when the law does not provide a procedure for the child to assert the same right with respect to a person with whom the child has a significant or substantial parent-like relationship. Since the Court holds that such a right is fundamental and constitutes a liberty interest under the Due Process Clause, the child must have an effective forum to assert that right.

III. Balancing the Fundamental Rights of a Parent and Child[30]

The Supreme Court has infrequently addressed the situation where constitutional interests between parents and their children compete, either with each other or with the state. In *Prince v Massachusetts* (321 US 158 [1944]), the Court held that the state's child labor laws trumped the parent's right to have her child engage in religious activity in public and the child's independent right to do so....*Prince* stands for the proposition that the state has *parens patriae* authority over children up to a point....

* * *

In *Santosky v Kramer* (455 US 745 [1982]), the Supreme Court held that New York's statutory scheme to terminate parental rights was flawed because due process required that the fact-finding determination be made by clear and convincing evidence, as opposed to a preponderance of the evidence standard. The majority decision, essentially parent-focused, held that the risk of fact-finding error should be distributed toward the Department of Social Services and away from the parents. In so holding, the decision assumes an alliance or unity of interest between the parents and the child. The minority, in finding that due process was served by a preponderance of the evidence standard, which allocated the risk of error evenly between the parents and the agency, left the children in a neutral position.

* * *

In *Michael H. v Gerald D* (491 US 110 [1989]), the Court was called upon to determine the constitutionality of a California statute that provided that a child born to a married woman living with her husband, who is neither impotent nor sterile, is presumed to be a child of the marriage and that this presumption may be rebutted only by the husband or the wife....

Read one way, *Gerald D* stands for the proposition that biology is not destiny and the court will look to the family relationships or unit that best serves the child's best interest, without regard to genetic parenthood.

* * *

The Court took 18 pages to dismiss the boyfriend/genetic-father's constitutional claims. It needed only three paragraphs to dismiss the child's....Justice Scalia does note that: "We have never had occasion to decide whether a child has a liberty interest, symmetrical with that of her parent in maintaining her filial relationship." (*Gerald D* at 110.) However, Justice Scalia also held that the child's claim must fail because there was no basis in law, history or tradition for a child to make a claim for multiple fatherhoods.

"In contrast, allowing a claim of illegitimacy to be pressed by the child...may *well disrupt an otherwise peaceful union*. Since it pursues a legitimate end by rational means, California's decision to treat Victoria differently from her parents is not a denial of equal protection." (*Gerald D* at 131-132 [emphasis added].)

This case, involving a married woman who had affairs of some duration with two other men and admittedly had a child out of wedlock, does not seem the best factual situation in which to raise an issue about disrupting "an otherwise peaceful union." Also, Justice Scalia, by inserting at the end the phrase, "legitimate end by rational means," puts the constitutional analysis of this case at the lowest level of scrutiny. However, the issues raised in this case and the precedents cited would support a higher level of constitutional scrutiny. Justice Stevens, concurring in the judgment, remarks....

"[Our] cases...demonstrate that enduring 'family' relationships may develop in unconventional settings. I therefore would not foreclose the possibility that a constitutionally protected relationship between a natural father and his child might exist in a case like this. Indeed, I am willing to assume for the purpose of deciding this case that Michael's relationship with Victoria is strong enough to give him a constitutional right to try to convince a trial judge that Victoria's best interest would be served by granting him visitation rights." (*Gerald D* at 133.)

* * *

The two cases that most directly impact the holding in this case are the Supreme Court's grandparents' visitation decision, handed down last year in *Troxel v Granville* (530 US 57 [2000]) and the New York Court of Appeals "*de facto*" parent visitation decision in *Matter of Alison D. v Virginia M.* (77 NY2d 651 [1991])....In *Troxel*,...the Supreme Court held that the Washington statute as applied was unconstitutional. The first deficiency they noted in the statute was that in allowing any person at any time to apply for visitation, the law was "breathtakingly broad." Secondly, the statute contained "no requirement that a court accord the parent's decision any presumption of validity or any weight whatsoever."...At the fact-finding stage, the trial court (1) presumed that grandparent visitation was in the child's best interest, (2) placed the burden on the parents to first articulate reasonable objections to the visits, and (3) the court articulated no "special factors" which would "justify the State's interference with [the parent's] fundamental right to make decisions concerning the rearing of her two daughters."...

...Justice Stevens is the only Justice to raise the issue of the child's constitutional rights....

* * *

Justice Kennedy, also in dissent, lends support to the concept that, under appropriate circumstances, court-ordered visitation between a child and a nonparent is constitutionally permissible.

"My principal concern is that the holding seems to proceed from the assumption that the parent or parents who resist visitation have always been the child's primary caregivers and that the third parties who seek visitation have no legitimate and established relationship with the child. That idea, in turn, appears influenced by the concept that the conventional nuclear family ought to establish the visitation standard for every domestic relations case....

Cases are sure to arise....in which a third party, by acting in a caregiving role over a significant period of time, has developed a relationship with a child which is not necessarily subject to absolute parental veto."...

* * *

In balancing the unquestionable constitutionally guaranteed right of a parent to raise his or her child on one hand and the constitutional right of a child to maintain contact with a parent-substitute (and the state intrusion in giving a court forum to voice that right) on the other hand, it will be helpful to examine other areas where a state does intrude into the parent's constitutional right to raise his or her child free of state interference. By examining these circumstances, we can gauge the level of intrusion into the parent's rights that are caused by recognizing this right for the parent's child.

The bedrock principle of *Troxel* is that "the liberty interest at issue in [this] case—the interest of parents in the care, custody, and control of their children—is perhaps the oldest of the fundamental liberty interests recognized by the [Supreme Court].".... While that is undoubtedly true, the pedigree for that claim was *Meyer v Nebraska* (262 US 390), decided in 1923. Starting more than 100 years earlier than that, state courts were establishing a substantial body of law in which the state's *parens patriae* authority was used to uphold child custodial rights of nonparents against the claims of parents....

* * *

These cases illustrate a well-established policy of the judiciary to manage conflicted family relations based on the best interest of the child. There is no mention of fundamental or constitutional rights in any of these cases, or any doubt expressed by the courts that they had the authority to make these decisions. This position was not limited to state courts. Supreme Court Justice Joseph Story, riding circuit, in *United States v Green* (3 Mason 482 [1824]) held as follows:

"As to the question of the right of the father to have custody of his infant child, in a general sense it is true. But this is not on account of any absolute right of the father, but for the benefit of the infant; the law presuming it to be for its interest to be under the nurture and care of its natural protector, both for maintenance and education. When, therefore, a court is asked to lend its aid to put the infant into the custody of the father and to withdraw him from other persons, it will look into all the circumstances, and ascertain whether it will be for the real, permanent interests of the infant...."

Accompanying the judiciary's foray into the management of parent and child family relationships has been the legislature's. There are any number of laws that restrict the activities of juveniles. Most, if not all, of those laws were passed without any mention that they restrict the child's parent's right to permit the child to engage in certain activities or engage in them in a fashion that the parent feels is appropriate. Looked at from this "parent restricting" point of view, we have the following laws which illustrate that point (citations omitted):

1. A parent may not let his child purchase, or consume alcohol outside a home setting, until the child is 21....

2. A parent may not allow his child to drive a car until age 16....

3. A parent may not permit his child to be a passenger in his car unless seat belted or, if less than four, in a car seat....

4. A parent may not permit his child to ride a bike or a scooter without a helmet....

5. A parent must submit his or her child to a series of vaccinations....

6. A parent may not permit his child less than 16 to possess a BB gun, handgun, shotgun or rifle....

7. A parent may not permit his child to purchase cigarettes....

8. A parent may not permit his child less than 16 to be employed in most occupations...

9. A parent may not permit a child to marry if the child is less than 14 or, if less than 16, without the permission of a judge....

10. A parent may not permit his child less than 16 to enter a bar without adult supervision....

11. A parent may not permit his child to get a tattoo....

12. A parent may not permit a child less than 18 to hunt bear or deer or less than 16 to hunt other wildlife with a firearm...

13. A parent may not permit his child to appear in a professional wrestling or boxing match if less than 18 and, if less than 16, the child may not attend such a performance....

14. A parent may not permit his child less than 10 to operate a snowmobile off the parent's land....

15. A parent must send his child to a full-time school from age six to 16....

...Today, mandatory schooling is universally accepted. This was not always so...

* * *

...All of the regulations of children listed above were based on the police power of the state exercised in the state's capacity as *parens patriae* (parent of the country). The laws needed to have only a rational basis to sustain constitutional muster. If the state can direct a parent to send his or her child to all day school for 180 days each year, how less an intrusion into parental rights is it to permit a court to order the parent to provide visitation to a *de facto* parent for, say, two days each month? When balanced with the child's constitutional right, this is a fairly modest incursion into the parent's constitutional right to direct the upbringing of his or her child.

There is also a significant body of statutory law that permits a Family Court to invade the fundamental right of a parent to the control of his or her child....

These statutes clearly illustrate the accepted authority of the state to intrude into a parent's custodial rights to his or her child when the child's best interests are at stake. An even more obvious example would be the several provisions of Family Court Act article 10, which provide for the removal of children from neglectful or abusive parents. For this entire statutory framework, there is no indication from the laws' words or context that any "special weight" must be given to a parent's wishes, as that point was made in *Troxel.*

Conclusion

The historical development of family law in America, and the expansion of individual constitutional rights by the Supreme Court of the United States and the Court of Appeals of the State of New York, give foundation to a holding that a child has a constitutional right to maintain contact with a person with whom the child has developed a parent-like relationship. Accompanying that right is also a right to the equal protection of the laws. This requires that the child have the due process necessary to claim his right. This claim can be given constitutional protection, while at the same time giving due recognition, respect and protection to a parent's constitutional right to the custody, care and control of his or her child. Accordingly, with this goal in mind, the Court holds the following:...

1.   That a child has certain enumerated and unenumerated constitutionally protected rights.

2.   That these rights are protected coextensively by the cited provisions of the Constitution of the United States and the Constitution of the State of New York.

3.   That the child's unenumerated rights include a fundamental right to maintain contact with a person with whom the child has developed a parent-like relationship.

4.   That the child also has an enumerated First Amendment freedom of association right under the State and Federal Constitutions to maintain personal relations with a nonbiologically related person.

5.   That the child's rights listed above are liberty interests protected by the Due Process Clauses of the Federal and State Constitutions.

6.   That the child is entitled to the equal protection of the laws to be similarly situated with other children who have a statutory procedure to enforce their constitutionally or statutorily protected association rights.

7.   That a child having such a right must be provided a process to enforce that right against unwarranted restrictions by the state or a third person, in this case a parent.

8.   That a parent has a fundamental right to direct the care, custody and guardianship of his or her child and is presumed to act in the child's best interest. (*Parham v J. R.,* 442 US 584 [1979].

9.   That this fundamental right of the parent must be balanced with the fundamental rights of the child....

[1] At the outset, the Court notes that the terms "custody" and "visitation" have outlived their usefulness. Indeed, their use tends to place any discussion and allocation of family rights into an oppositional framework. "Fighting for custody" directs the process towards determining winners and losers. The children, always in the middle, usually turn out to be losers. Churchill once said that we shape our buildings and afterwards our buildings shape us. The same can be said for our words. This Court has abandoned the use of the

word "visitation" in its orders, using the phrase "parenting time" instead. If the word "custody" did not so permeate our statutes and was not so ingrained into our psyches, that would be the next phrase to go. If our Domestic Relations Law, in both substance and process, was more child focused, as I believe this decision is, there would be a better framework for determining family rights. Instead, we focus on parental rights. This misplaced focus draws parents into contention and conflict, drawing the worst from them at a time when their children need their parents' best. The Court notes, for example, that the Family Court Act of Australia uses neither the word custody nor visitation, but refers only to "parenting orders" which can include "residence orders" and "contact orders."...

[2] See, for example, on the restraint side: Antonin Scalia, *A Matter of Interpretation, Federal Courts and the Law* (Princeton Univ 1997); Raoul Berger, *Government by Judiciary* (Liberty Fund, Law ed 1997); and Richard A. Posner, The Problems of Jurisprudence (Harv Univ Press 1990). On the expansionist side see: Charles L. Black, Jr., *A New Birth of Freedom* (Grosset/Putnam 1997); Laurence H. Tribe, *Constitutional Choices* (Harv Univ Press 1985); and William Lusser, *The Limits of Judicial Power, The Supreme Court in American Politics* (Univ of NC Press 1988). With a foot in both camps see: John Hart Ely, Democracy and Distrust, A Theory of Judicial Review (Harv Univ Press 1980); Cass R. Sunstein, *The Partial Constitution* (Harv Univ Press 1993); and Alexander M. Bickel, *The Supreme Court and The Idea of Progress* (Harper and Row 1970).

[3] ...[S]ome things that most people would probably consider as a constitutional (or fundamental) right are not so at all. For example, the right of a child to an education is not constitutionally protected. (*San Antonio Ind. School Dist. v Rodriguez,* 411 US 1 [1973].) One reason for this slow evolution of personal rights is that liberty rights follow property rights. Until a person's right to own and control property became protected by the Constitution, the rights to free speech, religion, and to assemble, were little more than lofty ideas. The Alien and Sedition Acts are a good example of how fragile and unprotected the rights of free speech and assembly were in 1798....

[4] The Court's use of the word Constitution in this decision includes both the New York State and Federal Constitutions. The Court finds that each Constitution's protective reach covers the right determined in this decision and should be interpreted identically.

[30] See Lawrence D. Houlgate, *Three Concepts of Children's Constitutional Rights: Reflections on the Enjoyment Theory,* 2 U Pa J Const L 77 (Dec. 1999); Melinda A. Roberts, *Parent and Child in Conflict: Between Liberty and Responsibility,*10 Notre Dame JL Ethics & Pub Poly 485 (1996); Justine Witkin, *A Time For Change: Reevaluating the Constitutional Status of Minors,* 47 Fla L Rev 113 (Jan. 1995); Gilbert A. Holmes, *The Tie that Binds: The Constitutional Right of Children to Maintain Relationships With Parent-Like Individuals,* 53 Md L Rev 358 (Winter 1994); Barbara Jones, *Do Siblings Possess Constitutional Rights?,* 78 Cornell L Rev 1187 (Sept. 1993).

Questions for Discussion

1. The court in *Webster* also holds that the court must give significant weight to the parent's determination as to what is in the child's best interest, including the decision to allow a certain level of contact. It holds that the child carries the burden of proof under a preponderance test. It also holds that there must be a "parent-like relationship," taking into account its "length, nature and quality." Can a three-year-old have such a relationship justifying court-ordered visitation? A six-month-old?

2. Will the (prior *de facto* parent) relationship be protected by court order until the child is 18 years of age? Will the court prevent the parent from moving the child geographically where it precludes contact from such a *de facto* parent—as in joint custody family court cases?

3. Note that an increasing number of cases recognize the rights of such *de facto* parents. These are parents who may not qualify as parents by virtue of biology, marriage, presumptive status (*e.g.*, under the Uniform Parentage Act), or *Kelsey* status by attempting to perform as a father. A number of these cases involve lesbian couples who agree to parent a child, so function, and then break up. The relationships are often complicated, with some of the claimants giving birth to the child, others contributing DNA material, *et al.* Some courts recognize the child's relationship with these parents as a critical factor and allow visitation for the

"parent" who does not have custody, and also impose child support obligations. See *Elisa B. v. Superior Court*, 37 Cal. 4th 108 (2005), with companion cases *K.M. v. E.G* and *Kristine H. v. Lisa R;* see also *Carvin v. Britain*, 155 Wn.2d 679 (2005). Other courts deny such status, ironically including the New York jurisdiction, as in *Alison D. v. Virginia M.*, 77 NY2d 651 (1991) (where a five-year relationship with a child did not confer any "parental" status warranting visitation). If a person functions as a parent and is reasonably so regarded by a child, *e.g.*, who provides shelter, changes diapers, feeds, medically tends, instructs, plays, nurtures, and worries—do traditional principles of equitable estoppel confer parental status? Is the parent's reliance on such a functional status relevant? Is the child's reliance?

4. As noted above, many of the cases recognizing *de facto* parental status do not involve foster parents. In *Smith v. OFFER* (discussed in Chapter 8), the Court denied any parental status whatever to foster parents, finding that they consent to a status as custodians for children pending parental return or other placement in the discretion of the local department of social services. The Court held that they lack any proper expectation of a relationship and denied them due process standing where such children are removed from their care. In *OFFER* the removal was not to return a child to a parent, but to move a child to a different placement with strangers. The *de facto* parent in *Webster* is such a foster parent. And here the child is to be placed with a natural father who had been wrongfully denied his child, is adjudged fit, and maintained an interest and consistent visitation through most of the child's tenure away. Does the *Webster* foster parent status and return of the child to a wronged parent make its judgment problematical given the *OFFER* precedent? On the other hand, did *OFFER* analyze or fully consider the rights of the child to a relationship with a parent? If there are such rights, as *Webster* holds, how can foster care status or implied waiver of parental claim foreclose the child's right?

Note on Expanding Concept of "Family" for Parental Rights and Obligations

Two intersecting trends complicate parental rights determination: artificial insemination advances and same sex unions seeking parental status. The first variable now permits acquisition of sperm from persons who have contracted to do so without any purported parental obligation. And it permits the implantation of sperm (or even developing embryos through *in vitro* fertilization) into "surrogate" mothers. These birth mothers may have allegedly disavowed by contract their parental rights. Science now allows a multitude of combinations: the relatively straightforward use of third-party sperm to impregnate a wife where the husband is unable to do so; the use of the husband's sperm to combine with the ovum of a third party (*in vitro* fertilization into an embryo) that may then be implanted in the wife; the above situation implanted in a third-party surrogate woman to carry the embryo to term; or a third-party surrogate accepting an ovum from a fourth-party female—which may or may not have been fertilized by a male seeking parental status. This fourth option of creating a child without the genes of the prospective parents, and which the erstwhile mother does not carry within her, appears a puzzling option (particularly given the hundreds of thousands of infants and children who would benefit from adoption). But the surrogates and genetic sources may well be relatives where genetic and emotional ties provide a bond to the baby for those seeking parenthood.

The variations from the new combinations above then play out in two superficially contrasting contexts: claimant parents seeking custody and enforcement of parental rights, or alleged parents disavowing parental status and rejecting support obligations. The conflicts here are resolved among the varying state statutes and court precedents serving as the predominant legal forum in this subject area.

The New Jersey case of *In the Matter of the Parentage of the Child by T.J.S. and A.L.S.*, 419 N.J. Super. 46 (2011) well illustrates the complexities now presented. Husband and wife were unable to have a child through "traditional" means because wife A.L.S. could not carry a child to term. Consequently, plaintiffs arranged for the *in vitro* fertilization of an ovum furnished by an anonymous donor using the sperm of husband T.J.S. This option means that the baby will carry his DNA, but have a third-party mother's DNA, and be carried by a fourth party—with wife A.L.S. neither contributing to the DNA nor carrying (giving birth) to the baby. The gestational surrogate was A.F., who so consented and who relinquished all rights within 72 hours of the birth.

The registrar of birth certificates refused to list A.L.S. as the birth mother and the court held that her status depended upon stepparent adoption (which normally requires consent of all biological parents and an involved home study, *et al.*, to determine appropriate placement). Applicable New Jersey law, fairly typical of state statutes defining parentage, is interpreted by the court *not* to "extend to a wife whose husband, while married, fathers a child with another woman,...or to a wife who simply acknowledges in writing her maternity of the child....On the contrary, where a husband has a child, born to another woman, while married to his wife, the wife may only establish a parental relationship with the child by adoption" (at 55). Interestingly, the Uniform Parentage Act will give a father parental status without biology or child birth simply by holding oneself out as the biological parent and bringing the child into the home and caring for him. This status is not adjudged applicable to females by New Jersey (and many other state courts), nor does the distinction apparently violate equal protection standards. Were the ovum to be that of claimant mother A.L.S., the court notes that equal protection issues would then arise. However, note that the male need not provide a scintilla of evidence of genetic contribution to be considered a father under the second prong of the Uniform Parentage Act's "presumed fatherhood" test.

Such strict application of the Uniform Parentage Act has been extended to non-parents who have, in fact, served as *de facto* parents. For example, in *Scott v. Superior Court*, 171 Cal. App. 4th 540 (2009), a California appellate court was confronted by the following: Rachael gave birth to three children from 1997–1999 fathered by William Scott, who lived elsewhere and by 2000 was living with Jan Forsberg. Rachael was a drug addict and her three children were removed in 2001. The children then began living with William and Jan. For the next seven years Jan acted as the mother of the three children, and they so regarded her. In 2008, Jan confronted William about his new infidelities. He abruptly left, removing the three children. Did her seven years of welcoming the children into her home, regarding them as hers, and functioning as a mother, qualify her as a presumed parent under the California's version of the Uniform Parentage Act? The evidence indicated that the children regarded her as their mother, called her "Mom" and had a positive parental relationship. The court remarkably held that it concurred with William Scott's position that "...she cannot be the children's presumed mother; thus, she is not an interested party and cannot be permitted to interfere with Bill's and Rachael's constitutionally protected right to make custody and visitation decisions for their children" (at 544). The court held that "there can only be two parents, not three," although prevaricating where a homosexual tie may be involved: "In a same-sex domestic partner relationship, a child may have two natural mothers (*i.e.*, a biological mother and a mother meeting the presumed parent criteria in Fam. Code § 7611) but in a heterosexual relationship, there can only be one mother." After mothering these children for seven years, Jan is viewed as a "non-parent"—essentially a "non-person"—lacking any standing whatever to appear or to otherwise participate in any placement decision regarding these three children.

These holdings seem to conflict with the growing weight given to *de facto* parental status discussed above (note the discussion of guardians now able to adopt children after two years so functioning—although lacking all parental status outside of the guardianship role), and with the trend toward some recognition of the child's right to a continued relationship with those he or she reasonably regards as a functioning parent, based perhaps on supervening notions of estoppel (*e.g.*, detrimental reliance of the new parent and the child on a continuing relationship that others have not challenged for years). The recognition of the right of a child to participate in a Uniform Parentage Act decision of parental status is rare, but is not without precedent. *See, e.g., J.A.R. v. Superior Court*, 179 Ariz. 267, 877 P.2d 1323 (1994), reversing a trial court's refusal to allow intervention by a child and the appointment of independent counsel in a family court custody battle. Indeed, increasing numbers of family courts are assigning independent counsel for children, particularly in cases where parents attempt to use children for advantage in their own dispute, or where one parent may threaten child abuse.

How do these issues play out in the same gender parent setting? In *Elisa B. v. Superior Court*, 37 Cal. 4th 108 (2005), a lesbian couple had agreed that each would be artificially inseminated from the same anonymous donor and both would raise the resulting children. Elisa B. earned substantially more, so she agreed to continue working while her partner (Emily) agreed to be the stay-at-home mother. Both gave birth within months, Elisa B. to a single child and Emily to twins (one of whom was a baby with Down syndrome). They created the baby's names by joining their names in various combinations. They each breast fed the infants. They named each other on insurance policies. The resulting three infants were held out by both as their children. But they did not adopt the children born to the other, nor did they register as "domestic partners" under California law.

The two women separated two years after these births. Elisa continued to provide some financial support for Emily and the twins for a year after separation, but stopped in 2001, claiming the loss of her full-time position. The district attorney filed an action for compelled child support by Elisa for the children birthed by Emily, and the trial court found that Elisa was making $95,000 at the time of the 2002 trial. What was Elisa's status? Could she be obligated to pay child support? Importantly, this decision on the "obligation" side of parenthood could have implications for the "rights" side—if Elisa desired to have visitation with Emily's twins as a parent under family law principles.

Elisa had no biological tie to Emily's twins. She was not married (nor even part of a civil union) with her. But if she were a man, she would be a presumptive father under the Uniform Parentage Act's second prong of "holding herself out" as the parent, welcoming the children into the home and functioning as a parent. The Court had already held that this "holding out" element could be satisfied even if the presumptive parent did not claim a biological tie. Note that the Court had already decided that where a father had agreed to artificial insemination from another man of his wife, that agreement bound him to enforceable child support on an estoppel basis (see *People v. Sorenson* discussed below). The Court then held in *Elisa B.* that a child could have two legally recognized parents of the same gender. The Court wrote: "By recognizing the value of determining paternity, the Legislature implicitly recognized the value of having two parents, rather than one, as a source of both emotional and financial support, especially when the obligation to support the child would otherwise fall to the public" (at 123).

The next question to be addressed is whether it is possible for a child to have three or perhaps more legally recognized and obligated parents in such a situation. While the artificial insemination donor in *Elisa B* neither had nor claimed parental rights, a three-parent dilemma was considered in California's *In Re M.C.*, 195 Cal. App. 4th 197 (2011). There, a lesbian couple legally married under California law which allowed such unions at the time. But one of them was impregnated by a man. The baby was born and the women treated her as the child of both. However, within a short time Child Protective Services intervened and removed the child after substantial evidence of birth mother meth amphetamine use and other problems indicating unfitness. The now separated wife of the birth mother and the biological father (now interested in exercising parental rights, and demonstrating some alleged *Kelsey* paternal commitment) sought permanent placement. The questions to be decided are: Can a child have a female father? Can a same gender "partner" supersede the rights of a biological parent who did not agree to their surrender through a surrogacy agreement or otherwise? Can all three of these persons have parental status? Most child advocacy amicus briefs in these cases argue for maximum reach of parental rights to all adults with a claim who may benefit the child.[7] In 2011, the *M.C.* court issued a somewhat confused decision, affirming the appropriateness of placement with the father as likely to be in the best interests of the child and supportable, but at the same time noting that legislative change was needed to allow parental status for three persons (here, biological mother, married lesbian partner, and biological father who qualified as a "*Kelsey*" father).

B. EMANCIPATION AND CHILD SUPPORT OBLIGATIONS

As a general rule, both parents are statutorily required to financially or directly support their children. State statutes that differentiate between paternal and maternal support obligations based strictly on gender raise equal protection infirmities given current case law. Most states require step-parent support of children, and the income of a step-parent living in the same household with a child is included in calculating eligibility for Temporary Aid to Needy Families (TANF) assistance, the primary cash safety-net program for children.

The obligation of support lasts until a child reaches "legal majority," which is 18 years of age in most states.[8] The obligation of support may end earlier if a child is "emancipated," has abandoned the parental home, or is receiving public aid for the totally disabled, or parental rights have been terminated. Emancipation generally requires that a child function apart from parents and have verifiable independent means of support. Such support must be legal, and some courts do not permit it to consist solely of public support. Marriage and military service are relevant bases for emancipation, and are sufficient standing alone in some jurisdictions. Some states require parental consent or non-consent to be considered by the court as a factor. In most states, the court is obligated to act in "the best interests of the child" and has substantial discretion to grant or deny emancipation.

Although such emancipation may appear to be intrinsically against the best interests of a child, since it may relieve parents of support obligations, it is often necessary where a youth has been effectively abandoned or victimized by parents and needs that status to authorize benefits (from medical coverage to education subsidies) which otherwise require parental signature. Emancipation is also sought where a youth wishes to enter into a binding contract.[9] The degree of emancipation implied in such an order varies somewhat between states, but it is not necessarily a "yes or no" proposition, and may relieve parents of some obligations and grant independent authority to a child—only within a range of decisions.

Post-majority support has become more important given the lowering of the age of majority from 21 to 18 years of age over the last forty years, and the growing importance of some higher education beyond high school. Such support may be enforceable where a parent has promised it and in some states courts have required parental contribution towards such advanced schooling.[10] Some courts have held that where a support statute refers to a "child" rather than a "minor" such obligations may be conferred past the age of majority.[11]

The obligation of support is normally enforced through child support agreements or orders upon separation or divorce. Courts rarely question financial commitment decisions made within an intact family, unless they rise to the level of child neglect. However, the high incidence of divorce has led to a substantial number of such support orders applicable to the non-custodial parent post-dissolution. Most are applicable to fathers, but an increasing proportion of fathers obtain custody and the incidence of orders applying to mothers has increased. In most states, such obligations are independent of visitation rights. Contrary to common belief, the noncustodial parent does not have the right to deny such support where visitation is improperly denied. Each obligation stands independently to serve the child and each is independently enforceable in most jurisdictions.

The amount of such post-divorce child support is set by family courts based on the needs of affected children principally for shelter, food, clothing, medical care, and education, in combination with the ability to pay of the respective parents.[12] One oft-cited standard is the right of a child to a standard of living that approximates predivorce conditions.[13] Courts will sometimes set amounts based on earning capacity rather than on income, particularly where the court suspects an obligor is working less in order to minimize payments due.

Substantial discretion is granted to family courts in setting support amounts. It may include required in-kind contributions—among them the important inclusion of child health and other insurance available to the non-custodial parent. During the 1970s and 1980s, total child support awards were criticized as inconsistent and inadequate.[14] Levels increased somewhat to 2006, and some states have adopted "child support formulas" by statute or rule to enhance consistency. However, rates of increase appeared to flatten in real money terms after 2000.[15] Monies received amount to a fraction of the direct costs of a child to custodial parents in the vast majority of cases.

Although many child support orders are agreed to by the involved parents, they are subject to independent court review and approval. That check is intended to preclude the bargaining away of the rights of a child. The most common example is the regrettable practice of a parent who will surrender child support for children in his or her custody in return for a surrender of visitation rights by the non-custodial parent. In such common circumstances, while the parents may be relieved of unpleasant contact between themselves, the child may be deprived of contact with one parent, and also of financial support properly due.

Child support obligations are subject to modification as circumstances change, and such circumstances increasingly involve a second family with new spouses and children imposing new obligations. Sometimes they involve new assets, more easily adding to established amounts where additional resources arise (*e.g.*, a new spouse with substantial income) but sometimes modifying downwards, particularly where the new obligations involve children.

Many children born to unwed parents are owed child support by the non-custodial parent. This population of obligors, usually fathers, are pursued primarily by the state (see child support enforcement discussion below). A large proportion of such children receive substantial cash assistance through the TANF program (prior to 1996 termed Aid to Families with Dependent Children (AFDC)). Accordingly, the state seeks recompense from the absent parent for payments made for such children. The child support obligation extant outside of marriage is normally determined by biology (*e.g.*, paternity test results or other evidence indicating a child is the biological issue of an obligor). Increasingly, custodial parents avail themselves of these resources to collect support even where monies are not due the state. That opportunity is important because such parents lack contact with family court (no divorce decree is entered since no marriage occurred) and lack resources for private enforcement. Over half of such sums collected now pass through to involved families and children.

County of Alameda v. Kaiser

238 Cal. App. 2d 815 (1965)

OPINION, **DRAPER, P.J.**: Does "emancipation" of a minor by agreement with his mother relieve her of liability for his support? Does a recent decision...bar recovery from her by the county for his treatment, in a county hospital, for physical ailments? These are the questions on this appeal.

Defendant, a widow, is the mother of Philip Kaiser, who was born August 3, 1942. He was seriously injured in an automobile accident August 13, 1962, and was treated for some time in a private hospital. On November 28, 1962, defendant made written application for county medical care for her son, representing that she had very little money or property. The next day, Philip was admitted to the county hospital, and remained hospitalized through March 28, 1963. Shortly after his admission, county officials learned that defendant had withdrawn a large amount from a bank account not listed in her financial statement. The board of supervisors then determined that defendant had financial ability to support her son (Welf. & Inst. Code, § 2576), and this action for $3,172.50 was filed in the municipal court.

At trial, defendant testified that Philip had left home in February 1962 and had resided with an aunt to the time of his injury. He had some employment while living with the aunt, but the record does not show the amount of his earnings or whether he paid the aunt for board or room. His mother had neither contributed to his support nor asked for any part of his earnings, and testified "He was living on his own, apart, permanently." The trial court concluded that the son had been "emancipated", and thus must be treated as an adult. On the theory that *Kirchner* barred recovery under these circumstances, judgment was entered for defendant. Hence, the evidence of defendant's financial ability is but sketchy. Plaintiff appealed. The appellate department expressed doubt as to the determination of "emancipation" but, assuming the son to be deemed an adult, held that *Kirchner* is inapplicable to treatment in a county hospital for physical ailments, and reversed the judgment. We accepted transfer on certification (Cal. Rules of Court, rules 62, 63).

The phrase "emancipation of a minor," as applied to agreements of parent and child, appears to have been rather loosely used. Frequently, emancipation of the minor is equated with release of the parent....In the decisions, most such statements are but dicta as to the parent's obligation, but some do hold that consensual "emancipation" of the child terminates the parent's liability....

Broad statements of this assumed rule appear infrequently in California decisions....But these cases dealt with relinquishment of the parent's rights—not with release from his liabilities. When the issue of the child's rights has been squarely presented, the California courts have held that "emancipation" by agreement does not terminate the right to support....

Logic and reason support this view. The term "emancipation" implies treatment of the individual as a chattel. Slavish adherence to definition of the word, perhaps carelessly adopted in the first place, has led some jurisdictions to infer that the obligations of the parent to his child are based wholly upon his right to the child's earnings, and that relinquishment of the right requires release from the liability. This "rule" has been contradicted or questioned by text writers (2 Armstrong, California Family Law, 1259–1260; Madden on Domestic Relations, 408–409; 5 Vernier, American Family Laws, 240). It seems apparent that the few decisions and the more frequent dicta relied upon by defendant mother confuse "emancipation" of the child with "emancipation" of the parent. The limitations upon the minor's right to make binding contracts with strangers emphasize the illogic of a rule that he may bind himself by a contractual release of his parent, the person most likely to have a strong influence upon him.

We conclude that Philip must be deemed a minor. Our question then is whether the recent ruling of our Supreme Court (*Department of Mental Hygiene v. Kirchner*, 60 Cal.2d 716) bars liability of defendant mother.

Parental liability for support of a minor child is of ancient origin. It was recognized by such writers as Coke and Blackstone (1 Schouler, Marriage, Divorce, Separation and Domestic Relations, 857), and was the subject of an old English statute (43 Eliz. I, c.2). It has long been statutory in California. One reason for imposing this obligation is to prevent the child from becoming a public charge....This long-recognized liability, often enforced, has not been held to be based upon an unreasonable classification. Thus *Kirchner's* proscription of denial of equal protection seems to have no application.

The statutes measuring liability for care and treatment of another in a county hospital...permit recovery by the county only to the extent of the responsible party's ability to pay. To the extent that *Kirchner* turns upon possible impoverishment of the party charged for another's care, its rule is thus inapplicable here.

This case differs from *Kirchner* in another respect. Here, hospitalization was for treatment of physical injuries, a treatment essentially for the benefit of the patient. It was apparently considered beneficial by the mother who sought her child's admission to the county hospital. The element of confinement for the protection of society from the mentally ill, present in Kirchner, is not a factor here.

We conclude that there is no constitutional bar to the recovery here sought.

Judgment reversed. The case is remanded for trial of the issue of defendant's pecuniary ability to pay for or contribute to her son's care for which recovery is sought.

Questions for Discussion

1. Would the decision be the same if aid were being sought directly by Philip Kaiser as a minor seeking medical assistance rather than by the state for recompense? By a doctor who incurred out-of-pocket expenses in treating Philip?

2. Is it fair to consider Phillip Kaiser "emancipated" based on his "agreement" when he is below the then age of majority? If a minor cannot agree to a contract which may be enforced against him, how can he agree to emancipation which deprives him of assured parental support?

3. Does the fact that Mrs. Kaiser sought hospital admission for her son contribute to her financial liability? Does maternal concern have to cease for emancipation to be effective?

Parker v. Stage
43 N.Y.2d 128 (1977)

OPINION OF THE COURT: JUDGE WACHTLER

The question on this appeal is whether the Department of Social Services can compel a father to pay for the support of his 18-year-old daughter after she has left his house, voluntarily and against his wishes, to live with her paramour and have a child. Both the Family Court and the Appellate Division held that, under the circumstances, the father should not be obligated to support his daughter even though she is receiving public assistance. The Commissioner of Social Services has appealed to this court by leave of the Appellate Division.

The facts developed at the Family Court hearing were not disputed. Respondent's daughter was born in September of 1956. Several years later the father and mother were divorced. After the divorce the girl remained in her father's custody. In early 1974 she informed her cousin that she intended to leave home to live with her paramour and have a child. Although neither she nor her boyfriend were employed, she said that she intended to support herself and her child by seeking public assistance. She did not return to school in the fall of 1974. In October, shortly after her 18th birthday, she left home while her father was at work. Nearly two weeks later he was able to locate her with the assistance of the police.

She returned home and for several months resided with her father, but only intermittently. For long periods of time she would "disappear." On each occasion her father accepted her back and continued to support her. He contacted her former guidance counselor and arranged for her to return to school. He informed her of this and continuously urged her to resume her schooling but she refused. She also refused to discuss her goals with him. At one point he helped her to obtain a job, but she quit after four weeks. For a time she was in a job training program but she quit that as well. Finally in the spring of 1975 she took up permanent residence with her paramour who was also unemployed.

In the fall of 1975 respondent's daughter gave birth to a child out of wedlock. She then applied for aid to dependent children and obtained public assistance for her child and for herself, as the mother of an eligible child (Social Services Law, § 349). In February, 1976 the Commissioner of Social Services of Orange County commenced this proceeding in the Family Court to compel the respondent to contribute toward his daughter's support.* The proceeding was brought pursuant to subdivision 3 of section 101-a of the Social Services Law which authorizes a social services official to institute a support proceeding against a parent or other responsible relative if the applicant or recipient of public assistance "fails" to do so.

At the conclusion of the hearing the Family Court Judge dismissed the petition on the ground that respondent's daughter, by leaving home to live with her paramour and have his child, had "emancipated herself from her father and his household...and...as a result of that emancipation, the respondent is relieved of any obligation to support" her.

* * *

Initially it should be noted that even in a case like *Matter of Roe v. Doe* (*supra*), when the suit is brought directly on the child's behalf pursuant to section 413 of the Family Court Act, the father's obligation to support is stated in mandatory terms. Our determination in that case, that a child who voluntarily and without good cause abandons the parent's home "forfeits her right to demand support" is not based on any express statutory exception. It rests on the State policy of fostering "the integrity of the family" by precluding the courts from interfering in the special relationship between parent and child, absent "a showing of misconduct, neglect or abuse"...It recognizes that the father's obligation to support includes the right to exercise parental control and guidance even though the child may be old enough "to elect not to comply" (*Matter of Roe v. Doe,...*).

The question then is whether a different policy applies when the suit is brought by a public welfare official to compel a father to support a child who would otherwise become a public charge.

It was once the policy of this State to place the financial burden of supporting needy individuals upon designated relatives, rather than the public, in order to reduce the amount of welfare expenditures....Thus the common-law obligation to support wife and minor children was expanded by statute to include adult children, grandchildren and parents when they would otherwise become public charges....

In recent years however the Legislature relented. The laws were amended to relieve individuals of the obligation to support grandchildren..., adult children and parents...who were unemployed and destitute. Thereafter the burden passed to the public. In a message accompanying the 1966 bill the Governor noted that this was in part prompted by the need to comply with Federal law in order to qualify for Federal financial assistance. But he also noted that "Experience has shown that the financial responsibility of a broad class of relatives, imposed by statute, is more often a destructive, rather than cohesive, factor in family unity"...Thus the legislative history shows that the current statutory scheme recognizes the need to preserve family unity even though the consequence is to place needy relatives on the public welfare rolls.

In addition the Legislature has expressly granted the courts discretionary powers in these cases. A father, of course, is still generally obligated to support his children until they are 21 years of age....And public welfare officials may seek to enforce the obligation if the child is an applicant for or recipient of public assistance....But in such cases the obligation is not absolute....

In sum we cannot agree with the commissioner that whenever an older child chooses to leave home, for any reason, the parents must pay for the child's separate maintenance, or contribute support, if the child applies for public assistance. The courts must still consider the impact on the family relationship and the possibility of injustice in the particular case. Of course the fact that the child is eligible for public assistance may, as is evident here, permit her to avoid her father's authority and demands however reasonable they may be. But it does not follow that the parent must then finish what has been begun by underwriting the lifestyle which his daughter chose against his reasonable wishes and repeated counsel.

It should be emphasized that this is not a case of an abandoned child, but of an abandoned parent. There is nothing to indicate that the respondent abused his daughter or placed unreasonable demands upon her. There is no showing that he actively drove her from her home or encouraged her to leave in order to have the public assume his obligation of support. Indeed the contrary appears to be true. The undisputed proof in this record establishes that the father continuously supported his daughter from birth; that he urged her to remain at home and continue her schooling; that he was a forgiving parent who always accepted her back after her absences and that he made efforts to obtain employment for her. We simply hold that under these circumstances the courts below could properly refuse to compel him to pay for her support when she chose to leave home to live with her paramour.

Accordingly, the order of the Appellate Division should be affirmed.

*It is conceded that respondent is not responsible for the support of his grandchild.

Questions for Discussion

1. Is Angelie's mother potentially liable for Angelie's support under these facts?

2. What if Angelie recants after leaving and having a child, and asks to return to her father's care and protection? Is she irretrievably emancipated because she defied his advice and left once? Would such a judgment apply to a 12-year-old who runs away from home? To a 14-year-old who is starving? To a teen who is mentally/emotionally troubled?

3. Would it matter if Angelie's father were a millionaire and the outcome is substantial public expense for Angelie and her child? Would it matter if Angelie's father had beaten her repeatedly? Engaged in mental or emotional cruelty? Does the broad discretion to trial courts granted in *Parker* compromise an important bright line for obligation, and invoke "who is at fault" within-the-family litigation? Before relieving a father of support obligations, should a court require at least one attempt to seek third party assistance where a child is incorrigible (*e.g.*, existing court services)?

4. Can emancipation be reversed, *i.e.*, can a child who is emancipated and economically independent then become financially dependent and again incur a parental support obligation? See *Wulff v. Wulff*, 243 Neb. 616 (1993). Note that New York law requires parental support until the child is 21 years of age. For application of support obligation up to age 21, even after consensual emancipation, see *In the Matter of Crimmins v. Crimmins,* 745 N.Y.S.2d 686 (2002).

C. CHILD SUPPORT COLLECTION

Where a traditional family court child support order is violated, it is enforced by contempt of court process—which can involve serious sanctions for a violator, including jail time. However, the American system's traditional aversion to "debtors' prisons" generally requires evidence of a willful violation of a support order to yield incarceration. Hence, such severity will require some demonstration of ability to pay (or self-manipulation so that such ability is foreclosed).

In addition to contempt of court, all states have separate statutes imposing criminal liability for "willful" non-support of children. Case law typically defines such willfulness to be a "deliberate or perverse design, malice, or an intentional or deliberate breach" of the child support duty "without just cause or excuse."[16] These laws are often invoked as a lever, with probation commonly granted pending compliance with outstanding support orders. From the perspective of most courts, a severe fine or jail time tends to undercut the purpose of the law (to provide support for affected children). The leverage of these statutes was enhanced by *Hicks v. Feiock*, 485 U.S. 624 (1988), where the Supreme Court upheld as constitutional a state law providing for civil contempt and "presuming" the ability to pay—thus shifting the burden to the parent to rebut that presumption. More recently, Congress has made willful failure to pay child support a federal crime punishable by a fine and/ or imprisonment for up to six months where a person willfully fails to pay a support obligation with respect to a child who resides in another state, if such obligation has remained unpaid for a period longer than one year, or is greater than $ 5,000. More severe punishment is applicable where a person travels in interstate or foreign commerce with the intent to evade a support obligation, if such obligation has remained unpaid for a period longer than one year, or is greater than $ 5,000, or willfully fails to pay a support obligation with respect to a child who resides in another state, if such obligation has remained unpaid for a period longer than two years, or is greater than $10,000.[17] Although the *Lopez* limitation on federal jurisdiction not involving "commerce" (see discussion in Chapter 1) might be invoked to void this statute, all eleven circuits have considered and upheld its jurisdiction as affecting interstate commerce (*e.g., see U.S. v. Faasse*, 265 F.3d 475 (6th Cir. 2001)). However, the U.S. Supreme Court has yet to address the question.

Apart from criminal enforcement of child neglect and the contempt enforcement of family court support orders, the federal government and states have created an extensive system to collect support from absent unwed fathers where mothers and children lack family court divorce jurisdiction. As noted above, states have historically established paternity and collected such child support primarily to recoup the TANF (AFDC pre-1996) payments made to children from their absent biological parents. As noted above, such efforts increasingly include child support orders for children in need who have *not* received public assistance.

A series of federal statutes led to the 2008 Uniform Interstate Family Support Act (UIFSA) to simplify collection between states (especially given interstate movement of obligors). All states are required by federal law to enact these uniform provisions as a condition for receiving federal funds for state child support collection. This statute has nine articles and incorporates the 2007 Hague Convention on the International Recovery of Child Support and Maintenance. The U.S. federal incorporation lagged behind until the 2014 Preventing Sex Trafficking and Strengthening Families Act was signed into law. All U.S. states have now adopted the 2008 UIFSA.

Providing a carrot as well as a stick, the federal 1998 Child Support Performance and Incentive Act provisions continue to incentivize state child support collection. These provisions require states to reinvest federal incentive funding in state programs stimulating collection efficacy, including parenting classes or employment services for non-custodial parents. In fiscal 2015, these federal incentive payments represented 10% of total program expenditures, widely ranging from 1% to 23% of expenditures in each state.[18]

The Federal Office of Child Support Enforcement operates pursuant to Social Security Act Title IV-D authority[19] to help states with collection and to direct incentive payments, as well as potential penalties (reductions in federal funding). Substantial reductions have been imposed (for example, against California in 1995–2002 for its failure to implement a statewide computer system to coordinate in-state collections).

Some states provide for the identification of biological fathers at time of birth. Under the Personal Responsibility and Work Opportunity Reconciliation Act of 1996 (the federal welfare reform statute) all birth mothers are required to make *bona fide* attempt to identify the biological father of the child, and to assist the state in finding him. Failure to so assist may yield grant reduction sanctions (see discussion in Chapter 3).

Most jurisdictions also provide assistance in establishing paternity where a woman seeks such an order, whether she is on welfare or not. Such paternity establishes fatherhood status for purposes of support obligations. Paternity can be established by a voluntary acknowledgment signed by both parents as part of an in-hospital or other acknowledgment program. States must have procedures that allow paternity to be established at least up to the child's eighteenth birthday. Child support paternities were established or acknowledged for 1.435 million children in 2017.[20]

Although states vary in their enforcement mechanisms, many assign child support collection to offices of district attorney or state's attorney (public prosecutors). If paternity is alleged, a test can be ordered and compliance enforced. The process then involves the establishment of an order, which includes a due process hearing right for the purported biological father, and for support collection—either in court or through an administrative hearing. In 2017, 935,948 child support orders were established.[21]

Following the entry of an order, states are engaging in extensive new enforcement strategies, including automatic garnishment of wages, capture of tax refunds and lottery winnings, and suspension of license renewals pending order compliance (including bar admission, trade licensure, and even driver's licenses in some states). Some states assign delinquent child support orders to state income tax agencies for collection and designation as high priority "tax liens."

The federal Office of Child Support Enforcement (OCSE) reported 14.2 million child support cases open in 2017. Total distributed child support collections stood at $28.6 billion in that year, with $24.4 million of that sum obtained through wage withholding.[22] The total collection amounts to $137 per month per child, with a percentage going to local, state, and government accounts to compensate them for TANF safety net assistance. However, these paltry figures exaggerate financial support levels from absent parents. The 14.2 million child support orders do not include an additional large number of children for whom support orders or even paternity identification are absent. As discussed in Chapter 2, this support per child per month amounts to less than one-fifth the average out-of-pocket cost of a child.[23]

People v. Sorensen

68 Cal. 2d 280 (1968)

OPINION BY: McComb

Defendant appeals from a judgment convicting him of violating section 270 of the Penal Code (willful failure to provide for his minor child), a misdemeanor.

The settled statement of facts recites that seven years after defendant's marriage it was medically determined that he was sterile. His wife desired a child, either by artificial insemination or by adoption, and at first defendant refused to consent. About 15 years after the marriage defendant agreed to the artificial insemination of his wife. Husband and wife, then residents of San Joaquin County, consulted a physician in San Francisco. They signed an agreement, which is on the letterhead of the physician, requesting the physician to inseminate the wife with the sperm of a white male. The semen was to be selected by the physician, and under no circumstances were the parties to demand the name of the donor. The agreement contains a recitation that the physician does not represent that pregnancy will occur. The physician treated Mrs. Sorensen, and she became pregnant. Defendant knew at the time he signed the consent that when his wife took the treatments she could become pregnant and that if a child was born it was to be treated as their child.

A male child was born to defendant's wife in San Joaquin County on October 14, 1960. The information for the birth certificate was given by the mother, who named defendant as the father. Defendant testified that he had not provided the information on the birth certificate and did not recall seeing it before the trial.

For about four years the family had a normal family relationship, defendant having represented to friends that he was the child's father and treated the boy as his son. In 1964, Mrs. Sorensen separated from defendant and moved to Sonoma County with the boy. At separation, Mrs. Sorensen told defendant that she wanted no support for the boy, and she consented that a divorce be granted to defendant. Defendant obtained a decree of divorce, which recites that the court retained "jurisdiction regarding the possible support obligation of plaintiff in regard to a minor child born to defendant."

In the summer of 1966 when Mrs. Sorensen became ill and could not work, she applied for public assistance under the Aid to Needy Children program. The County of Sonoma supplied this aid until Mrs. Sorensen was able to resume work. Defendant paid no support for the child since the separation in 1964, although demand therefor was made by the district attorney. The municipal court found defendant guilty of violating section 270 of the Penal Code and granted him probation for three years on condition that he make payments of $50 per month for support through the district attorney's office.

"From the record before us, this case could be disposed of on the ground that defendant has failed to overcome the presumption that "A child of a woman who is or has been married, born during the marriage or within 300 days after the dissolution thereof, is presumed to be a legitimate child of that marriage. This presumption may be disputed only by the people of the State of California in a criminal action brought under Section 270 of the Penal Code or by the husband or wife, or the descendant of one or both of them. In a civil action, this presumption may be rebutted only by clear and convincing proof." (Evid. Code, § 661,...)

...[T]he only question for our determination is: Is the husband of a woman, who with his consent was artificially inseminated with semen of a third-party donor, guilty of the crime of failing to support a child who is the product of such insemination, in violation of section 270 of the Penal Code?[1]

The law is that defendant is the lawful father of the child born to his wife, which child was conceived by artificial insemination to which he consented, and his conduct carries with it an obligation of support within the meaning of section 270 of the Penal Code.

Under the facts of this case, the term "father" as used in section 270 cannot be limited to the biologic or natural father as those terms are generally understood. The determinative factor is whether the legal relationship of father and child exists. A child conceived through heterologous artificial insemination...does not have a "natural father," as that term is commonly used. The anonymous donor of the sperm cannot be considered the "natural father," as he is no more responsible for the use made of his sperm than is the donor of blood or a kidney. Moreover, he could not dispute the presumption that the child is the legitimate issue of Mr. and Mrs. Sorensen, as that presumption "may be disputed only by the people of the State of California...or by the husband or wife, or the descendant of one or both of them." (Evid. Code, § 661,...) With the use of frozen semen, the donor may even be dead at the time the semen is used. Since there is no "natural father," we can only look for a lawful father.

It is doubtful that with the enactment of section 270 of the Penal Code and its amendments the Legislature considered the plight of a child conceived through artificial insemination. However, the intent of the Legislature obviously was to include every child, legitimate or illegitimate, born or unborn, and enforce the obligation of support against the person who could be determined to be the lawful parent.[3]

* * *

It is also essential to a conviction under section 270 that defendant's omission to support his child be willful. The statute provides that "Proof of...the omission by such father to furnish necessary food, clothing, shelter or medical attendance or other remedial care for his child is prima facie evidence that such...omission...is willful and without lawful excuse." This provision does not set forth a rule relating to proof but merely declares a rule of procedure that places upon defendant the duty of going forward with evidence that his omission to provide was not willful or was excusable....

Defendant failed to produce any evidence that his omission to provide for his minor child was not willful. The record shows that the district attorney requested defendant to pay $50 per month child support, but that defendant did not do so. When defendant and his wife separated she declared that she wanted no support for the child. The provisions of section 270, however, "are applicable whether the parents are married or divorced, and regardless of any decree made in any divorce action relative to alimony or to the support of the child." It is immaterial, therefore, that Mrs. Sorensen said that she wanted no support for the child, for she had no authority or power by agreement or release to deprive her child of the legal right to be supported by his father or to relieve defendant of the obligation imposed on him by law....

Rather than punishment of the neglectful parents, the principal statutory objectives are to secure support of the child and to protect the public from the burden of supporting a child who has a parent able to support him. Section 270d of the Penal Code provides that if a fine is imposed on a convicted defendant, the court shall direct its payment in whole or in part to the wife of the defendant or guardian of the child, except that if the child is receiving public assistance the fine imposed or funds collected from the defendant shall be paid to the county department either for current support of the child or as reimbursement for past support furnished from public assistance funds.

* * *

In the absence of legislation prohibiting artificial insemination, the offspring of defendant's valid marriage to the child's mother was lawfully begotten and was not the product of an illicit or adulterous relationship. Adultery is defined as "the voluntary sexual intercourse of a married person with a person other than the offender's husband or wife." (Civ. Code, § 93.) It has been suggested that the doctor and the wife commit adultery by the process of artificial insemination....Since the doctor may be a woman, or the husband himself may administer the insemination by a syringe, this is patently absurd; to consider it an act of adultery with the donor, who at the time of insemination may be a thousand miles away or may even be dead, is equally absurd. Nor are we persuaded that the concept of legitimacy demands that the child be the actual offspring of the husband of the mother and if semen of some other male is utilized the resulting child is illegitimate.

* * *

The judgment is affirmed.

[1] Section 270 of the Penal Code reads: "A father of either a legitimate or illegitimate minor child who...willfully omits without lawful excuse to furnish necessary clothing, food, shelter or medical attendance or other remedial care for his child is guilty of a misdemeanor and punishable by a fine not exceeding one thousand dollars ($1,000) or by imprisonment in a county jail not exceeding one year, or by both such fine and imprisonment. ...This statute shall not be construed so as to relieve such father from the criminal liability defined herein for such omission merely because the mother of such child is legally entitled to the custody of such child nor because the mother of such child, or any other person, or organization, voluntarily or involuntarily furnishes such necessary food, clothing, shelter or medical attendance or other remedial care for such child, or undertakes to do so.

"Proof of abandonment or desertion of a child by such father, or the omission by such father to furnish necessary food, clothing, shelter or medical attendance or other remedial care for his child is prima facie evidence that such abandonment or desertion or omission to furnish necessary food, clothing, shelter or medical attendance or other remedial care is...willful and without lawful excuse.

"The court, in determining the ability of the father to support his child, shall consider all income, including social insurance benefits and gifts....

"In the event that the father of either a legitimate or illegitimate minor child is dead or for any other reason whatsoever fails to furnish the necessary food, clothing, shelter or medical attendance or other remedial care for his minor child, the mother of said child shall become subject to the provisions of this section and be criminally liable for the support of said minor child during the period of failure on the part of the father to the same extent and in the same manner as the father.

"The provisions of this section are applicable whether the parents of such child are married or divorced, and regardless of any decree made in any divorce action relative to alimony or to the support of the child. A child conceived but not yet born is to be deemed an existing person insofar as this section is concerned."

[3] Section 270 was enacted in 1872. Prior to 1915, liability was imposed on the parents of only legitimate children. The section was then amended to include illegitimate minors as well. In the 1925 amendment a sentence was added declaring that a child conceived but not yet born was an existing person so far as this section was concerned.

Questions for Discussion

1. Can Mrs. Sorensen "agree" to forego all future support for her son from the child's father if the state does not step in to support her child? For example, would such an agreement be enforceable against a hypothetical petition by the child for such support?

2. Did it matter that Mr. Sorensen is not the biological father? Apart from specialized artificial insemination statutes, would he be a presumed father under the Uniform Parentage Act?

3. Would it be more efficient to simply garnish Mr. Sorensen's wages or attach his bank account to collect the $50 per month demanded? How much did a criminal prosecution cost the County, and what use would a jail sentence serve to provide assistance to the child? Does such a prosecution and possible incarceration "send a message" or otherwise deter the shirking of parental support obligations?

4. Sorensen may have consented to the use of another man's semen, estopping him from abandoning his support obligation. But what of the Pennsylvania case of *Vargo*—where a man thought he was the father of two daughters, only to then learn that they were the product of an affair by his wife.[24] He left the marriage and faced a now common dilemma—he could not countenance paying child support to and through the woman who betrayed him, and while the real biological father escaped liability. Child support obligation and visitation rights are separate, in theory. But what would be the consequences of a successful cancellation of all paternal status for Vargo? There are cases in which courts have ended child support obligations where the parent is defied in *extremis* (as in *Parker* above), or where the man is deceived about paternity and ends his paternal role immediately upon learning of it (obligations secured by fraud potentially may be rescinded). Vargo did not do so, but he successfully walked the tightrope—leaving the marriage shortly after discovering he was not the father of his two girls, while providing some support and visiting. Accordingly, the mother of the girls was able to obtain a child support order from the biological father, who attempted to substitute Vargo as the "presumptive father" of the girls based on his status at their birth and his failure to walk away dispositively having learned of the fraud. He failed and was effectively substituted as the obligor for Vargo. But what will that portend for his future rights of visitation if resisted by the mother? Moreover, why would courts not consider holding them both responsible? *E.g.*, what if Vargo was the best placement for custody? Or, alternatively, what if Mom and Vargo were meth addicts and the biological father was the optimum (or only kin) placement? What about the daughter's right to child support from someone she regarded as a father and for whom she has functioned as a loving daughter? Is her role acknowledged or discussed in relevant caselaw?[25]

5. Should paternity testing be conducted routinely as part of the post-birth inoculation regimen all children receive? Required where the mother is unmarried? Should it be available routinely upon the request of either listed parent? Upon the request of third parties? Upon the request of a youth?

Note on Child Custody and Visitation Enforcement

Separate from child emancipation rights and child support obligations are the "parental rights" issues of child custody and visitation where parental status is acknowledged. These rights are commonly litigated in family court. Regrettably, the context for these adjudications of parental rights to children (and child rights to parents) is an often emotional divorce proceeding where children may be caught in the vortex of hostility between their parents. Unlike juvenile court, children here rarely have their own counsel. Children are often used by feuding parents to gain advantage or to vindicate perceived wrongs *vis-a-vis* each other. The children's fate in terms of custody and visitation may be determined without their input to the court—and with a factual contest unhelpful to their future relationship with their parents. One trend in these disputes is to award "joint custody" to both parents—and to thusly limit the ability of one parent to move a child far away from the other parent. But problems of movement to another state to avoid court jurisdiction, or to defy the orders of a court pertaining to custody or visitation, have remained a continuing problem.

To address some of these difficulties, many states have enacted statutes to allow enforcement of court orders establishing custody and visitation in other states. The purpose is to subject these decisions to some judicial process, and not to delegate such decisions to the parent willing or able to physically remove a child across state or national lines. Such statutes have historically been guided by the Uniform Child Custody Jurisdiction Act (UCCJA), recommended in 1968 by the National Conference of Commissioners on Uniform State Laws. All fifty states enacted statutes generally conforming to its terms—although some included significant variations.

In 1980, Congress enacted the federal Parent Kidnapping Prevention Act (PKPA) (28 U.S.C. § 1738A) to give "full faith and credit" to the custody (and visitation) judgments of the respective courts among the several states. Section 1738(B) follows with similar terms for full faith and credit in the enforcement of child support orders between states. The crucial criterion of the statute defines the court of jurisdiction as the "home state" of the child, including a state that "had been the child's home state within six months before the date of the commencement of the proceeding and the child is absent from such State because of his removal or retention by a contestant or for other reasons, and a contestant continues to live in such State" (§ 1738A(c)(2)(A)(ii)). Allowance is made for the pick-up of jurisdiction in a non-home state where jurisdiction has not been asserted or has been rejected by other states and such jurisdiction is in the "best interest of the child"; no other state would qualify as a "home state" and there is some connection between the state and the child and at least one of the "contestants" for child custody, and the evidence as to the care and protection of the child is available in that state; the child is physically in the state and has been abandoned; or jurisdiction is necessary as an emergency to protect the child or a sibling has been "threatened with mistreatment or abuse." The most important provision of the statute is § 1738A(d), providing that the "jurisdiction of a court of a State which has made a child custody or visitation determination ... continues...[where] such State remains the residence of the child or of any contestant." Hence, the parent who remains in the jurisdiction where the court awarded custody/visitation should designedly be in a position to enforce that order in the locale of the child as moved. However, the provision applicable to where protection is necessary to prevent mistreatment or abuse of a child or sibling may be invoked if such an order has not yet been entered—perhaps encouraging movement *pendente lite.*

In 1993, the American Bar Association's Center on Children and the Law published its extensive report on the status of custody jurisdiction: *Obstacles to the Recovery and Return of Parentally Abducted Children* (1993), citing inconsistency of interpretation of the UCCJA and the technicalities of applying the PKPA and documenting a lack of consistency among the states—perhaps leading to some as destination "safe havens" for child movement in violation of adjudicated (or pending) orders. The *Obstacles* study suggested a number of amendments, some of which were recommended in a 1997 updated statute in a new model Uniform Child Custody Jurisdiction and Enforcement Act (UCJEA) by the National Conference of Commissioners on Uniform State Laws. The UCJEA clarifies the definition of a child's "home state," provides for emergency jurisdiction in another state only until the court with original jurisdiction can act, clarifies when a court has declined jurisdiction, and importantly includes a sweeping definition of covered orders to subsume neglect, dependency, wardship, guardianship and other decisions where they involve issues of custody and visitation. It also eliminates the "best interest" criteria as an overriding basis for jurisdiction given its open-ended nature.

One purpose of the UCCJA revision was to provide a remedy for interstate visitation and custody cases. As with child support, state borders have become one of the biggest obstacles to enforcement of custody and visitation orders. As the *Obstacles* study documents, the UCCJA does not effectively provide for a uniform method of enforcing custody and visitation orders validly entered in another state. One state might provide for a Motion to Enforce or a Motion to Grant Full Faith and Credit to initiate an enforcement proceeding. Another might require a Writ of Habeas Corpus or a Citation for Contempt. In some states, writs of mandamus or prohibition might be the norm. These variations increase costs and because burdens and elements of proof may vary, can create different outcomes—with some jurisdictions developing a reputation as an enforcement "safe haven," stimulating avoidance of properly litigated orders.

The provisions of Article 3 of the more recent UCCJEA provide several remedies for the enforcement of a custody determination. First, there is a simple procedure for registering a custody determination in another state to allow advance notice of its recognition. This alternative is important where a child is consistently sent to another jurisdiction—for example, visitation in another state where one parent now resides. The original court order will be honored by the state where the child is visiting. And such a provision could prove useful in international custody cases as well. The model Act provides a swift remedy along the lines of habeas corpus, preferred because time is of the essence in these adjudications—often triggered where a parent refuses to return a child after a vacation or visit. The scope of the enforcing court's inquiry is limited to the issue of whether the decree court had jurisdiction and complied with due process without further inquiry. The UCCJEA provides that the enforcing court will be able to use an extraordinary remedy. If the enforcing court is concerned that the parent, who has physical custody of the child, will flee or harm the child, a warrant allows the court to take physical possession of the child. And the new model statute provides a role for prosecutors, in the enforcement process to encourage compliance. Their involvement may be critical where the litigants are unable to afford counsel to privately enforce the law and obtain return of a child consistent with court command.

The issues are somewhat more complicated when movement of a child is across national boundaries, as discussed in Chapter 14. Some provisions of the UCCJEA pertaining to registration, *et al.*, may apply. Superimposed over the model is the Hague Convention on the Civil Aspects of International Child Abduction of 1986 and the International Child Abduction Remedies Act enacted by the Congress in 1988 to implement the Convention (42 U.S.C. § 11601 *et seq.*). Both establish administrative and judicial mechanisms to expedite the return of children (usually to their country of habitual residence) who have been abducted or wrongfully retained and to facilitate the exercise of visitation across international borders. Under the Hague Convention, children who are wrongfully removed from or retained in a contracting state (*i.e.*, a country that is party to the Convention) are subject to prompt return. The UCCJEA specifically provides for the enforcement of Hague Convention return orders and authorizes public officials to locate and secure the return of those children. As with other aspects of the rights of children, the theoretical protections of the UCCJEA—where enacted by the states—occurs in the context of continuing practicality problems: limited private resources, uncertain public authority priority, and lack of independent representation or access to the courts (or public prosecutors) by involved children.

ENDNOTES

[1] See https://www.cdc.gov/nchs/data/nvsr/nvsr67/nvsr67_01_tables.pdf#I26, Centers for Disease Control numbers at Table I-7, page 12.

[2] The UPA was adopted by the National Conference of Commissioners on Uniform State Laws in 1973. It was revised in 2000 to incorporate the Uniform Putative and Unknown Fathers Act and the Uniform Status of Children of Assisted Conception Act.

[3] 441 U.S. 380 (1979).

[4] For some indication that courts may apply some due diligence requirements for fathers to reach a parental rights threshold, see *In Re Baby Boy C*, 581 A.2d 1141 (D.C. App. 1990); see also *Robert O. v. Russell K.*, 604 N.E.2d 1999 (N.Y. 1992).

[5] The death of both parents would appear to be of some consequence to a child, and if the equivalent loss (from the child's perspective) were caused by the executive branch of the state, such a taking might be of some concern to the branch charged with checking the executive in the interests of potentially weak parties. Divorce usually involves retention by one parent and visitation by the other, and sometimes joint custody. However, as noted above, under the "winner take all" format of non-marital parental rights/custody law the child will likely lose all contact with the parents he has known since birth. Under current law, most jurisdictions do not acknowledge a constitutional dimension to Baby Richard's right to those he reasonably considers to be his parents—regardless of his age and passage of time, or his reliance on the state to provide parents. The issue is of particular importance given the common pattern in child abuse cases of allowing highly marginal parents to retain parental rights while children are placed into long-term foster care, sometimes in families licensed for that purpose, sometimes with relatives. After a substantial period, such an unterminated parent may win "reunification" return of the child into his or her custody. To what extent can he or she as the "parent" with custody then bar all contact with the responsible adult who had served as the child's "parent" during the interim? See *Troxel v. Granville* and related discussion below regarding the right of "parents" to exclude visitation from other persons—including grandparents, and at least in dicta, those who have functioned and have been regarded as the parents by the child, perhaps for many years.

[6] As a post script, in 1997, two years after the surrender of Baby Richard to Okatar and Daniella, she petitioned the court to be declared Richard's legal mother. Her approval of the adoption had extinguished her parental legal status and she sought its reinstatement. The new case led to Child Protective Services re-entry into the setting, and facing substantial opposition to parental rights restoration, Daniella subsequently withdrew her petition. Meanwhile, Okatar moved out of the house, taking up residence with another woman and leaving Richard with Daniella—the one parent who initially rejected him and whose parental status, at least on an adoption qualification basis, was apparently problematical.

[7] See, e.g., the *amicus* curiae brief of the Children's Advocacy Institute at http://www.caichildlaw.org/Misc/MC_Amicus_Brief_CAI.pdf.

[8] The passage of the 26th Amendment to the Constitution, lowering the voting age from 21 to 18 years, led to similar age reductions for adult status during the 1970s in almost all states. However, minimum age requirements for many privileges and rights—such as drinking alcohol, smoking, driving vehicles, etc.—are set at separately effective age levels by specific state statutes.

[9] Visible examples include youth sports stars or celebrities who seek to control their own affairs.

[10] See, e.g., *Risinger v. Risinger*, 253 S.E.2d. 652 (S.C. 1979); see also *Hinchey v. Hinchey*, 625 P.2d 297 (Alaska 1981).

[11] See *Wilkinson v. Wilkinson*, 585 P.2d 599 (Colo. 1978).

[12] See the guidelines in the Uniform Marriage and Divorce Act, Section 309, 9A ULA 167 (1967).

[13] Such support is affected by custody, with parents entitled to an offset of their support obligations if they have partial custody (since they are providing such support directly while the child is in their custody).

[14] See Bruch, *Developing Standards for Child Support, A Critique of Current Practice,* 16 UCD L. Rev. 49 (1982); see also Hunter, *Child Support Law and Policy: The Systemic Imposition of Costs on Women,* 6 Harv. L.J. 1 (1983).

[15] Average child support received in 2013 dollars was $3,902 in 1999 and $3,953 in 2013. It peaked in 2003 at $4,432 and has since regressed to historical levels; see Table 1 at https://fas.org/sgp/crs/misc/RS22499.pdf.

[16] *People v. Green*, 178 Colo. 77 (1972); see also *People v. Cressay*, 2 Cal. 3d 836 (1970).

[17] 18 U.S.C. § 228.

[18] See https://aspe.hhs.gov/system/files/pdf/260336/CSPIA-ASPE-MEF-Brief.pdf.

[19] 42 U.S.C. §§ 651–662.

[20] See https://www.acf.hhs.gov/sites/default/files/programs/css/fy_2017_preliminary_data_report.pdf?nocache=1529610354.

[21] *Id.*

[22] *Id.*

[23] See discussion in Chapter 1, and note that the *Wagner* case litigated by CAI included an extensive record of national data on child costs and foster care payments to provide relevant payments, including an extensive study by the University of Maryland. See http://www.caichildlaw.org/FC_Litig.htm.

[24] See *Vargo v. Schwartz*, 2007 Pa. Dist. & Cnty. Dec. LEXIS 74; 81 Pa. D. & C.4th 1 (2007). Note the substantial increase to over 400,000 annually in court admissible paternity DNA testing by 2011 in the United States; see also this theme of extraordinary pain and conflict portrayed in classic literature, *e.g.*, August Strindberg's play "The Father."

[25] See *Vargo v. Schwartz, supra* note 24.

CHAPTER TWELVE

Child Rights to Property, Contract and Tort Recovery

A. CHILD RIGHTS TO PROPERTY

1. Common Law Property Rights

Children have the right to "own" both personal and real property.[1] However, at common law they are considered incapable of managing it. Hence, parental authority generally includes the management of property owned by a child. Children can alienate and transmit title to property, but they are not permitted at common law to make irrevocable conveyances of realty without express judicial authority. Usually such a sale is approved for the maintenance or education of a minor.[2]

Parents do retain presumed title to property that they furnish to their children for support and education, such as clothing and toys. And parents have the right to earnings from their unemancipated children as concomitant to their obligation to support them. That right may take the form of child labor for a parent, or allowing children to work for others (within the limits of child labor laws) and collecting the earnings. If a parent abandons a child, the right to his or her earnings terminates.

Where parental guidance is lacking, a court may appoint a guardian for that purpose. More often, management of a child's assets is accomplished through use of trusts and gifts pursuant to the Uniform Gifts to Minors Act, which has been enacted in varying form in all fifty states. Gifts to children are presumed accepted if to their advantage. Upon receipt, the gift may be enforceable against attempted retrieval. An adult may confer gifts to a child tax-free up to the annual gift tax limit, which is $15,000 as of 2019.

Over the last thirty years, trusts have emerged as a common vehicle for transferring property to children, and for its maintenance until they reach majority. Named trustees are appointed by the trustor, are assigned duties by the trust instrument, and have a fiduciary duty to the child beneficiary and are liable for its breach.

2. Property Rights of Children of Unwed Parents

Much of the policy debate over child property rights over the past half-century has involved the rights of a particular subset of children: those born to unwed parents. What claim do such children have to property deriving from the biological parents (who owe them a duty of support)? How are such children to be treated in terms of government subsidies and payment due the children of married couples? Are such children a "suspect classification" entitled to "strict scrutiny" protection? To mid-level "heightened scrutiny"?

Levy v. Louisiana

391 U.S. 68 (1968)

MR. JUSTICE DOUGLAS delivered the opinion of the Court.

Appellant sued on behalf of five illegitimate children to recover, under a Louisiana statute[1] (La. Civ. Code Ann. Art. 2315...) for two kinds of damages as a result of the wrongful death of their mother: (1) the damages to them for the loss of their mother; and (2) those based on the survival of a cause of action which the mother had at the time of her death for pain and suffering. Appellees...are the doctor who treated her and the insurance company.

We assume in the present state of the pleadings that the mother, Louise Levy, gave birth to these five illegitimate children and that they lived with her; that she treated them as a parent would treat any other child; that she worked as a domestic servant to support them, taking them to church every Sunday and enrolling them, at her own expense, in a parochial school....

* * *

We start from the premise that illegitimate children are not "nonpersons." They are humans, live, and have their being....They are clearly "persons" within the meaning of the Equal Protection Clause of the Fourteenth Amendment....

While a State has broad power when it comes to making classifications..., it may not draw a line which constitutes an invidious discrimination against a particular class.... Though the test has been variously stated, the end result is whether the line drawn is a rational one....

In applying the Equal Protection Clause to social and economic legislation, we give great latitude to the legislature in making classifications....Even so, would a corporation, which is a "person," for certain purposes, within the meaning of the Equal Protection Clause...be required to forgo recovery for wrongs done its interests because its incorporators were all bastards? However that might be, we have been extremely sensitive when it comes to basic civil rights...and have not hesitated to strike down an invidious classification even though it had history and tradition on its side. (*Brown v. Board of Education*, 347 U.S. 483....) The rights asserted here involve the intimate, familial relationship between a child and his own mother. When the child's claim of damage for loss of his mother is in issue, why, in terms of "equal protection," should the tortfeasors go free merely because the child is illegitimate? Why should the illegitimate child be denied rights merely because of his birth out of wedlock? He certainly is subject to all the responsibilities of a citizen, including the payment of taxes and conscription under the Selective Service Act. How under our constitutional regime can he be denied correlative rights which other citizens enjoy?

Legitimacy or illegitimacy of birth has no relation to the nature of the wrong allegedly inflicted on the mother. These children, though illegitimate, were dependent on her; she cared for them and nurtured them; they were indeed hers in the biological and in the spiritual sense; in her death they suffered wrong in the sense that any dependent would.[5]

We conclude that it is invidious to discriminate against them when no action, conduct, or demeanor of theirs[6] is possibly relevant to the harm that was done the mother.[7]

Reversed.

[1] "Every act whatever of man that causes damage to another obliges him by whose fault it happened to repair it.

"The right to recover damages to property caused by an offense or quasi offense is a property right which, on the death of the obligee, is inherited by his legal, instituted, or irregular heirs, subject to the community rights of the surviving spouse.

"The right to recover all other damages caused by an offense or quasi offense, if the injured person dies, shall survive for a period of one year from the death of the deceased in favor of: (1) the surviving spouse and child or children of the deceased, or either such spouse or such child or children; (2) the surviving father and mother of the deceased, or either of them, if he left no spouse or child surviving; and (3) the surviving brothers and sisters of the deceased, or any of them, if he left no spouse, child, or parent surviving. The survivors in whose favor this right of action survives may also recover the damages which they sustained through the wrongful death of the deceased. A right to recover damages under the provisions of this paragraph is a property right which, on the death of the survivor in whose favor the right of action survived, is inherited by his legal, instituted, or irregular heirs, whether suit has been instituted thereon by the survivor or not.

"As used in this article, the words 'child,' 'brother,' 'sister,' 'father,' and 'mother' include a child, brother, sister, father, and mother, by adoption, respectively."

[5] Under Louisiana law both parents are under a duty to support their illegitimate children....

[6] We can say with Shakespeare: "Why bastard, wherefore base? When my dimensions are as well compact, My mind as generous, and my shape as true, As honest madam's issue? Why brand they us With base? with baseness? bastardy? base, base?" King Lear, Act I, Scene 2.

[7] Under Louisiana's Workmen's Compensation Act (...(1964)) an illegitimate child, who is a dependent member of the deceased parent's family, may recover compensation for his death....Employers are entitled to recover from a wrongdoer workmen's compensation payments they make to the deceased's dependent illegitimate children....

MR. JUSTICE HARLAN, whom **MR. JUSTICE BLACK** and **MR. JUSTICE STEWART** join, dissenting.

These decisions can only be classed as constitutional curiosities.

At common law, no person had a legally cognizable interest in the wrongful death of another person, and no person could inherit the personal right of another to recover for tortious injuries to his body....By statute, Louisiana has created both rights in favor of certain classes of persons. The question in these cases is whether the way in which Louisiana has defined the classes of persons who may recover is constitutionally permissible. The Court has reached a negative answer to this question by a process that can only be described as brute force.

One important reason why recovery for wrongful death had everywhere to await statutory delineation is that the interest one person has in the life of another is inherently intractable. Rather than hear offers of proof of love and affection and economic dependence from every person who might think or claim that the bell had tolled for him, the courts stayed their hands pending legislative action. Legislatures, responding to the same diffuseness of interests, generally defined classes of proper plaintiffs by highly arbitrary lines based on family relationships, excluding issues concerning the actual effect of the death on the plaintiff....

Louisiana has followed the traditional pattern. There the actions lie in favor of the surviving spouse and children of the deceased, if any; if none, then in favor of the surviving parents of the deceased, if any; if none, then in favor of the deceased's brothers and sisters, if any; if none, then no action lies. According to this scheme, a grown man may sue for the wrongful death of parents he did not love,[3] even if the death relieves him of a great economic burden or entitles him to a large inheritance. But an employee who loses a job because of the death of his employer has no cause of action, and a minor child cared for by neighbors or relatives "as if he were their own son" does not therefore have a right to sue for their death....Perhaps most dramatic, a surviving parent, for example, of a Louisiana deceased may sue if and only if there is no surviving spouse or child: it does not matter who loved or depended on whom, or what the economic situation of any survivor may be, or even whether the spouse or child elects to sue.[5] In short, the whole scheme of the Louisiana wrongful death statute, which is similar in this respect to that of most other States, makes everything the Court says about affection and nurture and dependence altogether irrelevant. The only question in any case is whether the plaintiff falls within the classes of persons to whom the State has accorded a right of action for the death of another.

* * *

The Court today, for some reason which I am at a loss to understand, rules that the State must base its arbitrary definition of the plaintiff class on biological rather than legal relationships. Exactly how this makes the Louisiana scheme even marginally more "rational" is not clear, for neither a biological relationship nor legal acknowledgment is indicative of the love or economic dependence that may exist between two persons. It is, frankly, preposterous to suggest that the State has made illegitimates into "nonpersons," or that, by analogy with what Louisiana has done here it might deny illegitimates constitutional rights or the benefits of doing business in corporate form.[8] The rights at issue here stem from the existence of a family relationship, and the State has decided only that it will not recognize the family relationship unless the formalities of marriage, or of the acknowledgment of children by the parent in question, have been complied with.

There is obvious justification for this decision....

The Equal Protection Clause states a complex and difficult principle. Certain classifications are "inherently suspect," which I take to mean that any reliance upon them in differentiating legal rights requires very strong affirmative justification. The difference between a child who has been formally acknowledged and one who has not is hardly one of these. Other classifications are impermissible because they bear no intelligible proper relation to the consequences that are made to flow from them. This does not mean that any classification this Court thinks could be better drawn is unconstitutional. But even if the power of this Court to improve on the lines that Congress and the States have drawn were very much broader than I consider it to be, I could not understand why a State which bases the right to recover for wrongful death strictly on family relationships could not demand that those relationships be formalized.

I would affirm the decisions of the state court and the Court of Appeals for the Fifth Circuit.

[3] He may even, like Shakespeare's Edmund, have spent his life contriving treachery against his family. Supposing that the Bard had any views on the law of legitimacy, they might more easily be discerned from Edmund's character than from the words he utters in defense of the only thing he cares for, himself.

[5] ...The Court speaks in *Levy* of tortfeasors going free. However, the deceased in that case left a legitimate parent. Under the Court's opinion, the right of legitimate and perhaps dependent parents to sue will henceforth be cut off by the mere existence of an illegitimate child, though the child be a self-supporting adult, and though the child elect not to sue. Incidentally, the burden of proving the nonexistence of such a child will be on the plaintiff parent....

[8] A more obvious analogy from the law of corporations than the rather farfetched example the Court has suggested is the elementary rule that the benefits of doing business in corporate form may be denied, to the willful, the negligent, and the innocent alike, if the formalities of incorporation have not been properly complied with.

Questions for Discussion

1. Should the children of unwed parents be a suspect classification invoking strict scrutiny? Generally, the courts have held that groups that are held in popular disregard, are politically weak, and have a history of discriminatory treatment warrant such status. Don't many refer to such children as "bastards"? Are they less politically weak than racial or religious minorities? Does the fact that such children have no choice in the circumstance of their birth commend such status?

2. Assuming the more generous "rational relation" test, what is the state interest here in differentiating these children from other children? Does it stimulate marriage? What is the evidence presented of that connection? Assuming it encourages marriage, can that encouragement be constitutionally accomplished through denial of benefits to third parties?

3. Louisiana may argue that children cannot collect when their absent father dies because they are not legal heirs, that parental status can determine property rights, and that marriage is a criterion for parental status. But when Louisiana seeks to collect child support for welfare it provided, does it restrict itself to married

fathers? Can it take from such a source for itself because of biological tie alone, but refuse to collect for the child under the same circumstance?

4. The dissent argues that Louisiana needs a bright line, and the status of marriage provides it. But failure to marry does not necessarily preclude the constitutional rights of unmarried biological fathers seeking parental rights (see Chapter 11). That bright line, however useful, was struck as underinclusive and abridging the parental rights of some fathers. Unlike these children, do not such fathers have the option to secure marriage prior to producing a child?

Mathews v. Lucas
427 U.S. 495 (1976)

MR. JUSTICE BLACKMUN delivered the opinion of the Court.

This case presents the issue of the constitutionality, under the Due Process Clause of the Fifth Amendment, of those provisions of the Social Security Act that condition the eligibility of certain illegitimate children for a surviving child's insurance benefits upon a showing that the deceased wage earner was the claimant child's parent and, at the time of his death, was living with the child or was contributing to his support.

I

Robert Cuffee, now deceased, lived with Belmira Lucas during the years 1948 through 1966, but they were never married. Two children were born to them during these years: Ruby M. Lucas, in 1953, and Darin E. Lucas, in 1960. In 1966 Cuffee and Lucas separated. Cuffee died in Providence, R.I., his home, in 1968. He died without ever having acknowledged in writing his paternity of either Ruby or Darin, and it was never determined in any judicial proceeding during his lifetime that he was the father of either child. After Cuffee's death, Mrs. Lucas filed an application on behalf of Ruby and Darin for surviving children's benefits under...the Social Security Act,...42 U.S.C. § 402(d)(1)..., based upon Cuffee's earnings record.

II

In operative terms, the Act provides that an unmarried son or daughter of an individual, who died fully or currently insured under the Act, may apply for and be entitled to a survivor's benefit, if the applicant is under 18 years of age at the time of application (or is a full-time student and under 22 years of age) and was dependent, within the meaning of the statute, at the time of the parent's death....A child is considered dependent for this purpose if the insured father was living with or contributing to the child's support at the time of death. Certain children, however, are relieved of the burden of such individualized proof of dependency. Unless the child has been adopted by some other individual, a child who is legitimate, or a child who would be entitled to inherit personal property from the insured parent's estate under the applicable state intestacy law, is considered to have been dependent at the time of the parent's death....Even lacking this relationship under state law, a child, unless adopted by some other individual, is entitled to a presumption of dependency if the decedent, before death, (a) had gone through a marriage ceremony with the other parent, resulting in a purported marriage between them which, but for a nonobvious legal defect, would have been valid, or (b) in writing had acknowledged the child to be his, or (c) had been decreed by a court to be the child's father, or (d) had been ordered by a court to support the child because the child was his....

An Examiner of the Social Security Administration, after hearings, determined that while Cuffee's paternity was established, the children had failed to demonstrate their dependency by proof that Cuffee either lived with them or was contributing to their support at the time of his death, or by any of the statutory presumptions of dependency, and thus that they were not entitled to survivorship benefits under the Act...

* * *

596

III

The Secretary does not disagree that the Lucas children and others similarly circumstanced are treated differently, as a class, from those children— legitimate and illegitimate—who are relieved by statutory presumption of any requirement of proving actual dependency at the time of death through cohabitation or contribution: for children in the advantaged classes may be statutorily entitled to benefits even if they have never been dependent upon the father through whom they claim.[7] Statutory classifications, of course, are not per se unconstitutional; the matter depends upon the character of the discrimination and its relation to legitimate legislative aims. "The essential inquiry...is... inevitably a dual one: What legitimate [governmental] interest does the classification promote? What fundamental personal rights might the classification endanger?"....

Although the District Court concluded that close judicial scrutiny of the statute's classifications was not necessary to its conclusion invalidating those classifications, it also concluded that legislation treating legitimate and illegitimate offspring differently is constitutionally suspect,[8] 390 F. Supp., at 1318–1319, and requires the judicial scrutiny traditionally devoted to cases involving discrimination along lines of race...or national origin....Appellees echo this approach. We disagree.[11]

It is true, of course, that the legal status of illegitimacy, however defined, is, like race or national origin, a characteristic determined by causes not within the control of the illegitimate individual, and it bears no relation to the individual's ability to participate in and contribute to society. The Court recognized in *Weber* that visiting condemnation upon the child in order to express society's disapproval of the parents' liaisons

> "is illogical and unjust. Moreover, imposing disabilities on the illegitimate child is contrary to the basic concept of our system that legal burdens should bear some relationship to individual responsibility or wrongdoing. Obviously, no child is responsible for his birth and penalizing the illegitimate child is an ineffectual—as well as an unjust—way of deterring the parent." 406 U.S., at 175. (Footnote omitted.)

But where the law is arbitrary in such a way, we have had no difficulty in finding the discrimination impermissible on less demanding standards than those advocated here....And such irrationality in some classifications does not in itself demonstrate that other, possibly rational, distinctions made in part on the basis of legitimacy are inherently untenable. Moreover, while the law has long placed the illegitimate child in an inferior position relative to the legitimate in certain circumstances, particularly in regard to obligations of support or other aspects of family law,...perhaps in part because the roots of the discrimination rest in the conduct of the parents rather than the child,[12] and perhaps in part because illegitimacy does not carry an obvious badge, as race or sex do, this discrimination against illegitimates has never approached the severity or pervasiveness of the historic legal and political discrimination against women and Negroes....

We therefore adhere to our earlier view,...that the Act's discrimination between individuals on the basis of their legitimacy does not "command extraordinary protection from the majoritarian political process," *San Antonio School Dist. v. Rodríguez*, 411 U.S. 1, 28 (1973), which our most exacting scrutiny would entail.[13]...

IV
***

...[W]e think it clear that conditioning entitlement upon dependency at the time of death is not impermissibly discriminatory in providing only for those children for whom the loss of the parent is an immediate source of the need....

But appellees contend that the actual design of the statute belies the Secretary's description, and that the statute was intended to provide support for insured decedents' children generally, if they had a "legitimate" claim to support, without regard to actual dependency at death; in any case, they assert, the statute's matrix of classifications bears no adequate relationship to actual dependency at death. Since such dependency does not justify the statute's discriminations, appellees argue, those classifications must fall under *Gomez v. Perez, supra*. These assertions are in effect one and the same.[14] The basis for appellees' argument is the obvious fact that each of the presumptions of dependency renders the class of benefit-recipients incrementally overinclusive, in the sense that some children within each class of presumptive dependents are automatically entitled to benefits under the statute although they could not in fact prove their economic dependence upon insured wage earners at the time of death. We conclude that the statutory classifications are permissible, however, because they are reasonably related to the likelihood of dependency at death.

* * *

B

Applying these principles, we think that the statutory classifications challenged here are justified as reasonable empirical judgments that are consistent with a design to qualify entitlement to benefits upon a child's dependency at the time of the parent's death. To begin with, we note that the statutory scheme is significantly different from the provisions confronted in cases in which the Court has invalidated legislative discriminations among children on the basis of legitimacy....These differences render those cases of little assistance to appellees. It could not have been fairly argued, with respect to any of the statutes struck down in those cases that the legitimacy of the child was simply taken as an indication of dependency, or of some other valid ground of qualification. Under all but one of the statutes, not only was the legitimate child automatically entitled to benefits, but an illegitimate child was denied benefits solely and finally on the basis of illegitimacy, and regardless of any demonstration of dependency or other legitimate factor....

* * *

...[W]here state intestacy law provides that a child may take personal property from a father's estate, it may reasonably be thought that the child will more likely be dependent during the parent's life and at his death.... For in its embodiment of the popular view within the jurisdiction of how a parent would have his property devolve among his children in the event of death, without specific directions, such legislation also reflects to some degree the popular conception within the jurisdiction of the felt parental obligation to such an "illegitimate" child in other circumstances, and thus something of the likelihood of actual parental support during, as well as after, life.[18]....

To be sure, none of these statutory criteria compels the extension of a presumption of dependency. But the constitutional question is not whether such a presumption is required, but whether it is permitted.... We conclude, in short, that, in failing to extend any presumption of dependency to appellees and others like them, the Act does not impermissibly discriminate against them as compared with legitimate children or those illegitimate children who are statutorily deemed dependent.

Reversed.

[7] It adds nothing to say that the illegitimate child is also saddled with the procedural burden of proving entitlement on the basis of facts the legitimate child need not prove. The legitimate child is required, like the illegitimate, to prove the facts upon which his statutory entitlement rests.

[8] Appellees do not suggest, nor could they successfully, that strict judicial scrutiny of the statutory classifications is required here because, in regulating entitlement to survivorship benefits, the statute discriminatorily interferes with interests of constitutional fundamentality....

The Court, of course, has found the privacy of familial relationships, to be entitled to procedural due process protections from disruption by the State, whether or not those relationships were legitimized by marriage under state law. *Stanley v. Illinois*, 405 U.S. 645 (1972). But the concerns relevant to that context are only tangential to the analysis here, since the statutory scheme does not interfere in any way with familial relations.

[11] That the statutory classifications challenged here discriminate among illegitimate children does not mean, of course, that they are not also properly described as discriminating between legitimate and illegitimate children In view of our conclusion regarding the applicable standard of judicial scrutiny, we need not consider how the classes of legitimate and illegitimate children would be constitutionally defined under appellees' approach.

[12] The significance of this consideration would seem to be suggested by provisions enabling the parents to legitimatize children born illegitimate. Compare *Weber*, 406 U.S., at 170–171, with *Labine v. Vincent*, 401 U.S. 532, 539 (1971). Of course, the status of "dependency" as recognized by the statute here is wholly within the control of the parent.

[13] In *Rodriguez* the Court identified a "suspect class" entitled to the protections of strict judicial scrutiny as one "saddled with such disabilities, or subjected to such a history of purposeful unequal treatment, or relegated to such a position of political powerlessness as to command extraordinary protection from the majoritarian political process." 411 U.S., at 28.

"We are not bound to agree with the Secretary's description of the legislative design if the legislative history and the structure of the provisions themselves belie it....Appellees are unable, however, to summon any meaningful legislative history to support their position regarding the congressional design....

"Appellees do not suggest, and we are unwilling to assume, that discrimination against children in appellees' class in state intestacy laws is constitutionally prohibited, see *Labine v. Vincent*, 401 U.S. 532 (1971), in which case appellees would be made eligible for benefits under § 216(h)(2)(A).

MR. JUSTICE STEVENS, with whom MR. JUSTICE BRENNAN and MR. JUSTICE MARSHALL join, dissenting.

The reason why the United States Government should not add to the burdens that illegitimate children inevitably acquire at birth is radiantly clear: We are committed to the proposition that all persons are created equal. The Court's reason for approving discrimination against this class—"administrative convenience"—is opaque and insufficient: opaque because the difference between this justification and the argument rejected in *Jimenez v. Weinberger*, 417 U.S. 628, is so difficult to discern; insufficient because it unfairly evaluates the competing interests at stake.

I

Jimenez involved a requirement that the wage earner must have contributed to the support of his illegitimate child prior to the onset of his disability; this case involves the requirement that the deceased wage earner was contributing to the support of his illegitimate child at the time of his death. The critical objections to the classification held invalid in *Jimenez* apply with equal force in this case.

The classification in *Jimenez* was "overinclusive" because it conclusively presumed that all legitimates and some illegitimates were dependent on the disabled wage earner when many such persons were not in fact dependent. Since legitimate as well as illegitimate children are sometimes abandoned by their father before his death, precisely the same objection applies to this statutory classification. Moreover, the *Jimenez* classification was "underinclusive" because it conclusively excluded some illegitimates who were in fact dependent on the wage earner.[1] In this case the two appellee children were conclusively excluded from the class of eligibles even though they had been supported by their father for 15 years and eight years respectively. If the underinclusiveness of the *Jimenez* classification was arbitrary, this classification is even more objectionable because it attaches greater weight to support at a particular moment in time than to support of several years' duration.

* * *

II

The Court recognizes "that the legal status of illegitimacy, however defined, is, like race or national origin, a characteristic determined by causes not within the control of the illegitimate individual, and it bears no relation to the individual's ability to participate in and contribute to society."....For that reason, as the Court also recognizes, "'imposing disabilities on the illegitimate child is contrary to the basic concept of our system that legal burdens should bear some relationship to individual responsibility or wrongdoing.'"....Thus the Court starts its analysis from the premise that the statutory classification is both "'illogical and unjust.'"....It seems rather plain to me that this premise demands a conclusion that the classification is invalid unless it is justified by a weightier governmental interest than merely "administrative convenience."

* * *

In this case, the "true" classification, according to the Court, is one between children dependent on their fathers and children who are not so dependent. All of the subsidiary classifications (which have the actual effect of allowing certain children to be eligible for benefits regardless of actual dependency) are supposedly justified by the increased convenience for the agency in not being required in every case to determine dependency. But do these classifications actually bear any substantial relationship to the fact of dependency?

In this statute, one or another of the criteria giving rise to a "presumption of dependency" exists to make almost all children of deceased wage earners eligible. If a child is legitimate, he qualifies. If the child is illegitimate only because of a nonobvious defect in his parents' marriage, he qualifies. If a court has declared his father to be in fact his father, or has issued an order of support against his father, or if the father has

599

acknowledged the child in writing, he qualifies. Apart from any of these qualifications, if the child is lucky enough to live in a State which allows him to inherit from his intestate father on a par with other children, he also qualifies. And in none of these situations need he allege, much less prove, actual dependency. Indeed, if the contrary fact is undisputed, he is nevertheless qualified.

The Court today attempts, at some length, to explain that each of these factors is rationally and substantially related to the actual fact of dependency, adopting even the somewhat tenuous rationalization of the District Court that "'[m]en do not customarily affirm in writing their responsibility for an illegitimate child unless the child is theirs and a man who has acknowledged a child is more likely to provide it support than one who does not,'"...without also noting that a man who lives with a woman for 18 years, during which two children are born, who has always orally acknowledged that the children are his, and who has lived with the children and supported them, may never perceive a need to make a formal written acknowledgment of paternity. Even more tenuous is the asserted relationship between the status of the illegitimate under state intestacy law and actual dependency. The Court asserts that "in its embodiment of the popular view within the jurisdiction of how a parent would have his property devolve among his children in the event of death, without specific directions, such legislation also reflects to some degree the popular conception within the jurisdiction of the felt parental obligation to such an 'illegitimate' child in other circumstances, and thus something of the likelihood of actual parental support during, as well as after, life."....That nebulous inference upon inference is treated as more acceptable evidence of actual dependency than proof of actual support for many years.[4]

* * *

I am persuaded that the classification which is sustained today in the name of "administrative convenience" is more probably the product of a tradition of thinking of illegitimates as less deserving persons than legitimates. The sovereign should firmly reject that tradition. The fact that illegitimacy is not as apparent to the observer as sex or race does not make this governmental classification any less odious. It cannot be denied that it is a source of social opprobrium, even if wholly unmerited, or that it is a circumstance for which the individual has no responsibility whatsoever.

A fair evaluation of the competing interests at stake in this litigation requires affirmance of the judgment of the District Court.

I respectfully dissent.

[1] "Even if children might rationally be classified on the basis of whether they are dependent upon their disabled parent, the Act's definition of these two subclasses of illegitimates is 'overinclusive' in that it benefits some children who are legitimated, or entitled to inherit, or illegitimate solely because of a defect in the marriage of their parents, but who are not dependent on their disabled parent. Conversely, the Act is 'underinclusive' in that it conclusively excludes some illegitimates in appellants' subclass who are, in fact, dependent upon their disabled parent. Thus, for all that is shown in this record, the two subclasses of illegitimates stand on equal footing, and the potential for spurious claims is the same as to both; hence to conclusively deny one subclass benefits presumptively available to the other denies the former the equal protection of the laws guaranteed by the due process provision of the Fifth Amendment." 417 U.S., at 637.

[4] If the relationship between an entitling presumption and the actual fact of dependency is so nebulous that the conclusion can be supported only by resort to a supposed popular conception within a jurisdiction, the classification must either be irrational, or serve a purpose other than the one by which it is assertedly justified.

Questions for Discussion

1. Isn't living with children and supporting them sufficient acknowledgment for these children to qualify? What would be Robert Cuffee's status if Ruby Lucas sought to give the children up for adoption? Would he be able to block the adoption? Would he be considered a "presumed father" under the Uniform Parentage Act (see cases and discussion in Chapter 11)?

2. Is the majority argument persuasive that illegitimate children are not a properly protected class because—unlike race and gender—they do not carry the physical "badge" of their difference? Do people reliably carry such badges of their religion, which is a basis for protected group strict scrutiny status?

3. Mr. Cuffee contributed to Social Security, which funds the child survivor benefits here at issue. If the federal jurisdiction were paying welfare to these children, would this biological father be assessed child support? If he has an obligation to support the children, which the federal government is prepared to enforce, aren't his children entitled to these benefits on the same biological basis? Is it fair for government to go beyond marriage to collect for itself, but to refuse to use the same criteria when paying out?

4. The Court argues that the marriage line is administratively convenient. Is that a convincing argument? Is a less restrictive alternative available, *e.g.*, an opportunity for an illegitimate child to show actual dependency? Is categorical exclusion necessary to accomplish the stated public purpose?

5. Is "support" at the moment of death an equitable criterion where marriage is lacking under the majority decision? What about parents who provide full support for a decade or more (*e.g.*, while funding their Social Security account), are the biological parents, and then die during a brief period when they are not supporting?

6. The children of unwed parents sometimes receive "heightened" or "intermediate" scrutiny when they are differentiated by the state. Would a statute stand that allows intestate succession to non-marital children as to their mothers' estates, but not as to their fathers'? Could the state argue that it has a compelling interest in timely and certain inheritance, and that paternal status is less certain? Could it argue more generally that such a policy properly furthers the compelling state interest in marriage as an institution? See the striking of such a statute in *Trimble v. Gordon*, 430 U.S. 762 (1977), with explicit court rejection of a policy to influence adult behavior through the "sanctioning of children." Given *Trimble*, can a state then permit non-marital children to intestate inheritance from their fathers only where a court has entered a "filiation order" prior to death? See the affirmance of this discrimination as consistent with the state's interest in providing for the "just and orderly disposition of property at death." *Lalli v. Lalli*, 439 U.S. 259 (1978). Are these two decisions consistent with each other? With *Levy*? With *Mathews*?

7. Do DNA and other advances undermine required "filiation orders" for non-marital child inheritance from fathers? Is uncertainty really a problem now? If timeliness is an issue, would not a time limit on claims filed satisfy such a state interest as a less restrictive alternative?

B. CHILD RIGHT OF CONTRACT

The common law acknowledges the immaturity of children to enter into the "meeting of the minds" which an enforceable contact requires.[3] Historically, contracts applied to children fell into three common law categories: (1) void (when clearly prejudicial to the child); (2) voidable (when possibly in the child's best interest); and (3) valid (when clearly in the child's best interest). The coalescence of these rules into the current "doctrine of incapacity" means that children may disaffirm contracts which are to their disadvantage, but enforce those which are of benefit. In other words, the law is not symmetrical in its application, but favors the child.

The child's disaffirmance may take place at any point during his or her minority, and perhaps for a short period after emancipation. There are some exceptions to the disaffirmance right, including contracts which are non-voidable by statute, or which provide a child with "necessaries" (e.g., food, clothing, medical care). And one consequence of disaffirmance may be the remedy of rescission—including the return of items possessed by the minor. The majority rule is that such return will be limited to actual property possessed, and does not extend to restoration of full value. However, disaffirmance may be denied by some courts where minors misrepresent their age—and such deceit may be a tort allowing full recovery for value received, in addition to possible damages (see tort discussion below).

C. CHILD TORT LIABILITY AND RECOVERY

1. Child Liability

Children generally are subject to the same tort rights and liabilities as adults. However, their immaturity may sometimes preclude liability for intentional torts where specific intent is required, as with slander, libel, trespass, or deceit. Such immunity is more likely where young children are implicated, with courts varying widely in their assignment of adequate capacity for liability. Some courts have formulated a "rule of 7," that children under seven years of age are presumptively unable to commit an intentional tort, those over 14 are presumed to have capacity, and liability for those 7 to 14 years of age depends on the facts. However, the majority rule is to use age simply as one factor to consider in measuring capacity. In general, courts are likely to apply the "reasonable man" standard as children exceed fourteen years of age.

With regard to a child's liability for negligence, state courts vary in their approach. Illinois and about a dozen other states maintain that children under seven are incapable of negligence; for those between seven and fourteen there is a rebuttable presumption that the child is incapable of negligence; and for children fourteen or above, there is a rebuttable presumption that the child is capable of negligence. With regard to very young defendants, some states apply a minimum age for liability, usually seven, six, or five, while other states reject such limits.

In 2010, four-year-old Juliet Breitman was racing her bicycle (with training wheels) against four-year-old Jacob Kohn on a New York sidewalk. She struck an 87-year-old woman, causing a hip fracture. The mothers of both children were sued for negligent supervision, but the four-year-old girl was also a named defendant. The trial court noted that she was three months from turning five and of sufficient age to be personally liable. The court held: "For infants above the age of four, there is no bright line rule, and 'in considering the conduct of an infant in relation to other persons or their property, the infant should be held to a standard of care...by what is expected of a reasonably prudent child of that age, experience, intelligence and degree of development and capacity.'"[4] The majority of states, however, adopted the rule articulated in the Restatement (Third) of Torts that children under the age of five may not be held liable for negligence.[5]

Parents are not automatically held liable for the intentional acts of their children simply by virtue of being a parent. Most states, however, have laws permitting such actions against parents, limited by certain conditions and only up to specified dollar limits. Furthermore, parents may incur liability when they have directed or consented to the child's act or failed to exercise reasonable care. For example, in the *Breitman* case above, the court noted that the parents' presence and failure to moderate was not necessarily a defense: "A parent's presence alone does not give a reasonable child *carte blanche* to engage in risky behavior such as running across a street. A reasonably prudent child, whom we may presume has been told repeatedly by the age of four to look both ways before crossing a street knows that running across a street is dangerous even if there is a parent nearby. Despite this, if a parent or other trusted adult actively directs a four year old child to cross a street at a certain time, the only logical inference is that the child will reasonably believe it is safe to cross the street at that time. Because a child above the age of four will only be *non sui juris* if it is impossible under the circumstances to draw any other inference, parental supervision is unlikely to affect the *sui juris* status of a child above the age of four unless the parent has taken an active role in encouraging the child's conduct."[6]

Questions for Discussion

1. A tort action may lie if a child is injured where there is an "attractive nuisance" (a setting that would attract a child to a hazard—such as a fall as in *Corson* below, a swimming pool, or vehicular danger). Does the "over the age of four" concept of *Breitman* mean that contributory negligence or assumption of risk may diminish or eliminate "attractive nuisance" liability? Will such a concept of imputed caution mean that although the bright lights and clowns and candy may have attracted the six-year-old, he really should have known better and exercised prudence? How are we to measure "a reasonably prudent child" of 14 for purposes of tort liability in failing to exercise "due care," or for the purposes of "assumption of risk" that might eliminate the liability of others for his injury? A child of the age of 10? A child of the age of 6?

2. Is the standard measured by acts which are subjectively deemed imprudent or prudent based on a child's individual upbringing? Is it based on his or her individual level of maturity—at a hypothetical age three years older or younger than the actual

age? Or is it based on an objective standard of the "reasonably prudent" child of his or her actual age? In either case, how is the standard measured and applied?

3. Are the courts rendering these decisions considering the body of modern literature on the capacity of young children, brain development, and behavioral influences? Is that possibly information anywhere in the relevant opinions or adduced in the record of cases making pronouncements such as those above?

4. How do such notions of responsibility and accountability correspond with (a) our categorical denial of a child's right (even at age 17) to enter into a contract enforceable against him or her, (b) our common requirement of mandatory education from five to eighteen, or (c) the mandatory duty of parents to care and protect their children (including criminal enforcement where such care is not provided)?

2. Child Recovery from Private Parties

a. Status of Children

As a general rule, children may recover where injured by the tortious acts of others. An exception is provided by the "parental immunity" doctrine which traditionally limits such suits against parents.[7] The rationale has been the importance of family harmony. The doctrine historically was extended so far as to bar suit for incestuous rape by a father.[8] And it was extended to provide immunity for stepparents and others performing a parental role. However, the doctrine has eroded over the last half century to the point where it no longer impedes child suit against a parent in most states.[9] The growth of liability insurance has spurred the doctrine's demise, since suit generally does not lead to collection from parents, but from insurance carriers. For example, children are almost universally allowed to sue carriers for their injuries resulting from negligent driving by their parents. Courts have also questioned the equity of denying recovery based on family harmony when many such torts are reflective of exploitive practices. Accordingly, courts rarely allow family harmony as a defense to "willful" or "wanton" (reckless) torts. Nevertheless, it may be invoked where negligence is alleged beyond the scope of insurance coverage, and its spirit is reflected in the understandable latitude afforded parents in exercising judgment about their children. "Parental discretion" stands as a formidable vestige of the parental immunity doctrine to protect good faith child rearing decisions of parents. Negligence by parents outside the penumbra of parenting, which violates the standards generally applicable, is not covered by this protection (e.g., gross negligence in starting a fire which injures a child).

Historically, children have not been allowed to recover damages for the loss of parental care and companionship occurring when a third party negligently injures or kills a parent. This omission is in contrast to the common damages for "loss of consortium" available to a spouse. However, since the 1980s, states have started to recognize this parental loss as a possible recoverable injury.[10]

Children were not able to recover for prenatal injuries at common law. They were viewed as a "person" only as to property rights (permitting the child-as-fetus to inherit and benefit from trusts). However, such rights of recovery have been increasingly recognized,[11] and now stand as the strong majority rule. Application does vary, with most jurisdictions confining it to prenatal injuries to infants born alive. A small and declining minority confine it to injuries incurred only after the child is "viable" (sometime during the second or early third trimester of pregnancy). With the exception of a single case brought before the Michigan Court of Appeals, children have not succeeded in actions brought against a mother for negligent infliction of prenatal injury.[12] However, where such injuries are the result of intentional harm (including possibly severe alcohol or drug contamination), such suits may be consistent with the trend discussed above.

b. The "Attractive Nuisance"

Perhaps the most advantageous tort doctrine applicable to children is the concept of "attractive nuisance," the liability which may attach to a person who creates a hazard where children are likely to be jeopardized, particularly one reasonably expected to attract their interest. That attraction is not limited to children known to the defendant, but to any child likely to appear. The longstanding doctrine imposes an implicit duty on the citizenry to safeguard children from dangerous conditions, even on their own property where child access may be predicted.

Corson v. Kosinski
3 F.3d 1146 (7th Cir. 1993)

OPINION: **BAUER**, Chief Judge.

Lynda Lontz filed a personal injury lawsuit for herself and on behalf of her son, Kenneth Corson. Corson and Lontz are citizens of Texas and the Kosinskis are citizens of Illinois. This case is in federal court under diversity jurisdiction. 28 U.S.C. § 1332. Lontz and Corson seek $750,000 in damages from the defendants, Bruno and Carolyn Kosinski. The Kosinskis filed a motion for summary judgment, which the district court granted. Lontz and Corson appeal. We affirm.

I.

Ten-year-old Kenneth Corson, who lived with his mother in Texas, was in Chicago to spend the summer of 1989 with his father. One day, eleven-year-old Evelyn Benitz invited Kenneth and three other children over to play. Evelyn lived in an apartment in a three-story building on North Hoyne Street in Chicago which was owned by Bruno and Carolyn Kosinski. She was the only child who lived in the building.

Like many in Chicago, the building Evelyn lived in is attached to another, similar building which is also owned by the Kosinskis. The buildings share a fire wall that extends from the foundation to approximately one and a half feet beyond the roof. Both roofs are the same height, but the perimeter of the adjoining roof does not squarely abut the fire wall. Instead, eighteen feet of the wall that starts at the front of the building borders an open shaft designed to allow light to reach the ground.

Evelyn, Kenneth, and the other boys were riding bicycles and went to the basement of Evelyn's apartment building for a drink of water. The children entered the basement through a locked door for which Evelyn and the other tenants had keys. After drinking, the children left the basement via a stairwell which connects the basement to the apartments. The stairwell extends beyond the apartments and adjoins an additional stairway that leads to the roof. One of the boys ventured all the way up the stairs and found an unlocked roof door. The children went out on the roof unnoticed, played, and left. They returned later the same day and played a game that involved jumping over the fire wall that sticks out of the roof. The children jumped over the center of the wall, but Kenneth moved towards the front of the building, not knowing that the light shaft, not the roof, was on the other side of the wall. When he jumped over the wall, he fell three stories to the ground. He sustained serious, permanent injuries.

II.

* * *

Corson and Lontz sued the Kosinskis for negligence resulting in Kenneth's injury. In Illinois, a landowner is liable for an injury to a child on the owner's property if the owner knew or should have known that young children frequent the premises and a dangerous condition exists, likely to cause a child injury if the child is incapable of appreciating the risk involved, and the expense or inconvenience of remedying the dangerous condition is slight relative to the risk....

* * *

1. Premises:

Initially we must determine what constitutes the premises in this case. The plaintiff argues that the basement, back stairwell, yard, and roof should be considered part of the premises because the stairwell opens to the yard and connects the basement, the apartments, and the roof. They further argue that because children are naturally curious they will seek adventure, ostensibly by roaming to the basement and the roof. Therefore, they conclude, all the areas common to the stairwell are the premises.

The evidence shows that a separate door led to the roof. The door was normally padlocked and the tenants did not have keys. The lock was to be closed at all times, and when the lock was closed, the roof was inaccessible to the tenants (and children). This was distinct from the basement, which was also secured by a locked door for which all the tenants had keys. The basement housed circuit breakers and storage, so that tenant access to the basement was necessary. In contrast, the tenants had no reason to go to the roof. Also, the other areas of the building, such as the front porch, the yard, and the stairwell were common and accessible to all tenants, unlike the roof. We believe that the roof was effectively separated from the rest of the apartment building.

* * *

Nor will the curiosity of children serve to provide the missing evidence. We agree that children are curious. Their curiosity on this occasion turned their trip for a drink of water into an ill-fated adventure. But we do not believe that this incident is enough to find that the roof is part of the premises. Benitz lived on the second floor of the building for eleven years. The evidence showed that the children had been on the back stairwell on fewer than six occasions during that time. Moreover, when on the stairwell the children's activities were confined to talking and whispering. The plaintiffs produced no evidence that children had ever played on the back stairwell or explored the area leading to the roof.

This is not to say that the children were wholly absent from the building. They occasionally played in the yard and gathered on the front porch....

2. Frequency:

Frequency is determined by the circumstances surrounding each case....This is a factual issue that is generally left for a jury.... But we have determined that the premises encompassed by our inquiry is the roof alone, and no other part of the building. The plaintiffs provided no evidence that Evelyn or any other child had ever been on the roof.

* * *

The district court decision is AFFIRMED.

Questions for Discussion

1. What would have been the cost to mitigate the hazard? What about a sign disclosing that a blind hole lay behind the wall?

2. Would the court's decision have been different if there had been a prior incident at the site? If there had been similar publicized incidents of such skylights causing injuries?

3. The case turns largely on whether the defendant knew or should have known if children were frequenting the site. Isn't it reasonable to assume a child would be in that location given the unlocked door to the roof and the presence of this building in the middle of a city with many thousands of children? Wouldn't a more sensible criteria be whether it is reasonable to assume anyone, including a child, would jump over the wall in question without looking behind it?

3. Child Tort Recovery from the State

a. The Duty of Care

Deshaney v. Winnebago County
489 U.S. 189 (1989)

CHIEF JUSTICE REHNQUIST delivered the opinion of the Court.

Petitioner is a boy who was beaten and permanently injured by his father, with whom he lived. Respondents are social workers and other local officials who received complaints that petitioner was being abused by his father and had reason to believe that this was the case, but nonetheless did not act to remove petitioner from his father's custody. Petitioner sued respondents claiming that their failure to act deprived him of his liberty in violation of the Due Process Clause of the Fourteenth Amendment to the United States Constitution. We hold that it did not.

I

The facts of this case are undeniably tragic. Petitioner Joshua DeShaney was born in 1979. In 1980, a Wyoming court granted his parents a divorce and awarded custody of Joshua to his father, Randy DeShaney. The father shortly thereafter moved to Neenah, a city located in Winnebago County, Wisconsin, taking the infant Joshua with him. There he entered into a second marriage, which also ended in divorce.

The Winnebago County authorities first learned that Joshua DeShaney might be a victim of child abuse in January 1982, when his father's second wife complained to the police, at the time of their divorce, that he had previously "hit the boy causing marks and [was] a prime case for child abuse."...The Winnebago County Department of Social Services (DSS) interviewed the father, but he denied the accusations, and DSS did not pursue them further. In January 1983, Joshua was admitted to a local hospital with multiple bruises and abrasions. The examining physician suspected child abuse and notified DSS, which immediately obtained an order from a Wisconsin juvenile court placing Joshua in the temporary custody of the hospital. Three days later, the county convened an ad hoc "Child Protection Team"—consisting of a pediatrician, a psychologist, a police detective, the county's lawyer, several DSS caseworkers, and various hospital personnel—to consider Joshua's situation. At this meeting, the Team decided that there was insufficient evidence of child abuse to retain Joshua in the custody of the court. The Team did, however, decide to recommend several measures to protect Joshua, including enrolling him in a preschool program, providing his father with certain counseling services, and encouraging his father's girlfriend to move out of the home. Randy DeShaney entered into a voluntary agreement with DSS in which he promised to cooperate with them in accomplishing these goals.

Based on the recommendation of the Child Protection Team, the juvenile court dismissed the child protection case and returned Joshua to the custody of his father. A month later, emergency room personnel called the DSS caseworker handling Joshua's case to report that he had once again been treated for suspicious injuries. The caseworker concluded that there was no basis for action. For the next six months, the caseworker made monthly visits to the DeShaney home, during which she observed a number of suspicious injuries on Joshua's head; she also noticed that he had not been enrolled in school, and that the girlfriend had not moved out. The caseworker dutifully recorded these incidents in her files, along with her continuing suspicions that someone in the DeShaney household was physically abusing Joshua, but she did nothing more. In November 1983, the emergency room notified DSS that Joshua had been treated once again for injuries that they believed to be caused by child abuse. On the caseworker's next two visits to the DeShaney home, she was told that Joshua was too ill to see her. Still DSS took no action.

In March 1984, Randy DeShaney beat 4-year-old Joshua so severely that he fell into a life-threatening coma. Emergency brain surgery revealed a series of hemorrhages caused by traumatic injuries to the head inflicted over a long period of time. Joshua did not die, but he suffered brain damage so severe that he is expected to spend the rest of his life confined to an institution for the profoundly retarded. Randy DeShaney was subsequently tried and convicted of child abuse.

Joshua and his mother brought this action under 42 U.S.C. § 1983 in the United States District Court for the Eastern District of Wisconsin against respondents Winnebago County, DSS, and various individual employees of DSS. The complaint alleged that respondents had deprived Joshua of his liberty without due process of law, in violation of his rights under the Fourteenth Amendment, by failing to intervene to protect him against a risk of violence at his father's hands of which they knew or should have known....

* * *

II

The Due Process Clause of the Fourteenth Amendment provides that "[n]o State shall...deprive any person of life, liberty, or property, without due process of law." Petitioners contend that the State...deprived Joshua of his liberty interest in "free[dom] from...unjustified intrusions on personal security,"...by failing to provide him with adequate protection against his father's violence. The claim is one invoking the substantive rather than the procedural component of the Due Process Clause; petitioners do not claim that the State denied Joshua protection without according him appropriate procedural safeguards, see *Morrissey v. Brewer*, 408 U.S. 471, 481 (1972), but that it was categorically obligated to protect him in these circumstances, *Youngberg v. Romeo*, 457 U.S. 307, 309 (1982).[2]

But nothing in the language of the Due Process Clause itself requires the State to protect the life, liberty, and property of its citizens against invasion by private actors. The Clause is phrased as a limitation on the State's power to act, not as a guarantee of certain minimal levels of safety and security....

...If the Due Process Clause does not require the State to provide its citizens with particular protective services, it follows that the State cannot be held liable under the Clause for injuries that could have been averted had it chosen to provide them.[3] As a general matter, then, we conclude that a State's failure to protect an individual against private violence simply does not constitute a violation of the Due Process Clause.

Petitioners contend, however, that even if the Due Process Clause imposes no affirmative obligation on the State to provide the general public with adequate protective services, such a duty may arise out of certain "special relationships" created or assumed by the State with respect to particular individuals....Petitioners argue that such a "special relationship" existed here because the State knew that Joshua faced a special danger of abuse at his father's hands, and specifically proclaimed, by word and by deed, its intention to protect him against that danger....Having actually undertaken to protect Joshua from this danger—which petitioners concede the State played no part in creating—the State acquired an affirmative "duty," enforceable through the Due Process Clause, to do so in a reasonably competent fashion. Its failure to discharge that duty, so the argument goes, was an abuse of governmental power that so "shocks the conscience," *Rochin v. California*, 342 U.S. 165, 172 (1952), as to constitute a substantive due process violation....[4]

We reject this argument. It is true that in certain limited circumstances the Constitution imposes upon the State affirmative duties of care and protection with respect to particular individuals. In *Estelle v. Gamble*, 429 U.S. 97 (1976), we recognized that the Eighth Amendment's prohibition against cruel and unusual punishment, made applicable to the States through the Fourteenth Amendment's Due Process Clause, *Robinson v. California*, 370 U.S. 660 (1962), requires the State to provide adequate medical care to incarcerated prisoners. 429 U.S., at 103–104.[5] We reasoned that because the prisoner is unable "'by reason of the deprivation of his liberty [to] care for himself,'" it is only "'just'" that the State be required to care for him....

* * *

But these cases afford petitioners no help. Taken together, they stand only for the proposition that when the State takes a person into its custody and holds him there against his will, the Constitution imposes upon it a corresponding duty to assume some responsibility for his safety and general well-being....

* * *

Affirmed.

[2] Petitioners also argue that the Wisconsin child protection statutes gave Joshua an "entitlement" to receive protective services in accordance with the terms of the statute, an entitlement which would enjoy due process protection against state deprivation under our decision in *Board of Regents of State Colleges v. Roth*, 408 U.S. 564 (1972)....But this argument is made for the first time in petitioners' brief to this Court: it was not pleaded in the complaint, argued to the Court of Appeals as a ground for reversing the District Court, or raised in the petition for certiorari. We therefore decline to consider it here....

[3] The State may not, of course, selectively deny its protective services to certain disfavored minorities without violating the Equal Protection Clause.... But no such argument has been made here.

[4] The genesis of this notion appears to lie in a statement in our opinion in *Martinez v. California*, 444 U.S. 277 (1980). In that case, we were asked to decide, *inter alia*, whether state officials could be held liable under the Due Process Clause of the Fourteenth Amendment for the death of a private citizen at the hands of a parolee. Rather than squarely confronting the question presented here—whether the Due Process Clause imposed upon the State an affirmative duty to protect—we affirmed the dismissal of the claim on the narrower ground that the causal connection between the state officials' decision to release the parolee from prison and the murder was too attenuated to establish a "deprivation" of constitutional rights within the meaning of § 1983. *Id.*, at 284–285. But we went on to say:

"[T]he parole board was not aware that appellants' decedent, as distinguished from the public at large, faced any special danger. We need not and do not decide that a parole officer could never be deemed to 'deprive' someone of life by action taken in connection with the release of a prisoner on parole. But we do hold that at least under the particular circumstances of this parole decision, appellants' decedent's death is too remote a consequence of the parole officers' action to hold them responsible under the federal civil rights law." *Id.*, at 285 (footnote omitted).

Several of the Courts of Appeals have read this language as implying that once the State learns that a third party poses a special danger to an identified victim, and indicates its willingness to protect the victim against that danger, a "special relationship" arises between State and victim, giving rise to an affirmative duty, enforceable through the Due Process Clause, to render adequate protection....

[5] To make out an Eighth Amendment claim based on the failure to provide adequate medical care, a prisoner must show that the state defendants exhibited "deliberate indifference" to his "serious" medical needs; the mere negligent or inadvertent failure to provide adequate care is not enough. *Estelle v. Gamble*, 429 U.S., at 105–106. In *Whitley v. Albers*, 475 U.S. 312 (1986), we suggested that a similar state of mind is required to make out a substantive due process claim in the prison setting. *Id.*, at 326–327.

JUSTICE BRENNAN, with whom **JUSTICE MARSHALL** and **JUSTICE BLACKMUN** join, dissenting.

"The most that can be said of the state functionaries in this case," the Court today concludes, "is that they stood by and did nothing when suspicious circumstances dictated a more active role for them."...Because I believe that this description of respondents' conduct tells only part of the story and that, accordingly, the Constitution itself "dictated a more active role" for respondents in the circumstances presented here, I cannot agree that respondents had no constitutional duty to help Joshua DeShaney.

* * *

The Court's baseline is the absence of positive rights in the Constitution and a concomitant suspicion of any claim that seems to depend on such rights. From this perspective, the DeShaneys' claim is first and foremost about inaction (the failure, here, of respondents to take steps to protect Joshua), and only tangentially about action (the establishment of a state program specifically designed to help children like Joshua). And from this perspective, holding these Wisconsin officials liable—where the only difference between this case and one involving a general claim to protective services is Wisconsin's establishment and operation of a program to protect children—would seem to punish an effort that we should seek to promote.

I would begin from the opposite direction. I would focus first on the action that Wisconsin *has* taken with respect to Joshua and children like him, rather than on the actions that the State failed to take. Such a method is not new to this Court. Both *Estelle v. Gamble*, 429 U.S. 97 (1976), and *Youngberg v. Romeo*, 457 U.S. 307 (1982), began by emphasizing that the States had confined J. W. Gamble to prison and Nicholas Romeo to a psychiatric hospital. This initial action rendered these people helpless to help themselves or to seek help from persons unconnected to the government....

* * *

Wisconsin has established a child-welfare system specifically designed to help children like Joshua. Wisconsin law places upon the local departments of social services such as respondent (DSS or Department) a duty to investigate reported instances of child abuse. See Wis. Stat. § 48.981(3) (1987–1988). While other governmental bodies and private persons are largely responsible for the reporting of possible cases of child abuse....Wisconsin law channels all such reports to the local departments of social services for evaluation and, if necessary, further action....Even when it is the sheriff's office or police department that receives a report of suspected child abuse, that report is referred to local social services departments for action, see § 48.981(3)(a); the only exception to this occurs when the reporter fears for the child's *immediate* safety. In this way, Wisconsin law invites—indeed, directs—citizens and other governmental entities to depend on local departments of social services such as respondent to protect children from abuse.

The specific facts before us bear out this view of Wisconsin's system of protecting children. Each time someone voiced a suspicion that Joshua was being abused, that information was relayed to the Department for investigation and possible action. When Randy DeShaney's second wife told the police that he had "'hit the boy causing marks and [was] a prime case for child abuse,'" the police referred her complaint to DSS.... When, on three separate occasions, emergency room personnel noticed suspicious injuries on Joshua's body, they went to DSS with this information....When neighbors informed the police that they had seen or heard Joshua's father or his father's lover beating or otherwise abusing Joshua, the police brought these reports to the attention of DSS....And when respondent Kemmeter, through these reports and through her own observations in the course of nearly 20 visits to the DeShaney home ...compiled growing evidence that Joshua was being abused, that information stayed within the Department—chronicled by the social worker in detail that seems almost eerie in light of her failure to act upon it. (As to the extent of the social worker's involvement in, and knowledge of, Joshua's predicament, her reaction to the news of Joshua's last and most devastating injuries is illuminating: "'I just knew the phone would ring some day and Joshua would be dead.'"...).

Even more telling than these examples is the Department's control over the decision whether to take steps to protect a particular child from suspected abuse. While many different people contributed information and advice to this decision, it was up to the people at DSS to make the ultimate decision (subject to the approval of the local government's corporation counsel) whether to disturb the family's current arrangements....When Joshua first appeared at a local hospital with injuries signaling physical abuse, for example, it was DSS that made the decision to take him into temporary custody for the purpose of studying his situation—and it was DSS, acting in conjunction with the corporation counsel, that returned him to his father....Unfortunately for Joshua DeShaney, the buck effectively stopped with the Department.

In these circumstances, a private citizen, or even a person working in a government agency other than DSS, would doubtless feel that her job was done as soon as she had reported her suspicions of child abuse to DSS. Through its child-welfare program, in other words, the State of Wisconsin has relieved ordinary citizens and governmental bodies other than the Department of any sense of obligation to do anything more than report their suspicions of child abuse to DSS. If DSS ignores or dismisses these suspicions, no one will step in to fill the gap. Wisconsin's child-protection program thus effectively confined Joshua DeShaney within the walls of Randy DeShaney's violent home until such time as DSS took action to remove him. Conceivably, then, children like Joshua are made worse off by the existence of this program when the persons and entities charged with carrying it out fail to do their jobs.

It simply belies reality, therefore, to contend that the State "stood by and did nothing" with respect to Joshua....Through its child-protection program, the State actively intervened in Joshua's life and, by virtue of this intervention, acquired ever more certain knowledge that Joshua was in grave danger. These circumstances, in my view, plant this case solidly within the tradition of cases like *Youngberg* and *Estelle*.

It will be meager comfort to Joshua and his mother to know that, if the State had "selectively den[ied] its protective services" to them because they were "disfavored minorities,"...their § 1983 suit might have stood on sturdier ground. Because of the posture of this case, we do not know why respondents did not take steps to protect Joshua; the Court, however, tells us that their reason is irrelevant so long as their inaction was not the product of invidious discrimination. Presumably, then, if respondents decided not to help Joshua because his name began with a "J," or because he was born in the spring, or because they did not care enough about him even to formulate an intent to discriminate against him based on an arbitrary reason, respondents would not be liable to the DeShaneys because they were not the ones who dealt the blows that destroyed Joshua's life.

* * *

As the Court today reminds us, "the Due Process Clause of the Fourteenth Amendment was intended to prevent government 'from abusing [its] power, or employing it as an instrument of oppression.'"....My disagreement with the Court arises from its failure to see that inaction can be every bit as abusive of power as action, that oppression can result when a State undertakes a vital duty and then ignores it. Today's opinion construes the Due Process Clause to permit a State to displace private sources of protection and then, at the critical moment, to shrug its shoulders and turn away from the harm that it has promised to try to prevent. Because I cannot agree that our Constitution is indifferent to such indifference, I respectfully dissent.

JUSTICE BLACKMUN, dissenting.

Today, the Court purports to be the dispassionate oracle of the law, unmoved by "natural sympathy."...But, in this pretense, the Court itself retreats into a sterile formalism which prevents it from recognizing either the facts of the case before it or the legal norms that should apply to those facts....

The Court fails to recognize this duty because it attempts to draw a sharp and rigid line between action and inaction. But such formalistic reasoning has no place in the interpretation of the broad and stirring Clauses of the Fourteenth Amendment. Indeed, I submit that these Clauses were designed, at least in part, to undo the formalistic legal reasoning that infected antebellum jurisprudence....

Like the antebellum judges who denied relief to fugitive slaves,...the Court today claims that its decision, however harsh, is compelled by existing legal doctrine. On the contrary, the question presented by this case is an open one, and our Fourteenth

Amendment precedents may be read more broadly or narrowly depending upon how one chooses to read them. Faced with the choice, I would adopt a "sympathetic" reading, one which comports with dictates of fundamental justice and recognizes that compassion need not be exiled from the province of judging....

Poor Joshua! Victim of repeated attacks by an irresponsible, bullying, cowardly, and intemperate father, and abandoned by respondents who placed him in a dangerous predicament and who knew or learned what was going on, and yet did essentially nothing except, as the Court revealingly observes, "dutifully recorded these incidents in [their] files." It is a sad commentary upon American life, and constitutional principles—so full of late of patriotic fervor and proud proclamations about "liberty and justice for all"—that this child, Joshua DeShaney, now is assigned to live out the remainder of his life profoundly retarded. Joshua and his mother, as petitioners here, deserve—but now are denied by this Court—the opportunity to have the facts of their case considered in the light of the constitutional protection that 42 U.S.C. § 1983 is meant to provide.

Questions for Discussion

1. The state's involvement with Joshua includes the creation of a mandated reporter system to detect child abuse, creation of a juvenile court system to protect the child, funding of a local agency to detect and monitor legal compliance, receipt of information indicating his abuse, physical custody and a decision to return Joshua to his father, monthly visits, and additional information of continuing abuse. Under these circumstances, is it reasonable to conclude that the state owes "no duty" to Joshua because at the time of the beating he was not in state custody?

2. The Court rules that the state is not responsible for private action, nor can the state be liable for failure to act without a "special relationship." Is there no special relationship between Joshua and the state? Are citizens reasonably relying on the state to affirmatively protect such children? Given the statutory commands to protect children and the system purportedly set up to provide that protection, should the state be equitably estopped from claiming lack of duty?

3. The remedy here might be to pay for Joshua's care from the local agency budget. Should the possible negative impact on its resources to protect other children be considered by the Court? On the other hand, what is the financial incentive to minimize negligence in child protection if there is no accountability?

4. In *Sniadach v. Family Finance Corp. of Bay View*, 395 U.S. 337 (1969), the Court ruled that there was sufficient "state action" to require due process hearings where a private creditor garnishes wages. Another case similarly found state action in the ministerial act of court marshals enforcing court judgments (see *Fuentes v. Shevin*, 407 U.S. 67 (1972)). Still other cases found "state action" where federal funding may be involved in what is otherwise private enterprise. How can such minor state involvement trigger a "state action" determination while the child protection regulatory system and Joshua's direct involvement with it is insufficient "state action" to confer liability to the state?

b. Child Tort Recovery Federal Liability Alternatives

DeShaney's denial of a state "duty of care" for children in parental custody does not preclude remedy where the state takes the child into custody and injury occurs during state-assumed care. Hence, suit may lie for injury suffered through the negligent acts of foster care providers, who function as state agents. Nor will the sovereign immunity barriers bar such suit given holdings that a child has a constitutionally (and statutorily) based right to a secure placement (see immunity bar discussion in Chapter 1).[13] However, such liability applies where removal is court ordered, and may not apply to parental voluntary placements of their children into foster care. See *Milburn v. Anne Arundel County Department of Social Services*, 871 F.2d 474 (4th Cir. 1989). Such a "voluntary surrender" category may be substantial given the common strategy of child welfare agencies seeking "stipulated agreements" from parents to foster care placement and even for parental rights termination. Such parents may be convinced that their chances of reunification are minimal and that a quick and voluntary agreement for state assistance for their child may be in the child's best interest.

Two alternative standards of care may apply to state actors subject to civil rights cases under § 1983: (1) the traditional professional malpractice standard of "departure from accepted standards of skill and judgment for that profession in the community," or (2) a stricter standard requiring officials to manifest a "deliberate indifference" to a risk actually known to them. The latter standard poses a significant burden on a plaintiff; the injured child must show indifference notwithstanding "actual knowledge." The difficult standard has been imposed by at least two circuits (*see, e.g., White v. Chambliss*, 112 F.3d 731 (4th Cir. 1997) and *K.H. ex rel. Murphy v. Morgan*, 914 F.2d 846 (7th Cir. 1990)).

Can a "special relationship" creating liability arise from the failure of the executive branch to enforce a specific court order intended to protect a child? In *Town of Castlerock v. Gonzales*, 545 U.S. 748 (2005), a court entered a restraining order preventing the violent father from contact with the plaintiff's three daughters (ages 7, 9, and 10) or from coming within 100 yards of their home. The father violated the order, entered the home, and took all three children. The plaintiff mother reported the taking and begged the police to enforce the order. They did not do so—nor attempt to do so. All three children were murdered. The complaint alleged that the police department had an official policy of not responding properly "to complaints of restraining order violations." Colorado state law makes the violation of a restraining order a crime. Colorado's law and those of other states in the domestic violence area are not comparable to "outstanding arrest warrants" issued by the court that may or may not be acted upon at a given time and place. The duty here is explicitly imposed on the police to "arrest" and to "use every reasonable means to enforce" the order—as is the case similarly in 18 other states. Nevertheless, writing for the majority, Justice Scalia held that even the direct instruction of the court to protect a child (not actually in state custody) does not create a "special relationship" creating a "duty" whose violation gives rise to damage liability under 42 USC § 1983. Rather, police have discretion and that discretion is not subject to liability based on police decisions to act or not to act. The dissent argued that a court order or judgment is a "property interest" that may be effectively "taken" from a possessor without due process by police breach of a duty to perform, and thus constitutes a valid § 1983 claim. And it complained about the Court ignoring the judgment of Colorado state courts that the failure of the police violated a mandatory duty. The majority rather focused on the "manner" of enforcement, positing discretion as to the means and methods (apparently even where there were no means or methods).

c. "State Official" Immunity Under Federal 42 U.S.C. § 1983

Children may suffer tort injury from the negligent acts of state officials where there is a "duty of care" under *DeShaney* above. That duty may not extend to the failure to remove a child such as Joshua, or his improvident return to parents. But it may include damage to children entrusted to (and under the direct care) of schools, public child care (such as Head Start), or foster care providers. However, there remains a second level of defense for state employees with such a duty of care: "state immunity" from federal court liability exposure. In *Miller v. Gammie* below, the Ninth Circuit discussed at length the criteria for absolute or for qualified immunity for state officials in light of Supreme Court tangential precedents.

Miller v. Gammie
335 F.3d 889 (9th Cir. 2003)

SCHROEDER, Chief Judge.

* * *

In December 1996, the Nevada Division of Child and Family Services (DCFS) removed twelve-year-old Earl Doe and his older brother from their home to protect them from the horrific physical and sexual abuse they had suffered, and to prevent them from inflicting abuse on other children. DCFS placed them in an emergency foster-care facility. Defendant-Appellant Nancy Gammie, a DCFS social worker, was responsible for Earl's case, and Defendant-Appellant Fran Zito, a DCFS social therapist, provided therapy to Earl.

Soon after removing Earl from his home, DCFS petitioned the Nevada Juvenile Court to declare Earl a ward of the State and to grant DCFS custody. The juvenile court approved the removal and placed Earl into the custody of DCFS. A clearly troubled youth, Earl stumbled through foster care and eventually came to live in a Volunteers of America (VOA) emergency shelter.

In her six-month report to the juvenile court, Gammie elaborated on the extent of Earl's sexual-abuse history, informed the court of his current placement, and of her plan to place Earl "into a more homelike setting within the next few weeks." The juvenile court approved Gammie's recommendations.

On December 2, 1997, Gammie placed Earl into John and Jane Roe's home as a foster child. John and Jane were the parents of two young children, but Gammie did not tell the Roes about Earl's abusiveness. The next day, Gammie submitted her second six-month report to the juvenile court. In it, she reported Earl's placement in the Roes' home; however, she did not mention the Roes' young children. Gammie noted that Earl still required extensive therapy in order to deal with his past sexual abuse "and to reach the point of being safe with other children."

Zito treated Earl during his placement with John and Jane, who accompanied him to therapy sessions. It was revealed to Zito that Earl had both suffered sexual abuse in prior placements and had sexually abused others. Jane asked Zito if her natural children were safe with Earl in their home. Zito assured Jane that she had nothing to worry about.

According to the complaint, Earl's placement with John and Jane Roe was tragically unsuccessful. Only two months after Earl's placement, the Roes' son, Joe, informed his parents that Earl had molested him. Two days later, Earl was arrested and admitted to sodomizing Joe three to five times.

* * *

The civil-rights statute, 42 U.S.C. § 1983, was enacted in 1871. It enables those individuals whose rights were deprived by persons acting under color of state law to bring their claims in federal court. On its face, § 1983 does not include any defense of immunity. Nevertheless, the Supreme Court has recognized that when Congress enacted § 1983, it was aware of a well-established and well-understood common-law tradition that extended absolute immunity to individuals performing functions necessary to the judicial process....Thus, it was presumed that if Congress had wished to abrogate common-law immunity, it would have done so expressly.

The Supreme Court in *Imbler* laid down an approach that granted state actors absolute immunity only for those functions that were critical to the judicial process itself. See *Imbler*, 424 U.S. at 430....At common law, judges, prosecutors, trial witnesses, and jurors were absolutely immune for such critical functions....*Imbler* also settled the general scope and rationale of a prosecutor's immunity. Only in "initiating a prosecution and in presenting the State's case" is the prosecutor absolutely immune....

Our court has recognized that family-service social workers, like appellant Gammie in this case, appear to perform some functions similar to those of prosecutors, but perform other functions as well....We were careful there, however, to distinguish between a social worker's activities performed as an advocate within the judicial decision-making process, a function for which there is common-law absolute immunity, and other actions taken by a social worker. *Id.* at 1157. We found that unless the social worker's activity has the requisite connection to the judicial process, only qualified immunity is available..., to enjoy absolute immunity for a particular action, the official must be performing a duty functionally comparable to one for which officials were rendered immune at common law....We look to functions that enjoyed absolute immunity at common law in 1871, because that is when Congress codified § 1983.

* * *

Our decision in *Meyers* is consistent with the controlling Supreme Court decisions and...recognized absolute immunity for social workers only for the discretionary, quasi-prosecutorial decisions to institute court dependency proceedings to take custody away from parents....At least two of our sister circuits have also recognized that the scope of absolute immunity for social workers is extremely narrow....

* * *

Here, the district court was obligated to examine the functions Gammie and Zito performed; however, those functions were unclear. Moreover, the defendants bear the burden of showing that their respective common-law functional counterparts were absolutely immune. It would appear that the critical decision to institute proceedings to make a child a ward of the state is functionally similar to the prosecutorial institution of a criminal proceeding....To the extent, however, that social workers also make discretionary decisions and recommendations that are not functionally similar to prosecutorial or judicial decisions, only qualified, not absolute immunity, is available. Examples of such functions may include decisions and recommendations as to the particular home where a child is to go or as to the particular foster parents who are to provide care. On this record, we cannot make that determination. However, such placement decisions may not be "judicial" or "prosecutorial" decisions of the type that would have enjoyed common-law absolute immunity.

> The district court, therefore, must apply the guiding principles to the allegations concerning the defendants in this case. The therapist, Zito, allegedly provided only treatment and diagnosis. She apparently is not alleged to have performed any quasi-judicial or prosecutorial function that enjoyed absolute immunity at common law, unless discovery discloses that she performed other functions more directly related to the prosecution of the dependency proceedings.
>
> With respect to the social worker, Gammie, the precise functions performed that allegedly give rise to liability are not clear from the existing complaint....

* * *

Note on Public Employee Accountability Notwithstanding the Immunity Defense

Even absolute immunity requires that the action complained of be within the scope of the official duties conferring that immunity. Hence, an off-duty act separate and apart from official function, and pursued for personal or ancillary reasons, may not yield immunity from tort liability. And "qualified immunity" does not extend to "reckless disregard," and will generally allow substantial discovery prior to dismissal. In addition, the immunity discussed in *Gammie* above only applies to the personal liability for damages in federal court. Tort immunity for damages may not bar a federal action in equity (injunctive or declaratory relief) that may compel an agency to provide restitution or public officials to change policies and future actions. In 2012, the Ninth Circuit reversed a district court's dismissal of claims brought by foster youth against defendants including Clark County, Nevada and administrators and caseworkers within the County's Division of Child and Family Services. The district court had ruled that the defendants were entitled to qualified immunity against claims for both damages and injunctive relief. The Ninth Circuit found that the district court was "clearly wrong" in its analysis. First, a municipality such as Clark County cannot claim qualified immunity. Furthermore, qualified immunity is not an available defense against a claim for injunctive relief. Qualified immunity could be asserted as a defense by individual defendants against the claims for money damages, but only if the right allegedly violated was not clearly established at the time of the conduct in question. The Ninth Circuit unequivocally stated that it was well established at the time of the conduct that foster youth have a right to "reasonable safety and minimally adequate care and treatment" while in government custody.[14]

An "immunity bar" in federal court will not apply to a tort action against state officials and agencies in state court. Such immunity provisions in that forum (discussed below) will turn on state immunity statutes—which vary. And at the state court level, other remedies may also apply. For example, state public employees may also be sanctioned by their state or local agency through job dismissal or other employment sanction. In fact, they may be prosecuted criminally by state prosecutors. During 2011, several New York social workers were charged with criminal manslaughter for gross negligence in allowing the death of a foster child, including the alleged deliberate falsification of their records pertaining to the child. It was revealed that "Marchella Brett-Pierce...died a horrific death in September

2010, after being starved, dehydrated, beaten with household items and poisoned with over-the-counter medications over a period of months while tied to a bed in her grandmother's room, according to an indictment."[15]

A final accountability check, one that may underlie others, is sufficient transparency of the child protection system so the public is aware of dangers—particularly in the foster care area, where the state and federal jurisdictions have claimed a responsibility, and where those children who have been removed are in the care of state court judges exercising parental authority. Child advocates argue that when children such as Joshua DeShaney are not removed, the major check on state nonfeasance is from public examination, and cite studies indicating the more than half of children who die from neglect and abuse have been the subject of prior reports to local child protective service agencies about the endangerment of that child[16] (see Chapter 8 for discussion of confidentiality).

d. Summary and Checklist for Child-Related Tort Actions in Federal Court

Tort actions for damages may arise from an alleged intentional tort (*e.g.,* assault), negligence, or negligent supervision of one to whom a duty of supervision is owed. They may be brought against state officials or agencies, or against private persons or corporations (often based on product liability). They may be brought on behalf of a single child or on behalf of a class of children. Such tort actions are generally for damages in an action "at law" involving a jury trial. The defendant may occasionally be a child, although the case of Juliet Breitman—discussed above—is unusual.

In every case where a child seeks recovery, some adult must bring the action for the child, usually a parent or guardian. Foster children usually have *guardians ad litem* (GALs, often attorneys) but their scope of representation is usually limited to juvenile dependency court issues. But those GALs, or another person with standing, may petition the court to appoint counsel for the child where such a tort cause of action may lie.

Beyond a factual basis and counsel, the following issues form the checklist for counsel pursuing such a tort remedy for a child in federal court:

a) If the basis for liability is statutory, does it include a remedy for the child victim (*e.g.,* is it a regulatory statute where compliance depends upon federal refusal to provide matching funds, or some other remedy)? If brought under a federal statute, is the invoked standard of care also a precondition for the receipt of federal funds, and does the federal executive or legislative branch have the option of cutting off that funding if its preconditions are not met? Although the federal Department of Health and Human Services very rarely threatens or deprives states of federal monies—notwithstanding egregious violations of Congressionally enacted standards—that possible remedy is theoretically at play. As *Suter v. Artist M* in Chapter 1 indicates, courts will sometimes view that cut-off remedy as the only intended enforcement option, particularly where the Congressional standard is not specifically concrete and requires judicial construction.

b) Does the child have standing to sue (is he or she intended to be protected by the statutory standard)?

c) If the injury is small but widespread across many children and requiring class status, does the child client serve as an appropriate class representative (e.g., with claims typical of the class), and is there requisite commonality among the class? These elements are more difficult to satisfy where seeking damages in an action at law. If the class is nationwide, is there sufficient commonality in standards among the states, do those common issues "predominate," and is the class action mechanism both "manageable" and "superior" to alternative redress? If a federal statute is not central, is there requisite diversity for jurisdiction on that basis?

d) Is the defendant a state agency or a state official, where the wrong is either the result of a discretionary decision, or one where that official is protected by absolute or qualified immunity?

e) If the negligence or wrong is not an affirmative act, but the result of a failure to act or supervise, does the potential defendant have a relevant duty to that child or those children, e.g., a "special relationship"? Is it a violation that constitutes a denial of rights under 42 U.S.C. § 1983?

f) Is the act or failure to act "foreseeable" as a cause of the injury that occurred?

g) What is the mechanism to pay counsel? If the action is based on violation of a statute, is it a "fee shifting" statute (such as § 1983)? If not, will a substantial fund be created to compensate counsel on a "percentage of common fund" basis? If neither of these options is available, attorneys' fees may not be available.

Importantly, these questions do not end the inquiry. As discussed above, other options include an action "in equity" for injunctive and declaratory relief—where class certification is much more easily achieved (see Chapter 1 discussion). And where the defendant is a state agency or official, options include public revelation and pressure on the federal jurisdiction to impose federal funding cuts as a sanction. Finally, one may pursue remedies in state court—where the impediments may be fewer, as discussed below.

e. Child-Related Tort Action in State Court

Many, but not all, of the checklist barriers listed above also apply to a tort action brought in state court. However, a remedy for a child victim may be more easily found to be implied in a statutory standard—because we do not here have the "fund cut-off" available to federal agencies as an alternative remedy. Similarly, states will not present the same immunity issues that suit against a state agency in federal court may pose, and immunity for public officials will turn on state law—which is often less protective than the federal standard discussed above.

Note also that most states will reproduce federal statutes, including applicable standards for state officials, within their own statutes—in order to be certain they qualify for the federal funds authorized by the federal version. Accordingly, a federal court may hold that the statute does not provide a private remedy, or that children are not specifically protected, or that the standard in the statute is too broad to permit federal judicial intervention and substitution of judicial judgment. But state courts are less constrained in the interpretation of their own statutes.

Similarly, a class action tort case involving an allegedly injurious or dangerous product, or state governmental policy, may enjoy easier certification. This is especially the case where the class is confined to the state where it is brought; *e.g.*, it need not confront variations between states undermining commonality. As noted above, class actions in state court generally allow certification much more liberally for those seeking injunctive or declaratory relief in equity than those that seek damages at law. Fees may be somewhat easier in the state jurisdiction, because in addition to the possible "fee shift" statute, and the generally allowed percentage from a "common fund" of monies collected for the class, some states have an additional source of fees: "attorney general" fees. This allows fees where the action involves risk, benefits a group beyond the named plaintiffs, and vindicates important public rights. This third option may allow not only market level fees, but sometimes a "multiplier" beyond that level to reward counsel who obtained an extraordinary result under difficult circumstances (see discussion in Chapter 1).

As with the federal court options, state court alternatives to a standard tort damage filing may include the equity class action noted above, or other options. One such option where the defendants are public officials is simply an individual action on behalf of a child or several named children in the form of a petition for mandamus or injunctive or declaratory relief action in equity that may function in practice as a broad remedy (binding a county or state). If a court order changes a public practice as to a named defendant, it may directly (or in practice) alter it in general. And options beyond direct court filing discussed above may also exist here: public pressure to force employee training, dismissals, ombudsman checks, or criminal prosecution by the state attorney general or a district attorney.

Two categories of defendants warrant special attention because they most often care for children: state and local child protection systems (including intake and foster and child care providers who are compensated by the state) and schools. Beyond federal court suit, class action formats, and options in equity, what are the obstacles to their tort liability from an individual tort action by a child for damages? The most formidable defenses to an individual child's action in tort for damages (from negligent supervision, violation of statutory standards, or other cause of injury) commonly involve issues of immunity, duty, and foreseeability.

Such standard tort suits may be brought in state court against state officials or foster care providers where children are harmed. However, the legal status of foster care providers whose negligence is often at issue is unclear. Some jurisdictions treat such providers as "state employees" or agents, affording access to public resources for compensation and treatment. Others regard foster parents as "independent contractors," in which case recovery may depend upon required or extant insurance coverage by these defendants. In addition, foster parents may receive the partial protection of "parental immunity" status given their parental role, as discussed above.[17]

But compare *DeShaney* to the subsequent New York appellate case of *Boland v. State*, 638 N.Y.S.2d 500 (1996), holding that the state had an intrinsic "special relationship" with the victims of child abuse and was not entitled to immunity for a failure to report child abuse for investigation. In *Boland*, a neighbor reported the suspected abuse of two children by a grandparent who was caring for them while their father was overseas. The report, made on the state's child protection "hotline" was assigned to the wrong county, and the investigation was delayed for two days— during which one of the children was beaten to death. The child's father filed an action and the appellate court held that there was a "special relationship" imposing a duty on the state to exercise due care through the enactment of a statutory scheme to protect children, and including its reporting investigation mechanism. When the state's child protective intake worker deemed the allegations a qualified "abuse report," she assumed a duty to protect the children (including a reliance by the person making the report), and a failure to discharge it could be a basis for state liability where a failure to act was a proximate cause of the child's injuries.

The injury or danger must be "foreseeable" for tort liability. An unforeseeable criminal act by a third party that injures a child in care may result in dismissal. For example, in *J.L. v. Children's Institute, Inc.*, 177 Cal. App. 4th 388 (2009), defendant CII arranged child care with licensed providers in Los Angeles County. The families selected the provider from among 45 alternative homes. In 1997, Yolanda Yglesias provided care for up to 6 children from 0–4 years of age. CII checked each provider, including Yglesias, twice a month. D.L placed her infant son J.L. there, but on one occasion noticed two older males on the premises, as well as a 14-year-old boy identified by Yglesias as her grandson. CII's caseworker Ramirez also saw the boy on the premises. On August 15, 2005, the teenage boy raped and sodomized J.L. Yglesias surrendered her day care license. The case against CII was dismissed not on the grounds of immunity or lack of duty, but because the tort was "unforeseeable" by CII—there was no information or basis for believing that the 14-year-old posed any danger, nor was there apparently any negligent supervision during the attack itself.

The other major group vulnerable to tort suit for injuries to children includes schools and school officials with whom children spend much of their time. One case (with multiple companion cases) illustrates the occasional extreme empathy lines of courts in the direction of school official dispensation. In *P.S. v. San Bernardino City Unified School District*, 174 Cal. App. 4th 953 (2009), and three other companion cases, the California Court of Appeal for the Fourth District specified a requirement that the minor be in the care of the school. P.S. was a first grade student within the Central School District in Rancho Cucamonga. A substitute teacher engaged in unlawful touching, including having her sit on his lap for sexual gratification. Three other students had similar complaints at the same school. The year prior, the same substitute teacher similarly touched another student in another school district and he was permanently barred there, and earlier in the same year he did it again in a second school district, where he was also banned. Rancho Cucamonga was then his third school in two years. The complaint alleged that the first two districts had a statutory, mandated duty to report the substitute teacher to child protective services so others could be warned, and failed to do so. The appellate court held that the mandated Reporting Act "reasonably construed,...was intended to protect only those children in the custodial care of the person charged with reporting the abuse and not all children who may at some future time be abused by the same offender" (at 961).

Questions for Discussion

1. Would it make a difference in the *J.L.* case above if the 14-year-old offender had a juvenile record of assaults? Foster care premises are required to engage in a records check of all persons who may have regular contact with the children in their care. Would the failure to make such a check confer liability if it would have yielded notice of a prior arrest or offense? Under what circumstances would that failure be properly imputed to CII, as the entity arranging, recommending, and monitoring the providers? Does it have a duty to supervise such compliance, and would such a failure constitute "negligent supervision?"

2. The *P.S.* decision above limits liability for failure to comply with a mandated reporting requirement—excluding all those outside of the reporting entity's care as an intended beneficiary of the system. These reporting statutes are common in all fifty states (see discussion of the *Stritzinger* case in Chapter 8). The court explains the purported legislative intent behind the reporting statute: "Under plaintiff's interpretation of the Reporting Act, a child care custodian that fails to report suspected child abuse could be held liable, perhaps years later, to any other children abused by the same offender..."(at 962). Query, isn't that the very purpose of a reporting system? What is its purpose if not to protect future and other children? What is the relevance of a reporting system to the originators of the report, who already know of the problem and have dismissed the offender—releasing him to other victims?

4. Child Tort Recovery—Insurance Coverage

J.C. Penney Casualty Insurance Co. v. M.K.
52 Cal. 3d 1009 (1991)

OPINION: EAGLESON, J.

* * *

FACTS

In September 1984, M.K., then a five-year-old girl, told her mother, S.K., that the girl had been sexually molested by an adult male neighbor, R.H....He was a friend of the mother and had often babysat the girl. R.H. was charged with eight counts of willfully committing lewd or lascivious acts with a child under the age of fourteen years in violation of Penal Code section 288, subdivision (a).[2] R.H. pled guilty to one count in a plea bargain that dismissed the other seven counts. He was sentenced to prison for six years.

Before the molestations, J.C. Penney Casualty Insurance Company (hereafter J.C. Penney) had issued to R.H. a comprehensive homeowner's policy that provided liability insurance....

* * *

The mother and child filed an action for damages against R.H. in June 1985, alleging causes of action in negligence and intentional tort. R.H. admitted to fondling the girl's genitals with his hands, holding the girl over his head with his thumb inserted into her vagina, and orally copulating her. A medical examination confirmed vaginal penetration, which caused a ruptured hymen, and possible anal penetration.

Before trial the mother and child dismissed all causes of action for intentional tort and proceeded to trial only on theories of negligence and negligent infliction of emotional distress. At the start of the mother and child's case, R.H. stipulated that he had been negligent as to the child. Based on that stipulation, the court entered a directed verdict in the child's action that R.H. was negligent. The issue of R.H.'s negligence as to the mother was submitted to the jury, which in special verdicts found that R.H. was negligent and that his negligence was a legal cause of damage to the mother.[3] The jury awarded $400,000 to the child and $100,000 to the mother.

J.C. Penney's declaratory relief action was tried in May 1987. The trial court received evidence as to R.H.'s state of mind when he molested the child. More specifically, R.H. testified in deposition, admitting the following: "*Question*: You intended to do what you did, correct? *Answer*: Yes....*Question*: And you knew at the time you were doing these things that they were wrong; Isn't that correct? *Answer*: Yes, I knew it was wrong *Question*: And after most of these incidents, you would generally go to the bathroom to relieve yourself? *Answer*: Generally, yes. *Question*: Sexually? *Answer*: Yes. *Question*: Because you were aroused by what had happened? *Answer*: Yes." R.H. also testified, however, that he did not intend to harm the child, and a psychologist testified likewise as to R.H.'s intent.

* * *

DISCUSSION

I. Effect of the underlying judgment against the insured

* * *

We reiterate the rule that an insurer that timely and adequately reserves its right to deny coverage and that does not subsequently intentionally waive its reservation of rights is not collaterally estopped by a judgment in favor of a third party against its insured. J.C. Penney is not collaterally estopped to deny coverage in this action for declaratory relief.

II. No coverage for sexual molestation of a child

We turn now to the primary issue addressed by the parties and numerous amici curiae: Is liability coverage for R.H.'s molestations of a child excluded by the terms of the insurance policy and Insurance Code section 533? J.C. Penney contends coverage is excluded because the molestations were intentional. Defendants respond that even an intentional and wrongful act is not excluded from coverage unless the insured acted with a "preconceived design to inflict injury." They contend psychiatric testimony shows that molesters, including R.H., often intend no harm despite the depravity of their acts, and that the molestation is often a misguided attempt to display love and affection for the child....

We conclude there is no coverage as a matter of law. No rational person can reasonably believe that sexual fondlings, penetration, and oral copulation of a five-year-old child are nothing more than acts of tender mercy. Except in the present case, every court to decide this issue under California law has held that a homeowner's insurance policy does not provide liability coverage for child molestation. The courts of many other states also have considered the issue and, almost without exception, have held there is no coverage.

A. Insurance Code section 533

Insurance Code section 533 provides that an insurer is not liable for a "wilful act of the insured."...Section 533 is "an implied exclusionary clause which by statute is to be read into all insurance policies."...As we will explain, section 533 excludes liability insurance coverage for child molestation.[8]

* * *

Section 533 states that, "An insurer is not liable for a loss caused by the *willful* act of the insured; but he is not exonerated by the negligence of the insured, or of the insured's agents or others." (Italics added.)...The statutory language sheds little light on the precise question before us. (Nor is there any legislative history to assist us.) Read literally, section 533 is internally inconsistent. Its first sentence purports to exclude coverage for all willful acts. The second sentence, however, expressly provides that the insured's negligence does not allow an insurer to disclaim coverage.

Negligence is often, perhaps generally, the result of a "willful act," as the term is commonly understood.[11] For example, "An ordinary consequence of driving an automobile without the exercise of ordinary care or an intentional violation of a statute (speed in excess of the maximum speed limit), is injury to the person or property of the driver or a third person. Certainly no one would contend that an injury occasioned by negligent or even reckless driving was not accidental within the meaning of a policy of accident insurance...." ..."It is settled that 'wilful act' in section 533 means 'something more than the mere intentional doing of an act constituting [ordinary] negligence.'"...A contrary rule would allow an insurer to deny coverage for a negligent act. That result is specifically prohibited by section 533. We long ago construed section 533's statutory predecessor (former Civ. Code, § 2629) as establishing that "[N]o form of negligence on the part of the insured, or his agents or others, leading to a loss avoids the policy, unless it amounts to a willful act on the part of the insured. The code thereby sets at rest a fruitful cause of litigation."....

In short, section 533 does not preclude coverage for acts that are negligent or reckless. We find nothing in the statute, however, to support defendants' view that a child molester can disclaim an intent to harm his victim. There is no such thing as negligent or even reckless sexual molestation. The very essence of child molestation is the gratification of sexual desire. The act is the harm. There cannot be one without the other. Thus, the intent to molest is, by itself, the same as the intent to harm.

B. Our prior decisions
The reasoning of prior decisions under section 533 also makes clear that the statute precludes coverage for child molestation. The public policy underlying section 533 is to discourage willful torts....In addition to being a crime, child molestation is indisputably a willful tort against the child. Defendants, however, contend our decision in *Clemmer v. Hartford Insurance Co., supra*, 22 Cal.3d 865 (*Clemmer*), mandates coverage unless the insurer can prove its insured acted with a "preconceived design to inflict injury."...Based on their view of *Clemmer* defendants contend psychiatric testimony should be allowed to establish that the insured lacked such a "preconceived design."...

Clemmer, supra, 22 Cal.3d 865, arose from the killing of a physician (Dr. Clemmer) by his employee (Dr. Lovelace) after an employment dispute between them. The court stated the key facts as follows: "[Dr. Lovelace] greeted Dr. Clemmer, then shot him twice. These shots were followed by two more shots. Finally, Dr. Lovelace knelt close to the victim and at close range shot him in the head. The gun was placed on the ground. Dr. Lovelace remarked that he knew what he was doing and that Dr. Clemmer was destroying him professionally." (*Id.* at p. 872.) Dr. Lovelace was convicted of second degree murder.

* * *

....We also stated, however, that even an intentional act is not excluded from coverage under section 533 unless the act is done with a "'preconceived design to inflict injury.'"...The quoted language is the linchpin of defendants' case. They argue that coverage for child sexual molestation is not excluded unless the insurer can show that the molester had a "preconceived design to inflict injury" on the child. In their view, the intent to molest is not enough.

Clemmer, supra, 22 Cal.3d 865, does not support defendants' contention. The brief reference in *Clemmer* to a "preconceived design to inflict injury" must be read in context. The inquiry in *Clemmer* was limited to the unresolved *mental capacity* of the insured, *i.e* , whether he was legally sane when he committed the killing. There was no issue as to whether the insured intended to shoot his victim five times (including once in the head at close range) but not to harm the victim....

* * *

[2] Penal Code section 288, subdivision (a), states: "Any person who shall willfully and lewdly commit any lewd or lascivious act including any of the acts constituting other crimes provided for in Part 1 of this code upon or with the body, or any part or member thereof, of a child under the age of 14 years, with the intent of arousing, appealing to, or gratifying the lust or passions or sexual desires of that person or of the child, shall be guilty of a felony and shall be imprisoned in the state prison for a term of three, six, or eight years."

[8] The insurance policy issued to R.H. also contains an explicit exclusion of "bodily injury or property damage which is either expected or intended from the standpoint of the insured."....J.C. Penney relies on both the explicit exclusion and section 533....Section 533 reflects a fundamental public policy of denying coverage for willful wrongs....The parties to an insurance policy therefore cannot contract for such coverage. (Civ. Code, § 1667.) We therefore need not and do not decide whether coverage would be excluded by the explicit policy exclusion in the absence of section 533.

[11] Indeed, it is hornbook tort law that an act "is a voluntary contraction of the muscles, and nothing more....When 'act' is used in this sense, it is tautological to speak of a 'voluntary act,' and self-contradictory to speak of an 'involuntary act,' since every act is voluntary." (Prosser & Keeton, The Law of Torts (5th ed. 1984) § 8, pp. 34–35.)

LUCAS, C.J., MOSK, J., PANELLI, J., KENNARD, J., and ARABIAN, J., concurred.

BROUSSARD, J. —I dissent.

Our courts have long enforced insurance contracts for intentional and criminal acts causing injury. Rather than read Insurance Code section 533...as precluding insurance for any willful act of the insured causing injury, such as intentionally speeding or running a red light, this court has interpreted the provision as only prohibiting enforcement of contracts insuring a person from losses intentionally caused. Thus in *Clemmer v. Hartford Insurance Co.* (1978) 22 Cal.3d 865..., this court pointed out the "clear line of authority in this state to the effect that even an act which is 'intentional' or 'willful' within the meaning of traditional tort principles will not exonerate the insurer from liability under Insurance Code section 533 unless it is done with a 'preconceived design to inflict injury.'...."

The majority repudiate *Clemmer.* They hold that section 533 prohibits a person from insuring against conduct that is "inherently harmful."...The opinion's construction of the provision finds no support in the language of the provision. Such a construction fails to give sufficient consideration to the interest and rights of the innocent victims of child abuse and other crimes. The construction flies in the face of our constitutional command for the "enactment of comprehensive provisions and laws ensuring a bill of rights for victims of crime..." (Cal. Const., art. I, § 28, subd. (a).) In addition, the majority's construction opens a Pandora's box such that insureds and insurers cannot know which promises of the insurer are enforceable.

The majority hold that the insured's intent to harm must be inferred from acts of child molestation because they are inherently harmful....In view of the undisputed expert testimony in this case as well as some others that the child molester may have intended no harm, the majority appear to be practicing psychiatry without a license and doing a terrible job of it.

* * *

A vague test based on degrees of blameworthiness would be so difficult to administer justly that it should be rejected out-of-hand. Attempting to draw a line between misdemeanors or between felonies on the basis of reprehensibility or repugnance on a case-by-case basis can only bring confusion and uncertainty to insurance law.

In any event, we rejected such a test in *Peterson v. Superior Court, supra,* 31 Cal.3d 147, 158–159. In that case we held that an intoxicated driver could be liable for punitive damages when it is shown that he performed an act from which he knows, or should know, it is highly probable that harm will result. Obviously, punitive damages are permitted only in cases involving the most reprehensible and repugnant conduct. In addition to the great likelihood of harm, which in fact occurred, the conduct was criminal. While we held that punitive damages may not be indemnified, we also held that section 533 would not be applicable to bar indemnification of compensatory damages for conduct involving an extreme degree of blameworthiness.

A "wilful" act or loss is a reference to subjective intent, and, absent a clear showing of legislative intent to the contrary, it cannot reasonably be interpreted to establish tests of "inherently harmful." In short, the test established by the majority opinion finds no support in the language of the code section and must be rejected for this reason alone. To read "inherently harmful" into this straightforward statute can only be categorized as judicial legislation.[1]

Since there is no history or strong public policy indicating that the Legislature inadvertently used the language it chose, the plain language of the code section should end the case.

Moreover, even if there was some ambiguity in the language of the code section permitting it to be reasonably construed to prohibit insurance of "inherently harmful" conduct, considerations of the interests and rights of the innocent victims of child abuse and other crimes should preclude our doing so.

Liability insurance serves two functions in our society. It not only provides a fund that the wrongdoer may resort to in order to meet his just obligation, but also provides compensation for the victims of wrongful and criminal conduct. Often, the wrongdoer's insurance is the only way the innocent victims of crime, including child molestation, may recover compensation for medical expenses, their disabilities and their injuries. Particularly as to child molesters, the wrongdoers are likely to be incarcerated for lengthy periods of time (see Pen. Code, §§ 288, subd. (a), 1170.1), and there is little likelihood that a judgment recovered against the wrongdoer can be collected out of the wrongdoer's earnings. The wrongdoer will ordinarily be faced with substantial legal expenses depleting whatever assets he may have had. Liability insurers ordinarily pay to the innocent victim rather than the insured, so there is little danger that the wrongdoer insured will fatten his pocket from the insurance.

Concern for the innocent victims of crime outweighs the policy of deterrence or penalizing the wrongdoer and strongly militates against an interpretation expanding section 533's prohibition of insurance coverage....

If there were any doubt as to the proper balance of competing policies, it is set at rest by our Constitution. Article I, section 28, subdivision (a) commands the "enactment of comprehensive provisions and laws ensuring a bill of rights for victims of crime." When we indulge in judicial legislation, we should observe the mandates of our Constitution applicable to legislation.

* * *

II

Upon analysis, the majority theory that we must infer intent to harm from child abuse fares no better. We cannot properly infer from child molestation the intent to harm as a matter of law in the face of an overwhelming record establishing that there was no intent to harm or even in the absence of such a record. Penal Code section 288, subdivision (a) provides: "Any person who shall willfully and lewdly commit any lewd or lascivious act including any of the acts constituting other crimes provided for in Part 1 of this code upon or with the body, or any part or member thereof, of a child under the age of 14 years, with the *intent* of arousing, appealing to, or gratifying the lust or passions or sexual desires of that *person or of the child* shall be guilty of a felony...." (Italics added.)

It is clear from the italicized portion of the code section that child molestation under the section is based on the intent of the wrongdoer and that the wrongdoer may be guilty of the crime on the basis of gratifying his lust or sexual desires without regard to those of the victim. Until today, at least, neither harm to the child nor intent to harm the child was an element of the offense. Accordingly, the insured's guilty plea to one count of child molestation does not establish intent to injure.

The physical acts of child molestation are not detailed in the statute; rather, the crucial factor is the intent of the actor. The physical acts may be of a wide variety, including acts which are commonly engaged in for medical or hygienic purposes by parents, siblings, and pediatricians. However, when such acts are done with the specified intent, the conduct is criminal. The point is illustrated by the instant case where 25 of the acts of child molestation occurred while the insured was playing with the child. He touched or fondled her vaginal area while she was fully clothed. Absent criminal intent, the physical conduct would be entirely innocent. I cannot agree that the physical conduct is "inherently harmful" or that we must as a matter of law infer from such conduct, even when coupled with an intent to gratify sexual desires, that there was an intent to harm.

The expert testimony was all to the effect that there was no intent to harm. The majority opinion quotes the statements from other cases that such testimony "flies 'in the face of all reason, common sense, and experience' and is 'inherently incredible.'"... There is nothing in our record to justify this shocking attack on the science of psychiatry. Neither the majority opinion nor the cited authorities provide any empirical evidence for such an attack, and the experience involved is that of child molesters and those who work with child molesters, not judges. In the absence of experience, judges should not undertake to practice psychiatry. The opinion also states that the psychiatric testimony was "irrelevant"...but, as pointed out above, much of the physical conduct was not inherently harmful. It consisted of physical acts which, if done without criminal intent, would be lawful and innocent and not harmful at all. I do not find any reasonable basis to reject the expert testimony, and we should not do so.

III
* * *

When insurers have collected premiums and agreed to indemnify liability imposed for child molestation, we should require them to perform their promises. The interests and rights of the innocent victims of child abuse preclude our exonerating such insurers.

[1] The majority tell us that they decide only the wrongdoing before us, child molestation....However, we can only expect that insurers will deny coverage in all or substantially all cases involving criminal conduct. All criminal conduct is "repugnant and reprehensible," and it will be for the courts to determine whether the particular conduct is so "repugnant and reprehensible" as to preclude insurance coverage.

Questions for Discussion

1. If an adult is raped by an insured person, recovery from the policy is not categorically barred. If an adult's house is burned to the ground in an act of apparent arson, recovery is not barred. If an adult (as in the *Clemmer* case) is shot twice in the head by the insured, and then twice more for good measure, insurance recovery may be possible. On what basis is the molestation of a child uniquely selected for coverage exclusion? Would such exclusion extend to sexual intercourse with a 17-year-old?

2. The statute and public policy impose an insurance coverage bar where there is a "preconceived design to inflict injury." Notwithstanding serious error, is it possible for a person to subjectively believe that fondling a child does not inflict injury? Is a "design to inflict injury" not more likely where the insured fires four bullets into a victim's head, as in *Clemmer*—where the court holds that coverage is possible?

3. One policy behind the coverage bar for intentional torts is to avoid indemnifying and perhaps stimulating tortious behavior. Is it likely that child molestation is driven by possible insurance coverage? Of all the possible tortious or criminal acts (arson, homicide, battery, *et al.*) is any of them less likely to be influenced one way or the other by insurance coverage than a lewd act on a child?

4. In *Minkler v. Safeco Insurance Company of America*, 49 Cal. 4th 315 (2010), the California Supreme Court held that coverage applies to a mother whose son molested a child, notwithstanding an exclusion for "intentional acts." The policy had a clause making the policy apply separately to each of several insureds. Accordingly, the bar for "intentional acts" may exclude coverage for the son, but not for the mother. Note that an insurance policy will not normally cover intentional torts—by the insured. But it will by third parties where the insured has negligently failed to supervise. Query, can the insurance industry undermine this coverage by refusing to provide policies that provide "separate" insurance coverage for those who are insured?

5. Note those implications after *Brandon S. v. State of California*, 174 Cal. App. 4th 815 (2009), where the Court of Appeal for the Second District foreclosed the application of the Foster Family Home and Small Family Home Insurance Fund based on a standard phrase excluding "intentional acts" that child advocates contend obviously refers to an exclusion for intentional acts *by the insured*. The case involved an intentional assault by the stepson of a foster parent on a foster child. Normally, negligent supervision is covered by policies and by such state funds, which are created because of now prevalent private insurer policies of blanket foster care liability exclusion. How is such negligent supervision insurable if it excludes any "intentional act" resulting in injury—by any third party at all? *E.g.*, assume a foster parent leaves an 11-year-old girl on a street corner in the highest crime area of a city overnight. She is assaulted by someone committing an intentional tort. If negligence is a basis for coverage, why should recovery for the child be denied because the injury was caused by an assault, rather than by, for example, the same child abandoned overnight under a bridge in 10 degree weather with a disabling injury occurring as a result? What is the policy rationale for a public fund's coverage of supervision negligence for the latter injury, but not the former?

6. In *Prince v. United National Insurance Company*, 142 Cal. App. 4th 233 (2006), the California Court of Appeal for the Second District upheld an insurance exclusion precluding coverage for two children who died after being left in a hot vehicle for six hours by their foster parent. The policy covers foster parent negligence resulting in injury to a child, but excludes injury "arising out of the ownership, maintenance, use or entrustment to others of any auto...operated by...any insured" (at 236). The court held that the deaths arose out of the "use" of the vehicle because they were in the car, and merely being in it was a form of "use." The cause of death was the dangerous confluence of sunlight on closed automobile windows, raising temperatures to fatal levels—a cause of many infant deaths in the United States. Did the characteristics of the car causing the deaths here have anything to do with the operation of the car as a "vehicle?" Should that have been relevant? Should the rule that adhesive provisions in contracts, particularly insurance policies, be interpreted strictly against the drafter apply to such an exclusion?

ENDNOTES

[1] *E.g.,* see discussion in *In Re Scott K.,* 24 Cal. 3d 395 (1979).

[2] *U.S. v. Morse,* 218 U.S. 493 (1910).

[3] For example: "'[M]inors are treated differently from adults in our laws, which reflects the simple truth derived from communal experience that juveniles as a class have not the level of maturation and responsibility that we presume in adults and consider desirable for full participation in the rights and duties of modern life.' ... Adolescents 'are more vulnerable, more impulsive, and less self-disciplined than adults,' and are without the same 'capacity to control their conduct and to think in long-range terms.'" *Stanford v. Kentucky,* 492 U.S. 361, 395 (1989) (dis. opn. of Brennan, J.).

[4] *Menagh v. Breitman,* 2010 NY Slip Op. 32892U, 2010 N.Y. Misc. LEXIS 5039 at 3, citing the 1928 case of *Camardo v. New York State Rys.,* 247 N.Y. 111, 159 N.E. 879 (1928).

[5] See discussion in *Nielsen v. Bell,* 2016 UT 14 (2016).

[6] *Id.*

[7] *Hewellette v. George,* 68 Miss. 703 (1891).

[8] *See, e.g., Roller v. Roller,* 37 Wash. 242 (1905).

[9] *See, e.g., Gibson v. Gibson,* 3 Cal. 3d 914 (1971).

[10] *See, e.g.,* the precedent set in *Ferriter v. Daniel O'Connell's Sons,* 381 Mass. 507 (1980).

[11] *See, e.g.,* federal recognition in *Bonbrest v. Kotz,* 65 F. Supp. 138 (D.D.C. 1946); note its incorporation into the 1977 Restatement of Torts.

[12] *Grodin v Grodin,* 102 Mich App 396 (1980).

[13] It is well established that once the state takes custody of a child, the state agency has a duty to ensure "reasonable safety and minimally adequate care and treatment..." *Lipscomb,* 962 F.2d 1379 (9th Cir. 1992) at 1379. See also *Doe v. New York City Department of Social Services,* 649 F.2d 134, 141-42 (2d Cir. 1981), *Taylor ex rel. Walker,* 818 F.2d at 797; *Meador v. Cabinet for Human Resources,* 902 F.2d 474, 476 (6th Cir. 1990); *Yvonne L. ex rel. Lewis v. N.M. Dep't of Human Servs.,* 959 F.2d 883, 892-93 (10th Cir. 1992); *Norfleet ex rel. Norfleet v. Ark. Dep't of Human Servs.,* 989 F.2d 289, 293 (8th Cir. 1993); *Nicini v. Morra,* 212 F.3d 798, 808 (3d Cir. 2000).

[14] *Henry A. v. Wilden,* 678 F. 3d 991 (9th Cir. 2012).

[15] See http://www.reuters.com/article/2011/03/23/us-child-abuse-idUSTRE72M9BE20110323.

[16] See Children's Advocacy Institute, *State Secrecy and Child Deaths in the United States,* 2nd edition (University of San Diego School of Law, San Diego, CA; 2012), available at http://www.caichildlaw.org/Misc/State_Secrecy_Final_Report_Apr24.pdf.

[17] However, note the contradictory limited status of foster care providers in leading cases (see *Smith v. OFFER* and related cases discussed in Chapter 8). Such providers are allegedly performing an "escrow holding" function for the state and are denied constitutional parental status, *e.g.,* denied the right to hearing where assigned foster children are removed from their custody.

CHAPTER THIRTEEN

Child Civil Liberties:
Speech and Religion

A. THE CONTEXT OF CONSTITUTIONAL LAW FOR CHILDREN

Children suffer from three disadvantages in securing constitution-based First Amendment protection: (1) "state action" asymmetry; (2) lack of access to court redress; and (3) child immaturity as a permitted distinction.

1. The "State Action" Requirement and Private Power Disadvantage

As discussed briefly in Chapter 1, the substantive constitutional guarantees of the first eight amendments originally focused on the feared federal government, seeking to limit it *vis-à-vis* the citizenry. They have been extended through the 14th Amendment also to assure individual liberties as against state governments. This requirement of "state action" to invoke protection necessarily excludes purely private parties and institutions. Some sources of such private power may operate with coercive force: from a one-company town monopoly to adult control of a child. Children suffer extraordinary disadvantage in their private bargaining power. They are subservient to the private power of adult parents, protectors, advocates, and others. Where suffering harm in their care, or from third parties or commercial exploitation or injury, children rely on the state for protection—via statutes or executive or judicial intervention. As noted above, federal and state constitutional prescriptions limit *this*, not the private power of the citizenry. Hence, the constitution functions substantially in a one-way direction for children: since they are most affected by private power abuse, constitutional limitations on the state may impede their sole remedy (state action against adults who may be their abusers). Although the state possesses extensive police powers properly subject to internal check, the state can also be a check itself to moderate private power abuse on behalf of an otherwise powerless population.

Related to "state action" asymmetry is the fact that constitutional doctrine tends to apply in the negative, to stop state intrusions rather than to compel state action. So, for example, if the basic economic or social rights of children were part of a nation's founding document (as is the case with many of the European constitutions, or would pertain if the U.S. were to ratify the Convention on the Rights of the Child), the state may be affirmatively compelled to act. For example, were children to be afforded the assured protection of minimal sustenance for survival, health care, or the right to a parental relationship, such rights could trigger an affirmative state action obligation. Our constitutional structure is not so framed.

2. Access to and Resources for Constitutional Enforcement

Even where constitutional concepts may apply to protect children, they are not effective without a mechanism to enforce them. Enforcement depends upon judicial action. As discussed in Chapter 1, the judiciary itself is passive, and depends upon public officials or private parties to bring matters before it for decision. Hence, access to its offices and the ability to obtain a judicial result substantially determine the efficacy of theoretical rights. Few public officials are assigned the task of vindicating the constitutional rights of children. And the federal courts have acted to limit constitutional enforcement where it has been attempted. The list of court-created impediments to constitutional court protection include:

- constitutional doctrines requiring justiciability, standing (a personal stake), and ripeness;[1]
- initial dismissal where moot, not a real "case or controversy," or where a dispute is in the nature of an "advisory opinion";[2]
- a series of decisions hostile to class certification, including requirements that common questions predominate, adequacy of representation, and "superiority" as a means of redress, et al. (see Chapter 1); and
- the refusal to grant "private attorney general" attorney's fees to counsel (provided by some states to counsel who prevail on behalf of a large group of persons where the outcome vindicates major constitutional principles in the public interest).[3]

Each of these doctrines has its own rationale, generally unrelated to child rights. When combined, they have a substantial impact on the access to the courts of those who are powerless, unorganized, inarticulate, and without resources. The interests of children are substantially affected by these limitations.

According to child advocates, constitutional private enforcement for children, including use of federal civil rights statutes, may be further limited by additional practical barriers discussed in Chapter 1, including the failure to include children as a "protected" group for equal protection purposes; state bar policies prohibiting "solicitation of clients" in the context of a client group often unable to solicit counsel; minimal budgets for legal aid attorneys (particularly where interest rates decline given legal aid dependency on interest income from state bar trust funds); some continuing restrictions on legal aid representation in class action formats; expansion of state "sovereign immunity" and contraction of "interstate commerce" definitions to inhibit federal jurisdiction; the lack of assigned legal representation for children outside of delinquency proceedings and some dependency proceedings; and the representation of many children in dependency proceedings by counsel for the county who, due to conflicts of interest, may be unable to mount a constitutional challenge to county or state policies.

Suggestions to improve access to the judiciary for children include creation of a federal, state, or independent agency with standing to represent children, including the vindication of their constitutional rights, and financed separately from other agencies that might require such judicial check. Also, constitutional or statutory provision could allow standing and attorney fee recompense for private vindication of constitutional rights (see Chapter 1 discussion of the *Serrano* private attorney general doctrine in California).

Child advocates argue that a judiciary cognizant of the elevated status of constitutional principles will bend toward their vindication, particularly on behalf of a population least able to provide its own remedy or to reach the court's protective jurisdiction by its own devices. The courts have reached far for some other groups to accomplish this end, for example, creating the exclusionary rule to sanction police acts violative of Fourth Amendment constitutional standards. Children have not often been the beneficiary of such judicial reach; child advocates contend that they have rather suffered from judicial "adult-centrism," and from antipathy toward large lawsuits, new and different parties, or unfamiliar functioning.

3. The Maturity Dilemma

The immaturity of children undeniably complicates the application of constitutional principles to them. Children are adults-in-progress. Even the most ardent child advocate acknowledges that the First Amendment rights of *any* two-year-old may not rise to the level of those accorded *any* adult. Indeed, many constitutional rights, *e.g.*, the right to worship the religion of our choice, may substantially be subsumed within a parental right. For example, most advocates would agree that such a parental right to require Sunday School might supersede the often child-preferred choice of morning cartoons. Even if constitutional religious rights (to worship or not to worship) applied to private action and could limit parents as such, the undeniable status of parents as having custody and control of their children within a family unit implies an authority to make decisions on their behalf.

Recognizing the immaturity of children does not, however, eliminate the application of constitutional principles for their benefit, nor does it necessarily mean that constitutional protections are only available through the vehicle of parental vindication. The constitution and courts have recognized that as children mature, their capacities and recognized rights may develop—evolving what is termed the "mature minor" doctrine. And the courts have begun to acknowledge the tragic but undeniable fact that assuring child protection through the surrogate application of parental rights does not work where parents are uncaring or absent, or where parents endanger their children. Once again, the courts may be caught in a two-party concept (state vs. adults), in a three-party setting (state vs. adults vs. children).

Further, many constitutional concepts do not involve the mature declaration of political grievances on the village green, but rather state deprivation of property, health and safety endangerment, invidious discrimination, or a host of other detriments which do not turn on maturity. For while the courts understandably discount at least by degree the speech, religion, and privacy rights of children, those rights which implicate the opportunity to develop may be arguably enhanced by the fact of immaturity.

B. FIRST AMENDMENT FREE SPEECH RIGHTS OF CHILDREN

1. Student First Amendment Rights in School

armband case [handwritten]

Tinker v. Des Moines Independent Community School District

393 U.S. 503 (1969)

MR. JUSTICE FORTAS delivered the opinion of the Court.

Petitioner John F. Tinker, 15 years old, and petitioner Christopher Eckhardt, 16 years old, attended high schools in Des Moines, Iowa. Petitioner Mary Beth Tinker, John's sister, was a 13-year-old student in junior high school.

In December 1965, a group of adults and students in Des Moines held a meeting at the Eckhardt home. The group determined to publicize their objections to the hostilities in Vietnam and their support for a truce by wearing black armbands during the holiday season and by fasting on December 16 and New Year's Eve. Petitioners and their parents had previously engaged in similar activities, and they decided to participate in the program.

The principals of the Des Moines schools became aware of the plan to wear armbands. On December 14, 1965, they met and adopted a policy that any student wearing an armband to school would be asked to remove it, and if he refused he would be suspended until he returned without the armband. Petitioners were aware of the regulation that the school authorities adopted.

On December 16, Mary Beth and Christopher wore black armbands to their schools. John Tinker wore his armband the next day. They were all sent home and suspended from school until they would come back without their armbands. They did not return to school until after the planned period for wearing armbands had expired—that is, until after New Year's Day.

* * *

I.

[handwritten: District court holding]
The District Court recognized that the wearing of an armband for the purpose of expressing certain views is the type of symbolic act that is within the Free Speech Clause of the First Amendment....As we shall discuss, the wearing of armbands in the circumstances of this case was entirely divorced from actually or potentially disruptive conduct by those participating in it. It was closely akin to "pure speech" which, we have repeatedly held, is entitled to comprehensive protection under the First Amendment...

First Amendment rights, applied in light of the special characteristics of the school environment, are available to teachers and students. It can hardly be argued that either students or teachers shed their constitutional rights to freedom of speech or expression at the schoolhouse gate. This has been the unmistakable holding of this Court for almost 50 years....

In *West Virginia v. Barnette...*, this Court held that under the First Amendment, the student in public school may not be compelled to salute the flag. Speaking through Mr. Justice Jackson, the Court said:

"The Fourteenth Amendment, as now applied to the States, protects the citizen against the State itself and all of its creatures—Boards of Education not excepted. These have, of course, important, delicate, and highly discretionary functions, but none that they may not perform within the limits of the Bill of Rights. That they are educating the young for citizenship is reason for scrupulous protection of Constitutional freedoms of the individual, if we are not to strangle the free mind at its source and teach youth to discount important principles of our government as mere platitudes." 319 U.S., at 637.

On the other hand, the Court has repeatedly emphasized the need for affirming the comprehensive authority of the States and of school officials, consistent with fundamental constitutional safeguards, to prescribe and control conduct in the schools.... Our problem lies in the area where students in the exercise of First Amendment rights collide with the rules of the school authorities.

II.

The problem posed by the present case does not relate to regulation of the length of skirts or the type of clothing, to hair style, or deportment....It does not concern aggressive, disruptive action or even group demonstrations. Our problem involves direct, primary First Amendment rights akin to "pure speech."

The school officials banned and sought to punish petitioners for a silent, passive expression of opinion, unaccompanied by any disorder or disturbance on the part of petitioners. There is here no evidence whatever of petitioners' interference, actual or nascent, with the schools' work or of collision with the rights of other students to be secure and to be let alone. Accordingly, this case does not concern speech or action that intrudes upon the work of the schools or the rights of other students.

Only a few of the 18,000 students in the school system wore the black armbands. Only five students were suspended for wearing them. There is no indication that the work of the schools or any class was disrupted. Outside the classrooms, a few students made hostile remarks to the children wearing armbands, but there were no threats or acts of violence on school premises.

The District Court concluded that the action of the school authorities was reasonable because it was based upon their fear of a disturbance from the wearing of the armbands. But, in our system, undifferentiated fear or apprehension of disturbance is not enough to overcome the right to freedom of expression. Any departure from absolute regimentation may cause trouble. Any variation from the majority's opinion may inspire fear. Any word spoken, in class, in the lunchroom, or on the campus, that deviates from the views of another person may start an argument or cause a disturbance. But our Constitution says we must take this risk, *Terminiello v. Chicago*, 337 U.S. 1 (1949); and our history says that it is this sort of hazardous freedom—this kind of openness—that is the basis of our national strength and of the independence and vigor of Americans who grow up and live in this relatively permissive, often disputatious, society.

In order for the State in the person of school officials to justify prohibition of a particular expression of opinion, it must be able to show that its action was caused by something more than a mere desire to avoid the discomfort and unpleasantness that always accompany an unpopular viewpoint. Certainly where there is no finding and no showing that engaging in the forbidden conduct would "materially and substantially interfere with the requirements of appropriate discipline in the operation of the school," the prohibition cannot be sustained....

* * *

It is also relevant that the school authorities did not purport to prohibit the wearing of all symbols of political or controversial significance. The record shows that students in some of the schools wore buttons relating to national political campaigns, and some even wore the Iron Cross, traditionally a symbol of Nazism. The order prohibiting the wearing of armbands did not extend to these. Instead, a particular symbol—black armbands worn to exhibit opposition to this Nation's involvement in Vietnam—was singled out for prohibition. Clearly, the prohibition of expression of one particular opinion, at least without evidence that it is necessary to avoid material and substantial interference with schoolwork or discipline, is not constitutionally permissible.

* * *

...The principal use to which the schools are dedicated is to accommodate students during prescribed hours for the purpose of certain types of activities. Among those activities is personal intercommunication among the students.[6] This is not only an inevitable part of the process of attending school; it is also an important part of the educational process. A student's rights, therefore, do not embrace merely the classroom hours. When he is in the cafeteria, or on the playing field, or on the campus during the authorized hours, he may express his opinions, even on controversial subjects like the conflict in Vietnam, if he does so without "materially and substantially interfer[ing] with the requirements of appropriate discipline in the operation of the school" and without colliding with the rights of others. *Burnside v. Byars, supra*, at 749. But conduct by the student, in class or out of it, which for any reason—whether it stems from time, place, or type of behavior—materially disrupts classwork or involves substantial disorder or invasion of the rights of others is, of course, not immunized by the constitutional guarantee of freedom of speech....

Under our Constitution, free speech is not a right that is given only to be so circumscribed that it exists in principle but not in fact. Freedom of expression would not truly exist if the right could be exercised only in an area that a benevolent government has provided as a safe haven for crackpots. The Constitution says that Congress (and the States) may not abridge the right to free speech. This provision means what it says. We properly read it to permit reasonable regulation of speech-connected activities in carefully restricted circumstances. But we do not confine the permissible exercise of First Amendment rights to a telephone booth or the four corners of a pamphlet, or to supervised and ordained discussion in a school classroom.

If a regulation were adopted by school officials forbidding discussion of the Vietnam conflict, or the expression by any student of opposition to it anywhere on school property except as part of a prescribed classroom exercise, it would be obvious that the regulation would violate the constitutional rights of students, at least if it could not be justified by a showing that the students' activities would materially and substantially disrupt the work and discipline of the school....In the circumstances of the present case, the prohibition of the silent, passive "witness of the armbands," as one of the children called it, is no less offensive to the Constitution's guarantees.

* * *

Reversed and remanded.

* * *

[6] In *Hammond v. South Carolina State College*, 272 F.Supp. 947 (D.C.S.C. 1967), District Judge Hemphill had before him a case involving a meeting on campus of 300 students to express their views on school practices. He pointed out that a school is not like a hospital or a jail enclosure. It is a public place, and its dedication to specific uses does not imply that the constitutional rights of persons entitled to be there are to be gauged as if the premises were purely private property....

MR. JUSTICE BLACK, dissenting.

The Court's holding in this case ushers in what I deem to be an entirely new era in which the power to control pupils by the elected "officials of state supported public schools..." in the United States is in ultimate effect transferred to the Supreme Court. The Court brought this particular case here on a petition for certiorari urging that the First and Fourteenth Amendments protect the right of school pupils to express their political views all the way "from kindergarten through high school." Here the constitutional right to "political expression" asserted was a right to wear black armbands during school hours and at classes in order to demonstrate to the other students that the petitioners were mourning because of the death of United States soldiers in Vietnam and to protest that war which they were against. Ordered to refrain from wearing the armbands in school by the elected school officials and the teachers vested with state authority to do so, apparently only seven out of the school system's 18,000 pupils deliberately refused to obey the order. One defying pupil was Paul Tinker, 8 years old, who was in the second grade; another, Hope Tinker, was 11 years old and in the fifth grade; a third member of the Tinker family was 13, in the eighth grade; and a fourth member of the same family was John Tinker, 15 years old, an 11th grade high school pupil. Their father, a Methodist minister without a church, is paid a salary by the American Friends Service Committee. Another student who defied the school order and insisted on wearing an armband in school was Christopher Eckhardt, an 11th grade pupil and a petitioner in this case. His mother is an official in the Women's International League for Peace and Freedom.

As I read the Court's opinion it relies upon the following grounds for holding unconstitutional the judgment of the Des Moines school officials and the two courts below. First, the Court concludes that the wearing of armbands is "symbolic speech" which is "akin to 'pure speech'" and therefore protected by the First and Fourteenth Amendments.

Secondly, the Court decides that the public schools are an appropriate place to exercise "symbolic speech" as long as normal school functions are not "unreasonably" disrupted. Finally, the Court arrogates to itself, rather than to the State's elected officials charged with running the schools, the decision as to which school disciplinary regulations are "reasonable."

Assuming that the Court is correct in holding that the conduct of wearing armbands for the purpose of conveying political ideas is protected by the First Amendment,...the crucial remaining questions are whether students and teachers may use the schools at their whim as a platform for the exercise of free speech— "symbolic" or "pure"—and whether the courts will allocate to themselves the function of deciding how the pupils' school day will be spent....

While the record does not show that any of these armband students shouted, used profane language, or were violent in any manner, detailed testimony by some of them shows their armbands caused comments, warnings by other students, the poking of fun at them, and a warning by an older football player that other, nonprotesting students had better let them alone. There is also evidence that a teacher of mathematics had his lesson period practically "wrecked" chiefly by disputes with Mary Beth Tinker, who wore her armband for her "demonstration." Even a casual reading of the record shows that this armband did divert students' minds from their regular lessons, and that talk, comments, etc., made John Tinker "self-conscious" in attending school with his armband. While the absence of obscene remarks or boisterous and loud disorder perhaps justifies the Court's statement that the few armband students did not actually "disrupt" the classwork, I think the record overwhelmingly shows that the armbands did exactly what the elected school officials and principals foresaw they would, that is, took the students' minds off their classwork and diverted them to thoughts about the highly emotional subject of the Vietnam war. And I repeat that if the time has come when pupils of state-supported schools, kindergartens, grammar schools, or high schools, can defy and flout orders of school officials to keep their minds on their own schoolwork, it is the beginning of a new revolutionary era of permissiveness in this country fostered by the judiciary. The next logical step, it appears to me, would be to hold unconstitutional laws that bar pupils under 21 or 18 from voting, or from being elected members of the boards of education....

* * *

In my view, teachers in state-controlled public schools are hired to teach there. Although MR. JUSTICE MCREYNOLDS may have intimated to the contrary in *Meyer v. Nebraska supra*, certainly a teacher is not paid to go into school and teach subjects the State does not hire him to teach as a part of its selected curriculum. Nor are public school students sent to the schools at public expense to broadcast political or any other views to educate and inform the public. The original idea of schools, which I do not believe is yet abandoned as worthless or out of date, was that children had not yet reached the point of experience and wisdom which enabled them to teach all of their elders. It may be that the Nation has outworn the old-fashioned slogan that "children are to be seen not heard," but one may, I hope, be permitted to harbor the thought that taxpayers send children to school on the premise that at their age they need to learn, not teach.

* * *

MR. JUSTICE HARLAN, dissenting.

I certainly agree that state public school authorities in the discharge of their responsibilities are not wholly exempt from the requirements of the Fourteenth Amendment respecting the freedoms of expression and association. At the same time I am reluctant to believe that there is any disagreement between the majority and myself on the proposition that school officials should be accorded the widest authority in maintaining discipline and good order in their institutions. To translate that proposition into a workable constitutional rule, I would, in cases like this, cast upon those complaining the burden of showing that a particular school measure was motivated by other than legitimate school concerns—for example, a desire to prohibit the expression of an unpopular point of view, while permitting expression of the dominant opinion.

Finding nothing in this record which impugns the good faith of respondents in promulgating the armband regulation, I would affirm the judgment below.

Questions for Discussion

1. How would the majority rule if the armbands signified gang membership (*e.g.*, red for Bloods and black for Crips)? Could such clothing also be considered "symbolic speech?" (See *Bivens v. Albuquerque Public Schools*, 899 F. Supp. 556 (D. N.M. 1995).)

2. The majority notes that these armbands are akin to "pure speech," a passive, silent opinion posing no disorder. Assume that a substantial number of the siblings of students had been killed in the Vietnam War, or the sons of teachers, would that make a difference in terms of "disruption" concern? Should such disruption justifying speech denial by the state focus on the reactions of others? If a black student wore an NAACP badge in the deep south in the 1960s and provoked disruption from white students, should such reaction form the basis for state denial of that expression? What if it is a white student wearing a confederate flag symbol? (See *Phillips v. Anderson County School District Five*, 987 F. Supp. 488 (D. S.C. 1997)).

3. If a school may require students to wear uniforms to school (which has been upheld[4]), does it have a lesser included right to prescribe clothing? If it is permissible to prohibit short dresses or halter tops because of the distraction they may cause, can the same rationale extend to armbands in *Tinker*?

4. Black argues that students need to learn under the guidance of school officials, who should make decisions free from court interference. Does he recognize any quantum of free speech right applicable to students? To youth in general? Is free expression effectively taught or manifest where the message is: "Sit and listen, the state's employees shall determine when you talk and what you should be saying?" Black notes that the teaching of discipline educates students to be good citizens. Does that include training students not to disrupt other students who express heartfelt political positions?

5. Harlan's dissent would find a constitutional breach if the motivation of the state is not education enhancement, but rather to favor a dominant opinion, which he finds absent in *Tinker*. Is it likely that students who wore American flags on their clothing or other symbols expressing support for the Vietnam War would have been treated to sanctions similar to those applied to *Tinker*?

newspaper case

Hazelwood School District v. Kuhlmeier

484 U.S. 260 (1988)

JUSTICE WHITE delivered the opinion of the Court.

This case concerns the extent to which educators may exercise editorial control over the contents of a high school newspaper produced as part of the school's journalism curriculum.

I
* * *

Spectrum was written and edited by the Journalism II class at Hazelwood East. The newspaper was published every three weeks or so during the 1982–1983 school year. More than 4,500 copies of the newspaper were distributed during that year to students, school personnel, and members of the community.

The Board of Education allocated funds from its annual budget for the printing of Spectrum. These funds were supplemented by proceeds from sales of the newspaper....

* * *

The practice at Hazelwood East during the spring 1983 semester was for the journalism teacher to submit page proofs of each Spectrum issue to Principal Reynolds for his review prior to publication. On May 10, Emerson delivered the proofs of the May 13 edition to Reynolds, who objected to two of the articles scheduled to appear in that edition. One of the stories described three Hazelwood East students' experiences with pregnancy; the other discussed the impact of divorce on students at the school.

Reynolds was concerned that, although the pregnancy story used false names "to keep the identity of these girls a secret," the pregnant students still might be identifiable from the text. He also believed that the article's references to sexual activity and birth control were inappropriate for some of the younger students at the school. In addition, Reynolds was concerned that a student identified by name in the divorce story had complained that her father "wasn't spending enough time with my mom, my sister and I" prior to the divorce, "was always out of town on business or out late playing cards with the guys," and "always argued about everything" with her mother....Reynolds believed that the student's parents should have been given an opportunity to respond to these remarks or to consent to their publication. He was unaware that Emerson had deleted the student's name from the final version of the article.

Reynolds believed that there was no time to make the necessary changes in the stories before the scheduled press run and that the newspaper would not appear before the end of the school year if printing were delayed to any significant extent. He concluded that his only options under the circumstances were to publish a four-page newspaper instead of the planned six-page newspaper, eliminating the two pages on which the offending stories appeared, or to publish no newspaper at all. Accordingly, he directed Emerson to withhold from publication the two pages containing the stories on pregnancy and divorce.[1] He informed his superiors of the decision, and they concurred.

* * *

II

Students in the public schools do not "shed their constitutional rights to freedom of speech or expression at the schoolhouse gate." Tinker supra, at 506. They cannot be punished merely for expressing their personal views on the school premises—whether "in the cafeteria, or on the playing field, or on the campus during the authorized hours,"...— unless school authorities have reason to believe that such expression will "substantially interfere with the work of the school or impinge upon the rights of other students." Id.....

We have nonetheless recognized that the First Amendment rights of students in the public schools "are not automatically coextensive with the rights of adults in other settings,"...and must be "applied in light of the special characteristics of the school environment." Tinker supra, at 506....A school need not tolerate student speech that is inconsistent with its "basic educational mission,"...even though the government could not censor similar speech outside the school. Accordingly, we held in Fraser that a student could be disciplined for having delivered a speech that was "sexually explicit" but not legally obscene at an official school assembly, because the school was entitled to "disassociate itself" from the speech in a manner that would demonstrate to others that such vulgarity is "wholly inconsistent with the 'fundamental values' of public school education."...We thus recognized that "[t]he determination of what manner of speech in the classroom or in school assembly is inappropriate properly rests with the school board,"...rather than with the federal courts. It is in this context that respondents' First Amendment claims must be considered.

A

We deal first with the question whether Spectrum may appropriately be characterized as a forum for public expression. The public schools do not possess all of the attributes of streets, parks, and other traditional public forums that "time out of mind, have been used for purposes of assembly, communicating thoughts between citizens, and discussing public questions."...Hence, school facilities may be deemed to be public forums only if school authorities have "by policy or by practice" opened those facilities "for indiscriminate use by the general public,"...or by some segment of the public, such as student organizations....If the facilities have instead been reserved for other intended purposes, "communicative or otherwise," then no public forum has been created, and school officials may impose reasonable restrictions on the speech of students, teachers, and other members of the school community...."The government does not create a public forum by inaction or by permitting limited discourse, but only by intentionally opening a nontraditional forum for public discourse."...

* * *

School officials did not deviate in practice from their policy that production of Spectrum was to be part of the educational curriculum and a "regular classroom activit[y]." The District Court found that Robert Stergos, the journalism teacher during most of the 1982–1983 school year, "both had the authority to exercise and in fact exercised a great deal of control over Spectrum."...

...In sum, the evidence relied upon by the Court of Appeals fails to demonstrate the "clear intent to create a public forum,"....School officials did not evince either "by policy or by practice," Perry Education Assn., 460 U.S., at 47, any intent to open the pages of Spectrum to "indiscriminate use," ibid., by its student reporters and editors, or by the student body generally. Instead, they "reserve[d] the forum for its intended purpos[e]," id., at 46, as a supervised learning experience for journalism students. Accordingly, school officials were entitled to regulate the contents of Spectrum in any reasonable manner....It is this standard, rather than our decision in Tinker, that governs this case.

B

The question whether the First Amendment requires a school to tolerate particular student speech—the question that we addressed in Tinker—is different from the question whether the First Amendment requires a school affirmatively to promote particular student speech. The former question addresses educators' ability to silence a student's personal expression that happens to occur on the school premises. The latter question concerns educators' authority over school-sponsored publications, theatrical productions, and other expressive activities that students, parents, and members of the public might reasonably perceive to bear the imprimatur of the school. These activities may fairly be characterized as part of the school curriculum, whether or not they occur in a traditional classroom setting, so long as they are supervised by faculty members and designed to impart particular knowledge or skills to student participants and audiences.[3]

Educators are entitled to exercise greater control over this second form of student expression to assure that participants learn whatever lessons the activity is designed to teach, that readers or listeners are not exposed to material that may be inappropriate for their level of maturity, and that the views of the individual speaker are not erroneously attributed to the school. Hence, a school may in its capacity as publisher of a school newspaper or producer of a school play "disassociate itself," Fraser, 478 U.S., at 685, not only from speech that would "substantially interfere with [its] work...or impinge upon the rights of other students," Tinker, 393 U.S., at 509, but also from speech that is, for example, ungrammatical, poorly written, inadequately researched, biased or prejudiced, vulgar or profane, or unsuitable for immature audiences.[4] A school must be able to set high standards for the student speech that is disseminated under its auspices—standards that may be higher than those demanded by some newspaper publishers or theatrical producers in the "real" world—and may refuse to disseminate student speech that does not meet those standards. In addition, a school must be able to take into account the emotional maturity of the intended audience in determining whether to disseminate student speech on potentially sensitive topics, which might range from the existence of Santa Claus in an elementary school setting to the particulars of teenage sexual activity in a high school setting. A school must also retain the authority to refuse to sponsor student speech that might reasonably be perceived to advocate drug

[handwritten: District Court holding]

or alcohol use, irresponsible sex, or conduct otherwise inconsistent with "the shared values of a civilized social order," *Fraser, supra,* at 683, or to associate the school with any position other than neutrality on matters of political controversy. Otherwise, the schools would be unduly constrained from fulfilling their role as "a principal instrument in awakening the child to cultural values, in preparing him for later professional training, and in helping him to adjust normally to his environment." *Brown v. Board of Education,* 347 U.S. 483, 493 (1954).

Accordingly, we conclude that the standard articulated in *Tinker* for determining when a school may punish student expression need not also be the standard for determining when a school may refuse to lend its name and resources to the dissemination of student expression....Instead, we hold that educators do not offend the First Amendment by exercising editorial control over the style and content of student speech in school-sponsored expressive activities so long as their actions are reasonably related to legitimate pedagogical concerns.[6] ~~*Holding*~~

* * *

The initial paragraph of the pregnancy article declared that "[a]ll names have been changed to keep the identity of these girls a secret." The principal concluded that the students' anonymity was not adequately protected, however, given the other identifying information in the article and the small number of pregnant students at the school. Indeed, a teacher at the school credibly testified that she could positively identify at least one of the girls and possibly all three. It is likely that many students at Hazelwood East would have been at least as successful in identifying the girls. Reynolds therefore could reasonably have feared that the article violated whatever pledge of anonymity had been given to the pregnant students. In addition, he could reasonably have been concerned that the article was not sufficiently sensitive to the privacy interests of the students' boyfriends and parents, who were discussed in the article but who were given no opportunity to consent to its publication or to offer a response. The article did not contain graphic accounts of sexual activity. The girls did comment in the article, however, concerning their sexual histories and their use or nonuse of birth control. It was not unreasonable for the principal to have concluded that such frank talk was inappropriate in a school-sponsored publication distributed to 14-year-old freshmen and presumably taken home to be read by students' even younger brothers and sisters.

The student who was quoted by name in the version of the divorce article seen by Principal Reynolds made comments sharply critical of her father. The principal could reasonably have concluded that an individual publicly identified as an inattentive parent— indeed, as one who chose "playing cards with the guys" over home and family—was entitled to an opportunity to defend himself as a matter of journalistic fairness. These concerns were shared by both of Spectrum's faculty advisers for the 1982–1983 school year, who testified that they would not have allowed the article to be printed without deletion of the student's name.[8]

* * *

In sum, we cannot reject as unreasonable Principal Reynolds' conclusion that neither the pregnancy article nor the divorce article was suitable for publication in Spectrum. Reynolds could reasonably have concluded that the students who had written and edited these articles had not sufficiently mastered those portions of the Journalism II curriculum that pertained to the treatment of controversial issues and personal attacks, the need to protect the privacy of individuals whose most intimate concerns are to be revealed in the newspaper, and "the legal, moral, and ethical restrictions imposed upon journalists within [a] school community" that includes adolescent subjects and readers. Finally, we conclude that the principal's decision to delete two pages of Spectrum, rather than to delete only the offending articles or to require that they be modified, was reasonable under the circumstances as he understood them. Accordingly, no violation of First Amendment rights occurred.[9]

The judgment of the Court of Appeals for the Eighth Circuit is therefore

Reversed.

[1] The two pages deleted from the newspaper also contained articles on teenage marriage, runaways, and juvenile delinquents, as well as a general article on teenage pregnancy. Reynolds testified that he had no objection to these articles and that they were deleted only because they appeared on the same pages as the two objectionable articles.

[3] The distinction that we draw between speech that is sponsored by the school and speech that is not is fully consistent with *Papish v. University of Missouri Board of Curators*, 410 U.S. 667 (1973) (*per curiam*), which involved an off-campus "underground" newspaper that school officials merely had allowed to be sold on a state university campus.

[4] The dissent perceives no difference between the First Amendment analysis applied in *Tinker* and that applied in *Fraser*. We disagree. The decision in *Fraser* rested on the "vulgar," "lewd," and "plainly offensive" character of a speech delivered at an official school assembly rather than on any propensity of the speech to "materially disrup[t] classwork or involv[e] substantial disorder or invasion of the rights of others." 393 U.S., at 513. Indeed, the *Fraser* Court cited as "especially relevant" a portion of JUSTICE BLACK'S dissenting opinion in *Tinker* "'disclaim[ing] any purpose...to hold that the Federal Constitution compels the teachers, parents, and elected school officials to surrender control of the American public school system to public school students.'" 478 U.S., at 686 (quoting 393 U.S., at 526). Of course, JUSTICE BLACK'S observations are equally relevant to the instant case.

[6] We reject respondents' suggestion that school officials be permitted to exercise prepublication control over school-sponsored publications only pursuant to specific written regulations. To require such regulations in the context of a curricular activity could unduly constrain the ability of educators to educate. We need not now decide whether such regulations are required before school officials may censor publications not sponsored by the school that students seek to distribute on school grounds....

[8] The reasonableness of Principal Reynolds' concerns about the two articles was further substantiated by the trial testimony of Martin Duggan, a former editorial page editor of the St. Louis Globe Democrat and a former college journalism instructor and newspaper adviser. Duggan testified that the divorce story did not meet journalistic standards of fairness and balance because the father was not given an opportunity to respond, and that the pregnancy story was not appropriate for publication in a high school newspaper because it was unduly intrusive into the privacy of the girls, their parents, and their boyfriends. The District Court found Duggan to be "an objective and independent witness" whose testimony was entitled to significant weight. 607 F. Supp. 1450, 1461 (ED Mo. 1985).

[9] It is likely that the approach urged by the dissent would as a practical matter have far more deleterious consequences for the student press than does the approach that we adopt today. The dissent correctly acknowledges "[t]he State's prerogative to dissolve the student newspaper entirely." *Post*, at 287. It is likely that many public schools would do just that rather than open their newspapers to all student expression that does not threaten "materia[l] disrup[tion of] classwork" or violation of "rights that are protected by law," *Post*, at 289, regardless of how sexually explicit, racially intemperate, or personally insulting that expression otherwise might be.

JUSTICE BRENNAN, with whom **JUSTICE MARSHALL** and **JUSTICE BLACKMUN** join, dissenting.

When the young men and women of Hazelwood East High School registered for Journalism II, they expected a civics lesson. Spectrum, the newspaper they were to publish, "was not just a class exercise in which students learned to prepare papers and hone writing skills, it was a...forum established to give students an opportunity to express their views while gaining an appreciation of their rights and responsibilities under the First Amendment to the United States Constitution...." 795 F. 2d 1368, 1373 (CA8 1986). "[A]t the beginning of each school year," *id.*, at 1372, the student journalists published a Statement of Policy—tacitly approved each year by school authorities—announcing their expectation that "*Spectrum* as a student-press publication, accepts all rights implied by the First Amendment....Only speech that 'materially and substantially interferes with the requirements of appropriate discipline' can be found unacceptable and therefore prohibited." App. 26 (quoting *Tinker v. Des Moines Independent Community School Dist.*, 393 U.S. 503, 513 (1969)).[1] The school board itself affirmatively guaranteed the students of Journalism II an atmosphere conducive to fostering such an appreciation and exercising the full panoply of rights associated with a free student press. "School sponsored student publications," it vowed, "will not restrict free expression or diverse viewpoints within the rules of responsible journalism."....

This case arose when the Hazelwood East administration breached its own promise, dashing its students' expectations. The school principal, without prior consultation or explanation, excised six articles—comprising two full pages—of the May 13, 1983, issue of Spectrum. He did so not because any of the articles would "materially and substantially interfere with the requirements of appropriate discipline," but simply because he considered two of the six "inappropriate, personal, sensitive, and unsuitable" for student consumption....

In my view the principal broke more than just a promise. He violated the First Amendment's prohibitions against censorship of any student expression that neither disrupts classwork nor invades the rights of others, and against any censorship that is not narrowly tailored to serve its purpose.

I

Public education serves vital national interests in preparing the Nation's youth for life in our increasingly complex society and for the duties of citizenship in our democratic Republic....The public school conveys to our young the information and tools required not merely to survive in, but to contribute to, civilized society. It also inculcates in tomorrow's leaders the "fundamental values necessary to the maintenance of a democratic political system...."....All the while, the public educator nurtures students' social and moral development by transmitting to them an official dogma of "'community values.'"....

The public educator's task is weighty and delicate indeed. It demands particularized and supremely subjective choices among diverse curricula, moral values, and political stances to teach or inculcate in students, and among various methodologies for doing so. Accordingly, we have traditionally reserved the "daily operation of school systems" to the States and their local school boards....We have not, however, hesitated to intervene where their decisions run afoul of the Constitution. *See e.g., Edwards v. Aguillard*, 482 U.S. 578 (1987) (striking state statute that forbade teaching of evolution in public school unless accompanied by instruction on theory of "creation science"); *Board of Education v. Pico supra* (school board may not remove books from library shelves merely because it disapproves of ideas they express); *Epperson v. Arkansas supra* (striking state-law prohibition against teaching Darwinian theory of evolution in public school); *West Virginia Board of Education v. Barnette*, 319 U.S. 624 (1943) (public school may not compel student to salute flag); *Meyer v. Nebraska*, 262 U.S. 390 (1923) (state law prohibiting the teaching of foreign languages in public or private schools is unconstitutional).

Free student expression undoubtedly sometimes interferes with the effectiveness of the school's pedagogical functions. Some brands of student expression do so by directly preventing the school from pursuing its pedagogical mission: The young polemic who stands on a soapbox during calculus class to deliver an eloquent political diatribe interferes with the legitimate teaching of calculus. And the student who delivers a lewd endorsement of a student-government candidate might so extremely distract an impressionable high school audience as to interfere with the orderly operation of the school. See *Bethel School Dist. No. 403 v. Fraser*, 478 U.S. 675 (1986). Other student speech, however, frustrates the school's legitimate pedagogical purposes merely by expressing a message that conflicts with the school's, without directly interfering with the school's expression of its message: A student who responds to a political science teacher's question with the retort, "socialism is good," subverts the school's inculcation of the message that capitalism is better. Even the maverick who sits in class passively sporting a symbol of protest against a government policy, cf. *Tinker v. Des Moines Independent Community School Dist.*, 393 U.S. 503 (1969), or the gossip who sits in the student commons swapping stories of sexual escapade could readily muddle a clear official message condoning the government policy or condemning teenage sex. Likewise, the student newspaper that, like Spectrum, conveys a moral position at odds with the school's official stance might subvert the administration's legitimate inculcation of its own perception of community values.

If mere incompatibility with the school's pedagogical message were a constitutionally sufficient justification for the suppression of student speech, school officials could censor each of the students or student organizations in the foregoing hypotheticals, converting our public schools into "enclaves of totalitarianism," *id*, at 511, that "strangle the free mind at its source," *West Virginia Board of Education v. Barnette supra*, at 637. The First Amendment permits no such blanket censorship authority. While the "constitutional rights of students in public school are not automatically coextensive with the rights of adults in other settings," *Fraser supra*, at 682, students in the public schools do not "shed their constitutional rights to freedom of speech or expression at the schoolhouse gate," *Tinker supra*, at 506. Just as the public on the street corner must, in the interest of fostering "enlightened opinion," *Cantwell v. Connecticut*, 310 U.S. 296, 310 (1940), tolerate speech that "tempt[s] [the listener] to throw [the speaker] off the street," *id.*, at 309, public educators must accommodate some student expression even if it offends them or offers views or values that contradict those the school wishes to inculcate *Tinker*, this Court struck the balance. We held that official censorship of student expression—there the suspension of several students until they removed their armbands protesting the Vietnam war—is unconstitutional unless the speech "materially disrupts classwork or involves substantial disorder or invasion of the rights of others" 393 U.S. at 513. School officials may not suppress "silent, passive expression of opinion, unaccompanied by any disorder or disturbance on the part of" the speaker. *Id.*, at 508. The "mere desire to avoid the discomfort and unpleasantness that always accompany an unpopular viewpoint," *id.*, at 509, or an unsavory subject, *Fraser, supra*, at 688–689 (BRENNAN, J., concurring in judgment), does not justify official suppression of student speech in the high school.

* * *

II

Even if we were writing on a clean slate, I would reject the Court's rationale for abandoning *Tinker* in this case. The Court offers no more than an obscure tangle of three excuses to afford educators "greater control" over school-sponsored speech than the *Tinker* test would permit: the public educator's prerogative to control curriculum; the pedagogical interest in shielding the high school audience from objectionable viewpoints and sensitive topics; and the school's need to dissociate itself from student expression....None of the excuses, once disentangled, supports the distinction that the Court draws. *Tinker* fully addresses the first concern; the second is illegitimate; and the third is readily achievable through less oppressive means.

A
* * *

The Court relies on bits of testimony to portray the principal's conduct as a pedagogical lesson to Journalism II students who "had not sufficiently mastered those portions of the...curriculum that pertained to the treatment of controversial issues and personal attacks, the need to protect the privacy of individuals..., and 'the legal, moral, and ethical restrictions imposed upon journalists....'"....In that regard, the Court attempts to justify censorship of the article on teenage pregnancy on the basis of the principal's judgment that (1) "the [pregnant] students' anonymity was not adequately protected," despite the article's use of aliases; and (2) the judgment that "the article was not sufficiently sensitive to the privacy interests of the students' boyfriends and parents...."....Similarly, the Court finds in the principal's decision to censor the divorce article a journalistic lesson that the author should have given the father of one student an "opportunity to defend himself" against her charge that (in the Court's words) he "chose 'playing cards with the guys' over home and family....".....

But the principal never consulted the students before censoring their work. "[T]hey learned of the deletions when the paper was released...." 795 F. 2d, at 1371. Further, he explained the deletions only in the broadest of generalities. In one meeting called at the behest of seven protesting Spectrum staff members (presumably a fraction of the full class), he characterized the articles as "'too sensitive' for 'our immature audience of readers,'"...and in a later meeting he deemed them simply "inappropriate, personal, sensitive and unsuitable for the newspaper"....The Court's supposition that the principal intended (or the protesters understood) those generalities as a lesson on the nuances of journalistic responsibility is utterly incredible. If he did, a fact that neither the District Court nor the Court of Appeals found, the lesson was lost on all but the psychic Spectrum staffer.

B

The Court's second excuse for deviating from precedent is the school's interest in shielding an impressionable high school audience from material whose substance is "unsuitable for immature audiences."....Specifically, the majority decrees that we must afford educators authority to shield high school students from exposure to "potentially sensitive topics" (like "the particulars of teen-age sexual activity") or unacceptable social viewpoints (like the advocacy of "irresponsible se[x] or conduct otherwise inconsistent with 'the shared values of a civilized social order'") through school-sponsored student activities....

Tinker teaches us that the state educator's undeniable, and undeniably vital, mandate to inculcate moral and political values is not a general warrant to act as "thought police" stifling discussion of all but state-approved topics and advocacy of all but the official position....Otherwise educators could transform students into "closed-circuit recipients of only that which the State chooses to communicate," *Tinker*, 393 U.S., at 511, and cast a perverse and impermissible "pall of orthodoxy over the classroom,"... Thus, the State cannot constitutionally prohibit its high school students from recounting in the locker room "the particulars of [their] teen-age sexual activity," nor even from advocating "irresponsible se[x]" or other presumed abominations of "the shared values of a civilized social order." Even in its capacity as educator the State may not assume an Orwellian "guardianship of the public mind,"...

The mere fact of school sponsorship does not, as the Court suggests, license such thought control in the high school, whether through school suppression of disfavored viewpoints or through official assessment of topic sensitivity.[2] The former would constitute unabashed and unconstitutional viewpoint discrimination,...as well as an impermissible infringement of the students' "'right to receive information and ideas,'"....Just as a school board may not purge its state-funded library of all books that "'offen[d] [its] social, political and moral tastes,'" 457 U.S. at 858–859 (plurality opinion) (citation omitted), school officials may not, out of like motivation, discriminatorily excise objectionable ideas from a student publication. The State's prerogative to dissolve the student newspaper entirely (or to limit its subject matter) no more entitles it to dictate which viewpoints students may express on its pages, than the State's prerogative to close down the schoolhouse entitles it to prohibit the nondisruptive expression of antiwar sentiment within its gates.

Official censorship of student speech on the ground that it addresses "potentially sensitive topics" is, for related reasons, equally impermissible. I would not begrudge an educator the authority to limit the substantive scope of a school-sponsored publication to a certain, objectively definable topic, such as literary criticism, school sports, or an overview of the school year. Unlike those determinate limitations, "potential topic sensitivity" is a vaporous nonstandard—like "'public welfare, peace, safety, health, decency, good order, morals or convenience,'"...—that invites manipulation to achieve ends that cannot permissibly be achieved through blatant viewpoint discrimination and chills student speech to which school officials might not object. In part because of those dangers, this Court has consistently condemned any scheme allowing a state official boundless discretion in licensing speech from a particular forum....

The case before us aptly illustrates how readily school officials (and courts) can camouflage viewpoint discrimination as the "mere" protection of students from sensitive topics....

C

The sole concomitant of school sponsorship that might conceivably justify the distinction that the Court draws between sponsored and nonsponsored student expression is the risk "that the views of the individual speaker [might be] erroneously attributed to the school."....Of course, the risk of erroneous attribution inheres in any student expression, including "personal expression" that, like the armbands in *Tinker*, "happens to occur on the school premises,"....Nevertheless, the majority is certainly correct that indicia of school sponsorship increase the likelihood of such attribution, and that state educators may therefore have a legitimate interest in dissociating themselves from student speech.

But "'[e]ven though the governmental purpose be legitimate and substantial, that purpose cannot be pursued by means that broadly stifle fundamental personal liberties when the end can be more narrowly achieved.'"...Dissociative means short of censorship are available to the school. It could, for example, require the student activity to publish a disclaimer, such as the "Statement of Policy" that Spectrum published each school year announcing that "[a]ll...editorials appearing in this newspaper reflect the opinions of the Spectrum staff, which are not necessarily shared by the administrators or faculty of Hazelwood East,"...; or it could simply issue its own response clarifying the official position on the matter and explaining why the student position is wrong. Yet, without so much as acknowledging the less oppressive alternatives, the Court approves of brutal censorship.

* * *

IV

....Instead of "teach[ing] children to respect the diversity of ideas that is fundamental to the American system,"...and "that our Constitution is a living reality, not parchment preserved under glass,"...the Court today "teach[es] youth to discount important principles of our government as mere platitudes."...The young men and women of Hazelwood East expected a civics lesson, but not the one the Court teaches them today.

I dissent.

[1] The Court suggests that the passage quoted in the text did not "exten[d] the *Tinker* standard to the news and feature articles contained in a school-sponsored newspaper" because the passage did not expressly mention them. *Ante*, at 269, n. 2. It is hard to imagine why the Court (or anyone else) might expect a passage that applies categorically to "a student-press publication," composed almost exclusively of "news and feature articles," to mention those categories expressly. Understandably, neither court below so limited the passage.

[2] The Court quotes language in *Bethel School Dist. No. 403 v. Fraser*, 478 U.S. 675 (1986), for the proposition that "'[t]he determination of what manner of speech in the classroom or in school assembly is inappropriate properly rests with the school board.'"....As the discussion immediately preceding that quotation makes clear, however, the Court was referring only to the appropriateness of the in which the message is conveyed, not of the message's content....

Questions for Discussion

1. Does the principal pass the *Harlan* "motivation" test? If the information published about the father was factually inaccurate and he did not have a chance to comment on it, is there a libel danger for the school? Why does the majority not discuss such a basis for non-publication?

2. Does Justice White's "special characteristics of the school environment" limiting student free speech rights apply only to kindergarten through twelfth grades? Does it apply to public colleges and universities as well?

3. The majority announces its agreement with the principal that "frank talk" about birth control is inappropriate for a 14-year-old. Surveys indicate that the incidence of ever having had sexual intercourse among high school students is as follows: 9th grade, 20.4%; 10th grade, 36.2%; 11th grade, 47.3%; 12th grade, 57.3%.[5] Is pregnancy appropriate for a 14-year-old? Does the Court believe that 14-year-olds are cut-off from sexual messages from the media or peers? Is the Court's decision partly driven by its own view of the subject matter? Isn't the point of the First Amendment that our own personal disagreement with a message is not itself determinative of its right to be published?

4. The Court denies "forum" status for the school newspaper. Does it analyze alternative available forums? Does it matter if there are no other realistic means for students to express themselves? Does it make sense for the majority to argue that the small number of persons controlling the primary means of communication at the school cuts against applying the First Amendment to that vehicle?

5. If the decision had been made by the teacher alone to cut these articles purely on grounds of poor journalism (failure to check sources, bad grammar, incomprehensible) would the dissenters join the majority? What would the dissenters say, were the teacher to determine that the article was not sufficiently "balanced" to

be in the news section, but would permit it in reduced form as a labeled "opinion" piece?

6. Does a school have a right to censor or sanction speech by a juvenile laced with "sexual innuendo," expressing "inappropriate" thoughts for minors? See *Bethel School District No. 403 v. Fraser,* 478 U.S. 675 (1986).

7. Would a Court holding more expansively protecting unfettered student free speech decrease the number of school publications like the *Spectrum,* which could pose public relations problems for administrators?

drug banner case

Morse v. Frederick

551 U.S. 393 (2007)

ROBERTS, C. J., delivered the opinion of the Court, in which SCALIA, KENNEDY, THOMAS, and ALITO, JJ., joined.

I.

On January 24, 2002, the Olympic Torch Relay passed through Juneau, Alaska, on its way to the winter games in Salt Lake City, Utah. The torchbearers were to proceed along a street in front of Juneau-Douglas High School (JDHS) while school was in session. Petitioner Deborah Morse, the school principal, decided to permit staff and students to participate in the Torch Relay as an approved social event or class trip.... Students were allowed to leave class to observe the relay from either side of the street. Teachers and administrative officials monitored the students' actions.

Respondent Joseph Frederick, a JDHS senior, was late to school that day. When he arrived, he joined his friends (all but one of whom were JDHS students) across the street from the school to watch the event. Not all the students waited patiently. Some became rambunctious, throwing plastic cola bottles and snowballs and scuffling with their classmates. As the torchbearers and camera crews passed by, Frederick and his friends unfurled a 14-foot banner bearing the phrase: "BONG HiTS 4 JESUS."... The large banner was easily readable by the students on the other side of the street.

Principal Morse immediately crossed the street and demanded that the banner be taken down. Everyone but Frederick complied. Morse confiscated the banner and told Frederick to report to her office, where she suspended him for 10 days. Morse later explained that she told Frederick to take the banner down because she thought it encouraged illegal drug use, in violation of established school policy.

II.

....[W]e agree with the superintendent that Frederick cannot "stand in the midst of his fellow students, during school hours, at a school-sanctioned activity and claim he is not at school.".....

III.

The message on Frederick's banner is cryptic. It is no doubt offensive to some, perhaps amusing to others. To still others, it probably means nothing at all. Frederick himself claimed "that the words were just nonsense meant to attract television cameras."... But Principal Morse thought the banner would be interpreted by those viewing it as promoting illegal drug use, and that interpretation is plainly a reasonable one.

* * *

The dissent mentions Frederick's "credible and uncontradicted explanation for the message—he just wanted to get on television."...But that is a description of Frederick's motive for displaying the banner; it is not an interpretation of what the banner says. The way Frederick was going to fulfill his ambition of appearing on television was by unfurling a pro-drug banner at a school event, in the presence of teachers and fellow students.

Elsewhere in its opinion, the dissent emphasizes the importance of political speech and the need to foster "national debate about a serious issue," as if to suggest that the banner is political speech. But not even Frederick argues that the banner conveys any sort of political or religious message. Contrary to the dissent's suggestion, this is plainly not a case about political debate over the criminalization of drug use or possession.

IV.

The question thus becomes whether a principal may, consistent with the First Amendment, restrict student speech at a school event, when that speech is reasonably viewed as promoting illegal drug use. We hold that she may.

* * *

JUSTICE THOMAS concurring (urging repudiation and reversal of *Tinker*).

I.

* * *

A.

During the colonial era, private schools and tutors offered the only educational opportunities for children, and teachers managed classrooms with an iron hand.... Because public schools were initially created as substitutes for private schools, when States developed public education systems in the early 1800's, no one doubted the government's ability to educate and discipline children as private schools did. Like their private counterparts, early public schools were not places for freewheeling debates or exploration of competing ideas. Rather, teachers instilled "a core of common values" in students and taught them self-control....

Teachers instilled these values not only by presenting ideas but also through strict discipline....Schools punished students for behavior the school considered disrespectful or wrong. Parkerson 65 (noting that children were punished for idleness, talking, profanity, and slovenliness). Rules of etiquette were enforced, and courteous behavior was demanded....To meet their educational objectives, schools required absolute obedience....

In short, in the earliest public schools, teachers taught, and students listened. Teachers commanded, and students obeyed. Teachers did not rely solely on the power of ideas to persuade; they relied on discipline to maintain order.

B.

Through the legal doctrine of *in loco parentis*, courts upheld the right of schools to discipline students, to enforce rules, and to maintain order. Rooted in the English common law, *in loco parentis* originally governed the legal rights and obligations of tutors and private schools. 1 W. Blackstone, Commentaries on the Laws of England 441 (1765) ("[A parent] may also delegate part of his parental authority, during his life, to the tutor or schoolmaster of his child; who is then in *loco parentis*, and has such a portion of the power of the parent committed to his charge, *viz.* that of restraint and correction, as may be necessary to answer the purposes for which he is employed"). Chancellor James Kent noted the acceptance of the doctrine as part of American law in the early 19th century. 2 J. Kent, Commentaries on American Law ("So the power allowed by law to the parent over the person of the child may be delegated to a tutor or instructor, the better to accomplish the purpose of education").

* * *

III.

In light of the history of American public education, it cannot seriously be suggested that the First Amendment "freedom of speech" encompasses a student's right to speak in public schools. Early public schools gave total control to teachers, who expected obedience and respect from students. And courts routinely deferred to schools' authority to make rules and to discipline students for violating those rules. Several points are clear: (1) Under *in loco parentis*, speech rules and other school rules were treated identically; (2) the *in loco parentis* doctrine imposed almost no limits on the types of rules that a school could set while students were in school; and (3) schools and teachers had tremendous discretion in imposing punishments for violations of those rules...

And because *Tinker* utterly ignored the history of public education, courts (including this one) routinely find it necessary to create ad hoc exceptions to its central premise. This doctrine of exceptions creates confusion without fixing the underlying problem by returning to first principles. Just as I cannot accept *Tinker's* standard, I cannot subscribe to *Kuhlmeier's* alternative. Local school boards, not the courts, should determine what pedagogical interests are "legitimate" and what rules "reasonably relat[e]" to those interests.

Justice Black may not have been "a prophet or the son of a prophet," but his dissent in *Tinker* has proved prophetic....In the name of the First Amendment, *Tinker* has undermined the traditional authority of teachers to maintain order in public schools. "Once a society that generally respected the authority of teachers, deferred to their judgment, and trusted them to act in the best interest of school children, we now accept defiance, disrespect, and disorder as daily occurrences in many of our public schools.".... We need look no further than this case for an example: Frederick asserts a constitutional right to utter at a school event what is either "[g]ibberish,"...or an open call to use illegal drugs. To elevate such impertinence to the status of constitutional protection would be farcical and would indeed be to "surrender control of the American public school system to public school students." *Tinker, supra*, at 526, (Black, J., dissenting).

* * *

[1] Even at the college level, strict obedience was required of students: "The English model fostered absolute institutional control of students by faculty both inside and outside the classroom. At all the early American schools, students lived and worked under a vast array of rules and restrictions. This one-sided relationship between the student and the college mirrored the situation at English schools where the emphasis on hierarchical authority stemmed from medieval Christian theology and the unique legal privileges afforded the university corporation."

JUSTICE STEVENS, joined by **JUSTICE SOUTER** and **JUSTICE GINSBURG**, dissenting.

* * *

...I would hold...that the school's interest in protecting its students from exposure to speech "reasonably regarded as promoting illegal drug use," cannot justify disciplining Frederick for his attempt to make an ambiguous statement to a television audience simply because it contained an oblique reference to drugs. The First Amendment demands more, indeed, much more.

* * *

....I take the Court's point that the message on Frederick's banner is not *necessarily* protected speech, even though it unquestionably would have been had the banner been unfurled elsewhere. [And] ...I am willing to assume that the Court is correct that the pressing need to deter drug use supports JDHS rule prohibiting willful conduct that expressly "advocates the use of substances that are illegal to minors." But it is a gross non sequitur to draw from these two unremarkable propositions the remarkable conclusion that the school may suppress student speech that was never meant to persuade anyone to do anything.

In my judgment, the First Amendment protects student speech if the message itself neither violates a permissible rule nor expressly advocates conduct that is illegal and harmful to students. This nonsense banner does neither, and the Court does serious violence to the First Amendment in upholding—indeed, lauding—a school's decision to punish Frederick for expressing a view with which it disagreed.

* * *

...Yet today the Court fashions a test that trivializes the two cardinal principles upon which *Tinker* rests....("[S]chools [may] restrict student expression that they reasonably regard as promoting illegal drug use"). The Court's test invites stark viewpoint discrimination. In this case, for example, the principal has unabashedly acknowledged that she disciplined Frederick because she disagreed with the pro-drug viewpoint she ascribed to the message on the banner....[T]he Court's holding in this case strikes at "the heart of the First Amendment" because it upholds a punishment meted out on the basis of a listener's disagreement with her understanding (or, more likely, misunderstanding) of the speaker's viewpoint. "If there is a bedrock principle underlying the First Amendment, it is that the government may not prohibit the expression of an idea simply because society finds the idea itself offensive or disagreeable.

It is also perfectly clear that "promoting illegal drug use,....comes nowhere close to proscribable "incitement to imminent lawless action."...Encouraging drug use might well increase the likelihood that a listener will try an illegal drug, but that hardly justifies censorship.

....No one seriously maintains that drug advocacy (much less Frederick's ridiculous sign) comes within the vanishingly small category of speech that can be prohibited because of its feared consequences. Such advocacy, to borrow from Justice Holmes, "ha[s] no chance of starting a present conflagration."...

II.

The Court rejects outright these twin foundations of *Tinker* because, in its view, the unusual importance of protecting children from the scourge of drugs supports a ban on all speech in the school environment that promotes drug use. Whether or not such a rule is sensible as a matter of policy, carving out pro-drug speech for uniquely harsh treatment finds no support in our case law and is inimical to the values protected by the First Amendment....

* * *

...[J]ust as we insisted in *Tinker* that the school establish some likely connection between the armbands and their feared consequences, so too JDHS must show that Frederick's supposed advocacy stands a meaningful chance of making otherwise-abstemious students try marijuana.

...But instead of demanding that the school make such a showing, the Court punts. Figuring out just *how* it punts is tricky; "[t]he mode of analysis [it] employ[s]...is not entirely clear,"....On occasion, the Court suggests it is deferring to the principal's "reasonable" judgment that Frederick's sign qualified as drug advocacy....At other times, the Court seems to say that it thinks the banner's message constitutes express advocacy....Either way, its approach is indefensible.

* * *

...That the Court believes such a silly message can be proscribed as advocacy underscores the novelty of its position, and suggests that the principle it articulates has no stopping point.

* * *

...Among other things, the Court's ham-handed, categorical approach is deaf to the constitutional imperative to permit unfettered debate, even among high-school students, about the wisdom of the war on drugs or of legalizing marijuana for medicinal use. ("[Students] may not be confined to the expression of those sentiments that are officially approved", [citing *Tinker*]). If Frederick's stupid reference to marijuana can in the Court's view justify censorship, then high school students everywhere could be forgiven for zipping their mouths about drugs at school lest some "reasonable" observer censor and then punish them for promoting drugs....

...While I find it hard to believe the Court would support punishing Frederick for flying a "WINE SiPS 4 JESUS" banner—which could quite reasonably be construed either as a protected religious message or as a pro-alcohol message—the breathtaking sweep of its opinion suggests it would.

III.

Although this case began with a silly, nonsensical banner, it ends with the Court inventing out of whole cloth a special First Amendment rule permitting the censorship of any student speech that mentions drugs, at least so long as someone could perceive that speech to contain a latent pro-drug message. Our First Amendment jurisprudence has identified some categories of expression that are less deserving of protection than others—fighting words, obscenity, and commercial speech, to name a few. Rather than reviewing our opinions discussing such categories, I mention two personal recollections that have no doubt influenced my conclusion that it would be profoundly unwise to create special rules for speech about drug and alcohol use.

* * *

...[J]ust as prohibition in the 1920's and early 1930's was secretly questioned by thousands of otherwise law-abiding patrons of bootleggers and speakeasies, today the actions of literally millions of otherwise law-abiding users of marijuana,... and of the majority of voters in each of the several States that tolerate medicinal uses of the product,...lead me to wonder whether the fear of disapproval by those in the majority is silencing opponents of the war on drugs. Surely our national experience with alcohol should make us wary of dampening speech suggesting—however inarticulately—that it would be better to tax and regulate marijuana than to persevere in a futile effort to ban its use entirely.

Even in high school, a rule that permits only one point of view to be expressed is less likely to produce correct answers than the open discussion of countervailing views.... In the national debate about a serious issue, it is the expression of the minority's viewpoint that most demands the protection of the First Amendment. Whatever the better policy may be, a full and frank discussion of the costs and benefits of the attempt to prohibit the use of marijuana is far wiser than suppression of speech because it is unpopular.

I respectfully dissent.

Questions for Discussion

1. The Court majority's rationale for First Amendment restriction is to uphold the policy not to "encourage drug use." How does a sign making a rather adolescent reference to "bongs"—indicating marijuana—provide an effective inducement to "light up"?

2. Mass advertisements directly target youth to drink hard alcohol (*e.g.*, the Captain Morgan rum ads, "alco pop" advertising hard liquor to young girls, *et al.*). Has the Court ever indicated that these sophisticated *inducements* to illegal and harmful alcohol consumption by minors cancel their commercial free speech status? What has been the Court's holdings on internet pornography (including pornography where actors are over 18 but appear to be younger, or where computer-generated effects are used to realistically depict children engaged in sexual acts)—which enjoys substantial First Amendment protection notwithstanding a rather more direct deleterious effect on children (see discussion in Chapter 14)?

3. Is it relevant that the banner was located on private property and was not on school grounds? Did the school contend that it really "interfered" with the school "event" (an Olympic torch procession)?

4. The majority opinion relies substantially on *Bethel School District # 403 v. Fraser*, 478 U.S. 675 (1986), which upheld a two-day suspension of a student who, at a school assembly, "delivered a speech nominating a fellow student for student elective office. During the entire speech, respondent referred to his candidate in terms of an elaborate, graphic, and explicit sexual metaphor." Similarly, the Court dismisses any political speech content to the "bong" message. However, note that Alaska has been debating the criminality of marijuana from 1996, with repeated statutes, court precedents, and electoral propositions on the subject. Would it protect

the banner had it ended with "vote for marijuana legalization now!" Or would that have added to the alarm of the five justices joining the majority opinion?

5. The Court makes the point that the message is brief and unclear (and certainly it is not even a complete sentence, much less a political commentary). But how many political messages take the form of sloganeering? How many banners or buttons discuss any issue in depth?

6. Would it have mattered if the student here did not contend he was trying to get TV attention and that the message was meaningless, but that the message was profound, important, and should be followed by the entire campus and city? Would those facets alter this majority's holding?

7. Are students allowed to comment on drug policies? Are such issues not relevant to political free speech, *e.g.*, given the public proposition elections to legalize marijuana, some of which have received millions of votes? Are students not allowed to discuss such issues because they might "encourage drug use" on campus? Write a letter to the school newspaper? To the community newspaper that is in the principal's office and available throughout the school?

8. If the banner had been held up by a 60-year-old ex-hippie, who believed that marijuana was much more benign than alcohol and the latter ought to be banned and not the former, could the principal remove his banner? What if the person unfurling the banner was a student, but from a rival school in another district and it read: "Juneau High students are Bong Heads—Beat Juneau!"? Or if that might be viewed as permissible because it implies criticism of drug use, what about the rival student's banner reading: "Eastside Eagles—Floating Like Happy Bongs Over You Sorry Juneau High Airheads!" Should the Juneau principal have the youth arrested? Should the Eastside principal suspend him from its campus across town?

9. The Thomas concurring opinion, expressing support for a somewhat "authoritarian/hierarchical" approach to student instruction, equates the school's function to parental authority. But is not the school rather a disparate entity as an agency of the state? Is it wise to ascribe to it parental authority as such? As one of many examples, can or should it decide the television shows watched by a child, with whom he may associate, when to go to bed, or what church to attend and when—all as a parent may? Is it possible that many parents, perhaps even most, would not want to delegate much of their parental authority to the state? Is it possible that many might have a very different view of education than the apparent "empty vessel, fill her" view of Thomas, and prefer that their children learn not only to listen, but to speak? If the latter is their view, how does the state justify First Amendment abridgement in the *in loco parentis* name of all parents?

Note on Student First Amendment Rights and Off-Campus Expression

The off-campus locus of the "BONG HiTS 4 JESUS" sign in *Morse, supra*, raises an important current issue—how far does the authority of a school extend to limit the speech of its students? The ubiquity of cell phones, the internet, Facebook, Twitter, *et al.* raises issues of the school's reach. Some of these issues arise in alleged "bullying" of students—often with regrettable consequences. Can a school address these communications? Some school officials argue, consistent with part of the *Morse* discussion, that a communication directed at fellow students may involve appropriate school authority. They argue that some of these bullying attacks arise from school relations, are addressed to classmates, and are read (and accompanied by photos sometimes) at the school.

A somewhat different but related issue is now reaching the federal appellate courts. During and after 2009, a number of cases confronted My Space or Facebook pages that attacked school officials. In December of 2005, Justin Layshock was a seventeen-year old senior at Hickory High School in Pennsylvania. The following is an excerpt from *Layshock v. Hermitage School District*, 593 F.3d 249, 251–252 (3d Cir. 2010):

> ...Sometime between December 10 and 14, 2005, while he was at his grandmother's house during non-school hours, he used her computer to create what he would later refer to as a "parody profile" of his principal, Eric Trosch. The only school resource that was even arguably involved in creating the profile was a photograph of Trosch that Justin copied from the school district's website. Justin copied that picture with a simple "cut and paste" operation using the computer's internet browser and mouse. Justin created the profile on "MySpace."...
>
> Justin created the profile by giving bogus answers to survey questions taken from various templates that were designed to assist in creating an online profile. The survey included questions about favorite shoes, weaknesses, fears, one's idea of a "perfect pizza," bedtime, etc. All of Justin's answers were based on a theme of "big," because Trosch is apparently a large man. For example, Justin answered the "tell me about yourself" questions as follows:
>
> Birthday: too drunk to remember
> Are you a health freak: big steroid freak
> In the past month have you smoked: big blunt....
> In the past month have you been on pills: big pills
> In the past month have you gone Skinny Dipping: big lake, not big dick
> In the past month have you Stolen Anything: big keg
> Ever been drunk: big number of times
> Ever been called a Tease: big whore
> Ever been Beaten up: big fag
> Ever Shoplifted: big bag of kmart
> Number of Drugs I have taken: big
> Under "Interests," Justin listed: "Transgender, Appreciators of Alcoholic Beverages." Justin also listed "Steroids International" as a club Trosch belonged to.
>
> Justin afforded access to the profile to other students in the District by listing them as "friends" on the MySpace website, thus allowing them to view the profile. Not surprisingly, word of the profile "spread like wildfire" and soon reached most, if not all, of Hickory High's student body....

This profile was one of four fake pages allegedly posing as the principal by other students at the school—the others being more profane and less amusing. After the principal complained to the school district, administrators worked for some months to block student access to the pages, but were apparently defeated by the student progenitors of the entries. School officials actually limited student computer use at school because of the entries. And Justin twice accessed his page to show to classmates while in school. Shortly thereafter, Justin was identified as the originator of the profile above, and he was summoned to the school district offices, admitted his creation, visited the principal personally, and apologized. That was followed up with a written letter of apology that the principal testified was "sincere." Although Justin was the only one of the four students posting such entries who was caught, the district proposed to place him in an alternative education placement (although Justin was classified as a "gifted" student, he would be sequestered with those adjudged delinquent), banishment from all extra-curricular activities (Justin had been a French tutor to middle school students needing help), and exclusion from the graduation ceremony.

The appellate court noted that this "prank" took place off campus, that it created no school disruption, and that Justin's copying of a photo from the school's website and access to the posting by those on campus was an insufficient nexus to the school to trigger its discipline.

However, in three other cases courts have held otherwise, finding sufficient school disruption from such postings. See *J.S. v. Bethlehem Area Sch. Dist.*, 807 A.2d 847 (Pa. 2002); *Wisniewski v. Bd. of Educ. of Weedsport Central Sch. Dist.*, 494 F.3d 34 (2d Cir. 2007); and *Doninger v. Niehoff*, 527 F.3d 41 (2d Cir. 2008). In *J.S.*, an eighth grade student created a threatening web site aimed at his algebra teacher that went so far as to explain "[w]hy Should She Die," and requested money to "to help pay for the hitman." The site frightened several students and parents and the algebra teacher was so badly frightened that she ended up having to take medical leave from her teaching responsibilities. As a result of her inability to return to teaching, "three substitute teachers were required to be utilized which disrupted the educational process of the students. In sum, the web site created disorder and significantly and adversely impacted the delivery of instruction." *J.S.*, *supra*, at 869. The Supreme Court of Pennsylvania concluded that the resulting disruption of instruction and the educational environment allowed the school to punish the student for his expressive conduct even though the student created the web site from his home.

In *Wisniewski*, the student created an image on the internet from his home computer that depicted a pistol firing a bullet at a teacher's head with dots representing splattered blood above the head. The words: "Kill Mr. VanderMolen" were printed beneath the drawing. VanderMolen was the student's English teacher. The student created the image a couple of weeks after his class was instructed that threats would not be tolerated at the school, and would be treated as acts of violence. The court of appeals reasoned that "[t]he fact that [the student's] creation and transmission of the icon occurred away from school property [did] not necessarily insulate him from school discipline." *Wisniewski, supra*, at 39. The court reasoned that it was not protected by the First Amendment because "it cross[ed] the boundary of protected speech and pose[d] a reasonably foreseeable risk [of] materially and substantially disrupting the work and discipline of the school." *Id.* at 38–39.

In *Doninger*, a student who was a class officer posted a message on her publicly accessible blog complaining about a school activity that was cancelled "due to douchebags in central office" and encouraged others to contact the central office to "piss [the district superintendent] off more." *Doninger, supra,* at 45. When the principal learned of the student's posting, she prohibited her from running for senior class secretary "because [the student's] conduct had failed to display the civility and good citizenship expected of class officers." *Id.* at 46. The student and her parents then sought a court order allowing her to run for class office. The court of appeals affirmed its denial because the student's out of school expressive conduct "created a foreseeable risk of substantial disruption to the work and discipline of the school." *Id.* at 53. The student herself testified that students were "all riled up" and that a sit-in was threatened. *Id.* at 51.

2. First Amendment Rights Outside of School: The State and Cyberbullying and Violent Video Games

a. Cyberbullying

Also related to child First Amendment rights and education is the broader issue of student "cyberbullying" via Facebook and other social networking platforms. This issue implicates the interests of children from two arguably competing angles—the interest of a child to be free from abuse, particularly when the abuse is compounded by the extraordinary ability of the internet to spread information widely and instantaneously; and the interest of a child in exercising his or her free speech rights. This issue was illuminated in *State of North Carolina v. Robert Bishop*, 368 N.C. 869 (2016), where the state supreme court case considered the constitutionality of North Carolina's cyberbullying statute. Under its terms, it is unlawful for "any person to use a computer or computer network to...post or encourage others to post on the internet private, personal, or sexual information pertaining to a minor...with the intent to intimidate or torment."

Four years before the final decision, the defendant and some of his friends posted negative photos and comments about victim Price, including on his Facebook page. The posts included sexually suggestive screenshots and accusations about sexual proclivities, with name-calling insults occurring between the youth involved. The victim's mother noticed self-destructive behavior by the victim and notified the police, spurring an undercover cyber investigation using fake Facebook accounts. The defendant and five of his friends were arrested and charged with violating the above law, and were subsequently convicted. The state court holding acknowledges that a crime may involve speech and not be subject to First Amendment protection, with the traditional law school example being the declaration "your money or your life" by a robber. It is a communication, but one that simply facilitates a crime without its own expressive character. It is possible the court could have distinguished these expressions as direct conduct properly prohibited given their effects when applied to children—given their potential vulnerability and the school milieu, which is often involved. It did not do so, holding that it criminalizes speech in a way that is "content based," triggering strict scrutiny, because the "statute defines regulated speech by its particular subject matter." It then holds it fails strict scrutiny notwithstanding that the governmental interest in protecting children from cyberbullying is a "compelling state interest." The court acknowledges that youth are indeed vulnerable to such abuses, but that the "least restrictive means" must be employed in addressing it, and a statute that criminalizes a posting, even if not harming a child or is even seen by the child is, overly broad. This holding is predictably consistent with longstanding U.S. Supreme Court analyses of the subject matter. They do not preclude a law protecting against cyber bullying of children, even one with criminal sanctions, but validity will depend upon its specificity.

b. Violent Video Games

A second modern example of outside-of-school freedom of speech protection involves video games. Can the state, citing the vulnerability of children and youth, prohibit video games that are extremely violent? Proponents argue that these games are not merely the receipt of communications, but involve active "playing" or interaction with the themes involved. This can and often does include assaults with knives, hatchets, spears, arrows, guns, mines, and explosives of every sort. In the recent U.S. Supreme Court case of *Brown v. Entertainment Merchants Assn.*, 564 U.S. 786 (2011), testing a California statute restricting the sale or rental of certain video games to minors, the Court found that such games qualify for First Amendment protection and noted that the state cannot create new "categories of unprotected speech simply by weighing (their) value against its social costs and then punishing it if it fails the test." The Court contends that California here wishes to "create a wholly new category of content-based regulation that is punishable as speech directed at children. That is unprecedented and mistaken."

Questions for Discussion:

1. Is not extortion a criminal offense based primarily on a message that threatens or intimidates? Would it make a difference if the North Carolina statute were not criminal at all, but simply provided for injunctive relief and perhaps civil penalties? Or a damages action by the victim? What of a statute without the admittedly (in the NC example) overly broad elements, including (a) a criminal sanction for any message which the originator "intends (subjectively) to intimidate" or (b) a prohibitory scope that includes even the "encouragement" to post a message? What of a statute that (a) is civil in format although allowing public prosecutor initiation as such, and (b) prohibits such postings concerning children that are "reasonably likely to generate extreme emotional and harmful response?"

2. Does a video game with interactive participation, including the depiction of death and destruction triggered by a child's shooting of a weapon-like instrument, not extend beyond "communications" with First Amendment focus? What substantive message is being transmitted here, if any? Does the brain development of the child have any relevance? Was not that factor determinative in the *Roper v. Simmons* U.S. Supreme Court case (see Chapter 10 above)? If a child's brain is in formation during these years, and if external influences can have profound effect, does that increase the justification for state protection? Would it matter if evidence were adduced that adolescents are substantially influenced by violent games and that they correlate with teen criminal or dangerous behavior? The Scalia majority opinion discounts such effects, noting that California has declined to regulate other child violence exposures, citing Saturday morning cartoons. Is there a difference between Popeye knocking down Bluto and a game where the child is actually shooting apparent bullets and explosives with rewards being generated for effective destruction? Is that difference discounted by the Court as non-existent not, in fact, rather profound?

3. Child Right to Privacy in Expressing and as Recipient of Communications

a. Control over the Message

Part of the First Amendment arguably includes not only the right of expression, but the right to choose who receives one's messages. Communications are often meant to be received by a specific person or group. This issue is particularly important in the modern era of internet communications, where messages can be transmitted to unintended recipients. Arguably, the right to choose who receives a message is part of the First Amendment right of free speech. This issue was raised poignantly in the case of *Fraley v. Facebook*. In that case, Facebook settled a class action filed against it by a class of subscribers for alleged violation of their privacy rights. Included within the class was a "subclass" of 10.5 million teen subscribers (children over 12 are allowed by Facebook to subscribe to its service). The settlement included some provisions for the adult class and some rewards, primarily to *cy pres* recipients connected to privacy issues. Both Public Citizen and the Children's Advocacy Institute (CAI) objected to the terms based on the consequences for child First Amendment privacy rights. Below is an excerpt of the CAI Reply Brief filed before the Ninth Circuit objecting to its terms.

Reply Brief: *Fraley v. Facebook*
INTRODUCTION

The red flags for this Honorable Court are many: The case settled before class certification; Facebook repeatedly threatened the class with millions of dollars to pay its counsel (due to an unusual California "reverse fee shift" provision), creating an unprecedented "forced collusion" contaminant; the Settlement was rejected by its own lead class representative for the minor subclass; it was rejected even by some *cy pres* award recipients; the primary legal contention of Facebook has drawn *amicus* opposition from the FTC and the California Attorney General—most knowledgeable about involved Congressional intent; and the case has drawn amicus opposition by America's most highly respected privacy and child rights institutions. But the central reason it is properly rejected involves the actual terms to be approved: the addition of the following to Facebook's lengthy legal (renamed) "Rights and Responsibilities" document, as follows:

> If you are under the age of eighteen (18), or under any other applicable age of majority, you represent that at least one of your parents or legal guardians has also agreed to the terms of this section (and the use of your name, profile picture, content, and information) on your behalf.

This addition purports to allow Facebook to seize any posting by a child subscriber, consisting of 10.5 million American teens, edit it and transmit it to whomever it chooses from among its 1.2 billion world subscribers without prior consent of the child or the parent, and even without prior notice to either that republication has occurred, what form it took and to whom it was sent.[Explanation of law pertaining to class action approval]...

Even more troublesome is the Court's failure to consider or comment upon in any way the application of California's information "privacy initiative" now in Article 1, Section 1 of the state Constitution, and extraordinarily applicable not just to "state action," but, unlike most constitutional measures, also applying directly to private actors such as Facebook.

* * *

III. The Settlement is Not "Fair, Adequate and Reasonable" for the Subclass of 10 Million American Children, For Whom No Settlement is Preferable

The Settlement Agreement places children in a position with less protection than they currently have. In fact, it purports to recruit the federal courts to enter an order that would effectively exempt Facebook from numerous statutes protecting privacy and children.

A. The Settlement Imposes an Unenforceable Contract—Even if All Involved Teens Were Somehow to Have Legal Capacity

Under the Settlement Agreement, the consent of more than ten million teen Facebook users will be effective simply via a notice from Facebook that the "Rights and Responsibilities" terms have been altered. This notice does not quote or show how this legal document has been altered nor does it explain what changes have occurred. Note that the original document "checked off" by teens and other subscribers was called "Terms and Conditions" and was routinely clicked-on without scrutiny and was

rarely if ever reviewed again. Those 10 million teens are now to receive a note that a "Rights and Responsibilities" document has been altered in some unspecified way (and even changing its name from its previous iteration)....This change is a significant and categorical waiver of rights to information control of teen postings to a commercial third party. How does it comply with the basic condition precedent that there be a meeting of the minds?

B. The Federal COPPA Statute Does Not Preempt State Laws Pertaining to the Privacy of Children Explicitly Excluded from its Coverage

Contrary to the assertions of both Appellees, the federal Children's Online Privacy Protection Act (COPPA) (15 U.S.C. §§ 6501-08), does not bar (or even address) teen privacy rights. Appellees make their arguments based on their interpretation of legislative intent coupled with the COPPA provision of 15 U.S.C. § 6502(d) which provides that "no state or local government may impose any liability for commercial activities or actions by operators ...in connection with an activity or action described in this title that is inconsistent with the treatment of those activities or actions under this section." But Congress explicitly removed a provision of the original bill that would have required parental consent for children up to the age of 17. Appellants seriously doubt that a single member of Congress from either party intended that this pro-privacy bill should overturn all of the relatively more permissive laws of the sovereign states that protect teens....

Appellees' dismissal of the *amicus curiae* briefs filed by the Federal Trade Commission ("FTC") and the State of California arguing that COPPA does not preempt state privacy laws is baffling. These are the two entities most intimately familiar and involved with the appropriate application of COPPA and California law, respectively. Appellees have no rebuttal to the detailed Congressional intent recitation of these public authorities who enforce and themselves interpret relevant statutory law.

C. The Settlement Terms Approved Below Impermissibly Violate Applicable California Law that Prohibits Children from Entering Into These Types of Contracts Without Clear Parental Consent

The Settlement Agreement purportedly gains the permission of children to use their names and photos for commercial purposes (or presumably, as written, for any purpose) through a contract to which children lack the capacity to consent under explicit California law....Facebook argues that it is not acting as "agents" for teens.... Appellees might be asked: "How is categorical conferral of this extraordinary discretion to a non-parent commercial third party not an effective grant of agency?" The only distinction is that this agent is taking not 10% of the compensation received, but 100%. But that overreach hardly affects the degree of discretion ceded to Facebook, nor any element of an agency relationship—which here exists as to every germane aspect of the agency concept.

* * *

...Contrary to the arguments of Facebook, continued use of a social networking service by a child does not constitute "implied consent" to participate in a separate commercial endorsement market.

CONCLUSION

...The nature of minors and the laws that apply to their privacy rights are issues of law. Accordingly, Appellants respectfully request that this Honorable Court specify that (a) COPPA does not preempt or void ANY common law or state privacy provision as to teens who are not a part of that federal statute; (b) the blanket waiver is not a valid "meeting of the minds" to effectuate an enforceable contract; (c) such a categorical waiver here violates the common law and provisions of the Civil and Family Code as noted above pertaining to the protection, capacity, and privacy of minors; and (d) the blanket waiver violates California Constitution Article I, Section 1 assuring informational privacy. [In note: "The waiver also raises serious issues pertaining to the federally guaranteed Constitutional "right to parent," a germane consideration not briefed below, see *Lassiter v. DSS*, 452 U.S. 18 (1981) and the role of the state here in sanctioning the private usurpation of parental rights as to the control over a child's information and property".]

Some special considerations apply to the momentous decision here....First, this is a case where the lead class representative for the class (Fraley) has withdrawn and publicly condemned the settlement (cite omitted). Two of the *cy pres* recipients have withdrawn—rejecting six figures for their own benefit. The FTC and Attorney General of California dispute the foundational legal assumption of both parties and the Court. And *amici* representing interests entitled to some respect, ranging from the highly regarded Center for Digital Democracy to the American Academy of Pediatrics, have contributed evidence and legal analysis that supports arguments made by Appellants.

Second, it is important for the judiciary to apply the broad constitutional principles and legislative intent in enactments to rapidly changing technology. Perhaps no example illustrates this need more than the case at hand. Privacy rights are now subject to threat beyond comprehension thirty years ago. This settlement for blanket expropriation occurs in the context of an Internet that goes into personal instruments inches from the faces of a child's friends and classmates, and possibly to millions. Any one of those receiving that post/photo can copy and paste and retransmit to large numbers (sometimes called "going viral"). The victim is unlikely to know who has seen it, and has no opportunity to rescind or correct or even comment on it. And it is all without any time limit—Google-ranked items can remain at the top for many years without meaningful recourse or opportunity to defend or deny. The cyber-bullying and teen suicide problems elucidated in *amicus* briefs before this Honorable Court are not merely theoretical dangers. They are real and documented....

b. Status of Privacy/First Amendment Law for Children

The arguments made in the *Fraley* case also included the underlying point that basic free speech rights include the discretion to choose who is to receive one's transmitted message or related personal information. The abridgement of that right is not confined to e-mail thefts by a foreign nation. Rather, civil libertarians argue that the "to whom" selection of a communication is a basic part of free speech exercise by the involved speaker. The right to speak and the right of privacy here interact. However, the advocacy in the *Fraley* case above did not focus on this argument because here the abridger was a private commercial interest rather than the state, to whom the First Amendment guarantees directly apply. That is why the argument here focused on a provision of the California Constitution that creates an "inalienable" right to privacy that properly extends to the exercise of speech, that—precedents have held applies to children, and critically, that also applies not merely to state actions as with federal constitutional rights, but also to privacy incursions by private actors. The end result of the *Fraley v. Facebook* litigation was mixed. The settlement was approved by the Ninth Circuit and the Supreme Court denied cert. However, the Circuit then took the unusual action of depublishing its decision to prevent its application as a precedent.

One way to safeguard privacy apart from direct constitutional bill of rights enforcement is the enactment of statutes that can indeed apply standards to private parties. Chief among these relevant to children is the federal Children's Online Privacy Protection Act (COPPA).[6] Enacted in 1998 and effective as of 2000, it provides some privacy safeguards for children under the age of 13. But, as noted above, it explicitly excludes teenagers. The COPPA statute is subject to the rulemaking and enforcement jurisdiction of the Federal Trade Commission (FTC). Briefly, it provides that web sites or online services directed to children under 13 years of age (or where there is actual knowledge that they are collecting personal information from such children) must provide notice to parents and obtain verifiable parental consent prior to collecting, using, or disclosing it. The FTC Rule also requires operators to keep secure the information they collect from children, and prohibits them from conditioning children's participation in activities on the collection of more personal information than is reasonably necessary to so participate. The Rule contains a "safe harbor" provision enabling industry groups or others to submit to the Commission a request for approval of their operational guidelines in disclosing personal information about children.[7]

Following the *Fraley* case, California took the lead on child privacy protection—of particular importance for teenagers not subject to COPPA and not able to protect themselves *vis-à-vis* private actors through federal Bill of Rights enforcement, whatever the level of market dominance involved. California already has the unusual constitutional right to privacy in its state constitution, albeit vague and not commonly enforced. But that policy has encouraged state legislators to seek First Amendment and privacy protections to the teens excluded from COPPA, and to add additional protective elements. California was the setting for a major privacy voter's initiative petition in 2018; however, it was withdrawn after the agreement by Facebook not to oppose a new state statute, the California Consumer Privacy Act. The Act was enacted on June 28, 2018, but does not go into effect until January 1, 2020, allowing 2019 for further changes. The new statute gives a consumer the right to request of any business the categories and sources of personal information collected about them, and the business purposes and third parties with whom that information is shared. The consumer then has the right to request deletion, which must occur where the request is verified. The consumer could alternatively "opt out" of the sale of personal information that is retained without any loss of product or service benefits for that decision—unless "reasonably related" to the value provided by that information (a provision causing some concern regarding protection efficacy).

Importantly, the law categorically prohibits selling any personal information of any person under 16 years of age unless affirmatively authorized. Teenagers from 13–16 can so authorize, and a parent/guardian must do so for children under 13. This required "opt in" is the system advocated by privacy advocates. As to children ages 16–18, removal would have to be by an inquiry and affirmative "opt out" available to a parent.

Enforcement of the statute rests with the Attorney General but also allows a private cause of action for violations, including statutory damages of from $100 to $750 for each incursion. Actions brought by the AG can yield civil penalties of up to $7,500 per violation. It also creates a Consumer Privacy Fund to support its enforcement, and gives rulemaking authority to the AG to implement it. Importantly, it voids the "term and condition" waivers relied upon by internet and other private interests to both cede privacy and preclude class action or court remedies for privacy incursions.[8]

Note that although a substantial new precedent, the "required opt-in" for those under 16 applies not only to all children, but to all adults as well throughout Europe. In 2018, the European Union adopted its General Data Protection Rule that requires an affirmative opt in from any person subject to personal information gathering and use or retransmission. The affirmative permission requirement sets a new standard that may eventually require replication by major internet players, with Facebook intimating it might apply its terms to United States' operations as well.[9]

c. Discretion to Receive or Discount Communications: Speaker Identity

Also related to destination choice is the right by the recipient of a message to know the identity of the source. That information informs the recipient's right to read or hear from sources of choice and the ability to judge the credibility of information now able to flow from millions into the hands of millions. This system is buttressed by the proliferation of cell phones, laptops, and other devices with easy accessibility via personal messages, video, and sound within inches of a recipient's face—including children for whom this First Amendment medium now dominates all communication. Arguably, knowing whether a communication is from a fifth grader, someone with a financial stake in the matter discussed, an extreme zealot, or the foreign intelligence, is a core part of the First Amendment. The purpose of free speech is not complete license to simply utter sounds pleasing to the source, but involves a core purpose to advance truth and understanding. While it operates with entry or content not circumscribed by the state, its purposes are undermined when it can be manipulated to deprive its participants of information about sources. This area of current legal absence is a proper issue for statutory and litigation attention, including as applied to the First Amendment rights of children.

C. CHILDREN AND FIRST AMENDMENT RELIGIOUS PRACTICE RIGHTS

amish case

Wisconsin v. Yoder

406 U.S. 205 (1972)

MR. CHIEF JUSTICE BURGER delivered the opinion of the Court.

On petition of the State of Wisconsin, we granted the writ of certiorari in this case to review a decision of the Wisconsin Supreme Court holding that respondents' convictions of violating the State's compulsory school-attendance law were invalid under the Free Exercise Clause of the First Amendment to the United States Constitution made applicable to the States by the Fourteenth Amendment. For the reasons hereafter stated we affirm the judgment of the Supreme Court of Wisconsin.

Respondents Jonas Yoder and Wallace Miller are members of the Old Order Amish religion, and respondent Adin Yutzy is a member of the Conservative Amish Mennonite Church. They and their families are residents of Green County, Wisconsin. Wisconsin's compulsory school-attendance law required them to cause their children to attend public or private school until reaching age 16 but the respondents declined to send their children, ages 14 and 15, to public school after they completed the eighth grade.[1] The children were not enrolled in any private school, or within any recognized exception to the compulsory-attendance law,.... and they are conceded to be subject to the Wisconsin statute.

On complaint of the school district administrator for the public schools, respondents were charged, tried, and convicted of violating the compulsory-attendance law in Green County Court and were fined the sum of $5 each....Respondents defended on the ground that the application of the compulsory-attendance law violated their rights under the First and Fourteenth Amendments.[4] The trial testimony showed that respondents believed, in accordance with the tenets of Old Order Amish communities generally, that their children's attendance at high school, public or private, was contrary to the Amish religion and way of life. They believed that by sending their children to high school, they would not only expose themselves to the danger of the censure of the church community, but, as found by the county court, also endanger their own salvation and that of their children. The State stipulated that respondents' religious beliefs were sincere.

In support of their position, respondents presented as expert witnesses scholars on religion and education whose testimony is uncontradicted. They expressed their opinions on the relationship of the Amish belief concerning school attendance to the more general tenets of their religion, and described the impact that compulsory high school attendance could have on the continued survival of Amish communities as they exist in the United States today. The history of the Amish sect was given in some detail, beginning with the Swiss Anabaptists of the 16th century who rejected institutionalized churches and sought to return to the early, simple, Christian life de-emphasizing material success, rejecting the competitive spirit, and seeking to insulate themselves from the modern world. As a result of their common heritage, Old Order Amish communities today are characterized by a fundamental belief that salvation requires life in a church community separate and apart from the world and worldly influence. This concept of life aloof from the world and its values is central to their faith.

A related feature of Old Order Amish communities is their devotion to a life in harmony with nature and the soil, as exemplified by the simple life of the early Christian era that continued in America during much of our early national life. Amish beliefs require members of the community to make their living by farming or closely related activities. Broadly speaking, the Old Order Amish religion pervades and determines the entire mode of life of its adherents. Their conduct is regulated in great detail by the *Ordnung*, or rules, of the church community. Adult baptism, which occurs in late adolescence, is the time at which Amish young people voluntarily undertake heavy obligations, not unlike the Bar Mitzvah of the Jews, to abide by the rules of the church community....

Amish objection to formal education beyond the eighth grade is firmly grounded in these central religious concepts. They object to the high school, and higher education generally, because the values they teach are in marked variance with Amish values and the Amish way of life; they view secondary school education as an impermissible exposure of their children to a "worldly" influence in conflict with their beliefs. The high school tends to emphasize intellectual and scientific accomplishments, self-distinction, competitiveness, worldly success, and social life with other students. Amish society emphasizes informal learning-through-doing; a life of "goodness," rather than a life of intellect; wisdom, rather than technical knowledge; community welfare, rather than competition; and separation from, rather than integration with, contemporary worldly society.

* * *

There is no doubt as to the power of a State, having a high responsibility for education of its citizens, to impose reasonable regulations for the control and duration of basic education. *See, e.g., Pierce v. Society of Sisters*, 268 U.S. 510, 534 (1925). Providing public schools ranks at the very apex of the function of a State. Yet even this paramount responsibility was, in *Pierce*, made to yield to the right of parents to provide an equivalent education in a privately operated system. There the Court held that Oregon's statute compelling attendance in a public school from age eight to age 16 unreasonably interfered with the interest of parents in directing the rearing of their offspring, including their education in church-operated schools. As that case suggests, the values of parental direction of the religious upbringing and education of their children in their early and formative years have a high place in our society....Thus, a State's interest in universal education, however highly we rank it, is not totally free from a balancing process when it impinges on fundamental rights and interests, such as those specifically protected by the Free Exercise Clause of the First Amendment, and the traditional interest of parents with respect to the religious upbringing of their children so long as they, in the words of *Pierce* "prepare [them] for additional obligations." 268 U.S., at 535.

* * *

The State advances two primary arguments in support of its system of compulsory education. It notes, as Thomas Jefferson pointed out early in our history, that some degree of education is necessary to prepare citizens to participate effectively and intelligently in our open political system if we are to preserve freedom and independence. Further, education prepares individuals to be self-reliant and self-sufficient participants in society. We accept these propositions.

State argument #1

However, the evidence adduced by the Amish in this case is persuasively to the effect that an additional one or two years of formal high school for Amish children in place of their long-established program of informal vocational education would do little to serve those interests. Respondents' experts testified at trial, without challenge, that the value of all education must be assessed in terms of its capacity to prepare the child for life. It is one thing to say that compulsory education for a year or two beyond the eighth grade may be necessary when its goal is the preparation of the child for life in modern society as the majority live, but it is quite another if the goal of education be viewed as the preparation of the child for life in the separated agrarian community that is the keystone of the Amish faith....

* * *

...There is no intimation that the Amish employment of their children on family farms is in any way deleterious to their health or that Amish parents exploit children at tender years. Any such inference would be contrary to the record before us. Moreover, employment of Amish children on the family farm does not present the undesirable economic aspects of eliminating jobs that might otherwise be held by adults.

* * *

Contrary to the suggestion of the dissenting opinion of MR. JUSTICE DOUGLAS, our holding today in no degree depends on the assertion of the religious interest of the child as contrasted with that of the parents. It is the parents who are subject to prosecution here for failing to cause their children to attend school, and it is their right of free exercise, not that of their children, that must determine Wisconsin's power to impose criminal penalties on the parent. The dissent argues that a child who expresses a desire to attend public high school in conflict with the wishes of his parents should not be prevented from doing so. There is no reason for the Court to consider that point since it is not an issue in the case. The children are not parties to this litigation. The State has at no point tried this case on the theory that respondents were preventing their children from attending school against their expressed desires, and indeed the record is to the contrary.[21] The State's position from the outset has been that it is empowered to apply its compulsory-attendance law to Amish parents in the same manner as to other parents—that is, without regard to the wishes of the child. That is the claim we reject today.

* * *

Indeed it seems clear that if the State is empowered, as *parens patriae* to "save" a child from himself or his Amish parents by requiring an additional two years of compulsory formal high school education, the State will in large measure influence, if not determine, the religious future of the child. Even more markedly than in *Prince*, therefore, this case involves the fundamental interest of parents, as contrasted with that of the State, to guide the religious future and education of their children. The history and culture of Western civilization reflect a strong tradition of parental concern for the nurture and upbringing of their children. This primary role of the parents in the upbringing of their children is now established beyond debate as an enduring American tradition....

* * *

Aided by a history of three centuries as an identifiable religious sect and a long history as a successful and self-sufficient segment of American society, the Amish in this case have convincingly demonstrated the sincerity of their religious beliefs, the interrelationship of belief with their mode of life, the vital role that belief and daily conduct play in the continued survival of Old Order Amish communities and their religious organization, and the hazards presented by the State's enforcement of a statute generally valid as to others. Beyond this, they have carried the even more difficult burden of demonstrating the adequacy of their alternative mode of continuing informal vocational education in terms of precisely those overall interests that the State advances in support of its program of compulsory high school education. In light of this convincing showing, one that probably few other religious groups or sects could make, and weighing the minimal difference between what the State would require and what the Amish already accept, it was incumbent on the State to show with more particularity how its admittedly strong interest in compulsory education would be adversely affected by granting an exemption to the Amish....

* * *

Affirmed.

[1]The children, Frieda Yoder, aged 15, Barbara Miller, aged 15, and Vernon Yutzy, aged 14, were all graduates of the eighth grade of public school.

[4] The First Amendment provides: "Congress shall make no law respecting an establishment of religion, or prohibiting the free exercise thereof...."

[21] The only relevant testimony in the record is to the effect that the wishes of the one child who testified corresponded with those of her parents. Testimony of Frieda Yoder, Tr. 92–94, to the effect that her personal religious beliefs guided her decision to discontinue school attendance after the eighth grade. The other children were not called by either side.

MR. JUSTICE POWELL and MR. JUSTICE REHNQUIST took no part in the consideration or decision of this case.

* * *

MR. JUSTICE DOUGLAS, dissenting in part.

I

I agree with the Court that the religious scruples of the Amish are opposed to the education of their children beyond the grade schools, yet I disagree with the Court's conclusion that the matter is within the dispensation of parents alone. The Court's analysis assumes that the only interests at stake in the case are those of the Amish parents on the one hand, and those of the State on the other. The difficulty with this approach is that, despite the Court's claim, the parents are seeking to vindicate not only their own free exercise claims, but also those of their high-school-age children.

It is argued that the right of the Amish children to religious freedom is not presented by the facts of the case, as the issue before the Court involves only the Amish parents' religious freedom to defy a state criminal statute imposing upon them an affirmative duty to cause their children to attend high school.

First, respondents' motion to dismiss in the trial court expressly asserts, not only the religious liberty of the adults, but also that of the children, as a defense to the prosecutions. It is, of course, beyond question that the parents have standing as defendants in a criminal prosecution to assert the religious interests of their children as a defense.[1] Although the lower courts and a majority of this Court assume an identity of interest between parent and child, it is clear that they have treated the religious interest of the child as a factor in the analysis.

Second, it is essential to reach the question to decide the case, not only because the question was squarely raised in the motion to dismiss, but also because no analysis of religious-liberty claims can take place in a vacuum. If the parents in this case are allowed a religious exemption, the inevitable effect is to impose the parents' notions of religious duty upon their children. Where the child is mature enough to express potentially conflicting desires, it would be an invasion of the child's rights to permit such an imposition without canvassing his views....

* * *

This issue has never been squarely presented before today. Our opinions are full of talk about the power of the parents over the child's education. See *Pierce v. Society of Sisters*, 268 U.S. 510; *Meyer v. Nebraska*, 262 U.S. 390. And we have in the past analyzed similar conflicts between parent and State with little regard for the views of the child. See *Prince v. Massachusetts, supra*. Recent cases, however, have clearly held that the children themselves have constitutionally protectible interests.

These children are "persons" within the meaning of the Bill of Rights. We have so held over and over again. In *Haley v. Ohio*, 332 U.S. 596, we extended the protection of the Fourteenth Amendment in a state trial of a 15-year-old boy. In *In re Gault*, 387 U.S. 1, 13, we held that "neither the Fourteenth Amendment nor the Bill of Rights is for adults alone." In *In re Winship*, 397 U.S. 358, we held that a 12-year-old boy, when charged with an act which would be a crime if committed by an adult, was entitled to procedural safeguards contained in the Sixth Amendment.

* * *

On this important and vital matter of education, I think the children should be entitled to be heard. While the parents, absent dissent, normally speak for the entire family, the education of the child is a matter on which the child will often have decided views. He may want to be a pianist or an astronaut or an oceanographer. To do so he will have to break from the Amish tradition.[2]

It is the future of the student, not the future of the parents, that is imperiled by today's decision. If a parent keeps his child out of school beyond the grade school, then the child will be forever barred from entry into the new and amazing world of diversity that we have today. The child may decide that that is the preferred course, or he may rebel. It is the student's judgment, not his parents', that is essential if we are to give full meaning to what we have said about the Bill of Rights and of the right of students to be masters of their own destiny.[3] If he is harnessed to the Amish way of life by those in authority over him and if his education is truncated, his entire life may be stunted and deformed. The child, therefore, should be given an opportunity to be heard before the State gives the exemption which we honor today.

> The views of the two children in question were not canvassed by the Wisconsin courts. The matter should be explicitly reserved so that new hearings can be held on remand of the case.[4]

*　*　*

[1] Thus, in *Prince v. Massachusetts*, 321 U.S. 158, a Jehovah's Witness was convicted for having violated a state child labor law by allowing her nine-year-old niece and ward to circulate religious literature on the public streets. There, as here, the narrow question was the religious liberty of the adult. There, as here, the Court analyzed the problem from the point of view of the State's conflicting interest in the welfare of the child. But, as MR. JUSTICE BRENNAN, speaking for the Court, has so recently pointed out, "The Court [in *Prince*] implicitly held that the custodian had standing to assert alleged freedom of religion...rights of the child that were threatened in the very litigation before the Court and that the child had no effective way of asserting herself." *Eisenstadt v. Baird*, 405 U.S. 438, 446 n. 6. Here, as in *Prince*, the children have no effective alternate means to vindicate their rights. The question, therefore, is squarely before us.

[2] A significant number of Amish children do leave the Old Order. Professor Hostetler notes that "the loss of members is very limited in some Amish districts and considerable in others." J. Hostetler, Amish Society 226 (1968). In one Pennsylvania church, he observed a defection rate of 30%. *Ibid.* Rates up to 50% have been reported by others....

[3] The court below brushed aside the students' interests with the offhand comment that "when a child reaches the age of judgment, he can choose for himself his religion."....But there is nothing in this record to indicate that the moral and intellectual judgment demanded of the student by the question in this case is beyond his capacity. Children far younger than the 14- and 15-year-olds involved here are regularly permitted to testify in custody and other proceedings. Indeed, the failure to call the affected child in a custody hearing is often reversible error...Moreover, there is substantial agreement among child psychologists and sociologists that the moral and intellectual maturity of the 14-year-old approaches that of the adult....

[4] Canvassing the views of all school-age Amish children in the State of Wisconsin would not present insurmountable difficulties. A 1968 survey indicated that there were at that time only 256 such children in the entire State....

Questions for Discussion

1. Would the Court reverse a legislatively-enacted minimum educational requirement if the group seeking exception were not the Amish, but Muslims?

2. Justice Douglas notes that 30% to 50% of Amish children leave their communities, although some data suggests that a majority appear to rejoin the Church in new locations. But where outside of the farms or work they learned as a child, where now needing employment in a wider setting, what are their prospects with no more than an 8th grade education? Does the state have a compelling state interest in assuring them opportunity? Does the court have adequate empirical data or appropriate breadth to reverse a legislative judgment that they warrant a minimum floor of public education beyond that level?

3. Is the state's policy to require minimum education standards for Amish children here a reflection of state *animus* toward the Amish? How would it react to a similar withdrawal from public education by other ethnic, linguistic, or religious groups?

4. Could the state require the Amish to provide students with a basic high school curriculum, giving them the option of controlling the school site? Does the *Yoder* decision conflict at all with the spirit of *Brown v. Board of Education* (Chapter 4 above) which determined that, in the racial context, "separate but equal" was inherently discriminatory? Do the Amish children have a right to intermix with and benefit from Wisconsin children who may differ from them, and vice versa? If not

constitutionally embodied, is such integration a "qualified compelling state interest"? Are the Amish regarded as having a collective right to seek to maintain their culture, apart from religion? Do American national minorities have this right? What about Native American tribes who combine culture and religion as do the Amish?

5. The majority opines that a child who desires a high school education is "not an issue." What happens where it is an issue? According to *Planned Parenthood v. Casey*, discussed in Chapter 2, the state may provide its own information about an abortion decision to all minors who seek that procedure. Can the state provide its own information to Amish 8th graders to inform their decision about whether they wish to stop schooling at the 8th grade level?

Christian club case

Board of Education of the Westside Community Schools v. Mergens

496 U.S. 226 (1990)

JUSTICE O'CONNOR delivered the opinion of the Court, except as to Part III.

This case requires us to decide whether the Equal Access Act..., 20 U.S.C. §§ 4071–4074, prohibits Westside High School from denying a student religious group permission to meet on school premises during noninstructional time, and if so, whether the Act, so construed, violates the Establishment Clause of the First Amendment.

I

Respondents are current and former students at Westside High School, a public secondary school in Omaha, Nebraska. At the time this suit was filed, the school enrolled about 1,450 students and included grades 10 to 12; in the 1987–1988 school year, ninth graders were added. Westside High School is part of the Westside Community School system, an independent public school district....

Students at Westside High School are permitted to join various student groups and clubs, all of which meet after school hours on school premises. The students may choose from approximately 30 recognized groups on a voluntary basis. A list of student groups, together with a brief description of each provided by the school, appears in the Appendix to this opinion.

School Board Policy 5610 concerning "Student Clubs and Organizations" recognizes these student clubs as a "vital part of the total education program as a means of developing citizenship, wholesome attitudes, good human relations, knowledge and skills."....Board Policy 5610 also provides that each club shall have faculty sponsorship and that "clubs and organizations shall not be sponsored by any political or religious organization, or by any organization which denies membership on the basis of race, color, creed, sex or political belief."....Board Policy 6180 on "Recognition of Religious Beliefs and Customs" requires that "students adhering to a specific set of religious beliefs or holding to little or no belief shall be alike respected."....In addition, Board Policy 5450 recognizes its students' "Freedom of Expression," consistent with the authority of the Board....

There is no written school board policy concerning the formation of students clubs. Rather, students wishing to form a club present their request to a school official who determines whether the proposed club's goals and objectives are consistent with school board policies and with the school district's "Mission and Goals"—a broadly worded "blueprint" that expresses the district's commitment to teaching academic, physical, civic, and personal skills and values....

In January 1985, respondent Bridget Mergens met with Westside's principal, Dr. Findley, and requested permission to form a Christian club at the school. The proposed club would have the same privileges and meet on the same terms and conditions as other Westside student groups, except that the proposed club would not have a faculty sponsor. According to the students' testimony at trial, the club's purpose would have

Background

2 Process to activate a club

665

been, among other things, to permit the students to read and discuss the Bible, to have fellowship, and to pray together. Membership would have been voluntary and open to all students regardless of religious affiliation.

Findley denied the request, as did associate superintendent Tangdell. In February 1985, Findley and Tangdell informed Mergens that they had discussed the matter with superintendent Hanson and that he had agreed that her request should be denied. The school officials explained that school policy required all student clubs to have a faculty sponsor, which the proposed religious club would not or could not have,...and that a religious club at the school would violate the Establishment Clause. In March 1985, Mergens appealed the denial of her request to the Board of Education, but the Board voted to uphold the denial.

* * *

II

A

In *Widmar v. Vincent*, 454 U.S. 263 (1981), we invalidated, on free speech grounds, a state university regulation that prohibited student use of school facilities "'for purposes of religious worship or religious teaching.'"....In doing so, we held that an "equal access" policy would not violate the Establishment Clause under our decision in *Lemon v. Kurtzman*, 403 U.S. 602, 612–613 (1971). In particular, we held that such a policy would have a secular purpose, would not have the primary effect of advancing religion, and would not result in excessive entanglement between government and religion....We noted, however, that "university students are, of course, young adults. They are less impressionable than younger students and should be able to appreciate that the University's policy is one of neutrality toward religion."....

In 1984, Congress extended the reasoning of *Widmar* to public secondary schools. Under the Equal Access Act, a public secondary school with a "limited open forum" is prohibited from discriminating against students who wish to conduct a meeting within that forum on the basis of the "religious, political, philosophical, or other content of the speech at such meetings."....A "limited open forum" exists whenever a public secondary school "grants an offering to or opportunity for one or more noncurriculum related student groups to meet on school premises during noninstructional time." § 4071(b). "Meeting" is defined to include "those activities of student groups which are permitted under a school's limited open forum and are not directly related to the school curriculum." § 4072(3). "Noninstructional time" is defined to mean "time set aside by the school before actual classroom instruction begins or after actual classroom instruction ends." § 4072(4). Thus, even if a public secondary school allows only one "noncurriculum related student group" to meet, the Act's obligations are triggered and the school may not deny other clubs, on the basis of the content of their speech, equal access to meet on school premises during noninstructional time.

The Act further specifies that "schools shall be deemed to offer a fair opportunity to students who wish to conduct a meeting within its limited open forum" if the school uniformly provides that the meetings are voluntary and student-initiated; are not sponsored by the school, the government, or its agents or employees; do not materially and substantially interfere with the orderly conduct of education activities within the

school; and are not directed, controlled, conducted, or regularly attended by "nonschool persons."....."Sponsorship" is defined to mean "the acting of promoting, leading, or participating in a meeting. The assignment of a teacher, administrator, or other school employee to a meeting for custodial purposes does not constitute sponsorship of the meeting." § 4072(2). If the meetings are religious, employees or agents of the school or government may attend only in a "nonparticipatory capacity." § 4071(c)(3). Moreover, a State may not influence the form of any religious activity, require any person to participate in such activity, or compel any school agent or employee to attend a meeting if the content of the speech at the meeting is contrary to that person's beliefs....

* * *

III

Petitioners contend that even if Westside has created a limited open forum within the meaning of the Act, its denial of official recognition to the proposed Christian club must nevertheless stand because the Act violates the Establishment Clause of the First Amendment, as applied to the States through the Fourteenth Amendment. Specifically, petitioners maintain that because the school's recognized student activities are an integral part of its educational mission, official recognition of respondents' proposed club would effectively incorporate religious activities into the school's official program, endorse participation in the religious club, and provide the club with an official platform to proselytize other students.

We disagree....

* * *

...First, although we have invalidated the use of public funds to pay for teaching state-required subjects at parochial schools, in part because of the risk of creating " a crucial symbolic link between government and religion, thereby enlisting—at least in the eyes of impressionable youngsters—the powers of government to the support of the religious denomination operating the school,"... there is a crucial difference between *government* speech endorsing religion, which the Establishment Clause forbids, and *private* speech endorsing religion, which the Free Speech and Free Exercise Clauses protect. We think that secondary school students are mature enough and are likely to understand that a school does not endorse or support student speech that it merely permits on a nondiscriminatory basis....

* * *

Second, we note the Act expressly limits participation by school officials at meetings of student religious groups, §§ 4071(c)(2) and (3), and that any such meetings must be held during "noninstructional time," § 4071(b). The Act therefore avoids the problems of "the students' emulation of teachers as role models" and "mandatory attendance requirements,"....To be sure, the possibility of *student* peer pressure remains, but there is little if any risk of official state endorsement or coercion where no formal classroom activities are involved and no school officials actively participate. Moreover, petitioners' fear of a mistaken inference of endorsement is largely self-imposed, because the school itself has control over any impressions it gives its students....

Third, the broad spectrum of officially recognized student clubs at Westside, and the fact that Westside students are free to initiate and organize additional student clubs,...counteract any possible message of official endorsement of or preference for religion or a particular religious belief. Although a school may not itself lead or direct a religious club, a school that permits a student-initiated and student-led religious club to meet after school, just as it permits any other student group to do, does not convey a message of state approval or endorsement of the particular religion....

Petitioners' final argument is that by complying with the Act's requirement, the school risks excessive entanglement between government and religion. The proposed club, petitioners urge, would be required to have a faculty sponsor who would be charged with actively directing the activities of the group, guiding its leaders, and ensuring balance in the presentation of controversial ideas....

Under the Act, however, faculty monitors may not participate in any religious meetings, and nonschool persons may not direct, control, or regularly attend activities of student groups....Moreover, the Act prohibits school "sponsorship" of any religious meetings,... which means that school officials may not promote, lead, or participate in any such meeting....Although the Act permits "the assignment of a teacher, administrator, or other school employee to the meeting for custodial purposes,"....

Accordingly, we hold that the Equal Access Act does not on its face contravene the Establishment Clause. Because we hold that petitioners have violated the Act, we do not decide respondents' claims under the Free Speech and Free Exercise Clauses. For the foregoing reasons, the judgment of the Court of Appeals is affirmed.

* * *

JUSTICE STEVENS, dissenting.

....Can Congress really have intended to issue an order to every public high school in the nation stating, in substance, that if you sponsor a chess club, a scuba diving club, or a French club—without having formal classes in those subjects—you must also open your doors to every religious, political, or social organization, no matter how controversial or distasteful its views may be? I think not. A fair review of the legislative history of the Equal Access Act (Act),....20 U.S.C. §§ 4071–4074, discloses that Congress intended to recognize a much narrower forum than the Court has legislated into existence today.

I

The Act's basic design is easily summarized: when a public high school has a "limited open forum," it must not deny any student group access to that forum on the basis of the religious, political, philosophical or other content of the speech of the group. Although the consequences of having a limited open forum are thus quite clear, the definition of such a forum is less so. Nevertheless, there is considerable agreement about how this difficulty must be resolved....

* * *

The forum at Westside is considerably different from that which existed at the University of Missouri. In *Widmar*, we held that the University had created "a generally open forum,"....Over 100 officially recognized student groups routinely participated in that forum....They included groups whose activities not only were unrelated to any specific courses, but also were of a kind that a state university could not properly sponsor or endorse. Thus, for example, they included such political organizations as the Young Socialist Alliance, the Women's Union, and the Young Democrats....The University permitted use of its facilities for speakers advocating transcendental meditation and

humanism. Since the University had allowed such organizations and speakers the use of campus facilities, we concluded that the University could not discriminate against a religious group on the basis of the content of its speech. The forum established by the state university accommodated participating groups that were "noncurriculum related" not only because they did not mirror the school's classroom instruction, but also because they advocated controversial positions that a state university's obligation of neutrality prevented it from endorsing.

* * *

Accordingly, as I would construe the Act, a high school could properly sponsor a French club, a chess club, or a scuba diving club simply because their activities are fully consistent with the school's curricular mission. It would not matter whether formal courses in any of those subjects—or in directly related subjects— were being offered as long as faculty encouragement of student participation in such groups would be consistent with both the school's obligation of neutrality and its legitimate pedagogical concerns. Nothing in *Widmar* implies that the existence of a French club, for example,

would create constitutional obligation to allow student members of the Ku Klux Klan or the Communist Party to have access to school facilities....More importantly, nothing in that case suggests that the constitutional issue should turn on whether French is being taught in a formal course while the club is functioning.

Conversely, if a high school decides to allow political groups to use its facilities, it plainly cannot discriminate among controversial groups because it agrees with the positions of some and disagrees with the ideas advocated by others. Again, the fact that the history of the Republican party might be taught in a political science course could not justify a decision to allow the young Republicans to form a club while denying Communists, white supremacists, or Christian Scientists the same privilege. In my judgment, the political activities of the young Republicans are "noncurriculum related" for reasons that have nothing to do with the content of the political science course. The statutory definition of what is "noncurriculum related" should depend on the constitutional concern that motivated our decision in *Widmar*.

* * *

...The Court focuses upon whether the Act might run afoul of the Establishment Clause because of the danger that some students will mistakenly believe that the student-initiated religious clubs are sponsored by the school....I believe that the plurality's construction of the statute obliges it to answer a further question: whether the Act violates the Establishment Clause by authorizing religious organizations to meet on high school grounds even when the high school's teachers and administrators deem it unwise to admit controversial or partisan organizations of any kind.

Under the Court's interpretation of the Act, Congress has imposed a difficult choice on public high schools receiving federal financial assistance. If such a school continues to allow students to participate in such familiar and innocuous activities as a school chess or scuba diving club, it must also allow religious groups to make use of school facilities. Indeed, it is hard to see how a cheerleading squad or a pep club, among the most common student groups in American high schools, could avoid being "noncurriculum related" under the majority's test. The Act, as construed by the majority, comes perilously close to an outright command to allow organized prayer, and perhaps the kind of religious ceremonies involved in *Widmar* on school premises.

* * *

Questions for Discussion

1. *Yoder* acknowledged the strength of "peer pressure" on children. The prospect of Amish defection based on the required immersion of their children into a public school system with a majority of school children possibly ridiculing the dress and customs of their children was a factor for the Court. What if *Yoder* had been decided differently and its students were integrated into public schools, typically making up 5% of the student body? What would be the consequence of widely attended non-Amish, or perhaps anti-Amish religious meetings right after school and in the same location, attended by teachers and announced by school media? Would it constitute a state (school) arranged or facilitated intrusion into parental religious direction of their children? If a parental fundamental liberty interest is invoked, is there a less restrictive alternative to the *Mergens* practice?

2. Would it matter if the club were to engage in social or charitable activities as opposed to the actual exercise of religious worship?

3. The dissent fears excessive state advancement of religion. The state already grants religion property tax subsidies and income tax subsidies (deductions) for any person who contributes to a church or religion, and our libraries spend substantial public funds on the literature and teachings of various religions. What is the distinction to prohibit public school buildings (which are otherwise unused) to be the site of such activities?

4. Justices Scalia and Kennedy concurred in *Mergens*, but would go further and allow the state to "endorse a religion" so long as it did not persecute or affirmatively discriminate against others. Would such a view be likely if such sponsorship were of the teachings and policies of a non-Christian religion? Do religions discriminate against members of other religious groups, agnostics, and atheists when they claim that their beliefs are valid and those of other religions are "false," and that those worshiping falsely are foreclosed from heaven and perhaps are affirmatively evil? Does the historical record of religious "tolerance" commend the assumption that state sponsorship would be benign for the unsponsored? Is

such persecution more likely to be prevented if the line is drawn to preclude state sponsorship of a religion, or to allow such sponsorship and to prohibit subsequent acts of discrimination or coercion?

5. If the school had an "atheists" or "agnostics" club, could it be denied access to school facilities under *Mergens*?

Christian deaf case

Zobrest v. Catalina Foothills School District
509 U.S. 1 (1993)

REHNQUIST, C. J., delivered the opinion of the Court, in which WHITE, SCALIA, KENNEDY, and THOMAS, JJ., joined.

Petitioner James Zobrest, who has been deaf since birth, asked respondent school district to provide a sign-language interpreter to accompany him to classes at a Roman Catholic high school in Tucson, Arizona, pursuant to the Individuals with Disabilities Education Act (IDEA), *20 U.S.C. § 1400* et seq., and its Arizona counterpart [cite omitted]. The United States Court of Appeals for the Ninth Circuit decided, however, that provision of such a publicly employed interpreter would violate the Establishment Clause of the First Amendment. We hold that the Establishment Clause does not bar the school district from providing the requested interpreter.

James Zobrest attended grades one through five in a school for the deaf, and grades six through eight in a public school operated by respondent. While he attended public school, respondent furnished him with a sign-language interpreter. For religious reasons, James' parents (also petitioners here) enrolled him for the ninth grade in Salpointe Catholic High School, a sectarian institution.[1] When petitioners requested that respondent supply James with an interpreter at Salpointe, respondent referred the matter to the County Attorney, who concluded that providing an interpreter on the school's premises would violate the United States Constitution....

* * *

We have never said that "religious institutions are disabled by the First Amendment from participating in publicly sponsored social welfare programs." *Bowen v. Kendrick,*...For if the Establishment Clause did bar religious groups from receiving general government benefits, then "a church could not be protected by the police and fire departments, or have its public sidewalk kept in repair."...Given that a contrary rule would lead to such absurd results, we have consistently held that government programs that neutrally provide benefits to a broad class of citizens defined without reference to religion are not readily subject to an Establishment Clause challenge just because sectarian institutions may also receive an attenuated financial benefit....

Respondent contends, however, that this case differs from *Mueller* and *Witters*, in that petitioners seek to have a public employee physically present in a sectarian school to assist in James' religious education. In light of this distinction, respondent argues that this case more closely resembles *Meek v. Pittenger,*...According to respondent, if the government could not place a tape recorder in a sectarian school in *Meek*, then it surely cannot place an interpreter in Salpointe. The statute in *Meek* also authorized state-paid personnel to furnish "auxiliary services" — which included remedial and accelerated instruction and guidance counseling — on the premises of religious schools. We determined that this part of the statute offended the First Amendment as well. *Id., at 372. Ball* similarly involved two public programs that provided services on private school premises; there, public employees taught classes to students in private school classrooms.[9]...

Respondent's reliance on *Meek* and *Ball* is misplaced for two reasons. First, the programs in *Meek* and *Ball* — through direct grants of government aid — relieved sectarian schools of costs they otherwise would have borne in educating their students. See *Witters, supra*, at 487 ("The State may not grant aid to a religious school, whether cash or in kind, where the effect of the aid is 'that of a direct subsidy to the religious school' from the State") (quoting *Ball, supra,* at 394). For example, the religious schools in *Meek* received teaching material and equipment from the State, relieving them of an otherwise necessary cost of performing their educational function. *421 U.S. at 365-366.* "Substantial aid to the educational function of such schools," we explained, "necessarily results in aid to the sectarian school enterprise as a whole," and therefore brings about "the direct and substantial advancement of religious activity." *Id., at 366.* So, too, was the case in *Ball:* The programs challenged there, which provided teachers in addition to instructional equipment and material, "in effect subsidized the religious functions of the parochial schools by taking over a substantial portion of their responsibility for teaching secular subjects." *473 U.S. at 397.* "This kind of direct aid," we determined, "is indistinguishable from the provision of a direct cash subsidy to the religious school." *Id.,* at 395. The extension of aid to petitioners, however, does not amount to "an impermissible 'direct subsidy'" of Salpointe. *Witters, 474 U.S. at 487.* For Salpointe is not relieved of an expense that it otherwise would have assumed in educating its students. And, as we noted above, any attenuated financial benefit that parochial schools do ultimately receive from the IDEA is attributable to "the private choices of individual parents." *Mueller, 463 U.S. at 400.* Handicapped children, not sectarian schools, are the primary beneficiaries of the IDEA; to the extent sectarian schools benefit at all from the IDEA, they are only incidental beneficiaries....

Second, the task of a sign-language interpreter seems to us quite different from that of a teacher or guidance counselor. Notwithstanding the Court of Appeals' intimations to the contrary, [citation omitted] the Establishment Clause lays down no absolute bar to the placing of a public employee in a sectarian school.[10] Such a flat rule, smacking of antiquated notions of "taint," would indeed exalt form over substance.[11] Nothing in

this record suggests that a sign-language interpreter would do more than accurately interpret whatever material is presented to the class as a whole. In fact, ethical guidelines require interpreters to "transmit everything that is said in exactly the same way it was intended." James' parents have chosen of their own free will to place him in a pervasively sectarian environment. The sign-language interpreter they have requested will neither add to nor subtract from that environment, and hence the provision of such assistance is not barred by the Establishment Clause.

The IDEA creates a neutral government program dispensing aid not to schools but to individual handicapped children. If a handicapped child chooses to enroll in a sectarian school, we hold that the Establishment Clause does not prevent the school district from furnishing him with a sign-language interpreter there in order to facilitate his education. The judgment of the Court of Appeals is therefore

Reversed.

[1] The parties have stipulated: "The two functions of secular education and advancement of religious values or beliefs are inextricably intertwined throughout the operations of Salpointe."

[9] Forty of the forty-one private schools in Ball were pervasively sectarian. 473 U.S. 384 at 384-385.

[10] For instance, in *Wolman v. Walter* [citation omitted] we made clear that "the provision of health services to all schoolchildren — public and nonpublic — does not have the primary effect of aiding religion," even when those services are provided within sectarian schools. We accordingly rejected a First Amendment challenge to the State's providing diagnostic speech and hearing services on sectarian school premises....

[11] Indeed, respondent readily admits, as it must, that there would be no problem under the Establishment Clause if the IDEA funds instead went directly to James' parents, who, in turn, hired the interpreter themselves. Brief for Respondent 11 ("If such were the case, then the sign language interpreter would be the student's employee, not the School District's, and governmental involvement in the enterprise would end with the disbursement of funds").

DISSENT: **JUSTICE BLACKMUN,** with whom **JUSTICE SOUTER** joins, and with whom **JUSTICE STEVENS** and **JUSTICE O'CONNOR** join as to Part I, dissenting.

Today, the Court unnecessarily addresses an important constitutional issue, disregarding longstanding principles of constitutional adjudication. In so doing, the Court holds that placement in a parochial school classroom of a public employee whose duty consists of relaying religious messages does not violate the Establishment Clause of the First Amendment. I disagree both with the Court's decision to reach this question and with its disposition on the merits. I therefore dissent.

* * *

II

* * *

Let us be clear about exactly what is going on here. The parties have stipulated to the following facts. Petitioner requested the State to supply him with a sign-language interpreter at Salpointe High School, a private Roman Catholic school operated by the Carmelite Order of the Catholic Church. Salpointe is a "pervasively religious" institution where "the two functions of secular education and advancement of religious values or beliefs are inextricably intertwined." Salpointe's overriding "objective" is to "instill a sense of Christian values." Its "distinguishing purpose" is "the inculcation in its students of the faith and morals of the Roman Catholic Church." Religion is a required subject at Salpointe, and Catholic students are "strongly encouraged" to attend daily Mass each morning. Salpointe's teachers must sign a Faculty Employment Agreement which requires them to promote the relationship among the religious, the academic, and the extracurricular....They are encouraged to do so by "assisting students in experiencing how the presence of God is manifest in nature, human history, in the struggles for economic and political justice, and other secular areas of the curriculum."... The Agreement also sets forth detailed rules of conduct teachers must follow in order to advance the school's Christian mission....

At Salpointe, where the secular and the sectarian are "inextricably intertwined," governmental assistance to the educational function of the school necessarily entails governmental participation in the school's inculcation of religion. A state-employed sign-language interpreter would be required to communicate the material covered in religion class, the nominally secular subjects that are taught from a religious perspective, and the daily Masses at which Salpointe encourages attendance for Catholic students. In an environment so pervaded by discussions of the divine, the interpreter's every gesture would be infused with religious significance. Indeed, petitioners willingly concede this point: "That the interpreter conveys religious messages is a given in the case."...By this concession, petitioners would seem to surrender their constitutional claim.

* * *

"Although Establishment Clause jurisprudence is characterized by few absolutes," at a minimum "the Clause does absolutely prohibit government-financed or government-sponsored indoctrination into the beliefs of a particular religious faith."...In keeping with this restriction, our cases consistently have rejected the provision by government of any resource capable of advancing a school's religious mission. Although the Court generally has permitted the provision of "secular and nonideological services unrelated to the primary, religion-oriented educational function of the sectarian school," *Meek*, 421 U.S. at 364, it has always proscribed the provision of benefits that afford even "the opportunity for the transmission of sectarian views," *Wolman*, 433 U.S. at 244.

Thus, the Court has upheld the use of public school buses to transport children to and from school, *Everson v. Board of Education*,...while striking down the employment of publicly funded buses for field trips controlled by parochial school teachers, *Wolman*, 433 U.S. at 254. Similarly, the Court has permitted the provision of secular textbooks whose content is immutable and can be ascertained in advance, *Board of Education v. Allen*,...while prohibiting the provision of any instructional materials or equipment that could be used to convey a religious message, such as slide projectors, tape recorders, record players, and the like, *Wolman*, 433 U.S. at 249. State-paid speech and hearing therapists have been allowed to administer diagnostic testing on the premises of parochial schools, *Wolman*, 433 U.S. at 241-242, whereas state-paid remedial teachers and counselors have not been authorized to offer their services because of the risk that they may inculcate religious beliefs, *Meek*, 421 U.S. at 371.

These distinctions perhaps are somewhat fine, but "'lines must be drawn.'" *Grand Rapids*, 473 U.S. at 398 (citation omitted). And our cases make clear that government crosses the boundary when it furnishes the medium for communication of a religious message. If petitioners receive the relief they seek, it is beyond question that a state-employed sign-language interpreter would serve as the conduit for petitioner's religious education, thereby assisting Salpointe in its mission of religious indoctrination. But the Establishment Clause is violated when a sectarian school enlists "the machinery of the State to enforce a religious orthodoxy."...

* * *

III

The Establishment Clause "rests upon the premise that both religion and government can best work to achieve their lofty aims if each is left free from the other within its respective sphere."...To this end, our cases have strived to "chart a course that preserves the autonomy and freedom of religious bodies while avoiding any semblance of established religion."...I would not stray, as the Court does today, from the course set by nearly five decades of Establishment Clause jurisprudence. Accordingly, I dissent.

* * *

Questions for Discussion

1. Does *Zobrest* signal the Court's acceptance of "voucher" financing of sectarian schools (each school-age child is assigned a sum of money which may be redeemed by parents in any school of choice: public, private, or sectarian)? Its discussion distinguishes *Zobrest* from prior cases prohibiting aid because the latter do not provide expenses they would otherwise have incurred, but merely allow additional sums not otherwise to be expended for religious or instructional purposes in furtherance of a non-sectarian policy of disability assistance. But it also distinguishes *Zobrest* from such prior cases by noting that the subsidy does not go to the schools, but essentially runs with the child or the parents, with the decision on where to spend it left to individuals. Footnote 11 indicates that this rationale alone provides an adequate distinction from prior law and makes such indirect funding of sectarian schools constitutional. What then is the constitutional bar to wholesale voucher funding?

2. The majority seems to be saying that the act of giving educational tax money back to parents and allowing them to decide where it is expended may not be a "public subsidy" violating the establishment clause. How would the majority answer the following: (1) if the gravamen of the wall between church and state is constitutional, it will apply even if a majority vote through their legislature, or directly, to publicly fund religion. How does the additional "vote" of individual allocation supersede constitutional bar? (2) Although individual parents may make decisions apart from state compulsion under the majority's discussion, are not the taxes collected and redistributed coercively by the state using its generic police power—deriving from the people at large? (3) Large numbers of Americans, who disagree with certain religious precepts, will be taxed and those sums redistributed to others to finance religious teaching. Does the fact that parents in the religious sects one finds abhorrent have made a decision to place their children in sectarian schools resolve one's objection?

Zelman v. Simmons-Harris

536 U.S. 639 (2002)

MR. JUSTICE REHNQUIST delivered the opinion of the Court:

The State of Ohio has established a pilot program designed to provide educational choices to families with children who reside in the Cleveland City School District. The question presented is whether this program offends the Establishment Clause of the United States Constitution. We hold that it does not.

There are more than 75,000 children enrolled in the Cleveland City School District. The majority of these children are from low-income and minority families. Few of these families enjoy the means to send their children to any school other than an inner-city public school. For more than a generation, however, Cleveland's public schools have been among the worst performing public schools in the Nation. In 1995, a Federal District Court declared a "crisis of magnitude" and placed the entire Cleveland school district under state control....The district had failed to meet any of the 18 state standards for minimal acceptable performance. Only 1 in 10 ninth graders could pass a basic proficiency examination, and students at all levels performed at a dismal rate compared with students in other Ohio public schools. More than two-thirds of high school students either dropped or failed out before graduation. Of those students who managed to reach their senior year, one of every four still failed to graduate. Of those students who did graduate, few could read, write, or compute at levels comparable to their counterparts in other cities.

It is against this backdrop that Ohio enacted...its Pilot Project Scholarship Program, financial assistance to families in any Ohio school district that is or has been "under federal court order requiring supervision and operational management of the district by the state superintendent."...The program provides two basic kinds of assistance to parents of children in a covered district. First, the program provides tuition aid for students in kindergarten through third grade, expanding each year through eighth grade, to attend a participating public or private school of their parent's choosing....Second, the program provides tutorial aid for students who choose to remain enrolled in public school. § 3313.975(A).

The tuition aid portion of the program is designed to provide educational choices to parents who reside in a covered district. Any private school, whether religious or nonreligious, may participate in the program and accept program students so long as the school is located within the boundaries of a covered district and meets statewide educational standards....Participating private schools must agree not to discriminate

on the basis of race, religion, or ethnic background, or to "advocate or foster unlawful behavior or teach hatred of any person or group on the basis of race, ethnicity, national origin, or religion." Any public school located in a school district adjacent to the covered district may also participate in the program. Adjacent public schools are eligible to receive a $ 2,250 tuition grant for each program student accepted in addition to the full amount of per-pupil state funding attributable to each additional student....

Tuition aid is distributed to parents according to financial need. Families with incomes below 200% of the poverty line are given priority and are eligible to receive 90% of private school tuition up to $ 2,250....For these lowest-income families, participating private schools may not charge a parental co-payment greater than $ 250....For all other families, the program pays 75% of tuition costs, up to $1,875, with no co-payment cap....

Where tuition aid is spent depends solely upon where parents who receive tuition aid choose to enroll their child. If parents choose a private school, checks are made payable to the parents who then endorse the checks over to the chosen school....

* * *

In *Mueller* (463 U.S. 397), we rejected an Establishment Clause challenge to a Minnesota program authorizing tax deductions for various educational expenses, including private school tuition costs, even though the great majority of the program's beneficiaries (96%) were parents of children in religious schools. We began by focusing on the class of beneficiaries, finding that because the class included "*all* parents," including parents with "children [who] attend nonsectarian private schools or sectarian private schools,"...viewing the program as a whole, we emphasized the principle of private choice, noting that public funds were made available to religious schools "only as a result of numerous, private choices of individual parents of school-age children." This, we said, ensured that "'no imprimatur of state approval' can be deemed to have been conferred on any particular religion, or on religion generally."...

* * *

Finally, in *Zobrest*, we applied *Mueller* and *Witters* to reject an Establishment Clause challenge to a federal program that permitted sign-language interpreters to assist deaf children enrolled in religious schools. Reviewing our earlier decisions, we stated that we observed that the program "distributes benefits neutrally to any child qualifying as 'disabled.'" Its "primary beneficiaries," we said, were "disabled children, not sectarian schools."...

We further observed that "by according parents freedom to select a school of their choice, the statute ensures that a government-paid interpreter will be present in a sectarian school only as a result of the private decision of individual parents....

* * *

MR. JUSTICE SOUTER, with whom JUSTICE STEVENS, JUSTICE GINSBURG, and JUSTICE BREYER join, dissenting:

The Court's majority holds that the Establishment Clause is no bar to Ohio's payment of tuition at private religious elementary and middle schools under a scheme that systematically provides tax money to support the schools' religious missions. The occasion for the legislation thus upheld is the condition of public education in the city of Cleveland. The record indicates that the schools are failing to serve their objective, and the vouchers in issue here are said to be needed to provide adequate alternatives to them. If there were an excuse for giving short shrift to the Establishment Clause, it would probably apply here. But there is no excuse. Constitutional limitations are placed on government to preserve constitutional values in hard cases, like these. "Constitutional lines have to be drawn, and on one side of every one of them is an otherwise sympathetic case that provokes impatience with the Constitution and with the line. But constitutional lines are the price of constitutional government."...

The applicability of the Establishment Clause[1] to public funding of benefits to religious schools was settled in *Everson Board of Ed. of Ewing*, 330 U.S. 1 (1947) which inaugurated the modern era of establishment doctrine. The Court stated the principle in words from which there was no dissent:

"No tax in any amount, large or small, can be levied to support any religious activities or institutions, whatever they may be called, or whatever form they may adopt to teach or practice religion." *Id.*, at 16. The Court has never in so many words repudiated this statement, let alone, in so many words, overruled *Everson*.

Today, however, the majority holds that the Establishment Clause is not offended by Ohio's Pilot Project Scholarship Program, under which students may be eligible to receive as much as $ 2,250 in the form of tuition vouchers transferable to religious schools. In the city of Cleveland the overwhelming proportion of large appropriations for voucher money must be spent on religious schools if it is to be spent at all, and will be spent in amounts that cover almost all of tuition. The money will thus pay for eligible students' instruction not only in secular subjects but in religion as well, in schools that can fairly be characterized as founded to teach religious doctrine and to imbue teaching in all subjects with a religious dimension.[2] Public tax money will pay at a systemic level for teaching the covenant with Israel and Mosaic law in Jewish schools, the primacy of the Apostle Peter and the Papacy in Catholic schools, the truth of reformed Christianity in Protestant schools, and the revelation to the Prophet in Muslim schools, to speak only of major religious groupings in the Republic. How can a Court consistently leave *Everson* on the books and approve the Ohio vouchers? The answer is that it cannot. It is only by ignoring *Everson* that the majority can claim to rest on traditional law in its invocation of neutral aid provisions and private choice to sanction the Ohio law. It is, moreover, only by ignoring the meaning of neutrality and private choice themselves that the majority can even pretend to rest today's decision on those criteria.

* * *

...it seems fair to say that it was not until today that substantiality of aid has clearly been rejected as irrelevant by a majority of this Court, just as it has not been until today that a majority, not a plurality, has held purely formal criteria to suffice for scrutinizing aid that ends up in the coffers of religious schools. Today's cases are notable for their stark illustration of the inadequacy of the majority's chosen formal analysis.

II

Although it has taken half a century since *Everson* to reach the majority's twin standards of neutrality and free choice, the facts show that, in the majority's hands, even these criteria cannot convincingly legitimize the Ohio scheme.

A

Consider first the criterion of neutrality. As recently as two Terms ago, a majority of the Court recognized that neutrality conceived of as evenhandedness toward aid recipients had never been treated as alone sufficient to satisfy the Establishment Clause....But at least in its limited significance, formal neutrality seemed to serve some purpose. Today, however, the majority employs the neutrality criterion in a way that renders it impossible to understand.

Neutrality in this sense refers, of course, to evenhandedness in setting eligibility as between potential religious and secular recipients of public money....Thus, for example, the aid scheme in *Witters* provided an eligible recipient with a scholarship to be used at any institution within a practically unlimited universe of schools....it did not tend to provide more or less aid depending on which one the scholarship recipient chose, and there was no indication that the maximum scholarship amount would be insufficient at secular schools. Neither did any condition of Zobrest's interpreter's subsidy favor religious education. See 509 U.S. at 10.

In order to apply the neutrality test, then, it makes sense to focus on a category of aid that may be directed to religious as well as secular schools, and ask whether the scheme favors a religious direction. Here, one would ask whether the voucher provisions, allowing for as much as $ 2,250 toward private school tuition (or a grant to a public school in an adjacent district), were written in a way that skewed the scheme toward benefiting religious schools.

This, however, is not what the majority asks. The majority looks not to the provisions for tuition vouchers,...but to every provision for educational opportunity: "The program permits the participation of *all* schools within the district, [as well as public schools in adjacent districts], religious or nonreligious." The majority then finds confirmation that "participation of *all* schools" satisfies neutrality by noting that the better part of total state educational expenditure goes to public schools, thus showing there is no favor of religion.

The illogic is patent. If regular, public schools (which can get no voucher payments) "participate" in a voucher scheme with schools that can, and public expenditure is still predominantly on public schools, then the majority's reasoning would find neutrality in a scheme of vouchers available for private tuition in districts with no secular private schools at all. "Neutrality" as the majority employs the term is, literally, verbal and nothing more. This, indeed, is the only way the majority can gloss over the very nonneutral feature of the total scheme covering "*all* schools": public tutors may receive from the State no more than $ 324 per child to support extra tutoring (that is, the State's 90% of a total

amount of $ 360),...whereas the tuition voucher schools (which turn out to be mostly religious) can receive up to $ 2,250....

* * *

B

The majority addresses the issue of choice the same way it addresses neutrality, by asking whether recipients or potential recipients of voucher aid have a choice of public schools among secular alternatives to religious schools. Again, however, the majority asks the wrong question and misapplies the criterion. The majority has confused choice in spending scholarships with choice from the entire menu of possible educational placements, most of them open to anyone willing to attend a public school. I say "confused" because the majority's new use of the choice criterion, which it frames negatively as "whether Ohio is coercing parents into sending their children to religious schools,"...ignores the reason for having a private choice enquiry in the first place. Cases since *Mueller* have found private choice relevant under a rule that aid to religious schools can be permissible so long as it first passes through the hands of students or parents.... The majority's view that all educational choices are comparable for purposes of choice thus ignores the whole point of the choice test: it is a criterion for deciding whether indirect aid to a religious school is legitimate because it passes through private hands that can spend or use the aid in a secular school. The question is whether the private hand is genuinely free to send the money in either a secular direction or a religious one. The majority now has transformed this question about private choice in channeling aid into a question about selecting from examples of state spending (on education) including direct spending on magnet and community public schools that goes through no private hands and could never reach a religious school under any circumstance. When the choice test is transformed from where to spend the money to where to go to school, it is cut loose from its very purpose.

* * *

There is, in any case, no way to interpret the 96.6% of current voucher money going to religious schools as reflecting a free and genuine choice by the families that apply for vouchers. The 96.6% reflects, instead, the fact that too few nonreligious school desks are available and few but religious schools can afford to accept more than a handful of voucher students. And contrary to the majority's assertion, public schools in adjacent districts hardly have a financial incentive to participate in the Ohio voucher program, and none has....For the overwhelming number of children in the voucher scheme, the only alternative to the public schools is religious. And it is entirely irrelevant that the State did not deliberately design the network of private schools for the sake of channeling money into religious institutions. The criterion is one of genuinely free choice on the part of the private individuals who choose, and a Hobson's choice is not a choice, whatever the reason for being Hobsonian.

III

* * *

A

The scale of the aid to religious schools approved today is unprecedented, both in the number of dollars and in the proportion of systemic school expenditure supported. Each measure has received attention in previous cases. On one hand, the sheer quantity of aid, when delivered to a class of religious primary and secondary schools, was suspect on the theory that the greater the aid, the greater its proportion to a religious school's existing expenditures, and the greater the likelihood that public money was supporting religious as well as secular instruction. As we said in *Meek*, "it would simply ignore reality to attempt to separate secular educational functions from the predominantly religious role" as the object of aid that comes in "substantial amounts."...

* * *

The gross amounts of public money contributed are symptomatic of the scope of what the taxpayers' money buys for a broad class of religious-school students. In paying for practically the full amount of tuition for thousands of qualifying students,...compare *Nyquist*, 413 U.S. at 781-783 (state aid amounting to 50% of tuition was unconstitutional), the scholarships purchase everything that tuition purchases, be it instruction in math or indoctrination in faith....[T]he majority makes no pretense that substantial amounts of tax money are not systematically underwriting religious practice and indoctrination.

B

It is virtually superfluous to point out that every objective underlying the prohibition of religious establishment is betrayed by this scheme, but something has to be said about the enormity of the violation. I anticipated these objectives earlier,...in discussing *Everson*, which cataloged them, the first being respect for freedom of conscience. Jefferson described it as the idea that no one "shall be compelled to...support any religious worship, place, or ministry whatsoever,"...even a "teacher of his own religious persuasion," and Madison thought it violated by any "'authority which can force a citizen to contribute three pence...of his property for the support of any... establishment.'"...

* * *

...Nor is the State's religious antidiscrimination restriction limited to student admission policies: by its terms, a participating religious school may well be forbidden to choose a member of its own clergy to serve as teacher or principal over a layperson of a different religion claiming equal qualification for the job....Indeed, a separate condition that "the school...not...teach hatred of any person or group on the basis of...religion,"... could be understood (or subsequently broadened) to prohibit religions from teaching traditionally legitimate articles of faith as to the error, sinfulness, or ignorance of others, if they want government money for their schools.

* * *

When government aid goes up, so does reliance on it; the only thing likely to go down is independence. If Justice Douglas in *Allen* was concerned with state agencies, influenced by powerful religious groups, choosing the textbooks that parochial schools would use, 392 U.S. at 265 (dissenting opinion), how much more is there reason to wonder when dependence will become great enough to give the State of Ohio an effective veto over basic decisions on the content of curriculums? A day will come when religious schools will learn what political leverage can do, just as Ohio's politicians are now getting a lesson in the leverage exercised by religion.

* * *

...Religious teaching at taxpayer expense simply cannot be cordoned from taxpayer politics, and every major religion currently espouses social positions that provoke intense opposition. Not all taxpaying Protestant citizens, for example, will be content to underwrite the teaching of the Roman Catholic Church condemning the death penalty....Nor will all of America's Muslims acquiesce in paying for the endorsement of the religious Zionism taught in many religious Jewish schools, which combines "a nationalistic sentiment" in support of Israel with a "deeply religious" element....Nor will every secular taxpayer be content to support Muslim views on differential treatment of the sexes,...or, for that matter, to fund the espousal of a wife's obligation of obedience to her husband, presumably taught in any schools adopting the articles of faith of the Southern Baptist Convention....Views like these, and innumerable others, have been safe in the sectarian pulpits and classrooms of this Nation not only because the Free Exercise Clause protects them directly, but because the ban on supporting religious establishment has protected free exercise, by keeping it relatively private. With the arrival

of vouchers in religious schools, that privacy will go, and along with it will go confidence that religious disagreement will stay moderate.

[1] "Congress shall make no law respecting an establishment of religion," U.S. Const., Amdt. 1.

[2] *See, e.g.,* App. 319a (Saint Jerome School Parent and Student Handbook 1999-2000, p. 1) ("FAITH must dominate the entire educational process so that the child can make decisions according to Catholic values and choose to lead a Christian life"); *id.* at 347a (Westside Baptist Christian School Parent-Student Handbook, p. 7) ("Christ is the basis of all learning. All subjects will be taught from the Biblical perspective that all truth is God's truth").

Questions for Discussion

1. What if the average expenditure in public school is $7,500 per student, and the vouchers (substantially going to parochial schools) amount to $8,000? What additional issues does such a format raise? What if the average expenditure in public school is $7,500 and the voucher amounts to $6,000, but those students who

remain in the public schools include a higher percentage of disabled or language deficient students who require $2,000 more per student than the previous population (prior to voucher departures) to educate? What if the vouchers amount to less than public school costs, but fail to count the parochial school public subsidy from tax deductible contributions they receive?

2. Is the state "establishing religion" constitutionally if it provides open competition and allows parents (or students) to choose public, private, or parochial as they desire and as is consistent with their religious belief? If parochial schools outperform public schools academically, why should the fact of religious teaching preclude subsidy?

3. What action should the state take, if any, where a voucher-financed parochial school admits persons of other religions, but requires them to learn and take examinations in the school's faith? What if it requires them to participate in the prayers and religious practice that is part of the parochial school's tradition? If state schools are permitted to take a "pledge of allegiance" including the group chant "under God," why cannot a parochial school impose similar faith-based practices? Can a Muslim school qualify for vouchers under *Zelman*? Can it include an opening group pledge of allegiance to "one nation under Allah?" Do we approve of the *Zelman* model in parts of the Middle East—where the education of young children is controlled by dogmatic Mullahs who purport to know how and why we were created and which people live in sin? Is our concern affected by the subsidy of those schools by the "civil" government that exercises taxation powers? Is it lessened by parental agreement to their child's attendance at such schools where financed by or through the state?

4. Ohio law purportedly prohibits schools from teaching "hatred of any person or group on the basis of race, ethnicity, national origin, or religion." Is it a violation of such a standard to teach that those of other religions live in sin? Is the definition of "hate" limited to personal *animus*, or does it include the teaching—through voucher (state tax sourced) finances—that other groups will not and cannot be "saved" and are bound to suffer everlasting perdition? How is the state to police its tolerance standards? Is Souter concerned about the public law pressure on parochial schools to limit their religious message—or the prospect that they will not limit it and the state will benignly tolerate that intolerance?

Note on Current Status of School Vouchers Under Establishment Clause: the *Winn* Case

In 2009, the Ninth Circuit issued an opinion that would void the Arizona school voucher system as an unconstitutional breach of the establishment clause. In *Winn v. Arizona Christian School Tuition Organization*, 562 F.3d 1002 (9th Cir. 2009), the court characterized the Arizona voucher system as one granting "income tax credits restricted to taxpayers who make contributions to nonprofit organizations that award private school scholarships to children. Plaintiffs, certain Arizona taxpayers, allege that some of the organizations funded under this program restrict the availability of their scholarships to religious schools, and that the program in effect deprives parents, the program's aid recipients, of a genuine choice between selecting scholarships to private secular schools or religious ones. We conclude that the plaintiffs' complaint sufficiently alleges that Arizona's tax-credit funded scholarship program lacks religious neutrality and true private choice in making scholarships available to parents. Although scholarship aid is allocated partially through the individual choices of Arizona taxpayers, overall the program in practice 'carries with it the *imprimatur* of government endorsement.'"

The Ninth Circuit explained that, Ariz. Rev. Stat. Ann. § 43-1089 gives individual taxpayers a dollar-for-dollar tax credit for contributions to school tuition organizations (STOs), private nonprofit organizations that allocate at least 90% of their funds to tuition grants or scholarships for students enrolled in a nongovernmental primary or secondary school or a preschool for handicapped students within the state. Individual taxpayers can claim a tax credit of up to $500 for such contributions and married couples filing jointly can claim a credit of up to $1,000, provided the allowable tax credit does not exceed the taxes otherwise. Taxpayers may designate their contribution to a STO that agrees to provide a scholarship to benefit a particular child, so long as the child is not the taxpayer's own dependent. The tax credit is available to all taxpayers in Arizona.

Plaintiffs alleged that, in practice, many STOs have opted to limit the schools to which they offer scholarships, and a number of STOs provide scholarships that may be used only at religious schools or schools of a particular denomination. For example, plaintiffs alleged that Arizona's three largest STOs, as measured by the amount of contributions reported in 1998, restrict their scholarships to use at religious schools. The largest of these, the Catholic Tuition Organization of the Diocese of Phoenix, restricts its scholarships to use at Catholic schools in the Phoenix Diocese such as St. Mary's, which advertises its mission as being "to provide a quality Catholic education by developing and sustaining a rich tradition grounded in Gospel and family values." The second largest STO, the Arizona Christian School Tuition Organization, expressly restricts scholarships to use at "evangelical" Christian Schools. The third largest, Brophy Community Foundation, restricts its scholarships to use at two Catholic schools, one of which advertises its goal to be "instill[ing] a knowledge of the truths of faith, enlightened by the post-Conciliar teachings of the Church," and the other of which promotes itself as offering students "an intimate relationship with God" through "the process of nurturing the soul."

Arizona does not specify scholarship eligibility criteria or dictate how STOs choose the students who receive scholarships, and STO-provided scholarships therefore vary considerably. Although STOs may choose to award scholarships primarily based on financial need, section 1089 does not require it. The availability of scholarships to particular students and particular schools thus depends on the amount of funding a STO receives, the range of schools to which it offers scholarships, and the STO's own scholarship allocation decisions and eligibility criteria. Therefore, plaintiffs allege, because the largest STOs restrict their scholarships to sectarian schools, students who wish to attend non-religious private schools are disadvantaged in terms of the STO-provided scholarships available to them. Thus, plaintiffs argued, the disparities in the availability and amount of scholarships for use at religious and secular schools show that the structure of section 1089, as applied, favors religious over secular schools, and thereby violates the Establishment Clause.

Allowing tax deductions or tax credits for private school education at an institution determined by the parent beneficiary seems to be permitted under *Zobrest* above. And, indeed, parents contributing to a religious school or to a church directly may deduct that amount from taxable income—effectuating what is sometimes termed a "tax expenditure" to a religion. But the Arizona allegations raise a wrinkle because of the intermediary of the "School Tuition Organization" getting direct funds through a "tax credit allocation." These STOs then contract with schools for the scholarship conferral—and 85% of the placements so subsidized are in religious institutions. The more subtle issue raised by these allegations is that it is not really a matter of subsidizing a "parental choice of schools," when parents will receive a subsidy only from existing STO beneficiaries—and which are providing slots overwhelmingly at religious institutions. Do you want a subsidy for your child to go to a private school? Your odds of receipt are rather better if you will direct him or her to a religious school that where the available slots predominate. On the other hand, the defendants argued that (a) taxpayers are free to direct their credits to any STO, and (b) parents are free to seek scholarships from a religious or non-sectarian private placement. Although not mentioned in the Ninth Circuit opinion, the amount of the scholarships afforded in Arizona through the STO scholarship alternative is approximately $2,000 per student per year, while the public school system receives $8,000 per student per year. This seemingly quantitative ratio is arguably relevant. For example, were the scholarships to be $10,000 per student, the state would be using state-arranged public monies to provide a clear cross-subsidy to the religious educational system.

Whatever the constitutional merits of the Arizona school subsidy for alternatives to public school, and the Ninth Circuit rejection of at least a demurrer to the complaint, the U.S. Supreme Court granted certiorari in the case, and decided it on April 5, 2011. In the now-titled *Arizona Christian School Tuition Organization v. Winn*, 563 U.S.125 (2011), the Court decided 5–4 that the petitioners lacked standing. The Court noted that taxpayer standing existed for direct state spending that violated separation of church and state, but not for tax expenditures. The dissent argued that much spending is accomplished through targeted tax forbearance, and that tax "credits" in particular redirected $350 million into accounts overwhelmingly subsidizing religious schools—and so allocating that amount of what would have been part of the state budget. Under the standing rationale of the Court, it is unclear how a challenge to such an alleged constitutional offense will reach federal court for effective constitutional compliance. However, it is likely that were the case to reach the Court, the same majority would uphold *Zelman* as applied in the Arizona scheme, relying on the taxpayer individual direction of the credit (not via legislative appropriations) and the relatively small public subsidy. The last factor means that the majority will likely argue that the system does not deprive the state of $350 million, but reduces public education expenditures needed by a much larger sum—adding to the net sums allocable by the Legislature on behalf of all taxpayers.

The worrisome question yet to addressed will be presented (if the Court's procedural barriers allow it) when such per student subsidies for primarily religion-controlled instruction approach or pass the amount expended for public school students.

ENDNOTES

[1] See, *e.g.*, *Baker v. Carr*, 369 U.S. 186 (1962).

[2] See, *e.g.*, *Flast v. Cohen*, 392 U.S. 83 (1968).

[3] See *Alyeska Pipeline v. Wilderness Society*, 421 U.S. 240 (1975), and discussion in Chapter 1.

[4] See *Canady v. Bossier Parish School Bd.*, 240 F.3d 437 (5th Cir. 2001), upholding uniform requirements where parents may "opt out." Note that most states have enacted statutes authorizing school districts to limit dress or prescribe uniforms.

[5] See https://www.cdc.gov/mmwr/volumes/67/ss/ss6708a1.htm?s_cid=ss6708a1_w.

[6] 15 U.S.C. § 6501 *et seq.*

[7] See https://www.ftc.gov/enforcement/rules/rulemaking-regulatory-reform-proceedings/childrens-online-privacy-protection-rule.

[8] See the Act's web site, explaining the 2018 initiative it supplanted and other details at https://www.caprivacy.org/.

[9] See https://www.nytimes.com/2018/05/06/technology/gdpr-european-privacy-law.html.

CHAPTER FOURTEEN

International Law and the Future of Child Rights and Remedies

A. THE STATUS OF CHILDREN INTERNATIONALLY

Due to advances in communications and transportation technology over the last fifty years, our world is a different place. Children who once seemed distant are now part of our consciousness. In particular, we now can visit and see more easily the children in less developed countries—who commonly are in more dire straits than are even the impoverished children of the United States. Indices of family wealth, health, and education are relatively high in North America, Western Europe, and Australia, and are in the process of improving moderately in parts of Latin America, China and India. In most of the rest of the world, children remain in jeopardy, notwithstanding some improvement. On a global scale, the mortality of children under five years old dropped from 12.5 million to 9 million annually between 1990 and 2010,[1] and then to 5.4 million in 2017.[2] But 5.4 million infant deaths, although a reduction, is substantial. And incidence of death widely varies, depending on where the child is located, reflecting the reality that a child's place of birth is a major determinant of health.

States understandably have focused their priorities on their own populations given the post-medieval rise of the nation-state. But advances in technology may be reducing the ability to draw negative caricatures of those from different places. That counterforce to millennia of sect/national/tribal loyalties can challenge the psychological basis of human cruelty based on groupings that discount commonality. And it may give force to one tradition of the world's major religions—the ethical imperative to alleviate human suffering—with special priority for children. National boundaries may still mitigate that obligation, but do not absolve it for religions that purport to transcend nations.

Overpopulation, illness, poverty, hunger, and illiteracy remain the prospect for a substantial number of the world's children. For America, a nation that remains perhaps the world's premier melting pot of diverse origins and cultures, the continuing disparities carry some special concern. Our nation includes those from virtually every place where children are in trouble. We may know their relatives. And the new world of instant contact from anyone to almost anyone makes unavoidable the confrontation between stated ideals and uncomfortable realities. Those realities are summarized in the special edition of the State of the World's Children by UNICEF—published at the end of 2009:

An estimated 1 billion children are still living with one or more forms of material deprivation. Millions of children, particularly in Africa and Asia, lack access to quality health care services, micronutrient supplementation, education, improved water sources and sanitation facilities, and adequate shelter. On average, more than 24,000 children under five still die every day from largely preventable causes. Between 500 million and 1.5 billion children are estimated to experience violence annually. Around 150 million children aged 5–14 are engaged in child labour, in excess of 140 million under-fives are underweight for their age, and about 100 million children of primary school age are not enrolled in primary school.[3]

B. POLICIES OF THE UNITED STATES AND CHILD RIGHTS

Within the international community, the United States exercises a leadership role on multiple levels. Our nation's scientific advances in electronics, biology and medicine, agriculture, and other technologies have produced profound worldwide change. The cultural and entertainment products of the U.S. proliferate the world's media. Advocates for children internationally concede that the political and moral leadership of the United States is important to worldwide child prospects. They contend that American leadership should include not just the ratification of international treaties and conventions advancing child rights, but the vigorous promotion of standards enforcement and of investment. Regrettably, the record to date does not match that expectation. As discussed in this Chapter, the United States is among the least supportive nations for international agreements for children—refusing to sign or ratify even those with widespread international support. But beyond "international rights" treaties, advocates point to three other important aspects of national commitment that can influence the fate of children: (a) our own example, (b) bilateral aid and investment, and (c) assistance to lessen child population increases beyond capacity.

1. Our Own Example

Setting an example *vis-a-vis* our own children would allow us to demand sacrifices by adults internationally without hypocrisy. Child advocates argue that it would include our own recognition of private reproductive responsibility, and of basic safety net and opportunity investment in our own children. U.S. data to date do not indicate such an exemplary national beacon—with other industrialized nations providing more assured health, safety, and educational opportunity. The United States has an unwed birth rate now reaching almost 40% of all births, a radical increase from previous generations. The average child support contribution received by children in single-parent families in the American culture is approximately $137 per month (see Chapters 2 and 11).

International rankings in 2015 measured the national performance of 179 countries along five maternal/child well-being criteria, including maternal health, child well-being, educational status, and political status. The United States ranked 33rd—and last among the industrial countries surveyed. The same study found that an American woman is, on average, "more than 10 times as likely to die in pregnancy and childbirth as is a Polish, Austrian, or Belarusian woman; and an American child under-five is just as likely to die as a child in Serbia or Slovakia."[4]

2. Bi-Lateral/International Aid and Spending Priorities

The second spect is our direct interaction with the children of other nations—bilateral aid from the United States varies substantially between regions and nations. In some spheres, such as AIDS assistance to Africa[5] and the 2010 response to the Haiti earthquake, America has responded with substantial official governmental generosity, and with charitable help directly from the citizenry and from its religious communities. But in general, the United States government focuses its assistance on strategic geopolitics, not investment in the world's children. Indeed, in 2013, the U.S. disbursed $37 billion in foreign assistance, $14 billion of it military and $23 billion economic. The military assistance does not include the much larger sum for direct U.S. military operations in the Middle East or the many U.S. military bases overseas. Israel, Egypt, Afghanistan, and Iraq accounted for just over $11 billion of the $14 billion in military assistance to other nations. The only other nations receiving substantial economic help are those with terrorist implications.[6]

The major object of United States economic assistance internationally has been military subsidy to its allies—and its own international military spending. Critics of U.S. priorities point out that, although the country makes up 4.5% of the world's population, it expends almost three times the military spending of all of the other NATO (relatively wealthy) nations—combined. In fact, the fiscal 2019 U.S. military budget of $686 billion dominates the world,[7] close to three times the budget of China and ten times the spending of Russia. In 2017 our traditional allies England, France, Germany, Italy, Canada, Australia, Japan, and South Korea added about another $300 million to the disproportionality. The remaining nations among the top fifteen spenders are India, Brazil, Saudi Arabia, and Turkey, not our major adversaries.[8] In addition to the contribution from allies, the United States maintains substantial military bases/installations in over 15 other nations, *e.g.*, Germany hosts 27 U.S. Air Force and Army bases—substantially financed by the U.S. military budget.[9]

The United States and other developed nations formally pledged to the United Nations in 1970 to devote 0.7% of their respective Gross National Incomes to the developing nations with most of the world's impoverished children. Neither the United States, nor most of the other nations so pledging, have fulfilled that promise. The most per capita and percentage of wealth generosity for the world's impoverished children comes from the Scandinavian nations of Europe.

In terms of bilateral economic aid to impoverished nations and children, the United States gives a credible amount, but not based on the gross national income proportion—the critical commitment indicator. The top ten nations based on the degree of generosity are, in order: Sweden, United Arab Emirates, Norway, Luxembourg, Denmark, Netherlands, the United Kingdom, Finland, Turkey, with Switzerland and Germany tied for tenth. The U.S. is not on the list. Only the top seven meet the agreed upon level of 0.7% of gross national income for these purposes.[10] Similarly, the proportion of World Bank or other international investment for impoverished children originating from the United States is insubstantial when compared to other developed nations. Importantly, the Trump Administration proposes for 2018 and 2019 to slash such foreign assistance substantially in order to fund military spending increases.[11] This decrease includes a 44% cut to economic aid relevant to children and a halving of the contribution to the United Nations. The UN is a major source of emergency aid for children, including the Office for the Coordination of Humanitarian Affairs (that distributes humanitarian aid), the World Food Program, UN Refugee Agency, the UN Children's Fund (UNICEF), and the UN Development Program.

Interestingly and in contrast, U.S. citizens rank extremely high in measures of individual and private charitable giving—reaching a record $410 billion in 2017—by far the leading source of private international charity. Individual Americans gave $287 billion (70%) of the total, with foundations contributing $66.9 billion, bequests $35.7 billion, and corporations $20.8 billion.[12]

3. Overpopulation and Future Child Health

Many nations lack a child safety net from public resources. A large proportion of child deaths and permanent disability come from those born to families unable to feed and provide for them in such locales. One strategy of amelioration internationally is assistance to prevent unintended children, particularly where they face immediate health and nutrition shortfalls. Beyond the short term, overpopulation represents an obvious problem for future generations. Earth's human population has reached its highest level in our evolution—with a 30-fold increase over the last millennium and now reaching 7.6 billion persons.[13] Rates of increase are particularly steep in underdeveloped nations lacking secure future resources. Even in the more developed nations where families are modest in size, zero population growth has not yet quite been achieved—with immigration in these nations from those with continuing high birth rates a major source of additional population increase.

Although the earth is able to accommodate a very large number of humans, the planet's size can be misleading. Most of it is ocean or is otherwise uninhabitable. Only a relatively small percentage of the earth's land area is fit for efficient human habitation, with temperate climate, arable land, and fresh water. Humans can extend into additional territory, but each new person requires water, food, and energy resources—with ever tightening capacity pressure.[14]

Increased efficiency and mass production have accommodated more than a doubling of the world's population over the past two generations. During the 1960s, Professor Paul Ehrlich wrote his best seller book "The Population Bomb," citing the many world assets in danger of depletion. Human ingenuity and additional discovery now moderate some of his fatalistic predictions—at least as to the precise timing of their diminution. But environmentalists argue that such ingenuity buys limited time. The doubling again of current population within the lifetimes of the newly born portends consequences. Complicating overall population growth is the expectation of more equitable energy and resource allocation among the nations—implying large energy and resource per capita increases for those in the populous countries of Southern Asia, South America, and Africa. Clearly, populous China and India are demanding their equitable share of the world's resources—one buttressed by growing economic power.

Substantial international programs under the title "Official Development Assistance" (ODA) include the "Global Fund" and a special fund to combat AIDS (PEPFAR). This international funding includes ten areas of health concern— two of which have special focus on children: Family Planning and Reproductive Health (FP/RH) and Maternal and Child Health (MCH). The former can help prevent maternal deaths and reduce unintended pregnancies. Each year, an estimated 303,000 women die from complications during pregnancy and childbirth, almost all in developing countries.[15] Approximately one-third of maternal deaths could be prevented annually if women who did not wish to become pregnant had access to and used effective contraception. Worldwide, 214 million women have an unmet need for modern contraception. Total U.S. funding for FP/RH, which includes the U.S. contribution to the United Nations Population Fund (UNFPA), was $608 million in FY 2018. The U.S. has been a funder of this account for 50 years, becoming its largest national contributor and is also the largest purchaser and distributors of contraceptives internationally.[16]

However, the longstanding goals for international family planning availability (referred to as the "Cairo goals") have not been met, and a new set of goals have emanated from the New Millennium Conference. The United States had pledged funds for population-related goal #5—a 75% reduction in global maternal mortality. In 2017, the Trump administration withheld the U.S. contribution, citing the Kemp-Kasten Amendment, although a relatively small sum may be proposed for fiscal 2019. The Trump Administration reinstated and expanded the absolutist Mexico City policy that had been terminated by the Obama Administration, to prohibit any assistance to birth control in any form—including assistance to non-abortion contraception by any entity that allows abortion. The proposed decrease for 2018 was rejected by Congress, but the 2019 and likely future proposed appropriations will seek major cuts.[17]

The other major international goal for children beyond the FP/RH is the Maternal and Child Health (MCH) category. That assistance is largely channeled through the United States Aid for International Development (USAID). Started in the 1970s and initially focusing on malaria that is child-centric, it introduced a newborn survival priority in 2012. The U.S. contributions here were at $1.046 billion in 2010, increasing to $1.4 billion to 2018, and with the Trump Administration proposal for 2019 at a substantially reduced $998 million.[18]

Questions for Discussion

1. A large percentage of current U.S. military spending is committed to nuclear submarines, aircraft carriers, vertical take-off planes (CV-22 Osprey), F-22 fighter jets, F-35 Stealth fighter costs, newly-developed sophisticated aircraft able to fly off of carriers without pilots, etc. The annual budget of the World Food Bank, the major international funding source for child starvation relief, is $3.2 billion. Each

U.S. B-2 bomber costs $2.2 billion to manufacture. Do these illustrative investment priorities reflect the values of the electorate that theoretically determine them? Or are such comparisons unfair, or explained by legitimate overriding self-protection needs of the nation, given the potential for nuclear proliferation or other threats?

2. Much military spending by developed nations worldwide was driven by the cold war. How much current military spending addresses the stated primary national security threat of terrorism? How many of the U.S. military bases overseas relate to current national security threats? Do the lobbying and campaign contribution powers of the defense industry compare to the political influence of those advocating for children domestically or internationally? How will policy changes from the Supreme Court's decision in *Citizens United* affect that political balance in the future (see Chapter 1 discussion)?

3. As noted above, nuclear proliferation remains a possible threat, with possible capacity in the hands of Israel, Pakistan, India, North Korea, and perhaps Iran. Defenders of military spending also note that oil and other resources come from specified nations, and that substantial diminution would disadvantage children whose nations depend upon their supply. To what extent do these concerns explain current U.S. foreign policy and defense spending?

4. While birth rates have slowed in developed nations, those rates in the less developed nations continue at high levels. What are the implications of another doubling of the earth's population to 15 billion? What are the implications of a human population of 30 billion? What policies and practices will achieve population stability—aside from resource limitations or exhaustion with implicit poverty and environmental implications?

5. Perhaps the most important single factor in child health is a reliable supply of clean water and basic sanitation. Each day more than 800 children die from the lack of such.[19] But the U.S. has not supported a declaration of the right of a child to clean water. What are the legal or political factors that distinguish assistance to children with AIDS and the stated commitment to a Global Health Initiative versus a commitment to the clean water and sanitation rights of children?

C. THE EVOLUTION OF INTERNATIONAL CHILD RIGHTS RECOGNITION

The following calendar tracks the major child-rights-related U.N agreements and declarations:

1924 The League of Nations adopts the Geneva Declaration on the Rights of the Child. Rights include means for material, moral and spiritual development; care when ill, disabled or orphaned; first call when in distress, and freedom from economic exploitation.

1948 U.N. General Assembly Passes the Universal Declaration of Human Rights; Article 25 identified "childhood" as entitled to "special care and assistance."

1959 U.N. General Assembly adopts the Declaration on the Rights of the Child, recognizing right to health care, education and special protection, and adding the right to a name and nationality and freedom from discrimination.

1966 The International Covenant on Civil and Political Rights and the International Covenant on Economic, Social and Cultural Rights are adopted, including protection of children from exploitation and affirming education rights.

1973 The International Labour Organization (ILO) adopts Convention No 138 on the Minimum Age for Admission to Employment, including eighteen years for any employment that might be hazardous to "health, safety, or morals."

1979 The U.N. General Assembly adopts the Convention on the Elimination of all Forms of Discrimination Against Women, which protects girls as well as adult women.

1989 The U.N. General Assembly unanimously approves the Convention on the Rights of the Child.

1990 The 1990 World Summit for Children adopts the World Declaration on the Survival, Protection and Development of Children.

1999 The ILO adopts Convention No. 182 "The Prohibition and Immediate Action for the Elimination of the Worst Forms of Child Labour.

2000 The U.C. General Assembly adopts two Optional Protocols to the Convention on the Rights of the Child, pertaining to (a) child pornography and sex trafficking and (b) child victimization in armed conflicts.

2002 The U.N. General Assembly holds its first Special Session on Children world leaders agree to a Compact on Child Rights: "A World Fit for Children."

2007 Five years after the 2002 Special Session (above), a declaration adopted by 140 governments reaffirms commitment to the 2002 Compact and the 1989 Convention and its two Optional Protocols.

1. Precursors to the International Convention on the Rights of the Child

All of the international agreements, covenants, and treaties discussed in this chapter must be both signed and ratified by a nation in order to effectively apply to it. In the U.S., the ratification process requires a two-thirds Senate vote. In practice, many nations (including the U.S.) may also need domestic implementing legislation to enforce the relevant standards. Accordingly, many child-related agreements that are ratified by the Senate also include subsequent federal follow-up legislation. But as discussed below, where international agreements become close to universally ratified, they may obtain the status of "international common law." In addition, treaties that have not been ratified and fall short of that status may have some influence in the interpretation of American law as discussed below. Or, an agreement may effectively redefine the terms of a treaty that is binding.

a. The Declaration of Human Rights

One non-treaty document that has binding effect, although not directly ratified itself, is the 1948 Declaration of Human Rights. This seminal Declaration was adopted to define the meaning of the phrases "fundamental freedoms" and "human rights" appearing in the United Nations Charter, which is itself binding on all member states. For this reason, the Universal Declaration is a fundamental constitutive document of the United Nations. Many international lawyers also argue that the Declaration forms part of customary or common international law, as noted above, and is a powerful tool in applying diplomatic and moral pressure to governments violating its articles. The 1968 United Nations International Conference on Human Rights advised that the 1948 Declaration "constitutes an obligation for the members of the international community" to all persons. The Declaration focuses on adult rights, but has relevance to children in many of its provisions pertaining to non-discrimination, medical coverage, safety, due process, personal rights (to travel, marry, own property), fair wages, and rights to an education, among others.

The three articles with particular impact on children include:

Article 16

Men and women of full age, without any limitation due to race, nationality or religion, have the right to marry and to found a family. They are entitled to equal rights as to marriage, during marriage and at its dissolution. Marriage shall be entered into only with the free and full consent of the intending spouses. The family is the natural and fundamental group unit of society and is entitled to protection by society and the State.

Article 25

Everyone has the right to a standard of living adequate for the health and well-being of himself and of his family, including food, clothing, housing and medical care and necessary social services, and the right to security in the event of unemployment, sickness, disability, widowhood, old age or other lack of livelihood in circumstances beyond his control. Motherhood and childhood are entitled to special care and assistance. All children, whether born in or out of wedlock, shall enjoy the same social protection.

Article 26

Everyone has the right to education. Education shall be free, at least in the elementary and fundamental stages. Elementary education shall be compulsory. Technical and professional education shall be made generally available and higher education shall be equally accessible to all on the basis of merit. Education shall be directed to the full development of the human personality and to the strengthening of respect for human rights and fundamental freedoms. It shall promote understanding, tolerance and friendship among all nations, racial or religious groups, and shall further the activities of the United Nations for the maintenance of peace. Parents have a prior right to choose the kind of education that shall be given to their children.

b. The International Covenant on Civil and Political Rights

In 1966, the United Nations adopted an "International Covenant on Civil and Political Rights." Entered into force in 1976, the Covenant included the theoretically binding provision that all children "shall have, without any discrimination as to race, colour, sex, language, religion, national or social origin, property or birth, the right to such measures of protection as are required by his status as a minor, on the part of his family, society and the State." The United States has signed and ratified the Covenant.

The Covenant includes several articles particularly relevant to child rights:

Article 10

1. All persons deprived of their liberty shall be treated with humanity and with respect for the inherent dignity of the human person.

2. (a) Accused persons shall, save in exceptional circumstances, be segregated from convicted persons and shall be subject to separate treatment appropriate to their status as unconvicted persons; (b) Accused juvenile persons shall be separated from adults and brought as speedily as possible for adjudication.

3. The penitentiary system shall comprise treatment of prisoners the essential aim of which shall be their reformation and social rehabilitation. Juvenile offenders shall be segregated from adults and be accorded treatment appropriate to their age and legal status.

Article 14

1. All persons shall be equal before the courts and tribunals. In the determination of any criminal charge against him, or of his rights and obligations in a suit at law, everyone shall be entitled to a fair and public hearing by a competent, independent and impartial tribunal established by law. The press and the public may be excluded from all or part of a trial for reasons of morals, public order (*ordre public*) or national security in a democratic society, or when the interest of the private lives of the parties so requires, or to the extent strictly necessary in the opinion of the court in special circumstances where publicity would prejudice the interests of justice; but any judgement rendered in a criminal case or in a suit at law shall be made public except where the interest of juvenile persons otherwise requires or the proceedings concern matrimonial disputes or the guardianship of children.

Article 18

1. Everyone shall have the right to freedom of thought, conscience and religion...

4.The States Parties to the present Covenant undertake to have respect for the liberty of parents and, when applicable, legal guardians to ensure the religious and moral education of their children in conformity with their own convictions.

Article 23

1. The family is the natural and fundamental group unit of society and is entitled to protection by society and the State.

2. The right of men and women of marriageable age to marry and to found a family shall be recognized.

3. No marriage shall be entered into without the free and full consent of the intending spouses.

4. States Parties to the present Covenant shall take appropriate steps to ensure equality of rights and responsibilities of spouses as to marriage, during marriage and at its dissolution. In the case of dissolution, provision shall be made for the necessary protection of any children.

Article 24

1. Every child shall have, without any discrimination as to race, colour, sex, language, religion, national or social origin, property or birth, the right to such measures of protection as are required by his status as a minor, on the part of his family, society and the State.

2. Every child shall be registered immediately after birth and shall have a name.

3. Every child has the right to acquire a nationality.

c. The International Covenant of Economic, Social and Cultural Rights

Also adopted in 1966, and effective in 1976, was the U.N.'s International Covenant on Economic, Social, and Cultural Rights, providing that "[s]pecial measures of protection and assistance should be taken on behalf of all children and young persons without any discrimination for reasons of parentage or other conditions." The U.S. has signed but not ratified this Covenant.[20] Other provisions of particular relevance to child rights include:

Article 10

1. The widest possible protection and assistance should be accorded to the family, which is the natural and fundamental group unit of society, particularly for its establishment and while it is responsible for the care and education of dependent children. Marriage must be entered into with the free consent of the intending spouses.

2. Special protection should be accorded to mothers during a reasonable period before and after childbirth. During such period working mothers should be accorded paid leave or leave with adequate social security benefits.

3. Special measures of protection and assistance should be taken on behalf of all children and young persons without any discrimination for reasons of parentage or other conditions. Children and young persons should be protected from economic and social exploitation. Their employment in work harmful to their morals or health or dangerous to life or likely to hamper their normal development should be punishable by law. States should also set age limits below which the paid employment of child labour should be prohibited and punishable by law.

Article 11

1. The States Parties to the present Covenant recognize the right of everyone to an adequate standard of living for himself and his family, including adequate food, clothing and housing, and to the continuous improvement of living conditions. The States Parties will take appropriate steps to ensure the realization of this right, recognizing to this effect the essential importance of international cooperation based on free consent.

2. The States Parties to the present Covenant, recognizing the fundamental right of everyone to be free from hunger, shall take, individually and through international co-operation, the measures, including specific programmes, which are needed:

(a) To improve methods of production, conservation and distribution of food by making full use of technical and scientific knowledge, by disseminating knowledge of the principles of nutrition and by developing or reforming agrarian systems in such a way as to achieve the most efficient development and utilization of natural resources;

(b) Taking into account the problems of both food-importing and food-exporting countries, to ensure an equitable distribution of world food supplies in relation to need.

Article 12

1. The States Parties to the present Covenant recognize the right of everyone to the enjoyment of the highest attainable standard of physical and mental health.

2. The steps to be taken by the States Parties to the present Covenant to achieve the full realization of this right shall include those necessary for:

(a) The provision for the reduction of the stillbirth-rate and of infant mortality and for the healthy development of the child;

(b) The improvement of all aspects of environmental and industrial hygiene;

(c) The prevention, treatment and control of epidemic, endemic, occupational and other diseases;

(d) The creation of conditions which would assure to all medical service and medical attention in the event of sickness.

Article 13

1. The States Parties to the present Covenant recognize the right of everyone to education. They agree that education shall be directed to the full development of the human personality and the sense of its dignity, and shall strengthen the respect for human rights and fundamental freedoms. They further agree that education shall enable all persons to participate effectively in a free society, promote understanding, tolerance and friendship among all nations and all racial, ethnic or religious groups, and further the activities of the United Nations for the maintenance of peace.

2. The States Parties to the present Covenant recognize that, with a view to achieving the full realization of this right:

(a) Primary education shall be compulsory and available free to all;

(b) Secondary education in its different forms, including technical and vocational secondary education, shall be made generally available and accessible to all by every appropriate means, and in particular by the progressive introduction of free education;

(c) Higher education shall be made equally accessible to all, on the basis of capacity, by every appropriate means, and in particular by the progressive introduction of free education;

(d) s who have not received or completed the whole period of their primary education;

(e) The development of a system of schools at all levels shall be actively pursued, an adequate fellowship system shall be established, and the material conditions of teaching staff shall be continuously improved.

3. The States Parties to the present Covenant undertake to have respect for the liberty of parents and, when applicable, legal guardians to choose for their children schools, other than those established by the public authorities, which conform to such minimum educational standards as may be laid down or approved by the State and to ensure the religious and moral education of their children in conformity with their own convictions.

4. No part of this article shall be construed so as to interfere with the liberty of individuals and bodies to establish and direct educational institutions, subject always to the observance of the principles set forth in paragraph I of this article and to the requirement that the education given in such institutions shall conform to such minimum standards as may be laid down by the State.

d. The Convention on the Elimination of all Forms of Discrimination Against Women

In 1979, the U.N. General Assembly adopted the Convention on the Elimination of all Forms of Discrimination Against Women, which protects girls as well as adult women in several respects. For example, the Convention includes a statement of purpose and several provisions of importance to child rights:

> ...Bearing in mind the great contribution of women to the welfare of the family and to the development of society, so far not fully recognized, the social significance of maternity and the role of both parents in the family and in the upbringing of children, and aware that the role of women in procreation should not be a basis for discrimination but that the upbringing of children requires a sharing of responsibility between men and women and society as a whole....

Article 5

States Parties shall take all appropriate measures:

(a) To modify the social and cultural patterns of conduct of men and women, with a view to achieving the elimination of prejudices and customary and all other practices which are based on the idea of the inferiority or the superiority of either of the sexes or on stereotyped roles for men and women;

(b) To ensure that family education includes a proper understanding of maternity as a social function and the recognition of the common responsibility of men and women in the upbringing and development of their children, it being understood that the interest of the children is the primordial consideration in all cases.

Article 9

1. States Parties shall grant women equal rights with men to acquire, change or retain their nationality. They shall ensure in particular that neither marriage to an alien nor change of nationality by the husband during marriage shall automatically change the nationality of the wife, render her stateless or force upon her the nationality of the husband.

2. States Parties shall grant women equal rights with men with respect to the nationality of their children.

Article 16

1. States Parties shall take all appropriate measures to eliminate discrimination against women in all matters relating to marriage and family relations and in particular shall ensure, on a basis of equality of men and women:

(a) The same right to enter into marriage;

(b) The same right freely to choose a spouse and to enter into marriage only with their free and full consent;

(c) The same rights and responsibilities during marriage and at its dissolution;

(d) The same rights and responsibilities as parents, irrespective of their marital status, in matters relating to their children; in all cases the interests of the children shall be paramount;

(e) The same rights to decide freely and responsibly on the number and spacing of their children and to have access to the information, education and means to enable them to exercise these rights;

(f) The same rights and responsibilities with regard to guardianship, wardship, trusteeship and adoption of children, or similar institutions where these concepts exist in national legislation; in all cases the interests of the children shall be paramount;

(g) The same personal rights as husband and wife, including the right to choose a family name, a profession and an occupation;

(h) The same rights for both spouses in respect of the ownership, acquisition, management, administration, enjoyment and disposition of property, whether free of charge or for a valuable consideration.

2. The betrothal and the marriage of a child shall have no legal effect, and all necessary action, including legislation, shall be taken to specify a minimum age for marriage and to make the registration of marriages in an official registry compulsory.

2. The Convention on the Rights of the Child

The agreements excerpted above addressed children as part of adult family rights. The first and still major international agreement focusing on children is the United Nations' Convention on the Rights of the Child. Drafting began on the Convention in 1979—which was declared the "Year of the Child" internationally. It was adopted by the General Assembly in 1989. The Convention has been signed and ratified by all but one U.N. member nation—the United States.

The Convention sets forth the rights of children in over 54 articles in three categories: (1) participation in society and in decisions affecting their future, (2) protection against discrimination, neglect, and exploitation, and (3) assistance for basic needs.[21]

Important provisions include the following:

Article 3

1. In all actions concerning children, whether undertaken by public or private social welfare institutions,...the best interests of the child shall be a primary consideration.

2. States Parties undertake to ensure the child such protection and care as is necessary for his or her well-being, taking into account the rights and duties of his or her parents, legal guardians, or other individuals legally responsible....

3. States Parties shall ensure that the institutions, services and facilities responsible for the care or protection of children shall conform with the standards established by competent authorities, particularly in the areas of safety, health, in the number and suitability of their staff, as well as competent supervision.

Article 6

1. States Parties recognize that every child has the inherent right to life.

2. States Parties shall ensure to the maximum extent possible the survival and development of the child.

Article 7

1. The child shall be registered immediately after birth and shall have the right from birth to a name, the right to acquire a nationality and, as far as possible, the right to know and be cared for by his or her parents.

Article 9

1. States Parties shall ensure that a child shall not be separated from his or her parents against their will, except when competent authorities subject to judicial review determine, in accordance with applicable law and procedures, that such separation is necessary for the best interests of the child. Such determination may be necessary in a particular case such as one involving abuse or neglect of the child by the parents, or one where the parents are living separately and a decision must be made as to the child's place of residence.

2. In any proceedings pursuant to paragraph 1 of the present article, all interested parties shall be given an opportunity to participate in the proceedings and make their views known.

3. States Parties shall respect the right of the child who is separated from one or both parents to maintain personal relations and direct contact with both parents on a regular basis, except if it is contrary to the child's best interests.

Article 12

1. States Parties shall assure to the child who is capable of forming his or her own views the right to express those views freely in all matters affecting the child, the views of the child being given due weight in accordance with the age and maturity of the child.

2. For this purpose, the child shall in particular be provided the opportunity to be heard in any judicial and administrative proceedings affecting the child, either directly, or through a representative or an appropriate body, in a manner consistent with the procedural rules of national law.

Article 13

1. The child shall have the right to freedom of expression; this right shall include

freedom to seek, receive and impart information and ideas of all kinds, regardless of frontiers, either orally, in writing or in print, in the form of art, or through any other media of the child's choice.

2. The exercise of this right may be subject to certain restrictions, but these shall only be such as are provided by law and are necessary:

(a) For respect of the rights or reputations of others; or

(b) For the protection of national security or of public order (ordre public), or of public health or morals.

Article 14

1. States Parties shall respect the right of the child to freedom of thought, conscience and religion.

2. States Parties shall respect the rights and duties of the parents and, when applicable, legal guardians, to provide direction to the child in the exercise of his or her right in a manner consistent with the evolving capacities of the child.

3. Freedom to manifest one's religion or beliefs may be subject only to such limitations as are prescribed by law and are necessary to protect public safety, order, health or morals, or the fundamental rights and freedoms of others.

Article 15

1. States Parties recognize the rights of the child to freedom of association and to freedom of peaceful assembly.

Article 18

1. States Parties shall use their best efforts to ensure recognition of the principle that both parents have common responsibilities for the upbringing and development of the child. Parents or, as the case may be, legal guardians, have the primary responsibility for the upbringing and development of the child. The best interests of the child will be their basic concern.

Article 19

1. States Parties shall take all appropriate legislative, administrative, social and educational measures to protect the child from all forms of physical or mental violence, injury or abuse, neglect or negligent treatment, maltreatment or exploitation, including sexual abuse, while in the care of parent(s), legal guardian(s) or any other person who has the care of the child.

Article 23

1. States Parties recognize that a mentally or physically disabled child should enjoy a full and decent life, in conditions which ensure dignity, promote self-reliance and facilitate the child's active participation in the community.

2. States Parties recognize the right of the disabled child to special care and shall encourage and ensure the extension, subject to available resources, to the eligible child and those responsible for his or her care, of assistance for which application is made and which is appropriate to the child's condition and to the circumstances of the parents or others caring for the child.

Article 24

1. States Parties recognize the right of the child to the enjoyment of the highest attainable standard of health and to facilities for the treatment of illness and rehabilitation of health. States Parties shall strive to ensure that no child is deprived of his or her right of access to such health care services.

Article 25

States Parties recognize the right of a child who has been placed by the competent authorities for the purposes of care, protection or treatment of his or her physical or mental health, to a periodic review of the treatment provided to the child and all other circumstances relevant to his or her placement.

Article 26

1. States Parties shall recognize for every child the right to benefit from social security, including social insurance...

Article 27

1. States Parties recognize the right of every child to a standard of living adequate for the child's physical, mental, spiritual, moral and social development.

2. The parent(s) or others responsible for the child have the primary responsibility to secure, within their abilities and financial capacities, the conditions of living necessary for the child's development.

3. States Parties, in accordance with national conditions and within their means, shall take appropriate measures to assist parents and others responsible for the child to implement this right and shall in case of need provide material assistance and support programmes, particularly with regard to nutrition, clothing and housing.

Article 28

1. States Parties recognize the right of the child to education, and with a view to achieving this right progressively and on the basis of equal opportunity, they shall, in particular:

(a) Make primary education compulsory and available free to all;

(b) Encourage the development of different forms of secondary education,...

(c) Make higher education accessible to all on the basis of capacity by every appropriate means;

Article 32

1. States Parties recognize the right of the child to be protected from economic exploitation and from performing any work that is likely to be hazardous or to interfere with the child's education, or to be harmful to the child's health or physical, mental, spiritual, moral or social development.

2. States Parties shall take legislative, administrative, social and educational measures to ensure the implementation of the present article. To this end, and having regard to the relevant provisions of other international instruments, States Parties shall in particular:

(a) Provide for a minimum age or minimum ages for admission to employment....

Article 34

States Parties undertake to protect the child from all forms of sexual exploitation and sexual abuse. For these purposes, States Parties shall in particular take all appropriate national, bilateral and multilateral measures to prevent:

(a) The inducement or coercion of a child to engage in any unlawful sexual activity;

(b) The exploitative use of children in prostitution or other unlawful sexual practices;

(c) The exploitative use of children in pornographic performances and materials.

Article 37

States Parties shall ensure that:

(a) No child shall be subjected to torture or other cruel, inhuman or degrading treatment or punishment. Neither capital punishment nor life imprisonment without possibility of release shall be imposed for offences committed by persons below eighteen years of age;

(b) No child shall be deprived of his or her liberty unlawfully or arbitrarily. The arrest, detention or imprisonment of a child shall be in conformity with the law and shall be used only as a measure of last resort and for the shortest appropriate period of time;

(c) Every child deprived of liberty shall be treated with humanity and respect for the inherent dignity of the human person, and in a manner which takes into account the needs of persons of his or her age. In particular, every child deprived of liberty shall be separated from adults unless it is considered in the child's best interest not to do so and shall have the right to maintain contact with his or her family through correspondence and visits, save in exceptional circumstances....

Note on U.S. Historical Opposition to the Convention

The U.S. government's opposition to the Convention centers on five of its aspects: (1) Article 37's prohibition on child capital punishment, which the U.S. uniquely imposed until 2005 (as discussed in Chapter 10); (2) the child labor limitations of Article 32, which some contend may be broader than current U.S. standards; (3) the promise of economic/health/special needs/education support from the state; (4) the possible application of minimum standards against the prerogatives of parents; and (5) the supersession of state sovereignty (including possible funding obligations) were its provisions to be ratified—since such ratification could incorporate its provisions into the body of federal law arguably entitled to constitutional supremacy over state discretion.

Although not ratified, some commentators contend that, given their virtual universal acceptance, the provisions of the Convention have achieved the status of "international common law," and as such are binding on the United States under international law theory, irrespective of its non-ratification by any single nation.

Questions for Discussion

1. What are the implications of the U.N. Convention on the Rights of the Child, *e.g.*, assured provision of health coverage, as to U.S. policies that omit or contradict them? Does such widespread adoption of the Convention not make it effective "international common law" effective in all nation-states? How are they to be enforced domestically (see discussion of international law weight in domestic court decisions below)?

2. The Convention on the Rights of the Child excludes some aspects of child deprivation, such as environmental rights and future indebtedness. But it includes many rights not secured in many parts of the world. Does it address the discrimination against girls in educational opportunity, *e.g.*, in nations guided by fundamentalist Muslim theocracies? Does it vary based on the culture and wealth of individual nations? Should it so vary, and how?

3. Addenda to the Convention on the Rights of the Child

In 2002, two optional protocols were added to the U.N. Convention on the Rights of the Child. Both have been ratified by the vast majority of nations.

a. Optional Protocol #1 on the Involvement of Children in Armed Conflict and Subsequent Enforcement

From 1997 to 2013, an estimated two million children died in armed conflict internationally, with six million permanently disabled. A 2019 report finds that from 2013 to 2017 another 550,000 babies are believed to have died due to armed conflict within the ten most volatile nations.[22] The author of the report noted that "…the way today's wars are being fought is causing more suffering to children. Almost one in five children are living in areas impacted by violence—more than at any time in the last two decades."[23] This cost is over and above the devastating effect of the loss of one or both parents in armed conflicts. Over fourteen million children have been forcibly displaced due to organized violence, including substantial numbers from the conflicts in Central Africa and in internecine conflicts such as those in Iraq and Yugoslavia.

Article 38 of the Convention of the Rights of the Child as entered into force in 1990 included four paragraphs addressing child involvement in the armed forces. The most important is the requirement to "take all feasible measures to ensure that persons who have not attained the age of fifteen years do not take a direct part in hostilities." It also provides that "State Parties shall refrain from recruiting" such persons into their armed forces. In recruiting among those persons who have attained the age of fifteen years but who have not attained the age of eighteen years, States Parties shall endeavour to give priority to those who are oldest."

Three relevant international agreements or declarations followed these limited provisions. In December of 1995, the 26th International Conference of the Red Cross and the Red Crescent recommended that parties to conflicts take steps to ensure that children under the age of eighteen do not take part in hostilities. The Rome Statute of the International Criminal Court of 1998 declared that the practice of conscripting or enlisting children under the age of fifteen years into the armed forces—or using them to "participate actively in hostilities"—is a war crime. That crime includes such conduct whether committed in an international or domestic dispute. In 1999, the International Labor Convention #182 was adopted on child labor abuse, and included within its ambit a prohibition on the forced recruitment of children for service in armed conflict.

These developments led to the 2002 Optional Protocol on the Involvement of Children in Armed Conflict to essentially strengthen Article 38 of the Convention. It requires nations to take "all feasible measures" to ensure that children under eighteen years of age do not take part in armed hostilities, and that such children are not involuntarily enlisted into their armed forces. Under Article 3, voluntary recruitment for those under eighteen must: (a) be "genuinely voluntary", (b) include the informed consent of parents or guardians, (c) fully inform the children of their duties, and (d) provide reliable proof of age.

Perhaps most important to the issues raised by this Optional Protocol is the evolution of the International Criminal Court (ICC). As noted above, the Rome Statute creating the International Criminal Court was created in 1998 to address child armed conflict issues (among others). It took full effect with sufficient signatories in 2002. The ICC is discussed below, including its armed conflict child abuse cases to date.

Most recently and following the Optional Protocol and effective date of the ICC, the United Nations unanimously adopted Resolution 1612 in 2005, condemning the use of child soldiers in military conflicts. More importantly, the Secretary General of the U.N. in that same year organized a program to more actively monitor national and intra-national military recruitment and practices, detailed in the Secretary General's 2005 Report. In theory, more than fifty nations and rebel groups were violating international law as of 2005, and recruiting children under age eighteen, with many of them violating the narrower prohibition on conscripting children under age fifteen. Current U.N. agencies, such as UNICEF, as well as nongovernmental groups, have been coordinated into a more active monitoring effort. While the ICC is restricted to a limited number of individual prosecutions, the Protocol, Resolution 1612, and the Secretary General's stated commitment may signal the direct involvement of a potent enforcement tool—the Security Council and authorized sanctions, including military assistance abatement, seizing of assets, prohibitions on travel, and other possibly effective measures.

Indeed, the subject of child soldiers has been one of the only areas of Security Council agreement for possible nation-state pressure on behalf of children. In 2006, the Secretary General appointed Radhika Coomaraswamy as Special Representative for Children and Armed Conflict, and she has led a task force, working with UNICEF, to reduce the number of children in armed conflict. Since then, a substantial number of leaders on a "name and shame" list have negotiated for their removal from that list—agreeing to action plans to keep children from military service. In 2014, the U.N. launched a campaign called "Children, Not Soldiers" in which it identified eight countries of concern: Afghanistan, Chad, the Democratic Republic of the Congo, Myanmar, Somalia, South Sudan, Sudan, and Yemen. When the campaign ended in 2016, each of the named governments had developed an action plan process with the U.N. and Chad and the Democratic Republic of the Congo have since been removed from the list of concern.[24]

Coomaraswamy worked to include within Security Council sanction ambit the sexual abuse of children by military forces, or where such abuses are part of a pattern that implicates political leadership. And the increasing activity of the International Criminal Court (discussed below) may impose personal accountability on leaders who ignore these international standards, as reflected in the prosecution of Thomas Lubanga in the Congo for military use of children in 2009. She has now been succeeded in this initiative by Virginia Gamba.

Questions for Discussion

1. One of the seminal international protections against war-related injury to children is the existing treaty banning the laying of mines and commanding their removal. Children are major victims of land mine explosions, including the vestigial effects of hundreds of thousands of mines left in place in areas of former hostility. The United States has substantial land mine assets dividing North and South Korea

and has refused to agree to the land mine treaty. Does the United States need this prophylactic defense measure to protect its ally? Are there alternatives? What weight is properly given to the child impact of an agreed universal subscription and precedent for land mine cessation and removal? Should those who insist on implanting such hazards have an obligation to prevent unintended detonations? How? Should such nations be required to fully fund the external costs borne by others from future unintended detonations of mines they have manufactured or implanted?

2. The armed conflict protocol deals with children, now defined as those under eighteen, who enter the armed forces and are trained to use weapons and explosives and to kill. Why does the protocol countenance with approval such entry of children if they are "informed of their duties" and service is "voluntary"? Are children generally considered fully competent to enter into contracts or otherwise make decisions in most nations? At seventeen years of age? At fifteen? Where such decisions subject them to danger? Are all of the "duties" to be imposed by military service permissible as long as they are "disclosed"? Presumably, those under eighteen would not be subject to actual fighting under UN standards, but is that an adequate safeguard for someone subject to military orders? Apparently, one of the forces opposing a more universal agreement on eighteen rather than fifteen for obligatory (non-fighting) military service is the tradition of Anglo-Saxon induction into military academies for younger children. Is that a sufficient interest to compromise child military entry? Can the British academies not have discipline and even military rituals without actual military service status?

b. Optional Protocol #2 on the Sale of Children, Child Prostitution, and Child Pornography

This protocol addition to the Convention was intended to strengthen the existing Convention on the Rights of the Child provisions addressing child sexual protection, particularly Articles 1, 11, 21, and 32–36. It was preceded by various international instruments after the creation of these Convention articles. These included ILO Convention #182 on child labor abuses in general also adopted in 1989, Provisions of the Hague Conventions in 1993 (discussed below), and the Stockholm World Conference of 1996—producing a Declaration and Agenda for Action for the "Prevention of the Sale of Children, Child Prostitution and Child Pornography." This was followed by the International Conference on Combating Child Pornography on the Internet held in Vienna in 1999. That conference called broadly for the worldwide "criminalization of the production, distribution, exportation, transmission, importation, intentional possession and advertising of child pornography."

The Optional Protocol on the Sale of Children, Child Prostitution and Child Pornography was then entered into force in 2002. The major specific provisions include the following.

Article 1

States Parties shall prohibit the sale of children, child prostitution and child pornography....

Article 2

For the purposes of the present Protocol:

(a) Sale of children means any act or transaction whereby a child is transferred by any person...to another for...consideration;

(b) Child prostitution means the use of a child in sexual activities for remuneration or any other form of consideration;

(c) Child pornography means any representation, by whatever means, of a child engaged in real or simulated explicit sexual activities or any representation of the sexual parts of a child for primarily sexual purposes.

Article 3

1. Each State Party shall ensure that, as a minimum, the following acts...are fully covered under its...penal law, whether these offences are committed domestically or transnationally....

(a) [The "sale of children" under Article 2 means] offering, delivering or accepting a child for the purposes of "sexual exploitation...; Engagement of the child in forced labor"; or "Improperly inducing consent...for the adoption of a child in violation of international legal instruments on adoption."

(b) Offering, obtaining, procuring or providing a child for prostitution as defined in article 2;

(c) Producing, distributing, disseminating, importing, exporting, offering, selling, or possessing for the above purposes child pornography as defined in article 2

Articles 2–4

[Attempts or complicity also constitute violations above, punishment shall be imposed taking into account the "grave nature" of the offenses, liability may be criminal, civil or administrative.]

Article 5

The offences referred to in Article 3, paragraph 1, shall be deemed to be included as extradictable offences....

Article 7

States Parties shall, subject to the provisions of their national law:

Take measures to provide for the seizure and confiscation...of (1) Goods, such as materials, assets and other instrumentalities used to commit or facilitate offences... and (2) proceeds derived from such offences....

Article 8

1. States Parties shall adopt appropriate measures to protect the rights and interests of child victims of the practices prohibited...at all stages of the criminal justice process, [including]

(a) Recognizing... their special needs;

(b) Informing child victims of their rights, their role and the scope, timing and progress of the proceedings and of the disposition of their cases;

(c) Allowing the views, needs and concerns of child victims to be presented...;

(d) Providing appropriate support services to child victims throughout the legal process;

(e) Protecting, as appropriate, the privacy and identity of child victims...;

(f) Providing...for the safety of child victims, as well as that of their families and witnesses on their behalf, from intimidation and retaliation;

(g) Avoiding unnecessary delay....

Article 9

States parties shall

(a) Adopt...measures to prevent the offences....

(b) Shall promote awareness in the public at large, including children,...about the preventive measures and harmful effects of the offences....[and] shall encourage participation of ...children and child victims in such information programmes...

(c) Shall take all feasible measures [for] appropriate assistance to victims... including their full social reintegration and...recovery.

(d) Shall ensure access to adequate procedures to seek...compensation for damages from those legally responsible.

(e) Effectively [prohibit] the production and dissemination of material advertising the offences....

Note on Optional Protocol #2: International Distribution of Pornography and U.S. Courts

New York v. Ferber, 458 U.S. 747 (1982) upheld a New York statute and conviction of a bookstore proprietor selling photos of young boys masturbating. More recently, and in order to address the growing problem of child pornography, Congress enacted the Communications Decency Act of 1996 to protect children from exposure to pornographic material in general on the internet. The statute was struck as overly broad under the First Amendment in *Reno v. ACLU*, 521 U.S. 844 (1997). Congress then enacted a more specific Child Online Protection Act (COPA) in 1998 to apply only to material on the worldwide web, covering only communications for "commercial purposes" and restricted only to material that is "harmful to minors," using the three part obscenity test upheld in *Miller v. California*, 413 U.S. 15 (1973). However, it was struck as also overly broad and infringing on the First Amendment in *ACLU v. Mukasey*, 534 F.3d 181 (3d Cir. 2008), *cert. denied* 2009 U.S. LEXIS 598 (2009).

The more limited PROTECT Act of 2003 (18 USC § 2252 *et seq.*) was upheld in *U.S. v. Williams*, 553 U.S. 285 (2008) because "offers to provide or requests to obtain child pornography" are categorically excluded from "strict scrutiny" restriction. However, the Court's holding upholds a very limited statute that requires actual "knowledge" for each of its elements, including a belief that the material being "advertised, promoted, presented, distributed, or solicited" is child pornography, an intent to make the consumer believe it was child pornography and advertise it as such, and that the material must be "sexually explicit" and cause the viewer "to believe that the actors actually engaged in that conduct on camera."

Child advocates argue that, as a practical matter, commercial purveyors may simply use actors who are eighteen years of age but appear to be much younger or alter the images artificially to portray explicit child sexual activity. This alteration removes the strict "intent with knowledge" of actual child sex acts. Such image gamesmanship means that those persons depicted may not be child victims, but effectively allows the protected depiction of child pornography images, including those that may be accessible to children. Some psychologists argue that the easy availability of such images could constitute a "safety valve" for some child sexual predators and lessen offense incidence. Others are concerned that pervasive publication will have the opposite effect and may both create more adult interest and stimulate sexual molestation by predisposed adults.

Questions for Discussion

1. The underlying prostitution offense in the United States requires the "*quid pro quo*" of money from a "john" for sex. Most prosecutions tend to involve sting operations where undercover "customers" tape the offer/acceptance elements of an explicit arrangement. Accordingly, enforcement tends to focus on the prostitute, rather than the customer or the third party "pimp" who may be arranging, managing, and profiting the most from the transaction. Some states currently treat exploited minors as criminal violators, not victims.[25] Prosecutors argue that many such young victims are drawn to reconnect with their pimps, with high recidivism, and that juvenile hall and/or incarceration are necessary for their own protection. Does such a regime comply with the international floor of the Convention protocol above? Are there remedies for the rehabilitation and protection of such children short of criminal prosecution and incarceration?[26]

2. Does current U.S. law effectively allow the depiction of explicit child sex on video, cable, or the internet unless the government can prove that it is (a) explicitly advertised as child sex, and (b) actual underage children are used by the purveyors with knowledge of that age? The U.N. Convention protocol above prohibits "any representation, by whatever means, of a child engaged in real or simulated explicit sexual activities." Do the statutes and court cases of the United States comply with this provision? Given the Court's recent *dictum* that "child pornography" is categorically not subject to strict scrutiny under First Amendment analysis (discussed above), can a statute be drafted that will comply with the Convention Protocol and not be struck as overly broad or otherwise infirm? Would greater breadth be permitted if the remedy were civil injunctions/penalties as opposed to criminal prosecution? What would such a statute prohibit?

D. DIRECT INTERNATIONAL ENFORCEMENT OF CHILD RIGHTS

1. History of U.N. Human Rights Standards and Administration

The international human rights modern origins are often traced to the United Nations General Assembly adoption of the Universal Declaration of Human Rights on December 10, 1948. Drafted as "a common standard of achievement for all peoples and nations," the Declaration set forth basic civil, political, economic, social and cultural rights that all human beings should enjoy. It has won substantial acceptance as a source of universally recognized, generic human rights. That Universal Declaration, together with the International Covenant on Civil and Political Rights and its two Optional Protocols, and the International Covenant on Economic, Social and Cultural Rights, form the modern "International Bill of Human Rights." From this base, the rights of children have been subject to United Nations and other international treaties and covenants, discussed and excerpted above.

2. The Office of High Commissioner for Human Rights (OHCHR)

Alongside the development of international human rights law, a number of United Nations human rights administrative bodies have been established to promote adopted standards applicable to all people, and implicitly including the separately enumerated rights of children. These provisions often depend upon the OHCHR for direct support and to coordinate nation-state efforts to comply. Such coordination may include other Charter-based or political bodies of State representatives with mandates established by the United Nations Charter. Alternatively, they may be committees with independent experts set up by international human rights treaties and mandated to monitor State parties' compliance with their treaty obligations. The United Nations Commission on Human Rights was established in 1946 as the key intergovernmental body responsible for human rights, until it was replaced by the Human Rights Council in 2006. In addition to assuming mandates and responsibilities previously entrusted to the Commission, the Council, reporting directly to the General Assembly, has expanded mandates. These include making recommendations to the General Assembly for further developing international law in the field of human rights, and undertaking a Universal Periodic Review of the fulfillment of each State of its human rights obligations and commitments.

3. Direct Enforcement and International Courts

The notion of international criminal prosecution for international offenses, including war crimes and genocide, was crystallized by the Nuremberg and Tokyo tribunals at the end of World War II. The offenses prosecuted included the murder of children, forced conscription of children, and medical experiments on child prisoners.

Two separate entities have evolved from the Nuremberg tradition, the International Court of Justice (sometimes called the "World Court") and the International Criminal Court, a more recent creation with significant potential jurisdiction.

a. The International Court of Justice (ICJ)

Established in 1945 by the U.N. Charter, the Court began work in 1946 as the successor to the Permanent Court of International Justice. The ICJ has not dealt with a large number of cases; it generally operates to adjudicate disputes between member nations submitted to it, or issues "advisory opinions." It has adjudicated only a few cases involving child rights.

In the 1980s the Court ruled that the involvement of the United States in the internal politics of Nicaragua (the covert Nicaraguan war) violated international law. The U.S. responded by withdrawing from Court recognition in 1986, and withdrawing dues for its financing. The U.S. now only accepts the court's jurisdiction on a case-by-case basis.

Chapter XIV of the United Nations Charter authorizes the U.N. Security Council to enforce World Court rulings. However, such enforcement is subject to the veto power of the five permanent members of the Council. Four of those five members also must be included among the home nations of fifteen justices, with one currently from the United States.

After the 1980s, the ICJ has convened in a number of cases tangentially involving child-related offenses. These include a case condemning practices in the Congo involving child conscription for armed combat and rape of women, including girls: "During the hearings, the Congo further observed that "the state of war and... occupation by foreign troops can hardly promote respect for women's rights" and it referred in this connection to the terrible suffering endured by women and children as a result of the presence of Rwandan troops, to "rapes and various acts of oppression," to "mutilations," and to "other forms of violence, including the burial of women alive," in violation of the Convention on the Elimination of All Forms of Discrimination against Women, pursuant to which the United Nations Commission on Human Rights deplored "the widespread use of sexual violence against women and children, including as a means of warfare."[27]

More recently, the ICJ condemned the construction of the Palestinian wall, partly based on its violation of provisions of the Convention on the Rights of the Child (Articles 16, 24, 27 and 28), and the International Covenant on Economic, Social and Cultural Rights (Articles 11–14). The Court concluded that the blockage of the wall violated those provisions of both assuring for children rights to food, clothing, housing, health, education, and to be free from hunger.[28]

Organizations, private enterprises, and individuals cannot have their cases taken to the International Court. It does not have jurisdiction to hear appeals from national supreme courts that may allegedly transgress international law (such as the U.S. Supreme Court decisions allowing Life without Possibility of Parole for juvenile offenders). Nor may U.N. agencies bring a case before the ICJ, except to seek a strictly non-binding "advisory opinion."

b. The International Criminal Court (ICC)

The International Court came into being on July 1, 2002—the date its founding treaty (the Rome Statute of the International Criminal Court) entered into force. It is an entirely separate entity from the ICJ. The Statute was in part the result of serious international crimes committed in Rwanda and the former Yugoslavia during the 1990s. The Court is located in The Hague, Netherlands, but its proceedings may take place anywhere. The ICC became effective in 2002, with an approval vote of 120 to 7.[29]

As of 2019, 123 states are members of the Court. An additional 31 countries, including Russia, have signed but not ratified the Rome Statute. The United States has generally refused to support the U.N. establishment of a War Crimes Tribunal or other entity similar to the ICC. Nevertheless, it signed the Treaty on December 31, 2000, but then withdrew its signature in 2002, during the second Bush administration. A number of important states with major child populations have refused to sign the Rome Statute, including China and India.

Unlike the ICJ focus on national policies, the ICC mandate is to prosecute individuals who have committed serious international crimes after its 2002 effective date. The ICC has jurisdiction where the alleged crime took place in the territory of a state party, the accused is a national, or the matter is referred to the Court by the Security Council. Importantly, the violation must be a serious and widespread offense—a "crime against humanity," requiring a magnitude or scope beyond a single or small number of offenses by an individual.

The court includes a President, eighteen judges divided into three divisions (Pre-Trial, Trial, and Appeals) and an Office of Prosecutor. It has a budget of approximately $170.5 million (150.8 million euros) as of 2019, and a staff of approximately 600 from over 80 nations. It is funded by member state (signatory) assessments and is more independent from the U.N. than is the ICJ, although the Security Council may refer cases to it, as occurred with Darfur. The Security Council may force the ICC to defer a matter for one year, with no limit on subsequent twelve-month deferral orders. It is designed to complement existing national judicial systems; it can exercise its jurisdiction only when national courts do not pursue the relevant crimes. Its jurisdiction may be seen as a limited "spillover" jurisdiction. Nevertheless, its Office of Prosecutor is empowered theoretically to investigate crimes on its own initiative, not merely based on referrals. And child rights have been much involved in many of its inquiries and prosecutions to date. ICC prosecutions of individuals (including political leaders) in Africa have alleged serious rape, genocide, forced conscription, and many other offenses in violation of the international laws discussed above. Such alleged crimes have been pursued in Northern Uganda, the Democratic Republic of the Congo, the Central African Republic, Darfur (Sudan), and the Republic of Kenya. The court has indicted seventeen people; seven of whom remain fugitives, two have died (or are believed to have died), five are in custody, and three have appeared voluntarily before the court (one of whose charges was dismissed). The ICC's first trial, of Congolese militia leader Thomas Lubanga, began in January of 2009. An important part of that successful prosecution regarded his conscription of children for armed conflict. In November of that year, the second trial began against Congolese militia leaders Germain Katanga and Mathieu Ngudjolo Chui. In 2011, the Office of the Prosecutor began investigating possible offenses in Afghanistan, Kenya, Chad, Georgia, and Libya. The focus of the Office in 2019 turned to the Central African Republic.[30]

Questions for Discussion

1. Does the position of the United States as one of the five permanent members of the Security Council able to block the ICJ alone, or in concert with its longstanding allies, properly ameliorate American fears of sovereign usurpation?

Is such usurpation likely given the jurisdiction of these bodies? What are the arguments for and against U.S. full recognition of each of them?

2. Critics contend that the ICC acts only *in extremis,* and where a (usually tribal) leader loses in an armed conflict and lacks any protection from an influential source. If those criticisms have merit, what additional powers might create more potent enforcement? Which of these will suffer continued rejection from the United States? From the two nations with the largest share of children in the world and who reject the jurisdiction of the ICC: China and India?

E. PARTICULARIZED INTERNATIONAL CONVENTIONS ADDRESSING CHILD ABDUCTION, ADOPTION, CUSTODY AND SUPPORT

The world's population is increasingly mobile. Some 44 million people in the United States—most of them legally here—were born abroad.[31] They have relatives, friends, and business in other nations. Americans are similarly visiting, working, and studying across the earth. The nations of Europe and Israel have experienced substantial immigration from North Africa, Eastern Europe, and elsewhere over the past thirty years. The peoples of Southern Asia and the Caribbean increasingly travel and immigrate in large numbers to other nations.

This movement has implications for children and families. What happens when a family suffers a divorce and a custody dispute ensues, with one spouse taking children to a previous (or new) nation? Who has jurisdiction to decide child custody issues? To what extent are the interests of the child relevant in such a situation? Similarly, a child who has been removed from unfit parents in one nation may properly be placed in the custody of a new parent (perhaps one of the biological parents, perhaps a grandparent or other relative) in another nation. How does the court with original jurisdiction—which has removed the child—evaluate placements in other nations? And where a child will benefit from an adoption by a citizen of another nation, how is that adoption applicant evaluated for parental competence from another nation's offices? How does one nation decide parental rights when another nation has already addressed the issue when one or both parents were located there? How does one nation collect child support from a parent who has moved alone to another country and is earning income there?

Many of these issues are not fully or clearly addressed in international or U.S. law, but some applicable treaties and precedents exist and are important to the rights of involved children.

1. The Hague Convention on Abduction and the Right to Parental Contact and Residence

The United States is a signatory to the Hague Convention on the Civil Aspects of International Child Abduction, along with 100 other states. However, the U.S. has signed with stated reservations regarding articles 24 and 26. The Convention is intended to protect children from "cross-border abductions" (and wrongful retention) by facilitating their prompt return (usually to the State of their "habitual residence"). The Convention is based on a presumption that, except in unusual circumstances, the wrongful removal or retention of a child across international boundaries is not in the best interests of the child. It assumes that the return of the child is more likely to vindicate the right of the child to have contact with both parents, and it supports continuity in the child's life. It is also intended to ensure that custody or access decisions are made by the most appropriate court, and that those decisions are honored by the courts of other signatory nations. And the effectuation of prompt return may serve as a deterrent to abductions and wrongful removals. The return order is designed to restore the *status quo ante* before the wrongful removal, and to deprive the wrongful parent of any advantage from the abduction. Reflecting the issue of reliance and the need for expedition, the Convention requires parents to apply for return within one year of a child's removal.

As is usual among the Hague Children's Conventions, central authorities in each contracting state are critical to its effective enforcement. The United States has enacted the International Child Abduction Remedies Act, effective in 1988 to govern its compliance,[32] has designated the State Department as its "Central Authority," and as of 2009 has assigned the Bureau of Consular Affairs, Office of Children's Issues as the responsible implementing agency.

Each nation a party to the Convention must provide assistance in locating the child and in achieving, if possible, a voluntary return of the child. Most importantly, every signatory nation's courts must issue enforceable mandatory orders applicable to the parent or custodian of the child in its jurisdiction—and compelling the child's return (usually to the "habitual residence" of a child under the age of 16) in another nation.[33] Such an order confers what U.S. courts refer to in matters between our sovereign states, as "full faith and credit" to the prior decisions of those other courts where applicable. For example, a court in the United States may be expected to order the return of a child improperly removed from another nation and now residing in the U.S. Such deference, as is the essence of international conventions in general, warrants the reciprocal return of children removed from the United States improperly back to the United States, and to the parent lawfully awarded custody under U.S. law. Most nations—but not the United States—provide free legal counsel to aggrieved parents from other nations seeking a child's return.

Abbott v. Abbott
130 S.Ct. 1983 (2010)

JUSTICE KENNEDY delivered the opinion of the Court.

This case presents,...a question of interpretation under the Hague Convention on the Civil Aspects of International Child Abduction (Convention), Oct. 24, 1980. The United States is a contracting state to the Convention; and Congress has implemented its provisions through the International Child Abduction Remedies Act (ICARA), 102 Stat. 437, 42 U.S.C. § 11601 et seq. The Convention provides that a child abducted in violation of "rights of custody" must be returned to the child's country of habitual residence, unless certain exceptions apply....The question is whether a parent has a "righ[t] of custody" by reason of that parent's exeat right: the authority to consent before the other parent may take the child to another country.

I.

Timothy Abbott and Jacquelyn Vaye Abbott married in England in 1992. He is a British citizen, and she is a citizen of the United States. Mr. Abbott's astronomy profession took the couple to Hawaii, where their son A. J. A. was born in 1995. The Abbotts moved to La Serena, Chile, in 2002. There was marital discord, and the parents separated in March 2003. The Chilean courts granted the mother daily care and control of the child, while awarding the father "direct and regular" visitation rights, including visitation every other weekend and for the whole month of February each year.

Chilean law conferred upon Mr. Abbott what is commonly known as a exeat right: a right to consent before Ms. Abbott could take A. J. A. out of Chile….After Mr. Abbott obtained a British passport for A. J. A., Ms. Abbott grew concerned that Mr. Abbott would take the boy to Britain. She sought and obtained a "*ne exeat* of the minor" order from the Chilean family court, prohibiting the boy from being taken out of Chile.

In August 2005, while proceedings before the Chilean court were pending, the mother removed the boy from Chile without permission from either the father or the court. A private investigator located the mother and the child in Texas. In February 2006, the mother filed for divorce in Texas state court. Part of the relief she sought was a modification of the father's rights, including full power in her to determine the boy's place of residence and an order limiting the father to supervised visitation in Texas. This litigation remains pending.

Mr. Abbott brought an action in Texas state court, asking for visitation rights and an order requiring Ms. Abbott to show cause why the court should not allow Mr. Abbott to return to Chile with A. J. A. In February 2006, the court denied Mr. Abbott's requested relief but granted him "liberal periods of possession" of A. J. A. throughout February 2006, provided Mr. Abbott remained in Texas....

In May 2006, Mr. Abbott filed the instant action in the United States District Court for the Western District of Texas. He sought an order requiring his son's return to Chile pursuant to the Convention and enforcement provisions of the ICARA. In July 2007, after holding a bench trial during which only Mr. Abbott testified, the District Court denied relief...[and the Fifth Circuit affirmed].

* * *

II.

The Convention was adopted in 1980 in response to the problem of international child abductions during domestic disputes. The Convention seeks "to secure the prompt return of children wrongfully removed to or retained in any Contracting State," and "to ensure that rights of custody and of access under the law of one Contracting State are effectively respected in the other Contracting States."....The provisions of the Convention of most relevance at the outset of this discussion are as follows:

"Article 3: The removal or the retention of the child is to be considered wrongful where—
a it is in breach of rights of custody attributed to a person, an institution or any other body, either jointly or alone, under the law of the State in which the child was habitually resident immediately before the removal or retention; and

b at the time of removal or retention those rights were actually exercised, either jointly or alone, or would have been so exercised but for the removal or retention."

* * *

"Article 5: For the purposes of this Convention —
a 'rights of custody' shall include rights relating to the care of the person of the child and, in particular, the right to determine the child's place of residence;
b 'rights of access' shall include the right to take a child for a limited period of time to a place other than the child's habitual residence."

* * *

"Article 12: Where a child has been wrongfully removed or retained in terms of Article 3...the authority concerned shall order the return of the child forthwith...."

* * *

Chilean law granted Mr. Abbott a joint right to decide his child's country of residence, otherwise known as a *ne exeat* right. [Chilean law] provides that "[o]nce the court has decreed" that one of the parents has visitation rights, that parent's "authorization...shall also be required" before the child may be taken out of the country, subject to court override only where authorization "cannot be granted or is denied without good reason." Mr. Abbott has "direct and regular" visitation rights and it follows from Chilean law, that he has a shared right to determine his son's country of residence under this provision. To support the conclusion that Mr. Abbott's right under Chilean law gives him a joint right to decide his son's country of residence, it is notable that a Chilean agency has explained that Minors Law 16,618 is a "right to authorize the minors' exit" from Chile and that this provision means that neither parent can "unilaterally" "establish the [child's] place of residence."...

The Convention recognizes that custody rights can be decreed jointly or alone,... and Mr. Abbott's joint right to determine his son's country of residence is best classified as a joint right of custody, as the Convention defines that term. The Convention defines "rights of custody" to "include rights relating to the care of the person of the child and, in particular, the right to determine the child's place of residence."...Mr. Abbott's *ne exeat* right gives him both the joint "right to determine the child's place of residence" and joint "rights relating to the care of the person of the child."

Mr. Abbott's joint right to decide A. J. A.'s country of residence allows him to "determine the child's place of residence." The phrase "place of residence" encompasses the child's country of residence, especially in light of the Convention's explicit purpose to prevent wrongful removal across international borders....And even if "place of residence" refers only to the child's street address within a country, a *ne exeat* right still entitles Mr. Abbott to "determine" that place. "[D]etermine" can mean "[t]o fix conclusively or authoritatively," Webster's New International Dictionary...but it can also mean "[t]o set bounds or limits to," ibid. (1st definition), which is what Mr. Abbott's *ne exeat* right allows by ensuring that A. J. A. cannot live at any street addresses outside of Chile. It follows that the Convention's protection of a parent's custodial "right to determine the child's place of residence" includes a *ne exeat* right.

Mr. Abbott's joint right to determine A. J. A.'s country of residence also gives him "rights relating to the care of the person of the child."...Few decisions are as significant as the language the child speaks, the identity he finds, or the culture and traditions she will come to absorb. These factors, so essential to self-definition, are linked in an inextricable way to the child's country of residence. One need only consider the different childhoods an adolescent will experience if he or she grows up in the United States, Chile, Germany, or North Korea, to understand how choosing a child's country of residence is a right "relating to the care of the person of the child." The Court of Appeals described Mr. Abbott's right to take part in making this decision as a mere "veto," but even by that truncated description, the father has an essential role in deciding the boy's country of residence. For example, Mr. Abbott could condition his consent to a change in country on A. J. A.'s moving to a city outside Chile where Mr. Abbott could obtain an astronomy position, thus allowing the father to have continued contact with the boy.

That a *ne exeat* right does not fit within traditional notions of physical custody is beside the point. The Convention defines "rights of custody," and it is that definition that a court must consult. This uniform, text-based approach ensures international consistency in interpreting the Convention. It forecloses courts from relying on definitions of custody confined by local law usage, definitions that may undermine recognition of custodial arrangements in other countries or in different legal traditions, including the civil-law tradition. And, in any case, our own legal system has adopted conceptions of custody that accord with the Convention's broad definition. Joint legal custody, in which one parent cares for the child while the other has joint decisionmaking authority concerning the child's welfare, has become increasingly common....("[A] recent study of child custody outcomes in North Carolina indicated that almost 70% of all custody resolutions included joint legal custody, as did over 90% of all mediated custody agreements")....

Ms. Abbott gets the analysis backwards in claiming that a ne exeat right is not a right of custody because the Convention requires that any right of custody must be capable of exercise. The Convention protects rights of custody when "at the time of removal or retention those rights were actually exercised, either jointly or alone, or would have been so exercised but for the removal or retention."...In cases like this one, a ne exeat right is by its nature inchoate and so has no operative force except when the other parent seeks to remove the child from the country. If that occurs, the parent can exercise the *ne exeat* right by declining consent to the exit or placing conditions to ensure the move will be in the child's best interests. When one parent removes the child without seeking the ne exeat holder's consent, it is an instance where the right would have been "exercised but for the removal or retention."...

The Court of Appeals' conclusion that a breach of a ne exeat right does not give rise to a return remedy would render the Convention meaningless in many cases where it is most needed. The Convention provides a return remedy when a parent takes a child across international borders in violation of a right of custody. The Convention provides no return remedy when a parent removes a child in violation of a right of access but requires contracting states "to promote the peaceful enjoyment of access rights."...For example, a court may force the custodial parent to pay the travel costs of visitation,... or make other provisions for the noncustodial parent to visit his or her child,...But unlike rights of access, *ne exeat* rights can only be honored with a return remedy because these rights depend on the child's location being the country of habitual residence.

Any suggestion that a *ne exeat* right is a "righ[t] of access" is illogical and atextual. The Convention defines "rights of access" as "includ[ing] the right to take a child for a limited period of time to a place other than the child's habitual residence,"...and ICARA defines that same term as "visitation rights,"...The joint right to decide a child's country of residence is not even arguably a "right to take a child for a limited period of time" or a "visitation righ[t]." Reaching the commonsense conclusion that a exeat right does not fit these definitions of "rights of access'" honors the Convention's distinction between rights of access and rights of custody.

* * *

B.

This Court's conclusion that Mr. Abbott possesses a right of custody under the Convention is supported and informed by the State Department's view on the issue. The United States has endorsed the view that *ne exeat* rights are rights of custody....It is well settled that the Executive Branch's interpretation of a treaty "is entitled to great weight."...There is no reason to doubt that this well-established canon of deference is appropriate here. The Executive is well informed concerning the diplomatic consequences resulting from this Court's interpretation of "rights of custody," including the likely reaction of other contracting states and the impact on the State Department's ability to reclaim children abducted from this country.

C.

This Court's conclusion that *ne exeat* rights are rights of custody is further informed by the views of other contracting states. In interpreting any treaty, "[t]he 'opinions of our sister signatories'...are 'entitled to considerable weight.'"...The principle applies with special force here, for Congress has directed that "uniform international interpretation of the Convention" is part of the Convention's framework....

A review of the international case law confirms broad acceptance of the rule that *ne exeat* rights are rights of custody. In an early decision, the English High Court of Justice explained that a father's "right to ensure that the child remain[ed] in Australia or live[d] anywhere outside Australia only with his approval" is a right of custody requiring return of the child to Australia....

* * *

Scholars agree that there is an emerging international consensus that *ne exeat* rights are rights of custody, even if that view was not generally formulated when the Convention was drafted in 1980. At that time, joint custodial arrangements were unknown in many of the contracting states, and the status of *ne exeat* rights was not yet well understood....A history of the Convention, known as the Perez-Vera Report, has been cited both by the parties and by Courts of Appeals that have considered this issue....We need not decide whether this Report should be given greater weight than a scholarly commentary....It suffices to note that the Report supports the conclusion that *ne exeat* rights are rights of custody.

* * *

D.

Adopting the view that the Convention provides a return remedy for violations of *ne exeat* rights accords with its objects and purposes. The Convention is based on the principle that the best interests of the child are well served when decisions regarding custody rights are made in the country of habitual residence....Ordering a return remedy does not alter the existing allocation of custody rights,...but does allow the courts of the home country to decide what is in the child's best interests. It is the Convention's premise that courts in contracting states will make this determination in a responsible manner.

Custody decisions are often difficult. Judges must strive always to avoid a common tendency to prefer their own society and culture, a tendency that ought not interfere with objective consideration of all the factors that should be weighed in determining the best interests of the child. This judicial neutrality is presumed from the mandate of the Convention, which affirms that the contracting states are "[f]irmly convinced that the interests of children are of paramount importance in matters relating to their custody."... International law serves a high purpose when it underwrites the determination by nations to rely upon their domestic courts to enforce just laws by legitimate and fair proceedings.

To interpret the Convention to permit an abducting parent to avoid a return remedy, even when the other parent holds a *ne exeat* right, would run counter to the Convention's purpose of deterring child abductions by parents who attempt to find a friendlier forum for deciding custodial disputes. Ms. Abbott removed A. J. A. from Chile while Mr. Abbott's request to enhance his relationship with his son was still pending before Chilean courts. After she landed in Texas, the mother asked the state court to diminish or eliminate the father's custodial and visitation rights. The Convention should not be interpreted to permit a parent to select which country will adjudicate these questions by bringing the child to a different country, in violation of a *ne exeat* right. Denying a return remedy for the violation of such rights would "legitimize the very action—removal of the child—that the home country, through its custody order [or other provision of law], sought to prevent" and would allow "parents to undermine the very purpose of the Convention."...This Court should be most reluctant to adopt an interpretation that gives an abducting parent an advantage by coming here to avoid a return remedy that is granted, for instance, in the United Kingdom, Israel, Germany, and South Africa....

Requiring a return remedy in cases like this one helps deter child abductions and respects the Convention's purpose to prevent harms resulting from abductions. An abduction can have devastating consequences for a child. "Some child psychologists believe that the trauma children suffer from these abductions is one of the worst forms of child abuse."...A child abducted by one parent is separated from the second parent and the child's support system. Studies have shown that separation by abduction can cause psychological problems ranging from depression and acute stress disorder to posttraumatic stress disorder and identity-formation issues....A child abducted at an early age can experience loss of community and stability, leading to loneliness, anger, and fear of abandonment....Abductions may prevent the child from forming a relationship with the left-behind parent, impairing the child's ability to mature....

IV.

While a parent possessing a *ne exeat* right has a right of custody and may seek a return remedy, a return order is not automatic. Return is not required if the abducting parent can establish that a Convention exception applies. One exception states return of the child is not required when "there is a grave risk that his or her return would expose the child to physical or psychological harm or otherwise place the child in an intolerable situation."...If, for example, Ms. Abbott could demonstrate that returning to Chile would put her own safety at grave risk, the court could consider whether this is sufficient to show that the child too would suffer "psychological harm" or be placed "in an intolerable situation."...The Convention also allows courts to decline to order removal if the child objects, if the child has reached a sufficient "age and degree of maturity at which it is appropriate to take account of its views."...The proper interpretation and application of these and other exceptions are not before this Court. These matters may be addressed on remand.

JUSTICE STEVENS, with whom **JUSTICE THOMAS** and **JUSTICE BREYER** join, dissenting.

Petitioner Timothy Abbott, the father of A. J. A., has no authority to decide whether his son undergoes a particular medical procedure; whether his son attends a school field trip; whether and in what manner his son has a religious upbringing; or whether his son can play a videogame before he completes his homework. These are all rights and responsibilities of A. J. A.'s mother, respondent Jacquelyn Abbott. It is she who received sole custody, or "daily care and control," of A. J. A. when the expatriate couple divorced while living in Chile in 2004....Mr. Abbott possesses only visitation rights.

On Ms. Abbott's custodial rights, Chilean law placed a restriction: She was not to travel with her son outside of Chile without either Mr. Abbott's or the court's consent. Put differently, Mr. Abbott had the opportunity to veto Ms. Abbott's decision to remove A. J. A. from Chile unless a Chilean court overrode that veto. The restriction on A. J. A.'s and Ms. Abbott's travel was an automatic, default provision of Chilean law operative upon the award of visitation rights under Article 48 of Chile's Minors Law 16,618. It is this travel restriction—also known as a *ne exeat* clause—that the Court today declares is a "'righ[t] of custody'" within the meaning of the Hague Convention on the Civil Aspects of International Child Abduction....

Because the Court concludes that this travel restriction constitutes a right of custody, and because Ms. Abbott indisputably violated the restriction when she took A. J. A. from Chile without either Mr. Abbott's or the court's permission, Mr. Abbott is now entitled to the return of A. J. A. to Chile under the terms of the Convention. Thus, absent a finding of an exception to the Convention's powerful return remedy,...and even if the return is contrary to the child's best interests, an American court *must* now order the return of A. J. A. to Mr. Abbott, who has no legal authority over A. J. A., based solely on his possessing a limited veto power over Ms. Abbott's ability to take A. J. A. from Chile. As I shall explain, use of the Convention's return remedy under these circumstances is contrary to the Convention's text and purpose.

I.

When the drafters of the Convention gathered in 1980, they sought an international solution to an emerging problem: transborder child abductions perpetrated by noncustodial parents "to establish artificial jurisdictional links...with a view to obtaining custody of a child."..."[F]undamental purpose" of the Convention is "to protect children from wrongful international removals or retention by persons bent on obtaining their physical and/or legal custody"). The drafters' primary concern was to remedy abuses by noncustodial parents who attempt to circumvent adverse custody decrees (*e.g.*, those granting sole custodial rights to the other parent) by seeking a more favorable judgment in a second nation's family court system....

Only when a removal is "wrongful" under Article 3 may the parent who possesses custody rights force the child's return to the country of habitual residence under the Convention's remedial procedures, pursuant to Articles 8 through 20. For those removals that frustrate a noncustodial parent's "rights of access," the Convention provides that the noncustodial parent may file an application "to make arrangements for organizing or securing the effective exercise of rights of access"; but he may not force the child's

return. A parent without "rights of custody," therefore, does not have the power granted by Article 3 to compel the child's return to his or her country of habitual residence. His rights are limited to those set forth in Article 21.

II.

* * *

...The Court concludes that the veto power Mr. Abbott has over Ms. Abbott's travel plans is equivalent to those rights "'relating to the care of the person of the child.'"...This is so, the Court tells us, because Mr. Abbott has a limited power to keep A. J. A. within Chile's bounds and, therefore, indirectly to influence "the language the child speaks, the identity he finds, or the culture and traditions she will come to absorb."...It is not nearly as self-evident as the Court assumes that Mr. Abbott's veto power carries with it any ability to decide the language A. J. A. speaks or the cultural experiences he will have....A. J. A.'s mere presence in Chile does not determine any number of issues, including: whether A. J. A. learns Spanish while there; whether he attends an American school or a British school or a local school; whether he participates in sports; whether he is raised Catholic or Jewish or Buddhist or atheist; whether he eats a vegetarian diet; and on and on. The travel restriction does *not* confer upon Mr. Abbott affirmative power to make any number of decisions that are vital to A. J. A.'s physical, psychological, and cultural development. To say that a limited power to veto a child's travel plans confers, also, a right "relating to the care" of that child devalues the great wealth of decisions a custodial parent makes on a daily basis to attend to a child's needs and development.

* * *

Such a view of the text obliterates the careful distinction the drafters drew between the rights of custody and the rights of access. Undoubtedly, they were aware of the concept of joint custody....But just because rights of custody can be shared by two parents, it does not follow that the drafters intended this limited veto power to be a right of custody. And yet this, it seems, is how the Court understands the case: Because the drafters intended to account for joint custodial arrangements, they intended for *this* travel restriction to be joint custody because it could be said, in some abstract sense, to relate to care of the child. I fail to understand how the Court's reading is faithful to the Convention's text and purpose, given that the text expressly contemplates two distinct classes of parental rights. Today's decision converts every noncustodial parent with access rights—at least in Chile—into a custodial parent for purposes of the Convention.

* * *

The Court's reading of this text depends on its substitution of the word "country" for the word "place." Such a substitution is not illogical, of course, in light of the Convention's international focus. But it is inconsistent with the Convention's text and purpose....

* * *

When the drafters wanted to refer to country, they did. For example, in Article 3, the drafters explained that rights of custody should be defined by looking to "the law of the State in which the child was habitually resident."...Had the drafters intended the definition of the child's "place of residence" in Article 5 to refer to his or her "State" or country of "residence," they could have defined the "right" at issue as "the right to determine the child's State of habitual residence." But they did not, even though they used the phrase "State of habitual residence" no fewer than four other times elsewhere within the Convention's text....

* * *

Accordingly, I would give "place of residence" the location-specific meaning its plain text connotes, irrespective of the fact that this Convention concerns international abduction. The right described by the Convention is the right to decide, conclusively, where a child's home will be. And this makes a good deal of sense. The child lives with the parent who has custodial rights or, in the language of the Convention, "care of the person of the child"....The child's home—his or her "place of residence"—is fixed by the custody arrangement. This comports too with the Convention's decision to privilege the rights of custodians over the rights of those parents with only visitation rights.

* * *

A reading as broad and flexible as the Court's eviscerates the distinction the Convention draws between rights of custody and rights of access. Indeed, the Court's reading essentially voids the Convention's Article 21, which provides a separate remedy for breaches of rights of access. If a violation of this type of provision were not a breach of the rights of access, I find it quite difficult to imagine what the Convention's drafters had in mind when they created a second, lesser remedy for the breach of access rights. The drafters obviously contemplated that some removals might be in violation of the law of the child's home nation, but not "wrongful" within the meaning of the Convention—i.e., not in breach of "rights of custody." This is precisely why Article 5 carefully delineates between the two types of parental rights in the first place. And this is precisely why Article 21 exists.

Nevertheless, the Court has now decreed that whenever an award of visitation rights triggers a statutory default travel restriction provision, or is accompanied by a travel restriction by judicial order, a parent possess a right of custody within the meaning of the Convention. Such a bright-line rule surely will not serve the best interests of the child in many cases. It will also have surprising results. In Chile, for example, as a result of this Court's decision, *all parents*—so long as they have the barest of visitation rights—now also have joint custody within the meaning of the Convention and the right to utilize the return remedy.

* * *

Putting aside any concerns arising from the fact that the Department's views are newly memorialized and changing, I would not in this case abdicate our responsibility to interpret the Convention's language. This does not seem to be a matter in which deference to the Executive on matters of foreign policy would avoid international conflict....Finally, and significantly, the State Department, as the Central Authority for administering the Convention in the United States, has failed to disclose to the Court whether t has facilitated the return of children to America when the shoe is on the other foot....

* * *

Views of foreign jurisdictions. The Court believes that the views of our sister signatories to the Convention deserve special attention when, in a case like this, "Congress has directed that 'uniform international interpretation' of the Convention is part of the Convention's framework."...This may well be correct, but we should not substitute the judgment of other courts for our own....

I also fail to see the international consensus—let alone the "broad acceptance," ...— that the Court finds among those varied decisions from foreign courts that have considered the effect of a similar travel restriction within the Convention's remedial scheme. The various decisions of the international courts are, at best, in equipoise. Indeed, the Court recognizes that courts in Canada and France have concluded that travel restrictions are not "rights of custody" within the meaning of the Convention....

V.

At bottom, the Convention aims to protect the best interests of the child.... Recognizing that not all removals in violation of the laws of the country of habitual residence are contrary to a child's best interests, the Convention provides a powerful but limited return remedy. The judgment of the Convention's drafters was that breaches of access rights, while significant (and thus expressly protected by Article 21), are secondary to protecting the child's interest in maintaining an existing custodial relationship.

Today, the Court has upended the considered judgment of the Convention's drafters in favor of protecting the rights of noncustodial parents. In my view, the bright-line rule the Court adopts today is particularly unwise in the context of a treaty intended to govern disputes affecting the welfare of children.

I, therefore, respectfully dissent.

Questions for Discussion

1. Article 13 of the Convention provides a crucial exception to a return obligation under the treaty where "there is a grave risk that his or her return would expose the child to physical or psychological harm or otherwise place the child in an intolerable situation."[34] The majority cites as an example some physical danger to Ms. Abbott should she return to Chile. In the widely publicized case of Elian Gonzalez, a young Cuban boy was removed by his mother and taken to Florida; when the mother died, Elian's father sought his return. Many commentators contended that forcing a child to return to a communist dictatorship should be considered

"intolerable" under international law. What would be the result of such a policy where the U.S. seeks the return to a U.S. parent of a child removed to Cuba in violation of U.S. court ordered custody rights?

2. Should the U.S. invoke the "intolerable" clause to bar a Christian child from transport to a nation deeply intolerant of that religion? Should a young girl with one Western parent and Western values be sent to Saudi Arabia or other Middle Eastern nations where endemic discrimination against women is allegedly a part of the legal system? Should a child be sent to Iraq or the Sudan or other places where war may endanger them? Would it be "intolerable" to take a child from the United States to a nation of abject poverty and little educational opportunity, such as Yemen or Somalia? On the other hand, what would Saudi Arabia, Iraq, the Sudan, Yemen, or Somalia then decide about returning children removed there from America in violation of U.S. court orders?

3. The dissent argues that the father does not have "custody," and his *ne exeat* status to block removal of the child from the nation falls far short of such status. Hence, it concludes that he is not covered by the Hague Convention and his child need not be returned to him. Does it matter whether Chile has a "joint custody" category to clearly confer mutual custody? What if the term "joint custody" in a nation simply means that the child may not be moved from a nation, or province or city, without court permission or consent of the other parent? While the father's explicit right to bar removal would not be equivalent to full custody, does it matter that it is here not an "implied right" from custody status, but a parental right specifically conferred to him by court order and violated?

4. If a court in the United States specifically ordered custody with one parent on the clear condition that such custody must be within the nation's territory unless the other parent consented—would we want other nations to return children removed in violation of that order?

5. If California (and not Chile) was the jurisdiction of a father with a court order requiring his permission to take the child from the state, and this Texas court refused to honor it, what would happen under the Interstate Compact on the Placement of Children (ICPC) or other applicable domestic law?

6. In another widely publicized case, Sean Goldman's wife removed their son from the United States following a divorce—and in violation of a U.S. family court order—settling in Brazil. She then married a Brazilian citizen and died from a fatal illness shortly thereafter. Sean Goldman was blocked in his efforts to secure the return of his son by the stepfather in Brazil over a five-year travail. The case was resolved with the return of Sean on Christmas Eve 2009, only after Congressman Smith introduced House Resolution 2701 to suspend special trade privileges on export goods worth $2.7 billion. What are the mechanisms for Hague Convention enforcement lacking the resources and extraordinarily skilled advocacy of Sean

Goldman (including 60 Minutes and major journalistic attention)? In how many cases are such trade sanctions a potent influence and imposed or effectively threatened? What would be the options for Brazil in an identical case where the United States refuses to return a child to a parent there in violation of a Brazilian court order?

Note on Juvenile Dependency Court Placement of Children in Foreign Nations

The Hague Convention on Abduction focuses on family court proceedings, *i.e.*, the removal of children in violation of custody orders. But there is another facet of international placements of children—the issue of dependency courts in a nation with jurisdiction over a parent and children and where those children have non-custodial parents, or other relatives, in other nations who may warrant custody. The Vienna Convention allows diplomatic cooperation between nations and certainly the embassy and diplomats of one country may inquire through those channels and seek assistance from another. But such a mechanism is not enforceable, reliable, or consistent. Under the laws of most nations, a second parent who does not have custody and lives in another country is an eligible (if not priority) candidate for custody where one parent has died, become incapacitated, or is judicially adjudged to be an unfit parent. But will a nation with jurisdiction over such a child surrender him or her to a nation where it is unable to ascertain the safety of the child in that placement, or compliance with its orders governing subsequent child custody?

Within the United States, an Interstate Compact on the Placement of Children (ICPC) governs cooperation in dependency court placements between the several states. It obliges states where eligible relatives live for placement to cooperate in the evaluation of such placements, including home visits and studies and other assistance similar to the normal practices in most states where the prospective placement is in the same state. The ICPC has been criticized in its execution for common delays and funding disputes in the out-of-state prospective placement locales (see discussion in Chapter 8). But internationally, there is no counterpart to the ICPC, whatever its flaws. Applying the principles of the Hague Convention on Abduction, or the ICPC, would presumably allow the court to surrender its jurisdiction, relying on the foreign nation's administration and courts to confirm the appropriate placement. However, a consistent international compact covering such children does not exist, and it requires a nation's court not to merely respect a pre-existing adjudicated order from another signatory nation (as with the Hague Convention on Abduction) but deference to an inspection and evaluation that has not occurred, may not occur, and may be contrary to the judgment and orders of the original court with jurisdiction over the child.

California courts have been most involved in addressing the issue of foreign nation placement of children under dependency court jurisdiction. *In Re Rosalinda C.*, 16 Cal.App.4th 274 (1993) confirmed the principle that a dependency court must not terminate its jurisdiction until or unless "a permanent and stable home is established." This judgment creates the catch-22 problem in placing a child, even with a grandfather in a neighboring nation (Mexico), where the U.S. must continue jurisdiction but is unable to evaluate the placement. In *Sabrina H.*, 149 Cal.App.4th 1403 (2007), the court decided that U.S. and California law does not prohibit the foreign placement of dependent children. Five children had been removed from an unfit mother and were placed with their grandfather in Mexico. However, the case was remanded to San Diego juvenile court with instructions to conduct a background check of the grandfather as an appropriate placement. The most important American case is the more recent case of *In re Karla C.*, 186 Cal. App.4th 1236 (2010). *Karla C.* was sexually abused by her stepfather while in her mother's home. The child was detained, the court took jurisdiction—supplanting parental authority—and the dispositional hearing placed the child with the father, who was not involved in the offense and was living in Peru. In the normal course, the California juvenile court must pursue "reasonable efforts" to reunify the child with the offending mother—a task that might be threatened if the child comes into Peruvian jurisdiction for custody outside of its reach *pendente lite*. On the other hand, a non-custodial parent has the presumed right to custody where that parent has not been adjudicated unfit. And under the domestic United States procedures between states under the ICPC, such a placement does not require a preliminary home visit and study to assure a proper placement.

Parents are presumed to be appropriate placements unless they demonstrate endangerment or otherwise disqualify. The appellate court ruled that during the consideration of reunification—and indeed short of the final and permanent placement of the child—the juvenile dependency court is the legal parent and as such cannot cede its jurisdiction. The appellate case requires the Peruvian authorities to explicitly acknowledge the continuing jurisdiction of the California dependency court. This controlling and relatively recent decision highlights the catch-22 structure created when there are no clear rules of coordination. The argument in favor of a treaty commending such deference is strong. It encounters the obvious objection—that it would require unusual deference by a nation and its courts in the location where the child would now reside. For although they now have direct contact with the child, the child is subject to their offices and her care must meet its national standards. Indeed, it is anathema in the eyes of some courts to be instructed about how to care for a child who is now in their territory, subject to care from their residents, and monitored by their social workers. On the other hand, the argument here is that the original court with jurisdiction (*e.g.*, the California juvenile dependency court) is different than the situation presented by family courts. For family courts adjudicate rights as between third-party parents, but the dependency court becomes the legal parent of the child himself. That parental obligation and status does not dissipate merely because "its" child has traveled across a national boundary—any more than a parent is less of a parent because a child is visiting a relative in Peru or France or Canada. The deference and respect for its jurisdiction as the effective legal "parent" is arguably similar to a request to honor a prior single order of a family court as to which third party is the custodial parent—including the one not in the nation where the child (and foreign courts) are located. A treaty is commended that builds on the Hague Convention on Abduction that allows the criteria of *Karla C.* to be met, requires international inquiry, response to questions and requests for interviews and evaluations, and acknowledges the authority of the original court—not unlike the theory behind the ICPC applicable within the United States. Lacking such a treaty or convention, decisions will be made on an *ad hoc* basis, and many children will not win placement with their optimum parental choice.

2. The Hague Convention on Intercountry Adoption

The United States and, as of 2018, 98 other nations are signatories to the 1993 Hague Convention on Intercountry Adoption. Many of the nations who are not signatories include all of Asia except for Hong Kong, Malaysia and Sri Lanka, virtually all of the Muslim world (except for Turkey) and virtually all of Africa (except for Zimbabwe and South Africa). Hence, nations expected to be source populations for adoption, and on whose behalf checks are properly conducted, are often not signatories. Even as to signatory nations, problems persist. Canada, for example, has variations in policies between provinces in the same way the United State varies its law between states. Mexico has a system of "amparo" that allows the constitutional review of an executive or lower court judgment, allowing a wealthy litigant to accomplish substantial delay. Other nations have similar impediments to actual effective performance.

The convention's rationale is the provision of a permanent family for a child unable to find one in his or her country of origin. Its stated purposes include cooperation between nations to prohibit improper financial gain (*e.g.*, selling of babies), and to stimulate predictability, security, and transparency for all parties to the adoption (including the prospective adoptive parents). The Convention purports to more specifically implement Article 21 of the United Nations Convention on the Rights of the Child (above).

While the Convention establishes minimum standards, it does not serve as a uniform law of adoption. Rather, it lists functions appropriate for the source and destination nation, respectively. It is guided by five paramount stated principles:

1) The best interests of the child are paramount.
2) Contracting States recognize that a child should be raised by his or her birth family or extended family whenever possible. If that is not possible or practicable, other forms of permanent care in the country of origin should be considered.
3) Safeguards must protect children from abduction, sale, and trafficking.
4) Co-operation must exist between States and within States.
5) Adoption decisions should be reciprocally recognized.

The Convention provides in its terms that consent to adoption must not be induced by payment and cannot be given until after birth; involved children must be given age-appropriate counseling and the child's wishes are entitled to "consideration"; compensation for those facilitating the adoption shall not be "unreasonably high" and no person shall realize "improper gain"; and the authorities of the receiving nation must assure that the adoptive parents are qualified and have been counseled.

Enforcement is essentially delegated to competent central authorities and accredited bodies. The treaty includes a related "Intercountry Adoption Technical Assistance Programme" (ICATAP). The United States enforcing statute is the Intercountry Adoption Act of 2000.

Note on the Case of Masha Allen

The United States is a major recipient nation for international adoptions. China, Ethiopia, and Ukraine are three leading source countries as of 2017. Previous leading sources Guatemala and Russia have banned adoptions to the United States. The turmoil regarding Russian adoptions, common before 2010, provides some important lessons involving Hague Convention efficacy in protecting children. American adoptions of Russian children started in 1991, with only twelve children. The policy allowing American adoptions was accelerated by the fall of the Iron Curtain and the Russian Education Ministry establishment of a division called "The Rights of the Child" to regulate them. The number accelerated through the 1990s, driven by publicity surrounding the large number of orphans in Russia (an estimated 260,000 by 2007) and Eastern Europe, and perceived advantages to foreign adoptions (less delay than domestic adoptions, and an added distance from biological parents who might at some point attempt rescission).

Problems in these adoptions indicate some possible weaknesses in the Hague Convention and in international safeguards. From 1995 to 2010, fourteen cases of adopted child murder by their American adoptive parents have been documented. But the publicity surrounding the case of Masha Allen brought popular media attention to the issue of adoptive child protection. Masha was born Mariya Nikoleavna Yashenkova on August 25, 1992. When she was three years old, her alcoholic Russian mother stabbed her and she was placed in an orphanage. In July of 1998 she was adopted by American Matthew Mancuso, a single Pennsylvania man. Mancuso had been married and had molested his biological daughter Rachelle from the age of five until she reached puberty, although the offense was not reported to authorities at the time, he had not been prosecuted, and was not on a sexual offender list. The night Masha arrived in the United States, at just under six years of age, Mancuso had sexual relations with her. She slept in his bed (the only bed in the apartment) during her entire childhood. Mancuso kept her under constant supervision and attempted to stunt her growth physically. He began to augment his molestation with nude and then erotic photography until Masha reached thirteen years of age. While Masha was between the ages of ten to thirteen, he exchanged photographs of her engaging in sex acts on the internet with other pedophiles. One such set of photographs was identified as coming from the Disney World hotel in Florida, and investigation led to Mancuso's identification, arrest, and conviction.

How did Mancuso obtain his victim? Have reforms and changes over the past fifteen years provided needed safeguards? The Russian regulations allowed a single parent to adopt. They required a dossier in support of the adoption applicant.

Information included required interviews prior to placement, and additional reports post-placement and prior to adoption finalization. In the case of Mancuso, nobody called his former wife—who likely would have reported the undesirability of child placement with him. There was one pre-placement interview at his residence, where there was no bed or furniture for the prospective child (Mancuso promised to provide it). The second pre-placement interview was at the American "agency" office. No checks of any kind were made of the recommendation letters submitted by Mancuso.

Mancuso finalized his paperwork and traveled to Russia and on July 9, 1998 and obtained guardianship of Masha from the Russian Court, arriving in the U.S. with Masha on July 11 and, as noted, starting his sexual abuse of her immediately. Russian procedure assumed a post-placement requirement of three "in-home" visits prior to adoption finalization. The first required date of November 1998 was missed, and after a Russian demand for compliance, the American agency located in New Jersey received the first post-placement report from "Social Services of Western Pennsylvania." Except no such entity exists, as an attempt to call the telephone number listed would have revealed (it was a non-existent number). It was a fraudulent document created by Mancuso. The second report was then conducted by a social worker for the New Jersey agency by telephone to Mancuso. There was no third visit. Mancuso then proceeded to continue with eight years of nightly molestation, even purporting to "marry" his pre-teen adoptive daughter.

The background law applicable to these events is complicated. By happenstance, Russia amended its Family Code just after Masha was taken by Mancuso. It would have required somewhat more pro-active judicial review, and by a higher Russian Regional Court, to approve the adoption. It would have at least facially required an evaluation of the "mental state" of the prospective parent. Starting in 1997, Russia began to require two to four post-placement reports involving visits (not phone calls) over a one- to four-year period. Then in 2006, Russia adopted "Decision #654," with somewhat stricter procedures for intercountry adoptions of Russian children, banning them entirely to the U.S. in 2013.

It is unclear whether the current state of the law prevents the Mancuso type of abuse, regardless of the national of origin. The Hague Convention differentiates between post-placement and post-adoption services for children adopted abroad. But American domestic procedure involves a home study and review before and after placement, but not after final adoption—when American checks stop. Hence, although Russia and other nations continuing to allow adoption exports to the U.S. may assume post-adoption visits, that is not the pattern and practice in the United States.

Questions for Discussion

1. What are the differences and dangers between adoptions pursuant to the Hague Convention and private adoptions? For adoptions from non-signatory countries?

2. Some nations are so impoverished and some families so overburdened that the solicitation of a child to live in a developed country for compensation can be a potent inducement, including possible claims that the "visit" to the wealthy nation will help the child and also produce compensation to assist other children who remain with the originating family. How do we reconcile the international dilemma posed by such economic hardships against our feelings that children should not be sold, and presumptively should not be removed from their friends, cultures, neighborhoods, and parents? How do we address the hardship and Hobson's choice that may be confronting these original parents?

3. What is the attraction of a child from an impoverished nation with the above removal issues over the similarly bereft 400,000 American child in foster care—many of whom will age out at eighteen without adoptive parents, are being raised by employees in group homes, and face disproportionate fates as unemployed, homeless, and incarcerated?

4. Why not create an international evaluation system that all prospective parents could confidently rely upon to secure selection of children who will clearly benefit from the proposed adoption, and will arrange secure clearance of applicant parents for parental skills and commitment? Does the current Hague Convention provide such assurance?

Note on Developments After Masha Allen

In the years since 2004, Americans have gradually abandoned international adoptions, reducing them by 81%, with numbers going from 22,989 in 2004 to 4,200 in 2018. Sources attribute this collapse to "crushing adoption regulations and refusal of the Office of Children's Issues within the State Department to collaborate with adoption service providers (ASPs)."[35] As of April 1, 2018 this function transitioned to the new Intercountry Adoption Accreditation and Maintenance Entity, Inc. (IAAME). This appears to be a violation of the Hague Convention requiring that the accrediting agency in a country not be an adoption agency itself, since IAAME is allegedly connected to the Partnership for Strong Families—such an agency. Meanwhile, the IAAME is imposing radically higher fees on Adoption Service Providers, increasing from $147,000 in fees collected to $2.5 million—to be borne by adoption agencies or adoptive families. While the Masha Allen case highlights the need for reforms, the responses noted above have led some sources to predict an effective end to American international adoptions by 2022.[36]

3. Hague Conventions on Parental Responsibility and Child Support

Two additional conventions address parental responsibility and the obligations of child support—including the 1996 Convention on Jurisdiction, Applicable Law, Recognition, Enforcement and Co-operation in Respect of Parental Responsibility and Measures for the Protection of Children (which was signed by the United

States in October of 2010, but has not yet been ratified by the Senate), and the 2007 Hague Convention on the International Recovery of Child Support and Other Forms of Family Maintenance (which was signed and ratified by the Senate in September of 2010).

As with other conventions and treaties, both ratification and, usually, domestic implementing legislation are necessary for their terms to be effectively enforced in the United States. However, as discussed below, their definitions and line drawing can be influential in court interpretations—particularly where current law is unclear.

The 1996 Convention is part of the Hague Conference on Private International Law and covers civil measures of child protection, such as orders imposing parental responsibility and contact, or providing for the public care and protection of children lacking parents, or measures to protect the property of children. The Convention's rules are intended to determine which nation has jurisdiction for rights delineation, and requires other signatory nations to honor those rules.[37] It complements the Abduction and Adoption Conventions above by covering the basic, often underlying issue of what law governs who has parental obligations. It applies particularly to parental disputes over custody and contact short of abduction and return issues, unaccompanied minors, and cross-frontier placements of children. The jurisdiction factor is driven largely by the respect for the place of "habitual residence" of the child and involved parents.

The 2007 Hague Convention on the International Recovery of Child Support and Other Forms of Family Maintenance is an area involving atypical American leadership. It is not unusual of those owing child support to avoid obligation when they move abroad. There is bipartisan support for the treaty in the United States. One expert estimates that only one percent of outstanding child support orders are stymied by international movement of obligors, but that proportion translates to 170,000 American children owed monies by such parents. Most U.S. obligors are in Canada, Central America ,or European Union nations.[38]

The convention compels individuals who move from one Contracting State to another to continue to remit payment by forcing the second Contracting State to enforce the child support agreement from the first Contracting State. Regrettably, as of 2019, the United States was joined by only twelve other signatory nations. However, the Convention is relatively new and it often takes a decade or more to collect a critical mass of ratifying nations. Meanwhile, the United States has had bilateral agreements to facilitate joint child support enforcement with fourteen nations and eleven Canadian provinces. However, outside of these territories, movement to another nation still allows relatively easy evasion.

F. U.S. CASES INTERPRETING CHILD RELATED INTERNA-
TIONAL AGREEMENTS AND CONVENTIONS

What variables are relevant to the weight given to international conventions and agreements within nations? Possible conflict between sovereign law and international mandates exists within every nation state. In the case of the United States, the influence of the international standard may turn on some of the following factors:

- What aspect of domestic law or precedent is at issue? Is it a phrase that may invite the relevance of an international standard, as the "cruel and unusual" prohibition on punishment under the U.S. Constitution's Eighth Amendment? Or is it a standard or obligation that may be *tabula rasa* in terms of existing domestic law? Or what if its terms are contrary to existing domestic statute, precedent, or constitutional mandate?
- What is the nature of the international provision? It is self-executing? Definitional? Or does it require affirmative action by nations domestically? Does it require their funding from domestic resources?
- What is the status of domestic approval of the agreement or convention? Has the domestic nation formally ratified the treaty or convention? If not, did the nation's executive participate in its negotiation and sign the document? If not, did the nation propose and negotiate the agreement, and obtain concessions from others, such that it is estopped from now violating it? Have so many nations approved of the agreement that it is now properly qualified as "customary international law" or "international common law" and is properly applied as such?

1. Interpreting the U.S. Constitution's Eighth Amendment

The majority opinion in *Roper v. Simmons*, 543 U.S. 551 (2005) (see discussion in Chapter 10) cites the Convention on the Rights of the Child and international standards as relevant to the "unusual" prohibition of the Constitution on punishment. The Court majority looked to a variety of factors, including the prevalence or rarity of executions for child victims among the fifty states, and the adoption of a categorical prohibition through the 192 nation ratification of the Convention. Other cases historically have cited international standards and practices as germane.[39] Even O'Connor's dissent in *Roper v. Simmons* acknowledges the possible relevance of an international norms argument and cases used to support the decision of the Court:

> Over the course of nearly half a century, the Court has consistently referred to foreign and international law as relevant to its assessment of evolving standards of decency....

Roper v. Simmons, at 604. Other Justices take a position markedly more critical of the consideration of international standards or practice in interpreting U.S. law, even where the term (here "unusual") may invite an expanse beyond domestic shores. Scalia wrote the majority opinion in *Stanford v. Kentucky*, 492 U.S. 361, that the *Roper* case reverses. It had held capital punishment of those who commit crimes before the age of eighteen not to be prohibited by the Eighth Amendment. Scalia writes in what is now a dissenting view in *Roper*:

> More fundamentally, however, the basic premise of the Court's argument—that American law should conform to the laws of the rest of the world—ought to be rejected out of hand. In fact the Court

itself does not believe it. In many significant respects the laws of most other countries differ from our law—including not only such explicit provisions of our Constitution as the right to jury trial and grand jury indictment, but even many interpretations of the Constitution prescribed by this Court itself. The Court-pronounced exclusionary rule, for example, is distinctively American....

The Court should either profess its willingness to reconsider all these matters in light of the views of foreigners, or else it should cease putting forth foreigners' views as part of the reasoned basis of its decisions. To invoke alien law when it agrees with one's own thinking, and ignore it otherwise, is not reasoned decisionmaking, but sophistry....

The Court responds that "[i]t does not lessen our fidelity to the Constitution or our pride in its origins to acknowledge that the express affirmation of certain fundamental rights by other nations and peoples simply underscores the centrality of those same rights within our own heritage of freedom.";...To begin with, I do not believe that approval by "other nations and peoples" should buttress our commitment to American principles any more than (what should logically follow) disapproval by "other nations and peoples" should weaken that commitment. More importantly, however, the Court's statement flatly misdescribes what is going on here.

Foreign sources are cited today, not to underscore our "fidelity" to the Constitution, our "pride in its origins," and "our own [American] heritage." To the contrary, they are cited to set aside the centuries-old American practice—a practice still engaged in by a large majority of the relevant States—of letting a jury of 12 citizens decide whether, in the particular case, youth should be the basis for withholding the death penalty....

Questions for Discussion

1. Is the extent of international judgment relevant to its inclusion as a factor? Is it relevant that the standard invoked by the court is joined by 192 nations making up more than seven billion of the earth's 7.6 billion people? For those nations that historically tolerated state-sponsored torture, the gassing of dissidents, the severing of hands as punishment for theft, child prostitution, and slavery—would we want U.S. standards of morality (and those of humanity in general) to be considered when they decide whether to continue such practices?

2. The Scalia dissent argues that the world's rejection of the death penalty should not be a factor because many nations have brutal "automatic" death penalty formulae (albeit for adults), and do not otherwise follow some of our civil libertarian traditions. It argues that it is hypocrisy to cite international practice banning child capital punishment when we do not follow it in these other respects. Do the Scalia examples of foreign practices we do not follow represent libertarian principles? Are they aspirational? Universally held?

3. Can the majority in *Roper* argue that world precedents are not symmetrical or otherwise require the rejection of all policies from any source that does not accept our policies? Are such policies all equivalent or fungible or part of a comprehensive

bargain that is properly rejected if not accepted as to all of its disparate parts? If a nation has a method of controlling police excesses separate and apart from the exclusionary rule of the American system, does that disqualify its standards as a laudatory example? Can the world's close-to-consensus agreement about minimal child rights form a floor of civilized practice notwithstanding some areas where we believe the United States has policies more favorable to children than do many of those other nations?

4. As discussed above, the Convention on the Rights of a Child has been signed and ratified by every nation of the world except the United States. Both it and the Second Optional Protocol to the International Convention on Civil and Political Rights ban capital punishment based on the acts of a child (under the age of eighteen). What would be the effect on the *Roper* dissenters if Congress were to ratify either of these two international agreements? Ratified treaties are the equivalent of federal statutes. Would *Lopez*, striking a federal gun statute as precluded by state prerogative (see Chapter 1), disallow federal supremacy and preclude such federal policy from supersession over state laws?

Following the *Roper* case, the Supreme Court considered the issue of Life Without the Possibility of Parole (LWOP) for juveniles in non-homicide cases in *Graham v. Florida*, 130 S.Ct. 2011 (2010) (see *Roper* and *Graham* discussion in Chapter 10). As with *Roper, Graham* has an international dimension because the U.N. Convention on the Rights of the Child prohibits not only capital punishment for juveniles, but also LWOP. That prohibition is based on widespread acceptance of a lifetime of confinement as an unacceptable penalty for crimes committed by children and juveniles. It applies to homicide and non-homicide offenses. The *Graham* holding did not test LWOP for homicides. The international dimension is relevant as a test of Convention weight, or a virtually universal "law of nations" principle or practice, on the interpretation of U.S. Constitutional meaning—here the interpretation of what is "cruel and unusual" under the Eighth Amendment.

The majority decision, by Justice Kennedy, addresses the international dimension:

> ....There is support for our conclusion in the fact that, in continuing to impose life without parole sentences on juveniles who did not commit homicide, the United States adheres to a sentencing practice rejected the world over. This observation does not control our decision. The judgments of other nations and the international community are not dispositive as to the meaning of the Eighth Amendment. But "'[t]he climate of international opinion concerning the acceptability of a particular punishment'" is also "'not irrelevant.'" The Court has looked beyond our Nation's borders for support for its independent conclusion that a particular punishment is cruel and unusual....

> Today we continue that longstanding practice in noting the global consensus against the sentencing practice in question. A recent study concluded that only 11 nations authorize life without parole for juvenile offenders under any circumstances; and only 2 of them, the United States and Israel, ever impose the punishment in practice....even if

Israel is counted as allowing life without parole for juvenile offenders, that nation does not appear to impose that sentence for nonhomicide crimes; all of the seven Israeli prisoners whom commentators have identified as serving life sentences for juvenile crimes were convicted of homicide or attempted homicide. Thus, as petitioner contends and respondent does not contest, the United States is the only Nation that imposes life without parole sentences on juvenile nonhomicide offenders. We also note, as petitioner and his amici emphasize, that Article 37(a) of the United Nations Convention on the Rights of the Child..., ratified by every nation except the United States and Somalia, prohibits the imposition of "life imprisonment without possibility of release...for offences committed by persons below eighteen years of age."...As we concluded in Roper with respect to the juvenile death penalty, "the United States now stands alone in a world that has turned its face against" life without parole for juvenile nonhomicide offenders.

"The State's amici stress that no international legal agreement that is binding on the United States prohibits life without parole for juvenile offenders and thus urge us to ignore the international consensus....

These arguments miss the mark. The question before us is not whether international law prohibits the United States from imposing the sentence at issue in this case. The question is whether that punishment is cruel and unusual. In that inquiry, "the overwhelming weight of international opinion against" life without parole for nonhomicide offenses committed by juveniles "provide[s] respected and significant confirmation for our own conclusions."....

"The debate between petitioner's and respondent's amici over whether there is a binding jus cogens norm against this sentencing practice is likewise of no import....The Court has treated the laws and practices of other nations and international agreements as relevant to the Eighth Amendment not because those norms are binding or controlling but because the judgment of the world's nations that a particular sentencing practice is inconsistent with basic principles of decency demonstrates that the Court's rationale has respected reasoning to support it."

2. International Standards and U.S. Common Law Application

In *Sosa v. Alvarez-Machain*, 542 U.S. 692 (2004) a Mexican citizen allegedly seized in Mexico and forcibly brought to the U.S. on charges of murdering an undercover agent sued the U.S. federal officials involved under the federal Tort Claims Act, citing international human rights law (The Universal Declaration of Human Rights and the International Covenant on Civil and Political Rights). The Court wrote:

...Whatever may be said for the broad principle Alvarez advances, in the present, imperfect world, it expresses an aspiration that exceeds any binding customary rule having the specificity we require. Creating a private cause of action to further that aspiration would go beyond any residual common law discretion we think it appropriate to exercise. It is enough to hold that a single illegal detention of less than a day, followed by the transfer of custody to lawful authorities and a prompt arraignment, violates no norm of customary international law so well defined as to support the creation of a federal remedy.

But although the facts removed the case from common law enforcement of international standards, extensive *dicta* represents a major recent Court discussion of the interplay between international treaties and law, and domestic law and enforcement. The majority decision of Souter reads:

> We think it is correct, then, to assume that the First Congress understood that the district courts would recognize private causes of action for certain torts in violation of the law of nations, though we have found no basis to suspect Congress had any examples in mind beyond those torts corresponding to Blackstone's three primary offenses: violation of safe conducts, infringement of the rights of ambassadors, and piracy. We assume, too, that no development in the two centuries from the...birth of the modern line of cases beginning with *Filartiga v. Pena-Irala*, 630 F.2d 876 (CA2 1980), has categorically precluded federal courts from recognizing a claim under the law of nations as an element of common law; Congress has not in any relevant way amended...or limited civil common law power by another statute. Still, there are good reasons for a restrained conception of the discretion a federal court should exercise in considering a new cause of action of this kind. Accordingly, we think courts should require any claim based on the present-day law of nations to rest on a norm of international character accepted by the civilized world and defined with a specificity comparable to the features of the 18th-century paradigms we have recognized.

However, the Court also recognized the need for legislative or other consent or affirmation for domestic enforcement, writing:

> ...Several times, indeed, the Senate has expressly declined to give the federal courts the task of interpreting and applying international human rights law, as when its ratification of the International Covenant on Civil and Political Rights declared that the substantive provisions of the document were not self-executing....

Justice Scalia, speaking for three justices, proposes to more substantially foreclose consideration of international norms, writing in his concurring opinion:

> ...The notion that a law of nations, redefined to mean the consensus of states on *any* subject, can be used by a private citizen to control a sovereign's treatment of its *own citizens* within its *own territory* is a 20th century invention of internationalist law professors and human rights advocates....The Framers would, I am confident, be appalled by the proposition that, for example, the American peoples' democratic adoption of the death penalty,...could be judicially nullified because of the disapproving views of foreigners.

* * *

> It would be bad enough if there were some assurance that future conversions of perceived international norms into American law would be approved by this Court itself. (Though we know ourselves to be eminently reasonable, self-awareness of eminent reasonableness is not really a substitute for democratic election.) But in this illegitimate lawmaking endeavor, the lower federal courts will be the principal actors; we review but a tiny fraction of their decisions. And no one thinks that all of them are eminently reasonable.

American law—the law made by the people's democratically elected representatives—does not recognize a category of activity that is so universally disapproved by other nations that it is automatically unlawful here, and automatically gives rise to a private action for money damages in federal court. That simple principle is what today's decision should have announced.

Responding to Justice Scalia, the majority writes:

...Justice Scalia...concludes, however, that two subsequent developments should be understood to preclude federal courts from recognizing any further international norms as judicially enforceable today, absent further congressional action. As described before, we now tend to understand common law not as a discoverable reflection of universal reason but, in a positivistic way, as a product of human choice. And we now adhere to a conception of limited judicial power first expressed in reorienting federal diversity jurisdiction, see *Erie R. Co. v. Tompkins*,...that federal courts have no authority to derive "general" common law.

Whereas Justice Scalia sees these developments as sufficient to close the door to further independent judicial recognition of actionable international norms, other considerations persuade us that the judicial power should be exercised on the understanding that the door is still ajar subject to vigilant doorkeeping, and thus open to a narrow class of international norms today. *Erie* did not in terms bar any judicial recognition of new substantive rules, no matter what the circumstances, and post-*Erie* understanding has identified limited enclaves in which federal courts may derive some substantive law in a common law way. For two centuries we have affirmed that the domestic law of the United States recognizes the law of nations.... It would take some explaining to say now that federal courts must avert their gaze entirely from any international norm intended to protect individuals.

3. International Child Standards and the Alien Torts Act

Abdullahi v. Pfizer
562 F.3d 163 (DC Cir. 2009)

PARKER, Circuit Judge:

...The central events at issue in these cases took place in 1996, during an epidemic of bacterial meningitis in northern Nigeria. The appellants allege that at that time, Pfizer, the world's largest pharmaceutical corporation, sought to gain the approval of the U.S. Food and Drug Administration ("FDA") for the use on children of its new antibiotic, Trovafloxacin Mesylate, marketed as "Trovan." They contend that [its]...team allegedly recruited two hundred sick children who sought treatment...and gave half of the children Trovan and the other half Ceftriaxone, an FDA-approved antibiotic the safety and efficacy of which was well-established. Appellants contend that Pfizer knew that Trovan had never previously been tested on children in the form being used and that animal tests showed that Trovan had life- threatening side effects, including joint disease, abnormal cartilage growth, liver damage, and a degenerative bone condition. Pfizer purportedly gave the children who were in the Ceftriaxone control group a deliberately low dose in order to misrepresent the effectiveness of Trovan in relation to Ceftriaxone. After approximately two weeks, Pfizer allegedly concluded the experiment and left without administering follow-up care. According to the appellants, the tests caused the deaths of eleven children, five of whom had taken Trovan and six of whom had taken the lowered dose of Ceftriaxone, and left many others blind, deaf, paralyzed, or brain-damaged.

Appellants claim that Pfizer, working in partnership with the Nigerian government, failed to secure the informed consent of either the children or their guardians and specifically failed to disclose or explain the experimental nature of the study or the serious risks involved. Although the treatment protocol required the researchers to offer or read the subjects documents requesting and facilitating their informed consent, this was allegedly not done in either English or the subjects' native language of Hausa... [and they did not inform the children that]...Doctors Without Borders...was providing a conventional and effective treatment for bacterial meningitis, free of charge, at the same site....

* * *

In 1998, the FDA approved Trovan for use on adult patients only. After reports of liver failure in patients who took Trovan, its use in America was eventually restricted to adult emergency care. In 1999, the European Union banned its use.

I. The Alien Tort Statute

The Alien Tort Statute, 28 U.S.C. § 1350, provides that "[t]he district courts shall have original jurisdiction of any civil action by an alien for a tort only, committed in violation of the law of nations or a treaty of the United States." Included in the Judiciary Act of 1789, the statute provided jurisdiction in just two cases during the first 191 years after its enactment...

We first extensively examined the ATS in *Filartiga v. Pena-Irala*, 630 F.2d 876 (2d Cir. 1980), where we held that conduct violating the law of nations is actionable under the ATS "only where the nations of the world have demonstrated that the wrong is of mutual, and not merely several, concern, by means of express international accords."... Following Filartiga, we concluded that ATS claims may sometimes be brought against private actors, and not only state officials,...when the tortious activities violate norms of "universal concern" that are recognized to extend to the conduct of private parties—for example, slavery, genocide, and war crimes....This case involves allegations of both state and individual action. In *Flores v. Southern Peru Copper Corp.*, 414 F.3d 233 (2d Cir. 2003), we clarified that "the law of nations" in the ATS context "refers to the body of law known as customary international law," which "is discerned from myriad decisions made in numerous and varied international and domestic arenas" and "does not stem from any single, definitive, readily-identifiable source."...These principles are rejected in their entirety by our dissenting colleague....

In 2004, the Supreme Court comprehensively addressed the ATS for the first time in *Sosa v. Alvarez-Machain*, 542 U.S. 692, [clarifying] that the ATS was enacted to create jurisdiction over "a relatively modest set of actions alleging violations of the law of nations" and with "the understanding that the common law would provide a cause of action."...The Supreme Court confirmed that federal courts retain a limited power to "adapt[] the law of nations to private rights" by recognizing "a narrow class of international norms" to be judicially enforceable through our residual common law discretion to create causes of action....

* * *

Turning now to this appeal, and remaining mindful of our obligation to proceed cautiously and self-consciously in this area, we determine whether the norm alleged (1) is a norm of international character that States universally abide by, or accede to, out of a sense of legal obligation; (2) is defined with a specificity comparable to the 18th-century paradigms discussed in Sosa; and (3) is of mutual concern to States.

A. The Prohibition of Nonconsensual Medical Experimentation on Humans

Appellants' ATS claims are premised on the existence of a norm of customary international law prohibiting medical experimentation on non-consenting human subjects. To determine whether this prohibition constitutes a universally accepted norm of customary international law, we examine the current state of international law by consulting the sources identified by Article 38 of the Statute of the International Court of Justice ("ICJ Statute"), to which the United States and all members of the United

Nations are parties. Article 38 identifies the authorities that provide "competent proof of the content of customary international law."...These sources consist of:

(a) international conventions, whether general or particular, establishing rules expressly recognized by the contesting states;
(b) international custom, as evidence of a general practice accepted as law;
(c) the general principles of law recognized by civilized nations;
(d) judicial decisions and the teachings of the most highly qualified publicists of the various nations, as subsidiary means for the determination of rules of law.

* * *

The appellants ground their claims in four sources of international law that categorically forbid medical experimentation on non-consenting human subjects: (1) the Nuremberg Code, which states as its first principle that "[t]he voluntary consent of the human subject is absolutely essential"; (2) the World Medical Association's Declaration of Helsinki, which sets forth ethical principles to guide physicians world-wide and provides that human subjects should be volunteers and grant their informed consent to participate in research; (3) the guidelines authored by the Council for International Organizations of Medical Services ("CIOMS"), which require "the voluntary informed consent of [a] prospective subject"; and (4) Article 7 of the International Covenant on Civil and Political Rights ("ICCPR"), which provides that "no one shall be subjected without his free consent to medical or scientific experimentation."

* * *

(i) Universality....since Nuremberg, states throughout the world have shown through international accords and domestic law-making that they consider the prohibition on nonconsensual medical experimentation identified at Nuremberg as a norm of customary international law....

* * *

It is clear that, as the court mentioned in Sosa, the Universal Declaration of Human Rights and the ICCPR themselves could not establish the relevant, applicable rule of international law in that case....Nonetheless, the ICCPR, when viewed as a reaffirmation of the norm as articulated in the Nuremberg Code, is potent authority for the universal acceptance of the prohibition on nonconsensual medical experimentation. As we discuss below,...the fact that the prohibition on medical experimentation on humans without consent has been consciously embedded by Congress in our law and reaffirmed on numerous occasions by the FDA demonstrates that the United States government views the norm as the source of a binding legal obligation even though the United States has not ratified the ICCPR in full.[11]

In 1964, the World Medical Association adopted the Declaration of Helsinki, which enunciated standards for obtaining informed consent from human subjects....The Declaration has since been amended five times. The informed consent provision now provides that "subjects must be volunteers and informed participants in the research project."...Although the Declaration itself is non-binding, since the 1960s, it has spurred States to regulate human experimentation, often by incorporating its informed consent requirement into domestic laws or regulations.

The history of the norm in United States law demonstrates that it has been firmly embedded for more than 45 years and—except for our dissenting colleague-its validity has never been seriously questioned by any court. Congress mandated patient-subject consent in drug research in 1962....the FDA promulgated its first regulations requiring the informed consent of human subjects. Tellingly, the sources on which our government relied in outlawing non-consensual human medical experimentation were the Nuremberg Code and the Declaration of Helsinki, which suggests the government conceived of these sources' articulation of the norm as a binding legal obligation....

he importance that the United States government attributes to this norm is demonstrated by its willingness to use domestic law to coerce compliance with the norm throughout the world. United States law requires that, as a predicate to FDA approval of any new drug, both American and foreign sponsors of drug research

Tinvolving clinical trials, whether conducted here or abroad, procure informed consent from human subjects....

(ii) Specificity

Sosa requires that we recognize causes of action only to enforce those customary international law norms that are no "less definite [in] content...than the historical paradigms familiar when [the ATS] was enacted."...The Nuremberg Code, Article 7 of the ICCPR, the Declaration of Helsinki, the Convention on Human Rights and Biomedicine, the Universal Declaration on Bioethics and Human Rights, the 2001 Clinical Trial Directive, and the domestic laws of at least eighty-four States all uniformly and unmistakably prohibit medical experiments on human beings without their consent, thereby providing concrete content for the norm....

(iii) Mutual Concern

Customary international law proscribes only transgressions that are of "mutual" concern to States—"those involving States' actions performed...towards or with regard to the other."...Conduct that States have prohibited through domestic legislation is also actionable under the ATS as a violation of customary international law when nations of the world have demonstrated "by means of express international accords" that the wrong is of mutual concern. An important, but not exclusive, component of this test is a showing that the conduct in question is "capable of impairing international peace and security."...Appellants have made both of these showings.

* * *

For these reasons, we hold that the appellants have pled facts sufficient to state a cause of action under the ATS for a violation of the norm of customary international law prohibiting medical experimentation on human subjects without their consent.... *Sosa* makes clear that the critical inquiry is whether the variety of sources that we are required to consult establishes a customary international law norm that is sufficiently specific, universally accepted, and obligatory for courts to recognize a cause of action to enforce the norm. Nothing in *Sosa* suggests that this inquiry can be halted if some of the sources of international law giving rise to the norm are found not to be binding or not to explicitly authorize a cause of action.

* * *

[11] *Khulumani* makes clear that treaties that the United States has neither signed nor ratified-let alone treaties like the ICCPR that the United States has signed but not ratified-may evidence a customary international law norm for ATS purposes where the treaty has been ratified widely and t is clear that the reason for the United States's failure to subscribe to the treaty was unrelated to the particular norm in question. See *Khulumani*, 504 F.3d at 276, 276 n.9 (Katzmann, J., concurring).

WESLEY, Dissenting:

The majority has undertaken to define a "firmly established" norm of international law, heretofore unrecognized by any American court or treaty obligation, on the basis of materials inadequate for the task. In deviating from our settled case law, the majority *identifies* no norm of customary international law, it creates a new norm out of whole cloth. Because the majority's analysis misconstrues—rather than vindicates—customary international law, I respectfully dissent.

* * *

The majority identifies three criteria that must be satisfied before a violation of international law can be actionable under the ATS: that the norm is (1) specific and definable, (2) universally adhered to out of a sense of legal obligation, and (3) a matter of mutual concern, namely a matter "involving States' actions performed towards or with regard to the other."...I agree with the methodology...[but not] their conclusion that a norm against non-consensual medical experimentation on humans by private actors is (1) universal and obligatory or (2) a matter of mutual concern.

The majority relies on eight sources of customary international law to support its determination that a norm against non-consensual medical experimentation on humans by private actors is universal and obligatory. However, this evidence falls far short of the quantum necessary to establish the existence of such a norm: (1) the International

Covenant on Civil and Political Rights has been described by the Supreme Court as a "well-known international agreement[] that despite [its] moral authority, ha[s] little utility," in defining international obligations,...and moreover, it does not apply to private actors, such as the Defendant in this action; (2) the Council of Europe's Convention on Human Rights and Biomedicine—a regional convention—was not ratified by the most influential nations in the region, such as France, Germany, Italy, the Netherlands, Russia and the United Kingdom, and it was promulgated on April 4, 1997, one year *after* the conduct at issue in this litigation; (3) the UNESCO Universal Declaration of Bioethics and Human Rights of 2005 and (4) the European Parliament Clinical Trial Directive of 2001 both also post-date the relevant time period by several years; (5) the Declaration of Helsinki issued by the World Medical Association, a private entity, and (6) the International Ethical Guidelines for Research Involving Human Subjects promulgated by the Council for International Organizations for Medical Sciences, another private entity, "express[] the sensibilities and the asserted aspirations and demands of some countries or organizations" but are not "statements of universally-recognized legal obligations,"...; (7) states' domestic laws, which, unsupported by express international accords, are not "significant or relevant for purposes of customary international law,"...; and (8) the so-called Nuremberg Code, a statement of principles that accompanied a criminal verdict, possesses at best "subsidiary" value as a judicial decision....Taken together, this evidence falls short of charting the existence of a universal and obligatory international norm actionable against non-government actors under the ATS....

In support of its determination that non-consensual medical experimentation by private actors is a matter of mutual concern, the majority reasons that non-consensual medical experiments breed distrust of medical interventions and thereby accelerate the spread of infectious diseases across international borders. It is not enough, however, that tortious conduct could create some sort of international consequence. In order for conduct to be a matter of mutual concern, it must "threaten[] serious consequences in international affairs."...Such is the case when an ambassador is assaulted, for example, because the assault "impinge[s] upon the sovereignty of the foreign nation and if not adequately redressed could rise to an issue of war."...Non-consensual medical experimentation by private actors simply does not present the same grave risk of serious consequences in international affairs and is therefore not a matter of mutual concern.

For these reasons, I conclude that non-consensual medical experimentation by private actors, though deplorable, is not actionable under international law and would therefore affirm the district court's dismissal of Plaintiffs' complaints.

* * *

Customary international law is discerned from myriad decisions made in numerous and varied international and domestic arenas. Furthermore, the relevant evidence of customary international law is widely dispersed and generally unfamiliar to lawyers and judges. These difficulties are compounded by the fact that customary international law...does not stem from any single, definitive, readily-identifiable source...the ability to pick and choose from this seemingly limitless menu of sources presents a real threat of 'creative interpretation'....

* * *

1. Treaties & Conventions

In *Flores*, we noted that treaties are the strongest evidence of customary international law because they 'create *legal obligations* akin to contractual obligations on the States parties to them.'..."[W]e look primarily to the formal lawmaking and official actions of States...as evidence of the established practices of States."...But not all treaties are equal. Although '[a]ll treaties that have been ratified by at least two States provide some evidence of the custom and practice of nations...a treaty will only constitute *sufficient proof* of a norm of customary international law if an overwhelming majority of States have ratified the treaty.'...Moreover, the 'evidentiary weight to be afforded to a given treaty varies greatly depending on (i) how many, and which, States have ratified the treaty, and (ii) the degree to which those States actually implement and abide by the principles set forth in the treaty.'...For instance, treaties ratified by the United States are of greater evidentiary value if they are either self-executing or executed through acts of Congress....

The majority relies primarily on two treaties.

a. International Covenant on Civil and Political Rights

* * *

The ICCPR is not appropriate evidence of customary international law for at least two reasons. First, the Supreme Court in Sosa explicitly described the ICCPR as a 'well-known international agreement[] that, despite [its] moral authority, ha[s] *little utility* under the standard set out in this opinion,' because the 'United States ratified [it] on the express understanding that it was not self-executing and so did not itself create obligations enforceable in the federal courts.'...

Second, whatever limited weight the ICCPR has with regard to state action, it does nothing to show that a norm prohibiting involuntary medical experimentation applies to non-state entities. In citing its seemingly universal language, the majority overlooks the ICCPR's operative section, which requires that "[e]ach State Party...undertake[] to respect and to ensure to all individuals within its territory and subject to its jurisdiction the rights recognized in the present Covenant."...Thus, despite its broad text, the ICCPR by its own terms, only governs "the relationship between a State and the individuals within the State's territory....whatever its evidentiary value had Plaintiffs sued the Nigerian government, the ICCPR clearly has none where the question is whether international law includes a norm actionable against a *private corporation*....

b. Convention on Human Rights and Biomedicine

The second treaty cited by the majority is the Convention on Human Rights and Biomedicine,...promulgated by the Council of Europe....Articles 5...and 16...of the Convention require that the subject of scientific research give his or her informed consent, which may be withdrawn at any time....[I]t is a regional agreement not signed by the most influential states in the region. Membership in the Council of Europe is limited to European states....

A second, more fundamental problem with the majority's reliance on the Convention is that it was promulgated *after* the conduct at issue here. I know of no authority for an international ex post facto definition of the law of nations by later signed treaties....

* * *

The majority centers its analysis around the Nuremberg Code, but, in the process, critically misstates its genesis and status in international law....Because the Code is a *sui generis* source of international law, its context is vital to understanding what it is—and what it is not.

* * *

The first of the American trials arising under Control Council Law No. 10 was the "Medical Case" against German doctors. On October 25, 1946, the American Office of Military Government for Germany enacted General Order 68, constituting Military Tribunal 1, comprised of three American military judges and one alternate judge. prisoners.... At the conclusion of the Medical Case, 16 of the 23 defendants were convicted of one or more of the charges, and seven were ultimately sentenced to death. Along with their verdict, the military judges enumerated ten principles that came to be known as the

Nuremberg Code, the first of which states that in medical experiments, the "voluntary consent of the human subject is absolutely essential."... the majority overlooks the fact that the Nuremberg Code dealt not with these general principles of law, but instead with the very specific issue of permissible medical experimentation. The ethical principles espoused in the Code had no forebears in either the London Charter or the judgment of the International Military Tribunal. They were developed exclusively in the Medical Case....

[Further], the Code is not a treaty and did not immediately bind any state. Under the framework of the ICJ Statute—and, accordingly, this Court—because it was part of a criminal verdict, its closest analogue is a judicial decision, but judicial decisions are only "subsidiary," rather than primary, sources of customary international law....

* * *

Simply put, the evidence here does not compare with the sources put forward in the few cases where we have held a principle to be a norm of customary international law. Exercising "extraordinary care and restraint"....In those cases, the evidence of international acceptance of each norm with respect to each defendant was "clear and unambiguous."...In each case, the nations of the world gathered to ratify in universal numbers treaties that specifically prohibited genocide, war crimes, torture, and attacks on neutral ships—not in generalized human rights agreements but in accords with those discrete norms as their exclusive subjects.

* * *

B. Restatement § 404

Nor does Plaintiffs' purported norm resemble the select few norms for which international law extends liability to private actors. Although the law of nations in general does not "confine[] its reach to state action,"...courts must still consider whether the specific norm at issue does. In *Kadic*, we noted that the Restatement (Third) of Foreign Relations Law of the United States differentiates between 'those violations that are actionable when committed by a state and a more limited category of violations' that apply with equal force to private actors....Section 404 of the Restatement authorizes universal criminal jurisdiction over non-state entities "for certain offenses recognized by the community of nations as of universal concern, such as piracy, slave trade, attacks on or hijacking of aircraft, genocide, war crimes, and perhaps certain acts of terrorism, even where [no other basis of jurisdiction] is present." Universal jurisdiction, not to be confused with universal acceptance of a norm for ATS purposes, "permits a State to prosecute an offender of any nationality for an offense committed outside of that State and without contacts to that State."...

* * *

...Section 404 lists only five specific acts for which universal criminal jurisdiction over private actors exists: piracy, genocide, slave trade, war crimes, and attacks on aircrafts....Plaintiffs argue that it is "sufficiently similar" to those acts to support its application to a private corporation....Non-consensual medical experimentation is not "sufficiently similar" to these crimes to warrant its incorporation into Section 404 by analogy....these crimes occur in locations where, or during times when, sovereignty, and *a fortiori* criminal jurisdiction, are incapable of being exercised. Because medical experimentation is entirely *intranational* and fully subject to domestic criminal jurisdiction, it is not "sufficiently similar" to those acts listed in section 404, and cannot be incorporated by analogy as to reach private, non-state actors.

* * *

The majority today authorizes the exercise of ATS jurisdiction over an entirely private corporation for violating a previously unrecognized norm of international law. In doing so, my colleagues accept proof far weaker than in any other case where this Court has identified a norm of customary international law, and, apparently, overlook the fact that this purported norm in no way resembles those few norms enforceable against private entities...

II. Mutuality

* * *

The majority concludes that non-consensual medical experimentation by one private party on another is a matter of mutual concern. I disagree.

"We have consistently held that the best evidence that states consider a matter to be of mutual concern is the fact that they have agreed to be bound "by means of express international accords.".....The majority points to the ICCPR, the Convention on Human Rights and Biomedicine, and the 2001 Clinical Trial Directive as evidence that "States throughout the world have entered into...express and binding international agreements prohibiting nonconsensual medical experimentation.".....But those agreements fail to demonstrate mutuality for the same reason they fail to demonstrate universality—the ICCPR does not address acts by non-state actors and the other two were not in force at the time of the alleged misconduct....

Questions for Discussion

1. If damages may lie against *Pfizer* for Nigerian medical experimentation abuses, can damages lie against *Lorillard* for misleadingly marketing addictive and health threatening cigarettes to much larger numbers of Nigerian youth?

2. If exporters of lead paint-coated toys in the People's Republic of China know that their product will seriously injure some infants, should they be liable to civil suit by American kids (or their parents) in China? What if they have virtually no assets in the United States other than the tainted toys and recovery is only available where the items were manufactured? What if the offending firm has its assets in Belgium, should suit be allowed there?

3. What if Nigeria is corruptly influenced by *Pfizer* bribery (as the pleadings here allege)? Should that be a factor in allowing suit outside that nation? What if Nigeria has the opposite bias, is politically outraged at the medical abuses of its children by *Pfizer* and the Nigerian state wishes to prosecute *Pfizer* and its executives criminally or civilly? What if it would countenance a private civil suit on behalf of its children within its own domain? What if *Pfizer* were viewed by Nigerian agencies and juries as a foreign, alien scofflaw appropriate for arbitrary assessment in order to achieve Western economic compensation for past grievances? What if *Pfizer* seeks preclusive jurisdiction in U.S. courts as a means of eliminating a Nigerian judgment?

4. What if the facts were somewhat different, and lacked any animus or deceit or medical maltreatment by *Pfizer*, but instead consisted of simply failing to provide adequate notice of all known information about the placebo, and each sample type to be tested? What if Nigerian law provided that as to certain serious illnesses such testing may take place given the harsh consequences of current treatment modalities and this illness so qualified?

5. The dissent argues that the agreements and treaties cited by the majority fail to establish universality, *et al.* It notes that the Council of Europe's Convention on Human Rights and Biomedicine is merely regional and some influential nations did not sign it. What would the dissent say about the universality of the U.N. Convention on the Rights of Children, signed by every nation of the world except for the U.S. (see above) and amounting to governments representing more than 95% of the world's population? Is that sufficiently universal to meet that criterion?

Note on 2018 Supreme Court Decision Shielding Foreign Corporations from the Alien Tort Statute

Undermining the scope of the Alien Tort Statute (ATS) is the recent seminal case of *Jesner et al. v. Arab Bank, PLC*, 138 S. Ct. 1386 (2018). This 5–4 decision, purporting to interpret *Sosa* above, instead charted new exempt grounds substantially voiding the major part of the law. The majority opinion acknowledged the theory of "torts" that may violate the "law of nations"—including wrongs committed against children as the *Sosa* facts indicated. But then the court cited its "general reluctance to extend judicially created private rights of action." It cited "foreign policy" concerns in allowing suit against a foreign corporation for wrongs committed—unless directly occurring in the United States. It then decided that "foreign corporations may not be defendants in suits brought under the ATS."[40] The context of the case involved a bank providing services to terrorist groups, with some transactions occurring in New York, that aided the Palestinian Intifada and injured 6,000 Israeli citizens. The case could have been distinguished narrowly based on the minor United States connection, and the lack of plaintiff connection to the United States, but the Court wrote a broader holding. That broad limitation on jurisdiction (based on the foreign policy concerns raised by court remedies against a foreign corporation) casts some doubt on the ability of the longstanding statute to provide a remedy. That limitation would apply to child exploitation and damage incurred by foreign corporations, even where there is a U.S. connection to the wrongs. Of particular concern over its breadth is the ease of any entity in the modern world to create corporations anywhere from Aruba to Russia. The Sotomayor dissent notes: "In categorically barring all suits against foreign corporations...entities capable of wrongdoing under our domestic law...remain immune from liability for human rights abuses, however egregious they may be."[41]

4. International Child Standards and Domestic Application in General

The application of the "law of nations" is complicated by widely disparate settings and applications. Those variables include the following relevant questions: (a) Is it a treaty or convention signed and/or ratified by the United States (or the nation-state where application is attempted)? (b) Is it within the ambit of subject areas such as ambassadorial privilege, genocide, or piracy that treaties and international comity may compel enforcement wherever necessary? (c) If not signed and ratified, is the principle related to basic international subject matter, or so universal it has achieved "law of nations" status? Is it universal, specific, and mutually applicable such that it achieves a kind of international "common law" ("law of nations") status? (d) Is the treaty or convention self-executing? (e) Is the party against whom the provision is enforced a private party, or a person acting under color or direction of a nation-state? (e) Does the enforcing party have jurisdiction over the defendant/respondent cognizable in the pursued forum? (f) Is there a domestic statute/rule in the pursued forum that repeats or enforces international tenets, or is the domestic provision subject to its interpretation based on such tenets?

Some of the following five cases involve immigration issues, including the effects on American citizen children of the deportation of their parents. Can you reconcile the following court language concerning the significance of international treaties and the "law of nations"?

- ***The Paquete Habana,*** 175 U.S. 677 (1900): "[W]here there is no treaty, and no controlling executive or legislative act or judicial decision, resort must be had to the customs and usages of civilized nations; and, as evidence of these, to the works of jurists and commentators, who by years of labor, research and experience, have made themselves peculiarly well acquainted with the subjects of which they treat. Such works are resorted to by judicial tribunals, not for the speculations of their authors concerning what the law ought to be, but for trustworthy evidence of what the law really is."

- ***Martinez-Lopez v. Gonzales,*** 454 F.3d 500 (5th Cir. 2006): "Martinez-Lopez argues that his removal violates two treaties, the Convention on the Rights of the Child ("CRC") and the International Covenant on Civil and Political Rights ("ICCPR"). The United States has not ratified the CRC, and, accordingly, the treaty cannot give rise to an individually enforceable right....[T]his Court cannot grant relief under the ICCPR because it is not a self-executing treaty."

  "Martinez-Lopez also argues that customary international law, including principles in the Universal Declaration of Human Rights, prevents his removal. International customs, however, cannot override congressional intent as expressed by statute."

- ***Cabrera-Alvarez v. Gonzales,*** 423 F.3d 1006, 1010–12 (9th Cir. 2005): "Although the [United Nations] Convention [on the Rights of the Child] is widely (indeed, almost universally) ratified, it has not been ratified by the United States....Therefore, the Convention is not 'the supreme law of the land' under the Treaty Clause of the United States Constitution. *See* U.S. Const. art. VI. For purposes of evaluating Petitioner's argument, however, we assume, without deciding, that the Convention has attained the status of 'customary international law.'"

  "...When an alien parent seeks cancellation of removal because of exceptional and extremely unusual hardship to a qualifying child, 8 U.S.C. § 1229b(b)(1)(D), that child's 'best interests' are precisely the issue before the agency, in the sense that 'best interests' are merely the converse of 'hardship.'...."

  "...[H]ardship to qualifying children is not the *only* factor that the agency must weigh in considering an application for cancellation of removal...."

  "...In short, no rule of statutory construction required the agency to elevate the qualifying child's best interests to a level that would effectively eliminate or alter the express comparative standard set forth in the statutory text...."

  "...[T]he agency's interpretation of the hardship standard, and its application of the standard in this case, are consistent with the 'best interests of the child' principle articulated in the Convention on the

Rights of the Child, even assuming that the Convention is 'customary international law' and that its dictates are relevant to a proceeding involving deportation of a parent...."

- **Naoum v. Attorney General of U.S.**, 300 F. Supp. 2d 521, 527–28 (N.D. Ohio 2004): "...[W]here there was no treaty, and no controlling executive or legislative act or judicial decision, courts must resort 'to the customs and usages of civilized nations.'...Customary international law is also an important tool of statutory construction as 'an act of congress ought never be construed to violate the law of nations if any other possible construction remains.'...Though it has constitutional authority to do so, Congress is generally presumed not to have acted in violation of customary international law...."

  "This Court need not resolve the extent to which customary international law is embodied in federal law....Assuming that ICCPR and CRC incorporates norms of customary international law as proposed by Mr. Naoum, these treaties express the following relevant principles: an alien shall 'be allowed to submit the reasons against his expulsion' (Article 13 of the ICCPR); 'No one shall be subjected to arbitrary or unlawful interference with his ... family' (Article 17 of the ICCPR); 'The family is the natural and fundamental group unit of society and is entitled to protection by society and the State' (Article 23 of the ICCPR); 'in all actions concerning children...the best interests of the child shall be a primary consideration' (Article 3 of the CRC); and a child shall have 'as far as possible, the right to know and be cared for by his or her parents' (Article 7 of the CRC")."

  "The above provisions do not prohibit the deportation of alien parents of citizen children, and the government, in this case, did nothing to violate any of these general principles...."

- **Beharry v. Reno,** 183 F. Supp. 2d 584, 595–599 (E.D. N.Y. 2002): "The [International Covenant on Civil and Political Rights] ICCPR... states that 'the family is the natural and fundamental group unit of society and is entitled to protection by society and the state.' ICCPR art. 23(1). Separating a parent from a citizen child by forced deportation can be considered a violation of the ICCPR if no adequate hearing is afforded. Article 7 of the ICCPR prohibits 'cruel, inhuman, or degrading treatment.' Arbitrary or capricious separation from one's family and longtime home can reasonably be interpreted to fall within that general category. The ICCPR is a signed, ratified treaty. It came with attached reservations of non-self-execution. This has led some courts to disregard some of its parts...."

  "The United States signed the CRC [Convention on the Rights of the Child] on February 16, 1995; it has never been sent to the Senate for ratification, but every other nation except Somalia-which is effectively without a government-has ratified the CRC. The CRC does not have the force of domestic law under the treaty clause of the Constitution. Non-ratification does not, however, eliminate its impact on American law...."

"While the UDHR [Universal Declaration of Human Rights] is not a treaty, it has an effect similar to a treaty....Provisions of the UDHR may be used in statutory construction....The UDHR is helpful in resolving questions of international human rights law....The UDHR has also been utilized in weighing the constitutionality of provisions of the [Antiterrorism and Effective Death Penalty Act and the Illegal Immigration Reform and Immigrant Responsibility Act]...."

"United States courts should interpret legislation in harmony with international law and norms wherever possible. 'An act of Congress ought never to be construed to violate the law of nations if any other possible construction remains.'..."

"Congress may override provisions of customary international law...but laws are to be read in conformity with international law where possible....it follows that in order to overrule customary international law, Congress must enact domestic legislation which both postdates the development of a customary international law norm, and which clearly has the intent of repealing that norm."

5. The Particular Issue of Child Rights and U.S. Immigration and Separation from Families

With the advent of the Trump Administration in January of 2017, a new issue arose involving the confluence of international law and U.S. immigration policies involving children. On April 6, 2018, Attorney General Jeff Sessions "notified the U.S. Attorney's Offices along the Southwest Border of a new 'zero-tolerance policy' for offenses under 8 U.S.C. § 1325(a), which prohibits both attempted illegal entry and illegal entry into the United States by an alien."[42] Although that prohibition has a possible criminal remedy, it specifies a civil process not involving confinement as the primary remedy. The new policy statement cited a 203% increase in "illegal crossings" along that border from March 2017 to March 2018 and hence required the arrest of all persons so entering, substantially in order to deter such crossing attempts. Part of that deterrence also involved the removal of any children from their respective accompanying families. The President justified the approach by characterizing immigrants, substantially families from the troubled nations of Guatemala, Honduras, and El Salvador, as invading aliens consisting largely of violent criminals and rapists, describing in detail the facts of such alleged attacks from such immigrants, including "the MS-13 violent gang," and contending that the last 170,000 deportation proceedings documented that stark criminality danger. He also declared the number of attempted entries along the Southern border to be at record levels threatening the security of the nation, and in early 2019 declared that circumstance to warrant a "declaration of emergency" to finance a wall across the South border of the nation, notwithstanding the Congressional rejection of that expenditure. The decision and its stated basis raised serious precedential issues given the explicit and exclusive constitutional authority of the Congress to determine public taxation and spending.

Before the "zero tolerance" memo purported justification was issued, the ACLU had filed an action in federal district court in San Diego against U.S. Immigration and Customs Enforcement (ICE) and other federal border agencies. The ACLU filed its Amended Complaint for Injunctive and Declaratory Relief in *Ms. L. and Ms. C. v. ICE* on March 9, 2018, seeking injunctive relief, an end to child removals and abductions, and the return of children already removed to their parents and families.[43] Proceedings revealed that over 2,000 children had been so separated during 2018 and later proceedings revealed another 1,000 previously undisclosed separations had occurred in 2017. The discovery and evidence adduced indicated erratic to non-existent tracking records of the children so removed, inhibiting compliance with Judge Dana Sabraw's subsequent order to effectuate their return.

The Trump Administration cited increasing numbers of Southern border crossings in early 2018, with the February count particularly high at 76,000. However, the increase in 2018 was a relatively temporary blip that did not approach the levels over the previous 20 years, particularly from 2000 to 2008, when annual and monthly levels were three to five times the 2017–19 numbers.[44] The crime contentions raise similar issues of balance and accuracy. If any immigrant not yet a citizen is arrested for a criminal offense, it is likely that they will be among the 170,000 deported persons cited by the President. But only 6% of such deportations concerned a criminal offense, and 1.76% involved violent felonies.[45] The Administration has cited persons incarcerated based on immigration offenses as "criminals" for rhetorical purposes. Texas is the only major state that routinely keeps data on the immigration status of criminal offenders. Its records and other studies suggest that the crime rate among recent immigrants is either lower than that of the longstanding native population, or that the correlation is too tenuous for conclusive judgment.[46] Meanwhile, the George W. Bush Presidential Center has gathered facts concerning immigrants and points out that: (1) Immigrants in 2018 make up 13.5% of the population, consistent with (not higher than) historical levels; and (2) Immigrants from Mexico are declining in percentage and are exceeded substantially by those from Asia.[47]

The argument for the removal of children presented in court includes the following primary argument: Those who enter the United States unlawfully commit a crime and are subject to arrest and incarceration pending the outcome of their respective cases. Such incarceration is inappropriate for children—so they are properly separated from those parents and placed with "sponsors" or otherwise accommodated by the Office of Refugee Relief within the Department of Health and Human Services. The longstanding historical tendency to vilify another human grouping in order to facilitate cohesion within one's own (sometimes referred to as the "wag the dog" approach inspired by the movie of that name) is not surprising. Moreover, there is an underlying issue that is not entirely bereft of merit: The United States has 4.5% of a world population of now over 7.6 billion persons. Entry and citizenship necessarily warrants barriers and restrictions given the laudable economic success that will attract more applicants than would be realistically accepted. On the other hand, we are a nation of immigrants and our statutes and their intent properly guide the executive branch, including those laws creating a "refugee" status entitled to *bona fide* consideration. Indeed, that refugee circumstance involving danger from current residence, is a major source of the American population, as well as a part of its cultural iconography.

Critics of the removal policy contend that it is not necessary to incarcerate persons who are seeking refugee status, nor does its theoretical allowance in the cited statute suggest it as an exclusive remedy given alternatives both allowed and historically employed. Moreover, the "illegality" justification is increasingly applied disingenuously by regarding the failure to follow a bureaucratic procedure to be a violation notwithstanding good faith to apply for refugee status. Immigrant advocates cite the high rate of appearances by refugee candidates for court proceedings, and the long wait of well over a year to schedule the critical hearing to decide that status. They cite the long history of confinement of immigrant parents *with* their children where such confinement is necessary—and where there is no child endangerment involved. And they object to the removal of children without proper records and their common dispersal to "sponsors" who are not screened or visited as is any American child removed from parental custody, and the resulting occurrence of alleged sexual abuse and human trafficking too often attending the removal of such children.[48] The major domestic law and international law arguments against this removal policy include the following written by the Children's Advocacy Institute for filing in the *Ms. L* case should it reach the Ninth Circuit.

LEGAL ARGUMENT AGAINST SEPARATION
Robert C. Fellmeth and Aaron X. Fellmeth

I. Immigrants Present in the United States are "Persons" Subject to Constitutional Protections

The U.S. Supreme Court has long held that the Constitution is not confined to U.S. citizens, but includes those within our national territory. See *Wong Wing v. United States*, 163 U.S.228, 238 (1896). In particular, a recent 9th Circuit holding clearly applied that inclusion to the 5th and 14th Amendment elements here at issue (See *Kwai Fun Wong v. U.S.*, 373 F.3d 952, 971 (9th Cir 2004) citing prior U.S. Supreme Court decisions on point.

II. Familial Association, and the "Right to Parent," are Fundamental Liberty Interests

There is a longstanding Constitutional "right to parent"—considered a fundamental liberty interest (FLI) entitled to "strict scrutiny." *Lassiter v. Department of Social Services*, 452 U.S. 18 (1981). But this seminal Constitutional right extends beyond the parental perspective. In addition, the relationship between parent and child has his or her own Constitutional protection, *Quillon v. Walcott*, 434 U.S. 246, 255 (1978); see also the leading case of *Troxel v. Granville*, 530 U.S. 57, 65 (2000). That relationship includes many aspects: the right to choose the education of the child, to specify where the child may go and with whom he or she may relate. It extends well beyond the right to continued contact and state removal of children from parental custody, control and in many cases—contact. This family integrity right "encompasses the reciprocal rights of both parent and children," *Duchesne v. Sugarman*, 566 F.2d817, 825 (2d Cir., 1977), with the Supreme Court adding more recently that these rights include freedom from "state interference" in their exercise. *Hodgson v. Minnesota*, 497 U.S. 417, 484 (1990).

As noted above, these underlying Constitutional rights apply to the immigrant appellees before this Honorable Court. In the leading case of *Plyler v. Doe*, 457 U.S. 202 (1982), the Court was presented with a Texas policy of refusing public school entry to illegal immigrant children. The Court noted: "Whatever his status under the immigration laws, an alien is surely a "person" in any ordinary sense of that term. Aliens, even aliens whose presence in this country is unlawful, have long been recognized as

"persons" guaranteed due process of law by the Fifth and Fourteenth Amendments. *Shaughnessv v. Mezei*, 345 U.S. 206, 212 (1953); *Wong Wing v. United States*, 163 U.S. 228, 238 (1896); *Yick Wo v. Hopkins*, 118 U.S. 356, 369 (1886). Indeed, we have clearly held that the Fifth Amendment protects aliens whose presence in this country is unlawful from invidious discrimination by the Federal Government. *Mathews v. Diaz*, 426 U.S. 67, 77 (1976)," at 210.[1]

The extent of abridgement here goes beyond any precedent, including *Plyler*. There, the Court focused not on the plight of the parent at all, but on the disadvantage such removal from school would portend for the involved children. The physical seizure of children at the border and their subsequent abduction is rather an extreme abridgement well beyond *Plyler*. Certainly it also involves deprivation of educational opportunity. There is little evidence indicating school classes in the normal course as *Plyler* assured. The separation affects the right to parent and the parent-child relationship. And it impacts the child's right to both opportunity and the continuation of that properly sacrosanct personal relationship between a child and his or her parent.

III. The Primacy of the Parent-Child FLI is Underlined by Recent Congressional Intent

The confluence of Supreme Court precedent and unmistakable Congressional intent exercised directly through statutes underlines the extraordinary due process and evidentiary elements here applicable. The requirements for the removal of parental authority and family integrity includes the following: (a) First, the basis for the abridgement of the right must center on the health and safety of the child and its protection (b) The state must manifest "reasonable efforts" not to remove a child. (c) An actual removal must be subject to an immediate court "detention" and then a "jurisdiction haring," with the burden on the state to justify removal and court jurisdiction for the protection of the child. (d) Parents must be appointed counsel unless it is clear that it could not be a factor in assisting the court's deliberations. (e) The child is appointed an adult *guardian ad litem* (GAL).[2] (f) Then there must be "reasonable efforts" to reunify the child with parents. (f) There are time limits on these proceedings.[3] (g) And the only way parental rights can be terminated is a court finding of "unfitness" by "clear and convincing" evidence.[4]

Underlining the above statutory implementation of this Constitutional right under the laws cited in note 4, is the enactment this year of the Bipartisan 2018 Family First Prevention Services Act.[5] At a time of regrettable partisan paralysis in our Congress, this issue bridged every divide. Congressional intent is clear to NOT remove children from parents unless absolutely necessary and after all other options to facilitate fitness of existing parents have been exhausted. And it has a second and particularly ardent co-equal purpose—to place children who are removed in a family setting and not in institutional placement of any kind—suffering care from strangers who are employees of provider entities. The Act specifies that, for the first time, the major SSA IV-E monies (amounting to $8.3 billion in 2018) be opened up for an additional purpose—to provide services to those even at risk of parental removal. To emphasize, this is not a symbolic gesture, it is an 11 section 40 page measure directing what will likely be hundreds of millions of dollars to inhibit child removal from parents and to prevent those who are removed from any congregate care setting.

Importantly, neither the plaintiffs below nor instant *amici* disagree with some of the Government's contentions, to wit: the nation properly limits immigration and requires refugee or other immigration qualification. In addition, there may be circumstances to justify separation of children from their parents. However, the "strict scrutiny" test which applies—requires a "compelling state interest" and no less restrictive alternatives to accomplish that interest.[6] These requirements may be met in a variety of hypothetical circumstances: *E.g.*, there is *probable cause* to believe that the alleged parent actually has no such status. Or as cited by the appellants, perhaps the parent is going to be removed into an incarceration setting for good cause that cannot accommodate children safely. Certainly many accused and convicted criminals suffer such separation from their children.[7] Under such circumstances (a) there is no reasonable, less restrictive alternative and (b) the factual justification elements have been adjudicated under procedural due process.

The court below notes the factual rationale of "deterring others from coming to the United States."[8] A presumptive policy of removing children for that or any other purpose proffered by the appellants has little clear connection to any compelling state interest,[9] without reaching the second test of no less restrictive alternative nor the underlying procedural due process requirements to ascertain the application of each.[10]

Any citation of compelling state interest with no less restrictive alternative is particularly egregious given the long tradition of not removing children, even when parents are confined during the pendency of their immigration claim. What new "compelling government interest" has appeared to justify a new and profound abrogation of long acknowledged parental rights?

How ironic to argue that the "compelling state interest" is here accomplished (a) without due process to determine whether it even applies, (b) in violation of the FLI of parents vis-à-vis their children, and (c) in a way that harms and traumatizes those children.[11] The U.S. has been a nation that separates children from parents only where it is necessary for the health and safety of those children, with many due process elements given the damage that erroneous removal can portend as outlined above.

IV. The Removal is Applied on a Racial/Ethnic Discriminatory Basis, Warranting Strict Scrutiny

As noted above, newly arrived persons seeking immigration into the United States properly face the potential denial of citizenship and deportation. But where such decisions are based on race or ethnic background most basic "suspect" classification for 14th Amendment application applies.

Note the title of the Exhibit 2 attached hereto, "Zero Tolerance Policy" from the Attorney General on April 6, 2018—to be applied only "Along the Southwest Border." *Amici* respectfully ask this Honorable Court to inquire of appellants the following:

1. The Southwestern border involves predominantly immigrants of Hispanic heritage. Have similar child removal or zero tolerance policies been implemented at any other border area? How many accompanied children coming from the Canadian border have been separated from their parents?

2. If the President repeatedly cites those coming across the Mexican-U.S. border as "rapists and murderers," what does that indicate in terms of racial prejudice and improper animus? Is the citation of a violent gang with Hispanic members properly indicative of the danger of the entire racial grouping?[12] What is the underlying implication of such a categorical denigration of a people based on their national origin or racial make-up.[13]

3. What is the factual basis for a judgment of universal lack of merit and appropriate rejection of any refugee claim based on the ethnicity of an applicant or his or her country of origin?

The incidence and stated purposes of the policies here at issue do not require a sociology study documenting that which is unconcealed. Because ethnic based prejudice is brazenly exposed hardly lessens its evidentiary strength or relevance.

V. The Removal and Related Practices Violate Applicable U.S. Immigration Law

The argument of the appellants involves the assertion of discretionary license, particularly applied to immigration enforcement. The implicit contention of appellants has been that separation of children from parents meets the strict scrutiny standard of a compelling state interest (discouragement of illegal immigration) with allegedly no effective alternatives. But in addition to the constitutional considerations above, and the lack of a defensible "fit" between the momentous impacts of removal and its stated purpose, another problem confronts appellants: The matter of executive branch authority. The Congress enacts the statutes that govern immigration policy. It is the function of the executive branch, as a general rule, to carry out Congressional intent. That is the constitutional lodestar of the executive branch. Certainly carrying out that intent involves discretion as to the "how," but not as much as to the "what."

As the *Plyler v. Doe* decision noted above holds: "The Constitution grants Congress the power to "establish a uniform Rule of Naturalization. Art. I., § 8, cl. 4. Drawing upon this power, upon its plenary authority with respect to foreign relations and international commerce, and upon the inherent power of a sovereign to close its borders, Congress has developed a complex scheme governing admission to our Nation and status within our borders. See *Mathews v. Diaz*, 426 U.S. 67 (1976); *Harisiades v. Shaughnessy*, 342 U.S. 580, 588-589 (1952)."[14]

The entire basis of the "zero tolerance" policy is purported to be 8 USC 1325(a) which does make it a misdemeanor with a fine and up to 6 months for attempting to enter at a location or time contrary to immigration instructions, and for making false statements relevant to qualification. But it does not mention 1325(b)—which then repeats the wrong location entry issue and designates its transgression as possibly warranting a civil penalty of $50 to $250. The Congressional intent to relax location of entry sanctions obviously flows from the realities of refugee entry. These include persons fleeing persecution and even death threats as to themselves and/or their children. They are often bereft of resources and are not tourists flying in from Paris able to flexibly arrange their entry.

In addition, federal law and Congressional intent binding the executive branch provides for an opportunity for refugees to obtain entry and possible citizenship. Congressional intent is clear that the basis or lack thereof for refugee states is to be individually ascertained, and in comportment with due process.[15] The practice of "zero

tolerance" where all persons meeting some category of perhaps unavoidable error are to be arrested criminally charged and incarcerated is problematical even before the pile-on of abduction of involved children. Basic due process is not consonant with an inflexible and categorical sanction without regard to applicable circumstances.

Federal law defines a "refugee" eligible for entry and possible citizenship as follows:

> The term 'refugee' means (A) any person who is outside any country of such person's nationality or, in the case of a person having no nationality, is outside any country in which such person last habitually resided, and who is unable or unwilling to return to, and is unable or unwilling to avail himself or herself of the protection of, that country because of persecution or a well-founded fear of persecution on account of race, religion, nationality, membership in a particular social group, or political opinion, or (B) in such special circumstances as the President after appropriate consultation (as defined in section 1157(e) of this title) may specify, any person who is within the country of such person's nationality or, in the case of a person having no nationality, within the country in which such person is habitually residing, and who is persecuted or who has a well-founded fear of persecution on account of race, religion, nationality, membership in a particular social group, or political opinion. (8 USC 1101).

How does that definition justify an executive branch decision to deny reasonable opportunity to qualify under these terms? The President has explicit authority to ADD to eligibility for persecution in a place of origin. How does that justify the abrogation of the statutory basis for entry? How does enacted law and its Congressional intent justify any kind of blanket and undifferentiated removal? Does it matter that even at designated "ports of entry" ICE has turned away many hundreds of refugee asylum seekers due to administrative inconvenience or other stated reasons?[16]

VI. The Acts at Issue Violate International Human Rights, Including Relevant Ratified Treaties and Customary International Law Subject to U.S. Compliance

A. International Law Is Relevant to Assessing the Legality of Executive Action

Ratified international treaties become a part of U.S. law enforceable in federal court under the Constitution. (Article VI, Cl. 2). Precedents establish that even beyond treaties, "customary international law" may be enforced in U.S. courts even in the absence of implementing legislation.[17] Several human rights treaty rules applicable under the instant facts also mirror customary international law.

B. International Asylum Seeker Rights

The United States has been bound by the terms of the 1951 Convention Relating to the Status of Refugees ("Refugee Convention") for over 50 years and codified the

Convention's provisions in the 1980 Refugee Act.[18] The Refugee Convention specifically forbids the unnecessary or punitive detention of asylum-seekers and the separation and detention of children from their families. Article 31 of the Convention states that nations "shall not impose penalties for illegal entry or presence...provided the applicants present themselves without delay to the authorities and show good cause for their illegal entry or presence." The applicable requirement contradicts the zero tolerance policy based entirely on the location of entry.

The United Nations High Commissioner for Human Rights (UNHCR) is opposed to the immigration detention of children and categorically calls on all states to end this practice.[19]   According to the Guidelines, children "should in principle not be detained at all."[20] The UNHCR has recently reiterated its understanding of state obligations as requiring that children should not be detained for immigration related purposes, irrespective of their legal/migratory status or that of their parents, and detention is never in their best interests. Appropriate care arrangements and community-based programmes need to be in place to ensure adequate reception of children and their families.[21] These provisions also reflect customary international law, [22] which, as noted, is directly binding on the United States and enforceable in our courts. Moreover, under the International Covenant on Civil and Political Rights (ICCPR), which the United States ratified in 1992 and is widely accepted as reflecting customary international law, states may not detain

children or treat them as criminals "solely for reasons of illegal entry or presence in the country."[23] A policy of detaining immigrant or refugee children or separating them from their families violates U.S. obligations under the ICCPR.

C. International Right to Family Preservation

The ICCPR also recognizes and protects a fundamental human right to family life. Article 17 of the ICCPR forbids any arbitrary or unlawful interference with a person's privacy or family and requires states to offer "the protection of the law against such interference." Article 23(1) states: "The family is the natural and fundamental group unit of society and is entitled to protection by society and the State." Article 24(1) provides: "Every child shall have, without any discrimination as to race [or] national or social origin...the right to such measures of protection as are required by his status as a minor, on the part of his family, society and the State." These provisions establish a human right that includes not being forcibly separated from one's family unnecessarily.

D. UN Convention on the Rights of the Child

The United States signed the UN Convention on the Rights of the Child ("CRC") but has not ratified it. However, every other nation on earth has ratified the treaty, which suggests that its provisions have become customary international law. The Convention provides 4 lodestar elements in the treatment of children: nondiscrimination, the best interests of the child, the right to life and development, and respect for the views of the child.[24] Recent separation and current detention practices violate its basic elements, in particular the best interests and nondiscrimination criteria.

[1] Supplementing these cases is the leading case of *Griswold v. Connecticut*, 381 U.S. 479 (1965), holding that the Ninth Amendment addresses "fundamental personal rights," including the right to raise a family, notwithstanding the fact that it is "not specifically mentioned in the Constitution." At 496.

[2] It is common for children to be appointed a Court Appointed Special Advocate (CASA), an adult to facilitate information to the court.

[3] See the Adoption Assistance and Child Welfare Act of 1980 (Pub.L. 96-276) and the Child Abuse Prevention and Treatment Act PL 93-247 as amended by PL 114-22 and 114-198.

[4] See *Santosky v. Kramer*, 455 U.S. 745 (1982). The *Santosky* Court quotes a leading case on point "As *parens patriae*, the State's goal is to provide the child with a permanent home....Yet while there is still reason to believe that positive, nurturing parent-child relationships exist, the parens patriae interest favors preservation, not severance, of natural familial bonds. ...[T]he State registers no gain towards its declared goals when it separates children from the custody of fit parents." *Stanley v. Illinois*, 405 U.S. 645 (1972) at 652. That cited case of Stanley involves is a longstanding holding that the constitutional right to parent included the unmarried fathers of children and even his right could not be abridged absent strict scrutiny justification.

[5] See pages 169-206 pf the 2018 Budget Act, See http://www.ncsl.org/research/human-services/family-first-prevention-services-act-ffpsa.aspx.

[6] See *United States v. Carolene Products Co.*, 304 U.S. 144 (1938).

[7] Although note that even in these extreme circumstances children retain visitation rights to see their parents and are not moved to distant locations without their responsible tracking.

[8] 6-6-18 Order below at 20.

[9] Such a stated "governmental interest" not only lacking "compelling" status, it is affirmatively in violation of the Refugee Act, PL. 96-212, 94 Stat. 102 (1980).

[10] The court below discusses the international law infirmities in the separation policy, 6-6-18 order at 18-20; see also the more detailed discussion in VI. below of the international law offenses subject to court enforcement herein.

[11] See the *amicus* of the American Academy of Pediatrics et al. re child harm.

[12] Although the cited gang is a problem, they are, in fact, not an immigrant population crossing the Southwest border. See also https://www.businessinsider.com/trump-doubles-down-on-calling-ms-13-gang-members-violent-animals-2018-5.

[13] https://www.newsday.com/news/nation/donald-trump-speech-debates-and-campaign-quotes-1.11206532.

[14] 457 U.S. 202 (1982) at 225.

[15] See Article II, Sec 3 of the Constitution re the Executive Branch obligation to "faithfully carry out the law."

[16] *E.g.*, https://www.americanimmigrationcouncil.org/content/us-customs-and-border-protections-systemic-denial-entry-asylum-seekers-ports-entry-us; see also a video showing blockage in real time at https://www.theatlantic.com/video/index/563084/us-border-asylum/.

[17] See *Filartiga v. Pena-Irala*, 630 F.2d 876, 886 (2d Cir. 1980) ("Appellees . . . advance the proposition that the law of nations forms a part of the laws of the United States only to the extent that Congress has acted to define it. This extravagant claim is amply refuted by the numerous decisions applying rules of international law uncodified by any act of Congress."). See also *The Paquete Habana*, 175 U.S. 677 (1900), the U.S. Supreme Court holding that "customary international law" in that case was part of U.S. law to be enforced by our courts.

[18] United States Refugee Act of 1980, Pub. L. 96-212 (Mar. 17, 1980), 94 Stat. 102, codified as amended at 8 U.S.C. ch. 12.

[19] See for instance UNHCR, "UN Refugee Agency calls on States to end the immigration detention of children on the 25th anniversary of the Convention on the Rights of the Child," Nov. 20, 2014, at http://www.unhcr.org/news/press/2014/11/546de88d9/un-refugee-agency-calls-states-end-immigration-detention-children-25th.html.

[20] Guidelines, para. 51.

[21] UNHCR, UNHCR's Position Regarding the Detention of Refugee and Migrant Children in the Migration Context, Jan. 2017, at http://www.refworld.org/docid/5885c2434.html.

[22] See I; Deborah Perluss & Joan F. Hartman, Temporary Refuge: Emergence of a Customary International Norm, 26 VIR. J. INT'L L. 551 (1986).

[23] CRC, GC No. 6, ¶ 63.

[24] See Committee on the Rights of the Children, General Comment No. 14, U.N. Doc. CRC/C/GC/14 (May 29, 2013), at 3 [hereinafter "CRC, GC No. 14"]. See also General Comment No. 5, U.N. Doc. CRC/GC/2003/5 (Nov. 27, 2003), ¶ 12 [hereinafter "CRC, GC No. 5"]

6. Reproductive Rights of Immigrant Children in Federal Custody

In 2017 the D.C. Circuit Court was confronted with a complaint that federal immigration authorities were aggressively preventing an immigrant child in their custody from an abortion she was seeking. In *Garza v. Hargan*, 874 F.3d 735 (D.C.Cir., 2017), the plaintiff filed a class action against the federal Department of Health and Human Services. The federal defense concedes that the victim has the right to an abortion and that the Texas decision to allow it was lawful, and that her status as an unlawful immigrant in custody did not properly inhibit that right. But, as noted in the concurring opinion, the government contended that the child in custody has "the burden of extracting herself from custody" if she wants to exercise that conceded right. The government contends that she must either find her own way out of detention by surrendering her claim of refugee or other legal status to remain in the United States or she must find a foster parent sponsor willing to (a) take custody of her and (b) agreeing not to interfere with her decision. The majority granted the order assuring the plaintiff the right to leave custody for the procedure without having to wait for a foster parent or other adult sponsor—an effort that had already consumed a fruitless seven weeks before the DC Circuit order.

G. INTERNATIONAL DANGERS AND THE FUTURE CHILD RIGHTS

1. International Endangerment from Abusive Labor and Safety Hazards

The growing economic interdependence of the world affects children. Three aspects of the evolving "flat earth" of particular relevance to children are the stimulation of abusive child labor through imports based strictly on cost factors in producing nations, the vulnerability of youth in impoverished nations to sex trafficking exploitation, and the export of dangerous products by nations that may be prohibited or regulated domestically.

a. Trade, Abusive Child Labor—Incidence

The most recent (2017) comprehensive survey[49] of International child labor found the following:

- Worldwide, 218 million children between 5 and 17 years are in employment—152 million are victims of child labour; almost half of them, 73 million, work in hazardous child labour.
- In absolute terms, almost half of child labour (72.1 million) is in Africa; 62.1 million in the Asia and the Pacific; 10.7 million in the Americas; 1.2 million in the Arab States and 5.5 million in Europe and Central Asia.
- In terms of prevalence, 1 in 5 children in Africa (19.6%) are in child labour, whilst prevalence in other regions is between 3% and 7%: 2.9% in the Arab States (1 in 35 children); 4.1% in Europe and Central Asia (1 in 25); 5.3% in the Americas (1 in 19) and 7.4% in Asia and the Pacific region (1 in 14).
- Almost half of all 152 million children victims of child labour are aged 5–11 years.42 million (28%) are 12-14 years old; and 37 million (24%) are 15-17 years old.
- Hazardous child labour is most prevalent among the 15–17 years old. Nevertheless up to a fourth of all hazardous child labour (19 million) is by children less than 12 years old.
- Among 152 million children in child labour, 88 million are boys and 64 million are girls.

- Child labour is concentrated primarily in agriculture (71%), which includes fishing, forestry, livestock herding and aquaculture, and comprises both subsistence and commercial farming; 17% in Services; and 12% in the Industrial sector, including mining.

In addition to this generic problem of hazardous work are the related dangers of children subject to little education, but rather involved in armed conflict, including their forced participation, as well as major problems of drug and sex trafficking (discussed below).[50]

b. Child Labor—International Law

Since 1957, several agreements, conferences or conventions have purportedly addressed child labor abuse:[51]

1957	The Supplemental Convention on the Abolition of Slavery, the Slave Trade, and Institutions and Practice Similar to Slavery
1957	The International Labor Organization Convention 105 Concerning the Abolition of Forced Labor
1975	The Conference on Security and Cooperation in Europe (Helsinki Accords)
1966	The International Covenant on Civil and Political Rights
1978	The American Convention on Human Rights
1989	The U.N. General Assembly Convention on the Rights of the Child
1990	World Summit for Children/World Declaration on the Survival, Protection and Development of Children
1999	ILO Convention No. 182: The Prohibition and Immediate Action for the Elimination of the Worst Forms of Child Labour
2000	Two Optional Protocols to the Convention on the Rights of the Child, pertaining to (a) child pornography and sex trafficking and (b) child victimization in armed conflicts
2002	The U.N. General Assembly Special Session on Children, "A World Fit for Children" Compact
2007	The Convention on the Protection of Children against Sexual Exploitation and Sexual Abuse

The International Labor Organization (ILO) 1999 Convention 182 focused on five forms of abusive child labor: slavery and sex trafficking, bondage/serfdom/compulsory labor, forced recruitment for armed conflict, pornography production, and illicit activity such as drug sales. Nations ratifying the convention are expected to implement national programs within a specified timeframe, which allegedly includes sanctions for non-compliance. However, there is no international regime of enforcement or sanctions—as with most other international remonstrations on child exploitation issues.

The United Nations International Children's Emergency Fund (UNICEF) and the ILO have been working to create conventions to check child labor abuse. However, arrayed against the common beneficent statements of intent in relevant conferences and covenants without enforcing features, is the economic reality of a world generally accepting a naked market approach to international trade. Eschewing tariffs or other national trade barriers, the underlying concept is for maximum production efficiency. Production accomplished by children may well undercut the costs of adult workers receiving traditional benefits and protections. Child labor critics argue that the long-term costs of such methods are not reflected in the operational cost of those employing children—allowing a form of "free ride" for such cost imposition on involved children or imposing other costs.

In theory, child labor may be addressed by a variety of economic remedies: outright prohibition along some set of international standards, refusal to engage in internationally subsidized investment in locales using such production, imposition of substantial fees and penalties for such use (to erase the economic incentive to exploit that source of labor), use of taxation or tariffs, identification or certification of items produced or not produced using child labor, and other measures.

U.S. Customs has had in place for many years a system of coding to signify products believed to be produced from abusive child labor, with yellow flags delineating "suspicion" that a product was produced by means "contravening local laws" pertaining to excessive hours, hazards, or denial of education. A stronger red flag indicates a "probable" offense in production involving "restraints, debt-based servitude, wages paid to third parties, physical abuse or employment of very young children." In theory, products with red flags are prohibited from importation.

Traditionally, importation bars (or alternatively, tariffs) have been the theoretical mechanism to deprive nations using child labor from the cost advantage it may afford. But, as noted, the trend has been in the direction not only of free entry and of tariff dispensation, but of a reversal of the prescription described above.[52] The post-World War II international evolution in world trade led to the General Agreement on Tariffs and Trade (GATT), the North American Free Trade Agreement (NAFTA), other regional no-tariff trade regimes, and the rise of the World Trade Organization (WTO). Developing nations have consistently opposed the imposition of child labor standards, contending that different standards of living require child contribution to the work force, and citing the dispensation the United States and other nations allow for child participation in agricultural harvests and in family restaurants and other businesses. They argue that the alternative for many of their families may be malnutrition and support the relaxed GATT regime, where a nation may bring a "claim" that products being imported enjoy cost-advantages from "unfair" child labor.

Hence, the U.S. Customs "red flags" discussed above may trigger sanctions from the WTO as a "barrier to trade" in violation of Article 11 of GATT. The WTO has become the potent enforcement agency where alleged barriers to trade occur. It increasingly serves as the effective arbiter of any enforceable floor for child labor, and for broader environmental protection. While every nation is free to adopt its own national protections for its children, those standards may not necessarily apply to the practices of other nations who export goods into their respective nations and which may be manufactured by methods violating stated international standards. The 1996 attempt to introduce a "social clause" standard including child labor floors in WTO decisions did not succeed.

The primary job of the WTO is to judge the laws of trading nations for compliance with its standards. The WTO now includes 164 nations, making close to 98% of all international trade. It conducts its business in Geneva, Switzerland without the public notice and public participation structure common to public bodies, and assured by law for such decisions within the United States. No outside appeal is available. Such disputes are determined by three panelists nominated to hear each such dispute. Once the WTO has declared a law that bars an import to be WTO-illegal, the nation must allow the import or face trade sanctions.

Article 20 of GATT, the "General Exceptions Clause," does allow "social value" or "public moral" conditions to take precedence over free trade. Such an exception is guided by what is referred to as the "Chapeau Requirements," which in turn require that the import bar or limitation not be "arbitrary or unjustifiable" or a "disguised restriction on international trade."[53] The WTO has not taken a child-protective stance in its GATT "social value" judgments, requiring a "universal standard," and failing to define an ascertainable floor. Children may work in developing nations for a fraction of an adult wage, and overall indigenous poverty may lead parents into the Hobson's choice of forsaking child education for desperately needed family income.

In over 80% of the cases brought to the WTO challenging domestic environmental, safety, and child labor practices since its creation in 1995, it has ruled those protections to be improper trade barriers, compelling their revocation or diminution.[54] Critics of the WTO contend that it has yet to create a clear body of law on the right of a nation to refuse goods based on child labor—or other child-related practices of the exporting nation. That failure is not the result of its recognition that such import exclusions are in compliance with their standards, but largely reflect the rarity of importation restrictions by the receiving nation based on such abuses in the nation of origin. Moreover, the focus of WTO policies and regional trade agreements on lowering barriers between nations elevates cost reduction as a determining market force—one that may make a child labor floor difficult to sustain.

Some attempts have been made within the United States to mandate national rejection of imports associated with abusive child labor production. The United States has attempted one possibly precedential mechanism in a U.S./Jordan treaty in 2000.[55] This bi-lateral trade agreement provided for child labor standards as a prerequisite to free trade relations under its terms, and included a mechanism for sanctions where violations occur. More recently, President Obama signed into law the Trade Facilitation and Trade Enforcement Act of 2015, effective in 2016, which can potentially create a sea change. Customs and Border Protection (CBP) has created a Forced Labor Enforcement Fact Sheet explaining that "merchandise mined, produced or manufactured, wholly or in part, in any foreign country by forced labor—including forced child labor…is subject to exclusion and/or seizure, and may lead to criminal investigation of the importer(s)."[56] Then in late 2016, the CBP issued three Withhold Release Orders (WROs) covering soda ash-calcium chloride caustic soda, potassium hydroxide, and nitrate and stevia related products—from China—based on failure to comply with this measure. However, enforcement is impeded by a lack of information and effective prosecutors to detect source violations for the millions of products imported; there is no indication that the Trump Administration gives priority to the enforcement of this statute.[57]

Given the issue of enforcement efficacy, another option that child advocates might consider is the use of a public or even a private certification system—where a respected group of independent examiners rates products on a scale according to how "child friendly" they are in their production and safe use.

c. International Child Sex Trafficking

Several forms of international child abuse involve problems beyond the exploitation of children as cheap labor for advantageous international trade. Those issues involve the movement of children across national borders for purposes of labor enslavement, for the movement of illicit drugs, and particularly for sexual exploitation. The last involves surprisingly large numbers of victims who are subject to degradation and serious sexually connected health risk and illness.

Actual prostitution and the movement of children to serve as sex slaves from underdeveloped nations to client developed nations have become common. It is driven largely by desperate economic circumstances in source nations, and a ready market of mostly men in wealthier nations who will pay to have sex with children. Some of the trade, particularly in places such as Southeast Asia, involves indigenous youth exploited by sex "tourists" from Europe and America. But it also includes the importation of youth into the exploiting nations where they are isolated and particularly helpless. Although this international trade has primarily victimized girls, it also includes boys. According to the United Nations Office on Drugs and Crime, the most common receiving/offending nations are Thailand, Japan, Israel, Belgium, the Netherlands, Germany, Italy, and Turkey, and the most common source nations are Thailand, China, Nigeria, Albania, Bulgaria, Belarus, Moldova, and Ukraine. The U.S. is also a major destination for sexual exploitation of minors (SEM) activity from Southeast Asia (*e.g.*, the Philippines, Taiwan), Mexico, and Central America.[58]

Some of the international covenants and conventions listed above and discussed below condemn such practices. A declaration of the World Congress against Commercial Sexual Exploitation of Children (CSEC), held in Stockholm in 1996, defined CSEC as: "sexual abuse by the adult and remuneration in cash or kind to the child or a third person or persons. The child is treated as a sexual object and as a commercial object." CSEC includes the prostitution of children, child pornography, child sex tourism, and other forms of transactional sex (survival sex) where a child engages in sexual activities to have key needs fulfilled, such as food, shelter, or access to education. Consistent with other efforts, the new Council of Europe has adopted "The Convention on the Protection of Children against Sexual Exploitation and Sexual Abuse" in 2007.[59]

One source of potential international intervention beyond remonstration may rest with international criminal prosecution of those engaging in and profiting from the movement of children across international borders for such purposes. One of the few precedents of international prosecution has been the International

Criminal Tribunal for the Former Yugoslavia. Those proceedings have acquired personal jurisdiction over some of the alleged perpetrators of the mass murders of large numbers of civilians based on their nationality or ethnic background during the Balkan hostilities of the early 1990s. This conflict was ended partly from U.N. intervention, and the subsequent prosecutions have included allegations of rape by soldiers under purported military control, of women and young girls. However, more widespread crimes against children, including the forced conscription of children in Africa, and the widespread practice of sex trafficking except for limited cases involving systemic rapes by soldiers, have not been the subject of international criminal prosecution.

It is possible that a broader range of future criminal proceedings against individuals could emanate from the International Criminal Court (ICC) created by the Rome Statute and in effect since 2002 (see ICC discussion above). In theory, crimes committed after that date may be subject to ICC prosecution—with penalties including imprisonment for up to 30 years. Enumerated crimes include Article VII(2) (c), condemning "sexual slavery," defined as the exercise of "rights of ownership" over a person and including "trafficking in persons, in particular women and children."[60]

The abatement of sex trafficking continues to depend upon international moralistic appeals for national enforcement—with no criminal prosecution and little trade or other sanction effectively applied through international offices to date.[61] Private international and national organizations have been active in bringing public attention to the issue.[62]

National laws in the United States have allowed some solicitude for immigrant child victims of exploitation, including possible eligibility for "Special Immigrant Juvenile Status" (referral to juvenile dependency court and possible citizenship). The Violence Against Women Act also allows for citizenship application where battering or abuse is committed by a U.S. citizen or permanent resident,[63] and "U Visas" may be available under the Trafficking Victims Protection Act[64] enacted by Congress in 2000. These allow victims who have suffered abuse, or who are helpful in the prosecution of traffickers, to remain in the U.S. for up to four years, and may be awarded permanent legal residence status after three years of U-Visa status.[65]

In terms of prevention and early detection, advocates have suggested compiling and providing lists of those convicted of prior sex offenses, particularly against children. Such notice of prior offender location and movement could deter some and allow for easier enforcement where violations occur. Domestically, U.S. law has increasingly provided for lists of sexual predators, including those engaging in underage solicitation, transportation, and pimping. In 1994, Congress enacted "The Wetterling Act" to provide guidelines for the tracking of sex offenders and mandated the confirmation of residence annually for ten years after their prison release—or quarterly if the offense were violent. It was treated as private data. But States have commonly created "Megan's Law" provisions and related statutes to provide public lists and information, including residence addresses, and now some controversial statutes inhibit those on the list from living within certain distances of schools, playgrounds, and other places where children congregate. In 2006, Congress enacted the Sex Offender Registration and Notification Act (SORNA) as Title I of the "Adam Walsh Act." It now specifies a three-tier system of national registration (including state, federal, and military sex-related convictions) and imposes criminal penalties for registration failure. Lengths of inclusion range from fifteen years to life for the third-tier more serious offenses. And the statute created the Sex Offender Sentencing, Monitoring, Apprehending, Registering, and Tracking (a "SMART" Office) within the Department of Justice. Efforts to challenge the constitutionality of SORNA have failed.

In contrast, the European Union's policies have reflected more deference to the privacy rights of former offenders. Its lists of sex offenders are available only to professionals and law enforcement. And attempts to unify EU sex offender laws have also not entirely succeeded. There is substantial cooperation between European (and other) nations and the United States on terrorist no-fly and other related suspect lists since 2001 and particularly since 2007, and in efforts through the FBI, Interpol, and other coordinating law enforcement agencies to apprehend wanted criminals. But post-conviction lists and post-release monitoring of sex offenders does not have an international counterpart to the U.S. system. And beyond Europe and the U.S., there is little coordination.

Child advocates argue that child-related sex offenses are subject to extremely high recidivism. And they contend that sex traffickers who know how to recruit and solicit enjoy substantial profit and do not always cease such practices upon release. Advocates cite five trends that commend international disclosure and interconnection: (a) the economic disparities and large families in undeveloped nations continues, (b) increased mobility makes it easier to move older children to developed "market" nations; (c) the increasing sexual "license" in America ("what happens in Vegas, stays in Vegas") and in much of Europe, (d) the rise of a popular culture that increases sexual demand and the sophistication of young girls from advertising, programming, and music that glorifies allure and well tolerates promiscuity; and (e) the rise of the internet as an advertising and "hook up" vehicle between buyers and sellers.

In 2015, Congress enacted HR 515 (Smith), which took effect in 2016. It was labelled the "International Megan's Law to Prevent Child Exploitation and Other Sexual Crimes Through Advanced Notification of Traveling Sex Offenders." It directs the Department of Homeland Security (DHS) to establish the Angel Watch Center within U.S. Immigration and Customs Enforcement. The law includes strict disclosure and notice requirements for international travel by any person subject to the Sex Offender Registration and Notification Act. That sex offender registry is also to include information on intended or actual international travel of any registrant. Failure to provide such information is a separate criminal offense, with a penalty of up to ten years in prison. The law also amends the William Wilberforce Trafficking Victims Reauthorization Act of 2008 to prohibit the issuance of a passport to any sex offender unless it includes a unique and visible identifier of registration status. And it cancels any law that limits international information or law enforcement cooperation.

The new Angel Watch Center must identify outbound sex offender travelers who failed to provide advance notice of international travel and provide their names to the U.S. Marshals Service to investigate. It expresses Congressional intent that the Department of State should negotiate reciprocal international agreements to facilitate its purposes.

d. Export and Import of Child-Dangerous Products

Related to the "lowest common denominator" problem of free trade and child labor as a trade advantage, or as a commodity, is the export of dangerous products that may injure children. Such products may be imported by the destination nation without safeguards, even where they might offend the domestic standards of the exporting nation. For example, the major American tobacco company Philip Morris has created an international corporation separate and apart from its U.S. counterpart (Philip Morris USA). All of its international operations involving production and sales to foreign nations are now entirely through the offices of its corporate operations outside of the U.S. Accordingly, the corporate "separate person" engaged in the production, advertising, and sales of tobacco will be free of any restriction that may be applicable in the United States. The abuses of deceptive advertising, denial of addiction effect, and purposeful marketing to children may occur throughout the world, subject only to restrictions that may be imposed by the receiving nations— assuming they are not challenged as an unfair trade barrier by the WTO. Tobacco is of particular concern to child advocates internationally, because historically the industry has depended upon advertising and promotion to youth, with the median age of addiction under 16 years of age.

The World Health Organization (WHO) reports that although smoking rates (and associated cancer, heart disease, and other consequences) are in decline in the United States, they are rising substantially throughout the developing world, and tobacco-related deaths are projected to increase to eight million per year by 2030, with 80% occurring in the developing world.[66] The vast majority of new addicts will be hooked via marketing designed to appeal to youth peer pressure. The projections led the WHO to propose the Framework Convention on Tobacco Control, which entered into force in 2005. The Convention is unusual in its explicit recognition not of the need for controls on state action, but for affirmative steps by nation-states against tobacco corporate marketing practices, including the contents of tobacco products, their disclosure, packaging and labeling, and restricting or banning tobacco advertising, promotion, and sponsorships. However, as with the other conventions discussed above, there is no international mechanism for enforcement, merely a delegation to nation-state signatories to enforce aspirational standards. Multinational corporation separation from prohibiting nations is not unlike the "Delaware" effect in the United States, allowing corporations to compete among states for the *situs* offering the least restrictive standards, possibly creating a competition to the "lowest common denominator" in public protection.

Beyond dangerous products exported from the U.S. to other nations is the counterpart concern of dangerous products from other nations imported into the United States. As discussed above, matters of contamination (*e.g.*, lead paint on child toys, mad cow disease danger in imported meat, egg and poultry difficulties, botulism, bacteria, and other hazards) may be presented into any nation from any exporting nation. The dangers here are accentuated by the degree of growing international mass marketing, and where there is a symptom delay that may allow a dangerous contaminant or epidemic to reach millions before the source is identified and addressed. Where applicable, each nation has its own system of vaccination that may moderate the severity of some outbreaks. During 2011, the United States enhanced FDA authority over tobacco, and buttressed its own food safety regulatory laws, reflecting increasing concern over the vulnerability of American markets—particularly where harm to children is threatened. Interest in the issue of child addiction led to the seminal *Castano* tobacco litigation and then to a Master Settlement Agreement requiring payment of $2 billion from 1998 to 2023, designed to prevent child tobacco addiction and ameliorate harm. However, most of these funds have been absorbed by state general funds.

Other mainstream lawful but dangerous products are subject to active international marketing to youth. As noted above, the U.S. has limited tobacco promotion domestically, but alcohol promotion is strongly on the upswing by Madison Avenue mainstream advertisers. An unwritten rule declining all mass advertising that might be accessible to youth, in effect for over fifty years, has ended over the last decade, as discussed below. Virtually every major hard liquor industry, joined in by wines and beers, have become dominant advertisers and product placers—with a strong and obvious appeal to youth. As the communications and commercially dominant nation on earth, that pattern will be reflected in international promotion. Similarly, the international mass marketing of U.S. fast food to children, including toys and prizes, contributes to record levels of child obesity, and to unbalanced ingestion of fat, sugar, and salt. No fees are assessed to adjust these markets to compensate for the external costs that will attend their ingestion over a lifetime. No international treaty addresses these child health issues, and as discussed above, an attempt to draw a line on the international origin of an unhealthy food or drink is more likely to yield a trade sanction as an "unjustified trade barrier" inhibiting any such limitation.[67]

International child health and safety child concerns arise from the marketing of illicit drugs: Marijuana, hashish, cocaine, PCP, heroin, and methamphetamine marketing targets youth. Drugs are commonly produced in nations other than where they are sold and ingested. These allegedly "controlled" substances are unlawful— it is often a crime in the nation of production and in the nation of importation to possess, possess for sale, transport, or use them. They are contraband subject to no lawful status under international commercial law. The contraband may be seized—and in the U.S., so may the assets used to make or carry the unlawful drugs. Participants are subject to criminal arrest.

The sociology of international illicit drug marketing involves the use of youth in two major capacities—for carriage/marketing, and for promotion as early and then repeated users. The use of children under eighteen as "mules" to transport large quantities of illegal drugs is a deliberate strategy to take advantage of the naiveté of the young, of their interest in the drug, their attraction of adult-defying adventure, and the fact that they are eligible for juvenile criminal status, involving confidential processes, lesser punishment, and greater sympathy. Indeed, use of youth in drug operations has reached levels in some drug producing nations where youth from twelve to eighteen are recruited as "hit men" for the syndicate. During late 2010, arrests were made of a fifteen-year-old hit man in Peru, who allegedly killed ten persons. One month later Mexican police arrested a twelve-year-old alleged hit man in Mexico ("El Ponchis"). Beyond its retail marketing, children are much involved internationally in its growing, harvest, production, and transport, from all of the major source nations: Bolivia, Peru, Mexico, Thailand, and Afghanistan, among others.

In American cities, the implications of illicit drug marketing for children is perhaps more stark. Much of the economy of impoverished areas—particularly where young minorities have dropped out of high school—focuses around drug manufacture, sale, and use. The incidence of arrest for drug sales and possession in these neighborhoods is high. Those sales and that world are directly tied to a violent gun-using culture. The often comic-book popular depiction of the American "peacock strutting" macho "make my day" male, occurs in the context of drug transactions, where the accepted means of line drawing is firearms use. The number of minority youth incarcerated as a result of this culture—built around unlawful acquisition, sales, protection and armed enforcement, is extraordinary. The consequences of their lack of alternative opportunity, drug use impact, and the prostitution/incarceration that results, exacts a high price on them and on the larger society seeking to enforce drug laws. It transforms hundreds of thousands of possibly contributing, tax-paying citizens into years of incarceration at a public per capita cost of $40,000 to $80,000 per year.[68]

Such incarceration rates are disturbingly high in impoverished and minority-dominated neighborhoods, and have been for many years. A 2000 report stated: "Our research shows that blacks comprise 62.7 percent and whites 36.7 percent of all drug offenders admitted to state prison, even though federal surveys and other data detailed in this report show clearly that this racial disparity bears scant relation to racial differences in drug offending. There are, for example, five times more white drug users than black. Relative to population, black men are admitted to state prison on drug charges at a rate that is 13.4 times greater than that of white men. In large part because of the extraordinary racial disparities in incarceration for drug offenses, blacks are incarcerated for all offenses at 8.2 times the rate of whites. One in every twenty black men over the age of eighteen in the U.S. is in state or federal prison, compared to one in 180 white men."[69]

Beyond illicit production and marketing, arrests, and economic consequences, is the problem of ingestion. Achieving addiction of youth has devastating physical health consequences for those who are involved. And the successful addiction of a parent, particularly to methamphetamine, carries with it implications more dangerous to children than arguably any other controlled substance. Even where youth avoid meth ingestion themselves, it has devastating consequences to those who care for children and become dependent on it. It is perhaps the most addictive drug available on the market. Importantly, it undermines basic maternal and paternal instinct. It does not place its users into a passive trance, but energizes them to commit often unspeakable acts upon children, and certainly to engage in common, severe neglect. A significant number of children removed from parents in San Diego County over the last twenty years for adult offenses other than molestation, have had parental involvement with methamphetamine, and more recently opioids. Incidence in other counties, especially in the Western United States, is not dissimilar. Virtually all major illicit drugs enjoy substantial production in foreign locales and pass through international barriers that are theoretically subject to drug interdiction policies.

Questions for Discussion

1. The United States has acceded to the jurisdiction of the WTO, an international body representing corporate and trade interests, as discussed above. This submission allows the WTO's commercial tribunals to perhaps override (or sanction) the democratically determined standards enacted by receiving nations to protect children where these are in conflict with "trade standards." As discussed below, is such a position consistent with insistence on sovereign prerogative where allegedly threatened by international supersession? Is accession to a WTO trade sanction (or abandonment of a national standard duly adopted in good faith for child protection) in conflict with Justice Scalia's position that the policies of foreign bodies outside of U.S. democratic domain should categorically not override U.S. sovereign laws?

2. Can exporting nations dismiss objections to their internal child labor standards as arrogant interference by developed nations who do not understand the harsh realities confronted by poorer nations? On the other hand, if those nations have ratified or are otherwise subject to ILO standards limiting such abusive child labor, can they then be held to those standards by receiving nations? If the WTO chooses not to enforce an ILO or U.N. Convention on the Rights of the Child, or other international standards, and chooses to impose sanctions on nations refusing goods for such alleged violations, what remedies are available to child advocates to contest that WTO judgment? What other check exists on WTO practical determination of standards that may violate or undermine child-related international conventions?

2. Public Debts/Deferred Obligations and Borrowing from Our Children

The world-wide economic collapse of 2007–10 underscores the increasing interdependence of nations—manifested in European common currency, the lowering of tariffs and the rise of free trade, and the emergence of multi-national large corporations. The U.S. bait-and-switch, sub-prime mortgage crisis,[70] aided by highly leveraged "derivatives" gambling, and by financial market concentration, had a world-wide impact.[71] The 2008–10 international financial crisis was stimulated by credit-default swaps and other "derivative" instruments with similar highly leveraged bets arranged in unregulated markets permitted by post-1981 U.S. deregulation. Critics contend that these markets have little justification in terms of economic efficiency and productivity, but serve as a source of high stakes gambling, with substantial percentage returns achievable with relatively small movement in the value of assets that are the subject of the bet. According to the Bank for International Settlements (BIS) in Basel, Switzerland—the central bankers' bank—the amount of outstanding derivatives worldwide as of December 2007 crossed $1.144 quadrillion in U.S. dollars ($1,144 trillion). This amount is more than the national budgets of every nation in the world combined. The total approximates $190,000 for every person on earth.[72] While the world economic disaster was averted, there were serious costs to homeowners and public budgets.

Critics of the real estate-based securities bubble contend that much of it has occurred in a "heads I win, tails you lose" scenario. A gambling win enriches, but a loss or a bubble collapse, might yield publicly provided insurance or state-provided coverage. The consequence of the derivatives and related bubble collapse that occurred in 2007–09 did produce large public payments to major financial institutions in the United States and Europe. It was joined by world-wide stimulative public spending to mitigate collapsing markets and an unemployment cycle that could accelerate the collapse into what some feared could have been a worldwide depression. One consequence of the public funding of failed financial firms, joined with (a) prior public deficit spending and (b) substantial unfunded liability for future retiree medical and pension benefits, has been increasing national debts/unfunded liability in many nations. Long-term projections remain dire. The fragility of nations such as Greece, Spain, and Portugal threatens the Euro—the common currency of much of the European continent. The decline of the Euro then reduces U.S. exports to Europe and adds to unemployment and recession in America. Currencies and trade make the developed and developing world increasingly interconnected. That interconnection includes the rise of India and China as major producing and consuming nations, and the role of the People's Republic of China as the largest single holder of U.S. national debt.

Debt levels have a central child interest dimension. Public employee and welfare spending in some European nations make up a large share of their present deficits, and of promised future obligations for taxpayers in later decades. A collapse from credit fragility, or debt excess and failure in one nation may affect the children in others. More directly, current and future deficits in each nation incurring them are paid by future taxpayers of those respective countries.

This problem of national debts does not just come from an economic downturn and necessary stimulative spending yielding resulting national budget deficits. Indeed, those deficits pale in comparison to largely undiscussed obligations separate and apart from immediate federal budget deficits. These larger obligations outside of the present budget have started to accrue well prior to the American-stimulated collapse of 2007–2009. Most unfunded liability imposed by current adults internationally on their children and grandchildren will come from (a) publicly-funded pensions and (b) extensive medical coverage and care for elderly adults. The United States example is particularly stark: Five percent of America's children, or 3.7 million, lacked any health coverage whatever in 2017, while all senior citizens are covered by a Medicare system at seven times the per capita cost of child coverage. The total unfunded liability projected over the next generation exceeds $35 trillion in current dollar shortfall. Several trends may increase such amounts: (a) the beneficially increasing longevity of the population which does add substantially to the time span of coverage; (b) the disproportionate expense of medical care for seniors; (c) advances in expensive procedures for the elderly, from now common joint replacements to organ transplants; and (d) the political power of the elderly as campaign contributors, organized voters and otherwise to increase coverage and publicly-financed procedures and benefits (see discussion in Chapter 1 above). Indeed, any limitation on medical spending for the elderly is considered politically incorrect by both political parties and yields sloganeering about public "death panels" for grandma in the nation's political milieu.

Public pensions form another unfunded liability throughout developed nations. Such pensions do not take the form of the child-friendly "defined contribution" format, where benefits to be paid are based on monies contributed by pensioners and employers into a fund. Rather, the common trend has been to interpose "defined benefit" pensions, where the amounts to be paid out are set, usually at levels substantially above amounts collected for (or from) those benefitting during their employment. In the U.S., Social Security unpaid projected liability is now at approximately $15 trillion, and the political power of American Association of Retired Persons and the elderly as a group inhibit adjustment of benefits—which increase with wage changes and generally outstrip the CPI (see discussion of comparative lobbying resources in Chapter 1). A Pew Center on the States study published in 2010 found the unfunded liability for state employee-promised pension and medical coverage already exceeded $1 trillion nationally. Added to that is a likely greater amount for local government employees, school teachers, utility workers, and others with benefits separate from state employees and from the generic Social Security and Medicare systems. Added to the above is potentially more substantial federal government liability for private pensions that fail.

The total liability within the next thirty years for Medicare, Social Security, and public pension/medical obligations, and to be imposed upon current children during their adult years, will conservatively exceed $52 trillion under current policies,[73] with a growing federal budget deficit adding to the total and reasonably projected into the $65 trillion range. The carrying charge on this burden at 4.5% will exceed $25,000 per American family per annum in current dollars before taxes. It appears likely to approach 50% of median gross family income. These numbers seem outlandish, but it is unclear how they are in error. Although some citizen groups have gathered to protest "government spending"—they focus on the federal budget deficit—an expenditure bringing some recession countering benefits and that may be diminished with recovery. But that total is less than 25% of the unfunded liability subject to an iron-clad promise, one that is more likely to grow than to enjoy reduction. The major progenitors of future liability are generally undiscussed in American politics, and will likely remain so until the progress payments and immediate obligations grow to untenable levels.

The national government power to print money and the temptation to defer costs down the line is not confined to the U.S. Much of Europe presents similarly deferred obligations, particularly from even more generously socialized pensions, medical coverage, and public employee benefits. Adding to these unfunded future liabilities are currently accruing national budget deficits. The IMF reported in 2010 that the gross national budget deficit as a percentage of the gross domestic product of developed nations have reached record levels across the international landscape. All are expected to increase markedly to 2020. Some child advocates and fiscal conservatives argue that the children of developed nations face an unprecedented burden of obligation imposed by and benefitting the current generation of adults.

Exacerbating the impact of future child burden is the population demographic throughout developed nations—the alteration of the traditional pyramid of population growth, where the population included three to five children and young adults for each elderly person receiving pension, medical, and other public subsidy. But the pyramid has grown narrower. It may appear increasingly more as the Washington monument than the broad-based Egyptian icons. There are fewer young at the base, and proportionally more elderly at the top. This structure provides substantially fewer persons in the next generation for the per capita support of the near-term elderly.

Accordingly, "defined benefit" systems have been interposed through most nations—particularly those influenced by public employee unions. The strong advocacy of such groups has been the rejection of "defined contribution" plans (common in the private sector)—where benefits come from monies forthcoming from the employees so benefitting, with a contribution from the taxpayer or employer as the same point in time.

Questions for Discussion

1. Traditionally, nations invest in the young and sacrifice for the future of their grandchildren. Some child advocates and independent commentators, such as former U.S. Comptroller David Walker, contend that the accumulating transfer of wealth from the young to the old through national deficits and unfunded medical coverage and pension liability is unprecedented in its extent, and is a major ethical issue. If those critics are factually correct about the current degree of public budget deficits and of medical and pension unfunded liability for the elderly, is there a precedent historically for such a generational reversal of obligation on the scale they contend is occurring? If the danger is accurate and predictable, why is its discussion not a major part of American political discourse?

2. What are the available tactics for child advocates to reduce what may be onerous burdens on the young and new generations for the benefit of the elderly, given the disproportionate political and organizational power of older citizens discussed in Chapter 1, and of public employee unions internationally?

3. International Free Competition, Markets, and Patents

As the world becomes more dominated by large international corporations, several trends are of concern to child advocates. The European Commission has prosecuted a number of alleged antitrust violations, but many offenses occur beyond the reach of its limited jurisdiction. The process of diminishing barriers in international trade, combined with outsourcing and mergers increasing economic concentration, is creating a group of powerful international corporations. As noted above, the failure of several major U.S. financial firms in 2007–09 reverberated across the world, causing international contraction, and leading to massive public bailouts. This process has multiple concerns for child advocates: (a) the debt incurred for future generations from such bail outs and by the stimulation of the economy from deficit financing throughout the world to ameliorate economic collapse; (b) the loss of influence by consumers "from the bottom of markets" and increased corporate top-down dictation that occurs where markets are not effectively competitive; and (c) the domination of public policy based on prior investment, discussed below and in Chapter 1.

Although the lowering of international trade barriers has increased world-wide competition and lowered the prices of many commodities and products, the trend since 1995 has been increasing mergers and concentration of international markets by multi-national corporations. Many of these combinations are not reflective of economy of scale justification and have implications for the viability of future markets. What economists call economic "concentration" (*e.g.*, the percentage of market share controlled by a small number of competitors) has grown with multinational corporation mergers. That concentration may lessen the "bottom up" influence of consumers. Where economic concentration is high, or antitrust violations exist, free market dynamics allowing consumer markets to determine product choice, and to stimulate producer efficiency, may suffer.

Beyond market concentration is the larger question of cartels among multinational corporations, often with associated involvement of nation-states. The precedent of the Organization of Petroleum Exporting Nations (OPEC) is an inducement to national involvement in supply control and price fixing. These arrangements would be a criminal felony offense were the participants private actors within the United States and would be subject to sanction in Europe if the actors were private. Antitrust advocates are concerned that such governmental combinations may well be expected for other commodity producers in the future. It is clearly to the advantage of producers (whether private or state involved) to control output and achieve substantially higher prices than the free market would yield. The price of oil and the channeling of substantial wealth to cartel participants indicate the efficacy of such arrangements—and to the inability of those who need such controlled resources to arrange for market competition. Children born in consuming nations are likely to suffer substantial wealth transfers to those in nations conspiring to jointly control output and prices.

Market diminution is not confined to organizations of nation-states. Multinational corporations have a similar motivation to dominate their respective markets. Even private interests may avoid market discipline without state sanction or participation. Antitrust and competition advocates contend that the growth of multinational corporations, oligopoly structures, and trade association participation by industry groupings, has grown beyond the control of current international oversight or national/multinational antitrust enforcement.

A final potential impediment to competition enjoyment for future generations involves intellectual property rights. The WTO and national policies led by the United States urge international respect for intellectual property. While trademark and trade name protection to assure consumer knowledge about who made what yields little objection from international scholars, there are concerns about the extension of such rights to include ancillary features of color and sound, and to limit even the mention of famous persons without their permission or commercial compensation ("reputation rights"). For example, note the 2009 case where a phone company mentioned (not in a sales context) that its disaster preparedness work included the construction of back-up facilities labeled "Mach One" and "Mach Two." It made reference by analogy to the historical accomplishment of "Chuck Yeager" in "breaking the sound barrier." The court upheld the right of Yeager to block the mention of his name—a limitation that will apparently last notwithstanding the publicly-funded nature of his feat, and for his lifetime and for his heirs for 70 years thereafter.[74]

Copyright protection implicates use of literature, music, computer software, and other creative work—not merely for profit reward for the artist, but of limited or barred uncompensated use, not merely for the exclusive marketing of a product over three to five years, but for more than a generation. In 1998, a statute in the United States added *another* twenty years to its protection.[75]

Patents, even more than trade names and copyrights, portend serious anticompetitive consequences for future generations. The idea behind patent protection is the encouragement of human invention. Society has sound reasons to provide incentives for investment in what patent law calls "advances over prior art." Hence, to assure that a novel and beneficial idea receives a reward, nations grant a legal monopoly for twenty years in the form of a "patent" allowing the holder to control production of its "advance" with some limitations. But two problems portend difficulties for future generations.

First is the connection between the goals of the patent system and its actual operation—the contrast between stimulating new invention and granting a lengthy legal monopoly with high transaction costs.[76] Patent applications totaled two million worldwide in 2008. Many applications are now filed in multiple countries for international enforcement, and backlogs have grown. The United States share of patent applications, once in the majority internationally, have now fallen, as Japan, Korea, and particularly China have increased numbers markedly. In 2016, for the first time, more than three million patent applications were filed worldwide. In 2016, the 1.3 million Chinese applications exceeded the total from the U.S., Japan, Korea, and Europe combined.[77]

United States applications come primarily from industry, with individual inventors or universities accounting for under 10%. Qualcomm, 3M, Intel, Motorola, Hewlett Packard, DuPont, Eastman Kodak, Procter and Gamble, and other Fortune 500 companies dominate. How many of these purported "advances over prior art" would have occurred without the proffered incentive? Critics of the patent system argue (a) its grant of a twenty-year monopoly bears little connection to the actual benefit conferred; (b) the system now favors large corporations able to afford specialized legal counsel; and (c) patent applications are less "new discoveries" and more attempts to foreclose competition by capturing marginally advantageous products or methods, or through infringement threats requiring high legal costs to contest.

Second, critics are concerned about the anticompetitive use of patents unrelated to invention stimulation purpose. One example cited is the automobile industry's notorious development or purchase of electric vehicle-related patents to protect sunk investment in the internal combustion engine. Others cite the development of seed patents to legitimately produce higher harvests with anti-disease features, but which include prohibitions on the seed purchasers' generation of seeds from their own crops, essentially creating a condition of continuous dependence on patented seeds from the corporate provider year after year. Other patent applicants have overreached by claiming monopoly rights to stem cell properties and DNA attributes.

Of particular concern to child advocates is the use of patents by pharmaceutical companies internationally in the dispensation of drugs for children, particularly newer discoveries that may be critical for childhood cancers, or serious nervous system illness, *et al.* The prices of pharmaceuticals internationally tend to be set based on the ability to pay—with prices highest in the United States.

Questions for Discussion

1. Are major U.S. and international financial institutions such as major banks and securities houses "natural monopolies" (*e.g.*, have a high initial fixed cost structure such as railroads or power line distribution requiring a single monopoly provider for efficient operation)? If such financial institutions are not large in size due to natural economies of scale, and such size creates market dysfunction and required public bailouts (*e.g.*, "too big to fail"), historical alternatives have been either regulatory controls or trust busting. The last involves breaking corporations into a greater number of competitors to preserve the market and allow for failure. Are either or both of these alternatives being pursued in the U.S. or internationally? If they were to be effectuated, who would compel such "antitrust" break-ups and how would it be accomplished?

2. How many patents, conferring a twenty-year monopoly, are truly "advances" that would not have occurred within months of the filed application? How many would not have been discovered during the twenty-year term of the patent? On the other hand, how many would not have attracted financing for their discovery but for the patent prospect? Are there alternative incentive options that would attract capital to R & D but confer incentive producing rewards more connected to the public benefit of the discovery?

3. Although drug companies cite the incentive produced by a prospective patent grant as necessary to attract financial investment, is it relevant that the same companies now spend more on advertising and marketing—including prescription

drugs previously banned from advertising promotion—than they do on research and development?

4. The Future of Media: Concentration and Reader/Listener Rights

Two aspects of this proliferation concern those projecting into the future: (a) the problem of a small number of entities able to occupy "chokepoints" in the seemingly diverse communications world so that effective access may be controlled by a few; and (b) the downside to facile communications—mass deception by persons able to flood those channels at little cost, and to hide their identity and interest.

a. Chokepoint Concentration of Mass Communications

On the private side, communications competition has opened up numerous avenues for more entertainment choices and easier and more varied expression. We have multiple fora with inexpensive access: traditional newspapers, magazines, telephone land lines, and radio stations have now been supplemented by international cell phone systems coordinated by land and satellite networks. Cable television allows a high speed entertainment and communications avenue. Satellite television transmission and the internet have all combined to allow unprecedented choice, access, and information.

Of special concern for the political rights of future generations is the increasing concentration of media, with implications for First Amendment diversity. On the one hand, cable television, satellite communications, cell phone networks, and the internet have produced easier access and much greater diversity and choice in media receipt than at any other point in human history. However, media critics express concern that concentration trends may present "chokepoints"—where a relatively few economic actors may control access by speakers/publishers to the bread spectrum avenues of discourse now extant. Even the First Amendment within the U.S. Constitution provides protection against *state* abridgement of free speech, not restrictions emanating from private interests controlling access. Indeed, that preservation may impede government intervention to assure diversity in media control.

The U.S. Newspaper Preservation Act, mergers, and economic changes have eliminated major newspaper competition in most cities of the United States. Worldwide as well, the changing economics of paper publishing have caused decline in circulation of newspapers and magazines, and investment for in-depth investigative reporting. Similar concentration in radio has been occurring, with many now merged into networks. Cable television is, in the normal course, a monopoly enterprise in each locality where it exists—with very few communities offering a choice of providers to residences. It is essentially unregulated, particularly as to pricing. Two firms now control most of these local monopolies in the United States. Two major satellite systems dominate television media by that mechanism, with one of them providing exclusive or dominant coverage over three continents. Telephony (telephone land lines) is a monopoly enterprise, with increasingly loose regulation by state public utility commissions. Three competing cell phone systems dominate the U.S. market. Internet service providers (ISPs) may control internet access—and concentration in that market is also substantial.[78]

The media structure internationally is dominated by U.S. corporations that are increasingly multinational in scope. Economic concentration has reached oligopoly levels—with three to five concerns controlling most of the relevant markets. The most effective competition may be intermodal—between telephony (land line telephones), cable, cell phone, satellites, and the internet. Such competition has limitations—some modes have inherent advantages in speed or locational availability giving them preclusive market power. Historically, competitors will price high where they have a competitive advantage to cross subsidize service where they face competition—with efficiency compromises and distorting effects.

There is a trend in intermodal, multinational mergers, apparently not limited effectively by traditional antitrust oversight.[79] Market leaders in publishing and broadcasting have become increasingly multi-modal and cross-own satellite, phone, cable, and internet assets. These combinations do not appear to be driven by notions of "economy of scale" efficiencies dictating only one railroad or power plant. Critics, such as the American Antitrust Institute, contend that they appear to be part of a process of competition absorption for enhancement of political/economic power.

b. Free Speech and Consumer Rights to Gauge Accuracy

The growth of mass communications has not included the disclosures required to facilitate truth-judgment by the listener/reader. Political reformers have succeeded in enacting disclosure of campaign contributor and lobbying identities so the body politic and public officials would be informed about who is speaking and weigh their economic interests. But current enhanced access now enables any person to achieve influence perhaps more politically potent than a typical campaign contribution. Any person able to type can reach millions. While a new freedom properly celebrated, these writers can be anonymous or misleadingly identified. The informational flood may become increasingly distorted in its selection, with messages that may suffer from undisclosed bias. Trade associations and individuals with narrow stakes are able to pose as consumer advocates contrary to their actual economic interests with little check. They are even able to pose as multiple parties, all seemingly transmitting the same factual message independent of one from the other. Nor do search engines filter or prioritize or assist in any truth seeking function. The result for future generations may be unprecedented diversity and access—with unprecedented volume—but with declining value for recipients. The dilemma is to achieve a balance between the rights of the listener to know who is talking as part of the truth seeking function of informed discourse—and the value of anonymous speech where identification would yield state retaliation that itself may prevent truth-telling to power.

5. Democracy and Public Integrity

Children are much affected by the governmental form of their respective nations. There is much room to argue about details—the merits of a bicameral legislature, direct election of a national leader or an "electoral college" system, and many others. But it is a consensus view of child advocates that children benefit from a system of bottom-up democracy, where there is open debate about public issues and elections conferring on political leaders the consent of the governed. In theory, such nations are less likely to engage in ego-based aggression. Elected leaders are more likely to make decisions from a broader range of facts and argument and to administer a system based on merit rather than family relationships. They are less likely to siphon off substantial national resources for their own benefit. Two factors in particular commend democracy for children: (a) the broad body politic cares about them; and (b) each of them will become an adult and aspire to have a voice in what they, in turn, will leave to their children.

The United States includes some important strengths along the Global Integrity scoring continuum, including a First Amendment particularly protective of political speech, three branches providing checks and balances, media independent from state control, a merit based civil service, voting rights, government transparency laws, and relatively accurate vote counts—with general respect for election outcomes. However, a number of troubling trends are cited by democracy reform groups: low electoral turnout (particularly by the young), party duopoly (impediments to third party challenges), the gerrymandering of district lines, supermajority requirements potentially frustrating the will of the majority, and private for-profit influence. The last concern is related to increases in privately-funded campaign costs, domination of lobbying, and job interchange between lobbyists and state positions. Such influence domination by those organized around a profit-stake in government decisions is of particular concern to the Center on Global Integrity, which identified that danger in 2009 as the most potent growing threat to its six indices—citing Bulgaria, South Africa, and especially the United States.[80]

Within the U.S., "horizontally-organized associations" continue to grow in number and influence. These associations include peer groupings of professionals, labor, and directly competing corporations. They dominate political influence in the United States, with over 20,000 registered lobbyists. The *Citizen's United* Supreme Court 2010 case gives them new opportunity to finance election campaigning—allegedly without limit or identification. Child advocates argue that such influence elevates the protection of prior invested capital. The interests of children may require long-term impact consideration, and some limitation on maximum return on invested capital—*e.g.*, where imposing such long-term costs to be suffered by future adults.[81] In some contrast, the values of the individual persons comprising the electorate may give more weight to the long-term and diffuse interests of children.

A political system that moves substantial influence over to short term outcomes, and the capital protection concerns of organized industries, may lead to a very different set of laws and public budgets. Nor is such a concern confined to corporate influence. Organizations of professions, trades and labor have a similar orientation, *e.g.*, as with the creation of unfunded long-term pension benefits for public employees discussed above.

Chapter 1 discusses the particular dangers to child-responsive government posed by trends and precedents over the past decade in the United States. The international aspect of that influence balance includes: (a) the direct impact on internationally influential U.S. foreign policy by multinational corporations now able to lobby and to finance campaigns without apparent limitation or secure public knowledge of their identity; and (b) similar trends likely in other nations—even those scoring high on the democracy scale—as the Center for Public Integrity warned in 2009.

Questions for Discussion

1. Does U.S. foreign policy toward Saudi Arabia, Kuwait, and the many nations lacking democracy and free speech, and who are guided by allegedly misogynist theocracies, comport with the stated American ethic of tolerance, freedom, and democracy?

2. The United States strongly supported the autocratic Shah of Iran, and after his removal, suffered the calumny of its population for that defense—and perhaps lessened influence to stimulate a secular, democratic succession. On the other hand, will such democratic structures espoused by U.S. leaders (*e.g.*, one stated basis for the Iraq intervention) produce religious intolerance, demagoguery, and violence to the disadvantage of children—particularly those in minority communities in those nations? Will an evolving international culture facilitated by instant mass communications limit destructive human tribalism, or stimulate it? How can international treaties, covenants, and incentives contribute to tolerance and lessen group persecution within nation-states?

6. International Cultural Values and Child-Related Commitment

Children do not become adults *tabula rasa*. The values, health, and character of an individual are determined by his or her families and cultures. Certainly during the 18th, 19th, and 20th centuries, a number of common cultural assumptions have served children well and have conferred wealth and comfort upon the current older adult generations of developed countries. Some social commentators cite in particular progress achieved through the luminary commitment of the so-called "Greatest Generation"—Americans born from 1900 to 1930. That generation overcame a devastating depression, defeated three fanatic totalitarian military powers, and rebuilt Europe. That reconstruction included the nations who attacked it—giving their children opportunity rarely offered a defeated people. It then enacted a GI Bill of Rights to give educational opportunity to its youth. It created a medical coverage and pension plan for its elderly. It built an infrastructure of highways and water projects throughout America, providing power and agricultural water to the breadbasket of the Midwest and to the source of much produce in the Central

Valley of California. It created parks and preserved wilderness. It allowed home ownership and middle class status to much of the nation. And it invested heavily in education, creating the world's finest public system of education and including affordable higher education chances for a large proportion of American youth.

The performance of the current American "Boomer" generation now ascendant may not match that intergenerational performance. A number of new trends distinguish it from the past record—and most of them have international reach. They include the issues of international tobacco and unhealthy food promotion to the young discussed above. Domestically, many states have created "marketing orders"—agricultural interests are allowed to collude and form promotional associations exempt from antitrust law. They use the power of the state to compel contribution from all producers to promote certain products; in California currently, that "state action" focuses on whole milk, cheese, avocados, eggs, beef, and wine marketing.

A related cultural issue is the growth of pornography, sexual abuse, and trafficking discussed above. Explicit sexual imagery is pervasively available via the internet, now supplemented with social networking and a trend toward photo exchanges. Meetings with persons of uncertain age and unclear background have become increasingly common—without the filtering from familiar and trusted sources. The problem here goes beyond the pervasive promotion in advertising and programming of allure as a primary aspiration for girls. There are accompanying cultural messages of some consequence for children. For example, the American culture increasingly portrays marriage as of little importance for children—and fathers as perhaps temporary happenstances who may or may not live with their children. Unfortunately, media cultural depictions may partly reflect our society, as art always does, but it may also help to shape it. American sitcoms include major characters having children without concern over single-mother family finances or the research suggesting that involved competent fathers do, in fact, contribute to the success of children (see Chapter 3).

The American trend of children born to unmarried parents has reached 40%, with child support collection from absent fathers an average of just $137 per month per child (see discussion in Chapters 2 and 3). A disproportionate number of these children have limited opportunities, and serious obstacles to success. Notwithstanding often remarkable maternal commitment, their incidence correlates with abuse, arrest, poverty, and drop outs. Europe, especially the Scandinavian nations, as well as Iceland—now have a higher incidence of unwed births than does the United States. Some of these nations have a more extensive social safety net system to assist single mothers, but that support is not permanently assured—as the retraction of the American support since 1996 for single mothers indicates and as the unfunded liabilities for the elderly may portend for much of the developed world, as discussed above.

Cultural factors for child opportunity also include more subtle issues. Much of America has long adopted the Calvinist ethic of hard work. One receives reward as one contributes. A citizen plants good corn, produces a bumper crop, and receives profit and success. But contrary signals are proliferating nationally and internationally. Television, a major factor of in popular culture, did not allow mass advertising of prescription drugs or hard liquor up to the end of the 20th century. American and European promotion of "alcopops," mentioned above, has been combined with mass television and other ads for rum, whiskey, and vodka openly appealing to youth. And, as noted in a question for discussion above, pharmaceutical companies (previously not advertising on television at all) are now advertising prescription drugs to such an extent that drug advertising and marketing now exceeds the amount committed to pharmaceutical research and development for the larger companies. Of concern to child advocates is the overall message conveyed by the accumulation of "let us please our respective pleasure centers" as a dominant cultural message.

In addition, child advocates are concerned about the societal message from newly-permissive and heavily-promoted mass gambling since the 1990s. The American cultural model through the 20th century has been to extol meritocracy and hard work. Historically, the public could gamble in Las Vegas in the U.S., Monte Carlo in Europe, and Macau in Asia. Horse races were the subject of betting. In the U.S., penny poker or bridge or an NCAA basketball pool would make up most popular gambling. After the 1980s, gambling has proliferated radically. Any sport event is the subject of bets from many locations. Poker contests run continuously on cable television. Internet gambling has proliferated as have self-promoting casinos.

Of greatest concern perhaps, the state, which purportedly sets the aspirational example, has adopted lotteries as a major funding source in multiple nations. The child-related implications of this shift are rarely discussed, but we know that a percentage of the citizenry is subject to gambling addiction. The gambling enterprise enriches primarily the house. Takings are highly regressive—the poor pay a much higher percentage of their income through losses. That means children and the opportunities their gambling parents are forsaking are major losers. State and regional lotteries in the United States now produce mega-million awards—where winnings of $250 million and $350 million and more, have been advertised and awarded. The outcome is the taking of substantial monies from impoverished parents in a system with high transaction costs (about one-third of revenues go toward administrative expenses) with an implicit message that extreme wealth is not the product of hard work or societal contribution, but blind luck. Such a message contrasts with the traditional cultural legacy of prior generations.

The United States is a major source of world culture. Its entertainment vehicles, music, and information technology have a wide reach—magnified by Microsoft and Apple, cell phones, satellite communications, Facebook, Linked In, YouTube, Twitter, et al. U.S. practices discussed above are being replicated in other nations. Almost all American schools are hooked up to the internet, with assets now including a record number of computers. That internet growth is international, with clear benefits for children including the chance to learn more efficiently, to read more, and to talk with more and different kinds of people. But in its present character it includes disadvantages beyond the issue of pornography and sex trafficking. It tends to lead to superficial responses, to "over communication" by children of events not warranting transmission—perhaps the vast majority of transmissions made. The culturally implicit values promoted here are self-absorbed and shallow discourse. Child advocates fear that they are not yet oriented toward child investment or health or child friendly values.

Joined to these cultural trends is the concern of some that a Western *hubris* may limit careful weighing of future consequences—the notion that human beings are so unique and special that they properly command the universe without consequence or limit. Such a "can do" spirit is part of the American tradition and may be commendable where prudently applied. But decisions ideally include the reality that human ingenuity has limits and thoughtless plunder may have consequences. The environmental discussion below includes some examples. A typical illustration is provided by the Ogallala Aquifer, also known as the High Plains Aquifer. It is a vast yet shallow undergroundwater table located beneath the Great Plains in the United States, covering 174,000 square miles and lying beneath eight Midwestern states, watering the farms through much of the most productive part of American agriculture. That asset—mass production of food—has been a key element allowing wealth, free time, and employment of millions in service industries because so few can produce so much for our sustenance. By itself, this one source of water provides 30% of our nation's agricultural groundwater, and drinking water for 82% of the people living above it. It is suffering depletion. Its future beyond the next two decades is unclear but facially dire.

This dramatic example is one of many, such as the Boomer dominant purchase of huge motor vehicles using three times the gas necessary in order to have 6 to 8 seats that are never used, and with performance features irrelevant to actual need. Or the prolific use of antibiotics on livestock with resistant strain implications. Or the pension/medical benefits discussed above, or the implications of radioactive waste dangerous for centuries noted below. These and other takings in the here and now have implications for our children and their children. These concerns, and others listed in the environment discussion below, are related to an underlying cultural question: How much do we care about the generations to follow us?

7. Preservation of the Earth

Important environmental issues extend beyond the scope of this text. But the rights of children include the maintenance of the uncontaminated resources of the earth. The international aspects of this child-right—to earth's assets, integrity, and health—passed down the line from previous generations, must involve multi-national practices that threaten despoliation. Hence, the reduction of plastics and other non-biodegradable waste, the restoration of habitat for endangered species survival, the health of the ocean and its reefs, the preservation of the world's forests and estuaries, and the limitation on carbon as an energy source—imply international participation.

One commonly discussed aspect of carbon consumption is the likelihood and impact on global warming over the next century. Climatologists generally agree that the human population, having increased from 200 million to over 7.5 billion in the blink of evolutionary time, combines with impressive per capita increases in fossil fuel-based emissions given modern power and transportation enhancements. This combination has created an increase in carbon dioxide in the atmosphere that accounts for gradual but measurable increases in ambient temperature, rising sea levels, and polar ice melt. That conclusion is supported by ice core analyses of atmospheric composition going back over 600,000 years, and by other evidence. Pre-industrial levels of carbon dioxide (prior to the start of the Industrial Revolution) were about 280 parts per million by volume (ppmv), and current levels are greater than 440 ppmv and increasing at a rate of 1.9 ppm yr.[82] The global concentration of CO_2 in our atmosphere today far exceeds the natural range over the last 650,000 years of 180 to 300 ppmv.[83] Of particular concern are so-called tipping points. For example, one such tipping point may occur due to temperature increases with white ice melting and reflective reduction (the albedo effect), combined with oxygen production decline. This would be exacerbated critically by extraordinary greenhouse producing methane—released from bodies of water with only slightly warmer temperatures. Most experts believe such a "tipping point" of danger short of actual final temperature increase is imminent—and beyond which amelioration may involve extraordinary cost or damage.[84]

Aside from global warming, child advocates focusing on earth as a generational legacy raise other consumption and waste issues. The oil, coal, and natural gas used for energy and transportation are the result of over one billion years of the earth's planetary evolution—much of it is composed of this accumulation of organic matter that lived and died. The earth still retains substantial reserves from these many millennia of previous life. But it is a limited asset. Environmentalists argue that the world's current adults are burning it—much of it wastefully—at a rate that promises the exhaustion of some assets for our children and more dire consequences for their legatees. That allegedly excessive (and often wasted or unnecessary) consumption raises a profound moral issue for the world's current adults. Similarly, generating power through nuclear fission at plants with typical lifespans of thirty to forty years, given limitations on fissionable material and the long-term contamination of substantial radioactive waste for centuries—raise similar issues of future cost and ethical obligation.

These concerns have been voiced in international fora. The number and range of international environmental agreements have increased markedly in recent years. An estimated 140 such agreements have been compiled by one source, more than half effectuated within the last forty years. Counting regional and bilateral agreements as well, the total now in effect exceeds 3,500.[85] The major international agreements on the global environment include bilateral, multilateral, international and UN agreements, conventions, and treaties. They cover transparency, the atmosphere, freshwater resources, hazardous substances, pollution liability, marine resources, nature, animal, and flora conservation and nuclear safety and liability from risk.[86]

Questions for Discussion

1. Do the above agreements address ocean acidification and reef diminution, rainforest destruction, pesticide practices, general overfishing (aside from porpoises, whales, and tuna), non-biodegradable refuse into the ocean, the survival of the vast majority of threatened flora and fauna, and the exhaustion of non-renewable resources beyond carbon—including exhaustion from wasteful or gratuitous exploitation and use?

2. Successful preservation of high atmosphere ozone (necessary for sun protection) has been cited as a major victory in international environmental protection (*e.g.*, the Montreal Protocol of 1989). The danger was clear and the cause of the depletion was emission at ground level of CFC compounds. However, those creating and selling those compounds represented a relatively minor economic force. Similarly, reductions in acid rain involved limitations on power generators and other isolated industry producers. What are the barriers to similar success which challenge massive investments in oil, coal, natural gas, nuclear power, ocean exploitation, and other areas of environmental concern? How would international incentives/disincentives/prohibitions be interposed given the wide disparities between nations?

3. Should nations such as Brazil, which provide substantial assets of value to future generations beyond their borders (*e.g.*, the oxygen producing, carbon absorbing, and rare species habitats of the Amazon), receive funds from nations and people indirectly benefitting from their long-term preservation? How should such payments be arranged? Under what conditions and with what monitoring of preservation performance?

4. Current carbon reduction efforts involve complex "cap and trade" proposals intended to allow the market to allocate emissions up to a tolerable level through market-based transactions (see the European Union Emission Trading Scheme). What are the difficulties in enforcing and administering such a regime?

5. If the permanent depletion of an earth asset is what economists call an "external cost" (a cost not borne by the market beneficiary but passed onto others), why not impose a fee that assesses that cost and allows the market to function without other intervention? Why not impose a very small fee at first, with a pre-announced schedule of increases year by year and decade by decade, with the proceeds allocated to some related subject with an "external benefit" (a gain that is not easily financed by its beneficiaries)?

6. Environmentalists argue that a major political roadblock to correction is the bias created by private and national investment in existing assets (*e.g.*, the oil industry investment in wells, tankers, pipelines and refineries, the coal industry investment in mines, railroad, and other assets, *et al.*). Some child advocates

argue that if an assessed fee were imposed at an initially very small level, but with a preannounced, gradual, and predictably enforced increase, existing investment could yield continued substantial profit. At the same time, knowledge of future fees inhibiting such profits in future decades could redirect future capital investment into solar, wind, or other renewable resources that did not impose future (or "external") costs. And such fees could be directed toward future-friendly investment.[87] Can the political imbalance between current asset owners and future interests discussed in Chapter 1 be addressed through such committed gradualism? Is it being implemented at the national level?[88] How would it be implemented at the international level?

7. The citizenry of the United States has special affection for its founding fathers, who risked much for the benefit of their legatees over the ensuing 243 years. What are the implications of the anticipated judgment of current adults in the year 2262—243 years in the future? The fossil fuels (natural gas, coal, oil) discussed above will be depleted by what percentage/amount in 2262? What are the implications of continuing population growth, resource exhaustion, earth temperature, ocean levels and ocean health, radioactive and non-biodegradable waste, and animal and plant diversity? Americans deeply treasure the sacrifices made by its founders in the late 18th century. What will be the judgment of our successors in 243 years about the 21st century American Boomer generation, its priorities, and its international leadership?

ENDNOTES

[1] See UNICEF, *The State of the World's Children—Special Edition—Celebrating 20 Years of the Convention on the Rights of the Child* (United Nations, November 2009) at Executive Summary, available at https://www.unicef.org/romania/SOWC_SpecEd_CRC_ExecutiveSummary_EN_091009.pdf.

[2] See https://www.who.int/gho/child_health/mortality/mortality_under_five_text/en/.

[3] UNICEF, *supra* note 1, at 5.

[4] See https://www.savethechildren.net/article/american-mothers-more-likely-die-peers-developed-countries-save-children.

[5] The United States has been the single most generous contributor to AIDS prevention and treatment in Africa.

[6] See 2000 through 2007 U.S. foreign economic and military aid by recipient nation at www.census.gov/compendia/statab/2010/tables/10s1263.pdf. The figures are for fiscal years ending September 30, for the 2013 figures see https://www.nationalpriorities.org/blog/2013/05/06/how-much-foreign-aid-does-us-give-away/.

[7] See https://dod.defense.gov/News/SpecialReports/Budget2019.aspx.

[8] See https://www.businessinsider.com/highest-military-budgets-countries-2018-5.

[9] See https://www.globalsecurity.org/military/facility/sites.htm.

[10] See https://www.weforum.org/agenda/2016/08/foreign-aid-these-countries-are-the-most-generous/.

[11] See https://www.globalcitizen.org/en/content/united-states-foreign-aid-history-trump/.

[12] See https://www.nptrust.org/philanthropic-resources/charitable-giving-statistics/.

[13] See http://www.worldometers.info/world-population/.

[14] See the discussion of environmental resources below, including continued reliance on non-renewable energy sources, as well as top soil diminution, and the threatened depletion of major fresh water agricultural underground supply.

[15] See https://www.who.int/news-room/fact-sheets/detail/maternal-mortality.

[16] See https://www.kff.org/global-health-policy/fact-sheet/the-u-s-government-and-international-family-planning-reproductive-health-efforts/.

[17] *Id.*

[18] See https://www.kff.org/global-health-policy/fact-sheet/the-u-s-government-and-global-maternal-and-child-health, for related data, see also https://www.kff.org/report-section/the-u-s-government-engagement-in-global-health-a-primer-report/.

[19] See https://www.unicef.org/wash/.

[20] This 1966 Covenant was ratified by 35 states by 1976 and has been in force since that date. The U.S. declined ratification, declaring opposition to its prohibitions on (a) child capital punishment, (b) the child labor limitations of Article 32, (c) the promise of state support for child "health, special needs and education," (d) the application of minimum standards supersession over parental prerogative and (e) the supersession of state sovereignty.

[21] For the full text of the Convention and related international agreements, see http://www.hrweb.org/legal/undocs.html.

[22] Save the Children, *Stop the War on Children* (2019) at https://www.stopwaronchildren.org/report.pdf.

[23] See https://zenit.org/articles/at-least-10000-children-die-each-yeardue-to-war-and-conflict/.

[24] See https://childrenandarmedconflict.un.org/six-grave-violations/child-soldiers/.

[25] It is not unusual for undocumented children to avoid such criminal prosecution, instead suffering deportation without appointed counsel or familial support.

[26] See discussion below of the 2009 enactment of the "Safe Harbor Act" in New York, making such a non-criminal option available for some alleged child prostitutes, and a similar new statute in Illinois. See also the G.E.M.S. organization in New York City working on alternative non-criminal therapies and remedies, at http://www.gems-girls.org.

[27] *Case Concerning Armed Activities on the Territory of the Congo*, 2 I.C.J. 219, 2002 WL 32912050 (I.C.J.) (2002).

[28] *Legal Consequences of the Construction of a Wall in the Occupied Palestinian Territory*, 2004 I.C.J. 136, 2004 WL 3587211 (I.C.J.) (2004).

[29] The seven nations casting negative votes were: Iraq, Israel, Libya, the People's Republic of China, Qatar, Yemen, and the United States.

[30] See https://www.icc-cpi.int/Pages/item.aspx?name=PR1439.

[31] Jie Zong, Jeanne Batalova, and Micayla Burrows, *Frequently Requested Statistics on Immigrants and Immigration in the United States* (Migration Policy Institute; March 14, 2019) at https://www.migrationpolicy.org/article/frequently-requestedstatistics-immigrants-and-immigration-united-states.

[32] Pub. L. No. 100-300, 102 Stat. 437.

[33] A free internet search tool includes the international caselaw interpreting the Convention, see http://www.incadat.com/.

[34] See Text of the Convention at https://www.hcch.net/en/instruments/conventions/full-text/?cid=24.

[35] See https://adoption.com/how-to-solve-the-us-international-adoption-crisis.

[36] *Id.*

[37] The measures referred to in Article 1 may deal in particular with (a) the attribution, exercise, termination or restriction of parental responsibility, as well as its delegation; (b) rights of custody, including rights relating to the care of the person of the child and, in particular, the right to determine the child's place of residence, as well as rights of access including the right to take a child for a limited period of time to a place other than the child's habitual residence; (c) guardianship, curatorship and analogous institutions; (d) the designation and functions of any person or body having charge of the child's person or property, representing or assisting the child; (e) the placement of the child in a foster family or in institutional care, or the provision of care by kafala or an analogous institution; (f) the supervision by a public authority of the care of a child by any person having charge of the child; and (g) the administration, conservation or disposal of the child's property.

[38] For detailed information, see www.acf.hhs.gov/css/resource/frequently-asked-questions-about-international-cases.

[39] "[The] climate of international opinion concerning the acceptability of a particular punishment" is an additional consideration which is "not irrelevant." *Coker v. Georgia*, 433 U.S. 584, 596, n. 10 (1977). "It is thus worth noting that the doctrine of felony murder has been abolished in England and India, severely restricted in Canada and a number of other Commonwealth countries, and is unknown in continental Europe." *Enmund v. Fla.*, 458 U.S. 782, 796 (1982). "We have previously recognized the relevance of the views of the international community in determining whether a punishment is cruel and unusual." *Thompson v. Okla*, 487 U.S. 815, 831 (1988). "Although these factors are by no means dispositive, their consistency with the legislative evidence lends further support to our conclusion that there is a consensus among those who have addressed the issue." *Atkins v. Virginia*, 536 U.S. 304, 316 (2002).

[40] *Jesner v. Arab Bank, PLC*, 138 S. Ct. 1386 (2018) at 1407.

[41] *Id.* at 1436.

[42] See https://www.justice.gov/opa/pr/attorney-general-announces-zero-tolerance-policy-criminal-illegal-entry.

[43] See *Ms. Li, et al v. U.S. Immigration and Customs Enforcement (ICE) et al.*, United States District Court for the Southern District of California, Case No.: 18cv00428 DMS (MDD).

[44] See census data, see also Brookings Institute gathered data pertaining to immigrants at https://www.brookings.edu/interactives/immigration-by-the-numbers/?gclid=EAIaIQobChMIntHOsqf24AIVbCCtBh21AAsAEAAYAiAAEgKLPfD_BwE.

[45] *Id.*

[46] See https://cis.org/Report/Examination-US-Immigration-Policy-and-Serious-Crime.

[47] See https://www.bushcenter.org/publications/resources-reports/resources/immigration-debunking-myths-infographic.html.

[48] See https://www.washingtonpost.com/national/failures-in-handling-unaccompanied-migrant-minors-have-led-to-trafficking/2016/01/26/c47de164-c138-11e5-9443-7074c3645405_story.html?utm_term=.822e8926d0c5.

[49] International Labour Organization, *Global Estimates of Child Labour: Results and trends, 2012–2016*, at http://www.ilo.org/global/topics/child-labour/lang--en/index.htm.

[50] See updated data at www.unicef.org.

[51] For full text of most of these documents, see http://www.hrweb.org/legal/undocs.html.

[52] The argument of free trade economists includes the contention that without a presumption against barriers, each nation's entrenched producers and labor interests will fabricate objections to products imported from genuinely more efficient outside producers.

[53] Another exception to GATT allows exception to free trade based on a need to "protect human, animal, or plant life or health" (Article 20(b)). However, it has been interpreted to apply to products with contaminants and toxins, such as Chinese toys with lead paint.

[54] For analyses of WTO and regional trade policies, transparency, governance and adverse impacts, see the work product of the Global Trade Watch division of Public Citizen, at http://www.citizen.org.

[55] See *e.g.*, Senator Harkin's Child Labor Deterrence Act of 1999, S. 1552 which would have banned products from the forced labor of children below the age of 15. The statute also would have provided economic relief and education resources for those displaced by the sales diminution, and would have provided for cooperative enforcement between the U.S., ILO and the UN Commission on Human Rights. It failed passage.

[56] See https://www.cbp.gov/trade/programs-administration/forced-labor.

[57] See https://www.dlapiper.com/en/us/insights/publications/2016/09/us-prohibits-imports-forced-labor/.

[58] See https://www.unodc.org/.

[59] The convention came into force on July 1, 2010, after five European nations ratified it. It creates a "Committee of the Parties" to the convention to (a) prevent and combat sexual exploitation of children, (b) protect the rights of child abuse victims, and (c) promote regional and international cooperation to enforce its provisions.

[60] Note that the focus of the Rome Treaty and the ICC's jurisdiction include sexual slavery as one of eleven other offenses: murder, extermination, enslavement, forced transfer of population, imprisonment involving "severe deprivation," torture, group "persecution," forced disappearance, apartheid, "other inhumane acts of similar character."

[61] A continuing issue within the United States is the criminalization of sexually exploited minors and the focus of enforcement on their punishment. Although international and federal definitions of "human trafficking" declare involved children to be victims, and focus criminal sanctions on the adults arranging and profiting from trafficking, some states continue to treat exploited children as criminals, and prosecute them as such. As noted above, New York and Illinois are among states that have enacted statutes recognizing the status of such children as victims, albeit possibly "persons in need of supervision" to effectively free them from the pimps or other adults upon whom they depend. See discussion in Chapter 8.

[62] These include the Coalition Against Trafficking in Women, and in the U.S.: the Protection Project at Johns Hopkins University, the San Francisco based Standing Against Sexual Exploitation, Children of the Night and Captive Daughters based in Southern California, the Polaris Project in Washington, D.C. and others.

[63] 8 U.S.C. § 1154(a)(1)A(iii), (B)(iii).

[64] Pub. L. No. 106-386, 114 Stat. 1463.

[65] See 8 U.S.C. § 1255(m)(1). A wide variety of crimes will qualify for U-Visa status for victims beyond trafficking, including incest, sexual assault, rape, torture, kidnapping, involuntary servitude, extortion, felonious assault, false imprisonment, witness tampering, obstruction of justice, perjury, *et al.* or conspiracy to violate any such criminal act; see 8 U.S.C. § 1101(a)(15)(u) et seq. The 2000 Protection Act also authorizes "T-Visas" on narrower grounds where a victim of human trafficking and is cooperating with law enforcement in related prosecutions. They are similar to "U-Visas", except with qualification for public benefits normally denied to non-citizens.

[66] See www.who.int/news-room/fact-sheets/detail/tobacco.

[67] Note that one legitimate objection of an importer of arguably unhealthy drink or food for children might be the failure of the receiving nation to develop standards applicable to products manufactured internally. Certainly the contrast between what is allowed domestically and what is barred from other sources raises the specter of disingenuous economic "protectionist" motivations. For a nation to be able to police imports, GATT standards may implicitly require it to treat its own production under similar standards. The problem that can occur may be driven by a fear to limit domestic production of unhealthy drink or food because of growing competition for its manufacture from outside the nation. Hence, one may limit one's own produced supply, and merely facilitate the same unhealthy substances coming from outside economic beneficiaries. The catch-22 dilemma requires a simultaneous imposition of standards, both domestically and as to imports. However, such coordination is difficult in a nation where substantial food standards policy may originate at local or state levels. For example, the removal of sugared soft drink machines from cafeterias and other school nutrition measures have generally occurred from policies of some states and some school districts, not from a federally coordinated school lunch regulation tied to the federal school lunch program.

[68] See http://drugwarfacts.org/cms/?q=node/64.

[69] See Human Rights Watch, *"Racial Disparities in the War on Drugs"* (Washington, DC: Human Rights Watch, 2000), www.hrw.org/legacy/reports/2000/usa/Rcedrg00.htm#P54_1086.

[70] Consumer advocates argue that the "subprime market" sales efforts of real property lenders from the 1990s offered artificially low interest rates (the "bait") to people who wanted to fulfill the American dream of home ownership—a status further incentivized by mortgage interest tax deductions. Lenders extended such credit, knowing that when the low interest "arm" of three to seven years expired, they could "switch" to interest rates requiring monthly payments substantially greater than borrowers would

likely afford—rates that often involved more than doubling monthly payments due. See http://www. inthesetimes.com/article/3276/thesubprime_bait_and_switch/.

[71] Historians and economists commonly cite speculative gambling "bubbles" as a precursor to major financial collapse. The depression of 1929 was substantially facilitated by highly leveraged purchase of stock on "margin"—with little money actually advanced for the purchase. Such investors risk the loss of what they have invested plus substantial sums beyond that investment (borrowed for the purchase) but may potentially gain enormous speculative profit—providing a strong net incentive. Post-1930 reforms increased the percentage of cash necessary to purchase (to ameliorate "margin call" collapse) and required major commercial banks to maintain reserves without speculative investment risk.

[72] As of 2007, the invested derivatives world-wide were itemized as follows (in U.S. dollars): (1) Listed credit derivatives of $548 trillion and (2) Over-The-Counter (OTC) derivatives of $596 trillion. Within the OTC category are (a) Interest Rate Derivatives of $393 trillion; (b) Credit Default Swaps of over $58 trillion; (c) Foreign Exchange Derivatives of over $56 trillion; (d) Commodity Derivatives of about $9 trillion; (e) Equity Linked Derivatives of $8.5 trillion; and (f) Unallocated Derivatives of over $71 trillion. See http://www. siliconvalleywatcher.com/mt/archives/2008/10/the_size_of_der.php. Query, what will prevent a future bubble with dramatic effects given the leverage of derivatives and the post-2016 removal of regulatory checks?

[73] For one discussion of some of these deferrals, particularly U.S. Medicare and Social Security, see the analysis by former U.S. Comptroller David M. Walker, *Comeback America: Turning the Country Around and Restoring Fiscal Responsibility*, Random House (2010).

[74] See, e.g., *Yeager v. Cingular Wireless LLC*, 673 F.Supp. 1089 (2009). Cingular's use of Yeager's name was as follows: "Nearly 60 years ago, the legendary test pilot Chuck Yeager broke the sound barrier and achieved Mach 1. Today, Cingular is breaking another kind of barrier with our MACH 1 AND MACH 2 mobile command centers, which will enable us to respond rapidly to hurricanes. " The mention concerned the firm's description of its disaster preparedness work, not for commercial sales. The district court denied summary judgment, supporting Yeager's right to permission/compensation because his name was used. Note that his fame was the product of taxpayer financed employment in an Army Air Force plane. The conferral of proprietary/advance permission rights to figures with historical relevance as a prerequisite to citing them by name, particularly in a non-sales context, may eventually be relevant to speech rights for multiple generations—given the extraordinary length of time such rights survive.

[75] See Sonny Bono Copyright Term Extension Act, Pub. L. No. 105-298, 112 Stat. 2827 (17 U.S.C.A. §§ 101 *et seq.*).

[76] Note that the twenty-year period runs from the application date. With a two- to three-year period for successful patent acquisition, the effective term post-approved patent is generally seventeen to eighteen years.

[77] See www.wipo.int/edocs/pubdocs/en/wipo_pub_941_2017-chapter2.pdf.

[78] UUNET Incorporated has access to 300,000 miles of fiber and cable and owns an estimated 30% of the Internet's infrastructure. UUNET emerged as WorldCom's brand, renaming itself MCI in 2004, and was then acquired by Verizon. Major players include AT&T, Sprint, Qwest, TeliaSonera, Tat, Savvis, L3, Global Crossing, as well as Verizon. Together, they form most of the internet backbone networks. See https://www.brighthub.com/computing/hardware/articles/85391.aspx.

[79] Even with traditional antitrust enforcement, oligopoly may be difficult to police or to prevent. One of the attendant fears where small groups of competitors dominate is the ease of "association" coordination among a small number of competitors. As discussed in Chapter 1, the "Noerr Pennington" doctrine within the United States allows horizontally competing enterprises to combine for purposes of political influence. And the *Citizens United* Supreme Court holding in 2010 now allows direct participation by corporations, and their organized associations, in political campaigns without clear limitation. Media interests are so organized in Washington D.C. and in most of the world's developed nations' capitals.

[80] Ti-Ping Chen, *Corruption: Political Finance is Top International Corruption Concern*, Center on Global Integrity (February 7, 2009).

[81] As discussed below, corporations invest private capital in resources and have a proper obligation to their investors to maximize profit from that investment for dividends and capital appreciation. That protection is the goal of corporate officers, who have a fiduciary duty to the governing stockholders providing that capital. *E.g.*, an investment in oil assets, refineries et al. leads to a strong interest in protecting the value of those assets without full calculation of the extern costs they may impose on others, nor the long range implications of resource exhaustion.

[82] See 400.350.org.

[83] *Id.*

[84] One source of such concern is the substantial supply of methane within the ocean and other bodies of water—now suppressed by the cold water temperatures but subject to substantial atmospheric emission with even small warming. Methane is twenty to thirty times more potent as a stimulator of global warming than carbon dioxide.

[85] See sources cited at http://www.ciesin.org/TG/PI/TREATY/envagree.html.

[86] A complete accounting and index by type, subject, and year is at iea.uoregon.edu.

[87] Free market economists, starting with progenitor Adam Smith in his seminal *The Wealth of Nations*, recognized that competitive markets require rules and prerequisites to function (*e.g.*, independent competitors, accurate information about products). And they are subject to "external cost" flaws—costs imposed on others and not subject to compensation from the market transaction. In addition, the market may not compensate for some "external benefits" (desirable ends not obtainable through market assessment—as with the classic example of the lighthouse). Proponents of fees for non-renewable asset depletion argue that such an "exhaustion" fee would create a more effective market, correcting for the external cost of asset deprivation to future generations, while possibly redirecting the fee to renewable investment—arguably an "external benefit."

[88] See discussion of U.S. environmentalists shifting support from "cap and trade" to a taxation approach at http://online.wsj.com/article/SB125011380094927137.html. Would not the proposed token initial assessment, with pre-determined gradual increase consonant with the growing effect over time, be more politically achievable?

Child Advocacy Resources

A. SELECTED CHILD ADVOCACY WEB SITES

ABA Center on Children and the Law
www.abanet.org/child

ABA Family Law Section
www.abanet.org/family

Alliance for Children and Families
www.alliance1.org

Alliance for Children's Rights
www.kids-alliance.org

American Academy of Pediatrics
www.aap.org

American Professional Society
on the Abuse of Children
www.apsac.org

America's Promise Alliance
www.americaspromise.org

Center for Law and Social Policy
www.clasp.org

Child Care Law Center
www.childcarelaw.org

Child Welfare League of America
www.cwla.org

Children Now
www.childrennow.org

Children's Advocacy Institute
www.caichildlaw.org

Children's Defense Fund
www.childrensdefense.org

The Children's Partnership
www.childrenspartnership.org

Children's Rights
www.childrensrights.org

Coalition for Juvenile Justice
www.juvjustice.org

Connecting for Kids
www.connectingforkids.org

Docs for Tots
www.docsfortots.org

Every Child Matters
www.everychildmatters.org

First Star
www.firststar.org

Foster Club
www.fosterclub.com

The Free Child Project
www.freechild.org

Fight Crime: Invest in Kids
www.fightcrime.org

First Focus
www.firstfocus.org

Forum for Youth Investment
www.forumfyi.org

Foster Care Alumni of America
www.fostercarealumni.org

International Society for the
Prevention of Child Abuse
and Neglect
www.ispcan.org

John Burton Advocates for Youth
www.jbaforyouth.org

Juvenile Law Center
www.jlc.org

Juvenile Law Society
www.juvenilelawsociety.org

Kempe Children's Center
www.kempecenter.org

National Association for Child Care
Resource and Referral Agencies
www.naccrra.org

National Association of Counsel for
Children
www.naccchildlaw.org

National Association for the
Education of Young Children
www.naeyc.org

National Center for Children
in Poverty
www.nccp.org

National Center for Missing and
Exploited Children
www.missingkids.org

National Center for Youth Law
www.youthlaw.org

National Network for Youth
www.nn4youth.org

National Head Start Association
www.nhsa.org

National Juvenile Defender Center
www.njdc.info

National Juvenile Justice Network
www.njjn.org

Partnership for America's Children
https://foramericaschildren.org

Pre-K Now
www.preknow.org

Prevent Child Abuse America
www.preventchildabuse.org

Robert F. Kennedy National
Resource Center for Juvenile Justice
www.rfknrcjj.org

Youth Law Center
www.ylc.org

B. KEY GOVERNMENT RESOURCES

Library of Congress, Legislative Information on the Internet
http://thomas.loc.gov

United Nations International Children's Emergency Fund (UNICEF)
www.unicef.org

U.S. Department of Education
www.ed.gov

U.S. Department of Health and Human Services' Children's Bureau
www.acf.hhs.gov/cb

U.S. Department of Health and Human Services' Family and Youth Services
Bureau
www.acf.hhs.gov/fysb

U.S. Department of Justice's Office of Juvenile Justice
and Delinquency Prevention
www.ojjdp.gov

U.S. Government Publishing Office
www.gpo.gov

U.S. Supreme Court
www.supremecourtus.gov

Index

C

Supplemental Security Income/State Supplementary Program (SSI/SSP) 265

T

Temporary Assistance to Needy Families (TANF) 22, 127
    assistance standards 127
    benefit levels 156
    eligibility 127
    state waivers 156

Tort liability and recovery
    child-related tort action in state court 618
    child-related tort actions in federal court 617
    children as tort defendants 602
    insurance coverage 621
    liability 602
    recovery from private parties 604
      attractive nuisance doctrine 605
      status of children 604
    recovery from the state 607
      duty of care 607
      liability alternatives 613
      public employee accountability notwithstanding the immunity defense 616
      state official immunity 614
    summary and checklist 617

U

Unwed births 81, 82

V

Victims/witnesses, child. See Child victims/witnesses

W

Women, Infants, and Children (WIC) 133